TRANSLATOR AND SENIOR EDITOR:
Rabbi Israel V. Berman

MANAGING EDITOR:
Baruch Goldberg

EDITOR:
Rabbi David Strauss

ASSOCIATE EDITOR:
Dr. Jeffrey M. Green

COPY EDITOR:
Alec Israel

ASSISTANT COPY EDITOR:
Abby Berman

BOOK DESIGNER:
Ben Gasner

GRAPHIC ARTIST:
Michael Etkin

TECHNICAL STAFF:
Moshe Greenvald
Inna Schwartzman

Random House Staff

PRODUCTION MANAGER:
Kathy Rosenbloom

ART DIRECTOR:
Bernard Klein

CHIEF COPY EDITOR:
Amy Edelman

The Talmud

The Steinsaltz Edition

Volume X

Tractate Ketubot

Part IV

VOLUME X
TRACTATE KETUBOT
PART IV

RANDOM HOUSE
NEW YORK

THE TALMUD

תלמוד בבלי

THE STEINSALTZ EDITION

Commentary by Rabbi Adin Steinsaltz (Even Yisrael)

Published in the United States by Times Books, a division of Random House, Inc., New York,
and simultaneously in Canada by Random House of Canada Limited, Toronto.

Library of Congress Cataloging-in-Publication Data
(Revised for volume X)
The Talmud.
English, Hebrew, and Aramaic.
Includes bibliographical references.
Contents: v. 1– Tractate Bava metzia–
v. 7. Tractate Ketubot, pt. 1. v. 10. Tractate Ketubot, pt. 4.
Accompanied by a reference guide.
I. Title.
BM499.5.E4 1989 89-842911
ISBN 0-394-57665-9 (guide)
ISBN 0-394-576667 (v. 1)
ISBN 0-394-57665-7 (v. 1)

Manufactured in the United States of America
9 8 7 6 5 4 3 2
First Edition

Dedicated in memory of

Joseph Nash
יוסף בן לעמעל

who taught us the values by which we live,

and in honor of

Ludwig and Lotte Bravmann,

our partners in conveying these values
to the next generation

Jack and Helen Nash

The Steinsaltz Talmud in English

The English edition of the Steinsaltz Talmud is a translation and adaptation of the Hebrew edition. It includes most of the additions and improvements that characterize the Hebrew version, but it has been adapted and expanded especially for the English reader. This edition has been designed to meet the needs of advanced students capable of studying from standard Talmud editions, as well as of beginners, who know little or no Hebrew and have had no prior training in studying the Talmud.

The overall structure of the page is similar to that of the traditional pages in the standard printed editions. The text is placed in the center of the page, and alongside it are the main auxiliary commentaries. At the bottom of the page and in the margins are additions and supplements.

The original Hebrew-Aramaic text, which is framed in the center of each page, is exactly the same as that in the traditional Talmud (although material that was removed by non-Jewish censors has been restored on the basis of manuscripts and old printed editions). The main innovation is that this Hebrew-Aramaic text has been completely vocalized and punctuated, and all the terms usually abbreviated have been fully spelled out. In order to retain the connection with the page numbers of the standard editions, these are indicated at the head of every page.

We have placed a *Literal Translation* on the right-hand side of the page, and its punctuation has been introduced into the Talmud text, further helping the student to orientate himself. The *Literal Translation* is intended to help the student to learn the meaning of specific Hebrew and Aramaic words. By comparing the original text with this translation, the reader develops an understanding of the Talmudic text and can follow the words and sentences in the original. Occasionally, however, it has not been possible to present an exact literal translation of the original text, because it is so different in structure from English. Therefore we have added certain auxiliary words, which are indicated in square brackets. In other cases it would make no sense to offer a literal translation of a Talmudic idiom, so we have provided a close English equivalent of the original meaning, while a note, marked "lit.," explaining the literal meaning of the words, appears in parentheses. Our purpose in presenting this literal translation was to give the student an appreciation of the terse and enigmatic nature of the Talmud itself, before the arguments are opened up by interpretation.

Nevertheless, no one can study the Talmud without the assistance of commentaries. The main aid to understanding the Talmud provided by this edition is the *Translation and Commentary,* appearing on the left side of the page. This is Rabbi Adin Steinsaltz's highly regarded Hebrew interpretation of the Talmud, translated into English, adapted and expanded.

This commentary is not merely an explanation of difficult passages. It is an integrated exposition of the entire text. It includes a full translation of the Talmud text, combined with explanatory remarks. Where the translation in the commentary reflects the literal translation, it has been set off in bold type. It has also been given the same reference numbers that are found both in the original text and in the literal translation. Moreover, each section of the commentary begins with a few words of the Hebrew-Aramaic text. These reference numbers and paragraph headings allow the reader to move from one part of the page to another with ease.

There are some slight variations between the literal translation and the words in bold face appearing in the *Translation and Commentary.* These variations are meant to enhance understanding, for a juxtaposition of the literal translation and the sometimes freer translation in the commentary will give the reader a firmer grasp of the meaning.

The expanded *Translation and Commentary* in the left-hand column is intended to provide a conceptual understanding of the arguments of the Talmud, their form, content, context, and significance. The commentary also brings out the logic of the questions asked by the Sages and the assumptions they made.

Rashi's traditional commentary has been included in the right-hand column, under the *Literal Translation.* We have left this commentary in the traditional "Rashi script," but all quotations of the Talmud text appear in standard square type, the abbreviated expressions have all been printed in full, and Rashi's commentary is fully punctuated.

Since the *Translation and Commentary* cannot remain cogent and still encompass all the complex issues that arise in the Talmudic discussion, we have included a number of other features, which are also found in Rabbi Steinsaltz's Hebrew edition.

At the bottom of the page, under the *Translation and Commentary*, is the *Notes* section, containing additional material on issues raised in the text. These notes deepen understanding of the Talmud in various ways. Some provide a deeper and more profound analysis of the issues discussed in the text, with regard to individual points and to the development of the entire discussion. Others explain Halakhic concepts and the terms of Talmudic discourse.

The *Notes* contain brief summaries of the opinions of many of the major commentators on the Talmud, from the period after the completion of the Talmud to the present. Frequently the *Notes* offer interpretations different from that presented in the commentary, illustrating the richness and depth of Rabbinic thought.

The *Halakhah* section appears below the *Notes.* This provides references to the authoritative legal decisions reached over the centuries by the Rabbis in their discussions of the matters dealt with in the Talmud. It explains what reasons led to these Halakhic decisions and the close connection between the Halakhah today and the Talmud and its various interpreters. It should be noted that the summary of the Halakhah presented here is not meant to serve as a reference source for actual religious practice but to introduce the reader to Halakhic conclusions drawn from the Talmudic text.

English commentary and expanded translation of the text, making it readable and comprehensible

Hebrew/Aramaic text of the Talmud, fully vocalized, and punctuated

REALIA

קַלְתָּהּ **Her basket.** The source of this word is the Greek κάλαθος, kalathos, and it means a basket with a narrow base.

Illustration from a Greek drawing depicting such a basket of fruit.

CONCEPTS

פֵּאָה ***Pe'ah.*** **One of the presents left for the poor** (מַתְּנוֹת עֲנִיִּים). The Torah forbids harvesting "the corners of your field," so that the produce left standing may be harvested and kept by the poor (Leviticus 19:9).
The Torah did not specify a minimum amount of produce to be left as *pe'ah*. But the Sages stipulated that it must be at least one-sixtieth of the crop.
Pe'ah is set aside only from crops that ripen at one time and are harvested at one time. The poor are allowed to use their own initiative to reap the *pe'ah* left in the fields. But the owner of an orchard must see to it that each of the poor gets a fixed share of the *pe'ah* from places that are difficult to reach. The poor come to collect *pe'ah* three times a day. The laws of *pe'ah* are discussed in detail in tractate *Pe'ah*.

TRANSLATION AND COMMENTARY

[1]**and her husband threw her a bill of divorce into her lap or into her basket**, which she was carrying on her head, [2]would you say **here, too,** that **she would not be divorced**? Surely we know that the law is that she *is* divorced in such a case, as the Mishnah (*Gittin* 77a) states explicitly!

אֲמַר לֵיהּ [3]Rav Ashi **said** in reply **to** Ravina: The woman's **basket is** considered to be **at rest, and it is she who walks beneath it.** Thus the basket is considered to be a "stationary courtyard," and the woman acquires whatever is thrown into it.

MISHNAH הָיָה רוֹכֵב [4]If **a person was riding on an animal and he saw an ownerless object** lying on the ground, **and he said to another person** standing nearby, **"Give that object to me,"** [5]if **the other person took** the ownerless object **and said, "I have acquired it for myself,"** [6]he has **acquired it** by lifting it up, even though he was not the first to see it, and the rider has no claim to it. [7]But **if, after he gave** the object **to** the rider, the person who picked it up **said, "I acquired** the object **first,"** [8]**he** in fact **said nothing**. His words are of no effect, and the rider may keep it. Since the person walking showed no intention of acquiring the object when he originally picked it up, he is not now believed when he claims that he acquired it first. Indeed, even if we maintain that when a person picks up an ownerless object on behalf of someone else, the latter does *not* acquire it automatically, here, by *giving* the object to the rider, he makes a gift of it to the rider.

GEMARA תְּנַן הָתָם [9]**We have learned elsewhere** in a Mishnah in tractate *Pe'ah* (4:9): **"Someone who gathered *pe'ah*** — produce which by Torah law [Leviticus 23:22] is left unharvested in the corner of a field by the owner of the field, to be gleaned by the poor — **and said, 'Behold, this *pe'ah*** which I have gleaned **is** intended **for so-and-so the poor man,'** [10]**Rabbi Eliezer says:** The person who gathered the *pe'ah* **has acquired it**

בִּרְשׁוּת הָרַבִּים [1]וְזָרַק לָהּ גֵּט לְתוֹךְ חֵיקָהּ אוֹ לְתוֹךְ קַלְתָּהּ — [2]הָכָא נַמִּי דְּלָא מִגָּרְשָׁה? [3]אֲמַר לֵיהּ: קַלְתָּהּ מֵינָח נַיְיחָא, וְאִיהִי דְּקָא מְסַגְּיָא מִתּוּתָהּ.

משנה [4]הָיָה רוֹכֵב עַל גַּבֵּי בְהֵמָה וְרָאָה אֶת הַמְּצִיאָה, וְאָמַר לַחֲבֵירוֹ "תְּנָה לִי", [5]נְטָלָהּ וְאָמַר, "אֲנִי זָכִיתִי בָּהּ", [6]זָכָה בָּהּ. [7]אִם, מִשֶּׁנְּתָנָהּ לוֹ, אָמַר, "אֲנִי זָכִיתִי בָּהּ תְּחִלָּה", [8]לֹא אָמַר כְּלוּם.

גמרא [9]תְּנַן הָתָם: "מִי שֶׁלִּיקֵּט אֶת הַפֵּאָה וְאָמַר, 'הֲרֵי זוֹ לִפְלוֹנִי עָנִי', [10]רַבִּי אֱלִיעֶזֶר

LITERAL TRANSLATION

in a public thoroughfare [1]and [her husband] threw her a bill of divorce into her lap or into her basket, [2]here, too, would she not be divorced?

[3]He said to him: Her basket is at rest, and it is she who walks beneath it.

MISHNAH [4][If a person] was riding on an animal and he saw a found object, and he said to another person, "Give it to me," [5][and the other person] took it and said, "I have acquired it," [6]he has acquired it. [7]If, after he gave it to him, he said, "I acquired it first," [8]he said nothing.

GEMARA [9]We have learned there: "Someone who gathered *pe'ah* and said, 'Behold this is for so-and-so the poor man,' [10]Rabbi Eliezer says:

RASHI

קלתה – סל שעל ראשה, שנותנת בה כלי מלאכתה וטווי שלה. הכי נמי דלא הוי גיטא – והאנן תנן במסכת גיטין (עז,א): זרק לה גיטה לתוך חיקה או לתוך קלתה – הרי זו מגורשת!

משנה לא אמר כלום – דאפילו אמרינן המגביה מציאה לחבירו לא קנה חבירו, כיון דיהבה ליה – קנייה ממה נפשך. אי קנייה קמא דלא מתכוין להקנות לחבירו – הא יהבה ניהליה במתנה. ואי לא קנייה קמא משום דלא היה מתכוין לקנות – הויא ליה הפקר עד דמטא לידיה דהאי, וקנייה האי כמאי דעקרה מידיה דקמא לשם קנייה.

גמרא מי שליקט את הפאה – אדם בעלמא שאינו בעל שדה. דאי בבעל שדה – לא אמר רבי אליעזר זכה. דליכא למימר "מגו דזכי לנפשיה", דאפילו הוא עני מוזהר הוא שלא ללקט פאה משדה שלו, כדאמר בשחיטת חולין (קלא,ב): "לא תלקט לעני" – להזהיר עני על שלו.

NOTES

מִי שֶׁלִּיקֵּט אֶת הַפֵּאָה **If a person gathered *pe'ah*.** According to *Rashi*, the Mishnah must be referring to someone other than the owner of the field. By Torah law the owner of a field is required to separate part of his field as *pe'ah*, even if he himself is poor, and he may not take the *pe'ah* for himself. Therefore the "since" (מגו) argument

HALAKHAH

קַלְתָּהּ **A woman's basket.** "If a man throws a bill of divorce into a container that his wife is holding, she thereby acquires the bill of divorce and the divorce takes effect." (*Shulḥan Arukh, Even HaEzer* 139:10.)

הַמְלַקֵּט פֵּאָה עֲבוּר אַחֵר **A person who gathered *pe'ah* for someone else.** "If a poor person, who is himself entitled to collect *pe'ah*, gathered *pe'ah* for another poor person, and said, 'This *pe'ah* is for X, the poor person,' he acquires the *pe'ah* on behalf of that other poor person. But if the person who collected the *peah* was wealthy, he does not acquire the *pe'ah* on behalf of the poor person. He must give it instead to the first poor person who appears in the field," following the opinion of the Sages, as explained by Rabbi Yehoshua ben Levi. (*Rambam, Sefer Zeraim, Hilkhot Mattenot Aniyyim* 2:19.)

Literal translation of the Talmud text into English

Marginal notes provide essential background information

Hebrew commentary of Rashi, the classic explanation that accompanies all editions of the Talmud

Numbers link the three main sections of the page and allow readers to refer rapidly from one to the other

Notes highlight points of interest in the text and expand the discussion by quoting other classical commentaries

On the outer margin of the page, factual information clarifying the meaning of the Talmudic discussion is presented. Entries under the heading *Language* explain unusual terms, often borrowed from Greek, Latin, or Persian. *Sages* gives brief biographies of the major figures whose opinions are presented in the Talmud. *Terminology* explains the terms used in the Talmudic discussion. *Concepts* gives information about fundamental Halakhic principles. *Background* provides historical, geographical, and other information needed to understand the text. *Realia* explains the artifacts mentioned in the text. These notes are sometimes accompanied by illustrations.

The best way of studying the Talmud is the way in which the Talmud itself evolved - a combination of frontal teaching and continuous interaction between teacher and pupil, and between pupils themselves.

This edition is meant for a broad spectrum of users, from those who have considerable prior background and who know how to study the Talmud from any standard edition to those who have never studied the Talmud and do not even know Hebrew.

The division of the page into various sections is designed to enable students of every kind to derive the greatest possible benefit from it.

For those who know how to study the Talmud, the book is intended to be a written Gemara lesson, so that, either alone, with partners, or in groups, they can have the sense of studying with a teacher who explains the difficult passages and deepens their understanding both of the development of the dialectic and also of the various approaches that have been taken by the Rabbis over the centuries in interpreting the material. A student of this kind can start with the Hebrew-Aramaic text, examine Rashi's commentary, and pass on from there to the expanded commentary. Afterwards the student can turn to the Notes section. Study of the *Halakhah* section will clarify the conclusions reached in the course of establishing the Halakhah, and the other items in the margins will be helpful whenever the need arises to clarify a concept or a word or to understand the background of the discussion.

For those who do not possess sufficient knowledge to be able to use a standard edition of the Talmud, but who know how to read Hebrew, a different method is proposed. Such students can begin by reading the Hebrew-Aramaic text and comparing it immediately to the *Literal Translation*. They can then move over to the *Translation and Commentary*, which refers both to the original text and to the *Literal Translation*. Such students would also do well to read through the *Notes* and choose those that explain matters at greater length. They will benefit, too, from the terms explained in the side margins.

The beginner who does not know Hebrew well enough to grapple with the original can start with the *Translation and Commentary*. The inclusion of a translation within the commentary permits the student to ignore the *Literal Translation*, since the commentary includes both the Talmudic text and an interpretation of it. The beginner can also benefit from the *Notes*, and it is important for him to go over the marginal notes on the concepts to improve his awareness of the juridical background and the methods of study characteristic of this text.

Apart from its use as study material, this book can also be useful to those well versed in the Talmud, as a source of additional knowledge in various areas, both for understanding the historical and archeological background and also for an explanation of words and concepts. The general reader, too, who might not plan to study the book from beginning to end, can find a great deal of interesting material in it regarding both the spiritual world of Judaism, practical Jewish law, and the life and customs of the Jewish people during the thousand years (500 B.C.E.–500 C.E.) of the Talmudic period.

Contents

The Talmud
The Steinsaltz Edition

Volume X
Tractate Ketubot
Part IV

Introduction to Chapter Four

נַעֲרָה שֶׁנִּתְפַּתְּתָה

"And if a man seduces a virgin who has not been betrothed and lies with her, he shall surely make her his wife. If her father will surely refuse to give her to him, he shall pay money according to the dowry of virgins." (Exodus 22:15–16.)

"If a man finds a virgin na'arah *who has not been betrothed, and seizes her and lies with her, and they are found, then the man who lay with her shall give to the father of the* na'arah *fifty pieces of silver, and she shall be his wife, for he has humbled her. He cannot let her go all his days."* (Deuteronomy 22:28–29.)

"If a man takes a wife, and he goes in to her, and hates her, and lays accusing speeches against her, and brings out an evil name upon her and says: 'I took this woman and I came near to her, and I did not find virginity in her,' then the father of the na'arah *and her mother take and bring out the tokens of the virginity of the* na'arah *to the elders of the city to the gate. And the father of the* na'arah *shall say to the elders: 'I gave my daughter to this man as a wife, and he hated her; and behold he has laid accusing speeches saying: "I have not found in your daughter virginity," and these are the tokens of my daughter's virginity.' And they shall spread the cloth before the elders of the city. And the elders of that city shall take the man and chastise him. And they shall fine him a hundred pieces of silver and they shall give them to the father of the* na'arah, *for he has brought out an evil name upon a virgin of Israel. And she shall be his wife; he may not send her away all his days. But if this thing was true, and the tokens of virginity were not found for the* na'arah, *then they shall bring out the* na'arah *to the door of her father's house, and the men of her city shall stone her with stones so that*

designates her for his son, he shall deal with her after the manner of daughters. If he takes another wife for himself, he shall not diminish her food, her clothing, and her conjugal rights. And if he does not do these three to her, then she shall go out free; there is no money." (Exodus 21:7-11)

In the section in the Torah dealing with the rape of a betrothed *na'arah*, it is stated that the fine imposed on the rapist is paid to the *na'arah*'s father. Our chapter opens with a clarification of the father's right to the fine paid for his daughter's rape, and then continues with a general discussion of the rights a father has with respect to his daughter until she reaches full adulthood or until she marries. A critical question posed is to what extent these rights are personal and belong only to the father, and to what extent they are monetary rights that can be passed on to the father's heirs. The father's rights with respect to his daughter are derived mostly from the verses dealing with a father's right to sell his daughter as a maidservant and his right to annul her vows. Some of a father's rights with respect to his daughter stem from enactments passed by the Sages.

A girl's father enjoys a special Halakhic status is if the girl's husband slanders his wife, falsely charging that she was not a virgin when she married him. Even though the laws pertaining to the slanderer are set out in detail in the Torah, there is still room for a clarification of the topic. The discussion focuses on the question of the extent to which the verses should be taken literally, and the extent to which they should be understood as metaphor. According to all opinions, the verses cannot be understood in an absolutely literal manner, for all agree that the presence or absence of a bloodstained sheet cannot serve as absolute proof about the wife's virginity one way or the other. Thus all must agree that the Torah is referring to a case in which both the husband and the father base their claims on the testimony of witnesses.

The discussion of a father's rights with respect to his daughter leads to the central theme of the chapter — the rights of a husband with respect to his wife, and the obligations he has toward her and her descendants. The Gemara begins its discussion of the conditions in the ketubah that define these rights and obligations, and the clarification of this subject which continues until the end of the tractate. In this chapter, the Gemara deals primarily with the husband's obligations by Torah law, which are also derived from the verses dealing with a maidservant who was taken by her master as his wife, as well as with the duties that were imposed on the husband by Rabbinic enactment.

TRANSLATION AND COMMENTARY

MISHNAH According to Jewish law, a girl is legally a minor until the end of her twelfth year. For six months after her twelfth birthday she remains under her father's guardianship and is called a *na'arah.* When she reaches the age of twelve-and-a-half she leaves her father's guardianship completely, is called a *bogeret,* and attains full legal majority. The ramifications of the father's guardianship over his daughter while she is a minor or a *na'arah* are discussed at length in this chapter.

נַעֲרָה שֶׁנִּתְפַּתְּתָה If a man seduces an unmarried girl between twelve and twelve-and-a-half years of age (a *na'arah*), he is liable for three payments: (1) An indemnity for the humiliation (בּוֹשֶׁת — literally "shame") he caused the girl; (2) compensation for her loss in value (פְּגָם — literally "blemish"), which is assessed according to the reduction in the girl's value caused by her loss of virginity; and (3) a fine (קְנָס) equivalent in value to "the virgins' dowry," i.e., two hundred zuz (see Exodus 22:16). If the man rapes the girl, he is liable for these three payments and in addition must pay an indemnity for the pain (צַעַר) suffered by the girl while being raped. [1]Our Mishnah explains that these payments are made to the father of the girl who was seduced or raped: **If a *na'arah* was seduced,** [2]**the payments for the humiliation** she suffered **and** for **her loss of value** now that she is no longer a virgin, **and** also **the fine** of two hundred zuz, are all paid by the seducer **to** the girl's **father.** [3]The father is **also** entitled to **the payment** made **for** the **pain** suffered by his daughter **in a case in which she was raped.**

עָמְדָה בַּדִּין [4]The Mishnah now considers who is entitled to receive these payments if the father dies after the seduction or the rape of his daughter: **If** the *na'arah* who was seduced or raped **came to court** to demand payment **before the father died,** [5]all the payments **belong to the father.** [6]Therefore, **if the father died** after his daughter sued the offender in court but before he could actually collect the money, the payments are made **to the** girl's **brothers,** who are their father's heirs. Once the father becomes entitled to the payments, the money is already considered to be his, so that it passes to his heirs in the event of his death.

LITERAL TRANSLATION

MISHNAH [1][Regarding] a *na'arah* who was seduced, [2][the payments for] her shame and her blemish, and her fine, belong to her father, [3]as well as the [payment for] pain in [the case of] a raped girl.

[4][If] she came to court (lit., "stood in judgment") before the father died, [5]they belong to [the] father. [6][If] the father died, they belong to [the] brothers.

נַעֲרָה

[1]שֶׁנִּתְפַּתְּתָה, [2]בּוֹשְׁתָּהּ וּפְגָמָהּ, וּקְנָסָהּ, שֶׁל אָבִיהָ, [3]וְהַצַּעַר בְּתְפוּסָה.
[4]עָמְדָה בַּדִּין עַד שֶׁלֹּא מֵת הָאָב, [5]הֲרֵי הֵן שֶׁל אָב. [6]מֵת הָאָב, הֲרֵי הֵן שֶׁל אַחִין.

RASHI

משנה נערה שנתפתתה. **והצער בתפוסה** – והצער נמי לאביה, באנוסה. **בתפוסה** – לישנא דקרא "ותפשה ושכב עמה" (דברים כב).

BACKGROUND

עָמְדָה בַּדִּין If she came to court. From the Mishnah's use of this term, *Rambam* infers that what is at issue is the fact that the claim has been made. If the girl has sued the rapist or the seducer, *even though the case has not been decided,* it is as though the father already has a right to the payment, and therefore his sons inherit it, as they inherit whatever else he leaves them.

NOTES

וְהַצַּעַר בְּתְפוּסָה As well as the payment for pain in the case of a raped girl. *Ramban* asks: Elsewhere (*Bava Kamma* 87b) the Gemara states that if someone causes a child a physical injury, the father of the child does not receive the compensation that must be paid for the child's pain and suffering. Why, then, is the father entitled to receive the payment for the pain suffered by his daughter when she was raped?

Ramban answers: Since the father is permitted to give his daughter in marriage to a man with whom she will find it painful to have sexual relations, he is also entitled to the monetary compensation for the pain she suffered during rape.

עָמְדָה בַּדִּין If she came to court. *Shittah Mekubbetzet* notes that the expression "if she came to court" does not imply that the *na'arah* alone can institute legal proceedings and demand compensation for her seduction or her rape. In fact, the father too is entitled to put forward a claim for compensation. The Mishnah speaks of the girl coming to court because it is about to consider the case in which the father has died and the girl alone can pursue the suit. Moreover, the Rishonim disagree about whether the girl by

HALAKHAH

נַעֲרָה שֶׁנִּתְפַּתְּתָה Regarding a *na'arah* who was seduced. "The three payments for which the seducer is liable (the payments for shame and blemish, and the fine) and the four payments for which the rapist is liable (the above-mentioned three and the payment for pain) are all made to the *na'arah*'s father. If she has no father, these payments belong to her," following the Mishnah. (*Rambam, Sefer Nashim, Hilkhot Na'arah Betulah* 2:14.)

עָמְדָה בַּדִּין If she came to court. "If a *na'arah* was seduced or raped, but did not sue the seducer or the rapist until after she reached full legal majority (at the age of twelve-and-a-half), or until after she married, or until after

TRANSLATION AND COMMENTARY

(According to Jewish law, a daughter only inherits her father's estate if he had no sons.) [1]But **if** the girl **did not go to court before her father died,** [2]and sued the seducer or the rapist only after her father's death, the payments **belong to** the girl **herself.** Since the father did not become entitled to the payments during his lifetime, he could not leave them to his sons. Sons inherit from their father those monies that have already been awarded to him, even if the father has not yet collected them. But they do not inherit from him *the right* to receive compensation from the girl's seducer or rapist.

עָמְדָה בַּדִּין [3]The Mishnah continues: **If** a *na'arah* who was seduced or raped **went to court** to demand payment **before she reached** full legal **majority,** i.e., before she reached the age of twelve-and-a-half and became a *bogeret,* [4]all the payments **belong to her father,** for until the girl becomes a *bogeret* she is considered to be under her father's guardianship. [5]Therefore, **if** the girl sued the seducer or the rapist before she became a *bogeret,* and then **her father died** before he could actually collect the money, the payments are made **to the** girl's **brothers,** even if in the meantime she has reached the age of twelve-and-a-half. Since the father had already become entitled to the payments before he died, the money is viewed as being his. Therefore, it passed to his heirs when he died. [6]But **if the girl did not go to court before she reached** full legal **majority,** and sued the seducer or the rapist only after she reached the age of twelve-and-a-half, [7]the payments **belong to** the girl **herself,** even if her father is still alive, for once a girl reaches full legal majority, at the age of twelve-and-a-half, she is no longer viewed as being under her father's guardianship.

[1]לֹא הִסְפִּיקָה לַעֲמוֹד בַּדִּין עַד שֶׁמֵּת הָאָב, [2]הֲרֵי הֵן שֶׁל עַצְמָהּ. [3]עָמְדָה בַּדִּין עַד שֶׁלֹּא בָּגְרָה, [4]הֲרֵי הֵן שֶׁל אָב. [5]מֵת הָאָב, הֲרֵי הֵן שֶׁל אַחִין. [6]לֹא הִסְפִּיקָה לַעֲמוֹד בַּדִּין עַד שֶׁבָּגְרָה, [7]הֲרֵי הֵן שֶׁל עַצְמָהּ.

LITERAL TRANSLATION

[1][If] she did not have time to come to court before the father died, [2]they belong to her. [3][If] she came to court before she matured, [4]they belong to [the] father. [5][If] the father died, they belong to [the] brothers. [6][If] she did not have time to come to court before she matured, [7]they belong to her.

RASHI

לא הספיקה לעמוד בדין כו׳ — כיון דלא עמדה בדין, לאו ממון הוא להורישו לבניו. ואמרינן לקמן (מג,א): אין אדם מוריש לבנו זכות שזכתה לו תורה בבתו, ויליף לה מקרא. **מת האב** — משעמדה בדין בנערותיה, בין בגרה קודם מיתה בין לא בגרה. **הרי הן של אחין** — דכיון דעמדה בדין זכה בהן אב.

BACKGROUND

הֲרֵי הֵן שֶׁל עַצְמָהּ They belong to her. A father's heirs have a right to inherit everything that comes to them from their father, whether the property actually exists (מוּחְזָק) at the time of his death or whether the father had a right to it but it had not yet come into his hands (רָאוּי). Only with respect to the double share to which the eldest son is entitled is there a difference between actual and potential property. However, as explained below (43a ff.), the father's right to the fine and the other damage payments that come to him through his daughter is not a normal property right that can be inherited; it is a personal right that is solely his own and cannot be transferred or left to others.

NOTES

herself has any standing before the court. *Ra'avad* argues that the girl cannot put forward the claim on her own behalf, because she is not viewed as the plaintiff in the case, since she will not receive the money if the suit succeeds (see *Rambam* and *Ra'avad, Sefer Nashim, Hilkhot Na'arah Betulah* 2:13).

הֲרֵי הֵן שֶׁל עַצְמָהּ They belong to her. Our commentary follows *Tosafot, Rosh* and *Rambam* (*Hilkhot Na'arah Betulah* 2:15), who explain that when the Mishnah says that if the girl was unable to go to court before her father died or before she reached full legal majority "they" belong to her, it means that *all* the payments mentioned in the Mishnah — the three payments for which the seducer is liable and the four payments for which the rapist is liable — belong to the girl.

Ramban, Rashba and others raise a number of objections against this position. They argue that if the girl was seduced, she herself is not entitled to any compensation whatsoever, for she engaged in sexual relations of her own free will, thus waiving all rights to compensation. If her father is alive and she has not yet reached full legal majority, he is entitled to compensation, for the girl cannot waive a payment to which her father is entitled. But if he died or she became a *bogeret* before the suit was brought, she cannot demand compensation on her own behalf. *Tosafot* and *Rosh* maintain that the girl is not viewed as having waived her rights for compensation, since at the time of her seduction these rights were not hers to waive, but rather her father's. Thus she herself can sue the seducer if a suit was not brought by her father before his death or before she came of age.

Ramban and *Rashba* argue that even in the case of rape the girl is entitled only to the fine and cannot demand the payments for shame, blemish or pain. The father's heirs do not inherit the fine if it was not awarded to him before he died, for until the fine has been awarded to him, it is not viewed as his to pass on as an inheritance. But the payments that the seducer or the rapist must make for the girl's shame, blemish and pain are ordinary financial obligations, and these are considered to exist even before

HALAKHAH

her father died, the payments awarded belong to her. If she sued the seducer or the rapist, and afterwards reached full legal majority or married, the payments belong to her father. If the father died after his daughter brought the suit, the payments belong to his sons who are his heirs, for the father became entitled to the money as soon as the suit was brought," following the Mishnah. (*Rambam, Sefer Nashim, Hilkhot Na'arah Betulah* 2:15.)

[1]רַבִּי שִׁמְעוֹן אוֹמֵר: אִם לֹא הִסְפִּיקָה לִגְבּוֹת עַד שֶׁמֵּת הָאָב, [2]הֲרֵי הֵן שֶׁל עַצְמָהּ.
[42A] [3]מַעֲשֵׂה יָדֶיהָ וּמְצִיאָתָהּ, [4]אַף עַל פִּי שֶׁלֹּא גָּבְתָה, [5]מֵת הָאָב, הֲרֵי הֵן שֶׁל אַחִין.

גמרא [6]מַאי קָא מַשְׁמַע לָן? [7]תְּנֵינָא: [8]"הַמְפַתֶּה נוֹתֵן שְׁלֹשָׁה דְּבָרִים, וְהָאוֹנֵס אַרְבָּעָה. [9]הַמְפַתֶּה נוֹתֵן בּוֹשֶׁת וּפְגָם וּקְנָס. [10]מוֹסִיף עָלָיו אוֹנֵס שֶׁנּוֹתֵן אֶת הַצַּעַר".

LITERAL TRANSLATION

[1]Rabbi Shimon says: If she did not have time to collect before the father died, [2]they belong to her. [42A] [3][Regarding] her handiwork and what she finds, [4]even though she has not [yet] collected, [5][if] the father has died, they belong to [the] brothers.

GEMARA [6]What is he teaching us? [7]We have [already] learned: [8]"The seducer gives three things, and the rapist four. [9]The seducer gives [payments for] shame and blemish and the fine. [10]A rapist adds to it in that he gives the [payment for] pain."

RASHI

רבי שמעון אומר — אף על פי שעמדה בדין לא הוי ממון דאב להורישו לבניו עד דמטי לידיה, ובגמרא יליף טעמא. **מעשה ידיה** — שעשתה בחיי אביה. **אף על פי שלא גבתה** — כגון שכר פעולה. **מת האב הרי הוא של אחים** — דמשבא לעולם זכה בו האב. ולא דמי לקנס, דלא הוי ממון עד שעמד בדין ויעידוהו, דהא אי מודה מיפטר. **מציאתה** — בגמרא פריך: ממאן גביא?

TRANSLATION AND COMMENTARY

רַבִּי שִׁמְעוֹן אוֹמֵר [1]**Rabbi Shimon** disagrees with the anonymous first Tanna of the Mishnah and **says:** Even if the *na'arah* went to court during her father's lifetime, and the seducer or the rapist was ordered to pay, **if she did not collect** the payments **before her father died,** [2]**they belong to** the girl **herself.** Even though the father became entitled to the payments before he died, the money is not considered his — so that it is passed on to his heirs — unless he received it during his lifetime.

מַעֲשֵׂה יָדֶיהָ [42A] [3]The Mishnah continues: Just as the father is entitled to the payments received from his daughter's seducer or rapist, so too is he entitled to her handiwork and to objects that she finds until she reaches full adulthood at the age of twelve-and-a-half. **The handiwork** produced by a young girl during her father's lifetime **and** the objects that **she finds** while her father is alive belong to her father, [4]**even if she has not yet collected** what she is owed. [5]Therefore, **if the father dies,** the payments for his daughter's handiwork and the objects that she has found **go to her brothers** as part of the legacy they inherit from their father. As soon as the girl picks up the lost object or produces the handiwork, it is already considered the father's property and passes to his heirs in the event of his death.

GEMARA מַאי קָא מַשְׁמַע לָן [6]The Gemara begins its analysis of the Mishnah by asking: **What does** the author of our Mishnah **teach us** that we would otherwise not have known? [7]Surely **we have already learned** elsewhere the principles laid down in our Mishnah, for there is an earlier Mishnah in our tractate (above, 39a) that states: [8]"A man who **seduces** a virgin *na'arah* must **give three things** in compensation, **whereas** a man who **rapes** a virgin *na'arah* must give **four.** [9]**The seducer pays** compensation **for** the girl's **shame** (her ruined reputation) **and blemish** (her loss of virginity) **in addition to the** fifty-shekel **fine** set by the Torah. [10]**A rapist must do more, in that he must** also **pay for** the **pain** suffered by the girl while being raped, in addition to the other three payments."

NOTES

the court orders they be paid. Thus the money is viewed as being the father's even before the matter comes before the court, and so it passes to his sons in the event of his death. According to *Tosafot,* an analogy is drawn by the Torah between the fine and the other payments, so that whenever the girl is entitled to the fine, she receives the other payments as well.

רַבִּי שִׁמְעוֹן אוֹמֵר **Rabbi Shimon says.** According to the straightforward reading of the Mishnah, we might draw the conclusion that Rabbi Shimon disagrees with the anonymous first Tanna on only one particular issue, but agrees with him about the rest. However, the Jerusalem Talmud and some Rishonim maintain that Rabbi Shimon also disagrees with the first clause of the Mishnah, which states that in the case of rape compensation must be made for the girl's pain, because Rabbi Shimon says elsewhere (above, 39a) that a rapist does not have to pay for the pain suffered by his victim. Some authorities (*Ramban* and others) suggest that the opinion that the rapist does not pay for pain is that of Rabbi Shimon as transmitted by his disciple Rabbi Shimon ben Yehudah, whereas the Tanna of our Mishnah had a different tradition about the opinion of Rabbi Shimon — that the rapist pays for pain as well.

אַף עַל פִּי שֶׁלֹּא גָּבְתָה **Even though she has not yet collected.** The phrase "even though she has not yet collected," as used in connection with something that a young girl finds, poses a certain difficulty, for a found object is not collected from anybody, but rather stumbled across and taken. The Gemara below (43a) discusses this point.

Our Mishnah rules that the girl's handiwork and what she finds belong to her brothers if her father has died, even though she did not collect what was due her during his

SAGES

רַבִּי שִׁמְעוֹן **Rabbi Shimon (bar Yoḥai).** See *Ketubot,* Part I, pp. 56–7.

TERMINOLOGY

מַאי קָא מַשְׁמַע לָן? תְּנֵינָא **What is he teaching us? We have already learned.** This expression is used when the Gemara is questioning a Mish- nah, a Baraita, or an Amoraic statement on the grounds that it is superfluous, having already been mentioned in a Mishnah.

CONCEPTS

בּוֹשֶׁת **Shame.** One of the five headings (חֲמִישָּׁה דְּבָרִים) under which a person may have to pay damages for an injury he caused another person. If the injured person has been shamed in the process, the person who caused the injury is obligated to compensate the person he injured for the shame he has caused him. The amount of the payment for בּוֹשֶׁת is evaluated according to the social standing of both the person who suffered the shame and the one who caused it. Payment is required under the heading of בּוֹשֶׁת, even if no physical injury was inflicted, provided that the shame was caused by a physical act. A person who verbally puts another to shame has no financial obligation to him under the heading of בּוֹשֶׁת.

פְּגָם **Blemish.** One of the categories of compensation that must be paid by a man who seduces or rapes a woman. פְּגָם is assessed according to the reduction in the woman's value caused by the loss of her virginity, if she were to be sold as a slave.

[1] לְאָבִיהָ אִיצְטְרִיךְ לֵיהּ.
[2] לְאָבִיהָ נַמִי פְּשִׁיטָא, [3] מִדְּקָא יָהֵיב מְפַתֶּה! [4] דְּאִי לְעַצְמָהּ, אַמַּאי יָהֵיב מְפַתֶּה? [5] מִדַּעְתָּהּ עֲבַד!
[6] עָמְדָה בַּדִּין אִיצְטְרִיכָא לֵיהּ, [7] פְּלוּגְתָּא דְּרַבִּי שִׁמְעוֹן וְרַבָּנַן.

LITERAL TRANSLATION

[1] It was necessary for him [to teach that the payments belong] to her father.

[2] [That they belong] to her father is also obvious, [3] from the fact that the seducer pays! [4] For if [the payments belong] to her, why does the seducer pay? [5] He acted with her consent!

[6] It was necessary for him [to teach the case where] she came to court, [7] [which is the subject of] a disagreement between Rabbi Shimon and the Rabbis.

TRANSLATION AND COMMENTARY

לְאָבִיהָ אִיצְטְרִיךְ לֵיהּ [1] In answer to this question, the Gemara now suggests that our Mishnah adds a provision of the law that was not specifically mentioned in the other Mishnah. The earlier Mishnah merely lists the various obligations that the seducer and the rapist must fulfill. Our Mishnah **was necessary** in order **to teach that the payments belong to** the girl's **father,** and not to the girl herself.

לְאָבִיהָ נַמִי פְּשִׁיטָא [2] The Gemara objects: **That** the payments **belong to** the girl's **father is also obvious,** [3] **from the fact that the seducer pays** anything at all! [4] **For if the payments belong to** the girl **herself, why should the seducer have to pay?** [5] Surely the girl **engaged in sexual relations** with the seducer **of her own free will,** and she therefore waived all rights to compensation! How, then, can she come later and demand compensation for her ruined reputation and for her loss of virginity, and require the seducer to pay a fine? If the seducer is required to make these payments, they can only be made to the girl's father, whose rights the girl cannot waive. Thus we return to our original question: What does our Mishnah teach us that we would otherwise not have known?

עָמְדָה בַּדִּין [6] The Gemara answers: Our Mishnah **was necessary** because it describes a situation in which the girl's **case was brought before the court,** and the seducer or the rapist was ordered to pay, but the father died before the payments were collected. [7] As the Mishnah explains, this case **is the subject of a disagreement between Rabbi Shimon and the Rabbis** as to whether the girl's brothers inherit the money from their father, or whether the money belongs to the girl herself.

RASHI

גמרא לאביה איצטריכא ליה – דלא תנן. **מדקא יהיב מפתה** – קנס ובושת ופגם – פשיטא דלאביה נינהו, דאי לדידה – הא אחלה גביה.

NOTES

lifetime. *Bah* (in his notes to *Rif*) points out that it would be wrong to infer from this that these things belong to the brothers only if during the father's lifetime she has already come to court and demanded payment, but that if she did not sue for the money before her father died, they belong to the girl herself. For the father is entitled to his daughter's handiwork as soon as it is produced, and so it passes to his heirs even if the girl did not come to court to demand payment before he died. The Mishnah does not go into detail about the case where the girl did not come to court to demand payment for her handiwork, because a person does not usually have to turn to the courts to collect his wages. By contrast, regarding the payments collected from the rapist or the seducer, the court must assess the compensation to which the girl is entitled for her pain and her shame.

Bet Aharon notes that the Mishnah's ruling regarding the girl's handiwork and what she finds follows the viewpoint of the anonymous first Tanna of the Mishnah. But Rabbi Shimon does not accept this ruling, for he maintains that the brothers inherit from their father only what has already been collected during his lifetime.

מִדַּעְתָּהּ עֲבַד He acted with her consent. The Gemara argues that even without our Mishnah we would have known that the payments mentioned in the Mishnah in the third chapter of *Ketubot* must be made to the father. The girl herself cannot have a claim against her seducer, because she waived her rights to compensation when she engaged in sexual relations with him of her own free will.

Tosafot and *Tosefot HaRosh* note that the Gemara could have argued that the other Mishnah speaks of the seduction of a minor and that it follows the opinion of the Sages (above, 40a), who maintain that the seducer pays a fine not only if he seduces a *na'arah* (a girl between twelve and twelve-and-a-half years of age), but also if he seduces a minor below the age of twelve. Were it not for our Mishnah we might have thought that the seducer must pay the fine to the girl, for a minor does not have the legal capacity to waive money to which she is entitled. But the Gemara does not make this suggestion because it assumes that this Mishnah in the third chapter speaks of the same case as the first Mishnah in that chapter, which refers explicitly to a *na'arah.*

Tosafot (*Sanhedrin* 73b) maintains that even a *na'arah* is entitled to compensation from her seducer, if before she agreed to have sexual relations with him she stated explicitly that she was not waiving her rights to the payments. According to this opinion, our Gemara's assumption that a *na'arah* waives her rights to compensation when she agrees to have sexual relations with the seducer is limited to the ordinary case in which the girl consents to the seducer's proposal without making such a stipulation (*Sukkat David*).

[1] תְּנַן הָתָם: [2] ״׳אָנַסְתָּ וּפִתִּיתָ אֶת בִּתִּי׳, [3] וְהוּא אוֹמֵר: ׳לֹא אָנַסְתִּי וְלֹא פִּתִּיתִי׳. [4] ׳מַשְׁבִּיעֲךָ אֲנִי׳, [5] וְאָמַר: ׳אָמֵן׳, [6] וְאַחַר כָּךְ הוֹדָה, חַיָּיב. [7] רַבִּי שִׁמְעוֹן פּוֹטֵר, שֶׁאֵינוֹ מְשַׁלֵּם קְנָס עַל פִּי עַצְמוֹ. [8] אָמְרוּ לוֹ: אַף עַל פִּי שֶׁאֵינוֹ מְשַׁלֵּם קְנָס עַל פִּי עַצְמוֹ, [9] אֲבָל מְשַׁלֵּם בּוֹשֶׁת וּפְגָם עַל פִּי עַצְמוֹ״.

LITERAL TRANSLATION

[1] We have learned elsewhere: [2] "[If the father says:] 'You raped or seduced my daughter,' [3] and he says: 'I did not rape [her] and I did not seduce [her],' [4] [and the father says:] 'I adjure you,' [5] and he said: 'Amen,' [6] and afterwards he confessed, he is liable. [7] Rabbi Shimon exempts [him], for he does not pay a fine on his own [confession]. [8] They said to him: Even though he does not pay a fine on his own [confession], [9] nevertheless he pays [for] shame and blemish on his own [confession]."

TRANSLATION AND COMMENTARY

תְּנַן הָתָם [1] The Gemara continues: If someone takes an oath, falsely denying a debt, and then later admits that his oath was false, he must pay the debt and add one-fifth to it, and must bring a ram as a guilt-offering. These regulations apply only if the person falsely denies an ordinary monetary obligation. But they are not applicable when a person falsely denies liability to pay a fine, for if a person admits to a transgression punishable by a fine before he is convicted in court, he is not liable to pay that fine. **We have learned elsewhere** in a Mishnah (*Shevuot* 36b) how these laws apply to the payments imposed on the seducer or the rapist. [2] The Mishnah states: **"If a father claims** in court: **'You raped or seduced my daughter,'** which is an allegation containing a claim for the payment of a fifty-shekel fine as well as compensation for the girl's ruined reputation and loss of virginity (and her pain, in the case of rape), [3] **and** the defendant **answers: 'I did not rape her nor did I seduce her,** and thus I owe you nothing,' [4] **and the father says: 'I demand that you swear** that you neither raped nor seduced my daughter,' [5] **and** the defendant **says: 'Amen,'** thus confirming his denial by taking an oath, [6] **and he afterwards confesses** that he did indeed rape or seduce the girl and that he swore falsely, **he is liable** and must pay the fine and the other monetary penalties for his crime, must add one-fifth, and must bring the guilt-offering that is brought for the false denial of a debt. This is the opinion of the Sages. [7] But **Rabbi Shimon exempts** the defendant from payment and from bringing the guilt-offering, **for he would not have had to pay the fine on** the basis of **his own confession.** If the defendant had admitted at the outset that he had raped or seduced the girl, he would not have been held liable to pay the fine. Thus, when he denied the offense, he did not deny a monetary obligation, and so he is not liable to make the payments or to bring the guilt-offering. [8] The Sages countered this argument and **said to** Rabbi Shimon: **Even though he would not have had to pay the fine on** the basis of **his own confession,** [9] **he would nevertheless have had to pay** compensation **for** the girl's **shame and blemish on** the basis of **his own confession."** If the defendant had admitted at the outset that he had raped or seduced the girl, he would indeed have been exempt from paying the fine. But he would still have had to pay for the girl's ruined reputation and for her loss of virginity, because those payments are not fines imposed by the court

RASHI

אנסת ופיתית = או פיתית. **חייב** — קרן וחומש ואשם, אם הודה אחרי כן, וזהו אשם גזילות. **שאינו משלם קנס על פי עצמו** — אלא על פי עדים. וכיון דאילו אודי ליה קמן כשתבעו הוה מיפטר, כי כפריה, נמי, אין זו שבועת כפירת ממון. **אבל משלם בושת ופגם** — דממונא הוא, ואשתכח דממונא כפריה. ולקמן מפרש טעמא דרבנן, דקא סברי: סתם טוען ״אנסת״ — לא תבעו אלא בושת ופגם, ולא נשבע זה על כפירת קנס.

TERMINOLOGY

תְּנַן הָתָם We have learned elsewhere. A term used to introduce a quotation from a Mishnah not at present under discussion (usually from another tractate or another chapter of the tractate being studied), but which has a bearing on the present discussion.

NOTES

״מַשְׁבִּיעֲךָ אֲנִי״ "I adjure you." The oath discussed here, known as "the oath of a deposit," is mentioned in Leviticus (5:20-26), and is discussed at length in tractate *Shevuot*. If one person owes something to another (for example, if he is holding a deposit which belongs to the other person, or if he stole something from him), and the other person demands it from him, and the debtor first takes an oath that he does not owe him anything and later admits that he swore falsely, he must make restitution for what he falsely denied, and in addition he must pay the injured party an extra one-fifth, as well as give a ram as a guilt-offering ("a guilt-offering for robbery"). Someone who falsely denies a debt is held liable to pay the extra one-fifth and to bring the guilt-offering only if certain conditions are met — for

HALAKHAH

״אָנַסְתָּ וּפִתִּיתָ אֶת בִּתִּי״ "You raped or seduced my daughter." "If someone brings a monetary suit against another person, and this suit includes a claim for the payment of a fine, as well as a claim for ordinary monetary compensation, and the defendant denies the entire claim under oath and then later admits that he swore falsely, he is liable for the guilt-offering that is brought for the false denial of a debt. How so? If a person claims that someone raped or seduced his daughter, and the defendant falsely denies the allegation under oath, he is held liable to make monetary

LITERAL TRANSLATION

[1] Abaye asked Rabbah: [2] [If] someone says to his fellow: "You raped or seduced my daughter, and I took you to court, and you were found liable to [pay] me money," [3] and he says: "I did not rape [her] and I did not seduce [her], and you did not take me to court, and I was not found liable to [pay] you money," [4] and he swore, and [later] confessed, [5] what [is the law] according to Rabbi Shimon? [6] Since he came to court, [7] is it money and he is liable for the sacrifice for an oath? [8] Or perhaps, even though he came to court, it is a fine?

[1] בְּעָא מִינֵּיהּ אַבַּיֵי מֵרַבָּה: [2] הָאוֹמֵר לַחֲבֵירוֹ: "אָנַסְתָּ וּפִיתִּיתָ אֶת בִּתִּי, וְהֶעֱמַדְתִּיךְ בַּדִּין, וְנִתְחַיַּיבְתָּ לִי מָמוֹן", [3] וְהוּא אוֹמֵר: "לֹא אָנַסְתִּי וְלֹא פִּיתִּיתִי, וְלֹא הֶעֱמַדְתַּנִי בַּדִּין, וְלֹא נִתְחַיַּיבְתִּי לְךָ מָמוֹן", [4] וְנִשְׁבַּע, וְהוֹדָה, [5] לְרַבִּי שִׁמְעוֹן מַאי? [6] כֵּיוָן דַּעֲמַד בַּדִּין, [7] מָמוֹנָא הֲוַאי וּמִיחַיַּיב עֲלֵיהּ קׇרְבַּן שְׁבוּעָה? [8] אוֹ דִּלְמָא, אַף עַל גַּב דַּעֲמַד בַּדִּין, קְנָס הָוֵי?

TRANSLATION AND COMMENTARY

but ordinary monetary obligations. Thus, when the defendant denied raping or seducing the girl, he was denying a monetary obligation, and he must therefore make the payments and bring the guilt-offering required for the false denial of a debt. The Gemara below (42b) will explain the two sides of the dispute.

בְּעָא מִינֵּיהּ [1] The Gemara now considers a variant of the case discussed in the Mishnah in tractate *Shevuot* just quoted. **Abaye asked Rabbah:** [2] **If one person says to another: "You raped or seduced my daughter, and I took you to court** and demanded the fine and the compensation to which I am entitled, **and** the court **found you liable to pay me,** but I have still not received the money," [3] **and** the defendant denies the allegation completely and **says: "I did not rape** your daughter **nor did I seduce her, nor did you** ever **take me to court** and demand me to make payments of any kind, **nor was I** ever **found liable to pay you** anything," [4] **and he takes an oath** to confirm his claim, **and later confesses** that he swore falsely, [5] **what is the law according to Rabbi Shimon?** Is he required to make the payments and to bring the guilt-offering for the false denial of a debt, or not? Abaye now examines both sides of the question: In the case of the Mishnah in tractate *Shevuot,* Rabbi Shimon exempted the defendant from making the payments and from bringing the guilt-offering, arguing that he did not deny an ordinary monetary obligation, but only a fine which he would not have had to pay had he admitted his offense at the outset. [6] But in this case, the father claims that the defendant **has** already **been taken to court** and has already been found liable to pay the fine. Now, once the court finds a person liable and orders him to pay, [7] even a fine **is** considered **an ordinary monetary obligation.** Therefore, when he now confesses that he lied when he denied the claim, **he should be liable for the sacrifice** that must be brought **for** falsely denying a debt under **oath.** [8] On the other hand, argues Abaye, **perhaps, even though** the defendant **has** already **been taken to court** and has been found liable to pay, he is still exempt, because he denied a debt that was originally imposed upon him as **a fine** and not as an ordinary monetary obligation.

RASHI

בעא מיניה אביי מרבה — בר נחמני, דרביה הוה. **כיון דעמד בדין** — כבר. ואי הוה מודי ליה קמן — הוה משלם, שכבר חייבוהו בית דין ראשון על פי עדים, השתא ממונא כפריה — וחייב. **או דלמא אף על גב דעמד בדין** — ואי מודה הוה מיחייב, אפילו הכי לא מיחייב בכפירתו קרבן שבועה, הואיל ועיקרו קנס, ולא חייבה תורה קרבן שבועה אלא על פקדון ותשומת יד וכיוצא בהן.

BACKGROUND

מָמוֹן וּקְנָס **Money and a fine.** The difference between a monetary payment and a fine is not expressed only in the fact that someone who admits to an offense punishable by a fine is exempt from paying the fine. The basis of the difference lies in the fact that monetary payments are legal obligations, so that in this respect the restoration of a deposit, or the payment of wages, or the payment of damages, are all legal obligations, and do not depend in themselves on a court decision. While a creditor may go to court to force a debtor to pay, and occasionally to fix the amount of payment, a fine is essentially a punishment imposed by the Torah upon a person who has committed a transgression either through his person or through his property, and the obligation to pay a fine derives not from the action but rather from the court's authority to impose punishments. Therefore fines may be imposed only by a court authorized to do so, in accordance with the conditions and limitations that apply to the imposition of punishments.

NOTES

example, if he denies a debt that he would have been required to pay had he admitted to it at the outset (to the exclusion of a fine). *Tosafot* notes that he is held liable to pay the extra one-fifth and to bring the guilt-offering only if the claim brought against him is related to a specific object from which the claimant was to receive payment. Even in cases where he is exempt from the "guilt-offering for robbery," he may still be liable for a sin-offering for having taken a false oath.

אוֹ דִּלְמָא, אַף עַל גַּב דַּעֲמַד בַּדִּין, קְנָס הָוֵי **Or perhaps, even though he came to court, it is a fine?** The texts of the Talmud used by the majority of the Rishonim add the words אוֹ דִּלְמָא אַף עַל פִּי דַּעֲמַד בַּדִּין קְנָס הָוֵי וּמוֹדֶה בִקְנָס פָּטוּר, so that the full sentence reads: "Or perhaps, even though he came to court, it is a fine, and someone who admits to a fine is exempt?" But *Rashi*'s reading omits these extra three words and reads: אוֹ דִּלְמָא אַף עַל גַּב דַּעֲמַד בַּדִּין קְנָס הָוֵי — "Or perhaps, even though he came to court, it is a fine?" Our text follows the standard text of the printed Talmud, which is in accordance with the reading adopted by *Rashi.*

HALAKHAH

restitution and to bring the guilt-offering. Since he would have been liable to offer compensation for the girl's shame and blemish, he is regarded as having falsely denied an ordinary monetary obligation which he was already liable to pay," following the Sages in the Mishnah in *Shevuot.* (*Rambam, Sefer Hafla'ah, Hilkhot Shevuot* 8:3.)

TRANSLATION AND COMMENTARY

אָמַר לֵיהּ [1] Rabbah **said to** Abaye: Since the defendant has been ordered to pay, the fine **is** considered **an ordinary monetary obligation.** [2] Thus, **he is liable for the sacrifice** that must be brought **for** taking **an oath** falsely denying a debt.

אֵיתִיבֵיהּ [3] Abaye **raised an objection against** Rabbah's position from the following Baraita: [4] **"Rabbi Shimon says: I might have thought that if one person says to another: 'You raped or seduced my daughter,'** [5] **and** the other person **answers: 'I did not rape** your daughter, **nor did I seduce her';** [6] **or if one person says to another: 'Your ox killed my** non-Jewish **slave,** and you are therefore liable to pay a fine of thirty shekalim [Exodus 21:32],' [7] **and** the owner of the ox **answers:** 'My ox **did not kill** your slave'; [8] **or if** someone's non-Jewish **slave says to him: 'You knocked out my tooth or you blinded my eye,** and you must therefore set me free [Exodus 21:26-27],' [9] **and** the master **replies: 'I did not knock out your tooth, nor did I blind you,'** [10] **and** the defendant in each of the cases **takes an oath** to confirm his claim, **and** he **later confesses** that he swore falsely — [11] in each of these cases **I might have thought that** the defendant **is** held **liable** to bring a guilt-offering for falsely denying an obligation that he has toward another person. [12] **Therefore the Torah states** in its discussion of the liability of someone who falsely denies a debt (Leviticus 5:21-22): 'If a person sinned, and committed a trespass against the Lord, **and lied to his neighbor regarding a deposit or regarding a loan or regarding something taken by violence,** [13] **or oppressed his neighbor, or found something that was lost and lied about it and swore**

[1] אָמַר לֵיהּ: מָמוֹנָא הָוֵי, [2] וּמִיחַיַּיב עֲלֵיהּ קָרְבַּן שְׁבוּעָה. [3] אֵיתִיבֵיהּ: [4] ״רַבִּי שִׁמְעוֹן אוֹמֵר: יָכוֹל הָאוֹמֵר לַחֲבֵירוֹ: ׳אָנַסְתָּ וּפִיתִּיתָ אֶת בִּתִּי׳, [5] וְהוּא אוֹמֵר: ׳לֹא אָנַסְתִּי וְלֹא פִיתִּיתִי׳; [6] ׳הֵמִית שׁוֹרְךָ אֶת עַבְדִּי׳, [7] וְהוּא אוֹמֵר: ׳לֹא הֵמִית׳; [8] אוֹ שֶׁאָמַר לוֹ עַבְדּוֹ: ׳הִפַּלְתָּ אֶת שִׁינִּי וְסִימִּיתָ אֶת עֵינִי׳, [9] וְהוּא אוֹמֵר: ׳לֹא הִפַּלְתִּי וְלֹא סִימִּיתִי׳, [10] וְנִשְׁבַּע, וְהוֹדָה — [11] יָכוֹל יְהֵא חַיָּיב. [12] תַּלְמוּד לוֹמַר: ׳וְכִחֵשׁ בַּעֲמִיתוֹ בְּפִקָּדוֹן אוֹ בִתְשׂוּמֶת יָד אוֹ בְגָזֵל, [13] אוֹ עָשַׁק אֶת עֲמִיתוֹ, אוֹ מָצָא אֲבֵדָה וְכִחֶשׁ בָּהּ וְנִשְׁבַּע

LITERAL TRANSLATION

[1] He said to him: It is money, [2] and he is liable for the sacrifice for an oath.

[3] He raised an objection against him: [4] "Rabbi Shimon says: I might have thought that [if] someone says to his fellow: 'You raped or seduced my daughter,' [5] and he says: 'I did not rape [her] and I did not seduce [her]'; [6] [or if someone claims]: 'Your ox killed my slave,' [7] and he says: 'It did not kill [him]'; [8] or if his slave said to him: 'You knocked out my tooth or you blinded my eye,' [9] and he says: 'I did not knock out [your tooth] and I did not blind [you],' [10] and he swore, and [later] confessed — [11] I might have thought that he is liable. [12] Therefore the Torah states: 'And he lied to his neighbor regarding a deposit or regarding a loan or regarding something taken by violence, [13] or oppressed his neighbor, or found something that was lost and lied about it and swore

RASHI

הפלת את שיני — נמי קנסא הוא, שהרי ממונו הוא, כאחד מן החמורים.

BACKGROUND

תְּשׂוּמֶת יָד וְעוֹשֶׁק A loan and oppression. The term תְּשׂוּמֶת יָד — the misappropriation of a loan — is interpreted by the Rabbis as being different from the illegal taking of a pledge (which is explicitly mentioned in the verse) that someone leaves or promises to leave with his fellow as security for a loan. The term עוֹשֶׁק — oppression — is also interpreted not as a general expression, but as a term with a narrow meaning based on its use in other verses such as Deuteronomy 24:14: "You shall not oppress a hired laborer who is poor and needy" (see also Malachi 3:5), meaning failure to pay a worker's wages.

NOTES

Which of the two readings is adopted leads to a vastly different understanding of Abaye's question and the discussion that follows. According to *Rashi,* Abaye's question is limited to one specific issue, liability to bring the guilt-offering for the false denial of a debt which had been originally imposed upon the defendant as a fine. Once the court finds the defendant liable to pay a fine, that fine is treated as any other monetary obligation, so that the defendant pays the fine on the basis of his own confession and must pay the claimant's sons, if the claimant himself dies before collecting the fine. The question therefore arises as to whether the defendant is held liable to bring a guilt-offering if he falsely denied such a debt, for he denied a debt that is now an ordinary monetary obligation. On the other hand, perhaps the defendant should be exempt from the guilt-offering, since the debt was originally imposed upon him as a fine.

But according to the reading accepted by most Rishonim, Abaye asks a much more fundamental question: After the court finds the defendant liable to pay a fine, is that fine treated as an ordinary monetary obligation, so that he is held liable to pay on the basis of his own confession, and he is held liable to bring a guilt-offering if he falsely denies the debt? Or is that fine still treated as a fine even after the defendant is ordered to pay by the court, so that he would be exempt from paying it on the basis of his own confession, and he would be exempt from bringing a guilt-offering for a false denial of the obligation?

Tosafot and many others try to explain what compelled *Rashi* to emend the text, and they point out the numerous difficulties with his position. Most Rishonim (*Ramban, Ra'ah, Rashba,* and *Ritva*) accept the reading that includes the extra three words, and they understand Abaye's question as it was explained above, though they differ slightly on certain details. This approach is adopted in our commentary.

עַל שָׁקֶר׳. [1]מָה אֵלּוּ מְיוּחָדִין שֶׁהֵן מָמוֹן, [2]אַף כָּל שֶׁהֵן מָמוֹן. [3]יָצְאוּ אֵלּוּ, שֶׁהֵן קְנָס״.

[42B] [4]מַאי לָאו בְּשֶׁעָמַד בַּדִּין? [5]לֹא, בְּשֶׁלֹּא עָמַד בַּדִּין.

LITERAL TRANSLATION

falsely.' [1]Just as these are special in that they are money, [2]so all [things] that are money [are included]. [3]These are excluded because they are fines."

[42B] [4]Is it not where he was brought (lit., "stood") to court? [5]No, it is where he was not brought to court.

TRANSLATION AND COMMENTARY

falsely.' It is from these verses that we learn in which cases a guilt-offering must be brought for falsely denying a debt. A guilt-offering must be brought not only in those cases mentioned specifically in the verses, but in any case analogous to them. [1]**Just as** the cases listed in these verses — deposit, loan, theft, wages, and found property — **are special in that they** involve **ordinary monetary claims,** and a guilt-offering must be brought if the claim was falsely denied, [2]**so** too in **all cases that** involve **ordinary monetary claims** the sacrifice must be offered if the defendant swore falsely to deny the claim. [3]This specifically **excludes those** cases that involve claims for the payment of **fines** — for example, the fines that must be paid by a rapist or a seducer, or by someone whose ox killed another person's slave."

מַאי לָאו [42B] [4]The Gemara now explains how this Baraita poses a difficulty for Rabbah: **Does** the Baraita **not** speak of a case **in which** the defendant **has** already **been taken to court** and has been found liable to pay, and then the plaintiff brings him back to court to demand payment and the defendant denies the claim? And yet Rabbi Shimon rules that the defendant is held liable to bring a guilt-offering only if he falsely denied an ordinary monetary obligation, but not if he lied under oath about an obligation that was originally imposed upon him as a fine; and surely this contradicts the viewpoint of Rabbah!

לֹא [5]Rabbah refutes this objection: **No,** the Baraita speaks of a case **in which** the defendant **has not** yet **been brought to court** and has not yet been ordered to pay by the court. Thus the defendant is held liable to bring a guilt-offering only if he falsely denied an ordinary monetary obligation, but not if he denied a fine, which he would not have had to pay had he admitted to the offense at the outset. But if the defendant has already been taken to court and has been found liable to pay, and later he falsely denies the claim when the plaintiff comes to demand payment, the defendant is indeed held liable to bring a guilt-offering

RASHI

מאי לאו בשעמד בדין — בבית דין אחד, ובאו עדים באותו בית דין, וחייבוהו בית דין על פיהם, ועכשיו זה תובעו מה שחייבוהו בית דין, וחזר וכפר, וקתני: פטור. **בשלא עמד בדין** — ועדיין לא העידו עדים.

NOTES

בְּשֶׁלֹּא עָמַד בַּדִּין Where he was not brought to court. *Tosafot* and other Rishonim ask: If the Baraita speaks of a case in which the defendant has not been brought to court and ordered to pay, Rabbi Shimon should not need a special verse to teach us that the defendant is not held liable to bring a guilt-offering if he denies an offense punishable by a fine. For in such a case even the Sages agree that there is no guilt-offering, because the defendant can exempt himself from paying the fine by admitting to his offense before the court finds him liable, and thus a situation will not arise in which he has denied money he already owes the plaintiff.

Ra'avad and *Ramban* answer: Rabbi Shimon needs the verse in order to teach us that the seducer and the rapist are exempt from the guilt-offering if they falsely deny their liability, even though they have not only denied a crime punishable by a fine, but have also denied ordinary monetary obligations, such as the compensation for the girl's ruined reputation and loss of virginity. *Ra'avad* infers from the case of a deposit that the defendant is held liable to bring the guilt-offering only if he denied a debt that was entirely an ordinary monetary obligation, but not if he denied a debt that was partly a fine and partly an ordinary monetary obligation.

Other authorities (*Rashba* and *Ritva*; but see *Rabbi Crescas Vidal* who rejects this explanation) add that Rabbi Shimon needed the verse for a case in which the defendant denied that his ox had killed someone else's slave or the defendant denied that he had knocked out his slave's tooth or blinded him. The fine takes the place of the defendant's ordinary monetary obligations, for when he pays the fine he does not have to pay the other person the slave's value or compensate his own slave for the loss of his tooth or his eyesight. But even so, the defendant is exempt from bringing a guilt-offering if he falsely denies his liability, for he is denying a fine that he would have been exempt from paying had he admitted to it at the outset.

HALAKHAH

יָצְאוּ אֵלּוּ, שֶׁהֵן קְנָס These are excluded, because they are fines. "If someone brings a monetary claim against another person which the defendant would not be required to pay if he admitted his transgression before being convicted by the court (e.g., if he claims the payment of a fine, which the defendant would not have to pay on the basis of his own confession), and the defendant falsely denies the claim under oath and later admits that he swore falsely, he is exempt from the guilt-offering that is brought for the false denial of a debt, but he is liable for having sworn falsely." (*Rambam, Sefer Hafla'ah, Hilkhot Shevuot* 7:2.)

TRANSLATION AND COMMENTARY

even in the case of a fine, for once a fine has been imposed on him, it is treated as an ordinary monetary obligation.

וְהָא מִדְּרֵישָׁא [1]Abaye now objects to this interpretation of the Baraita: **But surely since the first clause** of the Baraita **speaks of** a situation **in which** the defendant **has** already **been brought to court** and found liable to pay, [2]it is reasonable to assume that **the second clause** of the Baraita **also speaks of** a case **in which** the defendant **has** already **been brought to court** and ordered to pay. [3]The Gemara now quotes **the first clause** of the Baraita, which **states:** "Were it not for a special Biblical expression amplifying the scope of the law, **I would only know** that the defendant must bring a guilt-offering if he falsely denies a **claim for the payment of the principal,** for the verses speak of someone who falsely denies a deposit, or a loan, or something he has stolen, or wages that he owes his worker, or something he has found, and in all of these cases a claim is put forward for the return of the principal to its rightful owner. [4]But as for **the double payment** (when the thief must repay twice the value of the stolen article: the principal — the article itself or its value — and an additional payment equal to the value of the stolen article), or **the fourfold and fivefold payment** (when someone steals and then sells or slaughters a sheep, he is obliged to repay its owner four times the value of the sheep, and if the stolen animal is an ox, five times the value of the ox), **or the payments** made by **a rapist and** by **a seducer, and** the payment made by **a slanderer** (someone who falsely maintains that his wife was not a virgin when she married him and who brings false witnesses who testify that she committed adultery while betrothed to him, must pay his wife's father a fine of one hundred shekels) — [5]**from where do we know** that someone who falsely denies one of these obligations is also held liable to bring a guilt-offering? [6]**The verse states** (Leviticus 5:21): 'If a person sinned **and committed a trespass.'** This general term that precedes the detailed list of offenses for which the guilt-offering must be brought is intended to **include** other cases of sin and trespass, involving double payment, fourfold and fivefold payment, and the payments of the rapist, the seducer and the slanderer."

הֵיכִי דָּמֵי [7]The Gemara now demonstrates why the first clause of the Baraita must refer to a situation where the defendant has already been brought to court and found liable to pay. **How do we visualize the case** dealt with by the first clause of the Baraita? [8]**If** the defendant **has not** previously **been brought to court** and ordered to pay the fine, **is** he liable for the **double payment,** which would mean that his false

[1]וְהָא מִדְּרֵישָׁא בְּשֶׁעָמַד בַּדִּין, [2]סֵיפָא נַמִי בְּשֶׁעָמַד בַּדִּין. [3]דְּקָתָנֵי רֵישָׁא: ״אֵין לִי אֶלָּא דְּבָרִים שֶׁמְּשַׁלְּמִין עֲלֵיהֶם אֶת הַקֶּרֶן. [4]תַּשְׁלוּמֵי כֶפֶל, תַּשְׁלוּמֵי אַרְבָּעָה וַחֲמִשָּׁה, וְהָאוֹנֵס, וְהַמְפַתֶּה, וּמוֹצִיא שֵׁם רַע — [5]מִנַּיִן? [6]תַּלְמוּד לוֹמַר: ׳וּמָעֲלָה מַעַל׳ רִיבָּה״.

[7]הֵיכִי דָּמֵי? [8]אִי דְּלָא עָמַד בַּדִּין, כְּפֵילָא מִי אִיכָּא?

LITERAL TRANSLATION

[1]But surely since the first clause [refers to] where he was brought to court, [2]the last clause also [refers to] where he was brought to court. [3]For the first clause teaches: "I have only things for which they pay the principal. [4]The double payment, the fourfold and fivefold payments, and [the payments of] a rapist, and a seducer, and a slanderer — [5]from where [do I know about these]? [6]The Torah says: 'And committed a trespass,' [which] includes [them]."

[7]How do we visualize the case? [8]If he was not brought to court, is there double payment?

RASHI

והא מדרישא — מילתייהו דרבנן דאיפליגו עליה וחייבוהו קרבן שבועה איירי בשעמד בדין, מכלל דסיפא, כלומר רבי שמעון, דאתא לאיפלוגי עלייהו — בדכוותה איירי. **אין לי** — שיתחייב קרן וחומש ואשם. **כפילא מי איכא** — מי יימר דגנב, דתבעיה כפילא? **ועוד:** דלמא מודי ומיפטר.

CONCEPTS

תַּשְׁלוּמֵי כֶפֶל The double payment. A thief must repay twice the value of a stolen article (Exodus 22:3), i.e., he must restore the article itself to its legal owner and make an additional payment equal to the value of the article. This obligation is considered a fine (קְנָס). Accordingly, a thief is required to make this payment only if he is apprehended. If he voluntarily admits his wrongdoing and desires to restore the stolen article or its value, he does not have to make the additional payment. Similarly, a person who swears that something placed in his care was stolen, is also obligated to pay כֶּפֶל if the object is found to be still in his possession.

תַּשְׁלוּמֵי אַרְבָּעָה וַחֲמִשָּׁה The fourfold or fivefold payments. A person who steals an ox, and then sells or slaughters it, is obligated to reimburse its owner at the rate of five times the value of the stolen animal. If the stolen animal is a sheep, the restitution is four times the animal's worth (Exodus 21:37). The Sages offered various explanations as to why the thief must pay more for an ox than for a sheep: (1) The theft of an ox causes additional loss to its owner, who cannot use it for plowing. (2) Someone who steals a sheep carries it on his shoulders, and at least suffers fatigue while committing the crime. (3) Someone who steals an ox, which is large and difficult to lead away and hide, may be assumed to be an habitual thief.

NOTES

כְּפֵילָא מִי אִיכָּא? Is there double payment? *Rashi* first explains this expression as follows: If the defendant has not yet been brought to court, is there double payment? If he has not yet been convicted, what proof is there that he stole anything and is therefore held liable to make the double payment? *Ritva* (citing an objection by *Tosafot* which does not appear in the text of *Tosafot* in the standard edition of the Gemara) remarks that the same question can be asked about any other claim, and asks: If the court has not yet found in favor of the plaintiff, why should the defendant be held liable to pay anything? What, then, is special about the double payment?

Our commentary follows the second explanation offered by *Rashi*: If the defendant has not yet been brought to court, can he already be liable for the double payment, with the result that he must bring a guilt-offering if he denies the debt? Since he can still confess to his transgression and exempt himself from paying the fine, his denial of the claim is not to be viewed as a denial of money that he already owes the plaintiff.

[1]אֶלָּא פְּשִׁיטָא בְּשֶׁעָמַד בַּדִּין. [2]וּמִדְּרֵישָׁא בְּשֶׁעָמַד בַּדִּין, [3]סֵיפָא נַמִי בְּשֶׁעָמַד בַּדִּין!
[4]אֲמַר לֵיהּ: [5]יָכֵילְנָא לְשַׁנּוּיֵי לָךְ: רֵישָׁא בְּשֶׁעָמַד בַּדִּין, [6]וְסֵיפָא בְּשֶׁלֹּא עָמַד בַּדִּין, [7]וְכוּלָּהּ רַבִּי שִׁמְעוֹן הִיא. [8]וְשִׁינּוּיֵי דְּחִיקֵי לָא מְשַׁנֵּינַן לָךְ, [9]דְּאִם כֵּן, אָמְרַתְּ לִי: [10]לִיתְנֵי רֵישָׁא: ״רַבִּי שִׁמְעוֹן אוֹמֵר״, [11]אוֹ לִיתְנֵי סֵיפָא: ״דִּבְרֵי רַבִּי שִׁמְעוֹן״. [12]אֶלָּא, כּוּלָּהּ בְּשֶׁעָמַד בַּדִּין, [13]וְרֵישָׁא רַבָּנַן, [14]וְסֵיפָא רַבִּי שִׁמְעוֹן.

LITERAL TRANSLATION

[1]Rather it is obvious [that it is] where he was brought to court. [2]And since the first clause [refers to] where he was brought to court, [3]the last clause also [refers to] where he was brought to court!

[4]He said to him: [5]I could answer you: The first clause [refers to] where he was brought to court, [6]and the last clause [refers to] where he was not brought to court, [7]and all of it is [in accordance with] Rabbi Shimon. [8]But I will not answer you [with] forced answers, [9]for if so, you could say to me: [10]Let the first clause teach: "Rabbi Shimon says," [11]or let the last clause teach: "[These are] the words of Rabbi Shimon." [12]Rather, all of it is where he was brought to court, [13]and the first clause is [in accordance with] the Rabbis, [14]and the last clause is [in accordance with] Rabbi Shimon.

TRANSLATION AND COMMENTARY

denial of the debt renders him liable to bring a guilt-offering? Surely he could have exempted himself from the double payment by admitting to his offense before being convicted by the court. And all agree that a person is not held liable to bring a guilt-offering for having falsely denied a claim brought against him, if he could have exempted himself from payment by admitting the claim at the outset. [1]**Rather,** says the Gemara, **it is obvious that** the first clause of the Baraita must be dealing with a case **in which** the defendant **has** already **been brought to court** and found liable to pay the fine, which he later denies when the plaintiff brings him back to court and demands payment. [2]**And since the first clause** of the Baraita **speaks of** a case **in which** the defendant **has** already **been brought to court,** [3]it is reasonable to assume that **the second clause** of the Baraita **also speaks of** a case **in which** the defendant **has** already **been brought to court.** Nevertheless Rabbi Shimon rules that the defendant does not have to bring a guilt-offering if he falsely denied liability for a fine, and this surely contradicts the viewpoint of Rabbah!

אֲמַר לֵיהּ [4]Rabbah **said to** Abaye: If I wanted, **I could answer your** objection in the following way: [5]**The first clause** of the Baraita **speaks of** a case **in which** the defendant **has** already **been brought to court,** [6]**and the second clause speaks of** a case **in which he has not** yet **been brought to court.** [7]**And the entire** Baraita **is in accordance with** the viewpoint of **Rabbi Shimon.** Therefore, the first clause states that the defendant is held liable to bring a guilt-offering even when he denies a fine, for once he has been brought to court and ordered to pay, the fine is treated like any other monetary obligation. And the second clause states that he is exempt from bringing the guilt-offering if he denies a fine, because he could have exempted himself from paying the fine by his own admission. [8]**But it is not my intention to give you forced answers,** [9]**for if** I were to explain the Baraita in **such** a way, **you could** raise another objection and **say to me:** If the entire Baraita is in accordance with the viewpoint of Rabbi Shimon, why is the first clause stated anonymously and the attribution to Rabbi Shimon made at the beginning of the second clause, implying that only the second clause follows his view? [10]Either **let the first clause begin** with the words: **"Rabbi Shimon says,"** [11]**or let the second clause end** with the words: **"This is the opinion of Rabbi Shimon,"** implying that the entire Baraita is in accordance with his view! [12]**Rather,** I prefer to answer you that **the entire** Baraita does indeed speak of a case **in which** the defendant **has** already **been brought to court** and been ordered to pay, [13]**and the first clause is in accordance with** the viewpoint of **the Rabbis,** who maintain that the defendant is held liable to bring a guilt-offering for the false denial of any monetary obligation, even if it was originally imposed on him as a fine, [14]**and the last clause is in accordance with** the viewpoint

RASHI

אלא פשיטא בשעמד בדין — והא דקתני ״ואלו שהן קנס״ — לקמן מפרש לה: שעיקרן קנס. **או ליתני רישא** — דכולה, ״רבי שמעון אומר״. **או ליתני סיפא כו׳** — מאי שנא דאיפסיק ותנא ״רבי שמעון אומר״ בי מילעי?

NOTES

וְרֵישָׁא רַבָּנַן, וְסֵיפָא רַבִּי שִׁמְעוֹן And the first clause is in accordance with the Rabbis, and the last clause is in accordance with Rabbi Shimon. The Rishonim ask: Why did the Rabbis formulate their viewpoint about the fines paid by the seducer and the rapist in connection with the double payment and the fourfold and fivefold payments, whereas Rabbi Shimon stated his opposing viewpoint about the fines paid by the seducer and the rapist in connection with the fine paid by the master who knocked out his slave's tooth or blinded him?

According to *Tosafot Yeshanim,* Rabbi Shimon agrees with the Rabbis about the double, fourfold and fivefold

BACKGROUND

וְשִׁינּוּיֵי דְּחִיקֵי לָא מְשַׁנֵּינַן לָךְ But I will not answer you with forced answers. The term שִׁינּוּיָא is used to describe a certain way of reconciling contradictions, when it is argued that the two apparently contradictory cases are actually different from each other in some manner. For example, the explanation may be given that the cases are not dealing with exactly the same situation, or that they derive from two opposing Halakhic schools. Hence they cannot be compared. The approach of שִׁינּוּיָא (which was called חִילּוּק ["difference"] in the Middle Ages and later) makes it possible to explain and to reconcile a great number of difficulties — but not always convincingly. Consequently, we find in the Talmud that after such an explanation is proposed, further proof is often brought to show that the explanation is correct and not merely a formal dismissal of the difficulty. Here Rabbah says that he could have resolved the difficulty by means of a שִׁינּוּיָא דְּחִיקָא, but that he preferred not to do so, because the forced answer makes the difficult assumption that the author of the Baraita combined two statements which address two different subjects. Therefore he preferred to change his argument slightly in order to explain the Baraita better.

¹וּמוֹדֵינָא לָךְ לְעִנְיַן קָרְבַּן שְׁבוּעָה, ²דְּרַחֲמָנָא פְּטָרֵיהּ ³מִ״וְכִחֵשׁ״. ⁴וְכִי קָאָמֵינָא מָמוֹן הָוֵי, ⁵לְהוֹרִישׁוֹ לְבָנָיו.
⁶אֵיתִיבֵיהּ: ⁷״רַבִּי שִׁמְעוֹן אוֹמֵר: אִם לֹא הִסְפִּיקָה לִגְבּוֹת עַד שֶׁמֵּת הָאָב, הֲרֵי הֵן שֶׁל עַצְמָהּ״. ⁸וְאִי אָמְרַתְּ מָמוֹן הָוֵי לְהוֹרִישׁוֹ לְבָנָיו, ⁹לְעַצְמָהּ אַמַּאי? ¹⁰דְּאַחִין בָּעֵי מֵיהֱוֵי!
¹¹אֲמַר רָבָא: הַאי מִילְּתָא קָשַׁאי בָּהּ רַבָּה וְרַב יוֹסֵף עֶשְׂרִין וְתַרְתֵּין שְׁנִין, וְלָא אִיפְּרַק

LITERAL TRANSLATION

[1] And I agree with you concerning the matter of the sacrifice for [taking a false] oath, [2] that the Torah (lit., "the Merciful One") exempted him [3] [by derivation] from [the expression] "and lied." [4] And when I said it was money, [5] [that was] regarding [his right] to leave it to his sons.

[6] He raised an objection against him: [7] "Rabbi Shimon says: If she did not have sufficient time to collect before the father died, they belong to her." [8] But if you say it is money regarding [his right] to leave it to his sons, [9] why does it belong to her? [10] It should belong to the brothers!

[11] Rava said: Rabbah and Rav Yosef had difficulty with this matter for twenty-two years, and it was not solved

TRANSLATION AND COMMENTARY

of **Rabbi Shimon,** who disagrees. [1] **And,** continues Rabbah, **I agree with you,** Abaye, **about the sacrifice** that must be brought **for falsely** denying a debt under **oath,** [2] **that,** according to Rabbi Shimon, **the Torah exempts** from bringing the sacrifice someone whom the court has already found liable to pay the fine and who later denies the fine when the plaintiff brings him back to court to demand that it be paid. [3] He is exempt from the sacrifice **because of** the verse that states: "If a person sinned, and committed a trespass against the Lord, **and lied** to his neighbor regarding a deposit...." Rabbi Shimon derives from this that a person is only held liable to bring the guilt-offering if he falsely denies an obligation similar to those specified in the verse, to the exclusion of a case in which he falsely denies an obligation that was originally imposed on him as a fine. [4] **And when I said** that Rabbi Shimon maintains that even a fine **is** considered **an ordinary monetary obligation** once the defendant has been brought to court and found liable to pay, [5] **that was** only **regarding** the plaintiff's **right to leave** the fine as a legacy **to his sons.** If the defendant is found liable to pay a fine, and the plaintiff dies before he has had an opportunity to collect, the fine must be paid to the plaintiff's heirs, who inherit the fine just as they inherit any other money owed to the plaintiff.

אֵיתִיבֵיהּ [6] Abaye **raised an objection against** Rabbah's revised position from our Mishnah, which stated: [7] **"Rabbi Shimon says:** Even if the *na'arah* went to court during her father's lifetime, and the seducer or the rapist was ordered to pay, **if she did not have sufficient time to collect** the payments **before her father died, they belong to** the girl **herself."** [8] **But if you say** that once the defendant has been ordered by the court to pay a fine, **it is** treated as **an ordinary monetary obligation regarding** the plaintiff's **right to leave** the fine as a legacy **to his sons,** [9] **why do** the payments **belong to** the girl **herself?** [10] **They should belong to the** girl's **brothers,** who are their father's heirs!

אֲמַר רָבָא [11] **Rava said** in reply to Abaye's objection: **Rabbah and Rav Yosef had difficulty with this matter**

RASHI

ומודינא לך לענין קרבן שבועה — דלרבי שמעון אף על גב דעמד בדין לא מיחייב עליה קרבן שבועה. **להורישו לבניו** — משעמד בדין ומת עד שלא הספיק לגבות הרי הוא של אחיה ולא שלה. **עשרין ותרתין שנין** — הן היו ימי שררתו של רבה, ומת, וישב רב יוסף בראש, וסייעוהו מן השמים לפרקה, להיות לו לשם. לפי שהיה רבה חריף, ולכך קראוהו "עוקר הרים", ורב יוסף היה בעל שמועות ומשנה ובריית׳א לכך קראוהו "סיני".

SAGES

רָבָא Rava. A Babylonian Amora of the fourth generation. See *Ketubot,* Part I, p. 14.

רַבָּה Rabbah. A Babylonian Amora of the third generation. See *Ketubot,* Part II, p. 52.

רַב יוֹסֵף Rav Yosef. A Babylonian Amora of the third generation. See *Ketubot,* Part I, p. 102.

NOTES

payments, even if the defendant has not yet been brought to court — that he is held liable to bring the guilt-offering if he falsely denies his liability. For in these cases the plaintiff puts forward a claim for an ordinary monetary obligation, and the payment of a fine, both of which are clearly defined amounts, and he surely does not abandon his claim for the ordinary monetary obligation, which the defendant would not be exempt from paying if he admitted to it, and he does not have in mind only the fine, which the defendant can exempt himself from paying if he admits his liability at the outset. Thus, when the defendant denies the claim brought against him, he denies an ordinary monetary obligation (see Gemara below, 43a).

Ramban explains the different formulations as follows: The Rabbis and Rabbi Shimon disagree about the fines paid by the seducer and the rapist, even when the defendant has not yet been brought to court, and each of them compares the fines of the seducer and the rapist to the other fines that they each mention. Rabbi Shimon compares the fines paid by the seducer and the rapist to the fine paid by the master to his slave. In both cases the defendant denies a fine, and thus in both cases he is exempt from bringing a guilt-offering for his false denial. The Rabbis compare the fines paid by the seducer and the rapist to the double, fourfold, and fivefold payments. In all these cases, the defendant denies a claim that relates primarily to an ordinary monetary obligation, and he is therefore held liable to bring the guilt-offering.

LITERAL TRANSLATION

[1]until Rav Yosef sat at the head [of the Academy and solved it [as follows]: [2]It is different there, because the verse says: "And the man that lay with her shall *give* [*venatan*] to the father of the *na'arah* fifty pieces of silver." [3]The Torah transferred [it] to the father only from the time of giving. [4]And when Rabbah said it was money regarding [his right] to leave it to his sons, [5][he was referring] to other fines.

[1]עַד דְּיָתֵיב רַב יוֹסֵף בְּרֵישָׁא וּפֵירְקָהּ: [2]שָׁאנֵי הָתָם, דְּאָמַר קְרָא: "וְנָתַן הָאִישׁ הַשֹּׁכֵב עִמָּהּ לַאֲבִי הַנַּעֲרָה חֲמִשִּׁים כָּסֶף". [3]לֹא זִיכְּתָה תּוֹרָה לָאָב אֶלָּא מִשְּׁעַת נְתִינָה. [4]וְכִי קָאָמַר רַבָּה מָמוֹנָא הָוֵי לְהוֹרִישׁוֹ לְבָנָיו, [5]בִּשְׁאָר קְנָסוֹת.

RASHI

וכי אמר רבה ממונא הוי להורישו — משעמד בדין. **בשאר קנסות** — ולא מיפטר תו בהודאה.

TRANSLATION AND COMMENTARY

for twenty-two years, and it was not solved [1]**until** Rabbah died and **Rav Yosef became the head of the Academy and solved it as follows:** [2]The law **is different there** in the case of rape, **because the verse says** (Deuteronomy 22:29): **"And the man that lay with her shall *give* to the father of the *na'arah* fifty pieces of silver."** [3]In other words, **the Torah transfers** the money **to the father only from the time it is** actually **given** to him, but before he physically receives the money it is not yet his. Similarly in the case of seduction, the fine does not belong to the girl's father until he actually receives it, for the laws applying to rape are extended by analogy to a case of seduction. Therefore, ruled Rabbi Shimon in our Mishnah, if the girl has not yet collected her fine before her father dies, even though the court has already found the rapist or the seducer liable to pay, the money never became the father's to be passed on to his heirs when he died. Hence the money goes to the girl herself and not to her brothers. [4]**And when Rabbah said** that, according to Rabbi Shimon, once the court finds the defendant liable to pay a fine, that fine **is** considered **an ordinary monetary obligation regarding** the plaintiff's **right to leave it to his sons,** even if the plaintiff dies before he can collect the money, [5]Rabbi Shimon **was referring to other fines,** but not to the fines paid by the rapist or the seducer, which are governed by a special law.

BACKGROUND

עַד דְּיָתֵיב רַב יוֹסֵף בְּרֵישָׁא Until Rav Yosef sat at the head of the Academy. The details of how Rav Yosef was appointed head of the Pumbedita Yeshivah are given at the end of tractate *Berakhot* and at the end of tractate *Horayot*. After the death of Rav Yehudah, who was head of the Pumbedita Yeshivah, the two main candidates to succeed him were Rabbah and Rav Yosef. Rabbah, who was younger than Rav Yosef, was renowned for his sharp analytical powers, whereas Rav Yosef was renowned for his encyclopedic breadth of knowledge. Since the Rabbis of the yeshivah did not know which candidate to choose, they asked the Sages of Eretz Israel: "Between a 'Sinai' [someone possessing breadth of knowledge] and an 'Uprooter of Mountains' [someone possessing analytical power], which is preferable?" The Sages of Eretz Israel answered that a "Sinai" was preferable. The position was then offered to Rav Yosef, who for various reasons declined it, and during the twenty-two years in which Rabbah served as the head of the yeshivah Rav Yosef did not take on any position of authority. Only after the death of Rabbah was Rav Yosef appointed to succeed him. (See notes.)

NOTES

עַד דְּיָתֵיב רַב יוֹסֵף בְּרֵישָׁא וּפֵירְקָהּ Until Rav Yosef sat at the head of the Academy and solved it. *Rashi* explains that Rav Yosef was known for his wide erudition, whereas Rabbah's strength lay in the sharpness of his intellect. Nevertheless, it was only after Rabbah died and Rav Yosef replaced him as head of the Academy that a solution was found to the difficulty that both of them had tried to solve for twenty-two years. Rav Yosef was given divine help in finding a solution so that his stature as the new head of the Academy would be enhanced. *Sukkat David* adds that even though the Sages said that wide erudition is preferable to intellectual brilliance, the students at the Academy might not have accorded Rav Yosef the respect to which he was entitled. Therefore Rav Yosef was given this opportunity to display his own acuity and his ability to draw a distinction between the different fines.

וְכִי קָאָמַר רַבָּה מָמוֹנָא הָוֵי לְהוֹרִישׁוֹ לְבָנָיו, בִּשְׁאָר קְנָסוֹת And when Rabbah said it was money regarding his right to leave it to his sons, he was referring to other fines. Most Rishonim understand this final version of Rabbah's position as follows: Regarding all fines other than those paid by the rapist and the seducer, even Rabbi Shimon maintains that once the court finds the defendant liable to pay the fine, it is treated as an ordinary monetary obligation, so that if the plaintiff dies before collecting, the fine must be paid to the plaintiff's heirs, who inherit the fine just as they inherit any other money owed to the plaintiff. The fines paid by the rapist and by the seducer are governed by a special law, so that even after the defendant has been ordered by the court to pay the fine, the money is still not considered the father's (in which case it would pass to his heirs on his death) until the fine is actually given to him. But if the court has not yet found the defendant liable to pay a fine, then in no case is it considered an ordinary monetary obligation which the plaintiff passes on to his heirs as part of his estate, even according to the Rabbis who disagree with Rabbi Shimon. But this explanation leads to a difficulty, for there is a discussion between Rava and Rav Naḥman in tractate *Bava Kamma* (71b), from which it follows that they both agree that a person's sons do indeed inherit the fine to which their father was entitled, even if the father had not yet been awarded the fine by the court.

Ramban suggests that this issue is the subject of a dispute between the Amoraim. According to Rabbah, a fine does not pass to a person's heirs unless the court has already found the defendant liable to pay it, whereas according to Rava and Rav Naḥman a fine does indeed pass to a person's heirs, even if the defendant has not yet been found liable to pay it (with the exception of the fines paid by the rapist and the seducer). *Ramban* adds that the Jerusalem Talmud states explicitly that the Amoraim Rabbi Yonah and Rabbi Yose disagree on this matter.

Ri HaLavan understands our Gemara in an entirely different manner: When Rabbah says that only after the defendant is found liable to pay a fine is the fine treated as an ordinary monetary obligation so that it passes to the plaintiff's heirs, he does not mean to imply that if the plaintiff dies before the court has awarded him the fine, the fine does not pass to his heirs; for all — even Rabbah — agree that a fine does indeed pass to a person's heirs, even if the court has not yet found the defendant liable.

TRANSLATION AND COMMENTARY

אֶלָּא מֵעַתָּה [1]The Gemara asks: **But if so,** if we derive the special ruling in the case of the rapist from the Torah's use of the expression "give," then **with respect to** the fine that must be paid by a person whose ox has killed someone else's **slave,** [2]**about which the verse says** (Exodus 21:32): **"He shall *give* to his master thirty shekalim of silver,"** [3]**do we say that here too the Torah transfers** the money **to the master only from the time it is** actually **given** to him? We have just explained that the verse, "The man that lay with her shall *give* to the father of the *na'arah* fifty pieces of silver," implies that the money belongs to the father only when it is given to him, and therefore the money does not pass to his sons if he dies before receiving payment. On this basis, by analogy, we should infer from the verse, "He shall *give* to his master thirty shekalim," that this fine too does not belong to the master, so that it passes to his heirs, until it is actually received by him. How, then, can Rav Yosef say that all other fines other than those paid by the rapist and the seducer are considered ordinary monetary obligations once the court finds the defendant liable?

״יִתֵּן״ לְחוּד [4]The Gemara answers: A distinction is to be drawn between the two verses, in that the expression ***"yitten"*** (יִתֵּן — "he shall give"), in which the future form of the verb "to give" is used, **stands by itself, and** the expression ***"venatan"*** (וְנָתַן — "and he shall give"), in which the past form of the same root is used and which is understood as having a future sense only by virtue of the letter vav placed at the beginning of the word, also **stands by itself.** The past form of the verb "to give" is used with respect to the rapist in order to teach us that the fine he pays does not belong to the father until it is actually given to him. But it does not follow that the same law applies in the case of the slave, where the future form of that same verb is used.

[1]אֶלָּא מֵעַתָּה, גַּבֵּי עֶבֶד, [2]דִּכְתִיב: ״כֶּסֶף שְׁלֹשִׁים שְׁקָלִים יִתֵּן לַאדֹנָיו״, [3]הָכִי נַמִי לֹא זִיכְּתָה תּוֹרָה לָאָדוֹן אֶלָּא מִשְּׁעַת נְתִינָה? [4]״יִתֵּן״ לְחוּד, ״וְנָתַן״ לְחוּד.

LITERAL TRANSLATION

[1]But if so, with regard to a slave, [2][about whom] it is written: "He shall *give* [*yitten*] to his master thirty shekalim of silver," [3][do we say that] so too the Torah transferred [it] to the master only from the time of giving?

[4]*"Yitten"* is by itself, [and] *"venatan"* is by itself.

RASHI

יתן לחוד ונתן לחוד — ״יתן״ משמע לשון לווי, ולעולם. ״ונתן״ משמע דבר הנתון כבר.

NOTES

Rather, what Rabbah means to say is as follows: If the court has already found the defendant liable to pay the fine before the plaintiff dies, the fine is then treated as an ordinary monetary obligation, so that if his heirs demand the fine from the defendant, and the defendant falsely denies his liability on oath, he must bring a guilt-offering for the false denial of the debt. *Ramban* notes that while this explanation is in itself reasonable, it does not fit well with the expression: "It was money regarding his right to leave it to his sons," which implies that Rabbah is dealing with the question of whether or not the fine passes to the plaintiff's heirs. Nor does it fit well with the Jerusalem Talmud, which states explicitly that the Amoraim disagree about this matter.

״יִתֵּן״ לְחוּד ״וְנָתַן״ לְחוּד *"Yitten"* is by itself, and *"venatan"* is by itself. Our commentary follows *Rashi,* who understands that the Gemara distinguishes between the two fines on the basis of the verbal form used in each case. Regarding the fine paid by the rapist, the Torah uses a past form of the verb (וְנָתַן), implying that the fine does not belong to the father until the money is actually given to him. But regarding the fine paid in the case of the slave, the Torah uses a future form of the verb (יִתֵּן), implying that the fine already belongs to the master, even if the money will only be given to him at some point in the future.

Ritva understands the Gemara's distinction differently: The term *yitten* used in the case of the slave refers to the court, and means that the court will award the slave's master a fine of thirty shekalim and will order the ox's owner to pay it. Thus the fine belongs to the master as soon as the ox's owner comes to court and is found liable. But in the case of rape, the findings of the court are alluded to by the term *venimtza'u* (וְנִמְצָאוּ — "and they are found"), and thus the term *venatan* must refer to the rapist, and means that the rapist must give the fine to the girl's father. Thus the fine does not belong to the father until it is actually received by him.

Ramban offers a similar explanation as to why in the case of slander the fine belongs to the father of the slandered girl even before he actually receives it. *Ramban* distinguishes between the case of rape, where the Torah uses the term *venatan*, and the case of slander, where the Torah uses the term *venatenu* (וְנָתְנוּ — "and they shall give"). The term *venatan* in the case of rape refers to the rapist himself, and therefore the fine he pays does not belong to the father until it is actually received by him. But the term *venatenu* in the case of slander refers to the court, and means that the court awards the fine to the father of the slandered girl. Therefore the fine belongs to the father as soon as the court orders the slanderer to pay. *Ramban* also suggests as a possibility that the Gemara did not list all the cases in which the special law applies, for not only in the cases of rape and seduction but also in the case of slander the fine does not belong to the father until it actually reaches his hand.

[1]אִי הָכִי, ״תַּלְמוּד לוֹמַר: ׳וְכִחֵשׁ׳״? [2]״תַּלְמוּד לוֹמַר: ׳וְנָתַן׳״ מִיבָּעֵי לֵיהּ! [3]אֲמַר רָבָא: כִּי אִיצְטְרִיךְ ״וְכִחֵשׁ״, [4]כְּגוֹן שֶׁעָמְדָה בַּדִּין, וּבָגְרָה, וּמֵתָה. [5]דְּהָתָם, כִּי קָא יָרֵית אָבִיהָ, מִינָּהּ דִּידָהּ קָא יָרֵית. [6]אִי הָכִי, ״יָצְאוּ אֵלּוּ שֶׁהֵן

LITERAL TRANSLATION

[1]If so, [why does he say:] "The Torah says: 'And lied'"? [2]He should have [said]: "The Torah says: 'And he shall give'"!

[3]Rava said: When "and lied" was needed, [4][it was,] for example, where she came to court, and came of age, and died, [5]for there, when her father inherited, he inherited from her.

[6]If so, [why does it say:] "These are excluded, because they are

TRANSLATION AND COMMENTARY

אִי הָכִי [1]The Gemara asks: **If it is true** that the fines paid by the rapist and by the seducer are different from all other fines in that they are not treated as ordinary monetary obligations, even after the defendant has been brought to court and ordered to pay, **why did** the Baraita (above, 42a) **explain** that the rapist and the seducer do not bring guilt-offerings for having falsely denied the fines imposed on them by saying: "Therefore **the Torah states:** 'If a person sinned, and committed a trespass against the Lord, **and lied** to his neighbor'"? It is appropriate to cite that verse with respect to the other fines mentioned in the Baraita, for it teaches that a guilt-offering is not brought for the denial of a monetary obligation that was originally imposed as a fine, even if the fine is now treated like any other monetary obligation. [2]But with respect to the fines paid by the rapist and the seducer, the Baraita **should have said:** "Therefore **the Torah states: 'And** the man that lay with her **shall give,'**" for it is from that verse that we learn that these fines are not treated as ordinary monetary obligations, even after they have been imposed by the court!

אֲמַר רָבָא [3]**Rava said** in reply: The verse, "If a person sinned...**and lied,**" **was needed** to teach us a law even with respect to the fines paid by the rapist and the seducer, for there is a certain case in which the rapist and the seducer are exempt from bringing a guilt-offering, not because the fines are not considered ordinary monetary obligations after being imposed by the courts, but specifically because they were originally imposed as fines, even though they are now considered like any other monetary obligations. This is the case, [4]**for example, if** the girl who was raped or seduced **came to court** before she reached the age of twelve-and-a-half, **came of age** before she had time to collect the fine, **and** then **died,** so that payment of the fine must now be made to her father. Just as Rabbi Shimon disagrees with the anonymous first Tanna of our Mishnah about the case in which the girl came to court but did not collect the fine before her father died, he also disagrees with him about the case in which she came to court but did not collect the fine before coming of age. In both cases, Rabbi Shimon maintains that the payment of the fine must now be made to the girl herself, and not to the brothers (if the father died) or to the father (if she came of age). [5]Now, **if** the girl dies after coming of age, and **her father inherits** her estate, **he** also **inherits from her** the fine to be paid by the rapist or the seducer. With respect to the girl herself, once the fine has been imposed, it is considered like any other monetary payment to which she is entitled, and therefore it passes to her heirs when she dies, even if it has not yet been collected. Thus, if the father brought the rapist to court to demand payment from him, and the rapist took a false oath denying the claim against him, he remains exempt from the guilt-offering, not because the fine is not treated as an ordinary monetary obligation, but because it was originally imposed as a fine. Hence the Baraita includes the fines paid by the rapist and the seducer among the other fines for which there is no guilt-offering, because of the verse that states: "If a person sinned...and lied."

אִי הָכִי [6]The Gemara now asks: **If it is true** that the entire Baraita speaks of a case in which the defendant has already been brought to court and ordered to pay, **why does it state:** "This verse, 'If a person

RASHI

אי הכי — דשאני קנס דאונס ומפתה משאר קנסות, דאפילו עמד בדין נמי לאו ממונא הוא. **תלמוד לומר וכחש** — בתמיה: כלומר, מאי איריא דנסיב לה תלמודא לפטורא מ״וכחש״ כי היכי דיליף שאר קנסות? כלומר, מדלא דמי לתשומת יד למיהוי עיקר תחילתו ממון — תיפוק ליה דהשתא נמי לאו ממונא הוא, דרחמנא אמר ״ונתן״ דלא זיכתה לו תורה עד שעת נתינה. **כי איצטריך וכחש** — לקנס דאונס ופתוי, למילפינהו בהדי שאר קנסות לפטורא מ״וכחש״ משום דעיקרן קנס, ולא מצי למילף מ״ונתן״. **כגון שעמדה בדין ובגרה** — דלרבי שמעון דידה הוא. דכי היכי דפליג במתניתין ב״לא הספיקה לגבות עד שמת האב״ — הכי נמי פליג ב״לא הספיקה לגבות עד שבגרה״, דקאמר תנא קמא: הרי הן של אב, ולרבי שמעון הרי הוא של עצמה. ואם מתה אחרי כן — ירית לה אביה מכח דידה. והוי ממון גמור, ואף על גב דלא מטא לידה. דלגבי דידה לא הוה שאני משאר קנסות, דמשעת העמדה בדין ממונא הוא, וכי מייתא — ירית הוא כל זכות שהיה לה בו. הלכך מ״ונתן״ לא מצי למיפטריה, ונסיב תלמודא מ״וכחש״, ומשום דעיקרו קנס. **אי הכי** — דבשעמד בדין אוקימתה, וכבר נעשה ממון — היכי קתני ״יצאו אלו שהן קנס״? הא ממון נינהו!

קְנָס״? [1]מָמוֹן הוּא!
[2]אָמַר רַב נַחְמָן בַּר יִצְחָק: ״יָצְאוּ אֵלּוּ שֶׁעִיקָּרָן קְנָס״.
[3]אֵיתִיבֵיהּ: ״רַבִּי שִׁמְעוֹן פּוֹטֵר, [4]שֶׁאֵינוֹ מְשַׁלֵּם קְנָס עַל פִּי עַצְמוֹ״. [5]טַעֲמָא דְּלָא עָמַד בַּדִּין. [6]הָא עָמַד בַּדִּין, [7]דִּמְשַׁלֵּם עַל פִּי עַצְמוֹ, [8]קָרְבַּן שְׁבוּעָה נַמִי מִיחַיַּיב!
[9]רַבִּי שִׁמְעוֹן לְדִבְרֵיהֶם דְּרַבָּנַן קָאָמַר לְהוּ: [10]לְדִידִי, אַף עַל גַּב דַּעֲמַד בַּדִּין, [11]רַחֲמָנָא פְּטָרֵיהּ מִ״וְכִחֵשׁ״. [12]אֶלָּא לְדִידְכוּ, אוֹדוּ לִי מִיהַת הֵיכָא דְּלָא עָמַד בַּדִּין, [13]דְּכִי קָא תָּבַע, קְנָסָא

LITERAL TRANSLATION

fines"? [1]It is money!

[2]Rav Naḥman bar Yitzḥak said: [It means:] "These are excluded, because their basis was a fine."

[3]He raised an objection against him: "Rabbi Shimon exempts [him], [4]for he does not pay a fine on his own [confession]." [5]The reason is that he was not brought to court. [6]But if he was brought to court, [7]in which case he pays on his own [confession], [8]he is also liable for the sacrifice for [taking a false] oath!

[9]Rabbi Shimon spoke to the Rabbis according to their opinion: [10]According to me, even though he was brought to court, [11]the Torah exempted him [by derivation] from [the expression] "and lied." [12]But according to you, at least agree with me about where he was not brought to court, [13]that when he demands, he demands a fine,

TRANSLATION AND COMMENTARY

sinned...and lied' specifically **excludes those** cases that involve claims for the payment of **fines**"? [1]Surely, once the defendant has been ordered to pay, the fine **is** considered **an ordinary monetary obligation!**

אָמַר רַב נַחְמָן בַּר יִצְחָק [2]**Rav Naḥman bar Yitzḥak said** in reply: The Baraita **means** the following: "This verse specifically **excludes those** cases, **because** they involve claims for the payment of something that **was originally** imposed as **a fine,** even though the payment is now considered an ordinary monetary obligation."

אֵיתִיבֵיהּ [3]**A** further **objection was raised against** Rabbah from the Mishnah in tractate *Shevuot* cited above (42a), which stated: "If someone falsely denies under oath that he has raped or seduced a *na'arah*, **Rabbi Shimon exempts him** from bringing a guilt-offering, [4]**for he would not have had to pay the fine** of the rapist or the seducer **on** the basis of **his own confession."** If the defendant had admitted at the outset that he had raped or seduced the girl, he would not have been liable for the fine. Thus, when he denied the offense, he did not deny a monetary obligation, and thus he is not held liable to bring the guilt-offering. [5]Rabbi Shimon clearly states that **the reason** why the defendant is exempt from bringing the guilt-offering **is that he was not** previously **brought to court** and found liable to pay the fine. Since a person does not pay a fine if he confesses to an offense before being convicted in court, the defendant did not deny a monetary obligation for which he was already liable at the time of the denial. [6]**But** it follows from this that **if** the defendant **was** previously **brought to court** and a fine imposed — [7]**in which case he** *would* have to **pay on** the basis of **his own confession** if he were later to admit his liability to pay the fine, when the plaintiff takes him to court a second time and demands payment from him — [8]**he would also be liable to bring the sacrifice for taking a false oath,** if he were now falsely to deny that liability! How, then, can Rabbah say that according to Rabbi Shimon someone who falsely denies a fine is exempt from bringing the sacrifice, even if the court has already found him liable to pay, and he later denies the fine when the plaintiff takes him back to court to demand that it be paid?

רַבִּי שִׁמְעוֹן [9]To refute this objection the Gemara now suggests that Rabbi Shimon was not expressing his own viewpoint in that Mishnah, but was putting forward an argument based on the position of the Rabbis who disagreed with him. **Rabbi Shimon answered the Rabbis according to their** own **opinion,** saying to them as follows: [10]**According to my** opinion, **even** in the case **where** the defendant denies his liability after he **has** already **been brought to court** and found liable to pay the fine, [11]**the Torah exempted him** from bringing a guilt-offering **because of** the verse that states, "If a person sinned...**and lied."** For that verse teaches us that a person is only held liable to bring the guilt-offering if he falsely denies a monetary obligation similar to those specified in the verse, and this excludes the case in which he falsely denies an obligation that was originally imposed on him as a fine. [12]**But** even **according to your** opinion, you should **at least agree with me** that the defendant is exempt from bringing a guilt-offering in the case **where he was not** previously **brought to court,** [13]for in that case, **when** the plaintiff charges him with rape and **demands** to be

RASHI

שאינו משלם קנס בו׳ — ואי הוה מודי הוה מיפטר. אלמא, טעמא דרבי שמעון משום דאי הוה מודי מיפטר הוא, והא ליתא אלא כשלא עמד בדין. הכי גרסינן: והא עמד בדין דמשלם על פי עלמו קרבן שבועה נמי מיחייב. **רחמנא פטריה** — מקרבן שבועה. **מ״וכחש בעמיתו״** — שלא פירש בו אלא דברים שעיקרן ממון.

SAGES

רַב נַחְמָן בַּר יִצְחָק **Rav Naḥman bar Yitzḥak.** A Babylonian Amora of the fourth generation. See *Ketubot*, Part I, p. 52.

TERMINOLOGY

בְּמַאי קָא מִיפַּלְגִי About what do they disagree? When the practical difference between two conflicting points of view is clear, but the theoretical basis of the dispute is not, the Talmud may use this expression to inquire into the theoretical issue at the heart of the dispute.

SAGES

רַב פַּפָּא Rav Pappa. A Babylonian Amora of the fifth generation. See *Ketubot*, Part III, p. 11.

רַבִּי אָבִינָא Rabbi Avina. A Babylonian Amora of the third generation. See *Ketubot*, Part II, p. 179.

רַב שֵׁשֶׁת Rav Sheshet. A Babylonian Amora of the second and third generations. See *Ketubot*, Part I, p. 35.

TRANSLATION AND COMMENTARY

compensated, **he is demanding** the payment of **a fine.** [43A] [1]**And** the defendant could have exempted himself from paying that fine, for we have an established rule that **someone who admits to a fine** before his liability is established by a court **is exempt** from paying that fine. Therefore, if he takes a false oath and denies the charge, he should be exempt from bringing the guilt-offering, for he was not denying a monetary obligation for which he was liable at the time of the denial. [2]**But the Rabbis maintain: When** the father puts forward the charge of rape and **demands** compensation, [3]**he is** not only **demanding** the fine but he is also claiming the **payments** that must be paid **for** the **shame and blemish** suffered by his daughter. Thus, if the defendant falsely denies the charge, he is held liable to bring a guilt-offering, just as he would have to bring such a sacrifice if he falsely denied any other monetary obligation.

בְּמַאי קָא מִיפַּלְגִי [4]The Gemara now asks: If this is the dispute between Rabbi Shimon and the Rabbis, then **what** precisely is the issue **about which they disagree?**

אֲמַר רַב פַּפָּא [5]**Rav Pappa explained:** The Mishnah in *Shevuot* refers to a case in which the father accused the defendant of rape, without specifying what form of compensation he was demanding. The Tannaim disagree as to whether the father was demanding payment of the fine or whether he was suing the defendant for compensation for his daughter's ruined reputation and loss of virginity. [6]**Rabbi Shimon maintains: A person does not abandon something that is fixed** [7]**and demand something that is not fixed.** The rapist's fine is fixed at two hundred zuz, but the compensation he must pay for the girl's ruined reputation and loss of virginity must be assessed according to the real value of the damage suffered. Thus, when the father accused the defendant of rape, he was primarily interested in receiving the fine, the amount of which is fixed. And when the defendant denied the charge, he was only denying a fine, and he should therefore be exempt from bringing the guilt-offering. [8]**On the other hand, the Rabbis** disagree and **say: One person** suing another **does not abandon** a claim **which, if the defendant admits to it, he is not exempt** from paying, [9]**and demand something that, if the defendant admits to it, he is exempt** from paying. If the rapist admits his crime, his confession exempts him from paying the fine, but he must still pay compensation for the girl's ruined reputation and loss of virginity. Thus, when the father accused the defendant of rape, he was not only demanding the fine but also claiming the other payments. Hence, when the defendant denied raping the daughter, he was denying an ordinary monetary obligation, and is therefore held liable to bring the guilt-offering.

בְּעָא מִינֵּיהּ [10]The Gemara now proceeds to discuss a different topic — who has the rights to an orphan girl's handiwork? **Rabbi Avina asked Rav Sheshet: Regarding an orphan girl who is being maintained** from

קָא תָּבַע, [43A] [1]וּמוֹדֶה בִּקְנָס פָּטוּר. [2]וְרַבָּנַן סָבְרִי: כִּי קָא תָּבַע, [3]בּוֹשֶׁת וּפְגָם קָא תָּבַע.

[4]בְּמַאי קָא מִיפַּלְגִי?

[5]אֲמַר רַב פַּפָּא: [6]רַבִּי שִׁמְעוֹן סָבַר: לָא שָׁבֵיק אִינִישׁ מִידֵּי דְּקִיץ, [7]וְתָבַע מִידֵּי דְּלָא קִיץ. [8]וְרַבָּנַן סָבְרִי: לָא שָׁבֵיק אִינִישׁ מִידֵּי דְּכִי מוֹדֵי בֵּיהּ לָא מִיפַּטַר, [9]וְתָבַע מִידֵּי דְּכִי מוֹדֶה בֵּיהּ מִיפַּטַר.

[10]בְּעָא מִינֵּיהּ רַבִּי אָבִינָא מֵרַב שֵׁשֶׁת: בַּת הַנִּיזּוֹנֶת מִן הָאַחִין,

LITERAL TRANSLATION

[43A] [1]and he who admits to a fine is exempt. [2]But the Rabbis maintain: When he demands, [3]he demands [payment for] shame and blemish.

[4]About what do they disagree?

[5]Rav Pappa said: [6]Rabbi Shimon maintains: A person does not abandon something that is fixed, [7]and demand something that is not fixed. [8]But the Rabbis maintain: A person does not abandon something that when [the defendant] admits to it he is not exempt, [9]and demand something that when [the defendant] admits to it he is exempt.

[10]Rabbi Avina asked Rav Sheshet: [Regarding] a daughter who is maintained by the brothers,

RASHI

ומודה בקנס פטור — והרי לא תבעו אלא קנס לבדו, ועליו נשבע. וכיון דאי אודי ליה קמן לא משלם, כי כפריה נמי לאו ממונא כפריה. **בת הניזונית מן האחין** — שכך הוא תנאי כתובה בפרקין (כתובות נב,ב): בנן נוקבן דיהוויין ליכי מינאי אינון יהון יתבין בביתי ומיתזנן מנכסיי עד דתלקחון לגוברין.

NOTES

בַּת הַנִּיזּוֹנֶת מִן הָאַחִין Regarding a daughter who is maintained by the brothers. According to most Rishonim, the Amoraim agree that by Torah law the brothers are not entitled to the orphaned daughter's handiwork. The question posed to Rav Sheshet was whether or not the brothers are entitled to the orphan girl's handiwork by Rabbinic enactment. For just as the Rabbis awarded a husband certain rights regarding his wife, and a father certain rights regarding his daughter, they may similarly have enacted that after the father's death the brothers have certain rights

TRANSLATION AND COMMENTARY

her father's estate that has been inherited **by her brothers,** [1]**to whom does her handiwork belong?** As was explained in our Mishnah, a father is entitled to his daughter's handiwork until she reaches the age of twelve-and-a-half. What is the law if the father dies? A daughter is not entitled to a share of her father's estate if he is also survived by sons or by their descendants. But she is entitled to be maintained out of her father's estate until she reaches the age of majority or marries, whichever comes first. The daughter's right of maintenance stems from a stipulation attached to her mother's ketubah mortgaging her father's property for her support in the event of his death (*ketubat benan nukevan*, see below, 52b). The question arises as to whether her brothers are entitled to her handiwork during the period in which she receives this support, or whether she may keep it all for herself? [2]The Gemara examines the two sides of the question: **Do** the brothers **take the place of their father,** [3]**and just as there,** while the father was alive, the girl's **handiwork belonged to her father,** who maintained her, [4]**so too here** after his death **her handiwork** should **belong to her brothers,** from whose inheritance she is now being supported? [5]**Or perhaps** the brothers **are not like their father,** [6]**for there,** while the father was alive **she was maintained from his property,** and it was therefore appropriate that he benefit from her handiwork, [7]**whereas here** after his death **she is not** being **maintained from the property** of the brothers, but from her father's estate which had been mortgaged for her maintenance by the stipulation attached to her mother's ketubah, and the brothers should therefore have no right to her handiwork?

אֲמַר לֵיהּ [8]In reply to Rabbi Avina's question, Rav Sheshet **said to him:** [9]**You have** already **learned** the answer to your question in the following Mishnah (below, 95b): "After her husband's death, **a widow is maintained from the property** inherited by **his sons,** [10]**and her handiwork belongs to them."** Although a widow does not inherit her husband's estate, she is entitled to be maintained from it and to continue living in his house throughout her widowhood, as long as she has not yet received her ketubah (see below, 52b). The Mishnah rules that just as a husband is entitled to his wife's handiwork while he is supporting her, his sons

[1]מַעֲשֵׂה יָדֶיהָ לְמִי? [2]בִּמְקוֹם אָב קָיְימֵי, [3]מָה הָתָם מַעֲשֵׂה יָדֶיהָ לָאָב, [4]הָכָא נַמִי מַעֲשֵׂה יָדֶיהָ לָאַחִין? [5]אוֹ דִּלְמָא לָא דָּמֵי לָאָב, [6]הָתָם מִדִּידֵיהּ מִיתְזְנָא, [7]הָכָא לָאו מִדִּידְהוּ מִיתְזְנָא?

[8]אֲמַר לֵיהּ: [9]תְּנֵיתוּהָ: "אַלְמָנָה נִיזּוֹנֶת מִנִּכְסֵי יְתוֹמִים, [10]וּמַעֲשֵׂה יָדֶיהָ שֶׁלָּהֶן".

LITERAL TRANSLATION

[1]to whom [does] her handiwork belong? [2]Do they stand in the place of the father, [3][and] just as there her handiwork [belongs] to her father, [4]so too here her handiwork [belongs] to the brothers? [5]Or perhaps they are not like the father, [6][for] there she is maintained from what is his, [7][whereas] here she is not maintained from what is theirs?

[8]He said to him: [9]You have learned it: "A widow is maintained from the property of orphans, [10]and her handiwork belongs to them."

RASHI

לאו מדידהו — אלא מתנאי כתובת אמן. **אלמנה ניזונת מנכסי יתומים** — דהאי נמי תנאי כתובה הוא, בפרקין: את תהא יתבא בביתי ומיתזנא מנכסי כל ימי מיגר ארמלותיך. **ומעשה ידיה שלהן** — אלמא במקום אב קיימי.

TERMINOLOGY

תְּנֵיתוּהָ You have learned it. Sometimes an Amora may answer a question by noting that the answer is already found in a Tannaitic source. This term was often used by Rav Sheshet, and the sources it introduces were usually well known (e.g., Mishnayot).

NOTES

regarding the orphan daughter. The question here is whether the brothers take the place of their father by Rabbinic enactment, so that the daughter must now hand over her handiwork to them, or whether she is entitled to keep her handiwork for herself. The Rabbis may not have awarded her handiwork to the brothers, just as they did not require the brothers to maintain the daughter from their own property, but only from their father's estate (see *Tosafot, Ramban, Rashba, Ra'ah,* and others). But some Rishonim explain that according to Rav Sheshet it is by Torah law that the brothers are entitled to the orphan girl's handiwork (see *Rabbi Crescas Vidal* and *Ran*).

הָתָם מִדִּידֵיהּ מִיתְזְנָא There she is maintained from what is his. This passage seems to offer proof that the Gemara is dealing with the question of whether or not the brothers are entitled to the orphaned daughter's handiwork by Rabbinic enactment; for by Torah law the father is entitled to his daughter's handiwork even if he does not provide for her support, since there is a general principle that the father is entitled to all the profits earned by his daughter

HALAKHAH

אַלְמָנָה נִיזּוֹנֶת מִנִּכְסֵי יְתוֹמִים A widow is maintained from the property of orphans. "A widow is entitled to be maintained from her late husband's estate for the duration of her widowhood, provided that she has not yet claimed her ketubah. She is entitled to such maintenance even if it was not stipulated explicitly in her ketubah. And since the husband's heirs are liable for his widow's maintenance, they are entitled to her handiwork." (*Rambam, Sefer Nashim, Hilkhot Ishut* 18:1; *Shulḥan Arukh, Even HaEzer* 93:3 and 95:1.)

SAGES

רַבִּי אַבָּא Rabbi Abba. An Amora of the third generation. See *Ketubot,* Part II, p. 112.

רַבִּי יוֹסֵי Rabbi Yose. A Tanna of the generation before the completion of the Mishnah. See *Ketubot,* Part I, pp. 18–19.

BACKGROUND

יִשְׁאֲלוּ עַל הַפְּתָחִים Must beg at the doors. This is an extreme way of stating that the needs of the orphaned children are not to be supplied from the father's estate, and if the children are unable to support themselves by working, they must live on charity. The obligation to support the children thus passes from the estate to the general community, which must help them, either in an organized manner through the courts and the charity officials, or by having the children themselves beg from door to door if the community is not organized.

[1]מִי דָּמֵי? [2]אַלְמָנָתוֹ, לָא נִיחָא לֵיהּ בְּהַרְוָוחָה. [3]בִּתּוֹ, נִיחָא לֵיהּ בְּהַרְוָוחָה.
[4]לְמֵימְרָא דְּבִתּוֹ עֲדִיפָא לֵיהּ מֵאַלְמָנָתוֹ? [5]וְהָאָמַר רַבִּי אַבָּא אָמַר רַבִּי יוֹסֵי: [6]עָשׂוּ אַלְמָנָה אֵצֶל הַבַּת כְּבַת אֵצֶל אַחִין בִּנְכָסִין מוּעָטִין. [7]מָה הַבַּת אֵצֶל אַחִין, [8]הַבַּת נִיזּוֹנֶת וְהָאַחִין יִשְׁאֲלוּ עַל הַפְּתָחִים,

LITERAL TRANSLATION

[1]Is it comparable? [2][Regarding] his widow, he does not care about [her] comfort. [3][Regarding] his daughter, he cares about [her] comfort.
[4][Do you mean] to say that he prefers his daughter to his widow? [5]But surely Rabbi Abba said in the name of Rabbi Yose: [6]They made a widow in relation to (lit., "next to") the daughter like a daughter in relation to brothers when there are few properties. [7]Just as [in the case of] the daughter in relation to brothers, [8]the daughter is maintained and the brothers must beg at the doors,

TRANSLATION AND COMMENTARY

are entitled to his widow's handiwork while she is supported from the estate they have inherited. Rav Sheshet argues that just as the sons take their father's place with respect to his widow, so too should they take his place regarding his daughter. Thus they are entitled to the orphan girl's handiwork throughout the period she is maintained from the inheritance that has passed into their hands.

מִי דָּמֵי [1]The Gemara now rejects this argument: **Are the** two cases really **similar?** [2]A husband **does not care about the comfort of his widow.** He is not especially concerned that his widow should live comfortably and enjoy the earnings of her work in addition to the maintenance she will receive from his estate. Thus the widow is entitled only to her maintenance, but her handiwork goes to her husband's heirs, from whose inheritance she is supported. [3]But a father **does care about the comfort of his daughter.** He wants her to receive her basic maintenance out of his estate and to use her earnings for extras, so that she will be able to live in comfort. Thus she is entitled to her handiwork even while she is being maintained by her brothers.

לְמֵימְרָא [4]The Gemara asks: **Do you mean to say that** a man **cares more about his** orphaned **daughter than about his widow?** [5]**But surely Rabbi Abba said in the name of Rabbi Yose:** [6]The Sages **enacted** that the law that applies when a man leaves **a widow and a daughter** and only a small estate **is equivalent to** the law that applies when a man leaves **a daughter and sons and property that is insufficient** to provide for both the daughter's right of maintenance and the sons' rights of inheritance. [7]**Just as in the case** where a man is survived by **a daughter and** by **sons** and his estate is not large enough to meet their respective claims, [8]**the daughter is** first **given** whatever she needs for **her maintenance, and** if nothing remains

RASHI

בתו ניחא ליה בהרווחה — שתרויח מעשה ידיה לבד מפרנסתה. **אלמנה אצל הבת** — מי שמת והניח אלמנה ובת. **בנכסים מועטין** — שאין בהן כדי פרנסת שנים עשר חודש, כדאמר בפרק "מי שמת" בבבא בתרא, וקתני: הבנות יזונו והבנים ישאלו על הפתחים.

NOTES

before she reaches majority. The argument put forward here, that the father is entitled to his daughter's handiwork because it is he who maintains her, is valid only with respect to the rights and obligations of the father and daughter by Rabbinic law (see Rishonim cited in previous note, and *Ritva*; see also *Avnei Nezer* and other Aḥaronim).

אַלְמָנָתוֹ לָא נִיחָא לֵיהּ בְּהַרְוָוחָה Regarding his widow, he does not care about her comfort. The Aḥaronim offer an explanation of why a man cares more about his daughter's comfort than about his widow's comfort. A man wishes his daughter to marry, and so he arranges for her dowry during his lifetime, and he wants her to keep her earnings for herself after his death and add them to her dowry. But he does not particularly want his widow to remarry, and so he does not want her to enjoy the earnings provided by her work. On the other hand, if a man's estate is not large enough to maintain both his daughter and his widow, he prefers that his widow be maintained and his daughter go begging. Since he does not want his wife to remarry, he does not want her to fall into a state of degradation from which a second marriage will be her only escape. But he is ready to allow his daughter to be disgraced, for that will cause her to marry more quickly (*Ḥever ben Ḥayyim, Sukkat David*).

הַבַּת נִיזּוֹנֶת וְהָאַחִין יִשְׁאֲלוּ עַל הַפְּתָחִים The daughter is maintained and the brothers must beg at the doors. If the estate of the deceased is not large enough to satisfy both the daughter's right of maintenance and the sons'

HALAKHAH

הַבַּת נִיזּוֹנֶת וְהָאַחִין יִשְׁאֲלוּ עַל הַפְּתָחִים The daughter is maintained and the brothers must beg at the doors. "If a man dies and is survived by sons and daughters, the sons inherit his entire estate, and they maintain their sisters until the latter reach majority (at the age of twelve-and-a-half) or until they are betrothed, whichever comes first. This applies only if the father's estate contains assets sufficient to maintain both the sons and the daughters. But if there is only enough property to support the daughters, they are maintained from their father's estate, and the sons must, if necessary, live on charity." (*Rambam, Sefer Nashim, Hilkhot Ishut* 19:21; *Shulḥan Arukh, Even HaEzer* 112:11.)

TRANSLATION AND COMMENTARY

for **the sons,** they **must** go and **beg at** other people's doors, [1] so too if he is survived by **a widow and** by a **daughter** and the estate is not large enough to support them both, [2] **the widow is** first **given** whatever she needs for **her maintenance, and** if nothing is left, **the daughter must** go and **beg** for her food **at** other people's **doors.** Thus we see that if a choice has to be made between a man's daughter and his widow, preference is given to the widow. How, then, can the Gemara argue that a man cares more about his daughter's comfort than about that of his widow?

לְעִנְיָן זִילּוּתָא [3] The Gemara draws a distinction between the two issues. **Regarding disgrace,** a man **cares more about his widow** than about his daughter. If his estate is not large enough to support them both, and one of them will be forced to humiliate herself by asking for charity, he prefers that it be his daughter and not his widow. Thus his widow is given what she needs for her maintenance, and his daughter is sent out to beg for herself. [4] But **regarding comfort** and ease, a man **cares more about his daughter** than about his widow. Thus, nothing can be inferred with regard to the daughter's handiwork from the parallel law concerning the widow. The widow receives her maintenance from her late husband's heirs, but must hand over her earnings in exchange, whereas the daughter is entitled to keep her handiwork, even while she is maintained by her father's heirs, because it was her father's wish that she be able to live as comfortably as possible.

מְתִיב רַב יוֹסֵף [5] **Rav Yosef raised an objection** from our Mishnah against Rav Sheshet's ruling that the brothers are entitled to their orphan sister's handiwork. The Mishnah stated: **"The handiwork** produced by a young girl during her father's lifetime **and the objects that she finds** while her father is alive belong to the father even before he actually takes possession of them. [6] This is the case **even if she has not yet collected** what she is owed. [7] Therefore, **if the father dies, they go to her brothers** as part of the legacy that they inherit from their father." [8] Now, says Rav Yosef, **the reason** why the brothers receive the girl's uncollected earnings **is because** they were earned **during the lifetime of their father.** As soon as she completed her work, her earnings were already considered as belonging to her father, and they pass to his heirs in

LITERAL TRANSLATION

[1] so [in the case of] a widow in relation to the daughter, [2] a widow is maintained and the daughter must beg at the doors.
[3] Regarding disgrace, he prefers his widow; [4] regarding comfort, he prefers his daughter.
[5] Rav Yosef objected: "[Regarding] her handiwork and what she finds, [6] even though she has not [yet] collected, [7] [if] the father has died, they belong to [the] brothers." [8] The reason is that [she produced the handiwork] during the lifetime of the father.

אַף אַלְמָנָה אֵצֶל הַבַּת,
²אַלְמָנָה נִיזּוֹנֶת וְהַבַּת תִּשְׁאַל
עַל הַפְּתָחִים.
³לְעִנְיָן זִילּוּתָא, אַלְמָנָתוֹ עֲדִיפָא
לֵיהּ; ⁴לְעִנְיָן הַרְוָוחָה, בִּתּוֹ
עֲדִיפָא לֵיהּ.
⁵מְתִיב רַב יוֹסֵף: "מַעֲשֵׂה יָדֶיהָ
וּמְצִיאָתָהּ, ⁶אַף עַל פִּי שֶׁלֹּא
גָּבְתָה, ⁷מֵת הָאָב, הֲרֵי הֵן שֶׁל
אַחִין". ⁸טַעֲמָא דִּבְחַיֵּי הָאָב.

RASHI

טעמא דבחיי האב — עשתהו, וזכה
בו האב להוריש לבניו.

BACKGROUND

לְעִנְיָן זִילּוּתָא **Regarding disgrace.** Another explanation of the difference between disgrace and comfort lies in the assumption that if the widow must depend on charity, this is also a disgrace to her late husband, for she remains dependent on her husband's estate while she is a widow. But since in time the children ought to become independent, it is no disgrace to the father if he is unable to supply their needs. On the other hand, regarding comfort, we assume that a man is more attached to his children and wants to give them everything they need for a comfortable life, and so is interested in bequeathing them money for that purpose; but regarding his wife, it is sufficient if she has enough to subsist.

SAGES

רַב יוֹסֵף **Rav Yosef.** A Babylonian Amora of the third generation. See *Ketubot,* Part I, p. 102.

NOTES

rights of inheritance, the daughter is given preference. The daughter is preferred because her right of maintenance is based on a condition included in her mother's ketubah. Thus it is like any other financial obligation that falls upon the father and his estate. Even though it is the sons who inherit the estate, the assets of the estate are mortgaged for the payment of the daughter's maintenance, and so she

is given preference. As for the case where the estate of the deceased is not large enough to maintain both his daughter and his widow, both are entitled to maintenance by virtue of a condition in the ketubah. Thus it was necessary to consider other factors when deciding which of the two was to receive preference. See the Halakhah section, where the opinion of the Jerusalem Talmud on this issue is cited.

HALAKHAH

אַלְמָנָה אֵצֶל הַבַּת **The widow in relation to the daughter.** "If a man dies and is survived by a wife and a daughter, and his estate cannot maintain both of them, the widow is maintained from his property, and the daughter must live on charity (*Rambam,* following Rabbi Abba). Basing themselves on the Jerusalem Talmud (*Bava Batra* 9:1), *Tosafot* and *Rosh* explain that if a man with a small estate is survived by only a wife and a daughter, both are maintained from his property as long as something

remains of the estate. If he is survived by a wife, a daughter, and a son, only then do we say that the widow is given whatever she needs for her maintenance, and if nothing is left, the son and the daughter must live on charity. *Shulḥan Arukh* brings *Rambam*'s viewpoint as the primary ruling, and the viewpoint of *Tosafot* and *Rosh* as an alternative opinion." (*Rambam, Sefer Nashim, Hilkhot Ishut* 19:21; *Shulḥan Arukh, Even HaEzer* 93:4.)

TRANSLATION AND COMMENTARY

the event of his death. [1] **But** it follows from this that the earnings from the girl's handiwork that she produces **after her father's death belong to** the girl **herself,** for they never belonged to the father and they were therefore never included in his estate. [2] **Does this not apply** even in the case of **an** orphaned **daughter** who is being **maintained** out of the estate inherited **by her brothers?** Thus we see from our Mishnah that a girl may keep her handiwork for herself, even while receiving support from her brothers, and this refutes the ruling of Rav Sheshet!

לָא [3] The Gemara answers: **No,** the Mishnah is referring to a case **where** the girl **is not being maintained** out of her father's estate — for example, where her father died a poor man without any property. In such a case, the girl is forced to support herself, and she is therefore entitled to keep the earnings from her handiwork. But if she were to receive support from her brothers, they would be entitled to her handiwork, as argued by Rav Sheshet.

[1] הָא לְאַחַר מִיתַת הָאָב, לְעַצְמָהּ. [2] מַאי לָאו בְּנִיזּוֹנֶת? [3] לָא, בְּשֶׁאֵינָהּ נִיזּוֹנֶת. [4] אִי בְּשֶׁאֵינָהּ נִיזּוֹנֶת, [5] מַאי לְמֵימְרָא? [6] אֲפִילּוּ לְמַאן דְּאָמַר: [7] יָכוֹל הָרַב לוֹמַר לָעֶבֶד: ״עֲשֵׂה עִמִּי, וְאֵינִי זָנְךָ״, [8] הָנֵי מִילֵּי בְּעֶבֶד כְּנַעֲנִי, דְּלָא כְּתִיב בֵּיהּ ״עִמָּךְ״, [9] אֲבָל עֶבֶד עִבְרִי, דִּכְתִיב בֵּיהּ ״עִמָּךְ״, [10] לָא, כָּל שֶׁכֵּן בִּתּוֹ!

LITERAL TRANSLATION

[1] But after the death of the father, [2] it belongs to her. Is it not [referring] to [a daughter] maintained [by the brothers]?

[3] No, where she is not maintained.

[4] If [it is referring] to [a daughter] who is not maintained, [5] what [need is there] to say [this]? [6] Even according to the one who says: [7] A master can say to a slave: "Work for me, but I will not feed you," [8] this applies (lit., "these things") to a Canaanite slave, about whom "with you" is not written, [9] but not [to] a Hebrew slave, about whom "with you" *is* written, [10] [and] all the more so [to] his daughter!

RASHI

הא לאחר מיתת האב – עשתהו, הוי לעצמה, מדאצטריך לתנא לאשמועינן. **לא בשאינה ניזונת** – כגון שלא היו נכסים. **מאי למימרא** – דיוקא לא אצטריך לאשמועינן דעשתה לאחר מיתת האב לעצמה, ואי לאשמועינן היא גופה דמה שעשתה בחיי האב לאחים – פשיטא, דהא זכה ביה אב, דממונא הוא ולאו קנסא. **אפילו למאן דאמר** – במסכת גיטין (יב,א) פלוגתא.

אִי בְּשֶׁאֵינָהּ נִיזּוֹנֶת [4] The Gemara objects to this interpretation of the Mishnah. If the Mishnah is referring to a case in which the girl is being maintained by her brothers from her father's estate, then we can understand that its purpose is to teach us that the girl is entitled to keep her handiwork, even while receiving support from her brothers. But **if** the Mishnah **is referring** to a case **where** the girl **is not being maintained** by her brothers, [5] **what does it come to teach** us? The law stated explicitly in the Mishnah — that the brothers are entitled to the handiwork produced by the girl during her father's lifetime — is obvious, for the handiwork already belonged to the father before he died, so it must be included in his estate. And the law that can be inferred from this ruling — that the girl is entitled to keep for herself the handiwork she produces after her father's death — is also obvious. [6] For **even according to the** authority **who says** elsewhere (*Gittin* 12a): [7] **A master can say to** his **slave: "Work for me, but I will not feed you,"** for the master is not legally obliged to support his slave, [8] **this applies** only **in** the case of **a non-Jewish slave, about whom the verse does not use the expression: "With you."** [9] **But** as for **a Jewish slave, about whom the verse says** (Deuteronomy 15:16): "Because he is happy **with you,"** which teaches us that the slave must live in conditions comparable to those of his master, the master **cannot** demand that the slave work for him unless he provides him with his food. Now, if a slave cannot be forced to work without maintenance from his master, [10] then **surely an orphan girl** cannot be required to hand over her handiwork and earnings to her brothers if she is not being maintained by them!

NOTES

דִּכְתִיב בֵּיהּ ״עִמָּךְ״ **About whom "with you."** Our commentary follows *Meiri,* who explains that the Gemara here is referring to the verse (Deuteronomy 15:16), "Because he is happy with you," which teaches that a master must provide his Jewish slave with food and drink comparable to that he provides for himself. *Tosafot* argues that this verse merely describes the relationship between the slave and his master, but does not impose any normative obligation.

HALAKHAH

עֲשֵׂה עִמִּי וְאֵינִי זָנְךָ **"Work for me, but I will not feed you."** "A master can say to his non-Jewish slave: 'Work for me, but I will not feed you' (but if the slave was his wife's property, the husband is required to support him; *Rambam* and *Rif*). *Rema* notes that according to some authorities (*Tosafot, Rosh,* and *Tur,* basing themselves on *Gittin* 12b)

TRANSLATION AND COMMENTARY

אֲמַר רַבָּה בַּר עוּלָּא [1] **Rabbah bar Ulla said:** In fact, the Mishnah is referring to a case in which the girl is not being maintained by her brothers, and the ruling is needed to teach us that the girl may keep the handiwork she produces after her father's death. The objection that this is obvious, because the orphan girl should be no worse off than a Jewish slave who cannot be forced to work unless his master feeds him, can be rebutted as follows: From the law applying to a Jewish slave we know only that the girl is entitled to keep those earnings that she needs for her maintenance. [2] The Mishnah's ruling **was necessary** in order to teach us that she may even keep her **surplus** earnings, because the rights to her handiwork do not pass from her father to his heirs. But if the girl is supported by her brothers, they are indeed entitled to her handiwork, as argued by Rav Sheshet.

אֲמַר רָבָא [3] Responding to the argument put forward by Rabbah bar Ulla, **Rava said:** Is it possible that **a great man like Rav Yosef,** who raised an objection to Rav Sheshet's ruling from our Mishnah, **did not know that** Rav Sheshet could interpret the Mishnah as referring to the girl's **surplus** earnings, [4] **and** this was why **he raised his objection?** If Rav Yosef regarded our Mishnah as presenting a difficulty to the ruling of Rav Sheshet, he must have had something else in mind. [5] **Rather, Rava said: Rav Yosef had difficulty** in understanding **our Mishnah itself,** and this caused him to reach a conclusion that proves Rav Sheshet's position to be untenable. [6] **For** the Mishnah **states: "The handiwork** produced by a young girl during her father's lifetime **and** the objects **that she finds** while her father is alive belong to the father even before he actually takes possession of them. [7] This is the case **even if she has not yet collected** what she is owed." Now, says Rava, we can construct a case in which she has not yet received payment for the work she has already completed. [8] But with regard to **what she finds,** it is inappropriate to use the expression, "Even though she has not yet collected," for **from whom does she collect** anything when she finds a

[1] אֲמַר רַבָּה בַּר עוּלָּא: [2] לֹא נִצְרְכָה אֶלָּא לְהַעֲדָפָה. [3] אֲמַר רָבָא: גַּבְרָא רַבָּה כְּרַב יוֹסֵף לָא יָדַע דְּאִיכָּא הַעֲדָפָה, [4] וְקָמוֹתִיב תְּיוּבְתָּא? [5] אֶלָּא אֲמַר רָבָא: רַב יוֹסֵף מַתְנִיתִין גּוּפָא קַשְׁיָא לֵיהּ, [6] דְּקָתָנֵי: "מַעֲשֵׂה יָדֶיהָ וּמְצִיאָתָהּ, [7] אַף עַל פִּי שֶׁלֹּא גָּבְתָה". [8] מְצִיאָתָהּ מִמַּאן

LITERAL TRANSLATION

[1] Rabbah bar Ulla said: [2] It is needed only for the surplus.

[3] Rava said: Does a great man like Rav Yosef not know that there may be a surplus, [4] and [yet] he raises an objection? [5] Rather, Rava said: Rav Yosef has difficulty with our Mishnah itself, [6] for it teaches: "[Regarding] her handiwork and what she finds, [7] even though she has not [yet] collected." [8] From whom does she collect what she finds?

RASHI

להעדפה — לעולם לדיוקא דילה איצטריך, לאשמועינן דמעשה ידיה לאחר מיתת אב לעצמה, ובשאינה ניזונת. דלא תימא: זכות שזיכתה תורה לאב בבתו ממון הוא להורישו לבנים. ודקשיא לך במאי תיתזון, הא לא גרעה מעבד עברי? כי איצטריך לאשמועינן — להעדפה, שמעשה ידיה עודף על מזונותיה, איצטריך לאשמועינן. **אמר רבא וכי גברא רבה כרב יוסף** — דאותבה להא תיובתא, לא הוה ידע דאיכא העדפה, ומצי לדחויי ולשנויי בשאינה ניזונת ולהעדפה, ואפילו הכי אותבה? אלא על כרחך רב יוסף טעמא ידע, דתיובתא מעלייתא היא, והכי קשיא ליה ממתניתין אדרב ששת. **דקתני** — מתניתין "מציאתה עם מעשה ידיה", ולמה לי למתנייה? והא לא שייך למיתני "אף על גב שלא גבתה" — דממאן גבתה?

BACKGROUND

גַּבְרָא רַבָּה כְּרַב יוֹסֵף A great man like Rav Yosef. Although it is possible that an Amora may not have taken into account all the possibilities existing within the Halakhah, nevertheless, regarding an authority as great as Rav Yosef, it is unlikely that he would not have thought of this simple solution.

NOTES

Rather, says *Tosafot,* the Gemara here is referring to the verse (Leviticus 25:40), "He [the Jewish slave] shall be with you as a hired worker and as a sojourner," which instructs the master on how to treat his slave.

לֹא נִצְרְכָה אֶלָּא לְהַעֲדָפָה It is needed only for the surplus. According to most Rishonim, the father is entitled to his daughter's surplus earnings in excess of the amount she needs for her maintenance, even if he is providing nothing for her support. *Ra'avad* (cited by *Meiri* and by *Shittah Mekubbetzet* on *Bava Metzia*) maintains that the father acquires the surplus earnings only after his daughter's death, when she no longer needs to be maintained, or after she marries, when her husband becomes liable for her support. But while the girl is under her father's authority, if he fails to provide for her, he must not take her surplus earnings for himself, for the surplus that she earns one week she may need for her maintenance the next.

מְצִיאָתָהּ מִמַּאן גָּבְיָא From whom does she collect what she finds? *Ritva* explains that Rav Yosef's objection against the viewpoint of Rav Sheshet was not based on an inference drawn from our Mishnah — that the Mishnah's ruling that the girl's uncollected earings from the handi-

HALAKHAH

this ruling applies only under ordinary conditions, but in years of drought the master must support his slave, for nobody else will have compassion on him and offer him charity. But even then the master can say to his slave that he must support himself from his own handiwork, even if his handiwork does not suffice for his support." (*Rambam, Sefer Kinyan, Hilkhot Avadim* 9:7; *Shulḥan Arukh, Yoreh De'ah* 267:20.)

TRANSLATION AND COMMENTARY

lost object? Why, then, did the Mishnah mention what the girl finds in the same context as her handiwork? [1] **Rather, is it not that** the author of the Mishnah meant to **say as follows:** The young girl's **handiwork is** treated **like what she finds.** [2] **Just as** with respect to **what she finds,** objects that she comes across **during her father's lifetime belong to her father,** [3] **but** those that she comes across only **after her father's death belong to her,** even if she is maintained by her brothers from her father's estate, [4] **so too** with respect to **her handiwork,** what she produces **during her father's lifetime belongs to her father,** [5] **but** what she produces **after her father's death belongs to her,** even if she is being supported by her brothers. [6] Thus we can **conclude from this** that when the Mishnah speaks of the girl's handiwork, it is referring to the handiwork that the girl requires for her maintenance, and not to her surplus earnings. Hence it follows that the Mishnah must be referring to a case in which the girl is maintained by her brothers, and the Mishnah implies that she may keep her handiwork for herself even while being supported by her brothers, as was argued by Rav Yosef against the ruling of Rav Sheshet.

אִיתְּמַר נַמִי [7] The Gemara now reports the viewpoint of an Amora who disagreed with Rav Sheshet. **It was also stated that Rav Yehudah said in the name of Rav:** [8] Even if **an** orphan **daughter is maintained by her brothers** from their father's estate, [9] all **the handiwork** she produces after her father's death **belongs to her** and not to her brothers.

אָמַר רַב כָּהֲנָא [10] The Gemara now provides Scriptural support for this ruling. **Rav Kahana said: What is the reason** that the girl is entitled to keep her handiwork for herself? [11] It is **because the** Biblical **verse** dealing with non-Jewish slaves **says** (Leviticus 25:46): **"And you shall take them as an inheritance**

גָּבְיָא? [1] אֶלָּא לָאו הָכִי קָאָמַר: מַעֲשֵׂה יָדֶיהָ כִּמְצִיאָתָהּ. [2] מַה מְּצִיאָתָהּ בְּחַיֵּי הָאָב לָאָב, [3] לְאַחַר מִיתַת הָאָב לְעַצְמָהּ, [4] אַף מַעֲשֵׂה יָדֶיהָ נַמִי בְּחַיֵּי הָאָב לָאָב, [5] לְאַחַר מִיתַת הָאָב לְעַצְמָהּ. [6] שְׁמַע מִינָּהּ.

[7] אִיתְּמַר נַמִי, אָמַר רַב יְהוּדָה אָמַר רַב: [8] בַּת הַנִּיזּוֹנֶת מִן הָאַחִין, [9] מַעֲשֵׂה יָדֶיהָ לְעַצְמָהּ. [10] אָמַר רַב כָּהֲנָא: מַאי טַעֲמָא? [11] דִּכְתִיב: "וְהִתְנַחַלְתֶּם אֹתָם

LITERAL TRANSLATION

[1] Rather, is it not [that] he says as follows: Her handiwork is like what she finds. [2] Just as what she finds during the lifetime of the father belongs to the father, [3] [but] after the death of the father it belongs to her, [4] so too her handiwork during the lifetime of the father belongs to the father, [5] [but] after the death of the father it belongs to her. [6] Conclude from this.

[7] It was also stated [that] Rav Yehudah said in the name of Rav: [8] [Regarding] a daughter who is maintained by the brothers, [9] her handiwork [belongs] to her.

[10] Rav Kahana said: What is the reason? [11] Because it is written: "And you shall take them as an inheritance

RASHI

אלא לאו הכי קאמר מעשה ידיה כמציאתה — דמה שעשתה בחיי האב — לאב וליורשין, ומה שעשתה לאחר מיתת האב — לעצמה. **מה מציאתה כו'** — דמציאתה פשיטא לן דלעצמה, דהא אפילו בחיי האב לא זכי בהן אב אלא אם כן סמוכה על שלחנו, כדאמרינן בבבא מציעא (יב,ב), ומשום איבה, דכיון דאינו חייב במזונותיה בחייו, כדתנן בפרקין: האב אינו חייב במזונות בתו, ואי אמרת מציאתה לעצמה — תו לא יהיב לה מזונות. ולקמן בפירקין נמי אמרינן: זכאי במציאתה משום איבה. אבל אחין — על כרחייהו מתזנא מנכסי האב. **דכתיב והתנחלתם אותם** — עבדים כנענים.

SAGES

רַב כָּהֲנָא Rav Kahana. There were at least four Babylonian Amoraim bearing this name. It seems likely that the reference here is to Rav Kahana II, an Amora of the second generation who was a disciple of Rav and later of Rav Huna and Rav Yehudah.

NOTES

work she produced during her father's lifetime belong to the brothers implies that the earnings from the handiwork produced after his death belong to her. Rather, it was based on the fact that the Mishnah's words, "even though she has not yet collected," can apply only to her handiwork, but not to what she finds. Thus, the expression "what she finds" was unnecessary, and must have been included here to teach that a young girl is entitled to keep the handiwork she produces after her father's death, just as she may keep anything she finds after his death.

דִּכְתִיב "וְהִתְנַחַלְתֶּם" Because it is written: "And you shall take them as an inheritance." Many Rishonim have the reading: "Rav Kahana said: What is *Rav*'s reason?" — implying that Rav Kahana was seeking Scriptural support specifically for the position of Rav, but not for that of Rav Sheshet. But, as was explained in an earlier note, most Rishonim explain that Rav Sheshet agrees that the brothers are not entitled to the orphan daughter's handiwork by Torah law, but only by Rabbinic enactment.

Ramban suggests that Rav Kahana asked only about

HALAKHAH

בַּת הַנִּיזּוֹנֶת מִן הָאַחִין Regarding a daughter who is maintained by the brothers. "If an orphan girl is maintained by her brothers from her father's estate, all the handiwork she produces and the lost objects that she finds belong to her," following Rav Ashi who ruled in accordance with Rav. (*Rambam, Sefer Nashim, Hilkhot Ishut* 19:10; *Shulḥan Arukh, Even HaEzer* 112:2).

TRANSLATION AND COMMENTARY

for your sons after you," [1]implying that **them,** i.e., your slaves, **you can pass on to your sons,** [2]**but** the rights that you have in **your daughters** you **cannot** pass on **to your sons.** [3]**This** verse **teaches** us **that a man cannot pass on to his son a right** granted him by the Torah with respect **to his daughter.** The rights that a father has over his daughter, including the right to her handiwork, are personal privileges that are not subject to the laws of inheritance.

מַתְקִיף לָהּ רַבָּה [4]**Rabbah objected to this:** How do we know that this verse refers to the father's right to his daughter's handiwork? [5]Perhaps we can **say that the verse is speaking** here **of** the **payments** that a father receives as compensation if his **daughter** is **seduced** or raped, **and** the **fines** that he is paid in such circumstances, **and** the **payments** to which he is entitled if she suffers an **injury.** The right to all these payments is the personal privilege of a father with respect to his daughter, and this right cannot pass to his heirs. But the right to his daughter's handiwork may indeed pass from a father to his sons! [6]In support of Rabbah's objection, the Gemara notes that **Rav Ḥanina taught** a Baraita that came to a **similar** conclusion: [7]**"The verse is speaking** here **of** the **payments** that a father receives as compensation if his **daughter** is **seduced** or raped, **and** the **fines** that he is paid in such circumstances, **and** the **payments** to which he is entitled if she suffers an **injury."** The Gemara makes no attempt to rebut this objection.

לִבְנֵיכֶם אַחֲרֵיכֶם". [1]"אוֹתָם לִבְנֵיכֶם", [2]וְלֹא בְּנוֹתֵיכֶם לִבְנֵיכֶם. [3]מַגִּיד שֶׁאֵין אָדָם מוֹרִישׁ זְכוּת בִּתּוֹ לִבְנוֹ.
[4]מַתְקִיף לָהּ רַבָּה: [5]וְאֵימָא בְּפִיתּוּי הַבַּת וּקְנָסוֹת וַחֲבָלוֹת הַכָּתוּב מְדַבֵּר! [6]וְכֵן תָּנָא רַב חֲנִינָא: [7]"בְּפִתּוּי הַבַּת וּקְנָסוֹת וַחֲבָלוֹת הַכָּתוּב מְדַבֵּר".

LITERAL TRANSLATION

for your sons after you." [1]*"Them"* [you shall take] "for your sons," [2]but not your daughters for your sons. [3]It states that a man does not leave a right in his daughter to his son.

[4]Rabbah objected to this: [5]But say that the verse is speaking of [payments for] the seduction of the daughter and fines and [payments for] injuries! [6]And so did Rav Ḥanina teach: [7]"The verse is speaking of [payments for] the seduction of the daughter and fines and [payments for] injuries."

RASHI

זכות בתו — זכות שזיכתה לו תורה בבתו. **ואימא בפתוי הבת וקנסות** — דאונס וחבלות הכתוב מדבר, אבל מעשה ידיה, דמידי דשכיח וחסרי בה ממונא, דהא מיתזנא מינייהו — אימא דידהו הוי.

NOTES

Rav, because the Gemara has already explained why the Rabbis did not enact that the brothers are entitled to the daughter's handiwork — because she is not maintained from their property, but rather from the assets of their father's estate that had been mortgaged for her maintenance. Rav Kahana now comes to explain why the brothers do not take the place of their father by Torah law and inherit his right to their sister's handiwork, just as they inherit the rest of his estate.

Tosafot and others ask: Why does Rav Kahana have to derive the law that an orphan girl may keep her handiwork for herself from the verse regarding slaves? The father's right to his daughter's handiwork is derived by analogy from the master's right to his maidservant's handiwork. Thus it should follow that just as the master's right to his maidservant's handiwork does not pass to his heirs, so too should the father's right to his daughter's handiwork not be inherited by his sons.

Ritva answers: If this were the only source for the ruling that an orphan girl may keep her handiwork for herself, then the Rabbis could have enacted that the brothers are entitled to the handiwork, so as to prevent the brothers from hating their sister. But now that the law is derived from the verse regarding slaves, which teaches that the Torah was concerned that the daughter not be treated as a maidservant by her brothers, we can understand why the brothers are not entitled to her handiwork even by Rabbinic enactment. According to Rav Sheshet, the verse refers to the payments made for the girl's seduction and rape, and not to her handiwork. If Rav Sheshet were correct, the Rabbis could enact that her handiwork belongs to the brothers.

וְאֵימָא בְּפִיתּוּי But say that the verse is speaking of seduction. The Rishonim ask: Why should there be a difference between the right to the payments for the girl's seduction or rape, and the right to her handiwork? *Rashi* explains: Rabbah thought that the right to the daughter's handiwork might pass to the father's sons, even though the right to the payments for her seduction or rape does not, because girls often earn money by handiwork. If the brothers maintain her and receive nothing in return, they will suffer a substantial financial loss and hostility will develop between them and the orphan girl.

Rabbi Crescas Vidal adds that the Torah may have been concerned only that the sons should not gain a right in the daughter's person similar to the right they have in a slave they inherit from their father, and this right would be manifest in their claim to the payments for her seduction or rape. But perhaps they do indeed inherit their father's right to her handiwork, acquiring his lien on her earnings, for that is not considered a right to her person.

[1]חֲבָלוֹת צַעֲרָא דְּגוּפָא נִינְהוּ! [2]אָמַר רַבִּי יוֹסֵי בַּר חֲנִינָא: [43B] [3]שֶׁפְּצָעָהּ בְּפָנֶיהָ. [4]אָמַר רַב זֵירָא אָמַר רַב מַתְּנָה אָמַר רַב, [5]וְאָמְרִי לָהּ אָמַר רַבִּי זֵירָא אָמַר רַב מַתְּנָה אָמַר רַב:

LITERAL TRANSLATION

[1][But payments for] injuries are [for] bodily pain! [2]Rabbi Yose bar Ḥanina said: [43B] [3][It is] where he injured her in her face.

[4]Rav Zera said in the name of Rav Matenah who said in the name of Rav, [5]and some say [that] Rabbi Zera said in the name of Rav Matenah who said in the name of Rav:

TRANSLATION AND COMMENTARY

חֲבָלוֹת [1]The Gemara now raises a question about the reference made in the Baraita to the payments made for a young girl's personal injury. Surely, says the Gemara, **payments** in the case of personal **injury are** made in order to compensate **for** the **bodily pain** suffered by the injured party. It is well known that a father is not entitled to make use of the payments made for bodily pain suffered by his daughter, but must invest the money on her behalf until she comes of age. Why, then, did the Baraita include payments for the daughter's injuries among those rights that belong to the father but do not pass to his sons?

אָמַר רַבִּי יוֹסֵי בַּר חֲנִינָא [2]**Rabbi Yose bar Ḥanina said** in reply: [43B] [3]The Baraita is speaking here of a case **where someone injured** the girl **in the face,** thus reducing her value if she were to be sold as a maidservant or given away in marriage. Since it is the father who would suffer the loss, it is he who is entitled to the compensation. The Baraita establishes that this right to compensation is the father's personal privilege and does not pass to his heirs.

אָמַר רַב זֵירָא [4]The Gemara continues: According to one tradition, Rav himself used the Biblical verse dealing with non-Jewish slaves to support his opinion that an orphaned daughter maintained by her brothers is entitled to all her handiwork. **Rav Zera said in the name of Rav Matenah who said in the name of Rav,** [5]**and some** report the tradition differently and **say that Rabbi Zera** — after he was ordained in Eretz Israel and thereafter given the title of Rabbi — **said in the name of Rav Matenah who said in the name of Rav:**

RASHI

צערא דגופא הוא — ולצערא לא זכי ליה רחמנא לאב, כדתניא ב״החובל״ (בבא קמא פז,ב): בבנו ובבתו הקטנים — יעשה להם סגולה. **שפצעה בפניה** — דאפחתה מכספא. דאי איתיה לאב — דיליה הוא, דהא יש לו בה מכר. **אמר רב זירא ואמרי לה אמר רבי זירא** — הוא רבי זירא הוא רב זירא. אלא, בבבל מקמי דסליק לארעא דישראל לקמיה דרבי יוחנן, ואין סמיכה בבבל — הוו קרו ליה רב זירא. ובהא שמעתא, איכא למאן דאמר: מקמי דסמכוהו אמרה. ואיכא למאן דאמר: בתר דסמכוהו אמרה.

NOTES

חֲבָלוֹת צַעֲרָא דְּגוּפָא **But payments for injuries are for bodily pain.** *Ritva* points out that the Gemara's question regarding payments for injuries does not detract in any substantial way from the objection raised by Rabbah. The Gemara was concerned because Rabbah included compensation for the daughter's bodily injury among the rights that belong to the father. But Rabbah can still argue that the verse, "And you shall take them as an inheritance," refers only to the payments made to a father for his daughter's seduction or rape and the fine paid in such circumstances, and not to the father's right to her handiwork or to payments made as damages for her bodily injury.

שֶׁפְּצָעָהּ בְּפָנֶיהָ **It is where he injured her in her face.** *Rashi* explains that the Baraita is not referring to the damages paid for the girl's pain, but rather to the compensation to which she is entitled for being disfigured, which would reduce her value as a maidservant. Since the girl's father is entitled to sell her, he is the one who suffers the loss and receives the compensation. Thus we understand why the Baraita could have included such compensation among those rights that belong to the father but are not inherited by his sons.

Shittah Mekubbetzet records a different explanation of the Gemara's question and answer found in a manuscript of *Rashi*'s commentary: Responding to the suggestion that the verse refers to damages paid for bodily injury, the Gemara objects that it is obvious that damages for bodily injury are paid to the girl herself. Rabbi Yose bar Ḥanina answers that the verse speaks of a case in which the girl was injured in the face, in which case her entire family shares in her humiliation, and therefore we might have thought that the compensation paid for such humiliation is included in the property that passes from the father to his sons.

Ritva explains the Gemara's question as follows: How could it have been suggested that the verse speaks of

HALAKHAH

שֶׁפְּצָעָהּ בְּפָנֶיהָ **It is where he injured her in her face.** "If someone injures a minor girl in such a way that her value (were she to be sold as a maidservant or given away in marriage) is reduced, he must compensate the girl's father for her loss in value, as well as for any loss resulting from her inability to work because of her injury. But the compensation for her pain, her medical expenses, and her shame, as well as the compensation for any injury that does not cause her value to be reduced, must be paid to the girl herself. Similarly, if someone causes his own minor daughter a bodily injury, he must compensate her for her pain, her medical expenses and her shame," following Rabbi Yose bar Ḥanina here and Rabbi Yoḥanan in *Bava Kamma*. (*Rambam, Sefer Nezikin, Hilkhot Ḥovel U'Mazik* 4:14; *Shulḥan Arukh, Ḥoshen Mishpat* 424:6.)

SAGES

רַבִּי יוֹסֵי בַּר חֲנִינָא **Rabbi Yose bar Ḥanina.** A Palestinian Amora of the second generation, Rabbi Yose bar Ḥanina was a younger contemporary of Rabbi Yoḥanan and one of his first students. Rabbi Yoḥanan ordained him, and he grew in knowledge of Torah until he came to be regarded as Rabbi Yoḥanan's colleague. Many differences of opinion between the two are recorded (see *Bava Kamma* 39a). Rabbi Yose bar Ḥanina was also closely associated with Resh Lakish and Rabbi Elazar. Some of Rabbi Yoḥanan's pupils also studied with him. Many of them, especially Rabbi Abbahu and Rabbi Ḥama bar Ukva, transmitted teachings in his name. He is known to have had sons who died during his lifetime.

רַב מַתְּנָה **Rav Matenah.** A Babylonian Amora of the second generation. See *Ketubot*, Part III, p 120.

BACKGROUND

רַב זֵירָא...רַבִּי זֵירָא **Rav Zera...Rabbi Zera.** Only scholars who had been formally ordained by their teachers were qualified by Torah law to act as judges in all aspects of Jewish law. The ordination of scholars (סְמִיכָה) had to be conferred by three Sages, one of them himself ordained, who were given the authority to ordain others by the president (נָשִׂיא) of the Sanhedrin. By tradition, the chain of Rabbinic ordination stretched back to Moses himself.

Toward the end of the Second Temple period, the title "Rabbi" was used when referring to ordained scholars. Even the greatest of the Babylonian Sages did not receive ordination, since ordination was conferred only in Eretz Israel. Babylonian Sages were referred to by the title "Rav." Among the Babylonian Sages who immigrated to Eretz Israel, some did not receive ordination and continued to be called "Rav," whereas others did receive ordination (see above, 17b). Some of these scholars were young men when they came to Eretz Israel, and are therefore always mentioned with their full title (e.g., Rabbi Abba and

TRANSLATION AND COMMENTARY

[1]Even if **an** orphan **daughter is maintained by her brothers** from their father's estate, [2]all **the handiwork** she produces after her father's death **belongs to her** and not to her brothers. [3]**For the verse** dealing with non-Jewish slaves (Leviticus 25:46) **says: "And you shall take them as an inheritance for your sons after you."** [4]The use of the word **"them"** teaches that **you can pass** your slaves on **to your sons,** [5]**but** the rights that you have over **your daughters** you **cannot** pass on **to your sons.** [6]**This** verse **teaches us that a man cannot bequeath a right** granted him by the Torah with respect **to his daughter to his son.** Thus the right that a father has to his daughter's handiwork is considered a personal privilege that is not subject to the laws of inheritance.

אָמַר לֵיהּ [7]When **Avimi bar Pappi** heard the tradition reported by Rav Zera, he **said to him:** [8]It was **Shakud** who **issued** this ruling.

שָׁקוּד מַנּוּ [9]The Gemara clarifies what Avimi bar Pappi meant: **Who is** the scholar whom he referred to as **Shakud?** It is **Shmuel.** [10]But how could it be? **For surely** it was **Rav** who **said** this, as is indicated by the various reports of his position on the matter!

אֵימָא [11]The Gemara suggests: **Say** that this is what Avimi meant: **Shakud,** i.e., Shmuel, **also said** what Rav said — that a father's right to his daughter's handiwork does not pass to his sons with the rest of his estate when he dies.

אָמַר מָר בַּר אַמֵימָר [12]In conclusion, the Gemara now cites a number of decisions on the matter: **Mar bar Amemar said to Rav Ashi:** [13]**The** Sages of **Neharde'a say** as follows: **The law is in accordance with Rav Sheshet** that the brothers are entitled to their orphan sister's handiwork, if they are maintaining her from their father's estate. [14]**Rav Ashi** disagreed and **said: The law is in accordance with Rav** that the orphan girl can keep her handiwork for herself, even if she is being maintained by her brothers from their father's estate. [15]The Gemara ends with a final decision: **The law is in accordance with Rav** that the orphan girl can keep

[1]בַּת הַנִּיזּוֹנֶת מִן הָאַחִין, [2]מַעֲשֵׂה יָדֶיהָ לְעַצְמָהּ, [3]דִּכְתִיב: ״וְהִתְנַחַלְתֶּם אֹתָם לִבְנֵיכֶם אַחֲרֵיכֶם״. [4]״אוֹתָם לִבְנֵיכֶם״, [5]וְלֹא בְּנוֹתֵיכֶם לִבְנֵיכֶם. [6]מַגִּיד שֶׁאֵין אָדָם מוֹרִישׁ זְכוּת בִּתּוֹ לִבְנוֹ.

[7]אָמַר לֵיהּ אֲבִימִי בַּר פַּפִּי: [8]שָׁקוּד אֲמָרָהּ.

[9]שָׁקוּד מַנּוּ? שְׁמוּאֵל. [10]הָא רַב אֲמָרָהּ!

[11]אֵימָא: אַף שָׁקוּד אֲמָרָהּ.

[12]אָמַר מָר בַּר אַמֵימָר לְרַב אַשִׁי: [13]הָכִי אָמְרִי נְהַרְדְּעֵי: הִלְכְתָא כְּוָותֵיהּ דְּרַב שֵׁשֶׁת. [14]רַב אַשִׁי אָמַר: הִלְכְתָא כְּוָותֵיהּ דְּרַב. [15]וְהִלְכְתָא כְּוָותֵיהּ דְּרַב.

LITERAL TRANSLATION

[1][Regarding] a daughter who is maintained by the brothers, [2]her handiwork [belongs] to her, [3]for it is written: "And you shall take them as an inheritance for your sons after you." [4]*"Them"* [you shall take] "for your sons," [5]but not your daughters for your sons. [6]It teaches [us] that a man does not cause his son to inherit a right over his daughter.

[7]Avimi bar Pappi said to him: [8]Shakud said it.

[9]Who is Shakud? Shmuel. [10]But surely Rav said it!

[11]Say: Shakud also said it.

[12]Mar bar Amemar said to Rav Ashi: [13]The Neharde'ans say this: The law is in accordance with Rav Sheshet. [14]Rav Ashi said: The law is in accordance with Rav. [15]And the law is in accordance with Rav.

RASHI

שמואל – הוו קרו ליה שקוד על שום דהלכתא כוותיה בדיני, ושוקד על דבריו לאומרם כהלכתא. **הא רב אמרה** – לעיל. **כרב ששת** – דפשיט לעיל נתו מאלמנתו, ואמר: מעשה ידיה לאחין.

NOTES

compensation for bodily injury, implying that all the compensation paid for such an injury is made to the father? Surely all agree that the compensation for pain is paid to the girl herself, the medical expenses are paid to the doctor, and the compensation for her lost work is paid to the father, for it is he who is entitled to her handiwork. Rabbi Yose bar Ḥanina answers that the Baraita is referring to a case in which the only compensation to be paid is for the girl's loss of value if she is disfigured. In such a case, all the compensation is paid to the girl's father.

שָׁקוּד Shakud. *Rashi* explains that Shmuel was called Shakud, meaning "the industrious one," because of the care he took to formulate his statements and rulings in the most precise fashion (as evidenced by the fact that his pronouncements on all issues of civil law are authoritative). *Arukh* explains the name Shakud as meaning "the studious one," for Shmuel was extremely diligent in his study of Torah (see also Jerusalem Talmud, *Nedarim* 8:2, where Ben Azzai and Ben Zoma are referred to as *"shakdanim"*). Others explain that the term used here indicates speed, as in the verse (Jeremiah 1:12), "For I will hasten [שֹׁקֵד] my word," for Shmuel was quick in his studies (*Ramat Shmuel*). Another suggestion is that Shmuel was called Shakud because Rabbi Yehudah HaNasi was waiting (*"shoked"*) for a chance to ordain him, but the opportunity never presented itself (*Zuto Shel Yam*). Besides being called Shakud, Shmuel is in several places (*Shabbat* 53a, *Kiddushin* 39a, and elsewhere) referred to by the title *"Aryokh."*

Rabbi Elazar). There were also Sages who, even when they left Babylonia, were already well known and were called "Rav" there.

With reference to this last group there is no uniformity. Sometimes these scholars are referred to as "Rav" and sometimes as "Rabbi" (e.g., Rabbi/Rav Ammi and Rabbi/Rav Assi). Rabbi Zera, who is mentioned here, also belongs to this group. The Talmud attempts to distinguish between a law that Rabbi Zera stated while he was still in Babylonia and was called "Rav Zera," and a law that he stated after he had immigrated to Eretz Israel and was called "Rabbi Zera." See also *Ketubot*, Part I, p. 46.

SAGES

אֲבִימִי בַּר פַּפִּי Avimi bar Pappi. A Babylonian Amora of the second and third generations. Little is known of this Sage, though from other passages in the Talmud it seems that he was a colleague and contemporary of Rav Naḥman, with whom he discusses Halakhic issues.

שְׁמוּאֵל Shmuel. A Babylonian Amora of the first generation. See *Ketubot*, Part I, pp. 8–9.

מָר בַּר אַמֵימָר Mar bar Amemar. A Babylonian Amora of the seventh generation. Mar bar Amemar was the son of the well-known Amora, Amemar. Mar bar Amemar was a disciple of Rav Ashi and frequently reported his father's customs to Rav Ashi.

רַב אַשִׁי Rav Ashi. A Babylonian Amora of the sixth generation. See *Ketubot*, Part II, p 94.

TERMINOLOGY

אָמְרִי נְהַרְדְּעֵי The Neharde'ans say. Although this expression is a general one and refers to the Sages of the city of Neharde'a, nevertheless the Sages in the Talmud (*Sanhedrin* 17b) apply it to a particular Sage, Rav Ḥama, who was one of the most important Rabbis of that city. Occasionally this expression is used because the opinion expressed is not only Rav Ḥama's personal view, but reflects the approach taken by all the Sages of Neharde'a.

TRANSLATION AND COMMENTARY

her handiwork for herself, even if she is being maintained by her brothers from their father's estate.

MISHNAH הַמְאָרֵס אֶת בִּתּוֹ וְגֵרְשָׁהּ [1]According to Jewish law, a marriage is effected in two stages: (1) betrothal (*kiddushin,* also known as *erusin*), and (2) marriage (*nissu'in*). Though the marriage is not completed until after *nissu'in,* betrothal leads to a change in the personal status of the bride and the bridegroom and creates a tie between them which can only be dissolved by divorce or by the death of one of the parties. A father is entitled to arrange the betrothal of his daughter while she is a minor (below the age of twelve) or a *na'arah* (between twelve and twelve-and-a-half) and to give her away in marriage. This Mishnah discusses the right of the father to his daughter's ketubah, if she was betrothed or married while a minor or a *na'arah* and was then divorced or widowed before she reached the age of twelve-and-a-half. The Mishnah teaches: **If someone gave his daughter away in betrothal** while she was a minor or a *na'arah* **and the bridegroom divorced her** after their betrothal but before their marriage, [2]**and then** the father **gave** the girl **away in betrothal** a second time **and** the second bridegroom died and **she was left a widow,** [3]then even **the ketubah** to which she is entitled from her second betrothal — and certainly the one to which she is entitled from her first betrothal — **belongs to** her father, for until the girl reaches the age of twelve-and-a-half she remains under her father's authority. [4]But **if** the father **gave** his daughter **away in marriage and the husband divorced her,** [5]**and then** the father **gave** the girl **away in marriage** a second time **and** the second husband died and **she was left a widow,** [6]even **the ketubah** to which she is entitled from her first marriage — and certainly the one to which she is entitled from her second marriage — **belongs to** the girl **herself,** for once she was given away in marriage, she left her father's authority.

רַבִּי יְהוּדָה אוֹמֵר [7]**Rabbi Yehudah** disagreed with the first Tanna of the Mishnah and **said:** The payment of **the first** ketubah, which was drawn up before the girl's first marriage while she was still under her father's authority, **belongs to the father** of the girl. [8]The other Sages **said to him: Once he has given her**

משנה [1]הַמְאָרֵס אֶת בִּתּוֹ וְגֵרְשָׁהּ, [2]אֵירְסָהּ וְנִתְאַרְמְלָה, [3]כְּתוּבָּתָהּ שֶׁלּוֹ. [4]הִשִּׂיאָהּ וְגֵרְשָׁהּ. [5]הִשִּׂיאָהּ וְנִתְאַרְמְלָה, [6]כְּתוּבָּתָהּ שֶׁלָּהּ. [7]רַבִּי יְהוּדָה אוֹמֵר: הָרִאשׁוֹנָה שֶׁל אָב. [8]אָמְרוּ לוֹ: (אִם)

LITERAL TRANSLATION

MISHNAH [1][If] someone gave his daughter away in betrothal and [the bridegroom] divorced her, [2][and then] he gave her away in betrothal and she was widowed, [3]her ketubah belongs to him. [4][If] he gave her away in marriage and [the husband] divorced her, [5][and then] he gave her away in marriage and she was widowed, [6]her ketubah belongs to her. [7]Rabbi Yehudah says: The first belongs to the father. [8]They said to him: Once he has

RASHI

משנה כתובתה של אב — כתובה שהיא גובה משני ארוסין הללו. וקסבר: יש כתובה לארוסה, ובימי נערות וקטנות קאמר. **כתובתה שלה** — דמשהשיאה פקעה רשותו, ובתר גוביינא אזלינן, וגוביינא בתר הכי הוא. ולא אזלינן בתר כתיבה, לומר: הואיל והראשונה נכתבה בעודה ברשות האב תיהוי דאב. **הראשונה של אב** — טעמא מפרש בגמרא.

NOTES

אָמְרוּ לוֹ **They said to him.** *Tosafot Yom Tov* asks (as the Gemara asks in other places): What is the difference between the opinion of the Sages who replied to Rabbi Yehudah and the view of the anonymous first Tanna of the Mishnah? Both seem to agree that the father is entitled to his daughter's ketubah if she was betrothed, but loses his claim to the ketubah once she is married.

Tiferet Yisrael suggests that the first Tanna of the Mishnah speaks only of the girl's ketubah, and is of the opinion that once she is married, her father no longer has a claim to it. The Sages who disagreed with Rabbi Yehudah added that once the girl has been given away in marriage, her father no longer has any rights over her, and therefore cannot even recover the dowry he provided for her.

HALAKHAH

הַמְאָרֵס אֶת בִּתּוֹ וְגֵרְשָׁהּ **If someone gave his daughter away in betrothal and the bridegroom divorced her.** "A father may give his daughter away in betrothal while she is a minor or a *na'arah* (until she reaches the age of twelve-and-a-half), and he is entitled to her ketubah if she is widowed or divorced while betrothed. If the father then gives her away in betrothal a second time (or even many times), and she is widowed or divorced while betrothed, the father is entitled to her ketubah." (*Rambam, Sefer Nashim, Hilkhot Ishut* 3:11, 10:11; *Shulḥan Arukh, Even HaEzer* 37:1, 55:7.)

הִשִּׂיאָהּ וְגֵרְשָׁהּ **If he gave her away in marriage and the husband divorced her.** "If a minor (and certainly a *na'arah*) is given away in marriage by her father, and she is then widowed or divorced, her father no longer has any legal authority over her. Thus she is entitled to her ketubah

BACKGROUND

אֵירְסָהּ וְנִתְאַרְמְלָה **He gave her away in betrothal and she was widowed.** Though in certain respects אירוסין (betrothal) gives a bride the status of a married woman — she cannot separate from her betrothed except by divorce or on his death, and if she has sexual relations with another man, she is guilty of adultery — nevertheless we learn from the Torah (Numbers, chapter 30) that the father of a bride less than twelve-and-a-half years old still has certain authority over her after her betrothal. However, once the marriage has taken place and the girl has left her father's house, he no longer has authority over her, even if she is divorced or widowed while still a minor.

SAGES

רַבִּי יְהוּדָה **Rabbi Yehudah.** A Tanna of the fifth generation. See *Ketubot,* Part II, p. 30.

מִשֶּׁהִשִּׂיאָהּ, אֵין לְאָבִיהָ רְשׁוּת בָּהּ.

גמרא [1]טַעֲמָא דְּהִשִּׂיאָהּ וְגֵרְשָׁהּ, [2]הִשִּׂיאָהּ וְנִתְאַרְמְלָה, [3]אֲבָל נִתְאַרְמְלָה תְּרֵי זִמְנֵי, [4]תּוּ לָא חֲזְיָא לְאִינְסוּבֵי.

LITERAL TRANSLATION

given her away in marriage, her father has no authority over her.

GEMARA [1]The reason is that he gave her away in marriage and [the husband] divorced her, [2][and then] he gave her away in marriage and she was widowed. [3]But if she was widowed twice, [4]she is no longer fit to be married.

RASHI

גמרא **תו לא חזיא לאינסובי** – דהויא חזקה להיות בעליה מתים. ודק תנא במלתיה, דלא לינקוט בדרך פורענות.

TRANSLATION AND COMMENTARY

away in marriage, her father no longer **has** any **authority over her.**

GEMARA טַעֲמָא דְּהִשִּׂיאָהּ וְגֵרְשָׁהּ [1]The Gemara begins its analysis of the Mishnah by noting the precision with which it is worded. It constructs a case in which the first marriage ended in divorce and the second ended with the husband's death, even though the same law would apply if both marriages ended with his death. There is **a reason,** says the Gemara, why the Mishnah (specifically) referred to a case in which the father **gave** his daughter **away in marriage and the husband divorced her,** [2]**and then** the father **gave** the girl **away in marriage** for a second time **and** her second husband died and **she was left a widow.** [3]The Mishnah did not wish to deal with a case in which **she was widowed twice,** [4]for if this happens **she is no longer fit to be married** a third time, since a presumption has been established that she is a woman who in some way causes the person she

NOTES

מִשֶּׁהִשִּׂיאָהּ **Once he has given her away in marriage.** Some texts have the reading אִם מִשֶּׁהִשִּׂיאָהּ — "If from when he has given her away in marriage." *Hatam Sofer* explains this reading as follows: If the ketubah was written before she was married (in accordance with the viewpoint of *Rambam* and in accordance with common practice), the father is entitled to the ketubah, for it was drawn up while the girl was still under her father's authority. But if the ketubah was written only after she was married (in accordance with the viewpoint of *Ran*), the father is not entitled to the ketubah, for the girl was no longer under her father's authority when the ketubah was drawn up.

טַעֲמָא דְּהִשִּׂיאָהּ וְגֵרְשָׁהּ **The reason is that he gave her away in marriage and the husband divorced her.** According to *Rashi*, there is no direct connection between the law forbidding the third marriage of a woman whose first two husbands died and the law of our Mishnah concerning the father's right to his minor daughter's ketubah. But since the Tanna of our Mishnah agrees with Rabbi Yehudah HaNasi that a presumption is established after two occurrences, he preferred to construct a case in which the girl was divorced from her first husband and widowed from her second, to avoid the tragic case of a twice-widowed woman who is forbidden to remarry. But according to *Rabbi Moshe the son of Rabbi Yosef of Narbonne,* the two laws are directly connected, for if the woman is forbidden to remarry because her first two husbands died, she is not entitled to her ketubah from the estate of her second husband, since a woman is entitled to her ketubah only if she is fit to remarry (see *Ramban*, *Ritva*, and others, who considered this opinion but rejected it).

The Gemara infers that the Tanna of our Mishnah agrees with Rabbi Yehudah HaNasi, because he constructed a case in which the girl was divorced from her first husband and widowed from the second, rather than a case in which she was widowed from both. The Rishonim disagree as to whether a woman who was twice divorced is now forbidden to remarry. Some understand from *Rashi* elsewhere (*Yevamot* 26a) that such a woman is forbidden to remarry. *Ritva* rejects this opinion, arguing that since it is the husband who must decide on the divorce, a presumption cannot be established that a woman is destined for divorce, even if she has been divorced twice or even three times.

Elsewhere (*Yevamot* 64b), the Amoraim disagree about the presumption that a woman's third husband will also die: Are we afraid that he will die as a result of having sexual intercourse with her, or because he is married to a woman who is struck with bad fortune? One of the ramifications of this dispute concerns whether a woman who was betrothed twice, and on both occasions her bridegroom died, is permitted to remarry. It can be argued that her first two husbands did not die as a result of sexual intercourse; but it can also be argued that they died because of her bad fortune. According to *Rambam* and others who rule that it is the woman's bad fortune that is seen as responsible for her husbands' deaths, and therefore she may not remarry if she was widowed twice after betrothal, we can understand why the Tanna of our Mishnah constructed the case in the first clause as one in which the girl was betrothed and divorced, and then betrothed and widowed. *Tosafot* explains that, according to the opinion that a woman is not forbidden to remarry if she was twice widowed after betrothal, the Tanna formulated the first clause of the Mishnah in such a way that it would parallel the formulation of the second clause.

תּוּ לָא חֲזְיָא לְאִינְסוּבֵי **She is no longer fit to be married.** A woman about whom a presumption has been established

HALAKHAH

even after her first marriage, and certainly after her second marriage, if she remarries and is widowed or divorced a second time." (*Rambam, Sefer Nashim, Hilkhot Ishut* 3:12; *Shulhan Arukh, Even HaEzer* 37:3, 55:7.)

נִתְאַרְמְלָה תְּרֵי זִמְנֵי **If she was widowed twice.** "If a woman has been married twice (or even if she has been betrothed twice; *Rema*), and both her husbands have died, she may not marry a third time, for after the death of her second

LITERAL TRANSLATION

[1] And by the way the Tanna stated [the law] anonymously for us in accordance with Rabbi, [2] who says: Two occurrences established a presumption. [3] "Rabbi Yehudah says: The first belongs to the father." [4] What is the reason of Rabbi Yehudah?

[5] Rabbah and Rav Yosef both said: [It is] because the father acquired the right to them from the time of the betrothal.

[1] וְאַגַּב אוֹרְחֵיהּ קָא סָתֵים לָן תַּנָּא כְּרַבִּי, [2] דְּאָמַר: בִּתְרֵי זִמְנֵי הָוְיָא חֲזָקָה.

[3] "רַבִּי יְהוּדָה אוֹמֵר: הָרִאשׁוֹנָה שֶׁל אָב". [4] מַאי טַעְמָא דְּרַבִּי יְהוּדָה?

[5] רַבָּה וְרַב יוֹסֵף דְּאָמְרִי תַּרְוַיְיהוּ: הוֹאִיל וּמִשְּׁעַת אֵירוּסִין זָכָה בָּהֶן הָאָב.

RASHI

ואגב אורחיה — דבעי לאגמורינן משפט הכתובה. ומחלוקת רבי יהודה ורבנן, נקט לישנא דידיה למסתם לן כרבי דאמר במסכת יבמות (סד,ב): נשאת לראשון ומת, לשני ומת, לשלישי — לא תנשא. דבתרי זמני הויא חזקה. **דמשעת אירוסין** — של בעל הראשון, נתחייב לה כתובה וזכה בה אב. אבל באירוסין שני לא זכה, דמשנשאת לראשון פקעה זכותיה מינה.

TRANSLATION AND COMMENTARY

marries to die. [1] **The Tanna** of the Mishnah was primarily interested in teaching us about the right of the father to his daughter's ketubah. But **incidentally** he formulated the Mishnah in such a way as to teach us something else as well, for he **stated the law anonymously in accordance with** the viewpoint of **Rabbi** Yehudah HaNasi, [2] **who ruled** elsewhere (*Yevamot* 64b) that if a woman marries and her husband dies, and she then remarries and her second husband dies as well, she may not marry a third time, for Rabbi Yehudah HaNasi is of the opinion that if the same thing happens on **two occasions a presumption is established** that it will happen again. Rabban Shimon ben Gamliel disagrees with Rabbi Yehudah HaNasi on this matter and maintains that a woman whose first two husbands have died may marry a third time; but if she is widowed a third time, she may not marry again, for after the third occurrence a presumption is established that the same thing will happen again.

רַבִּי יְהוּדָה אוֹמֵר [3] The Gemara now proceeds to analyze the viewpoint of Rabbi Yehudah. We learned in our Mishnah: **"Rabbi Yehudah said:** The payment of **the first** ketubah, which was drawn up before the girl's first marriage while she was still under her father's guardianship, **belongs to the** girl's **father."** [4] The Gemara asks: **What is the reasoning of Rabbi Yehudah?**

רַבָּה וְרַב יוֹסֵף [5] **Rabbah and Rav Yosef both said** in reply: Payment of the first ketubah is made to the father **because the father acquired the right to it from the time of the** first **betrothal,** when the bridegroom accepted the obligations contained in the ketubah. The father acquired the right to the ketubah at that

NOTES

that her next husband will die is known as a *katlanit*, "a killer," and such a woman is forbidden to remarry. Rabbi Yehudah HaNasi and Rabban Shimon ben Gamliel disagree as to whether such a presumption is established after the deaths of her first two husbands, or only after the death of her third husband. The Amoraim disagree (*Yevamot* 64b) about the basis of the presumption. Rav Ashi maintains that her bad fortune was the cause of her husbands' deaths; Rav Huna maintains that this woman must have had some disease that was passed to her husbands through sexual intercourse. This dispute has a number of ramifications: First, whether the woman is forbidden to remarry if her first two husbands died while she was betrothed to them, in which case their deaths cannot be attributed to some sexually transmitted disease. Second, whether the woman is forbidden to remarry if her first two husbands died not of an illness, but as a result of some accident. See also Halakhah.

מַאי טַעְמָא דְּרַבִּי יְהוּדָה **What is the reason of Rabbi Yehudah?** Our Gemara understands the dispute between Rabbi Yehudah and the anonymous first Tanna of the Mishnah as based on two different opinions concerning the point in time at which the right to the ketubah is acquired. The Jerusalem Talmud explains Rabbi Yehudah's position differently: The Rabbis enacted that the father is entitled to his minor daughter's ketubah from her first husband — even if he has already given her away in marriage — in order to encourage him to give her a larger dowry. Since the father knows that he will get the dowry back if his daughter is divorced or widowed, he will be more inclined to endow her generously when she marries. In later generations, various communities (Toledo and others) instituted local enactments requiring the partial or total return of the dowry to the father of the bride in the event that the marriage was dissolved shortly after the wedding ceremony.

הוֹאִיל וּמִשְּׁעַת אֵירוּסִין זָכָה בָּהֶן הָאָב **It is because the father acquired the right to them from the time of the betrothal.** There is a fundamental disagreement among the

HALAKHAH

husband, a presumption has been established that she is a woman who causes her husbands to die (following Rabbi Yehudah HaNasi). But if nevertheless she does marry again, we do not compel her husband to divorce her. *Rema* states (in the name of *Ramban* cited by *Bet Yosef*) that this ruling does not apply if one of the woman's first two husbands was killed or died as the result of a widespread plague or an accident. Therefore many authorities exercise leniency on this matter, and permit marriage to a woman who has already been widowed twice." (*Rambam, Sefer Kedushah, Hilkhot Issurei Bi'ah* 21:31; *Shulḥan Arukh, Even HaEzer* 9:1.)

TRANSLATION AND COMMENTARY

time because his daughter was then still under his authority. Thus he is entitled to the ketubah, even if it is paid only after his daughter's marriage and divorce, when she is no longer under his authority. But the father is not entitled to his daughter's second ketubah, because she left his authority once she married the first time. Thus she was no longer under her father's authority at the time of the second betrothal when the second bridegroom accepted the obligations contained in the ketubah.

מְתִיב רָבָא [1]**Rava raised an objection** to this explanation of Rabbi Yehudah's viewpoint, citing the following Baraita: [2]**"Rabbi Yehudah says:** If someone gave his daughter away in marriage before she reached the age of twelve-and-a-half and she was then divorced or widowed, and the father gave her away in marriage a second time and she was again divorced or widowed, **the** girl's **first** ketubah **belongs to the father,** whereas the second belongs to the girl herself. [3]**But Rabbi Yehudah agrees** with the Sages **about** a case in which **someone gave his daughter away in betrothal while she was** still **a minor, and she** then **came of age,** i.e., she reached the age of twelve-and-a-half, **and** only **afterwards was she married, that her father has no authority over her.** Thus, if she is divorced or widowed, her father is not entitled to her ketubah." [4]Now, according to the explanation of Rabbi Yehudah's position offered by Rabbah and Rav Yosef, **why** should Rabbi Yehudah agree that in this second case the father is not entitled to his daughter's ketubah? [5]**Here, too, let** Rabbi Yehudah **say** that the father is entitled to it, **because the father acquired the right to it from the time of the betrothal,** when the bridegroom accepted the obligations contained in the ketubah. Since at that time the daughter was under her father's authority, he should be entitled to the ketubah, even if the daughter married only after she came of age and had left his authority!

אֶלָּא [6]The Gemara now suggests an emendation to the explanation of Rabbi Yehudah's viewpoint. **Rather,** says the Gemara, **if** something **was stated** on this matter, **it was stated in the following** form: [7]**Rabbah and Rav Yosef both said:** In the case of our Mishnah, Rabbi Yehudah maintains that the first ketubah belongs to the father, **because** that ketubah **was written while** his daughter **was** still **under his authority,** for the ketubah is ordinarily drawn up shortly before the marriage ceremony. Therefore the father receives the ketubah even if it is paid only after his daughter's marriage and divorce, when she is no longer under his authority. But the father is not entitled to his daughter's second ketubah, because that was drawn up before her second marriage, at a time when she was no longer under his authority. But Rabbi Yehudah agrees that the father is not entitled to his daughter's ketubah if she was betrothed as a minor but married only after she came of age. Since the girl came of age before she was married, the ketubah was drawn up only after she had already left her father's authority.

[1]מְתִיב רָבָא: [2]״רַבִּי יְהוּדָה אוֹמֵר: הָרִאשׁוֹנָה שֶׁל אָב. [3]וּמוֹדֶה רַבִּי יְהוּדָה בִּמְאָרֵס אֶת בִּתּוֹ כְּשֶׁהִיא קְטַנָּה, וּבָגְרָה, וְאַחַר כָּךְ נִשֵּׂאת, שֶׁאֵין לְאָבִיהָ רְשׁוּת בָּהּ״. [4]אַמַּאי? [5]הָכָא נַמִי לֵימָא: הוֹאִיל וּמִשְּׁעַת אֵירוּסִין זָכָה בָּהֶן הָאָב!

[6]אֶלָּא, אִי אִתְּמַר, הָכִי אִתְּמַר: [7]רַבָּה וְרַב יוֹסֵף דְּאָמְרִי תַּרְוַיְיהוּ: הוֹאִיל וּבִרְשׁוּתוֹ נִכְתָּבִין.

LITERAL TRANSLATION

[1]Rava objected: [2]"Rabbi Yehudah says: The first belongs to the father. [3]But Rabbi Yehudah agrees about someone who gave his daughter away in betrothal when she was a minor, and she came of age, and afterwards she was married, that her father has no authority over her." [4]Why? [5]Here too let him say: [It is] because the father acquired the right to them from the time of the betrothal!

[6]Rather, if it was said, it was said as follows: [7]Rabbah and Rav Yosef both said: [It is] because they were written [while she was] under his authority.

RASHI

הואיל וברשותו נכתבין — כתובה הראשונה שהיה לפני הנשואין. והלכך, בגרה קודם נשואין — לא נכתב ברשותו. הא דגרסינן "נכתבים" לשון רבים — אמנה ומאתים דכתובה קאי.

TERMINOLOGY

אֶלָּא אִי אִתְּמַר הָכִי אִתְּמַר Rather, if it was said, it was said as follows. Sometimes, when an objection has been raised against an Amoraic statement, the Talmud resolves this objection by suggesting that the Amora's remark was reported incorrectly, and hence must be amended: "If such a statement was made, it was made in the following form."

NOTES

Rishonim as to how to understand our Gemara. *Rashi* maintains that the Rabbis enacted that a woman is entitled to her ketubah from the time of betrothal, even if the bridegroom did not actually write out the ketubah at that time. Accordingly, the dispute about the lien on the husband's property revolves around the question of whether the lien is established when he becomes legally liable for his wife's ketubah, i.e., at the time of betrothal, or whether it is established only when the ketubah obligation is committed to writing, i.e., at the time of marriage.

Rabbenu Ḥananel maintains that a betrothed woman is only entitled to her ketubah if her bridegroom actually wrote out the ketubah at the time of betrothal. In his view, Rav Huna and Rav Assi disagree about the case in which the husband wrote one ketubah at the time of betrothal

SAGES

רַב הוּנָא Rav Huna. A Babylonian Amora of the second generation. See *Ketubot,* Part I, p. 38.

רַב (רַבִּי) אַסִּי Rav (Rabbi) Assi. A leading Amora of the third generation, Rav Assi was born and brought up in Babylonia, and studied there under Shmuel and Rav Yehudah. He immigrated to Eretz Israel, where his principal teacher was Rabbi Yoḥanan. He was a close colleague and friend of Rabbi Ammi.

BACKGROUND

מָנֶה מָאתַיִם מִן הָאֵירוּסִין The maneh and the 200 zuz are collected from the betrothal. Rav Huna's statement assumes that the husband's obligation to give his wife the minimum sum of the ketubah — 200 zuz for a virgin and a maneh for a non-virgin — is not derived from the written document, because the Sages decreed that the woman receives that sum even if there is no written ketubah. Therefore Rav Huna maintains that this obligation is incumbent on the husband from the moment of betrothal, and a woman may thus collect her ketubah as early as that date, even if the document itself was to be written later. However, the right to collect any amount beyond the basic settlement decreed by the Sages (עִיקַּר הַכְּתוּבָּה) takes effect only after the marriage.

TRANSLATION AND COMMENTARY

וּמִיגְבָּא מֵאֵימַת גָּבְיָא [1] A woman's ketubah creates a lien on all the real estate owned by her husband at the time of her marriage, and this lien allows her to recover the amount of her ketubah from that property, even if the property has in the meantime been transferred to a third party. The Gemara asks: **From when** precisely is the lien established that enables her to **collect** her ketubah from the husband's property which has been transferred to someone else? Is the lien established at the time of betrothal, even before the ketubah is drawn up, for it is at that time that the bridegroom accepts responsibility for his bride's ketubah? If so, the woman can collect her ketubah from any property owned by her husband at the time of betrothal, even if it was sold before her marriage. Or is the lien established only at the time of marriage, when the ketubah is actually written? In that case, the woman can only collect her ketubah from property in her husband's possession at that time.

אָמַר רַב הוּנָא [2] The Gemara records a controversy on this issue. **Rav Huna said:** With respect to **the maneh and the two hundred zuz** [dinarim] that constitute the main portion of the ketubah, a woman may collect these sums **from** the property owned by her husband at **the** time of her **betrothal.** [3] **But** with respect to **the additional amount** that the husband may add to the ketubah if he so wishes, the woman may collect only **from** the property in her husband's possession at **the** time of their **marriage.** The main portion of the ketubah is the basic amount that a woman is entitled to receive from her husband or his estate in the event of divorce or the death of her husband. By Rabbinic enactment, the minimum amount of a ketubah is two hundred zuz if the woman is a virgin at the time of marriage, and a maneh (one hundred zuz) if she is not. Since the groom assumes responsibility for the main portion of the ketubah at the time of betrothal, the lien on his property for the collection of that portion is established at that time. But responsibility for any additional amount that the groom chooses to add to the ketubah is assumed at the time that the ketubah is drawn up and the groom obligates himself to pay whatever is written therein. Hence the lien on his property for the collection of this additional amount is established only at the time of the marriage, when the ketubah is written. [4] **Rav Assi** disagreed with Rav Huna and **said:** With respect **both** to the main portion of the ketubah **and** to the additional amount, a woman may **collect** only **from** the property in her husband's possession at the time of **her marriage.** We assume that the woman waives the lien that was

[1] וּמִיגְבָּא מֵאֵימַת גָּבְיָא? [2] אָמַר רַב הוּנָא: מָנֶה מָאתַיִם מִן הָאֵירוּסִין, [3] וְתוֹסֶפֶת מִן הַנִּשּׂוּאִין. [4] וְרַב אַסִּי אָמַר: אֶחָד זֶה וְאֶחָד זֶה מִן הַנִּשּׂוּאִין.

LITERAL TRANSLATION

[1] And from when does she collect?

[2] Rav Huna said: The maneh [and] the two hundred [zuz are collected] from the betrothal, [3] and the additional amount from the marriage. [4] But Rav Assi said: Both this and that [are collected] from the marriage.

RASHI

ומגבא מאימת גביא — כלומר, לענין זכייה דאב, דהא חזינן דלאו בתר אירוסין אזלינן אפילו לרבי יהודה, כדקתני: ומודה רבי יהודה במארס את בתו ובגרה כו׳. אלמא בתר כתיבה אזיל. לענין מטרף לקוחות מאימת טרפא ממשעבדי? משעת אירוסין — דהא מההיא שעתא איחייב בתקנתא דרבנן, או דלמא עד שעת כתיבה, דהויא מלוה בשטר, לא טרפא. **מנה מאתים** — דמתקנתא דרבנן מחייב — טרפא מזמן אירוסין, אם מת או גרשה לאחר נשואין — טורפת לקוחות שלקחו מנכסיו מזמן אירוסין ואילך, דמההיא שעתא אשתעבד. **ותוספת** — שמעלמא היא באה לה — לא נשתעבד עד זמן כתיבת הכתובה, שקנו מידו וכתב. **אחד זה ואחד זה מן הנשואין** — דהיא גופה מחלה לשעבודא קמא, ונתרצתה בזמן הכתוב בשטר הכתובה ככל המפורש בה, בין עיקר בין תוספת.

NOTES

and another at the time of marriage. Does the ketubah written at the time of marriage cancel the lien established by the ketubah written at the time of betrothal, or does it add to it? The other Rishonim follow one or the other of these two approaches, bringing proofs and raising objections from our Gemara and other passages (see, for example, *Ra'ah* and *Ri HaLavan*).

אֶחָד זֶה וְאֶחָד זֶה מִן הַנִּשּׂוּאִין Both this and that are collected from the marriage. *Rav Sherira Gaon* (whose view was accepted by *Rambam*) goes even further than *Rabbenu Ḥananel*, whose position was explained in the previous note. According to *Rav Sherira Gaon,* a betrothed woman is entitled to her ketubah only if her bridegroom actually drew up a ketubah document for her. But even if

HALAKHAH

וּמִיגְבָּא מֵאֵימַת גָּבְיָא And from when does she collect? If someone betroths a woman and writes her a ketubah, but has not yet completed the marriage process by entering the bridal chamber with her before dying or before divorcing her, the woman may collect the main portion of her ketubah, but only from the assets in the bridegroom's possession. The additional amount that the bridegroom added on his own initiative she cannot collect at all. This is the opinion of *Rambam* (following *Rav Sherira Gaon*), based on the viewpoint of Rav Assi in our Gemara and the Gemara's final ruling (below, 44a). *Bet Shmuel* notes that according to *Rosh* the woman may collect the main portion of her

[1]וּמִי אֲמַר רַב הוּנָא הָכִי? [2]וְהָאִתְּמַר: הוֹצִיאָה עָלָיו שְׁתֵּי כְּתוּבּוֹת, אַחַת שֶׁל מָאתַיִם וְאַחַת שֶׁל שְׁלֹשׁ מֵאוֹת, [3]וְאָמַר רַב הוּנָא: בָּאתָה לִגְבּוֹת מָאתַיִם, [4]גּוֹבָה מִזְּמַן רִאשׁוֹן, [5]שְׁלֹשׁ מֵאוֹת, גּוֹבָה מִזְּמַן שֵׁנִי. [6]וְאִם אִיתָא, [7]תִּיגְבֵּי מָאתַיִם מִזְּמַן רִאשׁוֹן וּמֵאָה מִזְּמַן שֵׁנִי!

LITERAL TRANSLATION

[1]But did Rav Huna say thus? [2]But surely it was said: [If] she produced against him two ketubot, one for two hundred [zuz] and one for three hundred [zuz], [3]and Rav Huna said: [If] she came to collect the two hundred, [4]she collects from the first date, [5][and if she came to collect] the three hundred, she collects from the second date. [6]But if it is [true], [7]let her collect two hundred from the first date and one hundred from the second date!

RASHI

אחת של מאתים — והיא מוקדמת, דדוקא כסדר נקט. **ואמר רב הונא באתה לגבות מאתים כו׳** — כלומר, אין לה אלא אחד מהן, ויפה כחה לגבות איזה שתרצה. באתה לגבות מאתים, דניחא לה בהכי, וכגון שמכר נכסיו בין זמן ראשון לזמן שני, דאי מפקא למיגבי בשל שלש מאות — נמצאו שטרי הלקוחות קודמין. **גובה** — מאתים, וטורפת לקוחות מזמן הכתוב. **ואם איתא** — דסבר רב: הונא חוב ראשון מזמן ראשון, ותוספת מזמן שני — הכי נמי תיגבי מאתים מזמן ראשון, ומאה מזמן שני!

TRANSLATION AND COMMENTARY

established when she was betrothed, and relies thereafter on the lien established by the written document, not only for the additional amount recorded in it but also for the main portion of the ketubah.

וּמִי אֲמַר רַב הוּנָא הָכִי [1]The Gemara now asks: **But did Rav Huna** actually **say** that a woman may collect the main portion of her ketubah from property that was in her husband's possession at the time of betrothal? [2]**Surely it was stated** that the following case came under discussion: **If** a woman who is being divorced from her husband **presents him with two** different **ketubot** which were drawn up on two different dates, the earlier **one** obligating him to pay **two hundred zuz and** the later **one** obligating him to pay **three hundred zuz,** she is entitled to only one of the two amounts, but she can decide which one she wishes to collect. [3]**And Rav Huna said** about this case: **If she comes to collect the** ketubah obligating her husband to pay **two hundred zuz** — for she may prefer to collect the smaller amount, if it was dated earlier than the larger one, and her husband sold his property between the time he drew up the first, smaller ketubah and the time he wrote the second, larger ketubah — [4]**she collects** the two hundred zuz **from** those properties that her husband had in his possession **on the date** he wrote **the first** ketubah. [5]**But if she comes to collect the** ketubah obligating her husband to pay **three hundred zuz, she collects** only **from** the property that her husband owned **on the date** he drew up **the second** ketubah. [6]**Now,** says the Gemara, **if it is true** that Rav Huna maintains that a woman may collect the main portion of her ketubah from property that was in her husband's possession on a certain date, and may collect the additional amount from property which he owned on a later date, why did Rav Huna rule that if the woman comes to collect the ketubah of three hundred zuz, she may collect only from the property that her husband owned on the date he drew up the second ketubah? [7]**Let her collect two hundred zuz from** the property that was in her husband's possession **on the date** he wrote **the first** ketubah, for on that date she was already entitled to it, **and** let her collect **one hundred** zuz **from** the property he owned **on the date** he drew up **the second** ketubah, for this one hundred zuz should be considered the additional amount that the husband included in the ketubah!

NOTES

he wrote the document for her, she can collect the ketubah only from the free assets in the bridegroom's possession. No lien on his property is established by the ketubah written at the time of betrothal and she cannot therefore collect her ketubah from property later transferred by him to a third party. This applies not only if the betrothed couple later marry and the bridegroom writes his bride a second ketubah canceling the first, but also if he divorces her after betrothal before a second ketubah is ever written.

אַחַת שֶׁל מָאתַיִם One for two hundred zuz. *Rashi* emphasizes that it was the earlier ketubah that contained the sum of 200 zuz, and the later ketubah that contained the sum

HALAKHAH

ketubah even from property that has already been transferred by sale or gift to others." (*Rambam, Sefer Nashim, Hilkhot Ishut* 10:11; *Shulḥan Arukh, Even HaEzer* 55:6.)

הוֹצִיאָה עָלָיו שְׁתֵּי כְּתוּבּוֹת If she produced against him two ketubot. "If a woman presents her husband with two ketubot drawn up on different dates but for the same amount, the ketubah drawn up on the later date cancels the earlier one, so that she can collect only from property that belonged to her husband at the time he wrote the second ketubah. If one ketubah contains a larger amount than the other, she can collect whichever ketubah she chooses. If she opts for the first ketubah, she can collect from property owned by her husband at the time he wrote the first ketubah; if she prefers the later one, she can

BACKGROUND

שְׁתֵּי כְּתוּבּוֹת Two ketubot. The situation in which a woman can have two ketubot can arise in various ways. The first ketubah may have been lost, and, since it is forbidden for a man to live with a woman without a ketubah, the husband would have written another one for her. In such cases, a special version called כְּתוּבָּה דְּאִירְכְּסָא ("a lost ketubah") is supposed to be used. Sometimes a man may write a second ketubah because his economic situation has deteriorated, and, with his wife's agreement, he gives her a new ketubah. He may also wish to add to the sum mentioned in the original ketubah. It may also happen that the husband has divorced his wife and then remarried her before she has managed to collect the first divorce settlement from him, so that she now possesses two ketubot.

[1] But according to your opinion, [2] let her collect all five hundred [zuz], [3] two hundred from the first date [and] three hundred from the second date! [4] Rather, what is the reason that she does not collect the five hundred? [5] Since he did not write for her: "I chose to add for you three hundred to the two hundred," [6] this [is what] he said to her: "If you collect from the first date, you collect two hundred, [7] [and] if you collect from the second date, you collect three hundred." [44A] [8] Here too this is the reason that she does not collect — [9] since he did not write for her: [10] "I have added for you one hundred to the two hundred," she waived the first lien.

[1] וּלְטַעְמִיךְ, [2] תִּיגְבֵּי חֲמֵשׁ מֵאוֹת כּוּלָּם, [3] מָאתַיִם מִזְּמַן רִאשׁוֹן תְּלַת מֵאָה מִזְּמַן שֵׁנִי! [4] אֶלָּא, חֲמֵשׁ מֵאוֹת מַאי טַעֲמָא לָא גָּבְיָא? [5] כֵּיוָן דְּלָא כָּתַב לָהּ: "צָבִיתִי וְאוֹסִיפִית לָךְ תְּלַת מֵאָה אַמָּאתַיִם", [6] הָכִי קָאָמַר לָהּ: "אִי מִזְּמַן רִאשׁוֹן גְּבִיאַת, גָּבְיָא מָאתַיִם, [7] אִי מִזְּמַן שֵׁנִי גְּבִיאַת, גָּבְיָא תְּלַת מֵאָה". [44A] [8] הָכָא נַמִי הַיְינוּ טַעֲמָא דְּלָא גָּבְיָא — [9] מִדְּלָא כָּתַב לָהּ "אוֹסִיפִית לָךְ מֵאָה אַמָּאתַיִם", [10] אַחוּלֵי אַחִילְתֵּיהּ לְשִׁעְבּוּדָא קַמָּא.

TRANSLATION AND COMMENTARY

וּלְטַעְמִיךְ [1] The Gemara refutes this objection: **According to** the assumption that underlies **your objection** (that the second ketubah is seen as a separate obligation independent of the first ketubah), why should the woman collect no more than three hundred zuz? [2] **Let her collect** the total amount of the two ketubot, i.e., **all five hundred zuz,** [3] **two hundred from** the property that the husband owned **on the date** he wrote **the first** ketubah, **and three hundred from** the property in his possession **on the date** he drew up **the second!** [4] **Rather,** says the Gemara, we are forced to the following conclusion: **What is the reason that she does not collect the** combined total of the two ketubot — **five hundred** zuz? [5] The reason is this: **Since** the husband **did not write for** his wife in the second ketubah: **"I chose to add** an extra **three hundred** zuz **for you over** and above **the two hundred** zuz to which I obligated myself in the first ketubah," we can conclude that he did not wish to obligate himself to pay both ketubot. [6] In fact, **this is what he** meant to **say to her: "If you** prefer to **collect from** the property in my possession **on the date** I wrote **the first** ketubah, **you** may **collect** only **two hundred** zuz, because in the first ketubah I only obligated myself to pay a ketubah of two hundred zuz. [7] **And if you** prefer to **collect from** the property in my possession **on the date** I drew up **the second** ketubah, **you** may **collect three hundred** zuz, the amount stipulated in the second ketubah." [44A] [8] **Here, too, the reason why she cannot collect** two hundred zuz from the property that belonged to her husband at the time he wrote the first ketubah, and one hundred zuz from the property he owned at the time he wrote the second ketubah is this: [9] **Since** the husband **did not write for** his wife in the second ketubah: **"I have added an** extra **hundred** zuz **for you over** and above **the two hundred** zuz to which I obligated myself in the first ketubah," but instead wrote an entirely new ketubah on a different date for the entire three hundred zuz, we can conclude that the second ketubah did not add to the obligation undertaken by the husband in the first ketubah. [10] His wife **waived the first lien** completely when she agreed to accept the second ketubah. Thus, if she seeks to collect the three hundred zuz recorded in the second ketubah, she

RASHI

כיון דלא כתיב בה — בכתובה שניה. **צביתי ואוסיפית לך תלת מאה אמאתים** — שמע מינה לא להוסיף על הראשונה בא, ולא תגבה השניה אלא אם כן הראשונה בטלה. **הכא נמי** — מדלא כתב "ואוסיפית לה מאה אמאתים קמאי" אלא כתב זמן שני לכל השלש מאות, ולא בלשון מוסיף על השטר הראשון — שמע מינה אחילתיה לשעבודא קמא. ואם באת לגבות שטר השני — תגבה מזמן שני. אבל גבי תוספת, המוסיף בכל כתובות על מנה מאתים כותבין בו "ואוסיפית לה על מאי דתקון רבנן", הלכך לא אחילתיה לשעבודא קמא, וכדקאי קאי.

NOTES

of 300. *Rosh* explains that in the reverse case — where the earlier ketubah was for 300 zuz, and the later ketubah was for 200 — the woman would indeed be entitled to collect both ketubot, for a combined total of 500 zuz. In such a case there is no reason for her to prefer the second ketubah over the first, and so it must have been written as an addition to the first ketubah, and not in order to cancel it.

HALAKHAH

collect only from the property still belonging to him at the later date. If the husband wrote in the second ketubah: 'I have added for you over and above what I obligated myself with the first ketubah,' she collects the amount recorded in the first ketubah from property that belonged to her husband at the time he wrote the first ketubah, and she collects the additional amount recorded in the second ketubah from the property that belonged to him when he drew up the second ketubah," following Rav Huna. (*Rambam, Sefer Nashim, Hilkhot Ishut* 16:29; *Shulḥan Arukh, Even HaEzer* 100:14.)

אֲמַר מָר: 2 אִי בָּעֲיָא, בְּהַאי גָּבְיָא, 3 אִי בָּעֲיָא, בְּהַאי גָּבְיָא. 4 לֵימָא פְּלִיגָא דְּרַב נַחְמָן? 5 דְּאָמַר רַב נַחְמָן: שְׁנֵי שְׁטָרוֹת הַיּוֹצְאִין בָּזֶה אַחַר זֶה, 6 בִּיטֵּל שֵׁנִי אֶת הָרִאשׁוֹן. 7 לָאו מִי אִיתְּמַר עֲלָהּ: 8 אֲמַר רַב פַּפָּא: וּמוֹדֶה רַב נַחְמָן דְּאִי

LITERAL TRANSLATION

1 The master said: 2 If she wishes, she collects with this one, 3 [and] if she wishes, she collects with that one. 4 Shall we say [that] it disagrees with Rav Naḥman? 5 For Rav Naḥman said: [If] two deeds are issued one after the other, 6 the second canceled the first.
7 Was it not stated concerning this [ruling]: 8 Rav Pappa said: But Rav Naḥman agrees that if

RASHI

אמר מר — אדרב הונא קאי, דאמר: אם באת לגבות מאתים כו'. **שני שטרות** — של שדה אחת, של מכר או מתנה, וכתבן ראובן לשמעון, אחד בניסן ואחד בסיון. **ביטל שני את הראשון** — ואם כתב לו אחריות וטרפוה ממנו — אין גובה אלא מזמן שני. והכא נמי; נימא ראשון בטיל ליה, דאחליה לשעבודיה קמא.

TERMINOLOGY

אֲמַר מָר **The master said.** A term used to cite a passage from a Mishnah or a Baraita previously mentioned, which will now be elucidated at greater length by the Talmud (usually as the continuation of a previous discussion).

TRANSLATION AND COMMENTARY

can collect only from the property that belonged to her husband at the time he drew it up. And this ruling of Rav Huna does not contradict his other ruling that a woman may collect the main portion of her ketubah from the property owned by her husband at the time of her betrothal, but may collect the additional amount of the ketubah only from property belonging to him when the ketubah was committed to writing at the time of the marriage. For the husband writes in the ketubah: "And I have added such-and-such an amount to what I am obliged by law to provide for you." Thus the woman did not waive the lien that had been established when the bridegroom assumed responsibility for the main portion of the ketubah at the time of betrothal.

אֲמַר מָר 1 The Gemara now seeks to analyze in greater detail the ruling given by Rav Huna regarding the case in which a woman presented her husband with two different ketubot. **It was said above** that Rav Huna ruled: 2 **If** the woman **prefers, she can collect with the first** ketubah, 3 **and if she prefers** otherwise, **she** can **collect with the other** ketubah. 4 On this ruling the Gemara asks: **Must we say that** Rav Huna **disagrees with Rav Naḥman,** 5 **for Rav Naḥman said: If two deeds** of sale or gift **are issued** for the same transaction involving landed property, **one** deed dated **later than the other,** 6 **the second** deed **cancels the first?**

לָאו מִי אִיתְּמַר עֲלָהּ 7 The Gemara replies that there is no contradiction between the ruling of Rav Huna and that of Rav Naḥman. **Was not** the following clarification **stated with respect** to Rav Naḥman's ruling by **Rav Pappa:** 8 **Rav Naḥman agrees that if** something was added in the second deed — if, for example, the first

NOTES

שְׁנֵי שְׁטָרוֹת **Two deeds.** *Rif* notes that Rav Naḥman's ruling that the second deed cancels the first applies only to deeds of sale, deeds of gift, and a woman's ketubah. But if a creditor is holding two loan documents against the same debtor, even if the amounts recorded in the two documents are identical, we assume that two separate loans were extended, and the creditor is entitled to collect them both.

The Rishonim explain that a person does not ordinarily write two separate documents for the same transaction (sale or gift), and therefore, unless the second document adds something to the first, the second cancels the first. Similarly, a person does not ordinarily write his wife a second ketubah that does not add anything to the first, unless he intends that the first ketubah be canceled. As for loans, there is no reason to assume that the two documents refer to the same loan.

Rashi (below, 89b) notes that Rav Naḥman's ruling applies also to two loan documents that were drawn up with reference to the same loan. It is not clear whether *Rashi* agrees with *Rif* and refers only to a case in which we know that the two documents refer to the same loan, or whether he disagrees with him and maintains that unless we know differently we assume that the two documents were drawn up for the same loan (see *Ramban*).

The Rishonim (*Ramban, Ritva,* and others) cite the Jerusalem Talmud (*Ketubot* 9:10), which discusses whether a creditor who wishes to extend a second loan to the same debtor must write in the loan document that it is a second loan, and these Rishonim disagree as to whether the conclusion of the Jerusalem Talmud supports *Rif.*

HALAKHAH

שְׁנֵי שְׁטָרוֹת הַיּוֹצְאִין בָּזֶה אַחַר זֶה **If two deeds are issued one after the other.** "If two deeds of sale or two deeds of gift were issued for a transaction involving the same land, one dated later than the other, the second deed cancels the first. In such a case, the seller's guarantee to reimburse the buyer if the land is seized by the seller's creditors applies only from the date of the second deed. Furthermore, the seller is liable for any tax that is due on the land for the period between the dates recorded in the two deeds. Likewise, all of the usufruct enjoyed by the buyer during that interim period must be returned to the seller. According to *Tur* and others, the buyer may not take the usufruct during the interim period, but he is not required to reimburse the original owner for what he has already consumed." (*Rambam, Sefer Kinyan, Hilkhot Zekhiyyah U'Mattanah* 5:9; *Shulḥan Arukh, Ḥoshen Mishpat* 240:2.)

אוֹסֵיף בֵּיהּ דִּיקְלָא, [1]לְתוֹסֶפֶת כְּתָבֵיהּ? [2]הָכָא נַמִי, הָא אוֹסֵיף לָהּ מִידֵי.

[3]גּוּפָא: [4]"אָמַר רַב נַחְמָן: שְׁנֵי שְׁטָרוֹת הַיּוֹצְאִין בָּזֶה אַחַר זֶה, [5]בִּיטֵּל שֵׁנִי אֶת הָרִאשׁוֹן. [6]אֲמַר רַב פַּפָּא: וּמוֹדֶה רַב נַחְמָן דְּאִי אוֹסֵיף בֵּיהּ דִּיקְלָא, [7]לְתוֹסֶפֶת כְּתָבֵיהּ". [8]פְּשִׁיטָא רִאשׁוֹן בְּמֶכֶר וְשֵׁנִי בְּמַתָּנָה, [9]לְיַפּוֹת כֹּחוֹ הוּא

LITERAL TRANSLATION

he added a date palm, [1]he wrote it as an addition? [2]Here too, surely he added something for her.

[3]Returning to the statement quoted above (lit., "the thing itself"): [4]"Rav Naḥman said: [If] two deeds are issued one after the other, [5]the second canceled the first. [6]Rav Pappa said: But Rav Naḥman agrees that if he added a date palm, [7]he wrote it as an addition." [8]It is obvious [that if] the first [deed] was for a sale and the second was for a gift, [9]he wrote it to strengthen his

TRANSLATION AND COMMENTARY

document spoke only of the transfer of a field and in the second document the original owner **added a date palm** to the transaction — then the second deed does not cancel the first one completely? [1]Instead, we assume that the original owner **wrote** the second deed **for** the purpose of making **the addition** that was included in that second deed. [2]**Here too,** in Rav Huna's case regarding the woman who presented her husband with two different ketubot, **surely** the husband **added something for** his wife in the second ketubah, and thus the second did not cancel the first. Therefore Rav Naḥman would agree with Rav Huna's ruling that the woman can decide which of the two ketubot she wishes to use.

גּוּפָא [3]The Gemara now **returns to the statement** that was **quoted above** in the course of the previous discussion: [4]**"Rav Naḥman said: If two deeds** of sale or gift **are issued** for the same transaction involving landed property, **one** deed dated **later than the other,** [5]**the second** deed **cancels the first.** [6]**Rav Pappa said: Rav Naḥman agrees that if** the original owner **added** something in the second deed — if, for example, the first document spoke only of the transfer of a field and in the second document the owner added **a date palm** to the transaction — then the second deed does not cancel the first one. [7]Instead, we assume that the original owner **wrote** the second deed **for** the purpose of making **the addition** that was included in that second deed." [8]The Gemara proceeds to analyze this ruling in greater detail. **It is obvious that if the first document was a** deed of **sale, and the second was a** deed of **gift,** then even if nothing was added in the transaction recorded in the second document, that document does not cancel the first. [9]For in such a case we assume that the original owner **wrote** the second deed in order **to strengthen** the recipient's **position**

RASHI

דאי מוסיף בה דיקלא — בשטר בתרא. **לתוספת כתביה** — ולא לבטולי לקמא. אלא דאי מזמן שני אתי למגבי — ליקני עיקר ותוספת, ואי ניחא ליה בקמא משום דקדים — לא ליקני תוספת. **והכא נמי הא אוסיף לה** — דכתב לה שלש מאות. **ליפות כחו כתביה** — ואי נמי לא אוסיף ביה לא ביטל את הראשון, אלא דלא ליתו בני מצרא לערעורי עליה. דקיימא לן: מתנה לית בה משום דינא דבר מצרא.

TERMINOLOGY

גּוּפָא Returning to the statement quoted above (lit., "the thing itself"). An expression used to introduce a quotation from a source cited in passing in the previous discussion, which will now be analyzed at length. Generally, **גּוּפָא** introduces a new theme.

BACKGROUND

בִּיטֵּל שֵׁנִי אֶת הָרִאשׁוֹן The second canceled the first. In this instance the second document is identical to the first but was written at a later date. For if the second document refers to the existence of the first one, it is treated as an independent document on the basis of that reference. As the Gemara explains, the existence of two documents with different dates relating to the same matter arouses doubt as to their validity. Occasionally someone who holds two such deeds can explain the situation and produce evidence as to why the second document was written — for example, by proving that the first document was temporarily lost and that the seller agreed to replace it. However, where proof is lacking, we assume that the first document is no longer valid, either because of some inherent flaw in it or because the parties to the agreement decided to cancel it and put the transaction into effect from the later date.

NOTES

דְּאִי אוֹסֵיף בֵּיהּ דִּיקְלָא He added a date palm. *Rashi* and others point out that if two documents were written in connection with the same transaction, but the second document adds something, such as a date palm, to the transaction, and the land is later seized by the seller's creditors and the buyer demands to be reimbursed, the buyer has two options. He can collect the value of the land itself without the date palm from property that the seller possessed on the date recorded in the first document, or he can collect the value of the land together with the date palm from property possessed by the seller on the date recorded in the second document. Thus the law regarding two documents for the same transaction parallels exactly the law regarding a woman with two ketubot.

Arukh (cited by *Rashba* and *Ritva*, as well as *Rambam* according to *Maggid Mishneh*) argues that the law regarding the two documents parallels that regarding the two ketubot in that in both cases we say that the second document does not cancel the first if it adds something to it. But whereas in the case of the two ketubot the woman can collect either ketubah but not both, in the case of the two documents the buyer can collect on the basis of both documents — the value of the land itself from property possessed by the seller on the date of the first document, and the date palm from property he possessed on the date of the second document.

HALAKHAH

אוֹסֵיף בֵּיהּ דִּיקְלָא He added a date palm. "If two deeds of sale or two deeds of gift were issued for the same transaction, one dated later than the other, and something was added in the second deed, it does not cancel the first, for we assume that the second deed was drawn up for the purpose of including this specific addition," following Rav Pappa (*Rambam, Sefer Kinyan, Hilkhot Zekhiyah U'Mattanah* 5:9; *Shulḥan Arukh, Ḥoshen Mishpat* 240:2.)

רִאשׁוֹן בְּמֶכֶר If the first deed was for a sale. "If two deeds were issued for the same transaction, one dated later than the other, and the first was a deed of sale and the second was a deed of gift, or vice versa, the second deed does not

TRANSLATION AND COMMENTARY

[1] **with respect to the law regarding the neighbor's right of first refusal.** When land is sold, the neighbor who owns the adjacent property has the right of first refusal. Any other prospective buyer must yield to the neighbor if the latter wishes to exercise this right. The neighbor's right of first refusal is an application of the general principle of doing "what is right and good" (Deuteronomy 6:18). Hence the potential recipient is not obliged to yield to the neighbor if he himself will suffer a loss as a result. Moreover, the neighbor's right of first refusal does not apply if the land is given away. If the neighbor were to be accorded the right of first refusal, the recipient of the gift would suffer a loss, for he cannot get the equivalent gift somewhere else. Thus, if someone transfers property to someone else, first writing him a deed of sale and then giving him a deed of gift, the second document does not cancel the first, for we assume that the second document was drawn up specifically to counter a possible claim of first refusal on the part of a neighbor. [2] **And all the more so** does the second deed not cancel the first **if the first was a** deed of **gift, and the second was a** deed of **sale,** even if nothing was added in the transaction recorded in the second document. [3] **For** in such a case **we say that** the original owner **wrote** the second deed in order to protect the recipient of the gift **with respect to the law** entitling **a creditor** to seize his debtor's property, even if it has been transferred to someone else. A loan creates a lien on all of the borrower's landed property, so that if he defaults on the loan, the lender is entitled to seize his land, even if in the meantime it has been sold or given to someone else. To protect buyers against such an eventuality, a clause was inserted in the deed of sale relating to land, where the seller guaranteed to reimburse the buyer if the land was seized by the seller's creditors. Ordinarily, such a guarantee was not offered for a gift, as the donor was under no obligation to the recipient in the first place. Thus, if one person transfers property to another, first writing him a deed of gift and later giving him a deed of sale, the second document does not cancel the first, for we assume that the second document was drawn up specifically to protect the recipient of the gift in the event of seizure. [4] **But,** asks the Gemara, **if both** documents **were** deeds of **sale, or** if **both of them were** deeds of **gift,** [5] **what is the reason that** in such cases Rav Naḥman rules that **the second** deed **cancels the first?**

רַפְרָם אֲמַר [6] The Amoraim disagreed on how to explain this matter. **Rafram said:** If two deeds were

דְּכָתַב לֵיהּ, [1] מִשּׁוּם דִּינָא דְּבַר מִצְרָא. [2] וְכָל שֶׁכֵּן רִאשׁוֹן בְּמַתָּנָה וְשֵׁנִי בְּמֶכֶר, [3] דְּאָמְרִינַן מִשּׁוּם דִּינָא דְּבַעַל חוֹב הוּא דְּכָתַב כֵּן. [4] אֶלָּא, אִי שְׁנֵיהֶם בְּמֶכֶר, שְׁנֵיהֶם בְּמַתָּנָה, [5] בִּיטֵּל שֵׁנִי אֶת הָרִאשׁוֹן מַאי טַעֲמָא? [6] רַפְרָם אֲמַר: אֵימַר אוֹדוּיֵי

LITERAL TRANSLATION

[position], [1] because of the law of the one who borders. [2] And all the more so [if] the first was for a gift and the second was for a sale, [3] for we say [that] he wrote it in that way because of the law of the creditor. [4] But if the two of them were for sales, [or] the two of them were for gifts, [5] what is the reason [that] the second cancels the first?

[6] Rafram said: Say [that] he

RASHI

דינא דבעל חוב – דאי אתי בעל חוב וטריף ליה מיניה – קבל עליו אחריות בשטר השני, דנהדר וניגבי מיניה מעות הכתובים כאן. **מאי טעמא** – ביטל.

SAGES

רַפְרָם **Rafram.** A sixth-generation Babylonian Amora. See *Ketubot,* Part III, p. 127.

NOTES

מִשּׁוּם דִּינָא דְּבַר מִצְרָא **Because of the law of the one who borders.** According to most authorities (beginning with *Rav Hai Gaon*), the fact that the original owner wrote the buyer a deed of gift does not cancel the buyer's obligation to yield to the neighbor, if the latter wishes to purchase the field for himself. If a field is given away, and the donor writes the recipient of the gift a guarantee on the land, it is subject to the neighbor's right of first refusal (see *Bava Metzia* 108b), because we assume that the gift was really a sale. All the more so, if the field was indeed sold with a deed of sale, and then a deed of gift was drawn up, the field remains subject to the neighbor's right of first refusal. Thus, when the Gemara says that the deed of gift does not cancel the deed of sale, because we assume that the second deed was written to strengthen the recipient's position with respect to the law of the neighbor's right of first refusal, it means that the buyer thought he could hide the original document, and everybody would think that he had received the field as a gift.

Ritva adds that this assumption is valid even according to *Rambam* (*Hilkhot Shekhenim* 14:4), who implies that the neighbor can require the recipient of a gift to take an oath that no fraud was committed. The second deed does not cancel the first, because the buyer thought that the neighbor would be convinced that the field had been received as a gift and would not require him to take an oath to confirm that contention.

Tosafot argues that even if the deed of gift does not strengthen the recipient's position with respect to the neighbor's right of first refusal, it does in fact strengthen his position in other ways, and so the second deed does not cancel the first.

HALAKHAH

cancel the first, for we assume that the second deed was drawn up in order to endow the buyer with the advantages that the recipient of a gift has over a buyer, or in order to endow the recipient of the gift with the advantages that the buyer has over the recipient of a gift," following our Gemara. (*Rambam, Sefer Kinyan, Hilkhot Zekhiyyah U'Mattanah* 5:8; *Shulḥan Arukh, Ḥoshen Mishpat* 240:1.)

TRANSLATION AND COMMENTARY

issued for the same transaction, we **say that** the bearer of the deed may have **admitted to** the original owner that the document in his possession was forged, and it was therefore necessary for a second deed to be drawn up.

[1]**Rav Aḥa said:** If two deeds were issued for the same transaction, we **say that** the bearer of the deed must have **waived the lien** that he had on the original owner's property from the date of the first deed, and must have agreed that his lien would begin only on the date recorded in the second deed.

מַאי בֵּינַיְיהוּ [2]The Gemara asks: **What is** the practical **difference between these** two explanations of Rav Naḥman's ruling?

אִיכָּא בֵּינַיְיהוּ [3]The Gemara explains: **There are** a number of practical **differences between them.** [4]First, they differ **regarding the disqualification of the witnesses** who signed the first document. According to Rafram, since we suspect that the first document was forged, the testimony of the witnesses who attached their signatures to the false document is disqualified, and this disqualification applies even to testimony given by them regarding other matters. But according to Rav Aḥa, the witnesses who signed the first document are not disqualified. [5]Secondly, they differ regarding **compensation for the usufruct** derived from the property between the date recorded in the first document and that recorded in the second. According to Rafram, who maintains that we suspect that the first document was forged, the buyer must compensate the original owner for any benefit he derived from the property before the date recorded in the second document, because before that date the property did not belong to him. But according to Rav Aḥa, the buyer need not compensate the original owner for anything, as the property was his from the date recorded in the earlier document. **And** thirdly, they disagree regarding **the land tax** that must be paid for the period between the dates recorded in the two documents. According to Rafram, the tax must be paid by the original owner, for the property belonged to him during that period. But according to Rav Aḥa, it is the buyer who must pay the tax.

מַאי הָוֵי עֲלָהּ דִּכְתוּבָּה [6]The Gemara now returns to the controversy between Rav Huna and Rav Assi regarding the time at which the lien created by the ketubah is established, and seeks a decision on the matter. **What** Halakhic **conclusion,** asks the Gemara, **was** reached regarding this dispute **about the ketubah?**

LITERAL TRANSLATION

admitted to him. [1]Rav Aḥa said: Say [that] he waived his lien.

[2]What is [the difference] between them?

[3]There is [a difference] between them [4][regarding] disqualifying the witnesses, [5]and compensating for the usufruct, and for the land tax.

[6]What [conclusion] was there about the ketubah?

אוֹדֵי לֵיהּ. [1]רַב אַחָא אֲמַר: אֵימַר אַחוּלֵי אַחְלֵיהּ לְשִׁיעְבּוּדֵיהּ.

[2]מַאי בֵּינַיְיהוּ?

[3]אִיכָּא בֵּינַיְיהוּ [4]אוֹרוּעֵי סָהֲדֵי, [5]וּלְשַׁלּוּמֵי פֵּירֵי, וּלְטַסְקָא.

[6]מַאי הָוֵי עֲלָהּ דִּכְתוּבָּה?

RASHI

אודי ליה — בעל השטר שהראשון מזויף היה, ונתרצה על האחר לגבות מזמן שני. **אורועי סהדי** — החתומים בראשון. לרפרם — פסולים, לרב אחא — כשרים. **ולשלומי פירי** — שאכל לוקח בין זמן ראשון לזמן שני, לרפרם משלם. **ולטסקא** — לפרוע מס הקרקע למלך מזמן ראשון לזמן שני. לרפרם — על המוכר לפרוע, לרב אחא — על הלוקח לפרוע. **מאי הוי עלה דכתובה** — מאימת גביא.

SAGES

רַב אַחָא Rav Aḥa. This is Rav Aḥa the son of Rava, a Babylonian Amora of the sixth generation. He was a disciple of Rav Kahana, and a colleague of Ravina and Rav Ashi. He was head of the Pumbedita Yeshivah for five years.

TERMINOLOGY

מַאי בֵּינַיְיהוּ What is the difference between them? Where the Gemara records a difference of opinion about the reason for a law or the definition of a legal concept, it often asks: "What practical difference is there between the reasons or the definitions cited in the previous passage?" The answer to this question is introduced by the expression אִיכָּא בֵּינַיְיהוּ — "There is a difference between them...."

אִיכָּא בֵּינַיְיהוּ There is a difference between them.... This expression is used by the Gemara when there is a difference of opinion or of explanation between scholars, but the practical consequences of this difference are not clear. In explaining the distinction between the viewpoints, the Gemara introduces its answer by saying that "the practical difference between the conflicting viewpoints or the reasons mentioned in the previous passage is as follows."

מַאי הָוֵי עֲלָהּ What conclusion was here? I.e., what conclusion was reached about the matter? Or: What was the final Halakhic ruling in this case? This question is usually asked at the end of a lengthy discussion of a problem, in which different opinions have been expressed without being either proved or dismissed.

LANGUAGE

טַסְקָא Land tax. The term טַסְקָא mentioned here refers to a land tax. (A similar word is found in Arabic: طسق.) Payment of this tax was extremely important, because according to Persian law whoever paid it was regarded as the owner of the land, and non-payment could lead to the confiscation of the property.

NOTES

רַב אַחָא אֲמַר Rav Aḥa said. *Ramban* (followed by his disciples) argues that Rav Aḥa does not disagree with Rafram's explanation of Rav Naḥman's ruling, because he agrees that if both documents were deeds of gift, the second cancels the first, and regarding a gift there is nothing to waive (see *Ritva* and *Tosafot* who reject this argument). Rather, Rav Aḥa adds a second explanation, arguing that whenever it is possible to say that the bearer of the two documents may have waived the lien established by the first, we do not say that he must have admitted to the original owner that the first document was forged, for without proof we have no right to presume that forgery was committed.

אַחוּלֵי אַחְלֵיהּ לְשִׁיעְבּוּדֵיהּ He waived his lien. *Ramban* points out that Rav Aḥa says that if two documents were issued for the same transaction, we say that the bearer of the document must have waived the lien established by the first document, i.e, the lien he had on the rest of the original owner's property for reimbursement should the purchased field be seized by the original owner's creditor. If there are two documents recording the same transaction, we assume that the bearer of the documents waived the lien established on the date of the first document, and that he agreed that his lien would only begin on the date recorded in the second. But he cannot have waived his ownership of the property recorded in the document, for a valid act of acquisition cannot be undone by means of a waiver. But according to *Tosafot*, if there are two documents recording the same transaction, we assume that the bearer of the documents repudiated his ownership of the property granted him by the first document.

אוֹרוּעֵי סָהֲדֵי Disqualifying the witnesses. *Rashi*'s explanation, followed in our commentary, implies (and *Meiri* states this point explicitly) that according to Rafram all the

[1]תָּא שְׁמַע, דְּאָמַר רַב יְהוּדָה אָמַר שְׁמוּאֵל מִשּׁוּם רַבִּי אֶלְעָזָר בְּרַבִּי שִׁמְעוֹן: [2]מָנֶה מָאתַיִם מִן הָאֵירוּסִין, [3]וְתוֹסֶפֶת מִן הַנִּישּׂוּאִין. [4]וַחֲכָמִים אוֹמְרִים: אֶחָד זֶה וְאֶחָד זֶה מִן הַנִּישּׂוּאִין. [5]וְהִלְכְתָא: אֶחָד זֶה וְאֶחָד זֶה מִן הַנִּישּׂוּאִין.

משנה [6]הַגִּיּוֹרֶת שֶׁנִּתְגַּיְּירָה

LITERAL TRANSLATION

[1]Come [and] hear, for Rav Yehudah said in the name of Shmuel [who said] in the name of Rabbi Elazar the son of Rabbi Shimon: [2]The maneh [and] the two hundred [zuz] are from the betrothal, [3]and the additional amount is from the marriage. [4]But the Sages say: Both this and that are from the marriage. [5]And the law is: Both this and that are from the marriage.

MISHNAH [6][Regarding] a female convert whose daughter

TRANSLATION AND COMMENTARY

תָּא שְׁמַע [1]The Gemara answers: **Come and hear, for Rav Yehudah said in the name of Shmuel who said in the name of Rabbi Elazar the son of Rabbi Shimon:** [2]A woman may collect **the maneh or the two hundred zuz** that constitute the basic portion of her ketubah **from** the property owned by her husband at **the** time of her **betrothal,** [3]**but the additional amount** that the husband adds to the ketubah if he so wishes may be collected only **from** the property belonging to him at **the** time of their **marriage.** [4]**But the Sages say:** A woman may collect **both** the basic portion of the ketubah **and** the additional amount only **from** property owned by the husband at **the** time of their **marriage.** Thus the controversy between Rav Huna and Rav Assi is equivalent to the earlier Tannaitic dispute between Rabbi Elazar the son of Rabbi Shimon and the Sages. [5]Following the accepted rules about deciding the law, we may conclude that **the law is** in accordance with the view of the Sages that **both** the main portion of the ketubah **and** the additional amount may be collected only **from** property owned by the husband at the time of **the marriage.**

MISHNAH הַגִּיּוֹרֶת שֶׁנִּתְגַּיְּירָה [6]If a *na'arah* — a girl between twelve and twelve-and-a-half years of age — has been betrothed but not yet married, and she commits adultery, her offense is punishable by stoning. Regarding such a girl, the Torah states (Deuteronomy 22:21): "Then they shall bring out the *na'arah* to the door of her father's house, and the men of her city shall stone her with stones so that she dies, because she has perpetrated wantonness in Israel, to play the harlot in her father's house; and you shall put evil away from among you." If she is married, and her husband falsely maintains that he did not find her to be a virgin, and he brings false witnesses who testify that she committed adultery while betrothed to him, he is called a slanderer. He is flogged and ordered to pay a fine of one hundred shekalim, and he is permanently forbidden to divorce his wife. This Mishnah discusses whether these laws apply to a *na'arah* who is a convert or the daughter of a convert: If a non-Jewish **woman converted** to Judaism and **her daughter**

RASHI

משנה וזינתה – באירוסין, והיא נערה.

NOTES

testimony of the witnesses who signed the first document is disqualified. Most Rishonim (*Tosafot, Rid, Ramban,* and others) strongly object, arguing that the testimony of these witnesses is impaired only with respect to other documents bearing their signatures that are found in the hands of the buyer or the recipient of the gift. Since we assume that the buyer or the recipient of the gift is admitting that the first document was forged, he must also be admitting that the rest of his documents bearing the signatures of these witnesses are also invalid. *Rid* strengthens his argument by pointing out that the Gemara uses the expression אורועי, which can mean "impairment" and not necessarily "disqualification."

הַגִּיּוֹרֶת A female convert. *Melekhet Shlomo* seeks to suggest how the first Mishnayot of this chapter are connected to each other. The first Mishnah continues the theme of the previous chapter — the payments made by the seducer and the rapist — and discusses when they are paid to the victim's father and when they are paid to the girl herself. The second Mishnah deals with a related topic — when a minor's ketubah is paid to the girl's father and when it is paid to the girl herself. The third Mishnah turns its attention to the laws pertaining to a slanderous claim made by a husband that his wife was not a virgin when he married her, and these laws are in many ways similar to the laws regarding rape and seduction.

הַגִּיּוֹרֶת שֶׁנִּתְגַּיְּירָה בִּתָּהּ עִמָּהּ A female convert whose daughter converted with her. Most authorities explain that this law even applies to a girl who was converted to Judaism before the age of three. Even though the girl is assumed to have

HALAKHAH

אֶחָד זֶה וְאֶחָד זֶה מִן הַנִּישּׂוּאִין Both this and that are from the marriage. If a woman presents her husband with two ketubot, one drawn up when the couple were betrothed and the other drawn up when they were married, she can collect only from the property belonging to her husband at the time of their marriage." (*Shulḥan Arukh, Even HaEzer* 100:14.)

גִּיּוֹרֶת שֶׁנִּתְגַּיְּירָה בִּתָּהּ עִמָּהּ A female convert whose daughter converted with her. "If a female convert to Judaism was betrothed, and she committed adultery

TERMINOLOGY

תָּא שְׁמַע Come and hear. An expression used to introduce a source (usually Tannaitic, but sometimes Biblical or Amoraic) which will be used to support an opinion, prove a point, raise an objection, or resolve a problem. Where תָּא שְׁמַע introduces a suggested solution to a problem, if the solution is rejected, another solution is often introduced by the same expression. When a solution is finally accepted, the concluding expression שְׁמַע מִינָּהּ — "Prove it from this" — is often used.

וְהִלְכְתָא And the law is.... An expression used to introduce the Talmud's decision about a Halakhic issue left unresolved in the previous discussion.

SAGES

רַבִּי אֶלְעָזָר בְּרַבִּי שִׁמְעוֹן Rabbi Elazar the son of Rabbi Shimon. A contemporary of Rabbi Yehudah HaNasi, Rabbi Elazar the son of Rabbi Shimon was a distinguished scholar, like his father, Rabbi Shimon bar Yoḥai. Rabbi Elazar's remarkable personality was the subject of numerous anecdotes. When Rabbi Shimon bar Yoḥai, who was strongly opposed to Roman rule, was betrayed to the Roman authorities by informers, Rabbi Elazar fled with his father and lived with him in a cave for thirteen years. There the two subsisted on the barest essentials and spent their time studying Torah. During this period, Rabbi Elazar learned almost everything he knew from his father, who was his principal teacher (although Rabbi Elazar occasionally disagreed with his father's Halakhic decisions). Rabbi Elazar also studied with other scholars of his father's generation, e.g., Rabbi Yehudah, Rabbi Elazar (ben Shammua), and Rabbi Meir. Later, Rabbi Elazar was forced to accept the unpopular position of an enforcer of the law, and his acceptance of the post aroused opposition among the Sages. His spiritual independence led to friction between him and various other Rabbis, and to cooler relations with Rabbi Yehudah HaNasi, who was his boyhood friend. Nevertheless,

בִּתָּהּ עִמָּהּ וְזִינְּתָה, [1]הֲרֵי זוֹ בְּחֶנֶק. [2]אֵין לָהּ לֹא פֶּתַח בֵּית הָאָב, [3]וְלֹא מֵאָה סֶלַע. [4]הָיְתָה הוֹרָתָהּ שֶׁלֹּא בִּקְדוּשָּׁה וְלֵידָתָהּ בִּקְדוּשָּׁה, [5]הֲרֵי זוֹ בִּסְקִילָה, [6]וְאֵין לָהּ לֹא פֶּתַח בֵּית הָאָב, [7]וְלֹא מֵאָה סֶלַע.

LITERAL TRANSLATION

converted with her and [later] committed adultery, [1]she [the daughter] is subject to strangulation. [2]She is neither subject to [the law regarding] the door of her father's house, [3]nor to [the law regarding] the hundred sela'im. [4][If] her conception was not in holiness but her birth was in holiness, [5]she is subject to stoning, [6]but she is subject neither to [the law regarding] the door of her father's house, [7]nor to [the law regarding] the hundred sela'im.

TRANSLATION AND COMMENTARY

also **converted with her, and later** the daughter **commits adultery** after her betrothal but before her marriage, [1]**the daughter is subject to** the penalty of **strangulation,** but not to the penalty of stoning. Even if the girl was converted before she reached the age of three, so that she is presumed to have been a virgin at the time of her betrothal, she is not subject to the penalty of stoning, for the punishment of stoning was stipulated only in the case where the wantonness was perpetrated "in *Israel*," and this expression is understood to exclude the case of a convert. [2]Similarly, a *na'arah* who has been converted and later commits adultery while **she** is betrothed **is not subject to the law regarding the door of her father's house.** There is no need to bring her out to the door of her father's house before her execution, because the Torah requires this only in the case of a girl who was born Jewish. [3]**Nor** is such a girl subject **to the law regarding the hundred sela'im.** If the husband of a convert is found guilty of slandering her by falsely claiming that she was not a virgin when he married her, he is not required to pay the fine of one hundred shekalim, for regarding that penalty the Torah states (Deuteronomy 22:19): "For he has brought out an evil name upon a virgin of Israel," and this expression is understood to exclude the case of a convert. [4]**If** the girl's **conception was not in** a state of **holiness** — in other words, she was conceived before her mother converted — **but her birth was in** a state of **holiness,** her mother having converted during her pregnancy, [5]the daughter **is subject to** the penalty of **stoning** if she commits adultery while she is a betrothed *na'arah*. [6]**But** even **she is not subject to the law regarding the door of her father's house,** if she is sentenced to execution, [7]**or to the law regarding the hundred sela'im,** if her husband is found guilty of slander.

RASHI

הרי זו בחנק — ואפילו נתגיירה פחותה מבת שלש שנים, דבחזקת בתולה היא, דכי כתיבא סקילה בנערה המאורסה, בישראל כתיבא, דכתיב "כי עשתה נבלה בישראל". **אין לה לא פתח בית אביה** — אין צריך להוציאה אל פתח בית אביה. **ולא מאה סלע** — אם נמצא בעל שקרן ועדיו זוממין. דכולה פרשה בישראל כתיבא.

everyone acknowledged his personal piety, asceticism, and greatness in Torah knowledge. His father, Rabbi Shimon, considered him one of the most pious people of all time, and he was apparently considered exceptionally pious by the common people as well. Rabbi Elazar is also one of the most prominent figures in the *Zohar*. When he died, he was eulogized for his great achievements as a student of the Torah, both Written and Oral, as a preacher, and as a composer of liturgical poetry. The Talmud tells us that he was buried next to his father's grave in Meron.

Rabbi Elazar's teachings are quoted explicitly in several places in the Mishnah, while many other rulings of his apparently entered the Mishnah anonymously. He was therefore referred to as "Rabbi Elazar the son of Rabbi Shimon — the Anonymous Ruler" (סְתִימְתָאָה). Some of his teachings — which were also quoted by the early Amoraim — are cited in the Tosefta and in the Halakhic Midrashim.

NOTES

been a virgin at the time of her betrothal, the ordinary laws of adultery and slander do not apply, for she does not fall under the category of "Israel." *Tosafot* says that this is the reason why the Mishnah speaks of "a convert whose daughter converted with her" and not simply "a convert" — in order to teach us that it refers even to a girl who was converted before she reached the age of three, who would be converted only together with her mother. But *Rambam* (in his *Commentary to the Mishnah*) writes that the ordinary laws of adultery and slander do not apply here because we assume that the girl was not a virgin at the time of her betrothal. Thus the Mishnah must be limited to a case in which the girl converted after she had already reached her third birthday, and she is no longer presumed to be a virgin.

פֶּתַח בֵּית הָאָב The door of her father's house. *Rashi* and *Ritva* explain that there is no need to bring the convert out to the door of her father's house for execution, for that requirement was only stated with respect to a girl who was born a Jew. The Geonim (as well as *Rabbenu Yehonatan* and *Rid*) suggest that since by Jewish law a convert loses all her previous family ties, the girl is regarded as fatherless, and so the requirement of stoning at the door of her father's house does not apply.

HALAKHAH

between the age of twelve and twelve-and-a-half, she is subject to the penalty of strangulation (even if she was converted when she was less than three years old). If a man is found guilty of slandering his wife who was a convert to Judaism, he is exempt from the usual fine of 100 shekalim, as well as from flogging," following the Mishnah here. (*Rambam, Sefer Kedushah, Hilkhot Issurei Bi'ah* 3:7; *Sefer Nashim, Hilkhot Na'arah Betulah* 3:8.)

הָיְתָה הוֹרָתָהּ שֶׁלֹּא בִּקְדוּשָּׁה If her conception was not in holiness. "The following laws apply to a girl whose mother converted to Judaism while pregnant with her: If the girl is betrothed between the age of twelve and twelve-and-a-half, and she commits adultery, she is subject to the penalty of stoning. She is executed not at the door of her father's house, but at the city gate. If she is married, and her husband is found guilty of slandering her by falsely claiming that she was not a virgin when he married her, he is exempt from the usual fine of 100 shekalim, as well as from flogging," in accordance with the Mishnah. (*Rambam, Sefer Kedushah, Hilkhot Issurei Bi'ah* 3:11; *Sefer Nashim, Hilkhot Na'arah Betulah* 3:8.)

TRANSLATION AND COMMENTARY

(The Gemara will explain this distinction.) [1]But **if** both **her conception and her birth were in** a state of **holiness,** i.e., her mother converted to Judaism before she became pregnant with this girl, [2]the girl is treated **as Jewish in all respects** relating to adultery and slander. Thus she must be brought out to the door of her father's house for stoning, and her husband must pay the hundred shekalim if he is convicted of slander.

יֵשׁ לָהּ אָב [3]The Mishnah continues: **If** a girl who was born a Jew commits adultery, and **she has a father, but she has no door of her father's house,** because her father does not own a house of his own, [4]**or if she has a door of her father's house, but she has no father,** because her father is dead, [5]**she is** nevertheless **subject to** the penalty of **stoning.** [6]When the Torah referred to **"the door of her father's house,"** it **meant only** that it was **prescribed** that the girl be brought out to the door of her father's home for execution. But it did not mean to imply that her punishment is not carried out if she lacks a father or if her father lacks a door to his house.

[44B] **GEMARA** מְנָא הָנֵי מִילֵּי [7]Our Mishnah assumes that the special laws that govern adultery committed by a betrothed *na'arah* apply only to a girl of Jewish parentage, as the verse states: "She has perpetrated wantonness *in Israel.*" **What,** then, asks the Gemara, **is the** Biblical **source for the ruling** that a girl whose mother converted while pregnant is subject to the penalty of stoning if she commits adultery while she is a betrothed *na'arah?*

אֲמַר רֵישׁ לָקִישׁ [8]**Resh Lakish said** in reply: [9]We derive this law from **the verse** that **says** (Deuteronomy 22:21): "And the men of her city shall stone her with stones **so that she dies.**" The expression "so that she dies" is unnecessary, for if the men of the city stone her, she will surely die. [10]Thus we can infer that this

[1]הָיְתָה הוֹרָתָהּ וְלֵידָתָהּ בִּקְדוּשָּׁה, [2]הֲרֵי הִיא כְּבַת יִשְׂרָאֵל לְכָל דְּבָרֶיהָ. [3]יֵשׁ לָהּ אָב, וְאֵין לָהּ פֶּתַח בֵּית הָאָב, [4]יֵשׁ לָהּ פֶּתַח בֵּית הָאָב, וְאֵין לָהּ אָב, [5]הֲרֵי זוֹ בִּסְקִילָה. [6]לֹא נֶאֱמַר ״פֶּתַח בֵּית אָב״ אֶלָּא לְמִצְוָה.

[44B] **גמרא** [7]מְנָא הָנֵי מִילֵּי?

[8]אֲמַר רֵישׁ לָקִישׁ: [9]דְּאָמַר קְרָא: ״וָמֵתָה״ — [10]לְרַבּוֹת

LITERAL TRANSLATION

[1][If] her conception and her birth were in holiness, [2]she is like a daughter of Israel in all respects (lit., "in all her matters").

[3][If] she has a father, but she has no door of her father's house, [4][or if] she has a door of her father's house, but she has no father, [5]she is subject to stoning. [6]"The door of her father's house" was stated only as a precept.

[44B] GEMARA [7]From where are these things [derived]?

[8]Resh Lakish said: [9]For the verse said: "So that she dies" — [10]to include [where]

RASHI

הרי זו בסקילה — בגמרא יליף לה.

הרי היא כבת ישראל לכל דבריה — ויש לה פתח בית אב, ומאה סלעים.

יש לה אב ואין לה פתח בית אב — כגון שאין לו בית. ובישראלית קמיירי.

גמרא מנא הני מילי — שהורתה שלא בקדושה ולידתה בקדושה בסקילה. **ומתה** — ״וסקלוה (כל) אנשי עירה באבנים ומתה״, והאי ״ומתה״ קרא יתירא הוא.

TERMINOLOGY

מְנָא הָנֵי מִילֵּי From where are these things derived? I.e., what verse in the Torah is the source of the statement just made? This question by the Gemara is usually followed either by a Biblical text or by a Midrashic interpretation of Biblical verses from which the Halakhic ruling is derived.

NOTES

מְנָא הָנֵי מִילֵּי From where are these things derived? As mentioned by *Tosafot* (and expanded upon by the other Rishonim), the starting assumption of the entire discussion here in the Gemara is that the laws pertaining to the adultery of a betrothed girl do not apply to a convert, because she does not come into the category of "Israel." Thus we might have expected that a girl whose mother converted while pregnant should also be excluded from these laws. Accordingly, the Gemara's question is as follows (see *Rashi*): What is the Biblical source for the ruling that such a girl is indeed liable for stoning if she committed adultery during her betrothal?

But *Ḥatam Sofer* suggests that the Gemara is asking a more general question: What is the Biblical source for the difference in punishment meted out to the various girls mentioned in our Mishnah? Resh Lakish answers that the expression "so that she dies" teaches that all betrothed *ne'arot* are subject to the punishment of stoning. Only at the end of the passage does the Gemara infer from the expression "in Israel" that a *na'arah* who was converted as a child is excluded from these laws.

״וָמֵתָה״ — לְרַבּוֹת "So that she dies" — to include. A

HALAKHAH

הָיְתָה הוֹרָתָהּ וְלֵידָתָהּ בִּקְדוּשָּׁה If her conception and her birth were in holiness. "A girl whose mother converted to Judaism before the girl was conceived is treated as Jewish regarding all the laws of slander." (*Rambam, Sefer Nashim, Hilkhot Na'arah Betulah* 3:8.)

וְאֵין לָהּ אָב But she has no father. "If a *na'arah* commits adultery during her betrothal, and she has no father, or if she has a father, but he does not own a house, she is nevertheless subject to the penalty of stoning." (*Rambam, Sefer Kedushah, Hilkhot Issurei Bi'ah* 3:11.)

BACKGROUND

הַהִיא יִשְׂרְאֵלִית מְעַלְּיָיתָא הִיא **That girl is a proper Jew.** A girl who was not conceived as a Jew, even if she was born as a Jew, is regarded as not being of "Jewish seed." However, a girl whose mother converted before conceiving her was conceived and born in the sanctity of Judaism, and thus is of "Jewish seed." Although in certain matters, such as marriage to a priest, she may belong to the "community of converts" if both her father and her mother are converts, in principle she is fully Jewish according to law.

הוֹרָתָהּ שֶׁלֹּא בִּקְדוּשָּׁה [1] וְלֵידָתָהּ בִּקְדוּשָּׁה.
[2] אִי הָכִי, מִילְקָא נַמִי נִילְקֵי,
[3] וּמֵאָה סֶלַע נַמִי לְשַׁלֵּם!
[4] אֲמַר קְרָא: ״וָמֵתָה״. [5] לְמִיתָה נִתְרַבְּתָה, [6] וְלֹא לִקְנָס.
[7] וְאֵימָא: לְרַבּוֹת הוֹרָתָהּ וְלֵידָתָהּ בִּקְדוּשָּׁה!
[8] הַהִיא יִשְׂרְאֵלִית מְעַלְּיָיתָא הִיא.
[9] וְאֵימָא: לְרַבּוֹת הוֹרָתָהּ וְלֵידָתָהּ שֶׁלֹּא בִּקְדוּשָּׁה!

LITERAL TRANSLATION

her conception was not in holiness [1] and her birth was in holiness.
[2] If so, let him also be flogged, [3] and let him also pay the hundred sela'im!
[4] The verse said: "So that she dies." [5] For the death penalty she was included, [6] but not for the fine.
[7] But say: To include [where] her conception and her birth were in holiness!
[8] That [girl] is a proper Jew.
[9] But say: To include [where] her conception and her birth were not in holiness!

TRANSLATION AND COMMENTARY

seemingly unnecessary expression appears in the text in order **to include** a girl **whose conception was not in** a state of **holiness,** before her mother had converted, [1] **but whose birth was in** a state of **holiness,** after the mother had converted. This girl, too, is subject to stoning if she commits adultery while she is a *na'arah,* after her betrothal but before her marriage.

אִי הָכִי [2] The Gemara asks: **If it is true** that a girl whose mother converted while pregnant is governed by the same laws that apply to a girl of Jewish family, then **let** her husband **also be flogged,** [3] **and let him also pay the hundred-shekel** fine if he is found guilty of slandering her! Why does the Mishnah rule to the contrary?

אֲמַר קְרָא [4] The Gemara answers: **The verse says:** "And the men of her city shall stone her **so that she dies."** [5] The seemingly unnecessary expression, "so that she dies," teaches us that a girl whose mother converted while pregnant **is included** in the law **regarding the** special **death penalty** of stoning that is imposed on a betrothed *na'arah* who is found guilty of adultery. [6] **But** the expression does **not** imply that she is also included in the law **regarding the fine** imposed on the husband in the event that his claim concerning his wife's loss of virginity is found to have been slanderous.

וְאֵימָא [7] The Gemara now reconsiders the inference to be drawn from the superfluous expression "so that she dies": **But** let us **say** that its purpose is only **to include** a girl **whose conception** ***and*** **whose birth were in** a state of **holiness,** i.e., a girl whose mother had already converted to Judaism before her daughter was conceived. Perhaps, asks the Gemara, the special punishment of stoning applies only to such a girl, whereas a girl who was conceived before her mother converted is punished by strangulation if she commits adultery while she is a betrothed *na'arah*?

הַהִיא יִשְׂרְאֵלִית מְעַלְּיָיתָא הִיא [8] The Gemara answers: A **girl** whose mother had already converted to Judaism before the girl's conception **is a proper Jew!** There is no difference between such a girl and a girl born to a woman who was herself born Jewish. Thus no extra words are needed in order to extend the law of stoning to the daughter.

וְאֵימָא [9] The Gemara now suggests another derivation that can be made from the seemingly superfluous expression "so that she dies": **But** let us **say** that the purpose of this expression is **to include** even a girl **whose conception and birth were not in** a state of **holiness,** i.e., a girl who was born to a non-Jewish woman and who was later converted as a child. Perhaps she too is governed by the law that a betrothed *na'arah* who commits adultery is subject to the punishment of stoning?

NOTES

similar inference is found in the Jerusalem Talmud. But there the punishment of stoning is understood to have been extended to a girl whose conception was not in a state of holiness, but whose birth was in a state of holiness, by means of the repetition of the word "virgin." The expression "so that she dies" then implies that only the punishment of stoning is extended to such a girl, but not the 100-shekalim fine.

אִי הָכִי, מִילְקָא נַמִי נִילְקֵי **If so, let him also be flogged.** At this point in the argument the Gemara assumes that the application of the punishment of stoning to a *na'arah* whose mother converted while pregnant with her is not derived from the expression "so that she dies," because this expression is not a superfluous phrase that extends the law stated in the verse to a case not mentioned explicitly in it. Indeed, we find elsewhere that the instructions about stoning are coupled with the mention that the person sentenced to death will die (see Deuteronomy 17:5: "And you shall stone them with stones so that they die"), and this formula seems to be standard Biblical Hebrew. Alternatively, the expression "so that she dies" is needed for some other exposition (*Ritva*).

[1]אִם כֵּן, ״בְּיִשְׂרָאֵל״ מַאי אַהֲנֵי לֵיהּ?

[2]אָמַר רַבִּי יוֹסֵי בַּר חֲנִינָא: הַמּוֹצִיא שֵׁם רַע עַל הַיְּתוֹמָה פָּטוּר, [3]שֶׁנֶּאֱמַר: ״וְנָתְנוּ לַאֲבִי הַנַּעֲרָה״ — [4]פְּרָט לָזוֹ שֶׁאֵין לָהּ אָב.

[5]מְתִיב רַבִּי יוֹסֵי בַּר אָבִין, [6]וְאִיתֵּימָא רַבִּי יוֹסֵי בַּר זְבִידָא: ״׳וְאִם מָאֵן יְמָאֵן אָבִיהָ׳ — [7]לְרַבּוֹת יְתוֹמָה לִקְנָס.

LITERAL TRANSLATION

[1]If so, in what way was "in Israel" effective? [2]Rabbi Yose bar Ḥanina said: Someone who puts out a bad name about an orphan girl is exempt, [3]for it is said: "And they shall give to the father of the *na'arah*" — [4]to exclude this [girl] who has no father.

[5]Rabbi Yose bar Avin, [6]and there are [some] who say [it was] Rabbi Yose bar Zevida, objected: "'If her father will surely refuse' — [7]to include an orphan girl for the fine.

TRANSLATION AND COMMENTARY

אִם כֵּן [1]The Gemara answers: **If so,** then **for what reason was** the expression **"in Israel"** inserted? Surely, the words "she has perpetrated wantonness in Israel" come to teach us that the punishment of stoning was imposed only on a girl of Jewish parentage, to the exclusion of a convert. Hence the expression "so that she dies" specifically includes a girl whose mother converted while pregnant, and the expression "in Israel" specifically excludes a girl who was born before her mother converted. For if even a girl who was born to a non-Jewish mother and was later converted as a child is included in this regulation, nobody is left to be excluded.

אָמַר רַבִּי יוֹסֵי בַּר חֲנִינָא [2]Our Mishnah stated that a betrothed *na'arah* who is found guilty of adultery is subject to the penalty of stoning, even if she is an orphan. The Gemara now considers whether the husband of an orphan *na'arah* is subject to the laws of slander if he falsely accuses his wife of having committed adultery while betrothed to him. **Rabbi Yose bar Ḥanina said: If** a husband is found guilty of having **falsely accused** of adultery his wife who was **an orphan girl, he is exempt** from the fine of one hundred shekalim, [3]**for the verse says** (Deuteronomy 22:19): "And they shall fine him a hundred silver shekalim, **and give them to the father of the *na'arah*.**" [4]The mention here of "father" comes **to exclude** from **this** regulation a **girl who has no father.**

מְתִיב רַבִּי יוֹסֵי בַּר אָבִין [5]**Rabbi Yose bar Avin raised an objection** from a Baraita against the ruling of Rabbi Yose bar Ḥanina, [6]**and there are some who say** that **it was Rabbi Yose bar Zevida** who raised this objection: "Regarding the seducer of a *na'arah*, the verse states (Exodus 22:16): **'If her father will surely refuse** (אִם מָאֵן יְמָאֵן) to give her to him, he shall pay money according to the dowry of virgins.' The use of the double verb form — *im ma'en yema'en* — [7]comes **to include** the right of **an orphan girl to** receive **the fine.**

RASHI

בישראל — ״כי עשתה נבלה בישראל״. **מאן ימאן** — במפתה הכתוב מדבר, דמצי למיכתב ״(ו)אם ימאן״ וכתב ״(ו)אם מאן ימאן״ — בין אביה קיים וממאן, בין שאין אביה קיים והיא ממאנת. אלמא, אף על גב דכתיב באונס ״ונתן לאבי הנערה״, ואונס ומפתה מהדדי גמירי — מיחייב קנס ליתומה. וכי תימא שאני הכא דרבי רחמנא, [אבל לגבי מוציא שם רע לא אתרבאי] — הכא נמי לאו יתומה משמע מריבוי, אלא דבין היא ובין אביה

NOTES

״בְּיִשְׂרָאֵל״ מַאי אַהֲנֵי לֵיהּ **In what way was "in Israel" effective?** It has been noted that the expression, "Because she has perpetrated wantonness in Israel," does not necessarily exclude a convert; for now that she has converted and joined the Jewish people, her adultery can surely be categorized as "wantonness in Israel." Rather, it is the verse, "For he has brought out an evil name upon a virgin of Israel," that must be understood as excluding a convert. Even though that verse refers only to the slanderer's fine, it sheds light on the expression "in Israel," stated with respect to the adulteress's punishment, and teaches us that a convert is excluded from both these laws.

לְרַבּוֹת יְתוֹמָה לִקְנָס **To include an orphan girl for the fine.** The Rishonim raise numerous questions about the derivation of this law, and about how it poses a difficulty concerning the viewpoint of Rabbi Yose bar Ḥanina. First, the verse, "If her father will surely refuse to give her to him," is stated with respect to a girl who was seduced. Why, then, is an orphan girl entitled to the fine? When she engaged in sexual relations with the seducer, she did so of her own free will, thus waiving all rights to compensation!

Ramban suggests that we are not dealing here with a *na'arah*, but with a minor. Since a minor does not have the legal capacity to give her consent, her seduction is treated as rape, and she is therefore entitled to the fine. Second, it is legitimate to derive from the verse, "If her father will surely refuse to give her to him," that not only may the father refuse to give his daughter to the seducer, but the daughter too may refuse to be given to him. But how can anything be inferred from the verse about the fine (see *Ra'ah*)? Most Rishonim follow *Rashi* and explain that since a general analogy is drawn between the seducer and the rapist, we treat the verse, "If her father will surely refuse," as if it were written in the section dealing with a

HALAKHAH

הַמּוֹצִיא שֵׁם רַע עַל הַיְּתוֹמָה **Someone who puts out a bad name about an orphan girl.** "If a man falsely accuses his wife, who is an orphan girl, of adultery, he pays the fine of 100 shekalim to the girl herself," following Rava. (*Rambam, Sefer Nashim, Hilkhot Na'arah Betulah* 3:1.)

SAGES

רַבִּי יוֹסֵי בַּר אָבִין **Rabbi Yose bar Avin.** A Palestinian Amora of the fourth generation. See *Ketubot*, Part I, pp. 129-30.

רַבִּי יוֹסֵי בַּר זְבִידָא **Rabbi Yose bar Zevida.** When the Babylonian Talmud mentions Rabbi Yose with no further epithet, it is referring to the Tanna, Rabbi Yose ben Ḥalafta. But the Jerusalem Talmud frequently mentions an Amora named Rabbi Yose, whose full name was Rabbi Yose bar Zevida, and who is referred to by that name. This Amora belonged to the fourth generation of Palestinian Amoraim, and he studied under the students of Rabbi Yoḥanan. He seems to have spent almost his entire life in his native city of Tiberias, though he did spend a short time in Babylonia.

Rabbi Yose was one of the greatest Sages of his generation. He and his close friend Rabbi Yonah served as the leaders of the Jews of Eretz Israel in their generation. We also find them representing the Jewish population in contacts with the non-Jewish authorities. Sages abroad, both in Egypt and in Babylonia, heeded Rabbi Yose's directives in the letters he sent them. His ruling that the second day of Festivals should still be celebrated abroad, although the calendar was fixed, has remained in force to this day.

SAGES

רַבִּי יוֹסֵי הַגְּלִילִי Rabbi Yose HaGelili. A Tanna of the generation following the destruction of the Second Temple. See *Ketubot*, Part III, p. 163.

TERMINOLOGY

הוּא מוֹתִיב לָהּ וְהוּא מְפָרֵק לָהּ He raised the objection and he resolved it, i.e., the same Amora who raised the objection from a Mishnah or a Baraita resolved it.

TRANSLATION AND COMMENTARY

[1]**This is the opinion of Rabbi Yose HaGelili."** If an orphan *na'arah* is seduced, and she decides not to marry the seducer, she too is entitled to the fine. Thus we see that even when the Torah awards a fine to the girl's father, it does not mean to imply that the fine is not imposed if the father is dead. Just as a seducer is held liable to pay the fine if the girl's father is dead, so too should a slanderer be held liable to pay the fine if his wife is an orphan!

הוּא מוֹתִיב לָהּ [2]Rabbi Yose bar Avin **raised the objection and** then **resolved it** himself: When Rabbi Yose HaGelili said that even an orphan *na'arah* is entitled to the fine paid by the seducer, [3]he was speaking of a case **where** the seducer **had sexual relations with her and afterwards she was orphaned.** Since the father was alive at the time the offense was committed, the seducer must pay the fine, even if the father died before the fine was actually imposed by the court. But if the girl was already an orphan before she was seduced, the seducer is indeed exempt from paying the fine. Similarly, the slanderer is exempt from paying the fine, if his wife was an orphan when he falsely accused her of adultery.

רָבָא אָמַר [4]**Rava** disagreed with Rabbi Yose bar Ḥanina and **said:** If a husband falsely accuses his orphan wife of adultery, **he is** held **liable** to pay the fine of one hundred shekalim.

מִמַּאי [5]The Gemara asks: **From where did** Rava **reach** such a conclusion?

LITERAL TRANSLATION

[1][These are] the words of Rabbi Yose HaGelili."

[2]He raised the objection and he resolved it: [3][This applies] where he had sexual relations with her and afterwards she was orphaned.

[4]Rava said: He is liable.

[5]From where [does he infer this]?

[1]דִּבְרֵי רַבִּי יוֹסֵי הַגְּלִילִי״. [2]הוּא מוֹתִיב לָהּ וְהוּא מְפָרֵק לָהּ: [3]בְּבָא עָלֶיהָ וְאַחַר כָּךְ נִתְיַתְּמָה. [4]רָבָא אָמַר: חַיָּיב. [5]מִמַּאי?

RASHI

יכולין לעכב, כדאמרינן ב״אלו נערות״ (כתובות לט,ב). ויתומה לא אתרבאי הכא, אלא דסבירא ליה לתנא ד״אביה״ דקאמר קרא — לאו למעוטי יתומה, אלא למימרא דקנס לאביה ולא לעצמה, והוא הדין ל״אביה״ האמור במוציא שם רע. **הוא מותיב כו׳** — הא יתומה דקאמר תנא. **בבא עליה ואחר כך נתיתמה** — ולעולם ״אבי הנערה״ למעוטי יתומה, בין בקנס בין בהוצאת שם רע. **רבא אמר חייב** — המוציא שם רע על היתומה.

NOTES

girl who was raped, and it teaches us that an orphan girl is entitled to the fine paid by the rapist. Both of these questions fall away according to the reading of our text accepted by *Meiri*, "'For he has humbled her' (Deuteronomy 22:29) — to include an orphan girl for the fine," for that verse is stated with respect to a girl who was raped.

Even if it is granted that an orphan girl who was raped is entitled to the fine, how does it follow that the laws of slander apply to an orphan girl? An orphan girl who was raped is entitled to the fine, because of the verse, "If her father will surely refuse." But a husband who falsely accuses his wife, who is an orphan girl, of adultery may well be exempt from paying the fine, because the verse (Deuteronomy 22:19), "And they shall give them to the father of the girl," excludes from the laws of slander a girl who has no father!

Some suggest (see *Ramban*) that the Gemara here is applying the principle that when a law is discussed by the Torah in a certain context, and it can be shown that there is no need for this verse to appear in that context, the problematic verse may be interpreted as applying in another — similar — context where it *is* relevant. Here, the law derived from the verse, "If her father will surely refuse," is not needed with respect to a seduced girl, for an orphan girl is not entitled to a fine for her seduction. Thus the superfluity found in that verse teaches us that an orphan girl is also governed by the laws of slander. The difficulty with this explanation lies in the Gemara's failure to mention the most essential point of the derivation.

Most authorities follow *Rashi*, who explains that the verse, "If her father will surely refuse," teaches us a general rule that even when the Torah mentions the girl's father, the same law applies if the father is dead. Thus it should follow that the laws of slander apply even in the case of an orphan girl, although the verse says that the fine for slander is paid to the girl's father.

דִּבְרֵי רַבִּי יוֹסֵי הַגְּלִילִי These are the words of Rabbi Yose HaGelili. *Tosafot* and others ask: Why did Rabbi Yose bar Avin raise his objection against Rabbi Yose bar Ḥanina from Rabbi Yose HaGelili's ruling in the Baraita? This ruling is at best an indirect proof against him, for Rabbi Yose bar Ḥanina spoke of the fine paid by a slanderer, whereas Rabbi Yose HaGelili was ruling about the seducer's fine. Rabbi Yose bar Avin could have raised his objection from our Mishnah, since it states that a girl whose mother converted while pregnant is not entitled to the 100-shekel fine paid by the slanderer, and this implies that in the parallel case of a Jewish girl who has been orphaned, the husband *is* held liable to pay the fine, and this contradicts the viewpoint of Rabbi Yose bar Ḥanina.

Tosafot answers that our Mishnah may in fact follow the viewpoint of Rabbi Akiva (above, 38a), who says that if someone rapes a girl who was previously betrothed and then divorced, he is held liable to pay the rapist's fine, and that fine is paid to the girl herself. Just as Rabbi Akiva says that if the girl was not previously betrothed the rapist's fine is paid to her father, but if she was betrothed the fine is paid to the girl herself, he would similarly say that if the slandered girl has a father, the fine is paid to him, but if she is an orphan, the fine is paid to her; for according to Rabbi Akiva the fine need not necessarily be paid to the girl's father. Rabbi Yose bar Ḥanina issued his ruling in

TRANSLATION AND COMMENTARY

מִדְּתָנֵי אַמִּי [1]The Gemara answers that Rava derives his ruling **from** a Baraita **taught** by the Sage **Ammi,** which stated: "Regarding the fine paid by the slanderer, the verse states (Deuteronomy 22:19): 'For he has brought out an evil name upon **a virgin of Israel.**' The mention here of 'Israel' teaches us that he is liable for the fine only if he slandered a virgin of Jewish parentage, [2]**but not** if he slandered **a virgin** from among the **converts.**" [3]**Granted if you say that in the case** of an orphan who comes **from a Jewish family** the slanderer **is** held **liable** to pay the fine, [4]**this is why it was necessary for the verse to exclude** someone who slanders a virgin from among the **converts.** According to Jewish law, every convert is regarded as an orphan, for upon conversion all ties of kinship with the convert's biological parents are severed. Since the slanderer must pay the fine if he slanders an orphan of Jewish parentage, it was necessary to state that he is exempt if he slanders an "orphan" after her conversion. [5]**But if you say that in the case** of an orphan **from a Jewish family** the slanderer **is exempt** from paying the fine, there is a difficulty. [6]**For if** when he slanders an orphan **from a Jewish family, he is exempt** from paying the fine, [7]**is it necessary to mention** that he is exempt if he slanders a virgin from among the **converts?** It is obvious that he is exempt, for there is no reason why a convert should be more entitled to the fine than is an orphan of Jewish parentage!

אָמַר רֵישׁ לָקִישׁ [8]The Gemara now discusses another case in which the slanderer is exempt from paying the fine. **Resh Lakish said: If** a husband is found guilty of having **falsely accused** his wife of adultery when she is still **a minor** (less than twelve years old), **he is exempt** from paying the fine, [9]**for the verse says** (Deuteronomy 22:19): **"And they shall give** it **to the father of the *na'arah*"** — and not to the father of a minor. Resh Lakish explains: We know that the term *"na'arah"* is to be understood narrowly in this case, [10]because **the verse was speaking about a *"na'arah"* spelled in full.** The word *"na'arah"* is usually spelled in the Torah without its final Hebrew letter heh (ה). In this verse, however, the word is spelled in full, and this

[1]מִדְּתָנֵי אַמִּי: ״׳בְּתוּלַת יִשְׂרָאֵל׳ — [2]וְלֹא בְּתוּלַת גֵּרִים״. [3]אִי אָמְרַתְּ בִּשְׁלָמָא כִּי הַאי גַּוְונָא בְּיִשְׂרָאֵל מִיחַיַּיב, [4]הַיְינוּ דְּאִיצְטְרִיךְ קְרָא לְמַעוּטֵי גֵּרִים. [5]אֶלָּא אִי אָמְרַתְּ בְּיִשְׂרָאֵל כְּהַאי גַּוְונָא פָּטוּר, [6]הָשְׁתָּא בְּיִשְׂרָאֵל פָּטוּר, [7]בְּגֵרִים מִיבָּעֲיָא?

[8]אָמַר רֵישׁ לָקִישׁ: הַמּוֹצִיא שֵׁם רַע עַל הַקְּטַנָּה פָּטוּר, [9]שֶׁנֶּאֱמַר: ״וְנָתְנוּ לַאֲבִי הַנַּעֲרָה״. [10]״נַעֲרָה״ מָלֵא דִּבֵּר הַכָּתוּב.

LITERAL TRANSLATION

[1]From what Ammi taught: "'A virgin of Israel' — [2]but not a virgin of converts." [3]Granted if you say [that] in such a case in Israel he is liable, [4]this is why the verse was needed to exclude converts. [5]But if you say [that] in Israel in such a case he is exempt, [6]now [that] in Israel he is exempt, [7]is it necessary [to say this] regarding converts?

[8]Resh Lakish said: Someone who puts out a bad name about a minor is exempt, [9]for it is said: "And they shall give to the father of the *na'arah*." [10]The verse was speaking [about] a *"na'arah"* [spelled] in full.

RASHI

מדתני אמי כי הוציא שם רע על בתולת ישראל ולא בתולת גרים — והא בתולת גרים יתומה היא, דרחמנא אפקריה לזרעיה דנכרי כשל חמור, דכתיב (יחזקאל כג) "וזרמת סוסים זרמתם". והוא לשון שכבת זרע הזורם כזרם מים, ואצטריך קרא למעוטי. אי אמרת בשלמא כו'. **נערה מלא דבר הכתוב** — בכל מקום כתיב "נער" וכאן כתיב "נערה" מלא — להוציא את הקטנה.

NOTES

accordance with the viewpoint of Rabbi Yose HaGelili, who maintains that the rapist is exempt if his victim was previously betrothed and then divorced. Just as he says that no fine is paid if the raped girl was previously betrothed, he would similarly say that the slandered girl is not entitled to the fine if she is an orphan; for according to Rabbi Yose HaGelili, if the fine cannot be paid to the girl's father, it is not paid at all. Thus an objection was raised against Rabbi Yose bar Ḥanina from the other ruling of Rabbi Yose HaGelili — that an orphan girl is indeed entitled to the seducer's fine.

וְלֹא בְּתוּלַת גֵּרִים **But not a virgin of converts.** According to most Rishonim, every convert is treated as an orphan, because all the convert's ties of kinship are severed upon conversion. Since the phrase, "a virgin of Israel," was necessary in order to teach us that the slanderer is exempt from paying the fine if his wife is a convert, it follows that he *is* held liable to pay the fine if she is an orphaned Jew.

״נַעֲרָה״ מָלֵא דִּבֵּר הַכָּתוּב **The verse was speaking about a *"na'arah"* spelled in full.** The Jerusalem Talmud asks: The word *"na'arah"* appears several times in the Biblical passage dealing with the false accuser (Deuteronomy

HALAKHAH

הַמּוֹצִיא שֵׁם רַע עַל הַקְּטַנָּה **Someone who puts out a bad name about a minor.** "If someone falsely accuses his wife, who is a minor, of adultery, he is exempt from the fine and from lashes," following Resh Lakish. (*Rambam, Sefer Nashim, Hilkhot Na'arah Betulah* 3:2.)

SAGES

שִׁילָא Shila. Rav Shila was one of the first Babylonian Amoraim. After the death of Rabbi Yehuda HaNasi, Rav Shila became the spiritual leader of Babylonia. He lived in Neharde'a, and was head of the yeshivah there. When Rav came to Babylonia, Rav Shila did not recognize him at first, and used him as a translator. But after he learned who Rav was, he treated him with great honor and even accepted his authority. Nevertheless, Rav did not want to detract from Rav Shila's honor and moved to Sura, establishing his own yeshivah there.

Rav Shila's yeshivah apparently continued to exist for some time after his death, and various traditions are reported in its name. The Talmud reports several differences of opinion between Rav Shila and Rav, and various Halakhic teachings are transmitted in Rav Shila's name.

TRANSLATION AND COMMENTARY

informs us that the Torah was being very specific when it referred to this *na'arah*, and did not intend the law to apply to a minor or to an adult.

מַתְקִיף לָהּ רַב אַחָא בַּר אַבָּא [1] When **Rav Aḥa bar Abba** heard Resh Lakish's explanation, he **objected to it:** [2] We see from Resh Lakish's explanation that **the reason** why the law of the husband who falsely accuses his wife of adultery does not apply to a minor **is because** the Torah **wrote the word *"na'arah"* in full.** [3] **But** the implication is that **if this were not so we would have thought that** the verse **was referring even to a minor.** [4] **But surely** this is impossible, for the following **is written** in the next two verses: [5] **"But if this thing was true, and the signs of virginity were not found in the *na'arah*** [spelled defectively], [6] **then they shall bring the *na'arah*** [spelled defectively] **out to the door of her father's house and stone her."** [7] **But** surely the second verse cannot apply to a minor, since **a minor is not subject to punishment!** Even if his minor wife had committed adultery, she would not be stoned to death, since as a minor she was not legally competent. Hence the first verse must also not be referring to a minor. Why, then, do you need to learn this law from the spelling of the word *"na'arah"* in this verse?

אֶלָּא [8] **Rather,** Rav Aḥa bar Abba amended Resh Lakish's explanation to read as follows: **Here,** in the case of the husband who falsely accused his wife of adultery, where we know that the law does not apply to minors, the Torah (Deuteronomy 22:19) writes **"*na'arah*" spelling it in full.** Thus when the word *"na'arah"* is spelled in full, this means that the law does not apply to minors, [9] **but wherever** the word **"*na'arah*" is spelled defectively,** without its last letter, [10] we may infer that **a minor girl is** also **implied.** In all those cases, the word *"na'arah"* spelled defectively is used not to exclude a minor under the age of twelve, but rather to exclude a *bogeret*, who has already reached the age of twelve-and-a-half, and is legally an adult.

תָּנֵי שִׁילָא [11] The Sage **Shila taught** a Baraita, which stated: **"There are three punishments of execution**

[1] מַתְקִיף לָהּ רַב אַחָא בַּר אַבָּא:
[2] טַעֲמָא דִּכְתִיב בָּהּ ״הַנַּעֲרָה״.
[3] הָא לָאו הָכִי, הֲוָה אָמִינָא אֲפִילּוּ קְטַנָּה? [4] הָא כְּתִיב:
[5] ״וְאִם אֱמֶת הָיָה הַדָּבָר הַזֶּה, לֹא נִמְצְאוּ בְתוּלִים לַנַּעֲרָ,
[6] וְהוֹצִיאוּ אֶת הַנַּעֲרָ אֶל פֶּתַח בֵּית אָבִיהָ וּסְקָלוּהָ״. [7] וּקְטַנָּה לָאו בַּת עוֹנָשִׁין הִיא!
[8] אֶלָּא, כָּאן נַעֲרָה. [9] הָא כָּל מָקוֹם שֶׁנֶּאֱמַר ״נַעֲרָ״, [10] אֲפִילּוּ קְטַנָּה בְּמַשְׁמָע.
[11] תָּנֵי שִׁילָא: ״שָׁלֹשׁ מִדּוֹת

LITERAL TRANSLATION

[1] Rav Aḥa bar Abba objected to it: [2] The reason is that regarding her "the *na'arah*" is written [in full]. [3] But if this were not so, would I have thought [that] even a minor [was meant]? [4] But surely it is written: [5] "But if this thing was true, [and the signs of] virginity were not found in the *na'arah* [spelled defectively], [6] then they shall bring the *na'arah* [spelled defectively] out to the door of her father's house and stone her." [7] But a minor is not subject to punishment!

[8] Rather, here [it is spelled] *"na'arah"* [in full]. [9] But wherever *"na'arah"* is said [spelled defectively], [10] even a minor girl is within the meaning.

[11] Shila taught: "There are three punishments [of execution]

RASHI

אלא כאן נערה כו' — אלא האי דכתיב מלא — לא ללמד על עצמו בא ולהוציא את הקטנה, דאלמלא הך דרשא אמעיטא לה קטנה, כדאמרינן דלאו בת עונשין. אלא ללמד בא על כל נערה שבתורה שכתובין חסר — לומר שאף הקטנה במשמע. והכי יליף: כאן נערה, כאן שאי אפשר בקטנה — כתיב מלא, הא למדת שכל מקום שנכתב חסר — אף הקטנה במשמע, כגון באונס ומפתה.

שלש מדות — במיתת נערה המאורסה.

NOTES

22:13-21), and only once does it appear spelled in full. In the other cases, it is spelled without the final letter. But if the word *"na'arah"* spelled in full means a *na'arah* and not a minor, whereas the word spelled without the final letter includes a minor, why was it not spelled in full throughout the passage?

The Jerusalem Talmud answers that by spelling the word without the final letter, the Torah is teaching us that this law applies even if the wife was accused of committing adultery through anal intercourse, as if she were a male (the word *"na'arah"* spelled without the final letter is spelled the same way as the word for a young man).

שָׁלֹשׁ מִדּוֹת בְּנַעֲרָה There are three punishments of execution concerning a *na'arah*. *Shittah Mekubbetzet* notes that there are in fact more than three ways of carrying out the punishment imposed on a *na'arah* who is found guilty of adultery. To arrive at a complete set of rules, a number of additional factors must also be considered — for example, whether the girl's father has a house, and whether the town is mostly Jewish or non-Jewish. When the Baraita says that there are three punishments, it is referring only to those distinctions in the law that depend on the girl herself — her age and marital status at the time that the witnesses testify against her. But it ignores those distinctions in the law that depend on external factors — her father's house or the town's ethnic makeup.

TRANSLATION AND COMMENTARY

in cases of adultery **committed by a** ***na'arah:*** [1]**If witnesses come** after the girl is married, **when she is** already living **in her father-in-law's house, and testify that she committed adultery while** she was still only betrothed and living **in her** own **father's house,** [45A] **she is stoned** to death **at the door of her father's house,** as the verse says (Deuteronomy 22:21): 'Then they shall bring out the *na'arah* to the door of her father's house, and the men of her city shall stone her with stones.' This verse must be referring to a case in which the witnesses testified against her after she was married, because the Torah is dealing with a husband who accuses his wife of adultery committed before their marriage, while they were betrothed. If the *na'arah* is found guilty of adultery while she was betrothed, she is stoned at the door of her father's house, [2]**as if to say: 'See** what happened to **the plant you nurtured** in this house.' [3]**If witnesses come while** the girl **is** still living **in her father's house** after her betrothal but before her marriage, **and testify that she committed adultery** during her betrothal **while** she was living **in her father's house,** [4]**she is stoned at the**

בְּנַעֲרָה: [1]בָּאוּ לָהּ עֵדִים בְּבֵית חָמִיהָ שֶׁזִּינְּתָה בְּבֵית אָבִיהָ, [45A] סוֹקְלִין אוֹתָהּ עַל פֶּתַח בֵּית אָבִיהָ, [2]כְּלוֹמַר: 'רְאוּ גִּידּוּלִים שֶׁגִּידַּלְתֶּם'. [3]בָּאוּ לָהּ עֵדִים בְּבֵית אָבִיהָ שֶׁזִּינְּתָה בְּבֵית אָבִיהָ, [4]סוֹקְלִין אוֹתָהּ עַל

LITERAL TRANSLATION

concerning a *na'arah:* [1] [If] witnesses came [to testify] against her [while she was] in her father-in-law's house [and they said] that she committed adultery [while] in her father's house, [45A] they stone her at the door of her father's house, [2] as if to say: 'See the plants that you have nurtured.' [3] [If] witnesses came [to testify] against her [while she was] in her father's house [and they said] that she committed adultery [while] in her father's house, [4] they stone her at the

RASHI

באו לה עדים בבית חמיה — לאחר שניסת. **שזינתה בבית אביה** — באירוסין. **סוקלין אותה על פתח בית אביה** — דהכי כתיב "והוציאו את הנערה אל פתח בית אביה", והאי בבאו עדים בבית חמיה כתיב — דהא במוציא שם רע כתיב, דמפרש ביה קרא "ואקרב אליה", אלמא: כשניסת. **ראו גידולים שגידלתם** — כלומר, מבית זה יצאת הנבלה שבו זינתה. **באו לה עדים בבית אביה** — קודם שנשאת.

BACKGROUND

פֶּתַח בֵּית אָבִיהָ... פֶּתַח שַׁעַר הָעִיר The door of her father's house...the door of the gate of the city. The Torah does not usually specify where punishments are to be carried out, but the Sages said that the courts used to prepare a special place (outside the city) for capital punishment, and this is the "place of stoning" (בֵּית הַסְּקִילָה) mentioned in this passage. However, in some cases the Torah does emphasize where the guilty are to be executed. Usually the purpose of choosing a particular place is to deter potential transgressors and to publicize the punishment for the crime. Regarding the place of execution for the betrothed *na'arah* who committed adultery, the law has certain special features. Since adultery committed by a *na'arah* who has not yet reached legal majority is an exceptional case of moral corruption, both with respect to the *na'arah* and with respect to the man involved, she is punished in unusual locations — either at the door of her father's house, to indicate that the education she received in her father's house was faulty, or at the door of the gate of the city, to publicize the matter and to announce it to the residents of the city, including those who do not ordinarily attend executions at the place of stoning.

NOTES

בָּאוּ לָהּ עֵדִים בְּבֵית חָמִיהָ If witnesses came to testify against her while she was in her father-in-law's house. As *Ritva* points out, this is the standard case of a husband who accuses his wife of not having been a virgin at the time of their marriage. Witnesses are brought after the marriage to testify that the girl committed adultery during her betrothal. If the husband's accusation proves true, the girl is stoned at the door of her father's house, as if to say that it is the father's fault that his daughter sinned, so that people do not think that she committed adultery only after she entered her father-in-law's home. But the same law applies even if the witnesses come of their own volition, without the husband having accused his wife of not having been a virgin when she married him. (See also the next note, for a discussion of *Rambam*'s position on the matter.)

רְאוּ גִּידּוּלִים שֶׁגִּידַּלְתֶּם "See the plants that you have nurtured." If a *na'arah* commits adultery during the period of her betrothal, but witnesses come to testify against her only after she is already married, she is stoned at the door of her father's house. The sentence is carried out at her father's door in order to emphasize that the girl committed the offense while still under her father's authority. This serves to correct the possible misunderstanding that her father-in-law was in some way responsible for her transgression. However, the girl is not stoned at her father's door if the witnesses testify against her while she is still living in her father's house, for in such a case it is obvious that she sinned while under his authority. Hence, she is executed at the city gate, where her punishment will have the most publicity (*Ritva,* following *Rashi*).

According to *Rambam* (who has a different reading regarding the second case; see next note), the girl is stoned at her father's door, even if the witnesses come to testify against her while she is still living in his house. The Baraita refers to a case in which the witnesses came only after she went to live in her father-in-law's house, because witnesses usually come forward only after the girl is married and her husband accuses her of not having been a virgin at the time of their marriage (*Meiri*).

בָּאוּ לָהּ עֵדִים בְּבֵית אָבִיהָ If witnesses came to testify against her while she was in her father's house. The reading found in the standard text of the Talmud is as follows: "If witnesses came to testify against her while she was in her father's house and they said that she committed adultery while in her father's house." This reading is in

HALAKHAH

בָּאוּ לָהּ עֵדִים בְּבֵית חָמִיהָ If witnesses came to testify against her while she was in her father-in-law's house. "If a betrothed girl aged between twelve and twelve-and-a-half commits adultery while she is still living in her father's house, even though the witnesses come to testify against her only after she is already living in her father-in-law's house, she is stoned at the door of her father's house," in accordance with the Baraita taught by Shila. (*Rambam, Sefer Kedushah, Hilkhot Issurei Bi'ah* 3:9.)

בָּאוּ לָהּ עֵדִים בְּבֵית אָבִיהָ If witnesses came to testify against her while she was in her father's house. "If a betrothed girl aged between twelve and twelve-and-a-half

TRANSLATION AND COMMENTARY

door of the gate of the city, as the Torah states (Deuteronomy 22:23-24): 'If a *na'arah* who is a virgin is betrothed to a husband, and a man finds her in the city, and lies with her, then you shall bring them both out to the gate of that city, and you shall stone them with stones so that they die.' [1]**If the** *na'arah* **sins** and commits adultery while betrothed, **but** the witnesses come and testify against her only **afterwards,** when she **has** already **come of age,** i.e., when she has already reached the age of twelve-and-a-half, [2]**she is sentenced to death by strangulation,** just as if she had committed the offense after coming of age." Adultery is punishable by stoning only if the female partner was a betrothed virgin between twelve and twelve-and-a-half years of age. But if the female was an adult, she and the man are both subject to the penalty of strangulation. If the offense was committed before the *na'arah* came of age, but she was brought to trial only after she reached adulthood, she is liable to the same punishment that she would have received had she engaged in the adulterous relationship as an adult.

פֶּתַח שַׁעַר הָעִיר. [1]סָרְחָה וּלְבַסּוֹף בָּגְרָה, [2]תִּידּוֹן בְּחֶנֶק".

LITERAL TRANSLATION

door of the gate of the city. [1] [If] she sinned and afterwards came of age, [2] she is sentenced [to death] by strangulation."

RASHI

סוקלין אותה על שער העיר — דכתיב "כי יהיה נערה בתולה מאורסה וגו' והוצאתם את שניהם אל שער העיר ההיא". **תידון בחנק** — כי היכי דאילו זנאי השתא לאו סקילה איכא אלא חנק, דכי כתיב סקילה — בזינתה נערה כתיב, שנאמר "כי יהיה נערה בתולה וגו'" השתא נמי בחנק, דכיון דאשתני גופה בין חטא להעמדה בדין — אשתני קטלא לכדהשתא.

NOTES

accordance with the reading of *Rashi.* But different readings are found in the Talmudic texts available to other Rishonim. *Ra'avad* (cited by *Ritva*) has the following reading: "If witnesses came to testify against her while she was in her father's house and they said that she committed adultery while in her father-in-law's house." According to *Ra'avad,* if a betrothed *na'arah* commits adultery while on the way to her father-in-law's house (or, for that matter, anywhere outside her father's house), but before she actually enters the bridal chamber in marriage, she is executed at the city gate. But if she commits adultery in her father's house itself, she is executed at her father's door, even if the witnesses come and testify against her while she is still only betrothed, just as if they had come after she was already married. *Rambam* (see *Hilkhot Issurei Bi'ah* 3:9, *Maggid Mishneh,* and *Meiri*) seems also to have had the same reading. He, too, explains the Baraita as referring to a case in which the girl committed adultery while she was in her father-in-law's house (but before she married), and the witnesses came to testify against her after she had already returned to her father's house.

סָרְחָה וּלְבַסּוֹף בָּגְרָה If she sinned and afterwards came of age. A similar view is expressed by the Jerusalem Talmud in the name of Rav Adda bar Ahavah, who maintains that a *na'arah* who commits adultery while betrothed is subject to death by stoning only if the witnesses come and testify against her before she reaches adulthood. He derives this from the verse (Deuteronomy 22:21): "And they shall take the *na'arah* out...and stone her," which teaches us that she must still be a *na'arah* when she is put to death. There, too, a conflicting opinion is cited. Below in the Gemara (45b), Rabbi Il'a suggests that the term "the *na'arah*" can be understood as referring to someone who sinned while she was a *na'arah,* but who has now already reached adulthood.

Rabbi Akiva Eger objects: Capital punishment can be administered only if a formal warning was given to the person at the moment he was about to perform the transgression. The warning must state that the act is forbidden and it must include a description of the punishment the violator will receive if he indeed performs the transgression. This warning must be stated with certainty. If there is any doubt about the act itself or about the punishment, it is not considered a valid warning. How, then, can a betrothed *na'arah* who commits adultery ever become liable for capital punishment? There is always the possibility that she will come of age before she is sentenced, and she will then be subject to strangulation and not to stoning. Thus a warning cannot be issued which states with certainty the punishment to which she will be subject if she commits the offense! *Rabbi Akiva Eger* answers that our Gemara must follow the position of Rabbi Yehudah, according to whom the warning must include the fact that the offender will be subject to capital punishment, but need not specify the means of execution. (See also *Giddulei Shmuel,* who suggests another answer to this question.)

HALAKHAH

commits adultery while she is living in her father-in-law's house, but before she is handed over by her father for marriage, even though the witnesses come to testify against her only after she has returned to her own father's home, she is stoned at the city gate." This ruling follows *Rambam*'s reading in our Gemara; see notes. (*Rambam, Sefer Kedushah, Hilkhot Issurei Bi'ah* 3:9.)

סָרְחָה וּלְבַסּוֹף בָּגְרָה If she sinned and afterwards came of age. "If a betrothed girl between twelve and twelve-and-a-half years of age commits adultery, but the witnesses come to testify against her only after she has come of age or after she has married and has had sexual relations with her husband, she is stoned at the place of stoning," following Rabbi Yoḥanan (below, 45b) and contrary to the Baraita as taught by Shila. (*Rambam, Sefer Kedushah, Hilkhot Issurei Bi'ah* 3:10.)

[1] לְמֵימְרָא דְּכָל הֵיכָא דְּאִישְׁתַּנֵּי גּוּפָא, [2] אִישְׁתַּנֵּי קְטָלָא? [3] וּרְמִינְהִי: "נַעֲרָה הַמְאוֹרָסָה שֶׁזִּינְּתָה, [4] וּמִשֶּׁבָּגְרָה הוֹצִיא עָלֶיהָ שֵׁם רַע, [5] הוּא אֵינוֹ לוֹקֶה וְאֵינוֹ נוֹתֵן מֵאָה סֶלַע. [6] הִיא וְזוֹמְמֶיהָ מַקְדִּימִין לְבֵית הַסְּקִילָה".
[7] הִיא וְזוֹמְמֶיהָ סָלְקָא דַּעְתָּךְ?

LITERAL TRANSLATION

[1] [Do you mean] to say that wherever [someone's] person changes, [2] one's death [penalty] changes? [3] But a contradiction may be raised (lit., "cast them together"): "[Regarding] a betrothed *na'arah* who committed adultery, [4] and after she came of age [her husband] put out a bad name about her, [5] he is not flogged and he does not pay the hundred sela'im. [6] She and the witnesses who conspired against her hasten to the place of stoning."
[7] Can it enter your mind [that] she *and* the witnesses who conspired against her [are stoned]?

TRANSLATION AND COMMENTARY

לְמֵימְרָא [1] The Gemara now raises a question about the third rule cited here in the Baraita: **Do you mean to say that wherever** the girl **herself changes** and comes of age between the time she committed the adultery and the time she is brought to trial, [2] **the death penalty** to which she is liable also **changes?** [3] If this is so, then **a contradiction can be raised** between this ruling and another ruling found in a different Baraita, which states: **"Regarding a betrothed *na'arah*** who is accused by her husband of having **committed adultery,** [4] **if her husband falsely accuses her** only **after she has come of age,** i.e., he betrothed her while she was a *na'arah* and married her after she had already comes of age, and he then comes to court and claims that he found her not to be a virgin, [5] **he is not flogged** if his accusation is found to have been false, **nor does he pay the hundred-shekel** fine. The penalty of flogging and the payment of the fine apply only to someone who falsely accuses his wife while she is still a *na'arah,* not to someone who makes those false accusations after his wife has already come of age. [6] But even though the husband is not punished if his charges are found to have been false, if his wife is found guilty, **she and the witnesses who** are found to have **conspired** to give false testimony **against her are hastened to the place of stoning** for execution, even if the witnesses testified against her when she was already an adult."

הִיא וְזוֹמְמֶיהָ סָלְקָא דַּעְתָּךְ [7] Before considering the contradiction between this Baraita and the previously cited Baraita, the Gemara first raises an internal difficulty that is found in the second Baraita itself. **Do you really think,** asks the Gemara, **that** a case can occur in which both the girl **herself and the witnesses who conspired** to give false testimony **against her are hastened to the place of stoning?** Surely if the witnesses' testimony was upheld and the girl was found guilty of adultery, she alone is executed. And if the witnesses are proved to have conspired to give false testimony against her — a second pair of witnesses having testified that the first pair could not possibly have witnessed the girl's transgression, for at the time of the alleged offense the first pair of witnesses were elsewhere — the witnesses incur the penalty that they had sought to inflict on the girl. They are executed, and the girl is exonerated! How, then, can the Baraita speak of a case in which both the girl and the witnesses are executed?

RASHI

הוציא עליה שם רע — שכנסה משבגרה, ולא מצא לה בתולים, ובא לבית דין. **הוא אינו לוקה** — אם כיחש. **ואינו נותן מאה סלע** — דכי כתיב "ויסרו אותו" מלקות, "וענשו אותו" ממון — בנערה כתיב. וזה עקימת שפתיו גורמין לו ליענש, כדמתרץ לקמן, ועקימת שפתיו בבוגרת הואי. **היא** — אם אמת היה. **וזוממיה** — עדים שהיו מעידים על זנותה, ונמצאו זוממין. **מקדימין לבית הסקילה** — כלומר, ישכימו בבוקר לשם. כי אין להם נס והמלטה מן המיתה הזאת. **היא וזוממיה סלקא דעתך** — אם אמת היה אין שקר.

BACKGROUND

אִישְׁתַּנֵּי Changes. Although a person is punished for deeds he committed in the past, nevertheless if the transgressor has undergone an essential transformation, there is reason to clarify to what degree he is regarded as another person because of that change. There are certain changes, such as when a non-Jew converts, in which the person is seen as an entirely new creature with no connection to his past. But the changes in question here are smaller: bodily change (physical maturation) or change in status (appointment to office). Rabbi Shimon takes an extreme view of this matter, ruling that even a change in status transforms a person, so that he must be judged by his present status and not by what he was before.

TERMINOLOGY

וּרְמִינְהִי But a contradiction may be raised (lit., "cast them together"). An expression used by the Gemara to introduce a contradiction between the source about to be cited and the source that has just been cited, where both sources are of equal authority.

NOTES

הִיא וְזוֹמְמֶיהָ She and the witnesses who conspired against her. The Gemara resolves the difficulty it posed by interpreting the copulative vav in the word וְזוֹמְמֶיהָ as having the sense of "or," rather than "and." *Shittah Mekubbetzet* discusses why the Gemara did not suggest an alternative solution to the problem — that the Baraita is referring to the second pair of witnesses who refuted the testimony of the first pair of witnesses who testified against the girl, and teaches that if a third pair of witnesses come and refute the testimony of the second pair (thus reconfirming the testimony of the first pair of witnesses), the girl herself and the second pair (זוֹמְמֵי זוֹמְמֶיהָ) are hastened to the place of stoning for execution.

מַקְדִּימִין לְבֵית הַסְּקִילָה Hasten to the place of stoning. *Rashi* explains that the term מַקְדִּימִין is used here in the sense of going out early: The convicted parties go out early in the day to the place of stoning, for there is no way for them to escape their punishment. *Tosafot* (*Makkot* 2a, cited here by *Ritva*) suggests that the term signifies precedence. Stoning is the preferred means of execution, but if for some reason it is impossible to execute the girl or the witnesses by stoning, they are subjected to some other form of capital punishment.

CONCEPTS

חִידּוּשׁ An innovation. A unique law that differs from seemingly comparable laws in the Torah. For example, the law prohibiting the consumption of meat and milk mixtures is a חִידּוּשׁ, since each component of the mixture is itself permitted, and only when these components are mixed is the resulting food prohibited. Other prohibited foods, by contrast, are not produced by mixing permissible foods. And since a חִידּוּשׁ is by definition unique, no exegetical inferences (e.g., *kal vaḥomer, gezerah shavah*) can be drawn from it.

TRANSLATION AND COMMENTARY

אֶלָּא [1]**Rather,** answers the Gemara, the Baraita must be understood as follows: **Either** the girl **herself** is taken out *or* **the witnesses who conspired** to give false testimony **against her are hastened to the place of stoning** for execution.

This difficulty having been resolved, we are still left with a contradiction between this Baraita and the one cited above. For according to the earlier Baraita, if a *na'arah* commits adultery during the period of her betrothal, but the witnesses testify against her only after she has already reached adulthood, she is executed by strangulation. Since the status of the girl herself has changed, the death penalty to which she is liable also changes. But according to the second Baraita, the girl is executed by stoning. Even though she came of age between the time of her offense and the time her husband leveled his charges against her, the penalty to which she is liable remains the same!

אָמַר רָבָא [2]Addressing this contradiction, **Rava said: Are you speaking of** a case in which witnesses testify against the girl after she has come of age but before she marries, and comparing it to a case in which the husband **puts forward a charge of adultery** after he has married the girl and found her not to be a virgin? [3]But the law in the case where the husband **puts forward a charge of adultery** after he has married the girl **is different.** In such a case, if she committed adultery while she was a *na'arah,* she is stoned even if the accusation is leveled against her only after she has already come of age. [4]No analogy can be drawn between the two cases, **for the law** concerning the punishment inflicted on the girl if her husband's charge of adultery proves to be true **is a** Halakhic **innovation.** [5]**For** the law **in general** is that **any woman** — even if she has not yet reached the age of twelve-and-a-half — **who has** already **entered the bridal chamber** for

[1]אֶלָּא, אוֹ הִיא אוֹ זוֹמְמֶיהָ מַקְדִּימִין לְבֵית הַסְּקִילָה.
[2]אֲמַר רָבָא: מוֹצִיא שֵׁם רַע קָאָמְרַתְּ? [3]שָׁאנֵי מוֹצִיא שֵׁם רַע, [4]דְּחִידּוּשׁ הוּא. [5]דְּהָא נִכְנְסָה לַחוּפָּה וְלֹא נִבְעֲלָה

LITERAL TRANSLATION

[1] Rather, either she or the witnesses who conspired against her hasten to the place of stoning.

[2] Rava said: Do you speak of someone who puts out a bad name? [3] Someone who puts out a bad name is different, [4] for [this law] is an innovation. [5] For in general [a woman] who entered the bridal chamber but did not have sexual intercourse

RASHI

אלא או היא — אם אמת. **או זוממיה** — אם שקר. **לבית הסקילה** — אלמא, אף על גב דאשתני גופא, ואילו זנאי השתא בת חנק היא — לא אמרינן אישתני קטלא. **מוציא שם רע קאמרת** — לאותובי א״סרחה ולבסוף בגרה״, דתני תנא דאיירי בבאו לה עדים בבית אביה. **שאני** — מיתה הבאה על ידי הוצאת שם רע דבעל, משנשאת. **דחידוש הוא** — ולא אמרינן בה דמשום דאישתני דינא, דאי זנאי השתא — בת חנק היא, נימא אישתני קטלא דהך דזנאי בנערות. **דהא נכנסה לחופה ולא נבעלה בעלמא וזינתה**

NOTES

שָׁאנֵי מוֹצִיא שֵׁם רַע Someone who puts out a bad name is different. Our commentary follows *Rashi* and most Rishonim, who explained the Gemara as follows: According to the Baraita taught by Shila, once a betrothed *na'arah* who has committed adultery reaches the age of twelve-and-a-half, she is subject to strangulation, not stoning. Since the girl herself has changed between the time she committed adultery and the time she was brought to trial, the death penalty to which she is liable also changes. Thus the basic law governing the case in which the husband charges his wife after their marriage with having committed adultery during her betrothal is a Halakhic innovation. For if a betrothed *na'arah* enters the bridal chamber and then commits adultery, she is subject to strangulation as a married woman. But if at that stage her husband accuses her of having committed adultery during her betrothal and his accusation proves to be true, she is subject to death by stoning. Even though the punishment for adultery has changed from stoning to strangulation, the punishment for the adultery committed earlier remains the same. Thus it stands to reason that even if the girl was not married until after she reached adulthood, and only then did her husband charge her with having committed adultery before she reached adulthood, and the accusation proved to be true, she is also subject to stoning. On this point Rav Huna the son of Rav Yehoshua disagrees, arguing that all we can derive from the basic law governing the husband who accuses his

HALAKHAH

שָׁאנֵי מוֹצִיא שֵׁם רַע Someone who puts out a bad name is different. "The law pertaining to the case in which a husband puts forward the charge that his wife committed adultery during her betrothal, while she was a *na'arah,* is a Halakhic innovation. For if the husband's accusations prove to be true, and witnesses corroborate his claim that his wife committed adultery while she was betrothed to him, even if they say that she committed adultery only after she left her father's house, and even if they say that she committed adultery only after she entered the bridal chamber but before she had sexual intercourse with her husband, she is stoned at the gate of her father's house. This is so notwithstanding the fact that in general a betrothed girl who commits adultery after she has left her

TRANSLATION AND COMMENTARY

the purpose of marriage **but has not** yet **had sexual intercourse with her husband, and** then **commits adultery, is subject to** death by **strangulation.** But even though a *na'arah* is subject to strangulation if she commits adultery after having entered the bridal chamber, [1]if her husband **accuses her of having committed adultery** during her betrothal and the accusation proves to be true, **she is subject to** death by **stoning.** Even though the punishment for adultery changed from stoning to strangulation after the *na'arah* entered the bridal chamber, the punishment for adultery committed prior to the *na'arah's* entry into the bridal chamber is still death by stoning. Thus we see that the death penalty inflicted on a *na'arah* whose husband's charge of adultery during betrothal proves to be true is not the same as the punishment that would have been imposed on her had she committed adultery at the time the husband brought that charge against her. This being the case, the rulings found in the two Baraitot are not contradictory: If a *na'arah* commits adultery while she is betrothed, but the witnesses testify against her only after she has already attained adult status, she is sentenced to death by strangulation. But if she commits adultery during the period of her betrothal, and she marries after she comes of age, at which time her husband levels the charge of adultery against her, she is executed by stoning.

אֲמַר לֵיהּ [2]**Rav Huna the son of Rav Yehoshua said to Rava:** Your argument, that the law concerning a husband who puts forward a charge of adultery is a Halakhic innovation, does not necessarily resolve the contradiction between the two Baraitot. [3]For **perhaps the Torah made this innovation** — that the punishment for adultery committed during the period of betrothal does not change after the girl enters the bridal

בְּעָלְמָא וְזִינְּתָה בְּחֶנֶק, [1]וְאִילּוּ מוֹצִיא שֵׁם רַע בִּסְקִילָה.

[2]אֲמַר לֵיהּ רַב הוּנָא בְּרֵיהּ דְּרַב יְהוֹשֻׁעַ לְרָבָא: [3]דִּלְמָא כִּי חַדִּית

LITERAL TRANSLATION

[with her husband] and committed adultery is subject to strangulation, [1] whereas [in the case of] someone who puts out a bad name [she is] subject to stoning.

[2] Rav Huna the son of Rav Yehoshua said to Rava: [3] Perhaps when the Torah (lit., "the Merciful One") made the innovation,

RASHI

בחנק כו' – ותדע, דהא בלא בגרה נמי, [בלא] הוצאת שם רע, ואפילו בנערות – אשתני דינא הוא. דאילו זנאי השתא חנק הוא דאיכא, הואיל ונכנסה לחופה אף על פי שלא נבעלה, כדתניא [לקמן] (מח,ב): "נערה" – ולא בוגרת, "בתולה" – ולא בעולה, "מאורסה" – ולא נשואה. מאי "לא נשואה"? אי נימא נשואה ממש – היינו ו"לא בעולה", אלא לאו – נכנסה לחופה ולא נבעלה. אלמא, אילו זנאי השתא – בת חנק היא. **ואילו מוציא שם רע** – עליה השתא, וזנאי קודם כניסה לחופה – בסקילה. אלמא, בהוצאת שם רע לא אמרינן דמשום דאישתני דינא, אילו זנאי השתא – לישתני קטלא הבא על ידי זנות דמעיקרא. והילכך, כי בגרה נמי וניסת – לא אמרינן במוציא שם רע דמשום דאישתני דינא דהשתא אישתני קטלא דמעיקרא. **ודלמא כי חדית** – כלומר, הא ראייה דמייתינן מסתם מוציא שם רע לכאן – לאו ראייה היא לכאן. דהתם הוא דאף על גב דאישתני דינא, דאילו זנאי השתא לא אישתני קטלא דהא דזנאי מעיקרא – משום דלא אישתני גופא הוא, וחידוש שחידשה תורה, באישתני דינא – חדית, באישתני גופא – לא חדית. אבל בגרה – אישתני גופא היא, ואי באו לה עדים בבית אביה – אית לך למימר סרחה ולבסוף בגרה בחנק, במוציא שם רע נמי משבגרה הוה ליה למיתני חנק.

SAGES

רַב הוּנָא בְּרֵיהּ דְּרַב יְהוֹשֻׁעַ **Rav Huna the son of Rav Yehoshua.** A fifth-generation Babylonian Amora. See *Ketubot*, Part II, p. 80.

NOTES

wife of adultery is that the change in law that results from the girl's passing from the state of betrothal to the state of marriage does not affect the punishment to which she is subject if her husband's charges prove to be true. But if the girl herself has been transformed from a *na'arah* into an adult, it is indeed possible that her sentence changes as well. (*Rif* explains the entire passage at great length, apparently in accordance with the viewpoint of *Rashi*.)

Rashbam (cited by *Tosafot*) and *Rambam* understand the Gemara differently: The law governing the case in which a husband accuses his wife of having committed adultery is a Halakhic innovation. For if a betrothed *na'arah* enters the bridal chamber but does not engage in sexual relations with her husband, and then commits adultery, but it is not her husband who brings the charge of adultery against her, she is subject to strangulation as a married woman. But if her husband accuses her of adultery, she is subject to stoning, even though she committed her offense after she had already entered the bridal chamber. This explanation is rejected by most Rishonim, even though it fits well with the words of our passage, for the verses dealing with the laws of slander seem to imply that these laws apply only if the betrothed *na'arah* committed adultery in her father's house, i.e., before she entered the bridal chamber.

HALAKHAH

father's house is put to death by strangulation." This is the viewpoint of *Rambam* (and that of *Rabbenu Shmuel*, cited by *Tosafot*), following Rava. But *Rabbenu Ḥananel, Ra'avad* and others maintain that if the girl committed adultery after she was brought into the bridal chamber, she is executed by strangulation, even in a case where it was the husband who brought the charge of adultery against her. (*Rambam, Sefer Kedushah, Hilkhot Issurei Bi'ah* 3:8.)

רַחֲמָנָא, [1]הֵיכָא דְּלָא אִשְׁתַּנֵּי גּוּפָא, [2]אֲבָל הֵיכָא דְּאִשְׁתַּנֵּי גּוּפָא, לָא חַדֵּית רַחֲמָנָא! [3]אֶלָּא אֲמַר רַב נַחְמָן בַּר יִצְחָק: אִישְׁתַּנֵּי וְלָא אִשְׁתַּנֵּי תַּנָּאֵי הִיא, [4]דִּתְנַן: "חָטְאוּ עַד שֶׁלֹּא נִתְמַנּוּ, [5]וְנִתְמַנּוּ, הֲרֵי הֵן כְּהֶדְיוֹטוֹת. [6]רַבִּי שִׁמְעוֹן אוֹמֵר: אִם נוֹדַע לָהֶם עַד שֶׁלֹּא נִתְמַנּוּ, חַיָּיבִים; [7]מִשֶּׁנִּתְמַנּוּ, פְּטוּרִים".

LITERAL TRANSLATION

[1] it was where the [accused's] person did not change, [2] but where the [accused's] person changed, the Torah did not make the innovation!

[3] Rather, Rav Naḥman bar Yitzḥak said: [Whether we say that the penalty] changes or does not change is [a dispute between] Tannaim, [4] for we have learned: "[If] they sinned before they were appointed, [5] and they were [then] appointed, they are like ordinary people. [6] Rabbi Shimon says: If [their sin] became known to them before they were appointed, they are liable; [7] [if] after they were appointed, they are exempt."

TRANSLATION AND COMMENTARY

chamber — [1] only in a case **in which** the girl **herself has not changed** and has not yet reached adulthood. Even though the girl would be subject to strangulation if she committed adultery after she married, she remains subject to stoning if her husband's charge that she committed adultery during the period of her betrothal proves to be true. [2] **But where she herself has changed** and reached adulthood, **the Torah may not have made this innovation!**

אֶלָּא [3] **Rather, Rav Naḥman bar Yitzḥak said:** Indeed, the rulings found in the two Baraitot do contradict each other. The question **whether the** death **penalty** to which a betrothed *na'arah* is liable **changes** when she herself changes **or** whether **it does not change is** the subject of **a dispute between Tannaim.** [4] **For we have learned** elsewhere in a Mishnah (*Horayot* 10a): "The mandatory sin-offering brought by a High Priest or a king who unwittingly violates a prohibition requiring such a sacrifice differs from the sin-offering brought by an ordinary Jew under similar circumstances, for an ordinary Jew brings a lamb, a High Priest brings a bull, and a king brings a goat. **If** the High Priest or the king **commits the transgression before he is appointed** to the position of High Priest or of king, [5] **and then,** before he has brought his sin-offering, **he is appointed, he** must bring his offering **as an ordinary person.** This applies whether he became aware of his offense before he was appointed to his new position or only afterwards, since the sin-offering that must be brought is determined according to the sinner's status at the time of the offense. [6] **Rabbi Shimon** disagrees and **says: If** the future High Priest or king **becomes aware of his offense before he is appointed** to his new position, **he is** held **liable** to bring the sin-offering brought by an ordinary person. [7] But **if** he becomes aware of his transgression only **after he has been appointed, he is** totally **exempt** from bringing a sin-offering; for the sin-offering that must be brought is determined

RASHI

אלא אמר רב נחמן בר יצחק — הא דתני שילא תידון בחנק, הואיל ואישתני גופא אישתני קטלא, ותניא אחריתא בסקילה, ואף על גב דאישתני גופא לא אישתני קטלא — תנאי היא. **אישתני ולא אישתני** — אי אמרינן אישתני קטלא או לא אישתני קטלא — תנאי היא. **חטאו עד שלא נתמנו** — נשיא ומשוח, שאין קרבנם כשל יחיד, שהנשיא מביא שעיר, ומשוח מביא פר. **הרי הן כהדיוטות** — בכשבה ושעירה, שאף על פי שנשתנה גופם — לא נשתנה קרבנם. **אם נודע להם עד שלא נתמנו** — דהוה ליה ידיעה וחטאה בחד גופא — חייבין כהדיוטות. **משנתמנו** — דהוה ליה חטאה בשעת קרבן יחיד, וידיעה בשעת קרבן נשיא. **פטורין** — לגמרי. אלמא: דמשום דאישתני גופא — אישתני קרבן.

LANGUAGE

הֶדְיוֹט Layman. From the Greek ἰδιώτης, *idiotes,* meaning "common man," "layman," or "ordinary person." All these meanings are found in Rabbinic literature, although the word הֶדְיוֹט is used primarily to distinguish between common people and those in high office. Similarly, the Talmud uses this word to distinguish between consecrated property and unconsecrated property (שֶׁל הֶדְיוֹט), which belongs to a layman.

NOTES

חָטְאוּ עַד שֶׁלֹּא נִתְמַנּוּ If they sinned before they were appointed. The Rishonim ask: How can the Gemara draw a comparison between the case of the betrothed *na'arah* who comes of age and the case of the inadvertent sinner who was appointed High Priest or king? In the first case the girl herself undergoes a real physical change, whereas in the second case the sinner merely experiences a change in Halakhic status!

Rashi maintains that the appointment of a man as High Priest or as king is indeed considered a change in the person himself.

Tosafot suggests that the Gemara merely wishes to argue that the position of the Baraita taught by Shila is supported by the viewpoint of Rabbi Shimon. If the High Priest or the king does not bring the sin-offering of an ordinary person because he has undergone a change in his Halakhic status, then certainly a betrothed *na'arah* who commits adultery is not subject to stoning if the witnesses come and testify

HALAKHAH

חָטְאוּ עַד שֶׁלֹּא נִתְמַנּוּ If they sinned before they were appointed. "If, before he was appointed to his position, an anointed High Priest or a king unwittingly committed a transgression requiring a mandatory sin-offering, he must bring the same offering as is brought by an ordinary Jew who committed such a transgression, even if he became aware of his transgression only after he was appointed," following the anonymous Tanna of the Mishnah in *Horayot.* (*Rambam, Sefer Korbanot, Hilkhot Shegagot* 15:10.)

TRANSLATION AND COMMENTARY

according to the sinner's status both at the time of the offense and at the time he became aware of his transgression. He cannot bring the sin-offering brought by an ordinary person, because he is now held liable to bring the special sin-offering brought by a High Priest or a king. And he cannot bring that special sin-offering, because at the time of his offense he was an ordinary person." The anonymous first Tanna of the Mishnah maintains that the High Priest or the king brings the sin-offering of an ordinary person, even though he himself underwent a change in Halakhic status between the time he committed his offense and the time he brought his sacrifice. Hence this Tanna would say that a betrothed *na'arah* who committed adultery is subject to the penalty of stoning, even if she came of age between the time of her offense and the time the witnesses testified against her. By contrast, Rabbi Shimon maintains that the High Priest or the king does not bring the sin-offering of an ordinary person if he became aware of his transgression only after he was appointed to his position. Thus he would say that the punishment to which the girl is subject changes if she reaches adulthood between the time she committed adultery and the time she is brought to trial.

אֵימוּר דְּשָׁמְעִינַן לֵיהּ [45B] [1]The Gemara raises an objection: It does not follow from Rabbi Shimon's ruling that he would accept the position of the Baraita taught by Shila, that the death penalty changes if the betrothed girl has herself changed and reached adulthood when she is brought to trial. **Granted that we have established that Rabbi Shimon considers** not only the sinner's status at the time of his offense, but **also** his status at the time **he became aware** of his transgression. Thus, if the sinner is appointed High Priest or king after he has committed an offense requiring a sin-offering but before he has become aware of his transgression, he does not bring the sin-offering brought by an ordinary person. [2]**But have we established that** Rabbi Shimon **considers** only the status of the sinner as it was at the time **he became aware** of his transgression, **but does not consider** his status at the time of **his sin?** [3]**If** Rabbi Shimon maintains that the punishment changes when the status of the sinner changes, then he should have ruled that the High Priest or the king **must bring a sacrifice according to his status** at the time he became aware of his transgression — [4]if he is **an anointed High Priest,** he must sacrifice **a bull, and** if he is **a king,** he must sacrifice **a goat.** But Rabbi Shimon did not issue such a ruling. Instead, he said that the High Priest and the king are totally exempt from bringing a sin-offering! Thus the Mishnah in tractate *Horayot* offers no support for the position of the Baraita taught by Shila, that the betrothed *na'arah* is subject to strangulation if the witnesses testify against her only after she has come of age.

[45B] [1]אֵימוּר דְּשָׁמְעִינַן לֵיהּ לְרַבִּי שִׁמְעוֹן דְּאָזֵיל אַף בָּתַר יְדִיעָה. [2]דְּאָזֵיל בָּתַר יְדִיעָה וְלָא אָזֵיל בָּתַר חֲטָאָה מִי שָׁמְעַתְּ לֵיהּ? [3]אִם כֵּן, לֵיְיתֵי קָרְבָּן כִּי דְּהָשְׁתָּא — [4]מָשׁוּחַ פָּר, וְנָשִׂיא שָׂעִיר!

LITERAL TRANSLATION

[45B] [1]Granted (lit., "say") that we have heard that Rabbi Shimon also goes after knowledge. [2][But] have you heard that he goes after knowledge and does not go after the sin? [3]If so, let him bring a sacrifice according to his present [state] — [4]an anointed [High Priest] a bull, and a king (lit., "prince") a goat!

RASHI

אימור דשמעינן ליה כו׳ — כלומר, ליכא למאן דאמר הכא איטתני קרבן משום שינויא דגופא, מדלא מחייב להו רבי שמעון לנודע להם משנתמנו, לאיתויי כדהשתא. אלא פטורין לגמרי קאמר, וטעמא דידיה משום דבעי ידיעה וחטאה בחד גופה. **דאזיל אף בתר ידיעה** — כלומר, שעת החטא מחייבתו כשבה, ושעת ידיעה מחייבתו שעיר. לפיכך אין כאן אחד מכל הקרבנות שחייבתו תורה. **דאזיל בתר ידיעה** — דשינוי הגוף. **ולא אזיל בתר חטאה** — כי ההיא דתני שילא תידון בחנק, מי שמעת ליה? **אם כן** — דהכי שמעת ליה — לייתי כי השתא.

BACKGROUND

מָשׁוּחַ פָּר An anointed High Priest a bull. If a High Priest unwittingly made an erroneous Halakhic decision, and ruled that he was *permitted* to commit a transgression requiring a mandatory sin-offering if committed unwittingly, and if he also *acted* according to his mistaken ruling, he must offer a bull as a sacrifice. The blood of this sacrifice is sprinkled against the פָּרוֹכֶת — the curtain dividing the Sanctuary (הֵיכָל) from the Holy of Holies (קֹדֶשׁ הַקֳּדָשִׁים) — and on the Temple's inner altar (מִזְבַּח הַזָּהָב).

וְנָשִׂיא שָׂעִיר And a king a goat. If a King of Israel sins in a manner requiring a sin-offering (חַטָּאת), he does not bring a female goat or a lamb, like an ordinary person, but rather a young male goat. In all other respects, this sacrifice follows a procedure identical to that of the regular sin-offering.

NOTES

against her only after she has undergone a real physical change and reached adulthood.

Ritva argues that the Gemara here follows the viewpoint of Rava that there is no difference between a change in the person himself and a change in his Halakhic status. If someone's liability changes with a change in his person, then it should also change with a change in his Halakhic status.

אֵימוּר דְּשָׁמְעִינַן Granted that we have heard. *Ritva* asks: The question raised here by the Gemara is so obvious that it is difficult to understand how Rav Naḥman bar Yitzḥak could ever have suggested that the position of the Baraita taught by Shila is supported by the view of Rabbi Shimon in the Mishnah. He answers: It might have been argued that Rabbi Shimon is of the opinion that the reason why the High Priest and the king do not bring a sacrifice according to their present status is because the Torah stated specifically that those special offerings are imposed only "if the priest that is anointed sins" (Leviticus 4:3), or "when a ruler has sinned" (Leviticus 4:22). And here the High Priest or the king was an ordinary person at the time he committed his offense. But Rabbi Shimon would agree that the death penalty to which a betrothed *na'arah* who commits adultery is subject changes if she herself has

[1] הָאָמַר לֵיהּ רַבִּי יוֹחָנָן לְתַנָּא: [2] תְּנֵי: ״תִּידּוֹן בִּסְקִילָה״. [3] וְאַמַּאי? נַעֲרָה הַמְאוֹרָסָה אָמַר רַחֲמָנָא, [4] וְהָא בּוֹגֶרֶת הִיא! [5] אָמַר רַבִּי אִילְעָא: אָמַר קְרָא: ״הַנַּעֲרָה״ — [6] הַנַּעֲרָה שֶׁהָיְתָה כְּבָר. [7] אֲמַר לֵיהּ רַבִּי חֲנַנְיָא לְרַבִּי אִילְעָא: אִי הָכִי, מִילְקָא נַמִי לִילְקֵי, [8] וּמֵאָה סֶלַע נַמִי לִישַׁלֵּם!

LITERAL TRANSLATION

[1] Surely Rabbi Yoḥanan said to the Tanna: [2] State: "She is sentenced [to death] by stoning." [3] But why? The Torah (lit., "the Merciful One") spoke of a betrothed *na'arah*, [4] but this [girl] is an adult! [5] Rabbi Il'a said: The verse said: "The *na'arah*" — [6] she who has already been a *na'arah*. [7] Rabbi Ḥananya said to Rabbi Il'a: If so, let him also be flogged, [8] and let him also pay the hundred sela'im!

TRANSLATION AND COMMENTARY

הָאָמַר לֵיהּ [1] The Gemara now suggests that the Baraita taught by Shila should be amended. **Surely,** says the Gemara, **Rabbi Yoḥanan corrected the Tanna** (the reciter of Baraitot) who recited in his presence the Baraita taught by Shila: [2] **State** the third rule of the Baraita as follows: "If the *na'arah* sins and commits adultery during the period of her betrothal, but the witnesses come and testify against her only afterwards, when she has already come of age, **she is sentenced to death by stoning."** Thus, according to this Baraita as amended by Rabbi Yoḥanan, the death penalty to which the girl is subject does not change, even if the girl herself has changed between the time of her offense and the time she is brought to trial. Whereas the girl would be subject to death by strangulation if she committed adultery now, she is still subject to death by stoning for the adultery she committed before she came of age.

וְאַמַּאי [3] The Gemara now questions Rabbi Yoḥanan's amended version of the Baraita's ruling: **But why** should this girl be sentenced to death by stoning? **The Torah spoke of a *na'arah*,** a girl between twelve and twelve-and-a-half years of age, as being subject to stoning, [4] **but this girl** mentioned in the Baraita **has** already **become an adult** and is no longer a *na'arah!*

אָמַר רַבִּי אִילְעָא [5] **Rabbi Il'a said** in reply: **The verse** that **says** (Deuteronomy 22:21): "Then they shall bring out **the *na'arah***...and the men of her city shall stone her," does not mean to exclude from this punishment a girl who has come of age between the time of her offense and the time she is brought to trial. [6] Rather, the purpose of the expression "the *na'arah*" is to include in the punishment of stoning **someone who was a *na'arah*** at the time of her transgression, even though she is now no longer a *na'arah,* but an adult. Thus the verse teaches us that the death penalty to which the betrothed *na'arah* is subject does not change, even though the girl herself has changed and reached adulthood between the time she committed adultery and the time she was put on trial.

אֲמַר לֵיהּ [7] **Rabbi Ḥananya said to Rabbi Il'a: If so,** if the time when the transgression took place is the critical moment, then **let** the husband **also be flogged,** [8] **and let him also pay the hundred-shekel** fine if he betrothed his wife when she was still a *na'arah*, but married her and made his false accusations against her only after she had already come of age! Why does the Baraita cited above (45a) rule that the penalty

RASHI

האמר ליה כו׳ — שינויא הוא. **לתנא** — דתנא קמיה להא דתני שילא. **הנערה** — ״והוציאו את הנערה״ ולא כתב ״והוציאוה״. **שהיתה כבר** — ואף על פי שאינה עכשיו.

SAGES

רַבִּי אִילְעָא Rabbi Il'a. A third-generation Palestinian Amora. See *Ketubot,* Part III, p. 63.

NOTES

changed and reached adulthood before the witnesses testify against her.

Shittah Mekubbetzet argues that *Ritva*'s question can be answered in just the opposite way by the objection raised by *Tosafot. Tosafot* asks: Why does the Gemara conclude that the Baraita taught by Shila is not supported by the view of Rabbi Shimon? Perhaps Rabbi Shimon maintains that the High Priest or the king is totally exempt from bringing a sin-offering, because it cannot be decided which offering he must bring. He cannot bring the sin-offering brought by an ordinary person, because he is now the High Priest or the king. And he cannot bring the special offering of the High Priest or the king because he was an ordinary person at the time of his offense. But as for the betrothed *na'arah* who committed adultery, he would say that she is certainly subject to the death penalty, though there is a doubt whether she is subject to stoning or to strangulation. Hence she should be sentenced to strangulation, the more lenient of the two forms of execution.

תְּנֵי: תִּידּוֹן בִּסְקִילָה State: She is sentenced to death by stoning. *Ri HaLavan* argues that all the Tannaim — even Rabbi Shimon — may well agree with this reading of the Baraita. It is only with respect to the sin-offering brought for the inadvertent violation of a prohibition that we consider the status of the sinner at the time he became aware of his transgression, for with respect to a sin-offering, the sinner's awareness or lack of awareness of his transgression plays a role regarding his liability. But with respect to capital punishment, even Rabbi Shimon may agree that the only consideration is the sinner's liability at the time of his offense.

אִי הָכִי, מִילְקָא נַמִי לִילְקֵי If so, let him also be flogged. The Rishonim ask: Why was this question asked only according to Rabbi Yoḥanan's version of the Baraita? Even according to Shila's version, the following question may be

TRANSLATION AND COMMENTARY

of flogging and the payment of the fine apply only to someone who falsely accused his wife while she was still a *na'arah*, but not to someone who made those false accusations after she had already come of age?

אָמַר לֵיהּ [1]Rabbi Il'a **said to** Rabbi Ḥananya: **May God save us from this opinion!** The equation you have made between the girl's punishment for adultery and her husband's punishments for his false allegations is illogical!

אַדְּרַבָּה [2]Rabbi Ḥananya answered him: **On the contrary, may God save us from your opinion,** for it is your position that does not stand the test of logic!

וְטַעֲמָא מַאי [3]The Gemara now seeks to explain the distinction made by Rabbi Il'a between the girl's punishment for adultery and her husband's punishments for his false accusations, and asks: **What is the reason** why the girl is sentenced to death by stoning even if she has already come of age when she is convicted of adultery, but her husband is subject to flogging and to the hundred-shekel fine only if he falsely accused his wife before she came of age?

אָמַר רַבִּי יִצְחָק בַּר אָבִין [4]**Rabbi Yitzḥak bar Avin said (and there are some who say that it was Rabbi Yitzḥak bar Abba** who offered this explanation): [5]**In the case of this girl,** who committed adultery during the period of her betrothal, it was **her** adulterous **deeds** that **brought** her punishment **upon her.** Since the girl is punished for her adultery, we must consider whether or not she was a *na'arah* at the time of her offense. [6]**But in the case of this man,** the husband who falsely accused his wife of adultery, it was **his talk** that **brought** his punishment **upon him.** Since he is punished for his slanderous talk, we must consider whether or not his wife was a *na'arah* at the time he leveled his accusations against her. [7]**In the case of this girl,** it was **her** adulterous **deeds** that **brought** her punishment **upon her.** [8]**When she committed adultery, it was a *na'arah* who committed adultery,** and this is why she is sentenced to death by stoning as a *na'arah*. [9]**But in the case of** the husband, it was **his** slanderous **talk** that **brought** his punishment **upon him.** [10]**When does he become subject** to the punishment of flogging and to the hundred-shekel fine? [11]**At that time** when he brings the false charges against his wife. [12]But if **at that time she has** already **come of age,** the husband is exempt from punishment, for he did not falsely accuse a *na'arah*.

[1]אָמַר לֵיהּ: רַחֲמָנָא נִיצְּלַן מֵהַאי דַּעְתָּא!
[2]אַדְּרַבָּה, רַחֲמָנָא נִיצְּלַן מִדַּעְתָּא דִּידָךְ!
[3]וְטַעֲמָא מַאי?
[4]אָמַר רַבִּי יִצְחָק בַּר אָבִין, וְאִיתֵּימָא רַבִּי יִצְחָק בַּר אַבָּא: [5]זוֹ, מַעֲשֶׂיהָ גָּרְמוּ לָהּ; [6]וְזֶה, עֲקִימַת שְׂפָתָיו גָּרְמוּ לוֹ. [7]״זוֹ, מַעֲשֶׂיהָ גָּרְמוּ לָהּ״: [8]כְּשֶׁהִיא זִנַּאי, נַעֲרָה זִנַּאי. [9]״וְזֶה, עֲקִימַת שְׂפָתָיו גָּרְמוּ לוֹ״: [10]אֵימַת קָא מִיחַיַּיב? [11]הַהִיא שַׁעְתָּא. [12]וְהַהִיא שַׁעְתָּא בּוֹגֶרֶת הֲוַאי.

LITERAL TRANSLATION

[1]He said to him: May the Merciful One save us from this opinion!

[2]On the contrary, let the Merciful One save us from your opinion!

[3]But what is the reason?

[4]Rabbi Yitzḥak bar Avin said, and there are [some] who say [that it was] Rabbi Yitzḥak bar Abba: [5][In the case of] this [girl], her deeds brought [it] upon her; [6]but [in the case of] this [man], his talk (lit., "the cursing of his lips") brought [it] upon him. [7]"[In the case of] this [girl], her deeds brought [it] upon her": [8]When she committed adultery, [it was] a *na'arah* who committed adultery. [9]"But [in the case of] this [man], his words brought [it] upon him": [10]When does he become liable? [11]At that time. [12]And at that time she has come of age.

RASHI

רחמנא ניצלן מהאי דעתא – כיחד ממנו טעמו של דבר, מפני שתלוי בהבנת הלב, כדמפרש לקמן: זו מעשיה גרמו לה כו׳.

BACKGROUND

רַחֲמָנָא נִיצְּלַן מֵהַאי דַּעְתָּא May the Merciful One save us from this opinion! In this case the Gemara presents the very words of these Sages. In their agitation, each was convinced that the opinion of the other was so illogical that there was nothing to argue about, and they merely expressed their agitation: May the Lord preserve us from such an opinion, since it is devoid of logic! Rabbi Il'a's opinion is explained in the Gemara. However, the difficulty raised by Rabbi Ḥananya is not explained because it is simpler. If we say that the meaning of the word *na'arah* is specifically that the girl was a *na'arah* (between the ages of twelve and twelve-and-a-half), then the entire matter must be interpreted in that way, and it should not be limited to a single Halakhic item.

NOTES

raised: Why is a betrothed *na'arah* who is found guilty of adultery sentenced to stoning, even if her husband accuses her of the adultery only after she has come of age, but the husband is exempt from the penalty of flogging and the 100-shekel fine if the accusations he brings against his wife prove to have been false?

Ritva explains that, according to Shila, the law concerning the punishment inflicted on the girl if the husband's charge of adultery proves to be true is a Halakhic innovation. It is thus possible that the exceptional law was stated only with respect to the girl herself, but not with respect to her husband. But according to Rabbi Yoḥanan, the law is not an innovation, because the death penalty to which a betrothed *na'arah* who committed adultery is subject does not change, even if the girl herself changes between the time of her offense and the time she is brought to trial. If so, Rabbi Ḥananya suggests that the penalty of flogging and the fine should also apply to a husband who falsely accuses his wife after she has already come of age.

BACKGROUND

כַּיּוֹצֵא בַּדָּבָר אַתָּה אוֹמֵר Similarly you may say. Although the laws concerning a betrothed *na'arah* and those concerning an idol-worshiper are different from each other, it is noted here that they are at least similar with regard to the place of execution. Execution for these transgressions is not carried out as is usual at the place of stoning but rather at the gate of the city, or, if it is not possible to perform the execution at the city gate, at the gate of the court.

הָעוֹבֵד עֲבוֹדָה זָרָה Someone who worships idols. The assumption shared by these two rulings and by a few similar rulings is that when the Torah wishes to publicize a particularly grave sin, it punishes the sinner in a more public place, so that everyone will see the punishment and be deterred from committing that transgression. Regarding the betrothed *na'arah,* the grave aspect of the transgression is the combination of betrayal of the husband with the unusual corruption of such a young girl consenting to commit such a serious sin. As for idol-worship, it is an act of renunciation of the foundation of the entire Torah; as the Sages said: "Anyone who admits to idol- worship denies the entire Torah."

LITERAL TRANSLATION

1 Our Rabbis taught: "[Regarding] a betrothed *na'arah* who committed adultery, they stone her at the door of her father's house. 2 [If] she has no door of [her] father's house, they stone her at the door of the gate of that city. 3 And in a city in which the majority are non-Jews, they stone her at the door of the court. 4 Similarly you may say: [Regarding] someone who worships idols, they stone him at the gate at which he worshiped. 5 And in a city in which the majority are non-Jews, they stone him at the door of the court."

6 From where are these things [derived]?

7 For our Rabbis taught: "'Your gates' — this is the gate at which he worshiped. 8 You say the gate at which he worshiped; 9 but might it not be

1 תָּנוּ רַבָּנַן: ״נַעֲרָה הַמְאוֹרָסָה שֶׁזִּינְּתָה, סוֹקְלִין אוֹתָהּ עַל פֶּתַח בֵּית אָבִיהָ. 2 אֵין לָהּ פֶּתַח בֵּית הָאָב, סוֹקְלִין אוֹתָהּ עַל פֶּתַח שַׁעַר הָעִיר הַהִיא. 3 וּבְעִיר שֶׁרוּבָּהּ נָכְרִים, סוֹקְלִין אוֹתָהּ עַל פֶּתַח בֵּית דִּין. 4 כַּיּוֹצֵא בַּדָּבָר אַתָּה אוֹמֵר: הָעוֹבֵד עֲבוֹדָה זָרָה סוֹקְלִין אוֹתוֹ עַל שַׁעַר שֶׁעָבַד בּוֹ. 5 וּבְעִיר שֶׁרוּבָּהּ נָכְרִים, סוֹקְלִין אוֹתוֹ עַל פֶּתַח בֵּית דִּין״.

6 מְנָא הָנֵי מִילֵּי?

7 דְּתָנוּ רַבָּנַן: ״׳שְׁעָרֶיךָ׳ — זֶה שַׁעַר שֶׁעָבַד בּוֹ. 8 אַתָּה אוֹמֵר שַׁעַר שֶׁעָבַד בּוֹ; 9 אוֹ אֵינוֹ אֶלָּא

RASHI

על פתח בית אביה — אם באו עדים משניסת. **על שער העיר שעבד בה** — ואפילו נידון בעיר אחרת.

TRANSLATION AND COMMENTARY

תָּנוּ רַבָּנַן 1 The Gemara continues its discussion of the laws regarding a betrothed *na'arah* who committed adultery. **Our Rabbis taught** the following Baraita, which states: "If **a betrothed *na'arah* commits adultery, she is stoned at the door of her father's house,** as the verse says (Deuteronomy 22:21): 'Then they shall bring out the *na'arah* to the door of her father's house, and the men of her city shall stone her with stones so that she dies.' 2 **If there is no door to her father's house,** if, for example, the girl's father does not own a house of his own, the girl **is stoned at the door of the gate of that city.** 3 **And in a city in which the majority** of the inhabitants **are non-Jews,** so that it is not possible to carry out the execution at the door of the city gate, the girl **is stoned at the door of the court** that passed sentence on her." 4 The Baraita continues: **"Similarly you may say** that if **someone is found guilty of idolatry, he is stoned at the gate** of the city **in which he worshiped** the idols. 5 **And in a city in which the majority** of the inhabitants **are non-Jews, he is stoned at the door of the court** that passed sentence upon him."

מְנָא הָנֵי מִילֵּי 6 The Gemara asks: **What is the** Biblical source **for these rulings** concerning the idolater?

דְּתָנוּ רַבָּנַן 7 The Gemara answers: It is **as our Rabbis taught** in the following Baraita: "Regarding idolatry, the verse says (Deuteronomy 17:5): 'Then you shall bring forth that man or that woman, who have committed that wicked thing, to your gates.' The expression **'your gates'** refers here to **the gate** of the city **in which he worshiped** the idols." 8 Considering an alternative interpretation of the verse, the Baraita continues: **"You say** that the expression 'your gates' refers to **the gate** of the city **in which he worshiped** the idols, 9 **but might it not be** understood as referring to **the gate** of the court **at which he was judged?"** The

NOTES

עַל פֶּתַח בֵּית דִּין At the door of the court. The Rishonim point out that the execution does not take place directly outside the court but at some distance from it. *Tosafot* explains that the sentence is carried out away from the court so that it not be branded as a court that takes lives.

Ra'ah and *Ritva* explain that the punishment is carried out at some distance from the court in order to delay the execution, thereby allowing some extra time for new evidence to be brought before the court which may save the person who has been sentenced to death (see *Sanhedrin* 42b, where these two explanations are given).

שַׁעַר שֶׁעָבַד בּוֹ The gate at which he worshiped. The Rishonim note that the Baraita does not mean to say that the person who is convicted of idolatry is stoned at the

HALAKHAH

וּבְעִיר שֶׁרוּבָּהּ נָכְרִים And in a city in which the majority are non-Jews. "If a girl is sentenced to death by stoning, and the execution is supposed to be carried out at the door of the city gate, but the majority of the city's inhabitants are non-Jews, she is stoned at the door of the court that sentenced her to death," following the Baraita. (*Rambam, Sefer Kedushah, Hilkhot Issurei Bi'ah* 3:11.)

הָעוֹבֵד עֲבוֹדָה זָרָה Regarding someone who worships idols. "If someone is found guilty of idolatry, he is stoned at the gate of the city in which he worshiped the idols. In a city in which the majority of the inhabitants are non-Jews, he is stoned at the door of the court that sentenced him to death." (*Rambam, Sefer Shofetim, Hilkhot Sanhedrin* 15:2.)

TRANSLATION AND COMMENTARY

Baraita answers: [1]"When the verse **below** (v. 5) discusses the punishment meted out to an idolater, it **says:** 'Then you shall bring forth that man or that woman, who have committed that wicked thing, to **your gates.'** [2]**And** when the verse **above** (v. 2) first relates the offense of the idolater it **says:** 'If there is found among you, within any of **your gates** which the Lord your God gives you, a man or a woman, who has perpetrated wickedness in the sight of the Lord your God, in transgressing his covenant.' The expression 'your gates' mentioned in the earlier verse sheds light on the meaning of that same expression in the later verse. [3]**Just as** the expression **'your gates' that is mentioned** in the verse **above** describing the idolater's transgression **refers to the gate at which he worshiped** the idol, [4]**so** too the expression **'your gates' that is mentioned** in the verse **below** discussing his execution **refers to the gate at which he worshiped** that idol." [5]The Baraita continues: **"Another explanation** of the expression may also be suggested: The verse says: 'Then you shall bring forth that man or that woman, who have committed that wicked thing, to your gates.' You shall bring him 'to **your gates,'** [6]**but not** to **the gates of** a city in which the majority of the inhabitants are **non-Jews."** Thus, both rulings relating to the execution of an idolater are derived from the expression "your gates": An idolater is stoned at "your gates," at the gate of the city where he committed the offense, provided that it is "your gate," and not the gate of a city where most of the inhabitants are non-Jews.

הַאי ״שְׁעָרֶיךָ״ הָא אַפִּיקְתֵּיהּ [7]The Gemara now questions whether this one expression can serve as the source for both rulings: **Surely we have already used the expression "your gates" to derive** the law that an idolater is executed at the gate of the city where he worshiped the idol! How can we learn from the same expression that the law is different if most of the inhabitants of the city are non-Jews?

אִם כֵּן [8]The Gemara explains: **If it were true** that the expression "your gates" teaches us only the first law, then **the verse should have said:** "Then you shall bring forth that man or that woman, who have committed that wicked thing, to the **gate**"! [9]**What does** the verse **mean** to imply by specifying **"your gates"?** [10]It must mean that we are to **deduce two rulings from it:** Bring him to "the gate" of the city in which he worshiped the idol, provided that it is "your gate," and not the gate of a non-Jewish city.

אַשְׁכַּחַן [11]The Gemara now returns to the laws that apply to the execution of a betrothed *na'arah* who has committed adultery. **We have found a source regarding** the case of **idolatry,** stating that the offender is stoned at the gate of the city where he committed his transgression. [12]But **from where** in the Torah **do we know** that **a betrothed *na'arah*** who has committed adultery is stoned at the gate of the city where she committed her transgression, if she cannot be executed at the door of her father's house?

שַׁעַר שֶׁנִּידּוֹן בּוֹ? [1]נֶאֱמַר ׳שְׁעָרֶיךָ׳ לְמַטָּה, [2]וְנֶאֱמַר ׳שְׁעָרֶיךָ׳ לְמַעְלָה. [3]מַה ׳שְׁעָרֶיךָ׳ הָאָמוּר לְמַעְלָה שַׁעַר שֶׁעָבַד בּוֹ, [4]אַף ׳שְׁעָרֶיךָ׳ הָאָמוּר לְמַטָּה שַׁעַר שֶׁעָבַד בּוֹ. [5]דָּבָר אַחֵר: ׳שְׁעָרֶיךָ׳ — [6]וְלֹא שַׁעֲרֵי נָכְרִים״.

[7]הַאי ״שְׁעָרֶיךָ״ הָא אַפִּיקְתֵּיהּ! [8]אִם כֵּן, לֵימָא קְרָא ״שַׁעַר״. [9]מַאי ״שְׁעָרֶיךָ״? [10]שְׁמַע מִינָּהּ תַּרְתֵּי.

[11]אַשְׁכַּחַן עֲבוֹדָה זָרָה. [12]נַעֲרָה הַמְאוֹרָסָה מְנָא לַן?

LITERAL TRANSLATION

the gate at which he is judged? [1]'Your gates' was stated below, [2]and 'your gates' was stated above. [3]Just as 'your gates' that is mentioned above [refers to] the gate at which he worshiped, [4]so 'your gates' that is mentioned below [refers to] the gate at which he worshiped. [5]Another explanation (lit., 'matter'): 'Your gates' — [6]but not the gates of non-Jews."

[7]Surely you have [already] derived [something] from this [word] "your gates"!

[8]If so, let the verse say "gate." [9]What is [meant by] "your gates"? [10]Deduce two [things] from it.

[11]We have found [a source regarding] idolatry. [12]From where [do we know about] a betrothed *na'arah*?

RASHI

שעריך למעלה — ״כי ימצא בקרבך באחד שעריך וגו׳״ דהא ודאי באותו שער שעבד בו עבירה. **ונאמר שעריך למטה** — ״והוצאת את האיש ההוא אל שעריך וגו׳״. **שעריך** — בעבודה זרה כתיב (דברים יז) ״והוצאת את האיש ההוא או את האשה ההיא אשר עשו וגו׳״.

BACKGROUND

וְלֹא שַׁעֲרֵי נָכְרִים But not the gates of non-Jews. The presentation of a source for this Halakhah from the Torah proves that the reason for this ruling is not the impossibility of carrying out the verdict in a city inhabited mainly by non-Jews. For in such a case there is no need for a specific verse in the Torah. It is a general rule that whenever — for some external reason — a death sentence cannot be carried out as stipulated in the Torah, the transgressor is executed in another way. However, here it is explicitly ruled that this verdict must be carried out with conspicuous publicity only when the majority of the residents of the city are Jews. For in a city where the majority of the inhabitants are non-Jews, there is an element of profaning the name of God when Jewish sinners are executed with great publicity.

NOTES

entrance to the building in which he worshiped the idols, but rather that he is executed at the gate of the city where he committed his transgression. Even if he was sentenced in an another city, he is returned to the city in which he committed his crime, and is executed at the city gate (see *Rashi, Ra'ah, Rabbi Crescas Vidal,* and *Meiri*).

SAGES

רַבִּי אַבָּהוּ Rabbi Abbahu. A third-generation Palestinian Amora. See *Ketubot,* Part II, p. 20.

TRANSLATION AND COMMENTARY

אָמַר רַבִּי אַבָּהוּ [1]In reply to this question **Rabbi Abbahu said:** The law applying to the betrothed *na'arah* is derived from the law stated with respect to the idolater by means of a comparison of the expressions used in each case. The term **"door"** stated with respect to a betrothed *na'arah* ("Then they shall bring out the *na'arah* to the *door* of her father's house"; Deuteronomy 22:21) **is clarified by** the term **"door"** stated with respect to the Tabernacle in the wilderness ("And the screen for the *door* of the gate of the court"; Numbers 4:26). [2]That term **"door"** stated with respect to the Tabernacle is connected **to** the term **"gate"** mentioned in the same verse. Just as the word "door" regarding the Tabernacle is associated with the word "gate," so too should the word "door" regarding the execution of a betrothed *na'arah* be understood as being associated with the word "gate." Now that we have associated the term "door" that is used in connection with the betrothed *na'arah* with the term "gate," [3]the meaning of the word **"gate"** as it relates to the betrothed *na'arah* may be clarified **by** the term **"your gates"** stated with respect to the idolater. Just as the idolater is executed at the gate of the city in which he worshiped the idol, so too is the betrothed *na'arah* put to death at the gate of the city where she committed her transgression (if she cannot be executed at the door of her father's house).

תָּנוּ רַבָּנַן [4]The Gemara now cites another Baraita dealing with the laws that apply to a husband who falsely accuses his wife of adultery. **Our Rabbis taught** the following Baraita: **"Someone who falsely accuses his wife** of adultery **is flogged and pays** a fine of **a hundred sela'im.** [5]**Rabbi Yehudah says: As for** the penalty of **flogging,** the husband who falsely accuses his wife **is flogged in all cases,** whether he had intercourse with her and claimed that he found her not to be a virgin, or whether he did not have intercourse with her but brought false witnesses who testified that she had committed adultery during her betrothal. [6]But **as for the hundred-sela** fine — only **if he had intercourse** with his wife **does he pay** the fine; [7]**if he did not have intercourse** with her, **he does not pay** the fine."

[1]אָמַר רַבִּי אַבָּהוּ: גָּמַר "פֶּתַח" מִ"פֶּתַח", [2]וּ"פֶּתַח" מִ"שַּׁעַר", [3]וְ"שַׁעַר" מִ"שְּׁעָרֶיךָ". [4]תָּנוּ רַבָּנַן: "הַמּוֹצִיא שֵׁם רַע לוֹקֶה וְנוֹתֵן מֵאָה סֶלַע. [5]רַבִּי יְהוּדָה אוֹמֵר: לִלְקוֹת, לוֹקֶה מִכָּל מָקוֹם. [6]מֵאָה סֶלַע, בָּעַל, נוֹתֵן; [7]לֹא בָּעַל, אֵינוֹ נוֹתֵן".

LITERAL TRANSLATION

[1]Rabbi Abbahu said: He derived "door" from "door," [2]and "door" from "gate," [3]and "gate" from "your gates."

[4]Our Rabbis taught: "Someone who puts out a bad name [about his wife] is flogged and he pays a hundred sela'im. [5]Rabbi Yehudah says: As for flogging, he is flogged in all cases. [6][As for] the hundred sela'im, [if] he had intercourse, he pays; [7][if] he did not have intercourse, he does not pay."

RASHI

גמר פתח מפתח ופתח משער — אסמכתא דרבנן בעלמא, כתיב הכא "אל פתח בית אביה" וכתיב במשכן (במדבר ד) "מסך פתח שער החצר", מה "פתח" האמור במשכן — שער עמו, אף "פתח" האמור כאן — שער עמו. והדר גמר האי "שער" מ"שעריך" האמור בעבודה זרה. **ללקות** — מלקות במוציא שם רע, מ"ויסרו אותו". **לוקה מכל מקום** — בין בעל ובא לבית דין והוציא שם רע על ידי בעילתו, ואמר: לא מצאתי לבתך בתולים, בין לא בעל ובא לבית דין ואמר: באו לי עדים שזינתה בבית אביה, והרי היא לפניכם.

NOTES

לוֹקֶה מִכָּל מָקוֹם He is flogged in all cases. The Rishonim raise an objection: According to both explanations of the dispute between the Rabbis and Rabbi Yehudah, Rabbi Yehudah follows the opinion of Rabbi Eliezer ben Ya'akov, who says that the laws of slander apply only if the husband had intercourse with his wife. Why, then, does Rabbi Yehudah say that the husband is flogged even if he has not had intercourse with his wife?

Our commentary follows the explanation of *Rashi*, who maintains that at this point the Gemara understands that the husband is flogged because he violated the general prohibition against talebearing: "You shall not go as a talebearer among your people."

Tosafot and others raise a number of objections against *Rashi*: First, the Gemara below implies that the verse, "You shall not go as a talebearer," serves as a source that the Torah prohibits slander by an explicit negative precept, and not as a source for flogging. Second, according to *Rashi*'s explanation, a husband should be subject to flogging whenever he falsely accuses his wife of adultery, and not only if he married a *na'arah*. And third, according to Rabbi Yehudah, why does the Gemara below derive the punishment of flogging from the phrase, "And they shall chastise him"?

Rabbenu Tam explains that the Gemara understood from the outset that according to Rabbi Yehudah the husband is subject to lashes for rebelliousness if he slandered his wife without having had intercourse with her. Rav Naḥman bar Yitzḥak does not introduce a new interpretation of the Baraita, but merely reconciles the contradiction between the two Baraitot. According to *Rabbenu Tam*, this interpretation of Rabbi Yehudah's position is accepted by all, even by Rav Pappa who suggests a different resolution of the contradiction between the Baraitot.

[1]קָא מִיפַּלְגִי בִּפְלוּגְתָּא דְּרַבִּי אֱלִיעֶזֶר בֶּן יַעֲקֹב וְרַבָּנַן. [2]וְהָכִי קָאָמַר: הַמּוֹצִיא שֵׁם רַע לוֹקֶה וְנוֹתֵן מֵאָה סֶלַע, [3]בֵּין בָּעַל בֵּין שֶׁלֹּא בָּעַל, [4]כְּרַבָּנַן. [5]רַבִּי יְהוּדָה אוֹמֵר: לִלְקוֹת, לוֹקֶה מִכָּל מָקוֹם. [6]מֵאָה סֶלַע, בָּעַל, נוֹתֵן; [7]לֹא בָּעַל, אֵינוֹ נוֹתֵן, [8]כְּרַבִּי אֱלִיעֶזֶר בֶּן יַעֲקֹב.

[9]אִיכָּא דְּאָמְרִי: כּוּלָּהּ כְּרַבִּי אֱלִיעֶזֶר בֶּן יַעֲקֹב, [10]וְהָכִי קָאָמַר: הַמּוֹצִיא שֵׁם רַע לוֹקֶה וְנוֹתֵן מֵאָה סֶלַע, וְהוּא שֶׁבָּעַל.

LITERAL TRANSLATION

[1]They disagree about the [matter in] dispute between Rabbi Eliezer ben Ya'akov and the Rabbis. [2]And this [is what] it says: Someone who puts out a bad name [about his wife] is flogged and he pays a hundred sela'im, [3]whether he had intercourse or he did not have intercourse, [4]in accordance with the Rabbis. [5]Rabbi Yehudah says: As for flogging, he is flogged in all cases. [6][As for] the hundred sela'im, [if] he had intercourse, he pays; [7][if] he did not have intercourse, he does not pay, [8]in accordance with Rabbi Eliezer ben Ya'akov.

[9]There are [some] who say: It is all in accordance with Rabbi Eliezer ben Ya'akov, [10]and this [is what] it says: Someone who puts out a bad name [about his wife] is flogged and he pays a hundred sela'im, provided that he had intercourse.

TRANSLATION AND COMMENTARY

קָא מִיפַּלְגִי בִּפְלוּגְתָּא [1]The Gemara now suggests that the Rabbis and Rabbi Yehudah in the Baraita just quoted **disagree about the** same **matter** that was the subject of a **dispute between Rabbi Eliezer ben Ya'akov and the Rabbis,** which will be cited in full later in the Gemara (46a). Briefly put, the Rabbis maintain that all the laws of slander apply whether the husband had intercourse with his wife or not, whereas Rabbi Eliezer ben Ya'akov maintains that the laws of slander apply only if the husband had intercourse with his wife. [2]**And this is what** the Baraita **says: Someone who falsely accuses his wife** of adultery **is flogged and pays** a fine of **a hundred sela'im** in all cases, [3]**whether he had intercourse** with his wife and claimed that he found her not to be a virgin, **or** whether **he did not have intercourse** with her but brought false witnesses who testified that she had committed adultery while she was betrothed to him. [4]The anonymous first Tanna of the Baraita quoted above, representing the Rabbis who disagree with Rabbi Yehudah, **agrees with the Rabbis** in the Baraita quoted below, who maintain that the laws of slander apply in all cases, whether or not the husband had intercourse with his wife. [5]**Rabbi Yehudah** disagrees and **says: As for** the penalty of **flogging,** the husband who falsely accuses his wife of adultery **is flogged in all cases.** Even though the special laws concerning the slandering of one's wife apply only if the husband had intercourse with her and claimed that he did not find her to be a virgin, he is nevertheless subject to the punishment of flogging even if he did not have intercourse with her, because he violated the general prohibition against talebearing, "You shall not go as a talebearer among your people" (Leviticus 19:16). [6]But **as for the hundred-sela fine, if he had intercourse** with his wife, **he pays** the fine; [7]**if he did not have intercourse** with her, **he does not pay** the fine. [8]On these matters, Rabbi Yehudah **agrees with Rabbi Eliezer ben Ya'akov,** who limits the laws of slander to the case in which the husband, after having had intercourse with his wife, falsely accused her of adultery.

אִיכָּא דְּאָמְרִי [9]The Gemara now suggests that the dispute between the Rabbis and Rabbi Yehudah may be understood differently: **There are some who say** that the Baraita quoted above **is entirely in accordance with** the view of **Rabbi Eliezer ben Ya'akov,** who maintains that the laws of slander apply only if the husband had intercourse with his wife. [10]**And this is what** the Baraita **says: Someone who falsely accuses his wife** of adultery **is flogged and pays** a fine of **a hundred sela'im, provided** that **he had intercourse** with his wife and his charge of adultery was based on his claim that he did not find her to be a virgin. But if he did not have intercourse with his wife, he is neither flogged nor made to pay the fine, for the laws of slander apply only if the husband had intercourse with his wife, in accordance with the viewpoint of Rabbi Eliezer

SAGES

רַבִּי אֱלִיעֶזֶר בֶּן יַעֲקֹב Rabbi Eliezer ben Ya'akov. See *Ketubot,* Part II, p. 48.

RASHI

פלוגתא דרבי אליעזר בן יעקב ורבנן — לקמן בשמעתין. **כרבנן** — דאמרי: פרשת מוציא שם רע בין בעל בין לא בעל, וכתיב ביה "ויסרו...וענשו". **כרבי אליעזר בן יעקב** — דאמר לקמן: לא נאמר פרשת מוציא שם רע אלא כשבעל. הלכך מאה סלע לא מחייבינן ליה אלא כשבעל, אבל מלקות, דמשום אזהרת "לא תלך רכיל" (ויקרא יט) הוא — לקי ואפילו לא בעל, דהא הלך רכיל. ואי משום דהוי לאו שאין בו מעשה — רבי יהודה לטעמיה, דאמר: לאו שאין בו מעשה לוקין עליו, במסכת מכות (ג,ז) וב"שחיטת חולין" (פג,א). **והוא שבעל** — כרבי אליעזר בן יעקב. וקסבר תנא קמא אליבא דרבי אליעזר לאו שאין בו מעשה אין לוקין עליו. ומלקות דמוציא שם רע — חידוש הוא ומ"ויסרו אותו" נפקא, וההוא קרא כשבעל כתיב.

TRANSLATION AND COMMENTARY

ben Ya'akov. [1]**Rabbi Yehudah** disagrees and **says:** It is true that the laws of slander apply only if the husband had intercourse with his wife, and he is therefore not liable for the hundred-sela fine if he did not have intercourse with her. [2]But **as for** the penalty of **flogging,** the husband who falsely accuses his wife of adultery **is flogged in all cases,** even if he did not have intercourse with her, because he violated the general prohibition against talebearing.

וְסָבַר רַבִּי יְהוּדָה [3]The Gemara now points out a contradiction that appears to exist between two Baraitot as to the viewpoint of Rabbi Yehudah. **Does Rabbi Yehudah** really **maintain that "as for** the penalty of **flogging,** the husband who falsely accuses his wife of adultery **is flogged in all cases,"** even if he did not have intercourse with her? [4]**But surely it was taught** otherwise in another Baraita, which stated: [5]**"Rabbi Yehudah says: If** the husband who falsely accuses his wife of adultery **had intercourse** with her, **he is flogged;** [6]**if he did not have intercourse** with her, **he is not flogged"!**

אָמַר רַב נַחְמָן בַּר יִצְחָק [7]**Rav Naḥman bar Yitzḥak said:** Rabbi Yehudah agrees that by Torah law the husband who falsely accuses his wife is flogged only if he had intercourse with her. [8]And when Rabbi Yehudah says that the husband **is flogged** in all cases, even if he did not have intercourse with his wife, he means that the husband receives **lashes for rebelliousness,** a punishment that is administered **by Rabbinic enactment.** The Rabbis imposed this disciplinary measure upon the husband, because he falsely accused his wife of committing a capital offense.

[1]רַבִּי יְהוּדָה אוֹמֵר: [2]לִלְקוֹת, לוֹקֶה מִכָּל מָקוֹם.
[3]וְסָבַר רַבִּי יְהוּדָה "לִלְקוֹת, לוֹקֶה מִכָּל מָקוֹם"? [4]וְהָתַנְיָא:
[5]"רַבִּי יְהוּדָה אוֹמֵר: בָּעַל, לוֹקֶה; [6]לֹא בָּעַל, אֵינוֹ לוֹקֶה"!
[7]אָמַר רַב נַחְמָן בַּר יִצְחָק:
[8]לוֹקֶה מַכַּת מַרְדּוּת, מִדְּרַבָּנַן.

LITERAL TRANSLATION

[1]Rabbi Yehudah says: As for flogging, [2]he is flogged in all cases.

[3]But does Rabbi Yehudah maintain [that] "as for flogging, he is flogged in all cases"? [4]But surely it was taught: [5]"Rabbi Yehudah says: [If] he had intercourse, he is flogged; [6][if] he did not have intercourse, he is not flogged"!

[7]Rav Naḥman bar Yitzḥak said: [8]He is flogged lashes for rebelliousness, by Rabbinic enactment.

RASHI

רבי יהודה אומר ללקות לוקה מכל מקום – דמלקות משום אזהרת "לא תלך רכיל" הוא, ולאו שאין בו מעשה לוקין עליו. **אמר רב נחמן בר יצחק** – "לוקה מכל מקום" דקאמר – מכת מרדות, דרבנן.

CONCEPTS

מַכַּת מַרְדּוּת **Lashes for rebelliousness,** i.e., lashes administered by Rabbinic decree, rather than by Torah law. A disciplinary measure imposed to prevent or restrict social licence. In certain cases מַכַּת מַרְדּוּת comprised a set punishment imposed on anyone who violated specific Rabbinical prohibitions. מַכַּת מַרְדּוּת would also be imposed on people who were disobedient or disrespectful towards a Rabbinical Court. Similarly, people who refuse to fulfill positive Torah commandments may be given lashes, a type of מַכַּת מַרְדּוּת. The number of stripes administered is not fixed. The judges can increase or moderate the punishment, depending on the specific case (by contrast, when flogging is administered by Torah law, no more than thirty-nine lashes may be given). Even after Rabbinical Courts ceased imposing the penalty of Torah-ordained lashes, they continued to administer מַכַּת מַרְדּוּת, both in Eretz Israel and in the Diaspora.

NOTES

מַכַּת מַרְדּוּת **Lashes for rebelliousness.** Our rendering of the term *makkat mardut* (מַכַּת מַרְדּוּת) as "lashes for rebelliousness" follows *Arukh*, who (following *Rav Natronai Gaon*) explains that this punishment is called *makkat mardut* because it is imposed on a person who has rebelled against the words of the Torah and the Rabbis. *Arukh* (following *Rav Hai Gaon*) offers a second explanation, according to which the term should be understood as "disciplinary lashes" (compare with Leviticus 26:28, וְיִסַּרְתִּי אֶתְכֶם — "And I will discipline you," which Onkelos translates as וְאַרְדֵּי יָתְכוֹן). A Baraita is cited elsewhere (below, 86a-b), which states: "In the case of positive commandments — as when they say to him: 'Build a sukkah,' and he refuses; or: 'Take a lulav,' and he refuses — he is flogged until his soul departs." The Geonim inferred from this that the various provisions regarding the punishment of flogging as administered by Torah law — for example, that no more than thirty-nine lashes may be administered, and that the person to be flogged must be examined to determine whether he can bear that number of lashes — do not apply to the lashes for rebelliousness administered by Rabbinic law. According to this opinion, the Rabbinic penalty of lashes for rebelliousness can be more stringent than the Biblical penalty of flogging. According to another Geonic tradition, the Rabbinic penalty of lashes is limited to thirteen blows, one-third of the number of the Biblical punishment. Some Rishonim (*Remah* cited by *Ritva*; see also *Rambam, Commentary to the Mishnah, Nazir* 4:3) maintain that the number of lashes is left to the discretion of the court. *Ritva* and *Ran* distinguish between punitive lashes and disciplinary lashes. Whenever the Rabbis impose lashes as a punishment for a transgression that has already been committed, the penalty is less severe than that of flogging by Torah law, and the precise number of lashes is decided by the court according to the circumstances of the case. But whenever the Rabbis impose lashes as a disciplinary measure to force a person to perform a positive commandment or to desist from repeatedly violating a prohibition, the lashes continue until the offender dies or agrees to obey.

HALAKHAH

בָּעַל לוֹקֶה **If he had intercourse, he is flogged.** "A husband is not liable for slander unless he had intercourse with his wife in a natural manner and he falsely accuses her of having had intercourse with another man in a natural manner. If he did not have intercourse with her, or if he had intercourse with her in an unnatural manner, he is exempt by Torah law, but he receives lashes administered by Rabbinic decree," following Rabbi Eliezer ben Ya'akov and Rav Naḥman bar Yitzḥak. (*Rambam, Sefer Nashim, Hilkhot Na'arah Betulah* 3:10; *Tur, Even HaEzer* 177.)

[46A] [1]רַב פַּפָּא אֲמַר: [2]מַאי "בָּעַל, לוֹקֶה" דְּקָתָנֵי הָתָם? [3]מָמוֹן.
[4]וְקָרֵי לֵיהּ לְמָמוֹן מַלְקוֹת?
[5]אִין, וְהָא תְּנַן: [6]"הָאוֹמֵר: 'חֲצִי עֶרְכִּי עָלַי', נוֹתֵן חֲצִי עֶרְכּוֹ. [7]רַבִּי יוֹסֵי בְּרַבִּי יְהוּדָה אוֹמֵר: לוֹקֶה וְנוֹתֵן עֵרֶךְ שָׁלֵם". [8]לוֹקֶה אַמַּאי? [9]אֲמַר רַב פַּפָּא: לוֹקֶה בְּעֵרֶךְ שָׁלֵם. [10]מַאי טַעֲמָא?

LITERAL TRANSLATION

[46A] [1] Rav Pappa said: [2] What [is meant by] "if he had intercourse, he is flogged," which is taught there? [3] Money.

[4] But does he call money flogging?

[5] Yes, for we have learned: [6] "[If] someone says: 'I vow [lit., "upon me"] half of my value,' he pays half of his value. [7] Rabbi Yose the son of Rabbi Yehudah says: He is flogged and pays the full value." [8] Why is he flogged? [9] Rav Pappa said: He is punished by [paying] the full value. [10] What is the reason?

RASHI

רב פפא אמר – לעולם מלקות ממש, ומאי "בעל לוקה לא בעל אינו לוקה" דקאמר בהך ברייתא – ממון דמאה סלע קאמר. **חצי ערכו** – לפי שניו. דערך קצוב בפרשה לפי השנים.

TRANSLATION AND COMMENTARY

רַב פַּפָּא אֲמַר [46A] [1]**Rav Pappa suggested** a different solution to the apparent contradiction between the two Baraitot. Rabbi Yehudah does indeed maintain that a husband who falsely accuses his wife of adultery is subject to flogging by Torah law in all cases, even if he did not have intercourse with his wife, as was stated in the first Baraita. [2]And **what was meant by** the ruling: "Rabbi Yehudah says: **If** the husband who falsely accuses his wife of adultery **had intercourse** with her, **he is flogged;** if he did not have intercourse with her, he is not flogged," which **was taught** in the second Baraita? [3]That second Baraita refers to the **monetary** fine of a hundred shekalim (sela'im) that is imposed upon the husband. If he had intercourse with his wife, he pays the fine, but if he did not have intercourse with her, he is exempt from the fine.

וְקָרֵי לֵיהּ לְמָמוֹן מַלְקוֹת [4]The Gemara immediately challenges this interpretation. Is it possible to say that Rabbi Yehudah is **calling the monetary** fine imposed on the slanderer **flogging?** Surely the word "flogging" must be understood according to its plain sense as the penalty of lashes!

אִין [5]The Gemara answers: **Yes,** it is possible to refer to a monetary obligation when using the term *lokeh* (לוֹקֶה), even though that term usually denotes the penalty of flogging, **as we have learned** in the following Baraita (*Arakhin* 20a): [6]**"If someone says: 'I vow half of my value** to the Temple treasury,' **he pays half of his value** to the Temple treasury, according to the values set down in Leviticus, chapter 27, which vary according to the sex and the age of the person whose value is vowed. [7]**Rabbi Yose the son of Rabbi Yehudah** disagrees and **says: He is flogged** [*lokeh*] **and pays his full value."** [8]Concerning this Baraita, the Gemara in tractate *Arakhin* (ibid.) asks: **Why is he flogged?** What prohibition did he transgress that he should be subject to flogging? [9]**Rav Pappa said:** Rabbi Yose the son of Rabbi Yehudah did not mean to say that someone who vows half of his value is flogged, but rather that **he is punished** (*lokeh*) **by having to pay his full value.** [10]The Gemara explains: **What is the reasoning** of Rabbi Yose the son of Rabbi Yehudah?

BACKGROUND

עֶרֶךְ **Value.** Leviticus, chapter 27, describes the special vows made using the expressions, "I promise to pay the value [עֶרֶךְ] of so-and-so" or "I promise to pay my value." The sum to be paid is not calculated according to the presumed market value of the particular person if he were sold as a slave, but is established according to specific values set by the Torah. These depend only on the sex and the age of the person whose value was promised, and apply to all Jews over one month old. Vows in the form of "assessments" are like all other vows to the Temple, and the money pledged goes to the Temple treasury. If the person making the vow is unable to pay the full value set by the Torah, a priest evaluates his ability to pay and reduces his obligation accordingly.

NOTES

"חֲצִי עֶרְכִּי עָלַי" **"I vow half of my value."** The laws regarding vows of valuation are stated in Leviticus, chapter 27, and are explained in detail in tractate *Arakhin*. When a person uses the expression, "I vow the value (עֵרֶךְ) of so-and-so," the sum to be paid to the Temple treasury is not calculated according to the presumed value of the particular person if he were sold as a slave, but is set according to specific values laid down by the Torah. These values depend only on the sex and the age of the person whose value was vowed. Vows in the form of valuations are like all other vows to the Temple, and the money donated goes to the Temple treasury. If a person says, "I vow the value of my hand," he has not obligated himself to anything, because vows of valuation must relate to a whole person (as opposed to an ordinary vow of consecration, through which a person can consecrate the monetary value of a particular limb). But if he vows the value of his head or his heart, he is considered to have vowed his full value, for his life depends on those parts of his body.

HALAKHAH

הָאוֹמֵר: "חֲצִי עֶרְכִּי עָלַי" **If someone says: "I vow half of my value."** "If someone says: 'I vow half of my value to the Temple treasury,' he must pay the Temple treasury half of his value, according to the fixed values set down in the Torah for vows of valuation," following the anonymous first Tanna of the Baraita. (*Rambam, Sefer Hafla'ah, Hilkhot Arakhin* 2:2.)

¹גְּזֵירָה חֲצִי עֶרְכּוֹ אַטּוּ עֵרֶךְ חֶצְיוֹ, ²וְעֵרֶךְ חֶצְיוֹ הָוֵי לֵיהּ אֵבֶר שֶׁהַנְּשָׁמָה תְּלוּיָה בּוֹ.
³תָּנוּ רַבָּנַן: ⁴״׳וְעָנְשׁוּ אֹתוֹ׳ — זֶה מָמוֹן. ⁵׳וְיִסְּרוּ׳ — זֶה מַלְקוֹת״.
⁶בִּשְׁלָמָא ״וְעָנְשׁוּ״ זֶה מָמוֹן, ⁷דִּכְתִיב: ״וְעָנְשׁוּ אֹתוֹ מֵאָה כֶסֶף, וְנָתְנוּ לַאֲבִי הַנַּעֲרָה״. ⁸אֶלָּא ״וְיִסְּרוּ״ זֶה מַלְקוֹת מְנָלַן?

LITERAL TRANSLATION

[1] [It is] a preventive measure [where he vowed] half of his value on account of [the possibility that he would vow] the value of half of himself, [2] and the value of half of himself is [a vow of] a limb upon which one's life depends.

[3] Our Rabbis taught: [4] "'And they shall fine him' — this is money. [5] 'And they shall chastise [him]' — this is flogging."

[6] Granted that "and they shall fine [him]" is money, [7] for it is written: "And they shall fine him a hundred pieces of silver, and give them to the father of the *na'arah*." [8] But from where [do we know] that "and they shall chastise [him]" is flogging?

TRANSLATION AND COMMENTARY

[1] The Rabbis **instituted a preventive measure** that **where someone vows half of his value** he must pay his full value, **on account of the possibility that he might vow the value of half of himself.** By Torah law, someone who vows to pay half of his value to the Temple treasury only has to pay half of the value that is fixed in the Torah for a person of his sex and age. [2] **And** someone who vows **the value of half of himself is** in fact making **a vow** relating **to a part** of the body **upon which his life depends.** Therefore the Rabbis ruled that such a person is required to pay his full value, for he is considered as having vowed his full value. Thus we see that the term *lokeh* can be used in connection with a monetary obligation. Similarly, Rabbi Yehudah is referring to the hundred-shekel fine paid by the slanderer if he has had intercourse with his wife, and not to the penalty of flogging which is in fact imposed in all cases, even if he has not had intercourse with his wife.

תָּנוּ רַבָּנַן [3] The Gemara now establishes the Biblical source for the penalties of flogging and a fine which are imposed upon the husband who falsely accuses his wife of adultery. **Our Rabbis taught** the following Baraita: "Regarding the slanderer, the Torah says (Deuteronomy 22:18-19): 'And the elders of that city shall take the man and chastise him. And they shall fine him.' [4] The expression **'and they shall fine him' means** that he receives a **monetary** punishment, a fine. [5] The expression **'and they shall chastise him' means** that he is punished by **flogging."**

בִּשְׁלָמָא [6] The Gemara asks: **Granted that** the expression **"and they shall fine him"** refers to a **monetary** punishment, [7] **for the verse continues: "And they shall fine him a hundred pieces of silver, and give them to the father of the *na'arah*."** [8] **But from where do we know that** the expression **"and they shall chastise him"** refers to the penalty of **flogging?** Perhaps it refers to some other form of chastisement!

RASHI

גזירה חצי ערכו — דמשמע חצי ערך שלם, שקצוב לו לפי שנים. **אטו ערך חציו** — "עלי". והאומר "ערך חציו עלי" או "ערך ראשי" או "לבי עלי" — נותן ערך שלם. דהוה ליה מעריך אבר שהנשמה תלויה בו, וגבי ערכין כתיב (ויקרא כז) "בערכך נפשות", שהמעריך אבר שהנשמה תלויה בו — נותן קצבה שנתנה בו תורה.

BACKGROUND

אֵבֶר שֶׁהַנְּשָׁמָה תְּלוּיָה בּוֹ A limb upon which one's life depends. In the laws of valuation, if a person vows the value of an organ, it makes a difference whether the organ is one that could be removed without taking the donor's life, such as an arm or a leg. In such a case the vow is meaningless, and it is as if the person who made it said nothing. But if the donor vows the value of an organ upon which life depends, such as the heart or the liver, the donor is regarded as if he has vowed the value of a whole person, and he pays according to the standard valuations.

NOTES

וְעָנְשׁוּ אֹתוֹ״ — זֶה מָמוֹן״ "And they shall fine him" — this is money. *Shittah Mekubbetzet* asks a series of questions regarding this derivation of the penalties of flogging and a fine that are imposed on the slanderer. First, why does the Baraita explain the expression "and they shall fine him" (וְעָנְשׁוּ אֹתוֹ) before it explains the expression "and they shall chastise him" (וְיִסְּרוּ אֹתוֹ), when that second phrase appears first in the Biblical text? Second, why does the Baraita derive the fine from the expression "and they shall fine him" (lit., "and they shall punish him"), when the verse states explicitly that the slanderer must pay his wife's father 100 shekalim of silver? And third, why does the Gemara use the formula "granted that, etc.," which is ordinarily found in contexts in which some objection could have been raised against the assumption that follows? What other interpretation could possibly have been given to the expression "and they shall fine him 100 pieces of silver"?

Shittah Mekubbetzet answers that it might have been possible to understand the term וְעָנְשׁוּ אֹתוֹ in its broader sense as meaning "and they shall punish him." The verse then continues with a description of that punishment: The slanderer must pay 100 pieces of silver to the girl's father, and he must never divorce her. According to this explanation, the expression "and they shall chastise him" cannot refer to the punishment of flogging, for if it did, it should

HALAKHAH

עֵרֶךְ חֶצְיוֹ The value of half of himself. "If someone says: 'I vow the value of half of myself,' he must pay the Temple treasury his full value, for half of a person cannot be removed and the person continue to live." (*Rambam, Sefer Hafla'ah, Hilkhot Arakhin* 2:2.)

TRANSLATION AND COMMENTARY

אָמַר רַבִּי אַבָּהוּ [1]Rabbi Abbahu said in reply: **We learn** the meaning of the expression **"they shall chastise** him" stated with respect to the slanderer **from** the expression **"they shall chastise** him" (Deuteronomy 21:18) stated with respect to the rebellious son. [2]**And** the expression **"they shall chastise** him" stated with respect to the rebellious son is clarified **by** the word **"son"** mentioned in the same verse ("If a man has a stubborn and rebellious son, who will not obey the voice of his father or the voice of his mother, and they shall chastise him"). Having established that the chastisement of the slanderer can be compared to the chastisement of the rebellious son, we can infer that just as the latter is associated with the word "son," so too the former, the chastisement of the slanderer, is associated with the word "son." [3]**And** now that we have associated the chastisement of the slanderer with the word "son," the meaning of that word **"son"** (בֵּן) as it relates to the slanderer is clarified **by** the word **"worthy"** (בִּן — literally, "son of") mentioned in the section dealing with the penalty of flogging in the verse (Deuteronomy 25:2): [4]**"And it shall be, if the wicked man is worthy** (בִּן) **to be flogged."** Just as that wicked man is sentenced to be flogged, so too is the slanderer subject to chastisement by means of flogging. Thus it may be concluded that the expression "they shall chastise him," stated with respect to the slanderer, refers to the penalty of flogging.

אַזְהָרָה [5]There is a general rule that capital punishment may be imposed only if the offender committed a transgression that is forbidden by the Torah by an explicit negative precept. This leads to the following question: **Where do we find** such **a negative precept regarding someone who falsely accuses his wife** of adultery?

רַבִּי אֶלְעָזָר אָמַר [6]The Gemara offers two answers to this question. **Rabbi Elazar said:** Falsely accusing one's wife of not having been a virgin at the time of marriage is prohibited **by** the precept (Leviticus 19:16): **"You shall not go as a talebearer."** [7]**Rabbi Natan said:** Such a slanderer violates the precept (Deuteronomy 23:10): **"And you shall keep yourself from every evil thing."** The expression "evil thing" (דָּבָר רַע) is understood here as if it read "evil speech" (דִּבּוּר רַע). Following the principle that the term "you shall keep yourself" (וְנִשְׁמַרְתָּ) denotes a negative precept, Rabbi Natan explains the verse as prohibiting the "evil speech" of slander.

[1]אָמַר רַבִּי אַבָּהוּ: לָמַדְנוּ ״יִסְּרוּ״ מִ״יִסְּרוּ״, [2]וְ״יִסְּרוּ״ מִ״בֵּן״, [3]וּ״בֵּן״ מִ״בִּן״ — [4]״וְהָיָה אִם בִּן הַכּוֹת הָרָשָׁע״.
[5]אַזְהָרָה לְמוֹצִיא שֵׁם רַע מִנַּלַּן?
[6]רַבִּי אֶלְעָזָר אָמַר: מִ״לֹּא תֵלֵךְ רָכִיל״. [7]רַבִּי נָתָן אוֹמֵר: מִ״וְנִשְׁמַרְתָּ מִכֹּל דָּבָר רָע״.

LITERAL TRANSLATION

[1] Rabbi Abbahu said: We have learned "they shall chastise" from "they shall chastise," [2] and "they shall chastise" from "son," [3] and "son [בֵּן]" from "worthy [בִּן]" (lit., "son of") — [4] "And it shall be, if the wicked man is worthy [בִּן] to be flogged."

[5] From where do we [derive] the warning regarding someone who puts out a bad name [about his wife]?

[6] Rabbi Elazar said: From "you shall not go as a talebearer." [7] Rabbi Natan says: From "and you shall keep yourself from every evil thing."

RASHI

ויסרו מויסרו ויסרו מבן — כתיב הכא ״ויסרו אותו״ וכתיב גבי סורר ומורה ״ויסרו״, מה להלן בן עמו — אף כאן בן עמו, והיינו ״ויסרו״ דהכא מ״ויסרו״ דהתם. והאי ״ויסרו״ דהתם מ״בן״ שעמו, דלגמריה ל״בן״ שעמו על ״ויסרו״ דהכא, והדר יליף ״בן״ דאייתינן הכא מ״בן״ ״והיה אם בן הכות״, מה התם מלקות — אף הכא מלקות.

CONCEPTS

אַזְהָרָה Warning. There is a basic Halakhic principle that there cannot be punishment without prior warning. Corporal punishment is not imposed unless the potential transgressor has been warned that what he is about to do is forbidden. Hence we find that in the Torah itself a punishment is not decreed unless a warning also appears in the same place or elsewhere in the Torah, stating: Do not do this thing. For example, we find the warning: "You shall not commit adultery" (Exodus 20:13), and then the punishment: "The adulterer and the adulteress shall surely be put to death" (Leviticus 20:10). However, the Torah sometimes mentions the punishment for an act without explicitly stating that the act is forbidden. In such cases the Sages seek to find the warning that a person is forbidden to perform that action.

SAGES

רַבִּי אֶלְעָזָר Rabbi Elazar (ben Shammu'a). A Tanna of the fifth generation. See *Ketubot*, Part III, p. 193.

NOTES

have appeared after the expression "and they shall punish him." Therefore the Baraita states that the term וְעָנְשׁוּ אֹתוֹ refers specifically to the monetary punishment, and thus the expression "and they shall chastise him," which appears in the previous verse, can indeed refer to the punishment of flogging. The Gemara then asks: Granted that the expression וְעָנְשׁוּ אֹתוֹ refers specifically to the monetary punishment, for the verse states: "And they shall fine him 100 pieces of silver, and give them to the father of the girl," rather than: "And they shall punish him, and make him give 100 pieces of silver to the father of the girl." But how do we know that the phrase "And they shall chastise him" refers to the penalty of flogging?

HALAKHAH

אַזְהָרָה לְמוֹצִיא שֵׁם רַע The warning regarding someone who puts out a bad name about his wife. "If a man falsely accuses his wife of not having been a virgin at the time of their marriage, he is subject to flogging, because he has violated the negative commandment, 'You shall not go as a talebearer.'" (*Rambam, Sefer Nashim, Hilkhot Na'arah Betulah* 3:1.)

SAGES

רַבִּי נָתָן Rabbi Natan. One of the greatest Tannaim during the generation before the completion of the Mishnah. See *Ketubot,* Part II, p. 71.

[1]וְרַבִּי אֶלְעָזָר מַאי טַעֲמָא לָא אֲמַר מֵהַאי? [2]הַהוּא מִיבָּעֵי לֵיהּ לְכִדְרַבִּי פִּנְחָס בֶּן יָאִיר: [3]״׳וְנִשְׁמַרְתָּ מִכֹּל דָּבָר רָע׳. [4]מִכָּאן אָמַר רַבִּי פִּנְחָס בֶּן יָאִיר: [5]אַל יְהַרְהֵר אָדָם בַּיּוֹם וְיָבֹא לִידֵי טוּמְאָה בַּלַּיְלָה״.

[6]וְרַבִּי נָתָן מַאי טַעֲמָא לָא אֲמַר מֵהַאי?

[7]הַהוּא אַזְהָרָה לְבֵית דִּין, [8]שֶׁלֹּא יְהֵא רַךְ לָזֶה וְקָשֶׁה לָזֶה. [9]״לֹא אָמַר לְעֵדִים: ׳בּוֹאוּ וַהֲעִידוּנִי׳, [10]וְהֵן מְעִידִים אוֹתוֹ

LITERAL TRANSLATION

[1]And what is the reason [that] Rabbi Elazar did not derive (lit., "say") [it] from this [verse]?

[2]That [verse] is needed by him for [the teaching] of Rabbi Pineḥas ben Ya'ir: [3]"'And you shall keep yourself from every evil thing.' [4]From here Rabbi Pineḥas ben Ya'ir said: [5]A man should not have [impure] thoughts during the day and [thereby] come to impurity at night."

[6]And what is the reason [that] Rabbi Natan did not derive [it] from this [verse]?

[7]That is a warning to the court [8]that it should not be soft toward this one and hard toward that one.

[9]"[If] he did not say to the witnesses: 'Come and testify on my behalf,' [10]and they testify on his behalf on their own,

TRANSLATION AND COMMENTARY

וְרַבִּי אֶלְעָזָר מַאי טַעֲמָא [1]The Gemara asks: **What is the reason that Rabbi Elazar did not,** like Rabbi Natan, **derive** the prohibition **from the verse,** "And you shall keep yourself from every evil thing"?

הַהוּא מִיבָּעֵי לֵיהּ [2]The Gemara answers: Rabbi Elazar **required that verse for what was taught by Rabbi Pineḥas ben Ya'ir** in the following Baraita: [3]"The verse says: **'And you shall keep yourself from every evil thing.'** The 'evil thing' mentioned here is clarified by the next verse, which states: 'If there will be among you any man who is not ritually pure by reason of ritual impurity that happens by night.' [4]**From here Rabbi Pineḥas ben Yair said:** [5]**A man should not entertain impure** sexual **thoughts during the day, and thereby come to** ritual **impurity** through the emission of semen **at night.** A man who emits semen, whether voluntarily or involuntarily, during sexual relations or otherwise, becomes ritually impure. He must guard himself against sexual fantasies during the day, so that he does not defile himself at night."

וְרַבִּי נָתָן [6]The Gemara now turns to Rabbi Natan. **What is the reason that Rabbi Natan did not,** like Rabbi Elazar, **derive** the prohibition against slander **from the verse,** "You shall not go as a talebearer"?

הַהוּא אַזְהָרָה לְבֵית דִּין [7]The Gemara answers: Rabbi Natan interprets **that** verse **as a warning** directed **at the court** [8]**that it should not be lenient toward one** of the litigants **and hard toward the other,** but must treat the two parties equally. "You shall not go as a talebearer" (*rakhil* — רָכִיל) is understood by Rabbi Natan as if it read: You shall not go soft to this one (*rakh li* — רַךְ לִי), which literally means "soft to me."

לֹא אָמַר לְעֵדִים [9]The Gemara continues its discussion of various aspects of the laws of slander by citing the following Baraita: **"If the husband does not say to the witnesses: 'Come and testify on my behalf** that my wife committed adultery during the period of her betrothal,' [10]**but they** come and **testify on his behalf**

RASHI

ונשמרת מכל דבר רע — וכל מקום שנאמר "השמר" "פן" ו"אל" — אינו אלא לא תעשה. **לכדרבי פנחס** — במסכת עבודה זרה. **שלא יהרהר ביום ויבא לידי טומאה בלילה** — דסמיך ליה "כי יהיה בך איש וגו'". **רך לזה** — ורכיל, לשון: רך לי תהיה. **לא אמר לעדים** — המעידים על זנותה.

NOTES

שֶׁלֹּא יְהֵא רַךְ That it should not be soft. Rabbi Natan's novel interpretation of the verse seems to have been prompted by the fact that the precise meaning of the phrase לֹא תֵלֵךְ רָכִיל is not clear (for the root רכל is generally used in connection with business matters). The context also supports Rabbi Natan's interpretation, for the previous verse reads (Leviticus 19:15): "You shall do no unrighteousness in judgment; you shall not respect the person of the

HALAKHAH

אַל יְהַרְהֵר אָדָם בַּיּוֹם A man should not have impure thoughts during the day. "A man is required to guard himself from having impure sexual thoughts. He must not do anything or look at anything that will cause him to become sexually aroused." (*Rambam, Sefer Kedushah, Hilkhot Issurei Bi'ah* 21:5, 21; *Shulḥan Arukh, Even HaEzer* 23:3.)

שֶׁלֹּא יְהֵא רַךְ לָזֶה That it should not be soft toward this one. "A judge is required to treat each of the two litigants appearing before him as equals in all matters. He must not allow one of them to speak at length, if he cuts the other one short. He must not be friendly toward one and speak to him softly, if he is unfriendly to the other and speaks to him harshly." (*Rambam, Sefer Shofetim, Hilkhot Sanhedrin* 21:1; *Shulḥan Arukh, Ḥoshen Mishpat* 17:1.)

וְהֵן מְעִידִים אוֹתוֹ מֵאֲלֵיהֶן And they testify on his behalf

TRANSLATION AND COMMENTARY

on their own, and it is later proved that they testified falsely, [1]the husband **is not flogged** and **he does not pay the hundred-shekel** fine, because he did not prevail upon the witnesses to offer false testimony. [2]But even though the husband is not punished if he did not ask the witnesses to testify on his behalf, his wife **and the witnesses who** are found to have **conspired** to give false testimony **against her are hastened to the place of stoning** for execution."

היא וְזוֹמְמֶיהָ סָלְקָא דַּעְתָּךְ [3]Before considering the first clause and the ruling that applies to the husband, the Gemara raises an internal difficulty found in the second clause regarding the wife and the witnesses. **Do you really think,** asks the Gemara, that a case can occur in which both the wife **herself** ***and*** **the witnesses who conspired** to give false testimony **against her are hastened to the place of stoning?** Surely if the witnesses' testimony is upheld and the wife is found guilty of adultery, she alone is executed. And if the witnesses are proved to have conspired to give false testimony against her, they receive the penalty they had sought to inflict on the woman. They are executed, and she is exonerated! How, then, can the Baraita speak of a case in which both the wife and the witnesses are put to death?

אֶלָּא [4]**Rather,** answers the Gemara, the Baraita must be understood as follows: **Either** the wife **herself** (if the testimony is upheld) **or the witnesses who conspired** to give false testimony **against her** (if the witnesses are proved to have perjured themselves) **are hastened to the place of stoning** for execution.

טַעֲמָא דְּלָא אֲמַר לְהוּ [5]The Gemara now draws an inference from the first clause of the Baraita. It seems from the Baraita that **the reason** why the husband is not punished, even though the witnesses have been proved to have testified falsely, **is that he did not ask them** at the outset **to testify** against his wife. [6]**But** it follows from this that **if** the husband **did** in fact **ask them to testify** that his wife had committed adultery during the period of her betrothal, **even though he did not** offer to **pay them** for their testimony, then **he is subject** to both the flogging and the fine. [7]**This ruling** by the Baraita **comes to exclude the opinion of Rabbi Yehudah,** who maintains otherwise, [8]**as was taught** in another Baraita: **"Rabbi Yehudah says:** A husband who falsely accuses his wife of adultery **is not subject** to flogging or to the fine **unless he hired the witnesses** to testify against his wife."

מַאי טַעֲמָא דְּרַבִּי יְהוּדָה [9]The Gemara now seeks Scriptural support for Rabbi Yehudah's position and asks: **What is the reason** why **Rabbi Yehudah** exempts the husband from punishment if he did not hire the witnesses to testify against his wife?

מְאַלֵּיהֶן, [1]הוּא אֵינוֹ לוֹקֶה וְאֵינוֹ נוֹתֵן מֵאָה סְלָעִים. [2]הִיא וְזוֹמְמֶיהָ מַקְדִּימִין לְבֵית הַסְּקִילָה".

[3]הִיא וְזוֹמְמֶיהָ סָלְקָא דַּעְתָּךְ? [4]אֶלָּא, אוֹ הִיא אוֹ זוֹמְמֶיהָ מַקְדִּימִין לְבֵית הַסְּקִילָה. [5]טַעֲמָא דְּלָא אֲמַר לְהוּ. [6]הָא אֲמַר לְהוּ, אַף עַל גַּב דְּלָא אַגְרִינְהוּ. [7]לְאַפּוּקֵי מִדְּרַבִּי יְהוּדָה, [8]דְּתַנְיָא: "רַבִּי יְהוּדָה אוֹמֵר: אֵינוֹ חַיָּיב עַד שֶׁיִּשְׂכּוֹר עֵדִים".

[9]מַאי טַעֲמָא דְּרַבִּי יְהוּדָה?

LITERAL TRANSLATION

[1]he is not flogged and he does not pay the hundred sela'im. [2]She and the witnesses who conspired against her hasten to the place of stoning."

[3]Can it enter your mind [that] she *and* the witnesses who conspired against her [are stoned]?

[4]Rather, either she or the witnesses who conspired against her hasten to the place of stoning.

[5]The reason is that he did not tell them [to testify]. [6]But [if] he told them [to testify], even though he did not hire them, [he is liable]. [7][This ruling is] to exclude [the opinion of] Rabbi Yehudah, [8]for it was taught: "Rabbi Yehudah says: He is not liable unless he hires witnesses."

[9]What is the reason of Rabbi Yehudah?

BACKGROUND

עַד שֶׁיִּשְׂכּוֹר עֵדִים **Unless he hires witnesses.** If a husband accuses his wife of not having been a virgin when he married her, and witnesses come forward of their own accord and testify that she lost her virginity by committing adultery while she was betrothed to him, and if it is proved that the witnesses are false, they are punished. The husband is not responsible for their action, since he himself did not accuse her of the transgression of adultery but only of deceit (as clarified in the first chapter of this tractate).

Therefore, in order for the husband to be considered responsible for the false testimony by which the woman is placed in danger of execution, he must himself have caused the false witnesses to testify. This follows logically from the case itself, but in the opinion of Rabbi Yehudah it is not sufficient for the husband verbally to induce the witnesses to perjure themselves. He must also perform a physical action, such as paying them to testify falsely.

NOTES

poor, nor honor the person of the mighty; but in righteousness you shall judge your neighbor." Thus it is reasonable to interpret the next verse as being addressed to a judge, forbidding him to speak gently to one of the litigants and harshly to the other.

HALAKHAH

on their own. "If the husband did not ask the witnesses to come to testify against his wife, but they come to testify against her of their own volition, the witnesses are subject to the death penalty if they are found to have conspired against the woman, while the husband is exempt from all punishment." (*Rambam, Sefer Nashim, Hilkhot Na'arah Betulah* 3:11; *Tur, Even HaEzer* 177.)

SAGES

רַב יוֹסֵף צִידוֹנִי Rav Yosef of Sidon. From the context here it appears that this Sage was a Palestinian Amora, and that he transmitted a Baraita in the name of the Sages of the School of Rabbi Shimon ben Yoḥai. Some authorities suggest that he is to be identified with Rabbi Yose Zaidan, who is mentioned in the Jerusalem Talmud and was a Palestinian Amora of the third and fourth generation and a disciple of Rabbi Yirmeyah.

רַבִּי יִרְמְיָה Rabbi Yirmeyah. An Amora of the third and fourth generations. See *Ketubot*, Part II, p. 231.

LITERAL TRANSLATION

[1] Rabbi Abbahu said: "Laying" is derived from "laying." [2] It is written here: "And he lays accusing speeches against her," [3] and it is written there: "You shall not lay interest upon him." [4] Just as there [the verse refers to] money, [5] so too here [the verse refers to] money. [6] Rav Naḥman bar Yitzḥak said: [7] And similarly Rav Yosef of Sidon taught in the School of Rabbi Shimon ben Yoḥai: [8] "Laying" is derived from "laying."

[9] Rabbi Yirmeyah asked: [If] he hired them with land, what is [the law]? [10] With less than the value of a perutah, what is [the law]? [11] Both of them with a perutah, what is [the law]?

[12] Rav Ashi asked: [If] he put out a bad name

[1] אָמַר רַבִּי אַבָּהוּ: אָתְיָא ״שִׂימָה״ ״שִׂימָה״. [2] כְּתִיב הָכָא: ״וְשָׂם לָהּ עֲלִילֹת דְּבָרִים״, [3] וּכְתִיב הָתָם: ״לֹא תְשִׂימוּן עָלָיו נֶשֶׁךְ״. [4] מָה לְהַלָּן מָמוֹן, [5] אַף כָּאן מָמוֹן. [6] אָמַר רַב נַחְמָן בַּר יִצְחָק: [7] וְכֵן תָּנֵי רַב יוֹסֵף צִידוֹנִי בֵּי רַבִּי שִׁמְעוֹן בֶּן יוֹחַאי: [8] אָתְיָא ״שִׂימָה״ ״שִׂימָה״.

[9] בָּעֵי רַבִּי יִרְמְיָה: שְׂכָרָן בְּקַרְקַע, מַהוּ? [10] בְּפָחוֹת מִשָּׁוֶה פְּרוּטָה, מַהוּ? [11] שְׁנֵיהֶם בִּפְרוּטָה, מַהוּ?

[12] בָּעֵי רַב אַשִׁי: הוֹצִיא שֵׁם רַע

RASHI

שכרן בקרקע — לרבי יהודה, מהו? כיון דמרבית גמר — כסף או אוכל בעינן, דהוו מטלטלין, כדכתיב לענין רבית. או דלמא לממון הוא דגמר גזרה שוה, ואפילו מקרקעי.

TRANSLATION AND COMMENTARY

אָמַר רַבִּי אַבָּהוּ [1] The Gemara explains: The meaning of the term **"laying"** mentioned with respect to the husband who falsely accuses his wife **is derived from** another mention of the term **"laying"** found elsewhere. [2] **Here** (Deuteronomy 22:14) **the verse says: "And he lays [וְשָׂם] accusing speeches against her,"** [3] **and elsewhere** (Exodus 22:24) **the verse says: "You shall not lay [תְּשִׂימוּן] interest upon him."** [4] **Just as there,** with respect to forbidden interest, **the verse refers to** a "laying" of **money,** [5] **so too here,** with respect to the slanderer, **the verse refers to** the "laying" of accusations by means of **money** paid to the witnesses who were hired to offer false testimony. [6] Confirming that this is indeed the Scriptural source for Rabbi Yehudah's viewpoint, **Rav Naḥman bar Yitzḥak said:** [7] **And similarly** we find that **Rav Yosef of Sidon taught in the School of Rabbi Shimon ben Yoḥai:** [8] The meaning of the term **"laying"** mentioned with respect to the slanderer **is derived from** the mention of that same term **"laying"** with respect to the prohibition against charging interest.

בָּעֵי רַבִּי יִרְמְיָה [9] **Rabbi Yirmeyah asked:** According to the viewpoint of Rabbi Yehudah that the slanderer is only subject to punishment if he hired the witnesses who testified falsely against his wife, **what is the law if he hired them** to testify against her in exchange **for land?** Do we say that since this provision of the law is learned from the prohibition of interest, the slanderer is not liable unless he hired the witnesses and promised to pay them with money or movable goods, for these — and not land — are governed by the laws of interest? On the other hand, do we derive from the prohibition of interest that the witnesses must be hired by the husband, and it makes no difference what they are promised in exchange for their testimony? [10] Rabbi Yirmeyah raised two further questions regarding the viewpoint of Rabbi Yehudah: **What is the law** if the husband hired the witnesses **with less than the value of a perutah?** [11] And **what is the law** if he hired **both of them with a** single **perutah?** Do we say that the husband must hire the witnesses with what is considered money with respect to the prohibition of interest, and less than the value of a perutah is not considered money? Or do we derive from the prohibition of interest merely that the witnesses must be hired by the husband, but their pay does not have to meet the ordinary standards of what is considered money? The Gemara leaves Rabbi Yirmeyah's questions unanswered.

בָּעֵי רַב אַשִׁי [12] **Rav Ashi** also **asked** a number of questions regarding the laws of slander: **What is the law if** a man marries a woman and then divorces her, and, after marrying her a second time, **falsely accuses**

NOTES

אָתְיָא ״שִׂימָה״ ״שִׂימָה״ "Laying" is derived from "laying." *Tosafot* notes that this is not a real *gezerah shavah,* for if it were, there would be no justification for Rabbi Yirmeyah's questions regarding hiring the witnesses by paying them with land or with less than the value of a perutah. The same is implied by *Ritva,* who says that Rabbi Yehudah derives the husband's exemption from punishment — if he did not hire the witnesses to testify against his wife — from the unusual phrasing of the verse discussing the slanderer, "And he lays [וְשָׂם] accusing speeches against her." The term וְשָׂם, which is not usually used in connection with speech, teaches that the husband is only liable if he slandered his wife by means of the money laid before the witnesses as payment for their false testimony.

TRANSLATION AND COMMENTARY

her about their first marriage, claiming that when he married her the first time she was not a virgin, and that she committed adultery while betrothed to him? Furthermore, a man whose brother died without bearing children is obliged by Torah law to take his widowed sister-in-law as his levirate wife or to grant her *ḥalitzah*. [1] **What is the law** if a man marries the widow of his deceased brother and then falsely accuses her **about her marriage** to **his brother,** claiming that when his brother married her she was not a virgin, and that she committed adultery while she was betrothed to his brother? Is the slanderer subject to flogging and to the hundred-shekel fine in these cases?

פְּשׁוֹט מֵיהָא חֲדָא [2] The Gemara answers: We can **resolve** at least **one of the** two **questions** posed by Rav Ashi **from the following** Baraita **taught by Rabbi Yonah,** which stated: [3] "The verse says (Deuteronomy 22:16): 'And the father of the *na'arah* shall say to the elders: **"I gave my daughter to this man** as a wife."' The emphasis placed here on the man to whom the father gave his daughter in marriage teaches us that the laws of slander apply only if the false accusations were brought by [4] **'this man,'** the man to whom the *na'arah* was originally given in marriage, **but not** if the charge of adultery was later brought **by the *yavam*,** the brother-in-law who took her as his levirate wife after his brother's death."

מַאי רַבָּנַן [5] In the course of a previous discussion (above, 45b), reference was made to a difference of opinion between Rabbi Eliezer ben Ya'akov and the Rabbis. The Gemara now asks: **What are the opinions of the Rabbis and Rabbi Eliezer ben Ya'akov** alluded to earlier in the Gemara?

דְּתַנְיָא [6] The Gemara answers: The dispute **was recorded** in the following Baraita: **"How does** the transgression of **falsely accusing one's wife** of adultery **occur?** [7] **If the husband comes to court and says** to his father-in-law: **'So-and-so, I did not find your daughter a virgin** when I married her,' [8] and **there are witnesses that she committed adultery while** she was betrothed **to him, she is entitled to a ketubah of a maneh."**

עַל הַנִּישּׂוּאִין הָרִאשׁוֹנִים, מַהוּ? [1] עַל נִשּׂוּאֵי אָחִיו, מַהוּ? [2] פְּשׁוֹט מֵיהָא חֲדָא, דְּתָנֵי רַבִּי יוֹנָה: [3] "'אֶת בִּתִּי נָתַתִּי לָאִישׁ הַזֶּה'. [4] לָזֶה, וְלֹא לְיָבָם". [5] מַאי רַבָּנַן וּמַאי רַבִּי אֱלִיעֶזֶר בֶּן יַעֲקֹב? [6] דְּתַנְיָא: "כֵּיצַד הוֹצָאַת שֵׁם רַע? [7] בָּא לְבֵית דִּין וְאָמַר: 'פְּלוֹנִי, לֹא מָצָאתִי לְבִתְּךָ בְּתוּלִים', [8] אִם יֵשׁ עֵדִים שֶׁזִּינְּתָה תַּחְתָּיו, יֵשׁ לָהּ כְּתוּבָּה מָנֶה".

LITERAL TRANSLATION

about the first marriage, what is [the law]? [1] About his brother's marriage, what is [the law]? [2] Resolve one [of the questions] from the following, for Rabbi Yonah taught: [3] "'I gave my daughter to this man.' [4] To this [man], and not to a *yavam*." [5] What is [the opinion of] the Rabbis and what is [the opinion of] Rabbi Eliezer ben Ya'akov? [6] For it was taught: "How [does] putting out a bad name [about one's wife occur]? [7] [If the husband] came to court and said: 'So-and-so, I have not found in your daughter virginity,' [8] if there are witnesses that she committed adultery [while] with him, she has a ketubah of a maneh."

RASHI

על נשואין הראשונים — כנסה, ולא הוציא שם רע, וגרשה, והחזירה, ואחר כך מוציא שם רע: לא מצאתי בתולים לנישואין קמאי. **ולא ליבם** — אין יבם שהוציא שם רע על נישואי אחיו בכלל פרשה זו, לטעון טענת בתולים. איפשיטא ליה בעיא בתרייתא.

TERMINOLOGY

פְּשׁוֹט מֵיהָא חֲדָא Resolve one of the questions from the following. Sometimes, after posing a series of questions, the Gemara cites a source providing an answer to at least one of them. In such cases the Gemara may state: "Solve one of the questions just raised on the basis of this source."

SAGES

רַבִּי יוֹנָה Rabbi Yonah. A Palestinian Amora of the fourth generation. See *Ketubot*, Part II, p. 127.

NOTES

עַל הַנִּישּׂוּאִין הָרִאשׁוֹנִים About the first marriage. Our commentary follows *Rashi* and others, who explain that in this case the woman was fully married to her husband the first time, and similarly in the next case she was fully married to her husband before he died and she married his brother. *Rambam* and *Meiri* appear to understand the cases differently — that in the first case the woman had only been betrothed the first time, and similarly in the

HALAKHAH

עַל הַנִּישּׂוּאִין הָרִאשׁוֹנִים About the first marriage. "If a man betroths a girl and divorces her, and then remarries her and slanders her, bringing witnesses who testify that she committed adultery while she was betrothed to him the first time, and the witnesses are later refuted, the husband is exempt." Even though the Gemara did not decide on the matter, *Rambam* issued a lenient ruling. (*Rambam, Sefer Nashim, Hilkhot Na'arah Betulah* 3:9.)

עַל נִשּׂוּאֵי אָחִיו About his brother's marriage. "If a man marries (by levirate marriage) his deceased brother's widow and slanders her, bringing witnesses who testify that she committed adultery while she was betrothed to his brother, and the witnesses are later refuted, he is exempt," following the Gemara's conclusion. (*Rambam, Sefer Nashim, Hilkhot Na'arah Betulah* 3:9.)

כֵּיצַד הוֹצָאַת שֵׁם רַע How does putting out a bad name about one's wife occur? "How does a husband falsely accuse his wife of adultery? If he comes to court and

TRANSLATION AND COMMENTARY

אִם יֵשׁ עֵדִים [1]The Gemara interrupts its presentation of the Baraita and expresses its astonishment at the Baraita's ruling: **If there are witnesses** who testify **that she committed adultery while betrothed** to her husband, [2]how can the Baraita say that **she has a ketubah of a maneh?** [3]Surely such a woman **is punished by stoning!**

הָכִי קָאָמַר [4]The Gemara explains that the Baraita meant to **say as follows: If there are witnesses** who testify **that she committed adultery while betrothed** to her husband, **she is put to death by stoning.** [5]But **if** it turns out that she did not commit adultery but **she fornicated** with another man **before** her betrothal, and thus lost her virginity while she was still single, **she is entitled to a ketubah of a maneh** — the amount due to a woman who was not a virgin at the time of her marriage.

נִמְצָא [6]The Gemara now continues with its presentation of the Baraita: **"If it is found that the slander was baseless,** and that the girl was indeed a virgin at the time of her marriage, [7]the husband **is flogged and pays the** fine of a **hundred sela'im.** [8]He is subject to these punishments in all cases, **whether he had** sexual **intercourse** with his wife after he married her and then put forward the claim that he had not found physical evidence of her virginity, **or** whether **he did not have intercourse** with her and based his claim on the testimony of witnesses. [9]**Rabbi Eliezer ben Ya'akov** disagrees and **says:** [10]**These provisions** of the law — the flogging and the fine — **apply only if** the husband **had** sexual **intercourse** with his wife after he married her and then slandered her, claiming that he had found no signs of virginity and falsely accusing her of adultery."

[1]אִם יֵשׁ עֵדִים שֶׁזִּינְּתָה תַּחְתָּיו, [2]יֵשׁ לָהּ כְּתוּבָּה מָנֶה?! [3]בַּת סְקִילָה הִיא!

[4]הָכִי קָאָמַר: אִם יֵשׁ עֵדִים שֶׁזִּינְּתָה תַּחְתָּיו, בִּסְקִילָה. [5]זִינְּתָה מֵעִיקָּרָא, יֵשׁ לָהּ כְּתוּבָּה מָנֶה.

[6]״נִמְצָא שֶׁשֵּׁם רַע אֵינוֹ שֵׁם רַע, [7]הוּא לוֹקֶה וְנוֹתֵן מֵאָה סֶלַע, [8]בֵּין בָּעַל וּבֵין לֹא בָּעַל. [9]רַבִּי אֱלִיעֶזֶר בֶּן יַעֲקֹב אוֹמֵר: [10]לֹא נֶאֶמְרוּ דְּבָרִים הַלָּלוּ אֶלָּא כְּשֶׁבָּעַל״.

LITERAL TRANSLATION

[1]If there are witnesses that she committed adultery [while] with him, [2]she has a ketubah of a maneh?! [3]She is subject to stoning!

[4]Thus it said: If there are witnesses that she committed adultery [while] with him, [she is executed] by stoning. [5][If] she fornicated before that (lit., "from the beginning"), she has a ketubah of a maneh.

[6]"[If] it is found that the bad name was not a bad name, [7]he is flogged and he pays the hundred sela'im [8]whether he had intercourse or he did not have intercourse. [9]Rabbi Eliezer ben Ya'akov says: [10]These things were only said if he had intercourse."

RASHI

זינתה מעיקרא יש לה כתובה מנה — קסבר: כנסה בחזקת בתולה ונמצאת בעולה — יש לה כתובה מנה.

NOTES

second case, she had only been betrothed to her husband before he died and she then married his brother.

Even though the Gemara answered only the second of Rav Ashi's two questions, *Rambam* ruled that the husband is exempt from punishment in the first case as well (see Halakhah), prompting the later commentators to seek a source for that ruling. Some suggest that *Rambam* issued his ruling in accordance with the Jerusalem Talmud, even though the Jerusalem Talmud does not address itself directly to this case. Others argue that since the girl has left her father's authority, the laws of slander no longer apply. Others maintain that this ruling is inferred from the ruling in the case in which the husband died and his brother married his widow. Since the brother marries his sister-in-law as his brother's replacement, the case of the brother-in-law may be seen as parallel to that of a man who marries, divorces, and then marries the same woman a second time. And since the Gemara rules that the laws of slander do not apply to the brother-in-law, it follows that they also do not apply to the man who marries the same woman a second time (*Birkat Avraham*).

HALAKHAH

claims that he had intercourse with his wife (who is a *na'arah*) but found no signs of virginity, and after investigating the matter he finds witnesses who say that she committed adultery while betrothed to him, and the witnesses come and testify, and the court examines their testimony and it is found to be true, the wife is executed by stoning. But if the girl's father brings witnesses who refute the testimony of the husband's witnesses and give evidence that the husband's witnesses conspired to give false evidence against the girl, the first pair of witnesses are executed by stoning, and the husband is flogged and pays a 100 shekel fine." *Rambam* rules in accordance with the viewpoint of Rabbi Eliezer ben Ya'akov, following the general rule that the rulings of Rabbi Eliezer ben Ya'akov are authoritative, and because the Gemara's conclusion appears to support him. (*Rambam, Sefer Nashim, Hilkhot Na'arah Betulah* 3:6.)

[1]בִּשְׁלָמָא לְרַבִּי אֱלִיעֶזֶר בֶּן יַעֲקֹב, [2]הַיְינוּ דִּכְתִיב: ״וּבָא אֵלֶיהָ״ [3]״וָאֶקְרַב אֵלֶיהָ״. [4]אֶלָּא לְרַבָּנַן, מַאי: ״וּבָא אֵלֶיהָ״ [5]״וָאֶקְרַב אֵלֶיהָ״?

[6]״וּבָא אֵלֶיהָ״ — בַּעֲלִילוֹת. [7]״וָאֶקְרַב אֵלֶיהָ״ — בִּדְבָרִים.

[8]בִּשְׁלָמָא לְרַבִּי אֱלִיעֶזֶר בֶּן יַעֲקֹב, הַיְינוּ דִּכְתִיב ״לֹא מָצָאתִי לְבִתְּךָ בְּתוּלִים״. [9]אֶלָּא לְרַבָּנַן, מַאי: [10]״לֹא מָצָאתִי לְבִתְּךָ בְּתוּלִים״?

[11]״לֹא מָצָאתִי לְבִתְּךָ כְּשֵׁרֵי בְתוּלִים״.

[12]בִּשְׁלָמָא לְרַבִּי אֱלִיעֶזֶר בֶּן יַעֲקֹב, הַיְינוּ דִּכְתִיב: [13]״וְאֵלֶּה בְּתוּלֵי בִתִּי״. [14]אֶלָּא לְרַבָּנַן, מַאי: [15]״וְאֵלֶּה בְּתוּלֵי בִתִּי״?

LITERAL TRANSLATION

[1]Granted according to Rabbi Eliezer ben Ya'akov, [2]this is why it is written: "And he goes in to her" [and] [3]"and I came near to her." [4]But according to the Rabbis, what is [meant by]: "And he goes in to her" [and] [5]"and I came near to her"?

[6]"And he goes in to her" — with false accusations. [7]"And I came near to her" — with words.

[8]Granted according to Rabbi Eliezer ben Ya'akov, this is why it is written: "I have not found in your daughter virginity." [9]But according to the Rabbis, what is [meant by]: [10]"I have not found in your daughter virginity"?

[11]"I have not found for your daughter proofs to confirm her virginity."

[12]Granted according to Rabbi Eliezer ben Ya'akov, this is why it is written: [13]"And these are the tokens of my daughter's virginity." [14]But according to the Rabbis, what is [meant by]: [15]"And these are the tokens of my daughter's virginity"?

TRANSLATION AND COMMENTARY

בִּשְׁלָמָא [1]The Gemara now considers these two opinions in the light of the Biblical text upon which the laws of slander are based. **Granted that according to Rabbi Eliezer ben Ya'akov,** who maintains that the laws of slander apply only if the husband had intercourse with his wife, [2]we can understand **why the verse says** (Deuteronomy 22:13): "If a man takes a wife, **and he goes in to her"** [3]**and** why the next verse (verse 14) says: "I took this woman **and I came near to her."** Rabbi Eliezer ben Ya'akov explains the expressions "goes in" and "came near" that appear in these two verses according to their plain sense — as referring to sexual intercourse. [4]**But according to the Rabbis,** who maintain that the laws of slander apply even if the husband did not have intercourse with his wife, **what is meant by** the expressions **"and he goes in to her"** and [5]**"and I came near to her"?** What else can these expressions mean, if not sexual intercourse?

״וּבָא אֵלֶיהָ״ [6]The Gemara answers: The Rabbis interpret these expressions as follows: **"And he goes in to her"** means that he makes **accusations** regarding her virginity, even though he has never had intercourse with her. [7]**"And I came near to her"** means that he accuses **with words,** charging her with adultery, even though he has never had intercourse with her.

בִּשְׁלָמָא [8]The Gemara now considers the meaning of the latter part of this last verse according to Rabbi Eliezer ben Ya'akov and the Rabbis. **Granted that according to Rabbi Eliezer ben Ya'akov** we can understand **why the verse says: "I have not found in your daughter virginity."** According to Rabbi Eliezer ben Ya'akov, the husband maintained that he engaged in intercourse with his wife but did not find any physical evidence that she was a virgin at that time. [9]**But according to the Rabbis, what** does the husband **mean** when he says: [10]**"I have not found in your daughter virginity"?** If he has not had intercourse with her, how can he justify his claim that his wife was not a virgin?

לֹא מָצָאתִי [11]The Gemara explains: According to the Rabbis, what the husband means to say is as follows: "I have witnesses who claim that your daughter committed adultery during her betrothal, and **I have not found** other **witnesses for your daughter who can** refute their testimony and **confirm that she is** still **a virgin."**

בִּשְׁלָמָא [12]The Gemara now tries to understand the father-in-law's counterclaim according to the viewpoints of Rabbi Eliezer ben Ya'akov and of the Rabbis. **Granted that according to Rabbi Eliezer ben Ya'akov** we can understand **why the verse says** (verse 17): [13]**"And these are the tokens of my daughter's virginity."** According to Rabbi Eliezer ben Ya'akov, the girl's father counters the husband's accusation by saying that he has demonstrable proof that his daughter was a virgin at the time of her marriage, for he can produce the sheet that was soiled by her hymenal blood. [14]**But according to the Rabbis, what** does the father **mean** when he says: [15]**"And these are the tokens of my daughter's virginity"?** If the husband did not

RASHI

כשרי בתולים — עדים שיזימו לו יכחישו את אלו, ויכשירו את בתך לבתולה גמורה.

TRANSLATION AND COMMENTARY

have intercourse with his wife, what physical evidence can the father produce to defend his daughter against the charge of adultery?

וְאֵלֶּה כָּשְׁרֵי בְּתוּלֵי בִתִּי [1]The Gemara answers: The Rabbis interpret the father-in-law's claim in the following manner: The father says: **"And these witnesses can** refute the testimony of your witnesses and can **confirm that my daughter is** still **a virgin."**

בִּשְׁלָמָא [2]The Gemara now explains one last passage in accordance with each of the two views. **Granted that according to Rabbi Eliezer ben Ya'akov** we can understand **why the verse says** (verse 17): [3]**"And they shall spread the cloth."** Rabbi Eliezer ben Ya'akov explains the verse according to its plain sense — that the sheet on which the couple had intercourse is brought before the court and examined for traces of hymenal blood. [4]**But according to the Rabbis,** who maintain that the laws of slander apply even if the husband did not have intercourse with his wife, **what is the meaning of** the expression: [5]**"And they shall spread the cloth"?**

אָמַר רַבִּי אֲבָהוּ [6]**Rabbi Abbahu said:** The Rabbis interpret the passage as follows: The court **examines** the accusations **that** the husband **laid against her,** and investigates the credibility of the testimony of the husband's witnesses vis-à-vis the testimony of the witnesses brought by his father-in-law. Rabbi Abbahu cites a Baraita that elaborates on the two possible interpretations of this verse. [7]**For it was taught** in a Baraita: "The verse states: **'And they shall spread the cloth.'** [8]**This teaches that the** husband's **witnesses and the** father-in-law's **witnesses come, and** the court **clarifies the matter as if** it were examining **a new garment.** This is the meaning of the verse according to the Rabbis, who maintain that the laws of slander apply even if the husband brought his accusations against his wife without having had intercourse with her. They understand the spreading of the cloth as a metaphor for the careful examination of the various testimonies

[1]"וְאֵלֶּה כָּשְׁרֵי בְּתוּלֵי בִתִּי". [2]בִּשְׁלָמָא לְרַבִּי אֱלִיעֶזֶר בֶּן יַעֲקֹב, הַיְינוּ דִּכְתִיב: [3]"וּפָרְשׂוּ הַשִּׂמְלָה". [4]אֶלָּא לְרַבָּנַן, מַאי: [5]"וּפָרְשׂוּ הַשִּׂמְלָה"?
[6]אָמַר רַבִּי אֲבָהוּ: פָּרְשׂוּ מַה שֶּׁשָּׂם לָהּ. [7]כִּדְתַנְיָא: "'וּפָרְשׂוּ הַשִּׂמְלָה'. [8]מְלַמֵּד שֶׁבָּאִין עֵדִים שֶׁל זֶה וְעֵדִים שֶׁל זֶה, וּבוֹרְרִין אֶת הַדָּבָר כְּשִׂמְלָה חֲדָשָׁה.

LITERAL TRANSLATION

[1]"And these proofs can confirm my daughter's virginity."

[2]Granted according to Rabbi Eliezer ben Ya'akov, this is why it is written: [3]"And they shall spread the cloth." [4]But according to the Rabbis, what is [meant by]: [5]"And they shall spread the cloth"?

[6]Rabbi Abbahu said: They examine what he laid against her. [7]As it was taught: "'And they shall spread the cloth.' [8][This] teaches that the witnesses of this one come and the witnesses of that one come, and they clarify the matter like a new cloth.

RASHI

כשרי בתולי בתי — עדים המזימין את עדיו.

NOTES

פָּרְשׂוּ מַה שֶּׁשָּׂם לָהּ They examine what he laid against her. *Tosafot* and *Ritva* note that Rabbi Abbahu is not suggesting that the word שִׂמְלָה ("cloth, garment") is to be understood as if it were written as two words שָׂם לָהּ ("he laid against her"), for that is clearly not the way the word is understood in the Baraita that the Gemara immediately cites to support Rabbi Abbahu's interpretation. Rather, Rabbi Abbahu explains the verse as does the Baraita — that the court must clarify the matter as if it were examining a new garment. The phrase מַה שֶּׁשָּׂם לָהּ is merely an allusion to the earlier verse (verse 14): "And he laid against her [וְשָׂם לָהּ] accusing speeches." In any event, Rabbi Abbahu does not explain the verse according to its plain meaning. The Jerusalem Talmud cites a Baraita taught by Rabbi Yishmael, according to which this is one of three Scriptural verses that must be understood as metaphors. Here the spreading of the cloth must be taken as a metaphor for the clarification of the matter, or as *Rambam* puts it, "a discussion of the hidden aspects of the matter." It appears from the Jerusalem Talmud that this is the interpretation of the verse, not only according to the Rabbis, but also according to Rabbi Eliezer ben Ya'akov (see commentaries to the Jerusalem Talmud, *Kesef Mishneh* cited in the Halakhah section, and the next note).

HALAKHAH

"וּפָרְשׂוּ הַשִּׂמְלָה" "And they shall spread the cloth." "The expression, 'And they shall spread the cloth,' is an oblique way of saying that the court must investigate the covert aspects of the matter. Similarly, the verse, 'And these are the tokens of my daughter's virginity,' refers to the father-in-law's witnesses who refute the testimony of the witnesses brought by the husband." *Kesef Mishneh* notes that it is strange that *Rambam* explains these verses as did the Rabbis, while he rules in accordance with Rabbi Eliezer ben Ya'akov. *Kesef Mishneh* suggests that, according to *Rambam*, even Rabbi Eliezer ben Ya'akov agrees with the Rabbis' interpretation that the matter can only be clarified by the evidence of witnesses, and not by the examination of the bedsheet alone. (*Rambam, Sefer Nashim, Hilkhot Na'arah Betulah* 3:12.)

LITERAL TRANSLATION

[1] Rabbi Eliezer ben Ya'akov says: The words are [to be understood] as they were written — [2] a cloth, literally."

[3] Rabbi Yitzḥak the son of Rav Ya'akov bar Giyyore sent in the name of Rabbi Yoḥanan: [4] Even though we do not find in the entire Torah that Scripture distinguished between natural intercourse and unnatural intercourse with respect to flogging and punishments, [5] nevertheless [regarding] someone who puts out a bad name [about his wife] it distinguished. [6] [For] he is not liable unless he has intercourse [even] in an unnatural manner, [7] and he puts out a bad name [that she had intercourse] in a natural manner.

[1]רַבִּי אֱלִיעֶזֶר בֶּן יַעֲקֹב אוֹמֵר: דְּבָרִים כִּכְתָבָן, [2]שִׂמְלָה מַמָּשׁ״.
[3]שָׁלַח רַבִּי יִצְחָק בַּר רַב יַעֲקֹב בַּר גִּיּוֹרֵי מִשְּׁמֵיהּ דְּרַבִּי יוֹחָנָן:
[4]אַף עַל גַּב שֶׁלֹּא מָצִינוּ בְּכָל הַתּוֹרָה כּוּלָּהּ שֶׁחִלֵּק הַכָּתוּב בֵּין בִּיאָה כְּדַרְכָּהּ לְבִיאָה שֶׁלֹּא כְּדַרְכָּהּ לְמַכּוֹת וּלְעוֹנָשִׁין, [5]אֲבָל מוֹצִיא שֵׁם רַע חִלֵּק. [6]אֵינוֹ חַיָּיב עַד שֶׁיִּבְעוֹל שֶׁלֹּא כְּדַרְכָּהּ, [7]וְיוֹצִיא שֵׁם רַע כְּדַרְכָּהּ.

TRANSLATION AND COMMENTARY

brought before the court. [1] **Rabbi Eliezer ben Ya'akov says:** The laws of slander apply only if the husband had intercourse with his wife and claimed that he found no signs of her virginity. Hence **the words** of this verse **are to be understood as they were written.** [2] **'The cloth'** is to be understood **literally** — the court spreads out the cloth on which the couple had intercourse and examines it for physical evidence that can shed light on the matter."

שָׁלַח The Gemara continues: [3] **Rabbi Yitzḥak the son of Rav Ya'akov bar Giyyore sent** a ruling **in the name of Rabbi Yoḥanan** from Eretz Israel to Babylonia: [4] **Even though we do not find in the entire Torah that Scripture distinguishes between natural** (vaginal) **intercourse and unnatural** (anal) **intercourse,** neither **with respect to** the punishment of **flogging nor** with respect to any other **punishments,** [5] **nevertheless regarding slander** Scripture does indeed **distinguish.** The verse (Leviticus 18:22), "You shall not lie with a man in the *ways of lying* with a woman (מִשְׁכְּבֵי אִשָּׁה)," teaches that there are two ways of "lying with a woman" that can incur punishment by Torah law. Thus, in all cases of prohibited sexual intercourse, the offending parties are liable for punishment, whether the man had intercourse with the woman vaginally or anally. [6] But regarding the case of slander, the husband **is not liable unless he had intercourse** with his wife, **even** if it was **in an unnatural manner,** [7] **and he falsely accuses her about intercourse** that was performed **in a natural manner.** The husband is only liable if two conditions are met: He must have had intercourse with his wife (and it makes no

RASHI

שלא מצינו שחלק הכתוב — ״משכבי אשה״ כתיב, שני משכבותיה שוין לכל משפט עריות. **במוציא שם רע חלק** — שאם הביא עדים שנבעלה ארוסתו שלא כדרכה, ונמצאו זוממין — אינו נותן מאה סלע. ד״לא מצאתי בתולים״ כתיב, במקום בתולים. **אינו חייב עד שיבעול שלא כדרכה ויוציא שם רע בכדרכה** — כלומר כשבעל נאמרו דברים, ובעילתו אפילו היא שלא כדרכה. כי היכי דלא חלק בשאר עונשין. אבל ביאה של זנות שהוא מוציא לעז עליה — צריך שיאמר על ביאה כדרכה, ולקמן מפרש לה.

SAGES

רַבִּי יִצְחָק בַּר רַב יַעֲקֹב בַּר גִּיּוֹרֵי **Rabbi Yitzḥak the son of Rav Ya'akov bar Giyyore.** A Palestinian Amora of the second and third generations, this Sage was a disciple of Rabbi Yoḥanan and is mentioned in several places in the Talmud as sending responsa to Babylonia in the name of his teacher. The epithet "Bar Giyyore" indicates that his father came from a family of converts.

NOTES

דְּבָרִים כִּכְתָבָן The words are to be understood as they were written. According to the Jerusalem Talmud, even Rabbi Eliezer ben Ya'akov agrees that the verses cannot be taken absolutely literally. For certainly the presence or absence of a bloodstained cloth cannot serve as absolute proof about the wife's virginity one way or the other. Thus the girl cannot possibly be executed or the husband flogged and fined on that basis. Rabbi Eliezer ben Ya'akov must agree that the Torah is referring to a case in which both the husband and the father base their claims on the testimony of witnessess, and the court must decide between the conflicting testimonies. It therefore follows that the Tannaim disagree about whether the verses should be understood to any extent according to their literal sense. The Rabbis maintain that, since the matter must be decided on the basis of the testimony of the witnesses, the literal meaning of the verses should be ignored altogether. Rabbi Eliezer ben Ya'akov maintains that the literal meaning of the verses should be preserved as much as possible.

Most Rishonim explain that, according to Rabbi Eliezer, the husband must claim that he found no physical signs of his wife's virginity; and if he did not make such a claim the laws of slander do not apply. Why is such a claim necessary, if he must also bring witnesses to testify that she committed adultery during the period of her betrothal?

HALAKHAH

שֶׁחִלֵּק הַכָּתוּב בֵּין בִּיאָה כְּדַרְכָּהּ לְבִיאָה שֶׁלֹּא כְּדַרְכָּהּ That Scripture distinguished between natural intercourse and unnatural intercourse. "Someone who engaged in forbidden sexual intercourse is subject to the punishment stated for the particular offense, be it capital punishment, excision, flogging by Torah law, or flogging by Rabbinic enactment. He is subject to the stated punishment whether he had vaginal or anal intercourse," following our Gemara. (*Rambam, Sefer Kedushah, Hilkhot Issurei Bi'ah* 1:10; *Shulḥan Arukh, Even HaEzer* 20:1.)

TRANSLATION AND COMMENTARY

difference whether it was in a natural or in an unnatural manner); he must also have brought a false accusation of adultery against her, supporting that claim with the testimony of witnesses that while she was betrothed she engaged in intercourse with another man in a natural manner. But if the witnesses claim that she had sexual intercourse in an unnatural manner, the husband is not subject to any punishment, for the verse (Deuteronomy 22:14) — "I have not found virginity in her" — teaches us that the accusation brought by the husband against his wife must refer to natural vaginal intercourse.

[1] כְּמַאן? [2] אִי כְּרַבָּנַן, [3] אַף עַל גַּב דְּלָא בָּעַל. [4] אִי כְּרַבִּי אֱלִיעֶזֶר בֶּן יַעֲקֹב, [46B] [5] אִידִי וְאִידִי כְּדַרְכָּהּ בָּעֵינַן! [6] אֶלָּא שְׁלַח רַב כָּהֲנָא מִשְּׁמֵיהּ דְּרַבִּי יוֹחָנָן: [7] אֵינוֹ חַיָּיב עַד שֶׁיִּבְעוֹל כְּדַרְכָּהּ, [8] וְיוֹצִיא שֵׁם רַע בִּכְדַרְכָּהּ.

LITERAL TRANSLATION

[1] In accordance with whom [is this ruling]? [2] If it is in accordance with the Rabbis, [3] [the husband should be liable] even if he did not have intercourse. [4] If it is in accordance with Rabbi Eliezer ben Ya'akov, [46B] [5] [regarding] both this and that we require [intercourse] in a natural manner!

[6] Rather, Rav Kahana sent in the name of Rabbi Yoḥanan: [7] He is not liable unless he has intercourse in a natural manner, [8] and he puts out a bad name [about her that she had intercourse] in a natural manner.

RASHI

אידי ואידי בדרכה בעינן — כיון דלמר דברים ככתבן, היאך אתה קורא "לא מצאתי לה בתולים" אלא אם כן אמר: בעלתיה כדרכה ומצאתיה בעולה?

כְּמַאן [1] The Gemara now seeks to reconcile Rabbi Yoḥanan's ruling with one of the Tannaitic opinions cited above and asks: **In accordance with which** Tanna did Rabbi Yoḥanan issue his **ruling?** [2] **If it is in accordance with** the viewpoint of **the Rabbis,** why does he say that the husband is subject to punishment only if he had intercourse with his wife? [3] The Rabbis maintain that **the husband is liable, even if he did not have intercourse** with her. [4] And **if it is in accordance with** the viewpoint of **Rabbi Eliezer ben Ya'akov,** [46B] why does he say that the husband is liable even if he had intercourse with his wife in an unnatural manner, provided that he falsely accused her about intercourse that was performed in a natural manner? [5] **He should require** that **both** the adulterous **intercourse** and the intercourse between husband and wife had to have been performed **in a natural manner!** For, according to Rabbi Eliezer ben Ya'akov, the Scriptural verses are to be interpreted literally. Thus the husband's charge — "I did not find your daughter a virgin" — means that he failed to find physical evidence of his wife's virginity. The husband cannot make such an accusation unless he engaged in intercourse with his wife in a natural manner.

אֶלָּא [6] The Gemara answers that there is a different version of Rabbi Yoḥanan's ruling. **Rather, Rav Kahana sent** the following ruling **in the name of Rabbi Yoḥanan:** [7] The husband **is not subject** to flogging or to the fine **unless he had intercourse** with his wife **in a natural manner,** [8] **and he** also **falsely accuses her about intercourse** with another man that was performed **in a natural manner.** This ruling is in accordance with the opinion of Rabbi Eliezer ben Ya'akov.

NOTES

Tosafot and *Rosh* explain that the husband is liable if he had the audacity to bring the sheet as evidence that his wife was not a virgin, when in fact the sheet was stained with blood. *Ramban* explains that he is liable only if he compounded his offense, first by claiming that there was no physical evidence of his wife's virginity, and then by bringing false witnesses to support that claim.

According to some Rishonim (see *Rambam, Ra'ah, Ritva,* and *Nimmukei Yosef*), even Rabbi Eliezer ben Ya'akov agrees that the husband is liable if he claims that he did not find physical evidence of his wife's virginity but does not bring evidence to support his claim. "And they shall spread the cloth" merely teaches that the husband is liable only if he had intercourse with his wife.

וְיוֹצִיא שֵׁם רַע בִּכְדַרְכָּהּ And he puts out a bad name about her that she had intercourse in a natural manner. The husband is liable for slander only if he falsely accuses his wife of having committed adultery during the period of their betrothal, supporting that claim with the testimony of witnesses that she engaged in intercourse with another man in a natural manner. But if the witnesses say that she had sexual intercourse in an unnatural manner, and their

HALAKHAH

אֵינוֹ חַיָּיב עַד שֶׁיִּבְעוֹל כְּדַרְכָּהּ He is not liable unless he has intercourse in a natural manner. "A husband who falsely accuses his wife of adultery is not subject to punishment unless he had intercourse with her in a natural manner and also falsely accused her about intercourse performed in a natural manner," following Rabbi Yoḥanan according to the Gemara's conclusion. (*Rambam, Sefer Nashim, Hilkot Na'arah Betulah* 3:10.)

משנה

[1] הָאָב זַכַּאי בְּבִתּוֹ בְּקִידּוּשֶׁיהָ, [2] בְּכֶסֶף, בִּשְׁטָר, וּבְבִיאָה. [3] זַכַּאי בִּמְצִיאָתָהּ,

LITERAL TRANSLATION

MISHNAH [1] A father has authority over his daughter regarding her betrothal, [2] [whether it is] by money, by deed, or by intercourse. [3] He is entitled to what she finds,

RASHI

משנה האב זכאי בבתו — בקטנות ובנערות. בקידושיה בכסף — שכסף קידושיה שלו. ובשטר — שאם קבל שטר אירוסין עליה — הרי זו מקודשת. בביאה — רשאי למוסרה לביאה לשם קידושין.

TRANSLATION AND COMMENTARY

MISHNAH הָאָב זַכַּאי בְּבִתּוֹ [1] This Mishnah outlines the rights a father has with respect to his daughter until she reaches full adulthood or until she marries. **A father has authority over his daughter's betrothal** while she is a minor (under the age of twelve) and also while she is a *na'arah* (between twelve and twelve-and-a-half years of age). A woman may be betrothed in one of three ways: (1) By the transfer of money or something worth money (such as a ring) from the bridegroom to the bride; (2) by a document that the bridegroom hands over to the bride, in which he attests that he is betrothing her; (3) by sexual intercourse. Before a girl has reached majority, [2] her father may accept **money** from the bridegroom for her betrothal, and he may keep the money for himself. He may, alternatively, receive **a deed** of betrothal from the bridegroom on his daughter's behalf. **And** he may, as another possibility, hand his daughter over to the bridegroom so that the latter may betroth her by way of sexual **intercourse.** [3] The father **is** also

NOTES

testimony is refuted, the husband is not subject to any punishment. If, however, the witnesses' testimony is not refuted, the wife is subject to execution, even if she engaged in intercourse in an unnatural manner, for regarding the wife's adultery we follow the general rule that in all cases of prohibited sexual intercourse, the offending party is liable, and that includes intercourse performed in an unnatural manner. *Sifrei* derives this ruling from the Scriptural text, and it would seem to be in conformity even with the opinion of Rabbi Eliezer ben Ya'akov.

הָאָב זַכַּאי בְּבִתּוֹ A father has authority over his daughter. The Rishonim differ about the precise meaning of this sentence — whether the Mishnah is referring to the father's right to arrange his daughter's betrothal or whether it is referring to the financial benefit to which the father is entitled by virtue of that right. Our Gemara appears to understand the Mishnah as referring both to the father's right to arrange his daughter's betrothal and to the financial benefits accruing from this. *Rashi,* too, seems to understand that with respect to betrothal by means of money, the Mishnah is referring to the father's right to the money, whereas with respect to betrothal by means of a deed or by intercourse, it is referring to the father's right to give his daughter away in betrothal.

From the discussion of this Mishnah found in the Jerusalem Talmud, it is evident that the Jerusalem Talmud understood that in all three cases the father is entitled to a financial benefit. It asks: Granted that in the case in which the girl is betrothed by means of money or by means of a deed, the father is entitled to a financial benefit (in the case of a deed, the father may use the paper for his own purposes). But what financial benefit does he acquire when his daughter is betrothed by means of intercourse?

The Jerusalem Talmud explains that the father is entitled to the money that the bridegroom offers in exchange for his being allowed to betroth the girl by means of intercourse (see *Meiri* here, and *Tosafot* on *Kiddushin* 3b).

זַכַּאי בִּמְצִיאָתָהּ He is entitled to what she finds. *Meiri* maintains that the father is entitled to what his daughter finds, even after she is betrothed, provided that she is still a minor or a *na'arah,* i.e., she has not reached the age of twelve-and-a-half. This explains why the provisions of this clause of the Mishnah were not included in the previous clause. The first clause refers to the father's rights with respect to his daughter until she is betrothed, whereas the second clause refers to those rights that continue even after she is betrothed.

Shittah Mekubbetzet explains the matter differently: The father's right to what his daughter finds was not included in the first clause of the Mishnah because the father is not entitled to it by Torah law, but only by Rabbinic enactment. Moreover, the Mishnah put the father's rights to what his daughter finds, to her handiwork, and to the annulment of her vows in a separate clause, as an introduction to the later clause, which states: "If she marries, the husband has more than him." The husband is entitled not only to what his wife finds, to her handiwork, and to annul her vows, but to an additional right as well — the enjoyment of usufruct during his wife's lifetime. But the rights mentioned in the first clause of the Mishnah — the rights of betrothal — are of course not applicable to the husband.

HALAKHAH

הָאָב זַכַּאי בְּבִתּוֹ בְּקִידּוּשֶׁיהָ A father has authority over his daughter regarding her betrothal. "A father is entitled to arrange his daughter's betrothal while she is a minor or a *na'arah* (until the age of twelve-and-a-half). If she is betrothed by means of money, the father is entitled to the betrothal money. If the girl is more than three years old, he may arrange that she be betrothed by means of sexual intercourse." (*Rambam, Sefer Nashim, Hilkhot Ishut* 3:11; *Shulḥan Arukh, Even HaEzer* 37:1.)

זַכַּאי בִּמְצִיאָתָהּ וּבְמַעֲשֵׂה יָדֶיהָ He is entitled to what she finds and to her handiwork. "A father is entitled to what his daughter finds (even if she is not financially dependent upon him) and to her handiwork until she reaches full adulthood at the age of twelve-and-a-half," following the Mishnah. (*Rambam, Sefer Nashim, Hilkhot Ishut* 3:11, and *Sefer Nezikin, Hilkhot Avedah* 17:13; *Shulḥan Arukh, Even HaEzer* 37:1, and *Ḥoshen Mishpat* 270:2.)

CONCEPTS

הֲפָרַת נְדָרִים The annulment of vows. The Torah (Numbers 30) authorizes a father to nullify the vows of his daughter before she either attains majority or marries. Similarly, a husband is entitled to nullify any vows made by his wife. If a girl is betrothed before she attains majority, her vows may be nullified by her husband and father acting together. The vow must be nullified on the same day on which the father or husband heard of it. A husband is only empowered to nullify those vows which either directly or indirectly affect the personal relationship between him and his wife. According to many opinions, this restriction applies to the father as well.

TRANSLATION AND COMMENTARY

entitled to objects **that his daughter finds** while she is a minor or a *na'arah,* **as well as to the handiwork** she produces before she reaches full adulthood. [1]The father is also authorized to **annul the vows** made by his daughter before she reaches full adulthood or marries. If a father has arranged his daughter's betrothal, and the bridegroom wishes to dissolve the relationship, [2]the father **receives the bill of divorce** on his daughter's behalf, provided that she has not yet reached full adulthood (at the age of twelve-and-a-half) or married. If a girl who is a minor or a *na'arah* has inherited property from one of her mother's relatives, and the girl then dies, her father inherits the property from her. [3]**But he does not enjoy the usufruct** of that property **during her lifetime.**

נִשֵּׂאת [4]The Mishnah now considers the husband's rights with respect to his wife. **If** a girl **marries, her husband** is entitled to all those things to which the girl's father was previously entitled — to whatever she finds, and to her handiwork; and he is authorized to annul her vows. In fact, the husband **has more** rights **than** the father, **in that** not only does he inherit his wife's property when she dies, [5]but **he** also **enjoys the usufruct during her lifetime.** [6]The husband also accepts more obligations when he marries his wife: **He is liable for her maintenance** — her food, clothing, and lodging. [7]He is also obligated to provide the money **for her ransom** or to perform any other act that is required in order to redeem her should she be taken captive. [8]In addition, he must bear the costs **of her burial** and all related expenses. [9]**Rabbi Yehudah**

וּבְמַעֲשֵׂה יָדֶיהָ, [1]וּבַהֲפָרַת נְדָרֶיהָ, [2]וּמְקַבֵּל אֶת גִּיטָּהּ, [3]וְאֵינוֹ אוֹכֵל פֵּירוֹת בְּחַיֶּיהָ. [4]נִשֵּׂאת, יָתֵר עָלָיו הַבַּעַל, [5]שֶׁאוֹכֵל פֵּירוֹת בְּחַיֶּיהָ. [6]וְחַיָּיב בִּמְזוֹנוֹתֶיהָ, [7]וּבְפִרְקוֹנָהּ, [8]וּקְבוּרָתָהּ. [9]רַבִּי יְהוּדָה אוֹמֵר:

LITERAL TRANSLATION

and to her handiwork [1]and to the annulment of her vows, [2]and he receives her bill of divorce, [3]but he does not enjoy the usufruct during her lifetime.

[4][If] she marries, the husband has more than him, [5]in that he enjoys the usufruct during her lifetime. [6]And he is liable for her maintenance, [7]and for her ransom, [8]and [for] her burial. [9]Rabbi Yehudah says:

RASHI

ואינו אוכל פירות בחייה — אם נפלו לה קרקעות בירושה מבית אמה — אין אביה אוכל פירותיהן, אלא עושין לה סגולה. **בחייה** — אלא אם כן מתה והוא יורשה. **יתר עליו הבעל** — שהוא זוכה גם בכל השנויים למעלה, ואוכל פירות מנכסים שנפלו לה בירושה משניסת לו. **וחייב במזונותיה ובפרקונה** — אם נשבית, שהוא תנאי בית דין, כדתנן במתניתין. **בקבורתה** — דאמרינן לקמן: קבורתה תחת כתובתה שהכניסה לו מבית אביה, והוא יורשה במיתתה.

NOTES

וּבַהֲפָרַת נְדָרֶיהָ And to the annulment of her vows. According to *Rambam* (*Hilkhot Nedarim* 12:1), the father is entitled to annul all of his daughter's vows, whereas the husband is entitled to annul only those of his wife's vows that will deprive her of the necessities of life, or those that will affect their marital relations.

Rashash asks: According to *Rambam,* the formulation "the husband has more than him" is difficult, for the father's right to annul vows is greater than that of the husband. He answers (basing himself on *Rabbi Akiva Eger*): The Mishnah does not involve itself here with the details of each of the rights of the father and the husband, but with those rights in general. Thus it is justified in saying that the husband's rights are greater than those of the father, for in addition to all the father's rights the husband is also entitled to the usufruct of his wife's property during her lifetime.

HALAKHAH

וּבַהֲפָרַת נְדָרֶיהָ And to the annulment of her vows. "A father has the authority to annul the vows taken by his unmarried daughter while she is a minor or a *na'arah,"* following the Mishnah. (*Rambam, Sefer Hafla'ah, Hilkhot Nedarim* 11:6; *Shulḥan Arukh, Yoreh De'ah* 234:1.)

וּמְקַבֵּל אֶת גִּיטָּהּ And receives her bill of divorce. "If a father has effected the betrothal of his minor daughter, and the husband wishes to divorce her while she is still a minor, the father must receive the bill of divorce on her behalf. Once this reaches her father's hand, the girl is divorced (*Rif, Rambam* and others). According to some authorities (*Tosafot, Ba'al HaMa'or, Ran,* and others), the girl can also receive the bill of divorce on her own behalf. *Rosh* rules that it is preferable to be stringent and not allow the girl to receive her bill of divorce. If the husband wishes to divorce her when she is already a *na'arah,* then either the girl or her father can receive the bill of divorce." (*Rambam, Sefer Nashim, Hilkhot Gerushin* 2:18; *Shulḥan Arukh, Even HaEzer* 141:4.)

וְאֵינוֹ אוֹכֵל פֵּירוֹת בְּחַיֶּיהָ But he does not enjoy the usufruct during her lifetime. "A father is not entitled to the usufruct of the property belonging to his minor daughter." (See *Rambam, Sefer Nezikin, Hilkhot Ḥovel* 4:19; *Shulḥan Arukh, Ḥoshen Mishpat* 424:7.)

שֶׁאוֹכֵל פֵּירוֹת בְּחַיֶּיהָ In that he enjoys the usufruct during her lifetime. "A husband is entitled to the usufruct of his wife's property during her lifetime." (*Rambam, Sefer Nashim, Hilkhot Ishut* 12:3, 22:7; *Shulḥan Arukh, Even HaEzer* 69:3.)

וְחַיָּיב בִּמְזוֹנוֹתֶיהָ And he is liable for her maintenance. "A husband is liable for his wife's maintenance; he must ransom her if she is taken into captivity; and he must bear the costs of her burial if she dies." (*Rambam, Sefer Nashim, Hilkhot Ishut* 12:2; *Shulḥan Arukh, Even HaEzer* 69:2.)

[1]אֲפִילּוּ עָנִי שֶׁבְּיִשְׂרָאֵל לֹא יִפְחוֹת מִשְּׁנֵי חֲלִילִין וּמְקוֹנֶנֶת.

גמרא [2]״בְּכֶסֶף״. [3]מְנָלַן? [4]אָמַר רַב יְהוּדָה: אָמַר קְרָא: ״וְיָצְאָה חִנָּם; אֵין כָּסֶף״. [5]אֵין כֶּסֶף לְאָדוֹן זֶה, [6]וְיֵשׁ כֶּסֶף לְאָדוֹן אַחֵר. [7]וּמַנּוּ? [8]אָבִיהָ. [9]וְאֵימָא לְדִידָהּ! [10]הָשְׁתָּא אָבִיהָ מְקַבֵּל קִידּוּשֶׁיהָ, [11]דִּכְתִיב: ״אֶת בִּתִּי נָתַתִּי לָאִישׁ הַזֶּה״, [12]אִיהִי שָׁקְלָא כַּסְפָּא?

LITERAL TRANSLATION

[1]Even the poorest man in Israel must provide not less than two flutes and a lamenting woman.

GEMARA [2]"By money." [3]From where do we [know this]?

[4]Rav Yehudah says: The verse says: "And she shall go out free; there is no money." [5]There is no money for this master, [6]but there is money for another master. [7]And who is that? [8]Her father.

[9]But say [that the money belongs] to her!

[10]Now that her father receives her betrothal, [11]as it is written: "I gave my daughter to this man," [12]should she take the money?

TRANSLATION AND COMMENTARY

says: [1]**Even the poorest man in Israel must provide not less than two flute players and a lamenting woman** for his wife's funeral, for this too is included in the husband's obligation to provide for his wife's burial.

GEMARA בְּכֶסֶף [2]The Mishnah stated that the father is entitled to **"the money"** paid by the bridegroom for the daughter's betrothal. [3]The Gemara asks: **From where** in the Torah **do we know** that the father is entitled to **this** betrothal money?

אָמַר רַב יְהוּדָה [4]**Rav Yehudah said** in reply: Regarding a Hebrew maidservant, **the verse says** (Exodus 21:11): **"And she shall go out free; there is no money."** While his daughter is a minor, a father may sell her as a maidservant. She is freed after she has worked for six years, or at the advent of the Jubilee Year, or on the master's death, or by paying the master the value of the remainder of the term for which she was sold, or when she becomes a *na'arah,* whichever happens first. This verse teaches us that when the maidservant is freed upon becoming a *na'arah,* she is not required to give her master any money. [5]We may infer from this verse that **money is not** paid **to *this* master** when she leaves his authority, [6]**but money is** paid **to another master** when she leaves *his* authority. [7]**And who is that** master who is compensated when she leaves his authority? [8]It is **her father,** who is also considered her master. Thus, when a daughter leaves her father's authority upon her betrothal, the father is entitled to the betrothal money.

וְאֵימָא לְדִידָהּ [9]The Gemara suggests: **But** we can just as well **say that the** betrothal **money belongs to** the girl **herself,** and not to her father! The inference from the verse can be made as follows: The girl goes out free from *this* master, and no money is paid when she leaves his authority. But money *is* paid when she is betrothed and she leaves her *father's* authority. This teaches us that a girl may be betrothed by means of money paid by the bridegroom. But perhaps the money is paid to the girl herself!

הָשְׁתָּא אָבִיהָ מְקַבֵּל קִידּוּשֶׁיהָ [10]The Gemara rejects this suggestion: **Since her father** is entitled to **arrange her betrothal** and to choose the bridegroom, [11]**as the verse says** (Deuteronomy 22:16): **"I gave my daughter to this man,"** [12]is it reasonable that **she should take the money?** Surely the father, who arranges the betrothal, should be entitled to the betrothal money!

RASHI

משני חלילין — להספד, *קלמיל״ש.

גמרא בכסף מנלן — דכסף קידושיה לאביה. **אין כסף** — באמה העבריה כתיב. ובקידושין פריך: האי מבעי ליה לגופיה! **אין כסף לאדון זה** — בצאתה מרשותו בסימני נערות, כדילפינן בקידושין דיוצאה בסימנים משתעי קרא. **אבל יש כסף לאדון אחר** — כשיוצאה מרשותו. **ומנו אב** — שאין אדון לבת ישראל אלא אביה, חוץ מזה שנמכרה לו. **ואימא לדידה הוי** — וקרא כי אתא לאשמועינן אתא, שהיא נקנית לבעל בקדושי כסף. והכי תדרשיה: אין כסף ביציאה זו, אבל יש כסף ביציאה אחרת. ולעולם דידה הוי.

BACKGROUND

חֲלִילִין Flutes. During the Mishnaic period it was customary for flutes and other musical instruments to be played at funerals. Reference to this custom is found in another Mishnah (*Shabbat* 15a) which discusses whether a flute brought on Shabbat by a non-Jew can be played at the funeral of a Jew after the end of Shabbat. In later generations the custom of playing musical instruments at a funeral was discontinued as reflecting non-Jewish practice.

וּמְקוֹנֶנֶת And a lamenting woman. The Prophet Jeremiah (9:16) mentions the custom of hiring women to lament in times of mourning. These women sang dirges in tearful voices at a funeral about the great sorrow felt at the loss of the deceased and thereby intensified the emotion felt by those attending the funeral. According to Rabbi Yehudah, the presence of at least one lamenting woman was part of the proper way of conducting any funeral.

This custom, with some changes in form, remained in practice in Jewish communities until recent generations, although it was performed spontaneously and not by women whose profession it was to lament in public.

LANGUAGE (RASHI)

קלמיל״ש* From the Old French *chalemels,* meaning "flutes."

NOTES

הָשְׁתָּא אָבִיהָ מְקַבֵּל קִידּוּשֶׁיהָ Now that her father receives her betrothal. *Rashi* (*Kiddushin* 3b) explains the Gemara's argument as follows: Surely the Torah did not entitle the father to arrange his daughter's betrothal without also entitling him to the betrothal money! *Ritva* adds: The Torah entitled the father to arrange his daughter's betrothal even

HALAKHAH

לֹא יִפְחוֹת מִשְּׁנֵי חֲלִילִין Must provide no less than two flutes. "If a wife dies during her husband's lifetime, the husband is liable for her burial and all related expenses. He must arrange for a funeral in the manner customary in that place. If it is customary to have flutes at the funeral, he must provide at least two flute-players and one lamenting woman, even if he is poor," following Rabbi Yehudah, in accordance with whom the Gemara rules below (48a). (*Rambam, Sefer Nashim, Hilkhot Ishut* 14:23; *Shulḥan Arukh, Even HaEzer* 89:1.)

[1]וְאֵימָא: הָנֵי מִילֵּי קְטַנָּה, דְּלֵית לָהּ יָד. [2]אֲבָל נַעֲרָה, דְּאִית לָהּ יָד, [3]אִיהִי תְּקַדֵּשׁ נַפְשָׁהּ, וְאִיהִי תִּשְׁקוֹל כַּסְפָּא!

[4]אָמַר קְרָא: ״בִּנְעֻרֶיהָ בֵּית אָבִיהָ״. [5]כָּל שֶׁבַח נְעוּרִים לְאָבִיהָ.

[6]וְאֶלָּא הָא דְּאָמַר רַב הוּנָא אָמַר רַב: מִנַּיִן שֶׁמַּעֲשֵׂה הַבַּת לְאָבִיהָ? [7]שֶׁנֶּאֱמַר: ״וְכִי יִמְכֹּר אִישׁ אֶת בִּתּוֹ לְאָמָה״. [8]מָה אָמָה מַעֲשֵׂה יָדֶיהָ לְרַבָּהּ, [9]אַף בַּת מַעֲשֵׂה יָדֶיהָ לְאָבִיהָ.

LITERAL TRANSLATION

[1]But say: This applies (lit., "these words") [to] a minor, who has no legal capacity (lit., "hand"). [2]But [regarding] a *na'arah,* who does have legal capacity, [3]let her give herself in betrothal and let her take the money!

[4]The verse says: "While she is a *na'arah* in her father's house." [5]All the benefit of her being a *na'arah* [belongs] to her father.

[6]But [let us consider] what Rav Huna said in the name of Rav: From where [do we know] that the work of the daughter [belongs] to her father? [7]For it is said: "And if a man shall sell his daughter as a maidservant." [8]Just as the [in the case of] a maidservant, the work of her hands [belongs] to her master, [9]so too the work of a daughter's hands [belongs] to her father.

TRANSLATION AND COMMENTARY

וְאֵימָא [1]The Gemara raises an objection: **But it can be argued** that this verse, which allows the father to give his daughter away in betrothal, **applies** only **to** a girl who is still **a minor** (below the age of twelve), **who does not have** the **legal capacity** to change her personal status by becoming betrothed as a result of her own independent action. [2]**But as for a** ***na'arah*** (between twelve and twelve-and-a-half years of age), **who does have the legal capacity** to effect a change in her personal status, [3]**let her give herself** away **in betrothal and let her take the** betrothal **money** for herself!

אָמַר קְרָא [4]The Gemara now suggests a different source for this ruling: **The verse says** (Numbers 30:17): "These are the statutes that the Lord commanded Moses, between a man and his wife, between a father and his daughter, **while she is a** ***na'arah*** **in her father's house."** This verse implies that throughout the period of her youth, until the age of twelve-and-a-half, a girl remains under her father's authority, [5]so that **all the** monetary **benefits** she may receive **while she is a** ***na'arah*** **belong to her father.** Thus a father is entitled to the betrothal money given by the bridegroom for his daughter, even if she is already a *na'arah,* since that betrothal money is considered among the profits of the girl's youth.

וְאֶלָּא הָא דְּאָמַר [6]**But** the Gemara rejects this exegesis. All monetary benefits received by a *na'arah* do not go automatically to her father. **Let us consider what Rav Huna said in the name of Rav: From where do we know that the work of a daughter** (anything she makes or earns) while she is a *na'arah* **belongs to her father?** [7]Rav answers that **the verse** (Exodus 21:7) **says: "And if a man shall sell his daughter as a maidservant."** The word "maidservant" was inserted in this verse in juxtaposition to the word "daughter" so that we would compare the two situations and say: [8]**Just as the work of a maidservant** obviously **belongs to her master,** [9]**so too does the work of a daughter belong to her father.** But if all the monetary benefits

RASHI

ואימא הני מילי — דאמרה תורה ״את בתי נתתי״ — שבידו נתינתה. קטנה דלית לה יד — לקדש עצמה. ואף על גב דגבי מוציא שם רע כתיב, והיא נערה הוה — דלמא הכי קאמר: את בתי נתתי בקטנותה, ועתה נערה.

NOTES

without her knowledge or consent. Surely, then, he must be considered the party effecting the betrothal, and as such he must be entitled to the betrothal money. For if the girl were to be entitled to the money, she would be considered the party effecting the betrothal — the father acting only as her agent — and her consent to the betrothal would be necessary.

כָּל שֶׁבַח נְעוּרִים לְאָבִיהָ All the benefit of her being a *na'arah* belongs to her father. The Aḥaronim ask: Granted that we can infer from this verse that the father is entitled to the money given by the bridegroom to betroth his daughter. But how do we know from this verse that the father is entitled to arrange his daughter's betrothal to the bridegroom of his choice? *Ayyelet Ahavim* suggests that we can reverse the argument put forward earlier by the Gemara and argue that if the father is entitled to his daughter's betrothal money, then it stands to reason that he should also be entitled to arrange her betrothal.

אֶת בִּתּוֹ לְאָמָה His daughter as a maidservant. The expression "as a maidservant" is unnecessary, and it is understood here as teaching us that an analogy is to be drawn between a daughter and a maidservant (see *Rashi* below, 47a). The verse itself is referring to a girl who is still a minor, for a father may not sell his daughter as a maidservant once she has reached puberty. But the analogy drawn between the daughter and the maidservant relates to a daughter who is already a *na'arah.* As the Gemara explains below, there is no need for a special analogy to teach us that the handiwork of a minor daughter belongs to her father, for if a father can sell his minor daughter as

TRANSLATION AND COMMENTARY

that a girl may receive while she is a *na'arah* belong to her father, [1]**why do we need** a special exegetical argument to prove that her wages also belong to her father? [2]All we need to do is to **derive** this law **from** the general exegetical argument provided by the text, **"while she is a *na'arah* in her father's house"**!

אֶלָּא [3]**Rather,** says the Gemara, the exegetical argument presented above is incorrect. **The verse** in Numbers **deals** specifically **with the annulment of vows,** and it teaches us that a father has the power to annul his daughter's vows as long as she is a *na'arah.* Thus the verse cannot serve as the source for a general principle that all the benefits a girl may receive while she is a *na'arah* belong to her father.

וְכִי תֵּימָא [4]**And,** continues the Gemara, **if you say that we should derive from** the fact that the father has the power to annul his daughter's vows the principle that he is also entitled to keep any monetary benefits she receives, [5]we can object that **we do not derive monetary laws from ritual laws.** The laws governing ritual matters are different from those governing monetary matters. Hence we cannot extrapolate from the father's power to annul his daughter's vows the principle that he also has authority over her in monetary matters.

וְכִי תֵּימָא [6]**And,** continues the Gemara, **if you say that we should derive from** the father's right to **the** rapist's **fine** that he is also entitled to keep his daughter's betrothal money and any other monetary benefits she receives, [7]we can object that **we do not derive** regular **monetary laws from fines.** The money that a bridegroom gives to betroth a woman is ordinary monetary compensation, offered in exchange for the woman's consent to be his bride. But the money paid by the rapist or the seducer is a fine, which is not commensurate with anything he received or with the damage he caused. The imposition of a fine is viewed as an innovation made by the Torah. Thus the fine paid by the rapist or the seducer cannot serve as a model from which an inference may be drawn concerning the matter of betrothal money, which is a case of ordinary monetary compensation.

וְכִי תֵּימָא [8]**And,** continues the Gemara, **if you say that we should derive** the law that the father is entitled to his daughter's betrothal money **from** the fact that he is entitled to the indemnity paid by the rapist or the seducer for the **shame** his daughter suffered, **and** to the compensation for her **blemish** (her loss of value now that she is no longer a virgin), for these payments are instances of ordinary monetary compensation, since the amount paid is commensurate with the actual damage inflicted, we can object that the indemnities

[1]לָמָּה לִי? [2]תֵּיפּוֹק לֵיהּ מִ״בִּנְעֻרֶיהָ בֵּית אָבִיהָ״! [3]אֶלָּא, הַהוּא בַּהֲפָרַת נְדָרִים הוּא דִּכְתִיב. [4]וְכִי תֵּימָא: נֵילַף מִינָּהּ, [5]מָמוֹנָא מֵאִיסּוּרָא לָא יָלְפִינַן. [6]וְכִי תֵּימָא: נֵילַף מִקְּנָסָא, [7]מָמוֹנָא מִקְּנָסָא לָא יָלְפִינַן. [8]וְכִי תֵּימָא: נֵילַף מִבּוֹשֶׁת וּפְגָם,

LITERAL TRANSLATION

[1]Why do I need [this]? [2]Let him derive it from "while she is a *na'arah* in her father's house"!

[3]Rather, that is written about the annulment of vows.

[4]And if you say: Let us derive from it, [5]we do not derive monetary [laws] from ritual [laws].

[6]And if you say: Let us derive [it] from the fine, [7]we do not derive monetary [laws] from fines.

[8]And if you say: Let us derive [it] from shame and blemish,

RASHI

אלא ההיא בהפרת נדרים כתיב – מסקנא דקושיא היא, ולא שינויא הוא. **וכי תימא נילף** – כסף קידושיה מקנסה שזיכתה תורה לאב. **מבושת ופגם** – דאמרינן ב״אלו נערות״ (כתובות מ,ב) שהוא של אב.

NOTES

a maidservant, then he is surely entitled to her handiwork. Thus the analogy drawn between the daughter and the maidservant must come to teach us that even the handiwork of a daughter who is a *na'arah* belongs to her father.

נֵילַף מִבּוֹשֶׁת וּפְגָם Let us derive it from shame and blemish. The Rishonim ask: Elsewhere (above, 40b), the Gemara derives the ruling that the father is entitled to the payments made by the rapist or the seducer for the shame and the blemish suffered by his daughter from the fact that he can give her away in betrothal. How, then, can the Gemara here argue that the father's right to his daughter's betrothal money can be derived from his right to the payments for her shame and blemish?

Ramban, Rashba, and others suggest that the Gemara is referring here not to the shame and the blemish caused by the rapist or the seducer, but to the shame and the blemish suffered by the daughter as a result of having been betrothed to a despicable person. The Gemara's proposal is therefore as follows: Let us derive that the father is entitled to his daughter's betrothal money when she is betrothed as a *na'arah* from the fact that he may cause her to suffer shame and blemish as a *na'arah* by betrothing her to a despicable person when she is a minor.

¹שָׁאנֵי בּוֹשֶׁת וּפְגָם, דְּאָבִיהָ נַמִי שַׁיָּיךְ בֵּיהּ.
²אֶלָּא, מִסְתַּבְּרָא דְּכִי מְמַעֵט רַחֲמָנָא, ³יְצִיאָה דִּכְוָותָהּ קָא מְמַעֵט.
⁴וְהָא לָא דָּמְיָא הָא יְצִיאָה לְהָא יְצִיאָה. ⁵הָתָם, גַּבֵּי אָדוֹן, נָפְקָא לָהּ מֵרְשׁוּתֵיהּ לְגַמְרֵי.

LITERAL TRANSLATION

[1] shame and blemish are different, for her father too is involved with them.

[2] Rather, it stands to reason that when the Torah (lit., "the Merciful One") excluded [another leaving], [3] it excluded a leaving like it.

[4] But surely this leaving is not like that leaving. [5] There, regarding the master, she goes out from his authority completely.

TRANSLATION AND COMMENTARY

paid for the girl's [1] **shame and blemish are different, for her father too is involved with them.** The father suffers from his daughter's humiliation and loss of value, and so it is right that he should be entitled to those payments. But it cannot be inferred from this that he should also be entitled to his daughter's betrothal money. Thus we are still left without a source for the Mishnah's ruling that a father is entitled to arrange his daughter's betrothal even when she is a *na'arah*, and that he may keep the betrothal money for himself.

אֶלָּא [2] The Gemara now returns to its original argument that the father's right to his daughter's betrothal money is derived from the verse, "And she shall go out free; there is no money," which is stated with respect to a Hebrew maidservant. **Rather,** we may infer from this verse that "there is no money" to be paid to the maidservant's master when she leaves his authority, but there is money to be paid when a girl is betrothed and leaves her father's authority. As for the objection that may be raised, that the money should go to the girl herself and not to her father, the following rebuttal may be offered: **It stands to reason that when the Torah excluded** the case of a girl leaving her father's authority as a result of betrothal from the law that no money is paid when a maidservant leaves her master's authority, [3] **it excluded the** case of a girl **leaving** her father's authority in circumstances **similar to** those in the case of a maidservant leaving her master's authority. In the case of the maidservant, if money were to be paid, it would surely go to the master whose authority she is now leaving — just as the money goes to the master if she wishes to leave early by paying the value of the remainder of the term for which she was sold. Similarly in the case of the daughter, since money is paid when she leaves her father's authority upon betrothal, it is only reasonable that the money should go to her father, whose authority she is leaving.

וְהָא לָא דָּמְיָא [4] The Gemara asks: **But surely the** daughter's **leaving** her father's authority **is not similar to the** maidservant's **leaving** her master's authority? [5] **There, in the case of the master,** when the maidservant

RASHI

שייך בה — בידו ליטול ממון ולביישה בבושת זה, למוסרה לביאת קידושין למנוול ולמוכה שחין. **אלא** — כי פרכת אימא לדידה, הכי תשני: מסתברא כי קא ממעט קרא יציאתה מרשות אב בקידושין, מתורת יציאתה מרשות אדון בסימנין. **יציאה דכוותה קא ממעט** — מה כסף דיציאת אדון, אי הוה התם כסף, דאדון שהיא יוצאה ממנו בעי מהוי, כפדיון גרעונה, דמגרעת עמו ויוצאה, והמותר נותנת לו. אף כי קאמר נמי יש כסף ביציאה אחרת — דאדון שהיא יוצאה ממנו בעי למהוי, ולא לדידה. ואי אמרת לדידה הוה — לא קא ממעט יציאה דכוותה. כך מפורש בשאלתות דרב אחאי גאון. ואני שמעתי: יציאה דכוותה קא ממעט — מה התם נערה אף הכא נערה, וקשיא לי: אכתי אימא לדידה? ובמסכת קדושין פירשתיה בלשון שמועתי, ובקושי. **והא לא דמיא** — יציאה דקדושין ליציאת אמה העבריה, ולא יציאה דכוותה היא.

NOTES

דְּאָבִיהָ נַמִי שַׁיָּיךְ בֵּיהּ **For her father too is involved with them.** *Rashi* explains that the father is involved with his daughter's shame and blemish, because he is authorized to arrange a marriage for her that she will find humiliating.

Ramban and others explain that he is involved in that he too suffers from his daughter's shame and blemish. This second explanation is supported by the reading found in the parallel Gemara in *Kiddushin* 3b (as well as in some versions of our Gemara): "Her father too suffers pain on account of it." Even though a husband is not entitled to the full amount of the payments made for his wife's shame and blemish (see below, 65b), the father-daughter relationship is treated as closer than that between husband and wife, and therefore the daughter's shame and blemish are entirely her father's.

נָפְקָא לָהּ מֵרְשׁוּתֵיהּ **She goes out from his authority.** *Rosh* explains the Gemara's argument as follows: When the maidservant leaves her master's authority, she leaves it completely, and the master is no longer entitled to her handiwork. Thus, if money were to be paid when the girl left, it stands to reason that it would be paid to the master to compensate him for his loss. But when the daughter leaves her father's authority upon her betrothal, she does not leave it completely. The father does not lose anything by her departure from his authority, for he is still entitled to her handiwork. Thus there is no reason why the betrothal money should be awarded to the girl's father. It should go instead to the girl herself.

¹יְצִיאָה דְּאָב, אַכַּתִּי מִחַסְּרָא מְסִירָה לַחוּפָּה!
²מֵהֲפָרַת נְדָרִים מִיהָא, נָפְקָא לָהּ מֵרְשׁוּתֵיהּ. ³דִּתְנַן: ״נַעֲרָה הַמְאוֹרָסָה, אָבִיהָ וּבַעְלָהּ מְפִירִין לָהּ נְדָרֶיהָ״.
⁴״שְׁטָר וּבִיאָה״. ⁵מְנָא לָן?
⁶אָמַר קְרָא: ״וְהָיְתָה לְאִישׁ

LITERAL TRANSLATION

[1] [But regarding] the leaving from the father, delivery to the bridal chamber is still lacking!
[2] With respect to the annulment of vows at least, she goes out from his authority. [3] For we have learned: "[In the case of] a betrothed *na'arah*, her father and her husband annul her vows for her."
[4] "Deed and intercourse." [5] From where do we [know this]?
[6] The verse says: "And she shall be another man's wife."

RASHI

אכתי מיחסרא מסירה לחופה — ועדיין היא ברשות האב לירושתה ולמעשה ידיה. **נפקא לה מרשותיה** — דעד עכשיו היה מיפר לבדו, ועתה מיפר בשותפות עם בעלה. **בשטר ובביאה מנלן** — דביד אביה לקדשה ולמוסרה על כרחה.

TRANSLATION AND COMMENTARY

leaves his authority, **she leaves his authority completely.** [1] **But in the case of the** daughter's **leaving her father's** authority — even after she is betrothed, her **delivery to the bridal chamber is still lacking!** Until she enters the bridal chamber and completes the marriage process, she remains under her father's authority. During that period the father is still entitled to her handiwork, and he is her heir if she dies. How, then, can it be said that the verse dealing with the maidservant's leaving her master, "And she shall go out free; there is no money," comes to exclude the case of the daughter leaving her father, when in the latter case the girl does not really leave her father's authority until she is brought to the bridal chamber?

מֵהֲפָרַת נְדָרִים מִיהָא [2] The Gemara answers: Although a girl who is a minor or a *na'arah* does not leave her father's authority with respect to her handiwork and her inheritance until the marriage is completed, nevertheless **at least with respect to the annulment of** her **vows, she leaves his** exclusive **authority** as soon as she is betrothed. [3] **For we have learned** in a Mishnah (*Nedarim* 66b): **"In the case of a betrothed *na'arah*,** who has not yet entered the bridal chamber in marriage, **her father and her husband** may jointly **annul her vows."** When a girl who is a minor or a *na'arah* is betrothed, she comes under her bridegroom's authority for the annulment of her vows; but since she is still under her father's authority until she is delivered to the bridal chamber in marriage, she remains under her father's authority for the annulment of her vows as well. Thus the father and the husband must both agree to annul the girl's vow. If only the father annuls her vow but the husband is silent or confirms it, or vice versa, the vow is valid. Now, since the girl leaves her father's exclusive authority upon her betrothal with respect to the annulment of her vows, her betrothal is regarded as the moment when she leaves her father's authority. And thus the verse dealing with the maidservant's leaving her master, "And she shall go out free; there is no money," can indeed be understood as excluding the case of the daughter leaving her father upon her betrothal. Thus, whereas the master is not entitled to any money when his maidservant leaves his authority, the father *is* entitled to his daughter's betrothal money when she is betrothed and leaves his authority.

שְׁטָר וּבִיאָה [4] The Mishnah states that the father is entitled to arrange his daughter's betrothal while she is a minor or a *na'arah,* whether she is betrothed by means of money, by **document, or** by sexual **intercourse.** [5] The Gemara asks: **From where** in the Torah **do we know** that the father is entitled to arrange her betrothal by means of a document or by intercourse?

אָמַר קְרָא [6] The Gemara answers: **The verse** dealing with a case of divorce and remarriage **says** (Deuteronomy 24:2): "And she shall leave his house, and she shall go **and she shall be another man's wife."**

NOTES

מֵהֲפָרַת נְדָרִים מִיהָא **With respect to the annulment of vows at least.** The Gemara's answer poses a certain difficulty, for the Gemara seems to be arguing that, regarding at least one aspect of their relationship, the daughter leaves her father's authority completely upon her betrothal. But with respect to the annulment of her vows, the betrothed daughter remains under her father's authority, in that he is still authorized to annul her vows in conjunction with her bridegroom!

Rabbenu Ḥananel has a different reading: "With respect to this matter she leaves his authority completely." When a girl is betrothed, she leaves her father's authority completely with respect to her sale as a maidservant. After a father gives his daughter away in betrothal, he can no longer sell her as a maidservant, even if she is still a minor.

According to the standard text of the Gemara, which is referring here to the father's right to annul his daughter's vows, some Aḥaronim suggest: Here, too, the Gemara should have objected that we cannot derive a law regarding a monetary matter from a law regarding a ritual matter! *Pnei Yehoshua* answers that since the daughter may take a vow forbidding her father from deriving benefit from her property, the father's right to annul his daughter's vows comes under the category of monetary matters.

CONCEPTS

אֵיבָה Enmity. The avoidance of hostility among people is a consideration in various areas of the Halakhah, the ideal being the creation and fostering of peaceful and tranquil relations. This consideration is found mainly in the area of relations between Jews and non-Jews, in situations where insisting on the strict letter of the law and on scrupulous protection of a person's rights could result in misunderstanding and even hatred. In such cases a person is commanded to demand far less than his due (לִפְנִים מִשּׁוּרַת הַדִּין) and, in some cases, even to perform certain actions which by right he ought not to do, in order to avoid damaging the general fabric of relations. The Sages spoke often in praise of peace. For the sake of peace and to avoid hatred and envy, they even advocated stretching the truth and helping people one is not legally obligated to help.

TRANSLATION AND COMMENTARY

The verse does not specify the means by which the woman is betrothed to her second husband, but uses the general term "and she shall be." [1]This implies that **the** various **ways of entering** into **marriage are** all **compared to each other.** And just as the various methods of betrothal are alike with respect to the matter discussed in this verse, they are also all alike with respect to the father's authority over his daughter. Thus it follows that just as the father is entitled to arrange his daughter's betrothal by means of money, he is likewise entitled to arrange her betrothal by means of a document or by sexual intercourse.

זַכַּאי בִּמְצִיאָתָהּ [2]The next clause of our Mishnah states: "The father **is** also **entitled to what** his daughter **finds** while she is a minor or a *na'arah.*" [47A] [3]The Gemara explains the Mishnah's ruling: By Torah law the father is not entitled to what his daughter finds, but the Rabbis awarded him ownership of such things **so that** there would be no feelings of **enmity** between the father and the daughter. After a girl reaches the age of six, her father is under no legal obligation to support her. The Rabbis were concerned that if the father were not granted ownership of what his daughter found, he would harbor ill feelings toward her and might stop providing for her support.

בְּמַעֲשֵׂה יָדֶיהָ [4]The Mishnah continues: "The father is also entitled **to the handiwork** his daughter produces while she is a minor or a *na'arah.*" [5]The Gemara asks: **From where** in the Torah **do we know this?**

דְּאָמַר רַב הוּנָא [6]The Gemara answers: This question has already been asked and answered, **for Rav Huna said in the name of Rav: From where do we know that a daughter's handiwork belongs to her father?** [7]**For the verse says** (Exodus 21:7): **"And if a man shall sell his daughter as a maidservant."** The superfluous expression "as a maidservant" teaches us that an analogy is to be drawn between a maidservant and a daughter. [8]**Just as the handiwork of a maidservant** obviously **belongs to her master,** [9]**so too does the handiwork of a daughter belong to her father.**

וְאֵימָא [10]The Gemara now questions this exegesis: Let us say that **this** ruling entitling a father to his daughter's handiwork **applies** only **to a** girl who is still a **minor,** [11]**whom** the father **can sell** as a maidservant. Just as the father is authorized to sell his daughter as a maidservant while she is still a minor, so too is he entitled to her handiwork while she is still a minor. [12]**But as for** a girl who is already **a *na'arah,* whom** the father **can no** longer **sell** as a maidservant, [13]perhaps **her handiwork** should **belong to her!**

LITERAL TRANSLATION

[1]The ways of entering marriage (lit., "beings") are compared to each other.

[2]"He is entitled to what she finds." [47A] [3]Because of enmity.

[4]"To her handiwork." [5]From where do we [know this]?

[6]For Rav Huna said in the name of Rav: From where [do we know] that the work of the daughter [belongs] to the father? [7]For it is said: "And if a man shall sell his daughter as a maidservant." [8]Just as the handiwork of a maidservant [belongs] to her master, [9]so too [does] the handiwork of a daughter [belong] to her father.

[10]But say: This applies (lit., "these words") [to] a minor, [11]whom he can sell. [12]But [regarding] a *na'arah,* whom he cannot sell, [13]her handiwork belongs to her!

אַחֵר״. [1]אִיתְקוּשׁ הֲוָויוֹת לַהֲדָדֵי.
[2]״זַכַּאי בִּמְצִיאָתָהּ״. [47A]
[3]מִשּׁוּם אֵיבָה.
[4]״בְּמַעֲשֵׂה יָדֶיהָ״. [5]מְנָלַן?
[6]דְּאָמַר רַב הוּנָא אָמַר רַב: מִנַּיִן שֶׁמַּעֲשֵׂה הַבַּת לָאָב? [7]שֶׁנֶּאֱמַר: ״וְכִי יִמְכֹּר אִישׁ אֶת בִּתּוֹ לְאָמָה״. [8]מָה אָמָה מַעֲשֵׂה יָדֶיהָ לְרַבָּהּ, [9]אַף בַּת מַעֲשֵׂה יָדֶיהָ לְאָבִיהָ.
[10]וְאֵימָא: הָנֵי מִילֵּי קְטַנָּה, [11]דְּמָצֵי מְזַבֵּן לָהּ. [12]אֲבָל נַעֲרָה, דְּלָא מָצֵי מְזַבֵּן לָהּ, [13]מַעֲשֵׂה יָדֶיהָ דִּידָהּ הָווּ!

RASHI

איתקוש הוויות להדדי — מה כסף ברשות אביה — אף קידושי שטר וביאה ביד אביה, וקידושי שטר וביאה דמקדשת בהו ילפינן בקידושין. **משום איבה** — דכיון דאינו חייב במזונותיה, אי אמרת מציאתה שלה — איכא איבה ולא זיין לה תו.

NOTES

מִשּׁוּם אֵיבָה Because of enmity. Our commentary follows *Rashi,* who explains that the Rabbis enacted that the father is entitled to what his daughter finds so that ill feelings will not arise between them and cause him to withhold financial support from her.

Tosafot raises an objection that elsewhere (*Bava Metzia* 12b) the Gemara implies that the father is entitled to what his daughter finds, even if he does not provide for her support. Rather, says *Tosafot,* the Rabbis awarded what the girl finds to her father, so that the father will not bear ill feelings toward his daughter and give her away in betrothal to an unsuitable person whom she will detest. Alternatively, the father was granted the right to what his daughter finds, so that there would not be constant quarreling between the two.

TRANSLATION AND COMMENTARY

מִסְתַּבְּרָא [1] The Gemara answers: **It stands to reason that** even in the case of a *na'arah,* the daughter's handiwork **belongs to her father,** [2] **for if it were to enter your mind that her handiwork does not belong to her father,** [3] **then** how would you explain the fact **that the Torah entitles the father to deliver** his daughter **to the bridal chamber** even if she is a *na'arah*? [4] **How can he deliver her?** [5] **Surely he causes her to be idle from her handiwork** during the period of delivery! The father is entitled to arrange his daughter's betrothal and to complete the marriage process by delivering her to the bridal chamber, even if she is already a *na'arah.* Granted that if the father is entitled to his daughter's handiwork, he can forgo a day's income and deliver her to the bridal chamber. But if the father is not entitled to her handiwork, the daughter should be allowed to object to being taken to the bridal chamber, for she will be forced to set aside her work and will suffer a loss of income as a result.

פָּרֵיךְ רַב אַחַאי [6] **Rav Aḥai raised an objection** against this argument: The fact that the father is entitled to deliver his daughter to the bridal chamber even when she is a *na'arah* does not prove that he is entitled to her handiwork while she is a *na'arah.* We can **say that he must** indeed **pay her compensation for her enforced idleness** and the resulting financial loss. On this basis the daughter cannot object to being taken to the bridal chamber. [7] **Or else** we can **say that he must deliver her** to the bridal chamber **at night,** when she does not ordinarily work, and she will not suffer any loss of income as a result. [8] **Or else** we can **say that he must deliver her** to the bridal chamber **on a Shabbat or a Festival,** when in any case she cannot work. Thus the question raised earlier by the Gemara remains: How do we know that the father's right to his daughter's handiwork, which is derived from the verse dealing with a maidservant, applies to a daughter who is already a *na'arah*?

[1] מִסְתַּבְּרָא דְּאָבִיהָ הָווּ, [2] דְּאִי סָלְקָא דַּעְתָּךְ מַעֲשֵׂה יָדֶיהָ לָאו דְּאָבִיהָ, [3] אֶלָּא הָא דְּזַכֵּי לֵיהּ רַחֲמָנָא לָאָב לְמִימְסְרָהּ לְחוּפָּה, [4] הֵיכִי מָצֵי מָסַר לָהּ? [5] הָא קָמְבַטֵּל לָהּ מִמַּעֲשֵׂה יָדֶיהָ!

[6] פָּרֵיךְ רַב אַחַאי: אֵימָא דְּיָהֵיב לָהּ שְׂכַר פְּקַעְתָּהּ. [7] אִי נַמִי, דְּמָסַר לָהּ בְּלֵילְיָא. [8] אִי נַמִי, דְּמָסַר לָהּ בְּשַׁבָּתוֹת וְיָמִים טוֹבִים.

LITERAL TRANSLATION

[1] It stands to reason that it belongs to her father, [2] for if it enters your mind [that] her handiwork [does] not [belong] to her father, [3] then [regarding the fact] that the Torah (lit., "the Merciful One") entitled the father to deliver her to the bridal chamber, [4] how can he deliver her? [5] Surely he prevents her from [doing] her handiwork!

[6] Rav Aḥai objected: Say that he pays her compensation for her enforced idleness. [7] Or else [say] that he delivered her at night. [8] Or else [say] that he delivered her on a Shabbat or a Festival.

RASHI

הא דזכי ליה רחמנא לאב למימסרה לחופה — כדכתיב "את בתי נתתי" — כל נתינות שבה במשמע. ואותו היום אינה עושה מלאכה, היכי מצי כו'. **פקעתה** = בטילותה.

TERMINOLOGY

פָּרֵיךְ רַב אַחַאי Rav Aḥai objected. The expression פָּרֵיךְ — "he objected" — is often used to introduce the objections of certain specific scholars and is particularly associated with Rav Aḥai.

SAGES

רַב אַחַאי Rav Aḥai. From the most important historical document relating to the Talmudic period, the *Epistle of Rav Sherira Gaon,* we find that there were two Sages named Rav Aḥai, both of whom were active during the same period, and both of whom died in the early seventh century. This Rav Aḥai is apparently Rav Aḥai from Bei Ḥittim, who was one of the first of the Savoraim, the post-Talmudic Sages who prepared the final edition of the Talmud after the death of the last Amoraim.

Since Rav Aḥai was one of the first Savoraim, some of his teachings — mainly interpretations and clarifications of Talmudic statements — were included in the Talmud itself. In general they are introduced with opening phrases not common in the Talmud.

NOTES

דְּזַכֵּי לֵיהּ רַחֲמָנָא לָאָב לְמִימְסְרָהּ לְחוּפָּה That the Torah entitled the father to deliver her to the bridal chamber. *Rashi* brings proof that the father is entitled to deliver his daughter to the bridal chamber from the verse (Deuteronomy 22:16): "I gave my daughter to this man," which he understands as referring both to the father's giving of his daughter in betrothal and to his giving of her in marriage. Others (*Ramban, Rashba,* and others) argue that a verse is not needed in order to teach us that a father may give his daughter away in marriage. For it is obvious that if the father can give his daughter away in betrothal, he can certainly deliver her to the bridal chamber in marriage, for the bridegroom betrothed her on condition that she be given to him in marriage.

דְּמָסַר לָהּ בְּשַׁבָּתוֹת He delivered her on a Shabbat. *Tosafot* asks: There is a Halakhic rule that it is not permitted to mix one act of rejoicing with another (אֵין מְעָרְבִין שִׂמְחָה בְּשִׂמְחָה), and this is why a wedding may not be celebrated during the intermediate days of a Festival, and especially not on Shabbat or on a Festival itself (see *Mo'ed Katan* 8b). How, then, can our Gemara suggest that the father deliver his daughter to the bridal chamber on a Shabbat or a Festival?

Tosafot answers: The Gemara means to say that the father should deliver his daughter to the bridal chamber shortly before the beginning of Shabbat or the beginning of a Festival, when work is already forbidden, but before Shabbat or the Festival has actually begun. Indeed, some Rishonim have the reading: "He delivered her on the eve of Shabbat or on the eve of a Festival" (see *Mordekhai, Halakhot Gedolot*).

Some authorities point out that there is another reason why a wedding may not be celebrated on a Shabbat or on a Festival. The marriage ceremony includes elements of legal acquisition, and all forms of acquisition are forbidden on Shabbat and on Festivals. Others argue that the prohibition against effecting acquisitions on Shabbat or on Festivals is of Rabbinic origin, and weddings were never included in the prohibition (see *Ahavat Tzion, Rabbi Ya'akov Emden*). Nevertheless, all agree that weddings do not take place on Shabbat or on Festivals (see *Betzah* 36b).

TRANSLATION AND COMMENTARY

אֶלָּא [1] The Gemara answers: **Rather,** this is how to rebut the objection: **Regarding** a daughter who is **a minor, a verse is not required** to teach us that her handiwork belongs to her father. Even without a special analogy between a maidservant and a daughter, we would know by logical argument that the father is entitled to her handiwork. [2]**For since** the father **can sell her** as a maidservant, **is it necessary to mention** that he is also entitled to **her handiwork?** If the father has the authority to sell his daughter as a maidservant, thus transferring her handiwork to another person, then surely he is himself entitled to her handiwork! [3]**Rather, the verse was required** in order to teach us that even the handiwork of **a** ***na'arah,*** who cannot be sold as a maidservant, belongs to her father.

בַּהֲפָרַת נְדָרֶיהָ [4] The Gemara proceeds to discuss the next line of the Mishnah, which stated: "The father is also authorized **to annul the vows** made by his daughter while she is a minor or a *na'arah.*" [5]The Gemara asks: **From where** in the Torah **do we know** that the father is entitled to annul his daughter's vows?

דִּכְתִיב [6] The Gemara answers: **The verse** that concludes the passage dealing with the annulment of vows **says** (Numbers 30:17): "These are the statutes that the Lord commanded Moses, between a man and his wife, between a father and his daughter **while she is a** ***na'arah*** **in her father's house."** The verse teaches that until a girl reaches the age of twelve-and-a-half, she remains under the authority of her father with respect to the annulment of her vows.

וּמְקַבֵּל אֶת גִּיטָּהּ [7] We learned in our Mishnah: "If a father has arranged his daughter's betrothal and the bridegroom wishes to dissolve the relationship, the father **receives the bill of divorce** on his daughter's behalf, provided that she has not yet reached full adulthood [at the age of twelve-and-a-half] or married." [8]The Gemara asks: **From where** in the Torah **do we know this?**

דִּכְתִיב [9] The Gemara answers: **The verse** dealing with divorce and remarriage **says** (Deuteronomy 24:2): **"And she shall go out** from his house, a**nd she shall be** another man's wife." By mentioning the woman's divorce and her remarriage in the same verse, [10]the Torah teaches us that **divorce is compared to marriage,** so that the laws pertaining to the latter apply to the former as well. Just as the father is entitled to arrange his daughter's betrothal while she is still a *na'arah,* so too is he authorized to receive a bill of divorce on her behalf until she reaches the age of twelve-and-a-half.

[1]אֶלָּא, קְטַנָּה לָא צְרִיכָא קְרָא. [2]הָשְׁתָּא זַבּוּנֵי מְזַבֵּין לָהּ, מַעֲשֵׂה יָדֶיהָ מִיבָּעֵי? [3][אֶלָּא] כִּי אִיצְטְרִיךְ קְרָא, לְנַעֲרָה.
[4]״בַּהֲפָרַת נְדָרֶיהָ״. [5]מְנָלַן? [6]דִּכְתִיב: ״בִּנְעֻרֶיהָ בֵּית אָבִיהָ״.
[7]״וּמְקַבֵּל אֶת גִּיטָּהּ״. [8]מְנָלַן? [9]דִּכְתִיב: ״וְיָצְאָה...וְהָיְתָה״.
[10]אִיתְקוּשׁ יְצִיאָה לַהֲוָיָה.

LITERAL TRANSLATION

[1]Rather, a minor does not require a verse. [2]Now [that] he can sell her, is it necessary [to mention] her handiwork? [3]Rather, when the verse was required, [it was] for a *na'arah.*

[4]"To the annulment of her vows." [5]From where do we [know this]?

[6]For it is written: "While she is a *na'arah* in her father's house."

[7]"And he receives her bill of divorce." [8]From where do we [know this]?

[9]For it is written: "And she shall go out... and she shall be."

[10]Going out [from marriage] is compared to entering [marriage].

RASHI

אלא קטנה לא צריכא קרא — דקשיא לך לעיל: אימא הני מילי קטנה דמלי מזבן לה — לאו קושיא היא. **כי איצטריך קרא לנערה** — ואף על גב דעיקר קרא בקטנה כתיב, מיהו קרא יתירא הוא, דכתיב ״לאמה״ — לאקושי בת לאמה, להיקישא דנערה אתיא. **בנעוריה** — גבי הפרת נדרים כתיב. והכי קאמר: ״בנעוריה״ — ברשות אביה היא. וכי תימא: הא בהדיא כתיב ״כי הניא אביה אותה״! אי לאו האי — הוה אמינא בקטנה משתעי.

BACKGROUND

כִּי אִיצְטְרִיךְ קְרָא לְנַעֲרָה When the verse was required, it was for a ***na'arah.*** The Gemara'a exegesis here is similar to that used in the hermeneutic principle of אִם אֵינוֹ עִנְיָן — "if it does not refer to...." Since we have proved that the instance explicitly mentioned in the verse does not demand a special exegetical derivation from the word אָמָה ("maidservant"), we expand the meaning of the verse and infer from it that before a daughter comes of age she is in some sense her father's maidservant. Hence her handiwork belongs to him, even after she becomes a *na'arah* and he is no longer able to sell her.

NOTES

בַּהֲפָרַת נְדָרֶיהָ To the annulment of her vows. *Rashi* asks: Why did the Gemara derive the father's right to annul his daughter's vows from the verse that contains the expression "while she is a *na'arah* in her father's house," which at most is only an allusion to such a right? Why did the Gemara not cite the earlier verse (verse 6), "But if her father disallows her vow on the day that he hears, none of her vows or her bonds with which she has bound herself shall stand," which states explicitly that the father is authorized to annul his daughter's vows?

Rashi explains that without the expression "while she is a *na'arah*" we might have thought that the father's right to annul his daughter's vows is limited to the period during which she is a minor. The expression "while she is a *na'arah* [בִּנְעֻרֶיהָ — *bin'ureha*] in her father's house," teaches us that even while a girl is a *na'arah* her father is authorized to annul her vows.

Ritva points out that a difficulty still remains, for the first verse in the passage dealing with the annulment of vows states (verse 4): "And if a woman vows a vow to the Lord, and binds herself by a bond in her father's house while she is a *na'arah,*" clearly indicating that the father is authorized

[1]״וְאֵינוֹ אוֹכֵל פֵּירוֹת בְּחַיֶּיהָ״. [2]תָּנוּ רַבָּנַן: ״הָאָב אֵינוֹ אוֹכֵל פֵּירוֹת בְּחַיֵּי בִתּוֹ. [3]רַבִּי יוֹסֵי בְּרַבִּי יְהוּדָה אוֹמֵר: הָאָב אוֹכֵל פֵּירוֹת בְּחַיֵּי בִתּוֹ״.
[4]בְּמַאי קָמִיפַּלְגִי?
[5]תַּנָּא קַמָּא סָבַר: [6]בִּשְׁלָמָא בַּעַל תַּקִּינוּ לֵיהּ רַבָּנַן פֵּירֵי, [7]דְּאִם כֵּן מִימְנַע וְלָא פָּרֵיק. [8]אֶלָּא אָב, מַאי אִיכָּא לְמֵימַר? [9]דְּמִימְנַע וְלָא פָּרֵיק? [10]בְּלָאו הָכִי פָּרֵיק לָהּ! [11]וְרַבִּי יוֹסֵי בְּרַבִּי יְהוּדָה סָבַר: [12]אָב נַמִי מִימְנַע וְלָא פָּרֵיק. [13]סָבַר: כִּיסָא נְקִיטָא עִילָוָהּ. [14]תֵּיזִיל וְתִפְרוֹק נַפְשָׁהּ.

LITERAL TRANSLATION

[1]"But he does not enjoy the usufruct during her lifetime." [2]Our Rabbis taught: "The father does not enjoy the usufruct during the lifetime of his daughter. [3]Rabbi Yose the son of Rabbi Yehudah says: The father enjoys the usufruct during the lifetime of his daughter."
[4]About what do they disagree?
[5]The first Tanna maintains: [6]Granted that for the husband the Rabbis instituted usufruct, [7]for if [not] so, he would refrain and not redeem [her]. [8]But [regarding] the father, what is there to say? [9]That he would refrain and not redeem [her]? [10][Even] without this he would redeem her! [11]And Rabbi Yose the son of Rabbi Yehudah maintains: [12]The father would also refrain and not redeem [her]. [13][For] he thinks: A purse is held by her. [14]Let her go and redeem herself.

TRANSLATION AND COMMENTARY

וְאֵינוֹ אוֹכֵל פֵּירוֹת בְּחַיֶּיהָ [1]The Mishnah continued: **"But** the father of a daughter who is a minor or a *na'arah* **does not enjoy the usufruct** of her property **during her lifetime."** [2]However, in a related Baraita, **our Rabbis taught** that this ruling is the subject of a Tannaitic dispute. The Baraita states: "Although he inherits his daughter's property if she dies, **the father does not enjoy the usufruct** of that property **during the daughter's lifetime."** This is the opinion of the anonymous first Tanna of the Baraita, who is in agreement with the Tanna whose view is reflected in our Mishnah. [3]The Baraita continues: **"Rabbi Yose the son of Rabbi Yehudah** disagrees and **says: The father does** in fact **enjoy the usufruct** of his daughter's property **during her lifetime."**

בְּמַאי קָמִיפַּלְגִי [4]The Gemara now seeks to explain the dispute in the Baraita and asks: **About what do** these Tannaim **disagree?**

תַּנָּא קַמָּא סָבַר [5]The Gemara answers: **The** anonymous **first Tanna maintains** as follows: The Rabbis, as is stated in a Baraita below (47b), granted the husband the usufruct of his wife's property in return for his obligation to ransom her should she be taken captive. [6]**Granted that the Rabbis instituted usufruct for the husband,** [7]**for if** they had **not** done **so,** the husband **would refrain from redeeming her.** A husband might be unwilling to ransom his wife with his own funds, so they entitled him to all the usufruct of her property. In exchange, he became obligated to ransom his wife with all the means at his disposal. [8]**But** the Rabbis had no reason to grant the father the usufruct of his daughter's property. For **what argument can be brought** in favor of such an arrangement? [9]**That** the father **will refrain from redeeming** his own daughter? [10]Surely, **even without** being entitled to take the usufruct, the father will in any case not abandon his daughter, but **will redeem her!** [11]On the other hand, **Rabbi Yose the son of Rabbi Yehudah** disagrees with this assumption and **maintains:** The Rabbis granted the father the usufruct of his daughter's property, for if they had not done so, [12]**the father might also refrain from redeeming** his daughter if she were taken captive. [13]**For he** might **think** to himself: **She holds a purse** full of money to which I have no access and the usufruct of which I do not enjoy. [14]**Let her go and redeem herself** with her own money. Thus the Rabbis enacted that the father is entitled to the usufruct of his daughter's property, in exchange for which he is obligated to pay his daughter's full ransom.

RASHI

ומימנע ולא פריק – לפיכך תקנו לו פירות, כדאמר לקמן: ופירקונה תחת פירות, דליכלינהו בעל וכל פדיונה יהי עליו, אם רב אם מעט. דאי אמרת ליגחינהו, ויפדוה מהם אם תהיה שבוייה – ומנין דלא מלו. והשתא יהיב מדידיה. **כיסא נקיטא** – כיס מלא מעות יש לה בסגולה, ועד הנה לא נהניתי מהם – עתה תפדה את עצמה, ואם יחסר – אני לא אשלים.

SAGES

רַבִּי יוֹסֵי בְּרַבִּי יְהוּדָה Rabbi Yose the son of Rabbi Yehudah. A Tanna of the last generation, Rabbi Yose was the son of the Tanna Rabbi Yehudah (ben Il'ai). He was apparently a close disciple of his father, though he occasionally disagreed with him about the Halakhah, and he was a colleague of Rabbi Yehudah HaNasi. He also discussed the Halakhah with other Sages of his generation. In his activity as a Halakhic authority he was apparently closely associated with Rabbi Yehudah HaNasi, and his teachings are mentioned a number of times in the Mishnah, and very often in the Tosefta and elsewhere. He was also very prolific in the area of Aggadah, and some well-known sayings are transmitted in his name. He seems to have died before Rabbi Yehudah HaNasi, for he referred to him in his will.

NOTES

to annul his daughter's vows even when she is a *na'arah*. *Ritva* answers *Rashi's* question as follows: The Gemara often cites a particular verse even though a different verse could just as well have been cited, especially if the verse that it does cite is better known than the other.

וְאֵינוֹ אוֹכֵל פֵּירוֹת בְּחַיֶּיהָ But he does not enjoy the usufruct during her lifetime. According to the Baraita cited below (47b), the Rabbis enacted that a husband is entitled to the usufruct of his wife's property, in exchange for which he is obligated to ransom her if she falls into captivity. And our Gemara argues that a similar enactment was not made for the father, because even without being entitled to the usufruct of his daughter's property, the father will surely ransom his daughter from captivity.

The Jerusalem Talmud explains the enactment of usufruct differently. The Rabbis instituted that the husband is

BACKGROUND

כָּתַב לָהּ פֵּירוֹת If he wrote for her fruit. All the things mentioned here are movable property. According to Torah law, they are not acquired by their recipient until he performs a formal act of acquisition, such as pulling them. Thus the writing of a deed of transfer does not effect their transfer. It is a promise, and was made only on the assumption that the marriage would last for some time. Hence failure to keep such a promise does not entail even a moral blemish.

TRANSLATION AND COMMENTARY

נִיסֵּת [1] The next clause of the Mishnah stated: **"If** a girl **marries, her husband** is entitled to all those things to which her father was previously entitled. And the husband **has** one **more** entitlement **than** the father, **in that he** also **enjoys** the usufruct of his wife's property during her lifetime." [2] **Our Rabbis taught** the following Baraita, which deals with the husband's right to the property brought into the marriage by his wife: **"If a father** gives his daughter away in betrothal, and at the time of the betrothal he **assigns to her** movable goods, such as **fruit, clothing, and utensils,** [3] as part of the dowry **that will come with her** when she leaves **her father's house** and enters **her husband's house** in marriage, **and she dies** during the period of her betrothal, [4] **the husband does not acquire** any of **those things** mentioned above that were included in her dowry. [5] **In the name of Rabbi Natan they said:** If the girl dies during the period of her betrothal, **the husband acquires those things** that were promised to him as part of his wife's dowry."

[1] ״נִיסֵּת, יָתֵר עָלָיו הַבַּעַל שֶׁהוּא אוֹכֵל, כו׳״. [2] תָּנוּ רַבָּנַן: ״כָּתַב לָהּ פֵּירוֹת, כְּסוּת, וְכֵלִים, [3] שֶׁיָּבוֹאוּ עִמָּהּ מִבֵּית אָבִיהָ לְבֵית בַּעְלָהּ. מֵתָה, [4] לֹא זָכָה הַבַּעַל בַּדְּבָרִים הַלָּלוּ. [5] מִשּׁוּם רַבִּי נָתָן אָמְרוּ: זָכָה הַבַּעַל בַּדְּבָרִים הַלָּלוּ״.

LITERAL TRANSLATION

[1] "[If] she marries, the husband has more than him, in that he enjoys, etc." [2] Our Rabbis taught: "[If] he [the father] wrote for her fruit, clothing, and utensils, [3] which would come with her from the house of her father to the house of her husband, [and] she died, [4] the husband does not acquire these things. [5] In the name of Rabbi Natan they said: The husband acquires these things."

RASHI

כתב לה פירות כסות וכלים — פסק לה האב בנדונייתה שמכניס לבעלה מטלטלין, כגון פירות תלושין וכסות וכלים, וכתבן לה מן האירוסין. **ומתה** — באירוסין לא זכה כו׳.

NOTES

entitled to the usufruct, so that he will manage his wife's property properly. It was not necessary to make a similar enactment regarding the father, for even if he is not entitled to the usufruct of his daughter's property, he will surely manage her property in the best possible manner.

כָּתַב לָהּ פֵּירוֹת If he wrote for her fruit. According to *Rashi, Rabbenu Ḥananel, Rambam* and most other Rishonim, the Baraita is referring here to a girl who died during the period of her betrothal. But if she died after she was married, all agree that her husband acquires all those things that his father-in-law promised to provide as his daughter's dowry.

Rabbenu Tam and *Ba'al HaMa'or* raised several objections against this interpretation: First, this Baraita is cited by the Gemara in connection with the clause of the Mishnah that deals with the rights of a married man in his wife's property. Second, the law is that the bridegroom does not inherit anything from his betrothed bride before she enters the bridal chamber. And third, the term אִיחַתּוּנֵי — "getting married" — used by the Gemara in its discussion of this Baraita is inappropriate if we are dealing with a betrothed girl. Rather, the Gemara should have used the term אִיקְרוּבֵי דַּעְתָּא — "coming together" — (see below, 56a). For these and other reasons, *Rabbenu Tam* explains that the Baraita here must be referring to a girl who died after she was married. According to the anonymous first Tanna of the Baraita, the husband does not acquire those things that were promised as his wife's dowry, because his father-in-law obligated himself to the dowry only on condition that his daughter would derive some benefit from the dowry during her married life, and here the dowry has not yet been transferred to her husband's home.

The Rishonim deal at length with both approaches to the Gemara (see *Ramban, Ritva,* and others). As for the objections raised against *Rashi* and those who follow his explanation, the anonymous first Tanna of the Baraita maintains that the husband acquires the right to his wife's dowry only after they are married, and so the Baraita fits in well as part of the discussion surrounding our Mishnah. Even though the bridegroom does not ordinarily inherit from his betrothed bride, here the dowry has already been recorded in the ketubah that was drawn up at the time of the betrothal, the bridegroom inherits the bride's dowry even though she died before they were married. And lastly, the term אִיקְרוּבֵי דַּעְתָּא is the term used to describe the relationship between a bride and a bridegroom who are betrothed but not yet married; but as for the relationship between the father of the bride and his son-in-law, the term אִיחַתּוּנֵי is perfectly appropriate from the time of betrothal.

HALAKHAH

כָּתַב לָהּ פֵּירוֹת If he wrote for her fruit. "If a father promises to provide his daughter with a dowry, and she is married (or handed over to someone acting on behalf of the husband), but she dies before the dowry is actually transferred to her or to her husband, some authorities maintain that the husband is entitled to the full amount promised by the father-in-law (following *Rashi, Rambam,* and others). According to *Rabbenu Tam,* the husband is not entitled to the dowry, for the father-in-law only obligated himself to give the dowry on the basis that his daughter would derive some benefit from it. Since the law is in doubt, the husband cannot collect the dowry from his father-in-law. Various factors can influence the law — for example, whether or not the dowry was deposited in the hands

TRANSLATION AND COMMENTARY

לֵימָא בִּפְלוּגְתָּא [1] The Gemara now suggests that this Tannaitic dispute parallels another disagreement between Tannaim. **Shall we say that** the anonymous first Tanna of the Baraita and Rabbi Natan **disagree about the** same **matter** that was **in dispute between Rabbi Elazar ben Azaryah and the Rabbis?** [2] **For we have learned** in a Mishnah (below, 54b): "The Sages enacted that a virgin who marries is entitled to a ketubah of two hundred zuz, and a widow or a divorcee who remarries is entitled to a ketubah of only a maneh (one hundred zuz). Nevertheless, if the husband so wishes, he may obligate himself to the payment of an additional sum, no matter how high. [3] **If** the woman **was widowed or divorced,** [4] **whether after marriage or** even **after betrothal** (and the ketubah had already been drawn up at the time of betrothal), [5] she **collects the entire amount** recorded in the ketubah — both the standard, fixed ketubah payment and any addition to the basic sum which the husband had undertaken to pay. [6] **Rabbi Elazar ben Azaryah** disagrees and **says:** If she was widowed or divorced **after marriage, she collects the entire amount** recorded in the ketubah. [7] **But** if she was widowed or divorced **after betrothal,** she collects only the minimum amount — if she was **a virgin** at the time of her betrothal, she **collects two hundred** zuz, [8] **and** if she was **a widow** when she was betrothed, she collects **a maneh.** But she does not collect the additional sum [47B] **for** her husband **wrote the additional sum for her** in the ketubah **only on the basis that he would marry her,** and here she was widowed or divorced before the marriage process could be completed." The Gemara now explains how this dispute between the Rabbis and Rabbi Elazar ben Azaryah parallels the one found in the previously cited Baraita between the Rabbis (the anonymous first Tanna of the Baraita) and Rabbi Natan. [9] The Rabbis, **who say that** the husband **does not acquire** the movable goods that his father-in-law promised as part of his daughter's dowry, if his bride dies during betrothal, seem to **agree with Rabbi Elazar ben Azaryah,** who says that if a woman is widowed or divorced after betrothal, she is entitled only to the basic portion of her ketubah, but not to the additional sum.

[1] לֵימָא בִּפְלוּגְתָּא דְּרַבִּי אֶלְעָזָר בֶּן עֲזַרְיָה וְרַבָּנַן קָמִיפַּלְגִי? [2] דִּתְנַן: [3] ״נִתְאַרְמְלָה אוֹ נִתְגָּרְשָׁה, [4] בֵּין מִן הַנִּשּׂוּאִין בֵּין מִן הָאֵירוּסִין, [5] גּוֹבָה אֶת הַכֹּל. [6] רַבִּי אֶלְעָזָר בֶּן עֲזַרְיָה אוֹמֵר: מִן הַנִּשּׂוּאִין — גּוֹבָה אֶת הַכֹּל, [7] וּמִן הָאֵרוּסִין — בְּתוּלָה גּוֹבָה מָאתַיִם, [8] וְאַלְמָנָה מָנֶה, [47B] שֶׁלֹּא כָּתַב לָהּ אֶלָּא עַל מְנָת לְכוֹנְסָהּ״. [9] לְמַאן דְּאָמַר לֹא זָכָה כְּרַבִּי אֶלְעָזָר בֶּן

LITERAL TRANSLATION

[1] Shall we say that they disagree about the [matter in] dispute between Rabbi Elazar ben Azaryah and the Rabbis? [2] For we have learned: [3] "[If a woman] was widowed or divorced, [4] whether after marriage or after betrothal, [5] she collects everything. [6] Rabbi Elazar ben Azaryah says: After marriage, she collects everything, [7] but after betrothal, a virgin collects two hundred [zuz], [8] and a widow a maneh, [47B] for he only wrote [the addition] for her in order to marry her." [9] The one who says [that] he does not acquire is in accordance with Rabbi Elazar ben

RASHI

לימא בפלוגתא כו׳ — דמאן דאמר: בעלה יורש נדונייתה מן האירוסין — כרבנן, דאמרי: אם מת הוא — גובה את הכל: מנה, מאתים, ותוספת. אלמא כתובתה קיימא כאילו נישאת. אם מתה איהי — נמי ירית איהו נדוניא, שאף היא בתוך השטר נכתבה, דהכי כתבינן: דא נדוניא דהנעלת ליה מבי אבוה, כך וכך, וצבי ואוסיף לה מדיליה כך וכך. **מאן דאמר לא זכה כרבי אלעזר** — דאמר: לא כתב לה כתובה אלא על מנת לכונסה. ומנה מאתים דתקון לה רבנן הוא דאית לה. איהי נמי לא כתבה לו ״ודא נדוניא דהנעלת ליה״ אלא על מנת חיבת נשואין.

SAGES

רַבִּי אֶלְעָזָר בֶּן עֲזַרְיָה **Rabbi Elazar ben Azaryah.** A Tanna of the generation following the destruction of the Second Temple. See *Ketubot*, Part II, pp. 205-6.

NOTES

אֶלָּא עַל מְנָת לְכוֹנְסָהּ **In order to marry her.** Rabbi Elazar ben Azaryah rules that if a woman is widowed or divorced after betrothal, she collects only the basic portion of her ketubah, but not any additional sum for the husband obligated himself to pay the additional sum only if they were married. This ruling is not limited to a case in which the husband made an explicit stipulation to that effect, and we assume that this was his intention even if he made no mention of such a condition. For a condition does not necessarily have to be stated explicitly in order to be valid; it is sufficient that it be clear to all that such a condition was implicitly accepted by the parties to the agreement.

Tosafot asks: Why, then, do we not say that if a person buys an animal and it turns out to be *terefah* and therefore unfit to be eaten, the sale is void, for surely he bought it only on condition that it would be fit for him to eat?

HALAKHAH

of a third party. Numerous ordinances relating to a woman's dowry were instituted in various communities (Speyer, Worms, and Mainz; Toledo; and others), obliging the husband in certain circumstances to return part or all of his wife's dowry if she should die before or shortly after the marriage, even if the dowry was handed over to him during her lifetime." (*Rambam, Sefer Nashim, Hilkhot Ishut* 22:2, 23:15; *Shulḥan Arukh, Even HaEzer* 53:3; *Ḥoshen Mishpat* 253:16.)

עֲזַרְיָה. [1] וּמַאן דְּאָמַר זָכָה כְּרַבָּנַן.
[2] לָא, דְּכוּלֵּי עָלְמָא כְּרַבִּי אֶלְעָזָר בֶּן עֲזַרְיָה. [3] מַאן דְּאָמַר לֹא זָכָה כְּרַבִּי אֶלְעָזָר בֶּן עֲזַרְיָה. [4] וּמַאן דְּאָמַר זָכָה עַד כָּאן לָא קָאָמַר רַבִּי אֶלְעָזָר בֶּן עֲזַרְיָה אֶלָּא

LITERAL TRANSLATION

Azaryah. [1] And the one who says [that] he acquires is in accordance with the Rabbis.

[2] No, everyone is in accordance with Rabbi Elazar ben Azaryah. [3] The one who says [that] he does not acquire is in accordance with Rabbi Elazar ben Azaryah. [4] And the one who says [that] he acquires [maintains that] Rabbi Elazar ben Azaryah only

RASHI

כולי עלמא כרבי אלעזר בן עזריה — תרוייהו הנך תנאי דלעיל (תרוייהו) כרבי אלעזר בן עזריה, דפסקינן הלכתא כוותיה לקמן.

TRANSLATION AND COMMENTARY

Rabbi Elazar ben Azaryah maintains that the bride is not entitled to the additional sum in these circumstances, because the bridegroom obligated himself to pay it only if he married her. Similarly, the Rabbis in the previously cited Baraita maintain that the bridegroom does not acquire the movable goods promised as part of his bride's dowry, if she dies during betrothal, because the father-in-law obligates himself to give the dowry only if his daughter marries. [1] By contrast, Rabbi Natan, **who says that** the bridegroom **does** in fact **acquire** the movable goods promised as his bride's dowry, even if she dies during the betrothal, seems to **agree with the Rabbis** in the second Baraita, who say that a woman is entitled to her entire ketubah, the basic amount *and* the additional sum, even if she is widowed or divorced after betrothal. The Rabbis maintain that the obligations recorded in the ketubah take full effect from the time it is drawn up, even from the time of betrothal. Thus a woman is entitled to the additional sum contained in the ketubah drawn up by her bridegroom, even if she is widowed or divorced before the marriage is completed. Similarly, Rabbi Natan maintains that the bridegroom acquires the dowry recorded in the ketubah, even if his bride dies during their betrothal, for the obligations recorded in the ketubah take full effect from the time the ketubah is drawn up.

לָא [2] The Gemara now rejects the suggestion that the two Tannaitic disputes correspond to each other. **No,** says the Gemara, we can argue that, concerning the additional sum, **everyone** — both the Rabbis and Rabbi Natan — **agrees with Rabbi Elazar ben Azaryah** that if a woman is widowed or divorced after betrothal, she is entitled only to the basic portion of her ketubah, and not to any additional sum recorded in it. [3] As was explained above, it is obvious that the Rabbis in the first Baraita, **who say** that the bridegroom **does not acquire** the movable goods that his father-in-law promised as part of his daughter's dowry, if his bride dies during betrothal, **agree with Rabbi Elazar ben Azaryah.** Just as the bride is not entitled to the addition to her ketubah if she is widowed or divorced during betrothal, similarly the bridegroom does not acquire his bride's dowry if she dies during betrothal; for just as the bridegroom obligated himself to pay the additional sum only on the basis that he would marry her, so too the father-in-law obligated himself to give the dowry only on the basis that his daughter would be married. [4] **And** it is even possible to argue that Rabbi Natan, **who says that** the bridegroom **does** in fact **acquire** the movable goods promised as part of his bride's dowry, even if she dies during betrothal, will agree with Rabbi Elazar ben Azaryah regarding the additional sum in the ketubah. For he can argue that a distinction must be made between the two issues: It is possible **that Rabbi Elazar ben Azaryah stated** his opinion **only regarding property that goes from**

NOTES

Tosafot distinguishes between the two cases: In the case of the animal, the buyer bought it accepting the risk that it might be *terefah*, and he would have been willing to buy it even if the seller had insisted that he explicitly accept that risk. But in our case it is apparent to all that the bridegroom obligated himself to pay the additional sum only on condition that the betrothal would lead to marriage. The issue of implied conditions is widely discussed among the Aḥaronim (see *Eshel Avraham* and the responsa of *Rabbi Akiva Eger*).

דְּכוּלֵּי עָלְמָא כְּרַבִּי אֶלְעָזָר בֶּן עֲזַרְיָה Everyone is in accordance with Rabbi Elazar ben Azaryah. No logical argument compels us to say that the Rabbis and Rabbi Natan must agree with Rabbi Elazar ben Azaryah. It could equally have been argued that both the Rabbis and Rabbi Natan agree, against Rabbi Elazar ben Azaryah, that if a woman is widowed or divorced after betrothal, she is entitled not only to the basic portion of her ketubah but to the additional sum as well. It is obvious that Rabbi Natan — who maintains that the bridgroom acquires the goods promised by his father-in-law, even if his bride dies during betrothal — can agree with the Rabbis. It is even possible to say that the Rabbis in the one Baraita, who maintain that the bridegroom does not acquire the goods promised by his father-in-law, can agree with the Rabbis in the other Baraita, who maintain that the woman is entitled to the main portion of her ketubah as well as to the additional sum, even if she is widowed or divorced during betrothal. For they may well be of the opinion that the father-in-law obligates himself to pay the dowry only on condition that his daughter is married, whereas the bridegroom agrees that the obligations he accepts should take full effect from

TRANSLATION AND COMMENTARY

him to her, the sum that the bridegroom promises his bride as her marriage settlement. Rabbi Elazar ben Azaryah maintains that the bride is not entitled to the additional sum beyond the basic ketubah if she is widowed or divorced after betrothal, [1]**for** the bridegroom **wrote the additional sum for her** in the ketubah **on the basis that he would marry her.** [2]**But regarding property that goes from her to him** — the dowry that the father-in-law promises to provide for his daughter — [3]**even Rabbi Elazar ben Azaryah agrees** that the bridegroom acquires whatever was promised as his bride's dowry, even if the bride dies during the period of her betrothal. [4]**For** the father-in-law promises to provide his daughter with a dowry **because** he is interested in **creating a bond of marriage** with his future son-in-law. As soon as the bridegroom betroths the daughter, [5]**they have** already **created a bond of marriage,** and this is why the bridegroom acquires the dowry, even if the marriage process is never actually completed.

חַיָּיב בִּמְזוֹנוֹתֶיהָ [6]The Gemara now proceeds to the next clause of the Mishnah, which said: "The husband **is liable for** his wife's **maintenance,** for her ransom, and for her burial." [7]**Our Rabbis taught** a Baraita regarding these obligations, which states: "The Sages **instituted** that the husband is liable for his wife's **maintenance, in exchange for** which he is entitled to **her handiwork.** [8]Likewise, they instituted that the husband is liable for his wife's **burial, in exchange for** which he is entitled to the dowry recorded in **her ketubah** which he inherits upon her death. [9]**Therefore the husband enjoys the usufruct."**

פֵּירוֹת [10]The Gemara immediately objects: The last clause of the Baraita seems to be out of context. The Baraita refers to the husband's rights to his wife's handiwork and to her dowry. But **who mentioned** his right to the **usufruct** of her property, which is referred to at the end of the Baraita as if it had already been alluded to earlier?

חַסּוּרֵי מִחַסְּרָא [11]The Gemara answers: The text of **the Baraita is defective** — a sentence is missing from it — **and it should read as follows:** [12]"The Sages **instituted** that the husband is liable for his wife's **maintenance, in exchange for** which he is entitled to **her handiwork."** The Gemara now inserts the missing clause: [13]"Likewise, they instituted that the husband is obligated to provide the money for his wife's **ransom, in exchange for** which he is entitled to the **usufruct** of her property." [14]And the Baraita now continues: "The Sages also enacted that the husband must bear the costs of his wife's **burial, in exchange for** which he is entitled to the dowry recorded in **her ketubah,** which he inherits upon her death. [15]**Therefore the husband enjoys the usufruct."**

מִדִּידֵיהּ לְדִידָהּ, [1]שֶׁלֹּא כָּתַב לָהּ אֶלָּא עַל מְנָת לְכוֹנְסָהּ. [2]אֲבָל מִדִּידָהּ לְדִידֵיהּ, [3]אֲפִילּוּ רַבִּי אֶלְעָזָר בֶּן עֲזַרְיָה מוֹדֵי, [4]דְּמִשּׁוּם אִיחַתּוּנֵי הוּא, [5]וְהָא אִיחַתְּנֵי לְהוּ.

[6]"חַיָּיב בִּמְזוֹנוֹתֶיהָ וכו'". [7]תָּנוּ רַבָּנַן: "תִּיקְּנוּ מְזוֹנוֹתֶיהָ תַּחַת מַעֲשֵׂה יָדֶיהָ, [8]וּקְבוּרָתָהּ תַּחַת כְּתוּבָּתָהּ. [9]לְפִיכָךְ בַּעַל אוֹכֵל פֵּירוֹת".

[10]פֵּירוֹת, מַאן דְּכַר שְׁמַיְיהוּ? [11]חַסּוּרֵי מִחַסְּרָא, וְהָכִי קָתָנֵי: [12]"תִּיקְּנוּ מְזוֹנוֹתֶיהָ תַּחַת מַעֲשֵׂה יָדֶיהָ, [13]וּפִירְקוֹנָהּ תַּחַת פֵּירוֹת, [14]וּקְבוּרָתָהּ תַּחַת כְּתוּבָּתָהּ. [15]לְפִיכָךְ בַּעַל אוֹכֵל פֵּירוֹת".

LITERAL TRANSLATION

stated [his opinion regarding what goes] from him to her, [1]for he only wrote [the addition] for her in order to marry her. [2]But [regarding what goes] from her to him, [3]even Rabbi Elazar ben Azaryah agrees, [4]for it is [given] in order to create a bond of marriage, [5]and surely they did create a bond of marriage.

[6]He is liable for her maintenance, etc." [7]Our Rabbis taught: "They instituted her maintenance in exchange for her handiwork, [8]and her burial in exchange for her ketubah. [9]Therefore the husband enjoys the usufruct."

[10]Usufruct, who mentioned its name?

[11][The Baraita] is defective, and it teaches as follows: [12]"They instituted her maintenance in exchange for her handiwork, [13]and her ransom in exchange for usufruct, [14]and her burial in exchange for her ketubah. [15]Therefore the husband enjoys the usufruct."

RASHI

מדידיה לדידה – מה שחתן פוסק לכלה בכתובתה. **תחת כתובתה** – תחת הנדוניא שהכניסה לו, והיא כתובה בשטר הכתובה, והוא יורש. **תחת פירות** – שהוא אוכל מנכסי מלוג שלה, כגון נכסים שנפלו לה משניסת, או שהיו לה קודם לכן, שלא שמאתן לו בנדוניית כתובתה.

NOTES

the time the ketubah is drawn up. The Gemara preferred to say that both Rabbi Natan and the Rabbis agree with Rabbi Elazar ben Azaryah because the law is in accordance with the latter's view (*Rabbenu Crescas Vidal*).

וּפִירְקוֹנָהּ תַּחַת פֵּירוֹת **And her ransom in exchange for usufruct.** Even though the formulation "and her ransom in

BACKGROUND

מִשּׁוּם אִיחַתּוּנֵי **To create a bond of marriage.** In recent generations the Hebrew words לְהִנָּשֵׂא and לְהִתְחַתֵּן have been treated as synonymous, and both can be adequately translated as "to marry." However, both in the Bible and in Rabbinic literature the two concepts are quite distinct. The term נִישּׂוּאִין (derived from the verb לְהִנָּשֵׂא) refers to the personal bond between a man and his wife, which begins with betrothal and culminates in their living together. By contrast, the term לְהִתְחַתֵּן refers to the family tie that results from marriage, and it concerns the families of the bride and the bridegroom, which are now connected by marriage. While the tie of נִישּׂוּאִין is private and intimate, that of חֲתוּנָּה is familial and social. Consequently the family of one of the parties may be greatly interested in the familial and social connection created by the couple's agreement to marry (לְהִתְחַתֵּן), whereas the creation of the tie of marriage (נִישּׂוּאִין) is a matter between the husband and the wife and does not concern the entire family to the same degree.

תִּיקְּנוּ מְזוֹנוֹתֶיהָ **They instituted her maintenance.** This wording indicates that the Sages instituted this regulation in order to maintain a certain equilibrium within family life, to balance the obligations between the two parties. But these basic rights belong to the wife. Hence we can understand the approach of several Sages who argue that the wife, and only she, may waive some of these rights.

תַּחַת כְּתוּבָּתָהּ **In exchange for her ketubah.** *Rashi* and others explain that the term כְּתוּבָּתָהּ here does not refer to the ketubah itself, the sum that the husband is obliged to pay his wife if the marriage is dissolved by divorce or by his death, but, on the contrary, to the dowry, the sum that the wife's family gives the husband, which he has the right to use while he is married to her.

TERMINOLOGY

חַסּוּרֵי מִיחַסְּרָא, וְהָכִי קָתָנֵי **The Baraita is defective, and it teaches as follows.** Sometimes the Talmud resolves a difficulty regarding a

Mishnah (or a Baraita) by suggesting that a clause (or an entire sentence) was omitted from the text of the Mishnah: "The Mishnah lacks the following clause, and it states as follows...." Sometimes this phrase is used to propose a true emendation of the text of the Mishnah or the Baraita, when it is claimed that a sentence is actually missing from the text, and the difficulty in the passage is resolved by providing its wording in full. Indeed, errors of this kind are found in documents and are even more frequent in texts such as Baraitot, which were transmitted orally. However, in many cases the phrase does not introduce a true textual emendation, but rather a hypothetical explanation to the effect that if one were to supply certain words to complete a thought, it would be clearer and we could resolve the difficulty in the passage.

TRANSLATION AND COMMENTARY

מַאי ״לְפִיכָךְ״ [1] The Baraita's formulation is still difficult to understand, and the Gemara now asks: **What** does the Baraita **mean** when it states: **"Therefore** the husband enjoys the usufruct"? The Baraita has already explained that the husband is awarded the right to the usufruct of his wife's property in exchange for the obligation to ransom her should she fall into captivity. What, then, is added by the last clause of the Baraita?

מַהוּ דְּתֵימָא [2] The Gemara explains: **You might have thought that** when the Baraita says the Sages instituted that the husband is entitled to the usufruct of his wife's property, it does **not** mean that he is granted the right to **enjoy** the usufruct, [3] **but rather** that he **must let** the usufruct **lie** untouched, so that the money will be available for his wife's ransom; [4] **for if** this were **not so,** the husband **might refrain from ransoming her** with his own money. [5] **"Therefore,"** the Baraita concludes, "the husband enjoys the usufruct," thereby **telling us that it is preferable** that the husband be granted the right to enjoy the usufruct. [6] **For** if the Sages had enacted that the usufruct must be left untouched in a fund set aside for the wife's ransom, **the proceeds** so put aside **may sometimes not suffice** to ransom her and she will remain a captive. But now that the Sages have instituted that the husband is entitled to enjoy the usufruct of his wife's property, [7] **he must ransom her with his own money,** even if the amount that must be paid exceeds the value of the usufruct he has enjoyed.

וְאֵיפוּךְ אֲנָא [8] The Gemara now poses a more basic question regarding the Baraita: Why does the Baraita say that the Sages instituted the wife's maintenance in exchange for her handiwork, and her ransom in exchange for the usufruct of her property? **We can** just as well **reverse it** and argue that they instituted the wife's maintenance in exchange for the usufruct of her property, and her ransom in exchange for her handiwork!

LITERAL TRANSLATION

[1] What is [meant by] "therefore"?
[2] You might have said [that] he must not enjoy it, [3] [but rather] must let it lie, [4] for if [not] so, he will refrain and not ransom [her]. [5] [Therefore] he tells us that this is preferable. [6] [For] sometimes they [the proceeds] will not suffice, [7] and he will ransom [her] from his own [money].
[8] But I can reverse [it]!

[1] מַאי ״לְפִיכָךְ״?
[2] מַהוּ דְּתֵימָא מֵיכַל לָא נִכְלִינְהוּ, [3] אַנּוּחֵי נִנְחִינְהוּ, [4] דְּאִם כֵּן, מִימְנַע וְלָא פָּרֵיק. [5] קָא מַשְׁמַע לָן דְּהָא עֲדִיפָא. [6] זִימְנִין דְּלָא מָלוּ, [7] וּפָרֵיק לָהּ מִדִּידֵיהּ.
[8] וְאֵיפּוּךְ אֲנָא!

RASHI

דלא מלו — לא יהא בפירות כדי פרקונה. והשתא, כי אכלינהו ולא ידיע כמה הוה — פריק לה מדיליה, דהכי תיקון דאיהו אכיל בין רב בין מעט, והוא פריק כל כמה דהוי. ואיפוך אנא — מזונות תחת פירות, ופרקונה תחת מעשה ידיה. ונפקא מינה, דאי אמרה איני ניזונית ואיני עושה — לא כלום קאמרה. מזונות ומעשה ידיה מלוין, שבויה ואשה שיש לה נכסי מלוג — לא שכיחי.

NOTES

exchange for usufruct" could imply otherwise, most Rishonim explain that the Rabbis were primarily concerned with the woman's benefit and therefore they enacted that the husband is liable for his wife's ransom, and then in exchange they enacted that the husband is entitled to the usufruct of his wife's property (see *Tosafot* and *Ramban*). Since these measures were enacted for the wife's welfare, the husband cannot stipulate that he will waive his right to enjoy the usufruct of his wife's property, and in exchange his wife must waive her right to be ransomed. *Rashbam* (*Bava Batra* 49b) disagrees and says that the primary enactment was the one that entitled the husband to the usufruct of his wife's property. Therefore, if he wishes, he may waive his right to that usufruct and thereby release himself from the obligation to ransom his wife, if she is taken captive.

מַאי ״לְפִיכָךְ״ **What is meant by "therefore"?** *Tosafot* explains that the Baraita's formulation — "and her ransom in exchange for usufruct" — teaches us that a wife cannot stipulate that her husband will not be held liable to pay her ransom, and in return she will not be required to allow him to enjoy the usufruct of her property. On this basis we can understand why the word "therefore" introduces the last clause of the Baraita. Since the Rabbis enacted that the husband must ransom his wife, even if she has stipulated that he is exempt, *therefore* the husband always enjoys the usufruct of her property (*Bet Ya'akov*).

אַנּוּחֵי נִנְחִינְהוּ **But rather must let it lie.** The Rishonim ask: If the usufruct must be left untouched, then in what sense is the husband entitled to the usufruct of his wife's property? Surely the usufruct is not his if he cannot derive any benefit from it!

Tosafot answers that we might have thought that the husband must leave the usufruct untouched as long as he has some other means of support. But if he needs the usufruct to maintain himself, he is indeed entitled to enjoy it. *Ritva* (in the name of *Tosafot*) suggests that we might have thought that the husband must not consume the usufruct of his wife's property, but must purchase real estate with it, the principal of which must remain set aside for his wife's ransom, while its usufruct may be enjoyed by the husband himself.

וְאֵיפּוּךְ אֲנָא **But I can reverse it.** Our commentary follows *Rashi,* who explains that the Gemara is suggesting here that we can reverse the explanations regarding the enactments of ransom and maintenance and say that the Rabbis instituted the wife's maintenance in exchange for the usufruct of her property and her ransom in exchange for

TRANSLATION AND COMMENTARY

אָמַר אַבַּיֵי [1] **Abaye said** in reply: The Sages **instituted** the rights and duties of the husband and the wife in the following manner: They imposed **the more frequently** utilized obligation in exchange **for the more frequently** utilized right, [2] **and the less frequently** utilized obligation in exchange **for the less frequently** utilized right. The Sages obliged the husband to maintain his wife, and this is a regular need; in return they entitled him to her handiwork, and this is something that is regularly produced. And they enacted that the husband is liable for his wife's ransom in the unlikely event that she is taken captive, and in exchange they entitled him to the usufruct of her property, in the somewhat unusual case in which the wife has property of her own.

אָמַר רָבָא [3] According to the Baraita cited above, the husband's duty to maintain his wife is of Rabbinic origin, instituted by the Sages. **Rava said: The Tannaim** whose views are recorded in the following Baraita **are of the opinion that** the husband's duty **to maintain** his wife **is** an obligation imposed **by Torah law,** [4] **for** the following Baraita **was taught:** "The Torah says with regard to a Jewish maidservant (Exodus 21:9-10): 'And if he [the master] designates her for his son, he shall deal with her after the manner of daughters. If he takes another wife for himself, he shall not diminish her *she'er, kesut* or *onah* [שְׁאֵרָהּ, כְּסוּתָהּ, וְעֹנָתָהּ].' This verse states that a Jewish maidservant designated as a bride for her master or for his son is entitled to all the rights of a married woman, but the Tannaim disagree about the identification of those rights, which are referred to in this verse as *she'er, kesut,* and *onah.* [5] The anonymous first Tanna understands the verse as follows: **'*She'erah*' refers to** the girl's right to **maintenance.** [6] There is proof that the word *she'er* refers to food, for there is **another verse** that **says** (Micah 3:3): **'Who also eat the flesh** [*she'er*] **of my people.'** [7] **'*Kesutah*'** is to be understood **according to its plain sense** — that the husband is required to provide his wife with clothing, the usual meaning of the Hebrew word *kesut.* [8] **'*Onatah*' refers to** the girl's **conjugal rights,** her

[1] אָמַר אַבַּיֵי: תִּיקְנוּ מָצוּי לְמָצוּי, [2] וְשֶׁאֵינוֹ מָצוּי לְשֶׁאֵינוֹ מָצוּי.

[3] אָמַר רָבָא: הַאי תַּנָּא סָבַר מְזוֹנוֹת מִדְּאוֹרַיְיתָא, [4] דְּתַנְיָא: [5] "'שְׁאֵרָהּ' — אֵלּוּ מְזוֹנוֹת, [6] וְכֵן הוּא אוֹמֵר 'וַאֲשֶׁר אָכְלוּ שְׁאֵר עַמִּי'. [7] 'כְּסוּתָהּ' — כְּמַשְׁמָעוֹ. [8] 'עֹנָתָהּ' — זוֹ עוֹנָה הָאֲמוּרָה

LITERAL TRANSLATION

[1] Abaye said: They instituted the frequent for the frequent, [2] and the infrequent for the infrequent.

[3] Rava said: This Tanna maintains [that] maintenance is by Torah law, [4] for it was taught: [5] "'*She'erah*' — this is maintenance, [6] and similarly it says: 'Who also eat the flesh of my people.' [7] '*Kesutah*' — like its plain sense. [8] '*Onatah*' — this [means the wife's] conjugal rights that are mentioned in

RASHI

עונה האמורה בתורה — כמו שאמרה עונת תשמיש. ולקמן (כתובות סא,ב) תנן איזהו היא עונה.

NOTES

her handiwork. *Tosafot* (below, 52a) apparently understands this passage differently, and explains that the Gemara's question relates to the enactments of the wife's ransom and her burial: Why not say that the Rabbis instituted the wife's ransom in exchange for the dowry recorded in her ketubah, and her burial in exchange for the usufruct of her property? (See also *Maharshal.*)

שְׁאֵרָהּ — אֵלּוּ מְזוֹנוֹת *She'erah* — this is maintenance. According to the first two Tannaim mentioned in this Baraita, the husband's obligation to provide his wife with maintenance stems from Biblical law. As for the husband's duty to provide his wife with clothing, there seems to be unanimous agreement among the Tannaim of the Baraita that the obligation is of Torah origin. Following this Baraita, *Rambam* rules that the husband is indeed obligated by Torah law to maintain his wife and to clothe her (see Halakhah). But *Ramban* and others rule in accordance with the Baraita cited earlier that it is only by Rabbinic enactment that the husband is required to provide his wife with maintenance. Since the Mishnah does not list separately the husband's duty to clothe his wife, that duty must be included in the husband's obligation to provide for her maintenance. Hence it too is only of Rabbinic origin (*Ran*). According to *Ramban* (in his commentary to Exodus 21:10), all three terms — *she'er, kesut* and *onah* — refer to different aspects of the husband's obligation to engage in sexual relations with his wife. The verse teaches that there are three things that a husband may not withhold from his wife: Bodily contact (*she'er*), a properly made bed (*kesut*), and sexual relations at regular intervals (*onah*).

עֹנָתָהּ *Onatah.* Two etymologies have been suggested for the term *onah* used in reference to a wife's conjugal rights. The term may mean "time," or "interval," thus referring to the husband's obligation to engage in sexual relations at certain times, the frequently of which being determined by the nature of his work and the amount of time he

HALAKHAH

מְזוֹנוֹת מִדְּאוֹרַיְיתָא Maintenance is by Torah law. "Three of a husband's obligations toward his wife are imposed by Torah law: (1) To provide her with maintenance; (2) to provide her with clothing; and (3) to engage in sexual

LITERAL TRANSLATION

the Torah, [1]and similarly it says: 'If you shall afflict my daughters.' [2]Rabbi Elazar says: *'She'erah'* — this [means the wife's] conjugal rights, [3]and similarly it says: 'None of you shall come near to any that is near of kin to him to uncover her nakedness.' [4]*'Kesutah'* — like its plain sense. [5]*'Onatah'* — this is maintenance, [6]and similarly it says: 'And He humbled you and caused you hunger.' [48A] [7]Rabbi Eliezer ben Ya'akov says: *'She'erah kesutah'* [8]— according to her flesh give her clothing, [9]so that he will not give that of a young woman to an old woman, nor that of an old woman to a young woman.

בַּתּוֹרָה, [1]וְכֵן הוּא אוֹמֵר: ׳אִם תְּעַנֶּה אֶת בְּנֹתַי׳. [2]רַבִּי אֶלְעָזָר אוֹמֵר: ׳שְׁאֵרָהּ׳ — זוֹ עוֹנָה, [3]וְכֵן הוּא אוֹמֵר: ׳אִישׁ אִישׁ אֶל כָּל שְׁאֵר בְּשָׂרוֹ לֹא תִקְרְבוּ לְגַלּוֹת עֶרְוָה׳. [4]׳כְּסוּתָהּ׳ — כְּמַשְׁמָעוֹ. [5]׳עוֹנָתָהּ׳ — אֵלּוּ מְזוֹנוֹת, [6]וְכֵן הוּא אוֹמֵר: ׳וַיְעַנְּךָ וַיַּרְעִבֶךָ׳. [48A] [7]רַבִּי אֱלִיעֶזֶר בֶּן יַעֲקֹב אוֹמֵר: ׳שְׁאֵרָהּ כְּסוּתָהּ׳ — [8]לְפוּם שְׁאֵרָהּ תֵּן כְּסוּתָהּ, [9]שֶׁלֹּא יִתֵּן לָהּ לֹא שֶׁל יַלְדָּה לִזְקֵינָה, וְלֹא שֶׁל זְקֵינָה לְיַלְדָּה.

RASHI

לפום שארה — זקינה קשה לה משאוי, ואינה יכולה לסבול בגדים רחבים, וילדה צריכה בגדים רחבים להתנאות בהם.

TRANSLATION AND COMMENTARY

husband's obligation to engage in sexual relations with her at regular intervals, **that are mentioned** here **in the Torah.** [1]Proof that the word *onah* refers to sexual relations may be found in **another verse** that **says** (Genesis 31:50): **'If you shall afflict** [*te'anneh*] **my daughters** and refrain from cohabiting with them.' [2]**Rabbi Elazar** agrees that food, clothing and fulfilling his wife's conjugal rights are the husband's principal marital obligations, but he **says** that the verse from which these obligations are derived is to be understood differently: **'She'erah' refers to** the girl's **conjugal rights.** [3]As a proof text that the word *she'er* denotes sexual relations, he cites **another verse** that **says** (Leviticus 18:6): **'None of you shall come near to any that is near of kin to him** [*she'er besaro*] **to uncover her nakedness.'** [4]**'Kesutah'**, continues Rabbi Elazar, is to be understood **according to its plain sense,** and refers to the husband's duty to provide his wife with clothing. [5]**'Onatah' refers to** the girl's right to **maintenance,** [6]as is proved by the fact that a word with the same root is **similarly** used with respect to food in **the verse** that **says** (Deuteronomy 8:3): **'And He humbled you** [*vaye'annekha*] **and caused you to hunger** and fed you with manna.' [48A] [7]**Rabbi Eliezer ben Ya'akov says:** The entire verse speaks of the husband's obligation to provide his wife with clothing. The words ***'she'erah kesutah'*** (שְׁאֵרָהּ כְּסוּתָהּ — lit., her body, her clothing) inform us that the clothing that the husband provides for his wife must be appropriate for her. [8]This part of the verse is to be interpreted as follows: **According to** the wife's physical condition and **her age, give her clothing.** [9]**He must not give** the clothing **that** is suitable for **a young woman to an old woman, nor** the clothing **that** is fit for **an old woman**

NOTES

spends at home. Alternatively, the term is derived from the word עינוי — "affliction," or "distress." The husband is obligated to engage in sexual relations with his wife, because depriving her would cause her distress (see *Tosafot*). *Rashash* notes that it is not uncommon in Hebrew that the same root has two opposite meanings (e.g., דשן, שרש). Similarly, the root ענה has two opposite meanings: The root usually denotes the causing of distress, but in reference to a woman's conjugal rights it means the preventing of distress.

שְׁאֵרָהּ כְּסוּתָהּ *She'erah kesutah.* As it appears here, the ruling in the name of Rabbi Eliezer ben Ya'akov indicates that he views the husband's duties to provide his wife with maintenance and to engage in sexual relations with her as being of Rabbinic origin, for he explains all three terms in the verse as referring to the husband's obligation to provide his wife with clothing. But the end of the Baraita (found in *Mekhilta* and cited by the Jerusalem Talmud; see *Tosafot*) teaches that Rabbi Eliezer ben Ya'akov infers by means of a *kal vaḥomer* argument that both of these obligations stem from Torah law.

Tosafot asks: If so, who is the Tanna who maintains that it is only by Rabbinic enactment that the husband is obligated to support his wife? Some authorities answer that this is the view of the Baraita taught by Rav Yosef (below), for according to that Baraita the term *she'er* refers to bodily contact during sexual intercourse, and thus there is no source that teaches that the husband is required by Torah law to provide his wife with maintenance.

לְפוּם שְׁאֵרָהּ תֵּן כְּסוּתָהּ According to her flesh give her clothing. *Rabbenu Ḥananel* (cited by *Ritva*) has a different reading, but the position of Rabbi Eliezer ben Ya'akov

HALAKHAH

relations with her. This is the position of *Rambam,* who follows the anonymous Baraita. According to *Ramban,* the husband's duty to cohabit with his wife stems from the Torah, but his obligations to maintain and clothe her are only of Rabbinic origin. *Maggid Mishneh* rules that the wife's conjugal rights and her right to clothing are imposed by Torah law, but her right to maintenance derives from Rabbinic enactment (see *Bet Shmuel*)." (*Rambam, Sefer Nashim, Hilkhot Ishut* 12:2; *Shulḥan Arukh, Even HaEzer* 69:2.)

TRANSLATION AND COMMENTARY

to a young woman. [1]The words ***'kesutah ve'onatah'*** (כְּסוּתָהּ וְעֹנָתָהּ — lit., 'her clothing and her season') inform us that the clothing that the husband provides for his wife must be appropriate for the time of the year. [2]This phrase should be understood as follows: **According to the season** of the year, **give her clothing.** [3]The husband **should not give** his wife **new clothes during the summer.** [4]**Nor** should he give her **worn-out** clothing **during the winter."** Thus the first Tanna of the Baraita and Rabbi Elazar (and perhaps Rabbi Eliezer ben Ya'akov as well [see notes]), agree that the husband is obligated by Biblical law to maintain his wife, and therefore disagree with the Baraita that stated he is obligated to do so only by Rabbinic enactment.

תָּנֵי רַב יוֹסֵף [5]**Rav Yosef taught** the following Baraita, which offers yet another interpretation of the verse: "***'She'erah'* refers to** the husband's obligation to come into **bodily contact** with his wife when they engage in sexual relations, [6]and it informs us **that he should not act with her in the manner of the Persians, who engage in sexual relations** while **in their clothes."** [7]The Gemara adds that **this** Baraita **supports** the viewpoint of **Rav Huna, for Rav Huna said:** [8]**If someone says: "I refuse to engage in sexual relations unless I am in my clothing and** my wife **is in hers,"** [9]**he must divorce** his wife **and give her her ketubah.**

[1]'כְּסוּתָהּ וְעֹנָתָהּ' — [2]לְפוּם עוֹנָתָהּ תֵּן כְּסוּתָהּ, [3]שֶׁלֹּא יִתֵּן חֲדָשִׁים בִּימוֹת הַחַמָּה, [4]וְלֹא שְׁחָקִים בִּימוֹת הַגְּשָׁמִים". [5]תָּנֵי רַב יוֹסֵף: "'שְׁאֵרָהּ' — זוֹ קֵרוּב בָּשָׂר, [6]שֶׁלֹּא יִנְהַג בָּהּ מִנְהַג פָּרְסִיִּים, שֶׁמְּשַׁמְּשִׁין מִטּוֹתֵיהֶן בִּלְבוּשֵׁיהֶן". [7]מְסַיַּיע לֵיהּ לְרַב הוּנָא, דְּאָמַר רַב הוּנָא: [8]הָאוֹמֵר: "אִי אֶפְשִׁי אֶלָּא אֲנִי בְּבִגְדִי, וְהִיא בְּבִגְדָהּ" — [9]יוֹצִיא וְנוֹתֵן כְּתוּבָּה.

LITERAL TRANSLATION

[1]*'Kesutah ve'onatah'* — [2]according to her season give her clothing, [3]so that he will not give [her] new [clothes] during the summer (lit., 'in the days of the sun'), [4]nor worn-out [clothes] during the winter (lit., 'in the days of the rains')."

[5]Rav Yosef taught: "*'She'erah'* — this is bodily contact (lit., 'nearness of flesh'), [6]so that he will not behave toward her in the manner of the Persians, who engage in sexual relations in their clothes." [7][This] supports Rav Huna, for Rav Huna said: [8][If] someone says: "I do not want [to engage in sexual relations] unless I am in my garment and she is in her garment," [9]he must divorce [her] and give [her] her ketubah.

RASHI

לפום עונתה — לפי העת, אם חמה אם לנה. **חדשים** — חמים הם יותר מן השחקים.

BACKGROUND

מִנְהַג פָּרְסִיִּים The manner of the Persians. The commentators explain that the custom of remaining dressed during intercourse is contemptuous of women, since the husband appears to be treating his wife like a prostitute, using her body merely to satisfy his own bodily needs, without attributing importance to feelings of intimacy or to his wife's pleasure.

Though the Sages in Rabbinic literature warned that a couple must behave modestly, even during sexual intercourse, they also warned that a man is under an obligation to give his wife a feeling of intimacy, and to do so willingly and with enjoyment.

NOTES

remains the same: "According to her age give her clothing, so that he will not give her new clothes during the summer, etc." According to Rabbenu Ḥananel's reading, the words *she'erah kesutah* teach us that the clothes the husband provides for his wife must be suitable for her bodily needs. Thus he must not give her heavy clothing during the summer or light clothing during the winter. This version of the Baraita continues: "According to her season give her clothing, so that he will not give that of a young woman to an old woman, etc." The words *kesutah onatah* teach us that the clothing the husband provides for his wife must be appropriate according to her season, i.e., her years. Thus he must not give the clothes fashioned for a young woman to an old one, and vice versa.

מִנְהַג פָּרְסִיִּים The manner of the Persians. Some authorities suggest that this custom of the Persians is alluded to in a Baraita cited elsewhere (*Berakhot* 8b): "Rabban Gamliel said: There are three things that I like about the Persians: They are modest in their eating, modest in the bathroom, and modest in another matter [i.e., sexual relations]." But a certain difficulty presents itself: In that Baraita the Persians' modesty is praised, whereas here their custom is rejected. Moreover, *Ritva* maintains that a man who insists on remaining dressed while engaging in sexual relations must divorce his wife and give her her ketubah, even if his insistence is due to modesty. *Magen Avraham* (*Shulḥan Arukh, Oraḥ Ḥayyim* 240:8) mentions additional sources that imply that it is praiseworthy to be dressed while engaging in sexual relations. He concludes that a couple may jointly agree to conduct themselves modestly and to remain dressed during intercourse (see also *Mishnah Berurah* and *Sha'ar HaTziyyun, ad locum*).

HALAKHAH

שֶׁלֹּא יִתֵּן חֲדָשִׁים So that he will not give her new clothes. "A husband is required to provide his wife with clothing that is appropriate for the season, winter clothing during the winter and summer clothing during the summer," following the viewpoint of Rabbi Eliezer ben Ya'akov here in the Baraita, and that of the Mishnah (below, 64b). (*Rambam, Sefer Nashim, Hilkhot Ishut* 13:1; *Shulḥan Arukh, Even HaEzer* 73:1.)

אֶלָּא אֲנִי בְּבִגְדִי Unless I am in my garment. "If someone says: 'I refuse to cohabit with my wife unless we are both dressed in our clothing,' he must divorce her and give her her ketubah," following Rav Huna. (*Shulḥan Arukh, Even HaEzer* 76:13.)

[1]״רַבִּי יְהוּדָה אוֹמֵר: אֲפִילּוּ עָנִי שֶׁבְּיִשְׂרָאֵל, וכו׳״. [2]מִכְּלָל דְּתַנָּא קַמָּא סָבַר הָנֵי לָא. [3]הֵיכִי דָּמֵי? [4]אִי דְּאוֹרְחָהּ, מַאי טַעֲמָא דְּתַנָּא קַמָּא, דַּאֲמַר לָא? [5]וְאִי דְּלָאו אוֹרְחָהּ, מַאי טַעֲמָא דְּרַבִּי יְהוּדָה?

[6]לָא, צְרִיכָא, [7]כְּגוֹן דְּאוֹרְחֵיהּ דִּידֵיהּ וְלָאו אוֹרְחָהּ דִּידָהּ. [8]תַּנָּא קַמָּא סָבַר: כִּי אָמְרִינַן עוֹלָה עִמּוֹ וְאֵינָהּ יוֹרֶדֶת עִמּוֹ, הָנֵי מִילֵּי מֵחַיִּים, [9]אֲבָל לְאַחַר מִיתָה, לָא. [10]וְרַבִּי יְהוּדָה סָבַר: אֲפִילּוּ לְאַחַר מִיתָה.

LITERAL TRANSLATION

[1]"Rabbi Yehudah says: Even the poorest man in Israel, etc." [2][This proves] by implication that the first Tanna maintains [that] these are not [required]. [3]How do we visualize the case (lit., "how is it like")? [4]If it is her custom, what is the reason of the first Tanna, who said no? [5]And if it is not her custom, what is the reason of Rabbi Yehudah?

[6]No, it is necessary, [7]for example, where it is his custom but it is not her custom. [8]The first Tanna maintains: When we say [that] she rises with him but does not go down with him, this applies (lit., "these words") during [her] lifetime, [9]but after [her] death, not. [10]And Rabbi Yehudah maintains: Even after [her] death.

TRANSLATION AND COMMENTARY

רַבִּי יְהוּדָה אוֹמֵר [1]The Gemara now turns its attention to the last clause of the Mishnah, which stated: **"Rabbi Yehudah says: Even the poorest man in Israel** must provide not less than two flute players and a lamenting woman for his wife's funeral." [2]The Gemara notes that the attribution of this position to Rabbi Yehudah **proves by implication that the** anonymous **first Tanna** of the Mishnah **maintains that these requirements are not** included in the husband's obligation to provide for his wife's burial. [3]On this point the Gemara asks: **How do we visualize the case?** [4]**If it is the custom** in the wife's family to provide flute-players and a lamenting woman at funeral services, **what is the reasoning of the** anonymous **first Tanna, who maintains that** the husband is **not** obligated to do so? There is a general Halakhic principle (see below, 61a) that a woman is entitled to be maintained according to her husband's standard of living if it is above her own previous standard of living. But she is not required to suffer a decline in her standard of living below the level she enjoyed before she married. Thus, if it is customary in her family that flute players and a lamenting woman participate at family funerals, the anonymous first Tanna of the Mishnah should agree that the husband cannot deny his late wife this kind of burial, for he would be denying her the financial and social standards to which she was accustomed in her father's home. [5]**And,** continues the Gemara, **if** this **is not the custom** in her family, then **what is the reasoning of Rabbi Yehudah,** who maintains that the husband must provide flute players and a lamenting woman at his wife's funeral?

לָא, צְרִיכָא [6]The Gemara answers: **No, it was necessary** to state the disagreement between the anonymous first Tanna and Rabbi Yehudah — in order, [7]**for example,** to highlight the case **in which it is the custom** of the husband's family to provide flute players and a lamenting woman at family funerals, **but it is not the custom** of the wife's family to do so. [8]**The** anonymous **first Tanna maintains** that **when we say that** there is a general rule that a wife **rises with** her husband and is entitled to a standard of living in accordance with his means and social standing, **but** that she **does not go down with him** and cannot be forced to live at a standard of living lower than that to which she was accustomed in her father's home, **this** principle **applies** only **during her lifetime.** [9]**But after her death** she is **no** longer entitled to the benefits of her husband's elevated social status. [10]On the other hand, **Rabbi Yehudah maintains** that **even after her death** a husband must treat his wife in accordance with his social standing. Thus, if it is customary in his family that flute players and a lamenting woman participate at family funerals, the husband is obligated to arrange for a similar service when his wife dies.

RASHI

דאורחה — דרך בנות משפחתה בכך. **מאי טעמא דתנא קמא** — דאמר לא צריך. **אורחיה** — לבנות משפחתו עושין כן. **עולה עמו ואינה יורדת עמו** — מ״בעולת בעל״ נפקא לן: בעלייתו של בעל ולא בירידתו של בעל, בפרק ״אף על פי״ (שם). **הני מילי מחיים** — כגון: הוא אומר להניק את בנה והיא אומרת שלא להניק, ודרך בנות משפחתה להניק בניהם, ולא דרך משפחתו.

NOTES

כְּגוֹן דְּאוֹרְחֵיהּ **For example, where it is his custom.** Many Rishonim ask: The Gemara argues that the Tannaim in our Mishnah disagree about whether we follow the custom of the husband's family or that of the wife's family. Why, then, does Rabbi Yehudah state that the husband must provide not less than two flute-players and a lamenting woman? The husband's liability should be determined solely by the standard that is customary in his family!

Talmidei Rabbenu Yonah answers: The Mishnah speaks of a case in which it is the custom of the husband's family

[1]אָמַר רַב חִסְדָּא אָמַר מָר עוּקְבָא; הֲלָכָה כְּרַבִּי יְהוּדָה. [2]וְאָמַר רַב חִסְדָּא אָמַר מָר עוּקְבָא: [3]מִי שֶׁנִּשְׁתַּטָּה, בֵּית דִּין יוֹרְדִין לִנְכָסָיו, וְזָנִין וּמְפַרְנְסִין אֶת אִשְׁתּוֹ וּבָנָיו וּבְנוֹתָיו, [4]וְדָבָר אַחֵר. [5]אֲמַר לֵיהּ רָבִינָא לְרַב אַשִׁי: [6]מַאי שְׁנָא מֵהָא דְּתַנְיָא: ״מִי שֶׁהָלַךְ לִמְדִינַת הַיָּם וְאִשְׁתּוֹ תּוֹבַעַת מְזוֹנוֹת, [7]בֵּית דִּין יוֹרְדִין לִנְכָסָיו, וְזָנִין וּמְפַרְנְסִין אֶת אִשְׁתּוֹ, אֲבָל לֹא בָּנָיו וּבְנוֹתָיו, [8]וְלֹא דָּבָר אַחֵר״.

LITERAL TRANSLATION

[1]Rav Ḥisda said in the name of Mar Ukva: The Halakhah is in accordance with Rabbi Yehudah. [2]And Rav Ḥisda said in the name of Mar Ukva: [3][If] someone has gone mad, the court seizes (lit., "goes down to") his property, and maintains and supports his wife and his sons and his daughters, [4]and another matter.

[5]Ravina said to Rav Ashi: [6]Why is [this] different from what was taught: "[If] someone has gone abroad and his wife is demanding maintenance, [7]the court seizes his property, and maintains and supports his wife, but not his sons or his daughters, [8]and not another matter."

TRANSLATION AND COMMENTARY

אָמַר רַב חִסְדָּא [1]Having concluded its discussion of the Mishnah, the Gemara now records a Halakhic decision regarding the dispute between the anonymous first Tanna and Rabbi Yehudah: **Rav Ḥisda said in the name of Mar Ukva: The law is in accordance with Rabbi Yehudah.**

וְאָמַר רַב חִסְדָּא [2]The Gemara continues with another ruling that **Rav Ḥisda reported in the name of Mar Ukva: [3]If someone loses his sanity, the court seizes his property and maintains and supports his wife and his** young **sons and daughters.** [4]Besides food and clothing, it also provides for **another matter** (as will be explained below in the Gemara).

אֲמַר לֵיהּ רָבִינָא [5]**Ravina said to Rav Ashi:** [6]**Why is** the law in this case **different from** the law **taught** in the following Baraita: **"If someone goes abroad, and his wife** goes to court and **demands** her **maintenance, the court seizes** the husband's **property and maintains and supports his wife, but not his sons or his daughters.** Since the husband left home without arranging for his wife's support during his absence, the court takes control of his assets and provides her with the food and clothing she needs. But the court does not use its authority over his property in order to provide food or clothing for his children, for the father is not legally required to support them. [7]**Nor** does the court use its authority over the husband's property to provide for **another matter** [as will be explained below]." What difference does it make, says Ravina, whether the husband goes insane or goes abroad? Why does Mar Ukva rule in the former case that the court steps in and provides not only for his wife but also for his children, whereas in the latter case the Baraita states that the court provides only for the wife and not for the children?

RASHI

ודבר אחר – לקמן מפרש. **זנין** – מזונות. **מפרנסין** – לבוש וכסות. **אבל לא בניו ובנותיו** – שאינו חייב במזונותיהן בחייו.

TERMINOLOGY

דָּבָר אַחֵר Another matter. The term דָּבָר אַחֵר is sometimes used as a euphemism for things that the Talmud does not wish to mention explicitly, either for reasons of modesty or because they were considered repulsive. Here, however, both Rav Ḥisda and Rav Yosef explain the "other matter" literally, as meaning another gift — cosmetics or money for charity.

NOTES

to arrange a public funeral for all members of the family, but it is not the custom of the wife's family to arrange such a service. Rabbi Yehudah teaches us that in such a case the husband must arrange a public funeral for his wife, which must include at the very least two flute players and a lamenting woman. *Ritva* says: Since it is not the custom of the wife's family to provide any flute players or lamenting women at family funerals, the husband is only required to provide for his wife a funeral service which includes two flute players and one lamenting woman, even if it is customary in his family to arrange a more elaborate funeral.

אֲבָל לֹא בָּנָיו וּבְנוֹתָיו But not his sons or his daughters. The Gemara below (49a–b) discusses in detail the father's obligation to provide his minor children with maintenance. Opinions differ as to whether the father is legally obligated to maintain his children until they reach majority, or whether he is only liable for their maintenance until they reach the age of six. If the father is a man of means, another obligation stemming from the laws of charity may fall upon him to support his children. In the cases discussed in our Gemara an additional factor must be taken into consideration — whether or not we can assume that a father wants his children to be supported from his assets in a case where he is not legally obligated to provide for their support.

דָּבָר אַחֵר Another matter. There are a number of variant readings in our passage (see *Rashi* below), which lead to

HALAKHAH

מִי שֶׁנִּשְׁתַּטָּה If someone has gone mad. "If someone loses his sanity, the court takes control of his assets and provides for the maintenance of his wife and his children until they reach majority." This follows the viewpoint of *Tur* and *Ran*, but according to *Rambam* the court only supports his children until they reach the age of six, unless the father was wealthy, in which case it provides for their support until they reach majority (see *Maggid Mishneh* and *Ḥelkat Meḥokek*). (*Rambam, Sefer Nashim, Hilkhot Ishut* 12:17; *Shulḥan Arukh, Even HaEzer* 71:3.)

מִי שֶׁהָלַךְ לִמְדִינַת הַיָּם If someone has gone abroad. "If someone goes abroad and his wife goes to court and demands

LITERAL TRANSLATION

[1] He said to him: And is there no difference for you between someone who leaves wittingly and someone who leaves unwittingly?

[2] What is [meant by] "another matter"?

[3] Rav Ḥisda said: This [refers to] cosmetics.

[1] אֲמַר לֵיהּ: וְלָא שָׁאנֵי לָךְ בֵּין יוֹצֵא לְדַעַת לְיוֹצֵא שֶׁלֹּא לְדַעַת?

[2] מַאי "דָּבָר אַחֵר"?

[3] רַב חִסְדָּא אָמַר: זֶה תַּכְשִׁיט.

RASHI

ולא שאני לך כו' – יוצא מן המקום לדעת, היה בידו לצוות על מזונות בניו ובנותיו ואשתו, ולא צוה – גילה דעתו שאינו רוצה לזון. הילכך, אשתו דמיחייב לה בתנאי כתובה – אשתעבוד ניכסיה, בניו ובנותיו – לא. אבל נשתטה, דיצא מן העולם שלא לדעת – מסתמא ניחא ליה שיזונו בניו ובנותיו משלו. תבשיט – בשמים של אבקת רוכל, שהנשים מתקשטות בהם.

TRANSLATION AND COMMENTARY

אֲמַר לֵיהּ [1] Rav Ashi **said to** Ravina in reply: **Do you not see that there is a** profound **difference whether** the husband **left wittingly or left unwittingly?** The husband who went abroad left his family deliberately. If he had wished to provide for his family, he could have made the necessary arrangements before he left. His failure to make such arrangements indicates that he really did not want to support them. Thus, with respect to his wife whose maintenance he is obligated to provide, the court takes control of his assets and provides her with the necessary food and clothing. But it does not step in on behalf of the children, for the father is not obligated to maintain them. By contrast, the husband who lost his sanity was a victim of forces beyond his control. In such a case, we assume that he would want his children to be supported from his assets. Therefore the court takes control of his property and provides not only for his wife but also for his entire family.

מַאי "דָּבָר אַחֵר" [2] The Gemara asks: **What is the "other matter"** referred to both by the Baraita and by Mar Ukva?

רַב חִסְדָּא אָמַר [3] The Gemara presents two answers to this question. **Rav Ḥisda said:** The expression "another matter" **refers to** the wife's **cosmetics,** with which she adorns herself. If the husband loses his sanity, the court takes control of his assets and provides his wife not only with food and clothing but with cosmetics as well. However, if the husband goes abroad, she receives enough for her food and clothing,

NOTES

different explanations of the Talmudic text as well as to different Halakhic conclusions. According to the standard text, Rav Ḥisda, who says that the court does not provide the woman whose husband has gone abroad with money for cosmetics, will certainly agree that it does not allocate his money for charity. But Rav Yosef, who says that the court does not give his money to charity, might agree that it should give his wife money for her cosmetics. According to the variant reading cited by *Rashi,* Rav Yosef, who says that the court gives to charity the money of a man who has lost his sanity, will certainly agree that it should provide his wife with money for cosmetics. But Rav Ḥisda, who says that the court provides his wife with money for cosmetics, might agree that it should not allocate any of his money for charity. According to Rav Ḥisda, a woman whose husband has gone abroad is not given money for her cosmetics. Even though the Rabbis enacted that a woman must be given a certain allowance for cosmetics, since their intention was that the woman be given the means to make herself more attractive to her husband, it stands to reason that she should not receive money for cosmetics while her husband is abroad. Indeed, according to one of the variant readings, the husband who is abroad "is pleased that she should look repulsive," for when a man is away from home, he prefers that his wife should not adorn herself, so as not to make herself more desirable to other men.

Rid (whose reading of the Talmudic text is unclear) maintains that even in the case of the husband who has become insane, his wife is not awarded any money for her cosmetics, for her husband is not in a state to find his wife attractive. *Bet Shmuel* (following the standard reading) argues that a woman whose husband has become insane is given money for her cosmetics, for he may remain in that state permanently and it is not right that she be forced to forgo her cosmetics forever. But a woman whose husband has gone abroad is not given money for cosmetics, for he is expected to return and her deprivation will prove to have been temporary.

HALAKHAH

her maintenance, the court seizes his property after three months have passed and provides for the maintenance of the woman herself and her children under the age of six. But it does not provide anything for those children who have already reached their sixth birthday. *Rema* notes that, according to some authorities (*Mordekhai,* in the name of *Ri*), if the father began to support his children who were six or over, the court continues to provide for their support from the father's assets. And according to other authorities (*Tur,* against *Rambam*), if the father is a wealthy man, then in all cases the court maintains his children from his assets, even if they have already reached the age of six." (*Rambam, Sefer Nashim, Hilkhot Ishut* 12:16-17; *Shulḥan Arukh, Even HaEzer* 70:5, 71:2.)

תַּכְשִׁיט **Cosmetics.** "If a man has gone abroad without arranging for his wife's support, the courts provide for her maintenance from her husband's property, but they do not provide her with cosmetics. But if a woman's husband goes insane, the courts provide her with cosmetics as well." (*Rambam, Sefer Nashim, Hilkhot Ishut* 13:7; *Shulḥan Arukh, Even HaEzer* 70:5-6.)

TRANSLATION AND COMMENTARY

but she is not given anything for cosmetics. [1]**Rav Yosef said:** When the Baraita and Mar Ukva use the expression "another matter," they are referring to money for **charity.** If the husband loses his sanity, the court administers his property and allocates a certain sum for charity. But if he goes abroad, the court does not give any of his assets to charity.

מַאן דְּאָמַר תַּכְשִׁיט [2]The Gemara observes: Rav Ḥisda, **who says** that the court does not provide money for **cosmetics** to the woman whose husband went abroad, **would certainly agree** that it does not take his assets and allocate money for **charity.** [3]But Rav Yosef, **who says** that the court does not give any of the husband's assets to **charity,** may well distinguish between charity and cosmetics. [4]The court does not give any of the husband's property to charity, **but it does give** his wife enough for her **cosmetics.** Even though he left wittingly without making the necessary arrangements to provide for his wife during his absence, we assume that he would want her to be given enough money for cosmetics, [5]**because he does not want her to look repulsive** while he is away.

אָמַר רַב חִיָּיא בַּר אָבִין [6]The Gemara continues: **Rav Ḥiyya bar Avin said in the name of Rav Huna: If someone goes abroad and his wife dies** while he is away, [7]**the court seizes his property and buries her as befits** the husband's **dignity** and social standing. Just as the husband is required to provide his wife with food and clothing during her lifetime, he is likewise obligated to pay for her funeral when she dies.

[1]רַב יוֹסֵף אָמַר: צְדָקָה. [2]מַאן דְּאָמַר תַּכְשִׁיט כׇּל שֶׁכֵּן צְדָקָה. [3]מַאן דְּאָמַר צְדָקָה — [4]אֲבָל תַּכְשִׁיט יָהֲבִינַן לַהּ, [5]דְּלָא נִיחָא לֵיהּ דְּתִתְנַוָּול.

[6]אָמַר רַב חִיָּיא בַּר אָבִין אָמַר רַב הוּנָא: מִי שֶׁהָלַךְ לִמְדִינַת הַיָּם וּמֵתָה אִשְׁתּוֹ, [7]בֵּית דִּין יוֹרְדִין לִנְכָסָיו, וְקוֹבְרִין אוֹתָהּ לְפִי כְבוֹדוֹ.

LITERAL TRANSLATION

[1]Rav Yosef said: Charity.

[2]The one who said cosmetics [would] certainly [agree about] charity. [3]The one who said charity — [4]but we give her cosmetics, [5]because he does not want her to look repulsive.

[6]Rav Ḥiyya bar Avin said in the name of Rav Huna: [If] someone has gone abroad and his wife has died, [7]the court seizes his property, and buries her as befits his dignity.

RASHI

מאן דאמר תכשיט — לא יהבינן לאשתו, כל שכן שאין עלינו לעשות צדקה מנכסיו. ואמתניתא קיימי. **לא ניחא ליה דתינוול** — אף על פי שלא צוה בלכתו — עבדינן. ולי נראה: דאמר עוקבא קיימי, דאמר מי שנשתטה יורדין לנכסיו וזנין כו׳ ודבר אחר. ואיפכא גרסינן: מאן דאמר צדקה — כל שכן תכשיט, ומאן דאמר תכשיט אבל צדקה — לא. התם היינו טעמא דלא ניחא ליה דתינוול.

SAGES

רַב חִיָּיא בַּר אָבִין **Rav Ḥiyya bar Avin.** A Babylonian Amora of the third and fourth generations. See *Ketubot,* Part I, p. 62.

NOTES

צְדָקָה **Charity.** Rav Yosef maintains that if someone loses his sanity, the court administers his property and allocates a certain sum for charity. Two explanations have been offered for this position (see *Kesef Mishneh* on *Rambam, Hilkhot Naḥalot* 11:11): (1) It may be assumed that a person wishes to allocate a portion of his money for charitable purposes. If he is incapacitated, the court may act in his stead and give charity on his behalf. (2) An obligation rests on a person's assets that a certain portion be set aside as charity, and so the court may seize some of his assets and give them to charity even without his consent. (There are cases where there can be practical differences between these two explanations; see *Birkat Avraham.*) The court, however, does not seize the property of someone who has gone abroad and give some of his assets to charity, for that person may intend to fulfill his philanthropic obligations abroad.

וְקוֹבְרִין אוֹתָהּ לְפִי כְבוֹדוֹ **And buries her as befits his dignity.** Our Gemara rules that if a woman dies while her husband is abroad, the court may seize part of the husband's property to cover the costs of her burial. The Jerusalem Talmud discusses a case in which a woman's husband refuses to bury her, and someone else steps in and arranges for her burial. Rabbi Ḥaggai maintains that if that other person is the woman's father, he may recover his expenses from the husband. But if someone else buries her, that other person is not entitled to compensation. Rabbi Yose disagrees and says that whoever buries the woman may collect from her husband whatever was spent on her burial. *Rashba* argues that our Gemara supports the

HALAKHAH

צְדָקָה **Charity.** "If someone loses his sanity, the courts assess his obligation regarding charity and allocate a portion of his assets for that pupose." (*Rambam, Sefer Mishpatim, Hilkhot Naḥalot* 11:11; *Shulḥan Arukh, Ḥoshen Mishpat* 290:15.)

וְקוֹבְרִין אוֹתָהּ לְפִי כְבוֹדוֹ **And buries her as befits his dignity.** "If someone has gone abroad and his wife dies while he is away, the court seizes his property if necessary, sells it even without a public announcement, and uses the proceeds to bury the woman in a manner befitting the husband's social standing, or (if she came from a family with a higher social status) in a manner befitting her own social standing," following the Gemara's conclusion which is in accordance with the viewpoint of Rabbi Yehudah. (*Rambam, Sefer Nashim, Hilkhot Ishut* 14:24; *Shulḥan Arukh, Even HaEzer* 89:3.)

SAGES

רַב מַתְּנָה Rav Matenah. A second-generation Babylonian Amora. See *Ketubot*, Part III, p. 120.

TRANSLATION AND COMMENTARY

לְפִי כְּבוֹדוֹ [1]The Gemara raises a question about Rav Huna's statement: Did Rav Huna mean that the wife is buried **as befits** the husband's **dignity, but not as befits** the wife's **dignity?** This would mean that even if the wife comes from a family with a higher social standing than that of the husband, she is buried in accordance with the social norms of her husband's family. But surely this conflicts with the general rule that a woman's standard of living rises to match that of her husband, and does not go down to his level!

אֵימָא [2]The Gemara answers: We must **say** that this is what Rav Huna meant: If a woman comes from a socially more prominent family than that of her husband, she has to be buried as befits her dignity. But if the husband enjoys a higher social status than his wife's family, his wife is buried **even as befits** the husband's **dignity.** [3]And **this is what** Rav Huna **teaches us:** A woman **rises with** her husband, **but does not go down with him,** [4]not only during her lifetime but **even after her death.** We have now returned to the dispute between the Tannaim of our Mishnah, who disagreed about this very question — whether the rule that the wife rises with her husband applies only during her lifetime, or also after her death. Rav Huna teaches us that the rule applies even after her death, in accordance with the viewpoint of Rabbi Yehudah in our Mishnah.

אָמַר רַב מַתְּנָה [5]The Gemara concludes this discussion with one further ruling. **Rav Matenah said:** [6]**If someone says** before he dies: **"When** my wife **dies, do not use my assets to pay for her burial,"** [7]**we listen to him** and carry out his instructions. The husband's heirs (if they are not also the wife's heirs) are not required to pay for her burial. It is the wife's heirs — who collect her ketubah from the husband's heirs — who must pay all her funeral expenses.

מַאי שְׁנָא [8]The Gemara objects: Rav Matenah's statement seems to imply that only if the husband gives specific instructions that the expenses of his wife's funeral must not be paid from his estate are his heirs exempt from paying the costs of her funeral. But **what difference does it make that** the husband **said** that he does not want his wife's funeral expenses to be paid from his estate? [9]Are you going to suggest that we follow his instructions in such a case, **because** his **property falls to** the **orphans** as their inheritance and they are not held liable to pay for their father's wife's funeral (if they are not also her heirs)? [10]Surely the fact is that **even if** the husband **never said** that his estate should not be used to cover his wife's funeral expenses, [11]his **property** in any case **passes to the orphans** as their inheritance, and they are not liable for their father's wife's funeral. Why, then, should Rav Matenah's ruling be limited to a case in which the husband gave explicit instructions that his assets not be used to pay for his wife's funeral?

[1]לְפִי כְּבוֹדוֹ, וְלֹא לְפִי כְּבוֹדָהּ? [2]אֵימָא: אַף לְפִי כְּבוֹדוֹ. [3]הָא קָא מַשְׁמַע לָן: עוֹלָה עִמּוֹ וְאֵינָהּ יוֹרֶדֶת עִמּוֹ, [4]וַאֲפִילּוּ לְאַחַר מִיתָה.

[5]אָמַר רַב מַתְּנָה: [6]הָאוֹמֵר: ״אִם מֵתָה, לֹא תִּקְבְּרוּהָ מִנְּכָסָיו״, [7]שׁוֹמְעִין לוֹ.

[8]מַאי שְׁנָא כִּי אָמַר? [9]דְּנָפְלִי נִכְסֵי קַמֵּי יַתְמֵי? [10]כִּי לָא אָמַר נַמִי, [11]נִכְסֵי קַמֵּי יַתְמֵי רָמוּ!

LITERAL TRANSLATION

[1]As befits *his* dignity, and not as befits *her* dignity? [2]Say: Also as befits his dignity. [3]He tells us this: She rises with him but does not go down with him, [4]even after [her] death.

[5]Rav Matenah said: [6][If] someone says: "If she dies, do not bury her from his property," [7]we listen to him.

[8]Why is it different if he said [this]? [9]Because the property falls to (lit., "before") orphans? [10]Even if he did not say [this], [11]the property falls to the orphans!

RASHI

לפי כבודו ולא לפי כבודה — בתמיה: מידי דאורחה ולאו אורחיה מי לא בעי למיעבד לה? הא ודאי אינה יורדת עמו. ואפילו למאן דלית ליה עולה עמו לאחר מיתה — אינה יורדת אית ליה. **האומר** — בשעת מיתתו. **אם מתה אשתו כו׳ שומעין לו** — דכיון דהוא מת בחייה, והיא גובה כתובתה — אינו חייב לקוברה, דתנן (כתובות נה,ג): יורשיה, יורשי כתובתה, חייבין בקבורתה.

NOTES

view of Rabbi Ḥaggai, for it implies that only the court may order that the woman be buried, but if someone else buries her on his own initiative, he cannot recover his expenses. (The father, however, may recover his expenses, for it is inconceivable that a person must first receive the approval of the court before burying his own daughter.) But *Rambam* rules in accordance with Rabbi Yose that whoever buries the woman may demand compensation from the husband.

לְפִי כְּבוֹדוֹ, וְלֹא לְפִי כְּבוֹדָהּ? **As befits *his* dignity, and not as befits *her* dignity?** *Rid* points out that the Gemara raises this question even according to the opinion that the rule that a woman rises with her husband applies only during her lifetime but not after her death. For if a woman comes from a family with a higher social standing than

TRANSLATION AND COMMENTARY

אֶלָּא [1] **Rather,** answers the Gemara, whether the husband said anything about the matter or not, his heirs are never liable for his wife's burial. And Rav Matenah's statement must be amended so that it reads as follows: **If someone says:** [2] **"When I die, do not use my assets to pay for my burial,"** [3] **we do not listen to him.** Why do we not honor his request? [4] Because **it is not in his power to enrich his children** by [5] **casting himself** as a burden **on the** charity fund of his **community.**

MISHNAH לְעוֹלָם הִיא בִּרְשׁוּת הָאָב [6] As has already been explained, according to Jewish law the marriage process is effected in two stages: betrothal (*kiddushin* or *erusin*) and marriage (*nissu'in*). The act of betrothal leads to a change in the personal status of the bride and the bridegroom and creates a tie between them that can be dissolved only by divorce or by the death of one of the parties. But the marriage is not complete until after *nissu'in*, which is effected by bringing the bride and bridegroom together in the bridal chamber (ḥuppah). As a rule, the monetary rights and obligations applying to married couples (see the previous Mishnah, 46b) take effect only after the bride is handed over to the bridegroom for the purpose of *nissu'in*. This Mishnah establishes the point at which the bride is considered as having been handed over to her bridegroom, so that these rights and obligations take effect. The Mishnah states: Even after a *na'arah* has become betrothed, **she remains under her father's authority** regarding all of the rights of the father mentioned in the previous Mishnah **until she enters** [48B] **her bridegroom's authority** when she and her bridegroom are brought into the bridal chamber **for** the purpose of **marriage.**

[1] אֶלָּא, הָאוֹמֵר: [2] ״אִם מֵת הוּא, לֹא תִּקְבְּרוּהוּ מִנְּכָסָיו״, [3] אֵין שׁוֹמְעִין לוֹ. [4] לָאו כָּל הֵימֶנּוּ שֶׁיַּעֲשִׁיר אֶת בָּנָיו, [5] וְיַפִּיל עַצְמוֹ עַל הַצִּיבּוּר.

מִשְׁנָה [6] לְעוֹלָם הִיא בִּרְשׁוּת הָאָב עַד שֶׁתִּכָּנֵס [48B] לִרְשׁוּת הַבַּעַל לְנִשּׂוּאִין.

LITERAL TRANSLATION

[1] Rather, [if] someone says: [2] "If he dies, do not bury him from his property," [3] we do not listen to him. [4] It is not in his power to enrich his children, [5] and cast himself on the community.

MISHNAH [6] She is always under the authority of the father until she enters [48B] the authority of the husband for marriage.

RASHI

נכסי קמי יתמי רמו — ופשיטא דאין קבורתה עליהם. **אל תקברוהו מנכסיו** — אלא מן הצדקה.

משנה לעולם היא ברשות האב — ואם בת ישראל מאורסה לכהן היא — אינה אוכלת בתרומה, וזכאי בה בכל זכות אב בבתו. **לרשות הבעל לנשואין** — כלומר, שתכנס לחופה לשם נשואין, שתהא מסורה לרשות הבעל.

NOTES

that of her husband, all agree that she does not go down with her husband even after her death.

לִרְשׁוּת הַבַּעַל לְנִשּׂוּאִין **The authority of the husband for marriage.** The standard text of the Talmud follows *Rashi's* reading of the Mishnah, but many Rishonim have the reading: "She is always under the authority of the father until she enters the bridal chamber." Many consider this second reading superior, for it would appear that the Gemara raises its objection against Rav Assi on the basis of this Mishnah. Rav Assi argues that the girl may eat terumah as soon as she is handed over to her bridegroom, and this objection is valid only if the Mishnah means that she remains under her father's authority until she actually enters the bridal chamber with her bridegroom. But according to *Rashi*'s reading, the Mishnah can be interpreted as meaning that she only remains under her father's authority only until she is handed over to the bridegroom.

Ritva suggests that, according to *Rashi*, the unwieldy expression "until she enters the authority of the husband for marriage" implies that the Mishnah is referring to the

HALAKHAH

לֹא תִּקְבְּרוּהוּ מִנְּכָסָיו **Do not bury him from his property.** "If someone declares on his deathbed that he does not wish to be buried at his estate's expense, we do not listen to him. Rather, we compel the heirs to use the assets of the estate to cover the funeral expenses — the costs of the burial as well as any other expenses, including those relating to the erection of the tombstone," following Rav Matenah and the Gemara's conclusion. (*Rambam, Sefer Kinyan, Hilkhot Zekhiyah U'Matanah* 11:24; *Shulḥan Arukh, Yoreh De'ah* 348:2.)

עַד שֶׁתִּכָּנֵס לִרְשׁוּת הַבַּעַל לְנִשּׂוּאִין **Until she enters the authority of the husband for marriage.** "If a betrothed girl — a minor or a *na'arah* — is handed over by her father (or his agents) to her bridegroom (or his agents), and she dies on the journey to her bridegroom's house before she has entered the bridal chamber, her bridegroom is her heir, even if her dowry is still in her father's house. *Rema* notes that some authorities (*Tur*, in the name of *Rabbenu Tam*) disagree about the case in which the dowry has not yet reached the bridegroom. If the father (or his agents) should accompany the girl to her bridegroom's house, and on the journey the bridegroom and his bride enter a courtyard and seclude themselves inside for the purpose of marriage, and the bride dies, the bridegroom is her heir. But if the father (or his agents) should accompany the bridegroom (or his agents), and on the journey the bridegroom and his bride go into a courtyard to spend the night like travelers who spend the night in an inn, but they do not seclude themselves for the purpose of marriage, and the bride dies, her father is her heir, even if her dowry is already in her

TRANSLATION AND COMMENTARY

[1]**If the father hands over** his betrothed daughter **to her bridegroom's agents** who have been sent by the bridegroom to receive his bride and to bring her to him, **she is** already **under her bridegroom's authority** with respect to the rights and the obligations listed in the previous Mishnah. [2]But **if the father goes** along **with the bridegroom's agents,** [3]**or if the father's agents go** along **with the bridegroom's agents,** accompanying the girl until she reaches her bridegroom's house, [4]**she remains under her father's authority,** because she is not yet considered to have been handed over to the bridegroom. [5]But **if** the father sends his betrothed daughter with his agents, and on the journey **the father's agents hand her over to the bridegroom's agents** who have been sent to receive her, [6]**she is** from that time onward already considered **under her bridegroom's authority.**

GEMARA [7]מַאי ״לְעוֹלָם״ Our Mishnah stated that the betrothed *na'arah* "is always" under her father's authority until she enters her bridegroom's authority when she and her bridegroom are brought into the bridal chamber. The Gemara asks: **What** does the Mishnah **mean** to say when it emphasizes that the daughter **"is always"** under her father's authority?

לְאַפּוּקֵי מִמִּשְׁנָה רִאשׁוֹנָה [8]The Gemara answers: The expression "always" is used in order **to dissent from the** ruling given in another, **ancient, Mishnah,** [9]**for we have learned** elsewhere (below, 57a): "A betrothed virgin is given twelve months from the time her bridegroom asks for her in marriage, in order to prepare her trousseau. Between the betrothal and the marriage, the bride continues to live in her father's house and the bridegroom is not responsible for her support. [10]But **if the time** set for the marriage **comes and they are not married,** [11]**she** is entitled to **eat of** the bridegroom's **food**, for he is responsible for her support from the date on which the wedding was due to take place, **and she** is entitled to **eat terumah.** By Torah law, a woman who is betrothed to a priest is permitted to eat terumah, the portion of produce that is set aside for the priests and is forbidden to non-priests. But the Rabbis decreed that a betrothed woman may not eat terumah until after the marriage is completed. If, however, the time set for the marriage comes and the marriage does not take place, the bride is entitled to eat terumah." [12]**Therefore** our Mishnah **tells us** that a betrothed girl **remains** under her father's authority, even after the wedding date has arrived, until she

[1]מָסַר הָאָב לִשְׁלוּחֵי הַבַּעַל, הֲרֵי הִיא בִּרְשׁוּת הַבַּעַל. [2]הָלַךְ הָאָב עִם שְׁלוּחֵי הַבַּעַל, [3]אוֹ שֶׁהָלְכוּ שְׁלוּחֵי הָאָב עִם שְׁלוּחֵי הַבַּעַל, [4]הֲרֵי הִיא בִּרְשׁוּת הָאָב. [5]מָסְרוּ שְׁלוּחֵי הָאָב לִשְׁלוּחֵי הַבַּעַל, [6]הֲרֵי הִיא בִּרְשׁוּת הַבַּעַל.

גמרא [7]מַאי ״לְעוֹלָם״? [8]לְאַפּוּקֵי מִמִּשְׁנָה רִאשׁוֹנָה. [9]דִּתְנַן: [10]״הִגִּיעַ זְמַן וְלֹא נִישְּׂאוּ, [11]אוֹכְלוֹת מִשֶּׁלּוֹ וְאוֹכְלוֹת בִּתְרוּמָה. [12]קָא מַשְׁמַע לָן: ״לְעוֹלָם״.

LITERAL TRANSLATION

[1][If] the father handed [her] over to the husband's agents, she is under the authority of the husband. [2][If] the father went with the husband's agents, [3]or [if] the father's agents went with the husband's agents, [4]she is under the authority of the father. [5][If] the father's agents handed [her] over to the husband's agents, [6]she is under the authority of the husband.

GEMARA [7]What is [meant by] "always"?

[8]To exclude the ancient (lit., "first") Mishnah, [9]for we have learned: [10]"[If] the time came and they were not married, [11]they eat of his [food] and they eat terumah." [12][Therefore] it tells us: "Always."

RASHI

מסרו שלוחי האב — שהיה האב משלחה לו על ידי שלוחיו, ופגעו בשלוחי הבעל, ומסרוה להם.

גמרא ממשנה ראשונה — בפרק ״אף על פי״. **הגיע זמן** — שנים עשר חדש לבתולה, משתבעה הבעל להכין עצמה לנשואין, ולאלמנה שלשים יום. **ולא נישאו** — כגון שעכב החתן, או אונס שלו. **ואוכלות בתרומה** — אם בת ישראל מאורסת לכהן היא.

NOTES

actual completion of the marriage process when the couple enter the bridal chamber. As for the Gemara's objection, *Rashi* can argue either that it is based on a Baraita worded differently from our Mishnah, or that it is based on a paraphrase of the Mishnah.

מַאי ״לְעוֹלָם״ What is meant by "always"? *Talmidei*

HALAKHAH

bridegroom's house, in accordance with the Baraita and the ruling of Shmuel. *Rema* adds that if the couple enter the bridegroom's courtyard or into a courtyard belonging to the couple, but do not specify their reason for entering, we assume that they have entered for the purpose of marriage. But if they go into a courtyard belonging to the bride, or into one that does not belong to either of them, without specifying why they are going in, we assume that they have entered merely for the purpose of spending the night (*Maggid Mishneh* in the name of *Ramban* and *Rashba*)." (*Rambam, Sefer Nashim, Hilkhot Ishut* 22:2; *Shulḥan Arukh, Even HaEzer* 57.)

TRANSLATION AND COMMENTARY

actually enters her bridegroom's authority. Contrary to the ancient Mishnah just quoted, our Mishnah follows the ruling of a court of a later generation (see below, 57a-b) that a woman who is betrothed to a priest may not eat terumah until she is brought with her bridegroom into the bridal chamber.

מָסַר הָאָב לִשְׁלוּחֵי הַבַּעַל [1]The Gemara now proceeds to discuss the next clause of the Mishnah, which stated: **"If the father hands over** his betrothed daughter **to her bridegroom's agents** who have been sent by the bridegroom to receive his bride and to bring her to him, **she is** already **under her bridegroom's authority."** The Amoraim disagree about the scope of this statement. [2]**Rav said: Her being handed over** to the bridegroom's agents brings her under her bridegroom's authority **for everything, except terumah.** As soon as she is handed over to the bridegroom's agents, all the rights and obligations of marriage go into effect. The bridegroom is entitled to what his wife finds and to her handiwork, he inherits from her upon her death, and, if he is a priest, he is permitted to come into contact with her corpse and contract ritual impurity thereby. But if she is the daughter of a non-priest and she is betrothed to a priest, she may not partake of terumah until the marriage is actually completed. [3]**Rav Assi** disagreed and **said:** Her being handed over to the bridegroom's agents brings her under her bridegroom's authority for everything, **even for terumah.**

אֵיתִיבֵיהּ [4]**Rav Huna raised an objection** from a Tannaitic source very similar in language to our Mishnah **against** the viewpoint of **Rav Assi and some say that** it was **Ḥiyya bar Rav** who **raised the objection against Rav Assi:** [5]"A betrothed *na'arah* **is always under her father's authority until she enters the bridal chamber** with her bridegroom and completes the marriage." Now it has already been established that the expression "always" is used in this context to rule out the position of the ancient Mishnah, according to which a betrothed girl may eat terumah as soon as the date set for her marriage has arrived, even if the marriage has not yet taken place. The source quoted by Rav Huna informs us that, regarding the eating of terumah, the girl remains under her father's authority until she actually enters the bridal chamber with her bridegroom. This contradicts the position of Rav Assi, who maintains that the girl's being handed over to the bridegroom's agents brings her under his authority even with respect to terumah.

[1]״מָסַר הָאָב לִשְׁלוּחֵי הַבַּעַל, הֲרֵי הִיא בִּרְשׁוּת הַבַּעַל, וכו׳״. [2]אָמַר רַב: מְסִירָתָהּ לַכֹּל, חוּץ מִתְּרוּמָה. [3]וְרַב אַסִּי אָמַר: אַף לִתְרוּמָה.
[4]אֵיתִיבֵיהּ רַב הוּנָא לְרַב אַסִּי, וְאָמְרִי לָהּ חִיָּיא בַּר רַב לְרַב אַסִּי: [5]״לְעוֹלָם הִיא בִּרְשׁוּת הָאָב עַד שֶׁתִּכָּנֵס לַחוּפָּה״.

LITERAL TRANSLATION

[1]"[If] the father handed [her] over to the husband's agents, she is under the authority of the husband, etc." [2]Rav said: Her being handed over is for everything, except for terumah. [3]But Rav Assi said: Even for terumah.

[4]Rav Huna objected to Rav Assi and some say [that] Ḥiyya bar Rav [objected] to Rav Assi: [5]"She is always under the authority of the father until she enters the bridal chamber."

RASHI

מסירתה לכל – ליורשה, וליטמא לה, ולמעשה ידיה, ולכל דבר איש באשה – קיימא מסירת שלוחים במקום חופה. **חוץ מאכילת תרומה** – דטעמא דידה משום סימפון, כדלקמן בפרק "אף על פי" (נז,ב). ואכתי איכא למיחש להכי, שמא ימצאו בה מומין, ויהיו קידושיה ונישואיה טעות. **ורב אסי אמר אף לתרומה** – קסבר: הא דאמור רבנן ארוסה לא תאכל בתרומה – משום שמא ימזגו לה כוס בבית אביה ותשקה לאחיה ולאחיותיה, והשתא דאין אחיה ואחיותיה אצלה – שרי. **לעולם היא ברשות האב** – ואוקימנא דהאי לעולם משום אכילת תרומה נקט לה, וקתני: עד שתכנס לחופה.

NOTES

Rabbenu Yonah explains: The Gemara's question relates to the Mishnah's use of the emphatic word "always." For the Mishnah could simply have stated: "A girl is under her father's authority until she enters the bridal chamber," or, according to Rashi, "until she enters the authority of the husband for marriage." (See previous note.)

וְרַב אַסִּי אָמַר: אַף לִתְרוּמָה **But Rav Assi said: Even for terumah.** According to *Rashi,* Rav and Rav Assi disagree about why the Rabbis decreed that a woman who is betrothed to a priest may not partake of terumah — an issue that is elsewhere (below, 57b) the subject of a dispute between Ulla and Rav Shmuel bar Rav Yehudah. Rav's ruling is in agreement with the viewpoint of Rav Shmuel bar Rav Yehudah that a betrothed woman may not eat terumah because her bridegroom may find a reason to annul the betrothal. Thus she may not eat terumah until she enters the bridal chamber and the marriage is completed. And Rav Assi's ruling is in agreement with the

HALAKHAH

חוּץ מִתְּרוּמָה **Except for terumah.** "A woman who marries a priest is permitted to eat terumah. By Torah law she is permitted to eat terumah as soon as she is betrothed. But by Rabbinic enactment she may not partake of the terumah until she enters the bridal chamber for marriage," as is stated in our Gemara. (*Rambam, Sefer Zeraim, Hilkhot Terumot* 6:3.)

[1]אֲמַר לְהוּ רַב: לָאו אֲמִינָא לְכוּ: [2]לָא תֵּיזְלוּ בָּתַר אִיפְּכָא? [3]יָכוֹל לְשַׁנּוּיֵי לְכוּ: [4]מְסִירָתָהּ זוֹ הִיא כְּנִיסָתָהּ לַחוּפָּה. [5]וּשְׁמוּאֵל אָמַר: לִירוּשָּׁתָהּ.

LITERAL TRANSLATION

[1]Rav said to them: Did I not say to you: [2]Do not go after the opposite? [3]He can answer you: [4]Her being handed over is itself her entry into the bridal chamber.

[5]But Shmuel said: For her inheritance.

TRANSLATION AND COMMENTARY

אֲמַר לְהוּ רַב [1]**Rav said to them: Have I not** already **told you** [2]**not to raise an objection** based on a source that can be understood in **opposite** ways? [3]Rav Assi **can answer** the apparent contradiction between the Tannaitic source **you** have cited and his own view. The source you have quoted states that, regarding the eating of terumah, a *na'arah* remains under her father's authority until she enters the bridal chamber for marriage. [4]In the light of our interpretation of our Mishnah, Rav Assi can argue that **her being handed over** to the bridegroom's agents who were sent to receive her **is itself** equivalent to **her entering the bridal chamber** with her bridegroom.

וּשְׁמוּאֵל אָמַר [5]The Gemara now cites other opinions regarding the scope of our Mishnah's statement that the bride passes over to her bridegroom's authority when she is handed over to his agents. **Shmuel said:** Her being handed over to the bridegroom's agents brings her under the bridegroom's authority only **with regard to** his inheriting **her estate.** If the bride dies on the way to her bridegroom's house, the bridegroom inherits all the property in her estate. A Baraita cited later in this chapter (below, 53a) states that if someone betroths a woman and she dies, he does not inherit her property. Our Mishnah teaches us that, once the father hands his betrothed daughter over to the bridegroom's agents, she enters her bridegroom's authority regarding her estate as if she has already entered the bridal chamber and completed the marriage. Regarding all other matters, however, the girl remains under her father's authority until she actually enters the bridal chamber with her bridegroom.

RASHI

אמר להן רב – לתלמידו ובנו. לא תיזלו בתר איפכא – לא תשיבו בבית המדרש ממשנה הנהפכת לשני צדדים, שיוכל המתרץ לתרץ משמעה אחר דבריו. שמואל אמר לירושתה – הוא דמהניא מסירה, שאם מתה בדרך – בעל יורש נדונייתה. דאף על גב דאמר מר (כתובות נג,א): אשתו ארוסה, מתה – אינו יורשה. הכא, כיון דמסרה – אחולי אחיל אב מהשתא, מחמת קירוב נישואין. אבל לתרומה, ולהפרת נדריה שלא בשותפות, ולמציאתה דאינה אלא משום איבה ואכתי ליכא למיחש להכי – לא מהניא מסירה כי חופה.

BACKGROUND

לָא תֵּיזְלוּ בָּתַר אִיפְּכָא **Do not go after the opposite.** This expression is used by Rav in the Talmud on a number of occasions in discussion with his close disciple, Rav Huna, or with his own son, Ḥiyya bar Rav, when they try to adduce proofs in support of his approach, and he believes that in their desire to help him they have presented inadequate arguments.

The exact meaning of the expression can be explained in several ways. *Rashi* says here that בָּתַר אִיפְּכָא means "after something that can be reversed," i.e., after a proof from a source that can be understood in various ways and does not offer full support. Elsewhere, in tractate *Kiddushin* (46a), he explains that בָּתַר אִיפְּכָא means "after the opposite thing." In other words: "Why do you offer me support from something that cannot be proved; your Baraita offers nothing." Another interpretation, presented in the name of *Rabbenu Gershom,* is, "Why do you go in the opposite direction, and try to raise difficulties and reverse things?"

NOTES

viewpoint of Ulla that a betrothed woman may not eat terumah because she may happen to give the terumah to other members of her father's household who are forbidden to eat it. Thus, as soon as she is handed over to her bridegroom or to his agents, she is permitted to eat terumah, for she is no longer in the company of her family.

Tosafot objects to this explanation of the disagreement, arguing that subsequent Talmudic discussion shows that all agree that a betrothed woman is barred from eating terumah because of the concern that her bridegroom, the priest, may yet annul the marriage. Rather, says *Tosafot,* Rav Assi maintains that a betrothed woman is permitted to eat terumah as soon as she is handed over to her bridegroom or to his agents for marriage, for by then it is unlikely that he will later find a reason to annul the betrothal.

Rashba defends *Rashi's* explanation, arguing that Ulla is of the opinion that even according to the later Mishnah a betrothed woman is forbidden to eat terumah because she may happen to give some of it to other members of her father's household.

וּשְׁמוּאֵל אָמַר: לִירוּשָּׁתָהּ **But Shmuel said: For her inheritance.** The Rishonim disagree in their interpretation of Shmuel's viewpoint. Our commentary follows *Rashi,* who explains that, according to Shmuel, the girl passes to the bridegroom's authority only with regard to the matter of her inheritance when she is handed over to him or to his agents. But regarding all other matters — for example, her eating terumah, the bridegroom's right to annul her vows by himself, and his right to what she finds — she does not come under his authority until she actually enters the bridal chamber with him. Thus the viewpoint of Shmuel is diametrically opposed to that of Rav, who maintains that the girl's being handed over to her bridegroom brings her under his authority regarding all matters except for terumah.

According to *Rivan,* Shmuel maintains that the girl's being handed over to her bridegroom brings her under his authority with regard to the matter of her inheritance, but does not give her the right to eat terumah or allow her bridegroom, should he be a priest, to render himself ritually impure by coming into contact with her corpse.

Tosafot argues that Shmuel agrees with Rav that the girl's being handed over to her bridegroom brings her under his authority regarding all matters except terumah. When Shmuel says: "For her inheritance," he means: Even for her inheritance. Why, then, does Shmuel only mention the matter of her inheritance? Because we might have thought that since it was the Rabbis who enacted that a woman's estate passes to her husband (and not to her father, who is her heir by Torah law), they designated the husband as her heir only if the marriage process has been completed in the bridal chamber, but not if the girl's father has merely handed her over to the bridegroom or to his agents.

[1] רֵישׁ לָקִישׁ אָמַר: לִכְתוּבָּתָהּ. [2] ״כְּתוּבָּתָהּ״ מַאי הִיא? [3] דְּאִי מֵתָה, יָרֵית לָהּ? [4] הַיְינוּ דִּשְׁמוּאֵל!

[5] אָמַר רָבִינָא: לוֹמַר כְּתוּבָּתָהּ מֵאַחֵר מָנֶה.

[6] רַבִּי יוֹחָנָן וְרַבִּי חֲנִינָא דְּאָמְרִי תַּרְוַיְיהוּ: מְסִירָתָהּ לַכֹּל, אַף לִתְרוּמָה.

[7] מֵיתִיבֵי: ״הָלַךְ הָאָב עִם שְׁלוּחֵי הַבַּעַל, [8] אוֹ שֶׁהָלְכוּ שְׁלוּחֵי הָאָב עִם שְׁלוּחֵי הַבַּעַל, אוֹ שֶׁהָיְתָה לָהּ חָצֵר בַּדֶּרֶךְ וְנִכְנְסָה עִמּוֹ לָלִין, [9] אַף עַל פִּי שֶׁכְּתוּבָּתָהּ בְּבֵית בַּעְלָהּ, מֵתָה,

LITERAL TRANSLATION

[1] Resh Lakish said: For her ketubah.

[2] What is [meant by] "her ketubah"? [3] That if she dies, he inherits it? [4] That is the same as Shmuel!

[5] Ravina said: It is to say [that] her ketubah from someone else is a maneh.

[6] Rabbi Yoḥanan and Rabbi Ḥanina both said: Her being handed over is for everything, even for terumah.

[7] They raised an objection: "[If] the father went with the husband's agents, [8] or [if] the father's agents went with the husband's agents, or [if] she had a courtyard on the way and she went in with him to lodge, [9] even though her ketubah is in her husband's house, [if] she died,

RASHI

לכתובתה — הוא דמהניא מסירה. והשתא קא בעי תלמודא למילתיה. **מאי היא דאם מתה ירית** — בעל את הנדוניא, שפסק לה האב. **לומר כתובתה מאחר מנה** — לשוייה אלמנה מן הנשואין, שלא תיקנו לה חכמים אלא מנה מן הכונסה אחרי כן. **הלך האב כו׳** — אין מסירתו מסירה. **ונכנסה עמו** — עם בעלה ללון, כשאר לינה בדרך בעלמא, ולא לשם נשואין. **שכתובתה** — מטלטלין שייחד אביה לנדונייתה.

TRANSLATION AND COMMENTARY

רֵישׁ לָקִישׁ אָמַר [1] **Resh Lakish said:** Her being handed over to the bridegroom's agents brings her under the bridegroom's authority **with regard to her ketubah.**

כְּתוּבָּתָהּ [2] The Gemara now seeks to clarify the position of Resh Lakish. When he said that the girl enters her bridegroom's authority with regard to **her ketubah, what was it** that he had in mind? [3] If you say he meant **that if she dies** after being handed over to the bridegroom's agents, the bridegroom **inherits** the dowry recorded in her ketubah, there is a difficulty, [4] for **that is the same** point that **Shmuel** made!

אָמַר רָבִינָא [5] **Ravina said** in reply: Resh Lakish meant **to say that,** once a girl is handed over to her bridegroom's agents, she is viewed as having already been married, so that if the bridegroom dies or divorces her and she remarries, **her ketubah from her second husband is** only **a maneh.** A virgin who is widowed or divorced after she has been betrothed but before she is married to her first bridegroom is entitled to a ketubah of two hundred zuz when she remarries (see above, 10b). But if she is widowed or divorced after she has been married, she is entitled to a ketubah of only a maneh, which is one hundred zuz. According to Resh Lakish, our Mishnah teaches us that if a betrothed girl is widowed or divorced after being handed over to her bridegroom's agents, she is no longer considered a widow or a divorcee from after betrothal, who is entitled to a ketubah of two hundred zuz from her second husband, but is a widow or a divorcee after marriage, who is entitled to a ketubah of only a maneh.

רַבִּי יוֹחָנָן [6] The Gemara continues: Like Rav Assi, **Rabbi Yoḥanan and Rabbi Ḥanina both said** that a betrothed girl's **being handed over** to her bridegroom's agents brings her under her bridegroom's authority **for everything, even for terumah.**

מֵיתִיבֵי [7] **An objection was raised** from a Baraita that contradicts those Amoraim who maintain that the bride's being handed over to her bridegroom's agents brings her under his authority even with respect to the eating of terumah: **"If the father** of the bride **goes** together **with the bridegroom's agents** who have been sent to receive his daughter, [8] **or if the father's agents go** together **with the bridegroom's agents,** accompanying the girl until she reaches her bridegroom's house, **or if** the betrothed girl **owns a courtyard on the way** to the bridegroom's house **and she enters** the courtyard together **with** her bridegroom merely **to spend the night,** but not for the purpose of completing the marriage — in all these cases, [9] **even though** the dowry recorded in **her ketubah has** already **been transferred to her bridegroom's house, if she dies** before

NOTES

רֵישׁ לָקִישׁ אָמַר: לִכְתוּבָּתָהּ **Resh Lakish said: For her ketubah.** According to *Rabbenu Ḥananel* (cited by *Ramban*), Shmuel would agree with Resh Lakish that once a girl is handed over to her bridegroom's agents, she is already viewed as a married woman, so that if she is widowed or divorced and she remarries, she is entitled only to a ketubah of a maneh from her second husband. But Resh Lakish would not accept the viewpoint of Shmuel that the bridegroom inherits his bride's estate once she is handed over to him or to his agents for marriage. *Tosafot* suggests the possibility of the opposite view: Shmuel may not accept the viewpoint of Resh Lakish, but Resh Lakish may perhaps accept the viewpoint of Shmuel.

The Jerusalem Talmud also discusses the areas regarding

TRANSLATION AND COMMENTARY

she enters the bridal chamber, **her father inherits** from **her** and the dowry is returned to him, for she has not been handed over to her bridegroom. [1]But **if the father hands over** his betrothed daughter **to her bridegroom's agents, or if** the father sends her with his agents, and on the way **the father's agents hand her over to her bridegroom's agents** who have been sent to receive her, [2]**or if** the bridegroom **owns a courtyard on the way** to his house **and she enters** the courtyard together **with him for the purpose of** completing the **marriage** — in all these cases, [3]**even though** the dowry specified in **her ketubah** has not yet been transferred to her bridegroom, but **is** still **in her father's house,** [4]**if she dies, her bridegroom inherits her** estate and keeps the dowry for himself." [5]The Baraita now limits the scope of its ruling: **"Regarding which** area of the law **does this** ruling **apply?** [6]Only **with regard to inheriting her estate** does she pass over to the bridegroom's authority once she has been entrusted to his agents. [7]**But as for** the eating of **terumah, a woman** who is betrothed to a priest **may not eat terumah until she** and her bridegroom actually **enter the bridal chamber."** Now this Baraita states explicitly that a betrothed girl may not eat terumah until the marriage is completed when the bride and the bridegroom enter the bridal chamber. Does this not contradict the rulings of the Amoraim who stated above that under certain circumstances a bride may eat terumah, even before she is fully married to a priest?

תְּיוּבְתָּא דְּכוּלְּהוּ תְּיוּבְתָּא [8]The Gemara concludes that **this refutation of** the viewpoints of **all** the Amoraim who rule that a betrothed girl's being handed over to the bridegroom's agents brings her under his authority even with respect to her eating terumah, **is** indeed **a valid refutation.**

אָבִיהָ יוֹרְשָׁהּ. [1]מָסַר הָאָב לִשְׁלוּחֵי הַבַּעַל, אוֹ שֶׁמָּסְרוּ שְׁלוּחֵי הָאָב לִשְׁלוּחֵי הַבַּעַל, [2]אוֹ שֶׁהָיְתָה לוֹ חָצֵר בַּדֶּרֶךְ וְנִכְנְסָה עִמּוֹ לְשׁוּם נִישּׂוּאִין, [3]אַף עַל פִּי שֶׁכְּתוּבָּתָהּ בְּבֵית אָבִיהָ, [4]מֵתָה, בַּעְלָהּ יוֹרְשָׁהּ. [5]בַּמֶּה דְּבָרִים אֲמוּרִים? [6]לִירוּשָּׁתָהּ. [7]אֲבָל לִתְרוּמָה, אֵין אִשָּׁה אוֹכֶלֶת בִּתְרוּמָה עַד שֶׁתִּכָּנֵס לַחוּפָּה״.

[8]תְּיוּבְתָּא דְּכוּלְּהוּ תְּיוּבְתָּא.

LITERAL TRANSLATION

her father inherits her. [1][If] the father handed [her] over to the husband's agents, or [if] the father's agents handed [her] over to the husband's agents, [2]or [if] he had a courtyard on the way and she went in with him for the purpose of marriage, [3]even though her ketubah is in her father's house, [4][if] she died, her husband inherits her. [5]Regarding what are these things said? [6]For her inheritance. [7]But as for terumah, a woman does not eat terumah until she enters the bridal chamber."

[8]The refutation of everybody is a [valid] refutation!

RASHI

במה דברים אמורים — שמסירתה לשלוחים הוו נשואין. **ליורשה** — להא מילתא לחודא הוא דהויא נשואין. **תיובתא דכולהו** — הנך דפליגי אדשמואל.

NOTES

which the father's handing over of his daughter to her bridegroom's agents brings her under the bridegroom's authority. Rabbi Elazar says that she is brought under his authority to the extent that he inherits her estate if she dies before she can enter the bridal chamber. Resh Lakish says that she is brought under his authority regarding the annulment of her vows, so that the girl's father can no longer annul her vows together with her bridegroom.

תְּיוּבְתָּא דְּכוּלְּהוּ תְּיוּבְתָּא **The refutation of everybody is a valid refutation.** According to most of the Rishonim, this expression should not be taken literally, for the Baraita cited here does not actually refute all the Amoraic opinions mentioned earlier in the Gemara. *Rashi* maintains that the Baraita refutes the opinions of all the Amoraim who disagree with Shmuel, but not the opinion of Shmuel himself, for Shmuel agrees with the Baraita that the girl's being handed over to her bridegroom's agents brings her under the bridegroom's authority only with regard to her inheritance.

Tosafot argues that the Baraita refutes those Amoraim who accept the viewpoint of Rav Assi and say that the girl's being handed over to her bridegroom's agents brings her under his authority even with respect to terumah, for the Baraita states explicitly that she does not come under his authority regarding that matter.

Rabbenu Crescas Vidal maintains that the Baraita seems to contradict the viewpoint of Rav as well, for it implies that when the girl is handed over to her bridegroom's agents, she comes under his authority with respect to her inheritance, but in no other respect.

It can be argued that the Baraita does not refute the viewpoint of Resh Lakish that the girl is regarded as having been brought under her bridegroom's authority to the extent that if she is widowed or divorced and she remarries, she is entitled only to a ketubah of a maneh from her second husband, for the Baraita may be dealing only with issues that relate to the girl and her first husband (*Ritva*).

According to *Rabbenu Ḥananel,* however, the Baraita refutes the rulings of all the Amoraim cited above, even that of Shmuel. *Rabbenu Ḥananel* has a slightly different reading of the Baraita just quoted ("*and* he [the husband] had a courtyard," rather than "*or* if he had a courtyard"). According to that reading, the girl is not brought under her bridegroom's authority, even with regard to her inheritance, unless two conditions are met — she is handed over to

TRANSLATION AND COMMENTARY

הָא גּוּפָא קַשְׁיָא [1]The Gemara now turns its attention to an apparent contradiction between the two parts of the Baraita and observes: The Baraita **itself is difficult** to understand. [2]For in the first part of the Baraita, **it states:** "If the betrothed girl owns a courtyard on the way to her bridegroom's house and **she enters** the courtyard together **with** her bridegroom merely **to spend the night,** and she dies, her father inherits from her and the dowry is returned to him, for she has not entered the bridegroom's authority." [3]Now, if we read the Baraita precisely, we can infer that **the reason** she remains under her father's authority **is that** the two made it clear that they **entered** the courtyard together merely **to spend the night** there, and not for the purpose of completing the marriage process. [4]**This implies that if** the couple **entered** the courtyard **without specifying** why they went in, we assume that they entered it **for the purpose of** completing the **marriage,** so that the girl is no longer under her father's authority, but rather under that of her bridegroom. [5]**Contrast** this with what is stated in **the next clause** of the Baraita: "If the bridegroom owns a courtyard on the way to his house and his bride **enters** the courtyard **with him for the purpose of** completing the **marriage,** and she dies, her bridegroom inherits her estate and keeps the dowry specified in his bride's ketubah, for she is viewed as having already entered his authority." Now, again, if we read the Baraita precisely, we can infer that the reason the bride is viewed as having entered her bridegroom's authority is that the couple stated clearly that they were entering the courtyard for the purpose of completing the marriage. [6]**This implies that if** the couple **entered** the courtyard **without specifying** why they went in, we assume that they entered merely **to spend the night** there, and not for the purpose of completing the marriage! Thus, contradictory inferences can be drawn from the two clauses of the Baraita about how to treat the case in which the couple enter the courtyard without specifying their reason for doing so.

אָמַר רַב אַשִׁי [7]**Rav Ashi said:** In fact, there is no contradiction between the two parts of the Baraita. When the first clause speaks of the bride entering the courtyard together with her bridegroom merely in order to spend the night there, it does not refer to a case in which she announced that this was her intention. And, similarly, when the next clause speaks of the couple entering the courtyard for the purpose of completing the marriage, it does not refer to a case in which this was stated explicitly. [8]In fact, the author of the Baraita **describes two cases** in which the couple entered the courtyard **without specifying** why. [9]If it was **her courtyard** that they **entered,** we may assume that **when** they went in **without specifying** why, it was merely **to spend the night** there. [10]And if it was **his courtyard,** then we may assume that **when** they **went in without specifying** why, they entered **for** the purpose of completing the **marriage.** Thus the seeming contradiction between the two parts of the Baraita is resolved.

LITERAL TRANSLATION

[1]This itself is difficult. [2]You said: "She went in with him to lodge." [3]The reason is that [she went in] to lodge. [4]This [implies that if she went in] without specifying [it was] for the purpose of marriage. [5]Say the latter clause: "She went in with him for the purpose of marriage." [6]This [implies that if she went in] without specifying [it was] to lodge!

[7]Rav Ashi said: [8]It teaches [two] unspecified cases: [9][Entering] her courtyard, when unspecified, [means] to lodge; [10][entering] his courtyard, when unspecified, means for marriage.

[1]הָא גּוּפָא קַשְׁיָא. [2]אָמְרַתְּ: "נִכְנְסָה עִמּוֹ לָלִין". [3]טַעֲמָא דְּלָלִין. [4]הָא סְתָמָא לְשֵׁם נִישּׂוּאִין. [5]אֵימָא סֵיפָא: "נִכְנְסָה עִמּוֹ לְשֵׁם נִישּׂוּאִין". [6]הָא סְתָמָא לָלִין!

[7]אֲמַר רַב אַשִׁי: [8]סְתָמֵי סְתָמֵי קָתָנֵי: [9]סְתָם חָצֵר דִּידָהּ לָלִין; [10]סְתָם חָצֵר דִּידֵיהּ לְנִשּׂוּאִין.

BACKGROUND

סְתָמֵי סְתָמֵי קָתָנֵי It teaches two unspecified cases. According to Rav Ashi, neither the expression "and she went in with him to lodge," nor the expression "and she went in with him for the purpose of marriage," is included as an additional possibility in each of the clauses, but each is an explanation of what was written earlier. Since a true marriage is effected by the wife's entry into her husband's house, her entry into her own courtyard cannot be intended as entry into the husband's domain but rather as entry into a place for the simple purpose of lodging. Conversely, if she enters her husband's courtyard, this is similar to entering his home, and it can be understood that her intention is to complete the marriage.

RASHI

הא סתמא — אם נכנסה ושהתה עמו סתם, אמרינן: נשואין נינהו, וזו היא כניסת חופתה, ואף על פי שלא נבעלה — הוי נשואין. **סתמי סתמי קתני** — הא דקתני נכנסה עמו ללון — לא שפירשה "ללון אני נכנסת ולא לשם נשואין" והא דקתני נכנסה עמו לנשואין לא שפירשה "לנשואין אני נכנסת". אלא, זו וזו שנכנסה סתם. ותנא הוא דקאמר, דהיכא דחצר שלה — סתם כניסתה לא לנשואין הן אלא ללון, והיכא דחצר שלו — סתם כניסתה לשם נשואין.

NOTES

her bridegroom or to his agents, *and* she enters her bridegroom's courtyard for the purpose of marriage; whereas according to Shmuel she comes under her bridegroom's authority with respect to her inheritance as soon as she is handed over to her bridegroom's agents. (See *Ramban* and his disciples, who cite *Rabbenu Ḥananel's* view but reject it.)

חָצֵר דִּידָהּ...חָצֵר דִּידֵיהּ Her courtyard...his courtyard. There is no need for a formal "wedding ceremony" to make a marriage (*nissu'in*) valid. All that is necessary is that the bride be brought to her bridegroom under the ḥuppah (the bridal chamber) for the purpose of marriage, whether this is his home or a place symbolizing his domain — for example, a place where a canopy is spread across four

SAGES

רַב אַמִי בַּר חָמָא Rav Ammi bar Ḥama. This is the Babylonian Amora of the fourth generation who is often found in controversy with Rava, and is better known as Rami Bar Ḥama (see *Ketubot*, Part II, p. 57). "Rami" is not actually a name but an abbreviated form of "Rav Ammi." Indeed, in the Jerusalem Talmud, Rami bar Ḥama is usually called Rav Ammi bar Ḥama. Rava's comment later in the passage, "Ammi told me," also refers to Rami bar Ḥama. Since he was a close friend of Rava's, Rava did not refer to him by his title, but only by his first name, Ammi.

TRANSLATION AND COMMENTARY

תָּנָא [1]The Gemara continues: **A Tanna taught** the following Baraita: **"If the father hands over** his betrothed daughter **to her bridegroom's agents** who have been sent to receive the bride and bring her to him, **and she commits adultery** before she reaches her bridegroom, [2]**she is subject to** the penalty of execution by **strangulation** (under the category of a married woman who has committed adultery), rather than to execution by stoning (the punishment meted out to a betrothed *na'arah* guilty of adultery)."

מְנָא הָנֵי מִילֵּי [3]The Gemara asks: **From where** in the Torah **is this** ruling **derived?** In other words, what is the Biblical source for the Baraita's ruling?

אֲמַר רַב אַמִי בַּר חָמָא [4]**Rav Ammi bar Ḥama said** in reply: [5]This ruling is derived from **the verse** (Deuteronomy 22:21) that **says** that "the men of the city shall stone her with stones so that she dies, because she has perpetrated wantonness in Israel **to commit adultery in her father's house....**" The verse teaches us that a betrothed *na'arah* who commits adultery is only subject to the penalty of stoning if she committed the offense while she was still in her father's house. [6]This comes **to exclude** a case **where** she commits adultery after **her father** has already **handed her over to her bridegroom's agents,** so that she is no longer "in her father's house." In such a case she is subject to the penalty of execution by strangulation, because she has the status of a married woman.

וְאֵימָא [7]The Gemara raises an objection: **But** why not **say** that the verse comes **to exclude** a case **where** the betrothed girl has already **entered the bridal chamber** with her bridegroom, **but has not** yet **engaged in intercourse** with him? The verse may in fact be teaching us that in such a case she is treated as a married woman, even though she has not yet consummated her marriage and is still a virgin. But if she has not yet entered the bridal chamber, but has merely been handed over to her bridegroom's agents, perhaps she is still regarded as a betrothed *na'arah*, who, if she commits adultery, is punished by stoning!

[1]תָּנָא: ״מָסַר הָאָב לִשְׁלוּחֵי הַבַּעַל וְזִינְּתָה, [2]הֲרֵי זוֹ בְּחֶנֶק״.
[3]מְנָא הָנֵי מִילֵּי?
[4]אֲמַר רַב אַמִי בַּר חָמָא: [5]אֲמַר קְרָא: ״לִזְנוֹת בֵּית אָבִיהָ״ — [6]פְּרָט לְשֶׁמָּסַר הָאָב לִשְׁלוּחֵי הַבַּעַל.
[7]וְאֵימָא: פְּרָט שֶׁנִּכְנְסָה לַחוּפָּה וְלֹא נִבְעֲלָה!

LITERAL TRANSLATION

[1][A Tanna] taught: "[If] the father handed [her] over to the husband's agents, and she committed adultery, [2]she is subject to strangulation."

[3]From where are these things [derived]?

[4]Rav Ammi bar Ḥama said: [5]The verse says: "To commit adultery in her father's house" — [6]to exclude where the father handed [her] over to the husband's agents.

[7]But say: To exclude where she entered the bridal chamber but did not have intercourse!

RASHI

הרי זו בחנק — כנשואה, ולא בסקילה כארוסה. **ואימא פרט לכשנכנסה לחופה ולא נבעלה** — דייק אם מיעטת כגון זו, דלא תימא נערה בתולה כתיב גבי סקילה, והא אכתי בתולה הואי. אבל זו, שאף לחופה לא נכנסה — לא מיעטה הכתוב, ואכתי ״בית אביה״ קרינא ביה.

NOTES

poles and the bridegroom is waiting. Thus, if a betrothed girl enters a courtyard with her bridegroom in a manner that can be construed as entering the bridegroom's domain for the purpose of marriage, her entry into the courtyard can itself constitute *nissu'in*. Our Gemara considers the criteria whereby we can determine whether the couple entered the courtyard merely for lodging or for the purpose of marriage.

מָסַר הָאָב לִשְׁלוּחֵי הַבַּעַל וְזִינְּתָה, הֲרֵי זוֹ בְּחֶנֶק If the father handed her over to the husband's agents, and she committed adultery, she is subject to strangulation. *Shittah Mekubbetzet* argues that it does not follow from this Baraita that once a betrothed girl is handed over to her bridegroom's agents she is considered a married woman. Thus it has no bearing on the Amoraic dispute above regarding the scope of the Mishnah's statement that the bride comes under her bridegroom's authority when she is handed over to his agents. The only conclusion that may be drawn from the Baraita (as it is understood here by Rav Ammi bar Ḥama) is that once the betrothed girl is handed over to her bridegroom's agents, she is no longer governed by the laws that apply to a betrothed girl who is still in her father's house. A similar Baraita is recorded in the Jerusalem Talmud. There the Baraita is cited as support for the viewpoint of Resh Lakish that a girl passes over to her husband's authority regarding the annulment of her

HALAKHAH

מָסַר הָאָב לִשְׁלוּחֵי הַבַּעַל וְזִינְּתָה, הֲרֵי זוֹ בְּחֶנֶק If the father handed her over to the bridegroom's agents, and she committed adultery, she is subject to strangulation. "If a man other than her bridegroom has intercourse with a betrothed *na'arah*, both of them are subject to stoning, provided that the *na'arah* is a virgin, betrothed, and still in her father's house. If she has already reached majority, or if she has entered into the bridal chamber, even if she has not yet had intercourse with her bridegroom, or even if she has been handed over by her father to her bridegroom's agents, and she commits adultery, she is subject to strangulation," following our Gemara. (*Rambam, Sefer Kedushah, Hilkhot Issurei Bi'ah* 3:4.)

TRANSLATION AND COMMENTARY

אֲמַר רָבָא [1]**Rava said:** We cannot argue that the purpose of the verse is to exclude the case in which the betrothed girl has already entered the bridal chamber, [2]for the Sage **Ammi said to me** that the case in which the betrothed girl has already entered **the bridal chamber is mentioned explicitly** in another verse. For the Torah states (Deuteronomy 22:23-24): [3]**"If a *na'arah* who is a virgin is betrothed to a man,** and a man finds her in the city, and lies with her, then you shall bring them both out to the gate of that city, and you shall stone them with stones so that they die...." This text teaches us that adultery is punishable by stoning only if the offense was committed by "a *na'arah* who is a virgin" who is "betrothed." [4]A precise reading of the verse leads to the following conclusions: **"A *na'arah*"** who commits adultery is subject to the penalty of stoning, **but not** a girl **who has** already **come of age.** [5]**"A virgin"** who commits adultery is put to death by stoning, **but not** a **girl** who was **not a virgin** at the time of her offense. [6]A girl who is **"betrothed"** when she commits adultery is executed by stoning, **but not** one who is already **married** at the time of her transgression. [7]Now, **what is meant** here **by** the expression **"married** woman," who is excluded from the punishment of stoning? [8]**If we say** that the purpose of the verse is to exclude a case in which she is **actually married** to her bridegroom and the couple have consummated their marriage by intercourse, **that** case **is** already derived from the expression **"a virgin,"** which teaches us that only a girl who was a virgin when she committed adultery is subject to the penalty of stoning, **but not** a girl who was **not a virgin** at the time of her offense. [9]**Rather,** we must interpret the verse differently. Its purpose is to exclude the case **where** the girl commits adultery after **she** has already **entered the bridal chamber** with her bridegroom **but has not** yet **engaged in intercourse** with him, for in such a case she is subject to death by strangulation, as if she has already consummated her marriage. Thus the expression "to commit adultery in her father's house" must exclude a case in which the betrothed girl commits adultery after she has been handed over to her bridegroom's agents, even though she has not yet arrived at her bridegroom's house.

וְאֵימָא [49A] [10]The Gemara now raises a question regarding our Mishnah's ruling that once the father has handed over his betrothed daughter to the bridegroom's agents, she is already under her bridegroom's

[1]אֲמַר רָבָא: [2]אֲמַר לִי אַמִי: חוּפָּה בְּהֶדְיָא כְּתִיבָא: [3]״כִּי יִהְיֶה נַעֲרָה בְתוּלָה מְאֹרָשָׂה לְאִישׁ״. [4]״נַעֲרָה״ — וְלֹא בּוֹגֶרֶת. [5]״בְתוּלָה״ — וְלֹא בְּעוּלָה. [6]״מְאֹרָשָׂה״ — וְלֹא נְשׂוּאָה. [7]מַאי ״נְשׂוּאָה״? [8]אִילֵימָא נְשׂוּאָה מַמָּשׁ, הַיְינוּ ״׳בְּתוּלָה׳ — וְלֹא בְּעוּלָה״. [9]אֶלָּא לָאו שֶׁנִּכְנְסָה לַחוּפָּה וְלֹא נִבְעֲלָה?

[49A] [10]וְאֵימָא: הֵיכָא דְּהָדְרָא

LITERAL TRANSLATION

[1]Rava said: Ammi said to me: [2]The bridal chamber is mentioned explicitly: [3]"If a *na'arah* who is a virgin is betrothed to a man." [4]"A *na'arah*" — and not one who has come of age. [5]"A virgin" — and not a non-virgin. [6]"Betrothed" — and not married. [7]What is [meant by] "married"? [8]If we say actually married, that is the same as "'a virgin' — and not a non-virgin." [9]Rather, is it not that she entered the bridal chamber but did not have intercourse?

[49A] [10]But say: When she returns

RASHI

חופה — בלא בעילה בהדיא כתיבא דלאו בסקילה היא, וכי איצטריך האי למסירה. **אילימא נשואה ממש** — שנכנסה לחופה ונבעלה. הכי גרסינן: **ואימא היכא דהדרא לבי נשא תהדר למילתא קמייתא** — מי היא כמי שלא נמסרה. בעיא בעלמא היא, ואינה קושיא כל כך,

NOTES

vows when she is entrusted to his agents, so that the girl's father can no longer annul her vows together with her bridegroom. The Torah uses the expression "her father's house" both in connection with the annulment of a girl's vows and in connection with her execution by stoning. A betrothed girl leaves "her father's house" when she is handed over to her bridegroom's agents, and the father is no longer authorized to take part in the annulment of her vows; moreover, the girl would not be subject to stoning if she were now to commit adultery.

חוּפָּה בְּהֶדְיָא כְּתִיבָא The bridal chamber is mentioned explicitly. This expression cannot be taken literally, for nowhere does the Torah make explicit reference to the bridal chamber (though the word חוּפָּה is indeed found in the Bible). Rather, the Gemara is arguing that the Torah recognizes that a woman acquires the status of "being married" irrespective of whether she is still a virgin. Thus we are forced to conclude that there must be some act by which a woman passes from the state of betrothal to that of marriage, and this must be entry into the bridal chamber.

וְאֵימָא: הֵיכָא דְּהָדְרָא לְבֵי נָשָׂא But say: When she returns to her father's house. Our commentary follows *Rashi,* who explains the Gemara's question as referring back to the Mishnah: How does the Mishnah know that a girl who has been handed over to her bridegroom's agents remains permanently removed from her father's authority, even if she is divorced or widowed before reaching her bridegroom's house and then returns to her father's home? But most Rishonim read this question as directly connected to

SAGES

תַּנָּא דְּבֵי רַבִּי יִשְׁמָעֵאל A Tanna of the School of Rabbi Yishmael. See *Ketubot,* Part I, p. 54.

לְבֵי נָשָׂא, הָדְרָא לְמִילְּתָא קַמָּיְיתָא!

[1]אֲמַר רָבָא: הַהוּא כְּבָר פְּסָקָהּ תַּנָּא דְּבֵי רַבִּי יִשְׁמָעֵאל. [2]דְּתָנָא דְּבֵי רַבִּי יִשְׁמָעֵאל: [3]״׳וְנֵדֶר אַלְמָנָה וּגְרוּשָׁה, כֹּל אֲשֶׁר אָסְרָה עַל נַפְשָׁהּ, יָקוּם עָלֶיהָ׳. [4]מַה תַּלְמוּד לוֹמַר? [5]וַהֲלֹא מוּצֵאת מִכְּלַל אָב וּמוּצֵאת

LITERAL TRANSLATION

to her father's house, she returns to [her] original state (lit., "matter")!

[1]Rava said: That [point] a Tanna of the School of Rabbi Yishmael has already decided, [2]for [a Tanna] of the School of Rabbi Yishmael taught: [3]"'But a vow of a widow and of a divorcee, everything with which she has bound her soul, shall stand against her.' [4]What does the verse teach? [5]But has she not been taken out of her father's [authority] and been taken out

TRANSLATION AND COMMENTARY

authority regarding marital matters. The Mishnah implies that once a daughter has left her father's authority on being handed over to her bridegroom's agents, she never reverts to his authority even if she is widowed or divorced before she ever reaches her bridegroom. **But,** asks the Gemara, why do we not **say** that **if** the betrothed girl is widowed or divorced while in the hands of her bridegroom's agents, and **she** then **returns to her father's house, she returns to her original status** and is once again under her father's authority as if she has never left it?

אֲמַר רָבָא [1]**Rava said:** About **that matter a Tanna of the School of Rabbi Yishmael has already decided** that the girl does not return to her father's authority, [2]**for a Tanna of the School of Rabbi Yishmael taught** the following Baraita: [3]"The verse dealing with the annulment of vows says (Numbers 30:10): **'But a vow of a widow and of a divorcee, everything with which she has bound her soul, shall stand against her.'** [4]**What does this verse** come to **teach?** Is it not obvious that a vow taken by a widow or a divorcee cannot be annulled? [5]**Surely** a widow or a divorcee **was** already **taken out of her father's authority** when she married, **and she was taken out of her husband's authority** when he died or divorced her! Seeing that no one could possibly be authorized to annul the vows of a widow or a divorcee,

RASHI

אלא דקתני מתניתין הרי היא ברשות הבעל, ומשמע ואפילו חזרה מן הדרך לבית אביה כבר יצאה מרשות האב, וכיון דלא נפקא לן מסירת שלוחין אלא מקרא יתירא ד״בית אביה״ אימא היכא דהדרא — בית אביה קרינן ביה, ואם זינתה תהא בסקילה. **כבר פסקה תנא דבי רבי ישמעאל** — דלא הדרא למילתא קמייתא, למיהוי כמי שלא נמסרה. **מה תלמוד לומר** — למה הוצרך לכתוב ״יקום עליה״ וכי מי יפר לה? והלא לא נאמרו מפירים אלא אביה בבתו עד שלא ניסת, ובעלה משניסת. וזו שנתארמלה משניסת — מוצאת מכלל אב ומכלל בעל.

NOTES

the discussion that immediately precedes it in the Gemara. Indeed, many commentators have a reading according to which the Gemara's question is introduced by the words: "Rav Adda bar Matenah said to Rava: Say that this applies, etc.," a formulation which can only be understood as a continuation of the previous discussion. These Rishonim explain the Gemara's question as follows: It is still possible to argue that the verse, "To commit adultery in her father's house," excludes a case in which the betrothed girl has already entered the bridal chamber but has not yet engaged in intercourse with her bridegroom. As for the objection that we already know that the girl is not subject to stoning in such a case from the verse, "If a *na'arah* who is a virgin is betrothed to a man," this can be rebutted as follows: It is possible that that verse teaches only that the girl is not stoned if she commits adultery *while in her husband's house.* But if she is divorced or widowed and then returns to her father's house, and once again is betrothed and then commits adultery, she may indeed be subject to stoning. Thus the verse tells us: "To commit adultery in her father's house," to exclude a girl who has already entered the bridal chamber and has later returned to her father's house. How, then, do we know that a betrothed *na'arah* who commits adultery after she has been handed over to her bridegroom's agents is subject to strangulation and not to stoning? The Gemara answers: A verse is not needed to exclude the case in which the girl has already entered the bridal chamber but later returns to her father's house, for we have already learned from the verses dealing with the annulment of a girl's vows that a girl does not return to her original status if she returns to her father's house after having already entered the bridal chamber. Thus the expression, "To commit adultery in her father's house," must come to teach us that a betrothed girl who commits adultery after having been handed over to her bridegroom's agents is not subject to the penalty of stoning.

הָדְרָא לְמִילְּתָא קַמָּיְיתָא She returns to her original state. *Tur* (based on *Rabbenu Ḥananel*; see Halakhah) explains that a betrothed girl who has already been handed over to her bridegroom's agents, but later returns to her father's house, does in fact return to her original status regarding her father's right to annul the vows that she makes after she returns to his home. But most authorities maintain that when a father hands over his betrothed daughter to her bridegroom's agents, he permanently and absolutely severs the tie between himself and his daughter, so that he may never again annul any of the vows that she may make, even if she is later divorced or widowed and returns to his house.

וַהֲלֹא מוּצֵאת מִכְּלַל אָב But she has not been taken out of her father's authority. *Rabbi Avraham ben Isaac of Narbonne* asks: What is the Baraita's question? From where else but from this verse, "But a vow of a widow and of a divorcee, everything with which she has bound her soul, shall stand against her," would we know that a widowed

TRANSLATION AND COMMENTARY

why did the Torah find it necessary to teach us that their vows *cannot* be annulled? The verse cannot be referring to a widow or a divorcee after marriage. [1]**Rather,** it must be dealing with a case **where the father handed over** his betrothed daughter **to the bridegroom's agents** who had been sent to receive her, [2]**or where the father's agents,** who were taking the betrothed girl to her husband, **handed her over to the bridegroom's agents,** [3]**and** the girl **was widowed or divorced on the journey** to her bridegroom. The Torah has laid down the laws that apply to a girl who made a vow in her father's house or in her husband's house. [4]But we do not know **how to treat** this girl who was widowed or divorced while in the hands of her bridegroom's agents, and later made a vow after she returned to her father's house. [5]Do we say that she is once again governed by the law that applies to a girl who makes a vow in **her father's house or** is she considered someone who makes a vow in **her husband's house?** [6]**Therefore the verse comes to teach us** that **once** the girl **has left her father's authority for** even **one hour,** when the father handed her over to the bridegroom's agents, she never reverts to her father's authority. [7]Thus the father **can no longer annul her vows,** even if she is widowed or divorced while in the hands of her bridegroom's agents."

אָמַר רַב פַּפָּא [8]**Rav Pappa said: We have also learned** a ruling in a Mishnah corroborating the ruling found in the Baraita cited above (48b), that if a betrothed *na'arah* commits adultery after she has been handed over by her father to her bridegroom's agents, she is subject like a married woman to the penalty of execution by strangulation. [9]For the Mishnah states (*Sanhedrin* 66b): **"Someone who has intercourse with a**

מִכְּלַל בַּעַל? [1]אֶלָּא, הֲרֵי שֶׁמָּסַר הָאָב לִשְׁלוּחֵי הַבַּעַל, [2]אוֹ שֶׁמָּסְרוּ שְׁלוּחֵי הָאָב לִשְׁלוּחֵי הַבַּעַל, [3]וְנִתְאַרְמְלָה בַּדֶּרֶךְ אוֹ נִתְגָּרְשָׁה, [4]הֵיאָךְ אֲנִי קוֹרֵא בָּהּ? [5]בֵּית אָבִיהָ שֶׁל זוֹ אוֹ בֵּית בַּעְלָהּ שֶׁל זוֹ? [6]אֶלָּא לוֹמַר לְךָ: כֵּיוָן שֶׁיָּצְאָה שָׁעָה אַחַת מֵרְשׁוּת הָאָב, [7]שׁוּב אֵינוֹ יָכוֹל לְהָפֵר".

[8]אֲמַר רַב פַּפָּא: אַף אֲנַן נַמִי תְּנֵינָא: [9]"הַבָּא עַל נַעֲרָה

LITERAL TRANSLATION

of her husband's [authority]? [1]Rather, if the father handed [her] over to the husband's agents, [2]or if the father's agents handed [her] over to the husband's agents, [3]and she was widowed on the way or divorced, [4]how do I describe (lit., 'call') her? [5]Her father's house or her husband's house? [6]Rather [the verse comes] to tell you: Once she has left the father's authority for one hour, [7]he can no longer annul [her vows]."

[8]Rav Pappa said: We too have also learned [thus]: [9]"Someone who has intercourse with a betrothed *na'arah*

RASHI

אלא הרי שמסר כו' — כלומר, לא בא הכתוב לאלמנה ולגרושה מן נשואין — דהא כתיב בה "אם בית אישה נדרה אישה יפירנו" — והרי אין אישה קיים. אלא לאלמנה על ידי מסירת שלוחין. שעד עכשיו לא פירשו לך הכתובים אלא משפט נודרת בבית אביה ומשפט נודרת בבית אישה, וזו שנדרה בדרך משמסרוה לשלוחין — אין אני יודע היאך אני קורא בה, אם "בית אביה" אם "בית אישה", לפיכך בא כתוב זה ולמדך שלא תקרא לה "בית אביה" אלא "בית אישה", ולא נתרוקנה רשות לאב במיתתו של בעל, ושוב אינו יכול להפר. אלמא: לא הדרא למילתא קמייתא, דאילו נתארמלה מן האירוסין עד שלא נמסרה לשלוחין — תנן במסכת נדרים (ע,א): מת הבעל — נתרוקנה רשות לאב. וילפינן לה מקראי. **אף אנן נמי תנינא** — במתניתין, כי ההיא ברייתא דתניא לעיל "הרי זו בחנק".

TERMINOLOGY

אַף אֲנַן נַמִי תְּנֵינָא We too have also learned thus. This expression is used in the Gemara when proof is adduced for the ruling of an Amora from the words of a Mishnah or a Baraita. In general, the Tannaitic quotation does not deal directly with the subject at hand (for it would be surprising to have an Amora make a Halakhic ruling that had already appeared in a Mishnah); but the proof is usually more complex, stating that if one examined the matter closely one's conclusion would be the same as that of the Amora, although he did not base his ruling on the Mishnah.

NOTES

or a divorced girl has already left her father's authority regarding the annulment of her vows when she is married? He answers: The verse (Numbers 30:17), "While she is a *na'arah* in her father's house," teaches us that a girl remains under her father's authority only as long as she remains in his house. But when she leaves his house and marries, she also leaves his authority regarding the annulment of her vows, and she does not revert to that authority even if she is later widowed or divorced and returns to his house. Since the verse, "But a vow of a widow," is not needed to teach us about a widow or a divorcee after marriage, the Baraita understands it as referring to a girl who was widowed or divorced after having been handed over to her bridegroom's agents but before she actually entered the bridal chamber.

HALAKHAH

כֵּיוָן שֶׁיָּצְאָה שָׁעָה אַחַת מֵרְשׁוּת הָאָב, שׁוּב אֵינוֹ יָכוֹל לְהָפֵר Once she has left the father's authority for one hour, he can no longer annul her vows. "If the father accompanies (or his agents accompany) the bridegroom's agents to bring his betrothed daughter to the bridal chamber, she does not leave her father's authority until she actually enters the bridal chamber. During this period, her vows may be annulled by her father and her bridegroom acting together. But if the father hands his daughter over to the bridegroom's agents, of if the father's agents hand her over to the bridegroom's agents, she is no longer under her father's authority with respect to the annulment of her vows. (According to some authorities, the bridegroom cannot annul his bride's vows in such a case until she actually enters the bridal chamber.) If the betrothed girl has entered the bridal chamber, or if the father has handed her

TRANSLATION AND COMMENTARY

betrothed *na'arah* is not subject to the penalty of stoning **unless** certain conditions are met. The girl **must be a *na'arah*, a virgin, and betrothed, and she must** still **be in her father's house."** What, asks Rav Pappa, did the Mishnah mean to teach us when it listed all these conditions? [1]**Granted** that when it states that the girl must be **a *na'arah*** it means to inform us that she must be a *na'arah*, **and not a girl who has** already **come of age.** [2]And when it says that the girl must be **a virgin,** it means that the penalty of stoning is imposed only if the *na'arah* has never before engaged in sexual intercourse, **but not** if she is already **a non-virgin** at the time of the offense. [3]And when it says that she must be **betrothed,** it means that the offenders are only put to death by stoning if the bride is betrothed to her bridegroom, **but not** if she is **married** to him. [4]But, continues Rav Pappa, **what** case **does** the requirement that the betrothed girl must still be **"in her father's house"** come to **exclude?** [5]**Does it not** come to **exclude** a case **where the** girl's **father handed over** his betrothed daughter **to the bridegroom's agents,** and someone else had intercourse with her before she reached her bridegroom's house? Thus, concludes Rav Pappa, the Mishnah teaches us that in such a case the offender is not subject to stoning but rather to strangulation, for once the girl has been handed over to her bridegroom's agents, she is treated as a married woman.

אָמַר רַב נַחְמָן בַּר יִצְחָק [6]**Rav Naḥman bar Yitzḥak said: We have also learned** in another Mishnah a ruling that corroborates the ruling that once a betrothed girl has been handed over by her father to her bridegroom's agents, she is treated as a married woman. [7]For the Mishnah states (*Sanhedrin* 89a): **"Regarding someone who has intercourse with another man's wife,** the law is as follows: **Once** a betrothed *na'arah* **has entered her bridegroom's authority for** the purpose of **marriage, even if she has not** yet **had intercourse with him,** [8]if another man **has intercourse with her,** he **is subject to** execution by **strangulation,** as if he has had intercourse with a married woman." This Mishnah states that [9]**even if** the bride **has merely entered the authority of her bridegroom** but has not yet entered the bridal chamber, she and her partner in adultery are subject to execution by strangulation. [10]Therefore we can **conclude from here** that once a father has handed over his betrothed daughter to her bridegroom's agents for the purpose of marriage, she is treated as a married woman regarding the punishment that is inflicted if she is found guilty of adultery.

MISHNAH הָאָב אֵינוֹ חַיָּיב [11]Even though a minor daughter is entitled to be maintained from the estate of her deceased father until she reaches the age of majority or until she becomes betrothed (see below, 52b),

הַמְאוֹרָסָה אֵינוֹ חַיָּיב עַד שֶׁתְּהֵא נַעֲרָה, בְּתוּלָה, מְאוֹרָסָה, וְהִיא בְּבֵית אָבִיהָ״. [1]בִּשְׁלָמָא נַעֲרָה — וְלֹא בּוֹגֶרֶת; [2]בְּתוּלָה — וְלֹא בְּעוּלָה; [3]מְאוֹרָסָה — וְלֹא נְשׂוּאָה. [4]״בְּבֵית אָבִיהָ״ לְמַעוּטֵי מַאי? [5]לָאו לְמַעוּטֵי מָסַר הָאָב לִשְׁלוּחֵי הַבַּעַל?

[6]אָמַר רַב נַחְמָן בַּר יִצְחָק: אַף אֲנַן נַמִי תָּנֵינָא: [7]״הַבָּא עַל אֵשֶׁת אִישׁ, כֵּיוָן שֶׁנִּכְנְסָה לִרְשׁוּת הַבַּעַל לְנִשּׂוּאִין, אַף עַל פִּי שֶׁלֹּא נִבְעֲלָה, [8]הַבָּא עָלֶיהָ הֲרֵי זֶה בְּחֶנֶק״. [9]נִכְנְסָה לִרְשׁוּת הַבַּעַל בְּעָלְמָא. [10]שְׁמַע מִינָּהּ.

משנה [11]הָאָב אֵינוֹ חַיָּיב

LITERAL TRANSLATION

is not liable unless she is a *na'arah*, a virgin, [and] betrothed, and she is in her father's house." [1]Granted a *na'arah* — and not one who has come of age; [2]a virgin — and not a non-virgin; [3]betrothed — and not married. [4][But] what does "in her father's house" exclude? [5]Does it not exclude [where] the father handed [her] over to the husband's agents?

[6]Rav Naḥman bar Yitzḥak said: We too have also learned [thus]: [7]"[Regarding] someone who has intercourse with another man's wife, once she has entered the authority of the husband for marriage, even if she has not had intercourse [with him], [8]he who has intercourse with her is subject to strangulation." [9][This applies even if] she merely entered the authority of the husband. [10]Conclude from this.

MISHNAH [11]A father is not liable

RASHI

מאורסה ולא נשואה — נכנסה לחופה, ואף על פי שלא נבעלה. **דאי נבעלה** — הא תנא ליה בתולה. **נכנסה לרשות הבעל בעלמא** — תנן, ולא תנן בה ״נכנסה לחופה״.

משנה האב אינו חייב במזונות בתו — בחייו. ובגמרא מפרש אמאי נקט בתו.

HALAKHAH

over to the bridegroom's agents to bring her into the bridal chamber, and the bridegroom dies, she does not return to her father's authority with respect to the annulment of her vows. According to *Tur,* the girl returns to her father's authority with respect to the annulment of those vows she makes after her bridegroom's death. See *Bet Yosef, Shakh,* and *Taz,* who raise numerous objections against *Tur*'s position." (*Rambam, Sefer Hafla'ah, Hilkhot Nedarim* 11:22; *Shulḥan Arukh, Yoreh De'ah* 234:8,12.)

TRANSLATION AND COMMENTARY

a father is not legally **liable for his** minor **daughter's maintenance** during his lifetime. [1]**The following interpretation was expounded by Rabbi Elazar ben Azaryah before the Sages in the Academy at Yavneh** on the day he was appointed head of the Sanhedrin: Among the conditions specified in a woman's ketubah are the following two: (1) [2]**The sons** of the marriage **inherit** their mother's ketubah from their father (if their mother dies before their father, her ketubah passes to their father on her death), over and above their portion in their father's estate, which they must share equally with his sons by any other marriage. This enactment, known as *ketubat benin dikhrin* (כתובת בנין דיכרין — "the ketubah of male children"), was designed to ensure that the wife's property would pass to her descendants only, and thus to encourage the wife's father to give her a larger dowry. (2) [3]**The** minor **daughters** of the marriage **are entitled to maintenance** from the estate of their deceased father. Since by Torah law the existence of sons precludes daughters from being heirs of their father's estate, the Rabbis imposed an obligation on those who inherit the estate to maintain the daughters from that property until the daughters become betrothed. [4]Rabbi Elazar ben Azaryah taught that the one enactment sheds light on the other: **Just as the sons do not inherit** their mother's ketubah **until after their father's death,** since the sons do not inherit anything until after their father dies, [5]**similarly the** minor **daughters are not** entitled to be **maintained** from their father's estate **until after his death,** and during his lifetime he is not legally liable for their maintenance.

GEMARA בִּמְזוֹנוֹת בִּתּוֹ [6]The Mishnah stated that a father is not legally liable for his minor daughter's maintenance. A careful reading of this statement leads us to the following conclusions: The Mishnah emphasized that **it is for his daughter's maintenance that** the father **is not liable.** From the fact that the Mishnah specified that the father is not legally obligated to support his minor daughter, [7]it may be inferred that the father **is** indeed **liable for his son's maintenance.** [8]Furthermore, **even regarding his daughter,** the Mishnah says only that **there is no** legal **obligation** on the father to maintain his minor daughter, and therefore the courts cannot compel him to provide for her maintenance. **But** this formulation implies that

בִּמְזוֹנוֹת בִּתּוֹ. [1]זֶה מִדְרָשׁ דָּרַשׁ רַבִּי אֶלְעָזָר בֶּן עֲזַרְיָה לִפְנֵי חֲכָמִים בְּכֶרֶם בְּיַבְנֶה: [2]הַבָּנִים יִירְשׁוּ, [3]וְהַבָּנוֹת יִזּוֹנוּ. [4]מָה הַבָּנִים אֵינָן יוֹרְשִׁין אֶלָּא לְאַחַר מִיתַת הָאָב, [5]אַף הַבָּנוֹת אֵין נִיזּוֹנוֹת אֶלָּא לְאַחַר מִיתַת אֲבִיהֶן.

גמרא [6]בִּמְזוֹנוֹת בִּתּוֹ הוּא דְּאֵינוֹ חַיָּיב, [7]הָא בִּמְזוֹנוֹת בְּנוֹ חַיָּיב. [8]בִּתּוֹ נַמִי, חוֹבָה הוּא דְּלֵיכָּא, הָא מִצְוָה אִיכָּא.

LITERAL TRANSLATION

for his daughter's maintenance. [1]Rabbi Elazar ben Azaryah expounded this interpretation before the Sages in the Academy (lit., "vineyard") at Yavneh: [2]The sons will inherit, [3]and the daughters will be maintained. [4]Just as the sons do not inherit until after the father's death, [5]so too are the daughters not maintained until after their father's death.

GEMARA [6]It is for his daughter's maintenance that he is not liable, [7]but for his son's maintenance he is liable. [8][As for] his daughter too, there is no obligation, but there is a moral duty (lit., "commandment").

RASHI

זה מדרש דרש רבי אלעזר בן עזריה — ביום שמנוהו נשיא. **בכרם ביבנה** — על שם שהיו יושבין שורות שורות ככרם. **הבנים יירשו והבנות יזונו** — שתי תקנות תקנו בית דין בתנאי כתובה: הבנים יירשו כתובת בנין דכרין, דתנן במתניתין (כתובות נב,ב): "בנין דכרין דיהויין ליכי מינאי אינון ירתון כסף כתובתך יתר על חולקהון דעם אחוהון". והיינו הבנים יירשו — כתובת בנין דכרין, ולקמן בשמעתין מפרשינן לה מאי היא. **והבנות יזונו** — "בנן נוקבן די יהויין ליכי מינאי אינון יהוויין יתבן בביתי ומיתזנן מנכסי עד דתיבגרון או עד דתלקחון לגוברין". **מה הבנים אין יורשין** — כתובת אמן אלא לאחר מיתת אביהן, דהא "אינון ירתון" תנן, והכי מפרש לה ב"יש נוחלין" דהאי "הבנים יירשו" — אכתובת בנין דכרין קאי.

NOTES

זֶה מִדְרָשׁ דָּרַשׁ **Expounded this interpretation.** The Jerusalem Talmud cites a series of examples of Halakhot that were derived from or supported by interpretation of the text of the ketubah. The Rabbis applied to the ketubah and to other legal documents the same interpretative norms that were used in explaining Biblical and Rabbinic texts. In our Mishnah, Rabbi Elazar ben Azaryah applies the exegetical principle of *hekesh* (הֶיקֵּשׁ), by which legal inferences may be drawn by comparing two cases or laws that are juxtaposed in the same text. Since the enactment of *ketubat benin dikhrin* is mentioned together with the enactment regarding the maintenance of minor daughters, the law that applies to the one is extended to the other.

בְּכֶרֶם בְּיַבְנֶה **In the Academy at Yavneh.** *Rashi* and others explain that the academy of Yavneh was called *Kerem BeYavneh* (בְּכֶרֶם בְּיַבְנֶה — literally, "the vineyard at Yavneh") because the Rabbinic scholars at that Academy used to sit in rows that resembled rows of vines. After the destruction of the Second Temple, Yavneh achieved great prominence as the spiritual center of the entire Jewish population in Eretz Israel. The orderly arrangement of the seats in the Academy symbolized the fact that Yavneh had become the

BACKGROUND

זֶה מִדְרָשׁ דָּרַשׁ **Expounded this interpretation.** According to *Rashi*, mention of the place where this tradition was transmitted indicates that Rabbi Elazar ben Azaryah delivered it on the day he was appointed head of the Sanhedrin in Yavneh. This appointment came after the dismissal of the hereditary head of the Sanhedrin, Rabban Gamliel II, in response to pressure from many Sages there. Indeed, Rabbi Elazar ben Azaryah was appointed to this post as a very young man (considerations in his favor were his noble descent and his great wealth). Rabbi Elazar saw fit to deliver particularly important and innovative rulings so that his appointment would be accepted by everyone.

כֶּרֶם בְּיַבְנֶה **The Academy at Yavneh.**

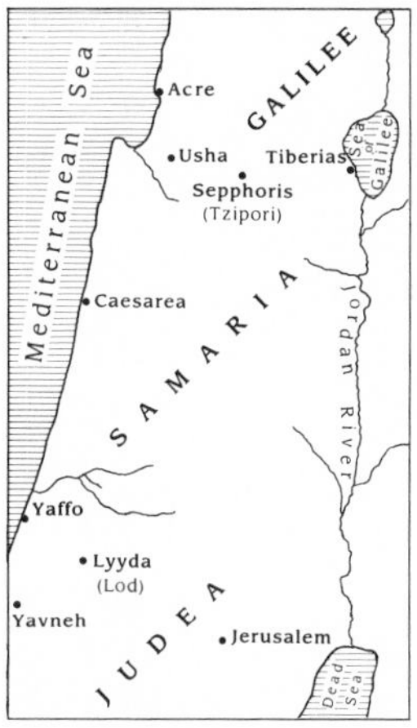

This term refers to the place in Yavneh where the Sanhedrin sat. According to an ancient tradition, the place was given the name כֶּרֶם בְּיַבְנֶה — literally, "the vineyard at Yavneh" — because both the Sages of the Sanhedrin and their disciples who sat before them were seated in rows like those of a vineyard, (Jerusalem Talmud). It could also be that the place was actually surrounded by vineyards, so that the term had a double meaning.

מְזוֹנוֹת **Maintenance.** This page and the following pages of the tractate deal extensively with the question of the obligations of parents, especially the father, to support their children. The Torah itself contains no explicit

TRANSLATION AND COMMENTARY

there ***is*** **a moral duty to support** one's minor daughter. [1]Now, asks the Gemara, if this interpretation of the Mishnah is correct, **who is the author of our Mishnah?** [2]The opinion expressed anonymously in the Mishnah does **not** seem to correspond with the known viewpoint **of Rabbi Meir, nor** with **that of Rabbi Yehudah, nor** with **that of Rabbi Yoḥanan ben Beroka.** [3]**For it was taught** in a Baraita: **"It is a moral duty to maintain** one's minor **daughters,** [4]**and all the more so** to maintain one's minor **sons, because they occupy themselves with** studying the **Torah** and cannot provide for themselves. [5]**This is the opinion of Rabbi Meir.** [6]**Rabbi Yehudah says: It is a moral duty to maintain** one's minor **sons,** [7]**and all the more so** to maintain one's minor **daughters, because of the disgrace** they will suffer if they are forced to go out and beg for charity. [8]**Rabbi Yoḥanan ben Beroka says: There is a** legal **obligation** on the father's heirs **to maintain** his **daughters** from his estate **after his death,** [9]**but during his lifetime neither** the sons **nor** the daughters **are maintained** by the father, for it is not even a moral duty to provide for the maintenance of one's minor children." [10]In the light of the viewpoints expressed by the three Tannaim mentioned in the Baraita, **who is the author of our Mishnah?** [11]**If** we say that the author **is Rabbi Meir,** there is a difficulty, for **surely he said** that **maintaining** one's **sons is** merely **a moral duty** and not a legal obligation, whereas according to the inference drawn from our Mishnah a father is legally obligated to support his minor sons. [12]And **if** we suggest that the Mishnah reflects the viewpoint of **Rabbi Yehudah,** this too is difficult to accept, for **surely he too said** that **maintaining** one's **sons is a moral duty** and not a legal obligation. [13]And **if** we argue that the Mishnah follows the opinion of **Rabbi Yoḥanan ben Beroka,** the

[1]מַנִּי מַתְנִיתִין? [2]לָא רַבִּי מֵאִיר, לָא רַבִּי יְהוּדָה, וְלָא רַבִּי יוֹחָנָן בֶּן בְּרוֹקָא. [3]דְּתַנְיָא: ״מִצְוָה לָזוּן אֶת הַבָּנוֹת, [4]קַל וָחוֹמֶר לַבָּנִים, דְּעָסְקֵי בַּתּוֹרָה. [5]דִּבְרֵי רַבִּי מֵאִיר. [6]רַבִּי יְהוּדָה אוֹמֵר: מִצְוָה לָזוּן אֶת הַבָּנִים, [7]וְקַל וָחוֹמֶר לַבָּנוֹת, מִשּׁוּם זִילוּתָא. [8]רַבִּי יוֹחָנָן בֶּן בְּרוֹקָא אוֹמֵר: חוֹבָה לָזוּן אֶת הַבָּנוֹת לְאַחַר מִיתַת אֲבִיהֶן, [9]אֲבָל בְּחַיֵּי אֲבִיהֶן אֵלּוּ וְאֵלּוּ אֵינָן נִיזּוֹנִין״. [10]מַנִּי מַתְנִיתִין? [11]אִי רַבִּי מֵאִיר, הָא אָמַר: בָּנִים מִצְוָה. [12]אִי רַבִּי יְהוּדָה, הָא אָמַר: בָּנִים נַמִי מִצְוָה. [13]אִי רַבִּי יוֹחָנָן בֶּן בְּרוֹקָא, אֲפִילּוּ מִצְוָה נַמִי לֵיכָּא!

LITERAL TRANSLATION

[1]Whose [viewpoint] is [reflected in] our Mishnah? [2]Not [that of] Rabbi Meir, not [that of] Rabbi Yehudah, and not [that of] Rabbi Yoḥanan ben Beroka. [3]For it was taught: "[It is] a moral duty to maintain daughters, [4][and] all the more so sons, because they occupy themselves with Torah. [5][These are] the words of Rabbi Meir. [6]Rabbi Yehudah says: [It is] a moral duty to maintain sons, [7]and all the more so daughters, because of the disgrace. [8]Rabbi Yoḥanan ben Beroka says: [There is] an obligation to maintain daughters after the death of their father, [9]but during their father's lifetime neither these nor those are maintained." [10]Who is [the author of] our Mishnah? [11]If it is Rabbi Meir, surely he said: [Maintaining] sons is a moral duty. [12]If it is Rabbi Yehudah, surely he said: [Maintaining] sons, too, is a moral duty. [13]If it is Rabbi Yoḥanan ben Beroka, it is not even a moral duty!

RASHI

גמרא חובה לזון הבנות — תנאי כתובה הוא. **אין נזונין** — אפילו מצוה אין כאן. **האמר בנים נמי מצוה** — ולא חובה. **אפילו מצוה ליכא** — לא בבנים ולא בבנות.

commandment to maintain one's children, though it is clear from many references throughout the Bible that this is the proper way for people to act. However, the legal issue is whether the obligation to support children is incumbent upon their parents, or whether it is a general obligation of the entire community.

This Mishnah discusses a secondary problems: Since the ketubah contains clauses obliging the father with respect to his sons and daughters, what is the legal meaning of these obligations, and when are they to be implemented?

הָא מִצְוָה אִיכָּא But there is a moral duty. Although the literal meaning of the word מִצְוָה is a divine commandment which must certainly be obeyed, when the word is used in contrast to the term חוֹבָה ("obligation"), it is understood as being less binding. A חוֹבָה is something that a person must do under all circumstances, and if it refers to a monetary obligation, the court can compel someone to obey. But, in the present context, a מִצְוָה is a good deed that a person should do, for which he is rewarded by Heaven; but it is not an absolute obligation, and the court cannot compel him to perform it.

SAGES

רַבִּי יוֹחָנָן בֶּן בְּרוֹקָה Rabbi Yoḥanan ben Beroka. A Tanna of the third and fourth generations. See *Ketubot,* Part II, pp. 5-6.

NOTES

official seat of the Sanhedrin and was empowered to legislate for all future generations. *Rambam* (*Commentary to the Mishnah, Eduyyot* 2:4) adds that the term "vineyard" is an allusion to the people of Israel, as in Isaiah 5:7: "For the vineyard of the Lord of hosts is the house of Israel."

מִצְוָה לָזוּן It is a moral duty to maintain. *Rashbam* (*Bava Batra* 141a) derives this from the verse (Isaiah 58:7): "And you shall not hide yourself from your own flesh," from which it may be inferred that there is a special obligation to provide for one's family, over and above the general obligation to give charity. Honoring this obligation is considered a moral duty, but the courts cannot compel a person to do so.

מִצְוָה לָזוּן אֶת הַבָּנוֹת It is a moral duty to maintain daughters. The Aḥaronim discuss whether there are any practical differences between the opinions of Rabbi Meir and of Rabbi Yehudah, for they both seem to agree that maintaining one's sons and daughters is a moral duty but is not compulsory. *Rabbi Akiva Eger* maintains that they disagree about the case in which the father has enough to provide either for his son or for his daughter, but not for both. According to Rabbi Meir, he should support his son, whereas according to Rabbi Yehudah, he should provide for his daughter. *Ḥatam Sofer* suggests that they disagree about the case in which the son does not apply himself to the study of the Torah. According to Rabbi Yehudah, the son is still deserving of support, whereas according to Rabbi Meir, he is not.

מִשּׁוּם זִילוּתָא Because of the disgrace. It is explained here that a father should maintain his minor daughters in order

TRANSLATION AND COMMENTARY

difficulty is even greater, for he said that maintaining one's minor children, whether they be sons or daughters, **is not even a moral duty!**

אִיבָּעֵית אֵימָא [1]The Gemara answers: In fact, the Mishnah can be interpreted according to any one of the three opinions recorded in the Baraita. **If you wish,** you can **say** that the Mishnah follows the viewpoint of **Rabbi Meir;** [2]and **if you wish,** you can **say** that **it reflects** the opinion of **Rabbi Yehudah;** [3]and **if you wish,** you can **say** that **it follows** the viewpoint of **Rabbi Yoḥanan ben Beroka.**

אִיבָּעֵית אֵימָא [4]The Gemara explains: **If you wish,** you can **say** that the Mishnah follows the viewpoint of **Rabbi Meir.** When the Mishnah states that the father is not liable for his daughter's maintenance, it does not mean to imply that he *is* liable for his son's maintenance. [5]**Rather, this is what** the Mishnah means to **say: A father is not** legally **liable for his** minor **daughter's maintenance** during his lifetime, **and the same law applies regarding his** minor **son.** [6]The courts cannot compel the father to provide for his children's maintenance, **but** supporting **one's daughter** ***is*** **a moral duty,** for which the father will receive his just reward, **and all the more so** is it a moral duty to support one's **sons,** for they are engaged in the study of the Torah. We cannot infer from the fact that the Mishnah speaks only of a daughter that the law is different with respect to a son. For if the Mishnah had stated that a father is not liable for the maintenance of his son or of his daughter, we might have inferred that the father is not legally obligated to provide for his son's support; but supporting him is indeed a moral duty, because the son is occupied in the study of the Torah; whereas supporting his daughter is not even a moral duty. [7]**And the fact that** the Mishnah **states** only that a father is not liable for the support of **his daughter teaches us** [49B] [8]**that even regarding his daughter,** who does not occupy herself with Torah study, **there is no** legal **obligation** incumbent on the father to maintain her, [9]**but** he **is** nevertheless bound by **a moral duty** to do so.

וְאִיבָּעֵית אֵימָא [10]The Gemara continues: **If you wish,** you can **say** that the Mishnah follows the viewpoint of **Rabbi Yehudah.** And as was explained above, the Mishnah did not single out the daughter in order to imply that the law regarding the son is different. [11]**Rather, this is what** the Mishnah means to **say: A father is not** legally **liable for his** minor **daughter's maintenance** during his lifetime, **and all the more so** is he not obligated to provide maintenance **for his son.** [12]**But** even though the courts cannot compel a father to maintain his children, supporting **one's son** ***is*** **a moral duty, and all the more so** is it a moral duty to support

LITERAL TRANSLATION

[1]If you wish, say it is Rabbi Meir; [2]if you wish, say it is Rabbi Yehudah; [3]if you wish, say it is Rabbi Yoḥanan ben Beroka.

[4]If you wish, say it is Rabbi Meir, [5]and this is what he says: A father is not liable for his daughter's maintenance, and that is [also] the law regarding his son. [6]But it *is* a moral duty regarding his daughter, [and] all the more so regarding sons. [7]And the fact that he teaches "his daughter" teaches us this — [49B] [8]that even [regarding] his daughter there is no obligation, [9]but there is a moral duty.

[10]And if you wish, say it is Rabbi Yehudah, and this is what he says: [11]A father is not liable for his daughter's maintenance, and all the more so for [that of] his son. [12]But it *is* a moral duty regarding his son,

[1]אִיבָּעֵית אֵימָא רַבִּי מֵאִיר; [2]אִיבָּעֵית אֵימָא רַבִּי יְהוּדָה; [3]אִיבָּעֵית אֵימָא רַבִּי יוֹחָנָן בֶּן בְּרוֹקָא.

[4]אִיבָּעֵית אֵימָא רַבִּי מֵאִיר, [5]וְהָכִי קָאָמַר: הָאָב אֵינוֹ חַיָּיב בִּמְזוֹנוֹת בִּתּוֹ, וְהוּא הַדִּין לִבְנוֹ. [6]הָא מִצְוָה בְּבִתּוֹ אִיכָּא, קַל וָחוֹמֶר לַבָּנִים. [7]וְהַאי דְּקָתָנֵי בִּתּוֹ הָא קָא מַשְׁמַע לָן — [49B] [8]דַּאֲפִילּוּ בִּתּוֹ חוֹבָה הוּא דְּלֵיכָּא, [9]הָא מִצְוָה אִיכָּא.

[10]וְאִיבָּעֵית אֵימָא רַבִּי יְהוּדָה, וְהָכִי קָאָמַר: [11]הָאָב אֵינוֹ חַיָּיב בִּמְזוֹנוֹת בִּתּוֹ, וְכָל שֶׁכֵּן לִבְנוֹ. [12]הָא מִצְוָה בִּבְנוֹ אִיכָּא,

RASHI

איבעית אימא רבי מאיר והכי קאמר כו' – כלומר, "בתו" דנקט לאו למידק: הא בנו חייב, אלא משום דרבי מאיר עדיף ליה בנו, אי נקט "אינו חייב במזונות בנו" – הוה אמינא: בנו הוא דחובה ליכא מצוה איכא, אבל בתו אפילו מצוה ליכא. להכי תנא "אינו חייב בבתו" – למימרא דמצוה מיהא איכא. **והוא הדין לבנו** – דחובה מיהא ליכא. **דאפילו בתו** – דקילא, דלא עסקא באורייתא.

NOTES

to preserve their dignity, for they will surely suffer disgrace if they are forced to beg for their maintenance. According to the Jerusalem Talmud, a father should maintain his minor daughters in order to safeguard their morals, for if the father does not support them, they may resort to prostitution or some other illicit activity to provide for their needs.

וְקַל וָחוֹמֶר לַבָּנוֹת. [1]וְהָא דְּקָתָנֵי "בִּתּוֹ" הָא קָא מַשְׁמַע לָן — [2]דַּאֲפִילּוּ בִּתּוֹ חוֹבָה לֵיכָּא. [3]וְאִיבָּעֵית אֵימָא רַבִּי יוֹחָנָן בֶּן בְּרוֹקָא, [4]וְהָכִי קָאָמַר: אֵינוֹ חַיָּיב בִּמְזוֹנוֹת בִּתּוֹ, [5]וְהוּא הַדִּין לִבְנוֹ. [6]וְהוּא הַדִּין דַּאֲפִילּוּ מִצְוָה נַמִי לֵיכָּא. [7]וְאַיְּידֵי דְּבָנוֹת לְאַחַר מִיתַת אֲבִיהֶן חוֹבָה, [8]תָּנָא נַמִי אֵינוֹ חַיָּיב. [9]אָמַר רַבִּי אִילְעָא אָמַר רֵישׁ לָקִישׁ מִשּׁוּם רַבִּי יְהוּדָה בַּר חֲנִינָא: [10]בְּאוּשָׁא הִתְקִינוּ שֶׁיְּהֵא אָדָם זָן אֶת בָּנָיו וְאֶת בְּנוֹתָיו כְּשֶׁהֵן קְטַנִּים.

LITERAL TRANSLATION

and all the more so regarding daughters. [1]And the fact that he teaches "his daughter" teaches us this — [2]that even [regarding] his daughter there is no obligation.

[3]And if you wish, say it is Rabbi Yoḥanan ben Beroka, [4]and this is what he says: He is not liable for his daughter's maintenance, [5]and that is [also] the law regarding his son. [6]And it is [also] the law that it is not even a moral duty. [7]And since [regarding] daughters after the death of their father there is an obligation, [8]he teaches also [that] he is not liable.

[9]Rabbi Il'a said in the name of Resh Lakish who said in the name of Rabbi Yehudah bar Ḥanina: [10]In Usha they enacted that a person must maintain his sons and his daughters while they are minors.

TRANSLATION AND COMMENTARY

one's **daughters.** We cannot infer that a father is obligated to provide for his son from the fact that the Mishnah exempts him from maintaining his daughter. [1]For **by stating** only that a father is not liable for the maintenance of **his daughter,** the Mishnah **teaches us that even regarding his daughter,** [2]**there is no** legal **obligation** on the father to maintain her.

וְאִיבָּעֵית אֵימָא [3]The Gemara now offers a third interpretation of the Mishnah: **If you wish,** you can **say** that the Mishnah can be explained even according to the opinion of **Rabbi Yoḥanan ben Beroka,** [4]**and this is what** the Mishnah means to **say:** A father **is not** legally **liable for his** minor **daughter's maintenance,** [5]**and the same law applies regarding his** minor **son.** [6]**And** just as there is no legal obligation to maintain one's children, **it is likewise not** considered **even a moral duty** to do so. Why, then, does the Mishnah state that there is no legal obligation to support one's minor children, and not mention that maintaining them is not even a moral duty? [7]The answer is this: **Since** the sons **are** in fact **obligated** to support **the daughters** from their father's estate **after the death of their father,** [8]the Mishnah **also teaches** us **that** the father **is not obligated** to support his daughters during his lifetime. The purpose of the Mishnah is to show that the law with respect to the father's liability during his lifetime is to be contrasted to the law regarding the sons' liability after their father's death.

אָמַר רַבִּי אִילְעָא [9]The Gemara now cites an Amoraic tradition about a Rabbinic enactment concerning the father's obligation to support his children. **Rabbi Il'a said in the name of Resh Lakish who said in the name of Rabbi Yehudah bar Ḥanina:** [10]When the Sanhedrin was sitting **in Usha** in Galilee (during the middle of the second century), the Sages **enacted that a person must maintain his sons and his daughters as long as they are minors.**

RASHI

ואיידי דתנא בנות כו׳ — לא גרסינן דתנא, דהא לא תני ליה במתניתין. אלא הכי גרסינן: ואיידי דבנות לאחר מיתת אביהן חובה כו׳. **באושא התקינו** — כשישבו סנהדרי גזית באושא, שהיא אחת מעשר גליות שגלתה סנהדרין, כדאמר בראש השנה (לא,א). **כשהן קטנים** — עד שיביאו שערות.

NOTES

כְּשֶׁהֵן קְטַנִּים **While they are minors.** *Rashi* explains that the term "minors" comes to set the upper limit of the enactment. In other words, the Sages in Usha enacted that a man must maintain his children until they reach puberty, after which they are treated as adults.

Tosafot maintains that the term "minors" comes to exclude very young children. The Sages of Usha enacted that a father must maintain his minor children who are six years of age and older, but, as our Gemara concludes, the law is not in accordance with that enactment, and the courts cannot compel a father to provide for his children after they have reached the age of six. But as for very young children, those below the age of six, all agree that the father is legally obligated to provide for their maintenance (see below, 65b).

HALAKHAH

שֶׁיְּהֵא אָדָם זָן אֶת בָּנָיו **That a person must maintain his sons.** "A father is liable for the maintenance of his minor children until they reach the age of six. From then on he should maintain them until they reach majority, in accordance with the Rabbinic enactment passed in Usha. If he refuses to do so, we upbraid him, shame him, and plead with him to support his children. If he remains adamant in his refusal, he is publicly proclaimed to be a cruel man

BACKGROUND

בְּאוּשָׁא הִתְקִינוּ **In Usha they enacted.** After the Sanhedrin was forced to move from Yavneh, the town of Usha (in Galilee) served as a center for Torah scholars, and for a period the Sanhedrin sat there. Numerous decrees were enacted there, primarily with regard to monetary matters within the family. The decrees of Usha were not included in the Mishnah, but were accepted in the Amoraic period.

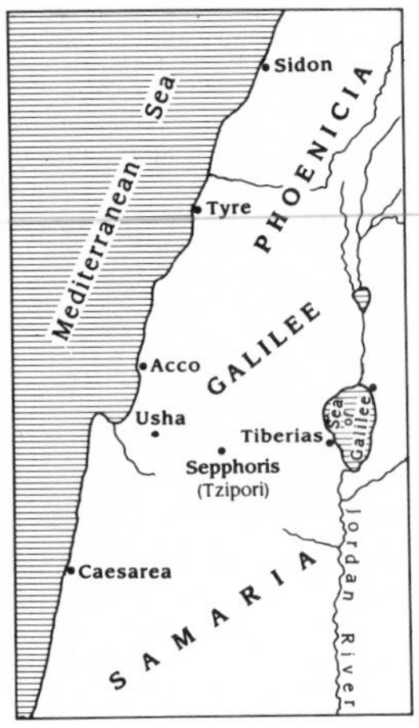

[1]אִיבַּעֲיָא לְהוּ: הִלְכְתָא כְּוָותֵיהּ אוֹ אֵין הִלְכְתָא כְּוָותֵיהּ? [2]תָּא שְׁמַע: כִּי הֲוָה אָתוּ לְקַמֵּיהּ דְּרַב יְהוּדָה, [3]אָמַר לְהוּ: "יָארוֹד יָלְדָה וְאַבְנֵי מָתָא שַׁדְיָא?!" [4]כִּי הֲוָה אָתוּ לְקַמֵּיהּ דְּרַב חִסְדָּא, [5]אָמַר לְהוּ: "כְּפוּ לֵיהּ אָסִיתָא בְּצִבּוּרָא, וְלֵיקוּם וְלֵימָא: [6]'עוּרְבָא בָּעֵי בְּנֵיהּ, וְהַהוּא גַּבְרָא לָא בָּעֵי בְּנֵיהּ'".

LITERAL TRANSLATION

[1]It was asked of them: Is the Halakhah in accordance with him or is the Halakhah not in accordance with him?

[2]Come [and] hear: When they used to come before Rav Yehudah, [3]he would say to them: "A jackal bears [children] and casts [them] on the people of the town?!" [4]When they used to come before Rav Ḥisda, [5]he would say to them: "Turn over a mortar for him in public, and let him stand and say: [6]'A raven looks after its young, but this man does not look after his children.'"

TRANSLATION AND COMMENTARY

אִיבַּעֲיָא לְהוּ [1]**The** following **question arose** in discussion among the Sages: **Is the Halakhah in accordance with** the enactment laid down at Usha that a father is liable for the maintenance of his minor children, **or is the Halakhah not in accordance with** that enactment, but rather in accordance with our Mishnah, which states that a father is under no obligation to support his children?

תָּא שְׁמַע [2]The Gemara answers: **Come and hear** the following anecdotes from which we can conclude that a father is under no legal obligation to provide for the support of his minor children: **When** people **used to come before Rav Yehudah** and report to him about a certain person who refused to support his children, [3]**he would say to them:** "Did **this 'jackal' bear children and** then **cast them on the people of the town** so that the townspeople should now maintain them from charity funds?!" Although Rav Yehudah was unable to take any legal action against the father to compel him to provide for his children's maintenance, he did condemn him strongly. [4]In a similar way, **when** people **used to come before Rav Ḥisda,** telling him about a father who was unwilling to maintain his children, [5]**he would say to them: "Turn over a mortar for him in public, and make him stand** there so that everybody can see and hear him, **and** have him **proclaim** himself to be less sensitive than a raven, [6]for **a raven looks after its young** and cares for them, **but this man does not look after his children** and is unwilling to assume financial responsibility for them." Rav Ḥisda's response indicates that a father who refuses to support his children may be put to public shame, but he cannot legally be forced to provide for their maintenance.

RASHI

תא שמע — דלית הלכתא כוותיה, אלא מימר אמרינן ליה, ואולי יכלכלם ויזון, אבל מיכף — לא כייפינן. **יארוד** = תנין. "מעון תנים" (ירמיה ט) מתרגמינן מדור יארודין. והוא אכזרי על בניו. **יארוד ילדה ואבני מתא שדיא** = התנין הוליד תולדותיו והטיל פרנסתן על בני העיר. **כפו ליה אסיתא** — כפו מכתשת על פיה, ויעמוד זה על גב שוליה בגובה, שישמעו קולו, ויכריז על עצמו שהוא רע מן העורבים, דעורבא בעי בני וההוא גברא לא בעי בני. ואית דמפרשי: שליח צבור יעמוד עליה ויאמר כן על אותו האיש.

LANGUAGE

יָארוֹד Jackal. This word (which *Arukh* and other sources spell יָרוֹד) is the Aramaic translation of the Hebrew word תַּנָּה or תַּנִּים. However, the meaning of the Hebrew word itself is uncertain. Some explain it as meaning "jackal," while others identify it as a type of night bird resembling an owl. The Tosefta states that the יָרוֹד is a species of bird, although this passage alone cannot decide the issue, since the word may have several meanings. *Rashi* does not interpret יָרוֹד consistently; sometimes he takes it as the name of a bird, and elsewhere he claims that it is some other type of animal.

BACKGROUND

כְּפוּ לֵיהּ אָסִיתָא Turn over a mortar for him. An אָסִיתָא was a large mortar and could be made of various materials, such as wood, stone, or brass. It was generally used for preparing large quantities of grain or legumes. Since it was a large vessel, a mortar was sometimes turned over and used for seating, or, as in our case, as a speaking platform so that the speaker could be heard. See the notes for various explanations of why this particular kind of vessel was used in this instance.

NOTES

הִלְכְתָא כְּוָותֵיהּ Is the Halakhah in accordance with him? *Rivan* explains that the Gemara is questioning the reliability of Rabbi Il'a's tradition that the Sages held a father liable for the maintenance of his minor children. Was such an enactment laid down in Usha, or not? In the Jerusalem Talmud, the matter is presented differently. After citing the enactment, the Jerusalem Talmud continues: "Rabbi Yoḥanan said: We know who was in that quorum [who passed that legislation] (or, perhaps: Do we know who was in that quorum?)." Whether we take Rabbi Yoḥanan's remark as a statement or as a question, he does not appear to dispute the fact that an enactment was passed in Usha. Rather, Rabbi Yoḥanan is questioning the authority of these Sages to institute such legislation compelling a man to support his children.

יָארוֹד יָלְדָה A jackal bears children. The Rishonim disagree as to the identification of the creature called *yarod* (יָארוֹד or יָרוֹד; see "language" section). Leaving that issue aside, we are left with two different explanations of the popular proverb cited here by Rav Yehudah. According to *Rashi,* the miserly father is compared to the *yarod* who bears its young and then acts cruelly toward them. *Ritva* suggests that the miserly father is contrasted with the *yarod.* Even the *yarod* shows mercy to its young, but this man cruelly casts his children on the charity of his townsmen.

כְּפוּ לֵיהּ אָסִיתָא Turn over a mortar for him. Our commentary follows the first explanation of *Rashi,* that the miserly father himself was made to stand on the mortar and proclaim that he was acting cruelly toward his children. According to *Rashi's* second explanation, it was a

HALAKHAH

who is unwilling to support his own children, and who is more despicable than an unclean bird that at least takes care of its young. But the courts cannot compel him to maintain his children once they have reached the age of six. This ruling applies only if the father is not wealthy; but if he is a man of means, he can be compelled to maintain his children until they reach majority, the obligation stemming from the laws of charity." (*Rambam, Sefer Nashim, Hilkhot Ishut* 12:14-15; *Shulḥan Arukh, Even HaEzer* 71:1.)

LANGUAGE

אֲמִיד Wealthy. The root of this word is apparently אמד, meaning to evaluate or estimate. The term אֲמִיד means someone who is assessed and valued. The Rishonim explain that when a man is wealthy, people customarily try to estimate his wealth. This is the derivation of the common use of this word for a wealthy man, a person of means.

[1] וְעוּרְבָא בָּעֵי בְּנֵיהּ? [2] וְהָכְתִיב: ״לִבְנֵי עֹרֵב אֲשֶׁר יִקְרָאוּ״!

[3] לָא קַשְׁיָא. [4] הָא בְּחִיוּרֵי, [5] הָא בְּאוּכָּמֵי.

[6] כִּי הֲוָה אָתֵי לְקַמֵּיהּ דְּרָבָא, אָמַר לֵיהּ: [7] ״נִיחָא לָךְ דְּמִיתַּזְנִי בָּנֶיךָ מִצְּדָקָה״?

[8] וְלָא אֲמָרַן אֶלָּא דְּלָא אֲמִיד, [9] אֲבָל אֲמִיד, כָּפֵינַן לֵיהּ עַל

LITERAL TRANSLATION

[1] But does a raven look after its young? [2] But surely it is written: "To the young ravens that cry"! [3] There is no difficulty. [4] Here [it refers] to white ones, [5] here [it refers] to black ones.

[6] When [such a case] used to come before Rava, he would say to him: [7] "Is it pleasing to you that your children should be maintained from charity?" [8] And we say this only if he is not wealthy. [9] But [if he is] wealthy, we compel him

TRANSLATION AND COMMENTARY

וְעוּרְבָא בָּעֵי בְּנֵיהּ [1] The Gemara now questions Rav Ḥisda's reference to the concern a raven shows for its young: **Does a raven** really **look after its young** and tend to their needs? [2] **But surely the verse says** (Psalms 147:9): "He gives the beast its food, and **to the young ravens that cry."** Thus we see that it is by the grace of God that the young ravens survive, and that their parents abandon them and let them cry.

לָא קַשְׁיָא [3] The Gemara answers: **There is** in fact **no difficulty,** for the Psalmist and Rav Ḥisda are referring to different types of birds? [4] **Here,** in the verse from Psalms, we are dealing **with white** ravens, which behave cruelly toward their young and abandon them, [5] whereas **here,** in the case of Rav Ḥisda, we are dealing **with black ones,** which take good care of their young.

כִּי הֲוָה אָתֵי לְקַמֵּיהּ דְּרָבָא [6] The Gemara now cites one more anecdote to prove that the law is not in accordance with the enactment laid down in Usha: **When a case** of refusal to provide support for children **used to come before Rava, he would say to** the father involved: [7] **"Is it pleasing to you that your children should be maintained from charity?"** Rava would try to persuade the father to maintain his children, even though he was not legally liable to support them. But it follows from this and the earlier stories that the courts cannot compel a father to maintain his children.

וְלָא אֲמָרַן [8] The Gemara continues: **We say** that the father cannot be compelled to maintain his children **only if he is not** sufficiently **wealthy** to provide for his own as well as for those of his children. [9] **But if** the father **is wealthy,** and can support himself and his family, **we compel him against his will**, if necessary, to provide for his children, for the courts can compel a person with means to give charity to the needy.

RASHI

לבני עורב אשר יקראו – אלמא לא זיין להו. **אוכמי** – כשגדל משחיר, והאם והאב אוהבין אותן. אבל מתחילתן – לבנים, ושונאין אותן. **ולא אמרן** – דלא כפינן. **אלא דלא אמיד** – שאינו עשיר. **בעל כרחו** – לא יהא אלא לדקה בעלמא, ואפילו אינן בניו.

NOTES

public official who stood on the mortar and made the public announcement that the man in question refused to assume financial responsibility for his children. According to the first explanation, the proclamation was made from on top of the mortar to add to the humiliation of the miserly father. According to the second, the mortar was needed to ensure that the announcement would be heard by all.

Ritva adds that the inverted mortar symbolized a reversal of fortune, and served as a warning that the father's failure to provide for his children would lead to a decline in his income.

Maharal suggests that the inverted mortar alluded to the fact that this father turned the laws of nature upside down when he failed to provide for the needs of his own children. It has also been argued that the inverted mortar hints at the verse (Proverbs 27:22): "Though you may grind a fool in a mortar among crushed grain with a pestle, his foolishness will not depart from him." In other words, all attempts to persuade the father to provide for his children have proved ineffective (*Ḥever ben Ḥayyim*). *Iyyun Ya'akov* suggests simply that Rav Ḥisda ordered the mortar to be overturned as a device to gain everybody's attention.

הָא בְּחִיוּרֵי, הָא בְּאוּכָּמֵי Here it refers to white ones, here it refers to black ones. According to *Rashi*, the Psalmist and Rav Ḥisda are referring to the same type of raven. The young raven is white and ignored by its parents, but as it grows it darkens and its parents begin to care for it. *Tosafot* argues that there are two different types of raven, the one that takes good care of its young, and the other that cruelly abandons them.

כָּפֵינַן לֵיהּ עַל כָּרְחֵיהּ We compel him against his will. The Gemara does not elaborate on the means by which the courts can compel a person to fulfill his obligation to give

HALAKHAH

אֲבָל אֲמִיד, כָּפֵינַן לֵיהּ עַל כָּרְחֵיהּ But if he is wealthy, we compel him against his will. "Everybody is obligated to give charity; even a pauper who is himself supported by charity must give charity from the money he receives. Anybody who gives less charity than is fitting for a person of his means may be compelled by the courts to give more, and he may be flogged until he agrees to give the full amount that he has been assessed to pay." (*Rambam, Sefer Zeraim, Hilkhot Mattenot Aniyyim* 7:10; *Shulḥan Arukh, Yoreh De'ah* 248:1.)

כָּרְחֵיהּ, [1]כִּי הָא דְּרָבָא כַּפְיֵיהּ לְרַב נָתָן בַּר אַמִי, [2]וְאַפֵּיק מִינֵּיהּ אַרְבַּע מֵאָה זוּזֵי לִצְדָקָה.

[3]אָמַר רַבִּי אִילְעָא אָמַר רֵישׁ לָקִישׁ: [4]בְּאוּשָׁא הִתְקִינוּ: הַכּוֹתֵב כָּל נְכָסָיו לְבָנָיו, [5]הוּא וְאִשְׁתּוֹ נִזּוֹנִים מֵהֶם.

[6]מַתְקִיף לָהּ רַבִּי זֵירָא, וְאִיתֵּימָא רַבִּי שְׁמוּאֵל בַּר נַחְמָנִי: [7]גְּדוֹלָה מִזּוֹ אָמְרוּ:

LITERAL TRANSLATION

against his will, [1]like that [case] where Rava compelled Rav Natan bar Ammi, [2]and extracted from him four hundred zuz for charity.

[3]Rabbi Il'a said in the name of Resh Lakish: In Usha they enacted: [4][If] someone assigns (lit., "writes") all his property to his sons, [5]he and his wife are maintained from it.

[6]Rabbi Zera objected to this, and some say [that it was] Rabbi Shmuel bar Naḥmani: [7]They said [something] greater than this:

TRANSLATION AND COMMENTARY

All the more so can a wealthy person be compelled to give charity to his own children, for the poor of one's own household take precedence over all other people. The Gemara supports this ruling with the following anecdote: [1]A wealthy man can be compelled to donate charity to the poor, **as in the case where Rava compelled Rav Natan bar Ammi,** who was a man of means, to fulfill his charitable obligations, [2]**and extracted four hundred zuz from him for charity.**

אָמַר רַבִּי אִילְעָא [3]Having mentioned the enactment laid down at Usha obligating a father to maintain his minor children, the Gemara now discusses a series of other enactments that were also instituted at Usha. **Rabbi Il'a said in the name of Resh Lakish:** [4]The Sages of the Sanhedrin sitting **in Usha enacted** that **if someone assigns all his property to his sons,** giving instructions that the property shall pass to the sons not as an inheritance after his death but rather as a gift during his lifetime, [5]**he and his wife are** nevertheless entitled to be **maintained from** the property during their lifetime. By Torah law, the owner of property gives up all his rights to it when he assigns it to someone else. But the Rabbis enacted that in the case of a father who assigns his property to his sons, the transfer of ownership is not absolute, and the father retains the right that he and his wife be maintained from the property for the rest of their lives.

מַתְקִיף לָהּ [6]**Rabbi Zera raised an objection against this** report by Rabbi Il'a in the name of Resh Lakish, **and some say that it was Rabbi Shmuel bar Naḥmani** who raised the objection: [7]What is added by this enactment? Surely the Sages **said something** much **greater than this,** for they said that a man's

RASHI

כי הא דרבא כפייה — על הצדקה. **הוא ואשתו נזונין מהן** — ואפילו כתבן מעכשיו. ולא מן הדין, אלא תקנת חכמים היא. **גדולה מזו אמרו** — בגדולה מזו אמרו. כגון אלמנה ובת, וניסת הבת. שאף על פי שהוא מת, והנכסים נשתעבדו ללוקח דרבנן, כגון בעל בנכסי אשתו, וקיימא לן (גיטין מח,ב): אין מוציאין למזון האשה מנכסים משועבדים — אפילו הכי, היכא דליכא למיחש לתיקון העולם, כגון כי האי לוקח שלא הוציא מעות — שויוהו רבנן כיורש, ואמרי: תזון האלמנה מנכסי בעלה.

SAGES

רַב נָתָן בַּר אַמִי Rav Natan bar Ammi. A Babylonian Amora of the fourth and fifth generations, Rav Natan bar Ammi was a disciple of Rava. He lived in Meḥoza and was a very wealthy man.

NOTES

charity. According to some authorities, the courts can upbraid him and publicly humiliate him, but they cannot actually force him to give charity or confiscate his property for that purpose (*Rav Hai Gaon;* see also *Tosafot*). *Rambam* (in his *Commentary to the Mishnah*) writes that the courts can force a wealthy person to give charity, even to the point of confiscating his assets or administering lashes.

Tosafot objects: There is a general rule that the courts cannot compel a person to fulfill a positive commandment the reward for which is stated explicitly in the Torah, and regarding charity the Torah promises (Deuteronomy 15:10): "For because of this thing the Lord your God will bless you in all your works"! Among the several solutions proposed by *Tosafot* is the suggestion that someone who fails to give charity violates the negative precepts (Deuteronomy 15:7), "You shall not harden your heart, nor shut your hand from your poor brother," and the courts are entitled to use force to prevent someone from violating a negative precept.

Ritva argues that the courts can compel a person to give charity in order to alleviate the distress of the poor.

Tosafot (*Bava Batra* 8b) suggests that the courts are not required to compel a person to fulfill a positive commandment the reward for which is stated explicitly in the Torah, nor are they held accountable if they fail to do so. But if the courts decide that such action is necessary, they may indeed compel a person to fulfill such an obligation.

הַכּוֹתֵב כָּל נְכָסָיו If someone assigns all his property. The Rishonim explain that the Rabbis enacted that the father

HALAKHAH

הַכּוֹתֵב כָּל נְכָסָיו לְבָנָיו If someone assigns all his property to his sons. "If someone transfers all his property to his son, retaining nothing for himself, he is not entitled to be maintained from the property, neither he himself nor his wife, following the Gemara's conclusion that the law is not in accordance with the enactment made in Usha. As for the story recorded in the Gemara about Rabbi Yonatan, who forced sons to maintain their father, the obligation there stemmed from the laws of charity, for a wealthy son is certainly obligated to support his father." (*Bet Yosef* on *Tur, Ḥoshen Mishpat* 257.)

LITERAL TRANSLATION

His widow is maintained from his property. [1] [So] was it necessary [to mention] him and his wife? For Ravin sent in his letter: [2] [If] someone died and left a widow and a daughter, [3] his widow is maintained from his property. [4] [If] the daughter marries, his widow is maintained from his property. [5] [If] the daughter dies, Rabbi Yehudah the son of the sister of Rabbi Yose bar Ḥanina said: [6] With me there was [such] a case, [7] and they said:

אַלְמָנָתוֹ נִזּוֹנֶת מִנְּכָסָיו. [1] הוּא וְאִשְׁתּוֹ מִיבָּעֲיָא? [2] דִּשְׁלַח רָבִין בְּאִיגַּרְתֵּיהּ: [3] מִי שֶׁמֵּת וְהִנִּיחַ אַלְמָנָה וּבַת, אַלְמָנָתוֹ נִיזּוֹנֶת מִנְּכָסָיו. [4] נִישֵּׂאת הַבַּת, אַלְמָנָתוֹ נִיזּוֹנֶת מִנְּכָסָיו. [5] מֵתָה הַבַּת, אָמַר רַבִּי יְהוּדָה בֶּן אֲחוֹתוֹ שֶׁל רַבִּי יוֹסֵי בַּר חֲנִינָא: [6] עַל יָדִי הָיָה מַעֲשֶׂה, [7] וְאָמְרוּ:

RASHI

כי הא דשלח רבין באיגרתיה כו׳ ניסת הבת — אף על גב דאמור רבנן בעל בנכסי אשתו לוקח הוי, וקיימא לן: אין מוציאין למזון האשה מנכסים משועבדים — הכא שוויהו רבנן כיורש, משום פסידא דאלמנה. והכי מפורש ב״יש נוחלין״.

TRANSLATION AND COMMENTARY

widow is entitled to be **maintained from the property** of her deceased husband, even if it has been inherited by his married daughter! A widow is entitled to be maintained from her late husband's estate by virtue of the provisions of her ketubah, as long as she has not received or claimed her ketubah. If a man has no sons but is survived by a widow and by a married daughter, the daughter inherits his estate and her husband gains the right to enjoy the usufruct of the property. The widow's right to be supported from her late husband's estate differs from other rights she possesses. She can recover her ketubah from property that her husband or his heirs have sold to others, but she cannot collect her maintenance from such property. The Rabbis enacted that she cannot collect her maintenance from the buyer, because the amount to be recovered is not fixed. However, she can collect her maintenance from her husband's estate if it has been inherited by his daughter, even if the daughter is married and the usufruct has automatically been transferred to the daughter's husband. Since the latter did not pay anything for the property, it does not matter that an indeterminate sum must be set aside for the widow's maintenance. Now, since a widow is entitled to maintenance from her husband's estate, even if the usufruct of the property has already passed to the daughter's husband, [1] **was it necessary to mention** that during their lifetime **a man and his wife** are entitled to maintenance from the man's property, even if he has already given it all as a gift to his children? There, too, the children have paid nothing for the property, and therefore they will suffer no loss if they have to forfeit the amount needed for their father's maintenance! [2] The Gemara now elaborates on the law underlying Rabbi Zera's objection: **For Ravin sent** the following rulings **in a letter** from Eretz Israel to Babylonia: [3] **If someone dies and leaves a widow and a daughter,** his daughter inherits his estate and **his widow is maintained from that property.** [4] **If the daughter marries, the widow** continues to be **maintained from** her late husband's **property,** even though the usufruct of that property now belongs to the daughter's husband. [5] **If the daughter dies,** and her husband inherits her estate, gaining full title to the property that the daughter inherited previously from her father, what is the law? **Rabbi Yehudah the son of the sister of Rabbi Yose bar Ḥanina said:** [6] **Such an incident was** brought **to my** attention, and I discussed it with the other Rabbis, [7] **and they said: The widow** continues to be **maintained from the property** of her late husband. Even though the daughter's husband inherited the property from his wife and not from her father, the father's widow retains her right to maintenance from his estate. The Gemara now restates its question:

SAGES

רָבִין **Ravin.** This is Rabbi Avin, an Amora of the third and fourth generations. He was born in Babylonia and immigrated to Eretz Israel. Ravin was one of Rabbi Yoḥanan's younger students, and also studied under Rabbi Yoḥanan's great disciples. He was apparently a merchant by profession and acted as an "Emissary of Zion," taking the Torah of Eretz Israel to Babylonia. Ravin was known to have transmitted the rulings of Rabbi Yoḥanan and his other teachers with great precision. The Talmud frequently mentions that Ravin's arrival in Babylonia followed that of another emissary, Rav Dimi, and that Ravin's ruling generally determined the Halakhah. The greatest of the Babylonian Sages also respected the teachings he transmitted, though they did not always consider him a great Sage in his own right. His teachings are also found frequently in the Jerusalem Talmud, where he is called Rabbi Boon.

Two Sages bearing the name Ravin (Rabbi Avin) are mentioned in the Talmud. The first Rabbi Avin was the father of the second, and died before the latter's birth.

BACKGROUND

דִּשְׁלַח רָבִין בְּאִיגַּרְתֵּיהּ **For Ravin sent in his letter.** Ravin was one of the great נְחוֹתֵי — the Sages who went to Babylonia from Eretz Israel and reported the Torah teachings they had learned in the Torah centers there. Because of his ties with Babylonia, Ravin also transmitted Halakhic decisions by means of letters. These letters, and similar ones sent by various other Sages, were considered authoritative, because they summed up the discussions of the principal Sages of Eretz Israel, whose influence at that time was still decisive.

עַל יָדִי הָיָה מַעֲשֶׂה **With me there was such a case.** In other words, this problem was brought before Rabbi Yose bar Ḥanina. He himself arranged to have it thoroughly discussed in the House of Study and was

NOTES

and his wife retain the right to be maintained for the rest of their lives from the property he has assigned to his children. He surely did not have in mind that his children should be given all his property, and that he and his wife would live on charity. The Jerusalem Talmud extends the enactment to the father's minor children — that they too are maintained from the property that their father has assigned to one or more of their older brothers.

HALAKHAH

אַלְמָנָה וּבַת **A widow and a daughter.** "If a man dies and leaves a widow and a daughter (whether from this wife or from a different one), the widow is entitled to maintenance from his estate, which the daughter inherits. Even if the daughter marries and her husband acquires the usufruct of the estate, the widow is still entitled to maintenance from the property of her late husband. Even if the daughter dies and the entire estate passes to her husband, the father's widow retains her right to maintenance from his estate." (*Shulḥan Arukh, Even HaEzer* 93:4.)

TRANSLATION AND COMMENTARY

If a widow is entitled to maintenance from her husband's estate, even if the estate has been inherited by his daughter, and even if the daughter has died and the estate has passed to her husband, [1] why **was it necessary to mention** that during their lifetime **a man and his wife** are entitled to maintenance from the man's property, even if he has already given it all as a gift to his children?

מַהוּ דְּתֵימָא הָתָם הוּא [2] The Gemara rebuts this objection: There is no difficulty, for we can easily distinguish between the two cases. **You might have said that there,** in the case of the widow, the Rabbis enacted that she continues to be maintained from her deceased husband's estate, even if the estate has been inherited by his daughter and has then passed to the daughter's husband, [3] **because there is nobody** else **who will exert himself** on her behalf. Since she was left a widow with nobody to look after her, the Rabbis entitled her to continue to receive maintenance from her late husband's estate. [4] **But here,** in the case where a man transferred all his property to his sons during his lifetime, you might have thought that he is not entitled to be maintained from that property, for he can **exert himself** and support **himself and his wife** by his own labors. [5] **Therefore** Rabbi Il'a **taught us** that **this** assumption **is incorrect,** for in Usha it was enacted that if someone assigns all his property to his sons, he retains the right to maintain himself and his wife from that property for the rest of their lives.

אִיבַּעְיָא לְהוּ [6] **The** following **question arose** in discussion among the Sages: **Is the Halakhah in accordance with** this enactment that a man may continue to maintain himself and his wife from the property that he has assigned to his sons, **or is the Halakhah not in accordance with** this enactment?

תָּא שְׁמַע [7] The Gemara answers: **Come and hear** the following story from which we can draw the conclusion that a father is not entitled to maintenance from the property that he has assigned to his sons: [8] Once **Rabbi Ḥanina and Rabbi Yonatan were standing** together, [9] **and a** certain **man came** over to them, **bent down and kissed Rabbi Yonatan on his foot.** [10] **Rabbi Ḥanina said to** Rabbi Yonatan: **"What is this** all about? Why does he feel so indebted to you that he is ready to kiss your feet?" [11] Rabbi Yonatan **said to him: "This is a man who** once **assigned** all **his property to his sons,** giving it to them as a gift during his lifetime.

אַלְמָנָתוֹ נִיזוֹנֶת מִנְּכָסָיו. [1] הוּא וְאִשְׁתּוֹ מִיבָּעֲיָא? [2] מַהוּ דְּתֵימָא הָתָם הוּא, [3] דְּלֵיכָּא דְּטָרַח, [4] אֲבָל הָכָא נִטְרַח לְדִידֵיהּ וּלְדִידָהּ. [5] קָא מַשְׁמַע לָן.
[6] אִיבַּעְיָא לְהוּ: הִלְכְתָא כְּוָותֵיהּ אוֹ לֵית הִלְכְתָא כְּוָותֵיהּ?
[7] תָּא שְׁמַע: [8] דְּרַבִּי חֲנִינָא וְרַבִּי יוֹנָתָן הָווּ קַיְּימֵי, [9] אֲתָא הַהוּא גַּבְרָא, גָּחִין וּנְשַׁקֵיהּ לְרַבִּי יוֹנָתָן אַכַּרְעֵיהּ. [10] אֲמַר לֵיהּ רַבִּי חֲנִינָא: "מַאי הַאי"? [11] אֲמַר לֵיהּ: "כּוֹתֵב נְכָסָיו לְבָנָיו הוּא,

LITERAL TRANSLATION

His widow is maintained from his property. [1] [So] was it necessary [to mention] him and his wife? [2] You might have said [that] there [the law] is [so], [3] because there is nobody to exert himself, [4] but here let him exert himself for himself and for her. [5] [Therefore] he tells us [that this is not so].

[6] It was asked of them: Is the Halakhah in accordance with him or is the Halakhah not in accordance with him?

[7] Come [and] hear: [8] For Rabbi Ḥanina and Rabbi Yonatan were standing, [9] [and] a man came, bent down and kissed Rabbi Yonatan on his foot. [10] Rabbi Ḥanina said to him: "What is this?" [11] He said to him: "He is someone who assigned his property to his sons,

RASHI

הוא ואשתו — שהוא קיים, ואלו בניו הם, ולא הוציאו מעות, אלא מתנה בעלמא. **מיבעיא** — ואף על גב דמתנה כמכר לענין שעבוד, התם הוא דאי לאו דעביד ליה ניחא לנפשיה — לא יהיב ליה מתנה, אבל בנו — ליכא למימר הכי. **מתה הבת** — ובעלה יורשה. **אלמנתו** — של אבי הבת. **ניזונת מנכסיו** — ולא אמרינן: איש נכרי הוא זה, ואינו יורשו של אב, אלא של אשתו וכלוקח בעלמא דמי, ואין מוציאין למזון האשה מנכסים משועבדין. **התם הוא דליכא דטרח קמה** — שמת בעלה, להכי עבוד רבנן תקנתא. **אבל הכא** — דקאי איהו, נטרח לדידיה ולדידה, קמשמע לן. **הלכתא כוותיה** — אדרבי אילעא קאי. **אברעיה** — על רגלו.

therefore extremely well-versed in the Halakhah on the subject. Moreover, Rabbi Yose bar Ḥanina was a leading expert on the ordinances instituted at Usha.

NOTES

דְּלֵיכָּא דְּטָרַח **Because there is nobody to exert himself.** *Maharam Schiff* infers from here that even though the law is not in accordance with the Ushan enactment that a man may continue to maintain himself and his wife from the property he has assigned to his sons, his widow *is* entitled to maintenance from that property, for after the husband's death we can invoke the argument that there is nobody else to exert himself on her behalf. *Bet Aharon* rejects this position, arguing that according to the Gemara's conclusion that the law is not in accordance with the Ushan enactment, the gift made by the father to his sons is treated as a total and irrevocable transfer of ownership during the father's lifetime, and therefore his widow has no claim to maintenance from the property after his death.

[50A] וְעַשִׂיתִינְהוּ לְזָנֵיהּ״. [1]אִי אָמְרַתְּ בִּשְׁלָמָא לָאו דִּינָא, [2]מִשּׁוּם הָכִי עַשְׂיִינְהוּ. [3]אֶלָּא אִי אָמְרַתְּ דִּינָא, [4]עַשְׂיִינְהוּ בָּעֵי? [5]אָמַר רַבִּי אִילְעָא: [6]בְּאוּשָׁא הִתְקִינוּ: הַמְבַזְבֵּז אַל יְבַזְבֵּז יוֹתֵר מֵחוֹמֶשׁ. [7]תַּנְיָא נַמִי הָכִי:

LITERAL TRANSLATION

[50A] and I forced them to maintain him." [1] Granted if you say [that this] is not the law, [2] it is for that [reason that] he forced them. [3] But if you say [that this] is the law, [4] did he need to force them?

[5] Rabbi Il'a said: In Usha they enacted: [6] Someone who spends [much in giving to charity] should not spend more than a fifth. [7] It was also taught thus:

RASHI

ועשיתינהו — כפיתי אותם בחזקה. ומפני שטרחתי עליו ליכנס לו לפנים משורת הדין — מחבביני. ואי דינא הוא — אין כאן גמילות טובה להחזיק לו טובה, שעל כרחו ישפוט אמת. המבזבז — לעניים. מחומש — שבנכסיו, שלא יצטרך לבריות.

TRANSLATION AND COMMENTARY

[50A] Later, when the sons showed an unwillingness to support their father, **I forced them to maintain him.** Ever since then, he has been extremely grateful to me, and kissing my feet is his way of showing it." [1]The Gemara now explains how it drew its conclusion from this story. **There is no problem if we say that the law is not** in accordance with the enactment of the Sages in Usha, and that the sons are under no legal obligation to maintain their father from the property he transferred to them. [2]We can **then** understand **why** Rabbi Yonatan had to **force them** to maintain their father. [3]**But if we say that the law is** in accordance with the enactment of the Sages in Usha, [4]why **was it necessary** for Rabbi Yonatan **to force** the sons to maintain their father? The judges should have confiscated the sons' property and compelled them to provide for their father. Thus we see that the enactment of the Sages in Usha could not have been accepted as the normative Halakhah.

אָמַר רַבִּי אִילְעָא [5]The Gemara now discusses another enactment of the Sages in Usha. **Rabbi Il'a said:** [6]When the Sanhedrin was sitting **in Usha,** the Sages **enacted** that even if **someone** wishes to **spend** his money **in giving to charity,** he **should not spend more than one-fifth** of his assets. [7]**The same** thing **was also**

BACKGROUND

אַל יְבַזְבֵּז יוֹתֵר מֵחוֹמֶשׁ Should not spend more than a fifth. The Talmud does not offer any inherent reason for this proportion aside from the allusion found in the Bible. Perhaps it is parallel to the normal proportion set aside from agricultural produce for the priests and the Levites, for when all of the donations are added together, they come to slightly more than one-fifth.

חוֹמֶשׁ A fifth. As mentioned in the notes, one-fifth of one's assets is not only the upper limit for charitable donation, but the recommended proportion for those who can afford it. This is not as large a share as it seems, for a man who is not wealthy can include within it his expenses for performing commandments, and, as noted here in the Gemara, the money he spends to support his small children and other members of his family, such as his parents, if they are in need.

NOTES

וְעַשִׂיתִינְהוּ לְזָנֵיהּ And I forced them to maintain him. A slightly different version of this story is cited in the Jerusalem Talmud (*Pe'ah* 1:1). There it is related how Rabbi Yonatan "forced" the son to support his father: He advised the father to assemble a group of people and to inform them that the son was refusing to support him. Publicly upbraided and humiliated, the son agreed to provide his father with the necessary support.

Elsewhere in the Gemara (*Kiddushin* 32a), the Rabbis differ about the expenses a son must incur in fulfilling the obligation of honoring his parents. The Halakhah is that the obligation must be fulfilled at the father's expense. *Rabbenu Tam* and others (*Tosafot, Kiddushin* 32a; *Sefer HaYashar* 141) maintain that if the father is poor, the son must use his own funds to fulfill his obligation. The courts can compel the son to provide for his father, for in such a case his obligation stems from the laws of charity. *Rabbenu Tam* bases his ruling on the passage in the Jerusalem Talmud cited above (which concludes that a son can be compelled to sustain his father), as well as on the anecdote cited earlier in our Gemara (49b) about Rava who compelled Rav Natan bar Ammi to give 400 zuz to charity.

עַשְׂיִינְהוּ בָּעֵי Did he need to force them? The Rishonim disagree about how Rabbi Yonatan forced the sons to provide for their father, and as a result they offer different explanations of the Gemara's argument. According to *Rashi,* Rabbi Yonatan used physical force to get the sons to provide for their father. Thus the Gemara's argument is as follows: There is no problem if you say that the law is not in accordance with the enactment made in Usha, for we can then understand why the father was so grateful. Rabbi Yonatan went beyond the letter of the law and compelled the sons to maintain the father. But if you say that the law is in accordance with the enactment made in Usha, then it was by right that Rabbi Yonatan compelled the sons to maintain their father, and there was no reason for the father to feel especially indebted to him. Others (*Tosafot;* see also *Ritva* and *Nimmukei Yosef*) explain that Rabbi Yonatan used verbal force — either the pressure of a public upbraiding or the pressure of a ban. Accordingly the Gemara's argument is as follows: There is no problem if you say that the law is not in accordance with the enactment made in Usha, and we can understand why Rabbi Yonatan only resorted to such relatively mild means of compulsion. But if you say that the law is in accordance with the enactment made in Usha, why did Rabbi Yonatan act in this way? He should have confiscated the sons' property or flogged them until they agreed to provide for their father.

אַל יְבַזְבֵּז יוֹתֵר מֵחוֹמֶשׁ Should not spend more than a fifth. *Rashi* explains that this enactment limits the amount of money that a person is permitted to give to charity.

HALAKHAH

אַל יְבַזְבֵּז יוֹתֵר מֵחוֹמֶשׁ Should not spend more than a fifth. "A person should not give away as charity more than one-fifth of his assets, so that he himself does not become dependent upon charity from others (*Rema* in the name of *Bet Yosef,* following the enactment made in Usha cited in our Gemara; see also commentaries, ad loc., which discuss whether or not this limitation applies to all people and in all circumstances)." (*Rambam, Sefer Hafla'ah, Hilkhot Arakhin* 8:13; *Shulḥan Arukh, Yoreh De'ah* 249:1.)

TRANSLATION AND COMMENTARY

taught in the following Baraita: "If **someone** wishes to **spend** his money **in giving to charity,** he **should not spend more than one-fifth** of his assets, [1]**lest he** himself **become** financially **dependent upon** the charity of other **people** after having given away his money. [2]**And it once happened that someone wished to spend more than one-fifth** of his money on charity for the poor, **but his colleague would not allow him** to give his money so liberally." [3]**And who was** the colleague who prevented the overgenerous benefactor from giving away too much of his money? It was **Rabbi Yeshevav.** [4]**And some report** this story in a slightly different manner: Once **Rabbi Yeshevav wished to spend** more than one-fifth of his money on charity for the poor, [5]**but his colleague would not allow him** to do so. [6]**And who was** the colleague who made Rabbi Yeshevav limit his gift to one-fifth of his assets? It was **Rabbi Akiva.**

"הַמְבַזְבֵּז אַל יְבַזְבֵּז יוֹתֵר מֵחוֹמֶשׁ, [1]שֶׁמָּא יִצְטָרֵךְ לַבְּרִיּוֹת. [2]וּמַעֲשֶׂה בְּאֶחָד שֶׁבִּקֵּשׁ לְבַזְבֵּז יוֹתֵר מֵחוֹמֶשׁ, וְלֹא הִנִּיחַ לוֹ חֲבֵירוֹ". [3]וּמַנּוּ? רַבִּי יְשֵׁבָב. [4]וְאָמְרִי לָהּ: רַבִּי יְשֵׁבָב, [5]וְלֹא הִנִּיחוֹ חֲבֵירוֹ. [6]וּמַנּוּ? רַבִּי עֲקִיבָא.

[7]אֲמַר רַב נַחְמָן, וְאִיתֵּימָא רַב אַחָא בַּר יַעֲקֹב: [8]מַאי קְרָא? [9]"וְכֹל אֲשֶׁר תִּתֶּן לִי עַשֵּׂר אֲעַשְּׂרֶנּוּ לָךְ". [10]וְהָא לָא דָּמֵי עִישּׂוּרָא בַּתְרָא לְעִישּׂוּרָא קַמָּא!

LITERAL TRANSLATION

"Someone who spends [much in giving to charity] should not spend more than a fifth, [1]lest he become dependent upon people. [2]And it once happened that someone wished to spend more than a fifth, and his fellow would not allow him." [3]And who was it? Rabbi Yeshevav. [4]And some say: Rabbi Yeshevav [wished to spend], [5]and his fellow would not allow him. [6]And who was it? Rabbi Akiva.

[7]Rav Naḥman, and some say [it was] Rav Aḥa bar Ya'akov, said: [8]What is the verse? [9]"And of all that You shall give me I will surely give a tenth of it to You." [10]But surely the latter tenth is not like the former tenth!

RASHI

עשר אעשרנו — שני עישורין, הוו להו חומש. **והא לא דמי בתרא לקמא** — דכי שקלת לקמא פשו להו תשעה, וכי הדרת מדלית מעשר דידהו — לאו כי קמא הוא, ואין כאן חומש בשניהם.

אֲמַר רַב נַחְמָן [7]**Rav Naḥman, and some say that it was Rav Aḥa bar Ya'akov, said:** [8]**Which verse** alludes to this law that a person should not give away more than one-fifth of his assets to charity? The enactment by the Sages in Usha is supported by the following verse (Genesis 28:22): [9]**"And of all that You shall give me I will surely give a tenth of it** (עַשֵּׂר אֲעַשְּׂרֶנּוּ) **to You."** The use of the double verb form עַשֵּׂר אֲעַשְּׂרֶנּוּ by the Patriarch Jacob in this verse is understood by Rav Naḥman as follows: "I will give a tenth and then I will give a second tenth." Thus the verse alludes to a gift of two-tenths, or one-fifth, of Jacob's total assets, and provides support for the enactment made in Usha that even if a person wishes to be generous with his money, he should not give away more than one-fifth of what he has.

וְהָא לָא דָּמֵי [10]The Gemara asks: **But surely the second tenth** mentioned in the verse **is not equal to the first tenth!** For if Jacob promised to tithe his assets and then tithe them a second time, the second tithe is a tenth of what is left after the first tithe has been removed. Thus the two tithes taken together constitute less than one-fifth of Jacob's total assets.

SAGES

רַבִּי יְשֵׁבָב **Rabbi Yeshevav.** A Tanna of the fourth generation. See *Ketubot,* Part III, p. 17.

רַבִּי עֲקִיבָא **Rabbi Akiva.** A Tanna of the fourth generation. See *Ketubot,* Part II, p. 206.

רַב אַחָא בַּר יַעֲקֹב **Rav Aḥa bar Ya'akov.** A Babylonian Amora of the third and fourth generations, Rav Aḥa bar Ya'akov was a disciple of Rav Huna and must have lived to a great age, for he also discusses the Halakhah with Abaye and Rava. Rav Aḥa bar Ya'akov lived in the city of Papunya (sometimes he is named "Papuna'i," after his place of residence). He was the leading Sage of that city and instituted various regulations.

In addition to his eminence as a Torah scholar — he was praised by Rava as a great man, and Rav Naḥman, too, acknowledged his intelligence — he was one of the most saintly members of his generation and a worker of miracles. Several of the Sages of the following generation studied under him.

His son, Ya'akov, is mentioned in tractate *Kiddushin,* and we also know of a nephew, Rav Aḥa the son of Rav Ika.

NOTES

Rambam (*Hilkhot Arakhin* 8:13) and *Rivan* maintain that this enactment also limits the amount of money that a person is permitted to consecrate to the Temple treasury. *Rambam* (*Hilkhot Mattenot Aniyyim* 7:5) implies that one-fifth of a person's money is not only the maximum amount but also the optimum amount of charity that he should give. Giving one-tenth of one's money as charity is considered to be an average virtue. Giving anything less than that is the sign of a miserly person. Elsewhere (below, 67b), the Gemara concludes that the limitation regarding how much money a person may give away as charity applies only during that person's lifetime, while there is a risk that he may become financially dependent upon others. But there is no limit on the amount of money a person may bequeath to charity. The Jerusalem Talmud explains that a person is not expected to give away one-fifth of his assets every year. Rather, a person should make a one-time contribution of one-fifth of his property. In subsequent years he should donate to charity one-fifth of the income generated by his remaining assets.

עַשֵּׂר אֲעַשְּׂרֶנּוּ **I will surely give a tenth of it.** *Shittah Mekubbetzet* writes that the formulation of Jacob's promise — that he would gave away two-tenths of his assets, rather than one fifth — supports the viewpoint of *Rambam* (*Commentary to the Mishnah, Avot* 3:18) that it is preferable to give a number of small gifts of charity to several people, rather than one large gift to a single person.

SAGES

רַב שִׁימִי בַּר אַשִׁי Rav Shimi bar Ashi. A Babylonian Amora of the fifth generation. See *Ketubot*, Part II, p. 91.

רַב יִצְחָק Rav (Rabbi) Yitzḥak. A prominent Palestinian Amora of the second and third generations, Rabbi Yitzḥak's full name was Rabbi Yitzḥak Nappaḥa. He was a disciple of Rabbi Yoḥanan and often presents teachings in the latter's name. He also spent part of his life in Babylonia, where he was an important source of information about the teachings and customs of Eretz Israel.

רַב Rav. A Babylonian Amora of the first generation. See *Ketubot*, Part I, pp. 42–3.

רַב שְׁמוּאֵל בַּר שִׁילַת Rav Shmuel bar Shilat. A Babylonian Amora of the first and second generations, Rav Shmuel bar Shilat was a schoolteacher in the city of Sura, where Rav lived. Rav himself had great respect for Rav Shmuel's educational activity, and he applied the verse (Daniel 12:3) to him: "And those who turn many to righteousness are as the stars." Rav also gave Rav Shmuel bar Shilat advice regarding educational methods. Rav Shmuel bar Shilat was also a Sage. He consulted Rav on Halakhic problems and transmitted rulings in the name of Rav and of Rav Kahana. His son, Rav Yehudah the son of Rav Shmuel bar Shilat, was also a Sage.

BACKGROUND

יוֹרֵד עִמּוֹ לְחַיָּיו He treats him harshly. Various sources in the Talmud and later literature attempt to define this expression more exactly, for it is used in other contexts as well. The common factor seems to be that it is permitted to harass someone in any fashion that will force him to change his ways or repent for the evil he has committed.

וּסְפֵי לֵיהּ כְּתוֹרָא And feed him like an ox. This advice reflects a widely held educational principle, that when a child is ready for studies, the teacher should not be afraid of overburdening him, but must try to teach him as

TRANSLATION AND COMMENTARY

אָמַר רַב אַשִׁי [1] **Rav Ashi said:** This is the way the verse must be understood: **"I will give a tenth"** of my assets [2] **the second time, just as** I will give a tenth **the first time.** Thus, Jacob promised to consecrate two equal tithes, the two together constituting one-fifth of his total assets.

אָמַר רַב שִׁימִי בַּר אַשִׁי [3] **Rav Shimi bar Ashi said: These** three **reports** about the enactments laid down in Usha **get shorter as they go on.** The first enactment, concerning the father's liability for the support of his minor children, was reported by Rabbi Il'a in the name of Resh Lakish, who reported it in the name of Rabbi Yehudah bar Ḥanina. The second enactment, concerning the father who assigns all his property to his sons, was reported by Rabbi Il'a in the name of Resh Lakish. And the third enactment, concerning the maximum amount to be spent on charity, was reported by Rabbi Il'a on his own. [4] **And here is a mnemonic** device to help you remember the order of the enactments and thus the length of the chain of tradition of each one: **"Minors wrote and spent."** "Minors" refers to the enactment concerning the father's obligation to maintain his minor children; "wrote" refers to the enactment about a father who assigns all his property to his children; "spent" refers to the enactment regarding a person who wishes to give his money away to charity. With the help of this mnemonic device, it is easy to remember which enactment was reported by a chain of three Amoraim, which by a chain of two, and which by a single Amora.

אָמַר רַב יִצְחָק [5] The Gemara now moves on to another enactment of the Sages in Usha: **Rav Yitzḥak said: In Usha** the Sages **enacted that a person should be patient with his son until he reaches the age of twelve.** Even if the child refuses to devote himself to his Torah studies, the father should bear with him and continue to deal with him gently. [6] But **from then onwards he should treat him harshly** if he does not begin to take his studies seriously.

אִינִי [7] The Gemara asks: **Is this really so?** [8] **But surely Rav said to Rav Shmuel bar Shilat,** who was a primary-school teacher: [9] If a child is **less than six years old, do not accept him** in your school; [10] but if he is already **six years old, accept him** as your pupil **and feed him** Torah **as** you would feed **an ox** his food! This simile implies that a child should be forced to learn Torah even before he reaches the age of twelve, and contradicts the enactment laid down in Usha.

[1] אָמַר רַב אַשִׁי: "אֲעַשְּׂרֶנּוּ" — [2] לְבַתְרָא כִּי קַמָּא.
[3] אָמַר רַב שִׁימִי בַּר אַשִׁי: וּשְׁמוּעוֹת הַלָּלוּ מִתְמַעֲטוֹת וְהוֹלְכוֹת. [4] וְסִימָנֵיךְ: "קְטַנִּים כָּתְבוּ וּבִזְבְּזוּ".
[5] אָמַר רַב יִצְחָק: בְּאוּשָׁא הִתְקִינוּ שֶׁיְּהֵא אָדָם מִתְגַּלְגֵּל עִם בְּנוֹ עַד שְׁתֵּים עֶשְׂרֵה שָׁנָה. [6] מִכָּאן וְאֵילָךְ יוֹרֵד עִמּוֹ לְחַיָּיו. [7] אִינִי? [8] וְהָא אֲמַר לֵיהּ רַב לְרַב שְׁמוּאֵל בַּר שִׁילַת: [9] בְּצִיר מִבַּר שִׁית לָא תְּקַבֵּיל; [10] בַּר שִׁית — קַבֵּיל וּסְפֵי לֵיהּ כְּתוֹרָא!

LITERAL TRANSLATION

[1] Rav Ashi said: "I will give a tenth of it" — [2] the latter one like the former one.

[3] Rav Shimi bar Ashi said: And these traditions get steadily shorter. [4] And your mnemonic is: "Minors wrote and spent."

[5] Rav Yitzḥak said: In Usha they enacted that a man should be patient with his son until [he is] twelve years [old]. [6] From then onwards he treats him harshly (lit., "descends with him to his life").

[7] Is that so? [8] But surely Rav said to Rav Shmuel bar Shilat: [9] Less than six years old — do not accept [him]; [10] six years old — accept [him] and feed him like an ox!

RASHI

אעשרנו — מדלא כתיב עשר אעשר לך — הכי קאמר: אעשרנו כראשון, כלומר: מעשר שני יהא כראשון. **שמועות הללו** — דרבי אילעא בתקנת אושא. **מתמעטות והולכות** — מאמוראים. הראשונה: אמר רבי אילעא אמר ריש לקיש משום דרבי יוסי בר חנינא, השניה: רבי אילעא אמר ריש לקיש, שלישית: רבי אילעא, לחודיה. **וסימניך** — בסדר ההלכות, ובו תדע סדר מיעוטן. **קטנים כתבו ובזבזו** — בניו ובנותיו כשהן קטנים, כותב נכסיו, המבזבז אל יבזבז. ומעתה לא תחליף באיזו שלשה ובאיזו שנים ובאיזו אחד. **מגלגל עם בנו** — אם מסרב מללמוד — יגלגל עמו בנחת ובדברים רכים. **יורד עמו לחייו** — לרדותו ברצועה ובחוסר לחם. **רב שמואל בר שילת** — מלמד תינוקות היה. **וספי ליה כי תורא** — הלעיטהו תורה, כשור שאתה מלעיטו ואובסו מאכל.

NOTES

וּסְפֵי לֵיהּ כְּתוֹרָא And feed him like an ox. This comparison between an ox and a child has been explained as follows: The ox first takes in a considerable amount of food, and then, after the food is swallowed, regurgitates it and chews it and chewed again. By analogy, a child should be taught a vast amount of material, for a child has the mental capacity to absorb a great number of facts. After he matures, he will have ample opportunity to examine the material more thoroughly and arrive at a deeper understanding (*Eshel Avraham*).

TRANSLATION AND COMMENTARY

אִין [1] The Gemara replies: There is really no contradiction between the enactment made in Usha that a father should be patient with his child until he is twelve years old and Rav's advice to Rav Shmuel bar Shilat about the proper way to teach a child. **Indeed,** one should **feed** a child Torah **as** one would feed **an ox,** allowing him to absorb as much Torah as he possibly can. [2] **Nevertheless,** if the child finds it difficult to devote himself properly to his studies, the father **should not treat him harshly until after he reaches the age of twelve.**

וְאִיבָּעֵית אֵימָא [3] The Gemara now suggests another solution to the apparent contradiction. **If you wish,** you can **say that there is** really **no difficulty,** for the two statements are dealing with different cases. [4] **This** statement by Rav, suggesting that the primary-school teacher should force his pupils to devote themselves to their studies, **refers to** the study of **Scripture.** From the age of six, a child should be forced to study Scripture. [5] But **this** enactment, that a father should be patient with his child until the child is twelve years old, **refers to** the study of **Mishnah.** [6] **For Abaye said: Mother** (the term used by Abaye to describe the nursemaid who brought him up) **used to tell me:** [7] When a child is **six years old, he is ready for** the study of **Scripture;** [8] **when he is ten years old,** he is ready **for** the study of **Mishnah,** but he should not be forced to study it until he is twelve; [9] when a boy is **in his thirteenth year,** he should begin **fasting** on the major fast days **for** a full **twenty-four hours,** just like an adult, [10] **and a girl** should begin fasting a full day **when she is in her twelfth year.**

אֲמַר אַבַּיֵי [11] The Gemara now cites another statement concerning young children which Abaye heard from his nursemaid. **Abaye said: Mother used to tell me** that **a six-year-old** child **who is stung by a scorpion on the day that he completes his sixth year will not survive** unless he receives proper medical attention. [12] **What is the remedy** that will save his life? **Mix the gall of a white vulture into beer, rub** some of the solution on the place where the child was stung, **and** then **give him** the rest **to drink.** Mother also used to tell

LITERAL TRANSLATION

[1] Yes, feed him like an ox. [2] Nevertheless, he does not treat him harshly until after [he is] twelve years [old].

[3] And if you wish, say: There is no difficulty. [4] This [refers] to Scripture; [5] this [refers] to Mishnah. [6] For Abaye said: Mother told me: [7] [At] six years old, [he is ready] for Scripture; [8] [at] ten years old, for Mishnah; [9] [at] thirteen years old, for a twenty-four-hour fast; [10] and as for a girl [the age is] twelve years old.

[11] Abaye said: Mother told me: A six-year-old whom a scorpion stings on the day that he completes his sixth [year] will not survive. [12] What is his remedy? [Put] the gall of a white vulture in beer, rub him [with it] and give [it] to him to drink.

[1] אִין, סְפֵי לֵיהּ כְּתוֹרָא. [2] מִיהוּ, אֵינוֹ יוֹרֵד עִמּוֹ לְחַיָּיו עַד לְאַחַר שְׁתֵּים עֶשְׂרֵה שָׁנָה.
[3] וְאִיבָּעֵית אֵימָא: לָא קַשְׁיָא. [4] הָא לְמִקְרָא; [5] הָא לְמִשְׁנָה. [6] דַּאֲמַר אַבַּיֵי: אָמְרָה לִי אֵם: [7] בַּר שִׁית, לְמִקְרָא; [8] בַּר עֶשֶׂר, לְמִשְׁנָה; [9] בַּר תְּלֵיסַר, לְתַעֲנִיתָא מֵעֵת לְעֵת; [10] וּבְתִינוֹקֶת בַּת תְּרֵיסַר.
[11] אֲמַר אַבַּיֵי: אָמְרָה לִי אֵם: הַאי בַּר שִׁית דְּטָרְקָא לֵיהּ עַקְרַבָּא בְּיוֹמָא דְּמִישְׁלַם שִׁית לָא חַיֵּי. [12] מַאי אַסּוּתֵיהּ? מְרִרְתָּא דְּדַיָּה חִיוַּרְתָּא בְּשִׁיכְרָא, נְשַׁפְיֵיהּ וְנַשְׁקְיֵיהּ.

RASHI

לתעניתא מעת לעת — להתענות כל היום. וחינוכא לשעות, מקודם לכן שנתיים, כדאמרינן ביומא (פב,א). **ובתינוקת** — שהיא ממהרת להביא כח, שאינה מתשת כח בלימוד תורה. ותרתי סרי דקאמר — שנת שתים עשרה גופא קאמר. דאי בת

ויום אחד — דאורייתא היא, שמביאה שתי שערות, ובת עונשים, ואין צורך לנו ללמוד ממניקתו של אביי. **לא חיי** — אם לא ברפואה בדוקה. **מררתא דדיה** — מרה של דיה, שקורין *וושט״ו. **נשפייה ונשקייה** — תמשחנו ממנו, ותשקנו ממנו בשכר.

NOTES

בַּר שִׁית לְמִקְרָא At six years old, he is ready for Scripture. This seems to contradict the Mishnah in *Avot* (5:21), which reads: "At five years old he is ready for Scripture." Some commentators reconcile the contradiction by suggesting that the term בַּר שִׁית used here should be understood as "in his sixth year," i.e., a child who is over five years old (*Talmidei Rabbenu Yonah* and others). Others (*Rashba, Ritva*) suggest that the Mishnah in *Avot* refers to the age at which a father should begin teaching his child Torah at home, whereas here we are dealing with the age when the child should enter school.

מַאי אַסּוּתֵיהּ What is his remedy? *Tosafot* argues that the remedies mentioned here will not cure a child who has already been stung by a scorpion or by a wasp, for the

HALAKHAH

בַּר שִׁית לְמִקְרָא At six years old he is ready for Scripture. "When should a father begin to teach his son Torah? When the child begins to speak, the father should teach him the verse, "Moses commanded us the Torah," and the verse,

much material as possible. A child's ability to absorb knowledge is very great, and things that are learned in childhood (גִּרְסָא דְּיַנְקוּתָא) are retained better than what is learned later.

BACKGROUND

בַּר שִׁית לְמִקְרָא At six years old, he is ready for Scripture. The study of Scripture on the elementary level in Talmudic times mainly involved the teaching of reading and writing, and learning to read out loud. This level of education was regarded as suitable for all. The store of knowledge and the skills acquired by a child during his elementary education were regarded as common to every Jew everywhere. Only a few children, just a tenth according to one source, apparently continued their education and studied Mishnah. There were also economic reasons for this, since parents needed their children's help at home and in the fields. At the same time there were intellectual reasons, since not every child is capable of learning Mishnah. Although the study of Mishnah in early times involved mainly learning by heart, it nevertheless required a high level of understanding and analytical ability.

לְתַעֲנִיתָא מֵעֵת לְעֵת For a twenty-four-hour fast. It is stated in tractate *Yoma* (82a) that children should be trained to fast a few years before reaching majority. The older children become, the more hours they are required to fast, especially on Yom Kippur. However, children are not required by law to fast for a full twenty-four hours until they come of age — at thirteen for boys, and at twelve for girls.

LANGUAGE (RASHI)

*וושט״ו (correct reading וולטו״ר). From the Old French *voltur,* meaning "vulture."

[1]הַאי בַּר שַׁתָּא דְּטָרֵיק לֵיהּ זִיבּוּרָא בְּיוֹמָא דְּמִישְׁלַם שַׁתָּא לָא חַיֵּי. [2]מַאי אֲסוּתֵיהּ? אַצְוָתָא דְּדִיקְלָא בְּמַיָּא, נְשַׁפְיֵיהּ וְנַשְׁקְיֵיהּ.

[3]אָמַר רַב קְטִינָא: כָּל הַמַּכְנִיס אֶת בְּנוֹ פָּחוֹת מִבֶּן שֵׁשׁ רָץ אַחֲרָיו וְאֵינוֹ מַגִּיעוֹ. [4]אִיכָּא דְּאָמְרִי: חֲבֵירָיו רָצִין אַחֲרָיו וְאֵין מַגִּיעִין אוֹתוֹ.

[5]וְתַרְוַיְיהוּ אִיתְנְהוּ: חֲלִישׁ וְגָמֵיר. [6]אִיבָּעֵית אֵימָא: הָא דִּכְחִישׁ; [7]הָא דְּבָרִיא.

LITERAL TRANSLATION

[1]A one-year-old whom a wasp stings on the day that he completes the year will not survive. [2]What is his remedy? [Put] the creeper [that grows] round a palm tree in water, rub him [with it] and give [it] to him to drink.

[3]Rav Ketina said: Whoever puts his son into [school when he is] less than six years old runs after him and does not reach him. [4]There are [some] who say: His fellows run after him and do not reach him.

[5]And both of them are [true]: He is weakened but he learns. [6]If you wish, say: This [refers to] where he is sickly; [7]this [refers to] where he is healthy.

TRANSLATION AND COMMENTARY

me that [1]**a one-year-old** child **who is stung by a wasp on the day that he completes the year will not survive** without the right medicine. [2]**What is the remedy** that will cure him? **Mix** a solution of **the creeper** that grows **round a palm tree in water, rub** some of the mixture on the spot where the child was stung, **and give him** the rest **to drink.**

אָמַר רַב קְטִינָא [3]The Gemara now returns to its discussion about when to begin a child's formal Torah education. **Rav Ketina said: Whoever enrolls his son in school when** the child **is less than six years old will run after him and not reach him.** The child's health will suffer as a result of his early entry into school; the father will have to worry about him and seek ways to repair the damage; and despite all the father's efforts, the child will remain sickly for a long time. [4]**There are some who report** a different version of Rav Ketina's statement: If someone enrolls his son in school when the child is less than six years old, the child's **friends will run after him and not reach him.** Since the child started school at an earlier age than his friends, he will have a head start in his studies, and his friends will find it difficult to catch up.

וְתַרְוַיְיהוּ אִיתְנְהוּ [5]The Gemara considers the two versions of Rav Ketina's statement. Though at first glance these two versions seem to contradict each other, **both** versions **are** in fact **correct.** A child who attends school before he reaches the age of six **is** apt to become **weakened** as a result, **but** at the same time **he will learn** more than his peers. [6]On the other hand, **if you wish,** you can **say** that the two versions of Rav Ketina's statement refer to different cases. The first version **deals with** a child **who is sickly** and has a weak constitution. If such a child starts school before the age of six, his health will suffer. [7]The second version **deals with** a child **who is healthy.** That child should indeed begin school at a younger age, for he will thrive there and gain a head start over the other children his age.

RASHI

אצותא דדיקלא — סיב שגדל סביב דקל תומר, כעין *ווילד״ה שכורך את עץ הגפן. **המכניס את בנו** — ללמוד תורה. **רץ אחריו** — להברותו ולהחיותו. **ואין מגיעו** — מסוכן הוא למות מרוב חולשו. **חביריו רצין אחריו** — להיות פקחין בתורה כמותו. **הא דכחיש** — אל יכניסנו, שמסוכן הוא פן יחלים וימות. **דבריא** — יכניסנו לפי שמתפקח.

NOTES

Gemara has just said that these children will not survive. Rather, the remedies are prophylactic measures to prevent the scorpion or the wasp from stinging the child. The Aḥaronim note that there is a certain difficulty with this explanation, for the vulture is a non-kosher bird, and the child should not be permitted to ingest the non-kosher solution unless there is an immediate threat to his life (*Porat Yosef*). Our commentary follows *Rashi,* who explains that these remedies will heal the stung child. When the Gemara says that these children will not survive the sting, it merely means that they will die if they do not receive immediate medical attention.

HALAKHAH

"Hear, O Israel." He should then continue to teach him a little at a time until he is six or seven (if he is a particularly sickly child; *Shakh*), at which point he should take him to a primary-school teacher. It is customary to begin teaching a child Scripture when he has completed his fifth year, but not before that. If he is a sickly child, he should begin to learn when he has completed his sixth year," following the rulings of Rav and Rav Ketina in our Gemara. (*Rambam, Sefer Mada, Hilkhot Talmud Torah* 1:6; *Shulḥan Arukh, Yoreh De'ah* 245:5,8.)

SAGES

רַב קְטִינָא Rav Ketina. A second-generation Babylonian Amora, Rav Ketina lived in Sura and was a disciple of Rav. Very little is known of his personal life. His teachings are cited by other Babylonian Amoraim of the second and third generations. These teachings include Halakhic and Aggadic dicta, as well as comments regarding ethical matters. The Talmud relates that Rav Ketina was a holy man and that the prophet Elijah and various angels appeared to him in visions.

BACKGROUND

דְּטָרְקָא לֵיהּ עַקְרַבָּא...דְּטָרֵיק לֵיהּ זִיבּוּרָא Whom a scorpion stings...whom a wasp stings. Scorpion stings are very painful (particularly the stings of certain species such as the yellow scorpion found in Israel), and can occasionally endanger the victim's life. Wasp stings, however, are usually not so dangerous, unless the victim is allergic to that particular poison. As a rule, the less the victim weighs, the more dangerous the sting, since the proportion of poison to body weight is greater, and this is apparently why the Gemara states that such stings are especially dangerous to young children.

פָּחוֹת מִבֶּן שֵׁשׁ Less than six years old. Modern psychologists disagree about the ideal age for starting school. To a certain extent, this depends on the child's physical and emotional maturity, and as such it varies from child to child. However, it is generally assumed today that by the age of six most children are sufficiently mature to begin studying on a regular basis.

LANGUAGE (RASHI)

ווילד״ה* (correct reading וידיל״ה). From the Old French *vedille,* meaning "soft branch."

TRANSLATION AND COMMENTARY

אָמַר רַבִּי יוֹסֵי בַּר חֲנִינָא [1] The Gemara now proceeds to discuss another enactment that was issued by the Sanhedrin sitting in Usha. **Rabbi Yose bar Ḥanina said:** [2] **In Usha** the Sages **enacted** that **if a wife sells her usufruct property during her husband's lifetime and** she subsequently **dies** before her husband, [3] **the husband can reclaim the property from the buyers.** Property that a woman brings into her marriage and is not recorded in her ketubah, or that she inherits or receives as a gift after she is married, is called usufruct property. Usufruct property belongs to the wife even after she is married. During her lifetime, her husband is entitled to use it as he sees fit, and upon her death he inherits it together with the rest of her estate. Now, since the wife retains ownership of the principal during her lifetime, she should be able to sell that principal to another person. Her husband would retain title to the usufruct for the rest of his life (because the wife cannot sell the usufruct), but once the husband dies, the buyer would gain full title to the land, both to the principal and to the usufruct, just as the woman regains title to the usufruct if her husband dies before her. However, the Rabbis enacted that the husband is viewed as having bought his wife's usufruct property at the time of the marriage, if she should die before him. Thus, after his wife's death, the husband is considered as the first buyer of the property, and therefore he can reclaim it from anyone who bought it from the woman while she was married.

אַשְׁכַּחֵיהּ [4] Concluding its discussion of the enactments passed in Usha, the Gemara relates that **Rav Yitzḥak bar Yosef** once **met Rabbi Abbahu standing in a crowd in Usha,** [5] and **said to him: "Who is an expert on the traditions of Usha?** Who has comprehensive and reliable knowledge of the enactments that were

[1] אָמַר רַבִּי יוֹסֵי בַּר חֲנִינָא: [2] בְּאוּשָׁא הִתְקִינוּ: הָאִשָּׁה שֶׁמָּכְרָה בְּנִכְסֵי מְלוֹג בְּחַיֵּי בַעְלָהּ וּמֵתָה — [3] הַבַּעַל מוֹצִיא מִיַּד הַלָּקוֹחוֹת.
[4] אַשְׁכַּחֵיהּ רַב יִצְחָק בַּר יוֹסֵף לְרַבִּי אַבָּהוּ דַּהֲוָה קָאֵי בְּאוּכְלוֹסָא דְּאוּשָׁא. [5] אֲמַר לֵיהּ: ״מַאן מָרֵה דִּשְׁמַעְתָּא דְּאוּשָׁא״?

LITERAL TRANSLATION

[1] Rabbi Yose bar Ḥanina said: In Usha they enacted: [2] [If] a woman sold part of her usufruct property in her husband's lifetime and died, [3] the husband may take [it] out from the hand of the buyers.

[4] Rav Yitzḥak bar Yosef met Rabbi Abbahu who was standing in a crowd in Usha. [5] He said to him: "Who is the master of the traditions of Usha?"

RASHI

שמכרה בנכסי מלוג — הקרן. **הבעל מוציא** — דשויוהו רבנן כלוקח, והוא לוקח ראשון. [**באוכלוסא** — אסיפת בני אדם].

LANGUAGE

אוּכְלוּסָא Crowd. From the Greek ὄχλος, *ochlos,* meaning "crowd," or "throng."

NOTES

הַבַּעַל מוֹצִיא מִיַּד הַלָּקוֹחוֹת **The husband may take it out from the hand of the buyers.** Most Rishonim maintain that the expression, "he may take it out from the hand of the buyers," does not imply that during the woman's lifetime the property passes into the ownership of the buyer, for a wife cannot transfer to another person property whose usufruct belongs to her husband. Rather, it means that the husband can remove the right that the buyer acquired in the woman's property — that the buyer would gain title to the property in the event that she predeceases her husband. But some authorities suggest that we are dealing here with a case where the husband had previously waived his right to the usufruct during his wife's lifetime. In such a case the buyer gains immediate title to the property, but by the Ushan enactment the husband can reclaim the property from him upon his wife's death (see *Ra'ah* and *Meiri*).

The Geonim disagree about whether the husband must compensate the buyer when he reclaims the property that was sold by his wife. Some maintain that since the sale became null and void when the woman died, the buyer can demand that the purchase money be returned to him. Others maintain that since the husband is considered the first buyer of the property, and since he is not responsible for his wife's debts, he may reclaim his wife's usufruct property without paying anything to the buyer.

Rabbenu Ḥananel and *Rif* (and most Rishonim) rule in accordance with the second view that the husband need not pay the buyer for the property. But if the money paid for the property was still in the wife's possession at the time of her death, the husband must return it to the buyer.

Ramban discusses the law in a case where the woman sold her usufruct property and pledged the rest of her assets to reimburse the buyer in the event that the property was seized by a creditor, and she later acquired property by way of a gift or an inheritance. In such a case the buyer may be entitled to compensation from the husband, for the husband's right to the property acquired by the woman after she sold her usufruct property did not precede that of the buyer.

HALAKHAH

הָאִשָּׁה שֶׁמָּכְרָה בְּנִכְסֵי מְלוֹג **If a woman sold part of her usufruct property.** "If a woman sells her usufruct property after she marries, and she dies during her husband's lifetime, her husband can reclaim the property from the buyers, in accordance with the enactment made in Usha." (*Rambam, Sefer Nashim, Hilkhot Ishut* 22:7; *Shulḥan Arukh, Even HaEzer* 90:9.)

TRANSLATION AND COMMENTARY

passed into law while the Sanhedrin was sitting in Usha?" [1] Rabbi Abbahu **said to him: "Rabbi Yose bar Ḥanina** is the greatest expert on the legislation passed in Usha." [2] Rav Yitzḥak bar Yosef then went to Rabbi Yose bar Ḥanina and **studied** the various enactments **with him forty times** over, [3] until he was so familiar with them that **it seemed to him as if they were resting in his pocket.**

אַשְׁרֵי שֹׁמְרֵי מִשְׁפָּט [4] Returning to the issue of maintaining one's children while they are minors, the Gemara now cites the following Midrashic exposition: The verse states (Psalms 106:3): **"Happy are they who keep justice, and do righteousness at all times."** [5] A question may be asked regarding this verse: **Is it** really **possible to do righteousness** — i.e., give charity — **at all times?** [6] Is a poor person who is deserving of charity always within easy reach? Therefore **our Rabbis who were in Yavneh expounded, and some say** that **it was Rabbi Eliezer** who suggested this interpretation: [7] **This** verse **refers to someone who maintains his sons and daughters while they are minors.** Since a father is not legally liable for the maintenance of his minor children, the support he provides for them is regarded as charity. And since children are constantly in need of financial support, a father who maintains his children acts charitably at all times. [8] **Rabbi Shmuel bar Naḥmani said: This** verse **refers to someone who raises an orphan boy or an orphan girl in his house and marries them off.** Since a person is under no legal obligation to raise someone else's children, bringing up orphan children can surely be regarded as being engaged in charitable activities at all times.

הוֹן וָעֹשֶׁר בְּבֵיתוֹ [9] The Gemara continues with another Midrashic exposition: The verse states (Psalms 112:3): **"Wealth and riches shall be in his house, and his righteousness endures forever."** How is it possible for a person's wealth to remain, and at the same time for his charity to endure forever? [10] **Rav Huna and Rav**

[1] אֲמַר לֵיהּ: ״רַבִּי יוֹסֵי בַּר חֲנִינָא״. [2] תָּנָא מִינֵּיהּ אַרְבְּעִין זִימְנִין, [3] וְדָמֵי לֵיהּ כְּמַאן דְּמַנְחָא לֵיהּ בְּכִיסְתֵּיהּ.

[4] ״אַשְׁרֵי שֹׁמְרֵי מִשְׁפָּט, עֹשֵׂה צְדָקָה בְכָל עֵת״. [5] וְכִי אֶפְשָׁר לַעֲשׂוֹת צְדָקָה בְּכָל עֵת? [6] דָּרְשׁוּ רַבּוֹתֵינוּ שֶׁבְּיַבְנֶה, וְאָמְרִי לָהּ רַבִּי אֱלִיעֶזֶר: [7] זֶה הַזָּן בָּנָיו וּבְנוֹתָיו כְּשֶׁהֵן קְטַנִּים. [8] רַבִּי שְׁמוּאֵל בַּר נַחְמָנִי אָמַר: זֶה הַמְגַדֵּל יָתוֹם וִיתוֹמָה בְּתוֹךְ בֵּיתוֹ וּמַשִּׂיאָן.

[9] ״הוֹן וָעֹשֶׁר בְּבֵיתוֹ, וְצִדְקָתוֹ עֹמֶדֶת לָעַד״. [10] רַב הוּנָא וְרַב

LITERAL TRANSLATION

[1] He said to him: "Rabbi Yose bar Ḥanina." [2] He learned [it] from him forty times, [3] and it seemed to him as if he had it lying in his pocket.

[4] "Happy are they who keep justice, and do righteousness at all times." [5] But is it possible to do righteousness at all times? [6] Our Rabbis who were in Yavneh, and some say [it was] Rabbi Eliezer, expounded: [7] This is someone who maintains his sons and his daughters while they are minors. [8] Rabbi Shmuel bar Naḥmani said: This is someone who brings up an orphan boy or an orphan girl in his house and marries them off.

[9] "Wealth and riches shall be in his house, and his righteousness endures forever." [10] Rav Huna and Rav

RASHI

תנא מיניה — דרבי יוסי בר חנינא מרה הוא. **זה הזן בניו ובנותיו קטנים** — שתמיד יום ולילה הן עליו, והיא צדקה, שאינו חיוב עליו בהם. **הון ועושר בביתו** — שאין הממון כלה, ואף על פי כן — צדקתו עומדת לעד.

NOTES

תָּנָא מִינֵּיהּ אַרְבְּעִין זִימְנִין **He learned it from him forty times.** *Rashi* explains that Rav Yitzḥak bar Yosef confirmed forty times that the source of the traditions concerning the Ushan enactments was Rabbi Yose bar Ḥanina.

Ḥatam Sofer suggests that Rav Yitzḥak bar Yosef originally thought that these traditions had been taught by Rabbi Yehudah bar Ḥanina. In order to fix the correction in his mind, so that he would not be confused about the matter in the future, it was necessary for Rav Yitzḥak bar Yosef to repeat the corrected version to himself forty times.

Maharshal (followed by our commentary) argues that it was not the source of the traditions that Rav Yitzḥak bar Yosef committed to memory, but rather the contents of those traditions. Once he heard that an authority of the stature of Rabbi Yose bar Ḥanina was the source of those traditions, he set his mind to studying them thoroughly.

הַזָּן בָּנָיו וּבְנוֹתָיו **Someone who maintains his sons and his daughters.** *Shittah Mekubbetzet* writes that the Gemara is referring here to a man of limited means who must struggle financially in order to provide for his children. But if a wealthy man maintains his minor children, he is not given the praise of "someone who does charity at all times," for he is supporting them in order to maintain his own social standing (see also *Maharsha*).

HALAKHAH

עֹשֵׂה צְדָקָה בְּכָל עֵת **And do righteousness at all times.** "If someone has sons or daughters over the age of six whom he is no longer obliged to support, but he maintains them in order to allow the sons to study Torah and the daughters to live in a dignified manner, the maintenance that he provides them is considered charity." (*Rambam, Sefer Zeraim, Hilkhot Mattenot Aniyyim* 10:16; *Shulḥan Arukh, Yoreh De'ah* 251:3.)

TRANSLATION AND COMMENTARY

Ḥisda disagreed about the matter. [1]**One said: This** verse **refers to someone who studies the Torah and teaches it** to others. His wealth remains with him even when he acts charitably and teaches Torah to others. [2]**And the other said: This** verse refers to **someone who writes** copies of **the Torah, the Prophets, and the Writings, and lends them to others.** His wealth remains in his house, for the scrolls that he writes remain his, but his charity endures forever, for the people who study those scrolls will continue to benefit from his acts of kindness.

וּרְאֵה בָנִים לְבָנֶיךָ [3]The Gemara cites one further Midrashic exposition: The verse states (Psalms 128:6): **"And you shall see your children's children, peace be upon Israel."** What is the connection between living to see one's grandchildren and peace for the Jewish people? [4]**Rabbi Yehoshua ben Levi said: Once your children have children** of their own, **there will be peace upon Israel,** [5]**for they will not come to *ḥalitzah*** or to **levirate marriage.** A man whose brother has died without children is obligated by Torah law to marry his deceased brother's widow or to grant her *ḥalitzah*, the ceremony that frees her from the obligation to marry her brother-in-law and allows her to marry someone else. If all one's children have their own children, there will never be a need for levirate marriage or for *ḥalitzah*, and the family will be spared the strife that sometimes arises when levirate marriage or *ḥalitzah* is necessary. [6]**Rabbi Shmuel bar Naḥmani said: Once your children have children** of their own, **there will be peace upon the judges of Israel, for** your estate will pass to your children, [7]and your other relatives **will not come to quarrel** with the judges about matters concerning the estate.

זֶה מִדְרָשׁ דָּרַשׁ [8]The Gemara now returns to our Mishnah, which stated: **"The following interpretation was expounded by Rabbi Elazar ben Azaryah before the Sages** in the Academy at Yavneh: Just as sons do

חִסְדָּא. [1]חַד אֲמַר: זֶה הַלּוֹמֵד תּוֹרָה וּמְלַמְּדָהּ. [2]וְחַד אֲמַר: זֶה הַכּוֹתֵב תּוֹרָה, נְבִיאִים, וּכְתוּבִים, וּמַשְׁאִילָן לַאֲחֵרִים. [3]״וּרְאֵה בָנִים לְבָנֶיךָ שָׁלוֹם עַל יִשְׂרָאֵל״. [4]אָמַר רַבִּי יְהוֹשֻׁעַ בֶּן לֵוִי: כֵּיוָן שֶׁבָּנִים לְבָנֶיךָ, שָׁלוֹם עַל יִשְׂרָאֵל, [5]דְּלָא אָתֵי לִידֵי חֲלִיצָה וְיִבּוּם. [6]רַבִּי שְׁמוּאֵל בַּר נַחְמָנִי אָמַר: כֵּיוָן שֶׁבָּנִים לְבָנֶיךָ, שָׁלוֹם עַל דַּיָּינֵי יִשְׂרָאֵל, [7]דְּלָא אָתֵי לְאִינְצוּיֵי. [8]״זֶה מִדְרָשׁ דָּרַשׁ רַבִּי אֶלְעָזָר

LITERAL TRANSLATION

Ḥisda [disagreed]. [1]One said: This is someone who studies the Torah and teaches it. [2]And one said: This is someone who writes the Torah, the Prophets, and the Writings, and lends them to others.

[3]"And you shall see your children's children, peace be upon Israel." [4]Rabbi Yehoshua ben Levi said: Once your children have children, there is peace upon Israel, [5]for they do not come to *ḥalitzah* or levirate marriage. [6]Rabbi Shmuel bar Naḥmani said: Once your children have children, there is peace upon the judges of Israel, [7]for they do not come to quarrel.

[8]"Rabbi Elazar ben Azaryah expounded this interpretation

RASHI

זה הלומד תורה ומלמדה – מתקיימת בו. הרי ״הון ועושר בביתו וצדקתו עומדת לעד״ – על שטרח ללמד לתלמידים. **זה הכותב כו׳** – הספרים קיימים לו, שאינם כלים, וצדקתו עומדת לעד. **לאינצויי** – מי קרוב וקודם בנחלה.

NOTES

שָׁלוֹם עַל דַּיָּינֵי יִשְׂרָאֵל There is peace upon the judges of Israel. *Rashi* explains that if someone is survived by children, his other relatives will not quarrel with the judges about the estate, for all will agree that it should pass to his children.

Tosafot (cited by *Ritva*) asks: Why, then, does the verse speak (literally) of "your sons' sons"? Would not the issue of the estate be settled just as amicably if the deceased were survived by a daughter, for all would agree that in the absence of male children the entire inheritance passes to the surviving daughter?

Ri answers: If all of a person's sons have sons of their own, he will leave an equal share to each of his children. But if one son has a son of his own, and another does not, the grandfather will leave a larger share to the one with a son of his own, and as a result the children will come to quarrel about the estate.

Hafla'ah suggests that what the Gemara means to say is as follows: If someone is survived by adult children who are old enough to have children of their own, there will be peace upon the judges of Israel, for the estate can be disposed of without any difficulties. But if the deceased is survived by minor children, the judges will have to act on behalf of the orphans and settle the disputes that may arise if anyone brings a claim against the estate.

Rabbenu Yeḥiel explains that if someone is survived by his son's daughter and by his own daughter, the judges will come to quarrel with the Sadducee judges, who maintain that in such a case the daughter is entitled to half of the estate, whereas according to the Halakhah the granddaughter receives the entire estate. But if the deceased is survived by his son's son and his own daughter, there will be peace upon the judges of Israel, for in such a case even the Sadducees agree that the entire estate passes to the grandson.

BACKGROUND

יְתֵיב רַב יוֹסֵף קַמֵּיהּ דְּרַב הַמְנוּנָא **Rav Yosef sat before Rav Hamnuna.** This statement provides interesting evidence about the structure of Babylonian academies during the Talmudic period. Specifically, the teacher sat and expounded Torah before the listeners. Usually, distinguished scholars sat in the front row of the audience, while other, less distinguished, scholars sat behind them. On days when no public lecture was held, the scholars who sat in the front commented on the lecture, and their discussions with the lecturer eventually became part of the Talmud.

LANGUAGE

אֲוַושׁ **Called out.** This word, which literally means "made a noise like the blowing of the wind," may possibly be derived from the Middle Persian *avac*, and it is often used to describe the noise made by a crowd.

TRANSLATION AND COMMENTARY

not inherit their mother's ketubah until after their father's death, similarly minor daughters are not entitled to be maintained from their father's estate until after his death." [50B] The Gemara notes that there is another point in common between the enactment that a woman's sons inherit their mother's ketubah from their father and the enactment that her minor daughters are entitled to maintenance from their father's estate. [1]It was related that **Rav Yosef** once **sat** in the Academy **before Rav Hamnuna** while the latter was giving a lecture, **and Rav Hamnuna sat** before his disciples **and said:** [2]**Just as sons inherit only land** and not movable property, [3]**so too are** minor **daughters** entitled to be **maintained only from** the **land** of their father's estate and not from the movable property. [4]**Everybody** hearing the lecture began to **call out** in protest: [5]Is it really true that if **someone** dies and **leaves land, his sons inherit** that land **from him,** [6]**but** if **he** dies and **does not leave** any **land, his sons do not inherit from him** the movable goods that make up his estate? Surely all of a person's property — both his real estate and his movable goods —

לִפְנֵי חֲכָמִים, כו׳״. [50B] [1]יְתֵיב רַב יוֹסֵף קַמֵּיהּ דְּרַב הַמְנוּנָא, וִיתֵיב רַב הַמְנוּנָא וְקָאָמַר: [2]כְּשֵׁם שֶׁאֵין הַבָּנִים יוֹרְשִׁין אֶלָּא מִן הַקַּרְקַע, [3]כָּךְ אֵין הַבָּנוֹת נִיזּוֹנוֹת אֶלָּא מִן הַקַּרְקַע. [4]אֲוַושׁ עֲלֵיהּ כּוּלֵּי עָלְמָא: [5]דְּשָׁבֵיק אַרְעָא — הוּא דְּיָרְתֵי לֵיהּ בְּנֵיהּ, [6]דְּלָא שָׁבֵיק אַרְעָא — לָא יָרְתֵי לֵיהּ בְּנֵיהּ?

LITERAL TRANSLATION

before the Sages, etc." [50B] [1]Rav Yosef sat before Rav Hamnuna, and Rav Hamnuna sat and said: [2]Just as the sons inherit only from land, [3]so too are the daughters maintained only from land. [4]Everyone (lit., "the whole world") called out at him: [5][Someone] who leaves land — his sons inherit from him, [6][but someone] who does not leave land — his sons do not inherit from him?

RASHI

אווש עליה כולי עלמא — והוא לא פירש ד״בנים יורשין״ דקאמר, כתובת בנין דיכרין היא, וסבורים שסתם ירושה קאמר, שאין הבנים יורשין מטלטלין.

NOTES

כָּךְ אֵין הַבָּנוֹת נִיזּוֹנוֹת אֶלָּא מִן הַקַּרְקַע **So too are the daughters maintained only from land.** *Shittah Mekubbetzet* notes that Rav Hamnuna's initial assumption is that sons inherit their mother's ketubah only from the landed property of their father's estate, and that Rav Hamnuna infers from this that the daughters likewise are entitled to collect their maintenance only from the landed property of the father's estate, but not from the movable goods. Why, asks *Shittah Mekubbetzet*, was the law regarding *ketubat benin dikhrin* clearer to Rav Hamnuna than the law concerning the daughters' maintenance? Both enactments are recorded in the woman's ketubah, but in neither case is such a limitation mentioned!

Shittah Mekubbetzet answers that, regarding the enactment of *ketubat benin dikhrin,* the Mishnah (below, 91a) states explicitly that the sons are only entitled to collect their mother's ketubah from the landed property of their father's estate. (This also explains why *Rashi* provides such a detailed explanation here of those Mishnayot which deal with that enactment.) Rav Hamnuna assumed that all his listeners were familiar with these Mishnayot, and drew an inference regarding the daughter's maintenance.

Hafla'ah asks: Is it not obvious that the sons collect their mother's ketubah and the daughters collect their maintenance only from the landed property of their father's estate? For the *ketubat benin dikhrin* and the daughters' right to maintenance stem from the conditions of their mother's ketubah. And since the ketubah itself can be collected only from landed property, it should follow that the ketubah stipulations should also be collected only from such property.

Hafla'ah explains that the ketubah stipulations are not always treated like the ketubah itself. For example, a woman is entitled to maintenance by virtue of a condition in her ketubah, and that maintenance may be collected even from the husband's movable goods.

דְּשָׁבֵיק אַרְעָא — הוּא דְּיָרְתֵי לֵיהּ בְּנֵיהּ **Someone who leaves land — his sons inherit from him.** Many commentators ask: How could Rav Hamnuna's disciples have possibly thought that their teacher was dealing with the sons' inheritance by Torah law and that he was ruling that they inherit only the landed property of their father's estate but not his movable goods?

Some suggest that Rav Hamnuna's disciples thought that

HALAKHAH

שֶׁאֵין הַבָּנִים יוֹרְשִׁין אֶלָּא מִן הַקַּרְקַע **Just as the sons inherit only from land.** "The sons who are entitled to their mother's ketubah by virtue of the enactment of *ketubat benin dikhrin* inherit it only from the landed property of their father's estate. According to *Rambam,* this ruling applies even after the Geonic enactment that the ketubah and the other rights that stem from conditions added to the ketubah can be satisfied from the husband's movable property. According to others, the *ketubat benin dikhrin* is treated like the rest of the conditions added to the ketubah, and can be collected from the movable property of the father's estate. *Rema* writes (*Even HaEzer* 111:16) that some authorities (*Rosh,* and *Maggid Mishneh* in the name of certain *Geonim*) maintain that the enactment of *ketubat benin dikhrin* does not apply at all today, for it has anyway become customary for fathers to give their daughters a substantial dowry." (*Rambam, Sefer Nashim, Hilkhot Ishut* 16:7; *Shulḥan Arukh, Even HaEzer* 111:14.)

TRANSLATION AND COMMENTARY

make up the estate that passes to his heirs! [1] **Rav Yosef said to** Rav Hamnuna: **"Perhaps, sir, you were speaking about** *ketubat benin dikhrin*, **the ketubah of male children,** the Rabbinic enactment that the sons of a marriage inherit their mother's ketubah (if she dies before her husband and leaves him her estate) over and above the portion of their father's estate that they must share equally with the sons from another marriage. And what you meant to say was that sons who are entitled to their mother's ketubah by virtue of the enactment of *ketubat benin dikhrin* inherit it only from the landed property in their father's estate, but not from the movable goods. Similarly, minor daughters who are entitled to maintenance from their father's estate may collect their maintenance only from the landed property of his estate, not from the movable goods. But as for inheritance in general, the sons certainly inherit both their father's movable property and his land." [2] Rav Hamnuna **said to** Rav Yosef: "You, **sir, being a great man,** [3] **understood what I** meant to **say,** but all the others misunderstood me."

אָמַר רַבִּי חִיָּיא בַּר יוֹסֵף [4] **Rabbi Ḥiyya bar Yosef said:** a case occurred in which orphan girls appeared before Rav, asking for maintenance from their father's estate. [5] When **Rav** saw that the father had not left any land, he ruled that **the daughters** were entitled to be **maintained from the wheat of the *aliyyah***, a term which refers to movable goods of some kind and which will be explained immediately by the Gemara.

אִיבַּעֲיָא לְהוּ [6] **The** following **question arose** when the Amoraim began to discuss Rav's ruling: Two different obligations are imposed on heirs with respect to the daughters of the deceased. First, daughters while they are minors are entitled to maintenance from their father's estate until they reach majority or until they are betrothed. Second, they are entitled to receive a portion of the estate as their dowry, as if the father were still alive. Now, which obligation was Rav talking about and what is the significance of the expression "wheat of the *aliyyah*"? [7] Perhaps Rav's ruling refers only to **the dowry.** This would mean that the daughters

[1] אֲמַר לֵיהּ רַב יוֹסֵף: ״וְדִלְמָא כְּתוּבַּת בְּנִין דִּכְרִין קָאָמַר מָר?״ [2] אֲמַר לֵיהּ: ״מָר, דְּגַבְרָא רַבָּא הוּא, [3] יָדַע מַאי קָאָמִינָא״.

[4] אֲמַר רַבִּי חִיָּיא בַּר יוֹסֵף: [5] רַב זָן מֵחִיטֵּי דַּעֲלִיָּיה.

[6] אִיבַּעֲיָא לְהוּ: [7] פַּרְנָסָה הָוְיָא,

LITERAL TRANSLATION

[1] Rav Yosef said to him: "Perhaps, master, you were speaking of the ketubah of male children?" [2] He said to him: "[You,] master, who are a great man, [3] understand what I said."

[4] Rabbi Ḥiyya bar Yosef said: [5] Rav maintained [orphan girls] from wheat of *aliyyah*.

[6] It was asked of them: [7] Was it [for] the dowry,

RASHI

דלמא כתובת בנין דיכרין קאמר מר — לפי ששתי תקנות הללו שתקנו חכמים בתנאי כתובה לומדות זו מזו, ובכתובת בנין דכרין תנן, בפרק "מי שהיה נשוי" (כתובות צא,א), דאין נגבית מן המטלטלין. דתנן: רבי שמעון אומר: אפילו יש שם נכסים שאין להם אחריות — אינן כלום, עד שיהא שם נכסים שיש להן אחריות מותר על שתי הכתובות דינר. והתם מפרש להילכתא כתובת בנין דיכרין. דתנן: מי שהיה נשוי שתי נשים ומתו, ואחר כך מת הוא, ויתומין של כל אחת מבקשין כתובת אמן. כגון שכתובת האחת מרובה, או אם שתיהן שוות — פעמים שבני האחת רבים ובני האחת מועטין, ואותן המועטין מבקשים כתובת אמן לחלקוה ביניהן, ובני השניה יחלקו את כתובת אמן ביניהן. ובאין עליהם מכח תנאי כתובת אמן, שכתוב בה "כתובת בנין דכרין דיהווין ליכי מינאי אינון ירתון כסף כתובתיך כו׳". אם יש מותר דינר על שתי הכתובות, שתתקיים בו נחלה דאורייתא — אלו נוטלין כתובת אמן, ואלו נוטלין כתובת אמן, ואם לאו — חולקין בשוה למנין גולגלותם, דבמקום דמיעקרא נחלה דאורייתא — לא תקון רבנן. **מר דגברא רבה הוא ידע** — שאין ללמוד מזון בנות מירושת בנים, אלא מירושת כתובת בנין דכרין, שבאה מכח תנאי כתובה כמותה. **רב זן מחיטי דעלייה** — יתומות באו לפניו ותובעות מזונות מחיטי דאביהן, שלא היו שם קרקעות אלא מטלטלין, ונתן להם. **פרנסה הואי** — לא מזונות היו, אלא פרנסת נדוניא לינשא, והיא גביא ממטלטלי.

SAGES

רַבִּי חִיָּיא בַּר יוֹסֵף **Rabbi Ḥiyya bar Yosef.** A second generation Babylonian Amora who later immigrated to Eretz Israel, Rabbi Ḥiyya bar Yosef was one of Rav's outstanding students and transmitted many of his teachings. After Rav's death, Rabbi Ḥiyya studied with Shmuel before moving to Eretz Israel, where he became a student-colleague of Rabbi Yoḥanan (with whom he had many Halakhic discussions). He may also have served as a Rabbinical judge in Tiberias.

NOTES

he was saying that the rule that the existence of sons precludes the daughters from inheriting their father's estate applies only to his landed property, for the verses that teach the Biblical laws of inheritance (Numbers 27:6-11) refer explicitly only to landed property. But the movable goods of the father's estate are divided equally between the sons and the daughters. It was against this mistaken understanding of Rav Hamnuna's ruling that his disciples raised their objection (*Ḥatam Sofer*).

מֵחִיטֵּי דַּעֲלִיָּיה **From wheat of *aliyyah*.** It is somewhat puzzling why the Gemara preferred to take the expression "wheat of *aliyyah*" as an allusion to the position of Shmuel or to the statement of Rav Yitzḥak bar Yosef, rather than to understand it according to its plain sense as referring to wheat stored in an attic. The answer may be based on the fact that the building practices in Babylonia were different from those in Eretz Israel. Unlike in Eretz Israel, where houses were built of stone and an upper story was often added to a building, in Babylonia it was not common practice to erect a structure with two floors, and if a second story was built, it was usually used as additional living space and not as a storage area. In that case, it is reasonable to assume that the ruling issued by the Babylonian Sage Rav was not referring to wheat stored in the attic of a house.

SAGES

רַב יִצְחָק בַּר יוֹסֵף Rav Yitzḥak bar Yosef. An Amora of the third and fourth generations, Rav Yitzḥak bar Yosef (who was known as Yitzḥak Sumka, which means Yitzḥak the Red) originally came from Babylonia and moved to Eretz Israel, where he studied with Rabbi Abbahu and Rabbi Yirmeyah and other members of their generation. After some time he seems to have returned to Babylonia and settled there.

Although his statements are often cited in the Talmud, he also transmits the teachings of his predecessors. He is one of the most important sources of the teachings of Rabbi Yoḥanan, though the accuracy of his reporting was sometimes doubted. He also cites the teachings of earlier generations.

רַבִּי בַּנַּאי אֲחוּהּ דְּרַבִּי חִיָּיא בַּר אַבָּא Rabbi Bannai (Rabbenai) the brother of Rabbi Ḥiyya bar Abba. A Babylonian Amora of the second and third generations. See *Ketubot,* Part II, p. 111.

TRANSLATION AND COMMENTARY

collect their actual maintenance only from the landed property of their father's estate, but that they collect their dowries even from his movable goods. **And what did** Rav **mean** when he said that they were to be maintained from wheat of the *aliyyah*? **"According to the status** [עִילּוּיָיא in Aramaic] **of the father"** and an assessment of what he would have given his daughter as a dowry had he still been alive. [1] If we interpret *aliyyah* in this way, Rav's ruling **is in accordance with** the viewpoint of **Shmuel, for Shmuel said:** [2] In order to determine the amount that an orphan daughter may collect **as her dowry, we assess** how much **the father** would have been willing to give his daughter as a dowry. We consider the father's means, his social standing, and his personal character, as well as whether his disposition was mean or generous. Since the dowry given to an orphan daughter is an assessment of what the father himself would have given her had he still been alive, she is entitled to collect it even from movable goods, if that is all that the father owned. This is one possible understanding of Rav's ruling. [3] On the other hand, we may **perhaps** say that when Rav ruled that the orphan daughters were to be maintained from their father's movable property, he **was** referring to their **actual maintenance.** [4] **And what did he mean** when he said that they were to be maintained from the wheat of the ***aliyyah?*** He meant that the orphan girls were to be maintained from the movable goods in their father's estate **"on the basis of the good things that were said in the upper room** [עֲלִיָּה — *aliyyah* in Hebrew]." [5] **For Rav Yitzḥak bar Yosef said:** When religious persecution prevented the Sages from convening in the House of Study and forced them to meet **in the upper room, they enacted that** orphan **daughters are to be maintained** not only from the landed property of their father's estate but **from** his **movable goods** as well.

תָּא שְׁמַע [6] The Gemara proposes an answer to its question. concerning the maintenance of orphan girls. **Come and hear** the following story: **In the hands of Rabbi Bannai, the brother of Rabbi Ḥiyya bar Abba,**

TALMUD

וּמַאי עֲלִיָּיה ״מֵעִילּוּיָיא דְּאָב״, [1] וּכְדִשְׁמוּאֵל, דְּאָמַר שְׁמוּאֵל: [2] לְפַרְנָסָה שָׁמִין בְּאָב? [3] אוֹ דִּלְמָא מְזוֹנֵי מַמָּשׁ הֲוָה, [4] וּמַאי עֲלִיָּיה ״מִדְּבָרִים טוֹבִים שֶׁנֶּאֶמְרוּ בַּעֲלִיָּיה״, [5] דְּאָמַר רַב יִצְחָק בַּר יוֹסֵף: בַּעֲלִיָּיה הִתְקִינוּ שֶׁיְּהוּ בָּנוֹת נִיזּוֹנוֹת מִן הַמִּטַּלְטְלִין?

[6] תָּא שְׁמַע: בִּידֵיהּ דְּרַבִּי בַּנַּאי, אֲחוּהּ דְּרַבִּי חִיָּיא בַּר אַבָּא,

LITERAL TRANSLATION

and what *aliyyah* [means is] "according to the status of the father," [1] and it is in accordance with Shmuel, for Shmuel said: [2] For the dowry we assess the father? [3] Or was it perhaps actual maintenance, [4] and what *aliyyah* [means is] "from the good things that were said in the upper room," [5] for Rav Yitzḥak bar Yosef said: In the upper room they enacted that daughters are to be maintained from movable goods?

[6] Come [and] hear: In the hands of Rabbi Bannai, the brother of Rabbi Ḥiyya bar Abba,

RASHI

וכדשמואל דאמר לפרנסה שמין באב — אומדין לפי וותרנותו של אב, או לפי קמצנותו, אם היה קיים — כך וכך היה נותן להם מנכסים הללו. וכיון דאומד דעתו שיימינן — מקרקעי ומטלטלי שוים בכך. **מעילווייא דאב** — לפי אומד עילוי דעת וותרנותו. **או דלמא מזוני ממש** — ואף על גב דתנאי כתובה כתובה, ואין נגבית ממטלטלי, דכל אסמכתא דשטרי אקרקעות היא לפי שעומדות בעין — רב סבר לה כתקנת עלייה, והיינו דקאמר: מחיטי דעלייה.

NOTES

מֵעִילּוּיָיא דְּאָב According to the status of the father. Elsewhere (below, 68a), a Baraita is cited which states that the father's heirs give the daughter one-tenth of the estate as her dowry. Shmuel rules that the daughter collects one-tenth of her father's estate only if it is impossible to assess how much the father would have been willing to give her as her dowry. But if such an assessment is possible, the heirs must give the daughter a dowry in accordance with this assessment.

Rashi explains that, according to Shmuel's ruling, we award the daughter more or less than one-tenth of the father's estate, depending on our assessment of his wishes.

According to *Rabbenu Ḥananel* (cited by *Tosafot* and other Rishonim), we assess how much the father would have given his daughter only so as to reduce the size of her dowry, but the daughter may never collect more than one-tenth of her father's estate, even if it is clear that he would have been willing to give her more. The Rishonim discuss these two positions at great length, adducing support for and raising objections against each view.

HALAKHAH

לְפַרְנָסָה שָׁמִין בְּאָב For the dowry we assess the father. "If a man dies and is survived by a daughter, the court assesses how much he would have wanted to give her as her dowry, and assigns her that amount from the property of his estate. The court considers his means, his social standing, and what his friends and acquaintances say about his disposition, as well as what he gave his other daughters when he married them off. If the court is unable to determine how much the father would have wanted to give his daughter, she is awarded one-tenth of his estate." (*Rambam, Sefer Nashim, Hilkhot Ishut* 20:3; *Shulḥan Arukh, Even HaEzer* 113:1.)

TRANSLATION AND COMMENTARY

were movable goods belonging to orphan boys, of whose father's estate Rabbi Bannai had been appointed administrator. [1]When the daughters of the deceased **came before Shmuel,** asking to be supported from their father's estate, Shmuel **said to** Rabbi Bannai: **"Go, and maintain** the daughters from the movable goods belonging to the sons." Now, when Shmuel instructed Rabbi Bannai to maintain the daughters from the movable goods entrusted to his care, [2]**was he not** referring **to** actual **maintenance,** so that we can conclude that Shmuel **agrees with Rav Yitzḥak bar Yosef** that an orphan daughter can collect her maintenance even from movable goods?

לָא [3]The Gemara rejects this argument: **No,** an orphan daughter may collect her maintenance only from the landed property of her deceased father. When Shmuel told Rabbi Bannai to maintain the daughters from the movable goods belonging to the orphan boys, he was **referring to the dowry,** which he maintains may be collected not only from the landed property of the father's estate but also from his movable goods. [4]**And Shmuel** issued his **ruling in accordance with his own opinion** mentioned above, [5]**for Shmuel said:** In order to determine the amount that an orphan daughter may collect **as her dowry, we assess** how much **the father** would have been willing to give his daughter as a dowry. She may collect the dowry even from movable goods, if that is all the father owned.

הֲוָה עוּבְדָא בִּנְהַרְדְּעָא [6]The Gemara relates that **a case occurred in Neharde'a** in which an orphan girl asked to be maintained from the movable goods of her father's estate, **and the judges of Neharde'a adjudicated the matter** in her favor, awarding her maintenance from her father's movable goods. [7]**A** similar **case occurred in Pumbedita, and** there too **Rav Ḥana bar Bizna let** orphan **daughters collect** maintenance from the movable property of the father's estate. [8]When he heard about these rulings, **Rav Naḥman said to** the judges: "The judgments you rendered were in error, for an orphan girl is not entitled to receive maintenance from the movable goods of her father's estate, but only from the landed property. [9]**Go** now and correct your mistakes, **and return** to the orphan boys whatever you collected from them on behalf of the daughters. [10]For **if** you do **not** do so, **I will order your mansions to be seized from you** and handed over to the orphans, for a judge who issues an incorrect ruling is liable for the financial loss that his ruling causes."

רַבִּי אַמִי [11]The Gemara relates further that when a similiar case was brought before **Rabbi Ammi and Rabbi Assi** for adjudication, they **thought** to rule that **the orphan girls were to be maintained from** the **movable goods** of their father's estate. [12]When **Rabbi Ya'akov bar Idi** heard that Rabbi Ammi and Rabbi Assi were

הָווּ מִטַּלְטְלִין דְּיָתְמֵי. [1]אָתוּ לְקַמֵּיהּ דִּשְׁמוּאֵל, אֲמַר לֵיהּ: "זִיל זוֹן". [2]מַאי לָאו לִמְזוֹנֵי, וּכְדְרַב יִצְחָק בַּר יוֹסֵף סְבִירָא לֵיהּ?

[3]לָא, הָתָם לְפַרְנָסָה הֲוַאי, [4]וּשְׁמוּאֵל לְטַעֲמֵיהּ. [5]דְּאָמַר שְׁמוּאֵל: לְפַרְנָסָה שָׁמִין בְּאָב.

[6]הֲוָה עוּבְדָא בִּנְהַרְדְּעָא, וְדוּן דַּיָּינֵי דִּנְהַרְדְּעָא. [7]בְּפוּמְבְּדִיתָא, וְאַגְבֵּי רַב חָנָא בַּר בִּיזְנָא. [8]אֲמַר לְהוּ רַב נַחְמָן: [9]"זִילוּ אַהַדְרוּ, [10]וְאִי לָא, מַגְבֵּינָא לְכוּ לְאַפַּדְנַיְיכוּ מִינַּיְיכוּ.

[11]רַבִּי אַמִי וְרַבִּי אַסִי סְבוּר לְמֵיזַן מִמִּטַּלְטְלֵי. [12]אֲמַר לְהוּ רַבִּי יַעֲקֹב בַּר אִידִי:

LITERAL TRANSLATION

were movable goods belonging to orphans. [1]They came before Shmuel, [and] he said to him: "Go [and] maintain [them]." [2]Was it not for maintenance, and he agrees with Rav Yitzḥak bar Yosef?

[3]No, there it was for the dowry, [4]and Shmuel [ruled] in accordance with his own opinion. [5]For Shmuel said: For the dowry we assess by the father.

[6]There was a case in Neharde'a, and the judges of Neharde'a judged [the matter]. [7][There was a case] in Pumbedita, and Rav Ḥana bar Bizna collected [for daughters]. [8]Rav Naḥman said to them: [9]"Go [and] return [it], [10]and if not, I will order your mansions to be seized from you."

[11]Rabbi Ammi and Rabbi Assi thought to maintain [orphan girls] from movable goods. [12]Rabbi Ya'akov ben Idi said to to them:

RASHI

זיל זון — את הבנות. **הוה עובדא ודון דייני** — לזון מן המטלטלין.

SAGES

רַב חָנָא בַּר בִּיזְנָא Rav Ḥana bar Bizna. A Babylonian Amora of the second and third generations, Rav Ḥana bar Bizna, who was a Rabbinical judge in Pumbedita, often transmitted the teachings of Rabbi Shimon Ḥasida. He was renowned among the scholars of his time both as an expert on Aggadah and as a Halakhic authority.

BACKGROUND

מַגְבֵּינָא לְכוּ לְאַפַּדְנַיְיכוּ מִינַּיְיכוּ I will order your mansions to be seized from you. Rav Naḥman was the greatest judge of his generation, and his decisions in civil suits were regarded as authoritative. Hence his influence was very great. Moreover, Rav Naḥman was connected by marriage to the House of the Exilarch, and he could use the power of the authorities to impose his judgments. Thus his threat bore considerable weight.

LANGUAGE

לְאַפַּדְנַיְיכוּ Your mansions. The word **אפדנא**, meaning "mansion" or "palace," appears in the Bible (Daniel 11:45), and is derived from the Old Persian *apadana.* Later it was borrowed by other ancient languages.

NOTES

מַגְבֵּינָא לְכוּ לְאַפַּדְנַיְיכוּ מִינַּיְיכוּ I will order your mansions to be seized from you. Rav Naḥman's demand that the judges return whatever had been collected from the orphan boys implies that he considered the judges' rulings to be contrary to the clear and established Halakhah, and thus invalid. Consequently, Rav Naḥman himself could have ordered that the rulings be set aside, but he thought that it would be more effective if the judges who issued the mistaken rulings reversed their decisions (*Tosafot*).

As for Rav Naḥman's threat that if the judges failed to correct their mistakes, he would collect their mansions and hand them over to the orphan boys, Rav Naḥman may have been of the opinion that a judge who delivers an erroneous decision is liable for the damage caused by that

1 ״מִילְּתָא דְּרַבִּי יוֹחָנָן וְרֵישׁ לָקִישׁ לָא עָבְדוּ בָּהּ עוּבְדָא אַתּוּן עָבְדִין בָּהּ עוּבְדָא?״
2 רַבִּי אֶלְעָזָר סָבַר לְמֵיזָן מִמְּטַלְטְלִין. 3 אָמַר לְפָנָיו רַבִּי שִׁמְעוֹן בֶּן אֶלְיָקִים: ״רַבִּי, יוֹדֵעַ אֲנִי בְּךָ שֶׁאֵין מִדַּת הַדִּין אַתָּה עוֹשֶׂה, 4 אֶלָּא מִדַּת רַחֲמָנוּת. 5 אֶלָּא שֶׁמָּא יִרְאוּ הַתַּלְמִידִים וְיִקְבְּעוּ הֲלָכָה לְדוֹרוֹת״.
6 הַהוּא דַּאֲתָא לְקַמֵּיהּ דְּרַב יוֹסֵף. 7 אֲמַר לְהוּ: ״הֲבוּ לָהּ מִתַּמְרֵי דְּעַל בּוּדְיָא״. 8 אֲמַר לֵיהּ אַבַּיֵי: ״אִילּוּ בַּעַל חוֹב הֲוָה, כִּי הַאי גַּוְונָא מִי הֲוָה יָהֵיב לֵיהּ מָר?״

TRANSLATION AND COMMENTARY

contemplating giving a decision in favor of the orphan girls, he **said to them:** 1 **"On a matter concerning which Rabbi Yoḥanan and Resh Lakish took no action are you** planning to **take action?** If great Sages like Rabbi Yoḥanan and Resh Lakish were unsure about the law, will you, Rabbi Ammi and Rabbi Assi, dare to take a decision on the matter?"

רַבִּי אֶלְעָזָר 2 When a similar case was brought before **Rabbi Elazar,** he too **thought** to rule that the **orphan girls were to be maintained from** the **movable goods** of their father's estate. 3 When **Rabbi Shimon ben Elyakim** was informed of Rabbi Elazar's impending decision, he **said to him: "Sir, I know that you are not acting in accordance with the** strict **rules of justice,** for you know that an orphan girl is not entitled to maintenance from her father's movable goods. 4 **But** you must be acting in accordance **with the rules of mercy.** You feel sorry for the orphan girls and you want to find a way to support them. 5 **But** I must warn you against issuing such a ruling, **lest the disciples see** how you acted **and establish** your decision as **the law for future generations."**

הַהוּא דַּאֲתָא לְקַמֵּיהּ 6 The Gemara now relates that there was **a certain person** who **came before Rav Yosef** with a question regarding the maintenance to which an orphan girl is entitled. After hearing the particulars of the case, 7 Rav Yosef turned to the orphan sons who had inherited their father's estate and **said to them: "Give** your sister **her** maintenance **from the dates** that are spread out **on the mats** for drying." 8 **Abaye,** who was present, thought that Rav Yosef was awarding the orphan girl maintenance from the movable property of her father's estate, and so he **said to him: "If the claimant had been a creditor, would you, Sir, have awarded him in this manner movable goods** that the debtor's sons inherited from their father? Surely not, for a creditor can recover his debt from the debtor's heirs only from the landed property they have inherited, but not from the movable goods." Now, a creditor's lien on the debtor's property is much stronger than a daughter's lien on her father's estate, for the creditor can recover his debt from the debtor's property even if it has been sold to a third party, whereas the daughter cannot collect her maintenance

LITERAL TRANSLATION

1 "[On] a matter concerning which Rabbi Yoḥanan and Resh Lakish took no action do you take action?"

2 Rabbi Elazar thought to maintain [orphan girls] from movable goods. 3 Rabbi Shimon ben Elyakim said before him: "My teacher, I know that you are not acting [in accordance with] the quality (lit., 'measure') of justice, 4 but [with] the quality of mercy. 5 But perhaps the disciples will see and will establish a Halakhah for [future] generations."

6 Someone came before Rav Yosef. 7 He said to them: "Give her from the dates on the mats." 8 Abaye said to him: "If [the claimant] had been a creditor, would the Master have given him [movable goods] in this manner?"

RASHI

מתמרי דעל בודיא — שהן מטלטלין. **בודיא** — מחצלות שנותנין תחת הדקלין כשגודרין התמרים. **אילו בעל חוב הוה** — כלומר אפילו בעל חוב שיפה כחו לטרוף ממשועבדין אינו גובה ממטלטלין של יתומים, וזו תגבה למזון הבנות שהורע כחן אלל משועבדים?

NOTES

decision, for such damage falls under the category of *garmi* — damage caused indirectly, for which the tortfeasor is liable. Alternatively, Rav Naḥman may not actually have been able to confiscate the judges' properties, but he made the threat anyway in order to intimidate the judges so that they would rectify their mistakes.

אִילּוּ בַּעַל חוֹב הֲוָה If the claimant had been a creditor. *Ḥatam Sofer* raises a number of questions: First, it is somewhat strange that Rav Yosef should award the orphan girl maintenance from the movable goods of her father's estate, for it was Rav Yosef himself who accepted Rav Hamnuna's ruling that an orphan daughter is entitled to maintenance only from the landed property of her father's estate. Furthermore, the analogy of the creditor is quite convincing. Why, then, was it not mentioned earlier in the discussion?

Ḥatam Sofer answers that there was never any doubt that Rav Yosef was of the opinion that an orphan girl is entitled to maintenance only from the landed property of her father's estate. Abaye understood that Rav Yosef was

SAGES

רַבִּי יַעֲקֹב בַּר אִידִי Rabbi Ya'akov bar Idi. A Palestinian Amora of the third generation. See *Ketubot,* Part I, p. 75.

רַבִּי שִׁמְעוֹן בֶּן אֶלְיָקִים Rabbi Shimon ben Elyakim. A Palestinian Amora of the third generation, Rabbi Shimon ben Elyakim is usually called Rabbi Shimon ben Yakim in the Jerusalem Talmud.

He was one of the most important disciples of Rabbi Yoḥanan and Resh Lakish, and he was a colleague of Rabbi Elazar. However, since Rabbi Elazar was the head of the yeshivah, Rabbi Shimon ben Elyakim deferred to him and called him his teacher.

BACKGROUND

שֶׁמָּא יִרְאוּ הַתַּלְמִידִים Perhaps the disciples will see. Practical Halakhic decisions normally serve as extremely important legal precedents, and their force exceeds theoretical decisions arrived at in the House of Study. Rabbi Shimon ben Elyakim was apprehensive lest the practical decision of an important Sage like Rabbi Elazar might serve as a precedent and determine the Halakhah for following generations. In this instance, as in other similar ones, it is suggested to a Sage that he should be cautious and avoid drawing general and permanent conclusions from a single instance in which special circumstances applied.

LANGUAGE

בּוּדְיָא Mats. Some manuscripts read בוריא, and similar forms are found in Persian and Arabic, as well as in late Latin (*buda*). All these words mean "mats made of reeds."

REALIA

מִתַּמְרֵי דְּעַל בּוּדְיָא From the dates on the mats. There are two varieties of dates, moist and dry. The former must be picked immediately after they ripen, so that they will not spoil. Dry dates, however, need not be picked immediately; hence people would spread mats (made of reeds) beneath the palm trees, so that the dates would

TRANSLATION AND COMMENTARY

from property that has been sold by her father or by his heirs. Thus it follows that a daughter is not entitled to maintenance from the movable property of her father's estate. For if a creditor, who is entitled to seize the debtor's property even if it has been transferred to a third party, cannot recover his debt from the movable goods in the hands of the debtor's heirs, then surely a daughter, who is not entitled to collect her maintenance from her father's property if it has been transferred to another person, cannot collect her maintenance from the movable goods belonging to her father's heirs!

אֲמַר לֵיהּ [1] Rav Yosef **said to** Abaye: "You are right that an orphan girl is not entitled to maintenance from the movable property of her father's estate. When I instructed the heirs to maintain the daughter from the dates on the mats, I was not referring to dates that had already been plucked from the trees and spread out on the mats. Rather, **I meant** that they should give her those **dates that** had already ripened and **were** therefore **ready to be** picked and **spread out on** the **mats** for drying. Since the dates have not yet been harvested, they are treated as landed property from which the daughter may collect her maintenance."

סוֹף סוֹף [51A] [2] Abaye still had difficulty in accepting Rav Yosef's ruling, and he said to him: "Your clarification notwithstanding, my objection **nevertheless** stands. For there is a general rule that **whatever is** fully ripened and **ready for harvesting is considered as if it has** already **been harvested,** even before it is detached from the ground. Thus it follows that dates that are ready to be picked should be regarded as if they have already been picked. The ripened fruit should therefore be considered as movable goods from which the orphan girl cannot collect her maintenance."

דִּצְרִיכָא לְדִיקְלָא קָאָמִינָא [3] Rav Yosef answered Abaye's objection, adding further clarification to his ruling: "I was not referring to fully ripened fruit. Rather, **I meant** that the father's heirs should maintain her from the **dates that** are almost ready to be picked and to be spread out on mats for drying, but which still **need** to be left on **the palm tree** a little longer to ripen completely. Since the dates are still attached to the tree, and continue to benefit from being attached, they are treated as landed property from which the orphan girl may collect her maintenance."

הַהוּא יָתוֹם וִיתוֹמָה [4] The Gemara now relates one more incident concerning the maintenance of an orphan girl. **An orphan boy and an orphan girl came before Rava** for a decision on the girl's maintenance. [5] **Rava said to** the boy's guardian, who was administering the estate left by the children's father: **"Give the orphan boy a larger** allowance from the movable goods of the father's estate, so that he will have enough

[1] אֲמַר לֵיהּ: ״דְּחַזְיָיא לְבוּדְיָא קָאָמִינָא״.
[51A] [2] ״סוֹף סוֹף, כָּל הָעוֹמֵד לִגָזוֹז כְּגָזוּז דָּמֵי״.
[3] ״דִּצְרִיכָא לְדִיקְלָא קָאָמִינָא״.
[4] הַהוּא יָתוֹם וִיתוֹמָה דְּאָתוּ לְקַמֵּיהּ דְּרָבָא. [5] אֲמַר לְהוּ רָבָא: ״הַעֲלוּ לַיָּתוֹם בִּשְׁבִיל יְתוֹמָה״.

LITERAL TRANSLATION

[1] He said to him: "I mean [dates] that are fit for [spreading on] mats."

[51A] [2] "At all events, whatever is ready for cutting is considered as having been cut."

[3] "I mean [dates] that need the palm tree."

[4] A certain orphan boy and an orphan girl came before Rava. [5] Rava said to them: "Give more to the orphan boy on behalf of the orphan girl."

RASHI

דחזו לבודיא — הקרובות לגדור ועדיין מחוברות. **יתום ויתומה** — אח ואחות ונכסיהם ביד אפוטרופוס. **העלו ליתום בשביל יתומה** — העלו ליתום מזונות יתירים, שמיזון אחותו עמו.

fall there after they had ripened. These dates, which were left on the mats until they had dried out completely, are the "dates on the mats" mentioned here.

TERMINOLOGY

סוֹף סוֹף At all events (lit., "the end," "finally"). In the course of a Talmudic discussion, after an objection has been made to a statement and a response has been offered to that objection, the Gemara may then restate its original objection by pointing out a weak point in the answer: "However much I wish to accept your answer, *nevertheless* my previous objection still stands."

NOTES

dealing with a case in which the dates were still attached to the tree at the time of the father's death, but were subsequently picked, and that Rav Yosef decided that those dates should be treated like landed property. Abaye argued that if a creditor had been in a similar situation, he would not have been entitled to collect from such produce, and therefore the daughter should also not be entitled to collect her maintenance from the dates.

כָּל הָעוֹמֵד לִגְזוֹז Whatever is ready for cutting. Elsewhere (*Shevuot* 43a), Rabbi Meir and the Sages disagree about whether grapes that are ready to be harvested are considered as having been harvested. According to *Tosafot*, Abaye's question assumes the position of Rabbi Meir that such grapes are indeed considered as harvested. Others (see *Ritva; Rambam, Hilkhot Mekhirah* 1:17) maintain that even the Sages agree that such produce is considered as if it has already been harvested, if it no longer benefits from being attached to the ground.

The rule stated here, that whatever is fully ripe and ready for harvesting is considered as harvested, even before it is detached from the ground, is related to another general principle formulated as follows: Whatever meal-offering is fit to be mixed, the fact that it has not been mixed does not invalidate it (כָּל הָרָאוּי לְבִילָה אֵין בִּילָה מְעַכֶּבֶת בּוֹ). Many

[1]אָמְרִי לֵיהּ רַבָּנַן לְרָבָא: ״וְהָא מָר הוּא דַּאֲמַר: [2]מִמְּקַרְקְעֵי וְלָא מִמְּטַלְטְלֵי, בֵּין לִמְזוֹנֵי, בֵּין לִכְתוּבָּה, וּבֵין לְפַרְנָסָה״! [3]אֲמַר לְהוּ: ״אִילּוּ רָצָה שִׁפְחָה לְשַׁמְּשׁוֹ, מִי לָא יָהֲבִינַן לֵיהּ? [4]כָּל שֶׁכֵּן הָכָא, דְּאִיכָּא תַּרְתֵּי״. [5]תָּנוּ רַבָּנַן: ״אֶחָד נְכָסִים שֶׁיֵּשׁ לָהֶן אַחֲרָיוּת וְאֶחָד נְכָסִים שֶׁאֵין לָהֶן אַחֲרָיוּת מוֹצִיאִין לִמְזוֹן אִשָּׁה וְלַבָּנוֹת. [6]דִּבְרֵי רַבִּי. [7]רַבִּי שִׁמְעוֹן בֶּן אֶלְעָזָר אוֹמֵר: נְכָסִים שֶׁיֵּשׁ לָהֶן אַחֲרָיוּת מוֹצִיאִין [8]לַבָּנוֹת מִן

LITERAL TRANSLATION

[1]The Rabbis said to Rava: "But surely it was the Master who said: [2][Payment is made] from land and not from movable goods, whether for maintenance, or for a ketubah, or for a dowry!" [3]He said to them: "If he wanted a maidservant to serve him, would we not give him [one]? [4]All the more so here, where there are two [reasons]."

[5]Our Rabbis taught: "We seize both immovable property (lit., 'property with responsibility') and movable property (lit., 'property without responsibility') for the maintenance of the wife and for the daughters. [6][These are] the words of Rabbi. [7]Rabbi Shimon ben Elazar says: We seize immovable property [8]for the daughters from the

TRANSLATION AND COMMENTARY

not only for himself but **for his orphan sister** as well." [1]When **the** other **Rabbis** heard this ruling, they **said to Rava: "But surely it was** you yourself, **Sir, who said:** [2]The Halakhah is that **payment is made from the landed property** left by the deceased, **but not from** his **movable goods, whether for** the **maintenance** of his minor daughters, **or for the ketubah** to which his widow is entitled, **or for the dowry** of his minor daughters! Why, then, did you award the orphan girl maintenance from the movable goods now belonging to the orphan boy?" [3]Defending his ruling, Rava **said to them: "If** the orphan boy **wanted a maidservant to serve him, would we not give him one** and have his guardian pay for her services from his father's estate, even if the father only left his son movable property? [4]**All the more so here** should the guardian of the estate give the boy a larger allowance so that he can maintain his sister, **for there are two reasons** to provide for her support — she is his sister, and she is fit to serve him." Since in any event money from the estate will have to be spent on the boy's care, it is appropriate that his sister be given the opportunity to serve him, in exchange for which she will be maintained from the movable property of her late father's estate.

תָּנוּ רַבָּנַן [5]The Gemara now cites a Baraita which teaches that there was a disagreement between Tannaim about whether an orphan girl is entitled to maintenance from the movable goods in her father's estate. **Our Rabbis taught** the following Baraita: "If a man dies and his estate passes to his sons, **we collect maintenance for the widow and** maintenance and dowries **for the** orphaned **daughters, both from immovable property and from movable property,** because the widow and the daughters are entitled to maintenance even from the movable goods of the estate. [6]**This is the opinion of Rabbi** Yehudah HaNasi. [7]**Rabbi Shimon ben Elazar** disagrees and **says: From immovable property we collect** the following: [8]If the father is survived by both sons and daughters, we collect maintenance and dowries **for the** minor **daughters from the sons** who

RASHI

דאיכא תרתי – אחותו, ותשמשנו. **מוציאין** – מן היתומים. **מוציאין לבנות מן הבנים** – למזונות ולפרנסה.

NOTES

meal-offerings have to be mixed with oil. However, as long as there is nothing to prevent the two substances from being mixed, the fact that they have not been mixed does not invalidate the offering. This principle was extended by the Sages to other Halakhic areas, in which the Sages stated that certain acts need not be carried out if the potential for their performance exists.

מוֹצִיאִין לַבָּנוֹת **We seize for the daughters.** A number of Halakhot come into play when the time comes to dispose of a person's estate. By Torah law, sons have priority over daughters as heirs. Hence the entire estate should pass into the hands of the sons of the deceased. But the Rabbis imposed an obligation on the sons to maintain their father's widow and daughters out of the property of the estate. These obligations stem from the conditions contained in the ketubah which impose a lien on the estate similar to the lien

HALAKHAH

בֵּין לִכְתוּבָּה **Whether for a ketubah.** "By Talmudic law, a woman may collect her ketubah, both the basic portion and any additional sum, from her husband's landed property, but not from his movable goods. But the *Geonim* enacted that she may collect even from his movable goods. It became the customary practice to write in the ketubah that all the husband's property is security for the ketubah, both his landed property and his movable goods." (*Rambam, Sefer Nashim, Hilkhot Ishut* 16:7; *Shulḥan Arukh, Even HaEzer* 100:1.)

בֵּין לִמְזוֹנֵי **Or for maintenance.** "By Talmudic law, maintenance — both that to which a widow is entitled and that

הַבָּנִים, [1] וְלַבָּנוֹת מִן הַבָּנוֹת, [2] וְלַבָּנִים מִן הַבָּנִים, [3] וְלַבָּנִים מִן הַבָּנוֹת בִּנְכָסִים מְרוּבִּין, [4] אֲבָל לֹא לַבָּנִים מִן הַבָּנוֹת בִּנְכָסִים מוּעָטִין. [5] נְכָסִים שֶׁאֵין לָהֶן אַחֲרָיוּת מוֹצִיאִין [6] לַבָּנִים מִן הַבָּנִים, [7] וְלַבָּנוֹת מִן הַבָּנוֹת, [8] וְלַבָּנִים מִן הַבָּנוֹת, [9] אֲבָל לֹא לַבָּנוֹת מִן הַבָּנִים״. [10] אַף עַל גַּב דְּקַיְימָא לָן הֲלָכָה כְּרַבִּי מֵחֲבֵירוֹ, [11] הָכָא הֲלָכָה

LITERAL TRANSLATION

sons, [1] and for the daughters from the daughters, [2] and for the sons from the sons, [3] and for the sons from the daughters where there are numerous properties, [4] but not for the sons from the daughters where there are few properties. [5] We seize movable property [6] for the sons from the sons, [7] and for the daughters from the daughters, [8] and for the sons from the daughters, [9] but not for the daughters from the sons."

[10] Although we maintain [that] the Halakhah is in accordance with Rabbi against his colleague, [11] here the Halakhah is

TRANSLATION AND COMMENTARY

have inherited the father's estate. If the father is survived only by daughters, they all share the estate equally, and none is awarded maintenance or dowries. [1] If the older daughters seize the entire estate for themselves, we collect **for the** minor **daughters** their portion of the estate **from the** older **daughters.** And, similarly, if the father had a number of sons, and the older sons seize the entire estate for themselves, [2] we collect **for the** minor **sons** their share of the estate **from the** older **sons.** If the father is survived by both sons and daughters, and the sons come to take the estate and the daughters demand their maintenance and dowries, [3] we collect the entire estate **for the sons from the daughters, provided that** the estate consists of **numerous properties,** which will be sufficient to maintain both the sons and the daughters until they reach adulthood. [4] **But** we do **not** collect the estate **for the sons from the daughters if** it consists of only **a few properties,** which will not be sufficient to maintain both the sons and the daughters. In such a case, the daughters are provided with maintenance from the estate, and the sons must seek charity elsewhere. [5] And if the father's estate consists of **movable property, we collect** the following: [6] If the older sons seize the entire estate for themselves, we collect **for the** minor **sons** their share of the estate **from the** older **sons.** If the father is survived by daughters only, and the older daughters seize the entire estate for themselves, [7] we collect **for the** minor **daughters** their portion of the estate **from the** older **daughters.** If the father is survived by both sons and daughters, [8] we collect the entire estate **for the sons from the daughters,** even if the estate is small, [9] **but** we do **not** collect maintenance or dowries **for the** minor **daughters from the sons** who inherited the estate, for the daughters are not entitled to maintenance from the movable goods of their father's estate."

אַף עַל גַּב [10] The Gemara concludes: **Although we maintain** in general **that the Halakhah is in accordance with** the viewpoint of **Rabbi** Yehudah HaNasi **rather than** with that of **a colleague** with whom he is in dispute, and therefore the law should be that an orphan girl is entitled to maintenance even from the movable goods of her late father's estate, [11] nevertheless **here the Halakhah is in accordance with** the viewpoint of

BACKGROUND

הֲלָכָה כְּרַבִּי מֵחֲבֵירוֹ The Halakhah is in accordance with Rabbi against his colleague. This is one of the principles laid down by the Gemara regarding Halakhic decision-making. According to this rule, whenever a contemporary of Rabbi Yehuda HaNasi disagrees with him (apart from a few exceptional cases, where there is a clear instruction to deviate from the rule), the Halakhah follows the viewpoint of Rabbi Yehudah HaNasi. He was the greatest Sage of his generation, and some Amoraim maintained that this rule applies even when many Sages disagree with him.

RASHI

ולבנות מן הבנות – לקטנות מן הגדולות. אם אין שם אלא בנות, והחזיקו גדולות בנכסים – מוציאין מידם וחולקות בשוה. והכא ליכא מזוני, שאין הבנות נזונות מן הבנות, לפי שכולן שוות בירושה. **ולבנים מן הבנים** – לקטנים מן הגדולים לחלוק בשוה. **אבל לא לבנים מן הבנות בנכסים מועטין** – שאין בהן כדי לזון אלו ואלו עד שיגדלו, דאמרי רבנן: הבנות יזונו, והבנים ישאלו על הפתחים.

NOTES

imposed on a person's property by a promissory note. Thus, the widow and the daughters may collect their maintenance from the sons who have inherited their father's estate. Moreover, if the assets of the estate are not sufficient to satisfy both the daughters' right of maintenance and the heirs' right of succession, the daughters' right takes preference. The matter is further complicated according to Rabbi Shimon ben Eliezer, who maintains that the ketubah conditions can be satisfied only from the landed property of the deceased, but not from his movable goods.

HALAKHAH

to which an orphaned daughter is entitled — may be collected only from the landed property left by the deceased to his heirs, but not from his movable goods. But since the *Geonim* enacted that a woman may collect her ketubah even from the movable goods of her late husband's estate, maintenance may also be collected from such property." (*Shulḥan Arukh, Even HaEzer* 112:7.)

TRANSLATION AND COMMENTARY

Rabbi Shimon ben Elazar, who disagrees with Rabbi Yehudah HaNasi about this issue. [1]**For Rava said: The Halakhah is** [2]that **payment is made from the landed property** left by the deceased to his heirs, **but not from his movable goods,** [3]**whether for the ketubah** to which his widow is entitled, **or for the maintenance or the dowry** to which his minor daughters are entitled.

MISHNAH לֹא כָּתַב לָהּ כְּתוּבָּה [4]The basic obligations imposed on a husband by virtue of the ketubah are the result of Rabbinic legislation. They do not derive from a contractual agreement reached between husband and wife. Thus the husband is held liable to meet those obligations, even if no ketubah was written, or if a particular obligation was omitted from the ketubah. This applies with respect to the amount of the main portion of the ketubah, the lien established on the husband's property to ensure payment of the ketubah, and the other obligations which are ordinarily specified in the ketubah, as the Mishnah now explains: A virgin who marries is entitled to a ketubah of two hundred zuz, whereas a widow or a divorcee who remarries is entitled to a ketubah of a maneh, which is equivalent to one hundred zuz, half the amount of a virgin's ketubah. Ordinarily these sums are recorded explicitly in the ketubah that the wife receives at the time of her marriage. **If** for some reason the husband **did not write** his wife **a ketubah,** and his wife was **a virgin** at the time she married, and later she was widowed or divorced, she still **collects two hundred zuz** as her ketubah, [5]**and** if she was **a widow** or a divorcee who remarried, she still collects her ketubah of **a maneh.** The husband (or his estate) is held liable for these amounts even though they were not recorded in the wife's ketubah, [6]**because** the woman's right to the main portion of her ketubah **is** based on **a condition laid down by the court.** In other words, her right is based on a Rabbinic enactment and does not depend on what was or was not written in her particular ketubah.

כָּתַב לָהּ שָׂדֶה [7]Our Mishnah teaches that all the husband's property becomes subject to the lien created by the ketubah, even if this stipulation was not included in the document: **If** the husband **wrote** in his wife's ketubah that he was assigning to her as security for the payment of her ketubah **a field worth** only **a maneh instead of the two hundred zuz** to which he was obligated by law, [8]**and he did not write** in the ketubah: **"All the property that I have is security for** the payment of **your ketubah," he is** nevertheless held **liable** to make up the difference between the value of the field (one hundred zuz) and the amount of the ketubah (two hundred zuz) from the rest of his property. He cannot claim that his wife is entitled to collect only from the field specified in the ketubah, [9]**because** the woman's right to collect her ketubah from all her husband's property **is** based on **a condition laid down by the court.**

כְּרַבִּי שִׁמְעוֹן בֶּן אֶלְעָזָר. [1]דְּאָמַר רָבָא: הִלְכְתָא: [2]מִמְּקַרְקְעֵי וְלָא מִמִּטַּלְטְלֵי, [3]בֵּין לִכְתוּבָּה, בֵּין לִמְזוֹנֵי, בֵּין לְפַרְנָסָה.

משנה [4]לֹא כָּתַב לָהּ כְּתוּבָּה, בְּתוּלָה גּוֹבָה מָאתַיִם, [5]וְאַלְמָנָה מָנֶה, [6]מִפְּנֵי שֶׁהוּא תְּנַאי בֵּית דִּין.

[7]כָּתַב לָהּ שָׂדֶה שָׁוֶה מָנֶה תַּחַת מָאתַיִם זוּז, [8]וְלֹא כָּתַב לָהּ: ״כָּל נְכָסִים דְּאִית לִי אַחֲרָאִין לִכְתוּבָּתִיךְ״, חַיָּיב, [9]שֶׁהוּא תְּנַאי בֵּית דִּין.

LITERAL TRANSLATION

in accordance with Rabbi Shimon ben Elazar. [1]For Rava said: The Halakhah is: [2][Payment is made] from land and not from movable goods, [3]whether for a ketubah, or for maintenance, or for a dowry.

MISHNAH [4][If] he did not write a ketubah for her, a virgin collects two hundred [zuz], [5]and a widow a maneh, [6]because it is a condition of the court.

[7][If] he assigned her a field worth a maneh instead of the two hundred zuz, [8]and he did not write for her: "All the properties that I have are security for your ketubah," he is liable, [9]for it is a condition of the court.

RASHI

לפרנסה – לנדוניא.

משנה ולא כתב לה כל נכסים כו׳ – חייב להיות כל הנכסים אחראין לה, ולא יכול לומר לה: אין ליך אלא שדה הכתובה לך בשטר כתובתיך.

NOTES

כָּתַב לָהּ שָׂדֶה שָׁוֶה מָנֶה **If he assigned her a field worth a maneh.** There is a general rule that the laws of *ona'ah* (overcharging and underpaying) do not apply to landed property, for land is not considered to have a set price.

HALAKHAH

לֹא כָּתַב לָהּ כְּתוּבָּה **If he did not write a ketubah for her.** "Even if a man did not write a ketubah for his wife, she is nevertheless entitled to the basic ketubah — two hundred zuz in the case of a virgin, and a maneh in the case of a widow." (*Rambam, Sefer Nashim, Hilkhot Ishut* 12:5; *Shulḥan Arukh, Even HaEzer* 69:1.)

כָּתַב לָהּ שָׂדֶה שָׁוֶה מָנֶה **If he assigned her a field worth a maneh.** "All a man's property is security for the payment

TRANSLATION AND COMMENTARY

לֹא כָּתַב לָהּ [1] A husband is obligated to ransom his wife if she is taken into captivity. But if he is a priest, he is forbidden to continue living with her, for a woman who was taken captive is assumed to have been raped, and a priest is forbidden to live with his wife if she has had sexual relations with another man since their marriage, even if she was the victim of rape. He must therefore ransom her, and send her back to her father's house, divorcing her and paying her ketubah. If the husband is not a priest, he must take her back as his wife, for an ordinary Jew is permitted to continue living with his wife if she has been raped. Even **if** the husband **did not write** in his wife's ketubah: **"If you are taken captive, I will ransom you and I will bring you back to me as my wife,"** he is required to ransom her and to take her back as his wife. [2] **And** similarly **in the case of a woman married to a priest, if** the husband **did not write** in his wife's ketubah: **"I will** ransom you and I will **return you to your city** and to your father's home," **he is** nevertheless held **liable** for her ransom and is required to maintain her until she returns to her father's home. The husband must fulfill these obligations even if they were not mentioned in his wife's ketubah, [3] **because** these obligations **are** based on **conditions laid down by the court.**

נִשְׁבֵּית [4] The Mishnah continues: If a woman **is taken captive,** her husband **is obligated to ransom her.** [5] **If** the husband **says:** "I am ready to divorce my wife and to pay her her ketubah. **Here is her bill of divorce**

[1] לֹא כָּתַב לָהּ: ״אִם תִּשְׁתַּבַּאי, אֶפְרְקִינֵךְ וְאוֹתְבִינֵךְ לִי לְאִינְתּוּ״, [2] וּבְכֹהֶנֶת: ״אַהַדְרִינָךְ לִמְדִינְתִּיךְ״, חַיָּיב, [3] שֶׁהוּא תְּנַאי בֵּית דִּין.
[4] נִשְׁבֵּית, חַיָּיב לִפְדּוֹתָהּ. [5] וְאִם אָמַר: ״הֲרֵי גִּיטָּהּ וּכְתוּבָּתָהּ,

LITERAL TRANSLATION

[1] [If] he did not write for her: "If you are taken captive, I will ransom you and I will bring you back to me as my wife," [2] or in [the case of] a priest's wife, [if he did not write:] "I will return you to your city," he is liable, [3] for it is a condition of the court.

[4] [If] she was taken captive, he is obligated to ransom her. [5] And if he said: "Here is her bill of divorce and her ketubah,

RASHI

ובכהנת – שאינו יכול לקיימה משנשבית, כותב לה: אפרקינך ואהדרינך למדינתך. לפי שאשת כהן אסורה לבעלה אם נאנסה.

NOTES

Thus, if someone sells a field worth 100 zuz for 200 zuz, the sale is valid, and the buyer cannot demand a refund of the money that he was overcharged. Here, however, where the husband wrote in his wife's ketubah that he was pledging to her as security for the payment of her ketubah a field that was worth only a maneh instead of 200 zuz, we do not say that the field should be treated as if it were worth 200 zuz. In this case, the field is assessed at its market value and the husband must make up the difference between the value of the field and the amount of the ketubah from the rest of his property. The Rishonim disagree about a case in which it is stipulated in the ketubah that the 100-zuz field is the only one from which the ketubah can be collected. It is not clear whether in such a case we say that the wife must accept the field as if it were worth 200 zuz (see *Ritva*).

נִשְׁבֵּית...וְלָקְתָה If she was taken captive...if she fell ill. If a woman is taken captive, her husband cannot evade his obligation to pay her ransom by divorcing her. But if she falls ill, he can free himself of his duty to pay her medical expenses by granting her a divorce. There is a further stringency regarding the husband's duty to ransom his wife, in that a woman cannot waive her right to be ransomed, but she can waive her right to have her medical expenses paid by her husband (see *Tosafot*, above, 47b).

Rashi and others explain that the husband's liability for his wife's medical expenses is part of his general obligation to pay for her maintenance, and therefore he can free

HALAKHAH

of his wife's ketubah, even if he did not write a stipulation to that effect in her ketubah, and even if he designated a particular field as security for the ketubah." (*Rambam, Sefer Nashim, Hilkhot Ishut* 16:10; *Shulḥan Arukh, Even HaEzer* 100:1.)

לֹא כָּתַב לָהּ: ״אִם תִּשְׁתַּבַּאי״ If he did not write for her: "If you are taken captive." "Even if a person did not write in his wife's ketubah that he will ransom her if she is taken captive, he is nevertheless held liable to pay her ransom." (*Rambam, Sefer Nashim, Hilkhot Ishut* 12:5; *Shulḥan Arukh, Even HaEzer* 69:1.)

וּבְכֹהֶנֶת: ״אַהַדְרִינָךְ״ Or in the case of a priest's wife, if he did not write: "I will return you." "If the wife of a priest is taken captive, the priest is obligated to ransom her and to return her to her father's house. This applies even if the clause obligating him to do so was omitted from the woman's ketubah, because the obligation is based on a condition laid down by the court." (*Rambam, Sefer Nashim, Hilkhot Ishut* 14:18; *Shulḥan Arukh, Even HaEzer* 78:6.)

נִשְׁבֵּית, חַיָּיב לִפְדּוֹתָהּ If she was taken captive, he is obligated to ransom her. "If a woman is taken captive, her husband is required to ransom her. He cannot divorce her and pay her her ketubah, and demand that she ransom herself." (*Rambam, Sefer Nashim, Hilkhot Ishut* 14:19; *Shulḥan Arukh, Even HaEzer* 78:1.)

LITERAL TRANSLATION

[1] and let her ransom herself," [2] he is not permitted. [3] If she has fallen ill, he is obligated to heal her. [4] [If] he said: "Here is her bill of divorce and her ketubah; [5] let her heal herself," [6] he is permitted.

GEMARA [7] Whose [viewpoint] is this]?

[1] וְתִפְדֶּה אֶת עַצְמָהּ", [2] אֵינוֹ רַשַּׁאי.
[3] לָקְתָה, חַיָּיב לְרַפְּאוֹתָהּ.
[4] אָמַר: "הֲרֵי גִּיטָּהּ וּכְתוּבָּתָהּ; [5] תְּרַפֵּא אֶת עַצְמָהּ", [6] רַשַּׁאי.
גמרא [7] מַנִּי?

RASHI

אינו רשאי — שכבר נתחייב בפדיונה משנשבית. חייב לרפואתה — שהרפואה כמזונות. רשאי — שאין אדם חייב לזון גרושתו.

TRANSLATION AND COMMENTARY

and her ketubah; [1] **let her** take the money and **ransom herself,"** he is still obligated to ransom her. [2] **He is not permitted** to divorce her in order to evade the responsibility of ransoming her.

לָקְתָה [3] The Mishnah concludes: If a woman **falls ill,** her husband **is obligated to pay her medical expenses** until she recovers, because a wife's medical care comes under the category of maintenance for which the husband is responsible. [4] **If** the husband **says:** "I am ready to divorce my wife and to pay her her ketubah. **Here is her bill of divorce and her ketubah;** [5] **let her pay for her medical expenses herself** with her ketubah money," [6] **he is permitted** to do so. Since the husband's liability for his wife's medical expenses is part of his general obligation to provide her with maintenance, he is required to pay for her medical expenses only so long as he is married to her and is liable for her maintenance. But once he divorces his wife, he is no longer required to pay her medical bills.

GEMARA מַנִּי [7] The Mishnah stated that the husband is liable for the amount of his wife's ketubah determined by law, even if he did not actually write her a ketubah for that amount. The Gemara asks: **Whose viewpoint** does **this** Mishnah reflect?

NOTES

himself of that liability by divorcing her, because a husband is not required to maintain his wife after he has given her a divorce. Similarly, he is freed of that liability if his wife stipulates that she waives her right to maintenance, in exchange for which she will keep her handiwork for herself. But the husband's liability for his wife's ransom was instituted as a separate obligation, and it does not depend on the husband's receiving anything in return.

Remah argues that the husband's obligation to ransom his wife takes effect the moment she is taken captive, and, once obligated, the husband can no longer evade this obligation. But the husband's duty to pay for his wife's medical care takes effect anew each day, just like the obligation to provide for her maintenance, and therefore he can free himself of that duty even after she becomes ill. Others add that the husband cannot free himself of his obligation to ransom his wife, for there is concern that if she is not ransomed she will become assimilated among her non-Jewish captors.

"תְּרַפֵּא אֶת עַצְמָהּ" "Let her heal herself." *Ra'avad* writes that the Mishnah's ruling that a husband may divorce his sick wife and tell her that she must attend to her medical needs on her own and pay for her care with the money from her ketubah applies only to a woman who is not seriously ill and bedridden. But if a woman is so ill that she is confined to bed, her husband may not divorce her until she recovers. *Ra'avad* adduces proof for his position from *Sifrei* to Deuteronomy 21:14, which speaks of the laws applying to a non-Jewish female prisoner of war. On the verse that says: "And you shall let her go where she will," *Sifrei* comments: "This teaches that if she is ill, he must wait until she recovers before he sends her away." If this is so regarding a non-Jewish female prisoner of war, argues *Ra'avad,* then all the more so is a husband not permitted to send his Jewish wife out of his house while she is ill (see also Halakhah).

מַנִּי? Whose viewpoint is this? The discussion of this question in the Jerusalem Talmud differs from that found in our Gemara. The Jerusalem Talmud maintains that the entire Mishnah, even the second clause, follows the opinion of Rabbi Meir. When our Gemara entertains that possibility (see below, 51b), it explains that when the Mishnah says that the woman can collect her ketubah from all of her husband's property, even if he failed to pledge her all his property in her ketubah, it means that she may collect from all her husband's free assets, but not from those that have been been transferred to a third party in the meantime. The Jerusalem Talmud maintains that the Mishnah can be understood according to its plain sense

HALAKHAH

לָקְתָה, חַיָּיב לְרַפְּאוֹתָהּ If she has fallen ill, he is obligated to heal her. "If a woman falls ill, her husband is required to pay her medical expenses. If he sees that his wife is very sick and that her medical care will be very costly, he can say to her: 'Either pay for your medical care out of your ketubah [i.e., from the additional amount he promised of his own volition, for he is not permitted to live with her if she does not have the main portion of her ketubah; *Perishah*], or I will divorce you and give you your ketubah.' But it is not proper for him to do this. *Maggid Mishneh* (in the name of *Rashba*) notes that if a woman is bedridden, her husband may not divorce her until she recovers. Today, when a man is not permitted to divorce his wife against her will because of the ban imposed by *Rabbenu Gershom,* a husband may certainly not compel his sick wife to accept a divorce (*Bet Shmuel* in the name of *Maharshal*; see also *Ḥelkat Meḥokek*)." (*Rambam, Sefer Nashim, Hilkhot Ishut* 14:17; *Shulḥan Arukh, Even HaEzer* 79:1,3.)

TRANSLATION AND COMMENTARY

רַבִּי מֵאִיר הִיא [1]The Gemara answers: Our Mishnah seems to **follow** the opinion of **Rabbi Meir, who said** elsewhere in the Mishnah (below, 54b): [2]"A man may not reduce the amount of his wife's ketubah to less than the legal minimum, even if the woman agrees to the reduction, for **whoever fixes the ketubah of a virgin at less than two hundred zuz, or that of a widow at less than a maneh,** [3]**his intercourse with her is** tantamount to **an act of prostitution.**" The ketubah not only defines the rights and the obligations of marriage, but it also sanctions the couple's sexual relations. The difference between casual sexual relations and those sanctified by the bond of marriage is that the latter take place within the framework of an agreement between the parties which defines their mutual obligations as long as they remain married, as well as the arrangements that are to be made if they separate. In the absence of a ketubah, even sexual relations between husband and wife are considered illicit. If the husband sets his wife's ketubah at less than the legal minimum, his stipulation is invalid, and his wife is still entitled to the full amount. But sexual relations between the two are nevertheless forbidden, for the woman thinks that she is entitled only to the reduced amount specified in her ketubah, and a ketubah of less than two hundred zuz (in the case of a virgin) or less than a maneh (in the case of a widow or divorcee) is not valid. Our Mishnah seems to reflect the viewpoint of Rabbi Meir expressed in the Mishnah below, for both Mishnayot maintain that the amount of the basic portion of a woman's ketubah is fixed by Rabbinic regulation, and not by what was actually written in the ketubah or was agreed upon by the parties. [4]**For if** we say that our Mishnah **reflects** the opinion of **Rabbi Yehudah,** who disagrees with Rabbi Meir, there is a difficulty, for **surely** Rabbi Yehudah **said** in that same Mishnah (below, 54b): [5]**"If** the husband **wishes** to reduce his obligation concerning his wife's ketubah, **he may write a** ketubah **document of two hundred zuz for** his wife who is **a virgin,** as is required of him by virtue of the Rabbinic enactment, [6]**and** then he can arrange to have his wife **write** him a receipt saying: **'I have** already **received a maneh** [one hundred zuz] **from you** in partial payment of my ketubah,' even though she has not received anything from him. [7]**Or he may write a** ketubah **document of a maneh for** his wife who is **a widow** or a divorcee, [8]**and** then he can arrange to have his wife **write** him a receipt saying: **'I have** already **received fifty zuz from you** in partial payment of my ketubah,' even though she has received nothing from him." According to Rabbi Yehudah, once the husband has complied with the formal requirement of writing his wife a ketubah of two hundred zuz or a maneh, she can then waive her

[1]רַבִּי מֵאִיר הִיא, דְּאָמַר: [2]"כָּל הַפּוֹחֵת לִבְתוּלָה מִמָּאתַיִם, וּלְאַלְמָנָה מִמָּנֶה, [3]הֲרֵי זוֹ בְּעִילַת זְנוּת". [4]דְּאִי רַבִּי יְהוּדָה, הָאָמַר: [5]"רָצָה, כּוֹתֵב לִבְתוּלָה שְׁטָר שֶׁל מָאתַיִם, [6]וְהִיא כּוֹתֶבֶת: 'הִתְקַבַּלְתִּי מִמְּךָ מָנֶה', [7]וּלְאַלְמָנָה מָנֶה, [8]וְהִיא כּוֹתֶבֶת: 'הִתְקַבַּלְתִּי מִמְּךָ חֲמִשִּׁים זוּז'".

LITERAL TRANSLATION

[1]It is Rabbi Meir, who said: [2]"Whoever fixes [the ketubah of] a virgin at less than two hundred [zuz], or [that] of a widow at less than a maneh, [3][his intercourse with her] is an act of prostitution." [4]For if it is Rabbi Yehudah, surely he said: [5]"[If] he wishes, he may write for a virgin a deed of two hundred [zuz], [6]and she may write: 'I have received from you a maneh,' [7]or [he may write] for a widow [a deed of] a maneh, [8]and she may write: 'I have received from you fifty zuz.'"

RASHI

גמרא פלוגתא דרבי מאיר ורבי יהודה — בפרק "אף על פי". והיא כותבת התקבלתי כו' — לשון שובר, ואפילו לא נתקבלה. ולרבי מאיר אינה יכולה למחול בעודה תחתיו. ומתניתין נמי, דקתני לא כתב לה כתובה — גובה כתובתה שלימה, קא סלקא דעתך ואפילו מחלה.

BACKGROUND

הֲרֵי זוֹ בְּעִילַת זְנוּת His intercourse with her is an act of prostitution. According to Rabbi Meir, any deviation from the precise phraseology instituted by the Sages in a document (מַטְבֵּעַ שֶׁטָּבְעוּ חֲכָמִים) invalidates that document. Therefore, if a man awards a woman less than the sum determined for her by the Sages, it is as if she has no ketubah at all. A woman without a ketubah is like a concubine and not a married woman.

NOTES

that the woman may collect her ketubah from all her husband's property, even property that is now in the hands of a third party, and that Rabbi Meir distinguishes between a ketubah and promissory notes. Regarding promissory notes, Rabbi Meir maintains that the omission of the clause in the document pledging the borrower's property as security for the loan is not assumed to be a scribal error, but in the case of a woman's ketubah such an omission *is* considered a scribal error.

HALAKHAH

כָּל הַפּוֹחֵת לִבְתוּלָה מִמָּאתַיִם Whoever fixes the ketubah of a virgin at less than 200 zuz. "If a man reduces his wife's ketubah below the legal minimum (200 zuz for a virgin, and a maneh for a widow), his intercourse with her is tantamount to an act of prostitution. This applies whether he reduced the amount below the legal mimimum when he first wrote the ketubah, or whether he wrote a proper ketubah and later had her write him a receipt saying that she had already received partial payment of her ketubah. The Rishonim disagree as to whether such a receipt has any legal validity. According to *Rambam,* the receipt is null and void, whereas according to *Tur,* it is binding." (*Rambam, Sefer Nashim, Hilkhot Ishut* 12:8; *Shulḥan Arukh, Even HaEzer* 66:9.)

TRANSLATION AND COMMENTARY

right to part of that sum by writing a fictitious receipt for part of the money. Thus the husband can reduce his liability, provided that his wife agrees to the reduction. The Gemara is now assuming that when our Mishnah says that a woman can always collect the two hundred zuz or the maneh to which she is entitled, no matter what sum is actually recorded, it is referring even to a case where the woman was willing to waive her right to part of her ketubah when she married. Hence our Mishnah cannot be in accordance with the viewpoint of Rabbi Yehudah.

אֵימָא סֵיפָא [1] The Gemara now raises an objection against the explanation that our Mishnah reflects the viewpoint of Rabbi Meir. The Gemara suggests that we **consider the next clause** of our Mishnah, which stated: **"If** the husband **wrote** in his wife's ketubah that he was assigning to her as security for the payment of her ketubah **a field worth** only **a maneh instead of the two hundred zuz** to which he is obligated by law, [2]**and he did not write** in the ketubah: **'All the property that I have is security for** the payment of **your ketubah,' he is** nevertheless held **liable** to make up the difference between the value of the field and the value of the ketubah from the rest of his property, [3]**because** the woman's right to collect from all her husband's property **is** based on **a condition laid down by the court."** At this point the Gemara is assuming that when the Mishnah says that the woman can collect from all of her husband's property, even if he assigned her a specific field and failed to write in her ketubah that all his property was security for her ketubah, it means to say that all the husband's property is subject to a lien, so that the wife can collect that property even from a third party who has acquired it, just as would be the case if the husband had explicitly assigned her all his property for the payment of her ketubah. [4]If this assumption is correct, says the Gemara, **we are adopting the viewpoint of Rabbi Yehudah, who said:** [5]**The omission of a clause** in a promissory note **mortgaging** the borrower's landed **property** as security for the loan **is an** accidental **error** on the part **of the scribe.** In Jewish law, a promissory note entitles the lender to recover payment from the borrower's landed property, even if the property has been transferred to a third party since the loan was given. Ordinarily, a clause is inserted into a promissory note stating explicitly that all the borrower's property is subject to the lender's lien. Rabbi Yehudah maintains that in the event that such a clause is omitted from the document, that omission is attributed to a scribal error, and the document is treated as if it contains such a clause. If the borrower does not want his property to

LITERAL TRANSLATION

[1]Say the last clause: "[If] he assigned her a field worth a maneh instead of the two hundred zuz, [2]and he did not write for her: 'All the properties that I have are security for your ketubah,' he is liable, [3]for it is a condition of the court." [4]We have come to [the viewpoint of] Rabbi Yehudah, who said: [5][Omission of a clause] mortgaging [property] is an error of the scribe.

[1]אֵימָא סֵיפָא: ״כָּתַב לָהּ שָׂדֶה שָׁוֶה מָנֶה תַּחַת מָאתַיִם זוּז, [2]וְלֹא כָּתַב לָהּ: ׳כָּל נְכָסִים דְּאִית לִי אַחֲרָאִין לִכְתוּבָּתֵיךְ׳, חַיָּיב, [3]שֶׁהוּא תְּנַאי בֵּית דִּין״. [4]אֲתָאַן לְרַבִּי יְהוּדָה, דְּאָמַר: [5]אַחֲרָיוּת טָעוּת סוֹפֵר הוּא.

RASHI

אחראין לכתובתיך חייב — שנשתעבדו נכסיו. וקסלקא דעתך, נשתעבדו בכל דין שעבוד כאילו נכתב בתוך השטר, ואם ימכור נכסיו תטרוף לקוחות. **אתאן לרבי יהודה** — דאמר: שטר שלא נכתב בו אחריות — לא מדעת המלוה נעשה, אלא סופר טעה, והרי הוא כמי שנכתב, וטורף מן המשועבדים.

TERMINOLOGY

אֲתָאַן לְרַבִּי יְהוּדָה We have come to the viewpoint of Rabbi Yehudah. Sometimes, part of a Mishnah follows the viewpoint of one scholar, while another part follows that of a different scholar. In such cases the Talmud may interject "We have come to the viewpoint of Rabbi X," i.e., the part of the Mishnah which follows is in accordance with the viewpoint of Rabbi X, as opposed to the previous part of the Mishnah, which follows the viewpoint of Rabbi Y.

CONCEPTS

אַחֲרָיוּת טָעוּת סוֹפֵר הוּא Omission of a clause mortgaging property is an error of the scribe. A Talmudic principle which maintains that it is taken for granted that in the case of a loan the debtor pledges his land as security for the repayment of the loan, and that in the case of a sale the seller pledges his other land as security in the event that a creditor should seize the land he is now selling to the purchaser. If the clause mentioning this pledge of security is omitted from the loan document or the deed of sale, that omission is attributed to a scribal error, and it is considered as if the clause was explicitly mentioned in the document. If the debtor, or the seller, does not wish to accept this responsibility, an explicit provision to that effect must be included in the document.

NOTES

אֲתָאַן לְרַבִּי יְהוּדָה We have come to the viewpoint of Rabbi Yehudah. The Rishonim object: The Gemara argues that the second clause of the Mishnah can best be understood as reflecting the viewpoint of Rabbi Yehudah, who says that the omission of the clause in a promissory note pledging the borrower's property as security for the loan is assumed to be a scribal error. But the Mishnah itself says that a woman can collect her ketubah from all of her husband's property, even if he has failed to write in her ketubah document that all of his property is pledged to her ketubah, because the woman's right to collect her ketubah from all of her husband's property is based on a condition laid down by the court, and not because the omission of the clause in a document pledging the borrower's property is assumed to be a scribal error.

Ramban answers that what the Mishnah means to say is as follows: Even if the husband pledged a field worth only a maneh, his wife can still collect 200 zuz, because she is entitled to a ketubah of 200 zuz by virtue of a condition laid down by the court. And since the husband is liable for 200 zuz, all of his property is pledged to that obligation, because the omission of the clause pledging the borrower's property is assumed to be a scribal error.

Ritva answers that we might have thought that the Rabbis were more lenient regarding a ketubah, so that an explicit clause pledging the husband's property to his wife's ketubah would be necessary. Therefore the Mishnah teaches that this is not so, and that by virtue of the condition laid down by the court the ketubah is treated like any other promissory note, and the omission of the clause pledging the husband's property to the ketubah is treated as a scribal error.

TRANSLATION AND COMMENTARY

be subject to such a lien, an explicit provision to that effect must be included in the document. Now, if our Mishnah reflects the viewpoint of Rabbi Yehudah, we can understand why the woman is entitled to collect her ketubah from her husband's property which has been transferred to a third party, even if the ketubah failed to mention that all the husband's property was security for the ketubah, for according to Rabbi Yehudah the omission of the clause mortgaging the property is assumed to be a mere scribal error. [1]**But if** we say that our Mishnah reflects **the viewpoint of Rabbi Meir,** who disagrees with Rabbi Yehudah, there is a difficulty, for **surely** Rabbi Meir **said:** [2]**The omission of a clause** in a promissory note **mortgaging** the borrower's landed **property** as security for the loan **is not** assumed to be **an** accidental **error** on the part **of the scribe.** According to Rabbi Meir, a lien is established on a borrower's property only if a clause to that effect was included in the promissory note that created the obligation. The Gemara now cites the source of this difference of opinion between Rabbi Yehudah and Rabbi Meir: [3]**For we have learned** in a Mishnah (*Bava Metzia* 12b): **"If someone finds a promissory note** recording a loan, and he does not know whether the loan has already been repaid and the document was lost by the borrower who took back the note when he repaid the loan, or whether the loan has not yet been repaid and the document was lost by the lender who was holding the note until he recovered his money, the following distinction applies: [4]**If** [51B] the promissory note **contains a clause mortgaging the borrower's landed property as security for the loan,** i.e., if the borrower stipulates in the promissory note that his landed property may be used for collection of the debt, [5]the finder **should not return** the note to the lender, **because the court may enforce payment** by means of that note **from** land sold by the borrower to a third party subsequent to the signing of the note. The finder should not return the note to the lender, even if the borrower admits that he has not repaid the loan, because we are concerned that the loan may actually have been repaid. The borrower may be admitting to the loan because he and the lender have formed a conspiracy to defraud the buyer. They may have arranged between themselves that the borrower will admit owing the money, the lender will seize the property sold by the borrower, and later the lender and the borrower will divide the property between themselves. [6]But **if** the promissory note **does not contain a clause mortgaging the borrower's landed property as security for the loan,** and the borrower admits that the loan has not yet been repaid, [7]the finder **should return** the note to the lender, **because the court cannot** use it to **enforce payment from** a third party who may have bought land from the borrower after the date of the loan, since the promissory note did not establish a lien on the borrower's property. [8]**This is the opinion of Rabbi Meir,** who maintains that the omission of the clause in a document mortgaging the borrower's property is not assumed to be a scribal error.

[1]דְּאִי רַבִּי מֵאִיר, הָאָמַר: [2]אַחֲרָיוּת לָאו טָעוּת סוֹפֵר הוּא. [3]דִּתְנַן: "מָצָא שְׁטָרֵי חוֹב, [4]אִם [51B] יֵשׁ בָּהֶן אַחֲרָיוּת נְכָסִים, [5]לֹא יַחֲזִיר, שֶׁבֵּית דִּין נִפְרָעִין מֵהֶן. [6]אֵין בָּהֶן אַחֲרָיוּת נְכָסִים, [7]יַחֲזִיר, שֶׁאֵין בֵּית דִּין נִפְרָעִין מֵהֶן. [8]דִּבְרֵי רַבִּי מֵאִיר.

LITERAL TRANSLATION

[1]For if it is [the viewpoint of] Rabbi Meir, surely he said: [2][Omission of a clause] mortgaging [property] is not an error of the scribe. [3]For we have learned: "If someone found promissory notes, [4]if [51B] they contain [a clause] mortgaging [the borrower's landed] property [as security for the loan], [5]he should not return [them], because the court will enforce payment from them. [6][If] they do not contain [a clause] mortgaging [the borrower's landed] property [as security for the loan], [7]he should return [them], because the court will not enforce payment from them. [8][These are] the words of Rabbi Meir.

RASHI

יש בהן אחריות נכסים — שמשעבד לוה נכסיו לאותה מלוה, לא יחזירנו מוצאו למלוה, ואפילו הלוה מודה שהוא חייב לו. ומפרש התם דחיישינן שמא פרעו, ומן הלוה נפל, וזה שהוא מודה — עצה קנוניא היא ביניהם, לטרוף לקוחות ויחלקו ביניהם.

HALAKHAH

מָצָא שְׁטָרֵי חוֹב If someone found promissory notes. "If someone finds a promissory note (even if it stipulates that the lender's claim that the loan has not yet been repaid will always be believed, and even if the loan recorded in the note is not yet due), even if the note does not include a clause mortgaging the borrower's property as security for repayment of the loan, and even if the borrower admits that the loan has not yet been repaid, the finder should not return the note to the lender, because we suspect that the borrower and the lender are conspiring to defraud the person who bought the borrower's property subsequent to the date on which the note was written (following the Sages). But if the note states explicitly that the borrower's property is not mortgaged as security for repayment of the loan, and the borrower admits that the loan has not yet been repaid, the finder may return the note to the lender." (*Rambam, Sefer Nezikin, Hilkhot Gezelah VaAvedah* 18:1; *Shulḥan Arukh, Ḥoshen Mishpat* 65:6.)

[1]וַחֲכָמִים אוֹמְרִים: אֶחָד זֶה וְאֶחָד זֶה לֹא יַחֲזִיר, שֶׁבֵּית דִּין נִפְרָעִין מֵהֶן". [2]רֵישָׁא רַבִּי מֵאִיר וְסֵיפָא רַבִּי יְהוּדָה!

[3]וְכִי תֵּימָא כּוּלָּהּ רַבִּי מֵאִיר הִיא, וְשָׁאנֵי לֵיהּ לְרַבִּי מֵאִיר בֵּין כְּתוּבָּה לִשְׁטָרֵי, וּמִי שָׁאנֵי לֵיהּ? [4]וְהָתַנְיָא: "חֲמִשָּׁה גּוֹבִין מִן הַמְּחוֹרָרִין, [5]וְאֵלּוּ הֵן: [6]פֵּירוֹת,

LITERAL TRANSLATION

[1]But the Sages say: In both cases he should not return [them], because the court will enforce payment from them." [2]The first clause [follows] Rabbi Meir and the last clause [follows] Rabbi Yehudah!

[3]And if you say [that] the entire [Mishnah follows] Rabbi Meir, and Rabbi Meir distinguishes between a ketubah and [promissory] notes, does he indeed make a distinction? [4]But surely it was taught: "Five collect from free property, [5]and they are: [6]Usufruct,

RASHI

וחכמים אומרים כו׳ — דאחריות טעות סופר הוא, וטריף ממשעבדי ומפסדי לקוחות, ובני פלוגתיה דרבי מאיר רבי יהודה הוה בהדייהו, שבדורו היה. **ושאני ליה כו׳** — דבכתובה אית ליה: אחריות טעות סופר הוא. **מן המחוררין** — אם יש נכסים בני חורין אלא החייב — נגבין, ואם לאו — אין נגבין מן המשועבדין. **פירות**

TRANSLATION AND COMMENTARY

[1]**But the Sages** — including Rabbi Yehudah — who disagree with Rabbi Meir **say: Both** in the case where the note includes a clause mortgaging the borrower's property as security for the loan **and** in the case where the note does not include such a clause, the finder **should not return** the note to the lender, **because** in both cases **the court may enforce payment from** landed property sold by the borrower to a third party, for, according to the Sages, the omission of the clause in a document mortgaging the borrower's property is assumed to be a scribal error. Thus the borrower and the lender could be conspiring to defraud the buyer and seize property from him illegally." [2]Hence it turns out that **the first clause** of our Mishnah **follows** the viewpoint of **Rabbi Meir, and the next clause** of our Mishnah **follows** the viewpoint of **Rabbi Yehudah!**

וְכִי תֵּימָא [3]The Gemara now suggests a way to explain our Mishnah as following the viewpoint of one single Tanna: **You can say that the entire Mishnah follows** the viewpoint of **Rabbi Meir, and** that **Rabbi Meir makes a distinction between a ketubah and** regular **promissory notes.** Regarding promissory notes, the omission of a clause mortgaging the borrower's property as security for the loan is not assumed to be a scribal error. But as for a ketubah, the omission of the clause mortgaging the husband's property *is* assumed to be a scribal error. Thus a woman can collect her ketubah from all her husband's property, even if he failed to write in her ketubah that all his property was mortgaged toward payment of her ketubah. But the problem with this explanation is this — **does** Rabbi Meir **in fact make** such **a distinction?** [4]**Surely it has been taught** otherwise in the following Baraita: "In **five** cases a creditor can **collect** only **from free property** still in the debtor's possession, but not from property that has already been transferred to a third party. [5]**These** five cases **are** as follows: (1) [6]If someone misappropriates a field and sells it to a third party, and the buyer cultivates the field and it yields produce, the person from whom the field has been stolen can reclaim the property from the buyer together with the produce that is growing there. Now, if the thief sold the field to the buyer and mortgaged his own property as security if the field should be seized, the buyer can collect the purchase money from all the thief's property, even from property that in the meantime has been transferred to a third party, but he can only collect the **usufruct** from the free assets that are still in the

NOTES

חֲמִשָּׁה גּוֹבִין מִן הַמְּחוֹרָרִין Five collect from free property. *Ritva* explains that the Baraita mentions only these five cases, even though there are other monetary obligations — for example, a loan that was not recorded in a written document — that can be collected only from free property, because in these five cases the obligation can be collected only from free assets even if the obligation was committed to writing. There are various reasons why a person is not entitled to collect money he is owed from property that has already been transferred from the person who owes the money to a third party. In some cases, a lien was never established on the debtor's property, and therefore the obligation can be collected only from the free assets that are in his possession at the time of collection. In other cases, the Rabbis enacted that the obligation cannot be collected from property that has already been transferred

HALAKHAH

פֵּירוֹת Usufruct. "If someone steals a field and causes damage or consumes the produce growing there, and the owner of the field comes to collect compensation from the thief for the damage or for the produce, he may only collect from the thief's free assets." (*Rambam, Sefer Nezikin, Hilkhot Gezelah VaAvedah* 9:5; *Shulḥan Arukh, Ḥoshen Mishpat* 372:1.)

TRANSLATION AND COMMENTARY

thief's possession. (2) [1]If someone misappropriates a field and sells it, and the buyer improves the field, and the original owner reclaims the property together with the improvements, the buyer can collect the money he paid for the field from all the thief's property, even from property that has been transferred to someone else, but **the improvements** made by the buyer **on the land** can be collected only from the free property that is still in the thief's possession. (3) [2]If **someone takes it upon himself to maintain his wife's son or daughter** from a previous marriage, and he dies, the son or the daughter may collect maintenance from the free property left by their step-father, but not from property that has already been transferred to a third party. (4) [3]If a lender is holding **a promissory note that does not contain a clause mortgaging the borrower's property** as security for repayment of the loan, he may not collect the debt from property that the borrower has already sold to someone else, but only from the free assets that are still in his possession. (5) [4]If **a woman** is holding **a ketubah that does not include a clause mortgaging the husband's property** as security for payment of the ketubah, she can collect her ketubah only from her husband's free assets, but not from property that has already been transferred to a third party." This Baraita is not attributed to a particular Tanna, but it is possible to deduce whose view is reflected here, since it states that if a lender is holding a promissory note that does not include a clause mortgaging the borrower's property as security for repayment of the loan, he may collect the debt only from the debtor's free assets. [5]**Of which** Tanna **have we heard that he maintains that the omission of the clause** in a document **mortgaging** the borrower's **property** as security for the loan **is not** assumed to be **a scribal error?** [6]Surely the Baraita must follow the position of **Rabbi Meir!** [7]**Yet** this same Baraita **states** that if a **woman** is holding **a ketubah** that does not include a clause mortgaging her husband's property as security for payment of the ketubah,

[1]וּשְׁבַח פֵּירוֹת, [2]וְהַמְקַבֵּל עָלָיו לָזוּן אֶת בֶּן אִשְׁתּוֹ וּבַת אִשְׁתּוֹ, [3]וְגֵט חוֹב שֶׁאֵין בּוֹ אַחֲרָיוּת, [4]וּכְתוּבַּת אִשָּׁה שֶׁאֵין בָּהּ אַחֲרָיוּת". [5]מַאן שָׁמְעַתְּ לֵיהּ דְּאָמַר אַחֲרָיוּת לָאו טָעוּת סוֹפֵר הוּא? [6]רַבִּי מֵאִיר. [7]וְקָתָנֵי: "כְּתוּבַּת אִשָּׁה"!

LITERAL TRANSLATION

[1]and the added value of usufruct, [2]and someone who takes [it] upon himself to maintain his wife's son or his wife's daughter, [3]and a promissory note that does not contain [a clause] mortgaging [the borrower's landed] property, [4]and a woman's ketubah that does not contain [a clause] mortgaging [the husband's landed] property." [5]Of whom have you heard that he says [that omission of a clause] mortgaging [property] is not an error of the scribe? [6]Rabbi Meir. [7]Yet it teaches: "A woman's ketubah"!

RASHI

ושבח פירות – כדתנן במסכת גיטין (מח,ב): אין מוציאין לאכילת פירות ולשבח קרקעות מנכסים משועבדים, מפני תיקון העולם. וב"שנים אוחזין בטלית" (בבא מציעא יד,ב) מפרש, לאכילת פירות ולשבח קרקעות כילד: הרי שגזל שדה מחבירו ומכרה לאחר והשביחה, והרי היא יוצאה בדין מתחת יד הלוקח, עם שבח שהשביח הלוקח בזבל ובניר ועם פירות שבה, שהנגזל טורפה ממנו. כשהוא חוזר על המוכר שמכרה לו באחריות – גובה קרן מנכסים משועבדין, ושבח מנכסים בני חורין ולא מן המשועבדין, מפני תיקון העולם, לפי שאין קצובין, ואין הלוקח יודע בכמה להזהר. **והמקבל עליו לזון בן אשתו ובת אשתו** – אף הוא אין גובה מן המשועבדים, לפי שאין קצובין ואין כתובים. והא דתנן ב"הנושא": והיא נזונית מנכסים משועבדין, מפני שהיא כבעל חוב – מוקמינן לה התם (כתובות קב,ב) בשקנו לה מידו, דסתם קנין לכתיבה עומד. **וגט חוב** – כל שטרות נקראין "גט".

NOTES

to a third party, in order to protect buyers against the seizure of their property. Certain obligations have no set limit and the buyers are therefore unable to know how much property to leave in the seller's hands to cover these obligations. In such cases, the Rabbis enacted that the obligation may be collected only from the free assets that are still in the possession of the person who owes the money.

HALAKHAH

וּשְׁבַח פֵּירוֹת And the added value of usufruct. "If someone steals a field and sells it to someone else, and the buyer makes improvements in the field, the value of which exceeds his expenditure, then when the original owner comes to reclaim his property, the buyer can collect his expenditure from the original owner, and can collect the purchase price and the rest of the value of the improvements from the thief from whom he bought the field. He can collect the purchase price from all the thief's property, even from property that has been transferred in the meantime to a third party, but he can collect the improvements only from the free assets that are still in the thief's possession." (*Rambam, Sefer Nezikin, Hilkhot Gezelah VaAvedah* 9:7; *Shulhan Arukh, Ḥoshen Mishpat* 373:1.)

וְהַמְקַבֵּל עָלָיו לָזוּן אֶת בֶּן אִשְׁתּוֹ And someone who takes it upon himself to maintain his wife's son. "If a man takes it upon himself to maintain his wife's children from a previous marriage, and he dies, the children can collect their maintenance even from property that their mother's

TRANSLATION AND COMMENTARY

the woman can collect it only from her husband's free assets! Thus we see that Rabbi Meir does not distinguish between a woman's ketubah and regular promissory notes, and in neither case is the omission of a clause mortgaging property as security for the debt attributed to scribal error. Hence we must conclude that the first clause of our Mishnah follows the viewpoint of Rabbi Meir, whereas the next clause of the Mishnah follows the viewoint of Rabbi Yehudah!

אִיבָּעֵית אֵימָא [1] The Gemara now suggests alternative ways of understanding our Mishnah as following the viewpoint of a single Tanna. **If you wish,** you can **say** that the entire Mishnah **follows** the viewpoint of **Rabbi Meir, and if you wish,** you can **say** that the entire Mishnah **follows** the viewpoint of **Rabbi Yehudah.** The Gemara explains: [2] **If you wish,** you can **say** that the entire Mishnah **follows** the viewpoint of **Rabbi Yehudah.** As for the argument put forward above — that the first clause of the Mishnah cannot reflect the viewpoint of Rabbi Yehudah because the Mishnah obligates the husband to pay his wife's ketubah to the full amount determined by the law, whereas Rabbi Yehudah said elsewhere that the husband can reduce his liability by having his wife write him a fictitious receipt for part of the money — the apparent contradiction can be reconciled as follows: [3] **There,** after the husband wrote his wife a ketubah of two hundred zuz or a maneh as required by law, **she wrote him** a receipt saying: **"I have** already **received** from you one hundred [or fifty] zuz as an advance on my ketubah." Rabbi Yehudah rules that in such a case the husband's liability is reduced, because his wife waived her right to part of her ketubah. [4] But **here** in our Mishnah we are dealing with a case in which the woman **did not write** her husband a receipt saying that **she had** already **received** part of her ketubah, but rather the husband failed to comply with his obligation to write his wife a ketubah of two hundred zuz or a maneh. In such a case, Rabbi Yehudah would agree that the woman is still entitled to the full amount, for we assume that she did not waive any part of her ketubah, but rather that she relied on the Rabbinic enactment guaranteeing her a ketubah of a certain amount. [5] On the other hand, **if you wish,** you can **say** that the entire Mishnah **follows** the viewpoint of **Rabbi Meir.** As for the objection raised earlier — that the second clause of the Mishnah cannot reflect the opinion of Rabbi Meir because the Mishnah states that even if the husband mortgaged a field worth only a maneh and not two hundred zuz as security for the payment of his wife's ketubah, he is still held liable to make up the difference between the value of the field and the amount of the ketubah from the rest of his property, whereas Rabbi Meir maintains that the omission of the clause mortgaging the husband's property as security for the payment of his wife's ketubah is not assumed to be the result of a scribal error — the apparent contradiction can be resolved as follows: The Mishnah does indeed agree that the omission of the clause mortgaging the husband's property is not a scribal error. [6] **What,** then, does the Mishnah **mean** when **it states** that if the husband mortgaged a field that was worth only a maneh and not two hundred zuz as security for the payment of his wife's ketubah, **"he is still liable"?** [7] It means to say that the woman can still collect the full value of her ketubah **from** the **free property** in her husband's possession, for the woman's right to collect her ketubah from all her husband's property is based on a condition laid down by the court.

[1] אִיבָּעֵית אֵימָא רַבִּי מֵאִיר, וְאִיבָּעֵית אֵימָא רַבִּי יְהוּדָה. [2] אִיבָּעֵית אֵימָא רַבִּי יְהוּדָה: [3] הָתָם, כָּתְבָה לֵיהּ: "הִתְקַבַּלְתִּי"; [4] הָכָא, לָא כָּתְבָה לֵיהּ: "הִתְקַבַּלְתִּי". [5] אִיבָּעֵית אֵימָא רַבִּי מֵאִיר: [6] מַאי "חַיָּיב" דְּקָתָנֵי? [7] מִן הַמְחוֹרָרִין.

LITERAL TRANSLATION

[1] If you wish, say it is Rabbi Meir, and if you wish, say it is Rabbi Yehudah. [2] If you wish, say it is Rabbi Yehudah: [3] There, she wrote for him: "I have received"; [4] here, she did not write for him: "I have received." [5] If you wish, say it is Rabbi Meir: [6] What [is meant by] "he is liable" that he teaches? [7] [He is liable to pay] from free property.

RASHI

הכא לא כתבה ליה התקבלתי — ואשמעינן מתניתין דאף על פי שלא כתב לה כתובה, לא אמרינן: מחלה לו עלה. אלא אמרינן: סמכה על תקנת בית דין שהכל יודעין שהנושא אשה יש לה כתובה. **מאי חייב נמי דקתני מן המחוררין** — אף על פי שלא כתב לה אחריות, תנאי בית דין הוא להיות כל נכסיו אחראין לה בעודם לפניו. אבל אם מכרם, אינה טורפת לקוחות, הואיל ולא נכתב בשטר, ולא אמרינן: אחריות טעות סופר הוא.

HALAKHAH

husband has already transferred to a third party, provided that he committed himself to their maintenance by means of a valid mode of acquisition or by a written document. But if there is only a verbal agreement to maintain these children, they can collect their maintenance only from his free assets." (*Rambam, Sefer Nashim, Hilkhot Ishut* 23:18; *Shulḥan Arukh, Even HaEzer* 114:4.)

TRANSLATION AND COMMENTARY

לֹא כָּתַב לָהּ [1] The Gemara now proceeds to analyze the next clause of the Mishnah, which stated: **"If the husband did not write** in his wife's ketubah: 'If you are taken captive, I will ransom you and I will bring you back to me as my wife,' he is nevertheless required to ransom her and to take her back as his wife, because the husband's duty to ransom his wife is based on a condition laid down by the court." [2] **The father of Shmuel said:** If **the wife of an ordinary Jew** (a non-priest) **was raped,** she **is forbidden to her husband,** [3] because **we suspect that** only at **the beginning** did she submit to the rapist **under duress, but** by **the end** she complied with him **willingly.**

אֵיתִיבֵיהּ [4] **Rav raised an objection against** the ruling of **Shmuel's father** from our Mishnah, which stated: "If the husband did not write in his wife's ketubah: [5] **'If you are taken captive, I will ransom you and I will bring you back to me as my wife,'** he is nevertheless required to ransom her and to take her back as his wife." Even though a woman who has been taken captive is presumed to have been raped, the husband is required to ransom her and to take her back as his wife. Thus we see that even when there is a presumption of rape, a woman remains permitted to her husband, and we do not suspect that by the final stages of the sexual act she responded willingly to her attacker.

אִישְׁתִּיק [6] The Gemara continues: When Shmuel's father heard Rav's objection, **he remained silent** and refrained from defending his position. [7] **Rav applied to Shmuel's father** the following verse (Job 29:9): **"The princes refrained from talking, and laid their hand on their mouth,"** implying that Shmuel's father was silent, even though he could have offered a convincing rebuttal of Rav's objection. [8] The Gemara explains: **What could** Shmuel's father **have said?** [9] He could have said: **In the case of a captured woman** the Sages **were lenient.** The Mishnah speaks of a woman who has been taken captive. She is presumed to have been raped, but there is no certainty about the matter. In such a case, the Sages were lenient, and did not add to the presumption of rape the suspicion that by the end of the sexual act the captured woman yielded to her attacker of her own free will.

וְלַאֲבוּהּ דִּשְׁמוּאֵל [10] The Gemara now raises another objection against the ruling given by Shmuel's father: **But according to Shmuel's father, how do we find a case of duress** regarding **which the Torah exempted** from punishment the person who acted under compulsion? The verse (Deuteronomy 22:26): "But to the *na'arah* you shall do nothing," teaches that the victim of rape is exempt from punishment, because she was

[1] ״לֹא כָּתַב לָהּ וכו׳״. [2] אָמַר אֲבוּהּ דִּשְׁמוּאֵל: אֵשֶׁת יִשְׂרָאֵל שֶׁנֶּאֶנְסָה, אֲסוּרָה לְבַעְלָהּ. [3] חָיְישִׁינַן שֶׁמָּא תְּחִלָּתָהּ בְּאוֹנֶס וְסוֹפָהּ בְּרָצוֹן.

[4] אֵיתִיבֵיהּ רַב לַאֲבוּהּ דִּשְׁמוּאֵל: [5] ״׳אִם תִּשְׁתַּבָּאִי, אֶפְרְקִינָךְ וְאוֹתְבִינָךְ לִי לְאִינְתּוּ׳״.

[6] אִישְׁתִּיק. [7] קְרֵי רַב עֲלֵיהּ דַּאֲבוּהּ דִּשְׁמוּאֵל: ״שָׂרִים עָצְרוּ בְמִלִּים, וְכַף יָשִׂימוּ לְפִיהֶם״. [8] מַאי אִית לֵיהּ לְמֵימַר? [9] בִּשְׁבוּיָה הֵקִילוּ.

[10] וְלַאֲבוּהּ דִּשְׁמוּאֵל, אוֹנֶס דְּשַׁרְיָא רַחֲמָנָא הֵיכִי מַשְׁכַּחַתְּ לָהּ?

LITERAL TRANSLATION

[1] "If he did not write for her, etc." [2] The father of Shmuel said: The wife of an Israelite who was raped is forbidden to her husband. [3] We suspect that perhaps its beginning was under duress, but its end was with consent.

[4] Rav raised an objection against the father of Shmuel: [5] "'If you are taken captive, I will ransom you and I will bring you back to me as my wife.'"

[6] He was silent. [7] Rav quoted (lit., "read") regarding the father of Shmuel: "The princes refrained from talking, and laid their hand on their mouth." [8] What does he have to say? [9] In [the case of] a captured woman they were lenient.

[10] But according to the father of Shmuel, how do you find a [case of] duress that the Torah (lit., "the Merciful One") permitted?

RASHI

תחלתה באונס – תחלתה של בעילה. **וסופה** – של בעילה. ולקמיה פריך: אונס דשריא רחמנא היכי משכחת לה? **בשבויה הקילו** – שלא ראינוה שנבעלה, וכי קאמר איהו בנבעלה.

SAGES

אֲבוּהּ דִּשְׁמוּאֵל The father of Shmuel. See *Ketubot*, Part II, p. 150.

NOTES

חָיְישִׁינַן שֶׁמָּא תְּחִלָּתָהּ בְּאוֹנֶס We suspect that perhaps its beginning was under duress. According to *Tosafot*, our suspicion that the rape victim yielded willingly to her assailant by the final stages of the sexual act is based on Torah law, for were it only based on a Rabbinic enactment, the woman would not be forbidden to her husband. But *Rid* and *Ritva* maintain that Shmuel's father agrees that by Torah law a woman who has been raped is permitted to her husband unless he is a priest. But by Rabbinic decree she is forbidden to him, because we suspect that by the end of the intercourse she complied with the rapist of her own free will. According to this explanation, the Gemara's

[1]כְּגוֹן דְּקָאָמְרִי עֵדִים שֶׁצָּוְוחָה מִתְּחִלָּה וְעַד סוֹף.
[2]וּפְלִיגָא דְּרָבָא, דְּאָמַר רָבָא: [3]כָּל שֶׁתְּחִלָּתָהּ בְּאוֹנֶס וְסוֹף בְּרָצוֹן, אֲפִילּוּ הִיא אוֹמֶרֶת: "הַנִּיחוּ לוֹ", [4]שֶׁאִלְמָלֵא לֹא נִזְקַק לָהּ, הִיא שׂוֹכַרְתּוֹ, מוּתֶּרֶת. [5]מַאי טַעֲמָא? [6]יֵצֶר אַלְבָּשָׁהּ.
[7]תַּנְיָא כְּוָותֵיהּ דְּרָבָא: "'וְהִיא

LITERAL TRANSLATION

[1]For example, where witnesses say that she cried out from beginning to end.

[2]And this [opinion] disagrees with [that of] Rava, for Rava said: [3]Wherever its beginning was under duress but its end was with consent, even if she says: "Let him be," [4]for if he had not attacked her, she would have hired him, she is permitted. [5]What is the reason? [6]Passion overcame her.

[7]It was taught in accordance with Rava: "'And she

TRANSLATION AND COMMENTARY

forced to submit to her attacker against her will. Why do we not say that she should be subject to punishment because we suspect that by the end of the sexual act she yielded willingly to her attacker?

כְּגוֹן [1]The Gemara answers: According to Shmuel's father, the Torah exempts the raped girl from punishment only if we are certain that she was acting under duress throughout the act — **for example, where witnesses** come and **testify that she cried out** and resisted her attacker **from the beginning** of intercourse **until the end.**

וּפְלִיגָא דְּרָבָא [2]The Gemara notes: **This opinion** expressed by Shmuel's father **is in disagreement with** the opinion **of Rava, for Rava said:** [3]**Wherever** a married woman is forced to have intercourse with a man other than her husband, even if only at **the beginning** does she submit to the rapist **under duress, but** by **the end** she complies with him **willingly,** and **even if** at the end **she says: "Let** the rapist **be,"** [4]**for if he had not attacked her, she** herself **would have** gone out and **hired him** for sexual relations, **she is permitted** to live with her husband. [5]**Why** is she permitted to her husband if she yielded willingly to the rapist? [6]Because we assume that her sexual **passion overpowered her.** During intercourse her natural impulses were aroused and she did not have the power to resist them. Thus we view her "willing" submission to the rapist as an act performed under duress.

תַּנְיָא כְּוָותֵיהּ [7]The Gemara now cites a Baraita that **was taught in accordance with** the viewpoint of **Rava:** "If a woman was warned by her husband against being alone with a certain man and she disobeyed her husband and was observed alone with that man, she is forbidden to her husband until she undergoes the test of 'the bitter waters' to determine whether or not she was guilty of adultery (see Numbers 5:11-31). Regarding

BACKGROUND

"וְהִיא לֹא נִתְפָּשָׂה" **"And she was not seized."** The expression "she was seized" (נִתְפָּשָׂה) is understood here as referring to her being raped, as in: "If a man finds a virgin *na'arah* who has not been betrothed, and seizes her [וּתְפָשָׂהּ], and lies with her..." (Deuteronomy 22:28). Hence the expression here, "she was not seized," is taken to mean that she was not raped.

RASHI

יצר אלבשה — וגם זה אונס. שבתחלת בעילה שהיא באונס הלבישה הבועל יצר. **והיא** — מיעוטא הוא. כלומר, בסתם אשה אמרתי לך טעם האיסור תלוי ב"לא נתפשה", הא נתפשה מותרת, ויש אשה שאף על פי שברצון — מותרת, ואיזו זו כו'.

NOTES

question should be understood as follows: In what case is the victim of rape exempt from punishment and permitted to her husband even according to Rabbinic law? Some strengthen this question by pointing to the rule set down by *Taz* that the Rabbis are not authorized to forbid something that the Torah explicitly permits. How, then, could the Rabbis have forbidden a rape victim to her husband, if the Torah states explicitly that she is not liable for her transgression (*Eshel Avraham*)?

כְּגוֹן דְּקָאָמְרִי עֵדִים שֶׁצָּוְוחָה מִתְּחִלָּה וְעַד סוֹף **For example, where witnesses say that she cried out from beginning to end.** The Aḥaronim argue that the Gemara could have suggested other cases in which we can apply the rule that if someone committed a transgression because of circumstances beyond his control, the Torah exempts him from punishment. For example, if a woman engaged in sexual relations with a man, mistakenly thinking that he was her husband (*Giddulei Shmuel*). Or else, if a woman remarried on the basis of the testimony of a single witness, and it later became known that her first husband was still alive (*Mitzpeh Eitan*). In both these cases, Shmuel's father would agree that the woman is exempt from punishment, for at the time of intercourse she was not violating the transgression of her own free will. The Gemara suggested the case in which the woman resisted her attacker from beginning to end, because the ruling issued by Shmuel's father relates to the case of rape, about which the Torah says that the victim is exempt from punishment because she cried out and nobody came to her rescue.

יֵצֶר אַלְבָּשָׁהּ **Passion overcame her.** *Rashi* explains the phrase as follows: "He clothed her with desire," meaning that the rapist filled her with desire when he violated her. *Rambam*'s explanation is slightly different: "Her desire took hold of her," meaning that the woman's natural desires

HALAKHAH

כָּל שֶׁתְּחִלָּתָהּ בְּאוֹנֶס, וְסוֹף בְּרָצוֹן **Wherever its beginning was under duress but its end was with consent.** "If the wife of a non-priest was raped, she is permitted to her husband. A woman is treated as a victim of rape if she was forced by another man to have intercourse with him, even if she yielded willingly to him during the final stages of the act," following Rava. (*Rambam, Sefer Kedushah, Hilkhot Issurei Bi'ah* 1:9; *Shulḥan Arukh, Even HaEzer* 6:11.)

TRANSLATION AND COMMENTARY

such a woman, the Torah says (ibid., verse 13): **'And she was not seized,'** [1]which teaches us that **only** if the woman is suspected of having been unfaithful and if she was not raped **is she forbidden** to her husband until her fidelity is established. [2]**But if she was** indeed **seized** against her will and raped, **she is permitted** to him. Now, the word 'she' (היא) is a term of limitation, teaching us that only in the ordinary case does the woman's fitness to continue living with her husband depend upon whether she was violated against her will or whether she yielded willingly to her attacker. [3]But **there is another** case **in which even though** the woman **was not violated** entirely against her will **she is** nevertheless **permitted** to her husband. [4]**And which** case **is that?** [5]**Wherever** at **the beginning** of the rape the woman **was under duress, but** by **the end** she complied with her attacker **willingly.** Even though she yielded willingly during the final stages of the act, she is still permitted to her husband, for she too is viewed as having acted under duress."

תַּנְיָא אִידָךְ [6]The Gemara now cites another Baraita, which interprets the verse differently. **It was taught in another Baraita:** "The verse states: **'And she was not seized,'** [7]which teaches us that **only** if the woman was not raped **is she forbidden** to her husband. [8]**But if she was** indeed **seized** against her will and raped, **she is permitted** to him. The word 'she' is a term of limitation, teaching us that [9]**there is another** case **in which even though** the woman **was seized** and forced to have relations with another man against her will, **she is** nevertheless **forbidden** to her husband. [10]**And which** case **is that?** [11]It is the case of **the wife of a priest,** for a priest is forbidden to continue living with his wife if she has had relations with another man, even if she was the victim of rape."

אָמַר רַב יְהוּדָה [12]The Gemara gives another interpretation of this verse. **Rav Yehudah said in the name of Shmuel who said in the name of Rabbi Yishmael:** "The verse states: **'And she was not seized,'** [13]which teaches us that **only** if the woman was not raped **is she forbidden** to her husband. [14]**But if she was** indeed **seized** and raped, **she is permitted** to him. The word 'she' is a term of limitation, teaching us that [15]**there is another** case **in which even though** the woman **was not seized** and forced to have sexual relations against her will, **she is** nevertheless **permitted** to continue living with her husband. [16]**And which** case **is that?**

לֹא נִתְפָּשָׂה׳. [1]אֲסוּרָה. [2]הָא נִתְפְּשָׂה, מוּתֶּרֶת. [3]וְיֵשׁ לְךָ אַחֶרֶת שֶׁאַף עַל פִּי שֶׁלֹּא נִתְפְּשָׂה מוּתֶּרֶת, [4]וְאֵיזוֹ? [5]זוֹ כָּל שֶׁתְּחִלָּתָהּ בְּאוֹנֶס, וְסוֹפָהּ בְּרָצוֹן״.

[6]תַּנְיָא אִידָךְ: ״׳וְהִיא לֹא נִתְפָּשָׂה׳. [7]אֲסוּרָה. [8]הָא נִתְפְּשָׂה, מוּתֶּרֶת. [9]וְיֵשׁ לְךָ אַחֶרֶת שֶׁאַף עַל פִּי שֶׁנִּתְפְּשָׂה אֲסוּרָה. [10]וְאֵיזוֹ? [11]זוֹ אֵשֶׁת כֹּהֵן״.

[12]אָמַר רַב יְהוּדָה אָמַר שְׁמוּאֵל מִשּׁוּם רַבִּי יִשְׁמָעֵאל: ״׳וְהִיא לֹא נִתְפָּשָׂה׳. [13]אֲסוּרָה. [14]הָא נִתְפְּשָׂה, מוּתֶּרֶת. [15]וְיֵשׁ לָהּ אַחֶרֶת שֶׁאַף עַל פִּי שֶׁלֹּא נִתְפְּשָׂה מוּתֶּרֶת. [16]וְאֵיזוֹ?

LITERAL TRANSLATION

was not seized.' [1][Only then] is she forbidden. [2]But [if] she was seized, she is permitted. [3]And you have another one who although she was not seized is permitted. [4]And who is this? [5]Wherever its beginning was under duress, but its end was with consent."

[6]Another [Baraita] was taught: "'And she was not seized.' [7][Only then] is she forbidden. [8]But [if] she was seized, she is permitted. [9]And you have another one who although she was seized is forbidden. [10]And who is this? [11]This is the wife of a priest."

[12]Rav Yehudah said in the name of Shmuel who said in the name of Rabbi Yishmael: "'And she was not seized.' [13][Only then] is she forbidden. [14]But [if] she was seized, she is permitted. [15]And you have another one who although she was not seized is permitted. [16]And who is this?

NOTES

compelled her to yield willingly. There may be a difference between these two explanations regarding the definition of compulsion: Is someone considered to be acting under compulsion only when the source of compulsion is external, or is he considered to be acting under compulsion even when he is being pressured by internal forces?

HALAKHAH

זוֹ אֵשֶׁת כֹּהֵן **This is the wife of a priest.** "If the wife of a priest has intercourse with another man, even if this intercourse was rape, she is forbidden to her husband." (*Rambam, Sefer Kedushah, Hilkhot Issurei Bi'ah* 18:7; *Shulḥan Arukh, Even HaEzer* 6:10.)

TRANSLATION AND COMMENTARY

[1]**It is** the case of a woman **whose betrothal was made in error** — for example, if the validity of her betrothal was made dependent upon the fulfillment of a certain condition, and that condition was never met. Such a woman, even if she has lived for years with her husband, [2]and **even if** she has **a child** by him who **is** now **riding on her shoulder, may** at any time **refuse** her husband **and leave** him without the need to receive a bill of divorce, for she was never legally married to him. In such a case, the woman is permitted to her husband even if she willingly engaged in sexual relations with another man, for only a married woman becomes forbidden to her husband when she commits adultery, and this woman was never legally married to her husband."

[1]זו שֶׁקִּידּוּשֶׁיהָ קִדּוּשֵׁי טָעוּת, [2]שֶׁאֲפִילּוּ בְּנָהּ מוּרְכָּב עַל כְּתֵיפָהּ מְמָאֶנֶת וְהוֹלֶכֶת לָהּ". [3]אָמַר רַב יְהוּדָה: הָנֵי נָשֵׁי דְּגַנְבוּ גַּנָּבֵי שַׁרְיָין לְגוּבְרַיְיהוּ. [4]אָמְרִי לֵיהּ רַבָּנַן לְרַב יְהוּדָה: "וְהָא קָא מַמְטִיאָן לְהוּ נַהֲמָא!" [5]"מֵחֲמַת יִרְאָה". [6]"וְהָא קָא מְשַׁלְּחָן לְהוּ גִּירֵי!" [7]"מֵחֲמַת יִרְאָה. [8]וַדַּאי שֶׁבַקִינְהוּ וְאָזְלָן מִנַּפְשַׁיְיהוּ, אֲסִירָן". [9]תָּנוּ רַבָּנַן: "שְׁבוּיֵי מַלְכוּת

LITERAL TRANSLATION

[1]This is she whose betrothal was a betrothal [made] in error, [2]who even if her son is riding on her shoulder may refuse and walk away."

[3]Rav Yehudah said: Those women whom thieves have abducted (lit., "stolen") are permitted to their husbands. [4]The Rabbis said to Rav Yehudah: "But surely they bring them bread!" [5]"Out of fear." [6]"But surely they send them arrows!" [7]"Out of fear. [8][But] certainly [if the thieves] left them and they went [back to them] on their own volition, they are forbidden."

[9]Our Rabbis taught: "Women captured by the government

RASHI

קידושי טעות – על תנאי, ולא נתקיים התנאי, אם זינתה תחתיו מותרת לו, לפי שאינה אשתו אלא פנויה בעלמא היא. **הני נשי דגנבו גנבי** – שלסטים גונבין מתחת בעליהן. **שריין לגברייהו** – לפי שבאונס הם באין עליהן. **והא קא ממטין להו נהמא** – והרי אנו רואים שבעודן אללן מוליכות להן לאותן גנבים לחם ומזון, אלמא רלון הוא! ומשני: מחמת יראה הוא דעבוד. **והא קא משלחן להו גירי** – כשנלחמין, מזמנות ומושיטות להם חילים לירות. **ודאי אי שבקינהו** – גנבים ללכת אל בעליהן, ואיהו אזלן מנפשייהו אל הגנבים – אסירן. **שבויי מלכות** – נשים ששבה המלך לתשמיש.

אָמַר רַב יְהוּדָה [3]The Gemara continues: **Rav Yehudah said: Women who have been abducted** from their husbands **by thieves are permitted to** continue living with **their husbands,** even if they have had sexual intercourse with their abductors, for they were certainly acting under duress. [4]**The Rabbis said to Rav Yehudah: "But surely** we see that in many cases the abducted women **bring** their abductors their **bread** and prepare their meals for them, and this indicates submission on their part. They should therefore be forbidden to their husbands." Rav Yehudah answered: "Although these women may appear to be serving their captors of their own free will, [5]they are acting solely **out of fear.** Thus, even if they engaged in sexual relations with their abductors, they are considered to have acted under duress." [6]The Rabbis raised another objection: **"But surely** we see that when the abductors are in battle, the women they have abducted often prepare their ammunition for them and **hand them** their **arrows!** This must be taken as a sign that the women have submitted to their captors of their own free will, for if not, they would refrain from helping them so that their captors may be killed in the fighting." [7]Rabbi Yehudah answered: "Even in such cases we assume that the women were acting solely **out of fear** for their lives, and so they are permitted to their husbands. [8]**But certainly, if the thieves leave** their captives behind and the women **return to them of their own free will, they are** thenceforth **forbidden** to their husbands, for in such cases they cannot argue that they were acting under compulsion."

תָּנוּ רַבָּנַן [9]**Our Rabbis taught** the following Baraita: **"Women who have been taken captive by government**

HALAKHAH

זו שֶׁקִּידּוּשֶׁיהָ קִדּוּשֵׁי טָעוּת This is she whose betrothal was a betrothal made in error. "If a woman is not married by Torah law, and she commits adultery, she is treated as a single woman who engaged in sexual relations, and so she is permitted to her husband, even if he is a priest (see *Maggid Mishneh*)." (*Rambam, Sefer Kedushah, Hilkhot Issurei Bi'ah* 3:2.)

נָשֵׁי דְּגַנְבוּ גַּנָּבֵי Those women whom thieves have abducted. "A woman who was abducted by thieves is treated as a captive, and is therefore permitted to her husband. But if the woman was released and chose to return to her abductors of her own free will, she is forbidden to her husband," following Rabbi Yehudah. (*Rambam, Sefer Nashim, Hilkhot Ishut* 24:20.)

הֲרֵי הֵן כִּשְׁבוּיִין. [1]גְּנוּבֵי לִיסְטוּת אֵינָן כִּשְׁבוּיִין״.
[2]וְהָתַנְיָא אִיפְּכָא!
[3]מַלְכוּת אַמַּלְכוּת לָא קַשְׁיָא.
[4]הָא בְּמַלְכוּת אֲחַשְׁוֵרוֹשׁ; [5]הָא בְּמַלְכוּת בֶּן נֶצֶר.
[6]לִיסְטוּת אַלִּיסְטוּת לָא קַשְׁיָא.
[7]הָא בְּבֶן נֶצֶר; [8]הָא בְּלִיסְטִים דְּעָלְמָא.

LITERAL TRANSLATION

are considered as captives. [1]Women abducted by bandits are not considered as captives."

[2]But surely the reverse was taught!

[3][From] government to government there is no difficulty. [4]This, [the former, refers] to the government of Ahasuerus; [5]this, [the latter, refers] to the government of Ben Netzer.

[6][From] banditry to banditry there is no difficulty. [7]This, [the former, refers] to Ben Netzer; [8]this, [the latter, refers] to an ordinary bandit.

RASHI

הרי הן כשבויין — ומותרין לבעליהן, כדתנן: ואותבינך לי לאינתו. **במלכות אחשורוש** — הן כשבויין, לפי שמלך גדול הוא, ויודעת שלא ישאנה, ובעילתה באונס. **בן נצר** — לסטים היה, ולכד עיירות ומלך עליהם, ונעשה ראש לסטים. ובדידיה תנן: שבויי מלכות אינן כשבויין, ואסורות לבעליהן. דסברה: מינסב קא נסיב לה, ונבעלת ברצון. **ליסטות אליסטות כו׳** — בבן נצר אסורות, כדאמרינן דסברה: מינסב נסיב לי והריני אשת מלך. **ליסטים דעלמא** — אפילו לקוחים שלו קשין לה, לפיכך אינה אלא אנוסה.

TRANSLATION AND COMMENTARY

officials **are considered as captives** who are permitted to continue living with their husbands, for if they have had sexual relations with their captors, it was certainly under duress. [1]But **women who have been abducted by bandits are not considered as captives.** They are forbidden to their husbands, for they are assumed to have submitted willingly to their abductors."

וְהָתַנְיָא אִיפְּכָא [2]The Gemara objects: **But surely** just **the reverse was taught** in a different Baraita — that women who have been abducted by bandits are treated as captives, who are permitted to their husbands, whereas women who have been taken captive by the king or by government officials are not treated as captives, and therefore they may not return to their husbands!

מַלְכוּת אַמַּלְכוּת [3]The Gemara now resolves the contradiction between the two Baraitot. **There is no difficulty** in reconciling **the two** rulings concerning a woman taken captive by a king or by a **government** official. [4]**The first** Baraita, which states that a woman taken captive by a government official is treated as a captive who is permitted to her husband, **refers to a government** like that **of Ahasuerus,** the king who reigned over the Persian empire in the days of Esther. If a woman is taken captive by a powerful king, she knows that he will not marry her; and therefore if she had sexual relations with him, it must have been under duress. [5]By contrast, **the second** Baraita, which states that a woman taken captive by a government official is not treated as a captive, **refers to a government** like that **of Ben Netzer,** a brigand who established himself as king over the territories that he captured. If a woman is taken captive by a minor king, she harbors the hope that he will take her as his wife and make her queen, and therefore she is ready to submit willingly to his advances.

לִיסְטוּת אַלִּיסְטוּת [6]The Gemara continues: **There is** also **no difficulty** in reconciling **the two** rulings concerning a woman who was abducted by **a bandit.** [7]**The first** Baraita, which states that the woman is not considered a captive, **refers to** a woman who was abducted by a bandit-king like **Ben Netzer.** As was explained above, we assume that she yielded to him of her own free will, hoping that he might marry her and make her queen. [8]**The second** Baraita, which states that the woman is considered a captive, **refers to** a woman who was abducted by **an ordinary bandit.** There we assume that if the woman engaged in sexual relations with her captor, it must have been under compulsion, for she certainly could not have had any desire to marry such a person.

NOTES

אֵינָן כִּשְׁבוּיִין Are not considered as captives. *Rabbi Shmuel HaNaggid* and many other Rishonim rule that whenever there are grounds for assuming that a woman submitted willingly to her captor, not only is she forbidden to her husband but her husband is not even required to ransom her. While there are cases in which the husband is obligated to ransom his wife even though she will be forbidden to him after she is released (for example, if the husband forbade her by a vow from benefiting from him, or if the husband was a priest; see below, 52a), here, if the woman submitted willingly, the Rabbis penalized her and freed her husband from paying her ransom.

הָא בְּבֶן נֶצֶר This refers to Ben Netzer. The Rishonim offer various explanations of why a woman taken captive by someone like the bandit-king Ben Netzer is not treated as a captive. Our commentary follows *Rashi* and others, who explain that if a woman is captured by a mighty king, she knows that he will not marry her, and therefore there is no reason to assume that she submitted to him willingly. Similarly, if she is captured by an ordinary bandit, we do not assume that she will have yielded to her captor willingly, for she will have had no desire to marry him. But if a woman is taken captive by a minor potentate like Ben Netzer, there is concern that she may have yielded to him

BACKGROUND

בֶּן נֶצֶר Ben Netzer. This was the original family name of Odenathus, who ruled over Palmyra — an area in Syria — during the middle of the third century C.E. Odenathus took advantage of the long, indecisive wars between Rome and Persia to expand his own authority and extend his sphere of influence well beyond the small desert region where Palmyra was located. After he joined forces with the Romans and fought against the Persian king, Shapur I, the Roman authorities appointed Odena-thus ruler of all the neighboring provinces. At the same time, he attempted to establish an independent, wide-ranging kingdom for himself. Ben Netzer was murdered in 267 C.E., and his grave was discovered among the ruins of Palmyra. His widow, Queen Zenobia, was later able to extend her influence to the boundaries of Egypt, until she was defeated by the Romans. The Rabbis strongly opposed Ben Netzer and his rule, presumably because of his hostility toward the Jews (which he manifested through the conquest and destruction of the Babylonian city of Neharde'a). Thus the Gemara here describes Ben Netzer as a combination of bandit and king.

LANGUAGE

לִיסְטִים Bandit. This word is derived from the Greek λῃστής, *lestes*, meaning a robber or pirate. The form ליסטים (rather than ליסטיס) owes its origin to an ancient spelling error (interchange between the letters ם and ס, which look alike), and this form eventually became standard.

BACKGROUND

גַּבֵּי אֲחַשְׁוֵרוֹשׁ Compared to Ahasuerus. In the opinion of most commentators, Ahasuerus was mentioned here only as an example of a mighty ruler ("who reigned from India to Ethiopia, a hundred and twenty seven provinces" [Esther 1:1]) as opposed to Ben Netzer, who was only a minor tribal leader and increased his power by various stratagems, ultimately declaring himself king. However, other commentators explain that Ahasuerus was mentioned here because he was particularly lecherous and took women by force.

TRANSLATION AND COMMENTARY

וּבֶן נֶצֶר [1] The Gemara asks: Why is it that **there,** in the first Baraita, **Ben Netzer is called a king, whereas here,** in the second Baraita, he **is called a bandit?**

אִין [2] The Gemara answers: **Indeed, compared to Ahasuerus,** Ben Netzer **is** considered **a bandit,** for he started his career as one. Thus in the first Baraita, which speaks of a woman captured by a king like Ahasuerus, Ben Netzer is called a bandit. [3] But **compared to ordinary bandits,** Ben Netzer **is a king,** for he ultimately became the sovereign ruler of a large dominion. Hence in the second Baraita, which refers to a woman who was abducted by ordinary bandits, Ben Netzer is called a king.

וּבְכֹהֶנֶת [4] The Gemara now proceeds to analyze the next clause of the Mishnah, which stated: **"And** similarly **in the case of a woman married to a priest, if** the husband **did not write** in his wife's ketubah: **'I will** ransom you and I will **return you to your city,'** he is nevertheless held liable for her ransom and is required to care for her until she returns to her father's home." [5] **Abaye said:** If **a widow was married to a High Priest** and she was taken captive, her husband **is obligated to ransom her.** A High Priest is forbidden to marry a widow, and if he does marry a widow, he is required to divorce her and to pay her her ketubah. If such a woman is taken captive, her husband is required to ransom her, [6] **for we can apply to her** what is stated in the ketubah of **a woman married to a priest: "I will** ransom you and I will **return you to your city."** Whenever a priest marries — even when he marries a woman who is not permitted to him — he obligates himself to ransom his wife. Thus, when a High Priest marries a widow, he obligates himself to ransom her from captivity, even though she was forbidden to him even before she was taken captive.

[1] וּבֶן נֶצֶר, הָתָם קָרֵי לֵיהּ מֶלֶךְ וְהָכָא קָרֵי לֵיהּ לִסְטִים!
[2] אִין. גַּבֵּי אֲחַשְׁוֵרוֹשׁ, לִסְטִים הוּא; [3] גַּבֵּי לִסְטִים דְּעָלְמָא, מֶלֶךְ הוּא.
[4] "וּבְכֹהֶנֶת, 'אַהַדְרִינָךְ לִמְדִינָתֵיךְ', וכו'". [5] אָמַר אַבַּיֵי: אַלְמָנָה לְכֹהֵן גָּדוֹל, חַיָּיב לִפְדּוֹתָהּ, [6] שֶׁאֲנִי קוֹרֵא בָּהּ: "וּבְכֹהֶנֶת, 'אַהַדְרִינָךְ לִמְדִינָתֵיךְ'".

LITERAL TRANSLATION

[1] And [regarding] Ben Netzer, there they call him a king and here they call him a bandit!

[2] Yes. Compared to Ahasuerus, he is a bandit; [3] compared to an ordinary bandit, he is a king.

[4] "Or in [the case of] a priest's wife, [if he did not write:] 'I will return you to your city, etc.'" [5] Abaye said: [In the case of] a widow [married] to a High Priest, he is obligated to ransom her, [6] for I apply (lit. "read") to her: "Or in [the case of] a priest's wife, [if he did not write:] 'I will return you to your city.'"

RASHI

לגבי אחשורוש לסטים הוא — הלכך מתניתין קמייתא דמיירי במלכות אחשורוש — קרי לבן נצר גנובי ליסטות. וברייתא דתנן איפכא דגנובי ליסטות איירי בליסטים דעלמא, קרי לבן נצר שבויי מלכות. **אלמנה לכהן גדול** — קיימא לן לקמן בפרק "אלמנה ניזונית" (כתובות ק,ב) יש לה כתובה ותנאי כתובה, ההוא דלמיסקל ולמיפק קאי. אבל תנאי כתובה דלמיקם קמיה, כגון מזונות ורפואה — אמרינן ביבמות דלית לה, בפרק "יש מותרות" (פה,א). והכא אשמעינן אביי דתנאי כתובה דפירקונה אית לה, דמעיקרא אישתעבד לה, שהרי אף לכשרה לא היה מתנה "ואותבינך לאינתו" אלא "אהדרינך למדינתך", והא נמי קרינן בה הכי. והאי תנאי נמי למיסקל ומיפק קאי.

NOTES

of her own free will, hoping that he would take her as his queen.

Ramban objects to this explanation, arguing that — unless her behavior indicates otherwise — we assume that a Jewish woman who is taken captive will remain faithful to her husband, and that she will not yield willingly to her captor even if he promises to marry her.

Rabbenu Ḥananel offers a different explanation: If a woman was captured by a mighty king like Ahasuerus, from whom she knows she will not be rescued, we can assume that she was acting under compulsion even if she did not protest against his advances. But if she was captured by a lesser potentate like Ben Netzer, she might have been rescued had she raised a protest, and therefore if she fails to protest, she is assumed to have yielded to her captor of her own free will.

Ramban also objects to this explanation, arguing that if the woman could have saved herself from Ben Netzer by protesting, then surely she could have saved herself from an ordinary bandit in the same way. Why, then, is a woman permitted to her husband if she was captured by an ordinary bandit? *Ramban* answers that, in the case of an ordinary bandit, we assume that the woman did not protest because she was afraid that she would be killed if she did so. But Ben Netzer, who was a king, would not have killed his captive if she had protested, and therefore her failure to protest is to be interpreted as a sign of willing submission.

Ramban himself prefers a third explanation: Unlike Ahasuerus, Ben Netzer was strongly opposed to rape, and therefore if a woman was taken captive in his kingdom and engaged in sexual relations with her captor, she is assumed to have acted of her own free will.

TRANSLATION AND COMMENTARY

מַמְזֶרֶת [52A] [1] But if **a *mamzeret*** (a woman born from an incestuous or adulterous relationship) **or a *netinah*** (a female descendant of the Gibeonites, a people who converted to Judaism during the days of Joshua but were later forbidden to marry other Jews) was **married to a non-priest** and was taken captive, her husband **is not obligated to ransom her.** An ordinary Jew of unblemished status is forbidden to marry a *mamzeret* or a *netinah*, and if he does marry one, he is required to divorce her and to give her her ketubah. But if she is taken captive, he is not obligated to ransom her, [2] **for we cannot apply to her** what is stated in the ketubah of an ordinary woman married to a non-priest: [3] "If you are taken captive, **I will** ransom you and I will **bring you back to me as my wife.**" Since the law requires that the marriage be dissolved, the obligation to ransom one's wife is not imposed.

רָבָא [4] **Rava** disagreed with Abaye about the first half of his ruling and **said: Whenever the prohibition** resulting **from** the priest's wife being taken into **captivity** is the only factor **causing her to be forbidden** to her husband, **he is obligated to ransom her.** [5] **But if** there is **some other prohibition** that also **causes her to be forbidden** to him, **he is not obligated to ransom her.** When a priest marries, he obligates himself to ransom his wife, even though she will be forbidden to him after she is released from captivity. This obligation applies only if the reason that she will be forbidden to her husband is that she has been taken captive. But if she is forbidden to her husband for some other reason — for example, if she is a widow married to a High Priest — then her husband is under no obligation to ransom her.

[52A] [1] מַמְזֶרֶת וּנְתִינָה לְיִשְׂרָאֵל, אֵינוֹ חַיָּיב לִפְדוֹתָהּ, [2] שֶׁאֵין אֲנִי קוֹרֵא בָּהּ: [3] "'וְאוֹתְבִינֵךְ לִי לְאִנְתּוּ'". [4] רָבָא אָמַר: כׇּל שֶׁאִיסּוּר שִׁבְיָיהּ גּוֹרֵם לָהּ, חַיָּיב לִפְדוֹתָהּ. [5] אִיסּוּר דָּבָר אַחֵר גּוֹרֵם לָהּ, אֵינוֹ חַיָּיב לִפְדוֹתָהּ.

LITERAL TRANSLATION

[52A] [1] [In the case of] a *mamzeret* or a *netinah* [married] to an Israelite, he is not obligated to ransom her, [2] for I do not apply (lit., "read") to her: [3] "'And I will bring you back to me as my wife.'" [4] Rava said: Whenever the prohibition of her captivity causes her [to be forbidden], he is obligated to ransom her. [5] [But if] a prohibition on account of something else causes her [to be forbidden], he is not obligated to ransom her.

RASHI

ממזרת ונתינה לישראל — אף על גב דאית לה כתובה ותנאי כתובה דלמשקל ומיפק, לית לה תנאי כתובה דפרקונה, דמעיקרא לא אשתעבד לה. **שאין אני קורא בה ואותבינך לאינתו** — שזהו תנאי כתובה לישראלית. **רבא אמר כו'** — בממזרת ונתינה כאביי סבירא ליה, דלא אשתעבד לה. אבל באלמנה לכהן גדול פליג עליה, ואמר: מעיקרא לא אשתעבד לכהנת "ואהדרינך למדינתך" אלא מחמת שאסרה השבויה עליו, אבל לנאסרה מחמת דבר אחר — לא נשתעבד, דתנאי כתובה דישראל וכהן שוין, אלא שהכהן מתנה עמה שאפילו תאסר עליו מחמת שבייתה — לא תפסיד כתובת פרקונה.

NOTES

כָּל שֶׁאִיסּוּר שִׁבְיָיה גּוֹרֵם לָהּ **Whenever the prohibition of her captivity causes her to be forbidden.** The disagreement between Abaye and Rava can be understood as follows: According to Abaye, the obligation of a non-priest to ransom his wife is substantially different from that of a priest. A non-priest obligates himself to ransom his wife, provided that she will be permitted to him after she is released from captivity. But a priest obligates himself to ransom his wife, without adding any proviso limiting his obligation. Thus the priest is required to ransom his wife, even though she will be forbidden to him — whether as a result of having been in captivity or for some other reason. According to Rava, the obligation of a priest to ransom his wife is essentially the same as that of a non-priest, except that the priest obligates himself to ransom his wife even though she will be forbidden to him as a result of her captivity. But the limitation on the obligation of the non-priest — that he is not liable for his wife's ransom if she is forbidden to him — applies to a priest as well. Thus the priest is not obligated to ransom his wife, if she will be forbidden to him for some reason other than that she has been in captivity (see *Maharam Schiff*).

HALAKHAH

כָּל שֶׁאִיסּוּר שִׁבְיָיה גּוֹרֵם לָהּ **Whenever the prohibition of her capitivity causes her to be forbidden.** "If someone marries a woman who is forbidden to him by a negative commandment, and she is taken captive, he is not obligated to ransom her. Rather, he may pay her her ketubah and she can then pay for her own ransom. But a priest is obligated to ransom his wife if her captivity is the only reason that she will be forbidden to him after her release," following Rava in his disagreement with Abaye. (*Rambam, Sefer Nashim, Hilkhot Ishut* 14:22; *Shulḥan Arukh, Even HaEzer* 78:6-7.)

CONCEPTS

מַמְזֶרֶת **A *mamzeret.*** A child born from relations between a married woman and someone other than her husband, or between relatives who are forbidden to marry by Torah law, where the participants in such a relationship are subject to excision. An exception to this rule is a menstruating woman, with whom sexual relations are forbidden under penalty of excision, but whose offspring is not a *mamzer*. The offspring of an unmarried couple is not a *mamzer*. A *mamzer* inherits from his natural father and is Halakhically considered his father's son in all respects. He may marry only a *mamzeret* or a convert to Judaism. Likewise, a *mamzeret* may marry only a *mamzer* or a convert. The offspring of any of these unions is also a *mamzer*.

נְתִינָה **A *netinah.*** In the Book of Joshua (9:3-27), the story is told that one of the Canaanite tribes living in the vicinity of the town of Gibeon approached Joshua and tricked him into signing a treaty of friendship with them. Even after the scheme was discovered, the treaty was honored. But the Gibeonites were punished for their ruse by being "given" (וַיִּתְּנֵם — *vayitenem*, from the Hebrew root נתן — *natan*, meaning "to give"; verse 27) to the Temple as hewers of wood and drawers of water for perpetuity. The *netinim* (from the same Hebrew root), the descendants of the Gibeonites, appear to have survived as a distinct group until well after the destruction of the Second Temple (see *Yevamot* 79b). The status of the *netinim* is mentioned in several places in the Talmud and is discussed in detail in tractate *Yevamot* (78b).

LITERAL TRANSLATION

[1] Shall we say that this is like the [following dispute between] Tannaim: [2] "[If] someone forbids his wife by a vow [from benefiting from him] and she is taken captive, [3] Rabbi Eliezer says: He ransoms [her] and gives her her ketubah. [4] Rabbi Yehoshua says: He gives her her ketubah but he does not ransom [her]. [5] Rabbi Natan said: I asked Summakhos: [6] When Rabbi Yehoshua said [that] he gives her her ketubah but he does not ransom [her], [7] [is that] where he forbade her by a vow and afterwards she was taken captive, [8] or [is it] where she was taken captive and afterwards he forbade her by a vow? [9] And he said to me: I did not hear, [10] but it seems [reasonable] that [it is] where he forbade her by a vow and afterwards she was taken captive." [11] For if you say that [it is where] she was taken captive and afterwards he forbade her by a vow, [12] he may come to circumvent [his obligation].

[1]לֵימָא כְּתַנָּאֵי: [2]״הַמַּדִּיר אֶת אִשְׁתּוֹ וְנִשְׁבֵּית, [3]רַבִּי אֱלִיעֶזֶר אוֹמֵר: פּוֹדֶה וְנוֹתֵן לָהּ כְּתוּבָּתָהּ. [4]רַבִּי יְהוֹשֻׁעַ אוֹמֵר: נוֹתֵן לָהּ כְּתוּבָּתָהּ וְאֵינוֹ פּוֹדֶה. [5]אָמַר רַבִּי נָתָן: שָׁאַלְתִּי אֶת סוּמָכוֹס: [6]כְּשֶׁאָמַר רַבִּי יְהוֹשֻׁעַ נוֹתֵן לָהּ כְּתוּבָּתָהּ וְאֵינוֹ פּוֹדֶה, [7]כְּשֶׁהִדִּירָהּ וּלְבַסּוֹף נִשְׁבֵּית, [8]אוֹ בְּנִשְׁבֵּית וּלְבַסּוֹף הִדִּירָהּ? [9]וְאָמַר לִי: לֹא שָׁמַעְתִּי, [10]וְנִרְאִין דְּבָרִים שֶׁהִדִּירָהּ וּלְבַסּוֹף נִשְׁבֵּית״. [11]דְּאִי אָמְרַתְּ נִשְׁבֵּית וּלְבַסּוֹף הִדִּירָהּ, [12]אָתֵי לְאִיעֲרוּמֵי.

TRANSLATION AND COMMENTARY

לֵימָא כְּתַנָּאֵי [1] The Gemara now asks: **Shall we say that this** dispute between Abaye and Rava **reflects an** earlier **Tannaitic dispute** recorded in the following Baraita? [2] **"If someone takes a vow forbidding his wife from deriving** any **benefit from him** — in which case he is required to grant her a divorce — **and** meanwhile **she is taken captive** and held for ransom, the Tannaim disagree about the husband's liability: [3] **Rabbi Eliezer says: He must pay her ransom and** then **give her her** full **ketubah** when he divorces her. [4] **Rabbi Yehoshua says: He must give her her ketubah, but he does not** have to **pay her ransom.** Instead, she must ransom herself with the money she receives as her ketubah." Before demonstrating how this dispute between Rabbi Eliezer and Rabbi Yehoshua is reflected in the disagreement between Abaye and Rava, the Gemara continues with the rest of the Baraita: [5] **"Rabbi Natan said: I asked Summakhos** the following question: [6] **When Rabbi Yehoshua said that** the husband who took a vow forbidding his wife from benefiting from him **must give her her ketubah but is not** obligated to **ransom her,** [7] was he referring to a case **where he** first **took a vow forbidding her** from benefiting from him **and** only **afterwards was she taken captive,** [8] **or** was he dealing even with a case **where she was** first **taken captive, and** only **afterwards did he take a vow forbidding her** from deriving any benefit from him? [9] **And** Summakhos **said to me: I have not heard** from my teachers the details of Rabbi Yehoshua's ruling, [10] **but it seems reasonable that** he exempted the husband from ransoming his wife only in the case **where he** first **took a vow forbidding her** from deriving benefit from him, **and afterwards she was taken captive."** [11] **If you say that** Rabbi Yehoshua's ruling applies even in the case **where** the man's wife **was taken captive and** only **afterwards did he take a vow forbidding her** from benefiting from him, [12] then whenever a woman is taken captive her husband **can circumvent his obligation** to ransom her by taking a vow forbidding her to derive any benefit from him.

RASHI

המדיר את אשתו — מליהנות לו. **פודה** — ואף על פי שסופו לגרשה מחמת נדר. **ואינו פודה** — לקמן מפרש טעמיה. **או בנשבית ולבסוף הדירה** — [כלומר: או אפילו כשנשבית ולבסוף הדירה] נמי אמר, ואף על גב דאיכא למימר לא הדירה אלא להפטר מן הפדיון.

NOTES

הַמַּדִּיר אֶת אִשְׁתּוֹ **If someone forbids his wife by a vow.** The laws pertaining to a husband who takes a vow forbidding his wife from benefiting from him are explained in detail at the beginning of the seventh chapter of *Ketubot*. As for the case discussed in our Gemara, *Rambam* rules that the husband is obligated to grant his wife a divorce as a consequence of taking the vow. *Rashi* explains that the husband took a vow forbidding his wife from deriving any benefit from him. *Meiri* says that the Baraita is referring to a case in which the husband took a vow forbidding his wife from engaging in sexual relations with him.

HALAKHAH

הַמַּדִּיר אֶת אִשְׁתּוֹ וְנִשְׁבֵּית **If someone forbids his wife by a vow from benefiting from him and she is taken captive.** "If a man takes a vow that requires him to divorce his wife and pay her her ketubah, and she is taken captive after he has taken the vow, he is not obligated to ransom her. But if she was taken captive before he took the vow, he must pay her ransom," following Rabbi Yehoshua (against Rabbi Eliezer) and Summakhos. (*Rambam, Sefer Nashim, Hilkhot Ishut* 14:21; *Shulḥan Arukh, Even HaEzer* 78:5.)

SAGES

רַבִּי נָתָן **Rabbi Natan.** One of the greatest Tannaim during the generation before the completion of the Mishnah. See *Ketubot*, Part II, p. 71.

סוּמָכוֹס **Summakhos.** His full name is Summakhos ben Yosef, and he was one of the fifth and last generation of Tannaim. Summakhos was Rabbi Meir's most distinguished disciple and was responsible for transmitting much of his master's legacy of teachings. Even after Rabbi Meir's death, Summakhos devoted much effort to resolving possible contradictions in those teachings.

Like Rabbi Meir, Summakhos was famous for his חֲרִיפוּת — his acute powers of reasoning. The Talmud (*Eruvin* 13b) praises him as being capable of providing 48 explanations to substantiate every ruling he made in matters of ritual purity.

He was apparently considered one of the leading Sages of his generation, for we even find him recorded as contesting the Halakhic opinions of the greatest of the contemporaries of Rabbi Meir, including Rabbi Yose and Rabbi Eliezer ben Ya'akov. As we see from the Gemara here, Summakhos's opinion was sought by the distinguished Sage, Rabbi Natan.

Summakhos appears to have lived to a great age, for even the Amora, Rav, met him and was taught by him.

רַבִּי יְהוֹשֻׁעַ **Rabbi Yehoshua (ben Ḥananyah the Levite).** One of the leading Tannaim of the generation following the destruction of the Second Temple. See *Ketubot*, Part II, pp. 6-7.

LANGUAGE

סוּמָכוֹס **Summakhos.** The source for this name is the Greek word σύμμαχος, *summakhos*, which means "ally."

BACKGROUND

שָׁאַלְתִּי אֶת סוּמָכוֹס **I asked Summakhos.** Rabbi Natan was a Babylonian who came to live in Eretz Israel. For that reason he was not familiar with all the oral traditions of the Sages of Eretz Israel. Therefore he asked Summakhos, Rabbi Meir's disciple, what was the tradition he had received on the subject under discussion.

¹מַאי לָאו בְּמַדִּיר אֵשֶׁת כֹּהֵן קָמִיפַּלְגִי, ²וְאַבַּיֵי דְּאָמַר כְּרַבִּי אֱלִיעֶזֶר, ³וְרָבָא דְּאָמַר כְּרַבִּי יְהוֹשֻׁעַ?

⁴לָא. ⁵הָכָא בְּמַאי עָסְקִינַן? כְּגוֹן שֶׁנָּדְרָה אִיהִי וְקִיֵּים לָהּ הוּא.

LITERAL TRANSLATION

[1] Do they not disagree about someone who forbade by a vow the wife of a priest, [2] and Abaye rules (lit., "says") in accordance with Rabbi Eliezer, [3] and Rava rules in accordance with Rabbi Yehoshua?

[4] No. [5] With what are we dealing here? For example, where she vowed and he confirmed

TRANSLATION AND COMMENTARY

מַאי לָאו [1] The Gemara now explains how the dispute between Abaye and Rava parallels the earlier dispute between Rabbi Eliezer and Rabbi Yehoshua: **Do not** the Tannaim **disagree about** a case in which **a priest took a vow forbidding his wife** from deriving benefit from him? They cannot disagree about the case of an ordinary Jew, because according to Rabbi Eliezer an ordinary Jew is only obligated to ransom his wife if he is permitted to live with her after her release. But if he has taken a vow forbidding her to benefit from him, he will be required to divorce her. Hence the Tannaim must disagree about the case in which a priest took a vow forbidding his wife from benefiting from him. Rabbi Eliezer maintains that the priest must ransom his wife, because he is obligated to do so even though she will be forbidden to him after she is released from captivity. And even though this woman will be forbidden to her husband not only because she has been taken captive, but also because her husband has taken a vow forbidding her from deriving any benefit from him, he is still responsible for her ransom. Rabbi Yehoshua disagrees and says that the priest must only pay his wife's ransom if the sole reason that she will be forbidden to him after her release is that she has been a captive. But here, where the woman is forbidden to her husband for another reason, he is not obligated to ransom her. May we not conclude, then, that **Abaye,** who says that a High Priest married to a widow must ransom his wife if she is taken captive, [2] **agrees with Rabbi Eliezer,** [3] **and** that **Rava,** who says that he is not required to ransom her, **agrees with Rabbi Yehoshua?**

לָא [4] The Gemara rejects this conclusion and suggests a different interpretation of the Tannaitic dispute: **No,** Rabbi Eliezer and Rabbi Yehoshua disagree about an entirely different matter. [5] **Here we are dealing with** the case of a woman married to a non-priest **who took a vow** forbidding herself from deriving any benefit from her husband, **and** her husband **confirmed the vow for her.** A husband is empowered to annul a vow made by his wife. But if he hears of the vow and explicitly confirms it, or if he lets a day pass without annulling it, the vow is confirmed and can no longer be annulled. Now, if a woman takes a vow forbidding herself from deriving any benefit from her husband, and the husband confirms the vow, he is no longer permitted to live with her and is required to divorce her. In such a case, the Tannaim disagree about

RASHI

מאי לאו במדיר אשת כהן – בכהן שהדיר את אשתו. דאי בישראל – לא אמר רבי אליעזר פודה, שהרי אין אני קורא בה תנאי כתובת ישראל "ואותבינך לי לאינתו". אלא בכהן קיימינן, ומשום שאני קורא בה "ואהדרינך למדינתך" קאמר רבי אליעזר פודה, ואף על גב דאיסור דבר אחר גרם לה. [ליאסר עליו. ואביי כרבי אליעזר, ורבא כרבי יהושע דאמר אינו פודה, הואיל ואיסור דבר אחר גרם לה]. **הכא במאי עסקינן כו׳** – כלומר לעולם רבי אליעזר ורבי יהושע לאו בפלוגתא דאביי ורבא פליגי. ואי באיסור דבר אחר שלא על ידי נדר, אי נמי בכהנת על ידי נדר – דכולי עלמא אי כאביי אי כרבא. והכא כגון שנדרה היא וקיים לה הוא, שאמר "יתקיים" או החריש ולא הפר ביום שמעו. ובישראל פליגי, וטעמא דרבי יהושע דקסבר – היא נתנה אצבע בין שיניה ונשכתו, כלומר: היא גרמה לעצמה לבטל תנאה, שאין אני יכול לקרות בישראל "ואותבינך לאינתו". ורבי אליעזר סבר: הוא נתן אצבעה בין שיניה לינשך, שלא הפר לה.

NOTES

לָא. הָכָא בְּמַאי עָסְקִינַן? **No. With what are we dealing here?** The Rishonim explain this passage of the Gemara in various ways. Our commentary follows *Rashi,* who explains that at this point the Gemara is saying that there is no way to determine the positions of Rabbi Eliezer and Rabbi Yehoshua on the matter in dispute between Abaye and Rava, for it is possible that they would both agree with Abaye, or that they would both agree with Rava. The disagreement between Rabbi Eliezer and Rabbi Yehoshua is limited to the case of a woman married to a non-priest who took a vow forbidding herself from deriving any benefit from her husband, and her husband confirmed the vow for her. They disagree about whether it is the woman's fault that she is now forbidden to her husband, or the fault of the husband; for if it is the husband's fault that she is forbidden to him, he is required to ransom her even though he cannot take her back as his wife.

Several objections were raised against this explanation of the Gemara: First, the Gemara does not state explicitly that Rabbi Eliezer and Rabbi Yehoshua disagree only about a woman who was married to a non-priest. If, as *Rashi* contends, this is an essential part of the Gemara's answer, the point should certainly have been mentioned. Second, if Rabbi Eliezer maintains that the husband is required to pay his wife's ransom because it is his fault that she is now forbidden to him, how could he agree with Rava with respect to the wife of a priest? The priest should certainly be required to ransom his wife, for it is his fault that she is now forbidden to him! Third, why was it necessary to say that, according to Rabbi Yehoshua, the husband is not

[1] רַבִּי אֱלִיעֶזֶר סָבַר: הוּא נוֹתֵן אֶצְבַּע בֵּין שִׁינֶּיהָ. [2] וְרַבִּי יְהוֹשֻׁעַ סָבַר: הִיא נָתְנָה אֶצְבַּע בֵּין שִׁינֶּיהָ.

[3] אִי הִיא נָתְנָה אֶצְבַּע בֵּין שִׁינֶּיהָ, כְּתוּבָּה מַאי עֲבִידְתָּהּ? [4] וְתוּ: ״אָמַר רַבִּי נָתָן: [5] שָׁאַלְתִּי אֶת סוּמָכוֹס: כְּשֶׁאָמַר רַבִּי יְהוֹשֻׁעַ נוֹתֵן לָהּ כְּתוּבָּתָהּ וְאֵינוֹ

LITERAL TRANSLATION

[the vow for her] [1] Rabbi Eliezer maintains: He puts a finger between her teeth. [2] But Rabbi Yehoshua maintains: She put a finger between her teeth.

[3] If she put a finger between her teeth, what is the ketubah's purpose (lit., "work")? [4] And furthermore: "Rabbi Natan said: [5] I asked Summakhos: When Rabbi Yehoshua said [that] he gives her her ketubah but he does not

TRANSLATION AND COMMENTARY

whether the husband is obligated to ransom her if she is taken captive before he gives her a divorce. [1] **Rabbi Eliezer maintains** that the husband is obligated to pay her ransom, for it is **he** who, as it were, **put his finger between her teeth** and caused her to bite him. By not annulling the vow on the day he heard it, the husband allowed the vow to be valid. Thus it is his fault that his wife is forbidden to him, and therefore he must ransom her even though he cannot take her back as his wife. [2] **Rabbi Yehoshua** disagrees and **maintains** that the husband is not obligated to pay his wife's ransom, for it is **she** who **put her finger between her** own **teeth,** and bit herself. It was she who took the vow that caused her to be forbidden to her husband. Thus her husband is exempt from paying her ransom, for it is her fault that he cannot fulfill the condition in her ketubah that he must ransom his wife if she is taken captive and must take her back as his wife.

אִי הִיא [3] The Gemara now raises two objections against this interpretation of the dispute between Rabbi Eliezer and Rabbi Yehoshua. **If** Rabbi Yehoshua maintains that the husband is not obligated to ransom his wife because it is **she** who **put her finger between her** own **teeth** and caused herself to be forbidden to her husband, then **why is it mentioned** here that he must pay her her **ketubah?** If it is his wife's fault that he is required to divorce her, the husband should be exempt from paying her her ketubah! [4] **And furthermore,** there is a second difficulty, for the Baraita continues: **"Rabbi Natan said: I asked Summakhos** the following question: [5] **When Rabbi Yehoshua said that** the husband who took a vow forbidding his wife from benefiting from him

NOTES

required to ransom his wife because it was her fault that she is forbidden to him? Why not say simply that he is not required to ransom her because he cannot take her back as his wife?

Ba'al HaMa'or has a slightly different reading of the Gemara: "With what are we dealing here? For example, where she vowed and he confirmed the vow for her. And Rabbi Yehoshua maintains: She put a finger between her teeth." *Ba'al HaMa'or* explains that Rava's position is certainly the subject of a Tannaitic dispute, for it can be reconciled with the normative view of Rabbi Yehoshua, but not with that of Rabbi Eliezer. The purpose of the Gemara is to demonstrate that the viewpoint of Abaye need not follow the viewpoint of any particular Tanna, for Abaye's ruling can even be reconciled with the position of Rabbi Yehoshua. Rabbi Yehoshua said that the husband is obligated to ransom his wife except when it is entirely her fault that she is forbidden to him. But he may well agree with Abaye that a priest must ransom his wife in all cases, even if she will be forbidden to him for a reason other than that she was taken captive.

Ra'ah explains the Gemara according to the reading found in the standard text in a manner similar to that of *Rashi*, except that according to *Ra'ah* Rabbi Eliezer and Rabbi Yehoshua disagree about the wife of a non-priest as well as about the wife of a priest. Rava can argue that his ruling is also consistent with Rabbi Eliezer's position, for Rabbi Eliezer said that the husband who confirmed his wife's oath is obligated to ransom her, because it is his fault that she is now forbidden to him. But in other cases, where it is not his fault that she is forbidden to him, and she is forbidden to him for some reason other than that she was taken captive, Rabbi Eliezer may well agree with Rava that the husband is not obligated to ransom his wife, even if he is a priest. And Abaye can argue that his ruling can also be reconciled with that of Rabbi Yehoshua, for Rabbi Yehoshua said that the husband who confirmed his wife's oath is not required to ransom his wife, because it is her fault that she is now forbidden to him, and therefore he is exempt from paying her ransom even if he is a priest. But in other cases, where it is not her fault that she is forbidden to him, Rabbi Yehoshua may well agree with Abaye that the priest is obligated to ransom his wife, even though she is forbidden to him for some reason other than that she was taken captive. (See also *Ramban* and *Ritva*, who defend the position of *Rashi*; *Meiri*, who follows *Ba'al HaMa'or*; and *Rabbi Crescas Vidal*, who follows *Ra'ah*.)

HALAKHAH

הוּא נוֹתֵן אֶצְבַּע He puts a finger. "If a woman takes a vow forbidding herself from enjoying certain benefits and her husband confirms it for her, or if she takes the vow and he fails to annul it, and then the husband claims that he does not want to be married to a woman who takes such a vow, he may divorce her, but he must pay her her ketubah, because he could have annulled the vow but instead allowed it to stand." (*Rambam, Sefer Nashim, Hilkhot Ishut* 12:24; *Shulḥan Arukh, Yoreh De'ah* 235:3.)

TRANSLATION AND COMMENTARY

must give her her ketubah but is **not** obligated to **ransom her,** [1]was he referring only to a case **where he** first **took a vow forbidding her** from benefiting from him **and** only **afterwards was she taken captive,** [2]**or** was he dealing even with a case **where she was** first **taken captive, and** only **afterwards did he take a vow forbidding her** from deriving any benefit from him? [3]**And** Summakhos **said to me: I have not heard** anything about this from my teachers, but it stands to reason that Rabbi Yehoshua exempted the husband from ransoming his wife only in the case where he first took a vow forbidding her from deriving benefit from him, and afterwards she was taken captive." [4]**Now,** says the Gemara, **if** Rabbi Yehoshua is referring to a case in which the wife **took the vow** forbidding herself to derive any benefit from her husband, and her husband merely confirmed it, [5]**what difference does it make whether he** first **confirmed the vow forbidding** her to benefit from him **and** only **afterwards was she taken captive,** [6]**or whether she was taken captive** first, **and** only **afterwards did he confirm the vow forbidding** her to derive any benefit from him? In both cases the husband should be exempt from paying his wife's ransom, for he merely confirmed the vow she took, and therefore he cannot be regarded as having taken deliberate action to evade his obligation to ransom her. Thus we must reject the suggestion that the Baraita is referring to a case in which the woman took the vow and her husband merely added his confirmation.

אֶלָּא [7]**But,** says the Gemara, the Baraita **is in fact referring** to a case **where** it was the husband who **took the vow forbidding** his wife to derive any benefit from him, as was suggested originally. Nevertheless, it does not necessarily follow that Abaye and Rava disagree about the same issue that was in dispute between Rabbi Eliezer and Rabbi Yehoshua. [8]For **Abaye** can **explain** the viewpoints of both Tannaim **in accordance with his** own **opinion,** [9]**and** similarly **Rava** can **explain** the two viewpoints **in accordance with his** own **opinion.**

אַבַּיֵי מְתָרֵץ [10]**Abaye** can **explain** the viewpoints of both Rabbi Eliezer and Rabbi Yehoshua **in accordance with his** own **opinion** in the following way: [11]If **a widow was married to a High Priest,** and she was taken captive, **both** Rabbi Eliezer and Rabbi Yehoshua **agree that** the husband **is obligated to ransom her,** for we can apply to her what is stated in the ketubah of a woman married to a priest: "If you are taken captive, I will ransom you and I will return you to your city." A High Priest who marries a widow is obligated to ransom her, because he is capable of fulfilling that stipulation at the time of marriage when the ketubah is drawn up and when she is actually taken captive. [12]But if **a *mamzeret* or a *netinah* was married to a non-priest** and she was taken captive, **both** Rabbi Eliezer and Rabbi Yehoshua **agree that** her husband **is not obligated to ransom her,** because we cannot apply to her what is stated in the ketubah of a woman married to a non-priest: "If you are taken captive, I will ransom you and I will bring you back to me as my wife." Neither

פּוֹדֶה, [1]כְּשֶׁהִדִּירָהּ וּלְבַסּוֹף נִשְׁבֵּית, [2]אוֹ בְּשֶׁנִּשְׁבֵּית וּלְבַסּוֹף הִדִּירָהּ? [3]וְאָמַר: לֹא שָׁמַעְתִּי״. [4]וְאִי דְּנָדְרָה אִיהִי, [5]מַה לִּי הִדִּירָהּ וּלְבַסּוֹף נִשְׁבֵּית, [6]מַה לִּי נִשְׁבֵּית וּלְבַסּוֹף הִדִּירָהּ? [7]אֶלָּא לְעוֹלָם דְּאַדְּרָהּ אִיהוּ, [8]וְאַבַּיֵי מְתָרֵץ לְטַעֲמֵיהּ, [9]וְרָבָא מְתָרֵץ לְטַעֲמֵיהּ.

[10]אַבַּיֵי מְתָרֵץ לְטַעֲמֵיהּ: [11]אַלְמָנָה לְכֹהֵן גָּדוֹל, כּוּלֵּי עָלְמָא לָא פְּלִיגִי דְּחַיָּיב לִפְדּוֹתָהּ. [12]מַמְזֶרֶת וּנְתִינָה לְיִשְׂרָאֵל, כּוּלֵּי עָלְמָא לָא פְּלִיגִי דְּאֵינוֹ חַיָּיב לִפְדּוֹתָהּ.

LITERAL TRANSLATION

ransom [her], [1][is that] where he forbade her by a vow, and afterwards she was taken captive, [2]or [is it] where she was taken captive and afterwards he forbade her by a vow? [3]And he said to me: I did not hear." [4]And if she took the vow, [5]what is [the difference] to me [whether] he forbade her by a vow and afterwards she was taken captive, [6][or whether] she was taken captive and afterwards he forbade her by a vow?

[7]But in fact [the Baraita refers to] where he forbade her by a vow, [8]and Abaye explains [it] according to his opinion, [9]and Rava explains [it] according to his opinion.

[10]Abaye explains [it] according to his opinion: [11][In the case of] a widow [married] to a High Priest, all agree (lit., "do not disagree") that he is obligated to ransom her. [12][In the case of] a *mamzeret* or a *netinah* [married] to an Israelite, all agree that he is not obligated to ransom her.

RASHI

מה לי הדירה ולבסוף נשבית — הא לא הערים מידי, שהרי היא התחילה בנדר. **ואביי מתרץ לטעמיה** — למימר: לאו תנאי היא, אלא דכולי עלמא כוותי קיימי. וכן רבא מתרץ לטעמיה. **דחייב לפדותה** — שהרי אני קורא בה בין בתחלת התנאי בין בסוף קיומו "ואהדרינך למדינתך", ואף על גב דאיסור דבר אחר גרם לה — אהדרינך למדינתך הוא. **ממזרת ונתינה לישראל אין חייב לפדותה** — שאין אני קורא בה לא בשעת התנאי ולא בסופו "ואותבינך לי לאינתו".

¹מַדִּיר אֵשֶׁת כֹּהֵן נַמִּי, כּוּלֵּי עָלְמָא לָא פְּלִיגִי דְּחַיָּיב לִפְדוֹתָהּ, ²דְּהַיְינוּ אַלְמָנָה לְכֹהֵן גָּדוֹל. ³כִּי פְּלִיגִי בְּמַדִּיר אֵשֶׁת יִשְׂרָאֵל. ⁴רַבִּי אֱלִיעֶזֶר אָזֵיל בָּתַר מֵעִיקָּרָא, ⁵וְרַבִּי יְהוֹשֻׁעַ אָזֵיל בָּתַר בַּסּוֹף.

⁶רָבָא מְתָרֵץ לְטַעֲמֵיהּ: ⁷אַלְמָנָה לְכֹהֵן גָּדוֹל, מַמְזֶרֶת וּנְתִינָה לְיִשְׂרָאֵל, ⁸כּוּלֵּי עָלְמָא לָא פְּלִיגִי דְּאֵינוֹ חַיָּיב לִפְדוֹתָהּ. ⁹כִּי פְּלִיגִי בְּמַדִּיר, בֵּין אֵשֶׁת כֹּהֵן וּבֵין אֵשֶׁת יִשְׂרָאֵל. ¹⁰רַבִּי אֱלִיעֶזֶר אָזֵיל בָּתַר מֵעִיקָּרָא,

LITERAL TRANSLATION

[1] [In the case of] one who forbids by a vow the wife of a priest also, all agree that he is obligated to ransom her, [2] for it is the same as a widow [married] to a High Priest. [3] Where they disagree is about one who forbids by a vow the wife of an Israelite. [4] Rabbi Eliezer goes after the beginning, [5] and Rabbi Yehoshua goes after the end.

[6] Rava explains [it] according to his opinion: [7] [In the case of] a widow [married] to a High Priest, or of a *mamzeret* or a *netinah* [married] to an Israelite, [8] all agree that he is not obligated to ransom her. [9] Where they disagree is about one who forbids [his wife] by a vow, whether [she is] the wife of a priest or the wife of an Israelite. [10] Rabbi Eliezer goes after the beginning,

TRANSLATION AND COMMENTARY

at the time of marriage nor at the time of his wife's capture is the husband capable of fulfilling this stipulation, for she is forbidden to him, and therefore he is exempt from the duty to pay her ransom. [1] And if **a priest took a vow forbidding his wife** from deriving any benefit from him, and she was captured, here too **both** Tannaim **agree that** the husband **is obligated to ransom** his wife, [2] **for this is** essentially **the same** case **as** that of **a widow** who was **married to a High Priest.** Here, too, the husband obligated himself to ransom his wife and to return her to her father's home, and he was capable of fulfilling this stipulation both at the time of the marriage and at the time she was taken captive. [3] Rabbi Eliezer and Rabbi Yehoshua **disagree** only **about** the case in which **a non-priest took a vow forbidding his wife** from benefiting from him, and she was taken captive. Here the husband originally obligated himself to ransom his wife and to take her back to live with him after she was released. At the time of the marriage, he was capable of fulfilling this obligation. But at the time of her capture, he was no longer capable of carrying out this stipulation, because his vow forbidding his wife to derive benefit from him compels the couple to divorce. [4] **Rabbi Eliezer** maintains that we **consider** the situation at **the beginning,** when the couple married. Since the husband could have taken his wife back had she then been taken captive, he remains liable for her ransom even though he cannot now take her back because of the vow he has taken. [5] **And Rabbi Yehoshua** maintains that we **consider** the situation at **the end,** when the woman was captured. Since the husband is no longer permitted to take his wife back to live with him, the stipulation is no longer valid and he is released from his obligation to pay her ransom.

רָבָא מְתָרֵץ [6] **Rava,** too, can **explain** the views of both Rabbi Eliezer and Rabbi Yehoshua **in accordance with his** own **opinion** in the following way: [7] If **a widow was married to a High Priest,** or if **a *mamzeret* or a *netinah* was married to a non-priest,** and the woman was taken captive, [8] **both** Rabbi Eliezer and Rabbi Yehoshua **agree that** the husband **is not obligated to ransom her.** The High Priest is exempt from paying his wife's ransom because a priest obligates himself to ransom his wife, despite the fact that she will be forbidden to him after her release, provided that the sole reason that she will be forbidden to him is that she has been taken captive. But here, she is forbidden to her husband because a High Priest is not permitted to marry a widow. The non-priest is exempt from ransoming his wife who is a *mamzeret* or a *netinah,* since he is not capable of fulfilling the stipulation that he will ransom her and take her back as his wife. [9] Rabbi Eliezer and Rabbi Yehoshua **disagree** only **about** the case in which **someone, whether a priest or a non-priest, took a vow forbidding his wife** from deriving benefit from him, and the wife was taken captive. [10] **Rabbi Eliezer** maintains that we **consider** the situation at **the beginning,** when the couple married and the ketubah was drawn up. At that time, the priest could have fulfilled the stipulation that he ransom his wife and return her to her father's home, because only the prohibition resulting from her being taken captive

RASHI

מדיר אשת כהן נמי — כהן שהדיר את אשתו נמי, שתנאי הראשון "ואהדרינך למדינתך" הוא, ואפשר לו לחול בשעת התנאי ואפשר לו לקיימו בסופו — חייב לפדותה, דהיינו כאלמנה לכהן גדול. **כי פליגי בישראל שהדיר את אשתו** — שתנאו הראשון "ואותבינך לאינתו" היה ראוי לחול, אבל בסופו אי אפשר לקיימו. רבי אליעזר אזל בתר מעיקרא כו'. **דאינו חייב לפדותה** — אלמנה שאין אני קורא בה "אהדרינך למדינתך" מחמת שבייה, אלא מחמת דבר אחר. וממזרת שאין אני קורא בה "ואותבינך לאינתו" לא בתחילה ולא בסוף. **כי פליגי במדיר בין אשת כהן** — דמעיקרא בשעת התנאי קרינן ביה "ואהדרינך" מחמת שבייה, ובסוף איכא איסור דבר אחר. וכן במדיר אשת ישראל, מעיקרא קרינן בה "ואותבינך לאינתו" ובסוף לא קרינן בה הכי.

¹וְרַבִּי יְהוֹשֻׁעַ אָזֵיל בָּתַר בַּסּוֹף.
²״נִשְׁבֵּית, חַיָּיב לִפְדּוֹתָהּ, וכו׳״.
³תָּנוּ רַבָּנַן: ״נִשְׁבֵּית בְּחַיֵּי בַעְלָהּ וְאַחַר כָּךְ מֵת בַּעְלָהּ, ⁴הִכִּיר בָּהּ בַּעְלָהּ, יוֹרְשִׁין חַיָּיבִין לִפְדּוֹתָהּ.
⁵לֹא הִכִּיר בָּהּ בַּעְלָהּ, אֵין יוֹרְשִׁין חַיָּיבִין לִפְדּוֹתָהּ״.
⁶לֵוִי סָבַר לְמֶיעֱבַד עוּבְדָא כִּי הָא מַתְנִיתָא. ⁷אֲמַר לֵיהּ רַב: הָכִי אֲמַר חֲבִיבִי: לֵית הִלְכְתָא כִּי הָא מַתְנִיתָא, ⁸אֶלָּא כִּי הָא

LITERAL TRANSLATION

¹and Rabbi Yehoshua goes after the end.

²"[If] she was taken captive, he is obligated to ransom her, etc." ³Our Rabbis taught: "[If] she was taken captive during her husband's lifetime and afterwards her husband died, ⁴if her husband knew about her, the heirs are obligated to ransom her. ⁵[If] her husband did not know about her, the heirs are not obligated to ransom her."

⁶Levi thought to take action in accordance with this Baraita. ⁷Rav said to him: My uncle said this: The law is not in accordance with this Baraita, ⁸but rather in accordance with

RASHI

הכיר בה בעלה — עד שלא מת נודע לו שנשבית, ונתחייב בפרקונה בחייו. **חביבי** — רבי חייא, שהוא דודו אחי אביו.

TRANSLATION AND COMMENTARY

caused her to be forbidden to her husband. Thus he is liable for his wife's ransom, even though at the end, when she was actually taken captive, she was already forbidden to her husband for another reason. Similarly, the non-priest could at the outset have fulfilled the stipulation that he ransom his wife and take her back to live with him. Thus he is liable for his wife's ransom, even though later, when she was taken captive, he was no longer capable of fulfilling that stipulation, for by then she was forbidden to him on account of the vow. ¹**And Rabbi Yehoshua** maintains that we **consider** the situation **at the end,** when the woman was actually taken captive. Since the husband can no longer fulfill the stipulation — if a priest, because his wife is now forbidden to him on account of another prohibition; and if an ordinary Jew, because his wife is now forbidden to return to him — he is exempt from paying her ransom.

נִשְׁבֵּית ²The Gemara now proceeds to discuss another aspect of the husband's obligation to ransom his wife. Our Mishnah stated: **"If** a woman **is taken captive,** her husband **is obligated to ransom her."** ³**Our Rabbis taught** a related Baraita: **"If** a woman **is taken captive during her husband's lifetime, and afterwards her husband dies** before her ransom is paid, the following distinction applies: ⁴**If her husband knew** that **she** had been taken captive, so that he was already liable for her ransom before he died, **his heirs are obligated to ransom her.** ⁵But **if her husband did not know** that **she** had been captured, so that he never actually became liable to pay her ransom, **his heirs are not obligated to ransom her."**

לֵוִי סָבַר ⁶The Gemara relates that **Levi** once **thought of taking action** and issuing a ruling **in accordance with this Baraita,** obligating the heirs of a man whose wife was taken captive during his lifetime to pay her ransom. ⁷**Rav said to** Levi: **My uncle,** Rabbi Ḥiyya, **said as follows: The law is not in accordance with this Baraita,** ⁸**but rather** it **is in accordance with** another Baraita, in **which** the following **was taught:**

NOTES

הִכִּיר בָּהּ בַּעְלָהּ **If her husband knew about her.** *Rivan* explains that once the husband learns that his wife has been taken captive, his property is mortgaged for her ransom, and so the husband's heirs are liable for the ransom if he dies before paying it. But if the husband dies without ever learning that his wife has been taken captive, his property never becomes mortgaged for her ransom, and therefore the obligation does not fall upon the heirs.

אֵין יוֹרְשִׁין חַיָּיבִין לִפְדּוֹתָהּ **The heirs are not obligated to ransom her.** *Rif, Rivan,* and others have a slightly different reading of the text: "If she was taken captive after her husband's death, her brother-in-law is not obligated to ransom her, etc." A man whose brother dies without children is called a *yavam* and is obligated by Torah law either to marry his deceased brother's widow or to grant her *ḥalitzah*, thereby releasing her from the levirate bond. Thus the Baraita rules that if a woman was taken captive after her husband's death (or even if she was taken captive during her husband's lifetime), her *yavam*, who is tied to her by the levirate bond and who inherits his brother's estate if he marries her, is not required to pay her ransom.

Talmidei Rabbenu Yonah notes that, even according to this reading, if the husband leaves children who inherit his estate, they are not obligated to ransom his wife, whether she was taken captive after his death or during his lifetime. The Baraita gave the ruling in relation to the *yavam* in order to teach us that even the *yavam,* who is tied to his sister-in-law by the levirate bond, is not obligated to pay her ransom.

HALAKHAH

נִשְׁבֵּית בְּחַיֵּי בַעְלָהּ **If she was taken captive during her husband's lifetime.** "A husband is obligated to ransom his wife during his lifetime, but his heirs are not obligated to ransom his widow from his estate. Even if the woman was taken captive during her husband's lifetime, and the husband did not manage to pay her ransom, his heirs are not obligated to ransom her," in accordance with the Baraita and the ruling of Rabbi Ḥiyya. (*Rambam, Sefer Nashim, Hilkhot Ishut* 18:5; *Shulḥan Arukh, Even HaEzer* 78:8.)

SAGES

לֵוִי **Levi.** A Palestinian Sage of the transitional generation between the Tannaitic and Amoraic periods. See *Ketubot*, Part I, p. 224.

LANGUAGE

חֲבִיבִי **My uncle.** The word used here, חָבִיב, means "beloved," or "uncle" (cf. the Hebrew word דּוֹד, which has the same meanings; cf. also the verb form חָבַב — "to like," "to be fond of"). However, חֲבִיבִי may simply be a contraction of אֲחִי אָבִי — "my father's brother." Indeed, this usage is attested in many of the ancient Aramaic Bible translations.

BACKGROUND

חֲבִיבִי אָמַר **My uncle said.** The bonds between Rav and Rabbi Ḥiyya were very close. Because of an unusual set of family relationships, Rabbi Ḥiyya was Rav's uncle both on his father's side and his mother's side. Moreover, Rabbi Ḥiyya also seems to have been Rav's first and most influential teacher. Although Rav studied under Rabbi Yehudah HaNasi (as did Rabbi Ḥiyya himself), it seems that he received most of his learning from his uncle. For this reason we very frequently find him quoting Rabbi Ḥiyya as a source of the highest authority.

BACKGROUND

עַד עֲשָׂרָה בְּדָמֶיהָ **Up to ten times her value.** When soldiers or bandits took captives, the captives were part of the booty and were sold as slaves. Thus there were standard prices for captives — the price of slaves in a given physical condition with a given capacity for work. However, since the Jews made every effort to redeem their captives, the captors would sometimes set a very high price for them, not according to their value as slaves, but according to what they could expect to extort from the captives' families or from Jewish communities.

TRANSLATION AND COMMENTARY

[1]**"If** a woman **is taken captive after her husband's death, the orphans** who inherit their father's estate **are not obligated to ransom her.** [2]**Furthermore, even if** the woman **was taken captive during her husband's lifetime** and he knew that she had been taken captive, **and afterwards her husband died** before he had the opportunity to pay her ransom, [3]**the orphans are not required to ransom her, for we cannot apply to her** what is stated in her ketubah: [4]'If you are taken captive, I will ransom you **and I will bring you back** to me **as my wife.'** Since the woman can no longer return to her husband, the obligation he undertook to ransom her is null and void."

תָּנוּ רַבָּנַן [5]**Our Rabbis taught** another Baraita on the subject of the husband's obligation to ransom his wife: **"If** a woman **is taken captive and** her captors **are demanding from** her husband an exorbitant amount **ten times her value,** [6]and it is **the first time** she has been taken captive, her husband is obligated to **ransom her.** He cannot divorce her, pay her her ketubah, and tell her to ransom herself. [7]But **from then on,** if she is taken captive again, the law is different. **If he wishes, he** may **ransom her** a second time, [8]**but if he wishes, he does not** have to **ransom her.** If he prefers, he can divorce her, pay her her ketubah, and relieve himself of his obligation to pay her ransom. [9]**Rabban Shimon ben Gamliel** disagrees and **says:**

דְּתַנְיָא: [1]״נִשְׁבֵּית לְאַחַר מִיתַת בַּעְלָהּ, אֵין הַיְתוֹמִין חַיָּיבִין לִפְדּוֹתָהּ. [2]וְלֹא עוֹד, אֶלָּא אֲפִילּוּ נִשְׁבֵּית בְּחַיֵּי בַעְלָהּ וְאַחַר כָּךְ מֵת בַּעְלָהּ, [3]אֵין הַיְתוֹמִין חַיָּיבִין לִפְדּוֹתָהּ, שֶׁאֵין אֲנִי קוֹרֵא בָּהּ: [4]׳וְאוֹתְבִינָךְ לְאִינְתּוּ׳״.

[5]תָּנוּ רַבָּנַן: ״נִשְׁבֵּית וְהָיוּ מְבַקְשִׁין מִמֶּנּוּ עַד עֲשָׂרָה בְּדָמֶיהָ, [6]פַּעַם רִאשׁוֹנָה, פּוֹדֶה. [7]מִכָּאן וְאֵילָךְ, רָצָה, פּוֹדֶה, [8]רָצָה, אֵינוֹ פּוֹדֶה. [9]רַבָּן שִׁמְעוֹן

LITERAL TRANSLATION

what was taught: [1]"[If] she was taken captive after her husband's death, the orphans are not obligated to ransom her. [2]And not only that, but even [if] she was taken captive during her husband's lifetime and afterwards her husband died, [3]the orphans are not obligated to ransom her, for I do not apply to her: [4]'And I will bring you back as my wife.'"

[5]Our Rabbis taught: "[If] she was taken captive and they were demanding from him up to ten times her value, [6]the first time, he ransoms [her]. [7]From then on, [if] he wishes, he ransoms [her], [8][and if] he wishes, he does not ransom [her]. [9]Rabban Shimon

RASHI

רצה אינו פודה — דלא תקינו בה רבנן אלא חד פדיון.

NOTES

אֲפִילּוּ נִשְׁבֵּית בְּחַיֵּי בַעְלָהּ **Even if she was taken captive during her husband's lifetime.** The Jerusalem Talmud reverses the argument: "Not only are the husband's heirs not liable for his wife's ransom if she was captured during his lifetime, but even if she was captured after his death, the heirs are not obligated to ransom her." (See *Korban HaEdah,* who amends the text so that it conforms with that found in our Gemara.) *Pnei Moshe* explains that the Jerusalem Talmud's ruling refers to a case in which the husband died without children, and his wife is now connected to her brother-in-law by the levirate bond, and is waiting for him to perform levirate marriage or *ḥalitzah.* Not only is the husband's heir, his brother, not liable for her ransom if she was taken captive during her husband's lifetime, for at that time her brother-in-law had no obligations toward her, but even if she was captured after the husband's death, when she was already tied to her brother-in-law by the levirate bond, the brother-in-law is not obligated to ransom her — for, not having been married to her before, he cannot fulfill the stipulation, "I will bring you back to me as my wife."

שֶׁאֵין אֲנִי קוֹרֵא בָּהּ: ״וְאוֹתְבִינָךְ לְאִינְתּוּ״ **For I do not apply to her: "And I will bring you back as my wife."** According to this second Baraita, the husband's heirs are not obligated to ransom his wife, even if she was taken captive during his lifetime, for they are unable to fulfill the stipulation, "I will ransom you and bring you back to me as my wife." One might perhaps argue that it follows from this that if the husband was a priest, his heirs should be obligated to ransom his wife, for the stipulation made by the priest, "I will ransom you and I will return you to your city," is still valid even if it cannot be fulfilled by the priest himself. For all the conditions in the ketubah are formulated in the first person and refer to the husband, and yet they fall upon the husband's heirs in the event of his death. But the law is in accordance with Rava, who maintains that a priest's obligation to ransom his wife is essentially the same as that of a non-priest, except that the priest obligates himself to ransom his wife even though she will be forbidden to him as a result of her captivity. Just as the husband's duty to ransom his wife does not pass to his heirs in the case of a non-priest, similarly it does not pass to the heirs in the case of a priest (*Maharam Schiff*).

מִכָּאן וְאֵילָךְ, רָצָה, פּוֹדֶה **From then on, if he wishes, he ransoms her.** Our commentary follows *Rashi,* who maintains that, according to the anonymous first Tanna of the

HALAKHAH

וְהָיוּ מְבַקְשִׁין מִמֶּנּוּ עַד עֲשָׂרָה בְּדָמֶיהָ **And they were demanding from him up to ten times her value.** "A husband is obligated to pay his wife's ransom, even if her captors demand a ransom ten times the value of her ketubah, and

TRANSLATION AND COMMENTARY

[52B] [1] **We do not** allow the **ransom** of **captives for more than their value, in** order to protect **the public interest.** Despite the great importance attached to the duty of ransoming Jewish prisoners, one must not ransom a prisoner for more than his value, so as not to encourage the taking of Jewish prisoners for ransom. Thus a husband is not obligated to ransom his wife, even the first time she is taken captive, if her captors are demanding an exorbitant amount for her release."

הָא בִּכְדֵי דְּמֵיהֶן פּוֹדִין [2] Now, observes the Gemara, this Baraita informs us that Rabban Shimon ben Gamliel exempts the husband from his duty to ransom his wife for more than her value. **But this implies that** if her captors are demanding a ransom **equal to her value,** Rabban Shimon ben Gamliel would agree that **we** require the husband to **ransom** his wife, [3] **even if the ransom** being demanded **exceeds** the amount of **her ketubah.**

בֶּן גַּמְלִיאֵל אוֹמֵר: [52B] [1] אֵין פּוֹדִין אֶת הַשְּׁבוּיִין יוֹתֵר עַל כְּדֵי דְמֵיהֶם, מִפְּנֵי תִּקּוּן הָעוֹלָם״.

[2] הָא בִּכְדֵי דְּמֵיהֶן פּוֹדִין, [3] אַף עַל גַּב דְּפִרְקוֹנָהּ יוֹתֵר עַל כְּתוּבָּתָהּ.

LITERAL TRANSLATION

ben Gamliel says: [52B] [1] We do not ransom captives for more than their value, in the public interest (lit., 'for the correction of the world')."

[2] But [this implies that] for their value we ransom, [3] even if her ransom exceeds her ketubah.

RASHI

מפני תיקון העולם – שלא ירגילו להעלות על דמיהן.

BACKGROUND

מִפְּנֵי תִּקּוּן הָעוֹלָם In the public interest. Many of the ordinances instituted by the Sages were stringencies intended to prevent people from inadvertently violating the laws of the Torah; others were intended to encourage meritorious deeds. Yet others were not instituted with respect to specific commandments but generally to "correct the world," to reform society in the public interest. The latter ordinances, some of which are listed in tractate *Gittin*, were given various justifications. Some were designed to prevent strife, others to encourage proper conduct, and yet others to prevent harm from coming to the community.

Although the Sages disagreed as to the reason for Rabban Shimon ben Gamliel's ordinance regarding the redemption of prisoners, it was clearly intended to avoid placing too heavy a burden on the Jewish community. The commandment to redeem prisoners is considered "a great commandment," one that is more important than others; but excessive zeal in performing it might cause indirect damage.

NOTES

Baraita, a husband is required to ransom his wife only the first time she is taken captive. But if he has already paid her ransom once, he is not required to pay anything toward her ransom if she is taken captive a second time.

According to *Rabbenu Ḥananel* (cited by *Tosafot*), the first Tanna of the Baraita maintains that the first time a man's wife is taken captive, he must pay her ransom, even if her captors demand an exorbitant amount for her release. But the second time she is taken captive, the husband is only required to ransom her if they are demanding a ransom equal to her value.

מִפְּנֵי תִּקּוּן הָעוֹלָם In the public interest. Elsewhere (*Gittin* 45a), the Gemara attempts to establish the precise meaning of this expression — whether a Jewish prisoner should not be ransomed at more than his value so as not to impose an excessive burden on the community, or so as not to encourage the taking of Jewish prisoners. In the passage in *Gittin* the Gemara does not arrive at a conclusive answer. It has been suggested that the anonymous first Tanna of our Baraita and Rabban Shimon ben Gamliel disagree about this very question. The anonymous first Tanna maintains that the Rabbis enacted that a Jewish prisoner should not be ransomed at more than his value so as not to impose an excessive burden on the community. But since the community is not involved in the case of a husband and wife, the husband is required to ransom his wife, even if her captors are demanding ten times her value. In contrast, Rabban Shimon ben Gamliel maintains that an exorbitant ransom must not be paid, so as not to encourage the taking of Jewish prisoners. Thus the Rabbinic enactment against paying a ransom exceeding the prisoner's value applies to a husband as well. Some Rishonim say that this is indeed the subject of the dispute between the Tannaim in our Baraita, and that the answer to the Gemara's question in *Gittin* depends on how we rule on the dispute here (*Ramban*, *Rashba*, and *Ra'ah*).

Rabbenu Tam (cited by *Ritva*) argues that our Baraita does not resolve the question posed by the Gemara in *Gittin*. The reason behind the ruling of the anonymous first Tanna of our Baraita may in fact be in order to discourage the taking of Jewish prisoners. But the Rabbis did not impose any restrictions on the amount that a man may

HALAKHAH

even if that is all the money he has. A husband is only required to ransom his wife the first time she is taken captive, but if he ransoms her and she is captured again, and he wants to divorce her, he is permitted to divorce her and pay her her ketubah, and she pays her own ransom." (*Rambam*, *Sefer Nashim*, *Hilkhot Ishut* 14:19; *Shulḥan Arukh*, *Even HaEzer* 78:3.)

אֵין פּוֹדִין אֶת הַשְּׁבוּיִין יוֹתֵר עַל כְּדֵי דְמֵיהֶם We do not ransom captives for more than their value. "We do not ransom a Jewish prisoner for more than his value, so as not to encourage the taking of Jewish prisoners for ransom, following Rabban Shimon ben Gamliel. But an individual may pay as much as he wants for his own ransom. A high ransom may also be paid for a great Talmudic scholar, and for a man who is not yet a great Talmudic scholar but demonstrates the potential of becoming one (*Tosafot* and *Rosh*). *Shakh* states in the name of *Baḥ* that someone may pay as much as he wants for the ransom of members of his family, and nobody may raise an objection, for this does not impose an extra burden on the community." (*Rambam*, *Sefer Zeraim*, *Hilkhot Mattenot Aniyyim* 8:12; *Shulḥan Arukh*, *Yoreh De'ah* 252:4.)

בִּכְדֵי דְּמֵיהֶן פּוֹדִין But this implies that for their value, we ransom. "A husband cannot be compelled to ransom his wife for more than her worth, but only for the amount that would be paid for other captives. *Rema* notes that, according to some authorities (*Tur*, and *Rosh* in the name of *Remah*), there is no limit to the amount that a husband may pay for his wife's ransom." (*Rambam*, *Sefer Nashim*, *Hilkhot Ishut* 14:19; *Shulḥan Arukh*, *Even HaEzer* 78:2.)

[1]וּרְמִינְהִי: ״נִשְׁבֵּית וְהָיוּ מְבַקְשִׁין מִמֶּנּוּ עַד עֲשָׂרָה בִּכְתוּבָּתָהּ, פַּעַם רִאשׁוֹנָה, פּוֹדֶה. [2]מִכָּאן וְאֵילָךְ, רָצָה, פּוֹדֶה, [3]רָצָה, אֵינוֹ פּוֹדֶה. [4]רַבָּן שִׁמְעוֹן בֶּן גַּמְלִיאֵל אוֹמֵר: אִם הָיָה פִּרְקוֹנָהּ כְּנֶגֶד כְּתוּבָּתָהּ, פּוֹדֶה. [5]אִם לָאו, אֵינוֹ פּוֹדֶה״! [6]רַבָּן שִׁמְעוֹן בֶּן גַּמְלִיאֵל תְּרֵי קוּלֵּי אִית לֵיהּ.

[7]״לָקְתָה, חַיָּיב לְרַפְּאוֹתָהּ״. [8]תָּנוּ רַבָּנַן: ״אַלְמָנָה נִיזּוֹנֶת מִנִּכְסֵי יְתוֹמִין, [9]וּצְרִיכָה רְפוּאָה,

LITERAL TRANSLATION

[1]A contradiction was raised (lit., "cast them together"): "[If] she was taken captive and they were demanding from him up to ten times her ketubah, the first time, he ransoms [her]. [2]From then on, [if] he wishes, he ransoms [her], [3][and if] he wishes, he does not ransom [her]. [4]Rabban Shimon ben Gamliel says: If her ransom was equal to her ketubah, he ransoms [her]. [5]If not, he does not ransom [her]!" [6]Rabban Shimon ben Gamliel makes (lit., "has") two leniencies.

[7]"[If] she fell ill, he is obligated to heal her." [8]Our Rabbis taught: "A widow is maintained from the property of the orphans, [9]and [if] she requires healing,

TRANSLATION AND COMMENTARY

וּרְמִינְהִי [1]A **contradiction was raised** by the Gemara between the Baraita just cited and another one that stated: **"If a woman is taken captive, and** her captors **are demanding from** her husband an exorbitant amount **ten times** that of **her ketubah,** and it is **the first time** she has been taken captive, her husband is obligated to **ransom her.** [2]But **from then on,** if she is taken captive again, the law is different. **If** the husband **wishes, he** may **ransom her,** [3]**but if he wishes, he does not** have to **ransom her.** If he prefers, he can divorce her, pay her her ketubah, and relieve himself of his obligation to pay her ransom. [4]**Rabban Shimon ben Gamliel** disagrees and **says: If the ransom** that the captors are demanding for the woman's release **is** less than or **equal to** the amount of **her ketubah,** the husband is obligated to **ransom her.** [5]But **if not,** if the ransom being demanded exceeds the amount of her ketubah, **he does not** have to **ransom her,** even the first time she is taken captive. The husband's liability for his wife's ransom, which is a right to which she is entitled under the conditions contained in the ketubah, cannot be greater than his liability for the ketubah itself." Thus there seems to be a contradiction between the two Baraitot regarding the viewpoint of Rabban Shimon ben Gamliel. Whereas the first Baraita implies that, according to Rabban Shimon ben Gamliel, the husband is obligated to ransom his wife, even if the ransom exceeds her ketubah, provided that it does not exceed her value, the second Baraita states explicitly that Rabban Shimon ben Gamliel exempts the husband from paying his wife's ransom if it exceeds the amount of her ketubah.

רַבָּן שִׁמְעוֹן בֶּן גַּמְלִיאֵל [6]The Gemara answers: There is in fact no contradiction, for **Rabban Shimon ben Gamliel makes two leniencies** regarding the husband's duty to ransom his wife. In the first Baraita he teaches us that the husband is not obligated to pay her ransom if the amount exceeds her value. And in the second Baraita he teaches us that the husband is not obligated to ransom his wife if the amount exceeds her ketubah. Thus the maximum amount that the husband need pay as ransom is his wife's value or the amount recorded in her ketubah, whichever is less.

לָקְתָה [7]The Gemara proceeds to discuss the final clause of our Mishnah, which stated: **"If a woman falls ill,** her husband **is obligated to pay her medical expenses** until she recovers." [8]**Our Rabbis taught** a related Baraita: **"A widow is** entitled to be **maintained from the property of the orphans** who inherited her late husband's estate. [9]**And if she requires medical care,** the expenses incurred must also be borne by her late

RASHI

כנגד כתובתה – אבל יותר מכתובתה. לא, דלא יהא טפל חמור מן העיקר תנאי כתובתה יתר על הכתובה. **תרי קולי** – לא יותר על דמיה שהיא ראויה לימכר בשוק, ולא יותר על כתובתה. **וצריכה רפואה הרי היא כמזונות** – ואם צריכה רפואה, הרי הרפואה

BACKGROUND

תְּרֵי קוּלֵּי אִית לֵיהּ Makes two leniencies. In other words, Rabban Shimon ben Gamliel's ruling implies two leniencies regarding the husband's duty to redeem his wife. As explained in the Talmud, these two leniencies do not have the same basis. The ruling that one should not ransom prisoners for more than their value applies to all Jewish prisoners, not simply to wives who have been taken captive. However, the second ruling, that a husband is not obligated to ransom his wife for more than the value of her ketubah, is based on a different consideration — that a husband cannot be required to pay more to ransom his wife than the total monetary obligation he has undertaken toward her.

NOTES

pay for his own ransom or for that of his wife, who is treated as himself. And the reason behind the ruling of Rabban Shimon ben Gamliel may in fact be to avoid overtaxing the community. Just as the Rabbis were concerned that a heavy burden not be placed on the community, they were similarly concerned that such a burden not be placed on the husband. Thus the husband may ransom his wife at more than her value if he so wishes, but he is not required to do so.

וּצְרִיכָה רְפוּאָה And if she requires healing. *Rashi, Rid,* and others explain that medical care is treated like maintenance because both are essential to good health. Other suggest

HALAKHAH

וּצְרִיכָה רְפוּאָה And if she requires healing. "If a widow falls ill and requires medical care that does not have a set limit, her care is treated like maintenance, the cost of which must be borne by the heirs who inherited her late

TRANSLATION AND COMMENTARY

husband's heirs, for a woman's medical care **is like** her **maintenance,** for which the husband's heirs are liable. [1]**Rabban Shimon ben Gamliel says** that the following distinction must be drawn: If **the medical care that** the woman requires **has a** set **limit,** the heirs are entitled to **pay for her medical expenses from her ketubah.** [2]But if the **medical care** that the woman requires **does not have a** set **limit** — in other words, if she suffers from a chronic disease that requires continual treatment — her medical care **is** treated **as maintenance,** and the heirs must bear the full cost without deducting anything from the amount she will receive as her ketubah."

אָמַר רַבִּי יוֹחָנָן [3]Accepting the distinction drawn by Rabban Shimon ben Gamliel, **Rabbi Yoḥanan said:** The Sages **treated bloodletting in Eretz Israel as medical care that has no** defined **limit.** Thus a widow is entitled to have the costs of her bloodletting borne by the heirs who inherited her late husband's estate.

קָרֵיבֵיהּ דְּרַבִּי יוֹחָנָן [4]The Gemara relates that the widowed **wife of the father of** certain **relatives of Rabbi Yoḥanan required daily medical care,** and this became a great burden on her late husband's family. [5]The relatives **came before Rabbi Yoḥanan** to seek his advice on the matter. Rabbi Yoḥanan **said to them:**

הֲרֵי הִיא כִּמְזוֹנוֹת. [1]רַבָּן שִׁמְעוֹן בֶּן גַּמְלִיאֵל אוֹמֵר: רְפוּאָה שֶׁיֵּשׁ לָהּ קִצְבָּה, נִתְרַפֵּאת מִכְּתוּבָּתָהּ. [2]שֶׁאֵין לָהּ קִצְבָּה, הֲרֵי הִיא כִּמְזוֹנוֹת".
[3]אָמַר רַבִּי יוֹחָנָן: עָשׂוּ הַקָּזַת דָּם בְּאֶרֶץ יִשְׂרָאֵל כִּרְפוּאָה שֶׁאֵין לָהּ קִצְבָּה.
[4]קָרֵיבֵיהּ דְּרַבִּי יוֹחָנָן הֲוָה לְהוּ אִיתַּת אַבָּא דַּהֲוַת צְרִיכָה רְפוּאָה כָּל יוֹמָא. [5]אֲתוּ לְקַמֵּיהּ דְּרַבִּי יוֹחָנָן, אֲמַר לְהוּ:

LITERAL TRANSLATION

it is like maintenance. [1]Rabban Shimon ben Gamliel says: [Regarding] healing that has a limit, she is healed from her ketubah. [2][Regarding healing] that does not have a limit, it is like maintenance."

[3]Rabbi Yoḥanan said: They made bloodletting in Eretz Israel like healing that does not have a limit.

[4]The relatives of Rabbi Yoḥanan had a father's wife who required healing every day. [5]They came before Rabbi Yoḥanan, [and] he said to them:

RASHI

כמזונות, דתרווייהו חיותא נינהו — מזונות אין להם קצבה, הלכך רפואה שיש לה קצבה, שאינה חולה תדיר — אינה בכלל מזונות.

NOTES

that food and medical care are alike in that both are needed continually. In contrast, medical care that requires a clearly defined outlay of funds cannot be compared to maintenance, which is distinguished by the absence of any such limit.

רְפוּאָה שֶׁיֵּשׁ לָהּ קִצְבָּה **Healing that has a limit.** With respect to a widow's right to have her medical expenses paid from her late husband's estate, the Baraita distinguishes between medical care that has a set limit and medical care that does not have such a limit. The Rishonim disagree about whether this distinction also applies to a married woman whose husband is still alive. *Rabbenu Ḥananel* and most other Rishonim maintain that during his lifetime a husband is liable for all of his wife's medical expenses, whether or not the care has a set limit. According to *Ittur,* the distinction drawn here regarding a widow applies also to a woman whose husband is still alive. Support for this position is brought from the Jerusalem Talmud (*Bava Batra* 9:4). Some authorities reject this proof from the Jerusalem Talmud, arguing that it is to be understood as referring to a widow and not to a woman whose husband is still alive (*Ra'ah*). Others accept that the Jerusalem Talmud is referring to a woman whose husband is still alive, but argue that the law is in accordance with our Gemara, which maintains that the distinction is limited to the case of a widow (*Ritva* and *Meiri*).

הַקָּזַת דָּם בְּאֶרֶץ יִשְׂרָאֵל **Bloodletting in Eretz Israel.** *Rivan* explains that the Sages treated bloodletting in Eretz Israel like medical care that has no defined limit, because there were at times shortages of bloodletters in Eretz Israel, and this caused dramatic increases in the price of bloodletting. *Talmidei Rabbenu Yonah* suggests that in Eretz Israel it was customary to let blood on a regular basis, and this is why the Sages ruled that bloodletting should be treated like maintenance, the total cost of which has no clearly defined limit.

קָרֵיבֵיהּ דְּרַבִּי יוֹחָנָן **The relatives of Rabbi Yoḥanan.** A similar story is related in the Jerusalem Talmud regarding a sick widow who approaches Rabbi Yoḥanan demanding that her medical expenses be paid by her late husband's heirs. Rabbi Yoḥanan warns her that if her medical costs are clearly defined they will be deducted from her ketubah. The woman assures Rabbi Yoḥanan that her medical costs are unlimited. An objection is raised against Rabbi Yoḥanan that the prohibition against making oneself like a lawyer forbids him from explaining the law to one of the litigants, since that litigant may come to present the court with a false plea. Rabbi Yoḥanan answers that he knows the woman to be honest, and that she will not misuse the information he has given her.

HALAKHAH

husband's estate. But if the widow requires medical care that has a set limit, she herself must pay for her medical expenses from her ketubah," following Rabban Shimon ben Gamliel. (*Rambam, Sefer Nashim, Hilkhot Ishut* 18:5; *Shulḥan Arukh, Even HaEzer* 79:1.)

TERMINOLOGY

מֵעִיקָּרָא מַאי סָבַר וּלְבַסּוֹף מַאי סָבַר Initially what did he think, and ultimately what did he think? In cases where a scholar changes his mind, the Talmud may ask what the Rabbi's reasoning was initially, and why he later changed his opinion.

TRANSLATION AND COMMENTARY

[1] **"Go and set a limit with the doctor,** and agree with him on a sum that will cover all the future medical care that he expects to give to your father's wife. Once that is done, her medical care will have a clearly defined limit, and you will be able to deduct your expenses from the amount she later receives as her ketubah." [2] After considering what he had done, **Rabbi Yoḥanan** regretted having offered his relatives this advice and **said** of himself: **We have made ourselves like lawyers** who seek to influence the judges to favor one litigant over another. Rabbi Yoḥanan had shown his relations how to avoid their obligation to pay for the medical expenses incurred by the father's wife, and his advice had given them an unfair advantage.

מֵעִיקָּרָא מַאי סָבַר [3] The Gemara asks: **Initially,** when Rabbi Yoḥanan advised his relatives to set a limit with the doctor, **what did he think, and ultimately,** [4] when Rabbi Yoḥanan expressed his regret for having offered this advice, **what did he think?**

מֵעִיקָּרָא סָבַר [5] The Gemara answers: **Initially Rabbi Yoḥanan thought:** The verse states (Isaiah 58:7): **"And do not hide yourself from your own flesh,"** which teaches us that a person must come to the assistance of his relatives. Thus Rabbi Yoḥanan felt justified in advising his relatives of a perfectly legal way of avoiding the obligation to pay for the medical expenses incurred by their father's wife. [6] **But ultimately** Rabbi Yoḥanan **thought:** Although it is perfectly acceptable that a person help his own relatives, the behavior of **an important person must be different.** A person in my position should never have offered his relatives counsel, for it made me too much like a lawyer advising a client.

[1] ״אֵיזִילוּ קוֹצוּ לֵיהּ מִידֵי לְרוֹפֵא״. [2] אָמַר רַבִּי יוֹחָנָן: עָשִׂינוּ עַצְמֵינוּ כְּעוֹרְכֵי הַדַּיָּינִין. [3] מֵעִיקָּרָא מַאי סָבַר, [4] וּלְבַסּוֹף מַאי סָבַר? [5] מֵעִיקָּרָא סָבַר: ״וּמִבְּשָׂרְךָ לֹא תִתְעַלָּם״. [6] וּלְבַסּוֹף סָבַר: אָדָם חָשׁוּב שָׁאנֵי.

LITERAL TRANSLATION

[1] "Go [and] fix a sum with the doctor." [2] Rabbi Yoḥanan said: We have made ourselves like lawyers (lit., "those who arrange [arguments before] the judges").

[3] Initially what did he think, [4] and ultimately what did he think?

[5] Initially he thought: "And do not hide yourself from your own flesh." [6] And ultimately he thought: An important person is different.

RASHI

קוצי ליה מידי לרופא — שיקבל עליו רפואתה עולמית בכך וכך. **בעורכי הדיינין** — אוהב אחד מבעלי דינין, ומטעים זכיותיו לדיין, ועורך [הדין לפני] הדיינין לזכותו — מיקרי עורכי הדיינין, שעורך את הדיינין להפוך לבם לטובתו של זה. **מעיקרא** — כשהשיא עצה. **ולבסוף** — כשנתחרט.

NOTES

כְּעוֹרְכֵי הַדַּיָּינִין Like lawyers. Rabbi Yoḥanan was concerned about the prohibition recorded in tractate *Avot* (1:8): "Yehudah ben Tabbai said: Do not make yourself like those who arrange arguments before the judges." Though the commentators to *Avot* interpret the words *orkhei hadayanim* (עוֹרְכֵי הַדַּיָּנִים) in different ways, the expression appears to be used in the same sense as in modern Hebrew, referring to lawyers who counsel a litigant about his legal position and the arguments that he will have to put forward in order to win his case. The Rishonim and the Aḥaronim discuss this prohibition at great length. Someone who advises a litigant to put forward a false plea is not only guilty of "arranging arguments before the judges," but is also a wicked sinner (*Tosefot Yom Tov*). Thus the prohibition discussed in *Avot* forbids certain types of counsel, even if the advice given is perfectly legal.

Ritva argues that two conclusions emerge from the anecdote regarding Rabbi Yoḥanan recorded in our Gemara: First, that the prohibition applies only if the counselor advises the litigant about a plea that he can put forward in order to circumvent an obligation that he would otherwise have to bear. But there is no prohibition against counseling a litigant about the merits of his case, if such advice is not offered. Second, the prohibition applies only if the litigant is unrelated to the counselor, or if the counselor is of elevated status. But a person of ordinary status is permitted to advise his relative as to how to present a plea before the court, even if that plea will exempt the relative from an obligation that he would otherwise have to bear.

אָדָם חָשׁוּב שָׁאנֵי An important person is different. In many places the Talmud cites this principle, that a person of elevated status is governed by different rules from those that govern ordinary people. An important person, whose actions influence the behavior of others, must conduct himself very scrupulously in all matters. There are times when a person of stature may not engage in an activity that is permitted to others. In general, the more prominent the person, the more careful he must be in all his actions. Someone who fails to live according to the standards required by his elevated position is guilty of a desecration of the name of God.

HALAKHAH

אֵיזִילוּ קוֹצוּ לֵיהּ מִידֵי לְרוֹפֵא Go and fix a sum with the doctor. "If a widow falls ill, the heirs of her husband's estate are permitted to agree with her doctor on a set sum that will cover all her medical care, so that she will have to pay for her care from her ketubah," following Rabbi Yoḥanan. (*Shulḥan Arukh, Even HaEzer* 79:2.)

TRANSLATION AND COMMENTARY

MISHNAH לֹא כָּתַב לָהּ [1] This Mishnah mentions several additional obligations imposed on the husband in the ketubah as conditions laid down by the court. **If** the husband **did not write for** his wife in her ketubah: [2] **"The male children that you will have from me will inherit the money of your ketubah** that I myself will inherit from you if you die before me, **in addition to their share** in the rest of my estate that they will share **with their brothers** from any another marriage," [3] **he is** nevertheless held **liable** to fulfill this stipulation, **for** the inheritance of the wife's ketubah by her sons **is** a right based on **a condition laid down by the court.** If a woman predeceases her husband, he inherits her entire estate, including the dowry she brought into the marriage. The Rabbis enacted that, when the husband dies, the ketubah and the dowry he inherited from his wife pass to the male children of that marriage, and only then is the rest of the man's estate divided up among all his heirs. Ordinarily, this provision was stated explicitly in the woman's ketubah. The Mishnah teaches us that the ketubah and the dowry are inherited by her sons, even if the document did not contain this clause.

בְּנָן נוּקְבָן [4] The Mishnah continues: **If** the husband **did not write** for his wife: **"The female children that you will have from me will live in my house and be maintained from my property** after my death **until they are taken in marriage by husbands,"** [5] the husband **is** still held **liable** to fulfill this obligation, **for** the right to have her daughters maintained from the estate of their deceased father **is based on a condition laid down by the court.** Since by Torah law the existence of sons excludes daughters as heirs of their father's estate, the Rabbis imposed an obligation on the sons who inherit the estate to maintain the minor daughters from it. A clause to this effect was usually inserted in the ketubah; but even if it is missing, the wife's daughters are still entitled to maintenance from their father's estate.

משנה [1] לֹא כָּתַב לָהּ:
[2] ״בְּנִין דִּכְרִין דְּיֶהֱווּ לֵיכִי מִינַּאי
אִינּוּן יִרְתוּן כֶּסֶף כְּתוּבָּתֵיךְ יָתֵר
עַל חוּלַקְהוֹן דְּעִם אֲחוּהוֹן״,
[3] חַיָּיב, שֶׁהוּא תְּנַאי בֵּית דִּין.
[4] ״בְּנָן נוּקְבָן דְּיֶהֶוְיָן לֵיכִי מִינַּאי
יֶהֶוְיָן יָתְבָן בְּבֵיתִי וּמִיתְזְנָן
מִנִּכְסַי עַד דְּתִלָּקְחוּן לְגוּבְרִין״,
[5] חַיָּיב, שֶׁהוּא תְּנַאי בֵּית דִּין.

LITERAL TRANSLATION

MISHNAH [1] [If] he did not write for her: [2] "The male children that you will have from me will inherit the money of your ketubah in addition to their share with their brothers," [3] he is liable, because it is a condition of the court.

[4] [If he did not write:] "The female children that you will have from me will live in my house and be maintained from my property until they are taken [in marriage] by men," [5] he is liable, because it is a condition of the court.

RASHI

משנה יתר על חולקהון דעם אחוהון – בני אשה אחרת. אם תמותי בחיי ואירשך – יטלו בניך כתובתיך. ונפקא מינה שמא מרובה היא, או שמא יהו בני אשה האחרת מרובים ובניך מועטים, וטוב להן שיטלו כתובת אמן והמרובים כתובת אמן, ואפי׳ הכתובות שוות.

BACKGROUND

תְּנַאי בֵּית דִּין A condition of the court. This term refers to a general ordinance instituted by the highest courts. These conditions were regarded as part of the Halakhah itself. A private individual may make any agreement dependent upon whatever conditions he chooses. However, the validity of those conditions must be clarified, both with respect to their wording and also with respect to their content. By contrast, conditions instituted by the court are the general law, applicable to all agreements of a certain type. Often such conditions may not be rescinded at all, or may be rescinded only with the explicit agreement of the parties concerned.

The ketubah is subject to a considerable number of conditions instituted by the court, regarding the clauses that it must contain, the sums of money involved, and the wording of the document.

NOTES

לֹא כָּתַב לָהּ: ״בְּנִין דִּכְרִין״ If he did not write for her: "The male children." During the period of the Geonim it was recognized by many authorities that the enactment of the *ketubat benin dikhrin* was no longer in force. Two explanations were offered as to why the enactment had become obsolete. First, because enforcing the enactment required a precise assessment of the estate of the deceased, and the judges no longer felt competent to decide on such matters. And second, because the Sages had originally instituted the *ketubat benin dikhrin* in order to encourage people to give their daughters larger dowries, and it had become customary for fathers to give their daughters such large dowries that there was concern that their sons would be left with nothing. Even those Rishonim who maintain that the enactment of the *ketubat benin dikhrin* is still in effect agree that the sons may collect their mother's ketubah only from real estate, even though the Geonim enacted that the ketubah and all of the conditions recorded in it may be collected from the estate's movable goods as well.

״וּמִיתְזְנָן מִנִּכְסַי״ "And be maintained from my property." *Ramban* maintains that the widow and the daughters are

HALAKHAH

לֹא כָּתַב לָהּ: ״בְּנִין דִּכְרִין״ If he did not write for her: "The male children." "One of the financial obligations undertaken by a husband by virtue of his wife's ketubah is that the sons of that marriage will inherit her ketubah (if the woman dies before her husband, and her ketubah passes to him) when their father dies, in addition to the share in the rest of his estate that they must share with all of their brothers. The sons inherit their mother's ketubah, even if the ketubah did not include a stipulation to that effect, for this right is based on a condition laid down by the court." (*Rambam, Sefer Nashim, Hilkhot Ishut* 12:2; *Shulḥan Arukh, Even HaEzer* 69:2.)

״בְּנָן נוּקְבָן״ "The female children." "A man's minor daughters are entitled to maintenance from his estate until

[1]״אַתְּ תְּהֵא יָתְבָא בְּבֵיתִי וּמִיתְזְנָא מִנִּכְסַי כָּל יְמֵי מֵיגַר אַלְמָנוּתֵיךְ בְּבֵיתִי״, [2]חַיָּיב, שֶׁהוּא תְּנַאי בֵּית דִּין. [3]כָּךְ הָיוּ אַנְשֵׁי יְרוּשָׁלַיִם כּוֹתְבִין. [4]אַנְשֵׁי גָּלִיל הָיוּ כּוֹתְבִין כְּאַנְשֵׁי יְרוּשָׁלַיִם. [5]אַנְשֵׁי יְהוּדָה הָיוּ כּוֹתְבִין: ״עַד שֶׁיִּרְצוּ הַיּוֹרְשִׁין לִיתֵּן לָךְ כְּתוּבָּתֵיךְ״. [6]לְפִיכָךְ, אִם רָצוּ יוֹרְשִׁין, נוֹתְנִין לָהּ כְּתוּבָּתָהּ, וּפוֹטְרִין אוֹתָהּ.

LITERAL TRANSLATION

[1] [If he did not write:] "You will live in my house and be maintained from my property all the days that you live in widowhood in my house," [2] he is liable, because it is a condition of the court. [3] This is how the people of Jerusalem used to write. [4] The people of Galilee used to write like the people of Jerusalem. [5] The people of Judea used to write: "Until the heirs wish to give you your ketubah." [6] Therefore, if the heirs wish, they give her her ketubah, and dismiss her.

TRANSLATION AND COMMENTARY

אַתְּ תְּהֵא יָתְבָא בְּבֵיתִי [1] The Mishnah now discusses another condition of a woman's ketubah. **If** the husband **did not write** in his wife's ketubah: "After I die, **you will live in my house and be maintained from my property all the days that you live in widowhood in my house,"** the husband **is** nevertheless held **liable** to fulfill this obligation, [2] for a woman's right to receive support from her deceased husband's estate **is** based on **a condition laid down by the court.** A widow is entitled to maintenance from her husband's estate, as well as to continue living in the same house in which she lived with her husband. The Mishnah teaches us that while these rights were usually mentioned explicitly in the ketubah, the widow does not forfeit anything if the document fails to refer to them explicitly. She retains these rights throughout her widowhood, unless she has remarried or received her ketubah. [3] The Mishnah notes that **the people of Jerusalem used to write** the ketubah **in this manner,** using the formula cited above: "You will live in my house and be maintained from my property all the days that you live in widowhood in my house." [4] **The people of Galilee,** too, **used to write** the ketubah using the same text **as the people of Jerusalem.** According to this formulation, the choice of receiving the ketubah lies entirely in the hands of the widow, and if she does not demand it, she is entitled to maintenance for the duration of her widowhood. The heirs cannot compel her to receive her ketubah and thereby be relieved of their obligation to maintain her. [5] But this was not the universal custom, for **the people of Judea used to write** the ketubah differently: "You will live in my house and be maintained from my property **until the heirs wish to give you your ketubah."** According to this formulation, the decision is placed in the hands of the heirs. [6] **If the heirs wish, they** can **give** the widow **her ketubah** even against her will **and** then **send her away** to provide for her own maintenance and housing.

RASHI

כל ימי מיגר ארמלותיך = כל ימי משך אלמנותיך.

NOTES

entitled to receive not only food ("maintenance" in the narrow sense of the word) but clothing as well from the estate of the deceased. Indeed, the formulation of the condition found in the Jerusalem Talmud (*Ketubot* 12:2) reads: "They will live in my house and be fitted out in my clothing." According to *Tosafot* (cited by *Ritva*), the Rabbinic enactment entitling the widow and the daughters to maintenance entitles them to food but nothing else.

״כָּל יְמֵי מֵיגַר אַלְמָנוּתֵיךְ״ **"All the days that you live in widowhood."** Our commentary follows the reading found in the standard texts — אַלְמָנוּתֵיךְ. Thus the husband stipulates that his wife will live in his house and be maintained from his property all the days that she *"lives"* (from the root גור) in widowhood in his house, or alternatively, all the days that she is *"dragged"* (from the root גרר) through widowhood (*Rivan*). A second reading is found in some talmudic manuscripts and cited by certain Rishonim — מֵיגַד אַלְמָנוּתֵיךְ. According to this reading, the husband promises his wife maintenance for the *"duration"* (from the root נגד) of her widowhood (*Talmidei Rabbenu Yonah*).

HALAKHAH

they are betrothed or reach majority, even if a stipulation to that effect was not recorded in their mother's ketubah, for this right is based on a condition laid down by the court." (*Rambam, Sefer Nashim, Hilkhot Ishut* 12:2; *Shulḥan Arukh, Even HaEzer* 69:2.)

״אַתְּ תְּהֵא יָתְבָא בְּבֵיתִי וּמִיתְזְנָא מִנְּכָסַי״ **"You will live in my house and be maintained from my property."** "A widow is entitled to receive maintenance from her late husband's estate and to continue living in the house in which she lived while they were married, even if a stipulation to that effect was not included in her ketubah, for these rights are based on a condition laid down by the court." (*Rambam, Sefer Nashim, Hilkhot Ishut* 12:2; *Shulḥan Arukh, Even HaEzer* 69:2.)

גמרא [1]אָמַר רַבִּי יוֹחָנָן מִשּׁוּם רַבִּי שִׁמְעוֹן בֶּן יוֹחַאי: [2]מִפְּנֵי מָה הִתְקִינוּ כְּתוּבַּת בְּנִין דִּכְרִין? [3]כְּדֵי שֶׁיִּקְפּוֹץ אָדָם וְיִכְתּוֹב לְבִתּוֹ כִּבְנוֹ.

[4]וּמִי אִיכָּא מִידֵּי דְּרַחֲמָנָא אָמַר בְּרָא לֵירוּת, בְּרַתָּא לָא תֵּירוּת, [5]וַאֲתוּ רַבָּנַן וּמְתַקְּנֵי דְּתֵירוּת בְּרַתָּא?

[6]הָא נַמִי דְּאוֹרַיְיתָא הוּא, דִּכְתִיב: [7]״קְחוּ נָשִׁים, וְהוֹלִידוּ בָּנִים וּבָנוֹת, וּקְחוּ לִבְנֵיכֶם נָשִׁים, וְאֶת בְּנוֹתֵיכֶם תְּנוּ לַאֲנָשִׁים״. [8]בִּשְׁלָמָא בָּנִים, בִּידֵיהּ קַיְימֵי, אֶלָּא בְּנָתֵיהּ מִי

LITERAL TRANSLATION

GEMARA [1]Rabbi Yoḥanan said in the name of Rabbi Shimon ben Yoḥai: [2]For what [reason] did they enact the ketubah of male children? [3]So that a man will be eager to (lit., "will jump and") write for his daughter as [for] his son.

[4]But is there anything that the Torah says [that] a son will inherit, [and] a daughter will not inherit, [5]and the Rabbis come and enact that the daughter will inherit?

[6]This too is [based on] the Torah, for it is written: [7]"Take wives, and beget sons and daughters, and take wives for your sons, and give your daughters to husbands." [8]Granted that sons are in his hand, but are his daughters

TRANSLATION AND COMMENTARY

GEMARA אָמַר רַבִּי יוֹחָנָן [1] **Rabbi Yoḥanan said in the name of Rabbi Shimon ben Yoḥai:** By Torah law, the ketubah and the dowry that the husband inherited from his wife should pass in equal shares to all his sons when he dies. [2]**Why,** then, **did** the Rabbis **enact** the ketubah condition, known as the *ketubat benin dikhrin,* whereby **the** wife's **ketubah** and dowry, inherited by her husband if she dies before him, are inherited by her **male children** when he dies? [3]It was **so that a man would be eager to give his daughter** as her dowry a share of his property **equal to** what he would give **his son.** Since the father is assured that the property he gives his daughter will pass only to her sons, he will be more generous when he decides on the size of her dowry.

וּמִי אִיכָּא [4]The Gemara asks: **But is there any case** that can serve as a precedent for such an enactment? Can it be that **the Torah said that** only **a son inherits** his father's estate, **and** that **a daughter does not inherit,** [5]**and the Rabbis came and enacted that the daughter would inherit?** This Rabbinic enactment encourages the father to give his daughter a share of his property that would otherwise belong to his estate and be passed to his sons as their inheritance!

הָא נַמִי דְּאוֹרַיְיתָא הוּא [6]The Gemara answers: **This** enactment, **too, is based on Torah law, for the verse says** (Jeremiah 29:6): [7]**"Take wives, and beget sons and daughters, and take wives for your sons, and give your daughters to husbands."** [8]This verse requires clarification: **Granted that it is within** a father's **power** to find a wife for his **son,** because it is generally the man who goes out in search of a wife, **but is it** really **within** the father's **power** to find a husband for his **daughter,** since fathers do not usually search for husbands

RASHI

גמרא מפני מה תקנו כתובת בנין דכרין – מאחר שהבעל יורש את אשתו, למה תקנו שיוריש לבניה מה שירש ממנה, דהיינו נדוניא שלה? **ויתן לבתו** – נדוניא יפה, דאילו מתה יירשו בניה. **דרחמנא אמר ברא לירות** – דכתיב (במדבר כז) ״איש כי ימות ובן אין לו וגו׳״ – הא יש לו – בנו יורשו, ולא בתו. **ותקון דתירות ברתא** – שיתן לה הא׳ ממונו שהיו בניו ראויין לירש. **בשלמא בנו בידו** – לבקש לו אשה, שדרכו של איש לחזור על אשה. **אלא בתו מי בידו** – וכי דרך אשה לחזור על איש?

NOTES

וּמִי אִיכָּא מִידֵּי But is there anything. The following question may be asked: The enactment of *ketubat benin dikhrin* seems to contradict the Torah's intention that a man's property should pass to his sons and not to his daughters. Why did the Gemara not also raise the objection that the enactment contradicts a fundamental principle of succession, that all the sons of the deceased (with the exception of the firstborn) receive an equal share of their father's estate? Apparently it was obvious to the Gemara that the law is in accordance with the viewpoint of Rabbi Yoḥanan ben Beroka (*Bava Batra* 130a) that a man may bequeath to one of his legal heirs a larger share of the estate than that to which he would otherwise have been entitled. But even Rabbi Yoḥanan ben Beroka agrees that a man may not leave any portion of his estate as an inheritance to someone who is not a legal heir — for example, to a daughter when there are also surviving sons (*Birkat Avraham*).

הָא נַמִי דְּאוֹרַיְיתָא הוּא This too is based on the Torah. *Ritva* explains this as follows: Giving one's daughter a dowry is recognized as a meritorious deed by Torah law (even though the Scriptural support that the Gemara adduces is found in the book of Jeremiah, and not in the Torah itself), but it is not obligatory even by Rabbinic law, and this is why the Baraita can rule (below, 68b): "If someone gives instructions on his deathbed that his daughters should not be provided a dowry out of his estate, these instructions are heeded."

קַיְימָן בִּידֵיהּ? [1]הָא קָא מַשְׁמַע לָן דְּנַלְבְּשָׁהּ, וְנִיכְסָהּ, וְנֵיתִיב לָהּ מִידֵי, [2]כִּי הֵיכִי דְּקָפְצֵי עֲלָהּ וְאָתוּ נָסְבִי לָהּ.
[3]וְעַד כַּמָּה?
[4]אַבַּיֵי וְרָבָא דְּאָמְרִי תַּרְוַיְיהוּ: עַד לְעִישּׂוּר נְכָסֵי.
[5]וְאֵימָא: דְּאָב לֵירוּת; [6]דְּבַעַל לָא לֵירוּת!
[7]אִם כֵּן, אָב נַמִי מִימְנָע וְלָא כָּתַב.

TRANSLATION AND COMMENTARY

for their daughters? [1]Thus **this** verse instructing a father to marry off his daughter must be understood as **teaching us that** the father **should fit** his daughter **out, dress her** appropriately, **and give her** a sizable dowry, [2]**so that** prospective bridegrooms **will be eager to offer to marry her.** Hence the Rabbis instituted the *ketubat benin dikhrin* in order to encourage fathers to be generous.

וְעַד כַּמָּה [3]The Gemara asks: **How much** of his property should a father give his daughter as her dowry?

אַבַּיֵי וְרָבָא [4]In reply, **Abaye and Rava both said:** A father should give his daughter **up to a tenth of his property** when she marries.

וְאֵימָא [5]The Gemara raises an objection: **But** if the reason why the Rabbis enacted the *ketubat benin dikhrin* was to encourage the father to give his daughter a sizable dowry, why did they enact that the woman's sons should inherit her entire ketubah when their father dies, both the portion that the woman's father gave his daughter as her dowry, and the portion that the husband obligated himself to give his wife from his own money? Let us **say** that **what the father gave** his daughter as her dowry her sons **should** indeed **inherit,** so that he will be encouraged to give the daughter a generous dowry; [6]but **what the husband** obligated himself to **give** her from his own money her **sons should not inherit!**

אִם כֵּן [7]The Gemara explains: **If it were the case** that the woman's sons did not inherit the main portion of their mother's ketubah together with her dowry, **the father would also refrain from giving** his daughter a sizable dowry. The father expects that his generosity will be matched by that of his son-in-law. If the father sees that his grandchildren will not inherit the portion of his daughter's ketubah that her husband obligates himself to pay from his own money, the father will not be willing to increase the size of the dowry he gives his daughter from *his* money.

LITERAL TRANSLATION

in his hand? [1]This teaches us that he should fit her out, and dress her, and give her something, [2]so that [people] will be eager to come [and] marry her.

[3]And how much?

[4]Abaye and Rava both said: Up to a tenth of his property.

[5]But say: What the father [gave] let [the sons] inherit; [6]what the husband [gave] let [the sons] not inherit!

[7]If so, the father also will refrain and will not write.

RASHI

ואימא דאב לירות דבעל לא לירות – כיון דטעמא כדי שיקפוץ ליתן לבתו הוא דתקון, נדוניא דיהב אב לבתו – לירתון בניס דילה, אבל שאר כתובות נכסי הבעל, כגון מנה מאתים ותוספת דבעל – לא לירתון. **אם כן** – דלא ירתי לשאר הכתובה. **אב נמי מימנע ולא כתב** – לבתו, אחרי שזה מקפיד על שלו מלהוריש לבני בתי – אף אני אמשוך ידי מלהרבות לו נדוניא.

NOTES

עַד לְעִישּׂוּר נְכָסֵי Up to a tenth of his property. *Rashi* and most Rishonim explain that this was a recommendation regarding how much a father ought to give his daughter as her dowry, and that this was the amount usually given. Thus, if the father has died, and we are unable to assess how large a dowry he would have given his daughter, we assume that he would have given her one-tenth of his property. But if the father wishes, he may give his daughter more than that amount. According to *Rabbenu Ḥananel* (cited by *Tosafot,* above, 50b), the father may not give his daughter a dowry that exceeds one-tenth of his property, to avoid giving her property that is supposed to pass to his sons as their inheritance. *Talmidei Rabbenu Yonah* explains that the Gemara does not mean to say that a man is required to give his daughter one-tenth of his property, but rather that he may give her as much as one-tenth of his property as her dowry, if he is unable to find a suitable husband who is ready to marry her for less.

HALAKHAH

דְּנַלְבְּשָׁהּ וְנִיכְסָהּ That he should fit her out, and dress her. "The Sages enacted that a man should give a small portion of his property to his daughter, so that suitors will be eager to marry her, and this is called her dowry." (*Rambam, Sefer Nashim, Hilkhot Ishut* 20:1; *Shulḥan Arukh, Even HaEzer* 58:1.)

עַד לְעִישּׂוּר נְכָסֵי Up to a tenth of his property. "If a man dies and is survived by a daughter, the court assesses how much the father would have been willing to give her as her dowry, and assigns her that amount from his estate. If the court is unable to determine how much the father would have wanted to give his daughter, she is awarded one-tenth of his estate (after deducting the funeral expenses; *Ba'er Hetev*)." (*Rambam, Sefer Nashim, Hilkhot Ishut* 20:3; *Shulḥan Arukh, Even HaEzer* 113:1.)

[1]וְאֵימָא: הֵיכָא דְּכָתַב אָב, לִכְתּוֹב בַּעַל; [2]הֵיכָא דְּלָא כָּתַב אָב, לָא לִכְתּוֹב בַּעַל!

[3]לָא פְּלוּג רַבָּנַן.

[4]בַּת בֵּין הַבָּנִים נַמִי תֵּירוֹת!

[5]כְּנַחֲלָה שַׁוְיוּהָ רַבָּנַן.

[6]בַּת בֵּין הַבָּנוֹת תֵּירוֹת!

[7]לָא פְּלוּג רַבָּנַן.

LITERAL TRANSLATION

[1]But say: Where the father wrote, let the husband write; [2]where the father did not write, let the husband not write!

[3]The Rabbis did not differentiate.

[4]A daughter among the sons should also inherit!

[5]The Rabbis made it like an inheritance.

[6]A daughter among the daughters should inherit!

[7]The Rabbis did not differentiate.

TRANSLATION AND COMMENTARY

וְאֵימָא [1]The Gemara now raises another objection: **But** if the reason why the Rabbis enacted the *ketubat benin dikhrin* was to encourage the father to give his daughter a sizable dowry, why did they enact that the husband must always insert that provision in the ketubah he gives his wife? Let us **say** that in cases **where the father gave** his daughter a dowry, **the husband must write** in the ketubah that the woman's sons will inherit the ketubah when he dies; [2]but in cases **where the father did not give** his daughter a dowry, **the husband does not have to include** such a provision in the ketubah!

לָא פְּלוּג רַבָּנַן [3]The Gemara answers: Indeed, the Rabbis did enact the *ketubat benin dikhrin* to encourage the bride's father to give his daughter a sizable dowry. But once **the Rabbis** enacted this, they **did not differentiate** between the different cases. Since most people do in fact provide their daughters with a dowry, the Rabbis enacted that the sons should inherit their mother's ketubah in all cases, even if a dowry was not given.

בַּת בֵּין הַבָּנִים [4]The Gemara now raises another objection: If the *ketubat benin dikhrin* was instituted in order to ensure that the dowry provided by the bride's father would remain in the hands of her descendants, why is it only the woman's sons who inherit her ketubah? If the woman had no sons but only a **daughter,** and her husband had **sons** from another marriage, the woman's daughter **should also** be eligible to **inherit** her ketubah! Why should the husband's sons from another marriage inherit it, forever depriving her descendants of the dowry provided by her father?

כְּנַחֲלָה שַׁוְיוּהָ רַבָּנַן [5]The Gemara answers: When **the Rabbis** enacted the *ketubat benin dikhrin,* they **gave it** the characteristics of **an inheritance.** When the sons receive their mother's ketubah, they receive it as an inheritance, as the condition inserted in the ketubah states: "The male children that you will have from me will *inherit* the money of your ketubah." Just as a man's sons exclude his daughters as heirs of their father's estate, so too in the case of a *ketubat benin dikhrin* do a man's sons exclude his daughters from inheriting their mother's ketubah.

בַּת בֵּין הַבָּנוֹת [6]The Gemara asks: If it is the case that the *ketubat benin dikhrin* has the characteristics of an inheritance, then if a woman had no sons but only **a daughter,** and her husband also had only **daughters** from his other marriage, the woman's daughter **should inherit** her mother's ketubah when her father dies! If a man is survived only by daughters, they each inherit an equal share of their father's estate. The Rabbis should have enacted that the woman's daughter inherits her mother's ketubah in addition to the part of her father's estate that she must share with his other daughters. Why, then, did they apply their enactment only to a case in which the woman had male children?

לָא פְּלוּג רַבָּנַן [7]The Gemara answers: **The Rabbis did not** wish to **differentiate** between the case in which the father had sons from his other marriage and the case in which he had only daughters. Even though they could have distinguished between the two cases in the light of the different circumstances, they preferred to make their enactment of general application, saying that the male children inherit their mother's ketubah but the female children do not.

RASHI

היכא דכתב אב כו' — כיון דטעמא משום שיקפוץ אב לתת נדוניא לבתו היא, היכא דכתב אב נדוניא לבתו — נכתוב בעל תנאי כתובת בנין דכרין, והיכא דלא כתב אב נדוניא לבתו — לא נכתוב בעל תנאי כתובת בנין דכרין. **לא פלוג רבנן** — לא חלקו בין כתובה לכתובה, אחרי שרוב כתובות יש בהן נדוניא לא חלקו. **בת בין הבנים תירות** — [כיון דטעמא משום נדוניא הוא, היכא דאין לו בנים ממנה אלא] יש לו בת מן אשה אחת, ובנים מן האחרת — תטול בת היחידה כתובת אמה לירש נדוניא שנתן אבי אמה, מאי שנא דתקון בנין דכרין? **כנחלה שויוה רבנן** — ד"ירתון" תנן, ואין בת יורשת בין הבנים. **בת בין הבנות תירות** — יש לו בת מן אשה אחת, ובנות מן האחרת — תטול בת היחידה כתובת אמה לירש נדונית אבי אמה. דהא אי נמי שויוה כנחלה — יש משפט נחלה לבת בין הבנות. **לא פלוג רבנן** — במשפט כתובת בנין דכרין, דבת בין הבנים לא תשקול, ובת בין הבנות תשקול.

TERMINOLOGY

לָא פְּלוּג רַבָּנַן **The Rabbis did not differentiate.** An argument occasionally used by the Gemara to explain why the law is the same in two slightly different situations. "The Rabbis wished to avoid possible confusion and therefore did not differentiate between the cases under discussion."

LITERAL TRANSLATION

[1] But let it be collected from movable goods!
[2] The Rabbis made it like a ketubah.
[3] Let it cause seizure from mortgaged property!
[4] We have learned: "They will inherit."
[5] But say: Even though there is not a surplus of a dinar!
[6] Where inheritance by Torah law would be uprooted, [7] the Rabbis did not pass an enactment.

[1]וְתִיגְבֵּי מִמִּטַּלְטְלֵי!
[2]כִּכְתוּבָּה שַׁוְיוּהָ רַבָּנַן.
[3]תִּטְרוֹף מִמְּשַׁעְבְּדֵי!
[4]״יִרְתּוּן״ תְּנַן.
[5]וְאֵימָא: אַף עַל גַּב דְּלֵיכָּא מוֹתַר דִּינָר!
[6]בְּמָקוֹם דְּקָא מִיעַקְרָא נַחֲלָה דְּאוֹרַיְיתָא, [7]לָא תַּקִּינוּ רַבָּנַן.

TRANSLATION AND COMMENTARY

וְתִיגְבֵּי מִמִּטַּלְטְלֵי [1] The Gemara raises another objection: **But** if it is the case that the sons receive their mother's ketubah as an inheritance, why did we learn earlier in the Gemara (above, 50b) that the sons inherit their mother's ketubah only from the landed property in their father's estate, but not from his movable goods. Since the Rabbis enacted the *ketubat benin dikhrin* in order to ensure that the dowry given to the bride by her father would remain in the hands of her descendants, **let** the *ketubat benin dikhrin* **be collected** even **from the movable goods** in the father's estate, so as not to alienate the woman's dowry from her descendants!

כִּכְתוּבָּה שַׁוְיוּהָ רַבָּנַן [2] The Gemara answers: When **the Rabbis** enacted the *ketubat benin dikhrin,* they **gave it** the characteristics of **a ketubah.** Just as a widow can collect her ketubah only from real estate, similarly the sons can collect their mother's ketubah by virtue of the enactment of the *ketubat benin dikhrin* only from real estate.

תִּטְרוֹף מִמְּשַׁעְבְּדֵי [3] This answer leads the Gemara to another question: If it is true that the sons collect their mother's ketubah in the same way as their mother would have collected her own ketubah, then **let** the sons be able to **seize** as payment **property that was mortgaged** as security for the ketubah and was later sold to a third party! All the husband's landed property is mortgaged toward payment of his wife's ketubah, so that she can recover it from real estate transferred to others by the husband or by his heirs. But when the sons come to collect their mother's ketubah by virtue of the enactment of the *ketubat benin dikhrin,* the Amoraim (below, 55a) disagree as to whether they are entitled to collect from property that has already been sold to a third party. Now, if the sons collect the ketubah in the same manner as does their mother, why do some authorities maintain that they cannot seize property sold to a third party?

״יִרְתּוּן״ תְּנַן [4] The Gemara answers: The sons cannot collect from a third party to whom the property has been sold because they do not have a direct claim. Instead, they inherit the ketubah that was due to their mother. This **we have learned** from our Mishnah, which records the formula included in the wording of the ketubah: "The male children that you will have from me **will *inherit*** the money of your ketubah." Since the sons are given the standing of heirs, their claim is limited by the laws of inheritance, and these laws state that an heir inherits only the property that is in his father's possession at the time of his death, and not property that has already been transferred to a third party.

וְאֵימָא [5] The Gemara concludes this discussion with a final question. **But** if the Rabbis enacted that the sons should inherit their mother's ketubah, let us **say** that the sons should inherit the ketubah **even if** the father did **not** leave an estate large enough so that, after the ketubah is collected, **a surplus of** at least **a dinar** will remain to be divided equally among all the brothers! Why, then, does the Mishnah rule elsewhere (below, 91a) that if the father's estate will not contain at least a dinar after the sons have collected their mother's ketubah, the enactment of the *ketubat benin dikhrin* does not apply, and all the sons take an equal share of their father's estate as laid down by Torah law?

בְּמָקוֹם [6] The Gemara answers: In cases **where inheritance by Torah law would be** totally **uprooted** by the Rabbinic enactment of the *ketubat benin dikhrin,* [7] **the Rabbis did not pass the enactment.**

RASHI

ותגבי ממטלטלי — כיון דטעמא משום נדוניית אבי האם הוא, אלמה אמרינן לעיל (נ,ב): כשם שאין הבנים אלא מקרקע, ואוקימנא בכתובת בנין דכרין. **בכתובה שויוה רבנן** — ומטלטלי דיתמי לא משתעבדי לשטרא. **תטרוף ממשעבדי** — אי ככתובה שויוה. ולקמן פליגי בה בריש פרק "אף על פי". **ירתון תנן** — ואין ירושה במשועבדין. **ואימא אף על גב דליכא מותר דינר** — יתר על שתי הכתובות — יטלו כתובת אמם, כדין כתובת בנין דכרין. אלמה תנן בפרק "מי שהיה נשוי" (לקמן צא,א): אין שם אלא שתי כתובות — חולקין בשוה. **מקום דמיעקרא נחלה דאורייתא** — משום נחלה דרבנן. **לא תקון רבנן** — נחלה דידהו לעקור נחלת חלוקה שוה לגמרי שהיא מן התורה. הלכך, כי איכא מותר דינר

HALAKHAH

בְּמָקוֹם דְּקָא מִיעַקְרָא נַחֲלָה דְּאוֹרַיְיתָא **Where inheritance by Torah law would be uprooted.** "The sons inherit their mother's ketubah only if, after they have collected the ketubah, at least a dinar's worth will remain of their father's estate,

TRANSLATION AND COMMENTARY

רַב פַּפָּא [1] The Gemara now relates that **Rav Pappa was** once **occupied with** arranging **the marriage of his son to the daughter of Abba of Sura.** [2] Rav Pappa **went** to Abba's house in order **to arrange for the writing of** his daughter-in-law's **ketubah,** planning to discuss with the bride's father the size of the dowry he would provide for his daughter. [3] When **Yehudah bar Maremar heard** that Rav Pappa was coming, he **went out and appeared before him** to greet him. [4] **When they arrived at the door** of Abba's house, Yehudah bar Maremar wished to **part** company **with** Rav Pappa, and asked for permission to be excused from entering the house with him. [5] Rav Pappa **said to him: "Please, Sir, come into** Abba's house **with me."** [53A] [6] When Rav Pappa **saw that** Yehudah bar Maremar **did not want** to go into Abba's house, [7] **he said to him: "What opinion do you** follow in not wanting to go into Abba's house? [8] Perhaps you are reluctant to enter **because** of what **Shmuel said to Rav Yehudah: 'You sharp-witted man!** [9] **Do not participate** in a transaction that will result **in the passing of an inheritance** from a legal heir, **even** if the inheritance will pass **from a bad son to a good son,** [10] **because one never knows what descendant will come from** the bad son. Perhaps his children or grandchildren will turn out to be righteous people, who fully deserve their rightful share of the inheritance. [11] **And all the more so,** do not take part in the passing of an inheritance **from a son to a daughter,** who is excluded by Torah law from inheriting a share of the estate.' Is this the reason why you, Yehudah bar Maremar, do not wish to go into Abba's house — because you do not want to be present when Abba obligates himself to provide his daughter with a dowry and promises to give her property that would otherwise be part of his estate and pass to his sons when he dies? [12] But surely providing one's daughter with a dowry **is also**

[1] רַב פַּפָּא אִיעֲסַק לֵיהּ לִבְרֵיהּ בֵּי אַבָּא סוּרָאָה. [2] אֲזֵיל לְמִיכְתַּב לָהּ כְּתוּבָּתָהּ. [3] שָׁמַע יְהוּדָה בַּר מָרֵימָר, נָפַק, אֲתָא, אִיתְחֲזִי לֵיהּ. [4] כִּי מָטוּ לְפִיתְחָא, הֲוָה קָא מִפַּטַּר מִינֵּיהּ. [5] אֲמַר לֵיהּ: ״נֵיעוּל מָר בַּהֲדַאי״. [53A] [6] חַזְיֵיהּ דְּלָא הֲוָה נִיחָא לֵיהּ. [7] אֲמַר לֵיהּ: ״מַאי דַּעְתֵּיךְ? [8] מִשּׁוּם דַּאֲמַר לֵיהּ שְׁמוּאֵל לְרַב יְהוּדָה: ׳שִׁינָּנָא! [9] לָא תֶּיהֱוֵי בְּעַבּוּרֵי אַחְסַנְתָּא אֲפִילּוּ מִבְּרָא בִּישָׁא לִבְרָא טָבָא, [10] דְּלָא יְדִיעָא מַאי זַרְעָא נָפֵיק מִינֵּיהּ, [11] וְכָל שֶׁכֵּן מִבְּרָא לִבְרַתָּא׳? [12] הַאי נַמִי

LITERAL TRANSLATION

[1] Rav Pappa was occupied with [the marriage of] his son [to a daughter of] the house of Abba of Sura. [2] He went to write her ketubah for her. [3] Yehudah bar Maremar heard, went out, came, [and] appeared before him. [4] When they arrived at the door, he parted from him. [5] He said to him: "Let the Master come in with me." [53A] [6] He saw that it was not pleasing to him. [7] He said to him: "What is your opinion? [8] [Is it] because Shmuel said to Rav Yehudah: 'You sharp-witted man! [9] Do not be [present] at the passing of an inheritance even from a bad son to a good son, [10] for it is not known what issue will come forth from him, [11] and all the more so from a son to a daughter'? [12] This too

RASHI

שיחלקוהו בשוה בנחלה דאורייתא — יטלו אלו כתובת אמן ואלו כתובת אמן משום נחלה דרבנן, ואי לא — לא. **בי אבא סוראה** — חמיו היה, והשיא רב פפא לבנו אחות אשתו. כדאמרינן ב״אלו נערות״ (לעיל לט,ב): אמרה לי בת אבא סוראה כי נהמא אקושא בחיגכי. ובסנהדרין (יד,ב) נמי אמרינן: איש ושתי נשים שאין מטילין לכים אחד — כגון רב פפא ובת אבא סוראה. **אזיל** — רב פפא לבית אבי הנערה לכתוב כתובתה, ושם יפסוק אביה ויכתוב לה בנדונייתה מה שיכתוב. **כי מטו לפתחא** — דאבא סוראה. **הוה מיפטר** — מיניה יהודה, נטל רשות מרב פפא לחזור לאחוריו. **חזא** — רב פפא דלא ניחא ליה ליהודה למיעל. **וכל שכן מברא לברתא** — והכא איעבורי אחסנתא הוא, שזה כותב לבתו מה שהיה ראוי להוריש לבניו.

SAGES

אַבָּא סוּרָאָה Abba of Sura. He was Rav Pappa's father-in-law; later, another daughter of Abba of Sura married Rav Pappa's son from a previous marriage, Abba Mari.

יְהוּדָה בַּר מָרֵימָר Yehudah bar Maremar. Several other Talmudic passages indicate that this scholar was a student of Rava and was Rav Pappa's contemporary and his colleague. Some manuscripts refer to this scholar as "Yehudah Mar bar Maremar," the title "Mar" frequently being appended to the names of members of the Exilarch's family. Thus, considering that Yehudah bar Maremar was himself a scholar and (apparently) a member of the Exilarch's family and a colleague of Rav Pappa, it was only natural that his arrival at Abba of Sura's house would be construed as a way of tacitly pressuring Abba of Sura to increase the dowry.

LANGUAGE

שִׁינָּנָא Sharp-witted one. This appellation for Rav Yehudah, which is found in several places in the Talmud, is understood by many commentators as meaning "sharp" or "acute," based on the analogy with the Hebrew word שָׁנּוּן, which has that meaning. However, the Geonim wrote that they were sure the term referred to a person with large teeth, based on the Aramaic and Hebrew word שֵׁן, meaning "tooth."

HALAKHAH

which can be divided among all the brothers. But if a dinar's worth of the father's estate will not remain after the sons have collected their mother's ketubah, all the sons take an equal share of the estate, so as not to negate the Biblical laws of inheritance." (*Rambam, Sefer Nashim, Hilkhot Ishut* 19:3; *Shulḥan Arukh, Even HaEzer* 111:2.)

לָא תֶּיהֱוֵי בְּעַבּוּרֵי אַחְסַנְתָּא Do not be present at the passing of an inheritance. "If someone bequeaths his estate to a beneficiary who is not his natural heir, the bequest is valid. The Rabbis, however, view such an action with disfavor, even if the testator's natural heirs treated him badly during his lifetime. It is an act of piety not to attach one's signature to a will through which a natural heir will be deprived of his inheritance, even if the estate will be passed from a bad son to a good one. *Rema* (in the name of *Mordekhai*) adds that if someone leaves instructions that his estate is to be disposed of in the best possible way, the estate is given to his natural heirs." (*Rambam, Sefer Mishpatim, Hilkhot Nahalot* 6:11; *Shulḥan Arukh, Ḥoshen Mishpat* 282:1.)

TRANSLATION AND COMMENTARY

required by virtue of **a Rabbinic enactment, as Rabbi Yoḥanan said in the name of Rabbi Shimon ben Yoḥai** that the Rabbis enacted the *ketubat benin dikhrin* so that a father would be encouraged to give his daughter a larger dowry!" [1]Yehudah bar Maremar **said to** Rav Pappa: **"This** enactment **applies if** the father **provides** for his daughter **of his own free will, but** does this mean that **it is also permitted to compel him** to provide her with a sizable dowry?" [2]Rav Pappa **said to him: "Did I** ever **suggest to you that you should go into** Abba's house with me **and compel him** to provide his daughter with a larger dowry? [3]All that **I asked** you to do was to **go into** Abba's house with me, **but not** that you should **compel him** to provide his daughter with more than he wants to give her." [4]Yehudah bar Maremar **said to him:** "But the very fact of **my going in** with you **is the same as compelling him** to provide his daughter with a larger dowry, for he will surely feel that he must increase the dowry on my account." [5]In the end Rav Pappa prevailed, and **he forced** Yehudah bar Maremar to **go into** Abba's house with him. [6]Throughout the negotiations, Yehudah bar Maremar **sat** there **silently,** without expressing any opinion about the size of the dowry. [7]Abba misinterpreted Yehudah bar Maremar's silence, **thinking that** he **was angry** with him for not providing a large enough dowry. **As a result, he assigned all** the property **he owned** for his daughter's dowry, hoping that this would please Yehudah bar Maremar. [8]**At the end,** when Abba saw that despite the large dowry that he had given his daughter, Yehudah bar Maremar persisted in his silence, **he said to him: "Will the Master not speak** to me **even now?** What more could I possibly have done to please you? [9]**By your life, Sir, I** have given my daughter everything I own, and **have left nothing** at all **for myself!"** [10]Yehudah bar Maremar then **said to him: "For my part, even that which you have assigned** for your daughter's dowry **does not please me,** for you did not decide to increase the size of the dowry of your own free will." Finally understanding

תַּקַּנְתָּא דְּרַבָּנַן הִיא, דְּאָמַר רַבִּי יוֹחָנָן מִשּׁוּם רַבִּי שִׁמְעוֹן בֶּן יוֹחַי". [1]אֲמַר לֵיהּ: "הָנֵי מִילֵּי מִדַּעְתֵּיהּ, לְעַשׂוּיֵיהּ נַמִי?" [2]אֲמַר לֵיהּ: "אַטּוּ מִי קָאָמִינָא לָךְ דְּעוּל וְעַשְׂיֵיהּ? [3]עוּל וְלָא תְּעַשְׂיֵיהּ קָאָמִינָא". [4]אֲמַר לֵיהּ: מֵעַלַּאי דִּידִי הַיְינוּ עַשְׂיֵיהּ". [5]אַכְפְּיֵיהּ וְעוּל. [6]אִישְׁתִּיק וִיתֵיב. [7]סָבַר הַהוּא מִירְתַּח רָתַח, כְּתָבֵיהּ לְכָל מַאי דַּהֲוָה לֵיהּ. [8]לְסוֹף אֲמַר לֵיהּ: "הָשְׁתָּא נַמִי לָא מִישְׁתַּעֵי מָר? [9]חַיֵּי דְּמָר, לָא שְׁבִיקִי מִידֵי לְנַפְשַׁאי!" [10]אֲמַר לֵיהּ: "אִי מִינַּאי דִּידִי, אֲפִילּוּ הַאי נַמִי דִּכְתַבְתְּ לָא נִיחָא לִי".

LITERAL TRANSLATION

is an enactment of the Rabbis, as Rabbi Yoḥanan said in the name of Rabbi Shimon ben Yoḥai." [1]He said to him: "This applies (lit., 'these things') [if he gives] of his own free will, [but is it permitted] to compel him also?" [2]He said to him: "Did I tell you to go in and compel him? [3]I said: Go in but do not compel him." [4]He said to him: "My going in is the same as compelling him." [5]He pressed him and he went in. [6]He was silent and sat. [7]He [Abba] thought [that] he was angry, [so] he assigned everything that he had. [8]At the end he said to him: "Now too does the Master not speak? [9]By the life of the Master, I have not left anything for myself!" [10]He said to him: "For my part (lit., 'if from me'), even this also that you have assigned is not pleasing to me."

RASHI

דאמר רבי יוחנן – לעיל, שיקפוץ אדם ויתן לבתו, ויליף לה מקרא. **לעשוייה נמי** – בתמיה. **מעלאי דידי היינו עשויי** – כניסתי עמך זהו עשוי, שירבה לפסוק בשביל כבודי. **אכפייה** – רב פפא ליהודה בדברים, ועל. **סבר איהו** – אבא סוראה, האי דשתיק יהודה – מרתח רתח, שאין הנדוניא הוגנת בעיניו. **אי מינאי דידי** – אם נטלת ממני עצה.

NOTES

תַּקַּנְתָּא דְּרַבָּנַן An enactment of the Rabbis. *Maharsha* asks: Why does the Gemara say that providing one's daughter with a dowry is required by Rabbinic enactment? It is true that a woman's sons inherit her ketubah from their father by virtue of the Rabbinic enactment of the *ketubat benin dikhrin*. But the Gemara stated earlier (52b) that providing one's daughter with a dowry is required by Torah law! *Maharsha* answers: In fact, it is only by Rabbinic enactment that one is required to provide one's daughter with a dowry. The verse from Jeremiah cited earlier, "Give your daughters to husbands," is merely an allusion to the law rather than its source.

HALAKHAH

הָנֵי מִילֵּי מִדַּעְתֵּיהּ This applies if he gives of his own free will. "A father cannot be compelled to marry off his daughter. Even though it is meritorious to provide one's daughter with a proper dowry, the father cannot be compelled to provide her with any specified amount. Rather, he may give her whatever he decides (*Rema*)." (*Shulḥan Arukh, Even HaEzer* 71:1.)

TRANSLATION AND COMMENTARY

Yehudah bar Maremar's position on the issue, [1] Abba **said to him: "Now** that I know that whatever I agreed to was based on a misunderstanding, **I will retract** and rewrite the terms of my daughter's dowry." [2] Yehudah bar Maremar **said to him:** "However displeased I was with the dowry you assigned to your daughter, **I did not say that you should** renege on your agreement and **make yourself someone who goes back on his word."**

בְּעָא מִינֵּיהּ רַב יֵימַר [3] The Gemara now turns to another aspect of the *ketubat benin dikhrin*. **Rav Yemar the Elder asked Rav Naḥman:** [4] **If** a woman **sells her ketubah to her husband, is she** still **entitled to** benefit from the enactment of **the *ketubat benin dikhrin*, or is she not** so **entitled?** A married woman may sell her ketubah to her husband. In exchange for a lesser sum that she receives immediately, she forfeits the right to receive her full ketubah in the event that she is widowed or divorced. The question arises as to whether, when she forfeits her right to her ketubah, she also forfeits her right to the condition in the ketubah by virtue of which her sons alone inherit her ketubah when their father dies. Do we say that when she sells her ketubah to her husband she loses all claim to her ketubah, so that it will no longer pass exclusively to her sons? Or does she perhaps only forfeit her own right to receive her ketubah, but not her sons' exclusive right to inherit it?

אֲמַר לֵיהּ רָבָא [5] **Rava said to Rav Yemar:** Why do you ask about a woman who sells her ketubah to her husband? **Ask about** a woman **who waives** her right to receive **her ketubah** without receiving anything in return! There, too, the question arises as to whether, when she waives her right to receive her ketubah, she also waives her right to the condition in the ketubah of the *ketubat benin dikhrin*.

[1] אֲמַר לֵיהּ: הָשְׁתָּא נַמִּי אֲהַדַר בִּי". [2] אֲמַר לֵיהּ: "שַׁוְיֵיה נַפְשָׁךְ הַדְּרָנָא לָא קָאָמֵינָא".

[3] בְּעָא מִינֵּיהּ רַב יֵימַר סָבָא מֵרַב נַחְמָן: [4] מָכְרָה כְּתוּבָּתָהּ לְבַעְלָהּ, יֵשׁ לָהּ כְּתוּבַּת בְּנִין דִּכְרִין אוֹ אֵין לָהּ כְּתוּבַּת בְּנִין דִּכְרִין?

[5] אֲמַר לֵיהּ רָבָא: וְתִבְעֵי לָךְ מוֹחֶלֶת!

LITERAL TRANSLATION

[1] He said to him: "If so (lit., 'now too'), I will retract." [2] He said to him: "[That] you should make yourself someone who goes back on his word I did not say." [3] Rav Yemar the Elder asked Rav Naḥman: [4] [If] she sold her ketubah to her husband, does she have the ketubah of male children or does she not have the ketubah of male children?

[5] Rava said to him: Rather, ask about one who waives [her ketubah]!

RASHI

או אין לה — מי אמרינן כיון דמכרה לבעלה פקעה לה תורת ירושת אביה מלהוריש נדוניא שלו לבני בתו, שהרי מכרתה, ואין כל הירושה באה מעכשיו אלא מכח הבעל — ויחלקו כל בניו בשוה בני שתי נשיו. **ותיבעי לך מוחלת** — שהוא דבר מצוי מן המכר. ואי משום דלא מטא הנאה לידה — מכל מקום פקעה זכותה בחייה.

SAGES

רַב יֵימַר סָבָא Rav Yemar the Elder. A Babylonian Amora of the third and fourth generations, Rav Yemar the Elder is mentioned in the Talmud as asking Rav Ḥisda and Rav Naḥman questions concerning the Halakhah. He was apparently called סָבָא (lit., "grandfather") to distinguish him from another Rav Yemar, a later Amora who was a contemporary of Rav Ashi.

רַב נַחְמָן Rav Naḥman. This is Rav Naḥman bar Ya'akov, a Babylonian Amora of the second and third generations. Rav Naḥman's father was a scribe at the court associated with the Amora Shmuel. Rav Naḥman studied with Shmuel, whose rulings he frequently cites, and with Rabbah bar Avuha, one of Rav's disciples and a member of the Exilarch's family (according to some opinions Rabbah bar Ahuva was himself the Exilarch).

Rav Naḥman married Rabbah bar Avuha's daughter, Yalta, a learned and firm-willed woman. By his marriage Rav Naḥman became connected with the House of the Exilarch, and after some time he was appointed judge of the House of the Exilarch in Neharde'a. Because of his status in the House of the Exilarch, and because of his profound knowledge of monetary law, Rav Naḥman was considered a greater authority than his colleagues in this field.

Rav Naḥman discusses Halakhic problems with a great many Sages, in particular Rav Huna, Rav Yehudah, Rav Sheshet, and Rav Ḥisda.

Although Rav Naḥman did not serve as an official head of a yeshivah, many members of his generation studied with him; the great Amora Rava was his outstanding disciple. Rav Naḥman seems to have been wealthy all his life. He was regarded as the greatest Sage of his generation and the authoritative teacher of Torah in his city. Several of Rav Naḥman's sons were scholars.

NOTES

הָשְׁתָּא נַמִּי אֲהַדַר If so, I will retract. The Gemara implies that had Abba wished to retract, he would have been permitted to do so. This poses a difficulty, for elsewhere (below, 102a) the Gemara says that the mutual promises made by the parents of the bride and the bridegroom are legally binding by mere oral agreement.

Tosafot answers that such promises become legally binding only after the bride and the bridegroom are actually betrothed. But here Abba considered retracting before the couple were betrothed. Alternatively, such promises are legally binding only if they are made before the couple are betrothed. But here the dowry arrangements were agreed upon only after the bride and the groom had already been betrothed.

מָכְרָה כְּתוּבָּתָהּ If she sold her ketubah. The Rishonim address a fundamental difficulty in this passage. Throughout its discussion of the topic, the Gemara considers the issue only from the perspective of the woman: When she sold her ketubah, did she or did she not intend to sell the right due her by virtue of the enactment of the *ketubat benin dikhrin*? But there is another party to consider here — the sons who are entitled to inherit their mother's ketubah. How can their mother sell a right that does not belong to her but to them?

Rid explains that since the sons are entitled to their mother's ketubah only by virtue of a stipulation in the document agreed upon by their mother and their father, their mother is entitled to sell that right as she wishes. *Ritva* and others explain that the Rabbis only enacted the *ketubat benin dikhrin* in a case where the woman had not already received her ketubah. Here, in the case of a woman who sold her ketubah to her husband, the Gemara is in doubt as to whether the transaction is treated as a sale or as the payment of her ketubah. If we conclude that the woman is viewed as having already received her ketubah, then there is no ketubah for the sons to inherit from their father.

וְתִבְעֵי לָךְ מוֹחֶלֶת Rather, ask about one who waives her ketubah. The Rishonim offer several explanations as to why it would have been preferable to ask about a woman who waives her ketubah rather than about a woman who sells it to her husband. *Rashi* and *Tosafot* suggest that it is more common for a woman to waive her ketubah than to sell it to her husband, and so the Gemara should have asked about the case that occurs more frequently.

Ra'ah and others argue that Rava meant to say that the question should also have been raised about a woman who waives her ketubah. Rava thought that Rav Yemar the Elder was asking specifically about a woman who sells her ketubah to her husband, because she receives something

LANGUAGE

עוּכְלֵי **Blows.** The Geonim explain that עוּכְלָא means "hammer"; thus, מֵאָה עוּכְלֵי בְּעוּכְלָא means "100 blows with a hammer" (see also *Rashi*).

BACKGROUND

מוֹכֶרֶת כְּתוּבָּתָהּ **If she sells her ketubah.** Since a ketubah is among other things a promissory note by which a husband obligates himself to pay his wife a certain sum, either that determined by the Halakhah or more, it can be sold like any other promissory note. Nevertheless, unlike other promissory notes, the ketubah does not constitute an absolute obligation, for if the woman predeceases her husband, the ketubah is null and void. The purchaser of a ketubah thus buys an option: If the woman is divorced or widowed, he will receive the ketubah. A woman may sell her ketubah to someone other than her husband if she requires cash immediately for needs for which her husband is not obliged to provide. For example, she may wish to give money to her parents or to her children from a previous marriage.

מוֹחֶלֶת כְּתוּבָּתָהּ **If she waives her ketubah.** Sometimes a woman may choose to waive the right to receive her ketubah from her husband, for by so doing she removes a lien on his property that prevents him from selling it.

TRANSLATION AND COMMENTARY

אָמַר לֵיהּ [1] Rav Yemar **said to** Rava: **Now that I am in doubt about** whether a woman **who sells her ketubah** to her husband also forfeits her right to the *ketubat benin dikhrin* — [2] **even though** there is good reason to say that she does not forfeit that right, for **it is possible to say that** some pressing **need** to raise **money forced her** to sell her ketubah to her husband, [3] **and I can** therefore **say that she was** acting under compulsion **like someone who is being struck a hundred strokes with a weighted lash** — [4] **was it necessary to mention** anything about a woman **who waives her ketubah?** If a woman who sells her ketubah under compulsion forfeits her right to the *ketubat benin dikhrin*, then it surely follows that a woman who waives her ketubah of her own free will also forfeits that right.

אָמַר רָבָא [5] **Rava said: It is obvious to me that if** a woman **sells her ketubah to someone other** than her husband, **she remains entitled to the *ketubat benin dikhrin*.** A married woman may sell the right to her ketubah to a third party. The buyer does not get anything for his money until the woman is divorced or widowed; and in the event that she dies before her husband, the buyer gets nothing at all. If the woman predeceases her husband, the husband inherits the ketubah, and when he dies the woman's sons inherit her ketubah from him. Even though the woman sold her ketubah to a third party, her sons still inherit her ketubah from their father, just as they would have inherited it had their mother never sold it. [6] **What is the reason** we do not say that when she sold her ketubah she also forfeited her right to the *ketubat benin dikhrin?* [7] It is because we assume that some pressing **need** to raise **money forced her** to sell her ketubah, and that she never intended to forgo her right to the *ketubat benin dikhrin*. [8] It is

[1] אֲמַר לֵיהּ הָשְׁתָּא מוֹכֶרֶת קָמִיבַּעֲיָא לִי, [2] דְּאַף עַל גַּב דְּאִיכָּא לְמֵימַר זוּזֵי אֲנָסוּהָ, [3] דְּאָמִינָא כְּמַאן דְּקָא מָחוּ לָהּ מֵאָה עוּכְלֵי בְּעוּכְלָא, [4] מוֹחֶלֶת מִיבַּעֲיָא?

[5] אֲמַר רָבָא: פְּשִׁיטָא לִי מוֹכֶרֶת כְּתוּבָּתָהּ לַאֲחֵרִים, יֵשׁ לָהּ כְּתוּבַּת בְּנִין דִּכְרִין. [6] מַאי טַעֲמָא? [7] זוּזֵי אֲנָסוּהָ. [8] מוֹחֶלֶת

LITERAL TRANSLATION

[1] He said to him: Now [that] I am in doubt about one who sells [her ketubah], [2] even though it is possible to say [that lack of] money forced her, [3] [for] I can say [that she is] like someone whom they are striking with a hundred strokes with [a lash bearing] a weight, [4] was it necessary [to mention] one who waives [her ketubah]?

[5] Rava said: It is obvious to me [that if] she sells her ketubah to others, she has the ketubah of male children. [6] What is the reason? [7] [Lack of] money forced her. [8] [If] she waives

RASHI

השתא מוכרת מבעיא לי — כלומר, מי סברת דמשום הנאה דמטא לידה תיסק אדעתאי דפקעה זכותה. **השתא מוכרת** — דאנוסה היא, סלקא אדעתאי דפקעה זכותה ומיבעיא לי, כל שכן מוחלת דלא אנוסה. **מחו לה מאה עוכלי בעוכלא** — מכין אותה מאה מכות ברצועה שבראשה ברזל, כמין משקולת קטנה ששמה עוכלא. **מוכרת כתובתה לאחרים** — בטובת הנאה, שאם נתארמלה או נתגרשה — יטלוה לקוחות, ואם מתה — ירשנה בעלה. ומתה וירשה בעלה. **יש לבניה כתובת בנין דכרין** — דהא כי לא זבניתה נמי ירית לה בעל, ותקון לה רבנן. השתא נמי לגבי בעל במוכרת — לא פקעה זכותה — ואי משום דהוקל בעיניה למוכרה ולהפסיד את בניה אם נתארמלה או נתגרשה — זוזי אנסוה, שהוצרכה להם.

NOTES

in exchange for it. But it was obvious to him that a woman who waives her ketubah does not waive her right regarding the *ketubat benin dikhrin*, for she does not receive anything in return for her ketubah. Rava therefore argued that the same question could be raised regarding a woman who waived her ketubah, for had she really not received anything from her husband, she would never have waived her ketubah.

Rabbi Yosef of Jerusalem (cited by *Ritva* and *Rosh*) explains that Rav Yemar the Elder should have asked about a woman who waived her ketubah, for he could have inferred from the answer he would have received from Rav Naḥman what the law is regarding a woman who sold her ketubah. For if Rav Naḥman answered that a woman who waives her ketubah is still entitled to the *ketubat benin dikhrin*, then it follows that a woman who sells her ketubah to her husband is certainly still entitled to the *ketubat benin dikhrin*. And if he answered that a woman who waives her ketubah forfeits her right to the *ketubat benin dikhrin*, then it follows that a woman who sells her ketubah is still entitled to the *ketubat benin dikhrin*, for if not, Rav Naḥman should have replied to Rav Yemar the Elder as follows: If a woman who sells her ketubah to her husband forfeits the *ketubat benin dikhrin*, is there any question about a woman who waives her ketubah?

מַאי טַעֲמָא? זוּזֵי אֲנָסוּהָ **What is the reason? Lack of money forced her.** According to Rava, a woman who sells her ketubah to a third party does not forfeit her right to the

HALAKHAH

מוֹכֶרֶת כְּתוּבָּתָהּ **If she sells her ketubah.** "If a woman sells her ketubah, whether to her husband or to someone else, her sons are still entitled to collect her ketubah by virtue of the enactment of the *ketubat benin dikhrin*. But if she waives her right to receive her ketubah from her husband, she also forfeits her sons' right to inherit her ketubah from their father," following Rava. (*Rambam, Sefer Nashim, Hilkhot Ishut* 17:19; *Shulḥan Arukh, Even HaEzer* 111:15.)

TRANSLATION AND COMMENTARY

equally obvious, said Rava, that **if** a woman **waives** her right to receive **her ketubah to her husband, she is no** longer **entitled to the *ketubat benin dikhrin*.** [1] **What is the reason** that her sons do not inherit her ketubah in this case? [2] It is because, when the woman waives her right to her ketubah, **she** also **waives** her right to the *ketubat benin dikhrin*.

בָּעֵי רָבָא [3] Having established the points about which he was certain, **Rava asked** about the following case: **If** a woman **sells her ketubah to her husband, is she** considered **like someone who sells** her ketubah **to a third party,** in which case she retains her right to the *ketubat benin dikhrin*? [4] **Or is she** considered **like** a woman **who waives** her right to receive her ketubah **from her husband,** in which case she also forfeits her right to the *ketubat benin dikhrin*?

בָּתַר דִּבְעָיָא [5] **After** Rava **had raised the question, he** himself **answered it: If** a woman **sells her ketubah to her husband, she is** considered **like someone who sold** her ketubah **to someone other** than her husband, for she must have been acting under dire financial necessity. Thus she remains entitled to the right due her by virtue of the enactment of the *ketubat benin dikhrin*.

כְּתוּבָּתָהּ לְבַעְלָהּ, אֵין לָהּ כְּתוּבַּת בְּנִין דִּכְרִין. [1] מַאי טַעֲמָא? [2] אַחוּלֵי אַחֵילְתָּא.
[3] בָּעֵי רָבָא: מוֹכֶרֶת כְּתוּבָּתָהּ לְבַעְלָהּ, כְּמוֹכֶרֶת לַאֲחֵרִים דָּמֵי, [4] אוֹ כְּמוֹחֶלֶת לְבַעְלָהּ דָּמֵי?
[5] בָּתַר דִּבְעָיָא, הֲדַר פָּשְׁטָא: מוֹכֶרֶת כְּתוּבָּה לְבַעְלָהּ כְּמוֹכֶרֶת לַאֲחֵרִים דָּמֵי.

LITERAL TRANSLATION

her ketubah to her husband, she does not have the ketubah of male children. [1] What is the reason? [2] She waived it.

[3] Rava asked: [If] she sells her ketubah to her husband, is she like one who sells [it] to others, [4] or is she like one who waives [it] to her husband?

[5] After having raised the question, he solved [it]: [If] she sells her ketubah to her husband, she is like one who sells [it] to others.

RASHI

אחולי אחילתה — ונקל בעיניה להפסיד בניה מכתובתה הנס. **מוכרת לבעלה** — נמי טובת הנאה בעלמא דבר מועט, שהרי אם מתה — יורשה, ואינו לוקח ממנה אלא שאם מת הוא לא תגבה. והרי לא מת, ובא לידי ירושה — הלכך כמוכרת לאחרים דמי. **או כמוחלת לבעלה דמי** — הואיל ובידו הכתובה, והוקל בעיניה להחליטה.

TERMINOLOGY

בָּתַר דִּבְעָיָא הֲדַר פָּשְׁטָא **After having raised the question, he solved it.** An expression used by the Gemara when the Amora who has raised a problem proceeds to solve it himself.

NOTES

ketubah condition regarding the *ketubat benin dikhrin*, for we assume that she sold her ketubah only because she needed the money. A number of Rishonim object (see *Rashba* and *Ritva*): The woman's sons should be entitled to her ketubah for another reason. All that the woman can sell is her right to the ketubah if she is widowed or divorced. But if she dies before her husband, the sale of her ketubah is null and void. Now, the enactment of the *ketubat benin dikhrin* applies only in a case in which the woman dies before her husband. Thus the woman's sons should be entitled to their mother's ketubah after their father's death, even if she sold it to someone else. For this reason, some authorities erase this line of the text of the Gemara altogether.

Rashi alludes to this difficulty, explaining that there was reason to think that a woman who sells her ketubah to a third party should lose the right due to her by virtue of the enactment of the *ketubat benin dikhrin*. Since the woman is ready to sell her ketubah if she is widowed or divorced, thus depriving her children of what is due to them, the Rabbis may have penalized her by causing her to forfeit the right she has by virtue of the *ketubat benin dikhrin*. Therefore it was necessary for the Gemara to say that the sons are still entitled to their mother's ketubah, for she sold her ketubah not because she treated it lightly but because she desperately needed the money.

מוֹחֶלֶת כְּתוּבָּתָהּ **If she waives her ketubah.** The Rishonim ask: How can a woman waive her ketubah? Surely the law follows the opinion of Rabbi Meir that a man is forbidden to live with his wife unless she has a ketubah!

Rif explains that we are dealing here with a case in which the woman did not waive her ketubah in favor of her husband, but waived it in favor of his heirs after he died.

Ra'avad and *Rosh* suggest that here the woman waived the addition to her ketubah, but not the basic portion (200 zuz in the case of a virgin and a maneh in the case of a non-virgin), or she waived the entire ketubah, and her husband then wrote her a new ketubah obligating himself only to the basic portion of the ketubah. Thus the woman is permitted to her husband, but her sons do not inherit from their father their mother's entire ketubah, but only the basic portion.

Ritva argues that there is in fact no difficulty. The woman is indeed forbidden to her husband, but we are dealing here solely with the monetary aspect of their relationship — whether or not the woman's sons are entitled to inherit their mother's ketubah upon their father's death.

The Rishonim raise another question: Why is the woman's waiving of her ketubah binding? Let her later argue that she only said that she was waiving her ketubah in order to appease her husband so that he would not be angry with her, but she never really intended to forfeit her claim to her ketubah, for we find elsewhere (below, 95b) that the Gemara accepts a similar argument.

Ramban, *Rashba* and others argue that a woman who waives the basic portion of her ketubah cannot later claim that she did so only to appease her husband, for all wives are entitled to a ketubah, and it is unlikely that a husband would hold a grudge against her because she did not waive hers. Thus we assume that when she waived her ketubah, she did so wholeheartedly.

[1] מְתִיב רַב אִידִי בַּר אָבִין: "מֵתָה, אֵין יוֹרְשִׁין שֶׁל זֶה וְאֵין יוֹרְשִׁין שֶׁל זֶה יוֹרְשִׁין כְּתוּבָּתָהּ". [2] וְהָוֵינַן בָּהּ: כְּתוּבָּתָהּ — [3] מַאי עֲבִידְתָּהּ? [4] וַאֲמַר רַב פַּפָּא: כְּתוּבַּת בְּנִין דִּכְרִין. [5] וְאַמַּאי? [6] הָכָא נַמִי לֵימָא יֵצֶר אֲנָסָהּ! [7] הָתָם קְנָסָא הוּא דִּקְנָסוּהָ רַבָּנַן.

LITERAL TRANSLATION

[1] Rav Idi bar Avin objected: "[If] she died, neither the heirs of this one nor the heirs of that one inherit her ketubah." [2] And we raised a difficulty about it: Her ketubah — [3] what is its purpose (lit., "its work")? [4] And Rav Pappa said: The ketubah of male children. [5] But why? [6] Here too let us say [that] passion overcame her! [7] There it is a fine that the Rabbis have fined her.

RASHI

אין יורשין של זה כו׳ — משנה היא ביבמות: האשה שהלך בעלה למדינת הים, ואמר לה עד אחד "מת בעליך", והתירוה לינשא, ונישאת, ואחר כך בא בעלה — תצא מזה ומזה, ואין לה כתובה לא מזה ולא מזה. ואם מתה — אין יורשין של זה וזה, בנים שיש לה מזה ומזה, יורשין כתובתה. **והוינן בה כתובתה מאי עבידתה** — הא אמרת אין לה כתובה. **ואמר רב פפא כתובת בנין דכרין** — והכי קאמר: מתה היא בחיי שניהם וירשוה הם, אין בנים שיש לה מזה ומזה נוטלין כתובת אמן כבנין דכרין, כשבאין לחלוק בנכסי אביהם, אלא חולקין בשוה. **ואמאי** — כיון דאמרינן כי אניסא לא מפסדא כתובת בנין דכרין. **נימא יצר אנסה** — שהיתה מתאוה לבעל. **קנסא** — משום דלא דייקא שפיר שמת בעלה, מקמי דתינסוב.

TRANSLATION AND COMMENTARY

מְתִיב רַב אִידִי בַּר אָבִין [1] **Rav Idi bar Avin raised an objection** against Rava's conclusion on the basis of the following Mishnah (*Yevamot* 87b): "If a woman's husband goes abroad, and a single witness comes and testifies that the husband is dead, and the woman remarries on the basis of that testimony, but later her first husband returns, she is forbidden to both husbands, for she is treated as a married woman who has committed adultery, and who is forbidden both to her husband and to the other man with whom she had sexual relations. She cannot collect her ketubah from either husband. Moreover, **if she dies, neither the heirs of the first** husband **nor the heirs of the second** husband **inherit her ketubah.**" [2] **And** elsewhere **we raised** the following **difficulty regarding** this Mishnah: The Mishnah states that if the woman dies, the heirs of the two husbands do not inherit **her ketubah.** [3] **Why was this mentioned here?** The Mishnah has just stated that the woman cannot collect her ketubah from either husband. What, then, can the heirs possibly inherit? [4] **And Rav Pappa explained:** The Mishnah is referring here to the enactment of **the *ketubat benin dikhrin.*** The Mishnah teaches us not only that the woman herself is not entitled to collect her ketubah from either husband, but that she even forfeits the condition contained in the ketubah by virtue of which her sons inherit her ketubah upon their father's death. The Gemara now explains how this Mishnah in *Yevamot* presents a difficulty to the viewpoint of Rava, who ruled that if a woman sells her ketubah to her husband, she is still entitled to the *ketubat benin dikhrin*: If we say that a woman does not forfeit the *ketubat benin dikhrin* when she sells her ketubah to her husband, because she was acting under financial compulsion when she sold it, [5] then **why** does the woman who remarries on the basis of the testimony of a single witness that her first husband has died forfeit the *ketubat benin dikhrin*? [6] **Here, too, let us say that** her **passion forced her** to remarry! This woman sincerely believed that she was a widow; her belief was supported by the testimony of a witness; and she desperately desired to remarry. Why should she lose her right to the *ketubat benin dikhrin* together with her ketubah, when the loss of her ketubah resulted from an act of adultery committed under compulsion?

הָתָם [7] The Gemara answers: **There** the woman's forfeiture of the *ketubat benin dikhrin* **is a** special **penalty that the Rabbis imposed upon her.** The Rabbis permitted the woman to remarry on the basis of the testimony of a single witness to her husband's death, assuming that the woman herself would make sure that her husband was indeed dead before she remarried. If the woman remarries without verifying that her first husband is dead, and it later transpires that he is in fact alive, she is subject to a number of penalties that affect the rights to which she is entitled by virtue of her marriage. And one of the penalties is the loss of her right to the *ketubat benin dikhrin.* But that special penalty has no bearing on Rava's ruling that a woman who sells her ketubah to her husband is still entitled to the *ketubat benin dikhrin.*

HALAKHAH

אֵין יוֹרְשִׁין שֶׁל זֶה **Neither the heirs of this one.** "If a woman marries another man while she is still married to her first husband (for example, if the bill of divorce from her first husband is discovered to have been invalid, or if her first husband, who was assumed to be dead, reappears), she is forbidden to both husbands, she must receive a bill of divorce from both of them, and she has no claim to her ketubah or to any of the ketubah conditions from either of them." (*Rambam, Sefer Nashim, Hilkhot Gerushin* 10:7; *Shulḥan Arukh, Even HaEzer* 17:56.)

TRANSLATION AND COMMENTARY

יְתֵיב [1] The Gemara now records another ruling about a woman who waives her right to receive her ketubah from her husband. **Ravin bar Ḥanina sat before Rav Ḥisda, and** as **he sat** there **he reported** the following ruling **in the name of Rabbi Elazar:** [2]**If** a woman **waives** her right to receive **her ketubah from her husband, she is not entitled to maintenance** from his estate when he dies, for when a woman waives her ketubah she also waives her right to benefit from any of the conditions contained in it. [3]Rav Ḥisda **said to** Ravin bar Ḥanina: **Had you not reported** this ruling **to me in the name of a great man,** Rabbi Elazar, [4]**I would have told you** that the ruling is unjust, as the verse says (Proverbs 17:13): **"Whoever rewards evil for good, evil shall not depart from his house."** It does not seem right that a woman who waives her ketubah of her own free will should be repaid with the loss of her right to be maintained from her husband's estate.

יְתֵיב רַב נַחְמָן [5] The Gemara now raises a new topic of discussion. It was related that **Rav Naḥman, Ulla and Avimi bar Rav Pappi were sitting** in the Academy, **and Rav Ḥiyya bar Ammi was sitting with them,** [6]when **a certain man whose betrothed bride had died came before them** for a ruling on how he should now act. [7]Rav Naḥman, Ulla, and Avimi bar Rav Pappa **said to him:** "You must either **go** and **bury her, or give her** heirs **her ketubah."** A Baraita cited earlier (47b) taught that the Sages instituted that a husband is held liable for his wife's burial in exchange for her ketubah. The Amoraim who were approached here for a ruling understood this Baraita as saying that the husband is liable for his wife's burial in exchange for the basic portion of her ketubah — the two hundred zuz or the maneh — which he may now keep for

[1]יְתֵיב רָבִין בַּר חֲנִינָא קַמֵּיהּ דְּרַב חִסְדָּא, וִיתֵיב וְקָאָמַר מִשְּׁמֵיהּ דְּרַבִּי אֶלְעָזָר: [2]מוֹחֶלֶת כְּתוּבָּתָהּ לְבַעְלָהּ, אֵין לָהּ מְזוֹנוֹת. [3]אֲמַר לֵיהּ: אִי לָאו דְּקָאָמְרַתְּ לִי מִשְּׁמֵיהּ דְּגַבְרָא רַבָּא, [4]הֲוָה אָמֵינָא לָךְ: ״מֵשִׁיב רָעָה תַּחַת טוֹבָה, לֹא תָמוּשׁ רָעָה מִבֵּיתוֹ״.

[5]יְתֵיב רַב נַחְמָן וְעוּלָּא וַאֲבִימִי בַּר רַב פַּפִּי, וִיתֵיב רַב חִיָּיא בַּר אַמִּי גַּבַּיְיהוּ. [6]אֲתָא הַהוּא גַּבְרָא דִּשְׁכִיבָא אֲרוּסְתּוֹ. [7]אָמְרִי לֵיהּ: ״זִיל קְבַר, אוֹ הַב לָהּ

LITERAL TRANSLATION

[1]Ravin bar Ḥanina sat before Rav Ḥisda, and he sat and said in the name of Rabbi Elazar: [2][If] she waives her ketubah to her husband, she does not have maintenance. [3]He said to him: Had you not said [it] to me in the name of a great man, [4]I would have said to you: "Whoever rewards evil for good, evil shall not depart from his house."

[5]Rav Naḥman and Ulla and Avimi bar Rav Pappi sat, and Rav Ḥiyya bar Ammi sat with them. [6]A certain man whose betrothed bride had died came [before them]. [7]They said to him: "Go and bury [her], or give her

RASHI

אין לה מזונות – באלמנותה, דתנאי כתובה ככתובה. **או הב לה כתובה** – דתקנו קבורתה תחת כתובתה. וסבר למימר: תחת מנה מאתים שתקנו לה חכמים.

SAGES

רָבִין בַּר חֲנִינָא Ravin bar Ḥanina (or Ḥinnana). A Babylonian Amora of the third generation, Ravin bar Ḥanina was a disciple of Rav Ḥisda. He emigrated from Babylonia to Eretz Israel, where he is mentioned among the students of Rabbi Zera. He apparently returned to Babylonia and reported there what he had learned in Eretz Israel.

רַב חִסְדָּא Rav Ḥisda. A Babylonian Amora of the second generation. See *Ketubot,* Part II, p. 64.

עוּלָּא Ulla. A Palestinian Amora of the second and third generations. See *Ketubot,* Part I, p. 103.

רַב חִיָּיא בַּר אַמִּי Rav Ḥiyya bar Ammi. A Babylonian Amora of the third generation, Rav Ḥiyya bar Ammi was a disciple of Ulla, in whose name he transmits many teachings. This Baraita regarding the status of a betrothed girl is quoted in his name in several places in the Talmud.

NOTES

מוֹחֶלֶת כְּתוּבָּתָהּ לְבַעְלָהּ, אֵין לָהּ מְזוֹנוֹת If she waives her ketubah to her husband, she does not have maintenance. According to most Rishonim, a woman who waives her ketubah is still entitled to maintenance from her husband during his lifetime. She may demand her maintenance from him not only for the reason put forward by Rav Ḥisda, that it is not right that a woman who waives her ketubah should be repaid with the forfeiture of her maintenance (though some Rishonim do base her claim on Rav Ḥisda's argument; see *Ra'ah*), but also because a woman's right to maintenance during her husband's lifetime does not derive from the conditions of her ketubah. Rather, it is a fixed obligation upon the husband, whether by Torah law or by Rabbinic enactment, in exchange for which he is entitled to his wife's handiwork. But *Rambam* maintains (see Halakhah) that a woman who waives her ketubah forfeits not only her right to maintenance from her husband's estate upon his death, but her right to maintenance from her husband during his lifetime as well.

The Jerusalem Talmud (*Ketubot* 11:2) records a ruling of Shmuel that a woman who waives her ketubah in favor of her husband's heirs is still entitled to maintenance from her husband's estate for the reason offered in our Gemara by Rav Ḥisda. The Rishonim differ about whether or not the Jerusalem Talmud agrees with the conclusion reached by the Babylonian Talmud (see *Ritva*).

HALAKHAH

מוֹחֶלֶת כְּתוּבָּתָהּ לְבַעְלָהּ, אֵין לָהּ מְזוֹנוֹת If she waives her ketubah to her husband, she does not have maintenance. "If a woman waives her ketubah to her husband, she forfeits her right to maintenance from his estate, but she is still entitled to maintenance during his lifetime. According to *Rambam*, she forfeits her right to maintenance even during her husband's lifetime." (*Rambam, Sefer Nashim, Hilkhot Ishut* 12:18, 17:19, 18:23; *Shulḥan Arukh, Even HaEzer* 93:9.)

TRANSLATION AND COMMENTARY

himself. Thus, if a man writes his wife a ketubah when he betroths her, and she dies, two options are open to him: If he wishes to keep her ketubah, he must bury her; if he does not wish to bury her, he must pay her ketubah to her heirs. [1]**Rav Ḥiyya** bar Ammi, who was sitting with his colleagues, **said to them:** But surely **we have learned** differently in the following Baraita: [2]**"If** a man's **betrothed bride dies, he does not observe *aninut*** (the laws of mourning observed on the day of death) **for her, nor does he become ritually impure for her** if he is a priest." A priest is ordinarily forbidden to become ritually impure by coming into contact with dead bodies, except for those of certain close relatives, including his wife. But the Baraita tells us that a priest is not permitted to become ritually impure for a woman who had been betrothed to him but not married. [3]**"Similarly,"** the Baraita continues, "**if** a man **dies,** his betrothed bride **does not observe *aninut* for him, and she does not** have to **become ritually impure for him.** In this case, she is not forbidden to become ritually impure, even if she is the daughter or the betrothed bride of a priest, but she need not do so unless she so desires. [4]**If** a betrothed woman **dies,** her bridegroom **does not inherit her** dowry, for a man does not inherit his wife's property unless she is considered fully married to him. [5]But **if** the bridegroom **dies,** his betrothed bride **collects her ketubah,** both the one hundred or the two hundred zuz that comprise the basic portion of her ketubah, and any additional amount that

כְּתוּבָּתָהּ״. [1]אֲמַר לְהוּ רַב חִיָּיא: תָּנֵינָא: [2]״אִשְׁתּוֹ אֲרוּסָה, לֹא אוֹנֵן, וְלֹא מִיטַּמֵּא לָהּ. [3]וְכֵן הִיא לֹא אוֹנֶנֶת, וְלֹא מִיטַּמְּאָה לוֹ. [4]מֵתָה, אֵינוֹ יוֹרְשָׁהּ. [5]מֵת הוּא, גּוֹבָה כְּתוּבָּתָהּ״.

LITERAL TRANSLATION

her ketubah." [1]Rav Ḥiyya said to them: We have learned: [2]"[If] one's betrothed bride [died], he does not observe *aninut* [for her], nor does he become ritually impure for her. [3]And similarly [if he died], she does not observe *aninut* [for him], and she does not become ritually impure for him. [4][If] she died, he does not inherit her. [5][If] he died, she collects her ketubah."

RASHI

תנינא — אני שונה שאין לארוסה שמתה משפט כתובה דהיינו קבורה. **לא אונן** — ליאסר בקדשים. **ולא מיטמא לה** — אם כהן הוא, דלאו שארו היא. **ולא מיטמאה לו** — אינה חייבת ליטמא לו, ואף על פי שמצוה להתעסק בששה מתי מצוה האמורים בפרשת כהנים (ויקרא כא), דכתיב "לה יטמא" — מצוה זו אינה מהם, דלאו שארו היא. אבל אם רוצה היא ליטמא — אינה מוזהרת מליטמא, אפילו כהנת. ד"בני אהרן" כתיב, ולא בנות אהרן. **אינו יורשה** — נדוניית בית אביה. דלא תקון ירושת הבעל עד שתכנס לחופה, או שתמסר לשלוחים. **מת הוא** — בחייה. **גובה כתובתה** — מנה מאתים, ותוספת אם כתב לה.

NOTES

אִשְׁתּוֹ אֲרוּסָה If one's betrothed bride died. Both with respect to the permission granted to a priest to contract ritual impurity, as well as with respect to the laws of succession, the Torah (Leviticus 21:2; Numbers 27:11) uses the term *she'er* (שְׁאֵר, meaning "kin"). A betrothed woman does not come under the category of her bridegroom's kin until after the marriage process is completed.

וְלֹא מִיטַּמְּאָה לוֹ And she does not become ritually impure for him. The Rishonim ask: What does the Baraita mean when it says that a betrothed bride does not become ritually impure for her bridegroom? Even if she is married to him, and even if she is the daughter of a priest, she should still not be barred from becoming ritually impure for the sake of her husband, for the prohibition against contracting ritual impurity through proximity with a corpse applies only to male priests and not to females!

Rashi and most Rishonim explain that the Baraita means to say that a betrothed woman is not required to become ritually impure for her bridegroom, because the obligation to arrange for the funeral of a close relative does not apply to a betrothed woman. But if she wishes to render herself ritually impure and to arrange for his funeral, she may indeed do so.

Others (*Tosefot Sens* and *Rosh*; *Rashi* and *Tosafot*, *Yevamot* 29b) explain that the Baraita is referring to the periods of the Jewish Festivals when all Jews must refrain

HALAKHAH

וְלֹא מִיטַּמֵּא לָהּ Nor does he become ritually impure for her. "If a betrothed woman dies, her bridegroom does not observe *aninut* for her, and if he is a priest, he may not become ritually impure. Similarly, if the man dies, his betrothed bride does not observe *aninut* for him, and she is not required to become ritually impure." (*Rambam*, *Sefer Shofetim*, *Hilkhot Avel* 2:7; *Shulḥan Arukh*, *Yoreh De'ah* 373:4.)

מֵתָה, אֵינוֹ יוֹרְשָׁהּ If she died, he does not inherit her. "If a betrothed woman dies, her bridegroom does not inherit her property." (*Rambam*, *Sefer Nashim*, *Hilkhot Ishut* 22:2; *Shulḥan Arukh*, *Even HaEzer* 55:5.)

מֵת הוּא, גּוֹבָה כְּתוּבָּתָהּ If he died, she collects her ketubah. "If a man betroths a woman and writes her a ketubah, but has not yet brought her into the bridal chamber, she is still considered betrothed, and not married. Thus, if he dies or divorces her, she can collect the basic portion of her ketubah, but only from his free assets, and she cannot collect the additional portion at all." (*Rambam*, *Sefer Nashim*, *Hilkhot Ishut* 10:11; *Shulḥan Arukh*, *Even HaEzer* 55:6.)

TRANSLATION AND COMMENTARY

he may have added to the ketubah." [1] Now a careful reading of the Baraita leads to the following conclusion: **The reason** why the betrothed bride collects her ketubah **is that** her bridegroom **died** during her lifetime. [2] **But if *she* dies** during *his* lifetime, **she is not entitled to her ketubah.** In other words, her heirs cannot collect her ketubah, and so her husband is not required to bury her if he wishes to keep the ketubah for himself. And when the Baraita stated (above, 47b) that the Sages instituted that a husband is liable for his wife's burial in exchange for her ketubah, they were referring to a married woman whose husband is liable for her burial in exchange for the dowry recorded in her ketubah which he inherits from her. [3] The Gemara asks: **Why** is the bridegroom not required to bury his betrothed bride in exchange for the ketubah that he inherits from her? [4] **Rav Hoshaya said:** It is **because we cannot apply to** the deceased bride the following clause that is written in her ketubah: [5] **"When you marry someone else, take** the amount **that is written for you** as your ketubah." A husband (or his estate) becomes liable to pay his wife's ketubah only when she becomes eligible to remarry. But if she dies first, he never becomes liable to pay her. Thus the Sages could not have enacted that the bridegroom is required to bury his betrothed bride in exchange for the ketubah he inherits from her, because he does not inherit what he never became liable to pay.

כִּי אֲתָא רָבִין [6] The Gemara relates further that **when Ravin came** to Babylonia from Eretz Israel, **he said in the name of Resh Lakish:** [7] If **a betrothed woman dies,** she **is not entitled to her ketubah.** Her heirs have no claim to the ketubah, and therefore her bridegroom is not required to bury her if he does not wish to pay her ketubah to them. [8] When **Abaye** heard this ruling, he **said to those** who reported it to him: **Go and tell** Ravin: [53B] [9] As the popular proverb goes, **your kindness is taken and cast into the thornbushes.** You thought we would be indebted to you for the kindness you showed when you transmitted to us Resh Lakish's statement on this matter, but the truth is that you reported something we already knew, [10] for **Rav Hoshaya has already explained this ruling in Babylonia.**

[1] טַעֲמָא דְּמֵת הוּא. [2] הָא מֵתָה הִיא, אֵין לָהּ כְּתוּבָּה. [3] מַאי טַעֲמָא? [4] אָמַר רַב הוֹשַׁעְיָא: שֶׁאֵין אֲנִי קוֹרֵא בָּהּ: [5] "לִכְשֶׁתִּנָּשְׂאִי לְאַחֵר, תִּטְלִי מַה שֶּׁכָּתוּב לֵיכִי".

[6] כִּי אֲתָא רָבִין, אָמַר רֵישׁ לָקִישׁ: [7] אֲרוּסָה שֶׁמֵּתָה אֵין לָהּ כְּתוּבָּה. [8] אֲמַר לְהוּ אַבַּיֵי: זִילוּ אָמְרִי לֵיהּ: [53B] [9] שְׁקִילָא טִיבוּתָךְ שַׁדְיָא אַחִיזְרֵי. [10] כְּבָר תַּרְגְּמָא רַב הוֹשַׁעְיָא לִשְׁמַעְתֵּיךְ בְּבָבֶל.

LITERAL TRANSLATION

[1] The reason is that *he* died. [2] But [if] *she* died, she does not have a ketubah. [3] What is the reason? [4] Rav Hoshaya said: Because I cannot apply (lit., "call") to her: [5] "When you marry someone else, you will take what is written for you."

[6] When Ravin came, [he said] in the name of Resh Lakish: [7] A betrothed woman who died does not have a ketubah. [8] Abaye said to them: Go [and] say to him: [53B] [9] Your favor is taken [and] cast into the thornbushes. [10] Rav Hoshaya has already explained your ruling in Babylonia.

RASHI

אין לה כתובה — דין כתובה. וקבורתה תחת כתובתה דתניא לעיל — בנשואה תניא, ותחת נדוניית בית אביה שהוא יורשה. אבל הכא, כיון דכי מתה אינו יורשה — אף הוא לא נתחייב לקוברה. **מאי טעמא** — דאמרינן כי מתה בחייו אין לה תביעת כתובה תקבר בשביל מנה מאתים שהוא יורש. **שאין אני קורא בו'** — וכך היו כותבין בשטר כתובתה. הלכך, כל זמן שלא מת ולא נתגרשה — לא נשתעבד לה, ולא יורש ממנה כלום. **שקילא טיבותיך** — חיזוק טובותיך, שאתה סבור שנחזיק לך טובה בזו — נטולה היא ממך ומוטלת על החרולים.

SAGES

רַב הוֹשַׁעְיָא Rav Hoshaya (or Oshaya — אוֹשַׁעְיָא). He belonged to the third generation of Babylonian Amoraim, and must be distinguished from the Sage known in the Jerusalem Talmud as Rabbi Oshaya Rabbah, a disciple of Rabbi Yehudah HaNasi. While living in Babylonia, Rav Hoshaya studied Torah with the greatest of the Amoraim, especially from Rav Yehudah. Some authorities claim that Rav Hoshaya and Rav Ḥananyah were brothers of the great Babylonian Amora Rabbah, and like Rabbah were priests who could trace their descent from the Biblical High Priest Eli.

Rav Hoshaya and Rav Ḥananyah immigrated to Eretz Israel, where they studied Torah with Rabbi Yoḥanan. The two brothers lived in Tiberias, where they eked out a meager living as cobblers. Rav Hoshaya married the daughter of the Amora Rabbi Shmuel bar Yitzḥak.

In the following generations, Rav Hoshaya is mentioned as a model of piety and modesty. Out of respect, the Babylonian Amora Rav Safra calls him "Moses."

NOTES

from coming into contact with a corpse, because they come on pilgrimage to the Temple. During those times, a betrothed bride is forbidden to render herself ritually impure for her bridegroom, because until she is married to him, her bridegroom is not included among those relatives for whom she may render herself ritually impure even on a Festival.

טַעֲמָא דְּמֵת הוּא The reason is that *he* died. *Shittah Mekubbetzet* explains the inference as follows: The Baraita could have stated simply: "And a betrothed woman collects her ketubah," for it is obvious that the woman collects her ketubah only if she is widowed (or divorced). The Baraita's formulation: "If he died, she collects her ketubah," must have been intended to imply that if she dies, her heirs cannot collect her ketubah, even if her husband does not bury her.

לִכְשֶׁתִּנָּשְׂאִי "When you marry." Even if a woman was already married to her husband when she died, we cannot apply what is written in her ketubah: "When you marry someone else, you will take what is written for you as your ketubah." But the husband is required to bury his wife in exchange for the dowry recorded in her ketubah, which he now inherits from her. It is only in the case of a betrothed bride that we free the bridegroom from the obligation to bury her. The bridegroom does not inherit his bride's dowry until she enters the bridal chamber, or she is handed over

TRANSLATION AND COMMENTARY

בְּנָן נוּקְבָן [1] We learned in our Mishnah that one of the conditions recorded in the ketubah states: **"The female children that you will have from me** will live in my house and be maintained from my property after my death until they are taken in marriage by husbands." The Amoraim disagreed about the precise wording of this stipulation. [2] **Rav taught** the Mishnah as it is in our texts: "The female children that you will have from me will be maintained from my property **until they are taken in marriage by husbands."** [3] **But Levi taught** that the Mishnah contained a slightly different version of the stipulation: "The female children that you will have from me will be maintained from my property **until they become adults."**

לְרַב [4] The Gemara asks: **Does Rav assert** that an orphan daughter is maintained from her father's estate until she is married, **even after she becomes an adult?** But surely such a girl would no longer be under her father's authority, even if he were still alive! Why, then, should she be entitled as an adult to maintenance from his estate now that he is dead? A similar objection can be raised against Levi's viewpoint: [5] **Does Levi assert** that an orphan daughter is maintained from her father's estate until she becomes an adult, **even after she is married?** She, too, would no longer be under her father's authority were he still alive, so why should she now be maintained from his estate?

אֶלָּא [6] **Rather,** says the Gemara, we must conclude that **if** the orphan girl **has reached adulthood,** even though **she is not** yet **married,** [7] **or if she is married,** even though **she has not** yet **reached adulthood,** [8] **both** Rav and Levi **agree** that she is no longer entitled to maintenance from her father's estate. [9] **They disagree** only **about** the case **where** the orphan **girl is betrothed, but has not** yet **reached adulthood.** According to Rav, an orphan girl is only entitled to maintenance until she is betrothed. According to Levi, she is entitled

[1] "בְּנָן נוּקְבָן דְּיֶהֶוְיָין לֵיכִי מִינַּאי, וכו׳". [2] רַב תָּנֵי: "עַד דְּתִלָּקְחָן לְגוּבְרִין". [3] וְלֵוִי תָּנֵי: "עַד דְּתִבָּגְרָן".
[4] לְרַב, אַף עַל גַּב דְּבָגַר, [5] וְלֵוִי, אַף עַל גַּב דְּאִינְסִיב?
[6] אֶלָּא, בָּגַר וְלָא אִינְסִיב, [7] אִינְסִיב וְלָא בָּגַר, [8] דְּכוּלֵּי עָלְמָא לָא פְּלִיגִי. [9] כִּי פְּלִיגִי בַּאֲרוּסָה וְלָא בָּגַר.

LITERAL TRANSLATION

[1] "The female children that you will have from me, etc." [2] Rav taught: "Until they are taken [in marriage] by men." [3] And Levi taught: "Until they become adults."

[4] According to Rav, even if she became an adult, [5] and according to Levi, even if she married?

[6] Rather, [if] she became an adult but was not married, [7] [or if] she was married but had not become an adult, [8] all agree (lit., "all the world do not disagree"). [9] They disagree about [a girl who was] betrothed but had not become an adult.

RASHI

לרב אף על גב דבגר – בתמיה, והלא בגרות מוציאה מרשות אב, ולמה תיזון מביתו? ובין לרבי בין לרבי אלעזר ברבי שמעון שנחלקו בדבר בפרק "מציאת האשה" (כתובות סח,ב) בעישור נכסים, מודים במזונות דבין נשאו בין בגרו – אבדו מזונות. **כי פליגי בארוסה** – רב אמר: "עד דתלקחן" – קיחה דאירוסין, ואפילו לא בגר. ולוי או תבגרן או ינשאו ויצאו מרשות אב לגמרי כי בגרות.

NOTES

to the husband's agents for marriage (see *Rashi, Shittah Mekubbetzet*).

Tosafot notes that the Gemara here arrives at a Halakhic conclusion based on the interpretation of the ketubah deed, even though it is Bet Shammai who say that such conclusions are valid, whereas Bet Hillel say that they are not (see *Yevamot* 116b). *Tosafot* concludes that in this matter the law must be in accordance with the viewpoint of Bet Shammai. Since we find elsewhere that the Rabbis interpret documents that evolved as a result of common usage, it must certainly be valid to interpret the ketubah document, which was specifically formulated by the Rabbis.

בָּגַר וְלָא אִינְסִיב **If she became an adult but was not married.** *Birkat Avraham* notes that two approaches to the dispute between Rav and Levi are found in the Rishonim. According to *Rashi* and *Tosafot,* the girl is entitled to maintenance from her father's estate as long as she would still be under her father's authority were he still alive. Thus she loses her right to maintenance when she becomes an adult or when she is married, for it is then that she would have left her father's authority. According to *Ramban,* the girl is entitled to maintenance from her father's estate as long as she does not have an alternative source of income. Thus she loses her right to maintenance when she becomes an adult and can find employment, or when she is married and is supported by her husband.

כִּי פְּלִיגִי בַּאֲרוּסָה **They disagree about a girl who was betrothed.** *Rabbenu Ḥananel* and *Ittur* explain that an

HALAKHAH

עַד דְּתִלָּקְחָן ... עַד דְּתִבָּגְרָן **Until they are taken...until they become adults.** "One of the financial obligations imposed on a husband by the conditions included in his wife's ketubah is that the minor daughters of the marriage are entitled to maintenance from his estate until they are betrothed or until they reach majority. If a daughter comes

TRANSLATION AND COMMENTARY

to maintenance even after she is betrothed, until she is married or reaches adulthood, at which time she would have left her father's authority, were he still alive.

וְכֵן תָּנֵי לֵוִי [1] **And similarly Levi taught** the following version of the stipulation **in his** version of the **Baraita:** [2]"The female children that you will have from me will be maintained from my property **until they become adults and the time comes for them to be married,"** which was ordinarily twelve months after their bridegrooms asked to marry them.

תַּרְתֵּי [3] The Gemara challenges Levi's version: But is it possible that the daughter is entitled to maintenance until **both** these conditions are met? Surely the girl would have left her father's authority as soon as *one* of those conditions was met!

אֶלָּא [4] **Rather,** says the Gemara, the Baraita must be understood as follows: The female children that you will have from me will be maintained from my property **until they either reach adulthood or the time comes for them to be married.** But if the orphaned daughter was betrothed but not yet married, she continues to be entitled to maintenance from her father's estate.

כְּתַנָּאֵי [5] The Gemara notes that **this** disagreement between Rav and Levi **was** already the subject of **a Tannaitic dispute,** as recorded in **the following** Baraita: **"Until when is an** orphaned **daughter** entitled to be **maintained** from her father's estate? [6]**Until she is betrothed,** but once she is betrothed, she is no longer entitled to maintenance." This is the opinion of the anonymous first Tanna of the Baraita. [7]The Baraita continues: "But **in the name of Rabbi Elazar they said:** An orphan girl is entitled to maintenance **until she becomes an adult."** Rav's opinion reflects that of the anonymous first Tanna of the Baraita, whereas Levi follows the viewpoint reported in the name of Rabbi Elazar.

תָּנֵי רַב יוֹסֵף [8] **Rav Yosef taught** another version of the stipulation entitling an orphaned daughter to maintenance: "The female children that you will have from me will be maintained from my property **until they become wives."**

[1]וְכֵן תָּנֵי לֵוִי בְּמַתְנִיתֵיהּ: [2]״עַד דְּתִבָּגְרָן וְיִמְטֵי זִמְנֵיהוֹן דְּאִינַסְּבָן״.
[3]תַּרְתֵּי?
[4]אֶלָּא, אוֹ תִּבָּגְרָן, אוֹ יִמְטֵי זִמְנֵיהוֹן לְאִיתְנַסְּבָא.
[5]כְּתַנָּאֵי: ״עַד מָתַי הַבַּת נִזּוֹנֵית? [6]עַד שֶׁתֵּאָרֵס. [7]מִשּׁוּם רַבִּי אֶלְעָזָר אָמְרוּ: עַד שֶׁתִּבָּגֵר״.
[8]תָּנֵי רַב יוֹסֵף: ״עַד דְּיֶהֶוְיָין״.

LITERAL TRANSLATION

[1]And similarly Levi taught in his Baraita: [2]"Until they become adults and their time comes for them to be married."

[3]Both?

[4]Rather, either [until] they become adults, or [until] their time comes for them to be married.

[5]It is like [the following dispute between] Tannaim: "Until when is a daughter maintained? [6]Until she is betrothed. [7]In the name of Rabbi Elazar they said: Until she becomes an adult."

[8]Rav Yosef taught: "Until they become [wives]."

TERMINOLOGY

תַּרְתֵּי **Both?** An expression indicating astonishment at an internal contradiction within a source.

RASHI

וכן תני לוי במתניתיה — דלוי סידר ברייתא ששה סדרים, כרבי חייא וכרבי אושעיא. **תרתי** — בתמיה. **ומטי זמניהון** — הגיע זמן שנים עשר חודש לבתולה, משתבעה הבעל, כדלקמן כתובות ב״אף על פי״ (נז,א).

NOTES

orphan daughter loses her right to maintenance upon her betrothal only if she was betrothed as a *na'arah*, after she had already reached the age of twelve, when her betrothal is valid by Torah law. But if she was betrothed as a minor, before she reached the age of twelve, in which case her betrothal is valid only by Rabbinic enactment, she is still entitled to maintenance from her father's estate. By Torah law, only the father is authorized to arrange the betrothal of his minor daughter, and therefore a minor girl cannot become betrothed if her father is dead. The Rabbis enacted that an orphan girl's mother or brothers can arrange a betrothal on her behalf. But this does not empower the mother or the brothers to cancel her right to maintenance from her father's estate. The girl still retains the right to her maintenance, for she does not have the legal capacity to waive it (*Rashba*). Moreover, since the girl may terminate the betrothal at any time before she reaches the age of twelve by simply declaring that she does not want it to continue, her betrothal is not considered strong enough to cancel her right to maintenance from her father's estate (*Ritva*).

HALAKHAH

of age but is not yet betrothed, or if she is betrothed but has not reached majority, she is no longer entitled to maintenance, following Rav and the anonymous first Tanna of the Baraita. Some authorities say that the daughter only loses her right to maintenance when she is betrothed if she does so as a *na'arah*; but if she was betrothed before she reached the age of twelve, she is still entitled to maintenance (*Rema* in the name of *Rabbenu Ḥananel* and *Rashba*)." (*Rambam, Sefer Ishut, Hilkhot Nashim* 19:10; *Shulḥan Arukh, Even HaEzer* 112:1,3.)

TRANSLATION AND COMMENTARY

אִיבַּעֲיָא לְהוּ [1] Since the meaning of this version is unclear, **the** following **problem arose** in discussion among the Sages: Does Rav Yosef's version of the stipulation refer to **the** daughters **becoming betrothed** and therefore follow the viewpoint of the anonymous first Tanna of the Baraita and that of Rav, namely that the orphaned daughter is entitled to maintenance only until she is betrothed? [2] **Or** does it refer to **the** daughters **becoming married,** and agree with the viewpoint of Rabbi Elazar and Levi that the girl continues to be maintained from her father's estate until she is married?

[1]אִיבַּעֲיָא לְהוּ: הֲוָיָה דְּאֵירוּסִין, [2]אוֹ הֲוָיָה דְּנִישׂוּאִין? [3]תֵּיקוּ. [4]אֲמַר לֵיהּ רַב חִסְדָּא לְרַב יוֹסֵף: [5]מִי שְׁמִיעַ לָךְ מִינֵּיהּ דְּרַב יְהוּדָה אֲרוּסָה יֵשׁ לָהּ מְזוֹנוֹת אוֹ אֵין לָהּ מְזוֹנוֹת? [6]אֲמַר לֵיהּ: מִשְּׁמַע לָא שְׁמִיעַ לִי, אֶלָּא מִסְּבָרָא לֵית לָהּ.

LITERAL TRANSLATION

[1] It was asked of them: The becoming of betrothal, [2] or the becoming of marriage?

[3] Let it stand.

[4] Rav Ḥisda said to Rav Yosef: [5] Did you hear from Rav Yehudah [whether] a betrothed [orphan] has maintenance or does not have maintenance? [6] He said to him: I did not hear [anything], but by reasoning she does not have.

RASHI

ארוסה יש לה מזונות — ארוסה יתומה יש לה מזונות מן האחין, או לא. הכי גרסינן: מסברא לית לה

BACKGROUND

מִי שְׁמִיעַ לָךְ Did you hear? It seems that Rav Ḥisda, who was a contemporary of Rav Yehudah, wanted Rav Yosef to tell him whether he had heard the ruling from Rav Yehudah, because not only had Rav Yehudah studied with Rav, but he was also a close disciple of Shmuel and his Halakhic rulings were extremely important in civil suits. Once Rav Yosef had said that he had not received a Halakhic ruling from his teacher on the subject, but that he could reply on the basis of his own reasoning, Rav Ḥisda answered that his logical explanation was unconvincing.

תֵּיקוּ [3] The Gemara does not find a solution to this problem and concludes: **The problem** raised here **remains unsolved.**

אֲמַר לֵיהּ רַב חִסְדָּא [4] The Gemara now seeks an authoritative ruling on the issue of whether the orphan girl is entitled to maintenance after she is betrothed. **Rav Ḥisda said to Rav Yosef:** [5] **Did you hear** anything **from Rav Yehudah,** your teacher, on **whether or not an orphaned** daughter who is **betrothed is** still **entitled to maintenance** from the property of her father's estate? [6] Rav Yosef **said to** Rav Ḥisda: **I did not hear anything** on this subject from Rav Yehudah, **but by** logical **reasoning** I would say that an orphan girl **is not entitled** to maintenance after she is betrothed. For why did the Rabbis enact that an orphaned daughter is entitled to maintenance from her father's estate? So that she should not have to demean herself and beg from door to door for her subsistence. But if she is betrothed, her bridegroom will maintain her. Even though the bridegroom is not legally obligated to maintain his bride until after they are married, nevertheless,

NOTES

אֲרוּסָה יֵשׁ לָהּ מְזוֹנוֹת A betrothed orphan has maintenance. The Rishonim give three main interpretations of this passage. Our commentary follows *Rashi,* who explains that the issue discussed here is whether or not an orphaned daughter is still entitled to maintenance from the property of her father's estate even after she is betrothed. Thus the question raised by Rav Ḥisda is the subject of the dispute between Rav and Levi, which parallels the dispute between the anonymous first Tanna of the Baraita and Rabbi Elazar. Either Rav Ḥisda was unfamiliar with the Baraita recording that dispute, or he was asking for a ruling on the matter (*Tosafot*). Rav Yosef adds an additional factor to the discussion by suggesting that the betrothed girl may not be entitled to maintenance from her father's estate, for her bridegroom will surely provide for her support. Several objections were raised against this explanation: First, it is valid only according to Rashi's reading (which is found in the standard edition of the Talmud), but many Rishonim (see *Rif*) have the following reading: "I did not hear anything, but by reasoning *she has.* Since he betrothed her, it is not pleasing to him that she be disgraced." Second, it is difficult to exempt the father's heirs from maintaining his daughter on the assumption that her bridegroom will maintain her, when the bridegroom is under no legal obligation to provide anything for her support (see *Ramban* and others).

Rif (as he is interpreted by most Rishonim) explains that Rav Ḥisda's question was whether a woman who is widowed after betrothal is entitled to maintenance from her bridegroom's estate. Such a woman is ordinarily not entitled to maintenance, but here we are dealing with a case in which the time set for the marriage had already arrived before the bridegroom died, but the couple had not yet been married. Once the date set for the marriage arrives, the bridegroom becomes responsible for his bride's support, as if they were already married. The question, therefore, arises as to whether the betrothed woman is now considered as if she were married, so that she should be entitled to maintenance from her bridegroom's estate, since he died after the planned date for the marriage. Rav Yosef argues that it stands to reason that the woman is in fact entitled to such maintenance. Since she was betrothed to her bridegroom, he would not have wished her to be forced to demean herself and beg for sustenance once the time

HALAKHAH

אֲרוּסָה יֵשׁ לָהּ מְזוֹנוֹת אוֹ אֵין לָהּ מְזוֹנוֹת Whether a betrothed orphan has maintenance or does not have maintenance. "If someone betroths a young orphan girl who has been maintained from her father's estate, he is liable for her maintenance from the time of her betrothal." (*Rambam, Sefer Nashim, Hilkhot Ishut* 19:15; *Shulḥan Arukh, Even HaEzer* 112:3.)

LITERAL TRANSLATION

[1]Since he betrothed her, it is not pleasing to him that she be disgraced. [2]He said to him: If you did not hear [anything], by reasoning she has. [3]Since he is not sure about [marrying] her, [4]he does not spend (lit., "throw") money for nothing.

[5]And there are [some] who say: He said to him: [6]I did not hear [anything, but] by reasoning she has. [7]Since he is not sure about [marrying] her, he does not spend money for nothing. [8]He said to him: If you did not hear [anything], by reasoning she does not have. [9]Since he betrothed her, it is not pleasing to him that she be disgraced.

[1]כֵּיוָן דְּאֵירְסָהּ, לָא נִיחָא לֵיהּ דְּתִיתְזִיל. [2]אֲמַר לֵיהּ: אִם מִשְׁמַע לָא שְׁמִיעַ לָךְ, מִסְּבָרָא אִית לָהּ. [3]כֵּיוָן דְּלָא קִים לֵיהּ בְּגַוָּהּ, [4]לָא שְׁדֵי זוּזֵי בִּכְדִי.
[5]וְאִיכָּא דְּאָמְרִי: אֲמַר לֵיהּ: [6]מִשְׁמַע לָא שְׁמִיעַ לִי, מִסְּבָרָא אִית לָהּ. [7]כֵּיוָן דְּלָא קִים לֵיהּ בְּגַוָּהּ, לָא שְׁדֵי זוּזֵי בִּכְדִי. [8]אֲמַר לֵיהּ: אִי מִשְׁמַע לָא שְׁמִיעַ לָךְ, מִסְּבָרָא לֵית לָהּ. [9]כֵּיוָן דְּאֵירְסָהּ, לָא נִיחָא לֵיהּ דְּתִיתְזִיל.

TRANSLATION AND COMMENTARY

[1]**since he has betrothed her, he does not want her to demean herself** and beg her family for her subsistence. [2]Rav Ḥisda **said to** Rav Yosef: **If you did not hear anything** on this matter from Rav Yehudah, then **by** logical **reasoning** you should say that an orphan girl **is** indeed **entitled** to maintenance from her father's estate even after she is betrothed. [3]**Since** the bridegroom does not know her very well, **he is** still **not sure** that the **marriage** will take place, for he may discover some problem that will lead him to divorce her. Hence it is unlikely that the bridegroom will maintain his betrothed bride, even if she has nothing to live on, [4]for **he does not** wish to **spend** his **money for nothing.** Thus it stands to reason that the Rabbis granted an orphaned daughter maintenance from her father's estate even after she is betrothed, so that she should not have to demean herself and beg for her food.

וְאִיכָּא דְּאָמְרִי [5]The Gemara now reports a different version of the previous discussion, in which the Sages' positions are reversed: **There are some** authorities **who say** that when Rav Yosef was asked by Rav Ḥisda about maintenance for a betrothed orphan girl, **he said to him**: [6]**I did not hear anything** on this subject from Rav Yehudah, **but by** logical **reasoning** I would say that an orphan girl **is** indeed **entitled** to maintenance from her father's estate even after she is betrothed. [7]**Since** the bridegroom does not know her very well and **is not sure** that the **marriage** will take place, **he will not spend** his **money for nothing** on her maintenance. [8]Rav Ḥisda **said to** Rav Yosef: **If you did not hear anything** on this matter from Rav Yehudah, then **by** logical **reasoning** you should say that an orphan girl **is not entitled** to maintenance from her father's estate once she is betrothed, for she is then maintained by her bridegroom. Even though by law the bridegroom is not required to support her until after they are married, nevertheless, [9]**since he has** already **betrothed her, he does not want her to demean herself** and go begging for her subsistence.

RASHI

כיון דאירסה לא ניחא ליה דתיתזיל – מסברא אני אומר שאין לה מזונות מן האחין, דמאי טעמא תקון רבנן מזונות לבת מנכסי האב, כי היכי דלא תיתזיל על הפתחים, הכא ליכא למיחש להכי. דכי חזי ארוס דמתזלא – זיין לה איהו מדידיה, ואף על פי שאינו מחויב לזונה, דכיון דאירסה – לא ניחא ליה דתיתזיל. **אמר ליה אי משמע לא שמיע לך** – בהדיא. **מסברא אית לה** – יש לך לומר שנזונת מן האחים, דארוס לא זיין לה. **כיון דלא קים ליה בגוה** – אם תינשא לו, שמא ימצא בה מום, לא שדי זוזי בכדי.

NOTES

for the marriage had already arrived and she was considered his wife. A number of objections were raised against *Rif's* interpretation of the Gemara: First, Rav Ḥisda should have specifically mentioned that he was asking about a betrothed woman who was widowed after the time had already arrived for her to be married. Second, his explanation of the phrase, "it is not pleasing to him that she be disgraced," is rather forced, considering that he is dead. And third, the context of Rav Ḥisda's question suggests that he is dealing with the maintenance due to an orphaned daughter, and not that due to a widow.

Rabbi Shmuel HaNaggid suggests a third interpretation, which is adopted by many Rishonim: Rav Ḥisda asked whether a betrothed orphan girl is entitled to maintenance from her bridegroom. Ordinarily, the bridegroom is not liable for his bride's maintenance before the time set for the marriage arrives. But here we are dealing with an orphan girl who was being maintained from her father's estate prior to her betrothal, and who, according to Rav, lost her right to that maintenance as a result of her betrothal. Thus the question arises as to whether the betrothed bride can demand maintenance from her bridegroom.

Some Rishonim (*Ra'ah, Ran,* and others) maintain that the bridegroom is liable for his bride's maintenance only until she reaches majority, for after that time he can argue that his bride would no longer be eligible for maintenance from her father's estate even if he had not betrothed her. *Ritva* maintains that once the bridegroom becomes liable for his bride's maintenance he must continue to maintain her even after she reaches majority.

BACKGROUND

סִימָן דְּגַבְרֵי **The sign of the men.** This mnemonic refers to five questions asked regarding the obligation to maintain a daughter in various doubtful cases. These questions are similar in that none of them receives an unequivocal answer.

CONCEPTS

שׁוֹמֶרֶת יָבָם **A woman who is waiting for her *yavam*.** As stated in the Torah (Deuteronomy 25:5-10), if a husband dies childless, his widow is not allowed to remarry immediately. She must marry one of her late husband's brothers (in a levirate marriage), or else the brother must release her from the obligation by performing the ḥalitzah ceremony.

In principle there is no reason to delay either the levirate marriage or the ḥalitzah, but the widow may be forced by circumstances to wait for a considerable time, either because her brother-in-law is abroad, or because he has not yet come of age and is not competent either to marry or to perform the ḥalitzah ceremony.

TRANSLATION AND COMMENTARY

סִימָן ¹The Gemara now proceeds to discuss a series of cases in which the orphaned daughter's right to maintenance from her father's estate is questioned. The discussion opens with **a mnemonic device** to help us remember **the authorities** who discussed each of the cases: **ShK ZRP,** i.e., Rav *Sh*eshet, Resh La*k*ish, Rabbi Elazar, *R*ava, and Rav *P*appa. As a second device to help us remember the five different cases treated here the Gemara lists the themes discussed: ²**"She refused"** and **"a yevamah"** of the **"second degree"** is **"betrothed"** and **"he raped her."** Now each case is discussed in detail.

בָּעוּ מִינֵּיהּ מֵרַב שֵׁשֶׁת ³**Rav Sheshet was asked** about the following case: By Torah law, only the father is authorized to arrange the marriage of his minor daughter. However, the Sages enacted that she may be given in marriage, with her consent, by her mother or her brothers. The girl may terminate such a marriage before she reaches the age of twelve by performing *me'un* (מִיאוּן — "refusal") and declaring that she does not want the marriage. When a girl refuses marriage in this way, she is called a *mema'enet* (מְמָאֶנֶת — "one who refuses"), the marriage is nullified retroactively, and she does not require a bill of divorce. ⁴Now, if an orphan **girl** was married off by her mother or her brothers, and she later **announced her refusal** and returned to her mother or her brothers, **is she** then again **entitled to maintenance** from her father's estate, **or is she not entitled to** such **maintenance?** Do we say that she is regarded as a minor who has been married, and has therefore forfeited her right to maintenance from her father's estate? Or do we say that since the marriage was nullified retroactively, she is considered as someone who has never been married, and is therefore entitled to maintenance from her father's estate until she becomes an adult?

אָמַר לְהוּ רַב שֵׁשֶׁת ⁵**Rav Sheshet replied to** those who posed the question: **You have already learned** the answer to your question from the ruling in the following Baraita: ⁶"If a minor girl was betrothed, and her bridegroom died, so that she is now **a widow** living **in her father's house,** or if she was betrothed, and her bridegroom divorced her, ⁷so that she is now **a divorcee** living **in her father's house;** or if she was betrothed, and her bridegroom died, and he is survived by a brother, ⁸**and** she is now **waiting for her** brother-in-law, the *yavam* (יָבָם), to perform levirate marriage while she is living **in her father's house,** and the father dies, ⁹in each of these cases the orphaned daughter **is entitled to maintenance** from her father's estate.

LITERAL TRANSLATION

¹The sign of the men: ShK ZRP. ²"She refused," and "a yevamah" [of the] "second degree" is "betrothed" and "he raped her."
³They asked Rav Sheshet: ⁴Does a girl who refuses [marriage] have maintenance or does she not have maintenance?
⁵Rav Sheshet said to them: You have [already] learned it: ⁶"A widow in her father's house, ⁷and a divorcee in her father's house, ⁸and a woman who is waiting for her *yavam* in her father's house, ⁹have maintenance.

¹סִימָן דְּגַבְרֵי: שַׁ״ךְ זַרַ״ף. ²מֵאֲנָה וִיבָמָה שְׁנִיָּה אֲרוּסָה וַאֲנָסָהּ. ³בָּעוּ מִינֵּיהּ מֵרַב שֵׁשֶׁת: ⁴מְמָאֶנֶת יֵשׁ לָהּ מְזוֹנוֹת אוֹ אֵין לָהּ מְזוֹנוֹת? ⁵אָמַר לְהוּ רַב שֵׁשֶׁת: תְּנֵיתוּהָ: ⁶"אַלְמָנָה בְּבֵית אָבִיהָ, ⁷וּגְרוּשָׁה בְּבֵית אָבִיהָ, ⁸וְשׁוֹמֶרֶת יָבָם בְּבֵית אָבִיהָ, ⁹יֵשׁ לָהּ מְזוֹנוֹת.

RASHI

מְמָאֶנֶת — קְטַנָּה יְתוֹמָה שֶׁהִשִּׂיאוּהָ אֶחֶיהָ, וּמֵיאֲנָה בְּבַעֲלָהּ, וְחָזְרָה אֶצְלָם. יֵשׁ לָהּ מְזוֹנוֹת — עַד שֶׁתִּתְגַּגֵּר, אוֹ לֹא? מִי אָמְרִינַן עַקַרְתִּינְהוּ לְנִישּׂוּאֵי מֵעִיקָּרָן, וַהֲוָה לָהּ כְּמִי שֶׁלֹּא נִיסַת, אוֹ דִּלְמָא — הָא נִיסַת וְיָצְאָה מֵרְשׁוּת אָב. אַלְמָנָה בְּבֵית אָבִיהָ — כְּלוֹמַר, מִן הָאֵירוּסִין. דְּאִי מִן הַנִּישּׂוּאִין — לֹא אָמְרִינַן יֵשׁ לָהּ מְזוֹנוֹת, דְּ״עַד דְּתַלְקְטָן" תְּנַן, וַאֲפִילּוּ לֵוִי — בְּנִישּׂוּאִין מוֹדֶה.

NOTES

אַלְמָנָה בְּבֵית אָבִיהָ **A widow in her father's house.** The Rishonim understand this Baraita in various ways. *Rashi* explains that the Baraita is referring to a minor girl who was widowed or divorced after betrothal, and that it follows the viewpoint of Levi, who maintains that a minor girl is entitled to maintenance from her father's estate even after she is betrothed. For if the girl lost or divorced her husband after marriage, even Levi agrees that she cannot collect maintenance from her father's estate.

Rabbenu Tam explains that the Baraita is referring to a minor girl who was widowed or divorced and returned to her father's home during his lifetime. Such a girl is entitled to maintenance from her father's estate, even if she was widowed or divorced after marriage, for at the time of her father's death she had already returned to his home. A minor girl forfeits her maintenance upon her betrothal (according to Rav) or her marriage (according to Levi), only if she was betrothed or married after her father's death.

Rabbenu Ḥananel agrees that the Baraita is referring to a girl who returned to her father's home during his lifetime,

HALAKHAH

מְמָאֶנֶת...אַלְמָנָה...וּגְרוּשָׁה **A girl who refuses marriage ...a widow...and a divorcee.** "If a minor girl is married and later refuses her husband, or if she is divorced, or if she is widowed (and even if she is waiting for her brother-in-law to perform levirate marriage), and she returns to her father's house before she reaches majority,

TRANSLATION AND COMMENTARY

[1] **Rabbi Yehudah says: If** the girl **is still in her father's house, she is entitled to maintenance** from her father's estate. [2] But **if she is no longer in her father's house, she is not entitled to** such **maintenance."** [3] Now this Baraita gives the impression that the viewpoint of **Rabbi Yehudah is the same as** that of **the** anonymous **first Tanna,** for they both seem to be saying that if the girl is still in her paternal home, she is entitled to maintenance from her father's estate! What, then, is the subject of their dispute? [4] **Rather,** we must conclude **that they disagree about** the case in which **an** orphan **girl** was married off by her mother or her brothers and later **refused** her husband and returned to her mother or her brothers. [5] **The first Tanna** of the Baraita **maintains** that **she is entitled** to maintenance from her father's estate. Since her refusal nullified her marriage retroactively, she is considered like a widow or a divorcee after betrothal, who, because she was never married, is entitled to maintenance from her father's estate. [6] **But Rabbi Yehudah maintains** that **she is not entitled** to maintenance. Only if the orphan girl always remained in her father's house — in other words, she was never married off, not even by her mother or her brothers — is she entitled to maintenance. But if she was married off by her mother or her brothers and left her father's house, she is no longer entitled to maintenance, not even after she refuses her husband and returns to her paternal home.

בָּעֵי רֵישׁ לָקִישׁ [7] The Gemara now proceeds to discuss a second case. **Resh Lakish asked:** If a man dies without offspring, and the brother of the deceased (known as the *yavam* — יָבָם) marries the widow (known as the *yevamah* — יְבָמָה) in accordance with the laws of levirate marriage (Deuteronomy 25:5–6), and a daughter is born of that marriage, **is the daughter of the *yevamah* entitled to maintenance** from her father's

[1] רַבִּי יְהוּדָה אוֹמֵר: עוֹדָהּ בְּבֵית אָבִיהָ, יֵשׁ לָהּ מְזוֹנוֹת. [2] אֵינָהּ בְּבֵית אָבִיהָ, אֵין לָהּ מְזוֹנוֹת״. [3] רַבִּי יְהוּדָה הַיְינוּ תַּנָּא קַמָּא! [4] אֶלָּא לָאו מְמָאֶנֶת אִיכָּא בֵּינַיְיהוּ? [5] דְּתַנָּא קַמָּא סָבַר: אִית לָהּ. [6] וְרַבִּי יְהוּדָה סָבַר: לֵית לָהּ.

[7] בָּעֵי רֵישׁ לָקִישׁ: בַּת יְבָמָה יֵשׁ לָהּ מְזוֹנוֹת אוֹ אֵין לָהּ מְזוֹנוֹת?

LITERAL TRANSLATION

[1] Rabbi Yehudah says: [If] she is still in her father's house, she has maintenance. [2] [If] she is not in her father's house, she does not have maintenance." [3] [Surely] Rabbi Yehudah is the same as the first Tanna! [4] Rather, is it not that there is [a dispute] between them [regarding] a girl who refuses [marriage]? [5] For the first Tanna maintains: She has. [6] But Rabbi Yehudah maintains: She does not have.

[7] Resh Lakish asked: Does the daughter of a *yevamah* have maintenance or does she not have maintenance?

RASHI

תנא קמא סבר ממאנת אית לה — והכי קאמר: אלמנה בבית אביה כו׳ והוא הדין לממאנת, דאין כאן נשואין, דהא עקרתינהו. ואתא רבי יהודה למימר: עודה בבית אביה בתחלתה, שלא יצתה משם בנשואין — יש לה מזונות, אבל משיצאה בנישואין — אין לה. **בת יבמה** — הכונס את יבמתו וילדה לו בת — יש לה מזונות לאחר מיתת האב, מן האחין, מנכסי אביה או לא?

NOTES

but he argues that she is entitled to maintenance from her father's estate only if she was widowed or divorced after betrothal but before marriage. But if the girl was married, she is not entitled to maintenance from her father's estate, even if she returned to his home during his lifetime, for when she married she left his authority permanently.

According to *Rambam,* a minor girl is entitled to maintenance from her father's estate even if she was widowed or divorced after marriage, and even if she returned to her father's house only after her father had already died.

בַּת יְבָמָה The daughter of a *yevamah*. The Gemara here is discussing whether or not the daughter of a *yevamah* is entitled to maintenance from her father's estate. The Rishonim ask: Why does the Gemara concern itself with the daughter of the *yevamah* when the same question can be raised with regard to the *yevamah* herself — is she entitled to maintenance from the estate of her second husband?

Most Rishonim maintain that it is obvious that if her first husband left an estate, the *yevamah* collects her maintenance from that estate. And if he did not leave an estate,

HALAKHAH

she is entitled to maintenance from her father's estate until she reaches majority or is betrothed again, following the anonymous first Tanna of the Baraita, according to Rav Sheshet. *Rema* notes that according to some authorities (*Rashi, Tosafot, Ran,* and *Tur*) the girl is entitled to maintenance only if she was divorced or widowed after betrothal, but if she was already married, she is no longer entitled to maintenance from her father's estate." (*Rambam, Sefer Nashim, Hilkhot Ishut* 19:16; *Shulḥan Arukh, Even HaEzer* 112:4.)

בַּת יְבָמָה The daughter of a *yevamah*. "If someone marries the widow of his deceased brother, and a daughter is born from this marriage, and the first husband left an estate from which his widow can collect her ketubah, the daughter is not entitled to maintenance (neither from the property of her mother's first husband, for he was not her

TERMINOLOGY

תֵּיקוּ Let it stand. I.e., the problem raised in the previous passage remains unresolved (lit., "standing") because we have no sources enabling us to resolve it, and there is no logical proof tending toward one solution rather than another. From a theoretical standpoint, therefore, the problem remains "standing" in its place. However, in Halakhic decision-making there are various principles as to what action is to be taken in such cases. If the unresolved problem relates to a Rabbinic decree, the decision leans toward leniency. In matters of civil law, where absolute degrees of stringency or leniency have no place, the decision is to leave the existing situation.

TRANSLATION AND COMMENTARY

estate upon his death, **or is she not entitled to** such **maintenance?** [1]The Gemara explains the two sides of the question: Elsewhere (*Yevamot* 38a), **the Master said** in a Mishnah: "Once the brother of the deceased marries the widow, she is considered his wife for all purposes, except that the *yevamah*'s **ketubah is a charge on the property of her first husband.**" The property of the first husband, and not that of the *yavam*, is security for the payment of the *yevamah*'s ketubah. Therefore it stands to reason that the *yevamah*'s daughter **is not entitled** to maintenance from her father's estate; for just as his property is not mortgaged for the payment of the *yevamah*'s ketubah, it is similarly not mortgaged for the payment of the conditions contained in the ketubah, including the daughter's right to maintenance from her father's estate. [2]On the other hand, **since** the law is that **if there is not** enough property in the estate **of the first** husband to cover the *yevamah*'s ketubah, **the Rabbis enacted** a ketubah **for her from her second** husband so that it should not be easy for the *yavam* to divorce her, **perhaps** the *yevamah*'s daughter **is** in fact **entitled** to maintenance from her father's estate. Just as the ketubah itself can be a charge on the *yavam*'s property, so are the ketubah conditions — including the daughter's right to maintenance — a charge on her father's estate.

תֵּיקוּ An answer to this question was not found, and so the Gemara concludes: [3]**The problem** raised here **remains unsolved.**

בָּעֵי רַבִּי אֶלְעָזָר [4]The Gemara now considers a third case. **Rabbi Elazar asked:** If someone marries a woman who is related to him in such a way that the marriage is forbidden by Rabbinic enactment as second-degree incest (if, for example, he marries his son's daughter-in-law), he is required to divorce her and need not pay her her ketubah. [5]Now, if **a daughter** is born **from** that marriage which is forbidden as **a secondary**

[1]כֵּיוָן דַּאֲמַר מָר: ״כְּתוּבָּתָהּ עַל נִכְסֵי בַּעְלָהּ הָרִאשׁוֹן״, לֵית לָהּ. [2]אוֹ דִּלְמָא, כֵּיוָן דְּאִי לֵית לָהּ מֵרִאשׁוֹן תַּקִּינוּ לָהּ רַבָּנַן מִשֵּׁנִי, אִית לָהּ.

[3]תֵּיקוּ.

[4]בָּעֵי רַבִּי אֶלְעָזָר: [5]בַּת שְׁנִיָּה

LITERAL TRANSLATION

[1]Since the Master has said: "Her ketubah is [a charge] on the property of her first husband," she does not have. [2]Or perhaps, since if she does not have from the first one the Rabbis enacted for her from the second one, she has.

[3]Let it stand.

[4]Rabbi Elazar asked: [5]Does the daughter from a secondary

RASHI

כיון דאמר מר — כתובתה אינה על נכסי יבם, תנאי כתובה דלה — נמי לאו על נכסיו הוא. **או דלמא** — כיון דאמרינן התם: אי לית ליה נכסים לראשון — תקינו לה רבנן משני, כדי שלא תהא קלה בעיניו להוציאה. **אית לה** — נמי תנאי כתובה, להיות בתו נזונת. **בת שניה** — מי שנשא שניה מדברי סופרים, דאמרי רבנן לקמן בפרק ״אלמנה״ (כתובות ק,ב): השניה אין לה כתובה ולא מזונות, בתה שילדה לו ומת.

NOTES

she is entitled to maintenance from the property of the *yavam*. For just as the ketubah itself is a charge on the property of the *yavam* if the *yevamah*'s first husband did not leave an estate with sufficient assets to cover it, so too is the *yevamah*'s right to maintenance, as well as to the other ketubah conditions, a charge on the property of the *yavam* if those obligations cannot be met by the first husband's estate.

Rivan and *Rid* argue that the Gemara did not ask about the *yevamah* herself because it is obvious that the *yevamah* is entitled to maintenance only from property left by her first husband, for after the *yavam*'s death she is treated as the widow of her first husband. Thus, if her first husband did not leave any property, she cannot collect her maintenance from the *yavam*'s estate.

The Rishonim ask: What is the law concerning the right of the *yevamah*'s sons to their mother's ketubah by virtue of the enactment of the *ketubat benin dikhrin*?

Rabbenu Crescas Vidal maintains that since the Rabbis instituted the *ketubat benin dikhrin* in order to encourage a father to give his daughter a generous dowry, that enactment applies to the *yevamah*'s sons as well. For if the *yevamah*'s sons cannot collect their mother's ketubah, a man will refrain from giving his daughter a sizeable dowry, knowing that whatever he gives her may be lost to his descendants if she becomes a widow and marries her brother-in-law.

Others (*Tosafot, Ra'ah,* and *Meiri*) maintain that the same question the Gemara posed with respect to the *yevamah*'s daughter's right to maintenance, can also be asked with respect to her sons' right to her ketubah.

HALAKHAH

father, nor from the property of the second husband, for he was not liable for her mother's ketubah). But if the first husband did not leave an estate from which his widow can collect her ketubah, and therefore the *yevamah* has a ketubah from her second husband, the daughter is entitled to maintenance from her father's estate (following *Tur, Rosh* and *Ran*). According to *Rambam,* since the issue was not resolved in the Gemara, the daughter of the *yevamah* is not entitled to maintenance from her father's estate." (*Rambam, Sefer Nashim, Hilkhot Ishut* 19:14; *Shulhan Arukh, Even HaEzer* 112:5.)

יֵשׁ לָהּ מְזוֹנוֹת אוֹ אֵין לָהּ מְזוֹנוֹת? [54A] [1]כֵּיוָן דְּלֵית לָהּ כְּתוּבָּה, לֵית לָהּ מְזוֹנֵי. [2]אוֹ דִּלְמָא, אִמָּהּ דַּעֲבָדָא אִיסּוּרָא קְנָסוּהָ רַבָּנַן; [3]אִיהִי, דְּלָא עֲבָדָא אִיסּוּרָא, לָא קְנָסוּהָ רַבָּנַן.
[4]תֵּיקוּ.
[5]בָּעֵי רָבָא: בַּת אֲרוּסָה יֵשׁ לָהּ מְזוֹנוֹת אוֹ אֵין לָהּ מְזוֹנוֹת?

LITERAL TRANSLATION

[forbidden] relationship have maintenance or does she not have maintenance? [54A] [1]Since she does not have a ketubah, she does not have maintenance. [2]Or perhaps, the Rabbis penalized her mother because she committed a transgression; [3]but the Rabbis did not penalize her, because she did not commit a transgression.
[4]Let it stand.
[5]Rava asked: Does the daughter of a betrothed woman have maintenance or does she not have maintenance?

TRANSLATION AND COMMENTARY

forbidden relationship, and her father dies, **is** the daughter **entitled to maintenance** from her father's estate, **or is she not entitled to** such **maintenance?** [54A] [1]The Gemara explains the two sides of the issue: Do we say that **since** the mother **is not entitled to her ketubah** because she entered into a forbidden marriage, similarly her daughter **should not be entitled to maintenance** from her father's estate, since the daughter's right to maintenance is one of the conditions of her mother's ketubah? [2]**Or perhaps** we should argue that it is only **the mother** whom **the Rabbis penalized because she transgressed a** Rabbinic **prohibition** and therefore is not entitled to her ketubah. [3]**But the Rabbis did not penalize** the daughter, **because she did not commit a transgression,** and therefore she retains her right to maintenance from her father's estate.

תֵּיקוּ [4]The Gemara concludes: The **problem** raised here **remains unsolved.**

בָּעֵי רָבָא [5]The Gemara now considers a fourth case. **Rava asked:** If a man betroths a woman and has intercourse with her before they are married, and a daughter is born from that union, and then the bridegroom dies, is **the daughter of the betrothed woman entitled to maintenance** from her father's estate **or is she not entitled to** such **maintenance?** The Gemara explains why the law in this case is in doubt:

RASHI

יש לה מזונות — מנכסיו, או לא? **כיון דלית לה כתובה** — לאם, לית לה מזוני דבת. דהא תנאי כתובה הוא. **בת ארוסה** — הבא על ארוסתו וילדה לו, ומת, ולא כניס יש לה מזונות מנכסיו, או לא?

NOTES

אִמָּהּ דַּעֲבָדָא אִיסּוּרָא **Her mother because she committed a transgression.** *Meiri* asks: How can the Gemara suggest that a daughter born from a marriage forbidden as a secondary forbidden relationship should be entitled to maintenance from her father's estate, and argue that only the mother should be penalized, because it was she who committed the transgression? Surely we learned above (53a) that if a woman remarries on the basis of the testimony of one witness to her first husband's death, and it later turns out that her first husband is still alive and that she has been guilty of adultery, the Rabbis penalize not only the woman but also the children of both marriages, so that they cannot collect their mother's ketubah by virtue of the enactment of the *ketubat benin dikhrin*! Thus we see that the Rabbis did in fact impose penalties upon the children for their mother's transgression.

Meiri distinguishes between the two cases: With respect to the woman who remarried without first verifying that her first husband was dead, only the woman did something wrong, and therefore it is fitting that her husband's estate should not be held liable to pay her ketubah or any of the ketubah's conditions. But in the case of the marriage forbidden as a secondary forbidden relationship, both the man and the woman were guilty of a transgression, and therefore it can be argued that the husband's estate should be subject to the ketubah condition entitling the woman's daughter to maintenance.

בַּת אֲרוּסָה **The daughter of a betrothed woman.** The Gemara argues that the daughter born to a betrothed woman should perhaps be entitled to maintenance from her father's estate because her mother is entitled to her ketubah. *Rashi* explains this in two ways: Either we are dealing with a case in which the bridegroom wrote his betrothed bride a ketubah of his own free will, or the Gemara is assuming that the Rabbis instituted a ketubah for a betrothed woman.

Rid argues that the Gemara must be assuming that a betrothed woman is entitled to a ketubah, for if we are dealing with a case in which the bridegroom wrote the ketubah of his own free will, the daughter's right to maintenance from her father's estate should depend on what is written in the document. If the ketubah stipulates that the daughter is entitled to maintenance, she should indeed receive maintenance, and if such a stipulation is not included, she should not.

Ra'avad explains that the Gemara is asking about a woman who gave birth to a daughter while she was betrothed to the girl's father, and she subsequently married him, and he later died. Do we say that, since the woman received her ketubah when she married the ketubah conditions apply retroactively to the daughter who was born during her mother's betrothal? Or do we say the daughter is not entitled to maintenance from her father's estate, for at the time of her birth her mother did not have a ketubah?

HALAKHAH

בַּת שְׁנִיָּה...בַּת אֲרוּסָה...בַּת אֲנוּסָה **The daughter from a secondary forbidden relationship...the daughter of a betrothed woman...the daughter of a raped girl.** "If a daughter is born from a marriage forbidden as a secondary

LITERAL TRANSLATION

[1]Since she has a ketubah, she has. [2]Or perhaps, since the Rabbis did not institute a ketubah [for her] until the time of marriage, she does not have. [3]Let it stand.

[4]Rav Pappa asked: Does the daughter of a raped girl have maintenance or does she not have maintenance? [5]According to Rabbi Yose the son of Rabbi Yehudah, there is no problem for you, [6]for he says: She has a ketubah [of] a maneh. [7]There is a problem for you according to the Rabbis, who say:

[1]כֵּיוָן דְּאִית לָהּ כְּתוּבָּה, אִית לָהּ. [2]אוֹ דִּלְמָא, כֵּיוָן דְּלָא תַקִּינוּ רַבָּנַן כְּתוּבָּה עַד שְׁעַת נִישּׂוּאִין, לֵית לָהּ.

[3]תֵּיקוּ.

[4]בָּעֵי רַב פַּפָּא: בַּת אֲנוּסָה יֵשׁ לָהּ מְזוֹנוֹת אוֹ אֵין לָהּ מְזוֹנוֹת? [5]אַלִּיבָּא דְּרַבִּי יוֹסֵי בְּרַבִּי יְהוּדָה, לָא תִּיבָּעֵי לָךְ, [6]דְּאָמַר: יֵשׁ לָהּ כְּתוּבָּה מָנֶה. [7]כִּי תִּיבָּעֵי לָךְ אַלִּיבָּא דְּרַבָּנַן, דְּאָמְרִי:

TRANSLATION AND COMMENTARY

[1]Do we say that **since** the betrothed woman **is entitled to her ketubah** if her bridegroom wrote her one when they became betrothed, therefore her daughter **should be entitled to** maintenance from her father's estate, seeing that this is one of the conditions of her mother's ketubah? [2]**Or** do we **perhaps** say that **since the Rabbis did not rule** that the bridegroom must write **a ketubah for** his bride **until the time of** their **marriage,** the daughter born to a woman during the period of her betrothal **is not entitled to** maintenance from her father's estate?

תֵּיקוּ [3]Here, too, the Gemara does not reach a conclusion and says: This **problem remains unsolved.**

בָּעֵי רַב פַּפָּא [4]The Gemara now considers one last case on this topic. **Rav Pappa asked:** If a man rapes a girl who is under twelve-and-a-half years of age, he is required by the Torah to marry her (provided that she and her father give their consent), and he cannot divorce her against her will. He is also obligated to pay a fine for raping her, as well as damages if she suffered physical injury. Now, if a man **rapes** such **a** young **girl** and then marries her, and a daughter is born, and the man dies, is **the daughter entitled to maintenance** from her father's estate **or is she not entitled to** such **maintenance?** [5]The Gemara notes that, **according to Rabbi Yose the son of Rabbi Yehudah, there is no problem,** [6]**for** Rabbi Yose the son of Rabbi Yehudah **said:** If a girl is raped, and the man who raped her marries her, **she is entitled to a ketubah of a maneh,** just like any other woman who is no longer a virgin when she marries. Even though her husband has already paid her father the fine for her rape, she is still entitled to receive her ketubah if she is widowed or divorced. Since, according to Rabbi Yose the son of Rabbi Yehudah, the mother is entitled to her ketubah, her daughter is obviously entitled to maintenance from her father's estate, since her right to maintenance is one of the conditions of any ketubah. [7]But **there is a problem according to the Rabbis, who** disagreed with Rabbi Yose the son of Rabbi Yehudah

RASHI

כיון דאית לה כתובה — כגון שכתב לה מן האירוסין. אי נמי — רבנן תקון נמי לארוסה. **או דלמא כיון דלא תקון רבנן** — למכתב עד שעת נשואין, תנאי כתובה נמי מקמי הכי לא חייל. **בת אנוסה** — אנס את הנערה ונשאה אחרי כן, כדכתיב ״ולו תהיה לאשה״ וילדה לו בת ומת, יש לה מזונות מן האחין או לא? **יש לה כתובה** — מנכסיו. **מנה** — אם מת, ואף על גב שכבר נתן כסף קנסה לאביה.

NOTES

לָא תַקִּינוּ רַבָּנַן כְּתוּבָּה עַד שְׁעַת נִישּׂוּאִין The Rabbis did not institute a ketubah for her until the time of marriage. At first glance, the Gemara appears to contradict itself, for it begins by saying that a betrothed woman has a ketubah, and it then argues that the Rabbis did not institute a ketubah until the time of marriage.

Rashi explains that even though a woman is entitled to her ketubah from the time of her betrothal (whether because the bridegroom wrote her a ketubah of his own free will, or because the Rabbis enacted that she is entitled to a ketubah; see previous note), the Rabbis did not enact that the ketubah be committed to writing until the time of her marriage.

Talmidei Rabbenu Yonah maintains that although the Rabbis enacted that a betrothed woman is entitled to a ketubah, the lien on the husband's property ensuring payment of the ketubah is not established until her marriage. (See also *Ra'avad* cited in the previous note.)

בַּת אֲנוּסָה The daughter of a raped girl. Some Rishonim note that the same question can be asked about the rape

HALAKHAH

forbidden relationship, or if a daughter is born to a young girl who was the victim of rape (even if the daughter was born after the girl was married), or if a daughter is born to a woman during her betrothal — in each of these cases the daughter is not entitled to maintenance from her father's estate. (But during the father's lifetime, he must maintain such daughters, just as he must maintain his other children.) The Gemara does not reach a conclusion about any of these cases, and therefore we follow the general principle that in cases of doubt the claimant cannot collect from the defendant." (*Rambam, Sefer Nashim, Hilkhot Ishut* 19:14; *Shulḥan Arukh, Even HaEzer* 112:5.)

TRANSLATION AND COMMENTARY

and **said:** [1]The rapist's **payment of the fine** to the girl's father **releases him** from the obligation to pay his wife **her ketubah.** [2]**What is the law** according to the Rabbis regarding the daughter? [3]Do we say that **since** the mother **is not entitled to** receive her **ketubah,** her daughter too **should not be entitled to maintenance** from her father's estate, for if there is no ketubah, there are also no ketubah conditions? [4]**Or** can we **perhaps** argue as follows? **The reason** why the Rabbis instituted **a ketubah** for an ordinary woman [5]**was in order that it should not be an easy matter** for a man **to divorce** his wife. In order to deter a husband from doing so, the Rabbis enacted that he must pay her the sum recorded in her ketubah if he ends the marriage. [6]**But in this** case, where a young girl was raped and then married by the man who raped her, the husband **cannot divorce** his wife against her will, for the verse says (Deuteronomy 22:29): "He cannot let her go all his days," and there was thus no need to institute a ketubah for her. It stands to reason that this applies only to the basic portion of the ketubah that a woman collects on her divorce. But the rest of the ketubah conditions apply to the victim of rape, just as they do to any other woman. Thus her daughter should be entitled to maintenance from her father's estate.

תֵּיקוּ [7]No decision was reached on this matter, and the Gemara concludes: Rav Pappa's **question remains unanswered,** together with the rest of the unsolved problems regarding a daughter's right to maintenance from her father's estate.

אַתְּ תְּהֵא [8]The Gemara now analyzes another of the ketubah conditions recorded in our Mishnah, which stated: "After I die, **you will live in my house** and be maintained from my property all the days that you live in widowhood in my house." [9]**Rav Yosef taught** the following Baraita: "The husband writes in his wife's ketubah: 'After I die, you will live **in my house but not in my hut.**' The widow is entitled to continue living in the same place as she lived with her husband provided that they had been living in a proper house, but not

[1]יָצָא כֶּסֶף קְנָסָהּ בִּכְתוּבָּתָהּ. [2]מַאי? [3]כֵּיוָן דְּלֵית לָהּ כְּתוּבָּה, לֵית לָהּ מְזוֹנֵי. [4]אוֹ דִּלְמָא, כְּתוּבָּה טַעֲמָא מַאי? [5]כְּדֵי שֶׁלֹּא תְּהֵא קַלָּה בְּעֵינָיו לְהוֹצִיאָהּ. [6]וְהָא לָא מָצֵי מַפֵּיק לָהּ.

[7]תֵּיקוּ.

[8]"אַתְּ תְּהֵא יָתְבָא בְּבֵיתִי, וכו'". [9]תָּנֵי רַב יוֹסֵף: בְּבֵיתִי וְלֹא

LITERAL TRANSLATION

[1]The money of her fine is in lieu of (lit., "went out in") her ketubah. [2]What [is the law]? [3]Since she does not have a ketubah, she does not have maintenance. [4]Or perhaps, what is the reason for a ketubah? [5]In order that she should not be light in his eyes to send her away. [6]But this one he cannot send away.

[7]Let it stand.

[8]"You will live in my house, etc." [9]Rav Yosef taught: In my house but not

RASHI

יצא כסף קנסה בכתובתה — ואין לה כתובה. **מאי** — מזונות הבת שהן תנאי כתובה פקעי בהכי, או לא? מי אמרינן: **כיון דלית לה כו'. או דלמא כתובה היינו טעמא** — דלא תקון לה רבנן, משום דכל כתובת אשה משום שלא תהא קלה בעיניו להוציאה תקנוה. **והא לא מצי מפיק** — כדכתיב "לא יוכל שלחה". כתובה דמשום אפוקי הוא — דלא תקון, דליכא למיחש לית לה. אבל שאר תנאי כתובה, דלאו משום שלא תהא קלה איתקון — אית לה. **בביתי ולא בביקתי** — אם יש לו בית כופין את היורשין לתת לה מדור לפי כבודה, ואין יכולין לומר לה: לכי לבית אביך ואנו זנין אותך שם. אבל אין לו בית אלא ביקתא בעלמא, צריך צר וקטן. ולשון ביקתא — בי עקתא (שבת עז,ב) יכולין לומר: לכי מאצלנו, ד"את תהא יתבא בביתי" כתב לך, ולא בביקתי.

NOTES

victim herself — whether or not she is entitled to maintenance from her husband's estate (*Tosafot*). The Gemara formulated its question in terms of the daughter to make it conform to the questions raised earlier in the Gemara, which relate to the maintenance due to an orphaned daughter (*Ra'ah, Rosh,* and *Ritva*). Other Rishonim maintain that the raped girl herself is certainly not entitled to maintenance from her husband's estate, for she is viewed as having already received her ketubah, in which case she is no longer entitled to any of the ketubah conditions (*Meiri* and *Ran*).

בְּבֵיתִי וְלֹא בְּבִיקְתִי In my house but not in my hut. Our commentary follows *Rashi,* who explains that the heirs of the deceased husband are not required to share living quarters with the widow if all that the husband left was a tiny hut. Instead, they can send her back to her father's home. According to this explanation, the heirs can certainly send the widow back to her paternal home if the husband did not leave a house at all. However, the Jerusalem Talmud rules that if the husband did not leave a house, his heirs must rent a house for his widow.

In order to reconcile this apparent contradiction, *Ramban* suggests that the Baraita in our Gemara means to say that if the deceased husband left only a tiny hut, the widow cannot demand that the heirs move out. Rather, the heirs can stay in the hut, which now belongs to them, but they must rent another house for the widow. And similarly, if the husband did not leave any house at all, his heirs must rent a house for the widow, as stated in the Jerusalem Talmud. Others explain that our Baraita teaches us that the widow cannot demand that the heirs set aside a residence where she alone will live, even if all she wants is a tiny hut, but the heirs can insist that she live in their house (*Meiri* and *Ramban*).

בְּבִיקְתִי. [1]אֲבָל מְזוֹנֵי אִית לָהּ. [2]מָר בַּר רַב אַשִׁי אֲמַר: אֲפִילּוּ מְזוֹנֵי נַמִי לֵית לָהּ. [3]וְלֵית הִלְכְתָא כְּמָר בַּר רַב אַשִׁי.

[4]אָמַר רַב נַחְמָן אָמַר שְׁמוּאֵל: [5]תְּבָעוּהָ לְהִנָּשֵׂא וְנִתְפַּיְּיסָה, אֵין לָהּ מְזוֹנוֹת.

[6]הָא לֹא נִתְפַּיְּיסָה, יֵשׁ לָהּ מְזוֹנוֹת?

[7]אֲמַר רַב עָנָן: לְדִידִי מִפָּרְשָׁא לִי מִינֵּיהּ דְּמָר שְׁמוּאֵל: [8]אָמְרָה ״מֵחֲמַת פְּלוֹנִי בַּעְלִי״, [9]יֵשׁ לָהּ מְזוֹנוֹת; [10]מֵחֲמַת בְּנֵי אָדָם שֶׁאֵינָן מְהוּגָּנִין לָהּ, אֵין לָהּ מְזוֹנוֹת.

[11]אָמַר רַב חִסְדָּא: זִינְּתָה, אֵין לָהּ מְזוֹנוֹת. [12]אָמַר רַב יוֹסֵף: כִּיחֲלָה וּפִירְכְּסָה, אֵין לָהּ

LITERAL TRANSLATION

in my hut. [1]But she does have maintenance. [2]Mar bar Rav Ashi said: Even maintenance too she does not have. [3]But the law is not in accordance with Mar bar Rav Ashi.

[4]Rav Naḥman said in the name of Shmuel: [5][If] they asked her to marry and she agreed, she does not have maintenance.

[6]But [if] she did not agree, does she have maintenance?

[7]Rav Anan said: It was explained to me personally by Mar Shmuel: [8][If] she said: "Because of So-and-so, my husband," [9]she has maintenance; [10][but if her refusal was] because of people who are not fit for her, she does not have maintenance.

[11]Rav Ḥisda said: [If] she fornicated she does not have maintenance. [12]Rav Yosef said: [If] she painted her eyelids or dyed her hair, she does not have

TRANSLATION AND COMMENTARY

if they had been living in a tiny hut. Therefore, if the husband left a house as part of his estate, his heirs cannot send his widow back to her father's home, even if they are willing to provide for her maintenance there. Instead, they must allocate a part of the house as a residence for their father's widow, the size of her apartment being determined by her social status. But if the husband left behind him only a tiny hut, the heirs are not obligated to maintain his widow in the hut, and they can send her back to her father's home." This Baraita limits the widow's right to continue living in the same house as she lived with her husband to a case in which they had been living in a house, and not in a hut. [1]**But** it follows that the widow **is entitled to maintenance** from her husband's estate even if she cannot exercise her right regarding her residence. Even though the widow's right to maintenance and her right to continue living in her husband's house are mentioned in the same clause in the ketubah, the one is not dependent on the other. [2]**Mar bar Rav Ashi** disagreed and **said:** The widow is entitled to maintenance from her husband's estate only if she is entitled to live in her husband's house. But if she cannot exercise this right, then **she is not even entitled to maintenance.** [3]The Gemara notes that **the law is not in accordance with** the opinion of **Mar bar Rav Ashi.**

אָמַר רַב נַחְמָן [4]According to the stipulation in the ketubah, a widow is entitled to maintenance from her late husband's estate as long as she remains his widow. The Gemara now proceeds to discuss the conditions under which a widow forfeits her right to maintenance. **Rav Naḥman said in the name of Shmuel:** [5]**If** a suitor **asks** a widow **to marry** him **and she agrees** to his proposal, **she is no** longer **entitled to maintenance** from her first husband's estate, even if she has not yet remarried, for she is no longer considered as living in widowhood.

הָא [6]The Gemara asks: Can we infer from Shmuel's ruling that **if** the widow **did not agree** to the suitor's proposal, **she is still entitled to maintenance,** even if her reason for rejecting the proposal was not due to lingering attachment to her late husband but because she felt that her suitor was not right for her?

אֲמַר רַב עָנָן [7]**Rav Anan said** in reply: **I myself personally heard Mar Shmuel explain** this law as follows: **If** a widow receives a proposal of marriage and rejects it, **saying:** [8]"I cannot marry you **because** I still feel an attachment to **So-and-so, my** late **husband,"** [9]**she is** still **entitled to maintenance** from her husband's estate. [10]But **if her refusal was because** her suitor **was unfit for her, she is no** longer **entitled to maintenance** from her late husband's estate, since she has demonstrated that she is ready to terminate her widowhood and remarry if she finds a suitable match.

אָמַר רַב חִסְדָּא [11]The Gemara continues: **Rav Ḥisda said: If** a widow does not remarry but **engages in sexual relations, she is no** longer **entitled to maintenance** from her late husband's estate, for she has shown that she no longer honors his memory. [12]**Rav Yosef said: If** a widow **applies paint to her eyelids or dyes her**

RASHI

אבל מזוני אית לה — בבית אביה מנכסיו, ולא אמרינן כיון דלא קרינן בה ״ואת תהא יתבא בביתי״ לא קרינן בה ״ומתזנא מנכסי״. ורב יוסף ״בביתי״ יתירא דריש, דתקון למכתב ״בביתי״ תרי זימני ״ואת תהא יתבא בביתי כל ימי מיגר ארמלותיך בביתי״. [**ונתפייסה** — תו לא קרינן בה ״מיגר אלמנותיך״]. **הא לא נתפייסה יש לה** — בתמיה, ואפילו אין העכבה מחמת כבוד בעלה, אלא שלא היה תובעה הגון לה? **ביחלה ופירכסה** — גליא דעתה דלא מחמת כבוד בעלה מעכבת לינשא.

LANGUAGE

בְּבִיקְתִי In my hut. The etymology of this word is unclear, although the Sages interpreted it as a contraction of בֵּי עָקְתָא, meaning "narrow house". At all events, the reference is to a house in which it is extremely difficult to live.

SAGES

מָר בַּר רַב אַשִׁי Mar bar Rav Ashi. A Babylonian Amora of the seventh generation, Mar bar Rav Ashi was the son of the famous Amora, Rav Ashi. His personal name was Tavyumi. He studied under his father, inheriting his position as head of the Mata Meḥasya Yeshivah twenty-four years after his father's death. He held this position for thirteen years.

רַב עָנָן Rav Anan. A Babylonian Amora of the second generation, Rav Anan was a disciple of Shmuel, many of whose teachings he transmitted. He also transmitted teachings in the name of Rav. After Shmuel's death, Rav Anan became one of the judges of the city of Neharde'a. Rav Anan was a younger contemporary of Rav Huna and an older contemporary of Rav Naḥman. Rav Anan's teachings, both in the name of Shmuel and in his own name, are found in several places in the Talmud, and several Sages of the following generation cite teachings in his name.

מְזוֹנוֹת. [1]מַאן דְּאָמַר: זִינְּתָה, כָּל שֶׁכֵּן כִּיחֲלָה וּפִירְכְּסָה. [2]מַאן דְּאָמַר: כִּיחֲלָה וּפִירְכְּסָה, [3]אֲבָל זִינְּתָה, אִית לָהּ. [4]מַאי טַעֲמָא? יֵצֶר אֲנָסָהּ.

[5]וְלֵית הִלְכְתָא כְּכָל הָנֵי שְׁמַעְתָּתָא, [6]אֶלָּא כִּי הָא דְּאָמַר רַב יְהוּדָה אָמַר שְׁמוּאֵל: הַתּוֹבַעַת כְּתוּבָּתָהּ בְּבֵית דִּין אֵין לָהּ מְזוֹנוֹת.

[7]וְלָא? [8]וְהָתַנְיָא: "מָכְרָה כְּתוּבָּתָהּ, וּמִשְׁכְּנָה כְּתוּבָּתָהּ,

LITERAL TRANSLATION

maintenance. [1][According to] the one who said: [If] she fornicated, how much more so [if] she painted her eyelids or dyed her hair. [2][According to] the one who said: [If] she painted her eyelids or dyed her hair, [3]but [if] she fornicated, she has [maintenance]. [4]What is the reason? Passion forced her.

[5]But the law is not in accordance with all these traditions, [6]but in accordance with what Rav Yehudah said in the name of Shmuel: She who claims her ketubah in court does not have maintenance.

[7]But [does she] not? [8]But surely it was taught: "[If] she sold her ketubah, or she pledged her ketubah,

TRANSLATION AND COMMENTARY

hair, in order to make herself more attractive to potential suitors, **she is no** longer **entitled to maintenance** from her late husband's estate. [1]The Gemara now considers what Rav Ḥisda and Rav Yosef would each say about the case discussed by the other. **According to** Rav Ḥisda, **who says** that a widow is no longer entitled to maintenance from her husband's estate **if she engages in sexual relations** with another man during her widowhood, **all the more so** would she not be entitled to maintenance from his estate **if she applied paint to her eyelids or dyed her hair,** for in the first case she did not indicate that she wished to remarry, whereas in the second she did. [2]But **according to** Rav Yosef, **who says** that a widow is no longer entitled to maintenance from her husband's estate **if she applies paint to her eyelids or dyes her hair,** [3]it is possible to say that **if she were to engage in sexual relations** during her widowhood, **she** would still **be entitled to maintenance.** [4]**What is the reason?** By putting on makeup in order to make herself more attractive, the widow demonstrated that she no longer wished to honor her late husband by remaining his widow, and thereby forfeited her right to maintenance. But if she engaged in sexual relations, she did not indicate that she wished to terminate her widowhood, for she may have been **overcome by** her sexual **passion.**

וְלֵית הִלְכְתָא [5]The Gemara rejects these rulings limiting a widow's right to maintenance, and concludes: **The law is not in accordance with any of these traditions,** [6]**but in accordance with what Rav Yehudah said in the name of Shmuel: If** a widow **claims her ketubah in court,** thereby demonstrating that she wishes to break off all ties with her late husband, **she is no** longer **entitled to maintenance** from his estate.

וְלָא [7]The Gemara asks: **But** is it really true that a widow **is not** entitled to maintenance from her late husband's estate once she has claimed her ketubah? [8]**Surely it was taught** in the following Baraita: **"If** a woman **sells her ketubah, or** if **she pledges her ketubah** as security for a debt that she owes,

NOTES

וְלֵית הִלְכְתָא כְּכָל הָנֵי שְׁמַעְתָּתָא **But the law is not in accordance with all these traditions.** According to *Tosafot,* this statement is imprecise, because the law is in fact in accordance with the viewpoint of Shmuel that if a suitor asks a widow to marry him and she accepts his proposal, she is no longer entitled to maintenance from her late husband's estate.

Rif and most other Rishonim maintain that the Gemara's statement is indeed precise, because the law is not in accordance with any of the views cited earlier, even that of Shmuel.

Ritva argues that the expression "with all these traditions" supports the viewpoint of *Rif,* for according to *Tosafot* the expression is inappropriate, since the Gemara wishes to exclude only two positions — that of Rav Ḥisda and that of Rav Yosef.

מָכְרָה כְּתוּבָּתָהּ, וּמִשְׁכְּנָה כְּתוּבָּתָהּ **If she sold her ketubah, or she pledged her ketubah.** A woman who sells or

HALAKHAH

הַתּוֹבַעַת כְּתוּבָּתָהּ בְּבֵית דִּין **She who claims her ketubah in court.** "Once a widow has claimed her ketubah in court, she is no longer entitled to maintenance from her husband's estate. She forfeits her right to maintenance the moment she puts forward her claim, even if she has not yet been paid her ketubah. According to some authorities (*Rosh,* following the Jerusalem Talmud), the widow does not forfeit her right to maintenance if she claims her ketubah because she is in serious financial difficulty (the maintenance she is receiving being insufficient), or if she is tricked into demanding her ketubah by her husband's heirs, who tell her that a certain man wishes to marry her." (*Rambam, Sefer Nashim, Hilkot Ishut* 18:1; *Shulḥan Arukh, Even HaEzer* 93:5.)

מָכְרָה כְּתוּבָּתָהּ **If she sold her ketubah.** "If a woman sells her ketubah, or pledges it as security for a debt, or makes

LANGUAGE

אַפּוֹתֵיקִי Hypothec. This word is derived from the Greek ὑποθήκη, *hypotheke,* meaning "mortgage," or "security." As used by the Sages, the word has a special meaning — a hypothec applying to a specific piece of property (unlike אַחֲרָיוּת — "responsibility," which is a generalized mortgage against all the borrower's property). The Sages also interpreted it as a compound of Aramaic words: אַפּוֹ תְּהֵי קָאֵי — "on this let it stand." If a specific piece of property has been mortgaged to guarantee a loan or some other obligation, the creditor has no right to claim other property owned by the debtor; nor may he demand an additional sum if the value of the property has fallen.

TRANSLATION AND COMMENTARY

or if she makes her ketubah a hypothec for a loan, specifying that the debt is to be collected from the ketubah alone, and her husband dies — [1]in all these cases the widow **is not entitled to maintenance** from her late husband's estate." [2]Now, this Baraita seems to imply that only in **these** cases does the widow **in fact** forfeit her right to maintenance, for in each of these cases she is viewed as having already received her ketubah. [3]**But if** the widow **were** merely **to claim** her ketubah, she would **not** forfeit her right to maintenance from her husband's estate. How, then, can Shmuel maintain the position that if a widow claims her ketubah, she is no longer entitled to maintenance from her late husband's estate?

הָנֵי [4]The Gemara answers: The inference drawn from the Baraita is incorrect, for a widow does in fact forfeit her right to maintenance when she claims her ketubah. Why, then, did the Baraita mention only those cases in which she sells or pledges her ketubah? It was because in **those** cases the widow forfeits her right to maintenance **whether** she comes **to court or not.** [5]But if the widow **claims** her ketubah, only if she comes **to court** does she forfeit her right to maintenance from her late husband's estate. [6]But if she claims her ketubah **without** going **to court,** she does **not** forfeit her right to maintenance.

וְכָךְ הָיוּ אַנְשֵׁי יְרוּשָׁלַיִם [7]The Gemara now discusses the last part of our Mishnah, which stated: **"The people of Jerusalem used to write** the ketubah using the following formula: 'You will live in my house and be maintained from my property all the days that you live in widowhood in my house.' The people of Galilee used to write the ketubah using the same text as the people of Jerusalem. But the people of Judea used to formulate the ketubah deed as follows: 'You will live in my house and be maintained from my property until my heirs wish to give you your ketubah.'" [8]**It was stated** that the Amoraim disagreed about which of the two customs should be followed. **Rav said: The law is in accordance with** the custom of **the people of Judea.** The husband's heirs can compel his widow to accept her ketubah and can then send her away ot provide her own maintenance and housing. [9]**But Shmuel said: The law is in accordance with** the custom of the people of Jerusalem and **Galilee,** and it is the widow who decides whether to collect her

עָשְׂתָה כְּתוּבָּתָהּ אַפּוֹתֵיקִי לְאַחֵר, [1]אֵין לָהּ מְזוֹנוֹת״. [2]הָנֵי — אִין; [3]אֲבָל תּוֹבַעַת — לָא! [4]הָנֵי — בֵּין בְּבֵית דִּין, בֵּין שֶׁלֹּא בְּבֵית דִּין. [5]תּוֹבַעַת, בְּבֵית דִּין — אִין; [6]שֶׁלֹּא בְּבֵית דִּין — לָא.

[7]״וְכָךְ הָיוּ אַנְשֵׁי יְרוּשָׁלַיִם, וכו׳״. [8]אִתְּמַר: רַב אָמַר: הֲלָכָה כְּאַנְשֵׁי יְהוּדָה. [9]וּשְׁמוּאֵל אָמַר: הֲלָכָה כְּאַנְשֵׁי גָּלִיל.

LITERAL TRANSLATION

[or] she made her ketubah a hypothec for someone else, [1]she does not have maintenance." [2]These — yes; [3]but she who claims — not!

[4]These — whether in the court or not in the court. [5]She who claims, in the court — yes; [6]not in the court — not.

[7]"And this is how the people of Jerusalem used to [write], etc." [8]It was stated: Rav said: The law is in accordance with the people of Judea. [9]But Shmuel said: The law is in accordance with the people of Galilee.

RASHI

עשתה כתובתה אפותיקי – קרקע המיוחדת לכתובתה, עשתה אפותיקי לבעל חוב שלה. **הני אין** – לפי שהן גיבוי כתובה, אבל תביעה – לא.

NOTES

pledges her ketubah forfeits her right to maintenance from her husband's estate, because she is viewed as having already received her ketubah. Thus she forfeits her right to maintenance only if she sells or pledges her entire ketubah; but if she sells or pledges only part of it, she is still entitled to maintenance. Even if she actually receives part of her ketubah money, she is still entitled to maintenance until the ketubah is paid in its entirety (see below, 97b).

כְּאַנְשֵׁי יְהוּדָה... כְּאַנְשֵׁי גָּלִיל In accordance with the people of Judea...in accordance with the people of Galilee. The Jerusalem Talmud explains the two customs as follows: "The people of Galilee were concerned about the widow's honor, but they were not concerned about the heirs' money. The people of Judea were concerned about the heirs' money, but they were not concerned about the widow's honor." The Galileans were more concerned about defending the widow's honor, and therefore they allowed her to choose to be maintained from her late husband's estate for the duration of her widowhood or until she claimed her ketubah. The Judeans were more concerned about the heirs' money, and therefore they stipulated that the heirs could decide to terminate the widow's maintenance by compelling her to accept her ketubah.

HALAKHAH

it a hypothec, whether she does one of these things during her husband's lifetime or only after he has died, and whether the transaction takes place before the court or not, she forfeits her right to maintenance from her husband's estate, following our Gemara's explanation of the Baraita. As for the case in which the woman sells her ketubah, but not in the presence of the court, *Shulḥan Arukh* implies that she forfeits her right to maintenance only if the sale takes place before three reliable people (see *Bet Shmuel* and *Ḥelkat Meḥokek,* who reject this position)." (*Rambam, Sefer Nashim, Hilkhot Ishut* 18:1; *Shulḥan Arukh, Even HaEzer* 93:8.)

TRANSLATION AND COMMENTARY

ketubah or to continue to receive maintenance from her late husband's heirs. [1] The Gemara notes that **in Babylon and the surrounding areas,** including the city of Sura where Rav was the head of the Academy, the people **acted in accordance with** the ruling of **Rav,** [2] whereas **in Neharde'a and the surrounding areas,** [3] the people **acted in accordance with** the ruling of **Shmuel,** the head of the Academy in Neharde'a.

הַהִיא בַּת מְחוֹזָא [4] It was related that **a certain woman from Meḥoza,** a city close to Babylon, **was** to be **married to a man from Neharde'a.** [5] When **they came before Rav Naḥman** to discuss matters relating to their ketubah, [6] **he could hear from her accent that she was from Meḥoza.** [7] Rav Naḥman **said to them: "In Babylon and the surrounding areas,** [8] the people **act in accordance with** the ruling of **Rav** that the ketubah deed is to be formulated according to the custom of the people of Judea." [9] Those who heard Rav Naḥman's ruling **said to him:** "It is true that the bride comes from Meḥoza, **but surely she is** to be **married to a man from Neharde'a,** and therefore we should consider the practice of his townsmen!" [10] Rav Naḥman **said to them: "If so,** then this is my decision: **In Neharde'a and the surrounding areas,** [11] the people **act in accordance with** the ruling of **Shmuel** that the ketubah is to be formulated according to the custom of the people of Galilee." [12] In conclusion, the Gemara asks: **How far** from **Neharde'a** do the Halakhic norms of that city **extend?** [13] The Gemara answers: **As far as the measure of Neharde'a is in use.** Places where people measure their grain using the measures of Neharde'a are governed by the Halakhic practices of Neharde'a.

אִיתְּמַר [14] **It was stated** that the Amoraim disagreed about a particular aspect **of a widow's** ketubah. **Rav said:** When the court awards a widow her ketubah, **it assesses the** value of the **clothing she is wearing** and deducts that amount from the sum due to her as her ketubah. [15] **But Shmuel said:** The court **does not assess** the value of **the clothing** the widow **is wearing** when they assess her ketubah.

[1] בָּבֶל וְכָל פַּרְוָודָהָא, נְהוּג כְּרַב. [2] נְהַרְדְּעָא וְכָל פַּרְוָודָהָא, [3] נְהוּג כִּשְׁמוּאֵל.
[4] הַהִיא בַּת מְחוֹזָא דַּהֲוַת נְסִיבָא לִנְהַרְדְּעָא. [5] אָתוּ לְקַמֵּיהּ דְּרַב נַחְמָן. [6] שְׁמָעָהּ לְקָלָהּ דְּבַת מְחוֹזָא הִיא. [7] אֲמַר לְהוּ: ״בָּבֶל וְכָל פַּרְוָודָהָא, [8] נְהוּג כְּרַב״. [9] אָמְרוּ לֵיהּ: ״וְהָא לִנְהַרְדְּעָא נְסִיבָא!״ [10] אֲמַר לְהוּ: ״אִי הָכִי, נְהַרְדְּעָא וְכָל פַּרְוָודָהָא, [11] נְהוּג כִּשְׁמוּאֵל״. [12] וְעַד הֵיכָא נְהַרְדְּעָא? [13] עַד הֵיכָא דְּסָגֵי קַבָּא דִּנְהַרְדְּעָא.
[14] אִיתְּמַר: אַלְמָנָה, רַב אָמַר: שָׁמִין מַה שֶּׁעָלֶיהָ. [15] וּשְׁמוּאֵל אָמַר: אֵין שָׁמִין מַה שֶּׁעָלֶיהָ.

LITERAL TRANSLATION

[1] [In] Babylon and all her outskirts, they act in accordance with Rav. [2] [In] Neharde'a and all her outskirts, [3] they act in accordance with Shmuel.

[4] [There was] a certain woman from Meḥoza who was married to a Neharde'an. [5] They came before Rav Naḥman. [6] He heard from her voice that she was from Meḥoza. [7] He said to them: "[In] Babylon and all her outskirts, [8] they act in accordance with Rav." [9] They said to him: "But surely she is married to a Neharde'an!" [10] He said to them: "If so, [in] Neharde'a and all her outskirts, [11] they act in accordance with Shmuel." [12] And how far [does] Neharde'a [extend]? [13] As far as the measure of Neharde'a is in use (lit., "spreads").

[14] It was stated: [In the case of] a widow, Rav said: [15] We assess what is on her. But Shmuel said: We do not assess what is on her.

RASHI

פרוודהא — כרכים הסמוכים לה. **מחוזא** — מפרוודי בבל. **דסגי קבא דנהרדעא** — כל מקום שמודדין תבואה במדת קב נהרדעא. **שמין מה שעליה** — כשמגבין לה בית דין כתובתה — שמין בגדיה בפרעון כתובה.

BACKGROUND

בָּבֶל, נְהַרְדְּעָא, וּמְחוֹזָא Babylon, Neharde'a, and Meḥoza.

קַבָּא דִּנְהַרְדְּעָא The measure of Neharde'a. In ancient times (and even today, in certain countries), different units of measurement (and units of weight and volume in particular) were used in different parts of the same country — sometimes even in neighboring cities. Apparently, these varying measurement units stemmed from different systems, which were originally used in once-independent municipalities. The Jewish community in Babylonia in the Talmudic period was divided into several districts, which differed in terms of local Halakhic practice and manners of speech (note how Rav Naḥman was able to determine the origins of the woman who appeared before him). Thus the boundaries of Neharde'a were determined (for the purpose of deciding which customs were binding) by the units of measurement used there.

HALAKHAH

הֲלָכָה כְּאַנְשֵׁי גָּלִיל The law is in accordance with the people of Galilee. "A widow is entitled to maintenance from the property of her husband's estate throughout her widowhood, even if this was not explicitly stipulated in her ketubah. As long as the widow does not claim her ketubah, her husband's heirs cannot compel her to take it and thus release themselves from their obligation to maintain her, unless this was stipulated in her ketubah or was the local custom. (*Bet Yosef* in the name of *Rivash* rules that the local courts can pass an enactment that the heirs can compel the widow to receive her ketubah.) Most of the Rishonim rule in accordance with Shmuel and against Rav that the law follows the people of Jerusalem and Galilee." (*Rambam, Sefer Nashim, Hilkhot Ishut* 18:1; *Shulḥan Arukh, Even HaEzer* 93:3.)

שָׁמִין מַה שֶּׁעָלֶיהָ We assess what is on her. "If a widow (or a *ḥalutzah*; *Bet Yosef* in the name of *Rivash*) comes to collect her ketubah, the court assesses the value of all the clothing that her husband gave her, both her weekday clothes and her Shabbat wear, and deducts that amount from the sum that is due to her as her ketubah," following Rav Naḥman who ruled in accordance with Rav. (*Rambam, Sefer Nashim, Hilkhot Ishut* 16:4; *Shulḥan Arukh, Even HaEzer* 99:1.)

TRANSLATION AND COMMENTARY

אָמַר רַב חִיָּיא בַּר אָבִין [1] **Rav Ḥiyya bar Avin said:** The dispute between Rav and Shmuel **is reversed in the case of a worker** who lives in his employer's house and receives clothing from him while he is living there. In that case, too, Rav and Shmuel disagree about whether we assess the value of the clothing that the worker is wearing when his employment ends and the employer pays him the balance of his salary. But in that case it is Shmuel who says that the value of the worker's clothing is assessed and that amount is deducted from the sum the employer owes his worker. And it is Rav who says that no such assessment is made. [2] **Rav Kahana taught** a different version of the dispute between Rav and Shmuel regarding a worker: Just as they disagree about a widow who comes to collect her ketubah, **so too** do they disagree **about a worker** who comes to collect his salary. Rav maintains that we assess the value of the clothing that the worker takes with him when his employment ends and we deduct that amount from his salary. But Shmuel maintains that we do not assess the value of his clothing. [3] **A mnemonic device was suggested** by Rav to make it easier to remember his position: **"Undress and send out the orphan and the widow."** According to Rav, when a worker (called an "orphan" here, because most workers are poor like orphans) comes to collect his salary or when a widow comes to collect her ketubah, we should "undress them" and assess the value of the clothing they are to take with them, and deduct that amount from the sum they receive.

אָמַר רַב נַחְמָן [4] Continuing the discussion about a widow's clothing, **Rav Naḥman said: Even though we have learned in a Mishnah** a ruling that is **in accordance with** the viewpoint of **Shmuel,** [5] **the law is in accordance with** the viewpoint of **Rav.** [6] **For we have learned** in the Mishnah (*Arakhin* 24a): **"Whether someone dedicates his property to the Temple** treasury **or takes a vow of valuation,** promising to pay the Temple treasury the specific value set down in the Torah for a person of his age and sex, [7] **the Temple treasurer has no right to** seize **his wife's clothing or his children's clothing,** for the clothing of a man's wife and children does not belong to him. [8] Nor may the Temple treasurer seize **the** new **clothing that** the dedicator **has dyed for** his wife or children, **or the new sandals that he has bought for them,** even if they have not

[1] אָמַר רַב חִיָּיא בַּר אָבִין: וְחִילוּפָה בְּלָקִיט. [2] רַב כָּהֲנָא מַתְנֵי: וְכֵן בְּלָקִיט. [3] וּמַנַּח בָּהּ סִימָנָא: ״יַתְמָא וְאַרְמַלְתָּא שַׁלַּח וּפוֹק״.

[4] אֲמַר רַב נַחְמָן: אַף עַל גַּב דִּתְנַן בְּמַתְנִיתִין כְּוָותֵיהּ דִּשְׁמוּאֵל, [5] הִלְכְתָא כְּוָותֵיהּ דְּרַב. [6] דִּתְנַן: ״אֶחָד הַמַּקְדִּישׁ נְכָסָיו, וְאֶחָד הַמַּעֲרִיךְ אֶת עַצְמוֹ, [7] אֵין לוֹ לֹא בִּכְסוּת אִשְׁתּוֹ, וְלֹא בִּכְסוּת בָּנָיו, וְלֹא בְּצֶבַע שֶׁצָּבַע לִשְׁמָן, [8] וְלֹא בְּסַנְדָּלִים חֲדָשִׁים שֶׁלָּקַח לִשְׁמָן״.

LITERAL TRANSLATION

[1] Rav Ḥiyya bar Avin said: And the reverse [is the case] regarding a worker (lit., "gleaner"). [2] Rav Kahana teaches: And so too regarding a worker. [3] And he laid down a mnemonic: "Undress and send out the orphan and the widow."

[4] Rav Naḥman said: Even though we have learned in a Mishnah in accordance with Shmuel, [5] the law is in accordance with Rav. [6] For we have learned: "Whether someone consecrates his property to the Temple, or consecrates his own value, [7] [the Temple treasurer] has no [right] either to his wife's clothing, or to his children's clothing, [8] or to the dyed [clothing] that he dyed for them, or to the new sandals that he bought for them."

RASHI

בלקיט — שכיר שגר בבית בעל הבית, ולקח לו בעל הבית בגדים. כשיוצא ממנו — שם אותן בגדים בשכרו לשמואל, ורב אמר: אין שמין. **וכן בלקיט** — לרב שמין, ולשמואל אין שמין. **ומנח בה** — רב סימנא במילתיה. **יתמא וארמלתא שלח ופוק** — הפשט בגדיהן וצא. **יתמא** — לקיט. **דתנן במתניתין** — בהך דערכין. **אחד המקדיש נכסיו כו׳ ואחד המעריך עצמו** — והגזבר בא למשכנו על ערכו הקצוב בפרשה, אין לו לגזבר לא בכסות אשתו כו׳. **לשמן** — בגדים שצבע לשם אשתו ולשם בניו, ואף על פי שלא לבשום עדיין. אלמא בגדיה שלה, כשמואל.

NOTES

יַתְמָא וְאַרְמַלְתָּא **The orphan and the widow.** *Rivan* explains that a worker is referred to here as an orphan because he is treated as an orphan who is sent out without proper clothing.

Rivan maintains that we assess the value of the clothing that the employer provided for his worker only if the worker's wages were not set before he started working. In such a case we say that the employer provided the worker with clothing as part of his wages. But if the parties agreed on the worker's wages from the outset, we do not deduct

HALAKHAH

אֵין לוֹ לֹא בִּכְסוּת אִשְׁתּוֹ **The Temple treasurer has no right either to his wife's clothing.** "If someone makes a vow of valuation, or vows his actual value to the Temple treasury, all of his property may be seized as a pledge or

¹אֲמַר לֵיהּ רָבָא לְרַב נַחְמָן: וְכִי מֵאַחַר דִּתְנַן מַתְנִיתִין כְּוָותֵיהּ דִּשְׁמוּאֵל, ²אַמַּאי הִלְכְתָא כְּוָותֵיהּ דְּרַב?
³אֲמַר לֵיהּ: לִכְאוֹרָה, כִּשְׁמוּאֵל רְהִיטָא. ⁴כִּי מְעַיְּינַתְּ בָּהּ, הִלְכְתָא כְּוָותֵיהּ דְּרַב. ⁵מַאי טַעֲמָא? ⁶כִּי אַקְנֵי לָהּ, אַדַּעְתָּא לְמֵיקַם קַמֵּיהּ. ⁷אַדַּעְתָּא לְמִשְׁקַל וּלְמֵיפַּק לָא אַקְנֵי לָהּ.
⁸כַּלְּתָא דְּבֵי בַּר אֶלְיָשִׁיב הֲוָה קָא תָּבְעָה כְּתוּבָּתָהּ מִיָּתְמֵי. ⁹הֲוָה קָא מַמְטֵי לְהוּ לְבֵי דִּינָא.

LITERAL TRANSLATION

¹Rava said to Rav Naḥman: But since we have learned a Mishnah in accordance with Shmuel, ²why is the law in accordance with Rav?

³He said to him: At first glance, it runs in accordance with Shmuel. ⁴When you look into it, the law is in accordance with Rav. ⁵What is the reason? ⁶When he transferred [the clothing] to her, it was with the intention that she would stay with him. ⁷He did not transfer [it] to her with the intention that she would take [it] and leave.

⁸A daughter-in-law of the house of Bar Eliashiv was claiming her ketubah from the orphans. ⁹She brought them to court.

TRANSLATION AND COMMENTARY

yet been worn, for they already belong to the wife or the children." This Mishnah supports the viewpoint of Shmuel that the clothing a man provides for his wife is not considered his property, and therefore there is no justification for deducting the value of the widow's clothing from the amount she is to receive as her ketubah. Nevertheless Rav Naḥman argues that the law follows the viewpoint of Rav.

אֲמַר לֵיהּ רָבָא לְרַב נַחְמָן ¹**Rava said to Rav Naḥman:** But since **we have learned** that **the Mishnah** in *Arakhin* is **in accordance with** the viewpoint of **Shmuel,** ²**why** do you rule that **the law is in accordance with** the viewpoint of **Rav?**

אֲמַר לֵיהּ ³Rav Naḥman **said to** Rava: **At first glance,** the Mishnah in *Arakhin* appears to **be in accordance with** the viewpoint of **Shmuel.** ⁴But **when you look into** the Mishnah more carefully, you will see that it implies that **the law is in accordance with** the viewpoint of **Rav.** ⁵**Why** do I say this? ⁶**When** a man **gives** his wife **clothing, it is with the intention that** the clothing will be hers **as long as they are married.** ⁷But **he does not give her** the clothing **with the intention that** it will permanently belong to her, so that **she can take it** with her if she **leaves him.** Thus the Mishnah teaches that the Temple treasurer cannot seize a woman's clothing as security for a vow taken by her husband, since as long as the couple are married the clothing belongs to the woman. But since the husband wants the clothing to belong to his wife only while she is with him, she is no longer entitled to it after she is widowed, and its value must be deducted from the amount paid to her as her ketubah, in accordance with the viewpoint of Rav.

כַּלְּתָא דְּבֵי בַּר אֶלְיָשִׁיב ⁸The Gemara now relates that **a** widowed **daughter-in-law of the family of Bar Eliashiv was claiming her ketubah from the orphans** who had inherited their father's estate. ⁹When **she asked**

RASHI

לכאורה כשמואל ריהטא — פתאום נראית משמעות המשנה כשמואל, אבל כי מעיינת בה — לא מסייעא לשמואל. דהא קמיה קיימא, ואינה יוצאה מביתו, ואדעתא דהכי מקני לה שיהו שלה כל זמן שהיא תחתיו.

LANGUAGE

לִכְאוֹרָה **At first glance.** The exact etymology of this word, which is common in modern Hebrew but appears in the Talmud only here, remains obscure. *Rivan* and *Rid* suggest that לִכְאוֹרָה is synonymous (and interchangeable) with לִכְעוּרָה, which they derive from the Hebrew root כער, meaning "to be repulsive." Thus the Gemara teaches us that only "to a repulsive person," i.e., to one who is not exacting, would it seem that the Halakhah follows Shmuel. Other authorities derive the word לִכְאוֹרָה from the Hebrew word אוֹרָה, meaning "light." Thus לִכְאוֹרָה means "at first light," "at first sight."

NOTES

from the worker's wages the value of the clothing he received from his employer, because the clothing is assumed to have been an outright gift.

According to *Meiri,* we assess the value of the worker's clothing even if the parties agreed on the worker's wages from the outset, for we assume that the employer gave his worker the clothing on the understanding that it would be regarded as partial payment of his wages.

אַדַּעְתָּא לְמִשְׁקַל וּלְמֵיפַּק **With the intention that she would take it and leave.** The Gemara explains that the court assesses the value of the widow's clothing and deducts that amount from the sum due to her as her ketubah, because her husband did not give her the clothing with the intention that she would take it with her when she left him. *Rif* infers from this that in the case of a divorcee the court does not assess the value of her clothing when she is awarded her ketubah, because the divorcee does not leave her husband of her own free will or as the result of *force majeure,* but rather it is her husband who sends her away.

Ba'al HaMa'or and *Ra'ah* disagree with this view, arguing that if we say that the husband does not give his wife her clothing with the intention that she keep it if she is widowed, when the separation between them is caused by *force majeure,* he certainly does not give her the clothing with the intention that she keep it if he himself brings about the separation and divorces her.

HALAKHAH

as payment of the vow. But the Temple treasurer may not seize his wife's clothing or his children's clothing, or the new clothing that he dyed for his wife or his children, or the new sandals that he bought for them. Similarly, if a man consecrates all his property to the Temple treasury, these articles are not included," following the Mishnah cited here. (*Rambam, Sefer Hafla'ah, Hilkhot Arakhin* 3:14.)

LANGUAGE

נְדוּנְיָא Dowry. This word is apparently related to the Biblical Hebrew נָדָן, meaning "gift" (cf. Ezekiel 16:33), which is synonymous with מוֹהַר, meaning "dowry," and denotes the property that a bride brings with her when she marries.

פּוּרְנָא Profit. This word is derived from the Greek φερνή, *pherne*, meaning "dowry."

SAGES

רַב אִידִי בַּר אָבִין Rav Idi bar Avin. A Babylonian Amora of the third and fourth generations. See *Ketubot*, Part II, p. 230.

TRANSLATION AND COMMENTARY

them to go to court with her to arrange a settlement, [1] **they** shrewdly **said** to her: **"It is degrading to us that you dress like that,** in your everyday clothes. Go and put on your most elegant garments." [2] **She went and dressed herself in all of her** finest **clothing.** [3] When **they came before Ravina** for a ruling on her ketubah, [4] **he said to them: The law is in accordance with** the view of **Rav,** [5] **who said** that **in the case of a widow** who comes to collect her ketubah, the court **assesses** the value of the clothing **she is wearing** and deducts that amount from the sum that is due to her as her ketubah. Thus the value of all of the clothing that the widow is wearing must be deducted from the final settlement of her ketubah.

הַהוּא דַּאֲמַר לְהוּ [6] The Gemara continues by relating that **there was a certain man who said to** those who were present while he was lying on his deathbed: **"Provide** from my property **a dowry for my daughter."** By Rabbinic decree, the gift of a person on his deathbed is valid even if no act of acquisition was performed. As a result, the daughter became entitled to the standard dowry given to a girl of her social standing in that particular locality. [7] But in the meantime **the** various items customarily provided as a girl's **dowry went down in price,** so that they could now be bought for less money than at the time the father issued his instructions. The question arose as to who was entitled to the difference between the amount that the father had intended to spend on his daughter's dowry and the amount that it would actually cost. [8] **Rav Idi bar Avin said:** The daughter is given the customary dowry, and **the saving goes to the orphans** who inherited their father's estate.

[1] אָמְרִי: ״זִילָא לָן מִילְּתָא דְּתֵיזְלִי הָכִי״. [2] אָזְלָא לְבִישְׁתִּינְהוּ וְאִיכַּסְתִּינְהוּ לְכוּלֵּיהּ מָנָא. [3] אָתוּ לְקַמֵּיהּ דְּרָבִינָא, [4] אֲמַר לְהוּ: הִלְכְתָא כְּוָותֵיהּ דְּרַב, [5] דְּאָמַר: אַלְמָנָה, שָׁמִין מַה שֶּׁעָלֶיהָ.

[6] הַהוּא דַּאֲמַר לְהוּ: ״נְדוּנְיָא לִבְרָת״. [7] זַל נְדוּנְיָא. [8] אֲמַר רַב אִידִי בַּר אָבִין: פּוּרְנָא לְיַתְמֵי.

LITERAL TRANSLATION

[1] They said: "It is degrading to us that you go like that." [2] She went [and] dressed and covered herself with all of her clothing. [3] They came before Ravina, [4] [and] he said to them: The law is in accordance with Rav, [5] who says: [In the case of] a widow, we assess what is on her.

[6] [There was] a certain [man] who said to them: "[Let] a dowry [be given] for my daughter." [7] The dowry went down in value. [8] Rav Idi bar Avin said: The profit is for the orphans.

RASHI

ההוא דאמר להו – צואת שכיב מרע. **נדוניא לברת** – קצובים היו תכשיטי הבנות, כך וכך לבושים. **פורנא ליתמי** – הריוח ליתומים. ולא אמרינן ניתיב לה דמי הנדוניא כיום הצוואה.

NOTES

זִילָא לָן מִילְּתָא It is degrading to us. *Rivan* explains that the heirs asked the widow to put on her finest garments when she went to court, so that the judges would see her most costly clothing and deduct their value from the final settlement of her ketubah.

Meiri asks: Why was it necessary for the heirs to trick the widow into appearing before the judges in her finest clothes? If the court assesses the value of the clothing that the widow is wearing, then it certainly assesses the value of the clothing hanging in her closet! Rather, the heirs tricked the widow into wearing her costly clothing in court so that she would not be able to deny having such garments when the court came to assess her clothing.

נְדוּנְיָא לִבְרָת "Let a dowry be given for my daughter." *Rosh* prefers the reading: "Let a dowry worth 400 zuz be given for my daughter," for if the father did not specify an amount, then the heirs can surely keep for themselves the difference between the amount that the father had intended to spend on his daughter's dowry and the amount that it actually cost. Rather, the novelty of Rav Idi bar Avin's ruling is that the heirs can keep such savings for themselves, even if the father specified the amount of his daughter's dowry. We assume that the father did not mean that that particular sum must be spent on the dowry, but that his daughter was to be provided with a dowry worth that amount on the day he issued his instructions.

פּוּרְנָא לְיַתְמֵי The profit is for the orphans. *Rosh* and *Meiri* note that orphans must also bear the loss if the cost of the dowry increased between the time the father gave his instructions and the time his heirs carried them out. In such a case the heirs must provide the daughter with the customary dowry, even though it will cost them more than the father had intended to spend.

HALAKHAH

נְדוּנְיָא לִבְרָת "Let a dowry be given for my daughter." "If someone gives instructions on his deathbed that his daughter is to be provided from his property with a dowry consisting of certain specified items, and in the meantime the cost of these items decreases, the heirs who inherit his estate are entitled to the saving, and they may provide her with the dowry at the lower cost," following Rav Idi bar Avin. (*Rambam, Sefer Kinyan, Hilkhot Zekhiyah U'Mattanah* 11:22; *Shulḥan Arukh, Ḥoshen Mishpat* 253:16.)

TRANSLATION AND COMMENTARY

הַהוּא דַּאֲמַר לְהוּ [1] The Gemara now relates that **there was a certain man who said to** those who were present when he was lying on his deathbed: [54B] [2] "Set aside **four hundred zuz of this wine for** the dowry of **my daughter."** [3] Meanwhile, before the daughter received her dowry, **the wine went up in value,** and what had been worth four hundred zuz was now worth more. The question arose as to who was entitled to the difference between the amount that the father had intended to provide as his daughter's dowry and the present value of the wine that had been set aside for that dowry. [4] **Rav Yosef said:** The daughter is given a dowry of four hundred zuz, and **the profit** from the appreciation in the value of the wine **belongs to the orphans** who inherited their father's estate.

קְרֵיבֵיהּ דְּרַבִּי יוֹחָנָן [5] The Gemara concludes this chapter with another story regarding a widow's maintenance. Certain **relatives of Rabbi Yoḥanan** thought that **their father's wife was spending** his money **wastefully on her maintenance.** They were concerned that after their father died the estate that they would inherit from him would be squandered on her maintenance. [6] **They came before Rabbi Yoḥanan** to ask his advice on the matter, **and he said to them:** [7] **"Go and tell your father that he should designate** a specific piece of **land for her maintenance.** If she agrees to such an arrangement, she will thereby waive her right to collect her maintenance from the rest of her husband's property." The father followed Rabbi Yoḥanan's

[1] הַהוּא דַּאֲמַר לְהוּ: [54B] [2] ״אַרְבַּע מֵאָה זוּזֵי מִן חַמְרָא לִבְרַת.״ [3] אִיַּיקַר חַמְרָא. [4] אֲמַר רַב יוֹסֵף: רַוְוחָא לְיָתְמֵי. [5] קְרֵיבֵיהּ דְּרַבִּי יוֹחָנָן הֲוָה לְהוּ אִיתַּת אַבָּא דַּהֲוָה קָמַפְסְדָה מְזוֹנֵי. [6] אֲתוּ לְקַמֵּיהּ דְּרַבִּי יוֹחָנָן, אֲמַר לְהוּ: [7] ״אֵיזִילוּ וְאִמְרוּ לֵיהּ לַאֲבוּכוֹן דְּנַיֵּיחֵד לָהּ אַרְעָא

LITERAL TRANSLATION

[1] [There was] a certain [man] who said to them: [54B] [2] "Four hundred zuz from [this] wine are for my daughter." [3] The wine went up in value. [4] Rav Yosef said: The profit is for the orphans.

[5] The relatives of Rabbi Yoḥanan had a father's wife who was wasting maintenance. [6] They came before Rabbi Yoḥanan, [and] he said to them: [7] "Go and tell your father that he should designate land for her

RASHI

ארבע מאה זוזי מן חמרא — משמע: אותו יין יהא משועבד לכך, אבל היין עצמו לא אמר ליתן לה כדמיו של יום הלוואה. **מפסדה מזוני** — מרבה לאכול. **דנייחד לה** — בלוואת שכיב מרע, ובעדים, אולי תקבל עליה. דאפילו גבי כתובה תנן (פאה פ״ג מ״ז): הכותב כל נכסיו לבניו וכתב לאשתו קרקע כל שהוא — אבדה כתובתה. רבי יוסי אומר: אם קבלה עליה, אף על פי שלא כתב לה. לישנא אחרינא: דהוי ליה כמחלק נכסיו על פיו, ונתן שאר הנכסים לבניו. והוה להו משעבדי, ואין הבנות והאשה ניזונות ממשעבדי.

NOTES

מִן חַמְרָא From this wine. In tractate *Gittin* (66a), the Gemara distinguishes between three formulations: חַמְרָא — "wine"; דְּמֵי חַמְרָא — "the monetary value of wine"; and מִן חַמְרָא — "from this wine." The Rishonim disagree about the Halakhic consequences of the various formulations. On the basis of their understanding of the conclusion of the Gemara in *Gittin, Ra'avad* and *Meiri* read in our Gemara: "400 zuz of the value of the wine [מִדְּמֵי חַמְרָא] are for my daughter." Only if the father formulates his instructions in this manner does the profit resulting from the wine's appreciation in value belong to the orphans who inherit their father's estate. But if the father says: "400 zuz from this wine [מִן חַמְרָא] are for my daughter," then the profit resulting from the wine's appreciation in value belongs to the daughter.

רַוְוחָא לְיָתְמֵי The profit is for the orphans. On the basis of his understanding of the conclusion of the Gemara in *Gittin* (see previous note), *Ritva* observes that the loss resulting from the wine's depreciation must also be borne by the orphans. Even if the wine goes down in value, the orphans must still provide the daughter with a dowry worth 400 zuz. Likewise, if some of the wine spills or turns sour, the daughter is not required to bear any of the loss, but is entitled to the full amount specified by her father.

דַּהֲוָה קָמַפְסְדָה מְזוֹנֵי Who was wasting maintenance. *Rashi* explains that Rabbi Yoḥanan's relatives were concerned because their father's wife ate too much. The Rishonim ask: Since a woman is entitled to eat as much as she requires, how could Rabbi Yoḥanan have advised his relatives to infringe that right?

Rivan suggests that the relatives were concerned because their father's wife was not frugal. She wasted her food allowance and expected that her husband's children would continue to provide for all her needs. Therefore they sought advice from Rabbi Yoḥanan as to how to get her to economize.

וְאִמְרוּ לֵיהּ לַאֲבוּכוֹן דְּנַיֵּיחֵד "Tell your father that he should designate." The Rishonim ask: Why did Rabbi Yoḥanan not say about himself here what he said about himself elsewhere (above, 52b) — that by giving his relatives legal advice he was in violation of the prohibition against a judge acting like a lawyer?

Tosafot explains that the prohibition does not apply here, for the arrangement which Rabbi Yoḥanan suggested to his relatives required the agreement of their father's wife. *Rivan* suggests that the incident reported in our Gemara occurred before the incident reported earlier. Only after he had advised his relatives a second time did he begin to be concerned that giving such advice might be forbidden. Others (*Ritva* and *Meiri*) argue that the prohibition does not apply here, for Rabbi Yoḥanan did not tell his relatives how to circumvent an obligation that they would otherwise have had to undertake. He only advised them how to

TERMINOLOGY

מַפֵּיקְנָא לְכוּ...מֵאוּנַיְיכוּ **I will take...out of your ears.** This expression is used in several places in the Talmud by a Sage who is reproaching someone for relying on the ruling of another authority. Since this is an idiomatic expression, it should not be interpreted literally. It means: You must ignore what you have heard and must accept the present ruling.

LITERAL TRANSLATION

for her maintenance." [1]They came before Resh Lakish, [and] he said to them: [2]"All the more so has he increased her maintenance!" [3]They said to him: "But surely Rabbi Yoḥanan did not say this!" [4]He said to them: "Go [and] give her, and if not, I will take Rabbi Yoḥanan out of your ears!" [5]They came before Rabbi Yoḥanan, [and] he said to them: "What can I do? [6]My equal (lit., 'opposite') disagrees with me." [7]Rabbi Abbahu said: It was explained to me [personally] by Rabbi Yoḥanan: [8][If] he said: "Toward maintenance," [9]he has increased her maintenance. [10][If] he said: "As maintenance," [11]he has limited her maintenance.

לִמְזוֹנָהּ״. [1]אָתוּ לְקַמֵּיהּ דְּרֵישׁ לָקִישׁ, אֲמַר לְהוּ: [2]״כָּל שֶׁכֵּן שֶׁרִיבָּה לָהּ מְזוֹנוֹת!״ [3]אָמְרוּ לֵיהּ: ״וְהָא רַבִּי יוֹחָנָן לָא אֲמַר הָכִי!״ [4]אֲמַר לְהוּ: ״זִילוּ הֲבוּ לָהּ, וְאִי לָא, מַפֵּיקְנָא לְכוּ רַבִּי יוֹחָנָן מֵאוּנַיְיכוּ״. [5]אָתוּ לְקַמֵּיהּ דְּרַבִּי יוֹחָנָן, אֲמַר לְהוּ: ״מָה אֶעֱשֶׂה? [6]שֶׁכְּנֶגְדִּי חָלוּק עָלַי״. [7]אֲמַר רַבִּי אַבָּהוּ: לְדִידִי מְפָרְשָׁא לִי מִינֵּיהּ דְּרַבִּי יוֹחָנָן: [8]אֲמַר: ״לִמְזוֹנוֹת״, [9]רִיבָּה לָהּ מְזוֹנוֹת. [10]אֲמַר: ״בִּמְזוֹנוֹת״, [11]קָצַץ לָהּ מְזוֹנוֹת.

הדרן עלך נערה

RASHI

כל שכן שריבה לה מזונות — אם אמר ״קרקע זו למזונותיך״ — אין זה אלא אם לא יתנו ליך מזונות מרווחים אלא מצומצמים, טלי קרקע זו להעדפה. דאי לשעבדה למזונותיה — הרי כל נכסיו משועבדים לכך. **שכנגדי** — אנוש כערכי, וראוי לחלוק עלי. **במזונות** — כחוב מזונות שיש ליך עלי. משמע שזו תהא פרעון לכך.

הדרן עלך נערה

TRANSLATION AND COMMENTARY

advice, and designated a particular field for his wife's maintenance. [1]After the father died, his heirs **came before Resh Lakish** for a ruling on the matter, **and he said to them:** "If your father designated a specific piece of land for his wife's maintenance, [2]then **all the more** so is she entitled to her usual maintenance, because **he has expanded** her right to collect **her maintenance."** For if the father had not designated a specific field, his widow would be entitled to collect her maintenance from all his property. Now that he has designated a field for her maintenance, he has thereby authorized her to collect *additional* maintenance from that property, if the maintenance provided by the heirs from the rest of the estate does not suffice for her. [3]The heirs **said** to Resh Lakish: **"But Rabbi Yoḥanan did not say this!"** [4]Resh Lakish **said to them: "Go and give her** as much maintenance as she needs, **for if not, I will take Rabbi Yoḥanan out of your ears** by force. I will deal so harshly with you that you will completely forget what you heard from Rabbi Yoḥanan." [5]**They returned to Rabbi Yoḥanan** to complain about Resh Lakish's decision, **and he said to them: "What can I do?** [6]**My** colleague who is my **equal disagrees with me.** There is nothing I can do to reverse his decision." [7]The Gemara adds a final note: **Rabbi Abbahu said: I myself personally heard Rabbi Yoḥanan explain** that there is a difference in the law depending on the precise formulation used by the husband in his stipulation. [8]**If** the husband **said** to his wife: "I am designating a specific field ***toward*** your **maintenance,"** [9]we understand that **he** meant to **increase her maintenance** and to give her the right to collect additional maintenance from that property, if the maintenance provided by the heirs from the rest of the property was insufficient. [10]But **if he said:** "I am designating a specific field ***as*** your **maintenance,"** [11]we understand that **he** meant to **set a limit on her maintenance,** and to give her the right to collect her maintenance from the produce of that field alone.

NOTES

protect themselves against a loss, while at the same time ensuring that their father's wife received all that was due to her.

אָתוּ לְקַמֵּיהּ דְּרֵישׁ לָקִישׁ **They came before Resh Lakish.** The heirs could not go to Rabbi Yoḥanan for a ruling because he was related to them and was therefore disqualified from rendering a decision about their case.

מַפֵּיקְנָא לְכוּ רַבִּי יוֹחָנָן מֵאוּנַיְיכוּ **"I will take Rabbi Yoḥanan out of your ears."** Some authorities understand the word אוּנַיְיכוּ as meaning "your ears." Resh Lakish warned Rabbi Yoḥanan's relatives to stop listening to Rabbi Yoḥanan. Others explain the word אוּנַיְיכוּ, as "your power." Resh Lakish warned Rabbi Yoḥanan's relatives that he would see to it that Rabbi Yoḥanan would not give them the power to object to his ruling. In several places, *Rashi* and *Tosafot* explain this expression as a threat of excommunication.

HALAKHAH

לִמְזוֹנוֹת...בִּמְזוֹנוֹת **Toward maintenance...as maintenance.** "If, before he dies, a man designates a specific field for his wife's maintenance, saying: 'This field shall be *toward* your maintenance,' we understand that he has extended his widow's right to maintenance. If the field does not suffice for her maintenance, she can collect the difference from the rest of his estate. If the field produces more than is due to her, she may keep it all. But if the husband says: 'This field shall be *as* your maintenance,' and she remains silent, she can collect her maintenance only from that specific field," following Rabbi Yoḥanan. (*Rambam, Sefer Nashim, Hilkhot Ishut* 18:18; *Shulḥan Arukh, Even HaEzer* 93:16.)

Conclusion to Chapter Four

The Sages summarized the rights of a father with respect to his daughter before she reaches majority with the rule that "all the benefits she may receive while she is a *na'arah* belong to her father." Thus the father is entitled to the money paid for his daughter's betrothal, the fines and the other payments made to her for her rape or seduction, her handiwork, and whatever she may find. But he is not entitled to the usufruct of the property that his daughter received as an inheritance or as a gift while she was a minor or a *na'arah*. The father is entitled to give his daughter away in betrothal, to receive her bill of divorce, and to annul her vows.

These rights with respect to a daughter are personal to her father, and are not passed on to his heirs. Thus the father's heirs are entitled only to those payments to which the father had already become entitled during his lifetime. The father has these rights with respect to his daughter only until she reaches full adulthood at the age of twelve-and-a-half or until she marries. But once she marries, she does not return to her father's authority, even if her marriage ends in divorce or in her husband's death (in which case the girl is considered "an orphan in her father's lifetime").

As for the regulations pertaining to the slanderer, the law is not in accordance with a literal understanding of the verses, but rather with the Rabbinic interpretation of the Scriptural text. These regulations can be summarized as follows: If someone marries a *na'arah* (and not a minor or an adult) and engages in sexual intercourse with her, and then goes to court and claims that he found her not to be a virgin, and later brings witnesses who testify that his wife committed adultery while she was betrothed to him, and the testimony of witnesses proves to be true, the girl is sentenced to death by stoning at the door of her father's house (if she has no father, or he has no house, she is stoned elsewhere). But if the father brings witnesses who prove that those brought by the husband conspired to give false testimony, the witnesses brought by the husband are sentenced to death by stoning, and the husband is flogged and required to pay a fine of one hundred shekalim to his wife's father. In addition, the husband is obligated to maintain the girl as his wife, and may not divorce her without her consent.

A husband's rights with respect to his wife are similar to a father's rights with respect to his daughter. Thus he may annul her vows, and is entitled to her handiwork and to what she finds, as well as to some of the payments that are paid to his wife in compensation for her personal injury. The husband has one right that the father does not have, for he is also entitled to the usufruct of the property brought into the marriage by his wife, even though the property itself remains in the wife's possession.

The husband also has various obligations toward his wife, for by Torah law she is entitled to maintenance, clothing, and her conjugal rights. By Rabbinic enactment, the husband is liable for his wife's medical care, her ransom, and her burial. After the husband's death, his widow is entitled to continue living in the house in which she was living during his lifetime, as well as to receive maintenance from his estate. Her daughters are entitled to maintenance from their father's estate until they come of age or until they are married (*ketubat benan nokvan*). The sons of the marriage are entitled to their mother's ketubah upon the father's death (if he inherited the ketubah when his wife predeceased him), in addition to the part of their father's estate that they must share with his sons from any other marriage (*ketubat benin dikhrin*).

In its discussion of a daughter's right to maintenance from her father's estate, the Gemara considers the father's obligation to maintain his minor children during his lifetime. The father is legally obligated to support his children as long as they are very young (until the age of six). After that and until they have reached adulthood, the court may pressure the father to maintain his children, but he is not legally obligated to do so. If the father is a man of means, the courts can compel him to maintain his children until they reach majority, the obligation stemming from the laws of charity.

Introduction to Chapter Five

אַף עַל פִּי

The present chapter continues the discussion that began in the previous one regarding the laws pertaining to the ketubah and conditions contained in it. One important issue is the size of a woman's ketubah: Is there a legal minimum to the amount a husband must obligate himself to include in his wife's ketubah? No less important is the issue of the additional sum that a husband may add to the basic portion of his wife's ketubah: To what extent do the laws applying to the basic portion of a woman's ketubah apply to the amount added by the husband at his own initiative?

Another issue discussed in this chapter relates to the time at which the obligations stemming from the conditions contained in the ketubah begin, especially the duty imposed on a married man to maintain his wife. There is one aspect of the question that goes beyond the context of civil law, for the daughter of a non-priest who is married to a priest is permitted to partake of terumah, the agricultural levy given to priests. It is necessary to ask and determine when the woman's right to terumah begins — from the time she is betrothed, from the time set for her wedding, or from the time she actually marries?

A married woman is required to perform certain household tasks on behalf of her husband, as well as to produce a certain amount of handiwork for him. In this chapter an attempt is made to define these duties more precisely, both with respect to the types of tasks that a woman is expected to perform for her husband and with respect to the quantity of handiwork she is expected to produce for him. The issue is raised as to what extent the standard of living and the social standing of the husband

and wife are to be considered when determining the wife's obligations in this area. Here, too, there is an aspect that goes beyond the strict boundaries of civil law — whether the husband or the wife can consecrate (or forbid by a vow) the woman's future handiwork.

One of the main obligations arising from marriage is the duty to engage in sexual relations with one's spouse. This chapter defines the husband's conjugal obligations, which vary according to his occupation and the frequency with which he is found at home. It considers the procedures that are to be adopted if a man or a woman persistently refuses to cohabit with his or her spouse.

Among the duties imposed on the husband by virtue of his marriage is the obligation to maintain his wife and to provide her with food and clothing. A precise listing is needed of the specific amounts of food and clothing that the husband must provide for his wife, particularly if the husband is living apart from his wife and supporting her through a third party. These and related issues are the main themes discussed in our chapter.

LITERAL TRANSLATION

MISHNAH [1]Although they said [that] a virgin collects two hundred [zuz] and a widow a maneh, [2]if he wished to add even a hundred maneh, he may add.

[3][If a woman] was widowed or divorced, whether after betrothal or after marriage,

אַף

[1]עַל פִּי שֶׁאָמְרוּ בְּתוּלָה גּוֹבָה מָאתַיִם וְאַלְמָנָה מָנֶה, [2]אִם רָצָה לְהוֹסִיף אֲפִילּוּ מֵאָה מָנֶה, יוֹסִיף.
[3]נִתְאַרְמְלָה אוֹ נִתְגָּרְשָׁה, בֵּין מִן הָאֵרוּסִין בֵּין מִן הַנִּשּׂוּאִין,

RASHI

משנה אף על פי. אם רצה — בגמרא פריך: פשיטא.

TRANSLATION AND COMMENTARY

MISHNAH אַף עַל פִּי A woman's ketubah records the obligations that the husband accepts with respect to his wife. The central feature of the ketubah is the amount of money that the husband or his heirs must pay the wife if she is divorced or widowed. Elsewhere (above, 10b), the Mishnah states that a woman who is a virgin when she marries is entitled to a ketubah of two hundred zuz, but a woman who is a widow or a divorcee at the time of marriage is entitled to a ketubah of only a maneh, which is equivalent to one hundred zuz. Our Mishnah teaches that these sums are the minimum amounts, and the husband may increase them if he so desires. [1]The Mishnah states: **Even though** the Sages **said** (above, 51a) that if the husband did not write his wife a ketubah, or if he wrote her a ketubah without specifying any amount, or if he specified a lesser amount, and his wife was **a virgin** when she married, she still **collects** a ketubah of **two hundred zuz, and** if she was a **widow** at the time of marriage, she still collects a ketubah of **a maneh,** [2]nevertheless **if** the husband **wishes to add** to his wife's ketubah **even a hundred maneh** (ten thousand zuz), **he may** indeed **add** as much as he wishes.

נִתְאַרְמְלָה אוֹ נִתְגָּרְשָׁה [3]According to Jewish law, a marriage is effected in two stages: (1) Betrothal (*kiddushin*, also known as *erusin*) and (2) marriage (*nissu'in*). If a woman **was widowed or divorced, whether**

NOTES

בְּתוּלָה גּוֹבָה מָאתַיִם A virgin collects two hundred zuz. *Shittah Mekubbetzet* asks: Why does the Mishnah say that the virgin *collects* 200 zuz as her ketubah? Since the Mishnah is dealing here with the writing of a woman's ketubah and not its collection, it should have said that a virgin *has* a ketubah of 200 zuz!

Shittah Mekubbetzet answers that the Mishnah should be understood as follows: Although a virgin collects 200 zuz as her ketubah, even if a ketubah document was never drawn up or was lost, whereas she can collect the additional sum only if she presents a ketubah explicitly obligating the husband to the payment of this addition, the husband may nevertheless add a further sum to the basic portion of the ketubah and fix the two as an aggregate amount.

Pnei Yehoshua explains that our Mishnah is referring back to the Mishnah in the previous chapter (above, 51a) which states: "If he did not write a ketubah for her, a virgin collects 200 zuz, and a widow a maneh, because it is a condition of the court." Thus our Mishnah teaches us that even though, as we have already learned, the husband may not reduce his wife's ketubah below the legal minimum, he may nevertheless add to it if he so wishes.

אִם רָצָה לְהוֹסִיף If he wished to add. The Jerusalem Talmud asks: If someone writes a promissory note for a debt which, as it later turns out, he did not really owe, he is not obligated to repay the note. Why, then, is the husband obligated to pay his wife the sum that he added on his own initiative to her ketubah? The Jerusalem Talmud answers that the husband wrote the additional sum in the ketubah so that his wife's family would consent to the marriage, or in order to appease his wife so that she should not leave him, or for some other such reason. Thus the husband derived a certain benefit, in exchange for which he accepted the obligation to pay his wife the addition to her ketubah.

אֲפִילּוּ מֵאָה מָנֶה Even a hundred maneh. *Shittah Mekubbetzet* notes that at first glance the expression "even 100 maneh" is superfluous, for if the husband is permitted to add an additional sum to the basic portion of his wife's ketubah, it should make no difference whether the sum is large or small. In fact, however, this apparently unnecessary phrase teaches us that the husband can obligate himself to a very large additional sum, even if at present he does not have the money *Tosafot* and other Rishonim discuss at length why such an obligation is binding.

HALAKHAH

אִם רָצָה לְהוֹסִיף If he wished to add. "If a husband wishes to add to the minimum amount of his wife's ketubah, he may do so. *Rema* notes that it is not necessary that the two amounts — the basic portion of the ketubah and the additional sum — be stated separately in the ketubah document (*Ran,* following *Ramban* and *Rashba*). But some authorities maintain that the basic portion of the ketubah as fixed by local custom and the additional sum must be stated separately in the ketubah document. Common practice follows the second opinion." (*Rambam, Sefer Nashim, Hilkhot Ishut* 10:7; *Shulḥan Arukh, Even HaEzer* 66:7.)

TRANSLATION AND COMMENTARY

after betrothal or after marriage, [1]**she collects the entire amount** recorded in the ketubah, both the standard, fixed, ketubah payment and any addition to the basic sum which the husband had undertaken to pay. This is the opinion of the anonymous first Tanna of the Mishnah. [2]**Rabbi Elazar ben Azaryah** disagrees and **says:** If she was widowed or divorced **after marriage, she collects the entire amount** recorded in the ketubah. [3]**But** if she was widowed or divorced **after betrothal,** she collects only the basic portion of her ketubah, the amount of which is determined by law: If she was **a virgin** at the time of her betrothal, she **collects two hundred zuz,** [4]**and** if she was **a widow** or a divorcee when she was betrothed, she collects **a maneh.** But she does not collect any additional sum that the husband added on his own initiative, [5]**for the** husband **wrote the additional sum for her** in the ketubah **only on the basis that he would marry her,** and here she was widowed or divorced before the marriage process was completed.

[1]גּוֹבָה אֶת הַכֹּל. [2]רַבִּי אֶלְעָזָר בֶּן עֲזַרְיָה אוֹמֵר: מִן הַנִּשּׂוּאִין, גּוֹבָה אֶת הַכֹּל, [3]מִן הָאֵירוּסִין, בְּתוּלָה גּוֹבָה מָאתַיִם, [4]וְאַלְמָנָה מָנֶה, [5]שֶׁלֹּא כָּתַב לָהּ אֶלָּא עַל מְנָת לְכוֹנְסָהּ.

[6]רַבִּי יְהוּדָה אוֹמֵר: אִם רָצָה, כּוֹתֵב לִבְתוּלָה שְׁטָר שֶׁל מָאתַיִם, [7]וְהִיא כּוֹתֶבֶת: ״הִתְקַבַּלְתִּי מִמְּךָ מָנֶה״, [8]וּלְאַלְמָנָה מָנֶה, [9]וְהִיא כּוֹתֶבֶת: ״הִתְקַבַּלְתִּי מִמְּךָ חֲמִשִּׁים זוּז״. [10]רַבִּי מֵאִיר אוֹמֵר: כָּל הַפּוֹחֵת לִבְתוּלָה מִמָּאתַיִם וּלְאַלְמָנָה מִמָּנֶה, [11]הֲרֵי זוֹ בְּעִילַת זְנוּת.

LITERAL TRANSLATION

[1]she collects everything. [2]Rabbi Elazar ben Azaryah says: After marriage, she collects everything, [3][but] after betrothal, a virgin collects two hundred [zuz], [4]and a widow a maneh, [5]for he only wrote [the addition] for her in order to marry her.

[6]Rabbi Yehudah says: If he wishes, he may write for a virgin a deed of two hundred [zuz], [7]and she may write: "I have received from you a maneh," [8]or [he may write] for a widow [a deed of] a maneh, [9]and she may write: "I have received from you fifty zuz." [10]Rabbi Meir says: Whoever makes [the ketubah of] a virgin less than two hundred [zuz], or [that] of a widow less than a maneh, [11][his intercourse with her] is an act of prostitution.

RASHI

שלא כתב לה – תוספת דמדעתו, אלא על מנת לכונסה. **והיא כותבת** – אף על פי שלא נתקבלה, מוחלת, וכותבת בלשון שובר.

רַבִּי יְהוּדָה אוֹמֵר [6]The last clause of our Mishnah discusses whether the husband can reduce his liability regarding his wife's ketubah below the minimum set by the Sages. **Rabbi Yehudah says: If** the husband **wishes** to reduce his obligation concerning his wife's ketubah, **he may write a** ketubah **document of two hundred zuz for** his wife who is **a virgin,** as is required of him by law, [7]**and** then he can arrange to have his wife **write** him a receipt saying: **"I have** already **received a maneh from you** in partial payment of my ketubah," even though she has not received anything from him. [8]**Or he may write a** ketubah **document of a maneh for** his wife who is **a widow** or a divorcee, [9]and then he can arrange to have his wife **write** him a receipt saying: **"I have** already **received fifty zuz from you** in partial payment of my ketubah," even though she has received nothing from him. According to Rabbi Yehudah, once the husband has complied with the formal requirement of writing his wife a ketubah of two hundred zuz or a maneh, his wife can then waive her right to part of that sum by writing a fictitious receipt for part of the money. [10]**Rabbi Meir** disagrees and **says:** A man may not reduce the amount of his wife's ketubah to less than the legal minimum, even if the woman agrees to the reduction, for **whoever fixes the ketubah of a virgin at less than two hundred zuz, or that of a widow at less than a maneh,** [11]**his intercourse with her is** tantamount to **an act of prostitution.** The difference between casual sexual relations and sexual relations sanctified by the bond of marriage is that the latter take place within the framework of an agreement between the parties that defines their mutual obligations as long as they remain married, as well as the arrangements that are to be made if they separate. If the husband sets his wife's ketubah at less than the legal minimum, his stipulation is invalid, and his wife is still entitled to the full amount that is rightfully hers. But sexual relations between

HALAKHAH

מִן הַנִּשּׂוּאִין גּוֹבָה אֶת הַכֹּל **After marriage, she collects everything.** "If a man betroths a woman and writes a ketubah for her, and then he dies or divorces her, the woman may collect the basic portion of her ketubah from her bridegroom's free assets only, and she may not collect any additional sum at all," following Rabbi Elazar ben Azaryah, whose opinion is accepted below (56a). (*Rambam, Sefer Nashim, Hilkhot Ishut* 10:11; *Shulḥan Arukh, Even HaEzer* 55:6.)

כָּל הַפּוֹחֵת לִבְתוּלָה מִמָּאתַיִם **Whoever makes the ketubah of a virgin less than two hundred zuz.** "Whoever fixes his wife's ketubah at less than the legal minimum, his intercourse with her is tantamount to an act of prostitution. This applies not only if the husband wrote his wife a

גמרא [1]פְּשִׁיטָא! [2]מַהוּ דְּתֵימָא: קִיצוּתָא עָבְדוּ רַבָּנַן, [3]שֶׁלֹּא לְבַיֵּישׁ אֶת מִי שֶׁאֵין לוֹ. [4]קָא מַשְׁמַע לָן. [5]״אִם רָצָה לְהוֹסִיף כו׳״. [6]״רָצָה לִכְתּוֹב לָהּ״ לָא קָתָנֵי, [7]אֶלָּא: ״רָצָה לְהוֹסִיף״. [8]מְסַיַּיע לֵיהּ לְרַבִּי אַיְבוּ אָמַר רַבִּי יַנַּאי.

LITERAL TRANSLATION

GEMARA [1]It is obvious!

[2]You might have said: The Rabbis set a definite amount, [3]so as not to shame someone who does not have. [4][Therefore] it tells us [that this is not so].

[5]"If he wished to add, etc." [6]It does not teach: "[If] he wished to write for her," [7]but rather: "[If] he wished to add." [8]It supports [what] Rabbi Aivu said in the name of Rabbi Yannai.

RASHI

גמרא רצה לכתוב לא קתני — אי תנא "לכתוב" לא הוה שמעינן מינה שיהיה התוספת קרוי כתובה. אלא כמתנה מדעתו, ואין שם כתובה עליו. השתא דתנן "להוסיף" — משמע נוסף על הכתובה שתקנו חכמים, ושם כתובה עליו, גם הוא מסייע ליה כו׳.

TRANSLATION AND COMMENTARY

them are nevertheless forbidden, for the woman thinks that she is entitled only to the reduced amount specified in her ketubah, and a ketubah of less than two hundred zuz (in the case of a virgin) or a maneh (in the case of a widow or a divorcee) is not considered valid.

GEMARA פְּשִׁיטָא [1]The Gemara asks: Why did the Mishnah need to inform us that the husband may add an additional sum to the basic amount of the ketubah? Surely **it is obvious** that he may accept any obligation that he so desires!

מַהוּ דְּתֵימָא [2]The Gemara answers: Had the Mishnah not stated that the husband may add an additional sum to the basic amount of the ketubah, **we might have said** that **the Rabbis fixed** the ketubah **at a definite amount,** [3]**so as not to shame someone who does not have** the means to obligate himself to more than the legal minimum. [4]It was **therefore** necessary for the Mishnah to **tell us that this is not so.** Although the minimum amount of a woman's ketubah is determined by law, the husband may add to it however much he desires.

אִם רָצָה לְהוֹסִיף [5]We learned in the Mishnah: **"If** the husband **wishes to add** to his wife's ketubah even a hundred maneh, he may do so." [6]The Gemara notes that the Mishnah **does not state: "If** the husband **wishes to write** a document **for** his wife in which he undertakes to pay her a certain amount in addition to the ketubah to which she is entitled by law, he may do so." Had the Mishnah been formulated in this way, we might have thought that the additional sum is treated as an independent obligation. [7]To avoid the possibility of such an inference, the Mishnah states **instead: "If** the husband **wishes to add** to his wife's ketubah, he may do so," implying that whatever the husband adds is considered an integral part of the ketubah. [8]**This** formulation — and the inference that may be drawn from it — **supports what Rabbi Aivu said in**

BACKGROUND

שֶׁלֹּא לְבַיֵּישׁ So as not to shame. This consideration — not to embarrass someone without means — is found in several regulations instituted by the Sages in Talmudic times and later. These regulations concern actions taken in public that could shame a person without means or cause poor people to give beyond their abilities (see above, 8b). Therefore it was conceivable that the Sages might have instituted a regulation of this kind in the case of ketubot as well.

SAGES

רַבִּי אַיְבוּ Rabbi Aivu. A Palestinian Amora of the third generation, Rabbi Aivu studied with the greatest Amoraim of the previous generation, and transmitted teachings in the name of Rabbi Yannai, Rabbi Yoḥanan, and others. In addition to his eminence in the area of Halakhah, Rabbi Aivu was also an outstanding preacher, and he is often quoted in the Palestinian Midrashim.

NOTES

פְּשִׁיטָא It is obvious! *Ritva* observes that the Gemara is not asking here why the Mishnah introduced the subject of the addition to the woman's ketubah, because it was necessary to mention the additional sum as an introduction to the dispute between the anonymous first Tanna and Rabbi Elazar ben Azaryah, or in order to teach us that the conditions contained in the ketubah are treated like the ketubah itself (see Gemara below). The Gemara is asking why the Mishnah had to say that, *if the husband so wishes,* he may add to his wife's ketubah. For it is surely obvious that if a person wants to accept an obligation, he may do so!

קִיצוּתָא עָבְדוּ רַבָּנַן The Rabbis set a definite amount. Many Geonim and Rishonim ask: Why would we have imagined that the Rabbis set a maximum amount to which the husband may obligate himself? They infer from this passage that the main portion of the ketubah and the addition need not be stated separately in the ketubah document, for were it necessary to record them separately, there would have been no reason to think that the husband is not permitted to add to his wife's ketubah so as not to shame someone who does not have the means to do so. For surely we do not say that a man may not give his wife a gift, or that a father may not provide his daughter with a large dowry, so as not to shame people of lesser means.

אֶלָּא: ״רָצָה לְהוֹסִיף״ But rather: "If he wished to add." The expression, "if he wished to write," would have implied that we view the addition to the ketubah as a separate gift, completely independent of the ketubah itself. But the expression, "if he wished to add," teaches us that the addition is an extension of the ketubah. The wording here is similar to the expression (*Sanhedrin* 2a), "adding to the city," which refers to the expansion of the boundaries of the city of Jerusalem, the added sections being granted the full sanctity of the rest of the city (*Geonim, Ritva*).

Some authorities maintain that the Mishnah was worded,

HALAKHAH

ketubah as required by law, and the woman later waived part or all of her ketubah (in which case, according to some authorities, the woman actually forfeits part or all of it), but even if the husband stipulated from the outset that his wife's ketubah would be less than the legal minimum (in which case the stipulation is null and void and she is entitled to the full amount as required by law)," following Rabbi Meir, whose opinion is accepted below, 57a. (*Rambam, Sefer Nashim, Hilkhot Ishut* 12:8; *Shulḥan Arukh, Even HaEzer* 66:9.)

TRANSLATION AND COMMENTARY

the name of Rabbi Yannai. [1]**For Rabbi Aivu said in the name of Rabbi Yannai: A condition added to the ketubah** — for example, the additional sum added by the husband, or any other financial obligation imposed on the husband and specified in the ketubah document — **is** treated **like** the main portion of **the ketubah.** Thus, whenever the woman is entitled to the basic portion of her ketubah, she is also entitled to the rights due to her under the ketubah conditions. Likewise, whenever she forfeits the basic portion of her ketubah, she also loses the rights due to her under the ketubah conditions.

נָפְקָא מִינָּהּ [2]The Gemara now lists fourteen **practical differences** that derive from the conclusion that the amount added to a woman's ketubah is considered part of the ketubah and not an independent obligation. (1) If **a woman sells her ketubah,** whether to her husband or to someone else, she cannot later argue that she sold only the basic portion of her ketubah — for when a woman sells her ketubah, the additional sum is included in the sale. (2) [3]If **a woman waives her ketubah** to her husband or to his heirs, the additional sum is included in the waiver. (3) [4]If **a woman rebels** against her husband, persistently refusing to cohabit with him, we deduct a certain sum each week from her ketubah (see below, 63a). Just as we deduct from the basic portion of her ketubah, so too do we deduct from the additional sum. (4) [5]If a divorced **woman impairs her ketubah,** acknowledging that she has already received a certain portion of the money due to her as her ketubah, and her husband claims that he has already paid her the entire amount, her husband has the right to require her to take an oath that she is not demanding more than the sum to which she is entitled (see below, 87a). If a woman admits that she has already received

[1]דַּאֲמַר רַבִּי אַיְבוּ אֲמַר רַבִּי יַנַּאי: תְּנַאי כְּתוּבָּה כִּכְתוּבָּה דָּמֵי.

[2]נָפְקָא מִינָּהּ לְמוֹכֶרֶת, [3]וּלְמוֹחֶלֶת, [4]לְמוֹרֶדֶת, [5]וּלְפוֹגֶמֶת,

LITERAL TRANSLATION

[1]For Rabbi Aivu said in the name of Rabbi Yannai: A condition [added to] the ketubah is like the ketubah.

[2]The practical difference is with regard to one who sells [her ketubah], [3]and to one who waives [it], [4][and] to one who rebels, [5]and to one who impairs [her ketubah],

RASHI

תנאי כתובה — תוספת שהוא מתנה להוסיף לה, וכן מזונות, וכל הנך דתנן בפרקין לעיל. **למוכרת ולמוחלת** — מוכרת כתובתה או מוחלת כתובתה — מחלה ומכרה את הכל, לפי שהכל קרוי כתובה, ולא אמרינן לא מיקרי כתובה אלא מנה מאתים. **למורדת** — דתנן בפרקין (לקמן כתובות סג,א): המורדת על בעלה — פוחתין לה מכתובתה כו׳, עד מתי הוא פוחת — עד כנגד כתובתה. לא תימא כנגד מנה מאתים לחודייהו, אלא אף התוספת פוחתין והולכין. **ולפוגמת** — בפרק ״הכותב״ (לקמן כתובות פז,א) תנן: הפוגמת כתובתה — לא תפרע אלא בשבועה. אם פגמה תוספת נמי, שאמרה לשם פרעון התוספות התקבלתי דינר — אף זו פוגמת כתובתה היא, ואם טוען בעלה התקבלת כל כתובתיך — לא תפרע אלא בשבועה.

NOTES

"if he wished to add," rather than, "if he wished to write," to teach us that the husband's promise of an addition to his wife's ketubah is binding even if it was not recorded in her ketubah document, for the woman's right to the additional sum can be established by a mere verbal agreement (*Rivan, Ra'ah,* and *Meiri*).

תְּנַאי כְּתוּבָּה כִּכְתוּבָּה דָּמֵי **A condition added to the ketubah is like the ketubah.** The Rishonim disagree about the scope of Rabbi Yannai's statement. Some authorities (*Rosh, Tosafot* cited by *Ritva*) explain that Rabbi Yannai was referring only to the addition to the ketubah, and not to any of the other ketubah conditions. Others (see *Rashi*) explain that all of the ketubah conditions are governed by the same laws as the basic portion of the ketubah, but the woman's dowry is not. *Ramban* argues that in most respects the woman's dowry is also included among the ketubah conditions, which are treated like the basic portion of the ketubah.

נָפְקָא מִינָּהּ לְמוֹכֶרֶת **The practical difference is with regard to one who sells her ketubah.** *Rabbenu Ḥananel* notes that since the Gemara lists fourteen areas regarding which the addition to a woman's ketubah is treated as part of the ketubah, it may be inferred that regarding other matters the basic portion of the ketubah and the addition are governed by different laws (see also Halakhah).

HALAKHAH

תְּנַאי כְּתוּבָּה כִּכְתוּבָּה דָּמֵי **A condition added to the ketubah is like the ketubah.** "In most matters, the law that applies to any sum added to a woman's ketubah is the same as the law that applies to the basic portion of her ketubah, although there are some instances in which the laws are different." (*Rambam, Sefer Nashim, Hilkhot Ishut* 10:7, 18:28; *Shulḥan Arukh, Even HaEzer* 66:7.)

לְמוֹכֶרֶת וּלְמוֹחֶלֶת **To one who sells her ketubah, and to one who waives it.** "If a woman sells or waives her ketubah without specifying the extent of the sale or the waiver, the addition to the ketubah is sold or waived along with the basic portion." (*Rambam, Sefer Nashim, Hilkhot Ishut* 18:28; *Shulḥan Arukh, Even HaEzer* 93:10.)

לְמוֹרֶדֶת **To one who rebels.** "A rebellious wife who forfeits her ketubah forfeits not only the basic portion but the additional sum as well." (*Rambam, Sefer Nashim, Hilkhot Ishut* 14:8-9; *Shulḥan Arukh, Even HaEzer* 77:2.)

וּלְפוֹגֶמֶת **And to one who impairs her ketubah.** "If a woman admits that she has already received part of her ketubah, whether from the basic portion of the ketubah or

TRANSLATION AND COMMENTARY

part or all of the additional sum, she must take an oath that she has not yet been paid the basic portion of her ketubah, and vice versa. [1](5) If **a widow claims** her ketubah in court, she forfeits her right to maintenance from her late husband's estate (see above, 54a). She loses that right to maintenance, even if she claims only the additional sum included as part of her ketubah. (6) [2]If a married **woman offends against** Mosaic law — if, for example, she feeds her husband food that has not been properly tithed, or if she engages in sexual relations with him during the time of the month that she is forbidden to him because of her menstrual period — or if she disregards **Jewish custom** by failing to adhere to the modest practices appropriate for a Jewish woman, her husband can divorce her without paying her her ketubah (below, 72a). She forfeits not only the basic portion of her ketubah, but the additional sum as well, if there is one. [55A] (7) [3]If a man dies and the assets of his estate do not suffice for the payment of his widow's ketubah, she cannot collect it from **improvements** to the estate effected by her husband's heirs after his death (*Bekhorot* 51b—52a). Just as she cannot collect the basic portion of her ketubah from these improvements, likewise she cannot collect the addition to her ketubah from such improvements. (8) [4]Wherever a woman is required to take **an oath** before she can collect the

[1]לְתוֹבַעַת, [2]וּלְעוֹבֶרֶת עַל דָּת, [55A] [3]לְשֶׁבַח, [4]לִשְׁבוּעָה,

LITERAL TRANSLATION

[1][and] to one who claims [it], [2]and to one who offends against Jewish law, [55A] [3][and] to improvement, [4][and] to an oath,

RASHI

לתובעת — שאמרו חכמים: התובעת כתובתה בבית דין — אין לה מזונות, תובעת תוספת — נמי אין לה מזונות. **עוברת על דת** — בפרק "המדיר" (לקמן כתובות עב,א) שאמרו עליה: תצא שלא בכתובה לא תימא כתובת מנה מאתים, אבל תוספת מתנה בעלמא הוא לא הפסידה. **לשבח** — שאמרו בבכורות (נא,ב): אין הבכור נוטל פי שנים בשבח ששבחו הנכסים לאחר מיתת אביהן, ולא האשה בכתובתה. ותוספת נמי לא גביא משבח ששבחו נכסים לאחר מיתת בעלה. **ולשבועה** — לכל מילי דשייכא לישבע על הכתובה, כגון הנפרעת שלא בפניו,

NOTES

לְתוֹבַעַת To one who claims it. Our commentary follows *Rashi* and *Rif*, who explain that the Gemara is saying that if a widow claims her ketubah in court, whether she claims the basic portion or the addition, she forfeits the right to maintenance from her late husband's estate.

Tosafot raises an objection: The law is in accordance with the viewpoint that a woman is entitled to maintenance, even if she has sold or mortgaged part of her ketubah, so long as she has retained part of the ketubah for herself. Why, then, should she forfeit her right to maintenance if all she did was claim the addition, and not her entire ketubah? Thus the Gemara must mean just the opposite: If a woman claims only the main portion of her ketubah, but not the addition, or vice versa, she is still entitled to maintenance.

Ramban argues that if this was the Gemara's intention, it should not have said that there is a practical difference with regard to one who claims her ketubah, but rather with regard to one who is being maintained from her husband's estate. What the Gemara means to say is that if a woman claims her ketubah without specifying further, she forfeits her right to maintenance, because we assume that she is claiming her entire ketubah, both the basic portion and the additional sum.

לְשֶׁבַח To improvement. Most Rishonim follow *Rashi*, who explains that we are dealing here with a case in which the husband's assets at the time of his death did not suffice for the payment of his widow's ketubah, but afterwards those assets increased in value (whether as a result of fluctuations in price or as a result of improvements effected on the estate by the husband's heirs). The woman may not collect any part of her ketubah from that increase in value — neither the basic portion nor the addition.

Rif cites another explanation, according to which the Gemara is referring here to a case in which the husband designated certain property for the payment of the addition to his wife's ketubah, and that property rose in value. Just as the increase in the value of the property designated for the payment of the basic portion of a woman's ketubah belongs to the husband, so too does the increase in value of the property designated for the payment of the addition belong to him.

לִשְׁבוּעָה To an oath. *Rashi* and *Rif* explain that the Gemara is informing us that whenever a woman is required

HALAKHAH

from the addition, she may not collect the rest unless she takes an oath that she has not already received her entire ketubah." (*Rambam, Sefer Nashim, Hilkhot Ishut* 16:14; *Shulḥan Arukh, Even HaEzer* 96:7.)

לְתוֹבַעַת To one who claims it. "If a widow claims her ketubah in court without specifying precisely what she is claiming, she forfeits her right to maintenance, because we assume that she is demanding her entire ketubah, both the basic portion and the addition. But if she claims only the basic portion of her ketubah or only the addition (and certainly if she claims only her dowry), she is still entitled to maintenance from her husband's estate (following *Tosafot;* see *Ba'er Hetev*)." (*Rambam, Sefer Nashim, Hilkhot Ishut* 18:1; *Shulḥan Arukh, Even HaEzer* 93:11.)

וּלְעוֹבֶרֶת עַל דָּת And to one who offends against Jewish law. "If a married woman disregards Mosaic law or Jewish custom, she is not entitled to her ketubah, neither the main portion nor the addition." (*Rambam, Sefer Nashim, Hilkhot Ishut* 24:16; *Shulḥan Arukh, Even HaEzer* 115:5.)

לְשֶׁבַח To improvement. "A widow cannot collect either the basic portion of her ketubah or the addition from improvements effected by her late husband's heirs on his estate. The authorities disagree about the law in a case in which the widow herself carried out the improvements." (*Rambam, Sefer Nashim, Hilkhot Ishut* 16:5; *Shulḥan Arukh, Even HaEzer* 95:7, 100:2.)

לִשְׁבוּעָה To an oath. "A widow cannot collect either the basic portion of her ketubah or the addition from her

[1] וְלַשְּׁבִיעִית, [2] וְלַכּוֹתֵב כָּל נְכָסָיו לְבָנָיו, [3] לִגְבּוֹת מִן הַקַּרְקַע,

LITERAL TRANSLATION

[1] and to the Sabbatical Year, [2] and to one who assigns all his property to his sons, [3] [and] to collecting from land,

RASHI

ועד אחד מעידה שהיא פרועה, והנפרעת מנכסים משועבדים ומנכסי יתומים, דתנן בפרק הכותב (כתובות פז,א) דבעו שבועה — אף תוספת נמי בעי שבועה. ואף על גב דפוגמת בהאי כללא איתיה — איצטריך למינקטיה בהדיא, לאשמועינן דפגימת תוספת מהניא להשביעה כפגימת כתובה. **ולשביעית** — שאין שביעית משמטת כתובה, כשאר שטרות, אלא אם כן פגמה וזקפה. כדאמרינן במסכת גיטין (יח,א). ותוספת נמי לא משמט. **לכותב נכסיו לבניו** — וכתב לאשתו קרקע כל שהוא — אבדה כתובתה, כדאיתא ב״יש נוחלין״ (בבא בתרא קלב,א), ותוספת ככתובה. אין כתובה נגבית אלא מן הקרקע ומן הזיבורית, כדתנן ב״הניזקין״ (גיטין מח,ב) וכן תוספת.

TRANSLATION AND COMMENTARY

basic portion of her ketubah — for example, if a single witness testifies that she has already received it, or if a widow comes to collect it from her late husband's heirs, or if a woman comes to collect it from property that her husband has transferred to a third party, or if a divorcee whose former husband has gone abroad wishes to collect her ketubah in his absence (see below, 87a) — she must also take an oath before she can collect the addition to her ketubah. (9) [1] All outstanding debts owed by Jews to each other are canceled by **the Sabbatical Year.** If a woman is widowed or divorced, and she has not yet collected her ketubah, the Sabbatical Year does not cancel the obligation — for the ketubah is an obligation imposed by the court, and is thus not affected by the Sabbatical Year (see *Gittin* 18a). Just as the Sabbatical Year does not cancel the husband's obligation regarding the basic portion of his wife's ketubah, likewise it does not cancel his obligation with regard to the addition. (10) [2] If someone **assigns all his property to his sons,** leaving his wife only a tiny parcel of land, and his wife does not raise any objections to the transaction, she forfeits the right to collect her ketubah from any of the property that has been transferred to the sons, for she has waived the lien that was established on that property (see *Pe'ah* 3:7). Just as the woman cannot collect the basic portion of her ketubah from the property that has been transferred to her husband's children, she likewise cannot collect the addition to her ketubah from that property. (11) [3] The addition to a woman's ketubah is similar to the main portion of her ketubah in that both may be **collected** only **from** the husband's **landed property.**

NOTES

to take an oath before she can collect the basic portion of her ketubah (as is explained below, 87a), she must also take an oath before she can collect the addition to her ketubah. The Rishonim ask: Why should this conclusion be based on the assumption that the addition to a woman's ketubah is considered part of her ketubah? The woman should be required to take an oath even if the addition is treated as an independent obligation that the husband accepts, for in such circumstances an oath is imposed on all creditors!

Ri Migash answers that we might have thought that the Rabbis are more lenient with respect to a woman coming to collect her ketubah, in order that women may be more willing to marry.

Tosafot suggests that the Gemara is informing us that if a woman takes an oath that she has not yet been paid her ketubah, she need not take another oath that she has not yet been paid the addition to her ketubah, for the addition is considered part of her ketubah.

According to *Ramban,* the Gemara means to say that if the husband stipulated that his wife would be believed when she saidthat she had not yet been paid her ketubah, even without taking an oath, he is understood as having exempted her from an oath not only with respect to the basic portion of the ketubah, but with respect to the addition as well.

Ra'avad argues that the Gemara is informing us that if the husband designated movable goods or landed property with specified boundaries for the payment of his wife's ketubah, she may collect without an oath not only the basic portion of her ketubah (see Gemara below), but the addition as well.

וְלַשְּׁבִיעִית And to the Sabbatical Year. Our commentary follows *Rashi,* who explains that the Gemara is informing us that just as the Sabbatical Year does not cancel the husband's obligation regarding the basic portion of his wife's ketubah, so too does it not cancel his obligation with respect to the addition.

HALAKHAH

husband's heirs unless she takes an oath that her husband did not assign property to her for the payment of her ketubah, and that she has not sold her ketubah to him or waived it." (*Rambam, Sefer Nashim, Hilkhot Ishut* 16:4; *Shulḥan Arukh, Even HaEzer* 96:1.)

וְלַשְּׁבִיעִית And to the Sabbatical Year. "A woman in possession of her ketubah document may collect her ketubah — the basic sum and the addition — at any time; even the Sabbatical Year does not cancel the financial obligations contained in it." (*Rambam, Sefer Zeraim, Hilkhot Shemittah* 9:13; *Shulḥan Arukh, Even HaEzer* 101:1.)

וְלַכּוֹתֵב כָּל נְכָסָיו לְבָנָיו And to one who assigns all his property to his sons. "If someone assigns all his property to his sons or his daughters, leaving his wife only a tiny parcel of land, and she does not object when she is informed of the arrangement, she forfeits the right to collect her ketubah, both the basic portion and the addition, from any of the property that has been transferred to her husband's children." (*Rambam, Sefer Kinyan, Hilkhot Zekhiyyah U'Mekhirah* 6:9; *Shulḥan Arukh, Even HaEzer* 106:1.)

לִגְבּוֹת מִן הַקַּרְקַע To collecting from land. "According to the law as laid down in the Talmud, the ketubah, both the

TRANSLATION AND COMMENTARY

(12) [1] If the husband has land of varying quality, his wife can **collect** both the basic portion of her ketubah and the addition only **from land of the poorest quality.** (13) [2] If a widow is living in her late husband's house, she may collect her ketubah at any time, no matter how long the period that has elapsed since her husband's death. If she returns to her paternal home, she may collect her ketubah during **the entire period that she lives in her father's house,** provided that twenty-five years have not passed since her husband died. After that, we assume that she has waived her right to the ketubah. Just as she may not collect the basic portion of her ketubah after twenty-five years, she may likewise not collect the addition to her ketubah after that time. (14) If a woman dies during her husband's lifetime, he inherits her entire estate, including her ketubah. The Rabbis enacted that when the husband dies, the ketubah he inherited from his wife passes to the male children of that marriage, and only then is the rest of his estate divided among all his heirs. [3] This enactment, known as the *ketubat benin dikhrin*, or **"the ketubah of male children,"** applies not only to the basic portion of a woman's ketubah, but also to the addition to her ketubah.

[1] וּמִן הַזִּיבּוּרִית, [2] וְכָל זְמַן שֶׁהִיא בְּבֵית אָבִיהָ, [3] וְלִכְתוּבַּת בְּנִין דִּכְרִין.

LITERAL TRANSLATION

[1] and [to collecting] from land of the poorest quality, [2] and [to] all the time that she is in her father's house, [3] and to the ketubah of male children.

RASHI

כל זמן שהיא בבית אביה — תנן ב"הנושא" (כתובות קד,א): כל זמן שהיא בבית בעלה במשך אלמנותה — גובה כתובתה לעולם. וכל זמן שהיא בבית אביה, שלא היו עודדים אותה היתומים ולא זנין אותה — גובה כתובתה עד עשרים וחמש שנים. ואם שתקה יתר על כן יום אחד — מחלתה, וכן תוספת. **כתובת בנין דכרין** — כשם שנוטלים נדוניית אבי אמם ומנה מאתים, כך נוטלים תוספת.

CONCEPTS

וּמִן הַזִּיבּוּרִית And to collecting from land of the poorest quality. Land was divided by quality into three categories: עִידִית — *iddit*, the best; בֵּינוֹנִית — *benonit*, average; and זִיבּוּרִית — *zibburit*, the worst. The division was not absolute — according to its objective value — but relative to the quality of other land in the area and to other property owned by the person in question. Poor-quality land was naturally worth less. Hence, since the wife received the worst land, she received a larger area of it. Although the monetary value of the woman's property (or that of any other creditor) was the same, people nevertheless preferred to collect their debts from the best land, because it took less effort to cultivate and was more fertile. The best land was also preferable because there were more prospective buyers for it.

NOTES

Tosafot and others object: The law is in accordance with the viewpoint that the Sabbatical Year only cancels debts created through a loan, but all other debts are unaffected by the Sabbatical Year. Thus it is obvious that neither the basic portion nor the addition to a woman's ketubah is canceled by the Sabbatical Year.

Rabbenu Ḥananel and *Rif* explain that the Gemara is informing us that if a woman impairs her ketubah, acknowledging that she has already received a certain portion of her ketubah money, or if she converts her ketubah into an ordinary loan, the ketubah — both the basic portion and the addition — is canceled by the Sabbatical Year.

מִן הַזִּיבּוּרִית From land of the poorest quality. *Ra'ah* notes that the Gemara means that the woman can collect the addition to her ketubah only from land of the poorest quality, even if she is a divorcee collecting her ketubah from the husband himself. For if she is a widow collecting her ketubah from her late husband's heirs, it is obvious that she can collect only from land of the poorest quality, just like any other creditor collecting from orphans.

וְכָל זְמַן שֶׁהִיא בְּבֵית אָבִיהָ And to all the time that she is in her father's house. This expression alludes to the distinction between a woman who continues to live in her late husband's home after his death, and a woman who returns to her father's house after her husband dies, with respect to the woman's permanent right to collect her ketubah (see below, 104a). According to Rabbi Meir, a woman who is living in her father's house may collect her ketubah at any time, whereas a woman who continues to live in her husband's home can only collect her ketubah within a period of twenty-five years. The Sages make the opposite distinction: A woman who continues to live in her husband's home may collect her ketubah at any time,

HALAKHAH

basic portion and the addition, may be collected only from the husband's landed property. But the Geonim enacted that a woman may collect her ketubah even from movable goods. This Geonic enactment was accepted in all communities." (*Rambam, Sefer Nashim, Hilkhot Ishut* 16:5,7-9; *Shulḥan Arukh, Even HaEzer* 100:1.)

מִן הַזִּיבּוּרִית From land of the poorest quality. "According to the law as laid down in the Talmud, if someone has land of varying quality, his wife may collect the basic portion of her ketubah, as well as the addition, only from that part of the land which is of the poorest quality. But it has long become common practice for the ketubah document to speak of 'the choicest of properties,' and thus the ketubah may be collected even from land of the highest quality." (*Rambam, Sefer Nashim, Hilkhot Ishut* 16:3; *Shulḥan Arukh, Even HaEzer* 100:2; *Tur, Ḥoshen Mishpat* 108.)

וְכָל זְמַן שֶׁהִיא בְּבֵית אָבִיהָ And to all the time that she is in her father's house. "In a place where it is not customary to write a ketubah document, a woman can collect her ketubah without presenting such a document, by virtue of the Rabbinic enactment entitling every woman to a ketubah. If a widow is living in her father's house, she must collect her ketubah within a period of twenty-five years after her husband's death. After that time, she forfeits her ketubah, for we assume that she has waived it. *Maggid Mishneh* and *Kesef Mishneh* note that the same law applies to the addition to the woman's ketubah, following our Gemara." (*Rambam, Sefer Nashim, Hilkhot Ishut* 16:23; *Shulḥan Arukh, Even HaEzer* 101:1.)

וְלִכְתוּבַּת בְּנִין דִּכְרִין And to the ketubah of male children. "Among the ketubah conditions is the stipulation that the woman's sons will inherit her ketubah from their father

[1]אִיתְּמַר כְּתוּבַּת בְּנִין דִּכְרִין,
[2]פּוּמְבְּדִיתָא אָמְרִי: לָא טָרְפָא
מִמְּשַׁעְבְּדֵי. [3]״יָרְתוּן״ תְּנַן. [4]בְּנֵי
מָתָא מְחַסְיָא אָמְרִי: טָרְפָא
מִמְּשַׁעְבְּדֵי. [5]״יִסְבּוּן״ תְּנַן.
[6]וְהִלְכְתָא: לָא טָרְפָא
מִמְּשַׁעְבְּדֵי. [7]״יָרְתוּן״ תְּנַן.

LITERAL TRANSLATION

[1]It was stated: [Regarding] the ketubah of male children, [2][the Sages of] Pumbedita say: It does not seize from mortgaged property. [3]We have learned: "They will inherit." [4]The Sages of (lit., "sons of") Mata Meḥasya say: It seizes from mortgaged property. [5]We have learned: "They will take." [6]And the law is: It does not seize from mortgaged property. [7]We have learned: "They will inherit."

RASHI

איתמר גרס, ולא גרס "דאיתמר".
ירתון תנן – "אינון ירתון כסף כתובתיך" וירושה לא טרפא לקוחות. **יסבון תנן** – לשון בעל חוב.

TRANSLATION AND COMMENTARY

אִיתְּמַר כְּתוּבַּת בְּנִין דִּכְרִין [1]Having mentioned the Rabbinic enactment of the *ketubat benin dikhrin*, the Gemara now cites an Amoraic dispute about the matter. **It was stated** that the Amoraim disagreed **about** the enactment of **the** *ketubat benin dikhrin*: [2]**The Sages of Pumbedita say:** The enactment **does not allow** the sons **to seize** as payment of their mother's ketubah **property that was pledged** as security for it and was later sold to a third party. All the husband's landed property is pledged as security for the payment of his wife's ketubah, so that she can recover it from real estate that the husband or his heirs have transferred to others. But the sons who come to collect their mother's ketubah by virtue of the enactment of the *ketubat benin dikhrin* cannot collect it from property that has already been sold to a third party. [3]For **we have learned** in the Mishnah (above, 52b) that the condition in the ketubah entitling the sons to their mother's ketubah is formulated as follows: "The male children that you will have from me ***will inherit*** the money of your ketubah in addition to the portion that they will share with their brothers from any other marriage." Since the sons were given the status of heirs, their claim to their mother's ketubah is limited by the laws of inheritance, and an heir inherits only the property that was in the testator's possession at the time of his death, and not property that had already been transferred to a third party. [4]**The Sages of Mata Meḥasya** disagree and **say:** The enactment of the *ketubat benin dikhrin* **allows** the sons **to seize** as payment of their mother's ketubah **property that was pledged** as security for it and was later sold to a third party. [5]For **we have learned** in that Mishnah that the ketubah condition is formulated as follows: "The male children that you will have from me ***will take*** the money of your ketubah in addition to the share that they will share with their brothers from any other marriage." According to the formulation of the ketubah accepted by the scholars of Mata Meḥasya, the sons are treated as creditors who have a prior claim to the property that was sold by their father to a third party. Just as a widow can recover her ketubah from real estate that the husband or his heirs have transferred to others, so too can her sons collect her ketubah from such property. [6]The Gemara concludes: **The law is** in accordance with the viewpoint of the Pumbeditan Sages, who maintain that the enactment of the *ketubat benin dikhrin* **does not allow** the sons **to seize** as payment of their mother's ketubah **property that was pledged** as security for it and was later sold to a third party, [7]for **we have learned** in the Mishnah that the ketubah deed is formulated as follows: "The male children that you will have from me ***will inherit*** the money of your ketubah in addition to the portion that they will share with their brothers from any other marriage."

NOTES

whereas a woman who is living in her father's house can only collect her ketubah within a twenty-five-year period. Most of the Rishonim explain that our Gemara assumes the position of the Sages. Just as a widow may not collect the basic portion of her ketubah after twenty-five years in her father's home, so too may she not collect the addition to her ketubah after that time.

Rivan explains our Gemara in accordance with the viewpoint of Rabbi Meir. Just as a widow who is living in her father's home may collect the basic portion of her ketubah even after twenty-five years have passed, so too may she collect the addition to her ketubah after that time.

HALAKHAH

(should she predecease her husband and her ketubah pass to him) over and above the portion of his estate that they must share with his sons from another marriage. *Shulḥan Arukh* writes that, according to some authorities, the addition to the woman's ketubah is governed by the same law. *Ḥelkat Meḥokek, Bet Shmuel,* and *Gra* all note that this formulation implies that some authorities disagree, whereas in fact our Gemara states explicitly that the enactment of the *ketubat benin dikhrin* also applies to the addition." (*Rambam, Sefer Nashim, Hilkhot Ishut* 19:1; *Shulḥan Arukh, Even HaEzer* 111:1.)

לָא טָרְפָא מִמְּשַׁעְבְּדֵי It does not seize from mortgaged property. "Someone who inherits his mother's ketubah by virtue of the enactment of the *ketubat benin dikhrin* may

TRANSLATION AND COMMENTARY

מְטַלְטְלֵי וְאִיתְנְהוּ בְּעֵינַיְיהוּ [1]The Gemara now continues with a series of disputes between the Sages of Pumbedita and Mata Meḥasya: If someone designates **movable goods** for the payment of his wife's ketubah, **and** when he dies those goods **are** still **intact,** all agree that **she may collect** her ketubah from those movable goods **without** taking **an oath.** Ordinarily a woman cannot collect her ketubah from her late husband's heirs unless she takes an oath that her husband did not deposit money or movable goods with her for the payment of her ketubah. But if the husband did designate movable goods for the payment of his wife's ketubah, and these goods are still in existence at the time of his death, we assume that he did not deposit any additional goods with her for the payment of her ketubah. [2]But the Amoraim disagree about the law in a case in which the goods that were designated for the payment of the ketubah **are no longer intact** when the husband dies. [3]**The Sages of Pumbedita say:** Since the husband designated movable goods for the payment of his wife's ketubah, we assume that he did not deposit any additional goods with her for that purpose, even if the designated goods are no longer intact. Thus the woman can **collect** her ketubah from the rest of her husband's property **without** having to take **an oath.** [4]**The Sages of Mata Meḥasya** disagree and **say:** She can collect her ketubah only if she takes **an oath** that her husband did not deposit other goods with her for the payment of her ketubah. [5]The Gemara concludes: **The law is** in accordance with the viewpoint of the Pumbeditan Sages, that the woman can collect her ketubah from the rest of her husband's property **without** taking **an oath.**

[1]מְטַלְטְלֵי וְאִיתְנְהוּ בְּעֵינַיְיהוּ — בְּלָא שְׁבוּעָה. [2]לֵיתְנְהוּ בְּעֵינַיְיהוּ, [3]פּוּמְבְּדִיתָא אָמְרִי: בְּלָא שְׁבוּעָה. [4]בְּנֵי מָתָא מְחַסְיָא אָמְרִי: בִּשְׁבוּעָה. [5]וְהִלְכְתָא: בְּלָא שְׁבוּעָה.

LITERAL TRANSLATION

[1]Movable goods and they are intact — [she collects] without an oath. [2][If] they are not intact, [3][the Sages of] Pumbedita say: [She collects] without an oath. [4]The Sages of Mata Meḥasya say: With an oath. [5]And the law is: Without an oath.

RASHI

מטלטלי ואיתנהו בעינייהו — המייחד מטלטלין לכתובת אשתו ומת, והן בעין, והיא נפרעת מהן — נוטלתן שלא בשבועה. דטעמא מאי אמור רבנן מנכסי יתומין לא תפרע אלא בשבועה — דחיישינן דלמא צררי אתפסה, והכא היינו צררי דאתפסה. **ליתנהו בעינייהו** — כגון שאבדו. **בלא שבועה** — דכיון דאבוד הני לא אתפסה אחריני, וכל נכסיו אחראין לכתובתה, ונפרעת מן הקרקעות.

BACKGROUND

פּוּמְבְּדִיתָא וּמָתָא מְחַסְיָא Pumbedita and Mata Meḥasya.

Mata Meḥasya was a small town near Sura which later became a suburb of Sura. The discussion in our Gemara apparently refers to a dispute that took place during Rav Ashi's time, when Mata Meḥasya first became an important center of Torah study, competing for primacy with the Pumbedita Yeshivah.

NOTES

לֵיתְנְהוּ בְּעֵינַיְיהוּ **If they are not intact.** Our commentary follows *Rashi,* who explains that the Sages of Pumbedita and Mata Meḥasya disagree about a case in which the husband designated movable goods for the payment of his wife's ketubah, and they were lost, or stolen, or for some other reason no longer intact when the husband died. By Rabbinic enactment, a woman cannot collect her ketubah from her husband's heirs without first taking an oath that she has not yet been paid, for we suspect that her husband may have deposited money or movable goods with her for the payment of her ketubah. But if the husband designated certain movable goods for the payment of his wife's ketubah, and they are still intact at the time of his death, we are not concerned that he may have deposited any additional goods with her. The Sages of Pumbedita and Mata Meḥasya disagree about the case in which the designated goods are no longer intact, as to whether or not there is reason to believe that the husband deposited other goods with his wife in their stead. The law follows the viewpoint of the Sages of Pumbedita that once the husband has designated certain movable goods for the payment of his wife's ketubah, there is no longer any concern that he has deposited other goods with her, even if the designated goods are no longer intact, and therefore the woman can collect her ketubah without taking an oath.

Rif, Rambam, and others (following *Rav Hai Gaon*) explain that the Sages of Pumbedita and Mata Meḥasya disagree about the case in which the particular movable goods that were designated by the husband for the payment of his wife's ketubah are no longer intact, but other goods have taken their place — for example, the designated goods were sold and other goods were bought with the proceeds of the sale. Only in such a case do the Sages of Pumbedita maintain that there is no concern that the husband may have deposited additional goods with his wife for the payment of her ketubah. But if the designated goods were lost, or stolen, or for some other reason not intact, all agree that we must be concerned that the

HALAKHAH

not collect the ketubah from property that his father has transferred to a third party, but only from the free assets in his father's estate, just like any other heir." (*Rambam, Sefer Nashim, Hilkhot Ishut* 19:9; *Shulḥan Arukh, Even HaEzer* 111:13.)

מְטַלְטְלֵי וְאִיתְנְהוּ בְּעֵינַיְיהוּ **Movable goods and they are intact.** "If a husband designated movable goods for the payment of his wife's ketubah, and those goods are still intact, or if they were sold and other goods bought with the proceeds, and those goods are still intact, the woman can collect her ketubah from the movable goods without taking an oath, following the Gemara's conclusion that the law is in accordance with the viewpoint of the Pumbeditan Sages." (*Rambam, Sefer Nashim, Hilkot Ishut* 16:13; *Shulḥan Arukh, Even HaEzer* 96:1.)

TRANSLATION AND COMMENTARY

יִיחֵד לָהּ אַרְעָא בְּאַרְבָּעָה מִצְרָנָהָא [1]The Gemara continues: **If** the husband **designates land for** the payment of his wife's ketubah, specifying the **four boundaries** of the designated land, and he dies, all agree that the woman may **collect** her ketubah **without** taking **an oath,** for in such a case we assume that the husband did not deposit either money or movable goods with her for the payment of her ketubah. [2]But the Amoraim disagree about a case in which the husband designates the land, but mentions only **one** of the four **boundaries.** [3]**The Sages of Pumbedita say** that **she** may **collect** her ketubah **without** taking **an oath,** for even in such a case we assume that the husband did not deposit any other property with his wife for the payment of her ketubah. [4]**The Sages of Mata Meḥasya** disagree and **say:** Since the husband mentioned only one of the four boundaries of the designated property, he may have meant to designate only a thin strip of land along that boundary as security for the payment of his wife's ketubah. Thus his wife may not have relied on that property as sufficient security for the payment of her ketubah, and the husband may well have deposited movable goods with her for the payment of her ketubah. Hence, in order to collect her ketubah the woman **must take an oath** that her husband did not deposit such property with her. [5]The Gemara concludes with the ruling that **the law is** in accordance with the viewpoint of the Sages of Pumbedita that the woman may collect her ketubah **without** taking **an oath,** even if her husband mentioned only one of the boundaries of the land he designated for the payment of her ketubah.

אֲמַר לְעֵדִים [6]The Gemara now records one more dispute between the Sages of Pumbedita and those of Mata Meḥasya: **If someone says to** the **witnesses** to a transaction: **"Write a document** that I am giving So-and-so

[1]יִיחֵד לָהּ אַרְעָא בְּאַרְבָּעָה מִצְרָנָהָא, בְּלָא שְׁבוּעָה. [2]בְּחַד מִצְרָא, [3]פּוּמְבְּדִיתָא אָמְרִי: בְּלָא שְׁבוּעָה. [4]בְּנֵי מָתָא מְחַסְיָא אָמְרִי: בִּשְׁבוּעָה. [5]וְהִלְכְתָא: בְּלָא שְׁבוּעָה. [6]אֲמַר לְעֵדִים: ״כְּתְבוּ וְחִתְמוּ

LITERAL TRANSLATION

[1][If] he designated land for her with four boundaries, [she collects] without an oath. [2][If] with one boundary, [3][the Sages of] Pumbedita say: [She collects] without an oath. [4]The Sages of Mata Meḥasya say: With an oath. [5]And the law is: Without an oath.

[6][If someone] said to witnesses: "Write and sign [a deed of gift]

RASHI

בארבעה מצרנהא — שייחד לה קרקע וכתב לה בארבעה המצרים שלה בחייו, לעשותה אפותיקי לכתובתה, ומת — נפרעת הימנה בלא שבועה, דודאי תו לא מתפיס לה צררי אחריני. **בשבועה** — דכיון דלא כתב לה ארבעה המצרים — אין זו סמיכה לסמוך עליה, והרי היא כמי שלא ייחד, ואיכא למיחש לצררי. **אמר לעדים כתבו וחתמו** — כגון מתנת קרקע.

NOTES

husband may have deposited other goods with his wife, and therefore she cannot collect her ketubah without first taking an oath. The Rishonim support this view by pointing out that the Gemara does not read לֵיתְנְהוּ — "they do not exist" — but rather לֵיתְנְהוּ בְּעֵינַיְיהוּ — "they do not exist in their original state."

כְּתְבוּ וְחִתְמוּ Write and sign. The Rishonim disagree about the nature of the case in dispute between the Sages of Pumbedita and those of Mata Meḥasya. Our commentary follows *Rashi* and most Rishonim, who explain that the Gemara is referring here to a case in which someone instructed two witnesses to draw up a deed of gift of landed property and to give it to the recipient. If a valid act of acquisition has been performed, all agree that the donor need not be consulted again, for the transfer of the gift has already been finalized by the act of acquisition. But if a valid act of acquisition has not yet been performed, the Amoraim disagree about whether the witnesses must consult the donor to make sure he has not changed his mind. But if someone instructs witnesses to draw up and deliver a deed testifying to a loan that he has received from another person or to an admission of indebtedness to another person, then all agree that the witnesses are not required to consult with him again before delivering the deed to the person in whose favor it was written, even if a valid act of acquisition has not been performed.

Rambam disagrees and states that even with respect to a deed testifying to a loan or an admission of indebtedness,

HALAKHAH

יִיחֵד לָהּ אַרְעָא בְּאַרְבָּעָה מִצְרָנָהָא If he designated land for her. "If a husband designated land for the payment of his wife's ketubah, whether he specified the four boundaries of the designated land or only a single boundary, the woman may collect her ketubah from that land without taking an oath, following the Gemara's conclusion that the law is in accordance with the view of the Pumbeditan Sages." (*Rambam, Sefer Nashim, Hilkot Ishut* 16:13; *Shulḥan Arukh, Even HaEzer* 96:1.)

אֲמַר לְעֵדִים: ״כְּתְבוּ וְחִתְמוּ״ If someone said to witnesses: "Write and sign." "If someone lends another person money in the presence of witnesses, they may not reduce their testimony to writing (so that the oral loan not be treated as a loan in writing), unless the debtor tells them to draw up a document, sign it and give it to the creditor. Even if the debtor gave the witnesses such instructions, they must consult with him again before handing the document over to the creditor. According to some authorities, it is not necessary to consult with the debtor again. If the debtor obligated himself with a *kinyan sudar* to repay the loan, the

TRANSLATION AND COMMENTARY

a certain field as **a gift, sign it and give** the deed **to him,"** [1] **and a** valid **act of acquisition has** already **been performed,** so that the donor can no longer withdraw from the transaction, all agree that **it is not necessary** for the witnesses **to consult with** the donor again before they actually draw up the deed of gift and present it to the recipient. Since a valid act of acquisition has already been performed, the gift is final and the deed of gift merely documents the transfer of ownership. But there is an Amoraic dispute about a case in which the donor tells the witnesses to draw up the deed, to sign it, and to give it to the recipient, [2] but **a** valid **act of acquisition** finalizing the transaction **has not** yet **been performed.** [3] **The Sages of Pumbedita say** that even in such a case **it is not necessary** for the witnesses **to consult with** the donor again before they draw up the deed of gift and give it to the recipient. [4] But **the Sages of Meḥasya** disagree and **say: It is necessary** for the witnesses **to consult with** the donor a second time before they draw up the deed. As long as a valid act of acquisition has not yet been performed, the donor can still retract. Thus the witnesses must consult again with the donor before drawing up the deed of gift, in order to verify that he has not changed his mind. [5] The Gemara ends this discussion with the ruling that **the law is** in accordance with the viewpoint of the Sages of Mata Meḥasya that **it is necessary** for the witnesses **to consult with** the donor again before they draw up the deed of gift.

רַבִּי אֶלְעָזָר בֶּן עֲזַרְיָה [6] The Gemara now resumes its analysis of our Mishnah, which stated: **"Rabbi Elazar ben Azaryah** says: If a woman was widowed or divorced after marriage, she collects the entire amount recorded in the ketubah, both the basic portion and any additional sum. But if she was widowed or divorced after betrothal, she collects only the basic portion of her ketubah, but not any additional sum, for the bridegroom obligated himself to pay the additional sum only on the basis that he would marry her." [7] **It was stated** that **Rav and Rabbi Natan disagreed** about the following question: **One of them said:**

וַהֲבוּ לֵיהּ", [1] קָנוּ מִינֵּיהּ, לָא צָרִיךְ אִימְּלוּכֵי בֵּיהּ. [2] לָא קָנוּ מִינֵּיהּ, [3] פּוּמְבְּדִיתָא אָמְרִי: לָא צָרִיךְ אִימְּלוּכֵי בֵּיהּ. [4] בְּנֵי מָתָא מְחַסְיָא אָמְרִי: צָרִיךְ אִימְּלוּכֵי בֵּיהּ. [5] וְהִלְכְתָא: צָרִיךְ אִימְּלוּכֵי בֵּיהּ.

[6] "רַבִּי אֶלְעָזָר בֶּן עֲזַרְיָה, וכו'".

[7] אִיתְּמַר: רַב וְרַבִּי נָתָן. חַד

LITERAL TRANSLATION

and give [it] to him," [1] [and] they performed an act of acquisition from him, it is not necessary to consult with him. [2] [If] they did not perform an act of acquisition from him, [3] [the Sages of] Pumbedita say: It is not necessary to consult with him. [4] The Sages of Mata Meḥasya say: It is necessary to consult with him. [5] And the law is: It is necessary to consult with him.

[6] "Rabbi Elazar ben Azaryah, etc." [7] It was stated: Rav and Rabbi Natan [disagreed]. One of

RASHI

לא צריך לאימלוכיביה – אם עדיין עומד בדבורו שיכתבו לו, דכיון דקנו ממנו – סתם קנין לכתיבה עומד.

NOTES

the Sages of Pumbedita and those of Mata Meḥasya disagree about whether the witnesses must consult the debtor before they transfer the deed to the creditor, if a valid act of acquisition has not been performed.

Ra'avad maintains that the case in question is one in which witnesses were instructed to draw up a ketubah with an addition, and the Amoraim disagree as to whether they must consult the husband again in order to verify that he still wants to obligate himself to that sum before they hand the ketubah over to the woman. According to *Ra'avad,* it is clear why this dispute is recorded in our Gemara. According to the other Rishonim, this dispute is brought here as an appendage to the other disagreements between the Sages of Pumbedita and those of Mata Meḥasya.

לָא צָרִיךְ אִימְּלוּכֵי בֵּיהּ **It is not necessary to consult with him.** *Rashi* maintains that all agree that once a valid act of acquisition has been performed, it is not necessary for the witnesses to consult with the donor again before they actually draw up the deed of gift and deliver it to the recipient, because we invoke the principle that an act of acquisition is intended to be committed to writing. When the Gemara speaks here of a valid act of acquisition, it is referring to a *kinyan sudar,* the symbolic transfer of a handkerchief or some other small article from one party to another, thereby formalizing the agreement that has been reached between them. Unless specified otherwise, an agreement formalized by a *kinyan sudar* is intended to be committed to writing. *Rashi* apparently understands from this that once a *kinyan sudar* has been performed, the parties cannot object to having the agreement committed

HALAKHAH

witnesses may commit the loan to writing, even if the debtor did not tell them to do so, for unless it is specified otherwise, a loan accompanied by a *kinyan sudar* is intended to be committed to writing. *Shakh* notes that the opinion requiring the witnesses to consult with the debtor reflects the view of *Rambam,* but most authorities (*Ra'avad, Ittur, Ran, Maggid Mishneh,* and others) disagree with him, maintaining that our Gemara's ruling refers to a case in which two witnesses were asked to draw up a deed of gift of land." (*Rambam, Sefer Mishpatim, Hilkhot Malveh VeLoveh* 11:1; *Shulḥan Arukh, Ḥoshen Mishpat* 39:2-3.)

TERMINOLOGY

תִּסְתַּיֵּים Conclude. Sometimes the Talmud notes that there was a controversy between two Sages concerning a certain issue, but it is not clear which Sage took what position. In such cases, the Talmud's initial attempt to attribute the views correctly is often introduced by the expression תִּסְתַּיֵּים דְּרַבִּי פְּלוֹנִי הוּא דְּאָמַר — "Conclude that it was Rabbi A who said...[and that Rabbi B holds the other view]."

SAGES

רַבִּי שִׁמְעוֹן שְׁזוּרִי Rabbi Shimon Shezuri. This Tanna lived during the period following the destruction of the Second Temple. He was a student of Rabbi Tarfon, and his colleagues were the principal students of Rabbi Akiva. His teachings are cited in the Mishnah and in Baraitot. We know nothing of his life, and his name "Shezuri" has been explained in various ways. Some authorities maintain that it refers to his profession, that he was a spinner of yarn or rope (לְשַׁזֵּר means "to spin"), but others link it to the village of Shazur on the border between Upper and Lower Galilee.

אֲמַר: [1]הֲלָכָה כְּרַבִּי אֶלְעָזָר בֶּן עֲזַרְיָה. [2]וְחַד אֲמַר: אֵין הֲלָכָה כְּרַבִּי אֶלְעָזָר בֶּן עֲזַרְיָה. [3]תִּסְתַּיֵּים דְּרַבִּי נָתָן הוּא דְּאָמַר הֲלָכָה כְּרַבִּי אֶלְעָזָר בֶּן עֲזַרְיָה, [4]דְּשָׁמְעִינַן לֵיהּ לְרַבִּי נָתָן דְּאָזֵיל בָּתַר אוּמְדָּנָא. [5]דְּאָמַר רַבִּי נָתָן: הֲלָכָה כְּרַבִּי שִׁמְעוֹן שְׁזוּרִי

LITERAL TRANSLATION

them] said: [1]The law is in accordance with Rabbi Elazar ben Azaryah. [2]And one said: The law is not in accordance with Rabbi Elazar ben Azaryah.

[3]Conclude that it was Rabbi Natan who said [that] the law is in accordance with Rabbi Elazar ben Azaryah, [4]for we have heard about Rabbi Natan that he follows an estimation. [5]For Rabbi Natan said: The law is in accordance with Rabbi Shimon Shezuri

RASHI

בתר אומדנא — אומד הדעת. בדבר שאינו מפורש אומדין בית דין, ואומרים: סתם אינש להכי איכוון, דלא כותב לה ממונו חנס אלא לחיבת ביאה.

TRANSLATION AND COMMENTARY

[1]**The law is in accordance with** the viewpoint of **Rabbi Elazar ben Azaryah,** who maintains that if a betrothed woman is widowed or divorced before her marriage, she collects only the basic portion of her ketubah, but not any additional sum promised by her bridegroom. [2]**And the other** Sage — Rav or Rabbi Natan — **said: The law is not in accordance with** the viewpoint of **Rabbi Elazar ben Azaryah,** but in accordance with the position of the anonymous first Tanna, who maintains that a woman is entitled to the entire amount recorded in her ketubah, both the basic portion and the addition, even if she was widowed or divorced after betrothal.

תִּסְתַּיֵּים [3]The Gemara has just stated that Rav and Rabbi Natan disagree about whether or not the law is in accordance with the viewpoint of Rabbi Elazar ben Azaryah. But the Gemara did not specify which of the viewpoints was that of Rav and which was that of Rabbi Natan. The Gemara now addresses this issue. We can **conclude that it was Rabbi Natan who said that the law is in accordance with** the viewpoint of **Rabbi Elazar ben Azaryah,** [4]**for we have heard that Rabbi Natan** ruled on an entirely different matter that if a person does not state his intentions in a clear manner, the court **estimates** what most people who find themselves in a similar situation have in mind. Thus Rabbi Natan must have ruled in accordance with Rabbi Elazar ben Azaryah that a woman who is widowed or divorced after betrothal is not entitled to the addition to her ketubah, for we assume that the husband obligated himself to give that additional sum only if the marriage actually took place. The Gemara now explains how we know that Rabbi Natan is of the opinion that the court estimates a person's intentions and issues rulings accordingly. [5]**For Rabbi Natan said: The law is in accordance with** the opinion of **Rabbi Shimon Shezuri in the case of someone who is dangerously ill.** We have learned elsewhere in the Mishnah (*Gittin* 65b): "At first the Sages said that if a person was being taken out to execution and he said to two people: 'Write a bill of divorce for my wife,' they should write the bill of divorce and give it to her. Even though the husband did not say that the bill of divorce should be given to the wife, we assume that he meant that it be given to her. Later the Sages said that the same law applies in the case of a person who is going out to sea or on some other long journey. Rabbi Shimon Shezuri said that the same law also applies in the case of a person who is mortally ill, for we assume that a person in such a situation would not have asked that a bill of divorce be written for his wife unless he intended that it be given to her." Now, just as Rabbi Natan ruled in accordance with the viewpoint of Rabbi Shimon Shezuri that we evaluate the intentions of a mortally ill person who asks two people to draw up a bill of divorce for his wife, he must likewise have ruled in accordance with the position of Rabbi Elazar ben Azaryah that we

NOTES

to writing, and therefore in our case the donor need not be consulted again about whether he still wishes the deed of gift to be drawn up and delivered to the recipient.

Ritva understands the matter differently. An agreement formalized by a *kinyan sudar* is intended to be committed to writing, but the parties to the agreement can still object to having a deed drawn up. However, unless we know otherwise, we assume that the parties have not changed their minds about wanting a written document, and therefore in our case the witnesses need not consult with the donor before they draw up the deed and deliver it to the recipient (see also *Tosafot*).

אוּמְדָּנָא Estimation. This is a Halakhic procedure in which a court bases its decision on an assumption about what a reasonable person would do in given circumstances, even when nothing explicit was stated about his intention, either orally or in writing. Since in monetary disputes one generally does not accept implicit intentions (אֵין הוֹלְכִים אַחַר דְּבָרִים שֶׁבַּלֵּב — lit., "one does not go after words in the heart", there is a dispute among the Sages regarding the degree to which it can be said that in a certain case a person's unexpressed intention was clear and understandable, and did not have to be stated explicitly.

TRANSLATION AND COMMENTARY

assess the intentions of a husband who obligates himself to make an addition to his wife's ketubah. [55B] Before questioning the conclusion to be drawn from Rabbi Natan's ruling that the law is in accordance with the viewpoint of Rabbi Shimon Shezuri in the case of someone who is dangerously ill, the Gemara first cites the second half of that ruling. [1] Rabbi Natan said: The law is also in accordance with the viewpoint of Rabbi Shimon Shezuri **about terumah of tithe from** doubtfully tithed produce, known as *demai* — produce which was bought from a person who, we suspect, may not have separated the various tithes, and from which the buyer must separate tithes by Rabbinic decree. The buyer must separate the first tithe (ten percent) from the produce, and from that first tithe he must separate one-tenth (called "terumah of tithe") and give it to a priest. On this point, we have learned elsewhere in the Mishnah (*Demai* 4:1): "If the terumah of tithe that a person has set aside from *demai* becomes mixed again with the produce from which it has been separated, so that the entire mixture is now forbidden to be eaten by an ordinary Jew on account of the terumah in it, which is permitted only to priests, Rabbi Shimon Shezuri says that the buyer can ask the seller whether or not he tithed his produce before he sold it, and can rely on his

בִּמְסוּכָּן, [55B] [1] וּבִתְרוּמַת מַעֲשֵׂר שֶׁל דְּמַאי.

LITERAL TRANSLATION

in [the case of] one who is dangerously ill, [55B] [1] and in [the case of] terumah of tithe from *demai*.

RASHI

במסוכן — במסכת גיטין (סה,ב): המפרש והיוצא בשיירא ואומר "כתבו גט לאשתי", אף על פי שלא אמר "תנו" — הרי אלו יכתבו ויתנו. דמחמת טרדתו, שהוא בהול על נפשו, לא הספיק לגמור דבריו, ומעיקרא לכתבו ותנו נתכוון. רבי שמעון שזורי אומר: אף המסוכן הגוסס, והיינו בתר אומדן דעתא, דאמרינן לא אמר כתבו אלא שיתנו, הואיל ומסוכן הוא — לא נתכוון לצחק בה. **ובתרומת מעשר של דמאי** — משנה היא במסכת דמאי (פרק ד משנה א): תרומת מעשר של דמאי שחזרה למקומה, ואסרה את החולין משום מדומע. רבי שמעון שזורי אומר: אף בחול שואלו לעם הארץ שלקח הימנו הפירות הללו, ואוכלן על פיו. אם אמר הפרשתי מעשרותיו כראוי עד שלא מכרתים לך — סומך עליו, דהואיל ומדרבנן הוא — הימנוהו רבנן במקום פסידא כי הכא, שאין לו תקנה לחזור ולהפריש, אלא למוכרה לכהנים בדמי תרומה, והפסד הוא לו. האי דנקט אף בחול — משום דקתני התם מילתא אחריתי. ויש בה חילוק, דבשבת שואלו ואוכלו על פיו מפני עונג שבת, ולמוצאי שבת לא יאכל עד שיעשר.

NOTES

בְּמְסוּכָּן In the case of one who is dangerously ill. *Rashi* explains that Rabbi Shimon Shezuri is referring to a dying person. Some Rishonim ask: If so, why do the Rabbis disagree? There is surely as much reason to assume that the dying man intended that the bill of divorce be given to his wife as there is in the case of a person who went out to sea or on some other long journey! They answer that Rabbi Shimon Shezuri is referring to a person who became ill suddenly, as is suggested in the Jerusalem Talmud, or to a person who thought he was dying but whose condition was actually not critical (see *Ritva, Meiri*).

ובִתְרוּמַת מַעֲשֵׂר And in the case of terumah of tithe. *Rivan* explains that Rabbi Shimon Shezuri's ruling regarding terumah of tithe of *demai* is mentioned here only incidentally. Having cited Rabbi Natan's ruling in accordance with the viewpoint of Rabbi Shimon Shezuri on one matter, the Gemara mentions incidentally that Rabbi Natan also ruled in accordance with the viewpoint of Rabbi Shimon Shezuri on a completely unrelated matter.

Shittah Mekubbetzet explains that, according to *Tosafot,* Rabbi Shimon Shezuri's ruling regarding terumah of tithe of *demai* is mentioned here because it, too, is based on the principle that we estimate a person's intentions and issue rulings accordingly. For Rabbi Shimon Shezuri maintains that if the terumah of tithe that a person has set aside from *demai* falls back into the produce from which it was separated, the buyer can rely on the seller's claim that the produce has already been tithed, because we estimate that even an *am ha'aretz*, an uneducated person who is not ordinarily believed when he claims that he has separated tithes, would not lie in a case in which terumah of tithe has already been separated from the produce.

וּבִתְרוּמַת מַעֲשֵׂר שֶׁל דְּמַאי And in the case of terumah of tithe from *demai*. Most Rishonim follow *Rashi*, who explains that we are dealing with a case in which terumah of tithe was set aside from produce that had been bought from an *am ha'aretz*, who is suspect about tithing, and it later fell back into the produce from which it had been separated. In such a case, the buyer can ask the seller whether he tithed his produce before he sold it, and can

HALAKHAH

בְּמְסוּכָּן In the case of one who is dangerously ill. "If someone asks two people to write his wife a bill of divorce, they should write it and give it to him. But they should not deliver the bill of divorce to his wife, unless he tells them explicitly to do so; and if they give her the bill of divorce without having received such instructions, it is not valid. This ruling applies to a healthy man in ordinary circumstances. But if a man was critically ill, or if he was being taken out to be executed, or if he was going out to sea or on some other long journey — in all these cases, even if he only said that the two should write his wife a bill of divorce, they should write the bill of divorce and deliver it to her, for it is clear that it was his intention that the bill of divorce be written and delivered to his wife," following Rabbi Natan's ruling in accordance with the viewpoint of Rabbi Shimon Shezuri. (*Rambam, Sefer Nashim, Hilkhot Gerushin* 2:12; *Shulḥan Arukh, Even HaEzer* 141:16.)

וּבִתְרוּמַת מַעֲשֵׂר שֶׁל דְּמַאי And in the case of terumah of tithe from *demai*. "If someone who is ordinarily not believed with respect to the separation of tithes is seen

TRANSLATION AND COMMENTARY

answer that he did indeed tithe the produce, even though the seller is a person who is not ordinarily believed when he claims that he has separated the tithes." Rabbi Natan ruled that the law is in accordance with this ruling of Rabbi Shimon Shezuri.

וְרַב [1]The Gemara objects: It was argued, above, that the Sage who said that the law is in accordance with the viewpoint of Rabbi Elazar ben Azaryah in our Mishnah must be Rabbi Natan, because we know that Rabbi Natan maintains that the court estimates a person's intentions and issues rulings accordingly. **But** does this mean that **Rav does not** maintain that the court **estimates** a person's intentions? [2]**Surely** we have learned otherwise, for **it was taught** that the Amoraim disagreed **about the gift of a person on his deathbed when the deed recording it states that an act of acquisition,** a *kinyan sudar* (a symbolic version of barter which is widely effective in transferring property), had been performed. The Rabbis enacted that the verbal instructions of a person on his deathbed have the same force as a formal deed written and delivered. But what is the law if a mortally ill person expresses his wish that a gift be given to another person and then records that gift in a document stating that a *kinyan sudar* has been performed? [3]**In the School of Rav they said in the name**

[1]וְרַב לָא אָזֵיל בָּתַר אוּמְדָּנָא? [2]וְהָא אִיתְּמַר: מַתְּנַת שְׁכִיב מְרַע שֶׁכָּתוּב בָּהּ קִנְיָן, [3]בְּבֵי רַב מִשְּׁמֵיהּ דְּרַב אָמְרִי: אַרְכְּבֵיהּ

LITERAL TRANSLATION

[1]But does Rav not follow an estimation? [2]But surely it was stated: [Regarding] the gift of a person on his deathbed in which an act of acquisition was written, [3]in the School of Rav they said in the name of Rav: He made him ride

RASHI

מתנת שכיב מרע – אינה לריכה קנין, שתקנו חכמים שדבריו ככתובים וכמסורים, שלא תטרף דעתו עליו.

CONCEPTS

מַתְּנַת שְׁכִיב מְרַע A gift of a person on his deathbed. By Rabbinic decree, gifts given by a person on his deathbed differ in several ways from those given in other circumstances. For example, the gift of a person on his deathbed is valid even if no act of acquisition (קִנְיָן) was performed, as long as the donor expressed his intention in words. Likewise, a mortally ill person may retract his gift as many times as he wishes, provided that he is of sound mind when he does so. All gifts given by a person on his deathbed are invalidated if he recovers.

NOTES

rely on his answer that the produce was indeed properly tithed. Since we believe the seller's claim that he tithed his produce, the buyer was not required to set aside terumah of tithe at all, and thus the produce into which it fell is permitted.

The Rishonim offer two explanations of why the seller is believed if he claims that his produce was properly tithed. *Rashi* argues that since the buyer would suffer a significant financial loss were the mixture to be declared forbidden — for nothing can be done with the mixture of terumah of tithe and ordinary produce, except to sell it to a priest at a discount price — the Rabbis were lenient and allowed the buyer to accept the seller's word that he had tithed his produce. According to *Tosafot* and others, the seller can be trusted because we assume that whereas an *am ha'aretz* is prepared to lie about his untithed produce and to claim that it was properly tithed (for he treats the prohibition against the consumption of untithed produce lightly), he is afraid to lie about the terumah of tithe that the buyer separated from his produce, and to claim falsely that the buyer had not been required to set it aside because he himself had properly tithed the produce (for he takes seriously the prohibition against eating terumah of tithe).

An entirely different explanation is offered by *Rambam* (*Hilkhot Ma'aser* 12:4): The Mishnah teaches that if an *am ha'aretz*, who is not ordinarily trusted about tithes, is seen setting aside terumah of tithe from his produce, and we then see that the terumah of tithe that he has set aside has fallen back into ordinary produce, and the *am ha'aretz* later claims that he set aside terumah of tithe from the mixture, he is believed, for even a person who is suspected of not tithing his produce is afraid to lie about mixtures of terumah of tithe and ordinary produce.

The Rishonim raise a number of objections against *Rambam's* ruling (see *Ra'avad, Kesef Mishneh*, and others). *Meiri* suggests that *Rambam* is referring to a case in which one part of the terumah of tithe fell into more than 100 parts of ordinary tithed produce. In such a case, the mixture is forbidden until an amount equal to the terumah of tithe that fell into the ordinary produce is removed from the mixture. The *am ha'aretz* is believed if he claims that he removed such an amount from the mixture, for we assume that he is afraid to lie about mixtures of terumah of tithe and ordinary produce. Alternatively, *Rambam* is referring to a case in which the seller insisted from the beginning that he had properly tithed his produce. But since his word was not accepted, he tithed the produce a second time so that people would buy it, and then the terumah of tithe fell into the tithed produce. In such a case we believe the seller with respect to his original claim that the produce had been properly tithed.

שֶׁכָּתוּב בָּהּ קִנְיָן In which an act of acquisition was written. *Tosafot* discusses at length the different opinions regarding the expression "in which an act of acquisition

HALAKHAH

setting aside terumah of tithe from his produce, and we see that the terumah of tithe that he set aside became mixed with ordinary produce, whether with the produce from which it was separated or with other tithed produce, and he claims that he has set aside terumah of tithe from the mixture, he is believed (not only on Shabbat, but even during the week), and we may eat of the produce on the basis of his claim. For even someone who we suspect may not have separated the various tithes is believed with respect to a mixture of terumah and ordinary produce. According to *Ra'avad,* if one part of terumah of tithe of *demai* falls into less than 100 parts of ordinary tithed produce, and the *am ha'aretz* from whom the *demai* was bought claims that he tithed his produce properly, so that it was unnecessary for the buyer to set aside terumah of tithe, the *am ha'aretz* is believed and the mixture may be eaten on the basis of his claim. *Radbaz* notes that *Rambam* agrees with *Ra'avad's* ruling (see also *Kesef Mishneh*)." (*Rambam, Sefer Zeraim, Hilkhot Ma'aser* 12:4.)

מַתְּנַת שְׁכִיב מְרַע שֶׁכָּתוּב בָּהּ קִנְיָן The gift of a person on his deathbed in which an act of acquisition was

TRANSLATION AND COMMENTARY

of Rav: The donor has **made** the recipient of the gift **ride on two horses.** In other words, the two separate acts of donation reinforce each other. [1]**But Shmuel said: I do not know how to rule on this,** for it is possible that the gift has no validity at all.

בְּבֵי רַב מִשְּׁמֵיהּ דְּרַב אָמְרִי [2]The Gemara now explains the position of Rav. **In the School of Rav they said in the name of Rav:** [3]The donor has **made** the recipient of the gift **ride on two horses.** [4]In some respects the gift **is like the gift of a healthy person,** for the donor employed one of the regular modes of acquisition, which is required only of a healthy person. [5]**But** in other respects **it is like the gift of a person on his deathbed,** for the donor was mortally ill when the gift was made. How so? [6]The gift **is like the gift of a healthy person,** [7]**in that if** the donor **recovers he cannot retract.** The gift of a healthy person takes effect immediately, and therefore, once a valid act of acquisition has been performed, the donor cannot withdraw from the transaction. But the gift of a person on his deathbed takes effect only upon his death, for the Rabbis enacted that such a gift is to be regarded as a form of bequest. If a critically ill person makes a gift and then recovers, the gift is invalidated. If, however, a person on his deathbed expresses his desire that a gift be made to someone, and he also effects one of the regular acts of acquisition, the gift remains in effect even if the donor recovers. [8]But such a gift **is** also treated **like the gift of a person on his deathbed,** [9]**in that if** the donor **said:** "Let **a loan owed to me** by So-and-so

אַתְּרֵי רִכְשֵׁי. [1]וּשְׁמוּאֵל אֲמַר: לָא יָדַעְנָא מַאי אֵידוּן בָּהּ. [2]בְּבֵי רַב מִשְּׁמֵיהּ דְּרַב אָמְרִי: [3]אַרְכְּבֵיהּ אַתְּרֵי רִכְשֵׁי. [4]הֲרֵי הִיא כְּמַתְּנַת בָּרִיא, [5]וַהֲרֵי הִיא כְּמַתְּנַת שְׁכִיב מְרַע. [6]הֲרֵי הִיא כְּמַתְּנַת בָּרִיא, [7]דְּאִם עָמַד אֵינוֹ יָכוֹל לַחֲזוֹר בּוֹ. [8]הֲרֵי הִיא כְּמַתְּנַת שְׁכִיב מְרַע, [9]שֶׁאִם

LITERAL TRANSLATION

on two horses. [1]But Shmuel said: I do not know how to rule on this.

[2]In the School of Rav they said in the name of Rav: [3]He made him ride on two horses. [4]It is like the gift of a healthy person, [5]and it is like the gift of a person on his deathbed. [6]It is like the gift of a healthy person, [7]in that if he recovered he cannot retract. [8]It is like the gift of a person on his deathbed, [9]in that if

RASHI

ואם כתוב בה קנין — אמר רב: ארכביה אתרי רכשי, כמו "רוכבי הרכש" (אסתר ח). כלומר, נתן בה שתי כחות. על ידי שכתוב בה "כדקליר ורמי בערסיה" וכל לשון שכיב מרע — נתן בה כח שכיב מרע, ועל ידי קנין שכתוב בה, שאינו נוהג אלא בבריא — נתן בה כח בריא. והשתא מפרש להו: כח מתנת בריא — שאם עמד מחוליו אינו חוזר ממתנתו, מה שאין כן בשכיב מרע. והרי היא כמתנת שכיב מרע שאין במתנת בריא אפילו בקנין, שאם כתב במתנה זו "הלואתי — שהלויתי לפלוני נתונה לפלוני זה" — הלואתו לפלוני, ואילו גבי בריא משום קנין לא קני ביה, שאין מטבע נקנה בחליפין אלא אגב קרקע, כדאמרינן ב"הזהב" (בבא מציעא מו,א). וזה קנה אם מת לא מחמת קנין אלא מחמת דברי שכיב מרע.

BACKGROUND

אַרְכְּבֵיהּ אַתְּרֵי רִכְשֵׁי **He made him ride on two horses.** This colorful expression means that the act of transferring the gift to the recipient had double validity, both as the gift of a healthy donor and also as the gift of a donor on his deathbed. The expression derives from the Persian army practice of getting troops to take two horses with them to war, in order to have a fresh horse when the first one tired. Here, too, the recipient benefits from the advantages of the doubly valid act of donation.

NOTES

was written." Does it mean that an act of acquisition, such as a *kinyan sudar*, was mentioned explicitly in the deed transferring the dying person's property to someone else, or does it mean that an act of acquisition was performed, even if it was not mentioned in the deed? All agree that if the deed was formulated in such a way that it is clear that a *kinyan sudar* was performed, not because the dying person did not want his gift to be effected by means of the special enactment allowing a person on his deathbed to dispose of his property without performing a valid act of acquisition, but in order to strengthen the recipient's claim to the property, the gift is treated as that of a person on his deathbed.

לָא יָדַעְנָא מַאי אֵידוּן בָּהּ **I do not know how to rule on this.** Most Rishonim (*Rashba*, *Ritva*, and *Meiri*) explain that since the validity of the gift is in question, the recipient is not entitled to the property, even if he seizes it, for unless it can be proved otherwise, the donor's heirs are assumed to be the rightful owners of his estate.

Ra'avad argues that since the validity of the gift is in doubt, neither the recipient of the gift nor the donor's heir is presumed to be the rightful owner. Thus, if the recipient of the gift seizes the property upon the donor's death, we do not remove it from his possession.

HALAKHAH

written. "If a dying person expresses the wish that his property be given to someone, and he records that gift in a deed stating that a *kinyan sudar* has been performed, the gift is not valid, for we are concerned that he may have intended to transfer the property only by means of the deed, and a deed of gift is not valid if it is to take effect only after the donor's death (following Shmuel, whose viewpoint is accepted in monetary matters). But if the dying person states explicitly (or it is clear from his actions) that the *kinyan sudar* was employed merely to strengthen the recipient's claim to the property, the gift is valid. Numerous factors must be taken into account when considering whether or not a *kinyan sudar* cancels a gift made by a person on his deathbed." (*Rambam, Sefer Kinyan, Hilkhot Zekhiyyah U'Mattanah* 8:10; *Shulḥan Arukh, Ḥoshen Mishpat* 250:17-19.)

TRANSLATION AND COMMENTARY

be transferred to So-and-so," [1]**the money owed him is** indeed **transferred to So-and-so.** Ordinarily, a creditor can assign a loan to someone who was not a party to the obligation only by means of a *ma'amad sheloshtan* (מַעֲמַד שְׁלָשְׁתָּן — "a meeting of the three"), which requires the physical presence of the debtor, the creditor and the assignee. But if the creditor is on his deathbed, this requirement is waived, and the mere expression of his desire that the loan be transferred to the other person is sufficient.

וּשְׁמוּאֵל אָמַר [2]The Gemara now proceeds to explain the viewpoint of Shmuel. **Shmuel said: I do not know how to rule on this** matter, [3]**for it is possible that** the gift has no validity at all. The dying person

אָמַר: ״הַלְוָאָתִי לִפְלוֹנִי״, [1]הַלְוָאָתוֹ לִפְלוֹנִי. [2]וּשְׁמוּאֵל אָמַר: לָא יָדַעְנָא מַאי אֵידוּן בָּהּ, [3]שֶׁמָּא לֹא גָּמַר

LITERAL TRANSLATION

he said: "My loan is [transferred] to So-and-so," [1]his loan is [transferred] to So-and-so.

[2]But Shmuel said: I do not know how to rule on this, [3]lest he did not intend

RASHI

שמא לא גמר בלבו להקנותו [אלא בשטר — שמאחר להכי כתב בה קנין, דלא גמר להקנותו] מתנה זו על ידי דברי שכיב מרע שהן ככתובים ומסורים דמי, אלא על ידי כתיבה וקנין, כבריא. דסתם קנין לכתיבה עומד, ושטר שכיב מרע אינו קונה מחיים,

NOTES

שֶׁאִם אָמַר: ״הַלְוָאָתִי לִפְלוֹנִי״ **In that if he said: "My loan is transferred to So-and-so."** *Rashi* understands the innovation contained in this law as follows: If a dying person expresses his desire that money owed to him be transferred to a third party, the gift is valid, even though a healthy person cannot transfer a loan even by means of *kinyan sudar*, for there is a rule that money cannot be acquired through barter, and *kinyan sudar* is a special case of barter. The mode of acquisition that is effective with respect to money, continues *Rashi*, is *agav karka* — acquiring it as an adjunct to land.

Tosafot and others raise a number of objections: First, according to *Rashi*, the Gemara should have said: "My coins are transferred to So-and-so," rather than: "My loan is transferred to him." Furthermore, the inference from *Rashi*'s explanation — that a loan can be transferred as an adjunct of land — is contradicted by the statement elsewhere (*Bava Batra* 148a) that a loan can be transferred only by means of *ma'amad sheloshtan* ("a meeting of the three"), a mode of acquisition requiring the physical presence of the debtor, the creditor, and the person to whom the loan is being assigned. Rather, says *Tosafot*, a healthy person cannot transfer a loan by means of a *kinyan sudar*, because a loan is viewed as an intangible obligation (there being no specific money that the debtor must return to the creditor), and a *kinyan sudar* cannot effect the acquisition of something intangible.

According to *Rav Hai Gaon*, the Gemara is referring here to a loan that had been committed to writing. Even though a healthy person can transfer such a loan only by delivering the deed attesting to the loan to the buyer, together with a second deed confirming that the buyer is to acquire the deed and the rights contained in it, a person on his deathbed can transfer such a loan without performing any act of acquisition.

הַלְוָאָתוֹ לִפְלוֹנִי **His loan is transferred to So-and-so.** According to *Rashi*, Rav maintains that the court may estimate a person's intentions and may issue rulings accordingly. We learn this from the fact that Rav says that the gift is treated both as the gift given by a healthy person, and as a gift given by a person on his deathbed. For if we do not estimate the dying man's intentions, Rav should have ruled — like Shmuel — that the gift has no validity at all.

Tosafot argues that Rav maintains that the court may estimate a person's intentions because he says that the gift is treated as a gift given by a person on his deathbed. Otherwise, the gift would be treated as a gift given by a healthy person.

Maharsha explains that the gift should have been treated as a gift given by a healthy person, even without estimating the donor's intentions, because he performed a valid act of acquisition. But it is only because we estimate his intentions that the gift is also treated as a gift given by a person on his deathbed; for if we do not estimate the donor's intentions, it might be argued that the deed mentions that the donor was on his deathbed, not because he wants the gift to be treated as the gift of a dying person, but because his situation is a relevant fact in the case.

Tosafot maintains that when the Gemara suggests that Rav is of the opinion that the court may estimate a person's intentions and issue rulings accordingly, it does not mean to imply that Shmuel does not maintain the same, for Shmuel himself rules in accordance with the viewpoint of Rabbi Elazar ben Azaryah in our Mishnah. *Tosafot* also raises the alternative argument that the Gemara is now suggesting that it is only Rav who maintains that the court may estimate a person's intentions, and that on the basis of that estimate it may extract money from someone who has physical possession of that money. Shmuel agrees that we may estimate a person's intentions, but only to allow him to retain money demanded of him by others.

Tosafot Yeshanim suggests that there is a special affinity between the estimate recognized by Rav and that recognized by Rabbi Elazar ben Azaryah.

Or Same'aḥ explains that just as in the case of the deed of gift of the dying person there is only a single deed, and yet we estimate that the donor wished it to be treated as the gift of a healthy person in some respects and as the gift of a dying person in others, so too in the case of the ketubah there is only a single deed, and yet we estimate that the husband wishes to accept liability for the basic portion immediately, but liability for the addition only from the time of marriage.

Rashash explains that both Rav and Rabbi Elazar ben Azaryah maintain that the court may estimate a person's intentions and may extract money from someone else on

TRANSLATION AND COMMENTARY

may have drawn up the document and stated therein that a *kinyan sudar* had been performed, because he did not want the gift to be effected by means of the special enactment allowing a dying person to dispose of his property without performing a valid act of acquisition, but rather by means of the deed and the *kinyan sudar*, as in the case of a healthy person. Now, if **he intended to transfer** the property **only by means of the deed,** the gift is not valid, for it is clear that he wanted the transfer to be effective only after his death, [1] and **a deed** of gift **is not valid** if it is to take effect only **after** the donor's **death.** Thus the gift has no validity — neither as the gift of a dying person, nor as the gift of a healthy person. We see that Rav maintains that the court may estimate a person's intentions and issue rulings accordingly. The dying person did not state explicitly that he wished to endow his gift with the strength of a gift given by a healthy person, as well as the strength of a gift given by a person on his deathbed. Nevertheless, Rav ruled that we estimate that this was indeed his intention. Thus Rav, too, may well have ruled that the law is in accordance with the viewpoint of Rabbi Elazar ben Azaryah in our Mishnah, that a woman who was widowed or divorced after betrothal collects only the basic portion of her ketubah but not the addition promised by her husband, because we estimate that the husband obligated himself to the addition only on the assumption that he would marry her. How, then, could we have concluded above that it must have been Rabbi Natan who said that the law is in accordance with the viewpoint of Rabbi Elazar ben Azaryah, and that it was Rav who said that the law is not in accordance with that viewpoint?

אֶלָּא [56A] [2] The Gemara now suggests that the dispute between Rav and Rabbi Natan is to be understood differently. **Rather,** we must say that **both** Rav and Rabbi Natan maintain that the court **estimates** a person's intentions and issues rulings accordingly. [3] Hence, **the one who says that the law is in accordance with** the viewpoint of **Rabbi Elazar ben Azaryah** in our Mishnah **is well** understood, for Rabbi Elazar ben Azaryah ruled that a woman who is widowed or divorced after betrothal is entitled only to the basic portion of her ketubah, because the court presumes that the husband accepted the obligation of providing the additional sum on the understanding that he would marry her. [3] **The other** authority — Rav or Rabbi Natan — **who says that the law is not in accordance with** the viewpoint of **Rabbi Elazar ben Azaryah,** but with that of the anonymous first Tanna who maintains that a woman is entitled to the entire amount recorded in her ketubah, both the basic portion of the ketubah and the addition, even if she is widowed or divorced

לְהַקְנוֹתוֹ אֶלָּא בִּשְׁטָר, [1] וְאֵין שְׁטָר לְאַחַר מִיתָה.
[56A] [2] אֶלָּא, תַּרְוַיְיהוּ אָזְלֵי בָּתַר אוּמְדָנָא. [3] מַאן דַּאֲמַר הֲלָכָה, שַׁפִּיר. [3] מַאן דַּאֲמַר אֵין הֲלָכָה,

LITERAL TRANSLATION

to transfer it except by means of the deed, [1] and a deed is not [valid] after death.

[56A] [2] Rather, both of them follow an estimation. [3] [According to] the one who says [that] the law [is in accordance with Rabbi Elazar ben Azaryah], it is well. [3] [According to] the one who says [that] the law is not [in accordance with Rabbi Elazar ben Azaryah],

RASHI

שהרי אין דעתו ליתן כלום אלא לאחר מיתה. ואפילו לרבי יוסי דאמר (גיטין עב,א): זמנו של שטר מוכיח עליו — הני מילי בבריא הכותב נכסיו לבנו לאחר מותו, דדעתו לאקנויי גוף הקרקע מהיום, ופירות לאחר מיתה. אבל זה — אין דעתו ליתן בחייו כלום, וכיון דמית — תו לא מצי לאקנויי מידי, דהא ליתיה דליקני ניהליה. ושמעינן מיהת דרב בתר אומדנא אזיל, שאומד דעתו של זה דלארכביה אתרי רכשי עבד, ואף על פי שלא פירש — מפיק רב ממונא בהכי. **אלא תרוייהו** — רב ורבי נתן.

NOTES

the basis of that estimate. For Rabbi Elazar ben Azaryah maintains that the court estimates that the husband meant to accept liability for the addition only from the time of marriage, so that even if the betrothed woman has already seized the addition, it can be reclaimed from her.

וְאֵין שְׁטָר לְאַחַר מִיתָה And a deed is not valid after death. *Rashi* explains that since the donor wrote the deed of gift on his deathbed, it is clear that he wants the property to be transferred to the recipient only after he dies. Thus the deed of gift is not valid, for after the donor's death there is nobody to effect the transfer of property.

Rashi himself raises an objection that the deed of gift should be valid, because we follow the opinion of Rabbi Yose HaGelili cited elsewhere (*Gittin* 72a) that the date recorded in a deed is informative as to when the deed is to take effect. *Rashi* argues that this rule is limited to a case in which a healthy person assigns his property to his son, stipulating that the transfer is to take effect only after

HALAKHAH

אָזְלֵי בָּתַר אוּמְדָנָא Follow an estimation. "Even if a donor did not state his intentions explicitly, the court may estimate what he must have had in mind when he made the gift, and may issue rulings according to that estimation." (*Rambam, Sefer Kinyan, Hilkhot Zekhiyyah U'Mattanah* 6:1; *Shulḥan Arukh, Ḥoshen Mishpat* 246:1.)

TRANSLATION AND COMMENTARY

between betrothal and marriage, [1]**also** bases his ruling on the court's **estimation regarding** the husband's **intention** when he obligated himself to the additional sum. [2]According to this interpretation of the dispute, the first Tanna of the Mishnah ruled that a woman is entitled to the addition to her ketubah from her betrothal, because we presume that the bridegroom **promised** his bride **the addition as a result of the attachment created** between them, [3]**and surely** such **an attachment was created** from the time of their betrothal.

יְתֵיב [4]The Gemara now cites a series of rulings about whether the law is in accordance with the viewpoint of Rabbi Elazar ben Azaryah in our Mishnah. **Rav Ḥanina** who was known as an expert on the Bible **sat before Rabbi Yannai and said: The Halakhah is in accordance with** the viewpoint of **Rabbi Elazar ben Azaryah.** [5]Rabbi Yannai **said to him: "Go out** of the study hall, **and recite your verses outside!** However knowledgeable you may be about Scriptural matters, your ruling on this Halakhic issue is not fit to be repeated within the walls of the Academy, [6]for **the Halakhah is not in accordance with** the viewpoint of **Rabbi Elazar ben Azaryah."** [7]**Rav Yitzḥak bar Avdimi said in the name of our Master,** Rabbi Yehudah HaNasi: **The Halakhah is in accordance with Rabbi Elazar ben Azaryah.** [8]Similarly, **Rav Naḥman said in the name of Shmuel: The Halakhah is in accordance with Rabbi Elazar ben Azaryah.** [9]**But Rav Naḥman himself,** expressing his own opinion, **said: The Halakhah is not in accordance with Rabbi Elazar ben Azaryah.** [10]**But the** Sages of **Neharde'a said in the name of Rav Naḥman: The Halakhah is in accordance with Rabbi Elazar ben Azaryah.** [11]**And even though Rav Naḥman uttered a curse, saying: "Any judge who rules in accordance with** the viewpoint of **Rabbi Elazar ben Azaryah,** [12]**such-and-such will happen to him,** for that judge has issued a grossly incorrect ruling," [13]**nevertheless the Halakhah is** in fact **in accordance with Rabbi Elazar ben Azaryah.**

[1]הָכָא נַמִי אוּמְדַּן דַּעְתָּא הוּא. [2]מִשּׁוּם אִיקְּרוּבֵי דַּעְתָּא הוּא, [3]וְהָא אִיקַּרְבָא לֵיהּ דַּעְתָּא. [4]יְתֵיב רַב חֲנִינָא קַמֵּיהּ דְּרַבִּי יַנַּאי, וְקָאָמַר: הֲלָכָה כְּרַבִּי אֶלְעָזָר בֶּן עֲזַרְיָה. [5]אֲמַר לֵיהּ: "פּוּק קְרֵי קְרָאָךְ לְבָרָא! [6]אֵין הֲלָכָה כְּרַבִּי אֶלְעָזָר בֶּן עֲזַרְיָה". [7]אָמַר רַב יִצְחָק בַּר אַבְדִּימִי מִשּׁוּם רַבֵּינוּ: הֲלָכָה כְּרַבִּי אֶלְעָזָר בֶּן עֲזַרְיָה. [8]אָמַר רַב נַחְמָן אָמַר שְׁמוּאֵל: הֲלָכָה כְּרַבִּי אֶלְעָזָר בֶּן עֲזַרְיָה. [9]וְרַב נַחְמָן דִּידֵיהּ אֲמַר: אֵין הֲלָכָה כְּרַבִּי אֶלְעָזָר בֶּן עֲזַרְיָה. [10]וּנְהַרְדְּעֵי מִשְּׁמֵיהּ דְּרַב נַחְמָן אָמְרִי: הֲלָכָה כְּרַבִּי אֶלְעָזָר בֶּן עֲזַרְיָה. [11]וְאַף עַל גַּב דְּלָט רַב נַחְמָן וַאֲמַר: "כָּל דַּיָּינָא דְּדָאֵין כְּרַבִּי אֶלְעָזָר בֶּן עֲזַרְיָה, [12]הָכִי וְהָכִי תֶּיהֱוֵי", [13]אֲפִילּוּ הָכִי הֲלָכָה כְּרַבִּי אֶלְעָזָר בֶּן עֲזַרְיָה.

LITERAL TRANSLATION

[1]here too it is an estimation regarding intention. [2][His promise of the addition] is because of the creation of an attachment (lit., "bringing the mind closer"), [3]and surely an attachment was created.

[4]Rav Ḥanina sat before Rabbi Yannai and said: The Halakhah is in accordance with Rabbi Elazar ben Azaryah. [5]He said to him: "Go out [and] recite your verse outside! [6]The Halakhah is not in accordance with Rabbi Elazar ben Azaryah." [7]Rav Yitzḥak bar Avdimi said in the name of our Master: The Halakhah is in accordance with Rabbi Elazar ben Azaryah. [8]Rav Naḥman said in the name of Shmuel: The Halakhah is in accordance with Rabbi Elazar ben Azaryah. [9]But Rav Naḥman himself said: The Halakhah is not in accordance with Rabbi Elazar ben Azaryah. [10]And the Neharde'ans said in the name of Rav Naḥman: The Halakhah is in accordance with Rabbi Elazar ben Azaryah. [11]And although Rav Naḥman cursed and said: "Any judge who rules in accordance with Rabbi Elazar ben Azaryah, [12]such-and-such will happen [to him]," [13]even so the Halakhah is in accordance with Rabbi Elazar ben Azaryah.

RASHI

משום רבינו — רב.

BACKGROUND

מִשּׁוּם אִיקְּרוּבֵי דַּעְתָּא Because of the creation of an attachment. A husband is not obliged to promise an additional amount in the ketubah, and when he does so it is a gift he makes because he is especially fond of his wife. At this stage of the discussion, the question is: At what point does the husband's special fondness develop, leading him to promise his wife the gift of an addition to the basic amount in the ketubah? In the opinion of Rabbi Elazar ben Azaryah, this fondness depends on actual marriage, whereas the first Tanna believes that betrothal itself creates this fondness and closeness, leading the bridegroom to decide to promise the additional amount as a gift from the moment of betrothal.

"פּוּק קְרֵי קְרָאָךְ לְבָרָא" "Go out and recite your verse outside!" The Talmud records various cases in which a Sage tells his student, "Go out and recite your verse outside," when he wishes to reject categorically a statement made by the student and to inform him that his conclusion is so unacceptable as to be unworthy of being pronounced within the House of Study. Since Rav Ḥanina was a Bible-teacher, the use of this expression conveys an element of contempt, as though he were expert only in the Bible and ought not to have offered a statement or anything else.

SAGES

רַב חֲנִינָא Rav Ḥanina. This Rav Ḥanina, a second-generation Palestinian Amora, is usually called Rabbi Ḥanina Kara — Rabbi Ḥanina the Bible-teacher. A student of Rabbi Ḥanina bar Ḥama and Rabbi Yannai, he apparently taught the Bible to schoolchildren and read the Torah in the synagogue. Therefore, when other scholars disagreed with him, they occasionally told him: "Go out and recite your verse outside!"

רַב יִצְחָק בַּר אַבְדִּימִי Rav (Rabbi) Yitzḥak bar Avdimi. There were two Sages named Yitzḥak bar Avdimi. The earlier one, referred to here, was

NOTES

his death. In such a case we assume that the father wishes to transfer the principal to his son during his lifetime, from the date recorded in the deed, but that he wishes to retain the usufruct for himself until his death. But in our case it is clear that the person on his deathbed does not want to transfer anything during his lifetime.

Some authorities (*Rivan, Rambam,* and *Rashba*) maintain that the Gemara is dealing here with a case in which the deed of gift was drawn up only after the donor's death, and in accordance with his deathbed instructions. According to this explanation, the date recorded in the deed of gift poses no problem.

TRANSLATION AND COMMENTARY

וַהֲלָכָה [1]The Gemara concludes with a definitive decision: **The Halakhah in** actual **practice is in accordance with** the viewpoint of **Rabbi Elazar ben Azaryah.**

בָּעֵי רָבִין [2]Having established that the Halakhah is in accordance with the opinion that a betrothed woman is not entitled to the addition to her ketubah until she marries, the Gemara continues: **Ravin asked: If a woman has** already **entered the bridal chamber** for marriage, **but has not** yet **engaged in sexual intercourse** with her husband, and at this point she is widowed or divorced, **what is the law** regarding the addition to her ketubah? [3]Do we say that it **is the affection** resulting **from** the bride's entering **the bridal chamber** that **effects the acquisition** of the right to the addition, and therefore she is entitled to the addition as soon as she enters the bridal chamber? [4]**Or** do we say that it is **the affection** resulting **from sexual intercourse** that **effects the acquisition** of that right, and therefore she cannot claim the addition to her ketubah until she has had sexual relations with her husband?

תָּא שְׁמַע [5]In answer to this question the Gemara says: **Come and hear** what we have learned in a Baraita, **for Rav Yosef taught** a Baraita which stated: "If a woman is widowed or divorced after betrothal, she is entitled only to the basic portion of her ketubah but not to the addition, **because** her husband **only assigned her** the addition **because of the affection** created **on the first night** of marriage." The Gemara now explains how this Baraita sheds light on the question posed by Ravin. [6]**Only if you say that** it is **the affection** resulting **from** the bride's entering **the bridal chamber** that **effects the acquisition** of the right to the addition, [7]can we understand **why** the Tanna of the Baraita **said:** "Because her husband only assigned her the addition to her ketubah because of the affection created on **the first night** of marriage," for the bride and the bridegroom enter the bridal chamber only once, on the first night of their marriage. [8]**But if you say that** it is **the affection** resulting

[1]וַהֲלָכָה לְמַעֲשֶׂה כְּרַבִּי אֶלְעָזָר בֶּן עֲזַרְיָה.
[2]בָּעֵי רָבִין: נִכְנְסָה לַחוּפָּה וְלֹא נִבְעֲלָה, מַהוּ? [3]חִיבַּת חוּפָּה קוֹנָה, [4]אוֹ חִיבַּת בִּיאָה קוֹנָה? [5]תָּא שְׁמַע, דְּתָנֵי רַב יוֹסֵף: "שֶׁלֹּא כָּתַב לָהּ אֶלָּא עַל חִיבַּת לַיְלָה הָרִאשׁוֹן". [6]אִי אָמְרַתְּ בִּשְׁלָמָא חִיבַּת חוּפָּה קוֹנָה — [7]הַיְינוּ דְּאָמַר "לַיְלָה הָרִאשׁוֹן". [8]אֶלָּא אִי אָמְרַתְּ חִיבַּת בִּיאָה

LITERAL TRANSLATION

[1]And the Halakhah in practice is in accordance with Rabbi Elazar ben Azaryah.

[2]Ravin asked: [If] she entered the bridal chamber but did not have sexual intercourse, what [is the law]? [3]Does the affection of the bridal chamber effect the acquisition, [4]or does the affection of sexual intercourse effect the acquisition?

[5]Come [and] hear, for Rav Yosef taught: "Because he did not assign [it] to her except for the affection of the first night." [6]Granted if you say [that] the affection of the bridal chamber effects the acquisition — [7]that is why he said "the first night." [8]But if you say [that] the affection of sexual intercourse

RASHI

והלכה למעשה כו׳ — התלמוד קא פסיק שכך נמנו וגמרו בני הישיבה. **מהו** — לרבי אלעזר בן עזריה.

a Palestinian Sage of the transitional generation between the Tannaim and the Amoraim. In the Jerusalem Talmud, he is known as Rabbi Yitzḥak Rubah ("the great"). Rabbi Yitzḥak was one of the youngest disciples of Rabbi Yehudah HaNasi, and he served as a Tanna (someone who memorized the Mishnah and recited it for the other scholars) in Rabbi Yehudah HaNasi's Academy. He was a very close friend of Rabbi Yehudah HaNasi and served him on many occasions. He both transmits Halakhic teachings in Rabbi Yehudah HaNasi's name and also recounts how the latter acted in practice.

Rabbi Yitzḥak bar Avdimi lived to a great age and taught Rabbi Yoḥanan's most senior disciples precise formulations of the Mishnah and of Baraitot.

BACKGROUND (p. 216)

הָכִי וְהָכִי תֶּיהֱוֵי **Such-and-such will happen to him.** Occasionally Sages express with great vehemence their negative opinion of a certain Halakhic approach, and even curse those who follow a certain custom. Wishing to avoid saying something negative, the Gemara does not cite Rav Naḥman's actual words. It prefers to use the general expression, "such-and-such," rather than to state exactly what Rav Naḥman himself said.

NOTES

וַהֲלָכָה לְמַעֲשֶׂה **And the Halakhah in practice.** Having cited a series of conflicting rulings regarding the issue in dispute between the anonymous first Tanna of our Mishnah and Rabbi Elazar ben Azaryah, the Gemara finds it necessary to conclude the discussion with a definite decision as to the law in actual practice. Similarly, the Jerusalem Talmud records a number of different rulings as to whether the law is in accordance with or contrary to the viewpoint of Rabbi Elazar ben Azaryah, and it too concludes that a practical decision was rendered in accordance with Rabbi Elazar ben Azaryah's viewpoint. *Rivan* adds that the Gemara emphasizes that its ruling in favor of the viewpoint of Rabbi Elazar ben Azaryah is the law in actual practice, so as not to leave the impression that, while the law is indeed in accordance with his viewpoint, the decision should not be made publicly known as a ruling that has practical application.

חִיבַּת לַיְלָה הָרִאשׁוֹן **The affection of the first night.** The discussion here of the precise meaning of the expression "the affection of the first night" is not found in the Jerusalem Talmud, for there the Baraita reads: "Because the husband did not assign the addition to her except for the affection on the first night when he had intercourse with his wife." It is clear from the discussion that follows the citing of this Baraita in the Jerusalem Talmud that it understands that the affection resulting from the sexual intercourse is what effects the acquisition of the woman's right to the addition to her ketubah.

HALAKHAH

וַהֲלָכָה לְמַעֲשֶׂה כְּרַבִּי אֶלְעָזָר בֶּן עֲזַרְיָה **And the Halakhah in practice is in accordance with Rabbi Elazar ben Azaryah.** "If a man betroths a woman and writes her a ketubah, and she is widowed or divorced after betrothal, she may collect the basic portion of her ketubah, but only from her husband's free assets. The addition to her ketubah she may not collect at all." (*Rambam, Sefer Nashim, Hilkhot Ishut* 10:11; *Shulḥan Arukh, Even HaEzer* 55:6.)

TRANSLATION AND COMMENTARY

from sexual intercourse that **effects the acquisition** of the woman's right to the addition to her ketubah, why did the Tanna of the Baraita speak of "the first night"? [1]**Does sexual intercourse take place** only **on the first night** of marriage, **but not from then on?**

וְאֶלָּא מַאי [2]The Gemara objects to this suggested proof. **But how** are we to understand the Baraita's reference to the affection created on the first night of marriage? [3]Are we to say that it refers to **the affection** resulting **from** the bride's entering **the bridal chamber** for marriage? This, too, is difficult to understand. [4]**Is** a woman brought into **the bridal chamber** only **at night, but not during the day?**

וּלְטַעְמִיךְ [5]The Gemara rebuts this objection: A similar question can be raised **according to your opinion** that the Baraita's mention of the affection created on the first night of marriage refers to the affection resulting from sexual intercourse. If the Baraita is referring to that affection, why does it speak of the first *night*? [6]**Does sexual intercourse take place** only **at night, and not during the day?** [7]**Surely Rava said:** Although a person is forbidden to engage in sexual relations during the day, **if he is in a dark room, it is permitted.**

הָא לָא קַשְׁיָא [8]The Gemara now rejects this rebuttal of its objection. The Baraita's mention of the first *night* **is not difficult** to understand if we assume that it is referring to the affection created by sexual intercourse. [9]For the Tanna **is** incidentally **informing us** that it is **proper behavior** for couples to engage in sexual **intercourse at night,** and not during the day.

אֶלָּא חוּפָּה קַשְׁיָא [10]**But,** objects the Gemara, if we say that the Baraita is referring to the affection created by the bride's entering **the bridal chamber, there is** still **a difficulty,** for surely a woman can be brought into the bridal chamber at any time of the day, and thus there was no reason for the Baraita to speak of "the first night" of marriage if it was not referring to sexual intercourse!

חוּפָּה נַמִי לָא קַשְׁיָא [11]The Gemara answers: Even if we say that the Baraita is referring to the affection created by the bride's entering **the bridal chamber, there is still no difficulty.** [12]**Since** entry into **the bridal chamber ordinarily leads to** sexual **intercourse,** which should take place at night, [13]the Tanna **informs us** that it is **proper behavior** for a woman to be brought into the bridal chamber **at night**, so that sexual intercourse can take place immediately afterwards.

קוֹנָה, [1]בִּיאָה בַּלַּיְלָה הָרִאשׁוֹן אִיתָא, מִכָּאן וְאֵילָךְ לֵיתָא? [2]וְאֶלָּא מַאי? [3]חוּפָּה? [4]חוּפָּה בַּלַּיְלָה אִיתָא, בִּימָמָא לֵיתָא? [5]וּלְטַעְמִיךְ, [6]בִּיאָה בַּלַּיְלָה אִיתָא, בִּימָמָא לֵיתָא? [7]הָא אָמַר רָבָא: אִם הָיָה בְּבֵית אָפֵל, מוּתָּר! [8]הָא לָא קַשְׁיָא. [9]אוֹרַח אַרְעָא קָא מַשְׁמַע לָן, דְּבִיאָה בַּלַּיְלָה. [10]אֶלָּא חוּפָּה קַשְׁיָא! [11]חוּפָּה נַמִי לָא קַשְׁיָא. [12]כֵּיוָן דִּסְתָם חוּפָּה לְבִיאָה קַיְימָא, [13]אוֹרַח אַרְעָא קָא מַשְׁמַע לָן, דְּבַלַּיְלָה.

LITERAL TRANSLATION

effects the acquisition, on the first night there is sexual intercourse, [1][but] from then on is there not? [2]But what then? [3][The affection of] the bridal chamber? [4]Is there a bridal chamber at night, [but] not during the day?

[5]And according to your opinion, [6]is there sexual intercourse at night, but not during the day? [7]Surely Rava said: If he was in a dark house, [intercourse] is permitted!

[8]This is not difficult. [9]He teaches us proper behavior (lit., "the way of the world") — that intercourse is at night.

[10]But the bridal chamber is difficult!

[11]The bridal chamber, too, is not difficult. [12]Since the bridal chamber ordinarily leads to intercourse, [13]he teaches us proper practice, that [it should be] at night.

NOTES

אִם הָיָה בְּבֵית אָפֵל **If he was in a dark house.** Elsewhere (*Niddah* 17a), the Gemara derives the prohibition against engaging in sexual relations during the day from the verse (Leviticus 19:18): "And you shall love your neighbor as yourself," which teaches that sexual relations are forbidden during the day, lest the husband detect something about his wife that he finds repulsive. *Meiri* supports this explanation of the prohibition by quoting the verse (Proverbs 3:29): "Do not devise evil against your neighbor." Alternatively, daytime sexual intercourse is forbidden because it is viewed as a breach of modesty. According to both explanations of the prohibition, it is clear that the critical factor is not the time of day, but rather the amount of light in the room at the time of intercourse.

HALAKHAH

אִם הָיָה בְּבֵית אָפֵל, מוּתָּר **If he was in a dark house, intercourse is permitted.** "A person is forbidden to engage in sexual relations during the day, but if he is in a dark room, it is permitted." (*Shulḥan Arukh, Oraḥ Ḥayyim* 240:11.)

[1] בָּעֵי רַב אַשִׁי: נִכְנְסָה לַחוּפָּה וּפֵירְסָה נִידָּה, מַהוּ? [2] אִם תִּימְצֵי לוֹמַר חִיבַּת חוּפָּה קוֹנָה, [3] חוּפָּה דְּחַזְיָא לְבִיאָה, [4] אֲבָל חוּפָּה דְּלָא חַזְיָא לְבִיאָה, לָא? [5] אוֹ דִּלְמָא לָא שְׁנָא? [6] תֵּיקוּ.

LITERAL TRANSLATION

[1] Rav Ashi asked: [If] she entered the bridal chamber and began to menstruate, what [is the law]? [2] If you say [that] the affection of the bridal chamber effects the acquisition, [3] [is it only] a bridal chamber that is fit for intercourse, [4] but a bridal chamber that is not fit for intercourse, not? [5] Or perhaps there is no difference? [6] Let it stand.

RASHI

ופירסה נדה — ופירש ממנה ומת.

TRANSLATION AND COMMENTARY

בָּעֵי רַב אַשִׁי [1] The Gemara continues with another question. **Rav Ashi asked: If a woman enters the bridal chamber** for marriage, **but** before she can engage in sexual relations with her bridegroom she **begins to menstruate**, so that she is forbidden to him, and then she is widowed or divorced, **what is the law** with respect to the addition to her ketubah? If we say that it is the affection of intercourse that effects the acquisition of a woman's right to the addition to her ketubah, then this woman is not entitled to the addition, because she never engaged in intercourse with her bridegroom. [2] But a question arises **if we say that** it is **the affection** resulting **from** the bride's entering **the bridal chamber** that **effects the acquisition** of her right to the addition to her ketubah. [3] Do we say that **it is only a bridal chamber that is fit for** sexual **intercourse** which effects the acquisition of a woman's right to the addition to her ketubah, [4] **but a bridal chamber that is not fit for** sexual **intercourse** does **not** effect the acquisition of that right? In this case, the woman who begins to menstruate while in the bridal chamber should not immediately be entitled to the addition to her ketubah, for the couple are now forbidden to have sexual intercourse. [5] **Or** do we **perhaps** say that **there is no difference?** Thus entry into the bridal chamber always effects the acquisition of a woman's right to the addition to her ketubah, whether or not the bridal chamber is fit for sexual intercourse.

תֵּיקוּ [6] The Gemara does not find a solution to Rav Ashi's problem and so it concludes: **The problem** raised here **remains unsolved.**

NOTES

נִכְנְסָה לַחוּפָּה וּפֵירְסָה נִידָּה If she entered the bridal chamber and began to menstruate. According to *Rambam* (see *Hilkhot Ishut* 10:2), Rav Ashi formulated his question precisely. In other words, he asked about the case in which a woman enters the bridal chamber for marriage when she is permitted to her bridegroom, and only *afterwards* does she begin to menstruate and thereby become forbidden to him. For if she has begun to menstruate before entering the bridal chamber, she is surely not entitled to the addition to her ketubah, for a bride who enters the bridal chamber while she is forbidden to her bridegroom on account of menstruation retains the status of a betrothed woman in all respects.

Many Rishonim reject *Rambam*'s position that the marriage process cannot be completed while a woman is ritually impure on account of menstrual bleeding. They must then find an alternative explanation for the way Rav Ashi posed his question, asking about a woman who enters jjthe bridal chamber when she is permitted to her bridegroom, and then begins to menstruate.

Ritva suggests that if a woman enters the bridal chamber after she has begun to menstruate, she is indeed regarded as a married woman in most respects; but it was obvious to Rav Ashi that she is still not entitled to the addition to her ketubah, his only question being whether or not she is entitled to the addition if she entered the bridal chamber before she began to menstruate.

Rosh maintains that Rav Ashi did not formulate his question precisely, because he could only have been asking about the case in which the woman entered the bridal chamber *after* she had begun to menstruate. For if she entered into the bridal chamber while she was permitted to her bridegroom, and only then did her menstrual bleeding begin, she is surely entitled to the addition, seeing that she acquired the right to the addition as soon as she entered the bridal chamber. The Rishonim and the Aḥaronim discuss at length the issue of the validity of a menstruating woman's entry into the bridal chamber, some distinguishing between a case in which the bridegroom knew at the time that his bride was forbidden to him and a case in which he had no such knowledge.

HALAKHAH

חִיבַּת חוּפָּה The affection of the bridal chamber. "Once a woman has been brought into the bridal chamber for marriage, even if she has not yet had sexual intercourse with her bridegroom, she is treated as a married woman in all respects. Thus she may collect both the basic portion of her ketubah and the addition, if she is then widowed or divorced. This ruling applies only if the woman was fit for intercourse at the time; but if she was brought into the bridal chamber during her menstrual period, she is still treated as a betrothed woman. According to some authorities (*Rosh*), she is regarded as a betrothed woman only with respect to the addition to her ketubah, but in all other respects she is treated as a married woman." (*Rambam*, *Sefer Nashim*, *Hilkhot Ishut* 10:2; *Shulḥan Arukh*, *Even HaEzer* 61:1.)

LITERAL TRANSLATION

[1] "Rabbi Yehudah says: If he wishes, he may write for a virgin, etc." [2] But does Rabbi Yehudah maintain that we write a receipt? [3] But surely we have learned: "[Regarding] someone who has repaid part of his debt, [4] Rabbi Yehudah says: He must exchange [the document]. [5] Rabbi Yose says: He must write a receipt for him."

[1] ״רַבִּי יְהוּדָה אוֹמֵר: רָצָה, כּוֹתֵב לִבְתוּלָה, וכו׳״. [2] וְסָבַר רַבִּי יְהוּדָה דְּכוֹתְבִין שׁוֹבֵר? [3] וְהָתְנַן: ״מִי שֶׁפָּרַע מִקְצָת חוֹבוֹ, [4] רַבִּי יְהוּדָה אוֹמֵר: יַחֲלִיף. [5] רַבִּי יוֹסֵי אוֹמֵר: יִכְתּוֹב לוֹ שׁוֹבֵר״.

RASHI

יחליף – יכתוב שטר אחר כדי חוב הנשאר, ויקרע הראשון. ולא יכתוב שובר להרע כח הלוה, שיצטרך לשמור שוברו מן העכברים. **רבי יוסי אומר יכתוב שובר** – ולא יחליף, להרע כח המלוה למחול שעבודו מזמן ראשון.

TRANSLATION AND COMMENTARY

רַבִּי יְהוּדָה אוֹמֵר [1] The Gemara now proceeds to analyze the next clause of our Mishnah, which stated: **"Rabbi Yehudah says: If** the husband **wishes** to reduce his obligation concerning his wife's ketubah, **he may write** a ketubah document of two hundred zuz **for** his wife who is **a virgin**, as is required of him by law, and then he can arrange to have his wife write him a receipt saying: 'I have already received a maneh from you in partial payment of my ketubah.'" [2] The Gemara asks: May it be inferred from this statement that **Rabbi Yehudah maintains that** if a debtor repays part of a loan that was attested to by a promissory note, he cannot demand that the original promissory note be replaced by another testifying to his current debt, but the creditor **writes** the debtor **a receipt** for the amount that he has already received from him, and may retain the original promissory note until the debt is entirely repaid? [3] **But surely we have learned** otherwise in a Mishnah (*Bava Batra* 170b), which states: **"If someone** receives a loan attested to by a promissory note and later **repays part of the debt,** the Tannaim disagree about the law: [4] **Rabbi Yehudah says:** The creditor **must replace** the original promissory note with another **document** testifying to the current balance. He must not retain the original document and write the debtor a receipt for the amount already received, because the debtor may lose his receipt and the creditor can then collect the entire amount recorded in the original document, even though part of that sum has already been repaid. [5] **Rabbi Yose** disagrees and **says:** The creditor may keep the original promissory note, but **he must write** the debtor **a receipt for** the money he has received from **him.** It is the debtor's responsibility to take care of that receipt, so that the creditor will not be able to collect again the amount that has already been repaid." Now, if Rabbi Yehudah maintains that the creditor does not write the debtor a receipt for the money he has already received, why does he say that the wife should write her husband a receipt saying that she has already received part of her ketubah?

CONCEPTS

שׁוֹבֵר Receipt. The Hebrew root **שבר** means "to break," and the word **שׁוֹבֵר** from this root means precisely a document meant to "break," i.e., to nullify, the validity of another document. A receipt in which the lender declares that he has received payment for his debt is thus a **שׁוֹבֵר**, in that it nullifies the original promissory note or other form of monetary obligation.

In a place where it is customary to rely upon a **שׁוֹבֵר**, the recipient is obliged to retain it for a long time, to forestall any possibility of his being required to pay the debt twice.

NOTES

וְסָבַר רַבִּי יְהוּדָה דְּכוֹתְבִין שׁוֹבֵר But does Rabbi Yehudah maintain that we write a receipt? Several Rishonim ask: What is the Gemara's difficulty? When Rabbi Yehudah says that the creditor must replace the original promissory note with another document testifying to the current balance, he surely does not mean that the creditor must not write the debtor a receipt for the amount already received if the debtor is willing to accept it and to allow the creditor to retain the original document! All that he means is that the creditor cannot compel the debtor to accept such a receipt. Here in our Mishnah, the husband is willing to accept a receipt. Why, then, should the woman not be allowed to write a fictitious receipt saying that she has already received partial payment of her ketubah?

They answer that if Rabbi Yehudah maintains that the creditor cannot compel the debtor to accept a receipt, lest the receipt be lost and the debtor suffer a loss, then he should not have instituted the practice whereby the husband writes his wife a proper ketubah and his wife writes him a fictitious receipt saying that she has already received part of her ketubah, lest it give rise to the mistaken notion that in general a creditor can compel the debtor to accept a receipt for partial payment. Rather, Rabbi Yehudah should have suggested that the husband first write his wife a proper ketubah, and then replace that ketubah with another for the lesser amount (*Rashba*, *Ritva*, *Rosh*).

מִי שֶׁפָּרַע מִקְצָת חוֹבוֹ Regarding someone who has repaid part of his debt. *Rashi* explains this Tannaitic dispute as follows: Rabbi Yehudah maintains that the creditor must replace the original promissory note with another stating the current balance, rather than write the debtor a receipt

HALAKHAH

מִי שֶׁפָּרַע מִקְצָת חוֹבוֹ Regarding someone who has repaid part of his debt. "If someone receives a loan attested to in writing and later repays part of the debt, the creditor, if he so wishes, may have the court replace the original promissory note with another that has the same date as the original document, but that states how much the debtor currently owes him. If the creditor prefers, he may retain the original promissory note and write the debtor a receipt for the amount he has received from him," following the Gemara's conclusion in *Bava Batra* 170b. (*Rambam*, *Sefer Mishpatim*, *Hilkhot Malveh Ve'Loveh* 23:15; *Shulhan Arukh*, *Hoshen Mishpat* 54:1.)

[1]אָמַר רַבִּי יִרְמְיָה: כְּשֶׁשּׁוֹבַרְתָּהּ מִתּוֹכָהּ.
[2]אַבַּיֵי אֲמַר: אֲפִילּוּ תֵּימָא בְּשֶׁאֵין שׁוֹבַרְתָּהּ מִתּוֹכָהּ.
[3]בִּשְׁלָמָא הָתָם, [4]וַדַּאי פְּרָעֵיהּ, דִּלְמָא מִירְכַּס תְּבַרְתָּא, [5]וּמַפֵּיק לֵיהּ לִשְׁטָרָא, וַהֲדַר גָּבֵי זִימְנָא אַחֲרִינָא. [6]הָכָא, וַדַּאי יָהַב לָהּ? [7]מִילְּתָא בְּעָלְמָא הִיא דְּאָמְרָה לֵיהּ. [8]אִי נָטְרֵיהּ, נָטְרֵיהּ. [9]אִי לָא נָטְרֵיהּ, אִיהוּ הוּא דְּאַפְסֵיד אַנַּפְשֵׁיהּ.

LITERAL TRANSLATION

[1]Rabbi Yirmeyah said: Where its receipt is in it. [2]Abaye said: You can even say where its receipt is not in it. [3]Granted there, [4][where] he has definitely repaid him, perhaps the receipt will be lost, [5]and he will take out the document, and collect again another time. [6]Here, did he definitely give her [anything]? [7]It was mere words that she said to him. [8]If he saved it, he saved it. [9]If he did not save it, it is he who caused himself the loss.

TRANSLATION AND COMMENTARY

אָמַר רַבִּי יִרְמְיָה [1]**Rabbi Yirmeyah said:** When Rabbi Yehudah says that the woman may write her husband a receipt for the portion of her ketubah that she says she has already received, he means that she may write **a receipt** for that sum **in** the ketubah document **itself.** There, in the Mishnah in *Bava Batra*, Rabbi Yehudah rules that the creditor must not write the debtor a receipt for the money that he has already received from him, because there is concern that the debtor may lose the receipt. But here, where the woman writes in the ketubah document itself that she has already received partial payment of her ketubah, there is no cause for concern that her husband may lose the receipt.

אַבַּיֵי אֲמַר [2]**Abaye said: You can even say** that Rabbi Yehudah did **not** mean that the woman must write **the receipt in** the ketubah document **itself,** but rather that she writes the receipt on a separate piece of paper. Yet there is no contradiction between Rabbi Yehudah's two rulings: [3]**Granted** that **there,** in the case in which the debtor repays part of his debt, Rabbi Yehudah rules that the creditor must not retain the original document. [4]For there the debtor **has actually repaid** part of the debt, and we are concerned that **the receipt may perhaps be lost,** [5]**and** that the creditor **will** then **take out the** original **promissory note and collect a second time** that portion of the debt that has already been repaid. [6]But **here,** in the case of our Mishnah, **did** the husband **actually give** his wife **any** portion of her ketubah? When the woman writes her husband the receipt saying that she has already received a portion of her ketubah, [7]**she is saying mere words to him,** indicating her willingness to forgo part of her ketubah. [8]Thus, **if** the husband **saves** the receipt, **he saves it,** [9]and **if** the husband **does not save** the receipt and it is lost, **it is he who has caused himself the loss,** and we are not concerned that he will now be held liable for the full amount recorded in his wife's ketubah.

RASHI

כששוברתה בתוכה — בתוך הכתובה עצמה יכתוב השובר: והיא אמרה בפנינו התקבלתי חציה. דטעמא מאי אמר רבי יהודה אין כותבין שובר — משום דלא יצטרך לוה לשומרו מן העכברים, דאי מרקב — הדר האי וגבי שטריה כוליה, הכא ליכא למיחש להכי. **אפילו תימא כו׳** — דהאי שובר לא חייש רבי יהודה לעכברים כי התם, דאילו התם מיפרע פרעיה דלמא כו׳. **הכא ודאי יהב לה** — בתמיה.

NOTES

for the amount that he has received from him, so that the debtor will not be obliged to preserve the receipt. Rabbi Yose maintains that it is preferable to place that additional burden on the debtor, so as not to cancel the lien on the debtor's property that was created by the original promissory note. For if the creditor replaces the original document with another stating the current balance, he will only be able to collect that sum from the property in the debtor's possession on the date recorded in the new document.

Tosafot notes that, according to the Gemara's conclusion in *Bava Batra* (171a), Rabbi Yehudah maintains that the new document is dated with the same date that appeared in the original document, and therefore the creditor's original lien on the debtor's property is not disturbed. Rabbi Yose argues that it is preferable to allow the creditor to retain the original document and to write the debtor a receipt for the amount he has repaid, for in that way the debtor will feel under pressure to pay the rest of his debt more quickly, since he will be afraid that he may lose the receipt and be required to pay the entire debt a second time.

כְּשֶׁשּׁוֹבַרְתָּהּ מִתּוֹכָהּ **Where its receipt is in it.** *Rashi* explains that, according to Rabbi Yehudah, the woman must write the receipt for the sum that she says she has already received from her husband in the ketubah itself, for this will ensure that she will be unable to collect that sum with her ketubah.

Ritva explains that *Rashi* means that the receipt must be written into the text of the ketubah itself above the witnesses' signatures, for if the receipt is written below their signatures, we should be concerned that the woman may erase or cut off the line saying that she has received part of her ketubah. Thus we can understand why the Gemara does not suggest anywhere that this device should be used in the case of an ordinary promissory note where the debtor has repaid part of his debt, but only in the case of a ketubah, where the woman is willing from the outset to waive part of her ketubah.

Tosafot and others ask: Even if the receipt is written into the ketubah document itself, should we not be concerned that the woman may perhaps hide or destroy the document and then seek to collect the full amount of her ketubah by

[1] בִּשְׁלָמָא אַבַּיֵי לָא אָמַר כְּרַבִּי יִרְמְיָה. [2] לָא קָתָנֵי שׁוֹבַרְתָּהּ מִתּוֹכָהּ. [3] אֶלָּא רַבִּי יִרְמְיָה מַאי טַעְמָא לָא אָמַר כְּאַבַּיֵי?

[4] גְּזֵירָה שׁוֹבֵר דְּהָכָא אַטּוּ שׁוֹבֵר דְּעָלְמָא.

[5] טַעְמָא דְּכָתְבָה לֵיהּ. [6] אֲבָל עַל פֶּה, לָא. [7] אַמַּאי? [8] דָּבָר שֶׁבְּמָמוֹן הוּא, וְשָׁמְעִינַן לֵיהּ לְרַבִּי יְהוּדָה דְּאָמַר: דָּבָר שֶׁבְּמָמוֹן, [9] תְּנָאוֹ קַיָּים!

LITERAL TRANSLATION

[1] Granted that Abaye did not say like Rabbi Yirmeyah. [2] It does not state [that] its receipt is in it. [3] But what is the reason [that] Rabbi Yirmeyah did not say like Abaye?

[4] The receipt here is a preventive measure on account of a receipt in general.

[5] The reason is that she wrote [a receipt] for him. [6] But by [word of] mouth, not. [7] Why? [8] It is a monetary matter, and we have heard that Rabbi Yehudah said: [In] a monetary matter, [9] his condition stands!

RASHI

אבל על פה – דהוה ליה תנאה בעלמא – לא הוי תנאה, דמתנה על מה שכתוב בתורה הוא.

TRANSLATION AND COMMENTARY

בִּשְׁלָמָא [1] The Gemara objects: **Granted** that **Abaye did not give the same explanation as Rabbi Yirmeyah**, who said that Rabbi Yehudah meant that the woman must write the receipt in the ketubah document itself, [2] for the Mishnah **does not state that the receipt** must **be** written **in** the ketubah **itself.** [3] **But** as for **Rabbi Yirmeyah, why did he not give the same explanation as Abaye,** that since the woman has not actually received any part of her ketubah, we are not concerned that the receipt may be lost and that her husband may have to pay her the full amount recorded in the ketubah?

גְּזֵירָה [4] The Gemara answers: Rabbi Yirmeyah did not explain Rabbi Yehudah's position in the same way as Abaye did, because he is of the opinion that, according to Rabbi Yehudah, **a safeguard** was enacted **regarding the receipt** discussed **here** in our Mishnah **on account of receipts in general.** Even though there is no reason to be concerned here about the receipt being lost, nevertheless, since in general we say that the creditor must not write the debtor a receipt for money he has already received from him but must replace the original loan document with another stating the current balance, in the same way the woman must not write a receipt on a separate sheet of paper, but must write the receipt in the ketubah document itself.

טַעְמָא דְּכָתְבָה לֵיהּ [5] The Gemara now continues its analysis of Rabbi Yehudah's position. The Mishnah seems to imply that **the reason**, according to Rabbi Yehudah, why the husband is not held liable for the full amount recorded in his wife's ketubah **is because she wrote him a receipt** saying that she had already received part of her ketubah. [6] **But** it follows from this that if the woman makes **an oral statement** that she has already received some of her ketubah money, her husband will **not** be exempted from paying his wife the full amount recorded in her ketubah document. [7] The Gemara now asks: But **why** should this be so? It is presumably because such a statement is treated like a condition contrary to Torah law; for by law every woman is entitled to the basic portion of her ketubah, but here the husband wishes to reduce his liability below the legal minimum by having his wife state that she is ready to waive her right to part of the money. And there is a general rule that a condition that runs counter to Torah law is null and void. [8] But this leads to a certain difficulty, for the woman's right to her ketubah **is a monetary matter,** [9] **and we have heard** elsewhere **that Rabbi Yehudah maintains** that **in monetary matters a condition** which is contrary to Torah law but which

NOTES

virtue of the Rabbinic enactment entitling every woman to a ketubah, even if she does not have a ketubah document? They answer that we are not concerned that the woman will hide or destroy the ketubah, because the dowry that she brought into the marriage is also recorded in it, and without the document she will be unable to collect her dowry upon the dissolution of her marriage. Alternatively, Rabbi Yehudah's ruling applies only where it is customary for all married women to receive a written ketubah, or where this is not the custom but witnesses can testify that the woman did in fact receive a written ketubah; for in such cases the woman cannot collect her ketubah without presenting her ketubah document, and there is therefore no reason to suspect that she will hide or destroy the document in order to collect the full amount of her ketubah.

טַעְמָא דְּכָתְבָה לֵיהּ **The reason is that she wrote a receipt for him.** *Rashi* seems to understand the text according to its plain sense — that the Gemara is distinguishing between a case in which the woman wrote her husband a receipt stating that she had already received part of her ketubah, and a case in which she made an oral statement to that effect. If the woman merely says that she has already received part of her ketubah money, her husband is still held liable to pay his wife the full amount recorded in the ketubah, because an oral statement is considered a condition, and a condition contrary to Torah law is void. Hence the Gemara raises the objection that Rabbi Yehudah is of the opinion that in monetary matters a condition that runs counter to Torah law is valid.

Ritva, *Rosh*, and others object to this interpretation, arguing that there should be no difference between a

TRANSLATION AND COMMENTARY

has nevertheless been accepted **is valid!** [1]**For it was taught** in a Baraita: **"If someone says to a woman: 'Behold, you are betrothed to me on condition that you have no claims against me for food, clothing, or conjugal relations,'** [2]**she is betrothed, but his condition is void,** because it runs counter to the Torah law requiring a husband to provide his wife with food and clothing and to have sexual relations with her. [3]**This is the opinion of Rabbi Meir.** [4]But **Rabbi Yehudah** disagrees and **says: Concerning monetary matters,** such as the husband's obligation to provide his wife with food and clothing, **a condition** that runs counter to Torah law but has nevertheless been accepted **is valid."** Thus Rabbi Yehudah should maintain that the husband is freed from his obligation to pay his wife the full amount recorded in her ketubah document, if she agrees to a condition whereby she waives a part of it!

[1]דְּתַנְיָא: "הָאוֹמֵר לְאִשָּׁה: 'הֲרֵי אַתְּ מְקוּדֶּשֶׁת לִי עַל מְנָת שֶׁאֵין לִיךְ עָלַי שְׁאֵר, כְּסוּת, וְעוֹנָה', [2]הֲרֵי זוֹ מְקוּדֶּשֶׁת, וּתְנָאוֹ בָּטֵל. [3]דִּבְרֵי רַבִּי מֵאִיר. [4]רַבִּי יְהוּדָה אוֹמֵר: בְּדָבָר שֶׁבְּמָמוֹן, תְּנָאוֹ קַיָּים".

LITERAL TRANSLATION

[1]For it was taught: "[If] someone says to a woman: 'Behold, you are betrothed to me on condition that you have no [claims] on me [for] food, clothing, or conjugal relations,' [2]she is betrothed, but his condition is void. [3][These are] the words of Rabbi Meir. [4]Rabbi Yehudah says: In a monetary matter, his condition stands."

RASHI

בדבר שבממון – שאר וכסות.

BACKGROUND

בְּדָבָר שֶׁבְּמָמוֹן תְּנָאוֹ קַיָּים **In a monetary matter, his condition is stands.** In the opinion of Rabbi Yehudah, since money may be given as a gift, there is no restriction regarding it; for if a person waives his monetary right as granted by the Torah, this is to be viewed as a voluntary gift, and there is nothing wrong with it. This is not the case with respect to non-monetary benefits. Since a person does not have the power to waive or alter these, the condition is invalid. By contrast, Rabbi Meir, who usually takes a more formalistic approach to contracts and agreements, maintains that the decision must depend on the precise wording of the agreement. If the agreement states or implies that Torah law will not apply in a certain situation, this is a transgression against the Torah, and the condition is not binding. However, if the condition is phrased in a different way, so that a person who is entitled to money gives it to someone else as a gift, the condition is valid.

NOTES

written receipt and an oral statement, for the woman's admission that she has already received part of her ketubah is just as contrary to Torah law when it is committed to writing as when it is stated orally. Rather, the Gemara must be understood as follows: The Mishnah seems to imply that the husband is not held liable for the full amount recorded in his wife's ketubah because he wrote her a proper ketubah as required by law, and she wrote him a receipt saying that she had already received part of her ketubah. But if he were to have stipulated with her from the outset — whether in writing or orally — that her ketubah would be less than the legal minimum, he would still be held liable for the full amount.

הֲרֵי זוֹ מְקוּדֶּשֶׁת, וּתְנָאוֹ בָּטֵל **She is betrothed, but his condition is void.** The Rishonim raise the following question: If a condition that runs counter to Torah law is void, why should the marriage not be void as well? The husband imposed certain conditions on his agreement to the marriage, and those conditions were not fulfilled. Thus the basic element of all transactions — mutual agreement — is lacking!

Rabbenu Tam (cited by *Tosafot Yeshanim* and *Tosefot Sens*; so too *Rashba, Ritva, Ran*, and others) suggests that a condition which runs counter to Torah law is treated like one that cannot possibly be fulfilled. Such a condition is assumed not to have been intended seriously. Thus the condition imposed by the man is disregarded, and we view his agreement to marry the woman as unconditional.

Ri argues that even if the condition was meant seriously, the marriage is still binding, even though the condition remains unfulfilled. Once a person agrees to a certain transaction, it is by no means self-evident that he can qualify that agreement with a condition. Had the Torah not stated otherwise, any condition attached to a transaction would always be void, and the transaction itself would be valid even though the condition was not or could not be fulfilled. We derive the law that a condition can qualify an agreement from the condition imposed by Moses concerning the land to be allocated to the tribes of Reuven and Gad (Numbers 32:29-30). However, the ability to qualify a transaction is limited to conditions similar to the condition imposed in that case. All other conditions (e.g., those that run counter to the Torah) are void. Nevertheless, the transactions to which they remain attached are valid. Therefore, when a condition that runs counter to Torah law is imposed on a marriage, the condition is void but the marriage is binding.

בְּדָבָר שֶׁבְּמָמוֹן, תְּנָאוֹ קַיָּים **In a monetary matter, his condition stands.** *Rashi* and *Rambam* explain that the wife's rights to food and clothing are considered "monetary matters" that can be canceled by a condition, but her right to conjugal relations is not.

Rabbenu Ḥananel (cited by *Ra'ah*) maintains that even a wife's right to conjugal relations is considered a "monetary matter," because anything that provides physical pleasure is treated as a "monetary matter" with respect to conditions. This viewpoint is in accordance with the Jerusalem Talmud (*Bava Metzia* 7:7), which includes a wife's right to conjugal relations among the monetary matters regarding which a condition is binding according to Rabbi Yehudah. As an example of a condition regarding a non-monetary matter, the Jerusalem Talmud suggests the case in which a man marries a woman on condition that if he dies without children she will not be required to

HALAKHAH

עַל מְנָת שֶׁאֵין לִיךְ עָלַי שְׁאֵר, כְּסוּת, וְעוֹנָה **On condition that you have no claims on me for food, clothing, or conjugal relations.** "If a man says to a woman: 'I am betrothing you on condition that I be exempt from providing you with food, clothing, and conjugal relations,' he is exempt from providing her with food and clothing, following Rabbi Yehudah that in monetary matters a condition made in violation of Torah law is binding. But he is not exempt from conjugal relations, for with regard to matters of a non-monetary nature, even Rabbi Yehudah agrees that a condition that runs counter to Torah law is null and void." (*Rambam, Sefer Nashim, Hilkhot Ishut* 6:9-10, 12:6; *Shulḥan Arukh, Even HaEzer* 38:5, 69:6.)

[1]קָסָבַר רַבִּי יְהוּדָה: כְּתוּבָּה דְּרַבָּנַן, [2]וַחֲכָמִים עָשׂוּ חִיזּוּק לְדִבְרֵיהֶם יוֹתֵר מִשֶּׁל תּוֹרָה. [3]הֲרֵי פֵּירוֹת דְּרַבָּנַן, [4]וְלָא עָבְדוּ לְהוּ רַבָּנַן חִיזּוּק. [5]דִּתְנַן: [6]"רַבִּי יְהוּדָה אוֹמֵר: לְעוֹלָם הוּא אוֹכֵל פֵּירֵי פֵּירוֹת, [7]עַד שֶׁיִּכְתּוֹב לָהּ: 'דִּין וּדְבָרִים אֵין לִי בִּנְכָסַיִךְ, וּבְפֵירוֹתֵיהֶן,

LITERAL TRANSLATION

[1]Rabbi Yehudah maintains: The ketubah is of Rabbinic [origin], [2]and the Sages made a reinforcement for their words greater than [for those] of the Torah.

[3][But] consider usufruct which is of Rabbinic [status], [4]and the Rabbis did not make a reinforcement for it. [5]For we have learned: [6]"Rabbi Yehudah says: He always enjoys the usufruct of usufruct, [7]until he writes for her: 'I have no legal claim to your property, or to its usufruct, or to the usufruct of

TRANSLATION AND COMMENTARY

קָסָבַר רַבִּי יְהוּדָה [1]The Gemara answers: Even though Rabbi Yehudah maintains that in monetary matters a condition that runs counter to Torah law is valid, here the condition is void unless it is reduced to writing. For **Rabbi Yehudah maintains** that the husband's obligation to give his wife **a ketubah is a Rabbinic enactment,** [2]**and the Sages reinforced their rulings** and were even **more** stringent about their own enactments **than** they were about the laws **of the Torah.** In order to strengthen their enactment, the Rabbis denied the possibility of stating any oral condition whereby the husband may seek to reduce his liability regarding the ketubah.

הֲרֵי פֵּירוֹת דְּרַבָּנַן [3]The Gemara now challenges this explanation: **But consider** the husband's right to enjoy the **usufruct** of his wife's property. [4]This right **is** granted only **by Rabbinic enactment, but the Rabbis did not reinforce** their ruling by decreeing that if a man stipulates that he will not enjoy the usufruct of his wife's property, the condition is void. [5]**For we have learned** in a Mishnah (below, 83a): "If someone writes to his betrothed bride: 'After we are married, I will have no claim to your property,' he still enjoys the usufruct of her property during her lifetime, and inherits her estate upon her death, for he never meant to waive his right to the usufruct or to her estate, but only his right to reclaim the property from a buyer if his wife sells the property during her lifetime. If a bridegroom writes to his betrothed bride: 'After we are married, I will have no claim to your property, nor to the usufruct of your property,' he does not enjoy the usufruct of her property during her lifetime, for he has explicitly waived that right; but if she dies, he inherits her estate, because he has not waived his right of succession. [6]**Rabbi Yehudah says:** Even if the husband waives his right to the usufruct of his wife's property, **he may always enjoy the usufruct of the usufruct** of that property, [7]**unless he writes** explicitly: **'I will not have a claim to your property, nor to its usufruct, nor to the usufruct of its usufruct forever.'** If the husband waives his right only to the usufruct of his wife's

RASHI

והרי פירות — דנכסי מלוג. **דרבנן** — האי דבעל אוכלן — תקנתא דרבנן היא, ולא עבוד רבנן חיזוק שיהא תנאו בטל, אם התנה למחול אכילתו. **פירי פירות** — אם כתב לה: "דין ודברים אין לי בנכסיך ובפירותיהן" — אוכל הוא פירי פירות, מוכר פירות ולוקח קרקע שיהא לה קרן, והוא אוכל פירות.

NOTES

undergo levirate marriage. Elsewhere, however, the Jerusalem Talmud (*Kiddushin* 1:2) maintains that the right to conjugal relations is not a monetary matter, and it suggests that the condition imposed by the husband that his wife will have no claim on him for conjugal relations is binding only if the bride is a minor.

Rashba notes that Rabbi Yehudah also agrees that a person cannot abrogate a Torah law, even one concerning a monetary matter, by means of a condition. Thus, if a man stipulates that he is marrying a woman on condition that the regulations regarding maintenance are not imposed, the condition is void. The dispute between Rabbi Yehudah and Rabbi Meir centers on the meaning of the condition: "You are betrothed to me on condition that you have no claims on me for food or clothing." Rabbi Meir maintains that this condition is to be understood as an attempt to abrogate a Torah law, and therefore it is void. Rabbi Yehudah argues that the husband is stipulating that he is marrying the woman on condition that she releases him from the obligations imposed on him by Torah law. Since the woman is capable of waiving her rights to food and clothing, the condition is valid.

HALAKHAH

כְּתוּבָּה דְּרַבָּנַן **The ketubah is of Rabbinic origin.** "According to most authorities (*Geonim, Rabbenu Ḥananel, Rif, Rambam, Ran, Maharam of Rothenburg*), it was the Rabbis who enacted that a woman is entitled to receive her ketubah from her husband or from his estate upon the dissolution of their marriage. Though there are some authorities who disagree (*Rabbenu Tam, Ri,* and others), the law is in accordance with the majority opinion (*Bet Yosef*)." (*Rambam, Sefer Nashim, Hilkhot Ishut* 10:7, 11:14, 12:2; *Shulḥan Arukh, Even HaEzer* 66:6.)

לְעוֹלָם הוּא אוֹכֵל פֵּירֵי פֵּירוֹת **He always enjoys the usufruct of usufruct.** "If someone writes to his betrothed bride (or

TRANSLATION AND COMMENTARY

property, he may sell the usufruct and buy land with the proceeds. That land will belong to his wife, but the husband will be entitled to enjoy its usufruct, for he only waived the right to enjoy the usufruct of his wife's property, but not the usufruct of the usufruct." [56B] [1]**And,** continues the Gemara, **we have an established tradition** with regard to the interpretation of the Mishnah just quoted: [2]**What does** Rabbi Yehudah **mean** when he says that the husband loses his right to all usufruct, if **he writes** that he will not have a claim to his wife's property, nor to its usufruct, nor to the usufruct of its usufruct forever? He does not mean that the husband must necessarily put this waiver in writing, [3]for even if **he** only **makes an oral statement** to this effect, his condition is binding. Now, if the husband can concede that he will not enjoy the usufruct of his wife's property to which he is entitled by Rabbinic enactment, why can the wife not concede that she is prepared to forfeit a part of her ketubah, which is hers only by Rabbinic enactment?

אָמַר אַבַּיֵי [4]To resolve this difficulty, **Abaye suggested** that a distinction is to be made between a woman's ketubah and a man's right to the usufruct of his wife's property. **All** married women, said Abaye, **have a ketubah, but not all** married men **have usufruct,** for not every woman brings to her marriage landed property, the usufruct of which belongs to her husband. [5]**In the case** of an enactment like a ketubah **that is common** to all, **the Rabbis reinforced** the enactment, ruling that it cannot be rendered void by a mere oral condition, but only by a written document. [6]But **in the case** of an enactment like the husband's right to the usufruct of his wife's property, something **that is not common** to all, **the Rabbis did not reinforce** the enactment. Thus the husband can give up his right to the usufruct by merely making an oral stipulation to that effect.

וּבְפֵירוֹת פֵּירוֹתֵיהֶן עַד עוֹלָם׳״.
[56B] [1]וְקַיְימָא לַן: [2]מַאי ״כּוֹתֵב״? [3]אוֹמֵר.
[4]אָמַר אַבַּיֵי: לַכֹּל יֵשׁ כְּתוּבָּה, וְלֹא לַכֹּל יֵשׁ פֵּירוֹת. [5]מִילְּתָא דִּשְׁכִיחָא עָבְדוּ בָּהּ רַבָּנַן חִיזּוּק; [6]מִילְּתָא דְּלָא שְׁכִיחָא לָא עָבְדוּ בָּהּ רַבָּנַן חִיזּוּק.

LITERAL TRANSLATION

its usufruct forever.'"

[56B] [1]And it is established for us: [2]What is [meant by] "he writes"? [3]He says.

[4]Abaye said: All have a ketubah, but not all have usufruct. [5]For a thing that is common the Rabbis made a reinforcement; [6]for a thing that is not common the Rabbis did not make a reinforcement.

RASHI

וקיימא לן — ב״הכותב״. מאי כותב אומר — אלמא: תנאיה תנאה.

NOTES

מַאי ״כּוֹתֵב״? אוֹמֵר **What is meant by "he writes"? He says.** Many Rishonim maintain that the Gemara never meant to distinguish between a written receipt and an oral statement, but rather between the waiver of an obligation that has already been accepted and a stipulation that the obligation will never take effect. According to those authorities, the Gemara is saying here that when Rabbi Yehudah ruled that the husband loses his right to all usufruct if he writes to his bride that he will have no claim to her property or to its usufruct forever, he did not mean that the husband forfeits his right to the usufruct only if he writes his wife a document transferring back to her the right to her property's usufruct that he attained by his marriage to her, for he can forfeit his right to the usufruct by making a stipulation to that effect at the time of the marriage (see *Ritva*).

מִילְּתָא דִּשְׁכִיחָא **A thing that is common.** *Maharsha* notes that this passage poses a difficulty for *Tosafot* (above 52a, s.v. רצה), who argues that the husband's right to the usufruct of his wife's property is considered a frequently utilized entitlement, because it remains in effect throughout their marriage, whereas the wife's right to her ketubah is regarded as an infrequently utilized right, for her ketubah is paid out only once.

Ayelet Ahavim explains that the issue here is whether or not the Rabbis reinforced their own enactment by decreeing that it could not be canceled by means of an oral condition. In this context, it is clear that an enactment like the ketubah, which applies to all women, is regarded as more common and is therefore in need of greater reinforcement than an enactment like the right to usufruct that applies to only some men.

HALAKHAH

says to her) that, after they are married, he will have no claim to her property or to the usufruct of that property, he may not enjoy the usufruct of his wife's property, but he may sell the usufruct, buy land with the proceeds, and then enjoy the usufruct of the land he has bought. Similarly, if he writes to her that he will have no claim to her property, or to the usufruct, or to the usufruct of the usufruct, he may sell the usufruct of her property, buy land with the proceeds, sell the usufruct of the land he has bought, buy more land with the proceeds, and then enjoy the usufruct of that property. This is the law, unless he waives his right to the usufruct and to the usufruct of the usufruct *ad infinitum*, in which case he is not entitled to any of the usufruct during his wife's lifetime," following Rabbi Yehudah. (*Rambam, Sefer Nashim, Hilkhot Ishut* 23:4; *Shulḥan Arukh, Even HaEzer* 92:4–5.)

TRANSLATION AND COMMENTARY

הֲרֵי [1] The Gemara now raises another objection against the assertion that, according to Rabbi Yehudah, the Rabbis reinforced their enactments by means of stringent rulings. **Surely** the case of two **ass-drivers who** bring *demai* (doubtfully tithed produce) to market and testify about each other's produce **is** a **common** occurrence, **and** yet, according to Rabbi Yehudah, **the Rabbis did not reinforce** their enactment regarding *demai* by means of a stringent ruling that the testimony of the one ass-driver about the other's produce is not believed. [2] **For we have learned** elsewhere in the Mishnah (*Demai* 4:7): **"If** two **ass-drivers enter a city,** each carrying grain for sale, [3] **and one of them says:** 'Buy my companion's grain, for it is better than mine. **My** grain **is new and my companion's is old** [grain improves with age], [4] and moreover **my** grain **has not** yet **been tithed and my companion's has been tithed** and is ready to eat,' [5] **he is not believed** and his companion's grain is still considered *demai*. Although we would ordinarily accept the ass-driver's testimony about someone else's produce, in this case we suspect that the two ass-drivers have conspired to further each other's interests, agreeing that in the first town they reach one will testify that his own grain has not yet been tithed, but the other's has indeed been tithed, and in the next town they will reverse roles. [6] **Rabbi Yehudah** disagrees with the first Tanna and **says:** The ass-driver **is believed**, because we are not concerned that he will testify falsely on behalf of his companion." Thus we see that, according to Rabbi Yehudah, the Rabbis did not reinforce their enactments even regarding matters that commonly occur. Why, then, did he rule that an oral condition reducing the husband's liability regarding his wife's ketubah is void?

[1] הֲרֵי חַמָּרִים דִּשְׁכִיחִי, וְלָא עָבְדוּ לָהּ רַבָּנַן חִיזּוּק. [2] דִּתְנַן: "הַחַמָּרִין שֶׁנִּכְנְסוּ לָעִיר, [3] וְאָמַר אֶחָד מֵהֶן: 'שֶׁלִּי חָדָשׁ וְשֶׁל חֲבֵרִי יָשָׁן; [4] שֶׁלִּי אֵינוֹ מְתוּקָּן וְשֶׁל חֲבֵרִי מְתוּקָּן', [5] אֵין נֶאֱמָנִים. [6] רַבִּי יְהוּדָה אוֹמֵר: נֶאֱמָנִים".

LITERAL TRANSLATION

[1] [But] consider ass-drivers who are common, but the Rabbis did not make a reinforcement. [2] For we have learned: "[If] ass-drivers entered a city, [3] and one of them said: 'Mine is new and my fellow's is old; [4] mine is not tithed (lit., "prepared") and my fellow's is tithed,' [5] they are not believed. [6] Rabbi Yehudah says: They are believed."

RASHI

והרי חמרים – גבי דמאי דרבנן הוא, ולא עבדו בהו חיזוק, למיחש לגומלין לרבי יהודה. **שלי חדש** – והישן טוב ממנו. שהחדש עדיין אינו יבש כל צרכו. והכי נמי אמרינן ב"איזהו נשך" (בבא מציעא עב,ב): היו חדשות מארבע וישנות משלש כו'. ויש מפרשים משום עומר. ולאו מילתא היא, דאם כן דמתרץ בדמאי הקילו – התינח דמאי, חדש מאי איכא למימר? ועוד: לא מצינו שנחשדו עמי הארץ על איסור חדש. ולא נקט לה אלא משום אין נאמנים לדמאי. ורבותא אשמועינן, דאף על גב דמשבח לה לדחבריה נמי במילי אחרנייתא – אינו נאמן על הדמאי, דחיישינן לגומלין.

BACKGROUND

שֶׁלִּי חָדָשׁ "Mine is new." The ass-drivers spoken of here are in fact merchants who peddle grain from place to place. *Tosafot* (above, 24a) explains that if one of them praises his comrade's wares and depreciates his own, we suspect that the two are conspiring. In the first town, one ass-driver praises the other's grain at his own expense, while his companion will do the same for him in the next town.

NOTES

הֲרֵי חַמָּרִים דִּשְׁכִיחִי But consider ass-drivers who are common. The Mishnah in *Demai* is cited and analyzed earlier in our tractate (above, 24a). *Ritva* (in the name of *Tosafot*) notes that the discussion in our Gemara assumes one of the positions proposed there — that with respect to matters of Torah law Rabbi Yehudah is concerned that people will give false testimony in each other's favor, and that it is only with respect to *demai*, which is a matter of Rabbinic law, that he does not have such concern. Basing itself on this assumption, the Gemara asks why Rabbi Yehudah does not suspect that the ass-drivers will give false testimony on each other's behalf, for it is Rabbi Yehudah who maintains that the Rabbis reinforced their enactments with stringencies. But according to the position that even with respect to matters of Torah law Rabbi Yehudah is not concerned that people will testify falsely in each other's favor, there is no cause for such a question, for in no case does Rabbi Yehudah have such a concern.

שֶׁלִּי חָדָשׁ "Mine is new." Our commentary follows *Rashi*, who explains that old grain is superior to new. According to this explanation, the only Halakhically significant statement of the ass-driver was his declaration that his companion's produce was tithed, whereas his own was not. The Mishnah inserted the other clause — in which the ass-driver praised the quality of his companion's grain — in order to sharpen the Mishnah's ruling: Even though the ass-driver sincerely admits that his grain is of poorer quality than his companion's and is not tithed, he is still not believed (according to the anonymous first Tanna of the Mishnah) when he testifies that his companion's grain is tithed, because we suspect a conspiracy between them.

Rashi cites another explanation, according to which the ass-driver testifies that his companion's grain is of the previous year's crop, whereas his own is new grain that ripened in the period before Pesaḥ and is now forbidden for consumption until after the offering of the Omer sacrifice on the sixteenth of Nisan (the second day of Pesaḥ). Even though the ass-driver testifies that his companion's grain is

HALAKHAH

הַחַמָּרִין שֶׁנִּכְנְסוּ לָעִיר If ass-drivers entered a city. "If two ass-drivers come to town carrying grain, and one of them says: 'My grain is untithed, but my companion's grain is tithed,' he is not believed, because we suspect that the two ass-drivers have conspired and that in the next town they will reverse their roles," following the anonymous first Tanna in the Mishnah in *Demai*. (*Rambam, Sefer Zeraim, Hilkhot Ma'aserot* 12:10.)

TRANSLATION AND COMMENTARY

אָמַר אַבַּיֵי [1] **Abaye answered** this difficulty by saying that a distinction can be made between the enactment of a woman's ketubah and the enactment regarding *demai*. In the case of **Rabbinic enactments** legislated **with regard to a certainty** (such as the legislation entitling every married woman to a ketubah), [2] **the Rabbis reinforced** their rulings by adding stringent requirements to them. Thus Rabbi Yehudah ruled that the enactment of a woman's ketubah cannot be canceled by a mere oral concession, but only by means of a written waiver. [3] But in the case of **Rabbinic enactments** passed into law **because of a doubt** — such as the decree that the produce of a person who we suspect may not have set aside the various tithes must be treated as of doubtful status — [4] **the Rabbis did not reinforce** their rulings with additional stringencies. Thus Rabbi Yehudah ruled that we do not suspect the ass driver of giving false testimony regarding the doubtfully tithed produce of his companion.

רָבָא אָמַר [5] **Rava proposed** a different answer: Even if in other cases of doubt the Rabbis reinforced their rulings with additional stringencies, **in the case of *demai* they were lenient.** When the Rabbis saw that a significant minority of people failed to separate all the tithes required by law, they enacted the laws of *demai*, ruling that a person who is not known to be scrupulously observant of the laws of tithing is not believed when he says that his own produce has been properly tithed. Hence produce purchased from someone who is suspected of not having set aside the required tithes must be tithed again by the buyer before it is permitted to be eaten. But since most people do in fact tithe their produce in the proper manner, various leniencies regarding *demai* were accepted. Thus Rabbi Yehudah was ready to accept the testimony of the ass-driver that his companion's grain had been properly tithed, even though there was reason to doubt it.

רַבִּי מֵאִיר אוֹמֵר [6] The Gemara now proceeds to analyze the next clause of our Mishnah, which stated: **"Rabbi Meir says:** A man may not reduce the amount of his wife's ketubah to less than the legal minimum, for **whoever reduces the ketubah of a virgin to less** than two hundred zuz, or that of a widow to less than a maneh, his intercourse with her is tantamount to an act of prostitution." [7] A precise reading of the clause that speaks of **"whoever reduces** his wife's ketubah to less than the legal minimum" teaches us that the

[1] אָמַר אַבַּיֵי: וַדַּאי דְּדִבְרֵיהֶם, [2] עָבְדוּ רַבָּנַן חִיזּוּק; [3] סָפֵק דְּדִבְרֵיהֶם, [4] לָא עָבְדוּ רַבָּנַן חִיזּוּק.

[5] רָבָא אֲמַר: בִּדְמַאי הֵקִילוּ.

[6] ״רַבִּי מֵאִיר אוֹמֵר: כָּל הַפּוֹחֵת, וכו׳״. [7] כָּל הַפּוֹחֵת אֲפִילּוּ

LITERAL TRANSLATION

[1] Abaye said: [Regarding] a certainty of a Rabbinic enactment (lit., "of their words"), [2] the Rabbis made a reinforcement; [3] [regarding] a matter in doubt of a Rabbinic enactment, [4] the Rabbis did not make a reinforcement.

[5] Rava said: In [the case of] *demai* they were lenient.

[6] "Rabbi Meir says: Whoever makes [the ketubah of a virgin] less, etc." [7] Whoever makes less [implies] even

RASHI

בדמאי הקילו — מאחר ספק דדבריהם. ואפילו ספק ליתיה, דרוב עמי הארץ מעשרין הן. **כל הפוחת אפילו בתנאה** — מדלא תנא כל בתולה שאין לה מאתים ואלמנה שאין לה מנה הרי זו בעילת זנות, שמע מינה דהכי

CONCEPTS

דְּמַאי *Demai.* This refers to produce (or food made from produce) which was purchased from a person who may not have separated the various tithes as required by law. The literal meaning of the word דְּמַאי is "suspicion," i.e., produce about which there is a suspicion that tithes were not properly taken from it. In the Second Temple period, the Sages decreed that such produce should be considered as being of doubtful status, even though the owner claimed that he had tithed it. The Sages further decreed that the buyer of such produce had to tithe it himself. Nevertheless, since the produce had probably been tithed, certain leniency was permitted concerning the use of *demai* for food and other purposes.

NOTES

of the previous year's crop, he is not believed, and his companion's grain is presumed to be new grain that is forbidden until the second day of Pesaḥ, for we suspect that the two-ass drivers are conspiring to further each other's interests. *Rashi* rejects this explanation, arguing that if this is our concern, why does Rabbi Yehudah maintain that the ass driver is believed? The argument put forward in the Gemara, that the Rabbis were lenient about *demai,* cannot be extended to the prohibition against new grain. Furthermore, we nowhere find that an *am ha'aretz* is suspected with respect to the prohibition against new grain.

Rashbam (cited by *Tosafot Sens*) suggests a third explanation, according to which the ass-driver testifies during the Sabbatical Year that his companion's grain is from the previous year's crop, whereas his own is grain that has grown during the Sabbatical Year, and thus may not be eaten after the last of the crop has been removed from the field. *Rabbenu Tam* rejects this explanation, arguing that an *am ha'aretz* is not suspect with respect to produce that grew during the Sabbatical Year.

בִּדְמַאי הֵקִילוּ In the case of *demai*, they were lenient. The Rishonim note that in the discussion concerning this Mishnah that is found above (24a), it is Abaye who argues that in the case of *demai* the Rabbis were more lenient, whereas here Abaye offers a different answer.

Ritva explains that there the Gemara is discussing the issue of whether we suspect people who testify in each other's favor of conspiring to further each other's interests. Abaye argues that, according to Rabbi Yehudah, the Rabbis were more lenient on that issue with respect to *demai* than they were regarding matters of Torah law. But here the issue is whether the Rabbis reinforced their enactments with stringencies. Here Abaye argues that, according to Rabbi Yehudah, the Rabbis imposed reinforcements to strengthen those enactments that were legislated with regard to a certainty, but they did not reinforce enactments that were legislated because of a doubt.

כָּל הַפּוֹחֵת אֲפִילּוּ בִּתְנָאָה Whoever makes less implies even with a condition. The Rishonim disagree about how

HALAKHAH

כָּל הַפּוֹחֵת אֲפִילּוּ בִּתְנָאָה Whoever makes less implies even with a condition. "If a man stipulates that his wife's ketubah

TRANSLATION AND COMMENTARY

couple's intercourse is considered an act of prostitution **even** if the husband reduced his wife's ketubah to less than the legal minimum **by means of a condition,** and the woman accepted the condition. [1]**It follows** that Rabbi Meir **maintains** that **the** husband's **condition** that his wife's ketubah will be less than what she is entitled to by law **is void,** [2]**and** that **she is** in fact still **entitled** to the **full** amount. [3]**But since** her husband **said to her: "You** will **have** a ketubah of **only a maneh,"** [4]**she does not rely on her ketubah** document, because she thinks that she is entitled only to the reduced amount. And since the woman thinks that her ketubah document does not guarantee her financial rights, [5]sexual **intercourse** between her and her husband **is** tantamount to **an act of prostitution.**

בִּתְנָאָה. [1]אַלְמָא קָסָבַר: תְּנָאוֹ בָּטֵל, [2]וְאִית לָהּ. [3]וְכֵיוָן דַּאֲמַר לָהּ: ״לֵית לֵיךְ אֶלָּא מָנֶה״, [4]לָא סָמְכָא דַּעְתָּהּ, [5]וְהָוְיָא לָהּ בְּעִילָתוֹ בְּעִילַת זְנוּת.

[6]וְהָא שָׁמְעִינַן לֵיהּ לְרַבִּי מֵאִיר דְּאָמַר: ״כָּל הַמַּתְנֶה עַל מַה שֶּׁכָּתוּב בַּתּוֹרָה תְּנָאוֹ בָּטֵל״. [7]הָא בִּדְרַבָּנַן, תְּנָאוֹ קַיָּים!

LITERAL TRANSLATION

with a condition. [1]Hence he maintains: His condition is void, [2]and she has [her full ketubah]. [3]But since he said to her: "You only have a maneh," [4]her mind does not rely [on her ketubah], [5]and his intercourse with her is an act of prostitution.

[6]But surely we have heard that Rabbi Meir said: "Whoever makes a condition contrary to what is written in the Torah, his condition is void." [7]But [if it is contrary] to [a law of] the Rabbis, his condition stands!

RASHI

אשמועינן: שאף על פי שהיא גובה לבסוף, דאין תנאו קיים — אפילו הכי, כיון דמעיקרא אתני — קרי לה בעילת זנות. משום דמשעת ביאה לא הוה סמכא דעתה אכתובה. אלמא קסבר תנאו בטל — דבלאו הכי לאו רבותא היא דנקט ״כל הפוחת״. והא שמעינן ליה — לעיל.

וְהָא [6]The Gemara asks: **But surely we have heard that Rabbi Meir said: "Whoever makes a condition** that is **contrary to what is written in the Torah, his condition is void,** and the agreement takes effect in accordance with Torah law"? Thus, says Rabbi Meir, if a man betroths a woman on condition that she will have no claims on him for food, clothing, or conjugal relations, she is betrothed, but his condition is void. [7]**But** we can infer from this that if someone makes a condition contrary **to a Rabbinic enactment, his condition is** indeed **valid,** and the agreement takes effect in accordance with the condition. Now, if a woman is only entitled to her ketubah by Rabbinic enactment, why does Rabbi Meir maintain that the husband cannot stipulate that his wife's ketubah will be less than the legal minimum?

NOTES

Rabbi Meir's statement — that whoever fixes the ketubah of a virgin at less than 200 zuz, his intercourse with her is tantamount to an act of prostitution — implies that the couple's intercourse is considered an act of prostitution even if the husband fixes his wife's ketubah at less than the legal minimum by means of a condition.

Rashi argues that the inference follows from the fact that Rabbi Meir does not speak of a woman whose ketubah is less than the legal amount, but rather of a woman whose ketubah is reduced to less than that amount, which implies that it was fixed at less than the legal amount by means of a condition.

Others suggest that the Gemara draws its conclusion from the fact that Rabbi Meir said: "Whoever *makes*," rather than: "Whoever *made*" (see *Nimmukei* Yosef). *Ra'ah* maintains that the argument is based on the fact that Rabbi Meir uses the sweeping formulation: "*Whoever* makes," which implies that his ruling applies whenever the woman thinks that she is entitled only to a reduced ketubah, even though she is in fact still entitled to the full amount, such as when her ketubah was reduced by means of a condition.

וְהָא שָׁמְעִינַן לֵיהּ לְרַבִּי מֵאִיר **But surely we have heard that Rabbi Meir said.** The Rishonim ask: How do we know that, according to Rabbi Meir, a condition that runs counter to a Rabbinic enactment is binding? Perhaps Rabbi Meir meant to say that if a person makes a condition that contradicts a provision set down in Torah law, the condition is invalid, and all the more so if he makes a condition that contradicts a Rabbinic enactment. For, as we saw above, Rabbi Yehudah, who maintains that a condition that runs counter to Torah law is binding, agrees that a condition that runs counter to a Rabbinic enactment is invalid!

Tosafot and *Ritva* explain that the Gemara draws its conclusion from the Baraita cited earlier, which taught that according to Rabbi Meir a condition made by the husband that his wife will have no claims against him for food, clothing, or conjugal relations is void. Rabbi Meir referred only to the woman's rights by Torah law, without mentioning any of her rights by Rabbinic enactment, which implies that he maintains that a condition denying a woman something to which she is entitled by Rabbinic enactment is binding.

HALAKHAH

will be less than the legal minimum — 200 zuz for a virgin, and a maneh for a non-virgin — the condition is null and void." (*Rambam, Sefer Nashim, Hilkhot Ishut* 12:8; *Shulḥan Arukh, Even HaEzer* 66:9, 69:6.)

[1]קָסָבַר רַבִּי מֵאִיר: כְּתוּבָּה דְּאוֹרַיְיתָא.
[2]תַּנְיָא: ״רַבִּי מֵאִיר אוֹמֵר: [3]כָּל הַפּוֹחֵת לִבְתוּלָה מִמָּאתַיִם, וּלְאַלְמָנָה מִמָּנֶה, [4]הֲרֵי זוֹ בְּעִילַת זְנוּת. [5]רַבִּי יוֹסֵי אוֹמֵר: רַשַּׁאי. [6]רַבִּי יְהוּדָה אוֹמֵר: [7]רָצָה, כּוֹתֵב לִבְתוּלָה שְׁטָר שֶׁל מָאתַיִם, [8]וְהִיא כּוֹתֶבֶת לוֹ: ׳הִתְקַבַּלְתִּי מִמְּךָ מָנֶה׳, וּלְאַלְמָנָה מָנֶה, [9]וְהִיא כּוֹתֶבֶת לוֹ: ׳הִתְקַבַּלְתִּי מִמְּךָ חֲמִשִּׁים זוּז׳״.
[10]וְסָבַר רַבִּי יוֹסֵי רַשַּׁאי?
[11]וּרְמִינְהִי: ״אֵין עוֹשִׂין כְּתוּבַּת

LITERAL TRANSLATION

[1]Rabbi Meir maintains: A ketubah is from the Torah. [2]It was taught: "Rabbi Meir says: [3]Whoever makes [the ketubah of] a virgin less than two hundred [zuz], or [that of] a widow less than a maneh, [4]it is an act of prostitution. [5]Rabbi Yose says: He is permitted. [6]Rabbi Yehudah says: [7][If] he wishes, he may write for a virgin a deed of two hundred [zuz], [8]and she may write for him: 'I have received from you a maneh,' or [he may write] for a widow [a deed of] a maneh, [9]and she may write for him: 'I have received from you fifty zuz.'"

[10]But does Rabbi Yose maintain [that] he is permitted? [11]A contradiction was raised (lit., "cast them together"): "We do not make a woman's ketubah

TRANSLATION AND COMMENTARY

קָסָבַר [1]The Gemara answers: **Rabbi Meir maintains** that a woman is entitled to her **ketubah by Torah law.** Thus a condition reducing a woman's ketubah to less than the legal minimum is invalid, because it is a condition that runs counter to Torah law.

תַּנְיָא [2]The Gemara continues with a related Baraita, in which **it was taught: "Rabbi Meir says:** A man may not reduce the amount of his wife's ketubah to less than the legal minimum, [3]for **whoever reduces the ketubah of a virgin to less than two hundred zuz, or that of a widow to less than a maneh,** [4]his intercourse with her **is** tantamount to **an act of prostitution.** [5]**Rabbi Yose says: He is permitted** to reduce his wife's ketubah to less than the legal minimum, even by way of an oral condition, provided that his wife agrees to the reduction. [6]**Rabbi Yehudah says:** The husband may not reduce his wife's ketubah by means of an oral condition, even if his wife agrees to the reduction, because the Rabbis reinforced their enactment of the ketubah by rendering such a condition void. [7]But **if he wishes** to reduce his obligation concerning his wife's ketubah, **he may write a** ketubah **document of two hundred zuz for** his wife who is **a virgin**, as is required of him by law, [8]**and** then he can arrange to have his wife **write him** a receipt saying: **'I have** already **received a maneh from you** in partial payment of my ketubah,' **or he may write** a ketubah **document** of **a maneh for** his wife who is **a widow** or a divorcee, [9]**and** then he can arrange to have his wife **write him** a receipt saying: **'I have** already **received fifty zuz from you** in partial payment of my ketubah,' even though she has received nothing from him."

וְסָבַר [10]The Gemara asks: **But does Rabbi Yose** really **maintain that** the husband **is permitted** to reduce his wife's ketubah to less than the legal minimum? [11]Surely **this is contradicted** by another Baraita in which it was taught: **"A person may not designate movable property for** the payment of **his wife's ketubah.** This

RASHI

רבי יוסי אומר רשאי — ואפילו על פה נמי תנאו קיים. ואתא רבי יהודה למימר נמי רשאי, כרבי יוסי, מיהו, **על פה** — תנאו בטל, כדאמרינן לעיל: חכמים עשו חיזוק לדבריהם יותר משל תורה. אבל באת למחול — תכתוב שובר. **אין עושין כתובה מטלטלין** — אין מייחדין מטלטלין לכתובה.

NOTES

קָסָבַר רַבִּי מֵאִיר: כְּתוּבָּה דְּאוֹרַיְיתָא Rabbi Meir maintains: A ketubah is from the Torah. *Rabbi Crescas Vidal* notes that even according to the opinion that the husband's obligation to pay his wife her ketubah is derived from the Torah, the amount of the ketubah is not fixed by Torah law but only by Rabbinic enactment. But since the Rabbis standardized what is essentially a Biblical obligation, a condition made by the husband to reduce his wife's ketubah is viewed as a condition that runs counter to Torah law.

The Gemara proposes here that Rabbi Meir is of the opinion that a woman is entitled to her ketubah by Torah law. The Rishonim object: All seem to agree that a widow's ketubah is a Rabbinic enactment (see above, 10a). Why, then, should Rabbi Meir invalidate a condition reducing a widow's ketubah to less than the legal minimum?

Ramban and others offer three answers: (1) Rabbi Meir maintains that even a widow is entitled to a ketubah by Torah law (following the Gemara's suggestion above [10b] that a widow is called an *almanah* because she has a ketubah of only a maneh). (2) Even though a widow's ketubah is indeed only a Rabbinic enactment, the Rabbis chose not to distinguish between a widow and a virgin in this respect, and declared invalid any condition reducing a woman's ketubah to less than the legal minimum. (3) According to Rabbi Meir, a condition fixing a virgin's ketubah at less than the legal minimum is invalid, because it runs counter to Torah law. But a condition reducing a widow's ketubah is indeed binding, for a widow is only entitled to her ketubah by Rabbinic enactment.

אֵין עוֹשִׂין כְּתוּבַּת אִשָּׁה מִטַּלְטְלִין We do not make a woman's ketubah a charge on movable property. The Rishonim ask: It is taught elsewhere in a Baraita (below, 82b) that Shimon ben Shetaḥ enacted that a person may not designate movable property for the payment of his wife's ketubah, in order that he not consider it easy to divorce

אִשָּׁה מִטַּלְטְלִין, מִפְּנֵי תִּיקּוּן הָעוֹלָם. ¹אָמַר רַבִּי יוֹסֵי: וְכִי מַה תִּיקּוּן הָעוֹלָם יֵשׁ בְּזוֹ? ²וַהֲלֹא אֵין קְצוּבִין, וּפוֹחֲתִין״! ³תַּנָּא קַמָּא נַמִי ״אֵין עוֹשִׂין״ קָאָמַר! ⁴אֶלָּא לָאו הָכִי קָאָמַר: בַּמֶּה דְּבָרִים אֲמוּרִים? ⁵בְּשֶׁלֹּא קִבֵּל עָלָיו אַחֲרָיוּת. ⁶אֲבָל קִבֵּל עָלָיו אַחֲרָיוּת, עוֹשִׂין. ⁷וַאֲתָא רַבִּי יוֹסֵי לְמֵימַר: כִּי קִיבֵּל עָלָיו אַחֲרָיוּת, ⁸אַמַּאי עוֹשִׂין? ⁹וַהֲלֹא אֵין קְצוּבִין, וּפוֹחֲתִין!

LITERAL TRANSLATION

[a charge on] movable property, for the benefit of the world. [1] Rabbi Yose said: But what benefit to the world is there in this? [2] But surely they are not fixed, and they depreciate!"

[3] The first Tanna also said: "We do not make"! Is it not that he says this: [4] In what [case] are these things said? [5] When he did not accept responsibility. [6] But [if] he accepted responsibility, we do make. [7] And Rabbi Yose came to say: If he accepted responsibility, [8] why do we make? [9] But surely they are not fixed, and they depreciate!

TRANSLATION AND COMMENTARY

ordinance was instituted **for the benefit of the world,** in order to prevent difficulties that might arise at a later date. For if a person were to designate his movable goods for the payment of his wife's ketubah, and they were to be lost or destroyed, or were to depreciate in value, the woman would be unable to collect the full amount of her ketubah. [1] **Rabbi Yose said: How does this** ordinance **operate for the benefit of the world?** [2] **Surely** movable goods **are not** permanently **fixed** in value, but are subject to fluctuations. Thus **they may depreciate** and the woman will not be able to collect the full amount to which she is entitled."

תַּנָּא [3] Before the Gemara explains how the viewpoint expressed here by Rabbi Yose contradicts what he said in the previous Baraita, the Gemara first explains the Tannaitic dispute within the Baraita itself. On what point does Rabbi Yose disagree with the first Tanna of the Baraita? **The first Tanna also said** that **a person may not designate** movable property for the payment of his wife's ketubah! [4] Rather, explains the Gemara, **this is** what the first Tanna meant to **say:** A person may not designate movable property for the payment of his wife's ketubah. **When does this apply?** [5] **When** the husband **does not accept responsibility** for the movable goods, should they be lost or destroyed. [6] **But if he does accept responsibility** for the movable goods, **he may** indeed **designate** such property for the payment of his wife's ketubah. [7] **And Rabbi Yose came and said:** Even **if** the husband **accepts responsibility** for the movable goods in the event that they are lost or destroyed, [8] **why** should **he** be allowed to **designate** movable property for the payment of his wife's ketubah? [9] **Surely** movable goods **are not fixed** in value, **and** therefore the goods that the husband designates for the payment of his wife's ketubah may **depreciate**, in which case the woman will be unable to collect the full amount to which she is entitled! Thus, argues Rabbi Yose, the husband may not designate movable goods for the payment of his wife's ketubah, even if he accepts responsibility for them should they be lost or destroyed.

RASHI

מפני תיקון העולם — שמא יאבדו, או יפחתו דמיהן. **אין קצובין** — אין דמיהן קצובין עולמית, דמוקרי ומוזלי, הלכך פעמים שפוחתין מכדי מה שמאוס. **אין עושין קאמר** — ופחיתה נמי, בכלל תיקון העולם היא. **שלא קבל עליו אחריות** — הבעל, אם יאבדו. ופריש ליה תנא דלא חייש לזולא אלא לאונסא, וקאמר ליה רבי יוסי: וכי קביל עליו אחריות נמי, מה נתקן העולם בכך? והלא אף כשהן קיימין אין קצובין ופוחתין.

BACKGROUND

מִפְּנֵי תִּיקּוּן הָעוֹלָם For the benefit of the world. The "benefit of the world" described here has the following aspects: (1) Linking the payment of the ketubah to real assets of stable value assures the full payment of the amount due; (2) it also makes the payment of the settlement more burdensome, and thereby prevents husbands from making a hasty decision to divorce their wives. Only in the generations after the Talmud, when many Jews no longer possessed real estate, was it declared that the ketubah could also be guaranteed by means of movable goods, with the husband's full personal guarantee for its payment.

NOTES

her. Rather, the husband must pledge all his property for the payment of her ketubah. How, then, can the anonymous first Tanna of the Baraita (who lived many years after Shimon ben Sheṭaḥ) maintain that the husband may designate movable property for the payment of his wife's ketubah, provided that he accepts responsibility for those goods should they be lost or destroyed?

Ramban and others answer: Shimon ben Sheṭaḥ's enactment applies only if the husband does not accept responsibility for the movable property that he designated for his wife's ketubah. Since he does not accept such responsibility, the woman will not allow him to use the goods. Therefore they will remain available for the payment of her ketubah, making it easy for the husband to divorce his wife. But if the husband accepts responsibility for the goods, his wife will allow him to use them as he sees fit, and therefore he will not regard it as easy to divorce her.

מִפְּנֵי תִּיקּוּן הָעוֹלָם For the benefit of the world. The Rishonim disagree as to how this ordinance benefits the world. *Rashi* and *Rivan* explain that if a person were permitted to designate his movable goods for the payment of his wife's ketubah, the goods might be lost or destroyed, and the woman would be left without a ketubah. *Ramban* suggests that this enactment benefits the world because without it women might refrain from getting married, fearing that they would not be able to collect the ketubah

HALAKHAH

אֲבָל קִבֵּל עָלָיו אַחֲרָיוּת, עוֹשִׂין But if he accepted responsibility, we do make. "If a man is unable to draw up a ketubah to give to his wife (for example, on Shabbat), or if he forgot to do so, he may give her movable property that

TRANSLATION AND COMMENTARY

הָשְׁתָּא [1]The Gemara now explains how this position of Rabbi Yose contradicts what he said in the other Baraita — that the husband may reduce his wife's ketubah to less than the legal minimum. **Now, if there** in the second Baraita, **where there is** merely **the possibility that** the movable goods **will depreciate,** [2]**Rabbi Yose is concerned** that the woman will not be able to collect the full amount of her ketubah, and he therefore rules that movable goods cannot be designated for the payment of a woman's ketubah, **here** in the first Baraita, **where** the woman **certainly reduces her ketubah** when she agrees to a condition fixing the amount promised her at less than the legal minimum, [3]**how much more so** should Rabbi Yose be concerned that the woman will not receive the full amount to which she is entitled; therefore he should rule that the condition is void and that the woman is still entitled to her full ketubah as determined by law!

הָכִי [4]The Gemara rejects the comparison between the two cases. **Now is it** really **true** that Rabbi Yose's two rulings contradict each other? How can you compare the two situations? [5]**There,** where the husband designates movable goods for the payment of his wife's ketubah, the woman **does not know** with certainty that the goods will depreciate, **and thus she** is not consciously **waiving** her right to collect the full amount of her ketubah. [6]But **here,** where the husband reduces his wife's ketubah by means of an oral condition, the woman **knows** that her ketubah is being reduced to less than the legal minimum, **and she is** consciously **waiving** her right to collect her full ketubah. Thus Rabbi Yose can maintain both positions: The husband may not designate movable goods for the payment of his wife's ketubah, but he may reduce her ketubah to less than the legal minimum by means of an oral condition.

אַחֲתֵיהּ [7]The Gemara now relates that **the sister of Rami bar Ḥama was married to Rav Ivya,** [57A] and **her ketubah** document **was lost.** [8]Rav Ivya and his wife **came before Rav Yosef** to ask him what should be done, [9]and **he said to them: This is what Rav Yehudah said in the name of Shmuel:** The statement in the Mishnah that if a man reduces his wife's ketubah to less than the legal minimum, his intercourse with her is tantamount to an act of prostitution, [10]**is the viewpoint of Rabbi Meir** alone. As was explained above,

[1]הָשְׁתָּא, וּמַה הָתָם דְּדִלְמָא פָּחֲתֵי, [2]חָיֵישׁ רַבִּי יוֹסֵי, הָכָא דְּוַדַּאי קָא פָּחֲתָה, [3]לֹא כָּל שֶׁכֵּן!

[4]הָכִי הָשְׁתָּא? [5]הָתָם לָא יָדְעָה דְּתָחֵיל; [6]הָכָא יָדְעָה וְקָא מָחֲלָה.

[7]אַחֲתֵיהּ דְּרָמֵי בַּר חָמָא הֲוַת נְסִיבָא לְרַב אִוְיָא. [57A] אִירְכַּס כְּתוּבָּתָהּ. [8]אָתוּ לְקַמֵּיהּ דְּרַב יוֹסֵף, [9]אֲמַר לְהוּ: ״הָכִי אֲמַר רַב יְהוּדָה אֲמַר שְׁמוּאֵל: [10]זוֹ דִּבְרֵי

LITERAL TRANSLATION

[1]Now, if there where they may possibly depreciate, [2]Rabbi Yose is concerned, here where she certainly reduces [her ketubah], [3]how much more so!

[4]Now is this so? [5]There she does not know that she should waive; [6]here she knows and she waives.

[7]The sister of Rami bar Ḥama was married to Rav Ivya. [57A] Her ketubah was lost. [8]They came before Rav Yosef, [9][and] he said to them: "Thus said Rav Yehudah in the name of Shmuel: [10]These are the words

RASHI

אירכס כתובתה – שטר כתובתה. **זו דברי רבי מאיר** – דאמר לעיל: כל הפוחת לבתולה ממאתים, ואפילו בתנאה, והתנאי בטל – קרי לה בעילת זנות, משום דלא סמכא דעתה. והכא נמי,

TERMINOLOGY

הָכִי הָשְׁתָּא Now is this so? The Talmud uses this expression in rejecting a comparison suggested previously: "Is this so? How can you compare? There, in case A, the circumstances are of type X, whereas here, in case B, the circumstances are different!"

SAGES

רָמִי בַּר חָמָא Rami bar Ḥama. A Babylonian Amora of the fourth generation. See *Ketubot*, Part II, p.57.

רַב אִוְיָא Rav Ivya. A Babylonian Amora of the fourth generation, Rav Ivya was a disciple of Rav Yosef and a colleague of Abaye and Rava. He lived for some time in Eretz Israel and we find him discussing Halakhic issues with Rabbi Ammi and Rabbi Abbahu. Some authorities believe that several of the Sages of the following generation were Rav Ivya's sons.

NOTES

to which they are entitled. *Meiri* explains that this ordinance is regarded as a benefit because it protects the woman, making it more difficult for her husband to divorce her.

לָא יָדְעָה דְּתָחֵיל She does not know that she should waive. *Meiri* explains that since the woman does not know with certainty that the goods will depreciate, she does not waive her right to collect the full amount of her ketubah, and even if she does waive her right to the ketubah, it is a waiver made in error.

Ritva suggests that the Gemara's argument is valid even according to the opinion that a waiver made in error is binding, because it is inappropriate for the Rabbis to allow a situation in which a woman may unwittingly waive her right to collect the full amount of her ketubah.

זוֹ דִּבְרֵי רַבִּי מֵאִיר These are the words of Rabbi Meir. Elsewhere (above, 51a) the Mishnah states that if a husband does not write his wife a ketubah, a virgin collects 200 zuz and a widow collects a maneh, and the Gemara argues that the Mishnah follows the opinion of Rabbi Meir. This would seem to contradict what is stated in our Gemara, that according to Rabbi Meir a man may

HALAKHAH

corresponds in value to the obligations mentioned in the ketubah, provided that he accepts responsibility for those goods should they be lost or depreciate. He is then permitted to have intercourse with his wife before he draws up a proper ketubah," following the Gemara above, 7a, and Rabbi Yose in our Gemara here. (*Shulḥan Arukh, Even HaEzer* 66:2.)

LITERAL TRANSLATION

of Rabbi Meir. [1]But the Sages say: A man may live with (lit., 'retain') his wife [for] two or three years without a ketubah." [2]Abaye said to him: "But surely Rav Naḥman said in the name of Shmuel: [3]The Halakhah is in accordance with Rabbi Meir in his enactments!" [4]"If so, go [and] write for her."

רַבִּי מֵאִיר. [1]אֲבָל חֲכָמִים אוֹמְרִים: מַשְׁהֶא אָדָם אֶת אִשְׁתּוֹ שְׁתַּיִם וְשָׁלֹשׁ שָׁנִים בְּלֹא כְּתוּבָּה". [2]אֲמַר לֵיהּ אַבָּיֵי: "וְהָא אָמַר רַב נַחְמָן אָמַר שְׁמוּאֵל: [3]הֲלָכָה כְּרַבִּי מֵאִיר בִּגְזֵירוֹתָיו!" [4]"אִי הָכִי, זִיל כְּתוֹב לַהּ".

TRANSLATION AND COMMENTARY

Rabbi Meir maintains that since the wife thinks that she is entitled only to the reduced amount as specified in the condition she allowed her husband to make, she does not rely on the ketubah document in her possession, and therefore the intercourse between the couple is considered an act of prostitution. Following the same logic, Rabbi Meir would also rule that a man may not live with his wife if her ketubah document has been lost or destroyed. Even though the woman is still entitled to her ketubah — for the woman's right to her ketubah is based on a Rabbinic enactment — she does not rely on the ketubah. Since the woman thinks that her financial rights are not guaranteed, sexual relations between the couple are forbidden. [1]**But the Sages** disagree with Rabbi Meir and **say: A man may live with his wife for two or three years without a ketubah** document, for even in the absence of such a document the woman is confident that she will receive everything that is rightfully hers. Thus Rav Ivya is not required to write his wife a new ketubah immediately. [2]**Abaye said to** Rav Yosef: **"But surely Rav Naḥman said in the name of Shmuel:** [3]There is a general rule that **the Halakhah is in accordance with Rabbi Meir when he makes an enactment.** Thus a woman who has lost her ketubah document should be forbidden to her husband until he writes her a new ketubah, in accordance with the position of Rabbi Meir!" Accepting Abaye's argument, Rav Yosef said to Rav Ivya: [4]**"If so, go and write** your wife a new ketubah, and until you have done so, you are forbidden to have sexual relations with her."

RASHI

לרבי מאיר הוא דאסור לשהות אשה שאבדה שטר כתובתה, ואפילו אית לה, דלא מפסדה בהכי, דגבייא בתנאי בית דין מיהא לא סמכא דעתה, דאמרה: כי תבענא ליה אמר "פרעתיך", הלכך בעילת זנות היא. **אבל חכמים אומרים כו׳** — דלית לן למיחש משום מסמך דעתה, דליהוי בעילת זנות. **בגזירותיו** — בדבר שהוא מחמיר על דבר תורה באיסור והיתר, על ידי גזירת דבריהם. **אי הכי זיל כתוב לה** — כתובה אחריתי, והא דאמרינן לעיל (כתובות נא,א): לא כתב לה כתובה — בתולה גובה מאתים, ואוקמינן כרבי מאיר — התם במקום שאין כותבין כתובה, דכולהו אתנאי קא סמכי. אי נמי: במקום שכותבין וגובה, לרבי מאיר מיהו, בעילת זנות באיסור היא.

BACKGROUND

מַשְׁהֶא אָדָם אֶת אִשְׁתּוֹ A man may live with his wife. Since according to Rabbinic ordinance every married woman is entitled to payment of the basic part of her ketubah if she is divorced or widowed, even if the husband did not write her a ketubah at all, in the view of the Sages the existence of a written ketubah document is of no Halakhic significance. However, if the husband obligated himself to pay her an additional settlement, the wife cannot demand it without producing evidence or a document.

הֲלָכָה כְּרַבִּי מֵאִיר בִּגְזֵירוֹתָיו The Halakhah is in accordance with Rabbi Meir in his enactments. The Talmud contains many rules for establishing the Halakhah. Some of these are quite general, such as: "The Halakhah is in accordance with Rabbi Yose as opposed to any other Sage who disagrees with him." Or: "The Halakhah agrees with whoever is lenient regarding a mourner." In other instances a rule distinguishes between types of cases, such as the rule that the Halakhah agrees with Rav in matters of ritual prohibitions but with Shmuel in monetary matters. There are also more detailed rules, such as the one that the Halakhah agrees with Rabbi Meir in his enactments, although there is another rule that almost everywhere that Rabbi Meir disagrees with one of his colleagues, the Halakhah does not agree with him.

NOTES

not live with his wife if she does not have a ketubah document in her possession.

Ritva explains that the ruling found in that Mishnah applied in places where it was customary to dispense with the writing of a ketubah document. In those places women certainly relied on the fact that the ketubah obligation is imposed by law and is not dependent on the ketubah document, and therefore in such circumstances a man was permitted to live with his wife even if she did not have a ketubah. Our Gemara is referring to those places where it was customary for the ketubah to be committed to writing. In such places, argues Rabbi Meir, sexual relations between a couple are forbidden if the woman is not in possession of her ketubah.

כְּרַבִּי מֵאִיר בִּגְזֵירוֹתָיו In accordance with Rabbi Meir in his enactments. *Rashi* and *Rivan* explain that when Shmuel says that the law is in accordance with Rabbi Meir with respect to his enactments (בִּגְזֵירוֹתָיו), he means that we follow the ruling of Rabbi Meir whenever he imposes a stringency prohibiting by Rabbinic decree something that is permitted by Torah law.

The Rishonim point out that the term *gezerah* is usually used in a more limited sense, referring to a Rabbinic prohibition imposed in order to prevent a more serious transgression or to avoid some undesirable outcome. Thus *Meiri* explains that the law is in accordance with Rabbi Meir with respect to matters like a woman's ketubah, which was instituted for the purpose of protecting her, so

HALAKHAH

זִיל כְּתוֹב לַהּ Go and write for her. "If someone writes his wife a ketubah and it is lost, or if the wife waives her right to her ketubah by writing her husband a receipt stating that it has already been paid her, he is required to write her a new document obligating himself at the very least to pay the basic portion of his wife's ketubah, for a man is forbidden to live with his wife even for a single hour if she is not in possession of a ketubah document (following Rabbi Meir, whose opinion is accepted whenever he prohibits by Rabbinic decree something that is permitted by Torah law). *Ḥelkat Meḥokek* and *Bet Shmuel* note that if the woman waives her right to her ketubah, her husband is required to write her a new document only for the amount of the basic portion of her ketubah, but if she loses her ketubah, he is required to write her a new one for the same amount as the original." (*Rambam, Sefer Nashim, Hilkhot Ishut* 10:10; *Shulḥan Arukh, Even HaEzer* 66:3.)

¹כִּי אֲתָא רַב דִּימִי אֲמַר רַבִּי שִׁמְעוֹן בֶּן פָּזִי אֲמַר רַבִּי יְהוֹשֻׁעַ בֶּן לֵוִי מִשּׁוּם בַּר קַפָּרָא: ²מַחֲלוֹקֶת בַּתְּחִלָּה, ³אֲבָל בַּסּוֹף לְדִבְרֵי הַכֹּל אֵינָהּ מוֹחֶלֶת. ⁴וְרַבִּי יוֹחָנָן אֲמַר: בֵּין בְּזוֹ וּבֵין בְּזוֹ מַחֲלוֹקֶת.

⁵אֲמַר רַבִּי אַבָּהוּ: לְדִידִי מִיפַּרְשָׁא לִי מִינֵּיהּ דְּרַבִּי יוֹחָנָן:

LITERAL TRANSLATION

[1]When Rav Dimi came, he said in the name of Rabbi Shimon ben Pazi who said in the name of Rabbi Yehoshua ben Levi who said in the name of Bar Kappara: [2]The dispute is regarding the beginning, [3]but regarding the end according to everybody she cannot waive. [4]But Rabbi Yoḥanan said: Both about this and about that there is a dispute.

[5]Rabbi Abbahu said: It was explained to me personally by Rabbi Yoḥanan:

RASHI

מחלוקת – דרבי יהודה ורבי יוסי, דאמר רבי יהודה על פה – לאו תנאה הוא, ורבי יוסי סבר: תנאה קיים. **בתחלה** – מפרש לקמן תחלת מאי. **דברי הכל אינה מוחלת** – שכבר זכתה, ואמירתה לאו כלום, אלא אם כן כתבה שובר "התקבלתי".

TRANSLATION AND COMMENTARY

כִּי אֲתָא רַב דִּימִי [1]The Gemara continues: **When Rav Dimi came** to Babylonia from Eretz Israel, **he reported in the name of Rabbi Shimon ben Pazi** that **Rabbi Yehoshua ben Levi said in the name of Bar Kappara:** [2]**The dispute** between Rabbi Yose and Rabbi Yehudah about whether a husband can reduce his wife's ketubah by means of an oral condition **is** only **regarding the beginning** (this expression will be explained immediately). [3]**But at the end, everybody agrees** that the woman **cannot waive** any portion of her ketubah by making an oral condition, but only by means of a written receipt stating that she has already received part of her ketubah. [4]**But Rabbi Yoḥanan said: Both** at the beginning **and** at the end Rabbi Yose and Rabbi Yehudah **disagree** about whether or not the husband can reduce his wife's ketubah by means of an oral condition.

אֲמַר רַבִּי אַבָּהוּ [5]The Gemara now clarifies these interpretations of the dispute between Rabbi Yose and Rabbi Yehudah. **Rabbi Abbahu said: I myself personally heard Rabbi Yoḥanan explain** his position and that

NOTES

that her husband should not consider it easy to divorce her.

Ritva and *Nimmukei Yosef* suggest that Rabbi Meir's ruling that a man may not live with his wife if he has fixed her ketubah at less than the legal minimum or if she has lost her ketubah document is indeed a *gezerah* in the strict sense of the word. For the Rabbis declared a couple's intercourse to be an act of prostitution if the woman thinks that she may not receive her full ketubah, even though she is in fact entitled to the full amount, because there are situations in which she is really not entitled to her ketubah (for example, if she waived her ketubah after she married), in which case the couple's intercourse is certainly regarded as an act of prostitution.

מַחֲלוֹקֶת בַּתְּחִלָּה The dispute is regarding the beginning. Two basic approaches (which to some extent are based on different versions of the text of the Talmud) are taken by the Rishonim in their interpretation of this passage. Our commentary follows *Rashi* and others (*Ritva* and *Meiri*), who explain that the Gemara is referring to the dispute between Rabbi Yose and Rabbi Yehudah cited in the Baraita as to whether a husband can reduce his wife's ketubah by means of an oral condition. But *Rivan*, *Ra'ah*, *Rashba*, and others maintain that the Gemara is referring to the dispute between Rabbi Meir and Rabbi Yehudah in our Mishnah as to whether a husband can reduce the amount of his wife's ketubah by having her write him a fictitious receipt saying that she has already received part of her ketubah. A similar discussion is found in the Jerusalem Talmud. There it is clear that the subject of the discussion is the dispute between Rabbi Meir and Rabbi Yehudah in the Mishnah.

אֲבָל בַּסּוֹף לְדִבְרֵי הַכֹּל אֵינָהּ מוֹחֶלֶת But regarding the end according to everybody she cannot waive. According to *Rashi,* who maintains that the Gemara is referring here to the dispute between Rabbi Yose and Rabbi Yehudah cited in the Baraita as to whether a husband can reduce his wife's ketubah by means of an oral condition (see previous note), this passage is to be understood as follows: Rabbi Yose and Rabbi Yehudah disagree only about the validity of an oral condition made at the beginning, before the woman has become entitled to her ketubah. But at the end, after the woman has already acquired the right to her ketubah, all agree that the husband cannot reduce his obligation without getting a receipt in writing.

Rivan, who explains that the Gemara is referring here to the dispute between Rabbi Meir and Rabbi Yehudah in our Mishnah as to whether a husband can reduce the amount of his wife's ketubah by having her write him a fictitious receipt saying that she has already received part of her ketubah, understands this passage differently: Rabbi Meir and Rabbi Yehudah disagree only about a waiver made at the beginning, before the couple have engaged in intercourse, for in such a case Rabbi Yehudah maintains that the woman has waived a portion of her ketubah wholeheartedly, and therefore her intercourse with her husband is not regarded as an act of prostitution. But at the end, after the woman has already engaged in intercourse on the assumption that she will be entitled to her full ketubah, even Rabbi Yehudah agrees that the husband cannot reduce his wife's ketubah by having her write him a fictitious receipt, because such a waiver would retroactively turn their intercourse into an act of prostitution.

[1]דַּאֲנָא וְרַבִּי יְהוֹשֻׁעַ בֶּן לֵוִי לָא פָּלְגִינַן אַהֲדָדֵי. [2]מַאי ״בַּתְּחִלָּה״ דְּקָאָמַר רַבִּי יְהוֹשֻׁעַ בֶּן לֵוִי? [3]תְּחִלַּת חוּפָּה. [4]וּמַאי ״סוֹף״? [5]סוֹף בִּיאָה. [6]וְכִי קָאָמִינָא אֲנָא בֵּין בְּזוֹ וּבֵין בְּזוֹ מַחֲלוֹקֶת. [7]תְּחִלַּת חוּפָּה וְסוֹף חוּפָּה, [8]דְּהִיא תְּחִילַּת בִּיאָה.

[9]כִּי אֲתָא רָבִין אֲמַר רַבִּי שִׁמְעוֹן בֶּן פָּזִי אֲמַר רַבִּי יְהוֹשֻׁעַ בֶּן לֵוִי מִשּׁוּם בַּר קַפָּרָא: [10]מַחֲלוֹקֶת לְבַסּוֹף, [11]אֲבָל בַּתְּחִלָּה דִּבְרֵי הַכֹּל מוֹחֶלֶת. [12]וְרַבִּי יוֹחָנָן אֲמַר: בֵּין בְּזוֹ וּבֵין בְּזוֹ מַחֲלוֹקֶת.

LITERAL TRANSLATION

[1]I and Rabbi Yehoshua ben Levi do not disagree with each other. [2]What is [meant by] "regarding the beginning" that Rabbi Yehoshua ben Levi said? [3]The beginning of the bridal chamber. [4]And what is [meant by] "the end"? [5]The end of intercourse. [6]And when I said [that] both about this and about that there is a dispute, [7][I meant] the beginning of the bridal chamber and the end of the bridal chamber, [8]which is the beginning of intercourse.

[9]When Ravin came, he said in the name of Rabbi Shimon ben Pazi who said in the name of Rabbi Yehoshua ben Levi who said in the name of Bar Kappara: [10]The dispute is regarding the end, [11]but regarding the beginning according to everybody she can waive. [12]But Rabbi Yoḥanan said: Both about this and about that there is a dispute.

TRANSLATION AND COMMENTARY

of Rabbi Yehoshua ben Levi as follows: [1]**Rabbi Yehoshua ben Levi and I do not** actually **disagree with each other.** We both maintain the same position; we just expressed that position differently. Now, Rabbi Yehoshua ben Levi said that Rabbi Yose and Rabbi Yehudah disagree regarding the beginning, but agree regarding the end. [2]**What did Rabbi Yehoshua ben Levi mean when he said "the beginning"?** [3]He meant **the beginning**, when the bride first enters **the bridal chamber.** [4]**And what did he mean** when he said **"the end"?** [5]He meant **the end of** sexual **intercourse.** According to Rabbi Yehoshua ben Levi, Rabbi Yose and Rabbi Yehudah disagree about whether the husband can reduce his wife's ketubah by means of a condition made after she has entered the bridal chamber, but before she has had intercourse with her husband. But after she has had intercourse, both agree that a mere oral condition is ineffective. [6]**And when I,** Rabbi Yoḥanan, **said that both** regarding the beginning **and** regarding the end Rabbi Yose and Rabbi Yehudah **disagree** about whether or not the husband can reduce his wife's ketubah by means of an oral condition, [7]I was referring to **the beginning,** when the bride first enters **the bridal chamber, and** to **the end**, when she is ready to leave **the bridal chamber,** [8]and to **begin** to engage in sexual **intercourse.** I, too, maintain that once the couple have had intercourse, both Rabbi Yose and Rabbi Yehudah agree that an oral condition is ineffective and that a written waiver is necessary.

כִּי אֲתָא רָבִין [9]**When Ravin came** to Babylonia from Eretz Israel, he transmitted a different tradition concerning these matters, for **he said in the name of Rabbi Shimon ben Pazi** that **Rabbi Yehoshua ben Levi said in the name of Bar Kappara** as follows: [10]**The dispute** between Rabbi Yose and Rabbi Yehudah about whether a husband can reduce his wife's ketubah by means of an oral condition **is** only **regarding the end** (this expression will be explained immediately). [11]**But at the beginning, everybody agrees** that the woman **can** indeed **waive** her right to collect the full amount of her ketubah by making an oral condition. [12]**But Rabbi Yoḥanan said: Both** at the beginning **and** at the end Rabbi Yose and Rabbi Yehudah **disagree** about whether or not the husband can reduce his wife's ketubah by means of an oral condition.

RASHI

תחלת חופה ומאי סוף סוף ביאה — והכי קאמר: מתחלת חופה ועד סוף חופה פליגי בה רבי יהודה ורבי יוסי, אבל משבא עליה מודה רבי יוסי דאין בדבריו כלום. **וכי אמינא אנא בין בזו ובין בזו מחלוקת** — לאו אסוף דרבי יהושע קאמינא, אלא אסוף חופה, דהיא קודם ביאה.

NOTES

אֲבָל בַּתְּחִלָּה דִּבְרֵי הַכֹּל מוֹחֶלֶת **But regarding the beginning according to everybody she can waive.** Relying on a parallel passage in the Jerusalem Talmud, *Ra'ah* suggests that the text of the Gemara should read as follows: "When Ravin came, he said...: The dispute is regarding the end, but regarding the beginning according to everybody she cannot waive." *Ra'ah* maintains that the Gemara is referring here to the dispute between Rabbi Meir and Rabbi Yehudah in our Mishnah. At the end, after the woman has already become entitled to her ketubah, both Rabbi Meir and Rabbi Yehudah agree that the woman can waive a portion of her ketubah. They disagree, however, about whether her waiver turns her intercourse into an act of prostitution. But at the beginning, before the woman has become entitled to her ketubah, in which case a waiver is treated as a condition, all agree that she cannot waive a part of her ketubah, because a condition that runs counter to Torah law is not binding.

[1]אֲמַר רַבִּי אַבָּהוּ: לְדִידִי מִיפַּרְשָׁא לִי מִינֵּיהּ דְּרַבִּי יוֹחָנָן: [2]דַּאֲנָא וְרַבִּי יְהוֹשֻׁעַ בֶּן לֵוִי לָא פָּלְגִינַן אַהֲדָדֵי. [3]מַאי ״לְבַסּוֹף״ דַּאֲמַר רַבִּי יְהוֹשֻׁעַ בֶּן לֵוִי? [4]סוֹף חוּפָּה. [5]וּמַאי ״תְּחִלָּה״? [6]תְּחִלַּת חוּפָּה. [7]וְכִי קָאָמִינָא אֲנָא בֵּין בְּזוֹ בֵּין בְּזוֹ מַחֲלוֹקֶת, [8]תְּחִלַּת בִּיאָה וְסוֹף בִּיאָה. [9]אֲמַר רַב פַּפָּא: אִי לָאו דַּאֲמַר רַבִּי אַבָּהוּ: [10]״לְדִידִי מִיפַּרְשָׁא לִי מִינֵּיהּ דְּרַבִּי יוֹחָנָן: [11]דַּאֲנָא וְרַבִּי יְהוֹשֻׁעַ בֶּן לֵוִי לָא פָּלְגִינַן אַהֲדָדֵי״, [12]הֲוָה אָמִינָא: רַבִּי יוֹחָנָן וְרַבִּי יְהוֹשֻׁעַ בֶּן לֵוִי

LITERAL TRANSLATION

[1]Rabbi Abbahu said: It was explained to me personally by Rabbi Yoḥanan: [2]I and Rabbi Yehoshua ben Levi do not disagree with each other. [3]What is [meant by] "regarding the end" that Rabbi Yehoshua ben Levi said? [4]The end of the bridal chamber. [5]And what is [meant by] "the beginning"? [6]The beginning of the bridal chamber. [7]And when I said [that] both about this and about that there is a dispute, [8][I meant] the beginning of intercourse and the end of intercourse.

[9]Rav Pappa said: If Rabbi Abbahu had not said: [10]"It was explained to me personally by Rabbi Yoḥanan: [11]I and Rabbi Yehoshua ben Levi do not disagree with each other," [12]I would have said: Rabbi Yoḥanan and Rabbi Yehoshua ben Levi

TRANSLATION AND COMMENTARY

אֲמַר רַבִּי אַבָּהוּ [1]The Gemara explains: **Rabbi Abbahu said: I myself personally heard Rabbi Yoḥanan** explain his position and that of Rabbi Yehoshua ben Levi as follows: [2]**Rabbi Yehoshua ben Levi and I do not** actually **disagree with each other.** We both meant to say the same thing, but we formulated our positions differently. Now, Rabbi Yehosuha ben Levi said that Rabbi Yose and Rabbi Yehudah disagree regarding the end, but agree regarding the beginning. [3]**What did Rabbi Yehoshua ben Levi mean when he said "the end"?** [4]He meant **the end** of the bride's stay in **the bridal chamber,** when the couple begin to engage in sexual intercourse. [5]**And what did he mean** when he said **"the beginning"?** [6]He meant **the beginning,** when the bride first enters **the bridal chamber.** According to Rabbi Yehoshua ben Levi, Rabbi Yose and Rabbi Yehudah disagree about whether the husband can reduce his wife's ketubah by means of an oral condition once the couple have begun to engage in sexual intercourse. But while the couple are in the bridal chamber before they engage in intercourse, both Rabbi Yose and Rabbi Yehudah agree that an oral condition is sufficient. [7]**And when I,** Rabbi Yoḥanan, **said that both** regarding the beginning **and** regarding the end Rabbi Yose and Rabbi Yehudah **disagree** about whether or not the husband can reduce his wife's ketubah by means of an oral condition, [8]**I was referring to the beginning and the end of** sexual **intercourse.** I, too, maintain that both Rabbi Yose and Rabbi Yehudah agree that during the time the couple are in the bridal chamber before they engage in intercourse, the woman can waive the right to collect the full amount of her ketubah by accepting an oral condition.

אֲמַר רַב פַּפָּא [9]Rav Dimi and Ravin disagree about how to understand the Tannaitic dispute between Rabbi Yose and Rabbi Yehudah. According to Rav Dimi, Rabbi Yose and Rabbi Yehudah disagree about whether the husband can reduce his wife's ketubah by means of an oral condition made after she has entered the bridal chamber but before she has had intercourse with him. But after she has had intercourse with her husband, both Sages agree that a mere oral condition is ineffective. According to Ravin, Rabbi Yose and Rabbi Yehudah disagree about whether the husband can reduce his wife's ketubah by means of an oral condition once the couple have begun to engage in sexual intercourse. But while the couple are in the bridal chamber before they engage in intercourse, both Rabbi Yose and Rabbi Yehudah agree that an oral condition is sufficient. The Gemara now suggests that theoretically the whole matter could have been understood differently. **Rav Pappa said: Were it not** for the fact **that Rabbi Abbahu said:** [10]**"I myself personally heard Rabbi Yoḥanan say** [11]that **he and Rabbi Yehoshua ben Levi do not** really **disagree with each other** in substance, but only in formulation," [12]**I would have said** that **Rabbi Yoḥanan and Rabbi Yehoshua ben Levi**

RASHI

אמר רב פפא אי לאו דאמר כו׳ — אנא לא הוה ניחא לי לפרושי מילתייהו הכי, דרבי יוחנן ורבי יהושע לא ליפלגו, ורב דימי ורבין ניפלגו בדרבי יהושע. אלא הכי הוה אמינא: רבי יוחנן ורבי יהושע בן לוי פליגי, דאההוא סוף דקאמר רבי יהושע בן לוי — דברי הכל אינה מוחלת, אתא רבי יוחנן למימר אף בזו מחלוקת. דרב דימי ורבין לא פליגי בדרבי יהושע, והכי הוה מפרישנא: לדרב דימי אמר רבי יהושע מחלוקת בתחלת ביאה, דהיא סוף חופה. אבל בסוף ביאה — דברי הכל אינה מוחלת. ורבי יוחנן פליג עליה דאפילו בסוף ביאה נמי פליגי. וכי אתא רבין אמר רבי יהושע בן לוי: מחלוקת בסוף חופה, והיא תחלת ביאה דקאמר נמי רב דימי, אבל בתחלת חופה — דברי הכל מוחלת. אבל השתא דפריש רבי אבהו לדרב דימי דבין לרבי יוחנן ובין לרבי יהושע בן לוי פליגי רבי יוסי ורבי יהודה בתחלת חופה ובסוף חופה, על כרחך פליגא דרבין אדרב דימי, דהא אמר רבין בתחלת חופה דברי הכל מוחלת.

TRANSLATION AND COMMENTARY

do in fact **disagree** with each other, but **Rav Dimi and Ravin do not disagree** with each other. Rather, they each relate to separate aspects of the dispute between Rabbi Yoḥanan and Rabbi Yehoshua ben Levi. For I could have said as follows: [1]**What did Ravin mean when he said "the end"?** [2]He meant **the end of** the bride's stay in **the bridal chamber,** which is when the couple begin to engage in sexual intercourse. [3]**And what did Rav Dimi mean when he said "the beginning"?** [4]He meant **the** time that the couple **begin** to engage in sexual **intercourse.** Thus, when Rav Dimi reported in the name of Rabbi Yehoshua ben Levi that the dispute between Rabbi Yose and Rabbi Yehudah about whether the husband can reduce his wife's ketubah by means of an oral condition is only regarding the beginning, he was referring to the beginning of intercourse at the end of the bride's stay in the bridal chamber. But at the end of intercourse, everybody agrees that the woman cannot waive any portion of her ketubah by means of an oral condition, but only by a written receipt stating that she has already received a portion of her ketubah. Rabbi Yoḥanan disagrees with Rabbi Yehoshua ben Levi and says that even regarding the end of intercourse Rabbi Yose and Rabbi Yehudah disagree about whether the husband can reduce his wife's ketubah by means of an oral condition. And when Ravin reported in the name of Rabbi Yehoshua ben Levi that the dispute between Rabbi Yose and Rabbi Yehudah about whether the husband can reduce his wife's ketubah by means of an oral condition is only regarding the end, he was referring to the end of the bride's stay in the bridal chamber, which is when the couple begin to engage in sexual intercourse. But at the beginning, when the bride first enters the bridal chamber, everybody agrees that the woman can indeed waive her right to collect the full amount of her ketubah by means of an oral condition. Rabbi Yoḥanan disagrees with Rabbi Yehoshua ben Levi and says that even regarding the beginning, when the woman first enters the bridal chamber, Rabbi Yose and Rabbi Yehudah disagree about whether or not an oral condition is effective. Thus there is no disagreement between Rav Dimi and Ravin. They both say that at the end of the bride's stay in the bridal chamber, which is also when the couple begin to engage in sexual intercourse, Rabbi Yose and Rabbi Yehudah disagree about whether an oral condition reducing a woman's ketubah is effective. Rav Dimi says that Rabbi Yehoshua ben Levi and Rabbi Yoḥanan disagree about whether the Tannaim are also in dispute regarding the end of sexual intercourse. And Ravin says that Rabbi Yehoshua ben Levi and Rabbi Yoḥanan disagree about whether the Tannaim are also in dispute regarding the beginning, when the bride first enters the bridal chamber.

מַאי קָא מַשְׁמַע לָן [5]The Gemara asks: **What is** Rav Pappa **teaching us** when he says that were it not for the fact that Rabbi Abbahu said that he heard directly from Rabbi Yoḥanan that he and Rabbi Yehoshua ben Levi do not actually disagree with each other in substance, he — Rav Pappa — would have said that Rabbi Yoḥanan and Rabbi Yehoshua ben Levi do in fact disagree with each other? Why did Rav Pappa tell us that theoretically the whole matter could have been understood differently, when he himself agrees that his proposed interpretation is wrong?

הָא [6]The Gemara answers: **This** is what Rav Pappa **teaches us:** If we wish to understand an early Amoraic dispute about which there are various traditions among the later Amoraim, it is preferable to understand

פְּלִיגִי, רַב דִּימִי וְרָבִין לָא פְּלִיגִי. [1]מַאי "סוֹף" דְּקָאָמַר רָבִין? [2]סוֹף חוּפָּה. [3]וּמַאי "תְּחִלָּה" דְּקָאָמַר רַב דִּימִי? [4]תְּחִלַּת בִּיאָה. [5]מַאי קָא מַשְׁמַע לָן? [6]הָא קָא מַשְׁמַע לָן: דִּפְלִיגִי

LITERAL TRANSLATION

disagree, [but] Rav Dimi and Ravin do not disagree. [1]What is [meant by] "the end" that Ravin said? [2]The end of the bridal chamber. [3]And what is [meant by] "the beginning" that Rav Dimi said? [4]The beginning of intercourse.

[5]What is he teaching us?

[6]He teaches us this: That

RASHI

מאי קא משמע לן — בהא דאמר אי לאו דקאמר רבי אבהו כו׳ האמר רבי אבהו ואיהו לא בעי לאיפלוגי עליה, ולמאי הלכתא אשמועינן? דאי לא אמרה רבי אבהו הוה ניחא ליה לדידיה לפרושי בענין אחר. **הא קא משמע לן** — דהיכא דאשכחן אמוראי דפליגי אהדדי. כל חד אליבא דנפשיה, ותרי אמוראי אחריני דפליגי בפלוגתא דהנך אמוראי, ואית לן לפרושי מילתא בתרי לישני, חדא מינייהו מיפלגי תרי אמוראי אליבא דנפשייהו, שכל אחד אומר סברא שלו, כגון רבי יוחנן ורבי יהושע, ואינך תרי אמוראי [אליבא דחד] לא מיפלגי, אלא אמרי חדא מלתא. וחדא מן לישנא מיפלגי תרי אמוראי אליבא דחד, כגון רב דימי ורבין, ומשויא מלתא דתרי אמוראי קמאי חדא מלתא — שבקינן ההיא לישנא דמיפלגי תרי אמוראי אליבא דחד, ונקטינן ההיא דמיפלגי תרי אמוראי אליבא דנפשייהו. דכי פליגי תרי אליבא דחד, מר אמר: הכי אמר פלוני, ומר אמר: הכי אמר פלוני — חד מינייהו משקר. אבל כי פליגי תרי אמוראי בדין או באיסור והיתר, כל חד אמר הכי מיסתבר טעמא — אין כאן שקר, כל חד וחד סברא דידיה קאמר, מר יהיב טעמא להיתירא, ומר יהיב טעמא לאיסורא. מר מדמי מילתא למילתא הכי, ומר מדמי ליה בענינא אחרינא. ואיכא למימר: אלו ואלו דברי אלהים חיים הם, זימנין דשייך האי טעמא וזימנין דשייך האי טעמא, שהטעם מתהפך לפי שינוי הדברים בשינוי מועט.

TRANSLATION AND COMMENTARY

that the two earlier **Amoraim disagree about their own positions,** [1]**and not that the two** later **Amoraim disagree about the position of a single** earlier **Amora.** It is preferable to assume that the two earlier Amoraim disagree in substance, each maintaining a different position, rather than to assume that the two earlier Amoraim are in agreement, and that the two later Amoraim disagree about what it was that the earlier Amoraim said. Jewish law recognizes the legitimacy of two conflicting opinions, and therefore if two Amoraim disagree in substance, both opinions can be valid. But if two Amoraim disagree about what was said by an earlier Amora, one of the opinions must be in error, the mistake arising as a result of faulty transmission of the point of view of the earlier Amora. Thus, says Rav Pappa, were it not for the fact that Rabbi Abbahu heard directly from Rabbi Yoḥanan that he and Rabbi Yehoshua ben Levi do not actually disagree with each other in substance, he — Rav Pappa — would have said that Rabbi Yoḥanan and Rabbi Yehoshua ben Levi do indeed disagree. For it is preferable to assume that Rabbi Yehoshua ben Levi and Rabbi Yoḥanan disagree with each other, rather than that they were in agreement, and that it was Rav Dimi and Ravin who disagreed about the positions of these earlier Amoraim.

MISHNAH נוֹתְנִין לִבְתוּלָה [2]It has already been explained that, under Jewish law, a marriage is effected in two stages — betrothal and marriage. Today, bethrothal and marriage are performed together, but in the time of the Mishnah and the Talmud the two ceremonies were ordinarily separated. After betrothal, the bride would remain in her father's house until the time agreed for the marriage, and only then would she be brought into the bridal chamber, at which time her married life would begin. Between betrothal and marriage, the bridegroom is not responsible for his bride's maintenance. Similarly, during this period the bride may not yet partake of terumah (the portion of produce that is set aside for priests and is forbidden to non-priests) if she is the daughter of a non-priest and is betrothed to a priest. Our Mishnah discusses how the wedding date is set, and the bride's right to receive maintenance and to eat terumah if the date set for the wedding has already arrived and the couple are not married. **A** betrothed **virgin is given twelve months from the time her bridegroom asks for her** in marriage, so that she will have ample opportunity **to provide for**

תְּרֵי אֲמוֹרָאֵי אַטַּעֲמָא דְּנַפְשַׁיְיהוּ, [1]וְלָא פְּלִיגִי תְּרֵי אֲמוֹרָאֵי אַלִּיבָּא דְּחַד אֲמוֹרָא.

מִשְׁנָה [2]נוֹתְנִין לִבְתוּלָה שְׁנֵים עָשָׂר חוֹדֶשׁ מִשֶּׁתְּבָעָהּ הַבַּעַל, לְפַרְנֵס אֶת עַצְמָהּ.

LITERAL TRANSLATION

two Amoraim disagree about their own reasoning, [1]and [that] two Amoraim do not disagree about the opinion of one Amora.

MISHNAH [2]We give a virgin twelve months from when her bridegroom claimed her, to provide for herself.

RASHI

משנה נותנין לבתולה – זמן לכניסתה לחופה מיום שתבעה הבעל, לאחר שקידשה, להזהירה על עסקי חופה, להכין תכשיטיה. **לפרנס עצמה** – בתכשיטין.

BACKGROUND

דִּפְלִיגִי תְּרֵי אֲמוֹרָאֵי אַטַּעֲמָא דְּנַפְשַׁיְיהוּ That two Amoraim disagree about their own reasoning. This interpretive preference of Rav Pappa is based on the difference in principle between a theoretical dispute and a dispute regarding the reliability of a tradition. A theoretical dispute is not only legitimate, but there is also no reason to assume that either disputant is in error (it is of cases like this that it was said, "Both these and these are the words of the living God"). However, when there is a dispute as to what a certain Sage said, this is a factual dispute, and in such a case one of the disputants is certainly in error.

NOTES

דִּפְלִיגִי תְּרֵי אֲמוֹרָאֵי אַטַּעֲמָא דְּנַפְשַׁיְיהוּ That two Amoraim disagree about their own reasonings. The Rishonim ask: Even if we assume that Rabbi Yehoshua ben Levi and Rabbi Yoḥanan do in fact disagree, the subject of their dispute is the Tannaitic disagreement found in the Mishnah or the Baraita. Why, then, is it preferable to assume that the two Amoraim disagree about what the Tannaim said, rather than that the two later Amoraim disagree about what the earlier Amoraim said? It would seem that, either way, one of the opinions must be in error!

Tosafot and *Ritva* answer that if Rav Dimi and Ravin disagree about what the earlier Amoraim said, they disagree about the validity of their traditions, one of which must of necessity be mistaken. But if indeed Rabbi Yehoshua ben Levi and Rabbi Yoḥanan disagree about what the Tannaim said, they disagree about something substantial and not about the authenticity of the traditions they have received. For neither Rabbi Yehoshua ben Levi nor Rabbi Yoḥanan bases his opinion on a tradition he has received as to the positions of the Tannaim. Each Amora argues that logically the Tannaitic dispute has to be understood in a certain way. Since the legitimacy of two conflicting opinions is recognized by Jewish law, both Amoraic opinions may have Halakhic validity.

נוֹתְנִין לִבְתוּלָה We give a virgin. *Melekhet Shlomo* explains the connection between this Mishnah and the preceding one. Rabbi Elazar ben Azaryah distinguished in the previous Mishnah between the ketubah to which a widow or a divorcee after betrothal is entitled and that to which a widow or a divorcee after marriage is entitled. Our Mishnah continues with a discussion regarding the laws that apply during the transitional period between betrothal and marriage.

HALAKHAH

נוֹתְנִין לִבְתוּלָה שְׁנֵים עָשָׂר חוֹדֶשׁ We give a virgin twelve months. "If a man betroths a minor, and their betrothal lasts a few years, and then when the bride is already a *na'arah* (aged between twelve and twelve-and-a-half) he asks for her in marriage, she is given twelve months from the time he asks for her in marriage to provide for herself and to prepare whatever she needs for married life, and afterwards she is married." (*Rambam, Sefer Nashim, Hilkhot Ishut* 10:17; *Shulḥan Arukh, Even HaEzer* 56:1.)

TRANSLATION AND COMMENTARY

herself and prepare her trousseau. [1]**And just as the woman is given** twelve months to prepare for her marriage, [2]**so** too **is the man given** twelve months **to provide for himself** and make the necessary preparations for the wedding feast and for his married life. [3]A betrothed **widow is given** only **thirty days** to provide for herself, for she still has the trousseau she prepared for her first marriage.

הִגִּיעַ זְמַן [4] The Mishnah continues: Between betrothal and marriage, the bride continues to live in her father's house and the bridegroom is not responsible for her support. But **if the time** set for marriage **came and they were not married,** [5]**she** is entitled to **eat of** the bridegroom's **food,** for he is responsible for her support from the date on which the wedding was to take place. Similarly, during the period between betrothal and marriage, the bride is not permitted to eat terumah if she is the daughter of a non-priest and is betrothed to a priest. But if the time set for marriage came and the marriage did not take place, [6]the bride is entitled to **eat terumah.** By Torah law the bride may eat terumah immediately upon her betrothal, but the Rabbis decreed that she may not eat terumah until the marriage process has been completed. Once the time set for the marriage has arrived, the reason for the decree no longer applies (as will be explained in the Gemara). [7]**Rabbi Tarfon says:** If the priest whose wedding date has

[1]וּכְשֵׁם שֶׁנּוֹתְנִין לְאִשָּׁה, [2]כָּךְ נוֹתְנִין לְאִישׁ לְפַרְנֵס אֶת עַצְמוֹ. [3]וּלְאַלְמָנָה שְׁלֹשִׁים יוֹם. [4]הִגִּיעַ זְמַן וְלֹא נִישְּׂאוּ, [5]אוֹכְלוֹת מִשֶּׁלּוֹ [6]וְאוֹכְלוֹת בִּתְרוּמָה. [7]רַבִּי טַרְפוֹן אוֹמֵר:

LITERAL TRANSLATION

[1]And just as we give a woman [time], [2]so we give a man [time] to provide for himself. [3]And to a widow [we give] thirty days.

[4][If] the time came and they were not married, [5]they eat of his [food] [6]and they eat terumah. [7]Rabbi Tarfon says:

RASHI

לפרנס עצמו – בצרכי סעודה וחופה. **ולאלמנה שלשים יום** – שאינה טורחת כל כך בתכשיטין, שכבר יש בידה. **ולא נישאו** – שהבעלים מעכבין. **ולאידי דתנא רישא בדידהי** – תנא סיפא נמי בדידהי. **ואוכלת בתרומה** – אם כהן הוא והיא ישראלית, שמשעה שקידשה אוכלת בתרומה מן התורה כדמפרש בגמרא, ורבנן גזור עד השתא.

NOTES

כָּךְ נוֹתְנִין לְאִישׁ **So we give a man.** Most Rishonim follow *Rambam*, who maintains that a bridegroom is given the same amount of time to prepare for his wedding as is his bride. Thus a man who marries a virgin is given twelve months for his preparations, whereas a man who marries a widow is given only thirty days. Some Rishonim (*Ra'ah*, *Rosh*, and *Tur*) accept the opinion of the Jerusalem Talmud that just as the Mishnah distinguishes between a virgin and a widow, so too must a distinction be made between a man marrying for the first time, who is given twelve months to prepare himself for the wedding (even if his bride is a widow), and a widower, who is given only thirty days to make his preparations (even if he is marrying a virgin).

וּלְאַלְמָנָה **And to a widow.** *Ra'avad* explains that when the whereas Mishnah says that a widow is given only thirty days to provide for herself, it is referring to a widow after marriage, a widow after betrothal is given a full year to prepare for her wedding. A widow after marriage is given only thirty days because she still has the trousseau she prepared for herself the first time she married.

Rashba agrees with *Ra'avad*'s position but rejects his reasoning, arguing that if the woman was married for some time, there may not be very much left of her first trousseau. Rather, a widow after marriage is given only thirty days to prepare for her wedding, because she holds herself in readiness for remarriage and prepares her trousseau in advance. Thus she is treated like a virgin who was betrothed

HALAKHAH

וּכְשֵׁם שֶׁנּוֹתְנִין לְאִשָּׁה **And just as we give a woman time.** "Just as when a bridegroom asks for his bride in marriage, the bride is given time to prepare herself for married life, so too when the bride asks that her wedding date be set, the bridegroom is given time to make his preparations. The bridegroom is given the same amount of time for his preparations as is the bride. If she is entitled to twelve months to prepare, he too is given twelve months, and if she is entitled to only thirty days, he too is given only thirty days. The Aḥaronim cite the opinion of *Rosh* and *Tur* (following the Jerusalem Talmud) that a man who is marrying for the first time is given twelve months even if his bride is a widow, whereas a man who has previously been married is given only thirty days even if he is marrying a virgin. *Ba'er Hetev* writes that nowadays, when it is customary for the bride's father to prepare the wedding celebration, the bridegroom is given less time to prepare himself, the precise amount of time being determined by the local court." (*Rambam, Sefer Nashim, Hilkhot Ishut* 10:18; *Shulḥan Arukh, Even HaEzer* 56:2.)

וּלְאַלְמָנָה שְׁלֹשִׁים יוֹם **And to a widow we give thirty days.** "A non-virgin is given only thirty days from the time her bridegroom asks for her in marriage to prepare herself for married life." (*Rambam, Sefer Nashim, Hilkhot Ishut* 10:17; *Shulḥan Arukh, Even HaEzer* 56:1.)

אוֹכְלוֹת מִשֶּׁלּוֹ **They eat of his food.** "If the time set for a couple's marriage has arrived but the marriage has not yet taken place, the bridegroom is nevertheless responsible for his bride's support," following the Mishnah. (*Rambam, Sefer Nashim, Hilkhot Ishut* 10:19; *Shulḥan Arukh, Even HaEzer* 56:3.)

נוֹתְנִין לָהּ הַכֹּל תְּרוּמָה. [1]רַבִּי עֲקִיבָא אוֹמֵר: מֶחֱצָה חוּלִּין [2]וּמֶחֱצָה תְּרוּמָה.
[3]הַיָּבָם אֵינוֹ מַאֲכִיל בִּתְרוּמָה. [4]עָשְׂתָה שִׁשָּׁה חֳדָשִׁים בִּפְנֵי הַבַּעַל וְשִׁשָּׁה חֳדָשִׁים בִּפְנֵי הַיָּבָם, [5]וַאֲפִילּוּ כּוּלָּן בִּפְנֵי הַבַּעַל חָסֵר יוֹם אֶחָד בִּפְנֵי הַיָּבָם, [6]אוֹ כּוּלָּן בִּפְנֵי הַיָּבָם חָסֵר יוֹם אֶחָד בִּפְנֵי הַבַּעַל,

LITERAL TRANSLATION

We give it all to her [from] terumah. [1]Rabbi Akiva says: Half [from] unconsecrated food [2]and half [from] terumah.

[3]A *yavam* does not feed [his sister-in-law] terumah. [4][If] she spent (lit., "did") six months with (lit., "before") the husband and six months with the *yavam*, [5]or even all of them with the husband less one day with the *yavam*, [6]or all of them with the *yavam* less one day with the husband,

TRANSLATION AND COMMENTARY

already passed wishes, **he may give** his bride **all** her maintenance **from terumah,** even though she is only permitted to eat the terumah while she is ritually pure. When she is ritually impure (for example, while she is menstruating) and is therefore forbidden to eat terumah, she may sell the terumah to someone who is fit to partake of it, and can then buy ordinary produce for herself with the proceeds. [1]**Rabbi Akiva** disagrees and **says:** The priest must give his bride **half** of her maintenance **from unconsecrated produce,** so that she will have food to eat while she is ritually impure and unfit to eat terumah, [2]**and** he is permitted to give her only **half** of her maintenance **from terumah,** which she can eat while she is ritually pure.

הַיָּבָם [3]The Mishnah now considers the case of a woman whose husband died childless. The brother of the deceased (called the *yavam*) is obligated to marry his late brother's widow through *yibbum* (levirate marriage) or to perform *ḥalitzah*, the ceremony that frees the widow from the obligation to marry her brother-in-law and allows her to marry someone else. **A *yavam* is not** entitled to **give his sister-in-law terumah to eat.** If a priest dies childless, and his widow is now waiting for his brother either to marry her or to free her through *ḥalitzah* to marry someone else, she may not eat terumah. Although the woman was permitted to eat terumah during her husband's lifetime, she may not eat terumah after his death by virtue of her bond to the *yavam* until the levirate marriage has been consummated by sexual intercourse. All the more so may the woman not eat terumah by virtue of her bond to the *yavam*, if she was betrothed but not yet married to his brother at the time of the latter's death, and had been permitted to eat terumah during her bridegroom's lifetime only because the date set for her marriage had come. And she may certainly not eat terumah because of her bond to the *yavam*, if her bridegroom died before their wedding date arrived, so that she was never permitted to eat terumah during her bridegroom's lifetime. The Mishnah now describes the various possibilities. [4]**If** the woman was given twelve months to prepare for her wedding, and **six months** passed while she was betrothed **to her bridegroom,** at which point the bridegroom died, **and** then another **six months** passed while she was Halakhically bound **to the *yavam*,** [5]or **even if the entire** twelve months passed while she was betrothed **to the bridegroom, except for one day** after her bridegroom's death during which she was bound **to the *yavam*,** [6]**or** if **the entire** twelve months passed while she was bound **to the *yavam*, except for one day** at the very beginning during which she was

RASHI

נותנין לה הכל תרומה — אם ירצה. וכשיגיעו ימי טומאתה — תמכרנה ותקח חולין. **מחצה חולין** — לאכול בימי טומאתה. **היבם אינו מאכיל בתרומה** — בעודה שומרת יבם. וטעמא יליף בגמרא. **עשתה ששה חדשים בפני הבעל** — מהנך שנים עשר חדש הקבועים לה משתבעה הבעל. או אפילו כולם בפני הבעל ואחד בפני היבם. אף על גב דרובא בפני הבעל — סוף סוף לא נתחייב במזונותיה בחייו, והוא הדין נמי אם נתחייב בחייו לא אכלה משמת, דקניין הבעל פקע. אלא דאי כולם בפני הבעל — הוה אכלה מיהא בחייו. **או כולן בפני היבם** — בגמרא פריך עלה: למאי תניא?

NOTES

after she reached majority, who is given only thirty days to prepare for her wedding, because we assume that she prepared her trousseau by the time she reached majority (see below, 57b). Alternatively, a thirty-day period of preparation suffices for a widow after marriage, because such a person does not ordinarily adorn herself to the same extent as a woman who has never been married.

עָשְׂתָה שִׁשָּׁה חֳדָשִׁים **If she spent six months.** Our commentary follows *Rashi*, who explains that a woman whose husband has died childless may not eat terumah by virtue of being bound to the *yavam*, even if she was permitted to eat terumah during her husband's lifetime, whether because she was already married to him or because the time set for her marriage had already arrived. Thus, when the Mishnah states: "Or even all of them with the husband less one day with the *yavam*," it does not

HALAKHAH

הַיָּבָם אֵינוֹ מַאֲכִיל בִּתְרוּמָה **A *yavam* does not feed his sister-in-law terumah.** "If a man dies childless, and his widow is waiting for his brother who is a priest to marry her, she may not eat terumah," following the Mishnah. (*Rambam, Sefer Zeraim, Hilkhot Terumot* 8:1,5.)

[1]אֵינָהּ אוֹכֶלֶת בִּתְרוּמָה. [2]זוֹ מִשְׁנָה רִאשׁוֹנָה. [3]בֵּית דִּין שֶׁל אַחֲרֵיהֶן אָמְרוּ: [57B] [4]אֵין הָאִשָּׁה אוֹכֶלֶת בִּתְרוּמָה עַד שֶׁתִּכָּנֵס לַחוּפָּה.

גמרא [5]מְנָא הָנֵי מִילֵּי? [6]אָמַר רַב חִסְדָּא: דְּאָמַר קְרָא: [7]"וַיֹּאמֶר אָחִיהָ וְאִמָּהּ: תֵּשֵׁב הַנַּעֲרָה אִתָּנוּ יָמִים אוֹ עָשׂוֹר". [8]מַאי "יָמִים"? [9]אִילֵימָא "תְּרֵי יוֹמֵי", [10]מִשְׁתַּעֵי אִינִישׁ הָכִי?

LITERAL TRANSLATION

[1]she does not eat terumah. [2]This was the first Mishnah. [3]The court after them said: [57B] [4]A woman does not eat terumah until she enters the bridal chamber.

GEMARA [5]From where are these things [derived]?

[6]Rav Ḥisda said: For the verse says: [7]"And her brother and her mother said: Let the girl stay with us *yamim* (lit., 'days') or ten." [8]What is [meant by] "*yamim*"? [9]If we say "two days," [10]does a person speak this way?

RASHI

זו משנה ראשונה – דמשהגיע זמן אוכלת בתרומה. **אין האשה אוכלת כו׳** – טעמא מפרש בגמרא.

TRANSLATION AND COMMENTARY

betrothed **to her bridegroom** before he died, [1]in all these cases **she does not eat terumah.** The Mishnah concludes: What was stated above — that a woman who is betrothed to a priest may eat terumah if the time set for their marriage has arrived, even if the marriage has not yet taken place — [2]**is** the position of **the early Mishnah.** [3]But **the court of a later** generation ruled differently, **saying:** [57B] [4]**A woman** who is betrothed to a priest **may not eat terumah until she** and her bridegroom actually **enter the bridal chamber** for marriage.

GEMARA מְנָא הָנֵי מִילֵּי [5]The Gemara begins its analysis of the Mishnah with the following question: **What is the** Biblical **source for the ruling** that a virgin is given twelve months, from the time her bridegroom asks for her in marriage, to prepare for her wedding?

אָמַר רַב חִסְדָּא [6]**Rav Ḥisda replied:** It is derived from **the verse** that **says** (Genesis 24:55): **"And her brother and her mother said:** [7]**Let the girl stay with us *yamim* or ten."** When Abraham's servant wanted to take Rebecca with him immediately to marry Isaac, her brother and her mother asked that she remain with them "*yamim* or ten." The Gemara first examines the meaning of the verse: [8]**What is meant** here **by** the word "***yamim***"? [9]**If we say** that the word is being used in its usual sense of "days," and it therefore means "**two days,**" for the smallest number of "days" is two, a difficulty arises. For according to this hypothesis, they were saying: "Let the girl stay with us two days or ten." [10]But **does a person speak this way?** For

BACKGROUND

מִשְׁנָה רִאשׁוֹנָה The first Mishnah. A "first Mishnah" is ancient Mishnah, from long before the time of Rabbi Yehudah HaNasi. Sometimes these "first Mishnayot" received their final form and wording in earlier generations. Occasionally a "first Mishnah" is cited in the Mishnah, and the sayings and formulations of later Sages are presented in contrast to it. Very often the "first Mishnah" differs from a teaching of Rabbi Akiva, for the version of the Mishnah formulated by him and his students, such as Rabbi Meir, is the basis of the Mishnah we possess. However, in some instances a "first Mishnah" can be detected by its context, when one sees later Sages disputing the meaning of statesments they received from their teachers. Some Mishnayot in the Gemara are attributed to the early Second Temple period, and occasionally Bet Hillel and Bet Shammai discuss the meaning of a "first Mishnah."

NOTES

mean to imply that if the entire twelve months passed while the woman was betrothed to her bridegroom, she would indeed be permitted to eat terumah while waiting for her brother-in-law to perform levirate marriage. All that it means to say is that if the entire twelve months passed while she was betrothed to her bridegroom, she would be permitted to eat terumah while he was alive, but upon his death terumah would once again be forbidden to her, for by Torah law the *yavam* does not cause his sister-in-law to be entitled to eat terumah.

Many Rishonim accept the opinion of *Rabbenu Tam* (cited by *Tosafot* below, 58a, s.v. ואפילו), who maintains that a widow may not eat terumah by virtue of being bound to the *yavam*, if the time set for her wedding had not yet arrived before her bridegroom died, so that she was never permitted to eat terumah during his lifetime. But if the time set for her wedding had already arrived, so that she was permitted to eat terumah during her bridegroom's lifetime, she is permitted (according to the viewpoint of the early Mishnah) to continue eating terumah by virtue of her bond to the *yavam*, because by Torah law a woman who is bound to her brother-in-law by the levirate bond may eat terumah, and it is only by Rabbinic decree that she may not do so. Thus the Mishnah's formulation, "less one day before the *yavam*," is precise.

מְנָא הָנֵי מִילֵּי From where are these things derived? *Ritva* and *Nimmukei Yosef* point out that it was the Rabbis who enacted that a virgin be given twelve months from the time her bridegroom asks for her in marriage, so that she will have sufficient time to provide herself with a proper trousseau. Thus the verse cited here is not the actual source of the regulation, but rather Biblical support for the Rabbinic enactment. *Nimmukei Yosef* adds that Biblical support was not sought for the regulation that a widow is given thirty days to prepare for her wedding, because there are practical reasons why a woman cannot make herself ready for marriage in less than thirty days. Alternatively, the verse cited here can also support the regulation regarding the time given to a widow to prepare for her wedding, for, as the Gemara argues, the word *yamim* can also be understood to mean "a month."

HALAKHAH

אֵין הָאִשָּׁה אוֹכֶלֶת A woman does not eat. "By Torah law, a woman who is betrothed to a priest may eat terumah, but the Rabbis forbade her to do so until she enters the bridal chamber for marriage." (*Rambam, Sefer Zeraim, Hilkhot Terumot* 6:3.)

TRANSLATION AND COMMENTARY

[1]**if** Rebecca's brother and mother **said to** the servant: "Let her stay with us **two days,"** [2]**and he said to them: "No,"** because he did not wish Rebecca to stay with her family for even the shortest period of time, [3]**would they** then **have said to him:** "Let her stay with us **ten days"?** [4]**Rather, what is meant** here **by** the word *yamim* **is a year,** [5]**as is stated in the verse** (Leviticus 25:29): "And if a man sells a dwelling house in a walled city, then he may redeem it within a whole year after it is sold; **within a full year [*yamim*] he may redeem it."** In the verse from Leviticus, the word *yamim* clearly means a year. Thus in Genesis, too, the word *yamim* is to be understood in the sense of a year, and this forces us to explain the word "ten" in the expression "*yamim* or ten" as meaning "ten months." Accordingly, Rebecca's relatives meant: "Let the girl stay with us for a year, or, at the very least, for a period of ten months."

[1]אָמְרוּ לֵיהּ: ״תְּרֵי יוֹמֵי״, [2]אֲמַר לְהוּ: ״לָא״, [3]אָמְרוּ לֵיהּ: ״עֲשָׂרָה יוֹמֵי״?! [4]אֶלָּא, מַאי ״יָמִים״? שָׁנָה, [5]דִּכְתִיב: ״יָמִים תִּהְיֶה גְּאֻלָּתוֹ״.
[6]וְאֵימָא ״חֹדֶשׁ״, [7]דִּכְתִיב: ״עַד חֹדֶשׁ יָמִים״!
[8]אָמְרִי: דָּנִין ״יָמִים״ סְתָם [9]מִ״יָּמִים״ סְתָם. [10]וְאֵין דָּנִין ״יָמִים״ סְתָם [11]מִ״יָּמִים״ שֶׁנֶּאֱמַר בָּהֶן ״חֹדֶשׁ״.
[12]אָמַר רַבִּי זֵירָא: תָּנָא: [13]״קְטַנָּה, בֵּין הִיא וּבֵין אָבִיהָ יְכוֹלִין לְעַכֵּב״.

LITERAL TRANSLATION

[1][If] they said to him: "Two days," [2][and] he said to them: "No," [3][would] they say to him: "Ten days"? [4]Rather, what is [meant by] *"yamim"*? A year, [5]as it is written: "Within a full year [*yamim*] he may redeem it."

[6]But say "a month," [7]as it is written: "Even a whole month [*hodesh yamim*]!"

[8]They say: We derive [the meaning of] *"yamim"* [stated] without specifying [9]from *"yamim"* [stated] without specifying. [10]But we do not derive [the meaning of] *"yamim"* [stated] without specifying [11]from *"yamim"* together with which [the word] "month" is stated.

[12]Rabbi Zera said: [A Tanna] taught: [13]"[Regarding] a minor, both she and her father can delay [the marriage]."

RASHI

גמרא ואימא – מאי ימים – חודש, ועשור – עשרה ימים.
יכולין לעכב – מלינשא עד שתגדל.

וְאֵימָא חֹדֶשׁ [6]The Gemara now suggests an alternative interpretation of the verse: **But** why not **say** that the word *yamim* here means **a month,** [7]just **as** it does **in the verse** (Numbers 11:20): **"Even a whole month [*hodesh yamim*]"!** According to this explanation, Rebecca's relatives said to Abraham's servant: "Let the girl stay with us for a month, or, at the very least, for a period of ten days."

אָמְרִי [8]The Gemara **answers:** It is legitimate to **derive the meaning of** the word ***yamim* stated without specification** — as in the verse: "Let the girl stay with us *yamim*" — [9]**from** another instance of the word ***yamim* stated without** any **specification** — as in the verse: "Within a full year [*yamim*] he may redeem it." [10]**But** it is **not** legitimate to **derive the meaning of** the word ***yamim* stated without specification** [11]**from** an instance of the word ***yamim* stated together with the word month,** as in the verse: "A whole month [*hodesh yamim*]." Thus Rebecca's relatives must have meant: "Let the girl stay with us for a year, or, at the very least, for a period of ten months." We may therefore infer from this verse that a virgin is ordinarily given a year, from the time her bridegroom asks for her in marriage, to provide herself with a trousseau and to prepare for her wedding.

אָמַר רַבִּי זֵירָא [12]The Gemara now qualifies the Mishnah's ruling that a betrothed virgin is given twelve months to prepare for her wedding, which implies that after twelve months she must agree to marriage or else she will be considered a rebellious wife who forfeits her right to her ketubah. **Rabbi Zera said: A Tanna taught** the following Baraita: [13]"If a father gives his daughter away in betrothal while she is **a minor,** and her bridegroom asks that she be handed over to him for marriage, **both she and her father can delay the marriage** until she reaches the age of twelve, even if more than twelve months will pass before then."

NOTES

בֵּין הִיא וּבֵין אָבִיהָ **Both she and her father.** If a minor girl is betrothed, she may delay her marriage, for she may not be ready to engage in sexual relations or to become a homemaker. *Rashbatz* adds that support for this regulation may be adduced from the verse (Genesis 24:57): "Let us call the girl, and ask her," which implies that Rebecca

HALAKHAH

קְטַנָּה, בֵּין הִיא וּבֵין אָבִיהָ **Regarding a minor, both she and her father.** "If a father gives his minor daughter away in betrothal, and her bridegroom asks that she be handed over to him for marriage, either the girl or her father can

TRANSLATION AND COMMENTARY

בִּשְׁלָמָא אִיהִי [1]The Gemara asks: **Granted that** the girl **can delay** her wedding until she reaches the age of twelve, for she may feel that she is not yet ready for marriage. [2]**But** why does **her father** have the right to delay the wedding? **If** the girl **is satisfied,** [3]**what difference does it make to her father?**

סָבַר [4]The Gemara answers: The father **thinks** as follows: "Although my daughter agrees to be married **now, she does not** really **know** the commitment she is making. But I know that she is not yet ready for married life. [5]**Tomorrow** or some time soon **she will rebel** against her husband **and leave him,** [6]**and** then **she will come and fall** back **upon me** for support." Since the father's concerns are legitimate, he too can delay his daughter's marriage until she reaches the age of twelve.

אָמַר רַבִּי אַבָּא בַּר לֵוִי [7]The Gemara continues its discussion of child marriage. **Rabbi Abba bar Levi said: A decision may not be made about marrying off a minor** girl **off while she is** still **a minor.** [8]**But a decision may be made now about marrying off a minor** girl **when she reaches majority.**

[1]בִּשְׁלָמָא אִיהִי מָצֵי מְעַכְּבָא. [2]אֶלָּא אָבִיהָ, אִי אִיהִי נִיחָא לָהּ, [3]אָבִיהָ מַאי נָפְקָא לֵיהּ מִינָּהּ?

[4]סָבַר: ״הָשְׁתָּא לָא יָדְעָה. [5]לְמָחָר מִימְרְדָא וְנָפְקָא, [6]וְאָתְיָא וְנָפְלָה עִילָּוַאי״.

[7]אָמַר רַבִּי אַבָּא בַּר לֵוִי: אֵין פּוֹסְקִין עַל הַקְּטַנָּה לְהַשִּׂיאָהּ כְּשֶׁהִיא קְטַנָּה. [8]אֲבָל פּוֹסְקִין עַל הַקְּטַנָּה לְהַשִּׂיאָהּ כְּשֶׁהִיא גְּדוֹלָה.

LITERAL TRANSLATION

[1]Granted [that] she can delay. [2]But [as for] her father, if she is satisfied, [3]what [benefit] comes out of it for her father?

[4]He thinks: "Now she does not know. [5]Tomorrow she will rebel and leave [him], [6]and she will come and fall upon me."

[7]Rabbi Abba bar Levi said: We do not decide regarding a minor to marry her off while she is a minor. [8]But we decide regarding a minor to marry her off when she becomes an adult.

RASHI

מימרדא ונפקא — תמרוד בבעלה, שלא תוכל לסבול, ותצא ותבא אלי עד שתגדל, ונמצאתי צריך לתכשיטין אחרים. **להשיאה כשהיא קטנה** — שטורח הוא לה. **אבל פוסקין כו׳** — ודוקא בלא קידושין. אבל קידושין בקטנות — לא, עד שתגדל ותאמר בפלוני אני רוצה.

SAGES

רַבִּי אַבָּא בַּר לֵוִי Rabbi Abba bar Levi. This Amora is quoted only here in the Talmud, and nothing is known of when he lived. Some manuscripts have the reading: Rabbah bar Levi (or Livai), who was a Babylonian Amora of the fourth generation and a colleague of Rava.

NOTES

would have been able to delay her marriage had she wished to do so. As for the length of the delay, most Rishonim follow *Rashi* (and this explanation is stated explicitly in the Jerusalem Talmud), who explains that both the girl and her father may delay her marriage until she reaches the age of twelve, even if more than twelve months will have passed in the meantime. *Rashba* cites an alternative explanation, according to which the Baraita teaches us that a girl who has been betrothed as a minor may delay her wedding for twelve months from the time her bridegroom asks for her in marriage.

אֵין פּוֹסְקִין עַל הַקְּטַנָּה We do not decide regarding a minor. The Rishonim disagree about the relationship between Rabbi Abba bar Levi's statement — that an agreement may be reached to marry off a minor girl once she reaches the age of twelve — and the ruling found elsewhere in the Gemara (*Kiddushin* 41a) that a father is forbidden to give his minor daughter away in betrothal until she has grown up and can say: "I wish to marry So-and-so."

Rashi and *Ritva* explain that when our Gemara speaks of an agreement for marriage, it does not refer to actual betrothal but only to a mutual promise made by the families of the bride and the bridegroom that the marriage will take place after the girl has grown up.

Ra'ah, *Rabbi Crescas Vidal*, and *Mordekhai* maintain that the two statements do in fact contradict each other.

Ritva cites another explanation, according to which the statement in *Kiddushin* refers to a minor girl who has a father, whereas the statement in our Gemara refers to an orphan girl. If the girl's father is alive, there is no reason why she should be betrothed while still a minor, for her father will see to it that she will be married off when she grows up. But if she is an orphan and has an opportunity to be betrothed, we do not delay the betrothal, for she does not have a father who will arrange her marriage when she grows up.

HALAKHAH

delay the marriage until she reaches the age of twelve, following Rabbi Zera. If both the girl and her father agree to the marriage, the bridegroom may complete the marriage process while she is still a minor, but it is not proper for him to do so." (*Rambam, Sefer Nashim, Hilkhot Ishut* 10:16; *Shulḥan Arukh, Even HaEzer* 56:4.)

אֵין פּוֹסְקִין עַל הַקְּטַנָּה We do not decide regarding a minor. "It is preferable that a father not give his minor daughter away in betrothal, but rather that he wait until she is grown up and can say: 'I wish to marry So-and-so,' following the Gemara in *Kiddushin* 41a. *Rema* (following *Tosafot* in *Kiddushin*) notes that because of the economic uncertainties prevailing in the Diaspora, it became common practice for parents to give their daughters away in betrothal while they were still minors — for if they were to delay their daughters' betrothal until they grew up, they might not be able to provide them with proper dowries or find them suitable husbands." (*Rambam, Sefer Nashim, Hilkhot Ishut* 3:19; *Shulḥan Arukh, Even HaEzer* 37:8.)

[1]פְּשִׁיטָא!
[2]מַהוּ דְּתֵימָא: לֵיחוּשׁ דִּלְמָא מְעַיְּילָא פַּחֲדָא מֵהָשְׁתָּא וְחָלְשָׁה. [3]קָא מַשְׁמַע לָן.
[4]אָמַר רַב הוּנָא: בָּגְרָה יוֹם אֶחָד וְנִתְקַדְּשָׁה, [5]נוֹתְנִין לָהּ שְׁלֹשִׁים יוֹם כְּאַלְמָנָה.
[6]מֵיתִיבֵי: ״בָּגְרָה, הֲרֵי הִיא כִּתְבוּעָה״. [7]מַאי לָאו: כִּתְבוּעָה דִּבְתוּלָה?
[8]לָא, כִּתְבוּעָה דְּאַלְמָנָה.
[9]תָּא שְׁמַע: ״בּוֹגֶרֶת שֶׁשָּׁהֲתָה

LITERAL TRANSLATION

[1]It is obvious!

[2]You might have said: We should be concerned lest fear enter [her mind] from now and she become sick. [3][Therefore] he tells us [that this is not so].

[4]Rav Huna said: [If] she reached majority one day and she was betrothed, [5]we give her thirty days like a widow.

[6]They raised an objection: "[If] she has reached majority, she is like one who has been asked for [in marriage]." [7]Does this not [mean]: Like a virgin who has been asked for [in marriage]?

[8]No, like a widow who has been asked for [in marriage].

[9]Come [and] hear: "[Regarding] an adult woman who has waited

TRANSLATION AND COMMENTARY

פְּשִׁיטָא [1]The Gemara objects to the second half of this ruling. **It is** surely **obvious** that a decision may be reached now to marry off a minor girl once she reaches the age of twelve!

מַהוּ דְּתֵימָא [2]The Gemara answers: **You might have said** that **we should be concerned lest** the minor girl **will** already **feel a sense of fear now**, when she hears that her father has decided to marry her off when she reaches the age of twelve, **and she will become sick** as a result. [3]**Therefore** Rabbi Abba bar Levi **tells us that there is no** room for **such concern**, and the father of a minor girl may enter into an agreement at this point to marry off his daughter when she reaches the age of twelve.

אָמַר רַב הוּנָא [4]The Gemara now cites a statement of **Rav Huna,** who **said: If** a young girl has reached full adulthood at the age of twelve-and-a-half, and **she has been an adult for** even **one day, and** then **she is betrothed,** [5]**she is given** only **thirty days** — from the time her bridegroom asks for her in marriage — to prepare for her wedding; in this she is just **like a widow,** for she has surely already prepared her trousseau by the time she has reached majority. According to Jewish law, a girl is legally a minor (קְטַנָּה — *ketannah*) until the end of her twelfth year. When she reaches her twelfth birthday, she becomes legally an adult (גְּדוֹלָה — *gedolah*). For six months, however, while she is between twelve and twelve-and-a-half, she remains under her father's authority and is called a *na'arah* (נַעֲרָה). When she reaches the age of twelve-and-a-half, she leaves her father's authority completely and is called a *bogeret* (בוגרת). Rav Huna maintains that when the Mishnah gives a betrothed virgin twelve months from the time her bridegroom asks for her in marriage, it is referring to a bride who was betrothed while she was a *na'arah*. But if she was betrothed after she became a *bogeret*, she is given only thirty days to make her preparations from the time her bridegroom asks for her in marriage.

מֵיתִיבֵי [6]**An objection was raised** against Rav Huna's ruling from the following Baraita: **"If** a girl **has reached** full **majority** at the age of twelve-and-a-half and is then betrothed, **she is** treated **like someone who has been asked for** by her bridegroom **in marriage."** [7]**Does this not mean** that she is treated **like a** betrothed **virgin who has been asked for in marriage,** who is given twelve months to prepare for her wedding, and does this not contradict the ruling of Rav Huna?

לָא [8]The Gemara answers: **No,** if a woman is betrothed after reaching full majority, she is treated **like a** betrothed **widow who has been asked for in marriage,** who is given only thirty days to prepare for her wedding.

תָּא שְׁמַע [9]The Gemara raises another objection against Rav Huna's ruling. **Come and hear** what we have learned in the following Mishnah (*Nedarim* 73b): "If a young girl **has reached** full **adulthood** and is then

RASHI

נותנין לה שלשים יום כאלמנה — משעת אירוסין. שכיון שבגרה היא מכינה תכשיטין קודם בגרות, שאינה רוצה לשהות עוד. **כתבועה** — כאילו תבעה להכין עצמה לנישואין. **דבתולה** — שנים עשר חודש משעת אירוסין.

HALAKHAH

בָּגְרָה, הֲרֵי הִיא כִּתְבוּעָה If she has reached majority, she is like one who has been asked for in marriage. "If the bridegroom asks for his bride to be given to him in marriage after she has already reached full adulthood, she is given twelve months from the day she reached adulthood to prepare for her marriage. Similarly, if he betroths his bride on the day that she reaches majority, she is given twelve months from that day to prepare for her marriage. But if he betroths his bride twelve months after she has reached majority, she is given only thirty days to make her preparations from the day he asks for her in marriage." (*Rambam, Sefer Nashim, Hilkhot Ishut* 10:17; *Shulḥan Arukh, Even HaEzer* 56:1.)

[1]שְׁנֵים עָשָׂר חֹדֶשׁ, [1]רַבִּי אֱלִיעֶזֶר אוֹמֵר: הוֹאִיל וְחַיָּיב בַּעְלָהּ בִּמְזוֹנוֹתֶיהָ, יָפֵר!״
[2]אֵימָא: בּוֹגֶרֶת וְשֶׁשָּׁהֲתָה שְׁנֵים עָשָׂר חוֹדֶשׁ, [3]רַבִּי אֱלִיעֶזֶר אוֹמֵר: הוֹאִיל וּבַעְלָהּ חַיָּיב בִּמְזוֹנוֹתֶיהָ, יָפֵר.
[4]תָּא שְׁמַע: ״הַמְאָרֵס אֶת הַבְּתוּלָה, [5]וּבֵין שֶׁתָּבְעָה הִיא וּבַעַל מְעַכֵּב, [6]נוֹתְנִין לָהּ שְׁנֵים עָשָׂר חֹדֶשׁ מִשְּׁעַת תְּבִיעָה, [7]אֲבָל לֹא מִשְּׁעַת אֵירוּסִין. [8]וּבָגְרָה, הֲרֵי הִיא כִּתְבוּעָה. [9]כֵּיצַד? [10]בָּגְרָה יוֹם אֶחָד וְנִתְקַדְּשָׁה, נוֹתְנִין לָהּ שְׁנֵים עָשָׂר חֹדֶשׁ, [11]וְלַאֲרוּסָה שְׁלֹשִׁים

LITERAL TRANSLATION

twelve months, [1]Rabbi Eliezer says: Since her husband is liable for her maintenance, he may annul [her vows]."

[2]Say: [Regarding] an adult woman or one who has waited twelve months, [3]Rabbi Eliezer says: Since her husband is liable for her maintenance, he may annul [her vows].

[4]Come [and] hear: "[If] someone has betrothed a virgin, [5]whether the husband has asked for her [in marriage] and she is delaying, [6]or she has asked [for marriage] and the husband is delaying, [7]we give her twelve months from the time of the request, [8]but not from the time of the betrothal. [9]And [if] she has reached majority, she is like one who has been asked for [in marriage]. [10]How so? [11][If] she reached majority one day and she was betrothed, we give her twelve months, [12]and to one who was betrothed [we give] thirty

TRANSLATION AND COMMENTARY

betrothed, and **twelve months** have **passed** but she is still not married, [1]**Rabbi Eliezer says: Since her bridegroom is** now **liable for her maintenance, he may annul her vows."** A husband is entitled to annul the vows taken by his wife. Rabbi Eliezer rules that once the bridegroom becomes liable for his wife's maintenance, he has the authority to annul her vows, even though the marriage is not yet completed. It is clear from Rabbi Eliezer's ruling that even in the case of an adult woman who is betrothed, twelve more months must pass before her bridegroom becomes liable for her maintenance. Thus we see that even if a girl is betrothed after she reaches full adulthood, she is given twelve months from the time she reached adulthood in order to prepare for her wedding, and this contradicts the ruling of Rav Huna!

אֵימָא [2]The Gemara answers that the text of the Mishnah in *Nedarim* must be emended, and we must **say** that it should read as follows: If a girl **has reached** full **adulthood** and is then betrothed, and thirty days have passed from the time her bridegroom asked for her in marriage, *or* if a girl was betrothed while still a *na'arah*, and **twelve months have passed,** [3]**Rabbi Eliezer says: Since her bridegroom is** now held **liable for her maintenance, he may annul her vows.** It is only in the case of a *na'arah* that twelve months must pass before her bridegroom is required to provide for her support. But if a *bogeret* is betrothed, she is entitled to support from her bridegroom thirty days after he asked for her in marriage, because a *bogeret* is given only thirty days to prepare for her wedding.

תָּא שְׁמַע [4]The Gemara now cites a final Tannaitic source in order to refute the viewpoint of Rav Huna. **Come and hear: "If someone has betrothed a virgin,** [5]**whether the bridegroom has asked for** his bride **in marriage and** it is **she** who **is causing a delay,** saying that she needs more time to get ready for the marriage, [6]**or** the bride **has asked** that the **marriage** take place **and** it is **the bridegroom** who **is causing the delay** — [7]in either case the bride and the bridegroom **are given twelve months** to prepare themselves for the marriage. These twelve months are counted **from the time that the request** for the marriage is made, [8]**and not from the time of the betrothal.** Thus, even if a couple have already been betrothed for several years, the twelve-month period of preparation for the marriage does not begin until the bride or the bridegroom asks for a date to be set for the wedding. [9]**And if** a young girl **has reached** full **adulthood** and is then betrothed, **she is** treated **like someone who has been asked for** by her bridegroom **in marriage.** [10]**How so?** [11]**If she has been an adult for** even **one day and she is** then **betrothed, she is given twelve months** to prepare for her wedding. [12]**And** there is a case in which **a betrothed** virgin **is given** only **thirty days** to provide for

RASHI

יפר — נדריה בלא שותפות דאב. שמעינן מיניה דבוגרת נמי אינו חייב במזונותיה עד שתשהה שנים עשר חודש. וששהתה — והכי קאמר: בוגרת לסוף שלשים, והנערה ששהתה שנים עשר חודש.

NOTES

רַבִּי אֱלִיעֶזֶר אוֹמֵר **Rabbi Eliezer says.** The Mishnah in tractate *Nedarim* concludes with the opinion of the Sages that the husband cannot annul his wife's vows on his own until she enters the bridal chamber for marriage. The law follows the viewpoint of the Sages.

יוֹם״. [1]תְּיוּבְתָּא דְּרַב הוּנָא תְּיוּבְתָּא.

[2]מַאי: ״וְלַאֲרוּסָה שְׁלֹשִׁים יוֹם״?

[3]אֲמַר רַב פַּפָּא: הָכִי קָאָמַר: [4]בּוֹגֶרֶת שֶׁעָבְרוּ עָלֶיהָ שְׁנֵים עָשָׂר חֹדֶשׁ בְּבַגְרוּת וְנִתְקַדְּשָׁה, [5]נוֹתְנִין לָהּ שְׁלֹשִׁים יוֹם כְּאַלְמָנָה.

[6]״הִגִּיעַ זְמַן וְלֹא נִישְּׂאוּ״. [7]אָמַר עוּלָּא: דְּבַר תּוֹרָה, אֲרוּסָה בַּת יִשְׂרָאֵל אוֹכֶלֶת בִּתְרוּמָה, [8]שֶׁנֶּאֱמַר: ״וְכֹהֵן כִּי יִקְנֶה נֶפֶשׁ קִנְיַן כַּסְפּוֹ״. [9]וְהַאי נַמִי קִנְיַן כַּסְפּוֹ הוּא. [10]מַה טַּעַם אָמְרוּ אֵינָהּ אוֹכֶלֶת? [11]שֶׁמָּא יִמְזְגוּ לָהּ כּוֹס בְּבֵית אָבִיהָ, [12]וְתַשְׁקֶה לְאָחִיהָ וְלַאֲחוֹתָהּ.

LITERAL TRANSLATION

days." [1]The refutation of Rav Huna is a refutation.

[2]What is [meant by]: "And to one who was betrothed [we give] thirty days"?

[3]Rav Pappa said: This is what he says: [4][Regarding] an adult over whom twelve months have passed in majority and she has been betrothed, [5]we give her thirty days like a widow.

[6]"If the time came and they were not married." [7]Ulla said: By Torah law (lit., "a word of Torah"), a betrothed woman [who is] the daughter of an Israelite eats terumah, [8]as it is said: "But if a priest acquires any person as the acquisition of his money, [he may eat of it]." [9]And this [woman] is also the acquisition of his money. [10]What is the reason they said [that] she does not eat? [11]Lest they pour (lit., "mix") a cup [of terumah wine] for her in her father's house, [12]and she give her brother or her sister to drink [from it].

TRANSLATION AND COMMENTARY

herself [as will be explained below]." [1]Now, **this refutation of Rav Huna is a** complete **refutation,** because it states explicitly that even if a woman was betrothed after reaching full adulthood, she is still given twelve months to prepare for her wedding.

מַאי [2]The Gemara now seeks to clarify the last clause of the Baraita just quoted, and asks: **What is the meaning of** the clause that states: **"And** there is a case in which a **betrothed** virgin **is given** only **thirty days"?**

אֲמַר רַב פַּפָּא [3]**Rav Pappa said: This is what** the Baraita **says:** [4]**Regarding a woman who has** already **reached** full **adulthood** and **over whom twelve months of adulthood have passed, if she is** then **betrothed,** [5]**she is given** only **thirty days** to prepare for her marriage, just **like a widow.**

הִגִּיעַ זְמַן [6]The Gemara now proceeds to analyze the next clause of the Mishnah, which stated: **"If the time** set for the marriage **came and** the couple **were not married,** the bride is entitled to eat of the bridegroom's food, and she is entitled to eat terumah." [7]**Ulla said: By Torah law, a betrothed woman who is the daughter of a non-priest** and is betrothed to a priest **may eat terumah** immediately upon her betrothal, [8]**because the verse states** (Leviticus 22:11): **"But if a priest acquires any person as the acquisition of his money, he may eat of it."** Terumah is permitted not only to a priest, but also to those members of his household who are considered acquisitions obtained by his money — for example, his non-Jewish slaves. [9]A man's bride **is also** considered **an acquisition** obtained **by his money,** in a sense, because one of the methods by which betrothal is effected is through the transfer of money or something worth money from the man to the woman. [10]**Why,** then, **did the** Rabbis **say that** a betrothed woman **may not eat** terumah until after the marriage process is completed? Because the bride still lives in her father's house during her betrothal. [11]The Rabbis were concerned that **a cup of terumah wine might be poured for her** while she was still **in her father's house,** [12]**and she might give her brother or her sister** or some other member of her father's household who is not permitted to partake of terumah **some of** the wine **to drink.** Because of their concern that the betrothed bride might give terumah to someone to whom it was forbidden, the Rabbis decreed that she must not eat terumah until she is married.

RASHI

נותנין לה שלשים יום – משעת אירוסין. שמא ימזגו לה כוס – של תרומה. בבית אביה – גרסינן.

NOTES

נוֹתְנִין לָהּ שְׁלֹשִׁים יוֹם כְּאַלְמָנָה **We give her thirty days like a widow.** *Rashi* states that if a woman is betrothed more than a year after reaching adulthood, she is given thirty days from the date of her betrothal to prepare herself for marriage. Most Rishonim disagree and say that she is given thirty days to make those preparations from the time her bridegroom asks to set a date for the marriage.

שֶׁמָּא יִמְזְגוּ לָהּ כּוֹס **Lest they pour a cup of terumah wine for her.** *Rashi* and most Rishonim have the reading found in our standard Talmudic texts: "Lest they pour a cup of terumah wine for her in her father's house, and she give her brother or her sister to drink from it." Since the bride is still living in her father's house during the period of her betrothal, there is concern that she may give some of the terumah to other members of her father's household.

Meiri and others have the following reading: "Lest they pour a cup of terumah wine for her in her *father-in-law's* house." The Rabbis decreed that a betrothed woman may

1 אִי הָכִי, הִגִּיעַ זְמַן וְלֹא נִישְּׂאוּ נַמִי!
2 הָתָם דּוּכְתָּא מְיַיחֵד לָהּ.
3 אֶלָּא מֵעַתָּה, 4 לָקִיט כֹּהֵן לְיִשְׂרָאֵל לָא לֵיכוּל בִּתְרוּמָה, 5 דִּלְמָא אָתוּ לְמֵיכַל בַּהֲדֵיהּ!
6 הָשְׁתָּא מִדִּידְהוּ סָפוּ לֵיהּ, מִדִּידֵיהּ אָכְלֵי?
7 רַב שְׁמוּאֵל בַּר רַב יְהוּדָה אֲמַר: מִשּׁוּם סִימְפּוֹן.

LITERAL TRANSLATION

[1] If so, if the time came and they were not married also!

[2] There he designates a place for her.

[3] But if so, [4] a priest who was hired out to an Israelite should not eat terumah, [5] lest they come to eat with him!

[6] Now [that] they feed him from their [food], will they eat from his [food]?

[7] Rav Shmuel bar Rav Yehudah said: Because of a condition annulling [the betrothal].

TRANSLATION AND COMMENTARY

אִי הָכִי [1] The Gemara asks: **If so,** then **if the time** set for the marriage **came but** the couple **were not married,** we should **also** be concerned about the same problem! Why does the Mishnah rule that once the time set for the marriage has come, the bride may eat terumah, even if the marriage has not yet taken place?

הָתָם [2] The Gemara answers: **There,** after the wedding date has passed, the bridegroom is already responsible for his bride's maintenance, and therefore **he sets aside a** special **place for her** to eat, because he does not want her to share the food he gives her with that of the other members of her family. Since she takes her meals in a designated area apart from the rest of her family, she may be given terumah to eat, for there is no concern that she will share it with her relatives.

אֶלָּא מֵעַתָּה [3] Another question is now posed: **But if it is true** that the Rabbis decreed that a woman betrothed to a priest may not eat terumah, lest she give some of the terumah to other members of her family, [4] then **a priest who is hired to** work for **a non-priest should** also **be forbidden to eat** his own **terumah** in his employer's house, [5] **lest** his employer and other people in the house **come to eat** the terumah **with him!**

הָשְׁתָּא [6] The Gemara answers: **Now that** the employer provides **his** worker **with food,** need we be concerned that the employer will come to **eat his** worker's **food?** There is no reason to fear that the employer will eat the employee's terumah.

רַב שְׁמוּאֵל בַּר רַב יְהוּדָה אֲמַר [7] **Rav Shmuel bar Rav Yehudah explained** in a different manner the Rabbinic decree forbidding a woman betrothed to a priest from eating terumah: By Torah law, a betrothed woman who is the daughter of a non-priest and is betrothed to a priest may eat terumah immediately upon her betrothal, even before she is married, and even before the time set for her marriage has arrived. But the Rabbis decreed that a betrothed woman is not permitted to eat terumah until she is married, **because** they feared that the bridegroom might find **some defect** in his bride that would give him grounds **to annul the betrothal** retroactively. It would then turn out that when she ate the terumah, she was not betrothed to the priest, and the terumah was thus forbidden to her, as it is to any other non-priest.

RASHI

דוכתא מייחד לה — אחר שהוא זן אותה תמיד, מוציאה מבית אביה ומייחד לה מקום, שלא תפסיד מזונותיו לחלקם לקרוביה. **לקיט** — ששוכרו ללקוט תבואתו. **לקיט כהן** — לקיט שהוא כהן, ונשכר לישראל. **משום סימפון** — הוא דאמר ארוסה לא תאכל תרומה עד שיגיע זמן שחייב במזונותיה. ולשון סימפון הוא ביטול, כגון שובר המבטל שטר קרוי סימפון, ומום באשה או בבהמה שמבטל המקח קרוי סימפון. והכא גזור בה שמא ימצא בה מום, ונמצאו קידושי טעות ובטלים, ונמצא שאכלה זרה בתרומה.

SAGES

רַב שְׁמוּאֵל בַּר רַב יְהוּדָה Rav Shmuel bar Rav Yehudah. A Babylonian Amora of the third generation, Rav Shmuel bar Yehudah was a disciple and close friend of the famous Amora Rav Yehudah (bar Yeḥekal). Rav Shmuel came from a family of proselytes and reached prominence as a Rabbinic scholar. He visited Eretz Israel and studied with Rabbi Yoḥanan and Rabbi Elazar in Tiberias, and transmitted to Babylonia many rulings of the Palestinian Amoraim. Abaye was one of his disciples.

LANGUAGE

סִימְפּוֹן A condition annulling the betrothal. This word may possibly be derived from the Greek σύμφωνον, *symphonon*, meaning "agreement," and, by extension, "cancellation of an agreement." Another possibility mentioned by scholars is that the word סימפון may be derived from the Greek σύμπτωμα, *symptoma*, meaning "a chance" or "a mishap."

NOTES

not eat terumah, lest she give some of the terumah to her younger brother or sister whom she brings with her to her father-in-law's house.

Ritva points out that we are not concerned that she will deliberately give the terumah to those to whom it is forbidden, but rather that she may come to give it to them inadvertently, or that they will take it themselves by mistake. For this reason Ulla speaks of wine, for a person ordinarily pays less attention to what he drinks than to what he eats.

Shittah Mekubbetzet adds that there is particular concern about wine, because the bridegroom sends his bride undiluted wine which must be mixed with water in her father's house before it can be drunk. Thus the Rabbis decreed that a betrothed woman may not eat terumah, lest her bridegroom send her more wine than she needs (for he does not know precisely with how much water the wine will be mixed), and she mistakenly give some of the terumah to the other members of her father's household. Moreover, there is concern that the other members of her family may test the wine to make sure that it has been mixed with the right quantity of water.

אֶלָּא מֵעַתָּה, לָקִיט כֹּהֵן But if so, a priest who was hired out. The Rishonim note that the Gemara does not propose that a priest should be forbidden to eat terumah if a non-priest is working for him in his house, lest the worker come to eat terumah with him. *Tosafot* explains that the Gemara is concerned that if a priest is working in the house of a non-priest, he may try to ingratiate himself with his employer by offering food to the members of his household, and he may inadvertently give them some of his terumah. But there is no concern about a non-priest

[1]אִי הָכִי, נִכְנְסָה לַחוּפָּה וְלֹא נִבְעֲלָה נַמִי! [2]הָתָם מִיבְדַּק בָּדֵיק לָהּ וַהֲדַר מְעַיֵּיל. [3]אֶלָּא מֵעַתָּה, עֶבֶד כֹּהֵן שֶׁלְּקָחוֹ מִיִּשְׂרָאֵל לָא לֵיכוּל בִּתְרוּמָה מִשּׁוּם סִימְפּוֹן! [4]סִימְפּוֹן בַּעֲבָדִים לֵיכָּא; [5]דְּאִי דְּאַבָּרָאֵי, הָא קָחֲזֵי לֵיהּ,

LITERAL TRANSLATION

[1]If so, if she entered the bridal chamber but did not have sexual intercourse also! [2]There he investigates her and afterwards brings [her] in.

[3]If so, a priest's slave whom he bought from an Israelite should not eat terumah because of a condition annulling [the purchase]!

[4]There is no condition annulling [the purchase] of slaves; [5]for if [the defect] is outside, surely he sees it,

TRANSLATION AND COMMENTARY

אִי הָכִי [1]The Gemara objects: **If so,** then even **if** the bride **has entered the bridal chamber, but has not** yet **had sexual intercourse** with her bridegroom, we should **also** be concerned that the bridegroom may find a defect that will retroactively annul the betrothal! Why, according to our Mishnah, did the later court rule that a woman who is betrothed to a priest may not eat terumah until she and her bridegroom enter the bridal chamber for marriage? This implies that as soon as they enter the bridal chamber, she is permitted to eat terumah, even before they engage in sexual intercourse. The ruling of the early Mishnah is even more difficult to understand, for according to the early Mishnah a priest's bride is permitted to eat terumah as soon as the time set for her marriage has arrived, even if the marriage has not yet taken place! In such a case, we should certainly be concerned that the groom may still find a flaw in his bride that will annul the betrothal retroactively.

הָתָם [2]The Gemara answers: **In that case,** after the bride has entered the bridal chamber, there is no longer any concern that the bridegroom will find a defect in his bride that will annul the betrothal, because he first **conducts an investigation** of his bride by way of his female relatives **and** only **afterwards does he bring her into** the bridal chamber for marriage. And even if the bride has not yet entered the bridal chamber, it can nevertheless be assumed that if the wedding date has arrived the bridegroom has already completed his investigation of his bride, and it is unlikely that he will now find any reason to annul the betrothal. Thus, according to the early Mishnah, the bride may eat terumah as soon as the time set for the marriage arrives, and according to the later court, she may eat terumah as soon as she enters the bridal chamber.

אֶלָּא מֵעַתָּה [3]The Gemara raises another question: **If it is true** that the Rabbis forbade terumah to a woman betrothed to a priest, because they feared that the groom might find a defect in his bride that would annul the betrothal, then **a priest's slave whom he bought from a non-priest should not** be permitted to **eat terumah, because** the priest may still find **a defect** in him **that annuls the purchase**! If the Rabbis were concerned that the priest might find a defect in his bride that would annul the betrothal, they should also have been concerned that a priest might find a defect in his slave that would invalidate his purchase, in which case it would turn out that when the slave ate the terumah, he was not a member of the priest's household, and the terumah was forbidden to him!

בַּעֲבָדִים לֵיכָּא סִימְפּוֹן [4]The Gemara answers: **There is no defect that can annul the purchase of a slave.** Thus the Rabbis had no reason to decree that a slave who is bought by a priest from a a non-priest is forbidden to eat terumah. The Gemara now explains why the purchase of a slave cannot be annulled on account of a defect discovered by the buyer. [5]**If the defect is external** and clearly visible to all, the buyer **surely saw it** before he agreed to buy the slave, and therefore he cannot later annul the purchase because

RASHI

אי הכי נכנסה לחופה ולא נבעלה — קא סלקא דעתך שעדיין אינו מכיר במומין שבה, ואמאי תני מתניתין אפילו, למשנה אחרונה עד שתכנס לחופה? וכל שכן דקשיא משהגיע זמן דמשנה ראשונה. **מיבדק בדיק לה** — ביד קרובותיו. **סימפון בעבדים ליכא** — אין מומין מבטל מקח.

NOTES

working in the house of a priest, for when the priest provides his worker with his meals, he will be careful not to give him terumah.

Ra'ah and *Ritva* add that the Gemara is concerned that an employer may eat his worker's food without his permission, and this is why it suggests that a priest working for a non-priest should be forbidden to eat terumah. But a worker is careful not to take anything from his employer without his permission, and there is thus no reason to forbid a priest from eating terumah just because a non-priest is working for him in his house.

HALAKHAH

סִימְפּוֹן בַּעֲבָדִים לֵיכָּא There is no condition annulling the purchase of slaves. "If someone buys a slave, he cannot invalidate the purchase on account of a defect in the slave that does not affect his capacity to work. For if the defect

LANGUAGE

קוּבְיוּסְטוּס A gambler. This word is derived from the Greek κυβευτής, *kubeutes*, meaning "gambler."

BACKGROUND

לִסְטִים מְזוּיָּין אוֹ מוּכְתָּב לְמַלְכוּת An armed bandit or one sentenced to death by the government. Now matter how the expression מוּכְתָּב לְמַלְכוּת is interpreted (see notes), it makes no difference from the buyer's point of view. The government will seize the slave from his owner, either to imprison him or to execute him. The buyer has a similar reason for not wishing to own a slave who is an armed bandit, since ultimately such a slave will be captured and taken away from his owner.

TRANSLATION AND COMMENTARY

[1] **And if** the defect **is internal,** so that it would not have been noticed by the buyer, surely the buyer **wants** the slave **for work,** [2] **and he does not care about a hidden defect,** provided that it does not affect the slave's capacity to work. [3] **If** the defect is not a physical flaw, but the slave **is** later **found to be a thief or** [58A] **a gambler, he is** nevertheless **acquired** by the buyer, for it is well known that most slaves steal and gamble, and therefore the buyer accepted the possibility that the slave he was buying might also have those characteristics. [4] **What** defect **is** left that could annul the purchase of a slave? [5] You might suggest that if the slave is found to be **an armed bandit or someone who has been sentenced to death by the government,** the buyer can annul the purchase, for this would be unusual and unexpected. In fact, however, even such a defect cannot annul the purchase, for if a slave is an armed bandit or someone who has been condemned to death, [6] that fact **is** surely **widely known,** and the buyer cannot later claim that he was ignorant of the slave's true nature at the time of the purchase.

[1] דְּאִי דְּאַבָּרָאֵי, הָא קָחֲזֵי לֵיהּ,
[2] וְאִי דְּגַוָּאֵי, לִמְלָאכָה קָא בָּעֵי,
[3] וְשֶׁבַּסֵּתֶר לָא אִיכְפַּת לֵיהּ.
[4] נִמְצָא גַּנָּב אוֹ [58A] קוּבְיוּסְטוּס, הִגִּיעוֹ. [5] מַאי אִיכָּא? [6] לִסְטִים מְזוּיָּין אוֹ מוּכְתָּב לְמַלְכוּת? [7] הָנְהוּ קָלָא אִית לְהוּ.

LITERAL TRANSLATION

[1] and if it is inside, he wants [him] for work, [2] and what is hidden he does not care about. [3] If he is found [to be] a thief or [58A] a gambler, he is acquired (lit., "he reached him"). [4] What is there? [5] An armed bandit or one sentenced (lit., "written") [to death] by the government? [6] These are talked about (lit., "have a voice").

RASHI

קוביוסטוס — גונב נפשות. **הגיעו** — ללוקח, ואין המקח בטל. וברייתא היא בבבא בתרא ב"המוכר פירות": המוכר עבד לחבירו ונמצא גנב או קוביוסטוס — הגיעו, שסתמן גנבים הן. **לסטים מזוין** — אין דרכו בכך. **מוכתב למלכות** — חטא למלכות, עד שלוה לגזור עליו שיהרגנו כל מוצאו. **קלא אית להו** — וסבר וקביל.

NOTES

קוּבְיוּסְטוּס A gambler. *Rabbenu Gershom* (*Bava Batra* 92b), *Rashi, Rivan,* and *Rambam* all explain that the term *kuvyustus* refers to a kidnapper. *Tosafot* argues that the term is also found in other places where it cannot possibly be understood as referring to a kidnapper. Moreover, as *Rashi* and *Rambam* themselves explain, the buyer cannot invalidate the purchase of a slave on account of his being a *kuvyustus,* because most slaves share this characteristic, and we therefore assume that the buyer accepted the possibility that his slave was a *kuvyustus.* But it does not stand to reason that most slaves are kidnappers. Thus *Tosafot* accepts the explanation of *Rabbenu Ḥananel* that the term *kuvyustus* refers to a gambler.

מוּכְתָּב לְמַלְכוּת Sentenced to death by the government. *Rashi, Rivan,* and others understand the term מוּכְתָּב לְמַלְכוּת (lit., "one who is written to the government") as referring to someone who has been sentenced to death by the government. According to *Rambam,* the term refers to someone who is registered as belonging to the king, so that the king can have him seized at any time and returned to his service.

הָנְהוּ קָלָא אִית לְהוּ These are talked about. Our commentary follows *Rashi* and others, who explain that if the slave is an armed bandit or someone facing the death penalty, surely that fact is widely known. Thus the buyer cannot annul the purchase because of such defects, for he too was surely aware of these defects when he bought the slave.

Rabbenu Tam explains that the Gemara means to say that if the slave is an armed bandit or is facing the death penalty, that fact is surely widely known, and it is therefore unlikely that a person would ever buy such a slave. Thus the Rabbis did not decree that a slave bought by a priest from a non-priest is forbidden to eat terumah, lest the priest discover that the slave is an armed bandit or is facing the death penalty, so that the purchase is void, for it is highly unlikely that such a slave would have been bought in the first place. (See also *Rambam* and *Ra'avad, Hilkhot Mekhirah* 15:13.)

HALAKHAH

is externally visible, the buyer was surely aware of it at the time of purchase. And if it is not externally visible, the buyer is surely not particular about such a defect, for he bought the slave to work. But if the buyer discovers a defect that affects the slave's capacity to work, the buyer can invalidate the purchase." (*Rambam, Sefer Kinyan, Hilkhot Mekhirah* 15:12; *Shulḥan Arukh, Ḥoshen Mishpat* 232:10.)

גַּנָּב אוֹ קוּבְיוּסְטוּס A thief or a gambler. "If someone buys a slave, and the slave is discovered to be an armed bandit or to be someone who has been condemned to death, such defects invalidate the entire purchase. But if the slave is discovered to be a thief or a kidnapper (following *Rashi*), the buyer cannot annul the purchase, for all slaves are assumed to have these characteristics. *Rema* notes that, according to some authorities, if the slave is found to be a kidnapper, he is treated as if he were found to be facing the death penalty, and therefore the sale is void. But the sale is not annulled if the slave is found to be a gambler (following *Rabbenu Ḥananel* and *Tosafot*)." (*Rambam, Sefer Kinyan, Hilkhot Mekhirah* 15:12-13; *Shulḥan Arukh, Ḥoshen Mishpat* 232:10.)

TRANSLATION AND COMMENTARY

מִכְּדֵי [1]The Gemara asks: **Now that both** Ulla **and** Rav Shmuel bar Rav Yehudah **agree that** by Rabbinic decree a woman who is betrothed to a priest **may not eat** terumah, [2]**what** practical **difference is there between** the reasons that they give for the decree?

אִיכָּא [3]The Gemara answers: **There are** practical **differences between** their reasons in the following cases: (1) [4]**Where** the priest **accepted** in advance any defect that he might find in his bride. In such a case there is no reason to be concerned that the betrothal will be annulled retroactively, and therefore, according to Rav Shmuel bar Rav Yehudah, the betrothed bride may eat terumah. But there is still room for concern that the bride's family will mistakenly eat terumah, and therefore, according to Ulla, the betrothed bride is not permitted to eat terumah. (2) [5]**Where** the bride's father **handed her over** to the bridegroom's agents who had been sent by the bridegroom to receive his bride, [6]**or** (3) **where** the father's agents **went** with the bridegroom's agents and accompanied the bride until she reached her bridegroom's house. In these last two cases, there is no reason to be concerned that the bride's family will inadvertently eat the terumah, since she is no longer living in her family home, and therefore, according to Ulla, the betrothed bride is permitted to eat terumah. But the possibility still exists that the bridegroom will find a defect in her that will cause him to annul the betrothal, and therefore, according to Rav Shmuel bar Rav Yehudah, the priest's bride is not permitted to eat terumah.

רַבִּי טַרְפוֹן אוֹמֵר [7]We learned in our Mishnah that there is a disagreement between the Tannaim about the maintenance that the priest must provide for his bride once the date set for their marriage has arrived. **"Rabbi Tarfon says:** If the priest wishes, **he may give** his bride **all** her maintenance **from terumah.** When she is ritually pure she can eat the terumah, and when she is not, she can sell some of the terumah and buy ordinary food for herself with the proceeds. Rabbi Akiva says: The priest must give his bride half of her

[1]מִכְּדֵי בֵּין לְמָר וּבֵין לְמָר לָא אָכְלָה, [2]מַאי בֵּינַיְיהוּ? [3]אִיכָּא בֵּינַיְיהוּ: [4]קִבֵּל, [5]מָסַר, [6]וְהָלַךְ.

[7]״רַבִּי טַרְפוֹן אוֹמֵר: נוֹתְנִין לָהּ

LITERAL TRANSLATION

[1]Now since both this Sage and that Sage [agree that] she does not eat, [2]what is [the difference] between them?

[3][The difference] between them is: [4][Where] he accepted, [5][where] he handed [her] over, [6]and [where] he went.

[7]"Rabbi Tarfon says: We give it

RASHI

קבל מסר והלך – קיבל עליו בעל את המומין, לסימפון – ליכא למיחש, לשמא תשקה לאחיה ולאחותה – איכא למיחש. **מסר** – האב לשלוחי הבעל, או שהלכו שלוחי האב עם שלוחי הבעל – ליכא למיחש שמא תשקה לאחיה ולאחותה, דהא ליתנהו גבה, ואיכא למיחש לסימפון.

NOTES

קִבֵּל, מָסַר, וְהָלַךְ **Where he accepted, where he handed her over, and where he went.** Because of its extreme brevity, this expression has received various interpretations. Our commentary follows *Rashi* and others, who explain that there are practical differences between the two rulings in three different cases. If the priest accepts any defect that he may find in his bride, there is no concern that the betrothal will be annulled retroactively, but there is concern that the bride's family may mistakenly eat terumah. And if the bride's father hands her over to the bridegroom's agents, or if the father's agents accompany the bridegroom's agents, there is no concern that the bride's family will mistakenly eat terumah, but there is concern that the bridegroom will find a defect that will annul the betrothal.

Ri (cited by *Tosafot* above, 48b, s.v. רב אסי) explains that in the last two cases as well there is no concern that the betrothal will be annulled retroactively, for once the bride has been handed over to the bridegroom's agents, there is little chance that the bridegroom will discover a defect that will annul the betrothal. But there is concern that the terumah may be eaten by someone to whom it is forbidden, for the bride may give some of the terumah to the agents who are accompanying her to her bridegroom's house.

Meiri maintains that the Gemara is referring here to two cases: (1) Where the priest accepted any defect that he might find in his bride, and (2) where the bride's father handed her over to the bridegroom's agents and went with them to the bridegroom's house. In the first case there is no concern that the betrothal will be annulled retroactively, whereas in the second case there is no concern that the bride's family will mistakenly partake of terumah, for her father, who is an adult, will take care not to eat her terumah.

Rabbenu Crescas Vidal also argues that the Gemara here is referring to only two cases: (1) Where the priest accepted any defect that he might find in his bride, so that there is no concern that the betrothal will be annulled retroactively, and (2) where the bride's father handed her over to the bridegroom's agents and then went on his way, so that there is no concern that that bride's family will mistakenly eat terumah.

Ra'avad explains that the Gemara is referring to a single case, in which the father accepted betrothal on behalf of his daughter, immediately handed her over to her bridegroom's agents, and then went on his way. In such a case, there is no room for concern that the bride's family will mistakenly eat terumah, but there is reason to suspect that some defect may still be discovered that will annul the betrothal retroactively.

הַכֹּל תְּרוּמָה, וכו׳״. [1]אָמַר אַבַּיֵי: מַחֲלוֹקֶת בְּבַת כֹּהֵן לְכֹהֵן. [2]אֲבָל בְּבַת יִשְׂרָאֵל לְכֹהֵן, [3]דִּבְרֵי הַכֹּל מֶחֱצָה חוּלִּין וּמֶחֱצָה תְּרוּמָה.

[4]וְאָמַר אַבַּיֵי: מַחֲלוֹקֶת בַּאֲרוּסָה. [5]אֲבָל בִּנְשׂוּאָה, [6]דִּבְרֵי הַכֹּל מֶחֱצָה חוּלִּין וּמֶחֱצָה תְּרוּמָה.

LITERAL TRANSLATION

all to her [from] terumah, etc." [1]Abaye said: The dispute is about the daughter of a priest [betrothed] to a priest. [2]But regarding the daughter of an Israelite [betrothed] to a priest, [3]all agree [that] half is [from] ordinary food and half [from] terumah.

[4]And Abaye said: The dispute is about one who is betrothed. [5]But regarding one who is married, [6]all agree [that] half is [from] unconsecrated food and half [from] terumah.

TRANSLATION AND COMMENTARY

maintenance from ordinary produce, so that she will have food to eat while she is ritually impure, and he is permitted to give her half of her maintenance from terumah, which she can eat while she is ritually pure."

[1]**Abaye said: The disagreement** between Rabbi Tarfon and Rabbi Akiva **is** specifically **about** a situation in which **the daughter of a priest** (who in any case is permitted to eat terumah when she is ritually pure) is **betrothed to a priest.** [2]**But regarding the daughter of a non-priest** who is **betrothed to a priest,** [3]**both** Tannaim **agree that** the priest must give his bride **half** of her maintenance **from ordinary produce and** that he may give her only **half** of her maintenance **from terumah.** The daughter of a priest is familiar with the precautions that must be taken to protect terumah from ritual defilement and with the practice of selling terumah during periods of ritual impurity. Therefore, argues Rabbi Tarfon, if the daughter of a priest is betrothed to a priest, and the time set for their marriage has arrived, the priest may give his bride all of her maintenance from terumah, for she will certainly deal with the terumah properly while she is ritually impure. But if the daughter of a non-priest is betrothed to a priest, even Rabbi Tarfon agrees that the bridegroom must give her half of her maintenance from ordinary produce, for she is not yet sufficiently familiar with the precautions that must be taken to protect terumah from defilement and should not be given all her maintenance from terumah.

וְאָמַר אַבַּיֵי [4]**Furthermore, Abaye said: The disagreement** between Rabbi Tarfon and Rabbi Akiva **is** specifically **about** the case of **a betrothed bride** whose wedding date has already arrived but whose marriage has not yet taken place. [5]**But if she is** already **married,** and is being maintained by her husband through a third party, [6]**both** Tannaim **agree that** the priest must give his wife **half** of her maintenance **from ordinary produce and** that he may not give her more than **half** of her maintenance **from terumah.** While the daughter of a priest is living in her father's house, her father is available to sell terumah and buy ordinary produce for her to eat while she is ritually impure. But once she is married and has left her father's house, there is

RASHI

בת כהן – בקיאה היא בשמירת תרומה, ולמוכרה בימי טומאתה. **בת ישראל** – אינה בקיאה בכך. **בארוסה** – ובת כהן, דהואיל והיא בבית אביה – טרח אביה למכור תרומה בחולין לימי טומאה, לפי שהוא רגיל בכך. **אבל בנשואה** – שנותן לה בעלה מזונות בביתה, כגון משרה אשתו על ידי שליש, דתנן במתניתין (כתובות סד,ב). **מחצה חולין** – לפי שכל כבודה בת מלך פנימה, ואביה ואחיה אינן אצלה שיתעסקו בצרכיה.

NOTES

מַחֲלוֹקֶת בְּבַת כֹּהֵן **The dispute is about the daughter of a priest.** Our commentary follows *Rashi* and most Rishonim, who explain that Rabbi Tarfon maintains that the daughter of a priest who was betrothed to a priest may be given all her maintenance from terumah because she is familiar with the precautions that must be taken to protect terumah from ritual impurity and with the practice of selling terumah during periods of ritual impurity. But the daughter of a non-priest who is betrothed to a priest must be given half of her maintenance from ordinary produce, because the laws of terumah are all new to her, and we are concerned that she will not handle the terumah properly while she is ritually impure.

Rivan and *Rid* explain the distinction differently: The daughter of a priest who is betrothed to a priest may be given all of her maintenance from terumah, because when she is ritually impure she can exchange the terumah with her father for ordinary produce and thus not suffer any loss. But the daughter of a non-priest who is betrothed to a priest must be given half of her maintenance from ordinary produce, so that when she is ritually impure she will not have to sell terumah at a discount to a priest and then buy ordinary produce at the full price, suffering a loss in the process.

HALAKHAH

מֶחֱצָה חוּלִּין **Half from unconsecrated food.** "If a woman is married to a priest and he is maintaining her through a third party, he must give her half of her maintenance from ordinary produce and may not give her more than half of her maintenance from terumah." (*Rambam, Sefer Nashim, Hilkhot Ishut* 12:13.)

TRANSLATION AND COMMENTARY

nobody to arrange that she has food to eat while she is ritually impure, and it is not fitting that the woman be required to go herself and sell the terumah in order to buy ordinary food with the proceeds. In such a case, even Rabbi Tarfon agrees that the priest must provide half of his wife's maintenance from ordinary produce, so that she can use it for her food during periods of ritual impurity.

תַּנְיָא [1]The Gemara notes that **the same** thing **was also taught** in the following Baraita: **"Rabbi Tarfon says:** If the priest whose wedding date has already passed wishes, **he may give** his bride **all** her maintenance **from terumah.** [2]**Rabbi Akiva** disagrees and **says:** The priest must give his bride **half** of her maintenance **from ordinary produce, and** only half **from terumah.** [3]**In what circumstances does this** dispute between Rabbi Tarfon and Rabbi Akiva **apply?** [4]**Where the daughter of a priest was betrothed to a priest.** [5]**But regarding the daughter of a non-priest** who is **betrothed to a priest,** [6]**both** Sages **agree that** the priest must give his bride **half** of her maintenance **from ordinary produce and** that he may give her only **half from terumah.** [7]**In what circumstances does this apply?** [8]**Where** the daughter of a priest **is betrothed** to a priest, and her wedding date has already arrived, but the marriage has not yet taken place. [9]**But if she is** already **married,** and is being maintained by her husband through a third party, [10]**both** Sages **agree that** the priest must give his wife **half** of her maintenance **from ordinary produce and** only **half from terumah."** [11]The Baraita now cites a number of opinions that do not appear in our Mishnah: **"Rabbi Yehudah ben Betera says:** The priest **may give** his bride **two-thirds** of her maintenance from **terumah and** only **one-third** from **ordinary produce.** [12]**Rabbi Yehudah says:** The priest **may give** his bride **all** her maintenance **from terumah,** and when she is ritually impure, [13]**she can sell** some of the terumah **and buy ordinary produce with the money.** [14]**Rabbi Shimon ben Gamliel says: Wherever it is stated** that the priest may give his bride all her maintenance from **terumah,** [15]it is on condition that **he gives her twice as much as** she would need if she were to receive her maintenance **from ordinary produce."**

[1]תַּנְיָא נַמִי הָכִי: ״רַבִּי טַרְפוֹן אוֹמֵר: נוֹתְנִין לָהּ הַכֹּל תְּרוּמָה. [2]רַבִּי עֲקִיבָא אוֹמֵר: מֶחֱצָה חוּלִּין וּמֶחֱצָה תְּרוּמָה. [3]בַּמֶּה דְּבָרִים אֲמוּרִים? [4]בְּבַת כֹּהֵן לְכֹהֵן. [5]אֲבָל בַּת יִשְׂרָאֵל לְכֹהֵן, [6]דִּבְרֵי הַכֹּל מֶחֱצָה חוּלִּין וּמֶחֱצָה תְּרוּמָה. [7]בַּמֶּה דְּבָרִים אֲמוּרִים? [8]בַּאֲרוּסָה. [9]אֲבָל בִּנְשׂוּאָה, [10]דִּבְרֵי הַכֹּל מֶחֱצָה חוּלִּין וּמֶחֱצָה תְּרוּמָה. [11]רַבִּי יְהוּדָה בֶּן בְּתֵירָא אוֹמֵר: נוֹתְנִין לָהּ שְׁתֵּי יָדוֹת שֶׁל תְּרוּמָה וְאַחַת שֶׁל חוּלִּין. [12]רַבִּי יְהוּדָה אוֹמֵר: נוֹתֵן לָהּ הַכֹּל תְּרוּמָה, [13]וְהִיא מוֹכֶרֶת וְלוֹקַחַת בַּדָּמִים חוּלִּין. [14]רַבָּן שִׁמְעוֹן בֶּן גַּמְלִיאֵל אוֹמֵר: כָּל מָקוֹם שֶׁהוּזְכְּרָה תְּרוּמָה, [15]נוֹתְנִין לָהּ כִּפְלַיִם בְּחוּלִּין״.

LITERAL TRANSLATION

[1]It was also taught thus: "Rabbi Tarfon says: We give it all to her [from] terumah. [2]Rabbi Akiva says: Half [from] unconsecrated food and half [from] terumah. [3]In what [case] are these things said? [4]Regarding the daughter of a priest [betrothed] to a priest. [5]But regarding the daughter of an Israelite [betrothed] to a priest, [6]all agree [that] half is [from] unconsecrated food and half [from] terumah. [7]In what [case] are these things said? [8]Regarding one who is betrothed. [9]But regarding one who is married, [10]all agree [that] half is [from] unconsecrated food and half [from] terumah. [11]Rabbi Yehudah ben Betera says: We give her two parts (lit., 'hands') of terumah and one of unconsecrated food. [12]Rabbi Yehudah says: He gives everything to her [from] terumah, [13]and she sells [it] and buys unconsecrated food with the money. [14]Rabban Shimon ben Gamliel says: Wherever terumah was mentioned, [15]we give her twice as much as from unconsecrated food."

RASHI

רבי יהודה אומר נותנין לה הכל תרומה כו׳ — בין רבי יהודה לרבי טרפון איכא, דאילו רבי טרפון סבר נותנין לה תרומה כדי מזונותיה, ואף על פי שהיא צריכה לחולין, ובאה למכור תרומה — אין דמי תרומה מגיעין ליקח בהן חולין, שהרי יקרים הם מן התרומה, שהכל קופצים עליהן. ולרבי יהודה נותנין לה תרומה כשיעור שהיא באה ליקח מחצה חולין לא תפחות מן דמי מחצית חולין, אבל טורח מכירה — מוטל עליה למכור, לתתה תחת חולין. **נותנין לה תרומה כפלים בחולין** — קסבר: לא מטרחינן לה למוכרה בשוייה, אלא נותן לה תרומה הרבה כדי שתתננה בזול, ותמצא לוקחין הרבה.

SAGES

רַבִּי יְהוּדָה בֶּן בְּתֵירָא Rabbi Yehudah ben Betera. See *Ketubot*, Part I, pp. 189-90.

NOTES

נוֹתְנִין לָהּ הַכֹּל תְּרוּמָה We give it all to her from terumah. The Jerusalem Talmud cites a Baraita that explains the dispute as follows: Rabbi Tarfon maintains that a priest may give his bride all her maintenance from terumah, for he has a great deal of terumah in his possession, and there is no reason to burden him with the obligation of providing his bride with ordinary produce. Rabbi Akiva maintains that the priest must give his bride half of her maintenance from ordinary produce, for a woman is often in a state of ritual impurity, and she might render the terumah in her possession ritually impure.

שְׁתֵּי יָדוֹת שֶׁל תְּרוּמָה Two parts of terumah. *Maharshal*

[1]מַאי בֵּינַיְיהוּ?
[2]אִיכָּא בֵּינַיְיהוּ טִירְחָא.
[3]״הַיָּבָם אֵינוֹ מַאֲכִיל בִּתְרוּמָה״.
[4]מַאי טַעֲמָא? ״קִנְיַן כַּסְפּוֹ״
[5]אָמַר רַחֲמָנָא. [6]וְהַאי קִנְיַן דְּאָחִיו הוּא.

LITERAL TRANSLATION

[1]What is [the difference] between them? [2][The difference] between them is effort. [3]"A *yavam* does not feed [his sister-in-law] terumah." [4]What is the reason? [5]The Torah (lit., "the Merciful One") said: "The acquisition of his money." [6]And this one is the acquisition of his brother.

TRANSLATION AND COMMENTARY

Terumah has a much narrower market than ordinary produce, for it is forbidden to most Jews. If the priest decides to give his bride all her maintenance from terumah, he must give her a much larger quantity of produce than she would need if he were to provide her with ordinary produce. Since she has more terumah to sell, she will still receive enough money to cover the cost of the ordinary produce she needs for her periods of ritual impurity.

מַאי בֵּינַיְיהוּ [1]The Gemara asks: **What is the** practical **difference between** the viewpoints of Rabbi Yehudah and Rabban Shimon ben Gamliel?

אִיכָּא [2]The Gemara answers: **The** practical **difference between** the two positions **is** as follows: According to Rabbi Yehudah, the priest's bride is required to make an **effort** to find a buyer who is willing to purchase the terumah at a high price. According to Rabban Shimon ben Gamliel, she is given a much larger quantity of terumah so that she will be able to lower the price and find a buyer with greater ease.

הַיָּבָם [3]The next clause of our Mishnah stated: **"A *yavam* does not give his sister-in-law terumah to eat."** [4]The Gemara asks: **What is the reason** that a widow who is tied to her deceased husband's brother by the levirate bond may not eat terumah? [5]It is because **the Torah says** (Leviticus 22:11): "But if a priest acquires any person as **the acquisition of his money,** he may eat of it [the terumah]." Terumah is permitted not only to a priest, but also to those members of his household who are considered acquisitions obtained by his money — for example, his non-Jewish slaves. For this reason a woman who is betrothed to a priest may eat terumah, because she too is in a sense an acquisition obtained by means of the priest's money. [6]**But this** woman who is tied to her brother-in-law by the levirate bond **was acquired by** the *yavam*'s **brother,**

RASHI

איכא בינייהו טירחא — בין רבי יהודה לרבן שמעון. והאי קנין אחיו הוא — וכי מיית ליה פקע ליה קניינו. אלא כנסה — הרי היא אשתו לכל דבר, והכתוב קראה אשתו,

NOTES

points out that the average menstrual cycle is thirty days and that a woman's menstrual bleeding usually lasts three days. Since the woman remains ritually impure until seven days have passed after her period has ended, the average woman is ritually impure for ten days in a month. Thus a woman who is betrothed to a priest must be given one-third of her maintenance from ordinary produce, so that she will have food to eat when terumah is forbidden to her.

מַאי בֵּינַיְיהוּ? **What is the difference between them?** At first glance, Rabbi Tarfon and Rabbi Yehudah are of the same opinion, for they both say that the priest is permitted to give his bride all her maintenance from terumah. *Rashi* explains the difference between the viewpoints of these Tannaim as follows: According to Rabbi Tarfon, when the priest gives his bride her maintenance from terumah, he need not give her any more than she would need if she were to receive her maintenance from ordinary produce. Even though she will have to sell some of the terumah when she is ritually impure, and even though she will have to sell the terumah at a discounted price, the bridegroom need not increase her maintenance when he provides it exclusively from terumah. Rabbi Yehudah disagrees and says that while the priest may give his bride all her maintenance from terumah, he must give her slightly more than she would need if he were to provide her with maintenance from ordinary produce, so that when she sells some of her terumah when she is ritually impure, she will be able to buy enough ordinary produce with the proceeds to satisfy her needs. *Talmidei Rabbenu Yonah* explains the two viewpoints in the opposite way. Rabbi Tarfon says that when the priest provides his bride with her maintenance exclusively from terumah, he must give her slightly more than he would if he were to give her ordinary produce. And Rabbi Yehudah apparently says that even when the priest gives his wife all her maintenance from terumah, he is not required to give her anything extra.

Rashi argues that when the Gemara asks what "the practical difference" is between the two positions, it is trying to explain the difference between the viewpoints of Rabbi Yehudah and Rabban Shimon ben Gamliel. It answers that they disagree about whether the priest's bride is required to exert herself to find a buyer for her terumah who will buy it at the market price. According to Rabbi Yehudah, the bride must make the effort, and the priest must give her only slightly more than she would need if he were to provide her with maintenance from ordinary produce. According to Rabban Shimon ben Gamliel, she is not required to exert herself, and the priest must therefore give her a much larger quantity of terumah, so that she will be able to lower the price significantly and find a buyer with ease.

In the view of *Ra'ah* and others, the Gemara is trying to explain the dispute between Rabbi Akiva and Rabbi Yehudah. Rabbi Akiva maintains that the bride is not required to exert herself and sell some of her terumah when she is ritually impure, and she must therefore be given half of her maintenance from ordinary produce. Rabbi Yehudah maintains that we obligate the bride to exert herself to sell some of her terumah, and the priest may therefore give her all her maintenance from terumah.

״קִנְיַן כַּסְפּוֹ״ אָמַר רַחֲמָנָא **The Torah said: "The acquisition of his money."** *Rashi* and *Rabbenu Tam* disagree about whether by Torah law a woman who is tied by the levirate

TRANSLATION AND COMMENTARY

and not by the *yavam* himself. She continues to be regarded as the acquisition of her deceased husband until the levirate marriage is consummated — i.e., completed by sexual intercourse.

עָשְׂתָה שִׁשָּׁה חֳדָשִׁים [1] The Gemara now proceeds to examine the next clause of our Mishnah, which stated: **"If a** woman was given twelve months to prepare for her wedding, and **six months** passed while she was betrothed **to her bridegroom,** at which point the bridegroom died, and then another six months passed while she was Halakhically tied to the *yavam*; or even if the entire twelve months passed while she was betrothed to the bridegroom, except for one day after her bridegroom's death during which she was tied to the *yavam*; or if the entire twelve months passed while she was tied to the *yavam*, except for one day at the very beginning during which she was betrothed to her bridegroom before he died, in all these cases she may not eat terumah." [2] The Gemara asks: **Now,** if the entire twelve months passed while the woman was betrothed **to the bridegroom,** except for one day after his death during which she was tied to the *yavam*, and the Mishnah **said** that in such a case the woman may **not** eat terumah, **was it necessary** for the Mishnah **to mention** that she may not eat terumah if the entire twelve months passed while the woman was tied **to the *yavam*** except for one day at the very beginning during which she was betrothed to her bridegroom before he died?

זוֹ וְאֵין צָרִיךְ [3] The Gemara answers: The Tanna **taught** the Mishnah in the style of **"this and it is unnecessary to say this."** It is true that the last part of the Mishnah's ruling is obvious, but the Mishnah was worded in this way for stylistic reasons. First the Tanna taught a case that he needed to discuss ("this"), and he then proceeded to a case that was obvious ("and it is not necessary to say this"). The latter case was not really needed, and was only introduced because of this accepted style of arranging cases in an anticlimactic way.

זוֹ מִשְׁנָה רִאשׁוֹנָה [4] The final clause of our Mishnah states: "The ruling that a woman who is betrothed to a priest may eat terumah if the time set for their marriage has arrived, even if the marriage has not yet taken place, **is** the position of **the early Mishnah.** But the court of a later generation ruled that she may not eat terumah until she and her bridegroom actually enter the bridal chamber for marriage." The Gemara asks: **What was the reasoning** of the later court?

[1] ״עָשְׂתָה שִׁשָּׁה חֳדָשִׁים בִּפְנֵי הַבַּעַל״. [2] הָשְׁתָּא בִּפְנֵי הַבַּעַל אָמְרַתְּ לָא, בִּפְנֵי הַיָּבָם מִיבַּעֲיָא? [3] ״זוֹ וְאֵין צָרִיךְ לוֹמַר זוֹ״ קָתָנֵי. [4] ״זוֹ מִשְׁנָה רִאשׁוֹנָה, כו׳״. מַאי טַעֲמָא?

LITERAL TRANSLATION

[1] "[If] she spent six months with the husband." [2] Now that with the husband you have said not, is it necessary [to mention] with the *yavam*?

[3] He teaches "this and it is unnecessary to say this."

[4] "This was the first Mishnah, etc." What is the reason?

RASHI

דכתיב (דברים כה) ״ולקחה לו לאשה״ — דקנייה בביאה. וכי היכי דקידושי ביאה מאכילין בארוסה, דאיתקוש הוויות להדדי — כך מאכילין ביבמה. השתא בפני הבעל — חוץ מיום אחד אמרת לא אכלה. כולם בפני היבם, דעל ידו אין לה לאכול, דלאו קנינו היא — מיבעיא ליה למימר דלא אכלה?

NOTES

bond to her brother-in-law who is a priest may eat terumah. *Rashi* explains that the verse cited here is the actual source of the law that a *yavam* does not enable his sister-in-law to eat terumah, for it is by Torah law that a woman may not eat terumah by virtue of the levirate bond.

According to *Rabbenu Tam,* who maintains that whenever a woman was entitled to eat terumah by virtue of the marital bond with her husband, she continues by Torah law to be entitled to eat terumah by virtue of the levirate bond to her brother-in-law, the verse cited here is not the actual source of the law, but merely a Biblical support for a Rabbinic enactment (see also *Ri HaLavan*).

זוֹ וְאֵין צָרִיךְ לוֹמַר זוֹ This and it is unnecessary to say this. Our commentary follows the reading and interpretation of *Rashi.* Several Rishonim object that even if the Mishnah was taught in the style of "this and it is unnecessary to say this," it should not have taught a case as obvious as that of the woman who was tied to the *yavam* for twelve months apart from the first day, during which she was betrothed to her bridegroom. A number of different readings and interpretations are suggested. *Tosafot* and others explain the Gemara's question as follows: If the entire twelve months passed while the woman was betrothed to the bridegroom, except for one day following the bridegroom's death during which she was tied to the *yavam*, and the Mishnah said that in such a case the woman may not eat terumah, was it necessary to mention that she may not eat terumah if she was betrothed to the

HALAKHAH

זוֹ מִשְׁנָה רִאשׁוֹנָה This was the first Mishnah. "By Torah law, a woman betrothed to a priest may eat terumah, but the Rabbis forbade her to do so until she enters the bridal chamber, lest she feed her father or siblings terumah while living in her father's house during the period of her betrothal." (*Rambam, Sefer Zeraim, Hilkhot Terumot* 6:3.)

[1]אֲמַר עוּלָּא, וְאִיתֵּימָא רַב שְׁמוּאֵל בַּר יְהוּדָה: [2]מִשּׁוּם סִימְפּוֹן.
[3]בִּשְׁלָמָא לְעוּלָּא, [4]קַמַּיְיתָא שֶׁמָּא יִמְזְגוּ לָהּ כּוֹס בְּבֵית אָבִיהָ, [5]וּבַתְרַיְיתָא מִשּׁוּם סִימְפּוֹן. [58B] [6]אֶלָּא לְרַב שְׁמוּאֵל בַּר יְהוּדָה, [7]קַמַּיְיתָא מִשּׁוּם סִימְפּוֹן [8]וּבַתְרַיְיתָא מִשּׁוּם סִימְפּוֹן! [9]מַאי בֵּינַיְיהוּ?

LITERAL TRANSLATION

[1]Ulla, and some say [it was] Rav Shmuel bar Yehudah, said: [2]Because of a condition annulling [the betrothal].

[3]Granted that according to Ulla, [4][the reason for] the first [ruling was] lest they pour a cup [of terumah wine] for her in her father's house, [5]and [the reason for] the last [ruling was] because of a condition annulling [the betrothal]. [58B] [6]But according to Rav Shmuel bar Yehudah, [7]the first [ruling was] because of a condition annulling [the betrothal] [8]and the last [ruling was] because of a condition annulling [the betrothal]! [9]What is [the difference] between them?

TRANSLATION AND COMMENTARY

אֲמַר עוּלָּא [1]**Ulla, and some say** that **it was Rav Shmuel bar Yehudah, said** in reply: The later court maintains that by Torah law a woman who is betrothed to a priest may eat terumah immediately upon her betrothal. But it decreed that she may not eat terumah until the marriage process has been completed, [2]**because** it feared that the bridegroom might find **some defect** in his bride **that would** retroactively **annul the betrothal.** It would then turn out that when she ate the terumah she was not betrothed to the priest and thus the terumah was forbidden to her. But if the bride has already entered the bridal chamber, she may eat terumah, even if she has not yet had sexual intercourse with her husband, for then there is no longer any concern that the groom will find a defect in his bride that will annul the betrothal.

בִּשְׁלָמָא לְעוּלָּא [3]The Gemara objects: **Granted that according to Ulla,** who disagreed with Rav Shmuel bar Rav Yehudah about the reasoning of the early Mishnah (above, 57b), we can understand the two rulings recorded in the Mishnah. [4]According to the **early** Mishnah, the Rabbis decreed that a betrothed woman should not eat terumah, **lest a cup of terumah wine would be poured for her** while she was still living **in her father's house,** and she might give the terumah to other members of her family. But if the time set for her marriage has already arrived, she may eat terumah even if the marriage has not yet taken place, for once the bridegroom is responsible for his bride's support, he sets aside a special place for her to eat, and there is no longer any concern that other members of her family will eat her terumah. [5]**And** according to **the later court,** the Rabbis made a second decree, prohibiting a betrothed woman to eat terumah until she and her bridegroom actually entered the bridal chamber, **because** they feared that until then the bridegroom might still find **some defect** in his bride that **would** give him grounds to **annul the betrothal** retroactively. [58B] [6]**But according to Rav Shmuel bar Yehudah,** there is a difficulty. [7]For Rav Shmuel bar Yehudah said, above, that the Sages who formulated **the early** Mishnah **decreed** that a betrothed woman was not permitted to eat terumah, **because** they were concerned that the bridegroom might find **some defect** in his bride that **would** retroactively **annul the betrothal.** [8]**And** here he says that **the later court** also based its decree on the fear that the bridegroom might find **some defect** in his bride **that would** retroactively **annul the betrothal.** [9]**What**, then, **is the** basis for the **difference between** the two decrees?

RASHI

קמייתא — משנה ראשונה שאוסרת משעת אירוסין, שהתורה התירתה והם גזרו עד שיגיע זמן — לא גזור מפני סימפון, אלא שמא תשקה, הלכך, משנתחייב לזונה, דמייחד לה דוכתא, וליכא למיחש לשמא תשקה — שריוה. **ובתרייתא** — משנה אחרונה, שחזרו וגזרו עד שתכנס לחופה — חשו לסימפון. **אלא לרב שמואל בר יהודה** — דאמר לעיל נמי טעם משנה ראשונה משום סימפון והשתא נמי מוקי טעם בית דין של אחריהם משום סימפון. **מאי בינייהו** — כלומר, מה ראו ראשונים להתירה מהגיע זמן ואילך, ומה ראו אחרונים לומר עד שתכנס לחופה?

NOTES

bridegroom for six months and then tied to the *yavam* for six months? The Gemara answers: The Tanna taught the Mishnah in the style of "not only this but also this [לֹא זוֹ אַף זוֹ קָתָנֵי]." The Mishnah began by mentioning a straightforward matter, and proceeded from there to a more complicated subject. Not only does the woman not eat terumah if she was betrothed to the bridegroom for six months and then tied to the *yavam* for a further six months, but she does not even eat terumah if she was betrothed to the bridegroom for the entire twelve months with the exception of the last day, during which she was tied to the *yavam* (see also *Ramban*, *Ra'ah*, and *Ritva*).

מִשּׁוּם סִימְפּוֹן **Because of a condition annulling the betrothal.** *Meiri* notes that, according to *Rambam* and others, the Rabbinic decree forbidding a woman who is betrothed to a priest from partaking of terumah was enacted solely because of the concern that she might give the terumah to other members of her family, and not because of the fear that some defect might be found that would retroactively annul the betrothal. The Jerusalem Talmud and *Sifrei* adduce Scriptural support for the law that a woman who is betrothed to a priest may not eat

TRANSLATION AND COMMENTARY

אִיכָּא [1]The Gemara explains: **There is** a dispute **between** the early Mishnah and the later court about **the external examination** of the bride conducted by the bridegroom's female relatives. Before the time set for the marriage arrives, the bridegroom arranges to have his bride examined by his female relatives to ensure that she is free of hidden defects. [2]The early Mishnah **maintains** that **an external examination,** even though it may be superficial, **is considered a** valid **examination,** and once it is completed, it is unlikely that the bridegroom will find a defect in his bride that will annul the betrothal. Thus the bride is permitted to eat terumah once the time set for her marriage has arrived. [3]**But** the later court **maintains** that **an external examination** of this kind **is not considered** a valid **examination.** Only after the bride and the bridegroom are alone in the bridal chamber, and the bridegroom himself has examined his bride, do we say that it is unlikely that he will find a defect that could annul the betrothal. Thus the bride is forbidden to eat terumah until she enters the bridal chamber.

MISHNAH הַמַּקְדִּישׁ [4]Elsewhere (above, 46b), the Mishnah establishes that a husband is obligated to maintain his wife and that he is entitled to the proceeds of her handiwork. In addition to providing for his wife's maintenance, the husband is required to give her a weekly allowance, in return for which he is entitled to her surplus handiwork — her earnings from tasks that she is not legally required to perform for her husband (see below, 64b). The present Mishnah discusses whether or not a husband is empowered to consecrate to the Temple treasury the proceeds of his wife's future handiwork or her future surplus earnings: **If someone consecrates** the proceeds of **his wife's** future **handiwork** to the Temple treasury, the wife's handiwork does not thereby become consecrated, [5]and **she may** do her **work and maintain herself** from the proceeds. [6]**If** the husband **consecrates** his wife's **surplus** earnings, **Rabbi Meir says:**

[1]אִיכָּא בֵּינַיְיהוּ בְּדִיקַת חוּץ. [2]מָר סָבַר: בְּדִיקַת חוּץ שְׁמָהּ בְּדִיקָה, [3]וּמָר סָבַר: בְּדִיקַת חוּץ לֹא שְׁמָהּ בְּדִיקָה.

מִשְׁנָה [4]הַמַּקְדִּישׁ מַעֲשֵׂה יְדֵי אִשְׁתּוֹ, [5]הֲרֵי זוֹ עוֹשָׂה וְאוֹכֶלֶת. [6]הַמּוֹתָר, רַבִּי מֵאִיר

LITERAL TRANSLATION

[1][The difference] between them is an external examination. [2]One Sage maintains: An external examination is considered an examination, [3]and one Sage maintains: An external examination is not considered an examination.

MISHNAH [4][If] someone consecrates the handiwork of his wife, [5]she works and eats. [6][If he consecrates] the surplus, Rabbi Meir

RASHI

מר סבר – משנה ראשונה. **בדיקת חוץ** – שבדקה ביד קרובותיו. **שמה בדיקה** – וקודם שיוציא מעותיו במזונותיה כבר בדקה. הלכך, תו לא חיישינן לסימפון. ובית דין של אחריהם סברי: אינה בדיקה עד שמתייחד עמה הוא עצמו ובודקה.

משנה מעשה ידי אשתו – במתניתין (כתובות סד,ב) מפרש: מה היא עושה לו – משקל חמש סלעים כו׳. **הרי זו עושה ואוכלת** – אין מעשה ידיה קדוש על פיו. ובגמרא מפרש לה. **המותר** – הקדיש את מותר מעשה ידי אשתו מה שהיא עושה לו יותר על הראוי שפסקו חכמים, ולא הקדיש מעשה ידיה עצמן.

BACKGROUND

בְּדִיקַת חוּץ An external examination. If a man discovers a defect in his wife that was hitherto unknown to him, he can have the marriage annulled. This provision refers to conspicuous physical flaws that can be seen upon inspection, and it is generally assumed that a man cannot be sexually intimate with a woman without noticing defects of this kind. In the opinion of Rav Shmuel bar Yehudah, the difficulty is whether an external examination (even if conducted by women) can discover these defects. He maintains that in the opinion of the later Mishnah, since a woman with a defect seeks to conceal it, dressing and behaving in such a way as to prevent the defect from being visible, we cannot be certain that an external examination will reveal a defect in the woman that will lead to the annulment of the marriage.

הַמַּקְדִּישׁ מַעֲשֵׂה יְדֵי אִשְׁתּוֹ If someone consecrates the handiwork of his wife. A person may consecrate things that belong to him to the Temple or for other sacred purposes. A husband's consecration of his wife's handiwork raises two problems. The first is how consecration can apply to something that does not yet exist, for the husband is not consecrating something that his wife has already made, but something that she will make in the future. And the second problem is whether a husband has full property rights over his wife's handiwork, or whether these rights depend on various conditions. If his rights can be withdrawn, they are insufficient to permit consecration.

NOTES

terumah until she actually enters the bridal chamber from the verse (Numbers 18:11): "Everyone who is ritually pure in your house shall eat of it," which teaches that only someone who is already "in your house" may eat terumah, and this excludes a betrothed woman who is still living in her paternal home.

בְּדִיקַת חוּץ An external examination. Most Rishonim follow *Rashi,* who explains that "an external examination" is one that is conducted by the female relatives of the bridegroom, who examine his bride for any hidden defects. *Rashba* notes that if there is a bathhouse in the town where a thorough examination of the bride can be made, then even an examination conducted by the bridegroom's female relatives is regarded as a valid examination, after which it is considered unlikely that the bridegroom will find a defect in his bride that will annul the betrothal (see below, 75b). Here we are dealing with a superficial examination conducted by the bridegroom's female relatives. *Rivan* cites an alternative explanation, according to which "an external examination" is one conducted by the bridegroom before he enters the bridal chamber. This lacks the thoroughness of the examination that he can conduct after the couple have entered the bridal chamber.

הַמַּקְדִּישׁ מַעֲשֵׂה יְדֵי אִשְׁתּוֹ If someone consecrates the handiwork of his wife. *Melekhet Shlomo* explains that since the previous Mishnah dealt with an issue involving terumah and ordinary produce, our Mishnah continues with a discussion of an issue involving consecrated property. Our Mishnah, which deals with the consecration of a wife's handiwork, also serves as an introduction to the next Mishnah, which lists the tasks that a married woman must perform for her husband.

הַמּוֹתָר The surplus. *Rashi, Rivan,* and others explain that this second clause of the Mishnah is unconnected to the first. The first clause of the Mishnah refers to a case in which the husband consecrates his wife's future handiwork,

HALAKHAH

הַמַּקְדִּישׁ מַעֲשֵׂה יְדֵי אִשְׁתּוֹ If someone consecrates the handiwork of his wife. "If a husband consecrates his wife's handiwork, she may do her handiwork and maintain herself from the proceeds. Her surplus earnings are not

TRANSLATION AND COMMENTARY

Her surplus earnings **become consecrated.** [1]**Rabbi Yoḥanan HaSandlar** disagrees and **says: They do not become consecrated.**

GEMARA **אָמַר רַב הוּנָא אָמַר רַב** [2]The Gemara begins with an Amoraic statement, the validity of which it will later judge in the light of our Mishnah. **Rav Huna said in the name of Rav: A woman can say to her husband:** [3]**"I will not** exercise my right to **be maintained** by you, **and I will not work** for you." By waiving her right to maintenance, the wife is able to deprive her husband of his right to the proceeds of her handiwork. [4]The Gemara explains the basis of Rav Huna's ruling: Rav Huna **maintains** that **when the Rabbis enacted** the rights and duties of husband and wife, the wife's right to **maintenance was the primary enactment,** instituted for the woman's benefit to guarantee her maintenance if she proved unable to support herself by her own earnings. [5]**And** in return for the husband's duty to maintain his wife, the Rabbis enacted that he should be entitled to **her handiwork, in order to avoid the enmity** that might arise between husband and wife if the husband were to be required to support his wife but were not to be entitled to the proceeds of her handiwork. Since the woman's right to maintenance is primary, she is entitled to surrender that right and keep for herself the proceeds of her handiwork, if she wishes. [6]Thus, **when she says: "I will not** exercise my right to **be maintained, and I will not work** for you," [7]**she is permitted to do so.**

אוֹמֵר: הֶקְדֵּשׁ. [1]רַבִּי יוֹחָנָן הַסַּנְדְּלָר אוֹמֵר: חוּלִּין.

גמרא [2]אָמַר רַב הוּנָא אָמַר רַב: יְכוֹלָה אִשָּׁה לוֹמַר לְבַעְלָהּ: [3]"אֵינִי נִיזּוֹנֶת וְאֵינִי עוֹשָׂה". [4]קָסָבַר: כִּי תַּקִּינוּ רַבָּנַן, מְזוֹנֵי עִיקָּר, [5]וּמַעֲשֵׂה יָדֶיהָ מִשּׁוּם אֵיבָה. [6]וְכִי אָמְרָה: "אֵינִי נִיזּוֹנֶת וְאֵינִי עוֹשָׂה", [7]הָרְשׁוּת בְּיָדָהּ.

LITERAL TRANSLATION

says: [It is] consecrated. [1]Rabbi Yoḥanan HaSandlar says: [It is] unconsecrated.

GEMARA [2]Rav Huna said in the name of Rav: A woman can say to her husband: [3]"I will not be maintained and I will not work." [4]He maintains: When the Rabbis made the enactment, [5]maintenance was the primary [enactment], and her handiwork was because of enmity. [6]And when she says: "I will not be maintained and I will not work," [7]she is permitted [to do so].

RASHI

והמותר קנוי לו במעה כסף שתקנו לה חכמים שיתן לה בכל שבת מעה כסף לצורכיה, לבד המזונות, כדתנן במתניתין. **רבי מאיר אומר הקדש כו׳** — מפרש בגמרא.

גמרא איני ניזונית — משלך. **ואיני עושה** — לך כלום, אלא לעצמי. **מזוני עיקר** — תחילת תקנתא לטובתה תקנוה, משום דזמנין דלא ספקה במעשה ידיה למזונות, ותקנו תחילה עיקר תקנתא שיזון את אשתו, והדר תקון לו מעשה ידיה משום איבה. וכיון דעיקר תקנתא לטובתה, ומשום דידה הוא, כי אמרה לא ניחא לי בהאי טיבותא — שומעין לה.

NOTES

which she is legally required to produce for him, and the second clause refers to a case in which he consecrated her surplus earnings.

Shittah Mekubbetzet notes that *Tosafot* gives a different explanation. *Rosh*, too, explains that the Mishnah is referring to a single case, in which the husband consecrates all of his wife's future handiwork to the Temple treasury, and that it distinguishes between the law that applies to the handiwork the wife is required to produce for her husband and the law that applies to her surplus earnings.

Meiri suggests that the second clause refers both to the case in which the husband consecrates his wife's surplus earnings as part of her total handiwork and to the case in which he consecrates only his wife's surplus earnings.

The term "surplus earnings" is also subject to a dispute between the Rishonim. *Rashi* and most Rishonim explain that the term refers to the wife's earnings from tasks that she is not legally required to perform for her husband because she has already met the quota of handiwork that she must produce for him (as is explained below, 64b). *Talmidei Rabbenu Yonah* and others explain that the term refers to those earnings that are left over when the woman maintains herself from her own handiwork (even if she does not produce more than is normally required of a married woman).

"אֵינִי נִיזּוֹנֶת" "I will not be maintained." The Gemara explains that, according to Rav Huna, a wife can waive her right to maintenance and deprive her husband of the proceeds of her handiwork, because the wife's right to maintenance was the primary enactment, in exchange for which the husband was granted the right to her handiwork. *Ra'ah* explains that, according to Resh Lakish, who disagrees with Rav Huna, neither right is treated as being primary, and neither spouse can deprive the other of his or her right. Thus the dispute between Rav Huna and Resh

HALAKHAH

consecrated," following Rabbi Yoḥanan HaSandlar, whose viewpoint was accepted as law by Shmuel (below, 59a). (*Rambam, Sefer Hafla'ah, Hilkhot Arakhin* 6:28; *Shulḥan Arukh, Even HaEzer* 81:1.)

"אֵינִי נִיזּוֹנֶת וְאֵינִי עוֹשָׂה" "I will not be maintained and I will not work." "If a wife says to her husband: 'I waive my right to maintenance, and I will keep my handiwork for myself,' we do not compel her to hand over her handiwork to her husband; for the wife's right to maintenance is primary, and the husband was granted the right to her

TRANSLATION AND COMMENTARY

מֵיתִיבֵי [1]**An objection was raised** against the viewpoint of Rav Huna from the following Baraita: [2]"The Sages **instituted** that the husband is liable for his wife's **maintenance in exchange for her handiwork.**" This Baraita implies that the husband's right to the proceeds of his wife's handiwork was the primary enactment, and that it was only because the woman was required to hand over her earnings to her husband that the Rabbis granted her the right of maintenance from her husband, and this is precisely the opposite of the ruling by Rav Huna!

אֵימָא [3]The Gemara explains that the Baraita must be amended: We must **say** that the Baraita should read as follows: The Sages **instituted** that the husband should be entitled to the proceeds of his wife's **handiwork in exchange for her maintenance.**

לֵימָא מְסַיֵּיע לֵיהּ [4]The Gemara now seeks to adduce support from our Mishnah for Rav Huna's ruling. **Shall we say that** Rav Huna's viewpoint **is supported** by our Mishnah, which stated: [5]**"If someone consecrates the** proceeds of **his wife's** future **handiwork,** the wife's handiwork does not become consecrated, and **she may** do her **work and maintain herself** from the proceeds"? [6]**Is** the Mishnah **not** referring to a case **where** the wife **is** being **maintained** by her husband, but the woman decides to waive her right to maintenance? By waiving this right, she deprives her husband of his right to the proceeds of her handiwork, and he is therefore unable to consecrate her earnings.

לָא [7]The Gemara rejects this argument: **No,** the Mishnah **is** referring to a case **where** the woman **is not** being **maintained** by her husband, because he does not have the means to support her. The husband loses his right to the proceeds of his wife's handiwork, if she does not actually receive her maintenance from

[1]מֵיתִיבֵי: [2]"תִּקְנוּ מְזוֹנוֹת תַּחַת מַעֲשֵׂה יָדֶיהָ".
[3]אֵימָא: תִּקְנוּ מַעֲשֵׂה יָדֶיהָ תַּחַת מְזוֹנוֹת.
[4]לֵימָא מְסַיֵּיע לֵיהּ: [5]"הַמַּקְדִּישׁ מַעֲשֵׂה יְדֵי אִשְׁתּוֹ, הֲרֵי הִיא עוֹשָׂה וְאוֹכֶלֶת"? [6]מַאי לָאו בְּנִיזּוֹנֶת?
[7]לָא, בְּשֶׁאֵינָהּ נִיזּוֹנֶת.

LITERAL TRANSLATION

[1]They raised an objection: [2]"They instituted maintenance in exchange for her handiwork."

[3]Say: They instituted her handiwork in exchange for her maintenance.

[4]Shall we say [that this] supports him: [5]"[If] someone consecrates the handiwork of his wife, she works and eats"? [6]Is it not where she is maintained? [7]No, it is where she is not maintained.

RASHI

מאי לאו בניזונת — שיש לו נכסים, ומבקש לזונה. ואפילו הכי תנן: אין מעשה ידיה ברשותו להקדישן. **בשאינה ניזונת** — שאין לו במה לזונה.

NOTES

Lakish is limited to the issue of handiwork. According to Rav Huna, a wife can waive her right to maintenance and keep her handiwork, whereas according to Resh Lakish she cannot. But both agree that a man cannot waive his right to his wife's handiwork and thus deprive her of her maintenance. The husband can, however, have his wife maintain herself from her own handiwork, provided that her earnings suffice for her support (see below, 70b).

The Rishonim disagree about whether a wife may reverse her decision and demand maintenance from her husband once she has waived her right to be maintained by him. *Tosafot* (above, 47b) argues that the wife can change her mind and demand maintenance, for the husband's duty to maintain his wife is regarded as an obligation that is renewed each day. *Ra'ah*, *Rashba*, *Ritva*, and others argue that once a wife comes before the court and waives her right to maintenance, the husband's obligation to maintain her is forever canceled, so that the Rabbinic enactment of maintenance does not become the object of derision.

אֵימָא: תִּקְנוּ מַעֲשֵׂה יָדֶיהָ Say: They instituted her handiwork. *Shittah Mekubbetzet* explains that the Gemara is not suggesting that the Baraita be amended, but only that it be understood differently. The Baraita does not mean that the Rabbis held the husband liable for his wife's maintenance in exchange for his previously established right to the proceeds of her handiwork, but rather that the Rabbis held the husband liable for his wife's maintenance, and in exchange they ruled that he is entitled to the proceeds of her handiwork. The Baraita is formulated the way it is because the main thing it wishes to teach is that a man is obligated to maintain his wife by Rabbinic enactment, and not by Torah law (as is argued by a number of Tannaim; see above, 47b). Had the Baraita stated that the Rabbis awarded the husband the proceeds of his wife's handiwork in exchange for her maintenance, we might have thought that the husband's obligation to maintain his wife derives from Torah law.

בְּשֶׁאֵינָהּ נִיזּוֹנֶת Where she is not maintained. Most Rishonim explain that, in suggesting that the Mishnah is referring to a case in which the wife is being maintained

HALAKHAH

handiwork in return for his duty to maintain her, following Rav Huna who reported the ruling of Rav. *Rema* writes that, according to *Bet Yosef* and *Maggid Mishneh*, this ruling applies only to those tasks that the wife performs in order to supplement the family income. But she is still required to perform the household duties that were imposed on a married woman, even if she waives her right to maintenance." (*Rambam, Sefer Nashim, Hilkhot Ishut* 12:4; *Shulḥan Arukh, Even HaEzer* 69:4; *Rema, Shulḥan Arukh, Even HaEzer* 80:15.)

[1]אִי בְּשֶׁאֵינָהּ נִיזּוֹנֶת, מַאי לְמֵימְרָא? [2]אֲפִילּוּ לְמַאן דְּאָמַר: יָכוֹל הָרַב לוֹמַר לְעֶבֶד: [3]״עֲשֵׂה עִמִּי, וְאֵינִי זָנְךָ״, [4]הָנֵי מִילֵּי בְּעֶבֶד כְּנַעֲנִי, דְּלָא כְּתִיב בֵּיהּ ״עִמָּךְ״, [5]אֲבָל עֶבֶד עִבְרִי, דִּכְתִיב בֵּיהּ ״עִמָּךְ״, לָא, [6]וְכָל שֶׁכֵּן אִשְׁתּוֹ!

[7]סֵיפָא אִיצְטְרִיךְ לֵיהּ: ״מוֹתָר, [8]רַבִּי מֵאִיר אוֹמֵר: הֶקְדֵּשׁ. [9]רַבִּי יוֹחָנָן הַסַּנְדְּלָר אוֹמֵר: חוּלִּין״.

LITERAL TRANSLATION

[1]If it is where she is not maintained, what [does it come] to say? [2]Even according to the one who says: A master can say to a slave: [3]"Work for me, but I will not feed you," [4]this applies (lit., "these words") to a Canaanite slave, about whom "with you" is not written, [5]but not [to] a Hebrew slave, about whom "with you" *is* written, [6][and] all the more so [to] his wife!

[7]He needed the last clause: "[If he consecrates] the surplus, [8]Rabbi Meir says: [It is] consecrated. [9]Rabbi Yoḥanan HaSandlar says: [It is] unconsecrated."

TRANSLATION AND COMMENTARY

him. In such a case the husband may not consecrate his wife's earnings, and the woman may therefore work and maintain herself from the proceeds. But if the husband is ready to support his wife, she may well be unable to waive her right to maintenance and thereby deprive her husband of his right to her handiwork.

אִי [1]The Gemara now challenges this explanation of our Mishnah. If the Mishnah is referring to a case in which the woman is being maintained by her husband, its purpose could be to teach us that she may waive her right to maintenance and thereby deprive her husband of his right to her handiwork. But **if** the Mishnah **is** referring to a case **where** the woman **is not** being **maintained** by her husband, **what does it come to teach** us? Is it not obvious that in such a case the husband is unable to consecrate the proceeds of his wife's handiwork? [2]For **even according to the** authority **who says** elsewhere (*Gittin* 12a): **A master can say to** his **slave:** [3]**"Work for me, but I will not maintain you,"** since the master is not legally obliged to support his slave, [4]**this applies** only in the case of **a non-Jewish slave, about whom the verse does not use the expression: "With you."** [5]**But** as for **a Jewish slave, about whom the verse says** (Deuteronomy 15:16): "Because he is happy **with you,"** which teaches us that the slave must live in conditions comparable to those of his master, the master **cannot** demand that the slave work for him unless he provides him with sustenance. Now if a Jewish slave cannot be forced to work for his master if he does not receive maintenance from him, [6]then **surely** a man's **wife** cannot be required to hand over the proceeds of her handiwork to her husband if she is not being maintained by him! And in such a case the husband can surely not consecrate his wife's earnings. What, then, does our Mishnah come to teach us?

סֵיפָא [7]The Gemara replies that the ruling contained in this part of the Mishnah is indeed obvious, but it was included as an introduction to what follows, for the Tanna **needed** to teach **the last clause** of the Mishnah, which states: **"If** the husband **consecrates** his wife's **surplus** earnings, [8]**Rabbi Meir says:** Her surplus earnings **become consecrated.** [9]**Rabbi Yoḥanan HaSandlar** disagrees and **says: They do not become consecrated."**

RASHI

אפילו למאן דאמר כו׳ — פלוגתא במסכת גיטין. **סיפא איצטריך ליה** — לאשמועינן פלוגתא במותר, דלא שייך אמזונות. ואף על גב דאינה נזונת איכא למאן דאמר קדוש לאחר מיתה כשיירשנה, וכדלקמן.

NOTES

by her husband, the Gemara does not mean that she is actually being maintained by him, for then it would be clear that the husband can consecrate his wife's handiwork. Rather the Gemara is suggesting that the Mishnah is referring to a case in which the husband is willing to maintain his wife, but she decides to waive her right to maintenance. Thus the Gemara understands that the Mishnah is advising a wife whose husband consecrates her handiwork to declare that she is waiving her right to maintenance, so that her handiwork will not become consecrated (see *Rashi*, *Meiri*). The Gemara then rejects this interpretation of the Mishnah, and suggests that it is referring to a case in which the wife is not being maintained by her husband, because he does not have the means to support her (*Rashi*), or because he does not wish to support her (*Rivan*). But if the husband is willing to support his wife, she may not deprive him of his right to her handiwork by waiving her right to maintenance.

HALAKHAH

״עֲשֵׂה עִמִּי, וְאֵינִי זָנְךָ״ "Work for me, but I will not feed you." "A master can say to his non-Jewish slave: 'Work for me, but I will not feed you.' In such a case, the slave must beg for food and support himself from charity." (*Rambam, Sefer Kinyan, Hilkhot Avadim* 9:7; *Shulḥan Arukh, Yoreh De'ah* 267:20.)

[1] וּפְלִיגָא דְּרֵישׁ לָקִישׁ, דַּאֲמַר רֵישׁ לָקִישׁ: [2] לָא תֵּימָא טַעֲמָא דְּרַבִּי מֵאִיר מִשּׁוּם דְּקָסָבַר אָדָם מַקְדִּישׁ דָּבָר שֶׁלֹּא בָּא לָעוֹלָם. [3] אֶלָּא טַעֲמָא דְּרַבִּי מֵאִיר: מִתּוֹךְ שֶׁיָּכוֹל לְכוֹפָהּ לְמַעֲשֵׂה יָדֶיהָ, [4] נַעֲשָׂה כְּאוֹמֵר לָהּ: ״יִקָּדְשׁוּ יָדַיִךְ לְעוֹשֵׂיהֶם״.

LITERAL TRANSLATION

[1] And it disagrees with Resh Lakish, for Resh Lakish said: [2] Do not say [that] the reason of Rabbi Meir is because he maintains that a man can consecrate something that has not [yet] come into the world. [3] Rather, the reason of Rabbi Meir is: Since he can compel her regarding her handiwork, [4] it is as if he says to her: "Let your hands be consecrated to Him who made them."

TRANSLATION AND COMMENTARY

וּפְלִיגָא [1] The Gemara now notes that the ruling by Rav Huna that a wife may waive her right to maintenance, and thus deprive her husband of his right to her handiwork, **is in disagreement with** the viewpoint of **Resh Lakish, for Resh Lakish said:** Just as Rabbi Meir disagrees with Rabbi Yoḥanan HaSandlar and says that a man can consecrate his wife's future surplus earnings, he likewise disagrees with the anonymous first Tanna of the Mishnah and says that a man can consecrate his wife's future handiwork. [2] **Do not say that the reason for Rabbi Meir's ruling** that a man can consecrate his wife's future handiwork and surplus earnings **is because he maintains that a person can consecrate something that has not yet come into existence.** We might have inferred from Rabbi Meir's rulings — that the wife's future handiwork and surplus earnings become consecrated — that he is of the opinion that a person can indeed consecrate something even though it is not yet in existence. [3] **But** this conclusion is incorrect, because **the reason for Rabbi Meir's ruling is** as follows: **Since** the husband **can compel** his wife to fulfill her obligation **regarding her handiwork,** he has a certain right to her hands. Therefore, when he consecrates his wife's handiwork, [4] **he is** regarded **as if he said to her: "Let your hands** — with respect to what they produce — **be consecrated to Him who made them."** Since his vow relates to something that is already in existence, her hands, the vow is valid and the woman's handiwork becomes consecrated. Now, since Resh Lakish says that the husband can compel his wife to fulfill her obligation regarding her handiwork, it follows that the wife cannot waive her right to maintenance and keep her handiwork. Thus Resh Lakish disagrees with Rav Huna, who says that a wife can indeed waive her right to maintenance and thereby deprive her husband of the proceeds of her handiwork.

RASHI

ופליגא — דרב הונא ארבי שמעון בן לקיש. **דבר שלא בא לעולם** — כגון מעשה ידיה, שהקדישן עד שלא עשאתן. **לעושיהן** — למי שבראן — וידים איתנהו בעולם. אלמא קסבר, יכול לכופה, ואינה יכולה לומר: איני ניזונית ואיני עושה.

NOTES

מִתּוֹךְ שֶׁיָּכוֹל לְכוֹפָהּ Since he can compel her. The Rishonim note that it follows from the Gemara here that when Resh Lakish says that a husband can compel his wife with respect to her handiwork, he is referring not only to her basic obligation, but to her surplus earnings as well. *Ra'ah* maintains that a wife is given the entire week to fill the weekly quota of handiwork that she must produce for her husband, but if she fills the quota early in the week, her husband can compel her to do additional work and deliver her surplus earnings to him. *Ritva* and others explain that a husband cannot compel his wife to produce more handiwork than she is required to do, but if she does produce surplus earnings, she can be compelled to hand them over to her husband.

The Rishonim also disagree as to whether Rav Huna's ruling, that a woman can waive her right to maintenance and thus deprive her husband of his right to her handiwork, can be extended to her surplus earnings as well. *Rabbenu Yonah* (cited by *Tur*) maintains that even Rav Huna agrees that a woman cannot deprive her husband of her surplus earnings by waiving her right to her weekly allowance. But most Rishonim (*Rav Aḥai Gaon*, *Ramban*, *Rashba*, and others) disagree. *Ran* justifies this position with the argument that if a wife can deprive her husband of the handiwork that all women produce for their husbands, then she should certainly be able to deprive him of her surplus earnings.

״יִקָּדְשׁוּ יָדַיִךְ לְעוֹשֵׂיהֶם״ "Let your hands be consecrated to Him who made them." The Rishonim explain that if a man consecrates his wife's hands to Him who made them,

HALAKHAH

מִתּוֹךְ שֶׁיָּכוֹל לְכוֹפָהּ לְמַעֲשֵׂה יָדֶיהָ Since he can compel her regarding her handiwork. "If a wife refuses to perform any one of the tasks that were imposed on a married woman, she can be compelled to perform the task. *Rema* writes that according to some authorities (*Rambam*; see also *Kesef Mishneh*) the wife can be physically forced to comply. He also notes that this ruling applies only if the wife insists on being maintained by her husband but refuses to perform the tasks that the Rabbis imposed on her. But if she is ready to waive her right to maintenance, she may keep her handiwork for herself." (*Rambam, Sefer Nashim, Hilkhot Ishut* 21:10; *Shulḥan Arukh, Even HaEzer* 80:15.)

״יִקָּדְשׁוּ יָדַיִךְ לְעוֹשֵׂיהֶם״ "Let your hands be consecrated to Him who made them." "If a man says to his wife: 'Let

BACKGROUND

אֵין אָדָם מוֹצִיא דְּבָרָיו לְבַטָּלָה A man does not utter his words in vain. Rabbi Meir is of the opinion that when a person says something that has no Halakhic or juridical meaning, we must assume that his statement was a slip of the tongue and not a meaningless utterance. Therefore we rephrase it so that it will entail Halakhic obligations.

TRANSLATION AND COMMENTARY

וְהָא [1]The Gemara objects to this explanation of Resh Lakish's position: **But surely** the husband **did not say to** his wife: "Let your hands be consecrated," but rather: "Let your handiwork be consecrated"!

כֵּיוָן [2]The Gemara replies: **We have heard** elsewhere **that Rabbi Meir stated** as a general principle that **a person does not utter his words in vain.** For it was taught in a Baraita (*Arakhin* 5a) that Rabbi Meir ruled that if someone makes a vow of valuation with respect to an infant less than a month old, he must pay the Temple treasury the infant's value as if he were being sold as a slave. The Torah fixes the amount a person must pay when he takes a vow of valuation according to the sex and the age of the assessed person, but there is no value set for a baby less than thirty days old. Nevertheless, we assume that the person uttering the vow must have meant the infant's actual value as if he were being sold as a slave, for if a person makes a Halakhically meaningless statement, we interpret the statement in such a way as to give it Halakhic significance. Here, too, in our case, the husband knows that he cannot consecrate something that has not yet come into existence, [3]and therefore we interpret his words **as if he had said to** his wife: **"Let your hands** — with respect to what they produce — **be consecrated to Him who made them."**

וְסָבַר רַבִּי מֵאִיר [4]The Gemara now asks: **But does Rabbi Meir** actually **maintain that a person cannot consecrate something that has not yet come into existence**, as was suggested by Resh Lakish? [5]**But surely**

[1]וְהָא לָא אֲמַר לָהּ הָכִי! [2]כֵּיוָן דִּשְׁמְעִינַן לֵיהּ לְרַבִּי מֵאִיר דְּאָמַר: אֵין אָדָם מוֹצִיא דְּבָרָיו לְבַטָּלָה, [3]נַעֲשֶׂה כְּאוֹמֵר לָהּ: "יִקָּדְשׁוּ יָדַיִךְ לְעוֹשֵׂיהֶם". [4]וְסָבַר רַבִּי מֵאִיר אֵין אָדָם מַקְדִּישׁ דָּבָר שֶׁלֹּא בָּא לָעוֹלָם? [5]וְהָתַנְיָא: "הָאוֹמֵר לְאִשָּׁה:

LITERAL TRANSLATION

[1]But surely he did not say so to her!

[2]Since we have heard that Rabbi Meir said: A man does not utter his words in vain, [3]it is as if he says to her: "Let your hands be consecrated to Him who made them."

[4]But does Rabbi Meir maintain [that] a man cannot consecrate something that has not [yet] come into the world?

[5]But surely it was taught: "[If] someone says to a woman:

RASHI

והא לא אמר — יקדשו ידיך, אלא "מעשה ידיך". **שמעינן ליה לרבי מאיר** — במסכת ערכין (ה,א), דאמר: אין אדם מוציא דבריו לבטלה. דתנן: המעריך פחות מבן חדש, רבי מאיר אומר: נותן דמיו, דאדם יודע שאין ערך לפחות מבן חדש, וגמר ואמר לשם דמים. הכא נמי, אדם יודע שאין אדם מקדיש דבר שלא בא לעולם, וגמר ואמר לשם ידים עצמן.

NOTES

her handiwork becomes consecrated, because the case is treated like that of someone who consecrates his tree with respect to its fruit, in which case the produce becomes consecrated. *Rashba* raises a question about this comparison. Consecration can indeed attach itself to a tree with respect to its fruit, because the tree belongs to its owner, and this is why the fruit becomes consecrated. But how can consecration attach itself to a wife's hands? Surely they do not belong to her husband, and he cannot consecrate them! If a person cannot consecrate even the hands of his Jewish slave, then all the more so should he not be able to consecrate his wife's hands.

דָּבָר שֶׁלֹּא בָּא לָעוֹלָם Something that has not yet come into the world. The issue of whether a person can consecrate something that has not yet come into existence is part of a more general question regarding the validity of any transaction involving something that has not yet come into existence. The concept of something that has not yet come into existence has several meanings: (1) Something that has not yet come into existence at all — for example, a woman's future handiwork. (2) Something that already exists but cannot in its present state be the object of the transaction in question — for example, a non-Jew or a slave with respect to betrothal. *Tosafot* alludes to what is stated elsewhere (*Gittin* 13b) — that even according to Rabbi Meir, who maintains that one can effect a transaction involving something that has not yet come into existence, one cannot effect a transaction with someone who has not yet come into existence. *Tosafot* also distinguishes between things that do not yet exist but will almost certainly come into existence — for example, the future fruit of a tree — and things about which there is no certainty that they will ever exist — for example, a non-Jew or a slave with respect to betrothal.

HALAKHAH

your hands be consecrated to Him who made them,' since those hands are obliged to work for him, all of his wife's handiwork becomes consecrated (following *Rambam*). *Rema* writes that according to some authorities (*Ran* and *Tur*) the wife's handiwork does not become consecrated, for she can waive her right to maintenance and keep her handiwork for herself." (*Rambam, Sefer Hafla'ah, Hilkhot Arakhin* 6:28; *Shulḥan Arukh, Even HaEzer* 81:1.)

אֵין אָדָם מַקְדִּישׁ דָּבָר שֶׁלֹּא בָּא לָעוֹלָם A man cannot consecrate something that has not yet come into the world. "A person cannot consecrate something that has not yet come into existence," following the Sages against Rabbi Meir. (*Rambam, Sefer Hafla'ah, Hilkhot Arakhin* 6:26.)

TRANSLATION AND COMMENTARY

it was taught in the following Baraita: **"If** a non-Jew **says to a woman:** [1]**'Be betrothed to me after I become a proselyte,'** [2]**or** if a Jew says to a non-Jewish woman: 'Be betrothed to me **after you become a proselyte,'** [3]**or** if a non-Jewish slave says to a woman: 'Be betrothed to me **after I am freed** from slavery,' [4]**or** if a free man says to a non-Jewish maidservant: 'Be betrothed to me **after you are freed** from slavery,' [5]**or** if a man says to a married woman: 'Be betrothed to me **after your husband dies,'** [6]**or** if a man says to his sister-in-law: 'Be betrothed to me **after** my wife, **your sister, dies,'** [7]**or** if a man says to a woman who is waiting for her *yavam* to perform levirate marriage or *ḥalitzah*: 'Be betrothed to me **after your *yavam* performs *ḥalitzah* with you,'** [8]in all these cases **Rabbi Meir says:** The woman **is betrothed** after the impediment to betrothal has been removed." Thus we see that Rabbi Meir maintains that a transaction involving something that has not yet come into existence — in these cases, a future status that will permit valid betrothal — has legal validity. Hence he should agree that a person can consecrate something that has not yet come into existence.

מֵהַהִיא [9]The Gemara answers: **From that Baraita** we may **indeed** conclude that Rabbi Meir is of the opinion that a person can consecrate something that has not yet come into existence. [10]But **from our Mishnah this** conclusion **cannot be inferred** for, as Resh Lakish explained, our Mishnah can be interpreted differently.

הַמּוֹתָר [11]The Gemara now proceeds to analyze the next clause of the Mishnah, which states: **"If the** husband **consecrates** his wife's **surplus** earnings, her earnings from tasks that she is not legally required to perform for her husband, **Rabbi Meir says:** Her surplus earnings **become consecrated.** Rabbi Yoḥanan HaSandlar disagrees and says: They do not become consecrated." [12]The Gemara asks: According to Rabbi Meir, **when do** the wife's surplus earnings **become consecrated?** [13]**Rav and Shmuel both said:** If a man consecrates his wife's **surplus** earnings, they **are consecrated** only **after her death**, when he becomes her heir. [14]**Rav Adda bar Ahavah said: The** wife's **surplus** earnings **are** already **consecrated during her lifetime**, as soon as they come into existence.

הֲוֵי בָּהּ רַב פַּפָּא [15]**Rav Pappa raised a question** regarding this matter when it arose in discussion. [16]**With which case**, he asked, is the Mishnah dealing? [17]**If we say** that the Mishnah is referring to a case **where** the husband **provides** his wife **with her maintenance, and he** also **provides her with** a weekly allowance of

[1]״הֲרֵי אַתְּ מְקוּדֶּשֶׁת לִי לְאַחַר שֶׁאֶתְגַּיֵּיר׳, [2]אוֹ ׳לְאַחַר שֶׁתִּתְגַּיְּירִי׳, [3]׳לְאַחַר שֶׁאֶשְׁתַּחְרֵר׳, [4]׳לְאַחַר שֶׁתִּשְׁתַּחְרְרִי׳, [5]׳לְאַחַר שֶׁיָּמוּת בַּעֲלֵיךְ׳, [6]אוֹ ׳שֶׁתָּמוּת אֲחוֹתֵיךְ׳, [7]אוֹ ׳לְאַחַר שֶׁיַּחֲלוֹץ לֵיךְ יְבָמֵיךְ׳, [8]רַבִּי מֵאִיר אוֹמֵר: מְקוּדֶּשֶׁת״. [9]מֵהַהִיא, אִין; [10]מֵהָא, לֵיכָּא לְמִשְׁמַע מִינָּהּ. [11]״הַמּוֹתָר, רַבִּי מֵאִיר אוֹמֵר: הֶקְדֵּשׁ״. [12]אֵימַת קָדוֹשׁ? [13]רַב וּשְׁמוּאֵל דְּאָמְרִי תַּרְוַויְיהוּ: מוֹתָר לְאַחַר מִיתָה קָדוֹשׁ. [14]רַב אַדָּא בַּר אַהֲבָה אָמַר: מוֹתָר מֵחַיִּים קָדוֹשׁ. [15]הֲוֵי בָּהּ רַב פַּפָּא: [16]בְּמַאי? [17]אִילֵימָא: בְּמַעֲלָה לָהּ מְזוֹנוֹת וּמַעֲלָה לָהּ מָעָה כֶּסֶף לִצְרָכֶיהָ,

LITERAL TRANSLATION

[1]'Be betrothed to me after I become a proselyte,' [2]or 'after you become a proselyte,' [3][or] 'after I am freed,' [4][or] 'after you are freed,' [5][or] 'after your husband dies,' [6][or] 'when your sister dies,' [7][or] 'after your *yavam* performs *ḥalitzah* with you,' [8]Rabbi Meir says: She is betrothed."

[9]From that [Baraita], yes; [10]from this [Mishnah], it is impossible to infer [this] from it.

[11]"[If he consecrates] the surplus, Rabbi Meir says: [It is] consecrated." [12]When is it consecrated? [13]Rav and Shmuel both say: The surplus is consecrated after [her] death. [14]Rav Adda bar Ahavah says: The surplus is consecrated during [her] lifetime.

[15]Rav Pappa discussed it: [16]In what [case]? [17]If we say: It is where he provides maintenance for her and he provides a silver ma'ah for her for her needs,

RASHI

לאחר מיתה — כשתמות היא, ויירשנה. **מחיים** — כשתעשנו.

TERMINOLOGY

מֵהָא לֵיכָּא לְמִשְׁמַע מִינָּהּ From this Mishnah, it is impossible to infer this from it. This expression is generally used after a failed attempt to prove a point using the method of דִּיּוּק — *diyyuk*, the precise examination of the wording of a Tannaitic statement. The essence of this method is that one subjects the wording of a Tannaitic statement to precise analysis, showing that everything not covered by the narrow definition of the source is subject to a different ruling. Proofs using this method of דִּיּוּק are often accepted, but they are sometimes refuted when it can be shown that application of the very same method of close analysis to another portion of the same Mishnah or Baraita leads to the opposite conclusion. In such cases the argument may be summed up with the phrase מֵהָא לֵיכָּא לְמִשְׁמַע מִינָּהּ, meaning that one cannot reach conclusions from this source by using the method of precise analysis, since we would thus draw inferences that are contradictory.

HALAKHAH

״הֲרֵי אַתְּ מְקוּדֶּשֶׁת לִי לְאַחַר שֶׁאֶתְגַּיֵּיר״ "Be betrothed to me after I become a proselyte." "If a man says to a woman: 'Be betrothed to me after I become a proselyte,' or 'after you become a proselyte,' or 'after I am emancipated,' or 'after you are emancipated,' or 'after your husband dies,' or 'after your sister dies,' the betrothal is not valid even after the condition is fulfilled, for he lacks the legal capacity to betroth the woman at the time he pronounces the betrothal formula, following the Sages who disagree with Rabbi Meir. If a man says to a woman whose husband has

TRANSLATION AND COMMENTARY

a silver ma'ah that she can spend on the various things that **she needs,** [1] **what is the reasoning of** Rav and Shmuel **who say** that the wife's surplus earnings **are consecrated** only **after her death?** Surely they should be consecrated as soon as they come into existence, for if the husband provides his wife with her maintenance and her weekly allowance, he is entitled to her surplus earnings. [2] **On the other hand, if** the Mishnah **is** referring to a case **where** the husband **does not provide** his wife **with her maintenance and does not provide her with a silver ma'ah for her** personal **needs,** [3] **what is the reasoning of** Rav Adda bar Ahavah **who says** that the wife's surplus earnings **are** already **consecrated during her lifetime**, as soon as they come into existence? If the husband is not providing his wife with her maintenance and her weekly allowance, then he is surely not entitled to her surplus earnings, and those surplus earnings cannot be consecrated by him!

לְעוֹלָם [4] The Gemara answers: **In fact,** the Mishnah **is** referring to a case **where** the husband **provides** his wife **with her maintenance, but does not provide her with a silver ma'ah for her** personal **needs.** And the Amoraic dispute about the time from which the wife's surplus earnings are consecrated must be understood as follows: [5] **Rav and Shmuel maintain** that when the Rabbis enacted that a husband is obliged to maintain his wife and to provide her with a weekly allowance, and that he is entitled to her earnings and surplus earnings, **they instituted** [59A] that the husband is held liable for his wife's **maintenance, in exchange for** which he is entitled to **her handiwork,** [6] **and** that he is required to provide her with a weekly allowance of **a silver ma'ah, in exchange for** which he is entitled to her **surplus** earnings. [7] This being the case, if the husband **does not provide** his wife **with** her weekly **silver ma'ah,** [8] **the surplus** earnings she produces **belong to her.** The husband has no right to her surplus earnings until she dies, and then whatever is left of her surplus earnings becomes part of her estate, which he inherits. Since the husband is not entitled to his wife's surplus earnings during her lifetime, they are not his to consecrate until after her death. [9] This is the viewpoint of Rav and Shmuel, but **Rav Adda bar Ahavah maintains** that when the Rabbis enacted the mutual rights and obligations of husband and wife, [10] **they instituted** that the husband be held liable for his wife's **maintenance, in exchange for** which he is entitled to her **surplus** earnings, [11] and that he be required to provide her with a weekly allowance of **a silver ma'ah, in exchange for** which he is entitled to **her handiwork.** [12] This being the case, if the husband **provides** his wife **with** her **maintenance, her surplus** earnings **belong to him** as soon as they come into existence, and therefore they can be consecrated during his wife's lifetime.

[1] מַאי טַעֲמָא דְּמַאן דְּאָמַר: לְאַחַר מִיתָה קָדוֹשׁ? [2] וְאֶלָּא כְּשֶׁאֵין מַעֲלֶה לָהּ מְזוֹנוֹת וְלֹא מַעֲלֶה לָהּ מָעָה כֶּסֶף לִצְרָכֶיהָ, [3] מַאי טַעֲמָא דְּמַאן דְּאָמַר: מֵחַיִּים קָדוֹשׁ?

[4] לְעוֹלָם בְּמַעֲלֶה לָהּ מְזוֹנוֹת וְאֵינוֹ מַעֲלֶה לָהּ מָעָה כֶּסֶף לִצְרָכֶיהָ. [5] רַב וּשְׁמוּאֵל סָבְרִי: תִּקְּנוּ [59A] מְזוֹנוֹת תַּחַת מַעֲשֵׂה יָדֶיהָ, [6] וּמָעָה כֶּסֶף תַּחַת מוֹתָר. [7] וְכֵיוָן דְּלָא קָא יָהֵיב לָהּ מָעָה כֶּסֶף, [8] מוֹתָר דִּידָהּ הָוֵי. [9] רַב אַדָּא בַּר אַהֲבָה סָבַר: [10] תִּקְּנוּ מְזוֹנוֹת תַּחַת מוֹתָר, [11] וּמָעָה כֶּסֶף תַּחְתָּךְ מַעֲשֵׂה יָדֶיהָ. [12] וְכֵיוָן דְּקָא יָהֵיב לָהּ מְזוֹנֵי, מוֹתָר דִּידֵיהּ הָוֵי.

LITERAL TRANSLATION

[1] what is the reason of the one who says: It is consecrated after [her] death? [2] But [if] it is where he does not provide maintenance for her and does not provide a silver ma'ah for her for her needs, [3] what is the reason of the one who says: It is consecrated during [her] lifetime?

[4] In fact, it is where he provides maintenance for her but does not provide a silver ma'ah for her for her needs. [5] Rav and Shmuel maintain: They instituted [59A] maintenance in exchange for her handiwork, [6] and a silver ma'ah in exchange for the surplus. [7] And since he does not give her the silver ma'ah, [8] the surplus is hers. [9] Rav Adda bar Ahavah maintains: [10] They instituted maintenance in exchange for the surplus, [11] and a silver ma'ah in exchange for her handiwork. [12] And since he gives her maintenance, the surplus is his.

RASHI

לעולם במעלה לה מזונות כו' — והוא הדין נמי דמצי לאוקמא כשאין מעלה לה מזונות ומעלה לה מעה, אלא משום רב דאית ליה יכולה אשה שתאמר "איני ניזונית ואיני עושה". ואוקי רישא דמתניתין דתני "עושה ואוכלת" בניזונת, להכי אוקי סיפא בניזונת. מזונות שכיחי ומעשה ידיה שכיח ומותר לא שכיח. מעה כסף קיץ, ומעשה ידיה קייץ, כדתנן (כתובות סד,ב): מה היא עושה משקל חמש סלעים.

HALAKHAH

died childless: 'Be betrothed to me after your *yavam* performs *ḥalitzah*,' the validity of the betrothal is in doubt." (*Rambam, Sefer Nashim, Hilkhot Ishut* 7:14; *Shulḥan Arukh, Even HaEzer* 40:5-6.)

[1]בְּמַאי קָמִיפַּלְגִי?
[2]מָר סָבַר: מִידֵי דִּשְׁכִיחַ מִמִּידֵי דִּשְׁכִיחַ. [3]וּמָר סָבַר: מִידֵי דְּקָיֵיץ מִמִּידֵי דְּקָיֵיץ.
[4]מֵיתִיבֵי: ״תִּקְּנוּ מְזוֹנוֹת תַּחַת מַעֲשֵׂה יָדֶיהָ״.
[5]אֵימָא: תַּחַת מוֹתַר מַעֲשֵׂה יָדֶיהָ.
[6]תָּא שְׁמַע: ״אִם אֵינוֹ נוֹתֵן לָהּ מָעָה כֶּסֶף לְצוֹרְכֶיהָ, [7]מַעֲשֵׂה יָדֶיהָ שֶׁלָּהּ״.
[8]אֵימָא: מוֹתַר מַעֲשֵׂה יָדֶיהָ שֶׁלָּהּ.
[9]וְהָא עֲלָהּ קָתָנֵי: ״מַה הִיא עוֹשָׂה לוֹ? [10]מִשְׁקַל חָמֵשׁ סְלָעִים שְׁתִי בִּיהוּדָה״.

LITERAL TRANSLATION

[1]About what do they disagree?
[2]This one maintains: [They instituted] something that is common [in exchange] for something that is common. [3]And that one maintains: [They instituted] something that is fixed [in exchange] for something that is fixed.
[4]They raised an objection: "They instituted maintenance in exchange for her handiwork."
[5]Say: In exchange for the surplus of her handiwork.
[6]Come [and] hear: "If he does not give her a silver ma'ah for her needs, [7]her handiwork is hers."
[8]Say: The surplus of her handiwork is hers.
[9]But surely in connection with this it teaches: "What does she do for him? [10]The weight of five sela'im of warp in Judea."

RASHI

והא עלה קתני — במתניתין. **ומה היא עושה לו** — ומדפרים בתר מעשה ידיה "ומה היא עושה לו" — מכלל דרישא במעשה ידיה איירי, ולא במותר. **שתי** — קשה לטוותו יותר מן הערב.

TRANSLATION AND COMMENTARY

בְּמַאי קָמִיפַּלְגִי? [1]The Gemara now inquires into the theoretical issue at the basis of the dispute. **About what** Halakhic principle **do** these Amoraim **disagree?**

מָר סָבַר [2]The Gemara answers: Rav and Shmuel **maintain** that when the Sages defined the rights and the duties of husband and wife, **they imposed** on the husband **the more frequently** applied obligation, to maintain his wife, **in exchange for the more frequently** utilized right to her handiwork, which is regularly produced. [3]Rav Adda bar Ahavah **maintains** that when the Sages enacted the mutual rights and obligations of husband and wife, **they imposed a fixed** obligation on the husband **in exchange for** which he is entitled to **a fixed right.** A wife's allowance for her personal needs is set at one silver ma'ah per week, but her maintenance is not similarly fixed. The obligatory handiwork that a wife must produce for her husband is also fixed at a specific amount (see below, 64b), but there is no limit to a wife's surplus earnings.

מֵיתִיבֵי [4]**An objection was raised** against Rav Adda bar Ahavah from the following Baraita, which directly contradicts his ruling: "The Sages **instituted** that the husband is held liable for his wife's **maintenance, in exchange for** which he is entitled to **her handiwork."**

אֵימָא [5]The Gemara suggests that according to Rav Adda bar Ahavah, the text of the Baraita must be slightly amended: **Say** that the Baraita should read as follows: The Sages instituted that the husband should be held liable for his wife's maintenance, **in exchange for** which he is entitled to **the surplus of her handiwork.**

תָּא שְׁמַע [6]The Gemara continues: **Come and hear** what we have learned in the following Mishnah (below, 64b): **"If** a man **does not provide** his wife **with a silver ma'ah** to spend **on her** personal **needs,** [7]**her handiwork belongs to her** to keep." The Mishnah seems to imply that in exchange for the husband's obligation to provide his wife with a weekly allowance, the Sages entitled him to keep her surplus earnings. This would support the viewpoint of Rav Adda Ada bar Ahavah and contradict that of Rav and Shmuel!

אֵימָא [8]The Gemara suggests that, according to Rav and Shmuel, the text of the Mishnah must be slightly amended: **Say** that the Mishnah should read as follows: If a man does not provide his wife with a silver ma'ah to spend on her personal needs, **the surplus of her handiwork belongs to her** to keep.

וְהָא עֲלָהּ קָתָנֵי [9]The Gemara questions this interpretation of the Mishnah: **But surely in connection with this** clause, the Mishnah itself **states: "What must** a wife **do for** her husband? [10]If she spins **warp** threads for weaving cloth, she must spin wool **weighing five Judean sela'im**, which are the equivalent of ten sela'im in Galilee." This clause of the Mishnah, fixing the amount of handiwork that a wife must produce for her husband, immediately follows the clause, that states what the wife may keep for herself if her husband

BACKGROUND

חָמֵשׁ סְלָעִים שְׁתִי Five sela'im of warp. Weaving is done on warp threads which are placed on a loom and can be raised and lowered to form patterns as the woof threads them. In general, the warp provides the foundation of the fabric, and the woof creates the pattern. Because the warp supports the fabric, it must be much sronger than the woof, though very often it is made of much finer threads. Hence the spinning of warp threads must be more precise than that of woof threads. Consequently the Sages ruled that a given weight of warp threads is worth twice as much as an equal weight of woof threads.

NOTES

מִידֵי דְּקָיֵיץ Something that is fixed. The Rishonim ask: The Mishnah below (64b) lists the specific amounts of food and clothing that a husband must provide for his wife when he supports her through a third party. That Mishnah goes on to say that the amounts listed comprise the minimal standards that apply to the poorest man in Israel, but a person of higher social standing must provide his wife with maintenance in accordance with his means and social position. Now it stands to reason that the same argument applies to a wife's allowance — that a person of higher social

[1]הָכִי קָאָמַר: מַעֲשֵׂה יָדֶיהָ כַּמָּה הָוֵי, דְּלֵידַע מוֹתַר דִּידָהּ כַּמָּה? [2]מִשְׁקַל חָמֵשׁ סְלָעִים שְׁתִי בִּיהוּדָה, שֶׁהֵן עֶשֶׂר סְלָעִים בַּגָּלִיל.

[3]אָמַר שְׁמוּאֵל: הֲלָכָה כְּרַבִּי יוֹחָנָן הַסַּנְדְּלָר.

[4]וּמִי אֲמַר שְׁמוּאֵל הָכִי? [5]וְהָתְנַן: "'קוֹנָם שֶׁאֲנִי עוֹשָׂה לְפִיךְ', אֵינוֹ צָרִיךְ לְהָפֵר.

LITERAL TRANSLATION

[1]He says thus: How much is her handiwork, so that we may know how much is her surplus? [2]The weight of five sela'im of warp in Judea, which are ten sela'im in Galilee.

[3]Shmuel said: The law is in accordance with Rabbi Yoḥanan HaSandlar.

[4]But did Shmuel say this? [5]But surely we have learned: "[If a wife says:] 'What I produce (lit., "do") is [forbidden] to you (lit., "to your mouth") [as] a *konam*,' he does not need to annul [it].

TRANSLATION AND COMMENTARY

does not provide her with her weekly allowance. Hence the former clause must also refer to her handiwork and not to her surplus earnings.

הָכִי קָאָמַר [1]The Gemara answers: The first clause of the Mishnah does refer to the wife's surplus earnings, which she may keep if her husband does not provide her with a weekly allowance. And **this is what** the Mishnah meant to **say** in the clause that follows immediately: In order to determine **what** handiwork **is surplus,** we must know **what is the** set **amount of handiwork** that a woman must produce for her husband. [2]If she spins warp threads, she must spin wool **weighing five Judean sela'im, which are** the equivalent of **ten sela'im in Galilee.**

אָמַר שְׁמוּאֵל [3]The Gemara now cites a ruling on the issue in dispute in our Mishnah: **Shmuel said: The law is in accordance with** the viewpoint of **Rabbi Yoḥanan HaSandlar** expressed in our Mishnah that a husband cannot consecrate his wife's surplus earnings.

וּמִי אֲמַר שְׁמוּאֵל הָכִי [4]The Gemara asks: **But did Shmuel** actually **say that** the law is in accordance with the viewpoint of Rabbi Yoḥanan HaSandlar? We saw above that Shmuel said that, according to Rabbi Yoḥanan HaSandlar, if a husband consecrates his wife's surplus earnings, they do not become consecrated even after her death, when he inherits them. Thus Shmuel's viewpoint must be that, according to Rabbi Yoḥanan HaSandlar, the wife's surplus earnings do not become consecrated because they did not belong to the husband at the time of consecration, and a person cannot consecrate something that does not belong to him. [5]**But surely** this leads to a difficulty, for **we have learned** in a Mishnah elsewhere (*Nedarim* 85a): **"If a wife says** to her husband: **'Whatever I produce is forbidden to you as a *konam*** [the word *konam* is used in vows as a substitute for the word *korban* — "sacrifice" — in order to avoid using the word *korban* itself],' **he does not need to annul** the vow, because the wife is obligated to produce handiwork for her

RASHI

הכי קאמר — [לעולם במותר איירי ברישא, והכי קאמר] סיפא: ומה היא עושה לו עיקר, דנדע מותר מאי ניהו. **משקל חמש סלעים** — סלע של יהודה כפליים במשקל סלע של גליל. **מי אמר שמואל הכי** — והאמר שמואל לעיל: במותר לאחר מיתה פליגי, ועלה אמר רבי יוחנן הסנדלר: חולין. ואף על פי דהשתא דידיה הוא, אלמא, טעמא דרבי יוחנן משום דבר שלא בא לעולם הוא, שעדיין לא מתה, ואין לו רשות במותר, הואיל ואינו מעלה לה מעה כסף, ובהא אמר שמואל הלכה! **והתנן קונם שאני עושה לפיך** — מה שאני עושה יהיה קונס לפיך — יהי עליך כהקדש מליהנות לו. **אינו צריך להפר** — נדר זה, שאין בה כח להקדישו, לפי שהוא שלו.

NOTES

standing must provide his wife with more than one silver ma'ah per week. Why, then, is a wife's allowance regarded as fixed, whereas her maintenance is not?

Rashba, *Ritva*, and others suggest that whereas the amount of maintenance that must be provided for a wife is fixed, the price of food is not, and therefore the husband's obligation is regarded as being undefined. Alternatively, the Mishnah fixes the amount of maintenance that the husband must provide for his wife when he supports her through a third party. But when she eats at his table there is no clearly defined amount of food that he must give her. But her allowance is fixed at a silver ma'ah per week, even if she is eating at his table.

קוֹנָם *Konam*. A *konam* is a type of vow whereby a person forbids himself to eat something or to derive benefit from something or someone by saying: "That person or thing is to me a *konam*." The word *konam* is a substitute for the word *korban* — "sacrifice" — and is used in order to avoid using the word *korban* itself. Forbidding something by a *konam* vow is similar to an act of consecration, although there are a number of significant differences. A consecrated object is forbidden to all, whereas a *konam* vow creates a private prohibition — to the person who made the vow or to another person. Furthermore, a consecrated object is no longer the private property of the donor, whereas something that has been forbidden by a *konam* vow remains the property of its owner.

"קוֹנָם שֶׁאֲנִי עוֹשָׂה לְפִיךְ" "What I do is forbidden to you as a *konam*." The reading found in the standard edition of the Talmud — קוֹנָם שֶׁאֲנִי עוֹשָׂה ("What I do shall be

HALAKHAH

קוֹנָם שֶׁאֲנִי עוֹשָׂה לְפִיךְ What I do is forbidden to you as a *konam*. "If a married woman says: 'Let my hands be consecrated to Him who made them,' or if she makes a vow that her husband may not derive benefit from her

1 רַבִּי עֲקִיבָא אוֹמֵר: יָפֵר, שֶׁמָּא תַּעֲדִיף עָלָיו יָתֵר מִן הָרָאוּי לוֹ. 2 רַבִּי יוֹחָנָן בֶּן נוּרִי אָמַר: יָפֵר, שֶׁמָּא יְגָרְשֶׁנָּה וּתְהֵא אֲסוּרָה לַחֲזוֹר". 3 וְאָמַר שְׁמוּאֵל: הֲלָכָה כְּרַבִּי יוֹחָנָן בֶּן נוּרִי!

LITERAL TRANSLATION

1 Rabbi Akiva says: He must annul [it], lest she do more work than is due to him. 2 Rabbi Yoḥanan ben Nuri said: He must annul [it], lest he divorce her and she will be forbidden to return [to him]." 3 And Shmuel said: The law is in accordance with Rabbi Yoḥanan ben Nuri!

TRANSLATION AND COMMENTARY

husband, and she cannot make a vow forbidding from benefiting from her handiwork. 1 **Rabbi Akiva** disagrees and **says:** The husband **must annul** the vow, **in case** his wife **produces more handiwork than is due to him.** The wife's surplus earnings do not belong to her husband, and therefore they are subject to her vow. 2 **Rabbi Yoḥanan ben Nuri said:** The husband **must annul** the vow for a different reason. Although at present the wife cannot forbid her husband from benefiting from her handiwork by means of a vow, **he may** at some point in the future **divorce her, and** then the vow will take effect, for then the woman will no longer be obligated to work for her former husband. But **she would** then **be forbidden to remarry him,** for a man cannot avoid deriving some benefit from what his wife does. 3 **And Shmuel** ruled on this matter and **said: The law is in accordance with** the viewpoint of **Rabbi Yoḥanan ben Nuri.** Now, Rabbi Yoḥanan ben Nuri says that a husband must annul his wife's vow, in case he divorces her and the vow takes effect. Thus we see that a woman can forbid by means of a vow something that is not yet in existence, for the handiwork that she will produce after her divorce is not yet in existence at the time she takes her vow. And since a vow forbidding another person from deriving benefit from something as if it were a sacrifice is similar to a vow of consecration, it follows that a person can indeed consecrate something that does not yet belong to him, or something that is not yet even in existence. This contradicts the viewpoint of Rabbi Yoḥanan HaSandlar with which Shmuel supposedly agreed!

RASHI

שמא תעדיף עליו — יותר ממה שפסקו לה חכמים, משקל חמש סלעים. דמותר זה אינו שלו, ויכולה להקדישו. **רבי יוחנן בן נורי אומר** — אף עיקר מעשה ידיה צריך הפרה. **שמא יגרשנה** — ויהא הנדר חל. שמשגרשה אינה משועבדת לו למעשה ידיה. **ותהא אסורה לחזור לו** — לפי שנאסר מעשה ידיה עליו, ואי אפשר לו ליזהר שלא תטחון ולא תאפה, וכל שאר מלאכות השנויות במשנתנו, שהאשה עושה לבעלה. **ואמר שמואל הלכה כו׳** — אלמא, לכשיגרשנה חל הנדר, אלמא: אדם מקדיש דבר שלא בא לעולם, שעדיין לא גירשה.

SAGES

רַבִּי יוֹחָנָן בֶּן נוּרִי **Rabbi Yoḥanan ben Nuri.** A Tanna of the third generation. See *Ketubot*, Part II, p. 198.

NOTES

forbidden as a *konam*") — is that of *Rashi* and most Rishonim. *Ra'ah* and others reject an alternative reading: קוֹנָם שֶׁאֵינִי עוֹשָׂה ("It shall be forbidden as a *konam* that I shall not do"), arguing that a *konam* is a type of vow that must relate to an object ("what I do"), and not to an activity that has no substance ("I shall not do"). Thus the wife's vow must be understood as follows: "Whatever I produce shall be forbidden to my husband as a *konam*." Some Rishonim accept the reading, קוֹנָם שֶׁאֵינִי עוֹשָׂה, arguing that a *konam* formulated with respect to an activity is also valid (see *Tosafot*).

יָפֵר, שֶׁמָּא יְגָרְשֶׁנָּה He must annul it, lest he divorce her. The Rishonim ask a number of questions regarding the position of Rabbi Yoḥanan ben Nuri: A husband is empowered to annul only those vows that cause his wife to suffer or that affect the personal relationship between him and his wife. How, then, can a husband annul his wife's vow forbidding him to derive benefit from her handiwork, if that vow is only to take effect after they are divorced? Such a vow does not cause her to suffer, nor does it affect the personal relationship between them!

Ritva answers that some authorities maintain that when Rabbi Yoḥanan ben Nuri said that the husband must annul the vow, he meant that a Sage must dissolve the vow. (A Sage's authority to dissolve a person's vows is not bound by the same restrictions as the husband's authority to annul the vows made by his wife.)

Ra'avad suggests that since the vow may deprive the husband of his wife's services, it affects the relationship between them.

Tosafot (cited by *Ritva)* argues that since the woman made the vow while she was married to her husband, and the vow can at some point affect the relationship between them, it affects the relationship between husband and wife.

Ritva himself explains that since the wife can waive her right to maintenance and can keep her handiwork for herself, and the vow would then take effect immediately and the husband would be forbidden to derive any benefit from what she produces, it is regarded as affecting the relationship between husband and wife.

Ra'ah argues that according to the Gemara's conclusion (below, 59b) there is no difficulty at all. For the Gemara

HALAKHAH

handiwork, her husband is not forbidden to derive benefit from her handiwork, for her hands are obligated to work for him. But the husband must annul the vow, lest he divorce his wife and the vow take effect, and he become barred from taking her back as his wife. *Rema* (following *Rosh, Ran,* and *Tur*) notes that the husband is only forbidden to derive benefit from his wife's handiwork if she says: 'Let my hands be consecrated to Him who made them.'" (*Rambam, Sefer Hafla'ah, Hilkhot Nedarim* 12:10; *Shulḥan Arukh, Yoreh De'ah* 234:71; *Even HaEzer* 81:2.)

TRANSLATION AND COMMENTARY

כִּי אֲמַר שְׁמוּאֵל [1] The Gemara answers: Shmuel does indeed maintain that a person cannot consecrate something that has not yet come into existence, or something that has come into existence but does not yet belong to him, and this is why Shmuel ruled in accordance with the viewpoint of Rabbi Yoḥanan HaSandlar. **When Shmuel said that the law is in accordance with** the viewpoint of **Rabbi Yoḥanan ben Nuri,** he meant only that the law is in accordance with his ruling that the husband must annul his wife's vow forbidding him to derive any benefit from what she produces, [2] in order to prevent her **surplus** earnings from becoming forbidden to him.

וְלֵימָא [3] The Gemara objects: **But** if so, Shmuel should have formulated his ruling differently. **He should have said** that **the law is in accordance with** the viewpoint of **Rabbi Yoḥanan ben Nuri,** but only **with respect to the** wife's **surplus** earnings. [4] **Or else** he should have said that **the law is not in accordance with** the viewpoint **of the first Tanna,** who says that the husband does not have to annul his wife's vow. [5] **Or else** he should have said that **the law is in accordance with** the viewpoint of **Rabbi Akiva,** who argues that the husband must annul his wife's vow to prevent her surplus earnings from becoming forbidden to him.

[1] כִּי אֲמַר שְׁמוּאֵל הֲלָכָה כְּרַבִּי יוֹחָנָן בֶּן נוּרִי, [2] לְהַעֲדָפָה. [3] וְלֵימָא: הֲלָכָה כְּרַבִּי יוֹחָנָן בֶּן נוּרִי לְהַעֲדָפָה. [4] אִי נַמִי: אֵין הֲלָכָה כְּתַנָּא קַמָּא. [5] אִי נַמִי: הֲלָכָה כְּרַבִּי עֲקִיבָא.

LITERAL TRANSLATION

[1] When Shmuel said [that] the law is in accordance with Rabbi Yoḥanan ben Nuri, [2] [it was] regarding the surplus.

[3] But let him say: The law is in accordance with Rabbi Yoḥanan ben Nuri regarding the surplus. [4] Or else: The law is not in accordance with the first Tanna. [5] Or else: The law is in accordance with Rabbi Akiva.

RASHI

כי אמר שמואל הלכה כרבי יוחנן בן נורי להעדפה — קאמר. כלומר, הלכה דיפר ולאו מטעמיה, דאילו לרבי יוחנן — עיקר מעשה ידיה צריך הפרה, ולשמואל משום העדפה, שמא תעדיף על הראוי, הוא דאמר יפר. והשתא נמי הוה מצי לאקשויי: סוף סוף לא בא לעולם, דהא לא נעשה! אלא אקשי ליה קושיא אחריתא. **אין הלכה כתנא קמא** — דאמר אין צריך להפר, אלא יפר.

NOTES

concludes that by Torah law the wife's vow should take effect immediately, but the Rabbis strengthened the husband's lien on his wife's handiwork, so that she cannot forbid it to him by means of a vow while they are still married. Thus it stands to reason that the Rabbis strengthened the husband's lien when it is to his advantage, so that the lien cannot be canceled by his wife's vow, but not when it is to his detriment, so that he will no longer be empowered to annul the vow.

The Rishonim ask: Why does the husband have to annul the vow now? Let him wait until after he is divorced, when the vow takes effect!

Tosafot (cited by *Ritva*) argues that after he divorces his wife he will not be able to annul the vow. Just as a husband cannot annul the vows made by his wife before they were married, after he is divorced he cannot annul those vows that his wife made while they were married.

Ritva cites another opinion, according to which the husband can indeed annul his wife's vow after he divorces her, but it is suggested that he annul the vow immediately so that he does not forget to do so later and inadvertently derive benefit from something that is forbidden to him.

כִּי אֲמַר שְׁמוּאֵל הֲלָכָה כְּרַבִּי יוֹחָנָן בֶּן נוּרִי, לְהַעֲדָפָה **When Shmuel said that the law is in accordance with Rabbi Yoḥanan ben Nuri, it was regarding the surplus.** Our commentary follows the reading and the interpretation of *Rashi*, who explains that Rabbi Yoḥanan ben Nuri agrees with Rabbi Akiva that the husband must annul his wife's vow so that her surplus earnings should not become forbidden to him while they are married, and he argues that there is an additional reason for annulling her vow, so that her handiwork should not become forbidden to him after he divorces her, in which case he will forever be forbidden to take her back as his wife (*Ri HaLavan*). Hence the Gemara can suggest that when Shmuel said that the law is in accordance with the viewpoint of Rabbi Yoḥanan ben Nuri, he meant that the law is in accordance with his viewpoint that the vow must be annulled — but not for his reason, but for Rabbi Akiva's reason. Thus the Gemara can object that, if this is what Shmuel meant, he should have said that the law is in accordance with the view of Rabbi Akiva.

However, most Rishonim accept the viewpoint of *Rabbenu Ḥananel* that Rabbi Yoḥanan ben Nuri disagrees with Rabbi Akiva. According to Rabbi Yoḥanan ben Nuri, the husband does not have to annul his wife's vow on account of her surplus earnings — for she cannot forbid her surplus earnings to him — but only on account of her handiwork, which would become forbidden to him should he divorce her. Thus, when the Gemara suggests that Shmuel meant that the law is in accordance with the viewpoint of Rabbi Yoḥanan ben Nuri regarding the woman's surplus earnings, it is saying that Shmuel agrees with Rabbi Yoḥanan ben Nuri that the wife cannot forbid her surplus earnings to her husband. These Rishonim accept a variant reading: "But let him say that the law is in accordance with the first Tanna. Or else: The law is not in accordance with Rabbi Akiva" (see *Tosafot*).

[1] אֶלָּא אֲמַר רַב יוֹסֵף: קוֹנָמוֹת קָאָמְרַתְּ? [2] שָׁאנֵי קוֹנָמוֹת. [3] מִתּוֹךְ שֶׁאָדָם אוֹסֵר פֵּירוֹת חֲבֵירוֹ עָלָיו, [4] אָדָם מַקְדִּישׁ דָּבָר שֶׁלֹּא בָּא לָעוֹלָם.

[5] אֲמַר לֵיהּ אַבַּיֵי: [6] בִּשְׁלָמָא אָדָם אוֹסֵר פֵּירוֹת חֲבֵירוֹ עָלָיו, שֶׁכֵּן אָדָם אוֹסֵר פֵּירוֹתָיו עַל חֲבֵירוֹ. [7] יֶאֱסֹר דָּבָר שֶׁלֹּא בָּא

LITERAL TRANSLATION

[1] Rather, Rav Yosef said: Do you speak of *konamot*? [2] *Konamot* are different. [3] Since a man can forbid his fellow's produce to himself, [4] a man can consecrate something that has not yet come into the world.

[5] Abaye said to him: [6] Granted that a man can forbid his fellow's produce to himself, since a man can forbid his own produce to his fellow. [7] Shall he forbid to his fellow something that has not yet come

RASHI

אלא אמר רב יוסף — לעולם הלכה ומטעמיה קאמר, ומשום שמא יגרשנה. **ושאני קונמות** — הקדש, שאינו הקדש לכל אלא על אדם אחד, בלשון קונם. **מתוך** — שהוא תופס במקום שאין סתם הקדש תופס. שאדם אוסר פירות חבירו עליו, ואומר: קונם פירות פלוני עלי. ובסתם הקדש אין אדם מקדיש דבר שאינו שלו. הלכך, אדם אוסר עליו נמי דבר שלא בא לעולם. אבל מתניתין — במקדיש הקדש גמור איירי, ואינו ממהר לתפוס כקונם. **אמר ליה אביי** — ומה ראיה פירות חבירו עליו לכאן? שהן פירות חבירו על חבירו, דעכשיו היא משועבדת לו למעשה ידיה, ואינה ראויה להתפיסו בקונם. ולכשיגרשנה קאמר דחייל. ועוד: שעדיין לא נעשית המלאכה עד לאחר גירושין וחזרה. **בשלמא אדם אוסר פירות חבירו עליו** — בקונם, שהרי אדם אוסר פירותיו על חבירו, בין בלשון קונם לחבירו לבדו בין שהקדישו סתם הקדש גמור. **יאסר דבר כו׳** — בתמיה.

TRANSLATION AND COMMENTARY

אֶלָּא אֲמַר רַב יוֹסֵף [1] The Gemara now suggests that the apparent contradiction between Shmuel's two rulings can be reconciled in a different manner. **Rather, Rav Yosef said: Do you cite** Shmuel's ruling regarding a ***konam*** vow to prove that Shmuel maintains that a person can consecrate something that is not yet in existence? It does not follow from that ruling that Shmuel is of the opinion that this is so, [2] because a ***konam*** vow by which one person forbids another from deriving benefit from something as if it were a sacrifice **is** governed by **different** rules from a vow of consecration by which a person forbids something to all other people. Rav Yosef proceeds to explain the difference: A *konam* vow can be binding even under circumstances where a vow of consecration is not binding. [3] **A person can forbid someone else's produce to himself** by means of a *konam* vow, but he cannot consecrate that produce to the Temple treasury. If someone says: "So-and-so's produce shall be forbidden to me as a *konam*," the vow is binding, even though the produce is not his. But if he says: "So-and-so's produce shall be consecrated to the Temple treasury," the consecration is not binding, for a person cannot consecrate property belonging to someone else. Just as a person can forbid to himself by means of a *konam* vow something that does not belong to him, [4] **he can** also **consecrate** — i.e., forbid to someone else by means of a *konam* vow — **something that has not yet come into existence.** Thus Shmuel ruled in accordance with the viewpoint of Rabbi Yoḥanan ben Nuri, that a husband must annul his wife's *konam* vow forbidding him to derive any benefit from what she produces, because that vow will take effect if he divorces her. But a person cannot consecrate to the Temple treasury something belonging to someone else, and likewise cannot consecrate something that has not yet come into existence. Thus Shmuel ruled in accordance with the viewpoint of Rabbi Yoḥanan HaSandlar in our Mishnah, that a man cannot consecrate his wife's future surplus earnings.

אֲמַר לֵיהּ אַבַּיֵי [5] The Gemara now questions the validity of Rav Yosef's argument. **Abaye said to** Rav Yosef: Does it really follow that since a person can forbid to himself something belonging to another person by means of a *konam* vow, he can likewise forbid to someone else by means of a *konam* vow something that has not yet come into existence? [6] **Granted that a person can forbid someone else's produce to himself, since he can forbid his own produce to someone else,** for in both cases he is in possession of at least one element — either the subject of the vow, his own produce, or the object of the vow, himself. [7] But does this mean that **a person can forbid to someone else** by means of a *konam* vow **something that has not**

NOTES

יֶאֱסֹר דָּבָר שֶׁלֹּא בָּא לָעוֹלָם **Shall he forbid to his fellow something that has not yet come into the world?** *Rabbi Shlomo of Montpellier* explains that Abaye is arguing with Rav Yosef on the basis of Rav Yosef's own position that something that does not yet exist is governed by the same laws as something belonging to another person, for something that does not yet exist cannot belong to anyone, and no one can forbid to someone else something that does not belong to him. But a person should be able to forbid to himself something that has not yet come into existence, for a person can indeed forbid to himself something that does not belong to him. But Abaye himself maintains that a person cannot forbid something that does not yet exist even to himself, for we cannot compare

לָעוֹלָם עַל חֲבֵירוֹ, [1] שֶׁכֵּן אֵין אָדָם אוֹסֵר פֵּירוֹת חֲבֵירוֹ עַל חֲבֵירוֹ?

[2] אֶלָּא אָמַר רַב הוּנָא בְּרֵיהּ דְּרַב יְהוֹשֻׁעַ: [3] בְּאוֹמֶרֶת: ״יִקָּדְשׁוּ יָדַי לְעוֹשֵׂיהֶם״, [4] דְּיָדַיִם אִיתְנְהוּ בָּעוֹלָם.

[5] וְכִי קָאָמְרָה הָכִי, מִי מִקַּדַּשׁ? [6] הָא מְשַׁעְבְּדָא לֵיהּ!

[7] דְּאָמְרָה: ״לְכִי מִיגַּרְשָׁה״.

LITERAL TRANSLATION

into the world, [1] since a man cannot forbid his fellow's produce to his fellow?

[2] Rather, Rav Huna the son of Rav Yehoshua said: [3] [It is] where she says: "Let my hands be consecrated to Him who made them," [4] for [her] hands are in the world.

[5] And when she says this, are they consecrated? [6] Surely she is obligated to him!

[7] [It is] where she says: "When I am divorced."

TRANSLATION AND COMMENTARY

yet come into existence, [1] **when one person cannot forbid someone else's produce to a third party** by means of such a vow? One person cannot forbid someone else's property to a third party by means of a *konam* vow, for in this case neither the subject of the vow nor the object of the vow belong to the person making it. Similarly, one should not be able to forbid something that has not yet come into existence to someone else by means of a *konam* vow, for here too neither element is in his possession. Thus the difficulty returns: If Shmuel did indeed rule in accordance with the viewpoint of Rabbi Yoḥanan HaSandlar that a husband cannot consecrate his wife's future surplus earnings because a person cannot consecrate something that has not yet come into existence, how could he have ruled in accordance with the viewpoint of Rabbi Yoḥanan ben Nuri that a wife can forbid her future handiwork to her husband by means of a *konam* vow, when that handiwork is not yet in existence and she herself is not entitled to her own handiwork until after she is divorced?

אֶלָּא [2] The Gemara now proposes another way to reconcile the apparent contradiction between Shmuel's two rulings. **Rather, Rav Huna the son of Rav Yehoshua said:** Our Mishnah refers to a case in which the husband consecrated his wife's future surplus earnings, and Shmuel ruled in accordance with the viewpoint of Rabbi Yoḥanan HaSandlar that the surplus earnings are not consecrated, because a person cannot consecrate something that has not yet come into existence. [3] But the Mishnah in *Nedarim* refers to a case **where** the wife **said** to her husband: **"Let my hands** with respect to what they produce **be** forbidden to you as a *konam*, as if they had been **consecrated to Him who made them."** There, Shmuel ruled in accordance with the viewpoint of Rabbi Yoḥanan ben Nuri that the vow is binding, [4] **because** there **the** woman's **hands were in existence** at the time she took the vow.

וְכִי קָאָמְרָה הָכִי [5] The Gemara raises an objection: **But when** the wife **formulates her vow in that manner, are** her hands indeed **forbidden** to her husband with respect to what they will produce? Such a formulation overcomes the problem that the wife's handiwork is not yet in existence. [6] But **surely** those hands are not entirely in her possession, because **she is obliged to** use them to work for her husband as long as she is married to him!

דְּאָמְרָה [7] The Gemara answers: The Mishnah in *Nedarim* refers to a case **where** the wife **said:** "Let my hands with respect to what they produce be forbidden to my husband **when I am divorced** from him." In

RASHI

דבר שלא בא לעולם — לא המלאכה באה, ולא הרשות באה לידה להתפיס, עד שתתגרש. **שכן אין אדם כו'** — שממקום שבאת אין אתה יכול ללמוד איסור, שהרי אף בקונם אין אוסר פירות חבירו על חבירו לומר: קונם פירותיך עליך. **באומרת יקדשו ידי כו'** — שהמלאכה כמי שבאת לעולם. ועל הגירושין שלא באו קא מסיק ואזיל ומתניתין באומר מעשה ידיך הקדש.

NOTES

something that exists but belongs to someone else with something that does not even exist.

Ra'ah, *Rashba*, and others disagree. They say that all agree that a person can forbid to himself by means of a *konam* vow something that has not yet come into existence.

״יִקָּדְשׁוּ יָדַי לְעוֹשֵׂיהֶם״ "Let my hands be consecrated to Him who made them." If someone consecrates his tree with respect to the fruit that it will produce, the fruit becomes consecrated; but if he consecrates his net with respect to the fish that will be caught in it, the fish do not become consecrated. The Rishonim argue that the case of the wife who forbids her hands to her husband with respect to what they will produce is similar to the case of the consecrated tree rather than to the case of the consecrated net. Even though the woman's handiwork does not actually issue from her hands, as the fruit issues from the tree, the woman's hands do produce the handiwork, just as the tree produces the fruit. But the fish do not issue from the net, nor are they produced by the net. They are simply caught in the net, and therefore they cannot become consecrated through a vow of consecration formulated in terms of the net (*Rashba*, *Ritva*, and others).

״לְכִי מִיגַּרְשָׁה״ "When I am divorced." The Rishonim ask: If the Mishnah in *Nedarim* refers to a case in which the wife says that her hands with respect to what they will

TRANSLATION AND COMMENTARY

such a case the vow is binding, because it will take effect only after the woman is divorced, when her hands and what they produce are already in her possession.

וּמִי אִיכָּא [1]The Gemara raises another objection: **But is there something that cannot become consecrated** or forbidden **at the present** time, **but can become consecrated** or forbidden at some **later** date?

אֲמַר רַבִּי אִלְעַאי [2]**Rabbi Il'ai said** in reply to this objection: **Why not?** [3]**If one person says to another** while negotiating the sale of a field with him: **"This field that I am selling to you** now **will be consecrated when I buy it back from you** in the future," [4]**will** the field **not become consecrated** when the original owner buys it back?

מַתְקִיף לַהּ רַבִּי יִרְמְיָה [5]**Rabbi Yirmeyah objected** to Rabbi Il'ai's argument: **Are** the two cases really **comparable?** [6]**There,** in the example suggested by Rabbi Il'ai, **it is in** the owner's **power to consecrate** the field which he still owns. Since he can consecrate the field now, he can also formulate his vow in such a way that the consecration will take effect at some point in the future when the field will once again be his. [7]But **here,** in our case, **it is not in** the wife's **power to grant herself a divorce** and thereby make herself entitled to her handiwork. Since she can do nothing to give herself the right to consecrate her handiwork at the present time, she is unable to consecrate her handiwork even if she formulates her vow in such a way that it only takes effect after she is divorced. [8]If anything, continues Rabbi Yirmeyah, our case **is comparable to** a case in which **one person says to another: "This field that I have** already **sold to you will be consecrated when I buy it back from you** in the future." [9]In such a case, the field **does not become consecrated,** even after the original owner

[1]וּמִי אִיכָּא מִידֵי דְּאִילּוּ הָשְׁתָּא לָא קָדֵישׁ, וּלְקַמֵּיהּ קָדֵישׁ? [2]אֲמַר רַבִּי אִלְעַאי: אַלְּמָה לָא? [3]אִילּוּ הָאוֹמֵר לַחֲבֵירוֹ: "שָׂדֶה זוֹ שֶׁאֲנִי מוֹכֵר לָךְ, לִכְשֶׁאֶקָּחֶנָּה מִמְּךָ, תִּיקָּדֵשׁ", [4]מִי לָא קָדְשָׁה? [5]מַתְקִיף לַהּ רַבִּי יִרְמְיָה: מִי דָּמֵי? [6]הָתָם, בְּיָדוֹ לְהַקְדִּישָׁהּ. [7]הָכָא, אֵין בְּיָדָהּ לְגָרֵשׁ אֶת עַצְמָהּ! [8]הָא לָא דָּמְיָא אֶלָּא לְאוֹמֵר לַחֲבֵירוֹ: "שָׂדֶה זוֹ שֶׁמָּכַרְתִּי לָךְ, לִכְשֶׁאֶקָּחֶנָּה מִמְּךָ, תִּיקָּדֵשׁ", [9]דְּלָא קָדְשָׁה.

LITERAL TRANSLATION

[1]But is there something that now would not be consecrated, but later is consecrated?

[2]Rabbi Il'ai said: Why not? [3]If someone says to his fellow: "This field that I am selling to you, when I buy it back from you, it shall be consecrated," [4]will it not be consecrated?

[5]Rabbi Yirmeyah objected to it: Is it comparable? [6]There, it is in his hand to consecrate it. [7]Here, it is not in her hand to divorce herself! [8]This, is only comparable (lit., "not comparable except") to someone who says to his fellow: "This field that I have sold to you, when I buy it back from you, it shall be consecrated," [9]where it is not consecrated.

RASHI

ומי איכא מידי כו׳ — כלומר, תירלת לא בא לעולם דמלאכה לא בא לעולם, דגירושין לא תירלת. דאילו השתא לית לה רשותא לאקדושיה, והיכי קדיש לקמיה? **אלמה לא** — בתמיה. **מי לא קדשה** — אם מכרה וחזר ולקחה. **בידו להקדישה** — שהרי עכשיו שלו, וכי היכי דאילו אקדשה השתא — קדשה, כי אמר נמי תיקדוש לקמיה — קדשה. **הא לא דמיא** — מסקנא דקושיא היא.

NOTES

produce will be forbidden to her husband when she is divorced from him, why did Rabbi Akiva say that the husband must annul the vow on account of her surplus earnings. As long as the woman is married to her husband, her surplus earnings are not forbidden to him, and after her divorce all her handiwork will be forbidden to him!

Rivan suggests that it is only according to Rabbi Yoḥanan ben Nuri that the Gemara interprets the Mishnah as referring to a case in which the woman forbids her hands to her husband only after she is divorced from him.

Others explain that the Mishnah is referring to all cases, when the wife forbids her hands to her husband without specifying when the vow is to take effect, or when she says that the vow is to take effect immediately, and also when she says that it is to take effect only after she is divorced from him. Rabbi Akiva says that the husband must annul the vow in all cases, on account of the wife's surplus earnings. Rabbi Yoḥanan ben Nuri says that the husband has to annul the vow only if she says that it is to take effect after she is divorced from him, when she is entitled to her handiwork (*Rashba, Ritva*).

HALAKHAH

"שָׂדֶה זוֹ שֶׁאֲנִי מוֹכֵר לָךְ" **"This field that I am selling to you."** "If one person says to another: 'This field that I am selling to you will be consecrated after I buy it back from you,' the field becomes consecrated when the original owner buys the field back, for when he took the vow of consecration, it was in his power to consecrate the field." (*Rambam, Sefer Hafla'ah, Hilkhot Arakhin* 6:29.)

"שָׂדֶה זוֹ שֶׁמָּכַרְתִּי לָךְ" **"This field that I have sold to you."** "If one person says to another: 'This field that I have already sold to you will be consecrated after I buy it back from you,' the field does not become consecrated even after the original owner buys it back, for when he took the vow of consecration, the field was not his to consecrate." (Ibid., 6:27.)

[1]מַתְקִיף לָהּ רַב פַּפָּא: מִי דָּמֵי? [2]הָתָם, גּוּפָא וּפֵירוֹת בְּיָדָא דְּלוֹקֵחַ. [3]הָכָא, גּוּפָהּ בְּיָדָהּ הוּא! [4]הָא לָא דָּמְיָא אֶלָּא לְאוֹמֵר לַחֲבֵירוֹ: [59B] [5]״שָׂדֶה זוֹ שֶׁמִּשְׁכַּנְתִּי לְךָ, לִכְשֶׁאֶפְדֶּנָּה מִמְּךָ, תִּיקָּדֵשׁ״, [6]דִּקְדְשָׁה. [7]מַתְקִיף לָהּ רַב שֵׁישָׁא בְּרֵיהּ דְּרַב אִידִי: [8]מִי דָּמֵי? [9]הָתָם, בְּיָדוֹ לִפְדוֹתָהּ. [10]הָכָא, אֵין בְּיָדָהּ לְגָרֵשׁ עַצְמָהּ! [11]הָא לָא

LITERAL TRANSLATION

[1]Rav Pappa objected to it: Is it comparable? [2]There, the field itself and the produce are in the hand of the buyer. [3]Here, her person is in her own hand! [4]This, this is only comparable to someone who says to his fellow: [59B] [5]"This field that I have pledged to you, when I redeem it from you, it shall be consecrated," [6]where it is consecrated.

[7]Rav Shesha the son of Rav Idi objected to it: [8]Is it comparable? [9]There, it is in his hand to redeem it. [10]Here, it is not in her hand to divorce herself! [11]This is only

TRANSLATION AND COMMENTARY

repurchases it from the buyer, for it did not belong to him when he made his vow of consecration.

מַתְקִיף לָהּ רַב פַּפָּא [1]**Rav Pappa objected to** the comparison drawn by Rabbi Yirmeyah between the case of the wife who forbids her handiwork to her husband, and the case of the man who consecrates a field that he has already sold to someone else: **Are** the two cases really **comparable?** [2]**There,** in the case of the field, both the **field itself and the** field's **produce are** now **in the hands of the buyer.** The original owner cannot consecrate the field, because the fact that he once owned the field is irrelevant to its present status. [3]But **here,** regarding the wife's handiwork, **her person is in her own possession!** Even though the husband is entitled to his wife's handiwork, the wife's hands themselves remain her own, and, as was explained earlier, the Mishnah is referring to a case in which the wife forbids her hands to her husband. Thus the *konam* vow taken by the wife forbidding her hands to her husband with respect to what they will produce should indeed be binding. [4]If anything, continues Rav Pappa, our case **is comparable to** a case in which **one person says to another:** [59B] [5]**"This field that I have** already **pledged to you will be consecrated when I redeem it from you** in the future." [6]In such a case, the field does in fact **become consecrated** as soon as it is redeemed by its owner. The owner cannot consecrate the field now, for it is pledged. But he can declare that the field will become consecrated after it is redeemed, for the field remains his property even while it is pledged to someone else.

מַתְקִיף לָהּ רַב שֵׁישָׁא בְּרֵיהּ דְּרַב אִידִי [7]**Rav Shesha the son of Rav Idi objected to** Rav Pappa's comparison between the case of the wife who forbids her handiwork to her husband and the case of the man who consecrates a field that he has already pledged to someone else: [8]**Are the two cases really comparable?** [9]**There,** in the case of the pledged field, **it is in** the owner's **power to redeem** the field immediately by repaying his debt, and therefore he can consecrate the field at once. Hence he can also formulate his vow to have the consecration take effect in the future when the pledge is redeemed. [10]But **here,** in our case, **it is not in** the wife's **power to grant herself a divorce,** which would entitle her to her own handiwork, so that she could consecrate it or forbid it to her husband by means of a *konam* vow! [11]If anything, our case **is**

SAGES

רַב שֵׁישָׁא בְּרֵיהּ דְּרַב אִידִי **Rav Shesha the son of Rav Idi.** A Babylonian Amora of the fourth and fifth generations, Rav Shesha (or, as he is sometimes called, Rav Sheshet) was the son of the Sage Rav Idi bar Avin, who belonged to the third generation of Babylonian Amoraim. Rav Shesha discusses Halakhic issues with Abaye and Rava and also with the greatest of their students.

RASHI

התם — גבי מכרתי לך אין לו עכשיו בה לא גוף ולא פירות, ואין אדם מקדיש דבר שאינו שלו. **הכא גופה בידה הוא** — והרי יקדשו ידי אמרה. **הא לא דמיא** — מסקנא דאתקפתיה היא.

NOTES

לִכְשֶׁאֶפְדֶּנָּה מִמְּךָ, תִּיקָּדֵשׁ" **"When I redeem it from you, it shall be consecrated."** *Tosafot* and others note that our Gemara implies that if one person pledges his field to another and then consecrates it, intending that the field be consecrated immediately, the field is not consecrated. But this poses a certain difficulty, for it would appear from other Talmudic passages that a debtor can consecrate property pledged for the repayment of his debt, provided that he has other property from which his debt can be repaid.

Rashba argues that there is really no difficulty, for the Gemara does not wish to say that there is no way to

HALAKHAH

שָׂדֶה זוֹ שֶׁמִּשְׁכַּנְתִּי לְךָ" **"This field that I have pledged to you."** "If one person says to another: 'This field that I have pledged to you shall be consecrated after I redeem it from you,' the field becomes consecrated after the owner has redeemed it, for it is in his power to redeem the field when he makes the statement. The field becomes consecrated after the owner has redeemed it, even if the field was pledged for a set period of time, for it is in the owner's power to redeem the field as soon as that period of time has passed." (*Rambam, Sefer Hafla'ah, Hilkhot Arakhin* 6:29.)

דָּמְיָא אֶלָּא לָאוֹמֵר לַחֲבֵירוֹ: [1]״שָׂדֶה זוֹ שֶׁמִּשְׁכַּנְתִּי לְךָ לְעֶשֶׂר שָׁנִים, לִכְשֶׁאֶפְדֶּנָּה מִמְּךָ, תִּיקָּדֵשׁ״, [2]דְּקָדְשָׁה.
[3]מַתְקִיף לָהּ רַב אַשִׁי: [4]מִי דָּמֵי? [5]הָתָם, לְעֶשֶׂר שָׁנִים מִיהָא בְּיָדוֹ לִפְדוֹתָהּ. [6]הָכָא, אֵין בְּיָדָהּ לְגָרֵשׁ עַצְמָהּ לְעוֹלָם.
[7]אֶלָּא אֲמַר רַב אַשִׁי: קוֹנָמוֹת קָא אָמְרַתְּ? [8]שָׁאנֵי קוֹנָמוֹת,

LITERAL TRANSLATION

comparable to someone who says to his fellow: [1]"This field that I have pledged to you for ten years, when I redeem it from you, it shall be consecrated," [2]where it is consecrated.

[3]Rav Ashi objected to it: [4]Is it comparable? [5]There, at least after ten years it is in his hand to redeem it. [6]Here, it is not in her hand to divorce herself ever.

[7]Rather, Rav Ashi said: Do you speak of *konamot*? [8]*Konamot* are different,

TRANSLATION AND COMMENTARY

comparable to a case in which **one person says to another:** [1]**"This field that I have** already **pledged to you for ten years will be consecrated when I redeem it from you** after the ten years have passed." Even though the owner cannot redeem his pledge and consecrate the field now, [2]the field does in fact **become consecrated** after the ten years have passed and the pledge is redeemed, for the field belongs to its owner even while it is pledged to someone else. This case is analogous to that of the wife who declares that her hands with respect to what they produce will be forbidden to her husband when she is divorced from him. Her vow is binding, for her hands remain in her possession while she is married and her husband is entitled to her handiwork.

מַתְקִיף לָהּ רַב אַשִׁי [3]**Rav Ashi objected to** the comparison drawn by Rav Shesha the son of Rav Idi between the case of the wife who forbids her handiwork to her husband, and the case of the man who consecrates a field that he has already pledged to someone else for ten years. [4]**Are** the two cases really **comparable?** [5]**There,** in the case of the pledged field, the owner cannot redeem his pledge for ten years, but **after** the **ten years** have passed **it will indeed be in** the owner's **power to redeem** his field. Thus the owner retains a certain control over his field even though it is pledged. [6]But **here,** in our case, **it will never be in** the wife's **power to grant herself a divorce.** Thus she should not be able to forbid her hands to her husband with respect to what they will produce, even if she states that her hands will only become forbidden to him after she is divorced.

אֶלָּא אֲמַר רַב אַשִׁי [7] The Gemara now proposes a different approach to the difficulties raised above. **Rather, Rav Ashi said: You cited** Shmuel's ruling regarding the ***konam*** vow taken by the wife forbidding her handiwork to her husband, in order to prove that Shmuel must maintain that a person can consecrate something that is not yet in his possession. [8]But that argument is invalid, because **a *konam*** vow, by which one person forbids another from deriving benefit from something as if it were a sacrifice, **is** governed by **different** rules from a vow of consecration, by which something is dedicated to the Temple treasury, **for** a *konam* vow **causes the** forbidden **object itself to be consecrated.** During the Temple period, a person could consecrate property either to the Temple treasury, in which case it would be used for the repair and upkeep of the Temple (קָדְשֵׁי בֶּדֶק הַבַּיִת — *kodshei bedek habayit*), or to the altar, in which case objects fit for sacrificial purposes, such as animals, flour, and oil, would be sacrificed, and all other objects would be used for the purchase of sacrifices (קָדְשֵׁי מִזְבֵּחַ — *kodshei mizbe'aḥ*). Consecrated property can have different degrees of sanctity: Objects that have been consecrated to the altar and are fit for sacrificial purposes have intrinsic sanctity, and cannot be redeemed. Objects that have been consecrated to the Temple treasury, or those that have been consecrated to the altar but are not fit for sacrificial purposes, have monetary sanctity,

RASHI

לא דמיא אלא להא — לא דמי לשדה זו שמשכנתי לך סתם, אלא לאומר ״שדה זו שמשכנתי לעשר שנים״ דאין בידו לפדותה ולהקדישה עכשיו. **דקדשה** — דהא שלו היא.

NOTES

consecrate a field while it is subject to a lien. The Gemara only formulated the case as it did, saying that the owner of the field stipulated that his field was to become consecrated after he redeemed it from his creditor, because it was meant to parallel the case of the wife who vowed that her hands with respect to what they would produce would be forbidden to her husband after she was divorced.

שָׁאנֵי קוֹנָמוֹת *Konamot* are different. Most authorities explain that Rav Ashi is referring to a case in which the wife said: "Let my hands be consecrated to Him who made them," but if she forbade her handiwork to her husband by means of a *konam* vow, the husband would not be forbidden to derive benefit from her handiwork even after he divorced her, for a person cannot forbid to another person something that is not yet in existence. *Rambam* (*Hilkhot Nedarim* 12:10) maintains that Rav Ashi is referring even to a case in which the wife forbade her handiwork to her husband by means of a *konam* vow (see *Kesef Mishneh* and *Leḥem Mishneh*).

TRANSLATION AND COMMENTARY

and can be redeemed. When one person forbids another by means of a *konam* vow from deriving benefit from something, the forbidden object is treated as if it has intrinsic sanctity, so that it cannot be redeemed and can never become permitted to the person to whom it has been forbidden. Now, since a *konam* vow imposes something akin to intrinsic sanctity upon the forbidden object, a wife can forbid her handiwork to her husband by means of a *konam* vow, even though she is obligated to hand over her handiwork to him, [1]**and this is in accordance with** the viewpoint of **Rava. For Rava said:** If someone has pledged his property to his creditor and later makes an irredeemable [2]**consecration** of that property — in other words, he consecrates it with intrinsic sanctity — [3]or the pledge is **leavened bread** and Pesaḥ arrives, during which no benefit may be derived from the leavened bread, [4]or the pledge is a slave and the owner grants him **emancipation,** in all these cases the creditor's **mortgage** on the pledge **is canceled.** The creditor's mortgage on the debtor's property is subject to the debtor's ownership of that property. If the debtor's ownership of the property ends, the debtor's mortgage is canceled. When someone makes an irredeemable consecration of his property, that property no longer

דִּקְדוּשַּׁת הַגּוּף נִינְהוּ. [1] וּכְדְרָבָא, דְּאָמַר רָבָא: [2] הֶקְדֵּשׁ, [3] חָמֵץ, [4] וְשִׁחְרוּר מַפְקִיעִין מִידֵי שִׁיעְבּוּד.

LITERAL TRANSLATION

for they are the consecration of the thing itself. [1]And it is in accordance with Rava, for Rava said: [2]Consecration, [3][the prohibition against] leavened bread, [4]and emancipation cancel a mortgage.

RASHI

דקדושת הגוף נינהו — כקדושת מזבח, שאין להן פדיון — כך אין פדיון לקונם להיות ניתר למי שנאסר עליו. שהרי אינו הקדש גמור לתפוס פדיונו, אלא אסור על אדם אחד. וכיון דקדושת הגוף הוא — מפקיע מידי שעבוד שהיא משועבדת לבעלה, וחייל. ולקמן פריך: אם כן מאי איריא שמא יגרשנה? מהשתא חייל! **הקדש** — כגון שיעבד שורו לבעל חוב, וחזר והקדישו — מפקיע שעבוד המלוה, וגובה חובו ממקום אחר. וזה כשר לקרבן, ואינו גזול. דלא הוה קני ליה אלא לגוביינא בעלמא. ודוקא קדושת הגוף, אבל קדושת דמים דבדק הבית — לא מפקיע שעבוד, כדתנן בערכין (כג,ב): מוסיף עוד דינר ופודה את הנכסים הללו כו׳. **חמץ** — עשה חמצו אפותיקי לנכרי, והגיע הפסח — איסור חמץ מפקיעו משעבוד הנכרי, ונאסר בהנאה. והא דתנן (פסחים ל,ב): נכרי שהלוה לישראל על חמצו, אחר הפסח מותר בהנאה אוקמינן לה התם כשהרהינו אצלו, שמסרו בידו משכון. **ושחרור** — עשה עבדו אפותיקי ושחררו הלוה — משוחרר, וזה גובה חובו ממקום אחר.

NOTES

הֶקְדֵּשׁ Consecration. Following the Gemara's remark that an object forbidden by means of a *konam* vow is treated as if it has intrinsic sanctity, *Rashi* and most Rishonim (see *Ramban* and *Rashba*) explain that consecration only cancels a lien if the pledged property was consecrated with intrinsic sanctity. But if the debtor consecrated the pledged property with monetary sanctity, the lien that was established on that property is not canceled. This position is supported by what the Gemara says elsewhere (*Arakhin* 23b) that if a person consecrates property that has been pledged to his creditor, he must redeem the property with a small amount of money, not because the property has actually become consecrated, but rather so that people do not wrongly conclude that consecrated property can lose its sacred status without any money being paid.

Rambam (*Hilkhot Arakhin* 7:14; *Hilkhot Malveh VeLoveh* 18:7) maintains that the creditor's lien is canceled even if the debtor consecrated the property with monetary sanctity. *Rambam's* position may perhaps be based on a different reading of the Gemara, according to which Rav Ashi said that *konamot* are different, without explaining that they have intrinsic sanctity.

Rabbenu Tam (*Sefer HaYashar* 113; *Tosafot, Gittin* 40b) argues that, in general, consecration cancels the creditor's lien, even if the pledged property was consecrated with monetary sanctity. The only exception is landed property, which cannot be consecrated if it has been pledged to a creditor, for a person can only consecrate property that is found in his possession, and pledged real estate is regarded as if it has already been collected and is now in the creditor's possession.

חָמֵץ Leavened bread. The Rishonim ask: Why does Rava

HALAKHAH

הֶקְדֵּשׁ Consecration. "If a debtor consecrates the property he has pledged to his creditor, the creditor's lien on that property is canceled, in accordance with the viewpoint of Rava. Most authorities follow *Rashi* and the Geonim, who say that this applies only if the debtor consecrated the property with intrinsic sanctity; but if he consecrated it with monetary sanctity, the creditor's lien is not canceled. In such a case, the debtor must redeem the property with a symbolic amount of money, so that people should not think that consecrated property can lose its sacred status without money being paid. According to *Rambam,* even if the debtor consecrated the property with monetary sanctity, the creditor's lien is canceled until the property is redeemed (see *Maggid Mishneh*)." (*Rambam, Sefer Mishpatim, Hilkhot Malveh VeLoveh* 18:6-7; *Sefer Hafla'ah, Hilkhot Arakhin* 7:14; *Tur, Ḥoshen Mishpat* 117; *Rema, Shulḥan Arukh, Ḥoshen Mishpat* 117:7.)

חָמֵץ Leavened bread. "If a Jew borrows money from a non-Jew and pledges his leavened bread as security for the repayment of the loan, and Pesaḥ arrives, the leavened bread is now forbidden (unless it was physically handed over to the non-Jew as a pledge), for the prohibition against leavened bread on Pesaḥ cancels the creditor's lien," following Rava. (*Rambam, Sefer Mishpatim, Hilkhot Malveh VeLoveh* 18:6; *Shulḥan Arukh, Oraḥ Ḥayyim* 441:1.)

וְשִׁחְרוּר And emancipation. "If someone pledges his slave

TRANSLATION AND COMMENTARY

belongs to him. A person's ownership of his leavened bread is canceled upon the advent of Pesaḥ, and his ownership of a slave ends when he sets him free. In all three cases, the creditor's mortgage is canceled when the debtor loses his ownership of the pledged property. Now, while a woman is married to her husband, her husband has a lien on her hands with respect to the handiwork they will produce. But since a *konam* vow imposes something akin to intrinsic sanctity upon the forbidden object, the husband's lien on his wife's hands is canceled when she forbids them to him by means of a *konam* vow, and thus the *konam* vow is binding.

וְנִקְדְּשׁוּ מֵהַשְׁתָּא [1] The Gemara objects: If the wife's *konam* vow does indeed cancel the husband's lien on his wife's hands, **let her handiwork be forbidden** to her husband **immediately!** Why did Rabbi Yoḥanan ben Nuri say that the husband must annul his wife's vow to prevent her handiwork from becoming forbidden to him after he divorces her?

אַלְמוּהָ רַבָּנַן לְשִׁיעְבּוּדֵיהּ דְּבַעַל [2] The Gemara answers: Rabbi Yoḥanan ben Nuri maintains that **the Rabbis made the husband's lien** on his wife's hands **stronger** than other liens, [3] **so that her handiwork cannot become forbidden** to him **now**, while the two are still married. But the *konam* vow does cancel the husband's lien on her hands, so that when she forbids them to her husband, she is not viewed as forbidding something that is not yet hers. Thus her vow is binding, and her handiwork becomes forbidden to her husband after their divorce.

MISHNAH וְאֵלּוּ [4] This Mishnah lists the household tasks that a married woman is obligated to perform. **These are the** seven **tasks that a wife** of limited means **must perform for her husband: She** must

[1] וְנִקְדְּשׁוּ מֵהַשְׁתָּא!
[2] אַלְמוּהָ רַבָּנַן לְשִׁיעְבּוּדֵיהּ דְּבַעַל, [3] כִּי הֵיכִי דְּלָא תִּיקָּדֵשׁ מֵהַשְׁתָּא.

מִשְׁנָה [4] וְאֵלּוּ מְלָאכוֹת שֶׁהָאִשָּׁה עוֹשָׂה לְבַעְלָהּ:

LITERAL TRANSLATION

[1] Then let [her handiwork] be consecrated from now!

[2] The Rabbis strengthened the lien of the husband, [3] so that [her handiwork] not be consecrated from now.

MISHNAH [4] And these are the tasks that a wife performs for her husband:

RASHI

ונקדשו מהשתא – מאי איריא דקתני שמא יגרשנה? מהשתא נמי קדיש. **אלמוה רבנן לשעבודיה דבעל** – בעודה תחתיו, דשויוהו רבנן כלוקח גמור, ולא כמלוה.

NOTES

mention only the case of leavened bread, and not other cases in which a prohibition against deriving benefit from the pledged property cancels the creditor's lien?

Some authorities explain that other items from which benefit may not be derived are included in the category of consecrated property (*Rabbenu Ḥananel*, *Rivan*). Others suggest that such items are included in the category of leavened bread (*Ra'ah*, *Ritva*).

אַלְמוּהָ רַבָּנַן לְשִׁיעְבּוּדֵיהּ דְּבַעַל The Rabbis strengthened the lien of the husband. *Rivan* explains that the Rabbis strengthened the husband's lien on his wife's handiwork because they were concerned that whenever a wife became angry with her husband, she would forbid her handiwork to him by means of a *konam* vow. Hence they enacted that the husband should be treated as if he has purchased his wife's handiwork, and therefore she cannot forbid it to him by means of a *konam* vow so long as the two are still married, for a *konam* vow can certainly not take effect upon property that has already been sold (*Rashi*, *Rivan*).

Some Rishonim explain that it is for this reason that the anonymous first Tanna of the Mishnah in *Nedarim* says that a man does not have to annul his wife's vow forbidding him to derive benefit from her handiwork. Since the Rabbis strengthened the husband's lien on his wife's hands, so that her handiwork cannot be forbidden to him while they are married, her handiwork also cannot be forbidden to him after they are divorced (*Ra'ah*, *Ritva*).

Others argue that the anonymous first Tanna disagrees with Rabbi Yoḥanan ben Nuri, and says that if one person forbids another from deriving benefit from something by means of a *konam* vow, the forbidden object is not treated as if it has intrinsic sanctity (*Rivan*, *Ramban*, and others).

וְאֵלּוּ מְלָאכוֹת And these are the tasks. The Jerusalem Talmud cites a Baraita which states: "Seven principal tasks were mentioned, but the others the Sages did not have to mention." The Mishnah's list does not exhaust the wife's responsibilities, for there are other obligations, both minor household tasks (for example, feeding his animals; see

HALAKHAH

to his creditor and then emancipates the slave, the creditor's lien is canceled and the slave becomes a free man," following Rava. (*Rambam, Sefer Mishpatim, Hilkhot Malveh VeLoveh* 18:6; *Sefer Kinyan, Hilkhot Avadim* 8:16; *Shulḥan Arukh, Yoreh De'ah* 267:68; *Ḥoshen Mishpat* 117:6.)

וְאֵלּוּ מְלָאכוֹת שֶׁהָאִשָּׁה עוֹשָׂה And these are the tasks that a wife performs. "There are certain tasks that a wife must perform for her husband if they are poor: She must grind his grain, bake his bread, cook his meals, launder his clothing, and nurse their child," following the Mishnah. (*Rambam, Sefer Nashim, Hilkhot Ishut* 21:5; *Shulḥan Arukh, Even HaEzer* 80:6.)

¹טוֹחֶנֶת, ²וְאוֹפָה, ³וּמְכַבֶּסֶת, ⁴מְבַשֶּׁלֶת, ⁵וּמֵנִיקָה אֶת בְּנָהּ, ⁶מַצַּעַת לוֹ הַמִּטָּה, ⁷וְעוֹשָׂה בַּצֶּמֶר.

⁸הִכְנִיסָה לוֹ שִׁפְחָה אַחַת, ⁹לֹא טוֹחֶנֶת, וְלֹא אוֹפָה, וְלֹא מְכַבֶּסֶת. ¹⁰שְׁתַּיִם — אֵין מְבַשֶּׁלֶת, ¹¹וְאֵין מֵנִיקָה אֶת בְּנָהּ. ¹²שָׁלֹשׁ — אֵין מַצַּעַת לוֹ הַמִּטָּה, ¹³וְאֵין עוֹשָׂה בַּצֶּמֶר.

LITERAL TRANSLATION

[1]She grinds, [2]and bakes, [3]and launders, [4][and] cooks, [5]and nurses her child, [6][and] makes his bed, [7]and works with wool.

[8]If she brought him one maidservant, [9]she does not grind, and she does not bake, and she does not launder. [10]Two — she does not cook, [11]and she does not nurse her child. [12]Three — she does not make his bed, [13]and she does not work with wool.

TRANSLATION AND COMMENTARY

(1) [1]**grind** his grain into flour, (2) [2]**bake** his bread, (3) [3]**launder** his clothing, (4) [4]**cook** his meals, (5) [5]**nurse** her infant **child, (6)** [6]**arrange** the mattress and pillows on her husband's **bed,** [7]**and** (7) **spin** a certain amount of **wool** each week, as will be specified later in the chapter (64b).

הִכְנִיסָה לוֹ שִׁפְחָה אַחַת [8] However, **if** a married woman **brought a maidservant** with her from her father's home, or a dowry sufficient for the purchase of a maidservant, or if the husband himself was sufficiently wealthy that he could afford to buy a maidservant, the wife is relieved of some of her domestic responsibilities, because the maidservant can carry out those duties for her. [9]**She is not required to grind** her husband's grain, **nor is she required to bake** his bread, **nor is she required to launder** his clothing. [10]If the wife brought **two** maidservants into the marriage, she is relieved of additional responsibilities. **She is not required to cook** her husband's meals, [11]**nor is she required to nurse her** infant **child**. [12]If she brought **three** maidservants into the marriage, she is exempt from all the domestic tasks listed in our Mishnah, for **she is not** even **required to arrange** the mattress and pillows on her husband's **bed,** [13]**nor is she required to spin** any **wool**.

RASHI

משנה אופה — פת. שתים אינה מבשלת כו׳ — בגמרא פריך: אמאי לא איפטרה מכולהו בחדא שפחה שהכניסה במקומה?

NOTES

below, 61b) and acts of intimacy (for example, pouring his cup; see below, 61a), which the Mishnah did not have to mention, it being obvious that they are included among the wife's duties (*Ra'ah*, *Rivan* and others).

Melekhet Shlomo notes that the seven tasks mentioned in the Mishnah are the principal categories of tasks that a wife must perform for her husband, and that each of them includes a number of subsidiary categories. For example, although the Mishnah only mentions the wife's duty to grind her husband's grain, she is also required to sift the flour. And similarly, although the Mishnah only refers to the wife's duty to bake her husband's bread, she must also knead the dough.

הִכְנִיסָה לוֹ שִׁפְחָה אַחַת If she brought him one maidservant. According to some authorities, a woman who brings a maidservant with her into the marriage is relieved of some of her domestic duties only if she assumes responsibility for the maidservant's maintenance. But if the husband has to maintain the maidservant, then his wife is still required to do all the tasks imposed on a married woman. Otherwise, the husband has gained nothing by having a maidservant in the house, since he now has two mouths to feed with no additional work being done (*Rashi* cited by *Ritva*; see also *Tosafot* 61a, s.v. הכניסה).

Others argue that the wife is relieved of her domestic duties even if the maidservant's maintenance falls upon the husband, for it was on the basis of this understanding that she brought the maidservant with her into the marriage (*Ritva*, and apparently *Rambam*).

HALAKHAH

מַצַּעַת לוֹ הַמִּטָּה And makes his bed. "A married woman is obligated to make her husband's bed. *Rema* adds that, according to some authorities (*Maggid Mishneh*, *Ran*), she is required to make all the beds in the house." (*Rambam*, *Sefer Nashim*, *Hilkhot Ishut* 21:3; *Shulḥan Arukh*, *Even HaEzer* 80:4.)

וְעוֹשָׂה בַּצֶּמֶר And works with wool. "A wife is required to produce handiwork for her husband in accordance with local custom. In a place where it is customary for women to weave, she must weave; where they embroider, she must embroider; where they spin wool, she must spin wool. In a place where women are not accustomed to doing any work, a husband can compel his wife to spin wool but nothing else." (*Rambam*, *Sefer Nashim*, *Hilkhot Ishut* 21:1; *Shulḥan Arukh*, *Even HaEzer* 80:1.)

הִכְנִיסָה לוֹ שִׁפְחָה אַחַת If she brought him one maidservant. "If a wife brings a maidservant with her into the marriage, or if she brings into the marriage a dowry large enough to buy a maidservant, or if her husband has a maidservant or enough money to buy one, the wife is not required to grind her husband's grain or to bake his bread, or to do his laundry, or to feed his animals." (*Rambam*, *Sefer Nashim*, *Hilkhot Ishut* 21:6; *Shulḥan Arukh*, *Even HaEzer* 80:7.)

שְׁתַּיִם Two. "If a wife brings two maidservants with her into the marriage, she is not required to cook her husband's meals or to nurse their child." (*Rambam*, *Sefer Nashim*, *Hilkhot Ishut* 21:6; *Shulḥan Arukh*, *Even HaEzer* 80:8.)

שָׁלֹשׁ Three. "*Rema* notes that if a wife brings three maidservants into the marriage, she is required only to make her husband's bed, but not the rest of the beds in the house (following *Ran*). According to some authorities (*Tur*), she is not even required to arrange the mattress and

TRANSLATION AND COMMENTARY

But she is still required to do some light housework. [1]And if the wife brought **four** maidservants into the marriage, **she may sit in a chair** as a lady of leisure. Since she came into the marriage with such a large staff of domestic servants, she is totally exempt from all housework.

רַבִּי אֱלִיעֶזֶר אוֹמֵר [2]**Rabbi Eliezer** disagrees with the first Tanna of the Mishnah and **says: Even if** the wife **brought a hundred maidservants** into the marriage, [3]her husband may **compel her to spin wool** or do other work, [4]**because idleness can lead** a person **to** sexual **promiscuity**, and therefore it is preferable that the wife be given work to keep her occupied.

רַבָּן שִׁמְעוֹן בֶּן גַּמְלִיאֵל אוֹמֵר [5]**Rabban Shimon ben Gamliel says: Similarly, if someone forbids** himself **by a vow** from deriving any benefit **from the work performed by his wife,** [6]he **must grant her a divorce and give her her ketubah,** [7]**for** the vow prevents her from doing any household work, and total **idleness can lead** a person **to insanity.**

GEMARA טוֹחֶנֶת סָלְקָא דַּעְתָּךְ [8]The Gemara asks first about the expression in the Mishnah which states that a wife must grind grain for her husband. **Do you really imagine that** the wife herself **must grind** the grain? Surely grain is ground by millstones that are operated by water or by animals!

אֶלָּא [9]The Gemara suggests that the wording of the Mishnah should be slightly amended: **Rather, say** that the Mishnah reads as follows: A married woman **must arrange for the grinding** of her husband's grain. She must bring the grain to the mill and collect the ground flour.

[1]אַרְבַּע — יוֹשֶׁבֶת בְּקַתֶּדְרָא. [2]רַבִּי אֱלִיעֶזֶר אוֹמֵר: אֲפִילּוּ הִכְנִיסָה לוֹ מֵאָה שְׁפָחוֹת, [3]כּוֹפָהּ לַעֲשׂוֹת בַּצֶּמֶר, [4]שֶׁהַבַּטָּלָה מְבִיאָה לִידֵי זִימָּה. [5]רַבָּן שִׁמְעוֹן בֶּן גַּמְלִיאֵל אוֹמֵר: אַף הַמַּדִּיר אֶת אִשְׁתּוֹ מִלַּעֲשׂוֹת מְלָאכָה, [6]יוֹצִיא וְיִתֵּן כְּתוּבָּה, [7]שֶׁהַבַּטָּלָה מְבִיאָה לִידֵי שִׁיעֲמוּם.

גמרא [8]טוֹחֶנֶת סָלְקָא דַּעְתָּךְ? [9]אֶלָּא אֵימָא: מַטְחֶנֶת.

LITERAL TRANSLATION

[1]Four — she sits in a chair.

[2]Rabbi Eliezer says: Even if she brought him a hundred maidservants, [3]he compels her to work with wool, [4]for idleness leads to promiscuity.

[5]Rabban Shimon ben Gamliel says: Even [if] someone forbids his wife with a vow from doing work, [6]he must divorce [her] and give [her] her ketubah, [7]for idleness leads to insanity.

GEMARA [8]Can it enter your mind that she grinds?

[9]Rather, say: She supervises the grinding.

RASHI

יושבת בקתדרא — לא תטרח בשבילו לילך בשליחות להביא לו חפץ מבית לעליה. **שעמום** — שיגעון.

גמרא טוחנת סלקא דעתך — המים מגלגלין האופן, וטוחן. **מטחנת** — מכינה צורכי טחינה, נותנתו באפרכסת וקולטת הקמח.

BACKGROUND

יוֹשֶׁבֶת בְּקַתֶּדְרָא She sits in a chair. A קַתֶּדְרָא — *katedra* — is not simply a chair, but rather a place of honor, like the throne on which rulers sit. Thus the phrase means that the wife sits like a queen who is not required to do any work at all.

LANGUAGE

קַתֶּדְרָא A chair. From the Greek καθέδρα, *kathedra*, meaning "a chair," and in particular the chair of a teacher or a ruler.

NOTES

יוֹשֶׁבֶת בְּקַתֶּדְרָא She sits in a chair. *Tosafot* notes that there is a difference between a woman who brings three maidservants into her marriage and one who brings in four. If a woman brings in three maidservants, she is exempt from all the domestic tasks mentioned in the Mishnah, but she is still required to do some light housework and to attend to the guests who visit her house (see below, 61a). But if she brings in four maidservants, she may sit back in her chair, for she is totally exempt from all housework.

כּוֹפָהּ לַעֲשׂוֹת בַּצֶּמֶר He compels her to work with wool. *Rashba*, *Ritva*, and others note that even Rabbi Eliezer agrees that a woman who brings a large number of maidservants into her marriage cannot be compelled to do the full quota of work that is ordinarily imposed on a

HALAKHAH

the pillows on her husband's bed, but only his sheet, the arrangement of which is considered an act of intimacy reserved for a man's wife." *Rambam* and *Shulḥan Arukh* do not include this ruling, because they rule in accordance with the viewpoint of Rabbi Eliezer, and because they do not distinguish between the different aspects of arranging beds. (*Shulḥan Arukh, Even HaEzer* 80:8, *Rema*.)

כּוֹפָהּ לַעֲשׂוֹת בַּצֶּמֶר He compels her to work with wool. "Even if a wife has many maidservants, she must not sit around idly without doing any work, according to the ruling of Rabbi Eliezer. She cannot, however, be compelled to work all day long, but only as much as is necessary so that she not be idle." (*Rambam, Sefer Nashim, Hilkhot Ishut* 21:2; *Shulḥan Arukh, Even HaEzer* 80:2.)

הַמַּדִּיר אֶת אִשְׁתּוֹ מִלַּעֲשׂוֹת מְלָאכָה If someone forbids his wife with a vow from doing work. "If someone takes a vow forbidding his wife from doing any work, he must grant her an immediate divorce and pay her her ketubah, for idleness can lead to promiscuity," following Rabbi Eliezer and against Rabban Shimon ben Gamliel, as will be explained below (61b). (*Rambam, Sefer Nashim, Hilkhot Ishut* 21:3; *Shulḥan Arukh, Even HaEzer* 80:3.)

מַטְחֶנֶת She supervises the grinding. "A wife is required to grind her husband's grain. How so? She must sit near the mill and collect the ground flour, or goad the animal moving the millstone, or operate a hand mill, if that is the local custom," in accordance with the two answers given by the Gemara. (*Rambam, Sefer Nashim, Hilkhot Ishut* 21:5; *Shulḥan Arukh, Even HaEzer* 80:6.)

¹וְאִיבָּעֵית אֵימָא: בְּרֵיחַיָּא דִּיָדָא.
²מַתְנִיתִין דְּלָא כְּרַבִּי חִיָּיא, דְּתָנֵי רַבִּי חִיָּיא: ³״אֵין אִשָּׁה אֶלָּא לְיוֹפִי; אֵין אִשָּׁה אֶלָּא לְבָנִים״. ⁴וְתָנֵי רַבִּי חִיָּיא: ״אֵין אִשָּׁה אֶלָּא לְתַכְשִׁיטֵי אִשָּׁה״. ⁵וְתָנֵי רַבִּי חִיָּיא: ״הָרוֹצֶה שֶׁיְּעַדֵּן אֶת אִשְׁתּוֹ, יַלְבִּישֶׁנָּה כְּלֵי פִשְׁתָּן. ⁶הָרוֹצֶה שֶׁיַּלְבִּין אֶת בִּתּוֹ, יַאֲכִילֶנָּה אֶפְרוֹחִים וְיַשְׁקֶנָּה חָלָב סָמוּךְ לְפִירְקָהּ״. ⁷״וּמֵנִיקָה אֶת בְּנָהּ״. ⁸לֵימָא מַתְנִיתִין דְּלָא כְּבֵית שַׁמַּאי,

LITERAL TRANSLATION

¹And if you wish, say: With a handmill. ²Our Mishnah is not in accordance with Rabbi Ḥiyya, for Rabbi Ḥiyya taught: ³"A wife is only for beauty; a wife is only for children." ⁴And Rabbi Ḥiyya taught: "A wife is only for a woman's ornaments." ⁵And Rabbi Ḥiyya taught: "[If] someone wishes to beautify his wife, he should clothe her [with] linen garments. ⁶[If] someone wishes to make his daughter's skin white, he should feed her chicks and give her milk to drink near her period [of puberty]." ⁷"And nurses her child." ⁸Shall we say that our Mishnah is not in accordance with Bet Shammai,

TRANSLATION AND COMMENTARY

וְאִיבָּעֵית ¹The Gemara also proposes a second solution. **And if you wish,** you can **say** that the Mishnah is referring to grain ground **by means of a hand mill**, in which case the woman herself must do the grinding.

מַתְנִיתִין ²The Gemara now notes: **Our Mishnah**, which lists a married woman's domestic responsibilities, **is not in accordance with** the viewpoint of **Rabbi Ḥiyya, for Rabbi Ḥiyya taught** the following Baraita: ³**"A wife is only for beauty; a wife is only for children,"** and not for the performance of household chores. ⁴**And Rabbi Ḥiyya taught** the following related Baraita: **"A wife is only for the ornaments** that her husband provides her to enhance her beauty." ⁵**And Rabbi Ḥiyya taught** yet another Baraita, which stated: **"If someone wishes to beautify his wife, he should clothe her with linen garments**, for these will set off her natural beauty to its best advantage. ⁶**If someone wishes to make his daughter's complexion white, he should feed her chicks and give her** plenty of **milk to drink** as she **nears puberty."**

וּמֵנִיקָה אֶת בְּנָהּ ⁷Among the wife's obligations toward her husband, the Mishnah records her duty to **nurse the** infant **child** born of the marriage. ⁸The Gemara asks: **Shall we say that our Mishnah is not in**

RASHI

ואיבעית אימא — לעולם טוחנת היא עצמה. **דידא** — רחיים של יד. **לתכשיטי אשה** — שיקנו לה תכשיטין להתנאות בהן. **שיעדן** — את זויה, *אישקלויי״ר בלעז. **לפירקה** — ימי הנעורים.

NOTES

married woman (as is explained below, 64b). Rather, she may do as much or as little work as she wishes, provided that she keeps herself busy with the work that she is doing. The Rishonim disagree about who is entitled to the profits from her work. Some say that the profits should be treated as surplus handiwork, i.e., earnings from those tasks that a wife is not legally required to perform for her husband, which ordinarily belong to the husband. Others argue that since by right the wife is totally exempt from doing any work, and whatever she does is only in order to keep herself occupied so that she not be led to promiscuity, any profit from the work belongs to her (see *Ritva* and *Ran*).

אֵין אִשָּׁה אֶלָּא לְיוֹפִי A wife is only for beauty. *Tosafot* notes that Rav Ḥiyya disagrees only about the household tasks mentioned in the Mishnah. In his opinion, a wife is not required to grind her husband's grain, bake his bread, cook his meals, nurse his child, or the like, for a man takes a woman as his wife for her beauty and in order to have children, and not to have her work as his housekeeper or his child's nursemaid. But even Rabbi Ḥiyya agrees that a wife must produce handiwork for her husband, for the Rabbis entitled the husband to his wife's handiwork in exchange for the maintenance that he must provide for her. *Ritva* adds that all agree that she must produce handiwork, so that she will not be led to promiscuity through idleness.

Melo HaRo'im distinguishes between the two halves of Rabbi Ḥiyya's Baraita: A wife is only for beauty, and therefore she is not required to grind, bake, cook, or launder, for these tasks detract from her beauty. A wife is only for children, and therefore she is not required to nurse, for she is less likely to conceive a child while she is nursing another. *Ḥever ben Ḥayyim* argues that if a wife is only for her beauty, then she is not required to nurse, for nursing detracts from her beauty. But if she is only required to produce children, she is indeed required to nurse her infant.

וּמֵנִיקָה אֶת בְּנָהּ And nurses her child. The Jerusalem Talmud explains that the Mishnah's wording is precise: A married woman is obligated to nurse her child, but her husband cannot compel her to nurse another woman's child. According to many authorities, he cannot even compel her to nurse his own child from another woman. According to most authorities (see *Meiri*), the Jerusalem Talmud rules that a woman who gives birth to twins is not obligated to nurse them both. *Rosh* maintains that the Jerusalem Talmud's discussion of the matter revolves around a rhetorical question, the law in fact being that the woman can be required to nurse both twins, if she is able to do so.

REALIA

בְּרֵיחַיָּא דִּיָדָא With a hand mill.

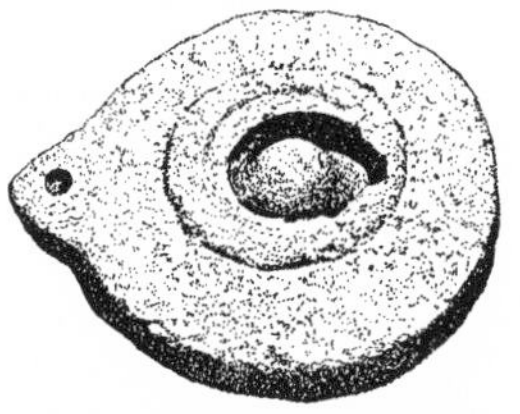

A millstone from a hand mill of the Talmudic period found in the synagogue in Jericho. There was a small hole on the side of the millstone, through which a rod to rotate the millstone was inserted. These millstones were the hand mills to which the Gemara refers here, and were used by women to grind flour for home use. When larger quantities were needed, the flour was ground in larger mills powered by water or by animals (see Judges 16:21). Such heavy work was not done by women, though women did supervise the grinding done in large mills.

BACKGROUND

הָרוֹצֶה שֶׁיַּלְבִּין אֶת בִּתּוֹ If someone wishes to make his daughter's skin white. In Eastern countries, white, unblemished skin is considered particularly beautiful (compare the verse in Song of Songs (1:6): "Do not look upon me, because I am black"). Rabbi Ḥiyya suggests feeding one's daughter nourishing and easily digestible foods, so that her skin will be soft and unblemished.

LANGUAGE (RASHI)

אישקלויי״ר* (correct reading: **אישקלריי״ר**). From the Old French *esclarier*, meaning "to brighten" or "to beautify."

TRANSLATION AND COMMENTARY

accordance with the viewpoint of **Bet Shammai, for it was taught** in a Baraita: [1] **"If a married woman vows not to nurse her** infant **child,** [2] **Bet Shammai say: She must remove her nipple from** the infant's **mouth,** for the vow is valid, and she is not permitted to nurse her baby. [3] **Bet Hillel say: Her husband can compel her to nurse** the infant, for she cannot take a vow that contradicts her marital obligations. [4] But **if she has been divorced,** her former husband **cannot compel her** to nurse their child, for this obligation is imposed upon a woman not as the child's mother but as the wife of the child's father. [5] **But if the baby** already **recognizes** his mother, so that he may refuse to accept milk from another woman, then even if his mother has been divorced, her former husband **can pay her the wage** of a wet nurse [6] **and** can **compel her to breast-feed** their child, **because of the danger** to the infant if she does not do so." Now, according to Bet Shammai, a vow taken by a woman not to nurse her child is binding. Thus it follows that a wife is under no obligation toward her husband to nurse their child.

אֲפִילּוּ [7] The Gemara answers: **You can even say that** the Mishnah **is in accordance with** the viewpoint of **Bet Shammai,** for even Bet Shammai agree that a wife has an obligation to her husband to nurse their

דְּתַנְיָא: [1] "נָדְרָה שֶׁלֹּא לְהָנִיק אֶת בְּנָהּ, [2] בֵּית שַׁמַּאי אוֹמְרִים: שׁוֹמֶטֶת דַּד מִפִּיו. [3] בֵּית הִלֵּל אוֹמְרִים: כּוֹפָה וּמְנִיקַתּוֹ. [4] נִתְגָּרְשָׁה, אֵינוֹ כּוֹפָה. [5] וְאִם הָיָה מַכִּירָהּ, נוֹתֵן לָהּ שְׂכָרָהּ, [6] וְכוֹפָהּ וּמְנִיקַתּוֹ, מִפְּנֵי הַסַּכָּנָה". [7] אֲפִילּוּ תֵּימָא בֵּית שַׁמַּאי.

LITERAL TRANSLATION

for it was taught: [1] "[If] she vowed not to nurse her child, [2] Bet Shammai say: She removes the nipple from his mouth. [3] Bet Hillel say: [Her husband] compels her and she nurses him. [4] [If] she has been divorced, he cannot compel her. [5] But [if the child] recognizes her, he gives her her wage, [6] and compels her and she nurses him, because of the danger."

[7] You can even say [that it is in accordance with] Bet Shammai.

RASHI

שומטת דד מפיו – לא תניקנו, שהל הנדר. **אלמא:** לא משעבדא ליה. **כופה ומניקה** – דמשעבדא ליה, ולא חל הנדר. **אם היה מכירה** – שאינו רוצה לינק מאחרת.

NOTES

נָדְרָה שֶׁלֹּא לְהָנִיק If she vowed not to nurse. The Rishonim point out that the Baraita cannot be understood according to its plain sense that the woman took a vow not to nurse, for a vow by which a person obligates himself to refrain from doing something must be formulated in relation to an object and not to an activity. Thus we must be dealing with a case in which the woman took a vow forbidding to herself the benefit derived from nursing (in other words, the relief from the pain she would feel if she did not nurse; *Tosafot*); or she took a vow forbidding her breasts to her husband with respect to nursing his child (*Rashba, Ritva*); or she took a vow forbidding her milk to her infant (*Talmidei Rabbenu Yonah*); or she took an *oath* forbidding herself from nursing her child (an activity can be forbidden by means of an oath; *Rashba*).

The Gemara argues that even Bet Shammai agree that a wife is obligated toward her husband to nurse their child. When Bet Shammai said that a woman must refrain from nursing her child if she took a vow forbidding herself to do so, they were referring to a case in which she took the vow and her husband confirmed it for her.

The Rishonim object: If a wife is obligated to nurse her infant, then even if her husband confirms the vow, it should not be valid, for a vow cannot release the person who made it from an obligation that he bears.

Ra'ah, *Ritva*, and others explain that we are dealing here with a case in which the wife took a vow forbidding to herself certain food if she nursed her child, and her husband confirmed the vow for her. Such a vow is indeed valid, for it does not release the woman from any obligation. But the question arises as to whether we can compel the woman to nurse the child, as a result of which the food will become forbidden to her. Bet Shammai maintain that the husband put his finger between his wife's teeth, and therefore she cannot be compelled to nurse the child. Bet Hillel maintain that the wife put her finger between her own teeth, and therefore she can be compelled to nurse the child, and the food becomes forbidden to her.

HALAKHAH

נָדְרָה שֶׁלֹּא לְהָנִיק If she vowed not to nurse. "If a married woman vows not to nurse her infant child, her husband may compel her to nurse the child until it reaches the age of two, whether it be a boy or a girl." (*Rambam, Sefer Nashim, Hilkhot Ishut* 21:13; *Shulḥan Arukh, Even HaEzer* 82:1.)

נִתְגָּרְשָׁה, אֵינוֹ כּוֹפָה If she has been divorced, he cannot compel her. "If a woman is divorced, her former husband cannot compel her to nurse their child. If she is willing to nurse it, her former husband must pay her the wage of a wet nurse. If she is not willing to do so, she must hand the child over to the father, and he must arrange for a wet nurse. But if the infant recognizes its mother (so that it will not take milk from anyone else; *Rema* in the name of *Tur*), the divorcee can be compelled to nurse her child until it reaches the age of two (during which time she must be paid as a wet nurse), so that the infant is not endangered." (*Rambam, Sefer Nashim, Hilkhot Ishut* 21:16; *Shulḥan Arukh, Even HaEzer* 82:5.)

[1]הָכָא בְּמַאי עָסְקִינַן? כְּגוֹן שֶׁנָּדְרָה הִיא וְקִיֵּים לָהּ הוּא. [2]וְקָסָבְרִי בֵּית שַׁמַּאי: הוּא נוֹתֵן אֶצְבַּע בֵּין שִׁינֶּיהָ. [3]וּבֵית הִלֵּל סָבְרִי: הִיא נָתְנָה אֶצְבַּע בֵּין שִׁינֶּיהָ.

[4]וְנִפְלְגוּ בִּכְתוּבָּה בְּעָלְמָא! [5]וְעוֹד, תַּנְיָא: ״בֵּית שַׁמַּאי אוֹמְרִים: [6]אֵינָהּ מֵנִיקָה״.

[7]אֶלָּא מְחַוַּורְתָּא מַתְנִיתִין דְּלָא כְּבֵית שַׁמַּאי.

[8]״אִם הָיָה מַכִּירָהּ״.

[60A] [9]עַד כַּמָּה?

LITERAL TRANSLATION

[1]With what are we dealing here? For example, where she vowed and he confirmed [the vow] for her. [2]And Bet Shammai maintain: He puts a finger between her teeth. [3]But Bet Hillel maintain: She put a finger between her teeth.

[4]Then let them disagree about a ketubah in general! [5]And furthermore, it was taught: [6]"Bet Shammai say: She does not nurse."

[7]Rather, it is clear [that] our Mishnah is not in accordance with Bet Shammai.

[8]"[If the child] recognizes her."

[60A] [9]At what age (lit., "until how much")?

RASHI

הכא במאי עסקינן — ברייתא. **ונפלגו בכתובה בעלמא** — נדרה מליהנות לו וקיים לה, בית שמאי אומרים: תצא ותטול כתובה, ובית הלל אומרים: תצא בלא כתובה. **ועוד תניא** — גבי כל הנשים, ואפילו בלא נדר. **אינה מניקה** — אם אינה רוצה. **עד כמה** — כמה חדשים אית לן למימר שיודע להכירה מלינק מאשה אחרת.

TRANSLATION AND COMMENTARY

infant child. [1]**What we are dealing with here** in the Baraita **is** a case of a married woman who **took a vow** not to nurse her infant child, **and** her husband **confirmed the vow for her.** A husband is empowered to annul a vow made by his wife on the day he hears of it. But if he confirms it, it can no longer be annulled. [2]**Bet Shammai maintain** that if a wife vows not to nurse her child, and her husband confirms the vow, the husband is regarded as having **put his finger between** his wife's **teeth** and having caused himself to be bitten. Since the husband could have invalidated the vow but chose not to, the wife is no longer obligated to nurse her child. [3]**But Bet Hillel** disagree and **maintain** that in such a case the wife is regarded as having **put her finger between her** own **teeth,** and caused herself to be bitten. It was she who vowed not to nurse her child. Even though her husband confirmed the vow for her, she alone is regarded as being responsible for it. Therefore, her obligation to nurse her child remains, even after she vows not to do so.

וְנִפְלְגוּ בִּכְתוּבָּה בְּעָלְמָא [4]The Gemara objects: If it is true that Bet Shammai and Bet Hillel disagree as to who must assume responsibility for a vow taken by a married woman and confirmed by her husband, **then let them disagree about a ketubah in general!** Let them disagree about a case in which a wife takes a vow denying herself any benefit from her husband, and he confirms the vow for her. If a wife takes such a vow and her husband confirms it, he is no longer permitted to live with his wife and must divorce her. In such a case, Bet Shammai should say that the husband must give his wife her ketubah, for it is he who is regarded as having "put his finger between his wife's teeth." And Bet Hillel should maintain that the husband is not required to give his wife her ketubah, for it is she who is regarded as having "put her finger between her own teeth." Why, then, did Bet Shammai and Bet Hillel disagree only about the wife's obligation to nurse her baby, and not about her right to her ketubah? [5]**And furthermore, it was** explicitly **taught** in the following Baraita: **"Bet Shammai say:** [6]If she does not wish to do so, a married woman **is not required to nurse** her child." This Baraita refers to women in general, and not just to a woman who took a vow not to nurse her child.

אֶלָּא מְחַוַּורְתָּא [7]The Gemara concludes: **Rather, it is clear**, as we said in the beginning, **that our Mishnah is not in accordance with** the viewpoint of **Bet Shammai.**

אִם [8]The Baraita that was cited above stated: **"If a baby already recognizes** his mother, so that he may refuse to accept milk from another woman, then even if his mother has been divorced, her former husband can pay her the wage of a wet nurse and compel her to nurse their child."

עַד כַּמָּה [60A] [9]The Gemara asks: **At what age** can we assume that an infant already recognizes his mother, so that he may refuse to accept milk from anyone else?

HALAKHAH

עַד כַּמָּה? At what age? "A mother can be compelled to nurse her child, even if she is divorced from her husband, whenever it is apparent that the baby recognizes her and will not nurse from another woman. This ruling follows Shmuel, who maintains that there is no set age at which we assume that a child recognizes his mother. *Rema* notes that, according to some authorities, if an infant recognizes his wet nurse and there is concern that he will not nurse from another woman, the wet nurse too can be compelled to continue nursing the child." (*Rambam, Sefer Nashim, Hilkhot Ishut* 21:16; *Shulḥan Arukh, Even HaEzer* 82:5.)

TRANSLATION AND COMMENTARY

אָמַר רָבָא [1] **Rava said in the name of Rav Yirmeyah bar Abba, who said in the name of Rav:** At the age of **three months.** [2] **But Shmuel said:** At the age of **thirty days.** [3] **And Rabbi Yitzḥak said in the name of Rabbi Yoḥanan:** An infant recognizes his mother at the age of **fifty days.**

אָמַר רַב שִׁימִי בַּר אַבַּיֵי [4] The Gemara now cites a ruling on this matter. **Rav Shimi bar Abaye said: The law is in accordance with** the viewpoint of **Rabbi Yitzḥak who stated in the name of Rabbi Yoḥanan** that at the age of fifty days an infant recognizes his mother, and therefore there is reason to think that he may refuse to nurse from another woman.

בִּשְׁלָמָא [5] The Gemara asks: **Granted** that we can understand the conflicting opinions of **Rav and Rabbi Yoḥanan,** the former maintaining that a child only recognizes his mother at the age of three months, and the latter maintaining that he already recognizes her at the age of fifty days. For **each** child recognizes his mother **according to his** own **intelligence** and personal development. A precocious child already recognizes his mother at the age of fifty days, whereas a less advanced child only recognizes her at the age of three months. [6] **But according to Shmuel,** who maintains that at the age of thirty days a child already recognizes his mother, there is a difficulty, for **do we** really **find a child** as precocious **as that?**

כִּי אֲתָא רָמִי בַּר יְחֶזְקֵאל [7] On this point the Gemara remarks: **When Rami bar Yeḥezkel came** to Babylonia from Eretz Israel, **he said:** [8] **Do not accept** as authoritative **those rules that my brother Yehudah stated in the name of Shmuel,** because some of them are not correct. [9] What **Shmuel said** was **this:** Each child must be assessed on an individual basis. **As soon as** it appears that the child already **recognizes** his mother, there is reason to be concerned that he may refuse to nurse from another woman.

[1] אָמַר רָבָא אָמַר רַב יִרְמְיָה בַּר אַבָּא אָמַר רַב: שְׁלֹשָׁה חֳדָשִׁים. [2] וּשְׁמוּאֵל אָמַר: שְׁלֹשִׁים יוֹם. [3] וְרַבִּי יִצְחָק אָמַר רַבִּי יוֹחָנָן: חֲמִשִּׁים יוֹם.

[4] אָמַר רַב שִׁימִי בַּר אַבַּיֵי: הֲלָכָה כְּרַבִּי יִצְחָק שֶׁאָמַר מִשּׁוּם רַבִּי יוֹחָנָן.

[5] בִּשְׁלָמָא רַב וְרַבִּי יוֹחָנָן — כָּל חַד וְחַד כִּי חוּרְפֵּיהּ. [6] אֶלָּא לִשְׁמוּאֵל, כִּי הַאי גַּוְונָא מִי מַשְׁכַּחַתְּ לָהּ?

[7] כִּי אֲתָא רָמִי בַּר יְחֶזְקֵאל, אֲמַר: [8] לָא תְּצַיְּיתִינְהוּ לְהָנֵי כְּלָלֵי דְּכָיֵיל יְהוּדָה אָחִי מִשְּׁמֵיהּ דִּשְׁמוּאֵל. [9] הָכִי אֲמַר שְׁמוּאֵל: כָּל זְמַן שֶׁמַּכִּירָהּ.

LITERAL TRANSLATION

[1] Rava said in the name of Rav Yirmeyah bar Abba who said in the name of Rav: Three months. [2] But Shmuel said: Thirty days. [3] And Rabbi Yitzḥak said in the name of Rabbi Yoḥanan: Fifty days.

[4] Rav Shimi bar Abaye said: The law is in accordance with Rabbi Yitzḥak who spoke in the name of Rabbi Yoḥanan.

[5] Granted [according to] Rav and Rabbi Yoḥanan — each one according to his intelligence (lit., "sharpness"). [6] But according to Shmuel, do you find [a child] like that?

[7] When Rami bar Yeḥezkel came, he said: [8] Do not listen to these rules that my brother Yehudah laid down in the name of Shmuel. [9] Shmuel said thus: As soon as he recognizes her.

RASHI

כל חד לפום חורפיה — יש תינוק חריף ומכירה בחמשים יום, ויש שאינו מכירה עד שלשה חדשים. **כל זמן שמכירה** — אין שיעור לדבר, אלא בבדיקה הדבר תלוי, אם אנו רואים שמכירה — כופה ומניקתו בשכר, [ואפילו גירשה].

SAGES

רָמִי בַּר יְחֶזְקֵאל Rami bar Yeḥezkel. Rami (an abbreviated form of "Rav Ammi") bar Yeḥezkel was a second-generation Babylonian Amora, and Rav Yehudah's younger brother. He apparently studied with Rav and Shmuel in his youth, although he later immigrated to Eretz Israel, where he learned many ancient teachings, particularly little-known Baraitot. In the Jerusalem Talmud he is referred to as Ammi (or Immi) bar Yeḥezkel. He returned later to Babylonia (and hence the Gemara's use of the term כִּי אֲתָא — "when he came"), and brought with him teachings he had learned in Eretz Israel. His versions of the ancient teachings were renowned for their accuracy and importance, and were even considered superior to the teachings of his older brother, Rav Yehudah.

BACKGROUND

כָּל זְמַן שֶׁמַּכִּירָהּ As soon as he recognizes her. Modern biologists and psychologists agree that infants begin developing relationships with people at the age of one month, while eight-week-old infants show interest in and act affectionately toward people they recognize. Six-month-old infants show a clearcut preference for their mothers over all other people. These ages are, of course, approximate, and vary from child to child. Even blind infants can distinguish between different people by the way they smell.

NOTES

אֶלָּא לִשְׁמוּאֵל, כִּי הַאי גַּוְונָא מִי מַשְׁכַּחַתְּ לָהּ? But according to Shmuel, do you find a child like that? The Jerusalem Talmud cites an even more extreme version of the viewpoint of Shmuel, according to which an infant is already able to recognize his mother at the age of three days. The Jerusalem Talmud argues that this opinion is consistent with the stories told by Shmuel himself and other Sages regarding their personal memories of events that occurred during the first few days of their lives.

כָּל זְמַן שֶׁמַּכִּירָהּ As soon as he recognizes her. Some Rishonim maintain that the Amoraim disagree about an infant whose attachment to his mother is not readily apparent. At what age do we assume that the infant does indeed recognize mother, so that we are concerned that he may refuse to nurse from anyone else? If the infant is less than a certain age, we assume that he does not recognize his mother, and if he has already reached that age we assume that he does. But if we see that the infant refuses to nurse from another woman, then we compel his mother to nurse him, even if he has not yet reached that age; and similarly, if we see that he is willing to nurse from another woman, then we do not compel his mother to nurse him, even if he has already reached that age (see *Rosh* and *Meiri*). Thus Shmuel (as reported by Rami bar Yeḥezkel), who maintains that we compel a woman to nurse her child whenever it is apparent that the child recognizes his mother, may not disagree with Rav and Rabbi Yoḥanan, who propose specific ages. This may explain why *Rambam* rules in accordance with Shmuel, even though the Gemara (followed by *Rif* and *Rosh*) states that the law is in accordance with the viewpoint of Rabbi Yoḥanan.

¹הַהִיא דַּאֲתַאי לְקַמֵּיהּ דִּשְׁמוּאֵל. ²אֲמַר לֵיהּ לְרַב דִּימִי בַּר יוֹסֵף: "זִיל בְּדַקָהּ". ³אֲזַל אוֹתְבָהּ בְּדָרֵי דְּנָשֵׁי, וּשְׁקַלֵיהּ לִבְרָהּ וְקָמְהַדַּר לֵיהּ עֲלַיְיהוּ. ⁴כִּי מָטָא לְגַבָּהּ, הֲוַת קָא מַסְוֵי לְאַפָּהּ. ⁵כְּבַשְׁתַּנְהִי לְעֵינָהּ מִינֵּיהּ. ⁶אֲמַר לָהּ: "נְטַף עֵינַיִךְ, קוּם, דְּרִי בְּרִיךְ".

⁷סוּמָא מְנָא יָדַע?

⁸אֲמַר רַב אַשִׁי: בְּרֵיחָא וּבְטַעֲמָא.

⁹תָּנוּ רַבָּנַן: ¹⁰"יוֹנֵק תִּינוֹק וְהוֹלֵךְ עַד עֶשְׂרִים וְאַרְבָּעָה חֹדֶשׁ. ¹¹מִכָּאן וְאֵילָךְ, כְּיוֹנֵק שֶׁקֶץ. ¹²דִּבְרֵי רַבִּי אֱלִיעֶזֶר. ¹³רַבִּי יְהוֹשֻׁעַ אוֹמֵר: אֲפִילוּ אַרְבַּע וְחָמֵשׁ שָׁנִים. ¹⁴פֵּירַשׁ לְאַחַר עֶשְׂרִים וְאַרְבָּעָה חֹדֶשׁ וְחָזַר, ¹⁵כְּיוֹנֵק שֶׁקֶץ".

LITERAL TRANSLATION

¹[There was] a certain [divorced] woman who came before Shmuel. ²He said to Rav Dimi bar Yosef: "Go [and] test her." ³He went [and] placed her in a row of women, and he took her son and passed him before them. ⁴When [the child] reached her, he looked up at her face. ⁵She hid her eyes from him. ⁶He said to her: "Raise your eyes, stand up, [and] take your child."

⁷How does a blind [child] know?

⁸Rav Ashi said: By smell and by taste.

⁹Our Rabbis taught: ¹⁰"An infant continues to nurse until [he is] twenty-four months [old]. ¹¹From then on, it is as if he is nursing from an unclean animal. ¹²[These are] the words of Rabbi Eliezer. ¹³Rabbi Yehoshua says: Even four or five years. ¹⁴[If] he stopped after twenty-four months and then started again, ¹⁵it is as if he is nursing from an unclean animal."

TRANSLATION AND COMMENTARY

הַהִיא דַּאֲתַאי ¹The Gemara now relates the following incident to illustrate Shmuel's ruling: **A certain divorcee** who did not wish to nurse her infant **came before Shmuel** for a ruling as to whether her former husband could compel her to nurse the child. ²After hearing her arguments, Shmuel **said to Rav Dimi bar Yosef: "Go** and **check** whether the infant recognizes his mother." ³Rav Dimi bar Yosef **went and placed** the child's mother **among a row of women, and he took her child** in his arms **and passed** with **him in front of** the women, to see how the child would react to each of them. ⁴**When the child reached** his mother, **he looked up at her face,** ⁵and the mother tried to **hide her eyes from him** in the hope that he would not recognize her. ⁶Rav Dimi bar Yosef then turned to the woman and **said to her: "Raise your eyes, stand up, and take your child** and nurse him, for it is clear that he recognizes you."

סוּמָא מְנָא יָדַע ⁷The Gemara asks: **How does a blind child know** which woman is his mother?

אֲמַר רַב אַשִׁי ⁸**Rav Ashi said: By** the **smell and** the **taste** of his mother's milk.

תָּנוּ רַבָּנַן ⁹The Gemara now discusses some of the Halakhic issues that arise in connection with nursing an infant. **Our Rabbis taught** the following Baraita: ¹⁰**"An infant may continue to nurse** from his mother **until he is twenty-four months old.** ¹¹But **from that age onward**, a child who nurses from his mother **is** regarded **as if he were nursing from an unclean animal.** ¹²**This is the opinion of Rabbi Eliezer.** ¹³But **Rabbi Yehoshua says:** A child may continue to nurse from his mother **even** if he is **four or five years** old. ¹⁴But **if** the child **stops** nursing **after** he is **twenty-four months** old, **and then** after a certain period **he starts** to nurse once **again,** ¹⁵**he is** regarded **as if he were nursing from an unclean animal."**

BACKGROUND

עַד עֶשְׂרִים וְאַרְבָּעָה חֹדֶשׁ Until he is twenty-four months old. In the Talmudic period, and for many generations thereafter, children continued to nurse for a long time, even after they were able to eat other foods. There were several reasons for this: mothers viewed prolonged nursing as a way of delaying another pregnancy, and it was difficult to find other food that would be as nourishing and provide for an infant's needs as completely as a woman's milk does.

כְּיוֹנֵק שֶׁקֶץ It is as if he is nursing from an unclean animal. Although, according to the Halakhah, man is not classified as an unclean animal, nevertheless a woman's milk is permitted only to infants; and just as an older child should be discouraged from nursing, all the more so must an adult refrain from doing so.

RASHI

ההיא דאתאי — גרושה, ולא היתה רוצה להניק. **זיל בדקה** — אם מכירה. **אותבה בדרא דנשי** — הושיבה בשורה של נשים. **מסוי** = מביט. **נטוף עיניך** = זקוף עיניך. כמו דשפיל ואזיל בר אווזא ועינוהי מטייפי דבבא קמא (נב,ב). **דרי בריך** = שאי בניך. **כיונק שקץ** — כאילו יונק דבר משוקץ.

NOTES

כְּבַשְׁתַּנְהִי לְעֵינָהּ מִינֵּיהּ She hid her eyes from him. It is possible that the child's mother was hiding her face in shame, being embarrassed that she had rejected her infant. But *Rivan* and *Talmidei Rabbenu Yonah* explain that she tried to hide her face from her infant in the hope that he would not recognize her if he did not look her directly in the eye. *Rivan* proposes that Shmuel's response — נְטַף עֵינַיִךְ — may be understood as a curse: "Let your eyes fall out," for the woman had acted cruelly to her child.

בְּרֵיחָא וּבְטַעֲמָא By smell and by taste. *Rivan* explains that a blind infant can recognize his mother by the smell and the taste of her milk. *Meiri* and *Talmidei Rabbenu Yonah*

HALAKHAH

סוּמָא A blind child. "A nursing infant who recognizes his mother may not be separated from her, even if he is blind." (*Rambam, Sefer Nashim, Hilkhot Ishut* 21:16; *Shulḥan Arukh, Even HaEzer* 82:5.)

יוֹנֵק תִּינוֹק וְהוֹלֵךְ An infant continues to nurse. "A sturdy child may continue to nurse until he is four years old, and a sickly child may continue to nurse until he is five," following Rabbi Yehoshua as understood by *Tosafot.* (*Rambam, Sefer Kedushah, Hilkhot Ma'akhalot Asurot* 3:5; *Shulḥan Arukh, Yoreh De'ah* 81:7.)

פֵּירַשׁ לְאַחַר עֶשְׂרִים וְאַרְבָּעָה חֹדֶשׁ If he stopped after twenty-four months. "If a child is weaned before he has

TRANSLATION AND COMMENTARY

אָמַר מָר [1] The Gemara now proceeds to analyze the Baraita in greater depth. **It was said above** in the Baraita: **"From** the age of two **onward**, a child who nurses from his mother **is** regarded **as if he were nursing from an unclean animal."** It would appear from this Baraita that human milk is treated as a forbidden food, and is no different from the milk of an unclean animal. [2] **A contradiction** to this ruling **may be raised** from another Baraita, which states: **"I might** mistakenly **have thought that human milk is unclean** and forbidden, just like the milk of an unclean animal. [3] **And this could have been logically inferred** by means of the following *a fortiori* argument: **If in the case of an unclean animal, regarding the touching of which** the Torah **was lenient** (an unclean animal does not impart ritual impurity during its lifetime), the Torah **was** nevertheless **stringent about its milk,** forbidding it for human consumption, [4] **how much more so in the case of a human being, regarding the touching of whom** the Torah **was stringent** (a person can impart ritual impurity during his or her lifetime), **should** the Torah **be stringent about his milk;** thus human milk should be forbidden. [5] **Therefore,** to prevent us from drawing this mistaken conclusion, **the Torah states** (Leviticus 11:4): 'Nevertheless these you shall not eat of those that chew the cud or of those that divide the hoof: **the camel, because it chews the cud,** but does not part the hoof; *it* is unclean to you.' [6] The emphatic word '*it*' [הוא] that is added here in the verse teaches us that **it**, the camel alone, **is unclean,** and its milk is forbidden for human consumption, **but human milk is not unclean,**

[1] אָמַר מָר: ״מִכָּאן וְאֵילָךְ, כְּיוֹנֵק שֶׁקֶץ״. [2] וּרְמִינְהִי: ״יָכוֹל יְהֵא חֲלַב מְהַלְּכֵי שְׁתַּיִם טָמֵא. [3] וְדִין הוּא: וּמַה בְּהֵמָה, שֶׁהֵקַלְתָּ בְּמַגָּעָהּ, הֶחְמַרְתָּ בַּחֲלָבָהּ, [4] אָדָם, שֶׁהֶחְמַרְתָּ בְּמַגָּעוֹ, אֵינוֹ דִּין שֶׁתַּחְמִיר בַּחֲלָבוֹ. [5] תַּלְמוּד לוֹמַר: ׳אֶת הַגָּמָל, כִּי מַעֲלֵה גֵרָה הוּא׳. [6] הוּא טָמֵא, וְאֵין חֲלַב מְהַלְּכֵי שְׁתַּיִם טָמֵא, אֶלָּא

LITERAL TRANSLATION

[1] The master said: "From then on, it is as if he is nursing from an unclean animal." [2] A contradiction was raised (lit., "cast them together"): "I might have thought that human milk (lit., 'the milk of those that walk on two [legs]') is unclean. [3] And it is a logical inference: If [in the case of] an [unclean] animal, regarding the touching of which you were lenient, you were stringent about its milk, [4] how much more so [in the case of] a human being, regarding the touching of whom you were stringent, should you be stringent about his milk. [5] Therefore the Torah states: 'The camel, because it chews the cud.' [6] It is unclean, but human milk is not unclean, but

RASHI

חלב מהלכי שתים — חלב של אשה, המהלכת בשתי רגלים. **טמא** — אסור. **שהקלת במגעה** — שאינה מטמאה מחיים. **החמרת בחלבה** — כדאמרינן בבכורות (ו,ב) ״גמל גמל״ שני פעמים — חד לאסור חלבו. **אדם שהחמרת במגעו** — נדה.

BACKGROUND

חֲלַב מְהַלְּכֵי שְׁתַּיִם...דַּם מְהַלְּכֵי שְׁתַּיִם Human milk...human blood. Although the eating of human flesh is regarded as an abominable offense by the Talmud, which not even the worst of nations commits publicly, nevertheless it is explained in the Talmud that since man is not classified as one of the animals, he is also not included in the prohibitions against unclean animals. Therefore, what comes from man, such as milk and blood, does not belong to the same legal category as the blood and milk of unclean animals. Hence the principal point is to avoid consuming them, either on the basis of a Rabbinic prohibition or else so as to avoid giving the appearance of violating the Halakhah (מַרְאִית עַיִן).

NOTES

explain that he knows his mother by her smell and by the taste of her milk.

בְּהֵמָה, שֶׁהֵקַלְתָּ בְּמַגָּעָהּ If in the case of an unclean animal, regarding the touching of which you were lenient. Our commentary follows *Rashi*, who explains that the Torah was lenient about an unclean animal, in that it does not impart ritual impurity during its lifetime but only after it is dead, and that the Torah was stringent about a human being, in that there are cases in which a living person can impart ritual impurity — for example, a menstruating woman.

Rabbenu Ḥananel proposes two other explanations: An unclean animal that comes into contact with a corpse does not contract ritual impurity and thereby impart ritual impurity to others, whereas a human being who touches a corpse contracts ritual impurity which can then be imparted to others. Alternatively, someone who touches the carcass of an unclean animal is ritually impure until nightfall, whereas someone who comes into physical contact with a human corpse is ritually impure for seven days.

Ri HaLavan explains that someone who touches the carcass of an unclean animal has the status of a רִאשׁוֹן לְטוּמְאָה, "the first level of ritual impurity," whereas someone who comes into physical contact with a human corpse has the status of an אַב הַטּוּמְאָה, "a primary source of ritual impurity," a more severe degree of ritual impurity than a רִאשׁוֹן לְטוּמְאָה.

HALAKHAH

reached his second birthday, his mother may resume nursing even if the child has not nursed for an extended period of time. But if he is weaned after he is two years old, he may not nurse again." (*Rambam, Sefer Kedushah, Hilkhot Ma'akhalot Asurot* 6:2; *Shulḥan Arukh, Yoreh De'ah* 81:7.)

חֲלַב מְהַלְּכֵי שְׁתַּיִם Human milk. "A woman's milk is a permitted food, provided that it has been expressed into a utensil (or even into one's hand; *Rema* in the name of *Bet Yosef*). But if an adult sucks milk directly from a woman's breast, he is regarded as having sucked milk from an unclean animal and is administered disciplinary lashes." (*Rambam, Sefer Kedushah, Hilkhot Ma'akhalot Asurot* 3:2,4; *Shulḥan Arukh, Yoreh De'ah* 81:7.)

טָהוֹר. [1]יָכוֹל אוֹצִיא אֶת הֶחָלָב, [2]שֶׁאֵינוֹ שָׁוֶה בַּכֹּל, [3]וְלֹא אוֹצִיא אֶת הַדָּם, שֶׁהוּא שָׁוֶה בַּכֹּל. [4]תַּלְמוּד לוֹמַר: ׳הוּא׳. [5]הוּא טָמֵא, וְאֵין דַּם מְהַלְּכֵי שְׁתַּיִם טָמֵא, אֶלָּא טָהוֹר״. [6]וְאָמַר רַב שֵׁשֶׁת: אֲפִילּוּ מִצְוַת פְּרִישָׁה אֵין בּוֹ.

LITERAL TRANSLATION

clean. [1]I might have thought that I should exclude milk, [2]which is not the same in all [cases], [3]but should not exclude blood, which is the same in all [cases]. [4]Therefore the Torah states: 'It.' [5]*It* is unclean, but human blood (lit., 'the blood of those that walk on two [legs]') is not unclean, but clean." [6]And Rav Sheshet said: There is not even an obligation of abstaining from it.

TRANSLATION AND COMMENTARY

but clean and permitted for human consumption." [1]The Baraita continues: **"I might** also mistakenly **have thought that** only human **milk is excluded** from the prohibition against milk from an unclean animal. [2]Since the law regarding animal milk **is not the same in all cases,** because the milk of a clean animal is permitted for human consumption, there is reason to assume that human milk is excluded from the prohibition as well. [3]**But I** might have imagined that we **do not exclude** human **blood** from the prohibition against the consumption of blood, because animal blood **is** governed by **the same** laws **in all cases,** and the blood of all animals is forbidden. [4]**Therefore the Torah states: 'It** is unclean to you.' The emphatic word *'it'* [5]teaches that **it,** the camel alone, **is unclean,** and its blood is forbidden for human consumption, **but human blood is not unclean, but clean** and permitted for human consumption." [6]Commenting on the first half of the Baraita, **Rav Sheshet said:** Not only is human milk permitted by Torah law, but **there is not even an obligation to abstain from it** by Rabbinic decree. Why, then, does Rabbi Eliezer rule in the first Baraita that a two-year-old child who nurses from his mother is regarded as if he were nursing from an unclean animal?

RASHI

שאינו שוה בכל – שהרי בטהורה טהור. **הוא טמא** – מחד קרא נפקא ליה. לשון אחרת: "זה" זה טמא כו׳, דכתיב ברישיה דקרא "אך את זה לא תאכלו" "זה" – מיעוטא הוא. ואמר רב ששת גרסינן. **אפילו מצות פרישה** – מדרבנן. **אין בו** – דמדאורייתא שרי. ורבנן נמי לא גזור ביה, דאמרינן: חלב מהלכי שתים טהור.

NOTES

דַּם מְהַלְּכֵי שְׁתַּיִם Human blood. According to the Gemara's conclusion, human milk and human blood are permitted by Torah law. By Rabbinic decree, human milk which has not first been expressed into a utensil is forbidden for human consumption (after a child reaches a certain age or stops nursing), as is human blood that has already left a person's body. The Rishonim disagree about whether by Torah law human flesh is permitted to be eaten. Most authorities accept the ruling found in *Sifra* (*Shemini* 4, 8), according to which human flesh is excluded from the prohibition applying to the flesh of non-kosher animals in much the same way as human milk and blood are excluded from the prohibition applying to the milk and blood of non-kosher animals. *Rambam* (*Hilkhot Ma'akhalot Asurot* 2:3) rules that although the negative precept forbidding the consumption of the flesh of non-kosher animals does not apply to human flesh, the positive commandment to eat kosher animals (Leviticus 11:2: "These are the animals that you shall eat") implicitly forbids the eating of human flesh. Thus someone who eats human flesh violates a positive Torah commandment, because the violation of an implicit prohibition is regarded as the violation of a positive commandment.

Ramban objects strongly to *Rambam's* position, arguing that we do not find such a prohibition anywhere in the Rabbinic sources. Moreover, human flesh must be permitted for human consumption, for if not, how can human milk and blood be permitted, since there is a general principle that whatever issues from what is forbidden is similarly forbidden? According to *Ramban,* human flesh is permitted to be eaten only if it is detached from a living person; but if it comes from a corpse, it is forbidden, because no benefit may be derived from a corpse, and therefore it certainly may not be eaten.

Ritva argues that the prohibition against eating the flesh of a living animal applies to human flesh as well (אֵבֶר מִן הַחַי — *evar min haḥai*), and thus there is no case in which human flesh is actually permitted to be eaten.

According to *Ra'ah*, human flesh is forbidden by Torah law because of the negative precept stated with respect to a non-kosher animal and extended to human flesh by means of the following *a fortiori* argument: If in the case of an unclean animal, regarding the touching of which the Torah was lenient, it was nevertheless stringent about its flesh, then surely in the case of a human being, regarding the touching of whom the Torah was stringent, it was stringent about human flesh. He rejects the ruling found in *Sifra* permitting human flesh, and argues that the *Sifra* is referring specifically to human milk and blood, as is our Gemara. According to *Ra'ah*, the principle that whatever issues from what is forbidden is similarly forbidden applies only to animals but not to human beings, and therefore the flesh of a human being can be forbidden while human milk and blood are permitted.

אֲפִילּוּ מִצְוַת פְּרִישָׁה אֵין בּוֹ There is not even an obligation of abstaining from it. *Rashi* explains that Rav Sheshet's

HALAKHAH

דַּם מְהַלְּכֵי שְׁתַּיִם Human blood. "Human blood that has left a person's body is forbidden, lest people confuse it with animal blood and falsely conclude that animal blood is permitted. Thus, if a person bites into bread and finds

TRANSLATION AND COMMENTARY

לָא קַשְׁיָא [1] The Gemara answers: **There is no difficulty**, because the two Baraitot deal with different cases. [2] The second Baraita, which rules that human milk is permitted, **is referring to** a case **where** the milk **has been expressed from the** woman's **breast** into a utensil. Such milk is permitted for human consumption even by Rabbinic law. [3] But the first Baraita, which implies that human milk is forbidden, **is referring to** a case **where** the milk **has not been expressed**, and the child is nursing directly from his mother's breast. According to Rabbi Eliezer, the Rabbis decreed that a two-year-old child may no longer nurse from his mother, for a two-year-old child who is still nursing from his mother is regarded as if he were nursing from an unclean animal.

וְחִלּוּפָא בְּדָם [4] The Gemara notes that the law **regarding** human **blood is** just **the opposite.** As stated in the Baraita above, there is no prohibition in Torah law against the consumption of human blood. But the Rabbis decreed that human blood is forbidden, lest people confuse it with animal blood and draw the mistaken conclusion that animal blood is also permitted. This decree applies only to blood that has already been separated from a person's body; but blood that has not yet been separated from a person's body is permitted, even according to Rabbinic law. [5] **For it was taught** in a Baraita: "If a person bites into bread and then finds traces of his **blood on the loaf, he** must **scrape off** the blood **and** only **then** may he **eat the** rest of the **loaf**, for the blood has already been separated from his body and is therefore forbidden to be eaten. [6] But if a person's mouth is bleeding and there is **blood between his teeth, he** may **suck** the blood out and swallow it, **and need not be concerned** that he is violating even a Rabbinic prohibition, because the Rabbis did not prohibit human blood that has not yet been separated from the person's body."

אָמַר מָר [7] The Gemara continues its analysis of the previously cited Baraita. **It was said above** in the Baraita: **"Rabbi Yehoshua says:** [8] A child may continue to nurse from his mother **even** if he is **four or five years** old." [9] The Gemara asks: **But surely** a different ruling by Rabbi Yehoshua **was taught** in the following Baraita: **"Rabbi Yehoshua says:** [10] A child may continue to nurse from his mother **even if** he is old enough to carry **his bundle on his shoulders."**

[1] לָא קַשְׁיָא. [2] הָא דְּפָרֵישׁ, [3] הָא דְּלָא פָּרֵישׁ.

[4] וְחִלּוּפָא בְּדָם, [5] כִּדְתַנְיָא: "דָּם שֶׁעַל גַּבֵּי כִּכָּר גּוֹרְרוֹ וְאוֹכְלוֹ. [6] שֶׁבֵּין הַשִּׁינַּיִם מוֹצְצוֹ וְאֵינוֹ חוֹשֵׁשׁ".

[7] אָמַר מָר: "רַבִּי יְהוֹשֻׁעַ אוֹמֵר: [8] אֲפִילּוּ אַרְבַּע וְחָמֵשׁ שָׁנִים". [9] וְהָתַנְיָא: "רַבִּי יְהוֹשֻׁעַ אוֹמֵר: [10] אֲפִילּוּ חֲבִילָתוֹ עַל כְּתֵיפָיו"!

LITERAL TRANSLATION

[1] There is no difficulty. [2] This [refers to] where it has left [the breast], [3] this [refers to] where it has not left [the breast].

[4] And it is the opposite regarding blood, [5] as it was taught: "Blood that is on a loaf he scrapes off and [then] eats [the bread]. [6] [Blood] that is between the teeth he sucks and is not concerned."

[7] The master said: "Rabbi Yehoshua says: [8] Even four or five years." [9] But surely it was taught: "Rabbi Yehoshua says: [10] Even [if] his bundle is on his shoulders"!

RASHI

הא דפריש — הא דקתני "מותר" — כשפירש מדדי האשה לכלי, והיונק מן הדד כיונק שקץ מדרבנן. **וחילופא בדם** — דמדפריש — אסור מדרבנן, דמיחלף בדם בהמה, ואתי למימר: דם בהמה אכל. **דם שעל גבי ככר** — כגון שנשכו וניכר בו דם השינים. **גוררו** — לדם. **מוצצו** — דהא ליכא דחזי ליה.

NOTES

ruling is that not only is human milk permitted by Torah law, but there is not even an obligation by Rabbinic law to abstain from it.

According to *Rivan*, Rav Sheshet was referring to human blood: Not only is there no Torah prohibition against consuming human blood, but even in Rabbinic law there is no prohibition against consuming blood that has not yet left a person's body. Thus a person who is bleeding in the mouth may suck the blood out from between his teeth and swallow it.

הָא דְּלָא פָּרֵישׁ This refers to where it has not left the breast. The Sages enacted that a woman's milk, consumed directly from the breast, is forbidden to anyone but an infant, lest people come to think that just as human milk is permitted even though a human being is not a kosher animal that has a cloven hoof and chews the cud, so too should an animal's milk be permitted even though the animal itself is not kosher. But there was no reason to forbid a woman's milk that has been expressed into a utensil, because anyone seeing a person drinking such milk

HALAKHAH

blood on the piece he is eating, he must scrape off the blood and throw it away. But the blood between his teeth, that has not yet left his body, he may suck out and swallow," following our Gemara. (*Rambam, Sefer Kedushah, Hilkhot Ma'akhalot Asurot* 3:5; *Shulḥan Arukh, Even HaEzer* 66:10.)

SAGES

רַבִּי מָרִינוּס Rabbi Marinus. He was a Tanna of the generation of Rabbi Yehudah HaNasi, and his teachings appear in the Tosefta and in Baraitot.

LANGUAGE (RASHI)

פליינדרי״א* From the Old French *plaindre*, meaning "to moan," or "to complain."

TRANSLATION AND COMMENTARY

אִידִי וְאִידִי [1] The Gemara answers: There is no contradiction between the two Baraitot, because they are **both** referring to the **same standard,** for a child who is four or five years old is mature enough to carry his bundle on his shoulders.

אָמַר רַב יוֹסֵף [2] The Gemara concludes this discussion with a ruling on the matter. **Rav Yosef said: The law is in accordance with** the viewpoint of **Rabbi Yehoshua** that a child may continue to nurse from his mother until he is four or five years old.

תַּנְיָא [3] The Gemara continues with a related matter, and cites a Baraita in which **it was taught: "Rabbi Marinus says:** [4] **Someone who is groaning** with severe chest pain and is in need of milk to alleviate his discomfort **may suck milk** directly from an animal's udder **on Shabbat,** even though he is forbidden to milk the animal on that day." [5] The Gemara asks: **What is the reason** for this ruling? The Gemara answers: The prohibition against milking an animal on Shabbat is derived from the prohibition against threshing. The purpose of threshing is to separate grain from chaff. Any activity by which food is extracted from unwanted matter to which it is connected — for example, the milking of an animal — is similarly prohibited. [6] But when a person **sucks** milk directly from an animal's udder, he **is extracting** the milk from the animal **in an unusual manner**, and such an action is forbidden on Shabbat only by Rabbinic decree. Thus, in the case of the Baraita, sucking milk directly from the animal's udder is permitted, [7] for **wherever** a person **is suffering** pain, even if his life is not in danger, **the Rabbis did not impose a prohibition.**

[1] אִידִי וְאִידִי חַד שִׁיעוּרָא הוּא. [2] אָמַר רַב יוֹסֵף: הֲלָכָה כְּרַבִּי יְהוֹשֻׁעַ.

[3] תַּנְיָא: ״רַבִּי מָרִינוּס אוֹמֵר: [4] גּוֹנֵחַ יוֹנֵק חָלָב בְּשַׁבָּת״. [5] מַאי טַעֲמָא? [6] יוֹנֵק מְפָרֵק כִּלְאַחַר יָד, [7] וּבִמְקוֹם צַעֲרָא לָא גָּזְרוּ רַבָּנַן.

LITERAL TRANSLATION

[1] This and that are one measure.

[2] Rav Yosef said: The law is in accordance with Rabbi Yehoshua.

[3] It was taught: "Rabbi Marinus says: [4] Someone who is groaning may suck milk on Shabbat." [5] What is the reason? [6] Sucking is separating in an unusual manner (lit., "as if with the back of the hand"), [7] and where there is suffering the Rabbis did not issue an enactment.

RASHI

גונח — המיילל מכאב לבו, *פליינדרי״א. **יונק חלב** — משום רפואה, ורפואתו חלב עז. **מפרק** — הנותק דבר ממקום שגדל בו, ולא מן המחובר אלא מן התלוש, ותולדה דדש הוא, שמפרק תבואה מקשיה (שבת עג,ב). **כלאחר יד** — שאין דרך בני אדם לינק, אלא לחלוב ביד. **ובמקום צערא** — שמצטער מכאבו.

NOTES

will assume that he is drinking the milk of a kosher animal. Just the opposite is true regarding human blood. The Sages enacted that human blood that has already left a person's body is forbidden for consumption, lest people confuse it with animal blood and come to permit the latter as well. But there was no reason to forbid human blood that has not yet left a person's body, for in such a case there is no cause for any confusion (*Rivan, Talmidei Rabbenu Yonah*).

מְפָרֵק Separating. The Gemara states that milking an animal is forbidden on account of מְפָרֵק — "separating." "Separating" is not listed among the thirty-nine primary categories of work forbidden on Shabbat. Our commentary follows *Rashi*, who explains that the "separating" of milk is forbidden because it constitutes a subcategory of "threshing." Milking an animal is similar to threshing in that in both activities food is extracted from the unwanted matter to which it is connected.

Tosafot and others raise the objection that the Gemara states elsewhere (*Shabbat* 75a), that the prohibition against threshing on Shabbat applies only to things that grow from the ground. *Rabbenu Tam* suggests (*Tosafot, Shabbat* 73b, s.v. מפרק) that milking is prohibited as a subcategory of "erasing," because during the course of milking, the animal's teat is "erased," is made flush with the rest of the udder.

Rashba suggests that milking is forbidden because it constitutes a subcategory of "shearing"; just as one is forbidden to remove an animal's wool on Shabbat, so too is one forbidden to remove its milk.

וּבִמְקוֹם צַעֲרָא And where there is suffering. The Rishonim discuss the apparent contradiction between the passage here and a discussion found elsewhere (*Yevamot* 114a), from which it emerges that, according to Abba Shaul, someone who is in distress may suck milk directly from an animal's udder on a Festival but may not do so on Shabbat.

Rabbenu Tam argues that the Gemara in *Yevamot* is referring to a person in distress because of hunger, who is

HALAKHAH

גּוֹנֵחַ יוֹנֵק חָלָב Someone who is groaning may suck milk. "Someone who is in distress may suck milk directly from an animal on Shabbat, for the Rabbis did not impose a prohibition in a situation where a person is in distress, following Rav Yosef's ruling in accordance with the viewpoint of Rabbi Marinus. Some authorities (*Rabbenu Tam, Rosh,* and *Tur*) maintain that a person who is in distress because of hunger is permitted to suck milk directly from an animal on a Festival, but not on Shabbat, following Abba Shaul in *Yevamot*." (*Rambam, Sefer Zemannim, Hilkhot Shabbat* 21:14; *Shulḥan Arukh, Oraḥ Ḥayyim* 328:33.)

TRANSLATION AND COMMENTARY

אָמַר רַב יוֹסֵף [1] The Gemara concludes this discussion with a ruling on the matter. **Rav Yosef said: The law is in accordance with** the viewpoint of **Rabbi Marinus** that if a person is in pain, he may suck milk directly from an animal's udder on Shabbat.

תַּנְיָא [2] The Gemara proceeds to discuss a similar ruling that **was taught** in the following Baraita: **"Naḥum of Gallia says:** [3] If someone has **a** drainpipe to clear the water from his roof, and it becomes blocked up by **rubbish that has entered** it causing the water to accumulate on his roof and then seep into his house, **he may crush** the rubbish **with his foot in private on Shabbat, and he need not be concerned** that he is violating the prohibition against repairing an article on Shabbat." [4] The Gemara asks: **What is the reason** for this permissive ruling? The Gemara answers: Repairs are generally made by using one's hands or by means of a tool held in one's hands. [5] When a person repairs something by using his foot, he **is repairing in an unusual manner,** and such an action is forbidden on Shabbat only by Rabbinic decree. Thus, in the case of the Baraita, repairing the drainpipe by crushing the rubbish with one's foot is permitted, [6] for **wherever** a Rabbinic decree **will cause a** financial **loss, the Rabbis did not impose a prohibition.**

אָמַר רַב יוֹסֵף [7] Once again the Gemara ends the discussion with a ruling on the matter. **Rav Yosef said: The law is in accordance with** the viewpoint of **Naḥum of Gallia** that a person may repair his drainpipe by means of his foot on Shabbat to prevent a blocked pipe from causing him financial loss.

[1] אָמַר רַב יוֹסֵף: הֲלָכָה כְּרַבִּי מָרִינוּס.

[2] תַּנְיָא: ״נַחוּם אִישׁ גַּלְיָא אוֹמֵר: [3] צִינּוֹר שֶׁעָלוּ בּוֹ קַשְׁקַשִּׁין, מְמַעֲכָן בְּרַגְלוֹ בְּצִנְעָא בְּשַׁבָּת וְאֵינוֹ חוֹשֵׁשׁ״. [4] מַאי טַעֲמָא? [5] מְתַקֵּן כִּלְאַחַר יָד הוּא, [6] וּבִמְקוֹם פְּסֵידָא לָא גָּזְרוּ בָּהּ רַבָּנַן.

[7] אָמַר רַב יוֹסֵף: הֲלָכָה כְּנַחוּם אִישׁ גַּלְיָא.

LITERAL TRANSLATION

[1] Rav Yosef said: The law is in accordance with Rabbi Marinus.

[2] It was taught: "Naḥum of Gallia says: [3] [Regarding] a gutter into which rubbish entered, he may crush it with his foot in private on Shabbat and need not be concerned." [4] What is the reason? [5] It is repairing in an unusual manner, [6] and where there is a loss the Rabbis did not issue an enactment.

[7] Rav Yosef said: The law is in accordance with Naḥum of Gallia.

RASHI

צנור – המקלח מים מן הגג. **קשקשים** – קשים ועשבים שסותמים ומעכבים את קלוחו, ומימיו יוצאים ומתפשטים לגג, ודולפין לבית. **כלאחר יד** – על ידי שינוי, ברגלו. **ומשום** דאמר רב יוסף הלכה בכולהו, נקט לה הכא.

SAGES

נַחוּם אִישׁ גַּלְיָא Naḥum of Gallia. This scholar is not mentioned anywhere else in the Talmud, and he was apparently one of the last Tannaim. He is described here as being from "Gallia." This may mean that he came originally from France ("Gallia" in Latin means "France"). But some scholars are of the opinion that the reference is to Gallia or Galatia in Asia Minor.

LANGUAGE

קַשְׁקַשִּׁין Rubbish. The word קַשְׁקַשִּׁין literally means "pieces of straw and other plants." Some authorities derive this word from the Hebrew root קשקש, meaning "to weed," and explain it as "weeding roots."

NOTES

permitted to suck milk directly from an animal on a Festival but not on Shabbat, whereas our Gemara is referring to a person in distress because of illness, who is permitted to suck directly from an animal even on Shabbat.

Rabbenu Ḥananel goes even further and says that our Gemara, which permits a person to suck directly from an animal even on Shabbat, is referring to a person who is *in danger* because of his illness. Most Rishonim reject this viewpoint and argue that if a person is dangerously ill, all activities ordinarily prohibited on Shabbat are permitted to him, and not merely an activity done in an unusual way.

Rif, *Ramban*, and others reconcile the two passages by arguing that there is a disagreement between Tannaim on the matter. The anonymous first Tanna of the Baraita in *Yevamot* maintains that an adult may not suck directly from an animal, neither on a Festival nor on Shabbat. Abba Shaul maintains that a person in distress may indeed suck directly from an animal on a Festival, but not on Shabbat. And Rabbi Marinus maintains that a person in distress may suck directly from an animal, even on Shabbat.

מְמַעֲכָן בְּרַגְלוֹ בְּצִנְעָא He may crush it with his foot in private. Naḥum of Gallia permits a person to repair his drainpipe with his foot on Shabbat, provided that the repairs are made in private and not in public. *Tosafot* considers this distinction in the light of Rav's principle that whenever the Sages forbade an activity because of the false conclusions that might be reached by those seeing someone engaged in that activity, they forbade that activity even in private. This principle, argues *Tosafot*, applies only when an observer might come to a mistaken conclusion about a Biblical prohibition, but not if he might come to a mistaken conclusion about a Rabbinic injunction. Thus a person may repair his drainpipe with his foot on Shabbat in private, if by not doing so he will suffer a substantial financial loss, because repairing something in an unusual manner is forbidden only by Rabbinic decree.

Ritva cites a viewpoint according to which our Baraita disagrees with Rav's principle, and according to which the law follows our Baraita, against Rav.

HALAKHAH

צִינּוֹר שֶׁעָלוּ בּוֹ קַשְׁקַשִּׁין A gutter into which rubbish entered. "If the drain pipe on a person's roof becomes blocked with rubbish, so that water is seeping into his house, he may remedy the problem even on Shabbat by pressing the rubbish down with his foot, provided that he does so in private, following Rav Yosef's ruling in accordance with the viewpoint of Naḥum of Gallia. *Ran* (cited by *Bet Yosef*) suggests that it is preferable that the pipe be cleared in private; but if that is not possible, it may be cleared even in public." (*Shulḥan Arukh, Oraḥ Ḥayyim* 336:9.)

SAGES

רַב יְהוּדָה בַּר חֲבִיבָא Rav Yehudah bar Ḥaviva. A Babylonian Amora of the second generation, Rav Yehudah bar Ḥaviva was a disciple of Shmuel, and his daughter married the son of Rav Yehudah bar Yeḥezkel. Rav Yehudah bar Ḥaviva's Halakhic teachings are found in a number of places in the Talmud.

TRANSLATION AND COMMENTARY

פֵּירַשׁ [1] The Gemara now proceeds to discuss the last clause of the previously cited Baraita, in which it was taught: **"If a child stops** nursing **after** he is **twenty-four months** old, **and then** after a certain period **he starts** once **again** to nurse, [2]**he is** regarded **as if he were nursing from an unclean animal."** The Gemara asks: The Baraita rules that a two-year-old child who has stopped nursing may not resume nursing. [3]**For how long** must the child have stopped nursing for this ruling to apply?

אָמַר רַב יְהוּדָה בַּר חֲבִיבָא [4]The Gemara answers: **Rav Yehudah bar Ḥaviva said in the name of Shmuel:** If the child stops nursing for **three days,** he may not start nursing again. [5]**There are some who** report this tradition in a slightly different manner and **say** that **Rav Yehudah bar Ḥaviva** did not report the statement of the Amora Shmuel, but **taught** the following Baraita **before Shmuel:** [6]"If the child stops nursing for **three days,** he may not start nursing again."

תָּנוּ רַבָּנַן [7] The Gemara now raises other Halakhic issues connected with a nursing mother. **Our Rabbis taught** the following Baraita: **"A nursing mother whose husband died within twenty-four months** after their baby was born [8]**may not accept betrothal** from another man **and may** certainly **not remarry** [60B] **until after** the baby is **twenty-four months** old, for by then most babies are weaned. If a nursing widow remarries before her infant reaches the age of two and she becomes pregnant by her new husband, her milk supply could be reduced, and she may be forced to wean her child. Her new husband may resent the child by her former husband and force her to neglect it. Out of concern for the child's welfare, the Rabbis therefore forbade the nursing widow not only from remarrying, but even from becoming betrothed to another man. [9]**This is the viewpoint of Rabbi Meir.** [10]**But Rabbi Yehudah** disagrees and **permits** a nursing widow to remarry **after** her infant is **eighteen months** old, for a child of one-and-a-half can be weaned without danger. [11]**Rabbi Natan bar Yosef said:** The viewpoint recorded here in the name of Rabbi Meir **is the very position maintained by Bet Shammai,** [12]and the viewpoint recorded in the name of Rabbi Yehudah **is the very position maintained by Bet Hillel.**

[1]״פֵּירַשׁ לְאַחַר עֶשְׂרִים וְאַרְבָּעָה חֹדֶשׁ וְחָזַר, [2]כְּיוֹנֵק שֶׁקֶץ״.
[3]וְכַמָּה?
[4]אָמַר רַב יְהוּדָה בַּר חֲבִיבָא אָמַר שְׁמוּאֵל: שְׁלֹשָׁה יָמִים.
[5]אִיכָּא דְאָמְרִי: תָּנֵי רַב יְהוּדָה בַּר חֲבִיבָא קַמֵּיהּ דִּשְׁמוּאֵל: [6]״שְׁלֹשָׁה יָמִים״.
[7]תָּנוּ רַבָּנַן: ״מֵינֶקֶת שֶׁמֵּת בַּעְלָהּ בְּתוֹךְ עֶשְׂרִים וְאַרְבָּעָה חֹדֶשׁ, [8]הֲרֵי זוֹ לֹא תִּתְאָרֵס וְלֹא תִּינָּשֵׂא [60B] עַד עֶשְׂרִים וְאַרְבָּעָה חֹדֶשׁ. [9]דִּבְרֵי רַבִּי מֵאִיר. [10]וְרַבִּי יְהוּדָה מַתִּיר בִּשְׁמוֹנָה עָשָׂר חֹדֶשׁ. [11]אָמַר רַבִּי נָתָן בַּר יוֹסֵף: הֵן הֵן דִּבְרֵי בֵּית שַׁמַּאי; [12]הֵן הֵן דִּבְרֵי בֵּית הִלֵּל.

LITERAL TRANSLATION

[1]"[If] he stopped after twenty-four months and then started again, [2]it is as if he is nursing from an unclean animal." [3]And for how long?

[4]Rav Yehudah bar Ḥaviva said in the name of Shmuel: Three days. [5]There are [some] who say: Rav Yehudah bar Ḥaviva taught before Shmuel: [6]"Three days."

[7]Our Rabbis taught: "A nursing mother whose husband died within twenty-four months [8]may not become betrothed and may not be married [60B] until [after the] twenty-four months. [9][These are] the words of Rabbi Meir. [10]But Rabbi Yehudah permits after eighteen months. [11]Rabbi Natan bar Yosef said: These are the very words of Bet Shammai; [12]these are the very words of Bet Hillel.

RASHI

וכמה — היא פרישה. **איכא דאמרי תני רב יהודה** — מתניתא ולא שמעתא. **בתוך עשרים וארבעה חדש** — שנולד בנה. **עד עשרים וארבעה חדש** — שמא תתעבר ותצטרך לגמול את בנה, ובעל זה אינו אביו שיקנה לו ביצים וחלב. **שמונה עשר חדש** — דיו לתינוק לינק בכך.

NOTES

שֶׁמֵּת בַּעְלָהּ Whose husband died. This Baraita teaches us that a nursing mother who is widowed may not remarry or even become betrothed until her infant is two years old. *Ramban, Rabbenu Tam, She'iltot*, and others maintain that the same law applies if the woman is divorced. *Rabbenu Shimshon* (cited by *Tosafot* below, 60b, s.v. והלכתא) argues that a nursing mother who is divorced may remarry immediately, for she is under no obligation to continue nursing her child.

HALAKHAH

שְׁלֹשָׁה יָמִים Three days. "If a two-year-old infant stopped nursing for three days, his mother may not resume nursing him. This ruling applies only if the child was healthy when he stopped nursing; but if the child stopped nursing because he was ill, his mother may nurse him again when he recovers. If there is a danger to the child's health, his mother may resume nursing him even if he has been weaned for more than three days (*Rosh*, following the Jerusalem Talmud)." (*Rambam, Sefer Kedushah, Hilkhot Ma'akhalot Asurot* 3:5; *Shulḥan Arukh, Yoreh De'ah* 81:7.)

TRANSLATION AND COMMENTARY

[1]**For Bet Shammai say** that a nursing widow may not remarry until her infant is **twenty-four months** old, [2]**and Bet Hillel** say that she may remarry when the infant is **eighteen months** old. [3]**Rabban Shimon ben Gamliel said: I say** that even [4]**according to** Bet Shammai, **who say** that a nursing widow may not remarry until after her infant is **twenty-four months** old, **she is** in fact **permitted to remarry as soon as** the infant **is twenty-one months** old. [5]And similarly, **according to** Bet Hillel, **who say** that a nursing widow may not remarry until her baby is **eighteen months** old, **she is** in fact **permitted to remarry as soon as** the baby is **fifteen months** old. [6]**For** even if she conceives immediately after she remarries, her **milk will not become turbid** and the supply will not be reduced **for** at least another **three months.** By that time the infant will be twenty-four months old (according to Bet Shammai) or eighteen months old (according to Bet Hillel) and ready for weaning."

אָמַר עוּלָּא [7]The Gemara continues: **Ulla said: The Halakhah is in accordance with** the viewpoint of **Rabbi Yehudah** that a nursing widow may remarry once her infant is eighteen months old. [8]**Mar Ukva reported** a practical ruling that he himself had received on this matter: **Rabbi Ḥanina allowed me to marry** a nursing widow **as soon as** her infant was **fifteen months** old, in accordance with Rabban Shimon ben Gamliel's interpretation of the viewpoint of Bet Hillel.

אֲרִיסֵיהּ דְּאַבַּיֵי [9]It was related that **Abaye's sharecropper** wished to betroth a nursing widow, and he **came before Abaye** for a ruling on the matter, [10]**saying: What is the law regarding betrothing** a nursing widow **once** her infant is **fifteen months** old? [11]Abaye **said to him**: Betrothing such a woman is permitted for several reasons: **First**, there is a general rule that **in a dispute between Rabbi Meir and Rabbi Yehudah,** [12]**the law is in accordance with** the viewpoint of **Rabbi Yehudah.** And, as was explained by Rabban Shimon ben Gamliel, this means that she may remarry when the child is fifteen months old. [13]**And furthermore,** there is a general rule that whenever there is **a dispute between Bet Shammai and Bet Hillel, the Halakhah is in accordance with** the viewpoint of **Bet Hillel.** And, following the interpretation of Rabban Shimon ben Gamliel, Bet Hillel were of the opinion that a nursing widow may remarry when her child reaches the age of fifteen months. [14]**And** furthermore, **Ulla said** that **the law is in accordance with** the viewpoint of **Rabbi Yehudah,**

[1]שֶׁבֵּית שַׁמַּאי אוֹמְרִים: עֶשְׂרִים וְאַרְבָּעָה חֹדֶשׁ, [2]וּבֵית הִלֵּל אוֹמְרִים: שְׁמוֹנָה עָשָׂר חֹדֶשׁ. [3]אָמַר רַבָּן שִׁמְעוֹן בֶּן גַּמְלִיאֵל: אֲנִי אַכְרִיעַ: [4]לְדִבְרֵי הָאוֹמֵר עֶשְׂרִים וְאַרְבָּעָה חֹדֶשׁ, מוּתֶּרֶת לִינָּשֵׂא בְּעֶשְׂרִים וְאֶחָד חֹדֶשׁ. [5]לְדִבְרֵי הָאוֹמֵר בִּשְׁמוֹנָה עָשָׂר חֹדֶשׁ, מוּתֶּרֶת לְהִנָּשֵׂא בַּחֲמִשָּׁה עָשָׂר חֹדֶשׁ, [6]לְפִי שֶׁאֵין הֶחָלָב נֶעְכָּר אֶלָּא לְאַחַר שְׁלֹשָׁה חֳדָשִׁים״.

[7]אָמַר עוּלָּא: הֲלָכָה כְּרַבִּי יְהוּדָה. [8]וְאָמַר מָר עוּקְבָא: לִי הִתִּיר רַבִּי חֲנִינָא לָשֵׂאת לְאַחַר חֲמִשָּׁה עָשָׂר חֹדֶשׁ.

[9]אֲרִיסֵיהּ דְּאַבַּיֵי אֲתָא לְקַמֵּיהּ דְּאַבַּיֵי, [10]אֲמַר לֵיהּ: מַהוּ לְאָרֵס בַּחֲמִשָּׁה עָשָׂר חֹדֶשׁ? [11]אֲמַר לֵיהּ: חֲדָא, דְּרַבִּי מֵאִיר וְרַבִּי יְהוּדָה, [12]הֲלָכָה כְּרַבִּי יְהוּדָה. [13]וְעוֹד, בֵּית שַׁמַּאי וּבֵית הִלֵּל, הֲלָכָה כְּבֵית הִלֵּל. [14]וַאֲמַר עוּלָּא: הֲלָכָה כְּרַבִּי יְהוּדָה,

LITERAL TRANSLATION

[1]For Bet Shammai say: Twenty-four months, [2]and Bet Hillel say: Eighteen months. [3]Rabban Shimon ben Gamliel said: I will decide: [4]According to the one who says twenty-four months, she is permitted to marry after twenty-one months. [5]According to the one who says eighteen months, she is permitted to marry after fifteen months, [6]for the milk does not become turbid until after three months."

[7]Ulla said: The Halakhah is in accordance with Rabbi Yehudah. [8]And Mar Ukva said: Rabbi Ḥanina permitted me to marry after fifteen months.

[9]Abaye's sharecropper came before Abaye, [10][and] said to him: What is [the law] regarding betrothal after fifteen months? [11]He said to him: First, [in a dispute] between Rabbi Meir and Rabbi Yehudah, [12]the Halakhah is in accordance with Rabbi Yehudah. [13]And furthermore, [in a dispute between] Bet Shammai and Bet Hillel, the Halakhah is in accordance with Bet Hillel. [14]And Ulla said: The Halakhah is in accordance with Rabbi Yehudah,

BACKGROUND

לְאַחַר שְׁלֹשָׁה חֳדָשִׁים **After three months.** During pregnancy, certain hormones (progesterone and estrogen) are secreted, which usually reduce lactation or cause it to cease completely. Until recently, these hormones were used by nursing women who wished to stop nursing. Moreover, the more the fetus grows, the more of the mother's food it consumes. Hence, the mother's milk is likely to cease shortly after she becomes pregnant, unless she is exceptionally well-nourished.

NOTES

אֲנִי אַכְרִיעַ **I will decide.** This term, used here by Rabban Shimon ben Gamliel, poses a certain difficulty, for it is usually used to introduce a Halakhic ruling, or to propose a middle position as a compromise between two more extreme opinions. A variant reading is found in *She'iltot*, as well as in certain Talmudic manuscripts: אֲנִי אֲפָרֵשׁ — "I will explain." According to this reading, Rabban Shimon ben Gamliel's statement is well understood — he did not intend to issue a ruling, or to propose a middle position, but merely to explain the Tannaitic dispute.

LANGUAGE

פַּרְסָא Parasang. A unit of length of Persian origin. The term derives from the middle-Persian *frasang*, which is *farsang* in modern Persian. The word was borrowed by Semitic languages (in Syrian פרסחא, *parsaha*) and by Greek (παρασάγγης, *parasanges*). A parasang is approximately four kilometers.

BACKGROUND

כּוּתְחָא Sour milk sauce. This food (called כּוּתָח in Hebrew) was a mixture of bread, sour milk, and salt, and was used as a dip for bread or as an appetizer. כּוּתָח was eaten mainly in Babylonia, and other Talmudic passages refer to it as כּוּתָח הַבַּבְלִי — "Babylonian *kutah*".

TRANSLATION AND COMMENTARY

[1] **and Mar Ukva said** that **Rabbi Ḥanina had allowed him to marry** a nursing widow **as soon as** her baby was **fifteen months** old. [2] And **how much more so** should an allowance be made in your case, for **you** have come **to betroth** the woman and not to marry her. [3] **When** Abaye later **came to** his teacher **Rav Yosef** and told him about the matter, Rav Yosef **said to him:** [4] The decision you gave was incorrect, for **Rav and Shmuel both said** that a nursing widow **must wait twenty-four months** before remarrying. She may not even become betrothed to another man until twenty-four months have passed from the time she gave birth, [5] **not including the day on which** her baby **was born and not including the day of her betrothal.** [6] When Abaye realized that his ruling was contrary to the opinion of Rav and Shmuel, **he ran after** his sharecropper, hoping to overtake **him** and to tell him not to rely on the ruling he had given, but to follow the more stringent viewpoint of Rav and Shmuel. Some say that he ran **three parasangs** after him, **and some say** that it was **one parasang in sand, but** in any event **he did not reach him** in time. [7] Commenting on this incident, **Abaye said: The Rabbis formulated a rule** that states: [8] **Even** about the simplest matter — for example, whether one is permitted to eat **an egg in** a **sauce** containing **sour milk** — a man should be careful **not to** give a Halakhic ruling **permitting** this if he is **in the vicinity of his teacher.** Even in a case that seems self-evident, such as the matter of the egg, in which it is clear that the egg may be eaten together with the dairy food, since an egg is not regarded as a meat product, one must consult one's teacher if he is nearby. The Rabbis said this

LITERAL TRANSLATION

[1] and Mar Ukva said: Rabbi Ḥanina permitted me to marry after fifteen months. [2] How much more so you [who want permission] be betrothed. [3] When he came before Rav Yosef, he said to him: Rav and Shmuel both said: [4] She must wait twenty-four months, [5] besides the day on which he was born and besides the day on which she is betrothed. [6] He ran after him three parasangs, and some say [it was one] parasang in sand, but he did not overtake him. [7] Abaye said: This statement that the Rabbis said — [8] [that] even an egg in sour milk sauce a person should not permit in the vicinity of his teacher —

[1] וַאֲמַר מָר עוּקְבָא: לִי הִתִּיר רַבִּי חֲנִינָא לָשֵׂאת לְאַחַר חֲמִשָּׁה עָשָׂר חֹדֶשׁ. [2] כָּל שֶׁכֵּן דְּאַתְּ לֵיאָרֵס. [3] כִּי אֲתָא לְקַמֵּיהּ דְּרַב יוֹסֵף, אֲמַר לֵיהּ: [4] רַב וּשְׁמוּאֵל דְּאָמְרִי תַּרְוַויְיהוּ צְרִיכָה לְהַמְתִּין עֶשְׂרִים וְאַרְבָּעָה חֹדֶשׁ, [5] חוּץ מִיּוֹם שֶׁנּוֹלַד בּוֹ וְחוּץ מִיּוֹם שֶׁנִּתְאָרְסָה בּוֹ. [6] רְהַט בַּתְרֵיהּ תְּלָתָא פַּרְסֵי, וְאָמְרִי לָהּ פַּרְסָא בְּחָלָא, וְלָא אַדְרְכֵיהּ. [7] אֲמַר אַבַּיֵּי: הַאי מִילְּתָא דַּאֲמוּר רַבָּנַן — [8] אֲפִילּוּ בֵּיעֲתָא בְּכוּתְחָא לָא לִישְׁרֵי אִינִישׁ בִּמְקוֹם רַבֵּיהּ —

NOTES

צְרִיכָה לְהַמְתִּין עֶשְׂרִים וְאַרְבָּעָה חֹדֶשׁ She must wait twenty-four months. A number of Rishonim (*Rivan, Ra'avan, Meiri*) cite a Midrash which finds a source for this ruling in the verse (Exodus 23:19): "You shall not seethe [תְבַשֵּׁל] a kid in its mother's milk." The numerical value of the word תְבַשֵּׁל is 732, and this alludes to the 732 days that a nursing widow must wait before she can accept betrothal from another man — twice 365 days (the number of days in a solar year) plus another two days (the day on which her baby was born and the day of her betrothal). *Meiri* argues that the law is not in accordance with this Midrash, for a nursing widow may not remarry until two years (according to the Hebrew lunar calendar) have passed since her baby was born, whether the years were intercalated, so that they have more than 365 days, or whether they were not intercalated, so that they have less.

אֲפִילּוּ בֵּיעֲתָא בְּכוּתְחָא Even an egg in sour milk sauce. *Rivan* explains that the Gemara is referring to an ordinary egg, and the legal issue involved is whether or not the egg may be eaten together with a dairy sauce.

Tosafot and others object that even the most unlearned person knows that an egg may be eaten together with milk, so that telling somebody that such is the law cannot be considered as issuing a ruling. These authorities prefer

HALAKHAH

צְרִיכָה לְהַמְתִּין עֶשְׂרִים וְאַרְבָּעָה חֹדֶשׁ She must wait twenty-four months. "The Sages enacted that a man may not marry or even betroth a pregnant woman or a nursing woman until the child is twenty-four months old, excluding the day that the child was born and the day that the man betroths the woman, following the ruling of Rav and Shmuel. *Rema* notes in the name of *Haggahot Mordekhai* that the twenty-four months are counted in sequence whether they contain twenty-nine or thirty days. According to some authorities (*Terumat HaDeshen*), an extra month must be counted in an intercalated year (see *Pitḥei Teshuvah*)." (*Rambam, Sefer Nashim, Hilkhot Gerushin* 11:25; *Shulḥan Arukh, Even HaEzer* 13:11.)

לָא לִישְׁרֵי אִינִישׁ בִּמְקוֹם רַבֵּיהּ A person should not permit in the vicinity of his teacher. "It is absolutely forbidden to issue a Halakhic ruling in the presence of one's teacher, and whoever issues such a ruling is liable to death at the hands of Heaven. *Rema* adds that if the disciple received most of his knowledge from one teacher, the disciple must not issue a ruling within three parasangs of this teacher, even if the teacher has granted him permission to do so." (*Rambam, Sefer Mada, Hilkhot Talmud Torah* 5:2; *Sefer Shofetim, Hilkhot Sanhedrin* 20:9; *Shulḥan Arukh, Yoreh De'ah* 242:4.)

TRANSLATION AND COMMENTARY

[1]**not because** they felt that issuing a ruling in one's teacher's vicinity would **seem** to others **like impudence,** [2]**but because** they knew that if a Sage rules in his teacher's vicinity, **he will not succeed in issuing** a correct ruling. [3]Abaye substantiated this conclusion from his own experience: **For I** myself had **learned this ruling of Rav and Shmuel**, that a nursing widow must wait until her child is twenty-four months old before remarrying. [4]**But even so,** when I was asked to issue a practical ruling on the matter, **I did not succeed in rendering** a correct decision. Rav and Shmuel's ruling escaped my memory, because I issued the ruling in the vicinity of my teacher, Rav Yosef.

תָּנוּ רַבָּנַן [5]The Gemara now cites a Baraita which qualifies the prohibition limiting a nursing mother's freedom to remarry. **Our Rabbis taught: "If** a nursing widow **gives her** infant **son to a wet nurse,** [6]**or if she weans him, or** if the infant **dies, she is permitted to remarry immediately,** even if twenty-four months (according to Rabbi Meir) or eighteen months (according to Rabbi Yehudah) have not yet passed from the date she gave birth, for in all these cases the woman's remarriage cannot endanger her child."

רַב פָּפָּא [7]It was related that **Rav Pappa and Rav Huna the son of Rav Yehoshua thought to issue a ruling in accordance with this Baraita,** and to allow a nursing widow to remarry after she had given her infant son to a wet nurse. [8]But **a certain old woman said to them: "I** myself **was in a similar situation, and Rav Naḥman forbade me** to remarry."

[1]לָא מִשּׁוּם דְּמִיחֲזֵי כְּאַפְקֵירוּתָא, [2]אֶלָּא מִשּׁוּם דְּלָא מִסְתַּיְּיעָא מִילְּתָא לְמֵימְרָא. [3]דְּהָא אֲנָא הֲוָה גְּמִירְנָא לֵיהּ לְהָא דְּרַב וּשְׁמוּאֵל, [4]אֲפִילּוּ הָכִי לָא מִסְתַּיְּיעָא לִי מִילְּתָא לְמֵימַר.

[5]תָּנוּ רַבָּנַן: "נָתְנָה בְּנָהּ לְמֵינֶקֶת, [6]אוֹ גְּמָלַתּוּ, אוֹ מֵת, מוּתֶּרֶת לִינָּשֵׂא מִיָּד".

[7]רַב פָּפָּא וְרַב הוּנָא בְּרֵיהּ דְּרַב יְהוֹשֻׁעַ סְבוּר לְמֶיעְבַּד עוּבְדָּא כִּי הָא מַתְנִיתָא. [8]אֲמַרָה לְהוּ הַהִיא סָבְתָא: "בְּדִידִי הֲוָה עוּבְדָּא, וַאֲסַר לִי רַב נַחְמָן".

LITERAL TRANSLATION

[1]is not because it looks like impudence, [2]but because he will not be successful in saying it. [3]For I learned this [ruling] of Rav and Shmuel, [4][but] even so I was not successful in saying it.

[5]Our Rabbis taught: "[If] she gave her son to a wet nurse, [6]or she weaned him, or he died, she is permitted to marry immediately."

[7]Rav Pappa and Rav Huna the son of Rav Yehoshua thought to give a practical ruling (lit., "to do a deed") in accordance with this Baraita. [8]A certain old woman said to them: "[Such] an incident happened to me, and Rav Naḥman forbade me [to remarry]."

RASHI

אפקירותא = חוצפא. **דלא מיסתייעא מילתא** — שיורה כהלכה. **נתנה בנה למינקת** — זו שמת בעלה, או גמלתו בתוך זמנו או מת.

BACKGROUND

לָא מִשּׁוּם דְּמִיחֲזֵי כְּאַפְקֵירוּתָא Not because it looks like impudence. In some instances a disciple who delivers Halakhic rulings in the vicinity of his teacher (up to a distance of three parasangs from him) is not regarded as showing impudence and coarseness. For example, the teacher may have given his disciple permission to deliver rulings, and he may not regard it as an impertinence. Nevertheless, if one does not consult one's teacher and takes Halakhic decisions when the teacher is available, this does indicate a lack of basic courtesy. Therefore Abaye said that, although the teacher is not particular about the matter, nevertheless Heaven does not permit a disciple to give a Halakhic ruling successfully when he does so in his teacher's place.

NOTES

the explanation offered by *Arukh* that the Gemara is referring here to a fully formed egg found inside a slaughtered chicken. Even though the egg was found inside the chicken, it is not treated as meat and may therefore be eaten together with a dairy sauce.

The Rishonim ask: Why is a fully formed egg that is found inside a properly slaughtered chicken not treated like the chicken itself and forbidden to be eaten with milk, when such an egg found inside an improperly slaughtered chicken is treated like the chicken itself and forbidden to be eaten altogether?

Tosafot (citing *Halakhot Gedolot*) answers: The improperly slaughtered chicken is forbidden for consumption by Torah law, and this is why the Rabbis were stringent about an egg found inside it. But a properly slaughtered chicken is only treated as meat by Rabbinic law, and this is why the Rabbis were lenient about its egg. According to *Rabbenu Tam*, the Rabbis were stringent about the egg found inside an improperly slaughtered chicken because the chicken itself is a forbidden food. But they were lenient about the egg found inside a properly slaughtered chicken because the chicken itself is a permitted food. *Sefer Yere'im* suggests that the prohibition imposed on an improperly slaughtered chicken applies to the bird itself and to everything found inside it, including its eggs. But the prohibition against eating chicken with milk was imposed only on the bird itself, but not on the eggs found inside it.

דְּהָא אֲנָא הֲוָה גְּמִירְנָא For I learned. *Rivan* explains that Abaye was referring to his own statement made elsewhere (above, 57a) that the law is in accordance with Rabbi Meir's decrees. Thus he should have known that the law is

HALAKHAH

נָתְנָה בְּנָהּ לְמֵינֶקֶת If she gave her son to a wet nurse. "A nursing mother may not remarry before her child is twenty-four months old, even if she entrusts the child to a wet nurse or weans him. This ruling applies even if the wet nurse took an oath promising not to go back on her agreement to nurse the child. Some authorities (*Rema* in the name of *Haggahot Mordekhai*) maintain that if the wet nurse took such an oath and the woman remarried, her husband need not divorce her." (*Rambam, Sefer Nashim, Hilkhot Gerushin* 11:27; *Shulḥan Arukh, Even HaEzer* 13:11.)

אֵינִי? ²וְהָא רַב נַחְמָן שְׁרָא לְהוּ לְבֵי רֵישׁ גָּלוּתָא!
³שָׁאנֵי בֵּי רֵישׁ גָּלוּתָא, ⁴דְּלָא הָדַר בְּהוּ.
⁵אֲמַר לְהוּ רַב פַּפִּי: ⁶וְאַתּוּן לָא תִּסְבְּרוּהָ מֵהָא דְּתַנְיָא: ⁷״הֲרֵי שֶׁהָיְתָה רְדוּפָה לֵילֵךְ לְבֵית אָבִיהָ, ⁸אוֹ שֶׁהָיָה לָהּ כַּעַס בְּבֵית בַּעְלָהּ, אוֹ שֶׁהָיָה בַּעְלָהּ חָבוּשׁ בְּבֵית הָאֲסוּרִין, אוֹ שֶׁהָלַךְ בַּעְלָהּ לִמְדִינַת הַיָּם, ⁹אוֹ שֶׁהָיָה בַּעְלָהּ זָקֵן אוֹ חוֹלֶה, אוֹ שֶׁהָיְתָה עֲקָרָה וּזְקֵנָה אַיְילוֹנִית וּקְטַנָּה, וְהַמַּפֶּלֶת אַחַר מִיתַת בַּעְלָהּ, וְשֶׁאֵינָהּ רְאוּיָה לֵילֵד — ¹⁰כּוּלָּן צְרִיכוֹת לְהַמְתִּין

LITERAL TRANSLATION

¹Is this so? ²But surely Rav Naḥman permitted them in the House of the Exilarch!
³The House of the Exilarch is different, ⁴for they do not retract.
⁵Rav Pappi said to them: ⁶But do you not maintain this from what was taught: ⁷"[If] she was accustomed to go to her father's house, ⁸or she had a quarrel in her husband's house, or her husband was imprisoned in jail, or her husband went abroad, ⁹or her husband was old or sick, or she was barren or old [or] an *aylonit* or a minor, or she miscarried after her husband's death, or she was unfit to conceive — ¹⁰all of them must wait

TRANSLATION AND COMMENTARY

אֵינִי ¹The Gemara asks: **Is it** really **true** that Rav Naḥman ruled against the Baraita? ²**But surely Rav Naḥman permitted** the nursing widows **in the House of the Exilarch** to remarry as soon as they gave their infants to a wet nurse!

שָׁאנֵי בֵּי רֵישׁ גָּלוּתָא ³The Gemara answers: The law that applies to a widow of **the House of the Exilarch is different, for** if a wet nurse agrees to care for such a child, ⁴**she will** certainly **not break the agreement** and return the child to his mother, for she fears the power of the House of the Exilarch. But in the case of an ordinary widow, the wet nurse who agrees to take her child may change her mind and return the child to his mother. The child will then be in danger if his mother has remarried in the meantime and is now unable to resume nursing or to secure adequate food for the child from her new husband.

אֲמַר לְהוּ רַב פַּפִּי ⁵**Rav Pappi said to** Rav Pappa and Rav Huna the son of Rav Yehoshua: ⁶**And** even if the old woman had not reported to you Rav Naḥman's ruling on the matter, **would you not maintain** that a nursing woman is forbidden to remarry even if she has given her infant to a wet nurse or if she has weaned him? But surely such a conclusion follows **from** what **was taught** in the following Baraita: ⁷"The Rabbis decreed that a widow or a divorcee is forbidden to remarry or even to accept betrothal during the first three months after her husband's death or the couple's divorce, in case she gives birth to a child six months later, and the identity of his father will be in doubt, for he may be the full-term child of the first husband or the prematurely born child of the second husband. Even **if** the woman **was accustomed** toward the end of her first marriage **to spend** most of her time **in her father's house,** ⁸**or** if **there was discord in her** first **husband's house, or** if **her** first **husband was in prison, or went abroad,** ⁹**or was old or sick, or** if the woman **was barren or old or an *aylonit*** [a sexually undeveloped woman incapable of bearing children] **or a minor, or** if **she miscarried after her husband died** or divorced her, **or** if **she was unfit to conceive** for some other reason — ¹⁰even in **these cases** the woman **is required to wait three**

RASHI

לבי ריש גלותא — אלמנות שהיו בהן מניקות, ונתנו בניהם למניקה, והתירום לינשא. **דלא הדרי בהו** — מניקה שפסקה להניק בניהם יראה לחזור בה, לפי שבני אדם מאוימים הם. אבל באינשי אחריני — דלמא הדרא בה המניקה, וחוזר הבן אצל האם ומסתכן. **לא תסברוה מהא** — אי לא אמרה לכו סבתא משמיה דרב נחמן לא הייתם יודעים ללמוד מתוך משנה זו שאסור? **הרי שהיתה רדופה** — רוב ימיה, להיות בבית אביה כו׳. כל אלו אין דרכן להתעבר. **שאינה ראויה לילד** — שנעקר בית הריון שלה.

BACKGROUND

רַב נַחְמָן שְׁרָא **Rav Naḥman permitted.** Rav Naḥman was related by marriage to the House of the Exilarch, and some maintain that his wife Yalta was the Exilarch's daughter. Therefore Rav Naḥman became in effect the Exilarch's Halakhic adviser, and would deliver Halakhic rulings to the Exilarch, to his household, and to everyone dependent on him.

CONCEPTS

אַיְילוֹנִית **An *aylonit*.** From the detailed discussions in the Talmud, especially in tractate *Yevamot*, it seems that an *aylonit* is a woman with a genetic flaw preventing her from giving birth. In contrast to a barren woman, who generally suffers from some secondary disability though her physical and sexual development is normal, an *aylonit* is characterized by abnormal physical development (such as the failure to develop secondary sexual traits). From the descriptions in Talmudic literature it seems that there are various kinds of *aylonit,* ranging from those with excess male hormones to those who suffer from Turner's syndrome. In the Halakhah there are many laws relating to the status of the *aylonit,* mainly because she either completely lacks secondary sexual traits or because these appear only at a later age. Consequently various questions arise regarding the age at which an *aylonit* reaches legal majority.

NOTES

in accordance with the viewpoint of Rabbi Meir that a nursing widow may not remarry until her child is twenty-four months old. Others explain that Abaye was referring to the specific ruling issued by Rav and Shmuel that a nursing widow must wait twenty-four months before she may remarry, which Abaye had once known but which had slipped his mind when he gave his ruling to his sharecropper (*Rid*).

שָׁאנֵי בֵּי רֵישׁ גָּלוּתָא **The House of the Exilarch is different.** Most authorities explain that the law applying to a widow of the family of the Exilarch is different, because a wet nurse who undertakes to nurse the child of such a woman will surely not dare to break an agreement she has reached with the House of the Exilarch. According to some readings (see also *She'iltot*), the Gemara is arguing that the law applying to the widow of the House of the Exilarch is

HALAKHAH

כּוּלָּן צְרִיכוֹת לְהַמְתִּין שְׁלֹשָׁה חֳדָשִׁים **All of them must wait three months.** "A widow or a divorcee is forbidden to remarry or even to become betrothed during the first ninety days after being widowed or divorced (not including the day her husband died or divorced her, and the day she accepts betrothal), in order to establish whether or not she

שְׁלֹשָׁה חֳדָשִׁים. [1]דִּבְרֵי רַבִּי מֵאִיר. [2]רַבִּי יוֹסֵי מַתִּיר לֵיאָרֵס וְלִינָּשֵׂא מִיָּד". [3]וְאָמַר רַב נַחְמָן אָמַר שְׁמוּאֵל: הֲלָכָה כְּרַבִּי מֵאִיר בִּגְזֵירוֹתָיו!

[4]אָמְרִי לֵיהּ: לָאו אַדַּעְתִּין.

[5]וְהִלְכְתָא: מֵת, מוּתָּר. [6]גְּמָלַתּוּ, אָסוּר.

LITERAL TRANSLATION

three months. [1][These are] the words of Rabbi Meir. [2]Rabbi Yose permits [them] to be betrothed and to be married immediately." [3]And Rav Naḥman said in the name of Shmuel: The Halakhah is in accordance with Rabbi Meir in his decrees!

[4]They said to him: It was not in our minds.

[5]And the Halakhah is: [If] he died, it is permitted. [6][If] she weaned him, it is forbidden.

TRANSLATION AND COMMENTARY

months before she remarries. Even though there is no concern that the woman may be pregnant by her first husband, she is still forbidden to remarry during the first three months after she is widowed or divorced. Once the Rabbis enacted that a widow or a divorcee may not remarry for three months, they did not make any exceptions [1]**This is the viewpoint of Rabbi Meir.** [2]But **Rabbi Yose** disagrees and **permits** the women mentioned above **to accept betrothal and** even **to remarry immediately** after they have become widowed or divorced, for in none of these cases is there any concern that the woman may be pregnant by her first husband." [3]**And Rav Naḥman said in the name of Shmuel:** There is a general rule that **the Halakhah is in accordance with Rabbi Meir in his decrees!** We follow the viewpoint of Rabbi Meir whenever he prohibits by Rabbinic decree something that is permitted by Torah law. Thus, in all cases, a widow or a divorcee is forbidden to remarry during the first three months after the death of the husband or the couple's divorce. Here, too, the law should be in accordance with Rabbi Meir's ruling that in all cases a nursing widow is forbidden to remarry before her infant reaches the age of twenty-four months, and no distinction should be made between a woman who is still nursing her child and a woman who has given her child to a wet nurse or has weaned him! Why, then, were you ready to rule in accordance with the Baraita that a nursing widow is permitted to remarry after she has given her infant son to a wet nurse or weaned him?

אָמְרִי לֵיהּ [4]Rav Pappa and Rav Huna the son of Rav Yehoshua **said to** Rav Pappi: When we were considering the matter, **we forgot about this** Baraita.

וְהִלְכְתָא [5]The Gemara notes in conclusion that **the Halakhah is** as follows: **If** a widow's infant child **dies, she is permitted** to remarry immediately, although twenty-four months have not passed from the time she gave birth to the child. [6]But **if** the woman **has weaned** her child, **she is** still **forbidden** to remarry until the child is two years old, lest she be tempted to wean her child prematurely.

RASHI

בגזירותיו — בכל מקום שהוא מחמיר מדרבנן. אלמא, אף על גב דאין כאן להבחין בין זרעו של ראשון לשל שני, דהא לא מיעברא — לא פלוג רבנן בתקנת גזירות שלהם בין אשה לאשה, וגזרו סתם שתמתין כל אשה שלשה חדשים. והכי נמי — לא פלוג רבנן במינקת שמת בעלה, בין שהיא מניקתו בין שאינה מניקתו. גמלתו אסור — שגמלתו מחמת שרוצה לינשא.

NOTES

different, for such a woman will surely not change her mind and resume nursing the child herself, and hence there need be no concern that the child will be endangered if its mother remarries. *Ḥatam Sofer* discusses this argument at length in order to justify the position of those who forbid a widow to remarry even after she has handed her child over to a wet nurse, and even if the wet nurse cannot break the agreement.

הֲלָכָה כְּרַבִּי מֵאִיר **The Halakhah is in accordance with Rabbi Meir.** The Rishonim ask: If Rav Naḥman maintains that the Halakhah is in accordance with Rabbi Meir in his decrees, so that a widow is forbidden to remarry before her infant is twenty-four months old, whether she is still nursing the child or not, why did Rav Naḥman issue a ruling allowing the widows in the House of the Exilarch to remarry as soon as they entrusted their infants to a wet nurse?

Rivan explains that since the widows in the House of the Exilarch always appointed wet nurses for their children, there was no concern that allowing them to remarry would lead to a situation where a nursing woman would be permitted to remarry.

Shittah Mekubbetzet argues that Rabbinic decrees are not ordinarily imposed in unusual situations, and the widows of the House of the Exilarch certainly fall into the category of uncommon cases. *Meiri* argues that Rav Naḥman's ruling was a special dispensation and is not to be taken as a precedent.

מֵת, מוּתָּר **If he died, it is permitted.** The Rishonim ask: It has been established that the Halakhah is in accordance

HALAKHAH

is pregnant by her first husband. The Sages decreed that a widow or a divorcee must wait these three months even if there is no actual concern that she is carrying her first husband's child — for example, if she is incapable of conceiving a child, or if she was widowed or divorced after betrothal," following Rabbi Meir. (*Rambam, Sefer Nashim, Hilkhot Gerushin* 11:18-19; *Shulḥan Arukh, Even HaEzer* 13:1.)

מֵת, מוּתָּר **If he died, it is permitted.** "If a woman with a young child is widowed and then her child dies, she is

BACKGROUND

דְּבָרִים הָרָעִים לֶחָלָב **Things that are bad for the milk.** The food eaten by a nursing woman affects her milk, although modern science has not determined precisely which foods affect lactation adversely and how they do so.

TRANSLATION AND COMMENTARY

מָר בַּר רַב אַשִׁי אָמַר [1] **Mar bar Rav Ashi said: Even if** the child **dies,** his mother **is forbidden** to remarry until two years have passed since his birth. For if she is allowed to remarry immediately, [2] there is concern that **she will perhaps murder** her baby in order to be allowed to **go and remarry.** [3] And **there was** indeed such **an incident,** in which a widow **strangled** her own baby in order to be granted permission to remarry.

וְלֹא הִיא [4] The Gemara rejects Mar bar Rav Ashi's viewpoint and says that support for **it** may **not** be brought from this appalling story. [5] **That woman was** clearly **insane, for women do not strangle their children.** Thus a widow whose infant child has died may remarry immediately, even if twenty-four months have not passed since the child was born.

תָּנוּ רַבָּנַן [6] The Gemara now proceeds to cite a Baraita that deals with some of the regulations regarding a wet nurse. **Our Rabbis taught: "If** a wet nurse **has been given an infant to nurse** and she is being paid for her nursing, **she must not nurse** another infant together **with him,** [7] **neither her own infant nor the infant of another woman,** so that she will have enough milk for the child she has been hired to nurse. [8] **If** a wet nurse is given an infant to nurse, and **she makes an agreement** with the infant's mother that the mother will provide her with a certain **amount of food** and this later proves **insufficient** for her, [9] the wet nurse **must eat a large amount** of food to ensure that she will have enough milk for the baby. A wet nurse **must not eat things that are bad for her milk."**

[1] מָר בַּר רַב אַשִׁי אָמַר: אֲפִילּוּ מֵת נַמִּי אָסוּר. [2] דִּלְמָא קָטְלָה לֵיהּ וְאָזְלָא וּמִינַּסְבָא. [3] הֲוָה עוּבְדָא וַחֲנַקְתֵּיהּ.

[4] וְלֹא הִיא. [5] הַהִיא שׁוֹטָה הֲוַאי, דְּלָא עָבְדֵי נָשֵׁי דְּחָנְקָן בְּנַיְיהוּ.

[6] תָּנוּ רַבָּנַן: ״הֲרֵי שֶׁנָּתְנוּ לָהּ בֵּן לְהָנִיק, [7] הֲרֵי זוֹ לֹא תָּנִיק עִמּוֹ לֹא בְּנָהּ וְלֹא בֶּן חֲבֶרְתָּהּ. [8] פָּסְקָה קִימְעָא, אוֹכֶלֶת הַרְבֵּה. [9] לֹא תֹּאכַל עִמּוֹ דְּבָרִים הָרָעִים לֶחָלָב״.

LITERAL TRANSLATION

[1] Mar bar Rav Ashi said: Even [if] he died, it is also forbidden. [2] Perhaps she will kill him and go and marry. [3] There was an incident and she strangled him.

[4] But it is not so. [5] That woman was insane, for women do not strangle their children.

[6] Our Rabbis taught: "[If] they gave her an infant to nurse, [7] she may not nurse with him her own infant or the infant of another woman. [8] [Even if] she agreed to a small amount [of food], she must eat a large amount. [9] She must not eat with him things that are bad for the milk."

RASHI

פסקה קימעא — פסקו ליתן לה מזונות מועטים. אוכלת הרבה — משלה, כדי שיהיה לה חלב הרבה ולא תמיתנו.

NOTES

with Rabbi Meir in his decrees, and a widow may not remarry during the first three months of her widowhood, even if she cannot possibly be pregnant by her first husband, in order that she not be confused with a woman who may be pregnant by her first husband. Why, then, does the Gemara conclude that a nursing woman whose infant has died is permitted to remarry, even if twenty-four months have not yet passed from the date she gave birth to the child? According to the logic of Rabbi Meir's decree, she should be forbidden to remarry, lest she be confused with a woman whose nursing child did not die!

Ritva and others explain that a woman who cannot possibly be pregnant by her late husband is forbidden to remarry during the first three months of her widowhood, because it is not clear to all that she cannot be pregnant. But a nursing mother whose infant has died is permitted to remarry immediately, because all can see that she has stopped nursing because her child has died.

הַהִיא שׁוֹטָה הֲוַאי **That woman was insane.** *Rid* writes that the widow who strangled her own baby was non-Jewish. Thus the incident cannot serve as support for Mar bar Rav Ashi's position.

פָּסְקָה קִימְעָא **Even if she agreed to a small amount of food.** Our commentary follows *Rivan* and *Meiri*, who explain this clause as referring to a wet nurse who has made an agreement with the mother of the infant whom she has been hired to nurse that the mother will provide her with a certain amount of food. If that amount proves insufficient for a nursing woman, the wet nurse must

HALAKHAH

permitted to remarry immediately, even if twenty-four months have not yet passed from the date she gave birth, for we are not concerned that she will be tempted to kill her child. Similarly, if the woman weaned her infant before her husband died, or if she was physically unable to nurse her infant, or if she handed her child over to a wet nurse three months before her husband's death and did not nurse afterwards, she is permitted to remarry immediately after her husband's death (following *Rosh*)." (*Rambam, Sefer Nashim, Hilkhot Gerushin* 11:27; *Shulḥan Arukh, Even HaEzer* 13:11.)

פָּסְקָה קִימְעָא, אוֹכֶלֶת הַרְבֵּה **Even if she agreed to a small amount of food, she must eat a large amount.** "While a woman is nursing, her husband must add to her maintenance and must provide her with foods that are beneficial for her milk. *Rema* adds that if her husband does not

TRANSLATION AND COMMENTARY

הָשְׁתָּא [1]Beginning its analysis of this Baraita, the Gemara asks: **Now that** the Baraita **has said that** a wet nurse **may not** even **nurse her own infant** together with the child she has been hired to nurse, [2]**was it necessary to mention** that she may not nurse together with him **the infant of another woman?**

מַהוּ דְּתֵימָא [3]The Gemara answers: Had the Baraita said only that the wet nurse may not nurse her own infant together with the child she was hired to nurse, we might have thought that it is only her own infant whom she may not nurse. For **we might have said that,** since **she has** a special maternal **affection for her** own **infant,** if she does not have enough milk for two babies **she will allow** her own infant **to nurse more** than the other infant whom she has been hired to nurse. [4]**But in the case of another woman's infant**, for whom she has no special affection, **were it not that she has extra** milk, so that she can nurse two children at the same time, [5]**she would not have allowed** the other woman's infant **to nurse.** [6]**Therefore** the Baraita **tells us** that a wet nurse may **not** nurse any other infant together with the infant whom she has been hired to nurse, for she may not have enough milk.

פָּסְקָה קִימְעָא [7]The next clause of the Baraita stated: **"If** a wet nurse is given an infant to nurse, and **she makes an agreement** with the infant's mother that the mother will provide her with a certain **amount of food,** and this later proves **insufficient** for her, the wet nurse **must eat a large amount** of food to ensure that she will have enough milk for the baby." [8]The Gemara asks: **From where** should the wet nurse procure the additional food she requires?

אָמַר רַב שֵׁשֶׁת [9]**Rav Sheshet said** in reply: She must purchase the food **with her own** money. The wet nurse agreed to receive a certain wage in return for which she is required to nurse the child and to prepare herself adequately for the task. If the food that the infant's mother agreed to provide her is insufficient, the wet nurse must go out and buy additional food for herself, in order to ensure that she will have enough milk for the baby.

לֹא תֹּאכַל [10]The Baraita concluded: "A wet nurse **must not eat things that are bad for her milk."** [11]The Gemara asks: **What are** those things that are bad for her milk?

[1]הָשְׁתָּא בְּנָהּ אָמַרְתְּ לָא, [2]בֶּן חֲבֶרְתָּהּ מִיבַּעְיָא?
[3]מַהוּ דְּתֵימָא בְּנָהּ הוּא דְּחָיֵיס עִילָּוֵיהּ, מְמַצְיָא לֵיהּ טְפֵי.
[4]אֲבָל בֶּן חֲבֶרְתָּהּ, אִי לָאו דַּהֲוָה לַהּ מוֹתָר, [5]לָא הֲוָה מְמַצְיָא לֵיהּ. [6]קָא מַשְׁמַע לַן.
[7]"פָּסְקָה קִימְעָא, אוֹכֶלֶת הַרְבֵּה". [8]מֵהֵיכָא?
[9]אָמַר רַב שֵׁשֶׁת: מִשֶּׁלָּהּ.
[10]"לֹא תֹּאכַל עִמּוֹ דְּבָרִים הָרָעִים". [11]מַאי נִינְהוּ?

LITERAL TRANSLATION

[1]Now [that] you say [that she may] not [nurse] her own infant, [2]was it necessary [to mention] the infant of another woman?

[3]You might have said [that in the case of] her own infant, for whom she has affection, she will allow him to suck more. [4]But [in the case of] the infant of another woman, if she did not have extra, [5]she would not have allowed him to suck. [6][Therefore] it tells us [that this is not so].

[7]"[Even if] she agreed to a small amount [of food], she must eat a large amount." [8]From where?

[9]Rav Sheshet said: From her own.

[10]"She must not eat with him things that are bad [for the milk]." [11]What are they?

NOTES

procure additional food for herself so that she will have enough milk for the baby.

Talmidei Rabbenu Yonah explains this clause as referring to a nursing mother who has come to an agreement with her husband about how much food he will provide her. If the stipulated amount proves insufficient, she cannot demand more from her husband but must increase her nutrition at her own expense so that she can meet the needs of her nursing infant.

Rambam (following *Rav Hai Gaon* and *Rabbenu Ḥananel*) understands this clause in an entirely different manner: If a nursing woman has been awarded an appropriate amount of maintenance, but she craves for more food on account of a certain stomach disorder from which she is suffering, she may eat as much as she wants at her own expense, and her husband cannot object and say that if she eats so much she will endanger the infant that she is nursing.

HALAKHAH

provide her with any extra food, she must eat more at her own expense. Some authorities (*Rambam*) maintain that if a nursing woman has been awarded an appropriate amount of food, but she craves for more or for different food, her husband cannot object by claiming that she is endangering her child. Others (*Ra'avad*) maintain that the husband can indeed object if his wife wishes to eat quantities or types of food that would endanger the child she is nursing." (*Rambam, Sefer Nashim, Hilkhot Ishut* 21:11; *Shulḥan Arukh, Even HaEzer* 80:11-12.)

[1]אָמַר רַב כָּהֲנָא: כְּגוֹן כְּשׁוּת, וְחָזִיז, וְדָגִים קְטַנִּים, וַאֲדָמָה. [2]אַבַּיֵי אֲמַר: אֲפִילוּ קָרָא וְחַבּוּשָׁא. [3]רַב פַּפָּא אֲמַר: אֲפִילוּ קָרָא וְכוּפְרָא. [4]רַב אַשִׁי אֲמַר: אֲפִילוּ כַּמְכָּא וְהַרְסְנָא. [5]מִינַּיְיהוּ פָּסְקֵי חַלְבָּא. [6]מִינַּיְיהוּ עָכְרִי חַלְבָּא.

[7]דִּמְשַׁמְּשָׁא בֵּי רֵיחַיָּא הָווּ לָהּ בְּנֵי נִכְפֵּי. [8]דִּמְשַׁמְּשָׁא עַל אַרְעָא הָווּ לָהּ בְּנֵי שְׁמוּטֵי. [9]דְּדָרְכָא עַל רְמָא דַּחֲמָרָא הָווּ לָהּ בְּנֵי גִּירְדָּנֵי. [10]דְּאָכְלָה חַרְדְּלָא הָווּ לָהּ בְּנֵי זַלְזְלָנֵי. [11]דְּאָכְלָה תַּחְלֵי הָווּ לָהּ בְּנֵי דוּלְפָּנֵי. [12]דְּאָכְלָה מוֹנִינֵי הָווּ לָהּ בְּנֵי מְצִיצֵי עֵינָא. [13]דְּאָכְלָה גַּרְגּוּשְׁתָּא הָווּ לָהּ בְּנֵי מְכוֹעָרֵי. [14]דְּשָׁתְיָא שִׁיכְרָא הָווּ לָהּ בְּנֵי אוּכָּמֵי. [15]דְּאָכְלָה בִּישְׂרָא וְשָׁתְיָא חַמְרָא הָווּ לָהּ בְּנֵי בְּרִיֵי. [61A] [16]דְּאָכְלָה בֵּיעֵי הָווּ לָהּ בְּנֵי עֵינָנֵי. [17]דְּאָכְלָה כַּוְורֵי

LITERAL TRANSLATION

[1]Rav Kahana said: For example, hops, and young blades of grain, and small fish, and earth. [2]Abaye said: Even a gourd and a quince. [3]Rav Pappa said: Even a gourd and an unripe date. [4]Rav Ashi said: Even sour milk sauce and fish-hash. [5]Some of them stop the milk. [6]Some of them turn the milk turbid.

[7]She who has sexual relations in a mill will have epileptic children. [8]She who has sexual relations on the ground will have long-necked children. [9]She who steps on the droppings of an ass will have bald children. [10]She who eats mustard will have gluttonous children. [11]She who eats cress will have children with tearful eyes. [12]She who eats fish brine will have children with blinking eyes. [13]She who eats clay will have ugly children. [14]She who drinks beer will have dark[-complexioned] children. [15]She who eats meat and drinks wine will have healthy children. [61A] [16]She who eats eggs will have children with big eyes. [17]She who eats fish

TRANSLATION AND COMMENTARY

אָמַר רַב כָּהֲנָא [1]A number of different answers to this question were provided by the Amoraim. **Rav Kahana said: Hops, young blades of grain, small fish, and earth** are bad for a woman's milk. [2]**Abaye said: Even a gourd or a quince.** [3]**Rav Pappa said: Even a gourd or an unripe date.** [4]**Rav Ashi said: Even** a **sauce** consisting of **sour milk** and bread, **and fish-hash.** [5]The Gemara notes that the various foods mentioned here affect a woman's milk in different ways: **Some of them cause** her **milk** supply **to be reduced,** [6]whereas **others cause the milk to turn turbid.**

דִּמְשַׁמְּשָׁא בֵּי רֵיחַיָּא [7]The Gemara continues with a discussion of the effects of a woman's diet and general behaviour upon her offspring. A woman **who engages in sexual relations in a mill will have epileptic children.** [8]A woman **who engages in sexual relations** while lying **on the ground will have long-necked children.** [9]A woman **who steps on the droppings of an ass** while she is pregnant **will have bald children.** [10]A woman **who eats mustard** during her pregnancy **will have gluttonous children.** [11]A woman **who eats cress** during her pregnancy **will have children with tearful eyes.** [12]A woman **who eats fish brine** while she is pregnant **will have children with** excessively **blinking eyes.** [13]A woman **who eats clay** during her pregnancy **will have ugly children.** [14]A woman **who drinks beer** while she is pregnant **will have children with dark complexions.** [15]A woman **who eats meat and drinks wine** during her pregnancy **will have healthy children.** [61A] [16]A woman **who eats eggs** while pregnant **will have children with big eyes.** [17]A woman **who eats fish** during her

RASHI

כשות — *הומלו״ן. **חזיז** — עשבים של זרע תבואה. **חבושא** — **קורליי״ה. **קורא** — רך הגדל בדקל, מה שנוסף על הענף בשנה זו. **כופרא** — תמרים בקטנותן. **כמכא** — כותח. **והרסנא** — דגים מטוגנין בקמח וליר ושומן שלהן. **מינייהו פסקי חלבא** — יש בדברים הללו שפוסקין חלב האשה, ויש בהן שאין מפסיקין אלא עוכרין. **בני נכפי** — ולדות שמתעברות שם — נופלים מחולי שמו ***פישיאו״ן. **שמוטי** — ארוכי צואר, והוא מום. **גירדני** — פירוש: אדם שנמרט שערות ראשו, או בעל גרב. **זלזלני** — רעבתנין. **דולפני** — עיניהם זולפות מים תמיד. **מוניני** — הורגלה לאכול דגים קטנים. **מציצי עינא** — עיניו פורחות ונעות תמיד. **גרגושתא** — אדמה, ****ארזילא״ה בלעז. **בריי** = בריאים. **עינני** — עיניהם גדולות.

NOTES

חָזִיז **Young blades of grain.** The *Geonim* explain that this term refers to wheat and barley shoots that are still green and not yet fully ripe.

אֲפִילוּ קָרָא **Even a gourd.** Most of the items mentioned here are not unhealthy foods in themselves. Indeed, some of them are considered to be delicacies. But they are said to be bad for a woman's milk, causing her supply to be diminished or her milk to become turbid.

רְמָא דַּחֲמָרָא **The droppings of an ass.** Our commentary follows *Rabbi Ya'akov Emden,* who explains this Aramaic term as referring to ass-droppings. *Rivan* has the reading דְּמָא דַּחֲמָרָא, which means "the blood of an ass."

דְּאָכְלָה תַּחְלֵי **She who eats cress.** The *Geonim* explain that it is during the first third of a woman's pregnancy that her diet determines the physical characteristics of her unborn child.

LANGUAGE

כַּמְכָּא Sour milk sauce. This word is apparently derived from the Middle Persian *kamak* and means a condiment used to stimulate the appetite. It apparently means the same as כותח referred to above.

הַרְסְנָא Fish-hash. From the Arabic حراس, meaning "small fish." In Rabbinic literature, this word usually refers to small fish fried in flour.

מוֹנִינֵי Fish brine. *Arukh* explains this as "brine," fish brine in particular (and by extension, "locust brine"). The word is apparently a contraction of the two words מֵי נוּנֵי, meaning "fish brine."

גַּרְגּוּשְׁתָּא Clay. This word refers to a type of high-quality clay used for making seals (on letters and packages).

LANGUAGE (RASHI)

*הומלו״ן From the Old French *homlon*, meaning "hops."

**קורציי״ה (correct reading: קודוינ״ץ) From the Old French *codoinz*, meaning "quince."

***פישיאו״ן From the Old French *paission*, meaning "illness," or "suffering," and used as a euphemism for epilepsy.

****ארזילא״ה From the Old French *arzile*, meaning "clay."

BACKGROUND

דְּאָכְלָה...הָווּ לָהּ בְּנֵי... She who eats... will have ...children. Modern science confirms the Gemara's assumption that the food eaten by a pregnant woman affects the fetus, although it is not clear precisely what effects different types of food have. It is known, however, that certain substances, such as drugs and alcohol, affect the fetus's general physical development, as well as its color and facial appearance. The effects of the foodstuffs mentioned in this passage of the Gemara have not been determined.

דְּאָכְלָה גַּרְגּוּשְׁתָּא She who eats clay. Pregnant women occasionally have cravings for strange foods, and they have sometimes been known to eat earth. In addition, certain types of earth (such as the גַּרְגּוּשְׁתָּא mentioned here) were believed to have medicinal value, and were taken to relieve heartburn.

TRANSLATION AND COMMENTARY

pregnancy **will have graceful children.** [1]A woman **who eats celery** while pregnant **will have handsome children.** [2]A woman **who eats coriander** during her pregnancy **will have fat children.** [3]A woman **who eats etrog** while pregnant **will have fragrant children.** [4]It was related **about the daughter of Shavor, the king** of Persia, that **her mother ate etrog while** she was **pregnant with her,** [5]**and** as a result her daughter had such a fragrant smell that **she would be brought in before her father at the head of the perfumes.**

אָמַר רַב הוּנָא [6]The Gemara now returns to its discussion of the Halakhic questions that arise in connection with a nursing woman. **Rav Huna said: Rav Huna bar Ḥinnana** once **tested us** with the following question: [7]**If** a woman **says** that she wants **to nurse** her child, **and** her husband **says** that he does **not** want her **to nurse** but wishes her to hand the infant over to a wet nurse, [8]**we listen to her** and allow her to nurse the baby herself. Why is this so? [9]If the woman is not allowed to nurse, **she will suffer** either physically or emotionally, and the husband has no right to cause her such suffering. [10]But **what is the law if** a man **says** that he wants his wife **to nurse** her child herself, **and** the woman **says** that she does **not** want **to nurse** but wishes to hand the baby over to a wet nurse? The scope of the question can be narrowed: [11]**Wherever it is not her** family's **custom** to nurse their babies, **we listen to** the woman and allow her to hand over her child to a wet nurse. [12]But **what is the law if it is her** family's **custom** for the women to nurse, **but it is not his** family's **custom** for the women to do so? [13]**Do we follow** the custom of **the husband's** family, [14]**or do we follow** the custom of **the wife's** family?

הָווּ לָהּ בְּנֵי חִינָּנֵי. [1]דְּאָכְלָה
כַּרְפָּסָא הָווּ לָהּ בְּנֵי זִיוְתָנֵי.
[2]דְּאָכְלָה כּוּסְבַּרְתָּא הָווּ לָהּ בְּנֵי
בִּישְׂרָנֵי. [3]דְּאָכְלָה אֶתְרוֹגָא הָווּ
לָהּ בְּנֵי רֵיחָנֵי. [4]בְּרַתֵּיהּ דְּשָׁבוֹר
מַלְכָּא, אָכְלָה בָּהּ אִמָּהּ
אֶתְרוֹגָא, [5]וְהָווּ מַסְּקֵי לָהּ
לְקַמֵּיהּ אֲבוּהּ בְּרֵישׁ רֵיחָנֵי.
[6]אֲמַר רַב הוּנָא: בָּדַק לָן רַב
הוּנָא בַּר חִינָּנָא: [7]הִיא אוֹמֶרֶת
לְהָנִיק, וְהוּא אוֹמֵר שֶׁלֹּא
לְהָנִיק, [8]שׁוֹמְעִין לָהּ; [9]צַעֲרָא
דִּידָהּ הוּא. [10]הוּא אוֹמֵר לְהָנִיק,
וְהִיא אוֹמֶרֶת שֶׁלֹּא לְהָנִיק,
מַהוּ? [11]כָּל הֵיכָא דְּלָאו
אוֹרְחָהּ, שׁוֹמְעִין לָהּ. [12]הִיא
אוֹרְחָהּ וְהוּא לָאו אוֹרְחֵיהּ,
מַאי? [13]בָּתַר דִּידֵיהּ אָזְלִינַן,
[14]אוֹ בָּתַר דִּידָהּ אָזְלִינַן?

LITERAL TRANSLATION

will have graceful children. [1]She who eats celery will have handsome children. [2]She who eats coriander will have fleshy children. [3]She who eats etrog will have fragrant children. [4][Regarding] the daughter of King Shavor, her mother ate etrog [while pregnant] with her, [5]and they would bring her in before her father at the head of the perfumes.

[6]Rav Huna said: Rav Huna bar Ḥinnana tested us: [7][If] she says to nurse, and he says not to nurse, [8]we listen to her; [9]it is her suffering. [10][If] he says to nurse, and she says not to nurse, what [is the law]? [11]Wherever it is not her custom, we listen to her. [12]Where it is her custom but it is not his custom, what [is the law]? [13]Do we go after his, [14]or do we go after hers?

RASHI

חנני = בעלי חן. **כרפסא** = *אפי״א. **כוסברתא** = **אליינדר״א בלעז. **צערא דידה הוא** – החלב רב בדדיה, ומצערה. **דלאו אורחה** – אין דרך משפחתה להניק.

REALIA

כַּרְפָּסָא Celery. The garden vegetable (*apium graveolens*) used in salads and as a condiment.

כּוּסְבַּרְתָּא Coriander. Coriander (כּוּסְבָּר in Rabbinic Hebrew, גַּד in Biblical Hebrew), which is used as a spice, has a distinctive flavor and aroma.

LANGUAGE (RASHI)

אפי״א* From the Old French *apie*, meaning "celery."

אליינדר״א** From the Old French *aliendre*, meaning "coriander."

BACKGROUND

שָׁבוֹר מַלְכָּא King Shavor. The "King Shavor" mentioned here was probably Shapur I (reigned 241–272 C.E.), the second ruler of the Sassanid dynasty. He extended the boundaries of the Persian Empire as far as Syria. He fought against the Romans and won large tracts of Roman territory (he even managed to take the Roman Emperor Valerian captive). However, not all of his battles against the Romans were successful.

Unlike most other members of the Sassanid dynasty, Shapur I was tolerant toward the members of other religions. The Talmud frequently mentions his close ties with the Jews (particularly with the Amora Shmuel), and his respect for Jewish tradition.

TERMINOLOGY

בָּדַק לָן Tested us. An introduction to a statement in which students relate how their teacher asked them a question in order to test their knowledge.

SAGES

רַב הוּנָא בַּר חִינָּנָא Rav Huna bar Ḥinnana. A Babylonian Amora of the third and fourth generations, Rav Huna bar Ḥinnana was a disciple of Rav Ḥisda and also studied under Rav Naḥman, Rav Sheshet, and Rav Yosef. Rava and Rav Safra were his colleagues. He lived in the city of Sikhra, near Meḥoza. He had a son who was a Sage in the following generation. The Rav Huna mentioned here as having "tested" Rav Huna bar Ḥinnana was not the great Amora, Rav Huna,

NOTES

בָּדַק לָן Tested us. This term is usually used to introduce a statement in which students relate how their teacher asked them a question in order to test their knowledge. Sometimes it expresses modesty on the part of the Sage relating the story. Rather than saying that his teacher could not resolve a certain difficulty on his own, he says that his teacher asked him the question in order to test him, implying that the teacher knew the answer.

צַעֲרָא דִּידָהּ הוּא It is her suffering. *Rashi* explains that if the woman is not allowed to nurse, she will suffer physical pain caused by the fullness of her breasts. *Rambam* explains that she will suffer emotional pain caused by her being separated from her infant. *Ri Migash* understands the matter differently: The Gemara argues that if a woman wishes to nurse, and her husband does not want her to do so, we allow her to nurse the baby because, if the woman is willing to suffer the difficulties of nursing, it is her business, and her husband should have no say in the matter. These different explanations can have practical legal ramifications.

הִיא אוֹרְחָהּ Where it is her custom. *Rosh* notes that the same principle applies with respect to the rest of a

HALAKHAH

הִיא אוֹמֶרֶת לְהָנִיק If she says to nurse. "If a woman wishes to nurse her infant, but her husband does not want her to do so, we listen to the woman and allow her to nurse the baby." (*Rambam, Sefer Nashim, Hilkhot Ishut* 21:13; *Shulḥan Arukh, Even HaEzer* 82:2.)

הוּא אוֹמֵר לְהָנִיק If he says to nurse. "If a woman from a poor family — the female members of which are accustomed to nurse their own infants — is married to a man of means, and she does not wish to nurse her infant, her husband must hire a wet nurse," following the Gemara's conclusion. (*Rambam, Sefer Nashim, Hilkhot Ishut* 21:14; *Shulḥan Arukh, Even HaEzer* 80:6,10; 82:3.)

but was probably Rav Huna the son of Rav Yehoshua, who was younger than Rav Huna bar Ḥinnana.

LANGUAGE

בַּחֲרִיקַאי In my place. *Arukh* and others read בהריקאי. The word בַּחֲרִיקַאי is apparently derived from the Middle Persian *bahrak* ("on behalf of, for the sake of"), although this meaning is inappropriate here, as the context calls for "in place of."

TRANSLATION AND COMMENTARY

Rav Huna continues: [1] **And we answered** Rav Huna bar Ḥinnana **on the basis of the following** accepted general principle: A woman **rises with** her husband and is entitled to a standard of living in accordance with her husband's means and social standing, **but she does not go down with him** and live according to a standard lower than that to which she was accustomed in her father's home. Thus, in our case, if it is not the custom of the women in the husband's family to nurse their own babies, the husband cannot force his wife to nurse her infant but must allow her to hand over her baby to a wet nurse in accordance with his family's custom.

אֲמַר רַב הוּנָא [2] **Rav Huna said: What is the Biblical source** that teaches us this principle? It is derived from the following verse (Genesis 20:3): [3] **"For she is a man's wife** [בְּעֻלַת בָּעַל — *be'ulat ba'al*]," [4] which teaches us that a woman rises **in** accordance with **the elevated status** [בַּעֲלִיָּיתוֹ — *ba'aliyyato*] of her husband, if her husband's standard of living is higher than hers, [5] **but** she does **not** go down to live in accordance **with** her husband's **lower status,** if hers was higher than his.

רַבִּי אֶלְעָזָר אֲמַר [6] **Rabbi Elazar said:** This principle **is derived from the following** verse (Genesis 3:20): [7] **"Because she was the mother of all living."** [8] A woman **is given** to a man in marriage **so that she may enjoy** a better **life,** [9] **but she is not given** to him as his wife **so that she will suffer.**

הִכְנִיסָה [10] The Gemara now proceeds to analyze the next clause of our Mishnah, which stated: **"If** a married woman **brought a maidservant** with her from her father's home, she is not required to grind her husband's grain into flour, or to bake his bread, or to launder his clothing." Now, since the Mishnah specifies the domestic responsibilities from which the wife is relieved, [11] it follows that **she must** still **do the rest** of the tasks incumbent upon a married woman. [12] The Gemara objects: **But let** the woman **say to** her husband: [13] "I should be relieved of all of my responsibilities, for **I have brought you** another **woman** to work **in my place."**

מִשּׁוּם [14] The Gemara answers: The wife is still required to perform certain tasks, **because** her husband **can say to her: "That maidservant** you have brought into the marriage **will serve me and herself.** [15] But if she is busy taking care of my needs and her own needs, **who will serve you?** Thus you, too, must do your share of the household tasks."

LITERAL TRANSLATION

[1] And we solved [it] for him from this: She rises with him but does not go down with him.

[2] Rav Huna said: What is its verse? [3] "For she is a man's wife [בְּעֻלַת בָּעַל — *be'ulat ba'al*]." [4] [She takes part] in the ascent [בַּעֲלִיָּיתוֹ — *ba'aliyyato*] of a husband, [5] but not in the descent of a husband.

[6] Rabbi Elazar said: [We derive it] from here: [7] "Because she was the mother of all living." [8] She was given for life, [9] but she was not given for suffering.

[10] "If she brought him one maidservant, etc." [11] But the rest she does. [12] But let her say to him: [13] "I have brought you a woman in my place"!

[14] Because he can say to her: "This [woman] works for me and for herself. [15] Who will work for you?"

[1] וּפְשִׁיטְנָא לֵיהּ מֵהָא: עוֹלָה עִמּוֹ וְאֵינָהּ יוֹרֶדֶת עִמּוֹ.

[2] אֲמַר רַב הוּנָא: מַאי קְרָאָה? [3] "וְהִיא בְּעֻלַת בָּעַל". [4] בַּעֲלִיָּיתוֹ שֶׁל בַּעַל, [5] וְלֹא בִּירִידָתוֹ שֶׁל בַּעַל.

[6] רַבִּי אֶלְעָזָר אֲמַר: מֵהָכָא: [7] "כִּי הִיא הָיְתָה אֵם כָּל חָי". [8] לְחַיִּים נִיתְּנָה, [9] וְלֹא לְצַעַר נִיתְּנָה.

[10] "הִכְנִיסָה לוֹ שִׁפְחָה, וכו׳". [11] הָא שְׁאָרָא עָבְדָא. [12] וְתֵימָא לֵיהּ: [13] "עַיְילִית לָךְ אִיתְּתָא בַּחֲרִיקַאי"!

[14] מִשּׁוּם דְּאָמַר לָהּ: "הָא טָרְחָא לְדִידִי וּלְדִידָהּ. [15] קַמֵּי דִּידָךְ מַאן טָרַח?"

RASHI

בחריקאי = במקומי. ולי נראה לשון סידקי — קרן, כלומר לשון פקידת מקום, בפקד מקומי ובפגמי.

NOTES

woman's domestic responsibilities — that a married woman cannot be compelled to do a particular task unless it was the custom of both her family and her husband's family that the wife performs that task for her husband. According to *Rosh,* the Gemara chose to single out nursing because it often happens that the wife wishes to nurse her infant, but her husband does not want her to do so.

וְתֵימָא לֵיהּ: "עַיְילִית לָךְ אִיתְּתָא" But let her say to him: "I have brought you a woman." The Jerusalem Talmud understands from the Mishnah that a woman who brings maidservants into her marriage is relieved of the domestic responsibilities listed in the Mishnah, but there are other things that she herself must do for her husband. The Jerusalem Talmud asks why the wife is not relieved of all her household responsibilities and answers that a maidservant does not have the physical strength to take over all the wife's tasks. Alternatively, the maidservant is given the baser work (the tasks listed in the Mishnah), but there are other tasks that should be done by the wife herself, and not assigned to a maidservant.

TRANSLATION AND COMMENTARY

שְׁתַּיִם [1] We learned in the next clause of our Mishnah: "If a married woman brought **two** maidservants into the marriage, she is relieved of additional responsibilities. **She is not required to cook** her husband's meals, **nor is she required to nurse** her infant child." [2] **But** the Mishnah implies that **she is** still **required to carry out the rest** of the tasks incumbent upon a married woman. [3] The Gemara objdects: **But let** the woman **say to** her husband: "I should be relieved of all my household responsibilities, for **I have brought you** two maidservants — one **other woman who will serve me and herself,** [4] **and one** woman **who will serve you and herself.** Thus there is nothing left that I have to do."

מִשּׁוּם [5] The Gemara answers: The woman is still required to perform certain tasks, **because** her husband **can say to her:** [6] **"Who will serve the guests and passing visitors** who frequent our house? Thus you, too, must take responsibility for some of the household tasks."

שָׁלֹשׁ [7] The Mishnah continues: "If a woman brought **three** maidservants into the marriage, **she is not** even **required to arrange** the mattress and pillows on her husband's **bed**, nor is she required to spin any wool." [8] **But the rest** of her domestic responsibilities — for example, the light housework that must be done in every house — **she must** still **perform.** [9] The Gemara objects: **But let** the woman **say to** her husband: "I should be relieved of all my responsibilities, for **I have brought you** three maidservants, one to serve me, one to serve you, and **another** to serve **the guests and passing visitors** to our house."

מִשּׁוּם [10] The Gemara answers: The woman is still required to perform certain tasks, **because** her husband **can say to her: "When there are many** permanent **members of the household,** [11] **there are** also **many guests and passing visitors.** Thus you, too, must help with some of the domestic tasks."

אִי הָכִי [12] The Gemara asks: **If so,** then **even** a woman who brings **four** maidservants into the marriage should **also** be required to perform some of the household tasks. Why does the Mishnah state that if a woman brings four maidservants into the marriage, she may sit in a chair as a lady of leisure?

אַרְבַּע [13] The Gemara answers: **If** the woman brought in **four** maidservants, she is relieved of all her household responsibilities. **Since there are** so **many** domestic helpers, **they will help each other** in all the housework, and there is no need for the wife to contribute her efforts.

[1] "שְׁתַּיִם — אֵינָהּ מְבַשֶּׁלֶת, וְאֵינָהּ מֵנִיקָה, וכו'". [2] הָא שְׁאָרָא עָבְדָא. [3] וְתֵימָא לֵיהּ: "עַיְילִית לָךְ אִיתְּתָא אַחֲרִיתִי דְּטָרְחָה לְדִידִי וּלְדִידָהּ, [4] וַחֲדָא לְדִידָךְ וּלְדִידָהּ"!
[5] מִשּׁוּם דְּאָמַר לָהּ: [6] "קַמֵּי אוֹרְחֵי וּפָרְחֵי מַאן טָרַח?"
[7] "שָׁלֹשׁ — אֵינָהּ מַצַּעַת הַמִּטָּה". [8] הָא שְׁאָרָא עָבְדָא. [9] וְתֵימָא לֵיהּ: "עַיְילִית לָךְ אַחֲרִיתֵי לְאוֹרְחֵי וּפָרְחֵי"!
[10] מִשּׁוּם דְּאָמַר לָהּ: "נְפִישׁ בְּנֵי בֵיתָא, [11] נְפִישׁ אוֹרְחֵי וּפָרְחֵי".
[12] אִי הָכִי, אֲפִילּוּ אַרְבַּע נַמִי!
[13] אַרְבַּע, כֵּיוָן דִּנְפִישֵׁי לְהוּ, מְסַיְּיעָן אַהֲדָדֵי.

LITERAL TRANSLATION

[1] "Two — she does not cook, and she does not nurse, etc." [2] But the rest she does. [3] But let her say to him: "I have brought you another woman who works for me and for herself, [4] and one [who works] for you and for herself"!
[5] Because he can say to her: [6] "Who will work for guests and passing visitors?"
[7] "Three — she does not make his bed." [8] But the rest she does. [9] But let her say to him: "I have brought you another [woman] for guests and passing visitors"!
[10] Because he can say to her: "[When there are] more members of the household, [11] there are more guests and passing visitors."
[12] If so, even four also!
[13] [When there are] four, since they are numerous, they help each other.

RASHI

אורחי — אורחים המשתהים שבת או חדש. **פרחי** — עוברים לדרכם. לפי שבמקום שיש בני בית רבים נוהגים להתארח עוברי דרך. **הא שארא** — כגון דברים קטנים.

NOTES

קַמֵּי אוֹרְחֵי וּפָרְחֵי **For guests and passing visitors.** Some authorities infer from here that a married woman is required to serve not only her husband but also those members of her husband's household who are financially dependent on him. Thus the Baraita cited below (61b), which states that a man cannot compel his wife to serve his father or his son, must be referring to members of the husband's family who are not dependent on him. Others maintain that our Gemara speaks only of guests and passing visitors, whose needs must be attended to by the woman of the house. But a woman is not required to serve the members of her husband's family who are living permanently in her house, even if they are financially dependent on him (*Ritva*).

SAGES

רַב יִצְחָק בַּר חֲנַנְיָא Rav Yitzḥak bar Ḥananya (bar Ḥanina, bar Ḥinnana). A Babylonian Amora of the third generation, Rav Yitzḥak bar Ḥananya was apparently a close disciple of Rav Huna, for in every place where he is mentioned in the Talmud he transmits the teachings of Rav Huna.

TRANSLATION AND COMMENTARY

אָמַר רַב חָנָא [1] The Gemara now clarifies what the Mishnah meant when it spoke of the maidservants whom the wife brought into the marriage. **Rav Ḥana, and some say** that **it was Rabbi Shmuel bar Naḥmani, said:** [2] The Mishnah **does not speak** only of a case in which the woman **actually brought** the **maidservants** with her from her father's house. [3] **Rather, whenever she is capable of bringing** in maidservants — for example, if she has a dowry that will suffice for the purchase of one or more maidservants — she is relieved of some or all of her domestic responsibilities, [4] **even if she has not** actually **brought** any maidservants into the marriage.

תָּנָא [5] **A Sage taught** the following Baraita: "A married woman is relieved of some or all of her domestic responsibilities, **whether she** actually **brought** maidservants with her into the marriage, [6] **or she economized with** the **money** that her husband gave her to spend on the household, thereby saving him enough money to buy one or more maidservants to help her with her domestic tasks."

אַרְבַּע [7] We learned in the next clause of the Mishnah: "If a woman brought **four** maidservants into her marriage, **she may sit in a chair,** for she is relieved of all her domestic responsibilities." [8] **Rav Yitzḥak bar Ḥananya said in the name of Rav Huna: Even though** the Sages **said** that a woman with four maidservants **may sit in a chair** and do nothing, [9] **she must nevertheless pour** the wine into her husband's **cup,**

[1] אָמַר רַב חָנָא, וְאִיתֵּימָא רַבִּי שְׁמוּאֵל בַּר נַחְמָנִי: [2] לֹא הִכְנִיסָה לוֹ מַמָּשׁ. [3] אֶלָּא, כֵּיוָן שֶׁרְאוּיָה לְהַכְנִיס, [4] אַף עַל פִּי שֶׁלֹּא הִכְנִיסָה.

[5] תָּנָא: "אֶחָד שֶׁהִכְנִיסָה לוֹ, [6] וְאֶחָד שֶׁצִּמְצְמָה לוֹ מִשֶּׁלָּהּ". [7] "אַרְבַּע — יוֹשֶׁבֶת בְּקַתֶּדְרָא". [8] אָמַר רַב יִצְחָק בַּר חֲנַנְיָא אָמַר רַב הוּנָא: אַף עַל פִּי שֶׁאָמְרוּ יוֹשֶׁבֶת בְּקַתֶּדְרָא, [9] אֲבָל מוֹזֶגֶת

LITERAL TRANSLATION

[1] Rav Ḥana said, and some say [it was] Rabbi Shmuel bar Naḥmani: [2] [It does] not [mean that] she actually brought him [maidservants]. [3] Rather, since she is able to bring [them], [4] even if she has not brought [them].

[5] [A Sage] taught: "Whether she brought [them] for him, [6] or she economized for him from her own [income]."

[7] "Four — she sits in a chair." [8] Rav Yitzḥak bar Ḥananya said in the name of Rav Huna: Even though they said she sits in a chair, [9] nevertheless she pours

RASHI

שראויה להכניס — שהכניסה נדוניא רבה, ויש כדאי למציאה נדוניא זו לקנות ממקלתה שפחות להכניס ולשמשה.

NOTES

כֵּיוָן שֶׁרְאוּיָה לְהַכְנִיס Since she is able to bring them. This expression used by Rav Ḥana has been interpreted in various ways. Our commentary follows *Rashi*, who takes it to mean that the Mishnah is referring not only to a case where the woman actually brought maidservants with her into the marriage, but also to a case where she is capable of bringing in maidservants because she has a large dowry. *Rabbenu Tam* explains that the Baraita extends the Mishnah's ruling to a case where the woman does not spend all the money that her husband is obligated to give her, saving him enough to pay for one or more maidservants. *Rif* and others have a different reading in the Baraita: שֶׁמָּצְאָה לוֹ מִשֶּׁלוֹ, meaning "where she found of his." According to this reading, the Mishnah's ruling applies not only to a case where the woman brings maidservants with her into the marriage, but also to a case where the husband is a wealthy man who has maidservants or can afford to buy them.

Ramban and his disciples understand Rav Ḥana's statement differently: A wife is relieved of her domestic responsibilities not only if she actually brought maidservants into the marriage, but also if she comes from a family that is accustomed to having maidservants. This explanation is supported by the Jerusalem Talmud, which provides proof for this ruling from the Baraita that states that a wife rises with her husband but does not go down with him.

אֲבָל מוֹזֶגֶת לוֹ כּוֹס Nevertheless she pours the cup for him. The Jerusalem Talmud poses the following question: Is a wife obligated to perform these tasks for her husband to endear herself to him, or must she do these intimate things because it would be immodest to assign them to a maidservant? One practical difference would be whether the wife must perform these tasks herself if she brought male servants into the marriage. The Jerusalem Talmud concludes that a married woman is personally obligated to

HALAKHAH

כֵּיוָן שֶׁרְאוּיָה לְהַכְנִיס Since she is able to bring them. "A married woman is relieved of some or all of her domestic responsibilities, if she brings one or more maidservants into the marriage, or if she has a dowry that will suffice for the purchase of such maidservants, or if her husband has maidservants or enough money to buy maidservants (following the reading of *Rif* and *Rosh*)." (*Rambam, Sefer Nashim, Hilkhot Ishut* 21:6; *Shulḥan Arukh, Even HaEzer* 80:8.)

אֲבָל מוֹזֶגֶת לוֹ כּוֹס Nevertheless she pours the cup for him. "Every woman is obligated to wash her husband's face, his hands, and his feet, to pour his cup, and to make his bed. These tasks must be performed by the wife herself, even if she has brought many maidservants into the marriage," following Rav Huna. (*Rambam, Sefer Nashim, Hilkhot Ishut* 21:3; *Shulḥan Arukh, Even HaEzer* 80:4-5.)

TRANSLATION AND COMMENTARY

arrange the sheets on **his bed, and wash his face, his hands, and his feet.** These three actions — pouring, arranging, and washing — are not regarded as domestic tasks, but as acts of intimacy that a wife personally performs for her husband. No matter how many maidservants a woman brings into her marriage, she may not assign these tasks to them.

אָמַר רַב יִצְחָק בַּר חֲנַנְיָא [1]The Gemara now cites a related ruling **stated** by **Rav Yitzḥak bar Ḥananya in the name of Rav Huna:** [2]**A menstruating woman may perform for her husband all** the **tasks that a woman** ordinarily **performs for her husband,** and there is no concern that the performance of her regular household duties will lead to sexual relations, which are forbidden while she is in a state of ritual impurity during and after menstruation. [3]There are, however, three **exceptions** to this general ruling: A menstruating woman may not **pour** wine into her husband's **cup,** nor may she **arrange** the sheets on **his bed,** nor may she **wash his face, his hands, or his feet,** for these three tasks — pouring, arranging, and washing — are acts of intimacy specifically performed by the wife for her husband. A woman may not perform these personal tasks while she is forbidden to her husband, for they may arouse desire and lead to forbidden sexual relations.

לוֹ כּוֹס, וּמַצַּעַת לוֹ אֶת הַמִּטָּה, וּמַרְחֶצֶת לוֹ פָּנָיו, יָדָיו, וְרַגְלָיו. [1]אָמַר רַב יִצְחָק בַּר חֲנַנְיָא אָמַר רַב הוּנָא: [2]כָּל מְלָאכוֹת שֶׁהָאִשָּׁה עוֹשָׂה לְבַעְלָהּ, נִדָּה עוֹשָׂה לְבַעְלָהּ, [3]חוּץ מִמְּזִיגַת הַכּוֹס, וְהַצָּעַת הַמִּטָּה, וְהַרְחָצַת פָּנָיו, יָדָיו, וְרַגְלָיו.

LITERAL TRANSLATION

the cup for him, and makes his bed, and washes his face, his hands, and his feet for him.

[1]Rav Yitzḥak bar Ḥananya said in the name of Rav Huna: [2]All tasks that a wife performs for her husband, a menstruating woman may perform for her husband, [3]except for the pouring of the cup, and the making of the bed, and the washing of his face, his hands, and his feet.

RASHI

אבל מוזגת לו כוס ומצעת לו מטה — לפרוס סדין ולבדין, דבר שאינו טורח. ומשום דמילי דחיבה נינהו, כדי שתתחבב עליו. ולא דמי למצעת דמתניתין דהוי דבר של טורח. ובכפייה הני לא כפי לה, אלא חכמים השיאוה עצה טובה להנהיג זאת בישראל. **חוץ ממזיגת כוס** — כל שהוא דברים של קירוב וחיבה, ומביאין לידי הרגל דבר.

NOTES

perform those intimate tasks that are intended to endear her to her husband.

Rashi notes, however, that a woman cannot be compelled to perform them. The Rabbis merely recommended that a woman perform these tasks for her husband in order to endear herself to him. The Jerusalem Talmud implies otherwise, that a woman can indeed be compelled to perform these intimate tasks for her husband.

וּמַצַּעַת לוֹ אֶת הַמִּטָּה And makes his bed. *Rivan* omits the words, "and makes his bed," apparently because we are dealing here with a woman who is exempt from the domestic duties ordinarily imposed upon a married woman, including the obligation to make her husband's bed. *Rashi* and *Tosafot* distinguish between the obligation mentioned in the Mishnah and the obligation mentioned here: The Mishnah requires a married woman to arrange the mattress and the pillows on her husband's bed, and exempts her from this task if she has brought three or more maidservants into the marriage. Here the Gemara requires a woman to arrange the sheets on her husband's bed, viewing the task as an act of intimacy that is imposed on a woman no matter how many maidservants she brings into the marriage. *Ra'ah* suggests that the Mishnah should read: וּמַצַּעַת אֶת הַמִּטָּה, "and she makes the bed," whereas here the Gemara should read: וּמַצַּעַת לוֹ אֶת הַמִּטָּה, "and she makes the bed for him." The Mishnah requires a wife to make all the beds in the house, and only exempts her from this task if she has brought a certain number of maidservants into the marriage. But here the Gemara speaks of a wife's duty to make her husband's bed as an act of intimacy, no matter how many maidservants she has brought into the marriage.

נִדָּה עוֹשָׂה לְבַעְלָהּ A menstruating woman may perform for her husband. In Eretz Israel and other places that adopted its customs a menstruating woman customarily refrained from all domestic activities when she was forbidden to her husband, to the point that permission was only reluctantly given for a menstruating woman to nurse her child. A number of factors contributed to the development of this custom: First, it evolved as an extension of the safeguards that had once been taken in order to prevent a menstruating woman from imparting ritual impurity. Second, it was developed in order to set up safeguards to prevent a menstruating woman from coming into forbidden physical contact with her husband. Karaite influences may also have left their mark on the practices accepted by normative Judaism. The Rishonim disagreed as to how to relate to this restrictive custom (see *Tosafot, Rid,*

HALAKHAH

נִדָּה עוֹשָׂה לְבַעְלָהּ A menstruating woman may perform for her husband. "A menstruating woman may perform for her husband all the tasks that a wife ordinarily performs for her husband, except for pouring his cup, making his bed, and washing his face, hands, and feet (or pouring him water for washing, even if she is careful not to touch him)." (*Rambam, Sefer Nashim, Hilkhot Ishut* 21:8; *Sefer Kedushah, Hilkhot Issurei Bi'ah* 11:19; *Shulḥan Arukh, Yoreh De'ah* 195:10-12.)

TRANSLATION AND COMMENTARY

וְהַצָּעַת הַמִּטָּה [1] The Gemara qualifies this last ruling: As for the ruling that a menstruating woman may not **arrange** the sheets on her husband's **bed, Rava said:** [2] The Rabbis **said** that **this is forbidden only** if it is done **in the presence** of the husband. [3] **But** if the wife makes his bed **in his absence, there is no objection to it,** for there is no concern that it will lead to forbidden sexual relations.

וּמְזִיגַת הַכּוֹס [4] The Gemara continues: **And** as for the ruling that a menstruating woman may not **pour** wine into her husband's **cup,** if she pours the wine an unusual manner, the prohibition does not apply, because the unusual manner of serving the wine will act as a reminder that she is forbidden to him. [5] Thus, while **Shmuel's wife** was in a state of ritual impurity, she **would change** the way she gave her husband wine **by pouring it with her left hand** instead of her right hand. [6] **Abaye's wife would place** the wine **on the mouth of a barrel,** and he would then take it into his hands by himself. [7] **Rava's wife would place** the poured wine **on his pillow,** [8] and **Rav Pappa's wife would place it on a stool.**

אָמַר רַב יִצְחָק בַּר חֲנַנְיָא [9] Since the Gemara has already cited two rulings issued by Rav Yitzḥak bar Ḥananya in the name of Rav Huna, it continues with another ruling by Rav Yitzḥak bar Ḥananya in the name of Rav Huna on a different issue. **Rav Yitzḥak bar Ḥananya said in the name of Rav Huna:** [10] **All foods may be kept from the waiter** until he has finished serving the meal and the diners have risen to leave, **except for meat and wine,** for the mere smell of meat or wine stimulates the appetite, and the

[1] וְהַצָּעַת הַמִּטָּה, אֲמַר רָבָא: [2] לָא אֲמָרַן אֶלָּא בְּפָנָיו, [3] אֲבָל שֶׁלֹּא בְּפָנָיו לֵית לָן בָּהּ. [4] וּמְזִיגַת הַכּוֹס, [5] שְׁמוּאֵל מְחַלְּפָא לֵיהּ דְּבֵיתְהוּ בִּידָא דִּשְׂמָאלָא. [6] אַבַּיֵי מַנְחָא לֵיהּ אַפּוּמָּא דְּכוּבָא. [7] רָבָא אַבֵּי סַדְיָא. [8] רַב פַּפָּא אַשַּׁרְשִׁיפָא. [9] אָמַר רַב יִצְחָק בַּר חֲנַנְיָא אָמַר רַב הוּנָא: [10] הַכֹּל מַשְׁהִין בִּפְנֵי הַשַּׁמָּשׁ, חוּץ מִבָּשָׂר וְיַיִן.

LITERAL TRANSLATION

[1] And [as for] making the bed, Rava said: [2] We only said [it is forbidden] in his presence, [3] but not in his presence we have no [objection] to it.

[4] And [as for] pouring the cup, [5] Shmuel's wife would make a change [and poured] for him with her left hand. [6] [The wife of] Abaye would place it on the mouth of the barrel. [7] [The wife of] Rava [would place it] on his pillow. [8] [The wife of] Rav Pappa [would place it] on a stool.

[9] Rav Yitzḥak bar Ḥananya said in the name of Rav Huna: [10] We delay all [foods] before the waiter, except for meat and wine.

RASHI

מיחלפא ליה – בימי ליבונה. **אבי סדיא** – מרגלותיו. **אשרשיפא** = ספסל. **הכל משהין לפני שמש** – המשמש בסעודה, ואוכלין בפניו, ושוהין מלהאכילו עד שיקומו הקרואים.

NOTES

Rambam's Responsa [Blau ed., nos. 114, 320]). It is generally agreed that it cannot be reconciled with our Gemara, which states explicitly that a menstruating woman may perform all those tasks that a woman ordinarily performs for her husband, with the exception of a few intimate ones.

מְחַלְּפָא **Would make a change.** *Rabbenu Ḥananel* explains that Shmuel's wife would pour her husband's wine in the ordinary manner with her right hand, but would present it to him in an unusual way with her left hand.

Rashi and *Rabbenu Ḥananel* explain that the wife can perform these tasks only after she has ceased menstruating but is not yet ritually pure, but not while she is actually menstruating. The Rishonim discuss this issue at length, the consensus being that since the stringency has been accepted that a menstruating woman must wait seven days after all bleeding has stopped before she may immerse herself in a *mikveh*, no distinction may be made between the days that she is actually menstruating and the days after she has ceased menstruating.

HALAKHAH

הַצָּעַת הַמִּטָּה **Making the bed.** "A menstruating woman may not make her husband's bed in his presence. This prohibition applies only to the spreading of his sheet, a task that is regarded as an act of intimacy. But she may arrange his mattress and pillows, for these tasks are chores rather than acts of intimacy. If her husband is not present, she may spread his sheet as well, even if he will know that it is she who made his bed." (*Rambam, Sefer Kedushah, Hilkhot Issurei Bi'ah* 11:19; *Shulḥan Arukh, Yoreh De'ah* 195:11.)

מְזִיגַת הַכּוֹס **Pouring the cup.** "A menstruating woman is forbidden to pour her husband's cup and to put it down before him in her usual manner. Instead, she must serve him his wine in a distinctively different way; for example, she must set the cup down before him with her left hand, or she must set it down on his pillow or mattress," as is explained in the Gemara. (*Rambam, Sefer Nashim, Hilkhot Nashim* 21:8; *Shulḥan Arukh, Yoreh De'ah* 195:10.)

הַכֹּל מַשְׁהִין בִּפְנֵי הַשַּׁמָּשׁ **We delay all foods before the waiter.** "If a waiter is serving someone a particularly aromatic food which whets the appetite, the diner must give the waiter a portion of the food immediately upon his being served. If he wishes to act piously, the diner should give the waiter a portion of each and every dish that is being served." (*Rambam, Sefer Ahavah, Hilkhot Berakhot* 7:7; *Sefer Kinyan, Hilkhot Avadim* 9:8; *Shulḥan Arukh, Oraḥ Ḥayyim* 169:1; *Yoreh De'ah* 267:17.)

TRANSLATION AND COMMENTARY

waiter will be distressed if he cannot eat any until the meal is over. [1] On this ruling **Rav Ḥisda said:** Rav Yitzḥak bar Ḥananya was referring specifically to **fat meat and** to **old wine**, because they strongly stimulate the appetite. [2] **Rava said**: The diners are barred from keeping **fat meat** from the waiter **throughout the year,** but they are forbidden to keep [3] **old wine** from him only **during the summer,** for heat intensifies the wine's bouquet and the waiter will suffer greatly if the wine is kept from him until the end of the meal.

אֲמַר רַב עֲנָן בַּר תַּחְלִיפָא [4] The Gemara illustrates the effects of strongly aromatic foods with the following two anecdotes. **Rav Anan bar Taḥlifa said:** [5] **I was** once **standing before Mar Shmuel, and he was brought a dish of mushrooms** which had a particularly strong aroma. [6] **Had he not given me some** of this food, **I would have become dangerously ill,** for I was overcome by a craving for it. [7] **Rav Ashi said: I was** once **standing before Rav Kahana, and he was brought slices of turnip in vinegar.** [8] **Had he not given me some, I would have become dangerously ill,** for the smell of the food made me crave to eat it.

רַב פַּפָּא אֲמַר [9] **Rav Pappa said: Even** if the waiter is serving **fragrant dates,** he must be allowed to eat some of them at the same time as the rest of the diners. [10] The Gemara summarizes these rules with **a general principle:** The diners may not deny the waiter **any food that has a strong smell or a pungent taste,** for he will suffer if he is prevented from eating such foods while serving them.

אֲבוּהּ בַּר אִיהִי [11] It was related that **Avuha bar Ihi and Minyamin bar Ihi** treated their waiters in different ways: [12] **One** of these Sages was accustomed to **feeding his waiter** at the beginning of the meal **from every type of food** that was to be served during the course of the meal. [13] **And the other** Sage **would** customarily **feed** his waiter at the beginning of the meal **from** only **one type** of food, but would keep the rest of the food from him until the meal was over. [14] The Prophet **Elijah would speak with the first Sage,** [13] **but would not speak with the second Sage,** for the first Sage went well beyond the requirements of the law in order to spare his waiter any discomfort.

[1] אָמַר רַב חִסְדָּא: בָּשָׂר שָׁמֵן וְיַיִן יָשָׁן. [2] אָמַר רָבָא: בָּשָׂר שָׁמֵן — כָּל הַשָּׁנָה כּוּלָּהּ. [3] יַיִן יָשָׁן — בִּתְקוּפַת תַּמּוּז.

[4] אֲמַר רַב עֲנָן בַּר תַּחְלִיפָא: [5] הֲוָה קָאֵימְנָא קַמֵּיהּ דְּמָר שְׁמוּאֵל, וְאַיְיתוּ לֵיהּ תַּבְשִׁילָא דְּאַרְדֵּי, [6] וְאִי לָאו דִּיהַב לִי, אִיסְתַּכְּנִי. [7] אֲמַר רַב אַשִׁי: הֲוָה קָאֵימְנָא קַמֵּיהּ דְּרַב כָּהֲנָא, וְאַיְיתוּ לֵיהּ גַּרְגְּלִידֵי דְּלִיפְתָּא בְּחָלָא, [8] וְאִי לָאו דִּיהַב לִי, אִיסְתַּכְּנִי.

[9] רַב פַּפָּא אֲמַר: אֲפִילּוּ תְּמַרְתָּא דְּהִנּוּנִיתָא. [10] כְּלָלָא דְּמִילְּתָא: כָּל דְּאִית לֵיהּ רֵיחָא וְאִית לֵיהּ קִיּוּהָא.

[11] אֲבוּהּ בַּר אִיהִי, וּמִנְיָמִין בַּר אִיהִי — [12] חַד סָפֵי מִכָּל מִינָא וּמִינָא, [13] וְחַד סָפֵי מֵחַד מִינָא. [14] מָר מִשְׁתָּעֵי אֵלִיָּהוּ בַּהֲדֵיהּ, [15] וּמָר לָא מִשְׁתָּעֵי אֵלִיָּהוּ בַּהֲדֵיהּ.

LITERAL TRANSLATION

[1] Rav Ḥisda said: Fat meat and old wine. [2] Rava said: Fat meat — throughout the year. [3] Old wine — in the summer (lit., "in the period of Tammuz").

[4] Rav Anan bar Taḥlifa said: [5] I was standing before Mar Shmuel, and they brought him a dish of mushrooms, [6] and had he not given [some] to me, I would have become dangerously ill. [7] Rav Ashi said: I was standing before Rav Kahana, and they brought him slices of turnip in vinegar, [8] and had he not given [some] to me, I would have become dangerously ill.

[9] Rav Pappa said: Even a fragrant date. [10] The general rule on the matter: Whatever has a [strong] smell or a pungent taste.

[11] Avuha bar Ihi and Minyamin bar Ihi — [12] one would feed [the waiter] from every type [of food], [13] and one would feed [him] from one type. [14] With the one [Sage] Elijah would speak, [15] but with the other Elijah would not speak.

RASHI

חוץ מבשר שמן כו׳ — שמתאוה להס, ומצטער. **בתקופת תמוז** — שריחו חזק, וחום היום מהרהר בו כארס. **תבשילא דארדי** — מין כמהין ופטריות. **אסתכני** — הייתי מסוכן לאחזני בולמוס, מחמת תאות רעבוני. **גרגלידי** — חתיכות דקות ועגולות, *מריר״א בלעז. **תמרתא דהנוניתא** = תמרה שמינה. כמו: קריב לגבי דהינא ואידהן (שבועות מז,ב). **קיוהא** = קיהיון שיניס, **איגרו״ר בלעז. **כל דאית ליה ריחא או קיוהא** — מזיק את מי שאוכלין לפניו ואינו אוכל. **חד ספי** — מאכיל את השמש מכל מין ומין. **וחד ספי ליה ממין אחד** — בתחלת סעודה לשובע, ומשאר המינין משהה עד שיגמור סעודתו.

SAGES

רַב עֲנָן בַּר תַּחְלִיפָא **Rav Anan bar Taḥlifa.** A Babylonian Amora of the second generation, Rav Anan bar Taḥlifa was a student of Shmuel, spent much time in his presence, and became familiar with many of his teacher's customs.

אֲבוּהּ בַּר אִיהִי וּמִנְיָמִין בַּר אִיהִי **Avuha bar Ihi and Minyamin bar Ihi.** These were Babylonian Amoraim of the first generation and lived in Neharde'a. Avuha bar Ihi was a student and a colleague of Shmuel, and also discussed his private matters with him. Both he and his brother Minyamin were famous for their piety.

LANGUAGE

גַּרְגְּלִידֵי דְּלִיפְתָּא **Slices of turnip.** From the Greek γογγυλις, *gongulis,* meaning "turnip."

LANGUAGE (RASHI)

מריר״א* (in some manuscripts רודיל״ש) From the Old French *rodeles,* meaning "round pieces."

איגרו״ר** From the Old French *aigror,* meaning "sourness."

NOTES

תְּמַרְתָּא דְּהִנּוּנִיתָא **A fragrant date.** Our translation and commentary follows *Rivan,* who explains that Rav Pappa is referring here to fragrant dates. *Talmidei Rabbenu Yonah* explains that the term refers to unripened dates that have a pungent taste. *Rashi* understands the term as meaning "fat dates." The Geonim suggest that the term refers to first-ripening fruit.

מִשְׁתָּעֵי אֵלִיָּהוּ **Elijah would speak.** *Maharsha* explains the

SAGES

רַב מָרִי וְרַב פִּנְחָס בְּנֵי רַב חִסְדָּא Rav Mari and Rav Pineḥas the sons of Rav Ḥisda. These two sons of the great second-generation Amora Rav Ḥisda are occasionally mentioned by the Talmud in discussion with Rava, who was their brother-in-law, having married Rav Ḥisda's daughter. These brothers were famous for their piety and good manners.

PEOPLE

אִיזְגּוּר King Izgur. This is one of the names used in the Talmud for King Yezdegerd I of Persia (ruled 399–420 C.E.). Yezdegerd I was a peacable king; during his reign, amicable relations existed between Persia and Rome. He was very tolerant toward members of other religions, and as a result the Persian priests condemned him as a sinner. The favorable conditions enjoyed by the Jews under his rule may have facilitated initial efforts at editing the Talmud during this period.

LANGUAGE

אַטוּרַנְגָּא Headwaiter. This is apparently a corruption of אַכְוַנְגְּרָא, which is derived from the Persian *chvangar*, meaning "waiter." The headwaiter was responsible for setting the table for kings and other high-ranking officials.

LANGUAGE (RASHI)

שינישקלאקו״ש* From the Old French *seneschal*, meaning "house steward."

שורשמי״ן** (correct reading probably שורשימי״ץ). From the Old French *sorsemez*, meaning "leprosy."

TRANSLATION AND COMMENTARY

הָנְהוּ תַּרְתֵּין חֲסִידֵי [1] The Gemara continues with a similar anecdote about **two pious men, whom some identify as Rav Mari and Rav Pineḥas the sons of Rav Ḥisda.** [2] **One** of these **Sages** was accustomed to **feed his waiter** even **before** he and his guests sat down to eat. [3] **And the other** Sage **would feed** his waiter only **after** the meal had been served. [4] The Prophet **Elijah would speak with** the Sage **who fed his waiter before** the meal was served, [5] but **he would not speak with** the other Sage, **who fed** his waiter only **after** the meal was over.

אֲמֵימָר [6] It was further related that **Amemar, Mar Zutra, and Rav Ashi were** once **sitting near the entrance to the palace of Izgur, the king** of Persia, [7] and they noticed that **the king's headwaiter was passing by,** carrying various dishes that he was bringing to the king and his men. [8] **Rav Ashi saw that Mar Zutra's** [61B] **face was turning pale,** as he was overcome by a craving for the king's food. [9] Rav Ashi immediately ran over to the waiter, **took some of the food with his finger and placed it in** Mar Zutra's **mouth.** [10] The waiter turned to Rav Ashi and **said to him: "You have spoiled the king's meal,** for he will not wish to eat any of this food now that you have put your fingers into it!" [11] Then the king's officers came over to Rav Ashi and **said to him: "How could you have acted** with such impertinence, touching the food intended for the king?" [12] Rav Ashi **said to them:** "It is not I who has spoiled the king's meal, for **whoever prepared this** dish **made food for the king** that is **unfit** to be eaten." [13] **They said to him: "Why** do you say such a thing?" [14] Rav Ashi **explained to them: "I saw leprosy** on the meat **in it.** [15] The king's men **examined** the food, **but did not find any** indication that something was wrong with the dish that had been

[1] הָנְהוּ תַּרְתֵּין חֲסִידֵי, וְאָמְרִי לַהּ רַב מָרִי וְרַב פִּנְחָס בְּנֵי רַב חִסְדָּא — [2] מָר קָדֵים סָפֵי, [3] וּמָר מְאַחֵר סָפֵי. [4] דְּקָדֵים סָפֵי אֵלִיָּהוּ מִשְׁתָּעֵי בַּהֲדֵיהּ, [5] דִּמְאַחֵר סָפֵי לָא מִשְׁתָּעֵי אֵלִיָּהוּ בַּהֲדֵיהּ.

[6] אֲמֵימָר וּמָר זוּטְרָא וְרַב אַשִׁי הָווּ קָא יָתְבִי אַפִּיתְחָא דְּבֵי אִזְגּוּר מַלְכָּא. [7] חָלֵיף וְאָזֵיל אַטוּרַנְגָּא דְּמַלְכָּא. [8] חַזְיֵיהּ רַב אַשִׁי לְמָר זוּטְרָא [61B] דַּחֲוַור אַפֵּיהּ. [9] שָׁקַל בְּאֶצְבְּעֲתֵיהּ, אַנַּח לֵיהּ בְּפוּמֵיהּ. [10] אֲמַר לֵיהּ: ״אַפְסַדְתְּ לִסְעוּדָתָא דְּמַלְכָּא״. [11] אֲמַרוּ לֵיהּ: ״אַמַּאי תֵּיעֲבִיד הָכִי״? [12] אֲמַר לְהוּ: ״מַאן דְּעָבֵיד הָכִי פָּסֵיל לְמַאֲכַל דְּמַלְכָּא״. [13] אָמְרוּ לֵיהּ: ״אַמַּאי״? [14] אֲמַר לְהוּ: ״דָּבָר אַחֵר חֲזַאי בֵּיהּ״. [15] בָּדְקוּ וְלָא

LITERAL TRANSLATION

[1] Two pious men, and some say [they were] Rav Mari and Rav Pineḥas the sons of Rav Ḥisda — [2] the one [Sage] would feed [the waiter] first, [3] and the other would feed [him] last. [4] With the one who fed [the waiter] first, Elijah would speak. [5] With the one who fed [him] last Elijah would not speak.

[6] Amemar and Mar Zutra and Rav Ashi were sitting at the entrance to the house of King Izgur. [7] The king's headwaiter was passing by. [8] Rav Ashi saw that Mar Zutra's [61B] face was turning white. [9] He took [some food] with his finger, [and] placed [it] in his mouth. [10] He said to him: "You have spoiled the king's meal." [11] They said to him: "Why did you do this?" [12] He said to them: "Whoever does thus makes the king's food unfit." [13] They said to him: "Why?" [14] He said to them: "I saw leprosy (lit., 'something else') in it." [15] They examined [it] but

RASHI

קדים ספי – קודם שיתן לפניו. **מאחר ספי** – מכל מין ומין, לאחר שנתן לפניו ולפני האורחין. **דקדים ספי משתעי אליהו בהדיה** – לפי שכשנותן לפניהן והוא רואה ומתאוה ומצטער, ופעמים שיש אורחין הרבה. **אזגור** – שם מלך פרס. **אטורנגא דמלכא** – מושיב המנות לפני השרים, ובלשונינו *שיניסקלאקוש. **דחוור אפיה** – פניו זועפים, שנתאוה לאכול. **אמר ליה** – אטורנגא לרב אשי. **אפסדתא לסעודתא** – לא יאכל המלך מעתה. **אמרו לו** – שוטרי המלך: אמאי תעביד הכי? **אמר להו** – רב אשי. **דעביד הכי פסיל למיכל למלכא** – העושה מאכל כזה אין ראוי שיאכל המלך מאכל מידו. **דבר אחר חזאי ביה** – בשר של חזיר מנורע, ובלשון לעז קורין לו **שורשמי״ן.

NOTES

connection between the way the various Sages treated their waiters and whether or not they merited a conversation with the Prophet Elijah as follows: The Sage who demonstrated greater concern for his waiter's discomfort commemorated the miracle by which Elijah was able to fast for forty days.

Hafla'ah connects the two by way of the incident involving the Prophet Elijah and the woman who provided him with cake to eat (I Kings 17). *Iyyun Ya'akov* argues that Elijah appears only to those who go well beyond the requirements of the law to act kindheartedly toward others.

אִזְגּוּר Izgur. *Rivan* explains that the Izgur mentioned here was a Jewish officer in the king's service. The assumption that Izgur was a Jew resolves a number of difficulties arising from this story — for example, how Rav Ashi could have fed Mar Zutra non-kosher food.

דַּחֲוַור אַפֵּיהּ Face was turning white. Mar Zutra turned white because he was overcome by an intense desire for the king's food, or because a patch of leprosy suddenly spread across his face (*Rivan*).

אַשְׁכְּחוּ. ¹שָׁקַל אֶצְבָּעֲתֵיהּ אַנַּח עֲלֵיהּ, אֲמַר לְהוּ: ²״הָכָא מִי בְּדַקִיתוּ״? ³בָּדְקוּ אַשְׁכַּחוּ. ⁴אָמְרוּ לֵיהּ רַבָּנַן: ״מַאי טַעֲמָא סָמְכַתְּ אַנִּיסָּא״? ⁵אֲמַר לְהוּ: ״חֲזַאי רוּחַ צָרַעַת דְּקָא פָּרְחָה עִילָּוֵיהּ״.

⁶הַהוּא רוּמָאָה דַּאֲמַר לָהּ לְהַהִיא אִיתְּתָא: ״מִינַּסְבַתְּ לִי״? ⁷אָמְרָה לֵיהּ: ״לָא״. ⁸אָזֵיל אַיְיתֵי רִימָּנֵי. פָּלֵי וַאֲכַל קַמָּהּ. ⁹כָּל מַיָּא דְּצָעֲרֵי לָהּ בְּלַעֲתֵיהּ, ¹⁰וְלָא הַב לָהּ, עַד דְּזָג לָהּ. ¹¹לְסוֹף אֲמַר לָהּ: ״אִי מָסֵינָא לָךְ, מִינַּסְבַתְּ לִי״? ¹²אָמְרָה לֵיהּ: ״אִין״. ¹³אָזֵיל אַיְיתֵי רִימָּנֵי. ¹⁴פָּלֵי וַאֲכַל קַמָּהּ. ¹⁵אֲמַר לָהּ: ״כָּל מַיָּא דְּצָעֲרֵי לָךְ תּוּף שְׁדַאי, תּוּף שְׁדַאי״, ¹⁶עַד דְּנָפְקָא מִינָּהּ כִּי הוּצָא יָרְקָא וְאִתַּסִּיאַת.

LITERAL TRANSLATION

did not find [anything]. [1]He took his finger [and] placed [it] on it, [2][and] said to them: "Did you examine here?" [3]They examined [and] found. [4]The Rabbis said to him: "What is the reason [that] you relied on a miracle?" [5]He said to them: "I saw that the spirit of leprosy was hovering over him."

[6]A certain Roman said to a certain woman: "Will you marry me?" [7]She said to him: "No." [8]He went [and] brought pomegranates. [9]He cut [them] open and ate [them] in front of her. [10]All the spittle (lit., "water") that was causing her distress she swallowed, but he did not give her [any fruit], until she swelled up. [11]Finally he said to her: "If I cure you, will you marry me?" [12]She said to him: "Yes." [13]He went [and] brought pomegranates. [14]He cut [them] open and ate [them] in front of her. [15]He said to her: "All the spittle that is causing you distress spit up [and] eject, spit up [and] eject," [16]until [something] like a green palm leaf came out from her and she was cured.

TRANSLATION AND COMMENTARY

prepared for the king. [1]Rav Ashi then **took his finger and placed it on** one of the pieces of meat, **and asked them:** [2]**"Did you examine this** piece carefully?" [3]**They examined** the piece again **and** this time they **found** signs of leprosy on the meat. [4]Later, after the king's officers left, **the Rabbis** who had witnessed the incident **said** to Rav Ashi: **"Why did you rely on a miracle?** How could you take the risk of offending the king, and then defend your actions by claiming that something was wrong with the food, relying on a miraculous appearance of leprosy to save you from punishment?" [5]Rav Ashi **said to them:** "I did not rely on a miracle, for when I replied to the king's officers, **I saw that the spirit of leprosy was hovering over** Mar Zutra, and I knew at once that something was wrong with the food."

הַהוּא רוּמָאָה [6]The Gemara concludes this discussion with another story: There was **a certain Roman** who **said to a woman: "Will you marry me?"** [7]**She answered: "No."** [8]The Roman **went** out, **brought pomegranates, cut them open, and** began to **eat them in front of her,** without offering her any of the fruit. The sight of the pomegranates made the woman crave for the fruit, and her mouth began to water until it was filled with saliva. [9]**She swallowed all the spittle that was causing her distress,** [10]**but** still her suitor **would not give her** any of the pomegranates, **even when** her face and stomach began to **swell up** as a result of all the saliva she had swallowed. [11]**Finally he said to her: "If I cure you, will you marry me?"** [12]The woman **said to him: "Yes,** I will marry you." [13]**He** then **went, brought** some more **pomegranates,** [14]**cut them open, and** once again began to **eat them in front of her.** [15]When the woman's mouth once again began to water, her suitor **said to her: "All the spittle that is causing you distress — cough up and spit out, cough up and spit out."** [16]She did as she was told **until** she spat out such a large quantity of spittle that it looked **as if a green palm leaf was coming out of her** mouth, **and** in the end **she recovered.**

RASHI

שקל אצבעתיה — רב אשי שקל אצבעתיה דקפילא. **אנח עליה** — על אחת החתיכות. אנחיריה לא גרסינן. **הכא מי בדקיתו** — כלומר, בדקתם את חתיכה הזו? **בדקו אשכחו** — נס נעשה לו. **דפרחה עילויה** — דמר זוטרא. **פלי** = מבקע. והרבה יש לו דומים במסכת נדה (כא,ב): דפלי פלויי. **מיא דצערי** — רוק שגדל בתוך הפה מחמת קיוהא דבר הנאכל בפניו, ואינו אוכל ממנו. **עד דזג** — נפחו פניה וכריסה, ונעשו כזכוכית, שכן דרכי הנפוחים. **תוף שדאי** — רקקי והשליכי.

NOTES

מַאי טַעֲמָא סָמְכַתְּ אַנִּיסָּא? What is the reason that you relied on a miracle? The Rabbis thought that Mar Zutra's sudden illness could not justify Rav Ashi's behavior, for by putting his finger into the king's food, Rav Ashi was placing himself in greater danger than the danger to which Mar Zutra had become exposed as a result of his illness (*Maharsha*).

חֲזַאי רוּחַ צָרַעַת I saw that the spirit of leprosy. *Rashi* and *Rivan* explain that Rav Ashi saw the spirit of leprosy hovering over Mar Zutra, and this was a sign that Mar Zutra was in critical danger. When Rav Ashi put his finger into the king's food, he was not relying on a miracle to be saved from punishment, but was ready to risk his life in order to save Mar Zutra.

TRANSLATION AND COMMENTARY

״וְעוֹשָׂה בַּצֶּמֶר״ [1] We learned in our Mishnah that together with the other domestic responsibilities that a married woman must undertake, **"she must spin** a certain amount of **wool** each week." [2] Now, since the Mishnah specifies wool, it follows that she must **indeed** work **with wool** and that she is **not** required to work **with flax.**

מַתְנִיתִין מַנִּי [3] On this point the Gemara asks: **Whose opinion** does **our Mishnah** follow?

רַבִּי יְהוּדָה הִיא [4] The Gemara answers: **It follows** the viewpoint of **Rabbi Yehudah, as was taught** in the following Baraita: [5] "A man **cannot compel** his wife **to serve his father or to serve his son.** [6] A man also **cannot** compel his wife **to place straw before his animals,** his horses and his asses, **but he can compel her to place straw before his cattle,** his cows and his oxen. [7] **Rabbi Yehudah says: He also cannot compel her to work with flax, because** whoever works with **flax** must constantly put the threads into his mouth to moisten them, and this procedure **causes the mouth to smell and the lips to stretch** and stiffen." [8] The Gemara notes that **this applies only to Roman flax,** which is particularly harsh on the mouth and lips.

[1] ״וְעוֹשָׂה בַּצֶּמֶר״. בַּצֶּמֶר — אִין; [2] בְּפִשְׁתִּים — לָא. [3] מַתְנִיתִין מַנִּי? [4] רַבִּי יְהוּדָה הִיא, דְּתַנְיָא: [5] ״אֵינוֹ כּוֹפָהּ לֹא לַעֲמוֹד לִפְנֵי אָבִיו, [6] וְלֹא לַעֲמוֹד לִפְנֵי בְּנוֹ, וְלֹא לִיתֵּן תֶּבֶן לִפְנֵי בְּהֶמְתּוֹ, אֲבָל כּוֹפָהּ לִיתֵּן תֶּבֶן לִפְנֵי בְּקָרוֹ. [7] רַבִּי יְהוּדָה אוֹמֵר: אַף אֵינוֹ כּוֹפָהּ לַעֲשׂוֹת בְּפִשְׁתָּן, מִפְּנֵי שֶׁפִּשְׁתָּן מַסְרִיחַ אֶת הַפֶּה וּמְשַׁרְבֵּט אֶת הַשְּׂפָתַיִם״. [8] וְהָנֵי מִילֵּי בְּכִיתָּנָא רוֹמָאָה.

LITERAL TRANSLATION

[1] "And works with wool." [2] With wool — yes; with flax — no.

[3] Whose [opinion] is our Mishnah?

[4] It is Rabbi Yehudah, as it was taught: [5] "He cannot compel her to stand before his father, nor to stand before his son, [6] nor to place straw before his animal, but he can compel her to place straw before his cattle. [7] Rabbi Yehudah says: He can also not compel her to work with flax, because flax causes the mouth to smell and causes the lips to stretch." [8] And these things [apply only] to Roman flax.

RASHI

לעמוד — לשרת. **בהמתו** — סוס וחמור, שהן מזויינין ורגילים לרביעה. אבל בקר אינו להוט אחר רביעת אשה, ואין יצרו ניכר כל כך, לפיכך אין אשה נפתית לו. ואני שמעתי: בקרו — נקבות, בהמתו — זכרים. **משרבט** — פושטן כמין שרביט עד שנעשין גדולות. ובלשונינו נקרא *אשא״ש. על ידי שהיא צריכה לשרות החוט תמיד ברוק.

BACKGROUND

מַסְרִיחַ אֶת הַפֶּה Causes the mouth to smell. Linen threads are often moistened in the mouth before being spun, to make weaving them easier. Thus they can produce mouth wounds, in addition to causing the lower lip, on which the threads are usually placed, to protrude. Moreover, linen fibers were usually prepared for spinning by allowing their stalks to decompose, and this created an unpleasant odor.

LANGUAGE (RASHI)

אשא״ש* Perhaps from the Old French *eseus*, meaning "groove," or "cut."

NOTES

Rivan suggests another interpretation, according to which Rav Ashi saw the spirit of leprosy hovering over the king's dish, so that he knew that the animal from which the meat had been taken was leprous.

בְּהֶמְתּוֹ...בְּקָרוֹ His animal...his cattle. Substantially different readings are found in the manuscripts and among the Rishonim. The French Rishonim have the same text as in our standard edition: "He cannot compel her to place straw before his animal [בְּהֶמְתּוֹ], but he can compel her to place straw before his cattle [בְּקָרוֹ]." The Spanish Rishonim have the reverse reading: "He cannot compel her to place straw before his cattle, but he can compel her to place straw before his animal." *Rashi* explains the French reading as follows: A man cannot compel his wife to place straw before his horse or his ass, because these animals are often sexually aroused;, but cattle, cows, and sheep are less eager to copulate, and so there is no room for such concern. *Rivan* adds that when a horse or an ass is aroused, it is liable to kick the woman and cause her injury. Others explain that a husband can compel his wife to place straw before his cattle, because they serve as work animals and as a source of food. But he cannot compel her to place straw before his horse or his ass, for these animals are only used for riding (*Ra'ah*, *Ritva*).

Talmidei Rabbenu Yonah explains the Spanish reading as follows: A man can compel his wife to place straw before the animal that he rides, for a wife is obligated to attend to her husband's personal needs. But he cannot compel her to place straw before his cattle, for she is not required to involve herself in the maintenance of his household. *Tosafot* has yet another reading, according to which a husband can neither compel his wife to place straw before his animals, nor compel her to place straw before his cattle.

וּמְשַׁרְבֵּט אֶת הַשְּׂפָתַיִם And causes the lips to stretch. *Rashi* and others explain that working with flax causes one's lips to become stretched. *Arukh* maintains that flax causes the

HALAKHAH

בַּצֶּמֶר — אִין; בְּפִשְׁתִּים — לָא With wool — yes; with flax — no. "Where it is customary for women to work with wool or flax, a husband can compel his wife to do so. Where it is not customary for women to do such work, a husband can compel his wife to work with wool but not with flax, for working with flax can cause injury to the lips." (*Rambam*, *Sefer Nashim*, *Hilkhot Ishut* 21:1; *Shulḥan Arukh*, *Even HaEzer* 80:1.)

לַעֲמוֹד לִפְנֵי אָבִיו To stand before his father. "A wife is not required to serve her husband's father or his son. *Rema* notes that some authorities (*Bet Yosef* in the name of *Ran*) maintain that this only applies if the husband's relatives are not living in his home." (*Rambam*, *Sefer Nashim*, *Hilkhot Ishut* 21:3; *Shulḥan Arukh*, *Even HaEzer* 80:4.)

לִיתֵּן תֶּבֶן לִפְנֵי בְּהֶמְתּוֹ To place straw before his animal. "A wife is obligated to place straw before her husband's

TRANSLATION AND COMMENTARY

רַבִּי אֱלִיעֶזֶר אוֹמֵר [1] Our Mishnah stated: **"Rabbi Eliezer** disagrees with the first Tanna of the Mishnah and **says: Even if** the wife **brought a hundred maidservants** into the marriage, her husband may still compel her to spin wool, because idleness can lead a person to promiscuity." [2] **Rav Malkiyu said in the name of Rav Adda bar Ahavah: The Halakhah is in accordance with** this ruling by **Rabbi Eliezer.**

אָמַר רַבִּי חֲנִינָא בְּרֵיהּ דְּרַב אִיקָא [3] There were two Amoraim with similar names — Rav Malkiyu and Rav Malkiya — and a certain confusion arose about the statements made by these two authorities. The Gemara now wishes to clarify which rulings were issued by which of these Sages: **Rabbi Ḥanina the son of Rav Ika said: The rulings regarding** moving **a spit** on a Festival (*Betzah* 28b), regarding a wife's domestic responsibilities in the case where she brings many **maidservants** into her marriage (here in *Ketubot*), **and** regarding hair **follicles** as a sign of puberty (*Niddah* 52a) were all issued by **Rav Malkiyu.** [4] **The rulings regarding a** non-Jew's **locks of hair** (*Avodah Zarah* 29a), regarding **ashes** placed on a wound, **and** regarding a non-Jew's **cheese** (*Avodah Zarah* 35b) were issued by **Rav Malkiya.** [5] **Rav Pappa said: Those rulings relating to** laws stated in **the Mishnah and the Baraita** were issued by **Rav Malkiya.** [6] **Those** rulings **relating to** Amoraic **traditions** were issued by **Rav Malkiyu.** [7] The Gemara suggests **a mnemonic device** to help the student remember Rav Pappa's rule: **The Mishnah is the queen.** In other words, the Tannaitic teachings found in Mishnayot and Baraitot reign as queens in comparison with the Amoraic traditions, for an Amoraic tradition must be rejected if it is contradicted by a Tannaitic teaching. The word "queen" (*malkata* in Aramaic) resembles the name Malkiya. Thus the mnemonic serves to teach us that the rulings relating to Mishnayot and Baraitot were issued by Rav Malkiya.

[1] ״רַבִּי אֱלִיעֶזֶר אוֹמֵר: אֲפִילּוּ הִכְנִיסָה לוֹ מֵאָה שְׁפָחוֹת״. [2] אָמַר רַב מַלְכִּיּוּ אָמַר רַב אַדָּא בַּר אַהֲבָה: הֲלָכָה כְּרַבִּי אֱלִיעֶזֶר.

[3] אָמַר רַבִּי חֲנִינָא בְּרֵיהּ דְּרַב אִיקָא: שְׁפּוּד, שְׁפָחוֹת, וְגוּמּוֹת רַב מַלְכִּיּוּ. [4] בְּלוֹרִית, אֵפֶר מִקְלֶה, וּגְבִינָה רַב מַלְכִּיָּא. [5] רַב פַּפָּא אֲמַר: מַתְנִיתִין וּמַתְנִיתָא רַב מַלְכִּיָּא. [6] שְׁמַעְתְּתָא רַב מַלְכִּיּוּ. [7] וְסִימָנָךְ: מַתְנִיתָא מַלְכְּתָא.

LITERAL TRANSLATION

[1] "Rabbi Eliezer says: Even if she brought him a hundred maidservants." [2] Rav Malkiyu said in the name of Rav Adda bar Ahavah: The Halakhah is in accordance with Rabbi Eliezer.

[3] Rabbi Ḥanina the son of Rav Ika said: [The rulings regarding] a spit, maidservants, and follicles [were transmitted by] Rav Malkiyu. [4] [The rulings regarding] a lock of hair, ashes, and cheese [were transmitted by] Rav Malkiya. [5] Rav Pappa said: [Those rulings relating to] a Mishnah and a Baraita [were transmitted by] Rav Malkiya. [6] [Those relating to Amoraic] traditions [were transmitted by] Rav Malkiyu. [7] And your sign is: The Mishnah is the queen.

RASHI

שפוד שפחות וגומות – סימני הלכות הן: שפוד – במסכת ביצה, שפחות – כאן, גומות – במסכת נדה. בלורית – במסכת עבודה זרה, אפר מקלה – במסכת מכות, גבינה – במסכת עבודה זרה. תלת מינייהו מתניתין: שפחות ובלורית וגבינה, ותלת מינייהו שמעתתא, ופרשינהו רב מלכיו ורב מלכיא. **רב פפא** – אסימנא דרב מלכיו פליג, דקאמר שפחות. רב מלכיו ליתא, דכל מתניתין ומתניתא דהכא – רב מלכיא פרשינהו. אבל שמעתתא דאמר ברב מלכיו – מודינא לך. וסימניך – שלא תחליף בגירסא. **מתניתא מלכתא** – לגבי שמעתא הויא מתניתא מלכתא, דהא מינה מותבינן תיובתא לשמעתא. וסימניך – מלכיא לשון נקבה, אבל מלכיו – לשון זכר.

NOTES

lips to become swollen. The Jerusalem Talmud reads מְשַׁלְבֶּקֶת אֶת הַשְּׂפָיוֹת — "it causes the lips to become blistered."

רַב מַלְכִּיּוּ...רַב מַלְכִּיָּא **Rav Malkiyu...Rav Malkiya.** Very few Talmudic statements are attributed either to Rav Malkiyu or to Rav Malkiya, but since they had such similar sounding names, it was necessary to clarify which rulings were issued by which one of them. Although it seems to make no Halakhic difference whether Rav Malkiyu or Rav Malkiya was the author of a particular statement, it is common for the Talmud to be precise not only about the Halakhic content of the material under discussion, but also about the names of the authorities who transmitted it. This effort reflects the Rabbinic dictum that whoever relates a statement in the name of its author brings redemption to the world.

HALAKHAH

animals (according to some, she is only obligated to place straw before the animal that her husband has designated as the animal he rides; *Ḥelkat Meḥokek*, following *Rosh* and others). But she is not required to place straw before his cattle (following *Rif*'s reading of our text)." (*Rambam, Sefer Nashim, Hilkhot Ishut* 21:5; *Shulḥan Arukh, Even HaEzer* 80:6.)

SAGES

רַבִּי חֲנִינָא בְּרֵיהּ דְּרַב אִיקָא **Rabbi** (Rav) **Ḥanina** (Ḥinnana) **the son of Rav Ika.** A Babylonian Amora of the fifth generation, he was a disciple of Abaye and of Rava and a colleague of Rav Pappa and of Rav Huna the son of Rav Yehoshua. His teachings are found in a few places in the Talmud.

רַב מַלְכִּיָּא וְרַב מַלְכִּיּוּ **Rav Malkiya and Rav Malkiyu.** These two Sages apparently lived in different generations, but the similarity of their names gave rise to some confusion even during the Amoraic period regarding the attribution of their teachings. Rav Malkiya was a Babylonian Amora of the second and third generations. He spent some time in Eretz Israel and visited the Palestinian Amora, Rabbi Simlai. Rav Malkiyu was a Babylonian Amora of the fourth generation and a contemporary of Rava, who praises him for his great wisdom.

REALIA

בְּלוֹרִית **Lock of hair.**

Head of a young soldier from a Greek drawing.

Many suggestions have been offered regarding the origin of this word, mainly from Greek or Latin, but none of them is exactly apt. The main point regarding this way of wearing one's hair is that tufts were left, mainly on the sides and back of the head, which were later shaved in a special, idolatrous ceremony.

LANGUAGE

נַרְדְּשִׁיר **Checkers.** This word, which some sources spell נַרְדָּשִׁיר, is cognate to similar words in Persian and Arabic (or to the abbreviated form *nard*). Our term is derived from the Middle Persian *new-artachser*, a game named after a Persian king (Ardeshir). A Persian source explains that the game was played on a board with thirty pieces, fifteen of which were black and fifteen white. It may have been somewhat similar to chess.

LANGUAGE (RASHI)

אישקקי״ש* From the old French *esjecs*, or the Italian *escacchi*, meaning "chess."

TRANSLATION AND COMMENTARY

מַאי בֵּינַיְיהוּ [1] The Gemara asks: **What is the difference between** Rav Pappa and Rabbi Ḥanina the son of Rav Ika on this matter?

אִיכָּא בֵּינַיְיהוּ שְׁפָחוֹת [2] The Gemara answers: **There is** a difference **between them regarding** a wife's responsibilities if she brings many **maidservants** into her marriage. According to Rabbi Ḥanina the son of Rav Ika, the ruling was stated by Rav Malkiyu. But according to Rav Pappa, the ruling was issued by Rav Malkiya, for it relates to a teaching found in our Mishnah.

רַבָּן שִׁמְעוֹן בֶּן גַּמְלִיאֵל [3] The Gemara now proceeds to discuss the last clause of our Mishnah, which stated: **"Rabban Shimon ben Gamliel says:** Similarly, if someone forbids himself by a vow from deriving any benefit from the work performed by his wife, he must grant her a divorce and pay her her ketubah, for the vow prevents her from doing any household work, and idleness can lead a person to insanity." [4] The Gemara asks: But **is this** not the same opinion as that of **the previous Tanna** in the Mishnah, Rabbi Eliezer, that a married woman must not be allowed to remain idle, for idleness can lead a person to promiscuity? And Rabban Shimon ben Gamliel teaches that she must not be allowed to remain idle, for idleness can lead a person to insanity. Is there any practical difference between these two rulings?

אִיכָּא בֵּינַיְיהוּ [5] The Gemara answers: **There is a difference between them** in a case **where** the woman is not totally idle but keeps herself busy **playing with small dogs or** a game such as **checkers.** As long as the woman keeps herself occupied with something, even if only with pets or games, she will not be led to insanity, for only total idleness can cause insanity. But she may still be led to promiscuity if she does not engage in some constructive activity. Thus, according to Rabbi Eliezer, a woman is required to spin wool, even if she has brought a hundred maidservants into the marriage. But according to Rabban Shimon ben Gamliel, a woman whose personal quota of work can be met by her maidservants is not required to spin any wool, provided that she can keep herself busy with pets or games.

MISHNAH הַמַּדִּיר אֶת אִשְׁתּוֹ [6] The previous Mishnah concluded with a ruling about a husband who forbids himself by a vow from deriving any benefit from his wife's work. The present Mishnah opens with a

LITERAL TRANSLATION

[1] What is [the difference] between them?

[2] There is between them [the ruling regarding] maidservants.

[3] "Rabban Shimon ben Gamliel says, etc." [4] This is the first Tanna!

[5] There is [a difference] between them where she plays with small dogs or checkers.

MISHNAH [6] [If] someone forbids his wife with a vow

[1] מַאי בֵּינַיְיהוּ?

[2] אִיכָּא בֵּינַיְיהוּ שְׁפָחוֹת.

[3] "רַבָּן שִׁמְעוֹן בֶּן גַּמְלִיאֵל אוֹמֵר, וכו׳". [4] הַיְינוּ תַּנָּא קַמָּא!

[5] אִיכָּא בֵּינַיְיהוּ דְּמִיטַּלְלָא בְּגוּרְיָיתָא קִיטַנְיָיתָא וְנַדְרַשִׁיר.

מִשְׁנָה [6] הַמַּדִּיר אֶת אִשְׁתּוֹ

RASHI

היינו תנא קמא — רבי אליעזר, מה לי לידי שעמום מה לי לידי זימה? **דמיטללא בגורייתא קיטנייתא ונדרשיר** — משחקת בכלבים דקים, ושחוק שקורין *אישקקי"ש. לידי זימה איכא, לידי שיעמום — ליכא. דאין שיעמום אלא ביושב ותוהא ובטל לגמרי. **משנה המדיר את אשתו** — כגון דאמר: יאסר הנאת תשמישך עלי. אבל הנאת תשמישי עליך — לא מיתסרא, דהא משועבד לה. דכתיב "ועונתה לא יגרע", והכי מוקמינן בנדרים בפרק "ואלו נדרים" (פא,ב).

NOTES

אִיכָּא בֵּינַיְיהוּ דְּמִיטַּלְלָא **There is a difference between them where she plays.** *Rif* records Rav Malkiyu's statement that the law is in accordance with Rabbi Eliezer. *Ran* and others understand from this that the law is in accordance with the viewpoint of Rabbi Eliezer, and against that of Rabban Shimon ben Gamliel. Thus a man who forbids himself from deriving any benefit from his wife's work must divorce her and pay her her ketubah, even if she can keep herself busy with other things, for we are concerned that her idleness may lead her to promiscuity.

As for the general rule that the law is in accordance with the rulings of Rabban Shimon ben Gamliel recorded in the Mishnah, *Tosafot* argues that the Tanna whose view is recorded in the Mishnah is a different Rabban Shimon ben Gamliel.

According to *Rosh,* the law is in accordance with the viewpoint of Rabbi Eliezer, and against that of the anonymous first Tanna of the Mishnah. Thus a woman can be compelled to work with wool, even if she has brought 100 maidservants into her marriage. But as for the issue in dispute between Rabbi Eliezer and Rabban Shimon ben Gamliel, we follow the general rule that the law is in accordance with the viewpoint of Rabban Shimon ben Gamliel.

הַמַּדִּיר אֶת אִשְׁתּוֹ **If someone forbids his wife with a vow.** *Rashi* and others note that the Mishnah cannot be referring

HALAKHAH

הַמַּדִּיר אֶת אִשְׁתּוֹ מִתַּשְׁמִישׁ הַמִּטָּה **If someone forbids his wife with a vow from sexual relations.** "If someone forbids himself by a vow from cohabiting with his wife, after seven days he must divorce her and give her her

TRANSLATION AND COMMENTARY

discussion of a husband who takes a vow forbidding himself from having sexual relations with his wife. **If someone forbids** himself **by a vow from** having **sexual relations with his wife,** the Tannaim disagree about how soon he can be compelled to grant her a divorce and to pay her her ketubah. [1]**Bet Shammai say:** The wife must wait **two weeks,** after which her husband must either go to a Sage and request the nullification of the vow, or he must grant her a divorce and pay her her ketubah. [2]**Bet Hillel** disagree and **say:** After **one week** the husband must take the necessary steps to release himself from the vow or else grant his wife a divorce.

הַתַּלְמִידִים יוֹצְאִין לְתַלְמוּד תּוֹרָה [3]The Mishnah continues its discussion of a husband's obligation to cohabit with his wife: Married Rabbinic **students may leave** their homes and go to another town **for the study of Torah without** their wives' **permission for** periods of up to **thirty days,** even though they will be unable to fulfill their conjugal obligations. [4]But **workers** may leave to work in another town without their wives' permission **for** only **one week** at a time.

הָעוֹנָה הָאֲמוּרָה בַּתּוֹרָה [5]The Mishnah now explains that **the** husband's **conjugal obligation,** which **stems from the Biblical verse** (Exodus 21:10): "And her duty of marriage he shall not diminish," varies according to the husband's occupation and how frequently he is found at home. [6]**Men of leisure,** who spend most of their time at home, are obliged to cohabit with their wives **every day.** [7]**Workers** who work in their home

מִתַּשְׁמִישׁ הַמִּטָּה, [1]בֵּית שַׁמַּאי אוֹמְרִים: שְׁתֵּי שַׁבָּתוֹת. [2]בֵּית הִלֵּל אוֹמְרִים: שַׁבָּת אַחַת. [3]הַתַּלְמִידִים יוֹצְאִין לְתַלְמוּד תּוֹרָה שֶׁלֹּא בִּרְשׁוּת שְׁלֹשִׁים יוֹם. [4]הַפּוֹעֲלִים שַׁבָּת אַחַת. [5]הָעוֹנָה הָאֲמוּרָה בַּתּוֹרָה: [6]הַטַּיָּילִין, בְּכָל יוֹם; [7]הַפּוֹעֲלִים,

LITERAL TRANSLATION

from sexual relations, [1]Bet Shammai say: Two weeks. [2]Bet Hillel say: One week.

[3]Students may leave for the study of Torah without permission [for] thirty days. [4]Workers [for] one week.

[5]The conjugal obligation stated in the Torah is [as follows]: [6]Men of leisure, every day; [7]workers,

RASHI

בית שמאי אומרים שתי שבתות — אם הדירה שתי שבתות — תמתין, ואם יותר — יוציא ויתן כתובה. **הטיילין** — מפרש בגמרא.

NOTES

to a case in which the husband took a vow forbidding his wife from sexual relations with him, for the husband is obligated by Torah law to cohabit with his wife, and so a vow intended to deny her that right is not effective. Rather, the Mishnah is referring to a case in which the husband formulated his vow in such a way that he forbade himself from deriving any enjoyment from sexual relations with his wife. Such a vow is valid because we cannot compel a person to derive benefit from something that is forbidden to him.

הַתַּלְמִידִים יוֹצְאִין **Students may leave.** *Ran* explains that the regulations mentioned here that Rabbinic students may leave their homes to study Torah for up to thirty days and workers may leave for a week at a time are additional examples of "the conjugal obligation stated in the Torah," which is discussed in the next clause of the Mishnah. Thus the Mishnah teaches us that the conjugal obligation of a Rabbinic student studying out of town must be carried out once in thirty days, and the marital duty of a worker employed out of town must be carried out once a week. The Mishnah did not teach these regulations under the heading of "the conjugal obligation stated in the Torah," so that it would not be understood as implying that the same laws apply even if the student and the worker study and work in their home towns.

Tosafot argues that these laws are not examples of "the conjugal obligation stated in the Torah." Otherwise, they should have been included in the next clause. Rather, the Mishnah teaches us that even though a Rabbinic student who is studying in his home town is obligated to cohabit with his wife once a week on Friday night, and a worker working in his own community is obligated to cohabit with his wife twice a week, a Rabbinic student and a worker may leave town without their wives' permission. A worker whose conjugal obligation involves relations twice a week may leave town and reduce his obligation to once a week. But someone whose conjugal obligation is less than once a week may not reduce his conjugal obligation any further without his wife's permission. Out of consideration for the important duty of Torah study, an exception was made for Rabbinic students, who were permitted to leave town without their wives' permission for up to thirty days.

הָעוֹנָה הָאֲמוּרָה בַּתּוֹרָה **The conjugal obligation stated in the Torah.** The plain sense of this expression is that the husband's conjugal obligation derives from the Biblical

HALAKHAH

ketubah. This ruling applies even if the husband is a sailor whose conjugal obligation is only once in six months." (*Rambam, Sefer Nashim, Hilkhot Ishut* 14:6; *Shulḥan Arukh, Even HaEzer* 76:9.)

הָעוֹנָה הָאֲמוּרָה בַּתּוֹרָה **The conjugal obligation stated in the Torah.** "A husband's conjugal obligation varies in accordance with his physical abilities and occupation. Unless otherwise stipulated by the parties, a man of leisure is obligated to have sexual relations with his wife every day of the week. The conjugal obligation of a worker (who works in his home town) is twice a week; that of an ass driver is once a week; that of a camel driver is once in thirty days; and that of a sailor is once in six months." (*Rambam, Sefer Nashim, Hilkhot Ishut* 14:1; *Shulḥan Arukh, Even HaEzer* 76:1-2.)

TRANSLATION AND COMMENTARY

town are obliged to cohabit with their wives **twice a week.** [1] **Ass drivers**, who leave their home towns and transport merchandise to the surrounding villages, but who are not ordinarily absent from their homes for more than a week at a time, are obligated to have sexual relations with their wives **once a week.** [2] **Camel drivers**, who transport merchandise greater distances, are required to cohabit with their wives **once in thirty days.** [3] **Sailors**, who are away from home for extended periods of time, are required to have sexual relations with their wives **once in six months.** [4] **These are** the husband's marital duties according to **the viewpoint of Rabbi Eliezer.**

שְׁתַּיִם בְּשַׁבָּת; [1] הַחַמָּרִים, אַחַת בְּשַׁבָּת; [2] הַגַּמָּלִים, אַחַת לִשְׁלֹשִׁים יוֹם; [3] הַסַּפָּנִים, אַחַת לְשִׁשָּׁה חֳדָשִׁים. [4] דִּבְרֵי רַבִּי אֱלִיעֶזֶר.

גמרא [5] מַאי טַעֲמָא דְּבֵית שַׁמַּאי?

[6] גָּמְרִי מִיּוֹלֶדֶת נְקֵבָה.

[7] וּבֵית הִלֵּל?

[8] גָּמְרִי מִיּוֹלֶדֶת זָכָר.

[9] וּבֵית הִלֵּל נָמֵי נִגְמְרוּ מִיּוֹלֶדֶת נְקֵבָה!

LITERAL TRANSLATION

twice a week; [1] ass drivers, once a week; [2] camel drivers, once in thirty days; [3] sailors, once in six months. [4] [These are] the words of Rabbi Eliezer.

GEMARA [5] What is the reason of Bet Shammai?

[6] They derive [it] from a woman who gives birth to a girl.

[7] And Bet Hillel?

[8] They derive [it] from a woman who gives birth to a boy.

[9] But let Bet Hillel also derive [it] from a woman who gives birth to a girl!

RASHI

החמרים – שיולאין לכפרים להביא תבואה למכור בשוק. **הגמלין** – סוחרי חבילות, ומביאין על הגמלים ממקום רחוק. **הספנים** – פורשין ליס הגדול לקצווי ארץ.

גמרא מיולדת נקבה – ששואה שבועיים מתשמיש. **נגמרו מיולדת נקבה** – כיון דאשכחן אורח ארעא לשהות כל כך – אין לנו לכופו להוציא.

GEMARA מַאי טַעֲמָא [5] The Gemara asks: **What is the reason** that **Bet Shammai** maintain that a wife must wait two weeks before she can demand a divorce from her husband, if he took a vow forbidding himself from engaging in sexual relations with her?

גָּמְרִי מִיּוֹלֶדֶת נְקֵבָה [6] The Gemara answers: **They derive** this law **from** the regulations governing **a woman who gives birth to a girl.** A woman is ritually impure for the first two weeks after giving birth to a girl, and is forbidden to engage in sexual relations with her husband. Bet Shammai infer from this that a two-week period of abstinence from sexual relations is not considered an unbearable hardship.

וּבֵית הִלֵּל [7] The Gemara continues: **And** what is the reason that **Bet Hillel** maintain that a woman need wait only a week before demanding a divorce from her husband?

גָּמְרִי מִיּוֹלֶדֶת זָכָר [8] The Gemara answers: **They derive** this law **from** the regulations governing **a woman who gives birth to a boy.** If a woman gives birth to a boy, she is ritually impure for a week, during which time she is forbidden to her husband.

וּבֵית הִלֵּל [9] An objection is now raised: **But let Bet Hillel also derive** the law regarding a man who forbids himself from having sexual relations with his wife **from** the laws applying to **a woman who gives birth to a girl,** as did Bet Shammai. Since there is a case in which the Torah forbids a woman from engaging in sexual relations with her husband for two weeks, Bet Hillel should agree with Bet Shammai that a woman whose husband forbids himself from cohabiting with her should not be able to demand a divorce before two weeks have passed.

NOTES

verse (Exodus 21:10), "And her duty of marriage he shall not diminish," which was understood by the Rabbis as varying according to the husband's occupation. *Bereshit Rabbah* and the Jerusalem Talmud find support for this supposition from the story regarding the peace-offering sent by Jacob to Esau (Genesis 32:15-16; see also *Rashi's* comment on the verses): "Two hundred she-goats, and twenty he-goats, two hundred ewes, and twenty rams, thirty milch camels with their colts, forty cows, and ten bulls, twenty she-asses, and ten foals." The animals were sent in different ratios between the males and the females of each kind, depending upon the difficulty of the work done by each species. The more tiring the work, the less available is the male for mating with the female. Just as animals' mating patterns vary according to the work imposed upon each different kind, so too do the husband's conjugal obligations vary according to his occupation and availability for sexual relations.

גָּמְרִי מִיּוֹלֶדֶת They derive it from a woman who gives birth. The Rishonim explain that the various derivations cited here for the positions of Bet Shammai and Bet Hillel are all based on the same principle that if the Torah prevents a woman from engaging in sexual relations with her husband for a certain period of time, then abstinence from sexual relations for that long cannot be considered an unbearable burden. Thus a husband who forbids himself from cohabiting with his wife cannot be compelled to divorce her until more time has passed.

Shittah Mekubbetzet notes that when the Gemara answers that Bet Hillel derive their position from the laws

[1]אִי מִיּוֹלֶדֶת גָּמְרִי לָהּ, הָכִי נַמִי. [2]אֶלָּא בֵּית הִלֵּל מִנִּדָּה גָּמְרֵי לָהּ.

[3]בְּמַאי קָמִיפַּלְגִי?

[4]מָר סָבַר: מִידֵי דִּשְׁכִיחַ מִמִּידֵי דִּשְׁכִיחַ. [5]וּמָר סָבַר: מִידֵי דְּהוּא גָּרֵים לָהּ מִמִּידֵי דְּהוּא גָּרֵים לָהּ.

[6]אָמַר רַב: מַחֲלוֹקֶת בִּמְפָרֵשׁ,

LITERAL TRANSLATION

[1]If they derived it from a woman who gives birth, [it would] indeed [be] so. [2]But Bet Hillel derive [it] from a menstruating woman.

[3]About what do they disagree?

[4]The one maintains: Something that is frequent [is derived] from something that is frequent. [5]And the other maintains: Something that he caused [is derived] from something that he caused.

[6]Rav said: The disagreement is where he specified,

RASHI

הכי גרסינן: אי מיולדת גמרי הכי נמי. **מידי דשכיח** – כעס, שכועס על אשתו ומדירה. **ממידי דשכיח** – נדות, לאפוקי לידה דלא שכיח כולי האי. **מידי דהוא גרים לה** – נדר האיש גורס לה לשהות, וכן לידה על ידו באה לה, לאפוקי נדה דממילא. ויש לנו ללמוד מן הדומה [אפילו לא שכיח כולי האי].

TRANSLATION AND COMMENTARY

אִי מִיּוֹלֶדֶת גָּמְרִי לָהּ [1]The Gemara answers: **If** Bet Hillel had **derived** their ruling regarding this matter **from** the regulations governing **a woman who gives birth, it would indeed be true** that they should have derived it from the regulations governing a woman who gives birth to a girl, and it would follow that two weeks must pass before the husband can be compelled to give his wife a divorce. [2]**But** in fact **Bet Hillel derived** their ruling **from** the laws that apply to **a menstruating woman.** Since by Torah law a menstruating woman is forbidden to her husband for seven days, a man who forbids himself from cohabiting with his wife cannot be compelled to divorce her until a week has passed during which she has been forbidden to him.

בְּמַאי קָמִיפַּלְגִי [3]The Gemara now seeks to clarify the dispute. **What** precisely is the issue **about** which Bet Shammai and Bet Hillel **disagree?**

מָר סָבַר [4]The Gemara explains: **The one** school of thought — Bet Hillel — **maintains** that laws applying to **a matter that occurs frequently** should **be derived from** laws applying to another **matter that occurs frequently.** Husbands often get angry with wives and take a vow against having sexual relations. Thus it is appropriate that the period of abstention from sexual relations resulting from such a vow, after which a husband may be compelled to divorce his wife, should be derived from the period of abstention following a woman's menstruation, which is a frequent occurrence, rather than from the period of abstention resulting from childbirth, which occurs much less frequently. [5]**And the other** school of thought — Bet Shammai — **maintains** that laws applying to **something that** the husband himself **has caused** should **be derived from** laws relating to **something** else **that** the husband himself **has caused.** When a man takes a vow forbidding himself from having sexual relations with his wife, he is responsible. Thus it is appropriate that the period of abstention after which he may be compelled to divorce his wife should be derived from the period of abstention following childbirth, for which the husband is also responsible, rather than from the period of abstention required by a woman's menstruation, for which the husband bears no responsibility.

אָמַר רַב [6]The Gemara now notes that the Amoraim disagreed about the scope of the dispute between Bet Shammai and Bet Hillel. **Rav said: The dispute** between Bet Shammai and Bet Hillel **is** limited to a case **where** the husband **specified** a certain period during which he would be forbidden to engage in sexual relations with his wife. Since he has set a limit on his period of abstinence, we assume that he plans to resume normal conjugal relations in the future. Therefore he is given a certain time to arrange for the nullification of his vow, and he can then resume such relations immediately. Bet Shammai maintain that

NOTES

applying to a menstruating woman, and not from those applying to a woman who gives birth, it means that nothing can be derived from the laws regarding a woman who has just had a baby, for a woman recovering from childbirth has little or no sexual desire. For such a woman two weeks of forced abstinence is not an intolerable burden, but for others it may indeed be an unbearable hardship and grounds for the woman to demand a divorce. (See also the Jerusalem Talmud which explains that Bet Hillel derive their position either from a woman who gives birth to a boy or from a menstruating woman.)

מַחֲלוֹקֶת בִּמְפָרֵשׁ **The disagreement is where he specified.** *Rashi* explains the Mishnah as saying that, according to Bet Shammai, if the husband forbids himself from cohabiting with his wife for two weeks, she must accept the abstinence forced upon her, but if he forbids himself from cohabiting with her for a longer period of time, he must divorce her immediately. And according to Bet Hillel, if the husband forbids himself from engaging in sexual relations with his wife for a week, she must accept it, but if he forbids himself from engaging in sexual relations with her for any longer than that, he must grant her an immediate

TRANSLATION AND COMMENTARY

he is given two weeks to release himself from the vow before he can be compelled to grant his wife a divorce, whereas Bet Hillel maintain that he is given only one week. [1]**But** in a case **where** the husband **took a vow** forbidding himself from cohabiting with his wife **without specifying** how long he would be forbidden to her, **all agree that he must divorce** his wife **immediately and pay** her **her ketubah,** because in such a case we assume that he will never seek a dispensation nullifying his vow. [2]**Shmuel** disagreed with Rav and **said: Even** in a case **where** the husband **took a vow** forbidding himself from engaging in sexual relations with his wife **without specifying** the length of time, **he is given** a certain amount of time — two weeks according to Bet Shammai, and one week according to Bet Hillel — before he can be compelled to grant his wife a divorce. Even in such a case the husband is not required to divorce his wife immediately, [3]**because he may** go to a Sage in order to **find a** Halakhic **justification for** nullifying **his vow.**

הָא פְּלִיגֵי [4] The Gemara raises an objection: But **surely** Rav and Shmuel have already **disagreed about this** matter **once before!** [5]**For we have learned** in a Mishnah (below, 70a): **"If someone forbids his wife by a vow from** deriving any material **benefit from him**, and tells her to spend what she earns from her handiwork on her maintenance, then **for** the first **thirty days** of the vow **he must appoint an administrator** to provide her with those extra things that she cannot afford on the basis of her earnings alone. [6]But **after this** initial

[1]אֲבָל בִּסְתָם, דִּבְרֵי הַכֹּל יוֹצִיא לְאַלְתַּר, וְיִתֵּן כְּתוּבָּה. [2]וּשְׁמוּאֵל אֲמַר: אֲפִילּוּ בִּסְתָם נַמִי יַמְתִּין, [3]שֶׁמָּא יִמְצָא פֶּתַח לְנִדְרוֹ.

[4]הָא פְּלִיגֵי בָּהּ חֲדָא זִימְנָא! [5]דִּתְנַן: "הַמַּדִּיר אֶת אִשְׁתּוֹ מִלֵּיהָנוֹת לוֹ, עַד שְׁלֹשִׁים יוֹם, יַעֲמִיד פַּרְנָס; [6]יוֹתֵר מִכָּאן,

LITERAL TRANSLATION

[1]but where [he vowed] without specifying, all agree [that] he must divorce [her] immediately, and pay [her] ketubah. [2]But Shmuel said: Even where [he vowed] without specifying, he should also wait, [3]in case he will find an opening for his vow.

[4]Surely they disagreed about this once [before]! [5]For we have learned: "[If] someone forbids his wife with a vow from benefiting from him, up to thirty days, he must appoint an administrator; [6]more than that,

RASHI

אפילו בסתם נמי ימתין — לבית שמאי שתי שבתות ולבית הלל שבת אחת. **שמא** — בתוך הזמן ילמוד למצוא פתח חרטה, לומר: אדעתא דהכי לא נדרי, ויתיר לו חכם נדרו. **מליהנות לו עד שלשים יום** — קונם את נהנית לי עד שלשים יום. ולא הדירה מהנאת תשמיש, דהא לא חייל, משום דמשועבד לה. וגבי מזונות נמי מוקמינן ליה לקמן (כתובות ע,א) באומר לה "צאי מעשה ידיך למזונותיך". ופרנס — משום דלא ספקא. ואית דמוקמא כגון שהוא מן הגמלים או מן הספנים, שאין לכופו בשביל תשמיש, ולאו מילתא היא, דהא מוקמא לקמן אכולהו קתני מתניתין לענין מדיר — שבוע אחת. **יעמיד פרנס** — שיזון אותה. והתם פריך: ואטו פרנס לאו שליחותיה עביד? תשמיש — לא אפשר בפרנס.

NOTES

divorce. This is what Rav means when he says that the dispute between Bet Shammai and Bet Hillel is limited to a case where the husband specified a time in his vow — two weeks according to Bet Shammai, and one week according to Bet Hillel.

Ritva argues that this is not the plain sense of the Mishnah. Moreover, if this is what the Mishnah meant to say, how could Shmuel have said that Bet Shammai and Bet Hillel disagree even about a case in which the husband took a vow forbidding himself from cohabiting with his wife without specifying the length of time during which such relations would be forbidden? In such a case, all would agree that the husband must divorce her immediately! Rather, the Mishnah merely teaches us that Bet Shammai and Bet Hillel disagree about how long a woman must wait before she is entitled to demand an immediate divorce. Rav remarks that the dispute is limited to a case in which the husband specified a time in his vow, even if it is longer than a week or two, for in such a case we assume that he plans to resume normal conjugal relations. But if the husband takes a vow without specifying how long he will be forbidden to his wife, all agree that he must divorce her immediately, for we assume that he will never seek a dispensation from his vow. Shmuel disagrees with Rav and says that Bet Shammai and Bet Hillel also disagree about a case in which the husband takes a vow without specifying any time, for even in such a case the husband may try to be released from his vow.

HALAKHAH

אֲפִילּוּ בִּסְתָם Even where he vowed without specifying. "If someone forbids himself by a vow from engaging in sexual relations with his wife, whether or not the vow specifies the period during which sexual relations will be forbidden, after seven days he must either seek a dispensation for his vow or grant his wife an immediate divorce and pay her her ketubah," following Shmuel, even though the law in matters of personal status is usually in accordance with the viewpoint of Rav. (*Rambam, Sefer Nashim, Hilkhot Ishut* 14:6; *Shulḥan Arukh, Even HaEzer* 76:9.)

TRANSLATION AND COMMENTARY

thirty-day period, the husband **must** take the necessary steps to release himself from the vow or must **grant her a divorce and pay** her **her ketubah."** [1]With reference to this Mishnah, **Rav said: This** ruling **applies only** in a case **where** the husband **specified** the time during which his wife would be forbidden to derive benefit from him. [2]**But** in a case **where he forbade** his wife from deriving benefit from him **without specifying** for how long such benefit would be forbidden to her, he **must divorce** his wife **immediately, and pay** her **her ketubah.** [3]**But Shmuel said: Even where** the husband **forbade** his wife from deriving benefit from him **without specifying** the length of time, **he is given** a certain amount of **time** before he is required to divorce her. Even in such a case we do not require the husband to divorce his wife immediately, **because he may** go to a Sage in order to **find a** Halakhic **justification** for nullifying **his vow.** Why, asks the Gemara, was this dispute between Rav and Shmuel taught twice?

צְרִיכָא [4]The Gemara answers: **It was necessary** for the dispute between Rav and Shmuel to be stated in both cases, **for if it had been stated** only **about** the case of our Mishnah, where the husband forbids himself from cohabiting with his wife, **I might have said that** only **in that** case **did Rav say** that the husband must divorce his wife immediately, **because** his marital duty **cannot** be fulfilled **through an administrator.** [5]**But in** the case of a husband who forbids his wife from deriving benefit from him, **where** her needs **can be** provided for her **through an administrator,** [6]**I might have said that** Rav **agrees with Shmuel** that the husband is not required to divorce his wife until a month has passed. [7]**And if** the dispute **had been stated** only **about that** case, **I might have said that** only **in that** case **did Shmuel say** that the husband is given thirty days before he can be compelled to divorce his wife, because her needs can be provided for her through an administrator. [8]**But in** the case of a husband who forbids himself from sexual relations, **I might have said that** Shmuel **agrees with Rav,** because his conjugal obligation cannot be fulfilled through an administrator. [9]**Thus it was necessary** for the dispute to be **stated twice,** to teach us that Rav and Shmuel do in fact disagree in both cases.

הַתַּלְמִידִים יוֹצְאִין לְתַלְמוּד [10]The Gemara now proceeds to analyze the next clause of the Mishnah, which stated: "Married Rabbinic **students may leave** their homes and go to another town **for the study** of Torah without their wives' permission for periods of up to thirty days." [11]The Gemara asks: And if these students go **with** their wives' **permission, for how long** may they absent themselves from their homes and avoid their conjugal obligations?

כַּמָּה דְּבָעֵי [12]The Gemara is puzzled by this question: If the students have their wives' permission, then surely they can stay away **for as long they want!** Why should they be required to return home if their wives have exempted them from their marital duties?

יוֹצִיא וְיִתֵּן כְּתוּבָּה״. [1]וְאָמַר רַב: לֹא שָׁנוּ אֶלָּא בִּמְפָרֵשׁ, [2]אֲבָל בִּסְתָם, יוֹצִיא לְאַלְתַּר וְיִתֵּן כְּתוּבָּה. [3]וּשְׁמוּאֵל אָמַר: אֲפִילּוּ בִּסְתָם נַמִי יַמְתִּין, שֶׁמָּא יִמְצָא פֶּתַח לְנִדְרוֹ.

[4]צְרִיכָא, דְּאִי אִיתְּמַר בְּהָא, בְּהָא קָאָמַר רַב, מִשּׁוּם דְּלָא אֶפְשָׁר בְּפַרְנָס. [5]אֲבָל בְּהַהִיא, דְּאֶפְשָׁר בְּפַרְנָס, [6]אֵימָא מוֹדֵי לֵיהּ לִשְׁמוּאֵל. [7]וְאִי אִיתְּמַר בְּהַהִיא, בְּהַהּ קָאָמַר שְׁמוּאֵל, [8]אֲבָל בְּהָא, אֵימָא מוֹדֵי לֵיהּ לְרַב. [9]צְרִיכָא.

[10]״הַתַּלְמִידִים יוֹצְאִין לְתַלְמוּד, וכו׳״. [11]בִּרְשׁוּת, כַּמָּה? [12]כַּמָּה דְּבָעֵי.

LITERAL TRANSLATION

he must divorce [her] and pay [her] ketubah." [1]And Rav said: They only taught [this] where he specified, [2]but where [he vowed] without specifying, he must divorce [her] immediately and pay [her] ketubah. [3]But Shmuel said: Even where [he vowed] without specifying, he should also wait, in case he will find an opening for his vow.

[4]It was necessary, for if it had been stated about this, [I might have said that] about this Rav made his statement, because it cannot [be done] through an administrator. [5]But about that, where it can [be done] through an administrator, [6]I might say [that] he agrees with Shmuel. [7]And if it had been stated about that, [I might have said that] about that Shmuel made his statement, [8]but about this, I might say [that] he agrees with Rav. [9][Therefore both statements were] necessary.

[10]"Students may leave for the study, etc." [11]With permission, for how long?

[12]For as long as he wants.

RASHI

ואי אתמר בהא – מליהנות לו. **בהא אמר שמואל** – משום דאפשר בפרנס.

[62A] [1]אוֹרְחָא דְּמִילְּתָא כַּמָּה? [2]אָמַר רַב: חֹדֶשׁ כָּאן וְחֹדֶשׁ בַּבַּיִת, [3]שֶׁנֶּאֱמַר: ״לְכֹל דְּבַר הַמַּחְלְקוֹת, הַבָּאָה וְהַיֹּצֵאת חֹדֶשׁ בְּחֹדֶשׁ לְכֹל חָדְשֵׁי הַשָּׁנָה״. [4]וְרַבִּי יוֹחָנָן אָמַר: חֹדֶשׁ כָּאן וּשְׁנַיִם בְּבֵיתוֹ, [5]שֶׁנֶּאֱמַר: ״חֹדֶשׁ יִהְיוּ בַלְּבָנוֹן, שְׁנַיִם חֳדָשִׁים בְּבֵיתוֹ״.

LITERAL TRANSLATION

[62A] [1]How long is the usual period (lit., "way")? [2]Rav said: A month here and a month at home, [3]as it is said: "In any matter of the divisions, who came in and went out month by month throughout all the months of the year." [4]But Rabbi Yoḥanan said: A month here and two months in his home, [5]as it is said: "A month they were in Lebanon, and two months at home."

TRANSLATION AND COMMENTARY

אוֹרְחָא [62A] [1]The Gemara explains: The question is how a Rabbinic student should behave if he wishes to act in **the proper way** and not take advantage of his wife's readiness to release him from his marital duties. **For how long** may he absent himself from his home and still be considered to be treating his wife fairly?

אָמַר רַב [2]**Rav said:** A married Rabbinic student may stay **a month here** in the Talmudic Academy **and** then must spend **a month at home** with his wife. Support for this opinion may be found in **the verse** relating to King David's army, [3]which **says** (I Chronicles 27:1): **"In any matter of the divisions, who came in and went out month by month throughout all the months of the year."** This teaches us that these troops spent one month in King David's service and the next month at home. [4]**Rabbi Yoḥanan** disagreed with Rav and **said:** A Rabbinic student may stay **a month here** in the Talmudic Academy **but** must then spend **two months at home** with his wife. [5]This opinion is supported by **the verse** relating to the work rotation used in the construction of the Temple, which **says** (I Kings 5:28): **"A month they were in Lebanon, and two months at home."**

RASHI

אורחא דמילתא — דרך ארץ, שלא ישא עליו חטא, ואפילו הוא יכול לפתותה שתתן לו רשות. **לכל דבר המחלקות הבאה והיוצאת חדש בחדש** — בדברי הימים במחלקות שהיו עובדים את דוד כל מחלקות חדש. ואף על גב דמשמעותא דעניינא משמע שלא היה פורש מביתו אלא חדש אחד בשנה, ואין ללמוד משם אלא חדש כאן ואחד עשר חדשים בביתו — רב קרא יתירא ד״הבאה״ והיוצאת דריש, דהוה ליה למכתב: ״המשרתים את המלך לכל דבר המחלקות חדשי השנה״, וכתב ״דבר המחלקות הבאה והיוצאת חדש בחדש לכל חדשי השנה״ משמע שהיו שתי מחלקות נלבים ומשרתים, שמשרתים עם השאר, זו ששה חדשים בדילוג וזו ששה חדשים בדילוג. זו באה וזו יוצאה מדי חדש בחדש, הרי חדש בבית המלך וחדש בביתו. ואף כאן — חדש בבית רבו וחדש בביתו. **ושנים חדשים בביתו** — האיש בביתו. שהרי שלשים אלף איש היה המס ״וישלחם לבנונה עשרת אלפים בחדש״ כשמחליפים אלו הולכין עשרת אלפים אחרים, ובחדש השלישי עשרת אלפים שלישים. נמצא שעמדו הראשונים בביתם שני חדשים. וכן כולם בחלופיהם כך.

NOTES

אוֹרְחָא דְּמִילְּתָא כַּמָּה **How long is the usual period?** Our commentary follows *Rashi*, who explains the Gemara's question as follows: How should a Rabbinic student conduct himself if he wishes to act in the proper way, and not abuse his wife's readiness to release him from his marital duties?

Ra'ah understood the question differently: For how long may a Rabbinic student absent himself from his home in order to study Torah, if his wife has granted him permission to leave but has not specified for how long? What is the normal length of time that a woman is willing to allow her husband to stay away from home?

The Rishonim ask: If a Rabbinic student should not stay away from home for more than thirty days, even if he has secured his wife's permission, how can we understand the various anecdotes related in the Gemara about Rabbinic students who were absent from their homes for years?

Some suggest that the Gemara's discussion here follows the viewpoint of Rabbi Eliezer, whereas the Rabbinic scholars who stayed away from home for extended periods of time acted in accordance with the view of the Sages (see below, 62b). *Tosafot* argues that the law is different if it was stipulated at the time of the marriage that the husband would absent himself for an extended period in order to study Torah. *Rabbenu Yitzḥak* (cited by *Tosafot*) maintains that the Gemara here is referring to workers, not to Rabbinic students. A worker may not leave home for more than thirty days at a time, even if he has his wife's permission, but there is no such limit on a Rabbinic student who goes away to study Torah with his wife's blessing. *Ra'avad* (cited by *Rosh*) distinguishes between an ordinary Talmudic student and a distinguished scholar about whom it may be said that "the Torah is his profession."

לְכֹל דְּבַר הַמַּחְלְקוֹת **In any matter of the divisions.** *Rashi* and others point out that, according to the plain sense of the Biblical text, there were twelve divisions, each of which served the king for one month during the year. Thus, if anything can be learned from the verse regarding the proper conduct of a Rabbinic student, it is that he may stay away at the Academy for a month but must then spend the next eleven months at home with his wife. *Rashi* suggests that Rav adduces support for his position that the Rabbinic student may leave home again after a month from the unnecessary phrase, "who came in and went out month by month," which implies that in addition to the twelve divisions there were two other divisions which rotated month by month in the king's service.

Maharsha argues that Rav only meant to prove from the verse that a Rabbinic student may absent himself from his home for a month at a time and not be considered as someone who mistreats his wife. But he does not use the verse to rule on how much time he must spend with

TRANSLATION AND COMMENTARY

וְרַב נַמִי [1] The Gemara now wishes to clarify how each of these Amoraim, Rav and Rabbi Yoḥanan, explains the Biblical verse cited by the other. **As for Rav, why did he not say** that the period of time that a Rabbinic student may absent himself from his home can be derived **from** the verse cited by Rabbi Yoḥanan concerning King Solomon's workers?

שָׁאנֵי [2] The Gemara answers: **The** regulations governing the work schedule of those involved in the **construction of the Temple were different, for** there were so many people involved in the project that the work started by one group of workers **could be** continued **by another** group. But a person cannot study Torah by means of a surrogate. Thus a Rabbinic student may study for a month at the Academy, and may then spend only one month at home with his wife before he resumes his studies for another month.

וְרַבִּי יוֹחָנָן [3] The Gemara now turns its attention to **Rabbi Yoḥanan** and asks: **Why did he not say** that the period of time that a Rabbinic scholar may absent himself from home is inferred **from** the verse cited by Rav relating to King David's army?

שָׁאנֵי [4] The Gemara answers: **There**, with respect to King David's army, the situation **was different, for** each of the soldiers **benefited materially** from being in the king's employ. For this reason the wives of King David's men were willing to accept that their husbands should go away for another month's army duty after being at home for only one month. But the wife of a Rabbinic student does not benefit materially from her husband's absence from home. Thus she wants her husband to spend two months at home for each month that he spends at the Academy.

אָמַר רַב [5] Having cited the disagreement between Rav and Rabbi Yoḥanan about the period of time that a Rabbinic student may absent himself from his home, the Gemara continues with another dispute between these two Amoraim. **Rav said: The sigh** that accompanies the receiving of bad news **breaks half a person's body,** [6] **as the verse says** (Ezekiel 21:11): **"And you, son of man, sigh; with the breaking of your loins and**

[1] וְרַב נַמִי, מַאי טַעֲמָא לָא אֲמַר מֵהַהִיא? [2] שָׁאנֵי בִּנְיַן בֵּית הַמִּקְדָּשׁ, דְּאֶפְשָׁר עַל יְדֵי אֲחֵרִים. [3] וְרַבִּי יוֹחָנָן, מַאי טַעֲמָא לָא אֲמַר מֵהַהִיא? [4] שָׁאנֵי הָתָם, דְּאִית לֵיהּ הַרְוָוחָה. [5] אָמַר רַב: אֲנָחָה שׁוֹבֶרֶת חֲצִי גּוּפוֹ שֶׁל אָדָם, [6] שֶׁנֶּאֱמַר:

LITERAL TRANSLATION

[1] And Rav also, what is the reason that he did not derive (lit., "say") [it] from that?

[2] The building of the Temple is different, for it could be [done] by others.

[3] And Rabbi Yoḥanan, what is the reason that he did not derive [it] from that?

[4] There it is different, for he has a liberal provision.

[5] Rav said: A sigh breaks half of a man's body, [6] as it is said:

RASHI

שאפשר על ידי אחרים — לפי מנין החליפות כך היו עולים. **שאני התם דאית ליה הרווחה** — שהיו נהנים מבית המלך, ואיכא רווח ביתא, לפיכך מקבלת עליה, שיהיה בבית המלך [חדש] אחד משני חדשים, שכיון שיש לו שכר יש לה מזונות מרווחים ותכשיטין. אבל תלמוד תורה — מלוה דיליה הוא. **אנחה שוברת כו'** — איידי דאיפלגו בה רב ורבי יוחנן בדרשא דקרא, נקט לה נמי הכא.

BACKGROUND

אֲנָחָה שׁוֹבֶרֶת A sigh breaks. The Talmud does not seem to be referring here to the fatigue caused by sighing itself but rather to the mood that causes one to sigh. When a person is worried or distressed, and when he expresses his sadness physically with a deep sigh, this can have a harmful effect on his health. The Sages are informing us here, as did *Rambam* long afterwards in his medical treatises, about the psychosomatic effects of worry and grief, how they have a direct influence on a person's vitality, and how they can lead to grave physical disturbances.

NOTES

his wife before returning to the Academy. This he infers by analogy from the period of time that the husband may stay away at the Academy.

בִּנְיַן בֵּית הַמִּקְדָּשׁ The building of the Temple. The Jerusalem Talmud cites the same verse, "a month they were in Lebanon," in its discussion of the proper conduct to be expected from a Rabbinic student. As an aside, the Jerusalem Talmud proves from the verse how great is the duty of procreation, for King Solomon's workmen would interrupt their work on the construction of the Temple in order to go home and be with their wives.

דְּאִית לֵיהּ הַרְוָוחָה For he has a liberal provision. The Gemara is arguing that, according to Rabbi Yoḥanan, a wife will let her husband stay away for a long time if she stands to benefit materially from his absence. *Rivan* notes that Rabbi Yoḥanan must therefore reject what the Gemara says below (62b) that a woman prefers a *kav* and frivolity to ten *kav*s and abstinence — in other words, a woman would rather live a frugal life with her husband at home than enjoy a higher standard of living with her husband away. *Tosafot* reconciles the two passages, arguing that the situation of a woman whose husband is in the king's employ is different, for she stands to gain a great deal.

Rosh notes that *Remah* rules in accordance with Rabbi Yoḥanan, whose position is usually accepted against that of Rav. *Rosh* himself argues that since we are not dealing here with a matter of law, but only with an issue of proper behavior, we may follow the more lenient viewpoint of Rav. *Rambam,* who does not refer to the issue at all, apparently understood that Rabbi Yoḥanan and Rav were stating their views according to Rabbi Eliezer, but maintained that the law follows the opinion of the Sages that a Rabbinic student may leave home for the study of Torah for several years at a time without receiving his wife's permission (see below, 62b).

אֲנָחָה שׁוֹבֶרֶת A sigh breaks. *Rashi* explains that the discussion between Rav and Rabbi Yoḥanan regarding the injurious effects of a sigh was recorded here immediately after the dispute between these same two Amoraim

BACKGROUND

שָׁאנֵי שְׁמוּעָה דְּבֵית הַמִּקְדָּשׁ Tidings about the Temple are different. The destruction of the Second Temple by the Romans in 70 C.E. caused a severe spiritual crisis, for every Jew was deprived of the spiritual center to which he had turned and from which he had received support and assistance. Not only did the destruction change the Jewish way of life and the observance of the commandments, but people felt that the center of their lives had been cut off. Therefore, during the first generations after the destruction, reference to this event was an extremely grave matter, serving as a reminder of a general and individual disaster whose severity transcended the problems and concerns of the individual Jew.

TRANSLATION AND COMMENTARY

with bitterness you shall sigh before their eyes." This teaches us that a sigh breaks a person's body in half at the loins. [1] **Rabbi Yoḥanan** disagreed and **said:** A sigh **breaks a person's entire body,** [2] **as the** next **verse says** (Ezekiel 21:12): **"And it will be, when they say to you, Why do you sigh? then you will say, Because of the tidings, for it comes;** [3] **and every heart will melt, and all hands will be feeble, and every spirit will faint, and all knees will turn to water."** From this verse we can infer that bad tidings may cause a person's total physical collapse.

וְרַבִּי יוֹחָנָן נַמִי [4] The Gemara now tries to understand how each of these Sages explains the Biblical verse cited by the other. **Rabbi Yoḥanan** should **also** say that a sigh breaks half a person's body, [5] for **surely the verse says:** "Sigh... **with the breaking of your loins,"** but not with the breaking of the entire body!

הַהִיא [6] The Gemara reconciles the verse with Rabbi Yoḥanan's position: **That** verse teaches that **when** a sigh **starts** to affect a person, [7] **it starts from the loins.** But in the end its harmful effects reach the whole body.

וְרַב נַמִי [8] The Gemara now turns its attention to **Rav** with the following argument: He **too** should agree with Rabbi Yoḥanan, for **surely the verse says:** [9] **"And every heart will melt, and all hands will be feeble, and every spirit will faint,"** which implies that a sigh breaks a person's entire body!

שָׁאנֵי [10] The Gemara answers: That verse speaks of bad tidings about the destruction of the Temple. Bad **tidings about the Temple are different, for they** have a **very harsh** effect. A sigh that accompanies bad news about the Temple may cause a person's total physical collapse. But in most cases the injury that results from bad news is limited to half of a person's body.

הַהוּא [11] It was related that **a Jew and a non-Jew were** once **traveling on the road together,** [12] but **the non-Jew was unable to keep up with the Jew.** The non-Jew tried to slow the Jew down by distressing him, [13] and so **he reminded him about the destruction of the Temple.** [14] When he was reminded of the Temple's destruction, the Jew **became faint and sighed, but even so the non-Jew was unable to keep up with him.** [15] The non-Jew then **said to him: "Did your** Sages **not say that a sigh** that accompanies bad tidings **breaks**

"וְאַתָּה בֶן אָדָם, הֵאָנַח; בְּשִׁבְרוֹן מָתְנַיִם וּבִמְרִירוּת תֵּאָנַח". [1] וְרַבִּי יוֹחָנָן אָמַר: אַף כָּל גּוּפוֹ שֶׁל אָדָם, [2] שֶׁנֶּאֱמַר: "וְהָיָה כִּי יֹאמְרוּ אֵלֶיךָ, עַל מָה אַתָּה נֶאֱנָח? וְאָמַרְתָּ, אֶל שְׁמוּעָה, כִּי בָאָה; [3] וְנָמֵס כָּל לֵב, וְרָפוּ כָל יָדַיִם, וְכִהֲתָה כָל רוּחַ, וְכָל בִּרְכַּיִם תֵּלַכְנָה מַּיִם".

[4] וְרַבִּי יוֹחָנָן נַמִי, [5] הָכְתִיב: "בְּשִׁבְרוֹן מָתְנַיִם"!

[6] הַהִיא דְּכִי מַתְחָלָא, [7] מִמָּתְנַיִם מַתְחָלָא.

[8] וְרַב נַמִי, הָכְתִיב: [9] "וְנָמֵס כָּל לֵב, וְרָפוּ כָּל יָדַיִם, וְכִהֲתָה כָּל רוּחַ"!

[10] שָׁאנֵי שְׁמוּעָה דְּבֵית הַמִּקְדָּשׁ, דְּתַקִּיפָא טוּבָא.

[11] הַהוּא יִשְׂרָאֵל וְנָכְרִי דַּהֲווּ קָאָזְלֵי בְּאוֹרְחָא בַּהֲדֵי הֲדָדֵי. [12] לָא אִימְצֵי נָכְרִי לְסַגּוּיֵי בַּהֲדֵי יִשְׂרָאֵל. [13] אַדְכְּרֵיהּ חוּרְבַּן בֵּית הַמִּקְדָּשׁ. [14] נְגִיד וְאִיתְנַח, וַאֲפִילּוּ הָכִי לָא אִימְצֵי נָכְרִי לְסַגּוּיֵי בַּהֲדֵיהּ. [15] אֲמַר לֵיהּ:

LITERAL TRANSLATION

"And you, son of man, sigh; with the breaking of your loins and with bitterness you shall sigh [before their eyes]." [1] But Rabbi Yoḥanan said: [It] even [breaks] a man's entire body, [2] as it is said: "And it will be, when they say to you, Why do you sigh? then you will say, Because of the tidings, for it comes; [3] and every heart will melt, and all hands will be feeble, and every spirit will faint, and all knees will turn to water."

[4] And Rabbi Yoḥanan also, [5] surely it is written: "With the breaking of your loins"!

[6] That is because when it starts, [7] it starts from the loins.

[8] And Rav also, surely it is written: [9] "And every heart will melt, and all hands will be feeble, and every spirit will faint"!

[10] Tidings about the Temple are different, for they are very harsh.

[11] A Jew and a non-Jew were going on the road together. [12] The non-Jew was unable to keep up with the Jew. [13] He reminded him about the destruction of the Temple. [14] He became faint and sighed, but even so the non-Jew was unable to keep up with him. [15] He said to him:

RASHI

מתנים – כאמצע הגוף.

NOTES

regarding the length of time that a Rabbinic student may absent himself from his home, because regarding both matters the Amoraim disagree about the proper interpretation of Biblical texts. *Rabbi Ya'akov Emden* adds that the discussion regarding the injurious effects of bad news on a person's well-being is related to the previous passage in a more substantive way, for bad news can impair a person's sexual capacity.

"לָאו אָמְרִיתוּ אֲנָחָה שׁוֹבֶרֶת חֲצִי גּוּפוֹ שֶׁל אָדָם"? [1]אֲמַר לֵיהּ: "הָנֵי מִילֵּי מִילְּתָא חַדְתִּי, [2]אֲבָל הָא דִּשְׁנַן בָּהּ לָא, [3]דְּאָמְרִי אֱינָשֵׁי: [4]דְּמַלְפֵי תִּכְלֵי לָא בָּהֲתָה".

[5]"הַטַּיָּילִין בְּכָל יוֹם". [6]מַאי "טַיָּילִין"?

[7]אֲמַר רָבָא: בְּנֵי פִּירְקֵי.

[8]אֲמַר לֵיהּ אַבַּיֵי: מַאן דִּכְתִיב בְּהוּ: [9]"שָׁוְא לָכֶם מַשְׁכִּימֵי קוּם, מְאַחֲרֵי שֶׁבֶת, אֹכְלֵי לֶחֶם הָעֲצָבִים, כֵּן יִתֵּן לִידִידוֹ שֵׁנָא", [10]וְאָמַר רַב יִצְחָק: אֵלּוּ נְשׁוֹתֵיהֶן שֶׁל תַּלְמִידֵי חֲכָמִים שֶׁמְּנַדְּדוֹת שֵׁינָה מֵעֵינֵיהֶם

LITERAL TRANSLATION

"Do you not say [that] a sigh breaks half of a man's body?" [1]He said to him: "This applies (lit., 'these words') to a new thing, [2]but not to something with which we are familiar (lit., 'which we have repeated'), [3]as people say: [4]She who is accustomed to bereavement is not confounded." [5]"Men of leisure, every day." [6]What is [meant by] "*tayyalin*"? [7]Rava said: Those who study locally. [8]Abaye said to him: About whom is it written: [9]"It is vain for you that rise up early, that sit up late, that eat the bread of toil, for truly to His beloved He gives sleep," [10]and Rav Yitzḥak said: These are the wives of Rabbinic scholars who make sleep flee from their eyes

TRANSLATION AND COMMENTARY

half a person's body? Why, then, were you not physically affected by my mention of the destruction of the Temple?" [1]The Jew **said to him: "That** statement of our Sages **applies** only **to new** bad **tidings.** [2]**But** repeated mention of **something with which we are** already **familiar** does **not** have the same effect. [3]This corresponds to the idea expressed by **the popular proverb,** which **states:** [4]A woman **who is accustomed to the loss of her children is not confounded** when another of her children passes away. In similar fashion, a person who has become accustomed to a calamitous event does not break down every time it is mentioned."

הַטַּיָּילִין [5]The next clause of our Mishnah stated: **"Men of leisure,** who spend most of their time at home, are obliged to cohabit with their wives **every day."** [6]The Gemara asks: **What does** the Mishnah **mean** when it speaks of **"men of leisure"** (in Hebrew, טַיָּילִין — *tayyalin*)?

אֲמַר רָבָא [7]**Rava said:** The Mishnah is referring to **those** Rabbinic students **who study locally.** Since they return home every night to sleep in their own beds, they are obliged to cohabit with their wives every day.

אֲמַר לֵיהּ אַבַּיֵי [8]**Abaye** raised an objection against Rava's interpretation of the Mishnah and **said to him: About whom does the verse say** (Psalms 127:2): [9]**"It is vain for you that rise up early, that sit up late, that eat the bread of toil, for truly to His beloved He gives sleep"?** [10]Surely **Rav Yitzḥak said** that the verse is referring to **the wives of Rabbinic scholars who make sleep flee from their eyes in this world,** waiting up until late in the night for their husbands to return from their studies, for these women will surely **come to life in the World to Come.** Rav Yitzḥak understood the verse containing the expression, כֵּן יִתֵּן לִידִידוֹ שֵׁנָא, which is customarily translated as "for truly to His beloved He gives sleep," as meaning: It is vain for you — those who toil for a living — to rise up early in the morning and go out to work, or to stay up late at night to earn some extra money, for it is those who make sleep flee from their eyes — the wives of Rabbinic students who wait up late for their husbands (and certainly the Rabbinic students themselves) — whom God will reward in the World to Come. Rav Yitzḥak explained the word יְדִידוֹ as being derived

RASHI

דשנן בה — הורגלנו בה. כמו "כיון דדש דש" (גיטין נו,ב). **דמלפא תכלי לא בהתה** — אשה הלימודת לשכל בניה לקוברם אינה תמיהה ומפחדת במות אחד מהם, שכבר לימודת. **בני פירקי** — תלמידים שהרב מצוי להם בעירן, ושונים פרקם, ולנים בביתם. **מאן דכתיב בהן** — בשבילם נאמר לבעלי אומניות. **שוא לכם משכימי קום מאחרי שבת** — למלאכת הרשות, אוכלי לחם בעצב — "כן יתן" הקדוש ברוך הוא "לידידו שנא" — למי שמנדד לכבודו ולמצותו שינה. **מנדדות שינה** — ממתינות את בעליהן שהן בבית רבם ושונים פירקם. אלמא, בשעת שינה עודן בבית רבן. ואת אמרת יש להן פנאי לעונה בכל לילה!

LANGUAGE

בָּהֲתָה Confounded. *Arukh* explains this as "embarrassed." Rashi, however, interprets this word as "confounded and frightened."

NOTES

בְּנֵי פִּירְקֵי Those who study locally. A similar suggestion is found in the Jerusalem Talmud, that a Rabbinic student should be treated as a man of leisure who is obligated to cohabit with his wife every day. The Jerusalem Talmud rejects the suggestion, arguing that, on the contrary, intensive Torah study is so gruelling that by the end of the day a Rabbinic student is too exhausted to engage in sexual relations with his wife.

HALAKHAH

הַטַּיָּילִין בְּכָל יוֹם Men of leisure, every day. "Healthy men who do not work and have no public responsibilities are obliged to cohabit with their wives every day." (*Rambam, Sefer Nashim, Hilkhot Ishut* 14:1; *Shulḥan Arukh, Even HaEzer* 76:1.)

LANGUAGE

פְּרִיסְתָּקָא Officer. From the Middle Persian *frestak*, meaning "courier" or "messenger" sent to collect taxes and the like.

BACKGROUND

אִיפְּחִית בֵּי בָּאנֵי The bathhouse collapsed. Large bathhouses in Talmudic times were modeled on those built by the Romans. Upstairs was a big pool where people bathed, and downstairs was a room used to heat the water. Sometimes the heat and the weight of the water on the upper floor caused it to collapse into the room below.

TRANSLATION AND COMMENTARY

from the root נדד meaning "to drive away sleep." Thus, continues Abaye, it seems that Rabbinic students, even those who study in a local Academy, keep very long hours and are ordinarily absent from their homes. [1]How then can **you**, Rava, **say** that when the Mishnah speaks of "men of leisure," it is referring to **those** Rabbinic students **who study locally?**

אֶלָּא [2]**Rather, said Abaye,** The Mishnah should be understood **as Rav explained** it, [3]**for Rav said:** When the Mishnah speaks of "men of leisure," it refers to people who earn a comfortable living without having to engage in difficult physical labor. It speaks of a person **like Rav Shmuel bar Shilat,** a well-known schoolteacher, who earned enough to maintain himself, [4]and could afford to **eat and drink of his own** earnings, **and sleep under the roof of his** own **house,** [5]**but** lived so modestly that **a royal agent never passed** through **his door** to collect taxes from him. Such a person, who stays at home and does not have to worry about his finances, is obligated to cohabit with his wife every day.

כִּי אֲתָא רָבִין [6]**When Ravin came** to Babylonia from Eretz Israel, **he said:** When the Mishnah speaks of "men of leisure," [7]it is referring to people **like the gentlemen** who live **in Eretz Israel.** Such people maintain themselves in good physical condition. Since they are so strong in body, they are obligated to fulfill their marital duty every day.

רַבִּי אַבָּהוּ [8]The Gemara now recounts two anecdotes illustrating the physical prowess of those living in Eretz Israel. It was related that **Rabbi Abbahu was** once **standing in the bathhouse, and two servants were** there with him **supporting him** as he walked about. [9]Suddenly, the floor of **the bathhouse collapsed under** Rabbi Abbahu, and he and the two servants fell into the cavity under the floor through which the water flowed. [10]**There happened to be a pillar close by, and** Rabbi Abbahu **climbed** up holding on to the pillar with one hand, and **pulled up** the two servants with the other. [11]Similarly, it was related that **Rabbi Yoḥanan was**

בָּעוֹלָם הַזֶּה, וּבָאוֹת לְחַיֵּי הָעוֹלָם הַבָּא, [1]וְאַתְּ אָמְרַתְּ: בְּנֵי פִּירְקֵי?!

[2]אֶלָּא, אֲמַר אַבַּיֵי: כִּדְרַב, [3]דַּאֲמַר רַב: כְּגוֹן רַב שְׁמוּאֵל בַּר שִׁילַת, [4]דְּאָכֵיל מִדִּידֵיהּ וְשָׁתֵי מִדִּידֵיהּ, וְגָנֵי בְּטוּלָּא דְּאַפַּדְנֵיהּ, [5]וְלָא חָלֵיף פְּרִיסְתָּקָא דְּמַלְכָּא אַבָּבֵיהּ.

[6]כִּי אֲתָא רָבִין, אֲמַר: [7]כְּגוֹן מְפַנְּקֵי דְּמַעֲרָבָא.

[8]רַבִּי אַבָּהוּ הֲוָה קָאֵי בֵּי בָּאנֵי, הָווּ סָמְכֵי לֵיהּ תְּרֵי עַבְדֵי. [9]אִיפְּחִית בֵּי בָּאנֵי מִתּוּתֵיהּ. [10]אִיתְרְמִי לֵיהּ עַמּוּדָא, סָלֵיק וְאַסְקִינְהוּ. [11]רַבִּי יוֹחָנָן הֲוָה

LITERAL TRANSLATION

in this world, and come to the life of the World to Come, [1]and you say: Those who study locally?!

[2]Rather, Abaye said: [It is] as Rav [said], [3]for Rav said: Like Rav Shmuel bar Shilat, [4]who eats of his own and drinks of his own, and sleeps in the shade of his palace, [5]and an officer of the king never passes his door.

[6]When Ravin came, he said: [7]Like the gentlemen of Eretz Israel (lit., "the west").

[8]Rabbi Abbahu was standing in the bathhouse, [and] two servants were supporting him. [9]The bathhouse collapsed under him. [10]A pillar happened [to be close] to him, [and] he climbed [it] and pulled them up. [11]Rabbi Yoḥanan was

RASHI

רב שמואל בר שילת — מלמד תינוקות היה, ומתפרנס מהן. כדאמרינן ב"נערה שנתפתתה" (לעיל כתובות נ,א). **ולא חליף פריסתקא דמלכא אבביה** — אין שליח מלך פרס עובר על פתחו לשאול לו עבודת המלך. שאין עין המלך עליו, שאינו עשיר בעיניהם. **מפנקי דמערבא** — בני ארץ ישראל מעונגים במאכל ומשתה, לכך הם בריאים ובעלי כח לתשמיש. **איפחית בי באני** — תחת המרחצאות יש חלל שהמים נופלים שם. **אסקינהו** — העלה את העבדים בידו אחת, ובשניה היה מטפס ועולה בעמוד.

NOTES

כְּגוֹן רַב שְׁמוּאֵל בַּר שִׁילַת Like Rav Shmuel bar Shilat. Elsewhere (above, 50a), the Gemara says that Rav Shmuel bar Shilat was a schoolteacher. *Rashi* explains that Rav Shmuel bar Shilat was able to support himself from the tuition fees he received from his students. A royal agent never passed through his door to collect taxes from him, because the authorities did not think of him as a wealthy man. Such a person, argued Rav, is obligated to cohabit with his wife every night.

Talmidei Rabbenu Yonah asks: How could anyone imagine that a person who ekes out a living teaching Torah to young children falls under the category of "a man of leisure"? Rather, Rav Shmuel bar Shilat was independently wealthy and volunteered his services as a teacher. A royal agent never passed through his door because, being a Rabbinic scholar, Rav Shmuel bar Shilat was exempt from paying taxes. Rav argued that since Rav Shmuel bar Shilat did not become a teacher to earn a living, but rather because he enjoyed being involved in sacred work, he may indeed be treated as a man of leisure who is obligated to cohabit with his wife every night.

A number of authorities maintain that Rav could not have meant that Rav Shmuel bar Shilat was obligated to cohabit with his wife every day, for he was a Rabbinic scholar who is obligated to engage in sexual relations once a week on Friday night. Rather, Rav cited Rav Shmuel bar Shilat as an example of a person who is not involved in difficult work (*Bnei Ahuvah*, *Ayelet Ahavim*).

TRANSLATION AND COMMENTARY

once **going up** a flight of **stairs, and Rav Ammi and Rav Assi were** directly behind him, **supporting him** as he went up the stairs. [1]Suddenly, **the stairs collapsed under** Rabbi Yoḥanan. **He** managed to **climb up, and** he **pulled** the others **up** with him. [2]**The Rabbis said to** Rabbi Yoḥanan: **"Now that** you have demonstrated how strong you really are, **why do you need to be supported** as you climb up the stairs?" [3]Rabbi Yoḥanan **said to them:** "I prefer to conserve my strength and allow myself to be assisted by others, for **if** I use up all of my vigor now, **what** strength **will I leave for my old age?"**

וְהַפּוֹעֲלִים [4]The Gemara now proceeds to the next clause of our Mishnah, which stated: **"Workers** are obligated to cohabit with their wives **twice a week."** [5]The Gemara asks: **But surely it was taught** in a Baraita: **"Workers** are obligated to engage in sexual relations with their wives **once a week"!**

אָמַר רַבִּי יוֹסֵי בְּרַבִּי חֲנִינָא [6]Rabbi Yose the son of Rabbi Ḥanina said: **There is no difficulty** in reconciling this seeming contradiction, because the two sources deal with different cases. [7]**Here** in the Mishnah we are dealing with workers **who work in their** home **town.** [8]But **there** in the Baraita we are dealing with workers **who work in another town.** Such workers usually return home only once a week, and their conjugal obligations are reduced accordingly.

תַּנְיָא [9]The Gemara notes that **the same** distinction **was also taught** in another Baraita, which stated: **"Workers** are obliged to cohabit with their wives **twice a week.** [10]**When does this apply?** [11]**When** the workers **work in their** home **town.** [12]**But when they work in another town,** they are obligated to cohabit with their wives **once a week."**

קָסָלֵיק בְּדַרְגָּא, הֲווֹ סָמְכֵי לֵיהּ רַב אַמֵּי וְרַב אַסִּי. [1]אִיפַּחְתָּא דַּרְגָּא תּוּתֵיהּ. סָלֵיק וְאַסְּקִינְהוּ. [2]אָמְרִי לֵיהּ רַבָּנַן: ״וְכִי מֵאַחַר דְּהָכִי, לָמָּה לֵיהּ לְמִיסְמְכֵיהּ?״ [3]אֲמַר לְהוּ: ״אִם כֵּן, מָה אַנִּיחַ לְעֵת זִקְנָה?״

[4]״וְהַפּוֹעֲלִים, שְׁתַּיִם בְּשַׁבָּת״. [5]וְהָתַנְיָא: ״הַפּוֹעֲלִים, אַחַת בְּשַׁבָּת״!

[6]אָמַר רַבִּי יוֹסֵי בְּרַבִּי חֲנִינָא: לָא קַשְׁיָא. [7]כָּאן בְּעוֹשִׂין מְלָאכָה בְּעִירָן, [8]כָּאן בְּעוֹשִׂין מְלָאכָה בְּעִיר אַחֶרֶת.

[9]תַּנְיָא נַמִי הָכִי: ״הַפּוֹעֲלִים, שְׁתַּיִם בְּשַׁבָּת. [10]בַּמֶּה דְּבָרִים אֲמוּרִים? [11]בְּעוֹשִׂין מְלָאכָה בְּעִירָן. [12]אֲבָל בְּעוֹשִׂין מְלָאכָה בְּעִיר אַחֶרֶת, אַחַת בְּשַׁבָּת״.

LITERAL TRANSLATION

going up stairs, [and] Rav Ammi and Rav Assi were supporting him. [1]The stairs collapsed under him. He climbed up, and pulled them up. [2]The Rabbis said to him: "Now since this is so, why do you (lit., 'does he') need to be supported?" [3]He said to them: "If so, what will I leave for [my] old age?"

[4]"And workers, twice a week." [5]But surely it was taught: "Workers, once a week"!

[6]Rabbi Yose the son of Rabbi Ḥanina said: There is no difficulty. [7]Here [it is] where they do work in their town, [8]here [it is] where they do work in another town.

[9]It was also taught thus: "Workers, twice a week. [10]In what [case] are these things said? [11]When they do work in their town. [12]But when they do work in another town, once a week."

RASHI

מאחר דהכי – שבעל כח אתה. **אם כן** – שאתיש את כחי, ולא יסמכוני. **מה אניח** – כח בעצמי להשתמש בו לעת זקנה. **בעירם** – שתים בשבת.

NOTES

וְהָתַנְיָא: ״הַפּוֹעֲלִים, אַחַת בְּשַׁבָּת״ But surely it was taught: "Workers, once a week." The Rishonim ask: Why does the Gemara not object to the Mishnah's ruling that a worker must cohabit with his wife twice a week from another ruling found in the very same Mishnah, that a worker may leave town without his wife's permission for a week at a time? They answer that the earlier clause of the Mishnah is not relevant, for it refers to a case in which the worker deviates from his usual behavior and leaves town without his wife's permission. But as long as the worker is at home, his conjugal obligation remains twice a week. Therefore the Gemara asks its question from the Baraita, which teaches that a worker's conjugal obligation is only once a week (*Tosafot*, *Ra'ah* and *Ritva*; see also Jerusalem Talmud).

HALAKHAH

וְהַפּוֹעֲלִים And workers. "A worker who works in his home town is obligated to cohabit with his wife twice a week, but one who works in another town is obligated to cohabit with his wife only once a week. *Rema* notes that some authorities (*Rabbenu Yitzḥak the son of Rabbi Barukh*, cited by *Tosafot*) maintain that this applies only if the worker returns home every night. But if the worker does not sleep at home every night, he is obligated to cohabit with his wife only once every eight days." (*Rambam, Sefer Nashim, Hilkhot Ishut* 14:1; *Shulḥan Arukh, Even HaEzer* 76:2.)

TERMINOLOGY

איכפל תנא Did the Tanna go to the trouble. This expression appears in several places in the Talmud. It means that the Gemara considers it unreasonable for a Mishnah to describe a Halakhah in general terms when it refers to a very specific and unusual situation. The word איכפל literally means "doubled-up," or "bent over," and implies that the Tanna was pressed and forced to do something.

TRANSLATION AND COMMENTARY

הַחַמָּרִים [1] We learned in the next clause of the Mishnah: **"Ass drivers** are obligated to engage in sexual relations with their wives **once a week.** Camel drivers and sailors are obligated to cohabit with their wives even less frequently." [2] **Rabbah bar Rav Ḥanan said to Abaye:** In the first part of the Mishnah, the Tanna recorded the viewpoint of Bet Hillel that if a person forbids himself by a vow from sexual relations with his wife, he must take steps to release himself from the vow within a week or grant her a divorce. It stands to reason that the husband cannot be compelled to divorce his wife before his vow actually interferes with his wife's conjugal rights. But often it does not interfere with his wife's conjugal rights at all, for in many cases the husband's conjugal obligation is less than once a week. [3] **Did the Tanna go to the trouble of teaching us** a law which applies only to **a man of leisure or** to **a worker** who works in his home town, both of whom are obligated to cohabit with their wives twice a week?

אָמַר לֵיהּ [4] Abaye **said to** Rabbah bar Rav Ḥanan: **No,** the Mishnah's ruling about the husband who took a vow forbidding himself from sexual relations with his wife is not limited to a man of leisure or to someone who works in his home town. [62B] [5] **It applies to all of** the people mentioned in the Mishnah, even those whose conjugal obligation is less frequent than once a week. Even if the husband's vow does not actually interfere with his wife's conjugal rights, nevertheless since he took a vow forbidding himself from having sexual relations with her, he can be compelled to divorce her after a week has passed.

וְהָא "שִׁשָּׁה חֳדָשִׁים" קָאָמַר [6] The Gemara objects: **But surely** the Tanna of our Mishnah **said:** "Sailors, who are away from home for extended periods of time, are required to have sexual relations with their wives once in **six months."** Why, then, should a sailor who forbids himself by a vow from enjoying sexual relations with his wife be compelled to divorce her after the first week?

[1] "הַחַמָּרִים, אַחַת בְּשַׁבָּת". [2] אֲמַר לֵיהּ רַבָּה בַּר רַב חָנָן לְאַבַּיֵי: [3] אִיכְּפַל תַּנָּא לְאַשְׁמוּעִינַן טַיָּיל וּפוֹעֵל? [4] אֲמַר לֵיהּ: לָא. [62B] [5] אַכּוּלְּהוּ. [6] וְהָא "שִׁשָּׁה חֳדָשִׁים" קָאָמַר!

LITERAL TRANSLATION

[1] "Ass drivers, once a week." [2] Rabbah bar Rav Ḥanan said to Abaye: [3] Did the Tanna go to the trouble of teaching us [about] a man of leisure and a worker?

[4] He said to him: No. [62B] [5] [It applies] to all of them.

[6] But surely it says: "Six months"!

RASHI

איכפל תנא לאשמועינן טייל ופועל – תנא דסתם לעיל: המדיר את אשתו, בית הלל אומרים שבת אחת – אין לו לומר זאת לא בספן ולא בגמל ולא בחמר ולא בתלמידי חכמים, שהרי [אף החמר] עונתו אחת בשבת, ובשביל יום אחד יוציא ויתן כתובה? הרי עונתו משבעה לשבעה, וכל שכן גמל וספן. אין בכלל הזה אלא טייל ופועל העושה מלאכה בעירו, שדרכו לשמש שתים בשבת. **אבולהו** – נמי קאמר, דעל ידי נדר יותר משבת אחת – לא. **והא** – בלא נדר ששה חדשים קאמר בספנים.

NOTES

לְאַשְׁמוּעִינַן טַיָּיל וּפוֹעֵל Of teaching us about a man of leisure and a worker. The Rishonim ask: Why does the Gemara not include an ass driver in this list, for an ass driver is obligated to engage in sexual relations with his wife once a week, and a vow forbidding him from engaging in sexual relations with his wife interferes with his wife's conjugal rights during the first week after he makes the vow?

Rivan argues that an ass driver is indeed included here under the category of a worker. *Rashi* argues that it stands to reason that the husband cannot be compelled to divorce his wife if his vow interferes with his wife's conjugal rights for just one day. The Geonim explain that since an ass driver is required to cohabit with his wife only once a week, he can fulfill his obligation at the conclusion of the week, and so a vow forbidding him to cohabit with his wife will not interfere with her conjugal rights during the first week after he makes such a vow.

וְהָא "שִׁשָּׁה חֳדָשִׁים" קָאָמַר! But surely it says: "Six months"! The Gemara could equally have asked its question regarding a camel driver, whose conjugal obligation is once in thirty days. But it chose to use the example of a sailor, because here the difficulty is even more pronounced, for a sailor's conjugal obligation is once in six months (*Rivan*).

HALAKHAH

אַכּוּלְּהוּ To all of them. "If someone forbids himself by a vow from cohabiting with his wife, whether he took the vow without specifying the period for which sexual relations would be forbidden or whether he took a vow forbidding cohabitation for seven days or more, we wait seven days, after which he must either seek a release from his vow or grant his wife an immediate divorce and pay her her ketubah. This ruling applies in all cases, even if the husband is a sailor whose conjugal obligation is once in six months," following Abaye. (*Rambam, Sefer Nashim, Hilkhot Ishut* 14:6; *Shulḥan Arukh, Even HaEzer* 76:9.)

[1] אֵינוֹ דּוֹמֶה מִי שֶׁיֵּשׁ לוֹ פַּת בְּסַלּוֹ לְמִי שֶׁאֵין לוֹ פַּת בְּסַלּוֹ. [2] אֲמַר לֵיהּ רַבָּה בַּר רַב חָנָן לְאַבַּיֵי: חַמָּר וְנַעֲשֶׂה גַּמָּל, מַאי? [3] אֲמַר לֵיהּ: רוֹצָה אִשָּׁה בְּקַב וְתִיפְלוּת מֵעֲשָׂרָה קַבִּין וּפְרִישׁוּת. [4] ״הַסַּפָּנִים, אַחַת לְשִׁשָּׁה חֳדָשִׁים. [5] דִּבְרֵי רַבִּי אֱלִיעֶזֶר״. [6] אָמַר רַב בְּרוֹנָא אָמַר רַב: הֲלָכָה כְּרַבִּי אֱלִיעֶזֶר. [7] אָמַר רַב אַדָּא בַּר אַהֲבָה אָמַר רַב:

LITERAL TRANSLATION

[1] One who has bread in his basket is not like one who does not have bread in his basket.

[2] Rabbah bar Rav Ḥanan said to Abaye: [If] an ass driver became a camel driver, what [is the law]?

[3] He said to him: A woman prefers a *kav* and frivolity to ten *kabbin* and abstinence.

[4] "Sailors, once in six months. [5] [These are] the words of Rabbi Eliezer." [6] Rav Brona said in the name of Rav: The Halakhah is in accordance with Rabbi Eliezer. [7] Rav Adda bar Ahavah said in the name of Rav:

TRANSLATION AND COMMENTARY

אֵינוֹ דּוֹמֶה [1] The Gemara answers with a proverb: It is well known that **someone who** is fasting and **has** a loaf of **bread** ready for him **in his basket is not like someone who** is fasting and **does not have** a loaf of **bread** ready for him **in his basket.** It is comforting to know that one has food at hand. Similarly, a woman who is forced to abstain from sexual relations because her husband's occupation keeps him away from home for extended periods of time, but who always harbors the hope that her husband may return earlier than expected and cohabit with her, suffers far less from the lack of sexual relations than a woman who is forced to abstain because her husband has forbidden himself by a vow from cohabiting with her. Thus a husband who takes such a vow can be compelled to divorce his wife after the first week.

אֲמַר לֵיהּ [2] The Gemara continues: **Rabbah bar Rav Ḥanan said to Abaye: What is the law** regarding a man who was **an ass driver** when he married but now wants to change his work and **become a camel driver?** A camel driver earns more money than an ass driver, but has to be absent from home for longer periods of time. May a husband make a career change without his wife's permission in order to better his financial situation, if that change will reduce his conjugal obligation?

אֲמַר לֵיהּ [3] Abaye **said to** Rabbah bar Rav Ḥanan: **A woman prefers a** ***kav*** **and frivolity to ten** ***kabbin*** **and abstinence.** A woman would rather be poor and enjoy frequent sexual intercourse with her husband than be rich and be without him. So he cannot change his work without her permission.

הַסַּפָּנִים, אַחַת לְשִׁשָּׁה חֳדָשִׁים [4] The final sentence of our Mishnah stated: **"Sailors,** who are away from home for extended periods of time, are required to have sexual relations with their wives **once in six months.** [5] **These are** the husband's marital duties according to **the viewpoint of Rabbi Eliezer."** [6] **Rav Brona said in the name of Rav: The Halakhah is in accordance with** the viewpoint of **Rabbi Eliezer.** [7] **Rav Adda bar Ahavah**

RASHI

אינו דומה – לענין תענית מי שיש לו כו׳ – אף כאן, בלא נדר דעתה נוחה לבעלה, שמא יבא בתוך הזמן. אבל זו, משהדירה הרי היא כמי שאינה מלפה לבעל. **חמור ונעשה גמל מאי** – נישאת לו כשהוא חמר. מהו ליעשות גמל שלא ברשות? הרווחה עדיפא לה שיתעשר, או עונה עדיפא לה? **בקב ותיפלות** – להיות בעלה עמה. **מעשרה קבין** – להתעשר. **דברי רבי אליעזר** – אמתניתין קאי. וסיפא דמתניתין נקיט.

SAGES

רַבָּה בַּר רַב חָנָן Rabbah bar Rav Ḥanan. He is occasionally called Rava (רָבָא) bar Rav Ḥanan, for both the names Rabbah and Rava are abbreviations of Rav Abba. He was a Babylonian Amora of the fourth generation. He and Abaye studied together under the great Amora Rabbah (bar Naḥmani). Rabbah bar Rav Ḥanan is quoted on many occasions in the Talmud as a colleague of Abaye and also of Rava. He lived in or near Pumbedita and earned his living as a farmer.

רַב בְּרוֹנָא Rav Brona. A Babylonian Amora of the second generation, Rav Brona was a disciple of Rav and transmitted several rulings in the name of his teacher. He was a close friend of the Palestinian Amora Rabbi Elazar (ben Pedat).

NOTES

קַב וְתִיפְלוּת A *kav* and frivolity. The word תִּיפְלוּת in Rabbinic literature usually means "frivolity," and is used in the sense of sexual license. A number of Rishonim (*Rivan, Talmidei Rabbenu Yonah*) explain that the word here has the same meaning as טִיפְלוּת, which means "dependence" or "attachment," and some manuscripts actually have that reading. A woman prefers to live a more frugal life and to be attached to and dependent on a husband who is always with her than to live a more extravagant life alone and separated from her husband.

מֵעֲשָׂרָה קַבִּין To ten *kabbin*. Many Rishonim and Talmudic manuscripts have the reading "nine *kabbin*." Whether the text reads nine or ten, the number seems to be a mere figure of speech without any specific significance. As *Rav Hai Gaon* writes in his *Sefer Mikkaḥ U'Mimkar,* the Rabbis used the number nine, and especially the term "nine *kabbin,*" as a hyperbolic expression indicating a large number or quantity (much as the number "seven" is used in the Bible). But other Geonim and *Arukh* (cited by *Tosafot* and other Rishonim) explain that the number nine is used here in its literal sense. For later in the chapter (below, 64b) we learn that if a husband is supporting his wife

HALAKHAH

חַמָּר וְנַעֲשֶׂה גַּמָּל If an ass driver became a camel driver. "A woman may object to her husband changing his line of work, even if he will earn more from his new job, if the change will reduce his conjugal obligation," following Abaye. (*Rambam, Sefer Nashim, Hilkhot Ishut* 14:2; *Shulḥan Arukh, Even HaEzer* 76:5.)

SAGES

רַב רְחוּמִי **Rav Reḥumi.** A Babylonian Amora of the fifth generation, Rav Reḥumi was a student of Abaye and Rava, and he is mentioned in several places of the Talmud discussing Halakhah with Abaye.

TRANSLATION AND COMMENTARY

said in the name of Rav: The various regulations recorded in the Mishnah were stated in accordance with **the viewpoint of Rabbi Eliezer.** [1]**But the Sages** disagree with Rabbi Eliezer and **say:** Married Rabbinic **students may leave to study Torah** in another town **for** up to **two or three years** at a time **without** their wives' **permission.**

אָמַר רָבָא [2]**Rava said: The Rabbis relied on** the opinion of **Rav Adda bar Ahavah** that Rabbinic students are allowed to leave their homes for the purpose of study for two or three years at a time even without their wives' permission, **and they themselves followed this viewpoint** in actual practice. But this practice sometimes led to tragedies, [3]**as happened in the case of Rav Reḥumi, who studied with Rava in Meḥoza.** [4]Rav Reḥumi **was accustomed to** spending all his time in the Academy with his teacher, and **going home** once a year **on the eve of Yom Kippur.** [5]**On one occasion his studies** so **engrossed** his attention that he stayed in the Academy later than usual, and he was unable to reach his home before Yom Kippur for his annual visit. [6]But **his wife kept looking out for him, saying: "Now he must** surely **be coming, now he must** surely **be coming,"** until in the end she realized that **he was not coming.** [7]**She became** so **distressed and** disappointed that **tears came to her eyes.** [8]At that very moment, her husband Rav Reḥumi **was sitting on a roof, and the roof collapsed under him, and he died.**

זוֹ דִּבְרֵי רַבִּי אֱלִיעֶזֶר, [1]אֲבָל חֲכָמִים אוֹמְרִים: הַתַּלְמִידִים יוֹצְאִין לְתַלְמוּד תּוֹרָה שְׁתַּיִם וְשָׁלֹשׁ שָׁנִים שֶׁלֹּא בִּרְשׁוּת. [2]אָמַר רָבָא: סָמְכוּ רַבָּנַן אַדְּרַב אַדָּא בַּר אַהֲבָה וְעָבְדֵי עוּבְדָא בְּנַפְשַׁיְיהוּ. [3]כִּי הָא דְּרַב רְחוּמִי הֲוָה שְׁכִיחַ קַמֵּיהּ דְּרָבָא בִּמְחוֹזָא. [4]הֲוָה רָגִיל דַּהֲוָה אָתֵי לְבֵיתֵיהּ כָּל מַעֲלֵי [5]יוֹמָא דְּכִיפּוּרֵי. יוֹמָא חַד מְשַׁכְתֵּיהּ שְׁמַעְתָּא. [6]הֲוָה מְסַכְיָא דְּבֵיתְהוּ: "הָשְׁתָּא אָתֵי, הָשְׁתָּא אָתֵי", לָא אֲתָא. [7]חֲלַשׁ דַּעְתָּהּ, אַחֵית דִּמְעֲתָא מֵעֵינָהּ. [8]הֲוָה יָתֵיב בְּאִיגְּרָא, אִפְּחִית אִיגְּרָא מִתּוּתֵיהּ, וְנָח נַפְשֵׁיהּ.

LITERAL TRANSLATION

These are the words of Rabbi Eliezer, [1]but the Sages say: Students may leave for the study of Torah [for] two or three years without permission. [2]Rava said: The Rabbis relied on Rav Adda bar Ahavah and acted [in this way] for themselves. [3]As [happened in the case] of Rav Reḥumi [who] was in regular attendance before Rava in Meḥoza. [4]He was accustomed to go to his house every eve of Yom Kippur. [5]One day his studies engrossed him. [6]His wife was looking out [for him, saying]: "Now he is coming, now he is coming," [but] he did not come. [7]She became distressed [and] shed a tear from her eye. [8]He was sitting on a roof, [and] the roof collapsed under him, and he died.

RASHI

זו דברי רבי אליעזר — הנך עונות ויציאות שלא ברשות דמתניתין, דקתני: התלמידים יוצאים לתלמוד תורה שלא ברשות שלשים יום. **סמכו רבנן** — תלמידים שבדורנו סומכים על דבריו, ויוצאין שלא ברשות. **ועבדי עובדא** — כוותיה. **בנפשייהו** — והוא בא להם ליטול מהם נפשות, שנענשים ומתים. **מסכיא** — תרגום של מצפה.

NOTES

through a third party, he must provide her with two *kabbin* of wheat a week and must cohabit with her once a week on Friday night. And we learn elsewhere (below, 63a) that if a husband rebels against his wife, and refuses to engage in sexual relations with her, he is made to pay three dinarim a week, a sum that buys eighteen *kabbin* of wheat. Thus it turns out that a woman who is denied her conjugal rights is given nine *kabbin* for every *kav* received by a woman who has sexual relations with her husband.

וְעָבְדֵי עוּבְדָא בְּנַפְשַׁיְיהוּ **And acted in this way for themselves.** *Rashi* and *Rivan* explain the term בְּנַפְשַׁיְיהוּ as meaning "with their lives." The Rabbis acted in accordance with the viewpoint of the Sages, leaving their homes for extended periods in order to study Torah, and thereby placed themselves in mortal danger, as is evidenced by the case involving Rav Reḥumi. *Rid* explains that Rava's purpose was to condemn the practice, and therefore he concludes that the law is not in accordance with the viewpoint of Rav Adda bar Ahavah.

Rambam (*Hilkhot Ishut* 14:2) rules that the law follows the viewpoint of Rav Adda bar Ahavah, and most authorities agree. They apparently understood that Rava meant to inform us that the Rabbis accepted the viewpoint of Rav Adda bar Ahavah in actual practice. *Talmidei Rabbi Yonah* adds that the Gemara relates the story regarding Rav Reḥumi in order to teach us that although a Rabbinic scholar is entitled to leave home for two or three years for the study of Torah, even without his wife's permission, he should always consider how she feels about his prolonged absence; and if he fails to do so, he is liable to suffer divine punishment for the pain he causes her.

HALAKHAH

הַתַּלְמִידִים יוֹצְאִין **Students may leave.** "Rabbinic scholars may move to another town for the study of Torah for up to two or three years at a time without their wives' permission, following Rav Adda bar Ahavah. *Rema* adds that a Rabbinic scholar may stay at the Academy for as long as his wife permits him to be away from home." (*Rambam, Sefer Nashim, Hilkhot Ishut* 14:2; *Shulḥan Arukh, Even HaEzer* 76:5.)

TRANSLATION AND COMMENTARY

עוֹנָה שֶׁל תַּלְמִידֵי חֲכָמִים אֵימַת [1] The Gemara asks: **What are the conjugal obligations of Rabbinic scholars?**

אָמַר רַב יְהוּדָה [2] **Rav Yehudah said in the name of Shmuel:** A Rabbinic scholar should engage in sexual relations with his wife once a week **on Friday night.**

אֲשֶׁר פִּרְיוֹ יִתֵּן בְּעִתּוֹ [3] The same idea was expressed in connection with the following verse (Psalms 1:3): "And he shall be like a tree planted by streams of water, **that brings forth its fruit in its season."** [4] **Rav Yehudah said and some say** that **it was Rav Huna,** [5] **and some say** that **it was Rav Naḥman: This** verse **refers to someone who has sexual relations** with his wife once a week **on Friday night.**

יְהוּדָה בְּרֵיהּ דְּרַבִּי חִיָּיא [6] It was related that **Yehudah** who was **the son of Rabbi Ḥiyya and the son-in-law of Rabbi Yannai would go and sit in the Academy** all week long, studying Torah with his teacher, [7] **and every Friday evening at dusk he would come home** and visit his wife. [8] **Whenever** Yehudah **came** home, his father-in-law **Rabbi Yannai would see before him a pillar of fire** signalling his son-in-law's arrival. [9] **On one occasion** Yehudah's **studies** so **engrossed him** that he remained in the Academy later than usual, and was unable to reach home before Shabbat. [10] **When** Rabbi Yannai **did not see the** usual **sign** signalling his son-in-law's return, **he said to** the members of his household: **"Overturn** Yehudah's **bed** as a sign of mourning, [11] **for if Yehudah were alive, he would not have neglected his conjugal obligation.** Since he has not returned home, he must surely be dead!" [12] The Gemara relates that Rabbi Yannai's declaration of Yehudah's death **was "as an error which proceeds from the ruler"** (Ecclesiastes 10:5). Once Rabbi Yannai declared him dead, "the ruler's error" became reality, **and** Yehudah **died.**

[1] עוֹנָה שֶׁל תַּלְמִידֵי חֲכָמִים אֵימַת?
[2] אָמַר רַב יְהוּדָה אָמַר שְׁמוּאֵל: מֵעֶרֶב שַׁבָּת לְעֶרֶב שַׁבָּת.
[3] ״אֲשֶׁר פִּרְיוֹ יִתֵּן בְּעִתּוֹ״. [4] אָמַר רַב יְהוּדָה, וְאִיתֵּימָא רַב הוּנָא, [5] וְאִיתֵּימָא רַב נַחְמָן: זֶה הַמְשַׁמֵּשׁ מִטָּתוֹ מֵעֶרֶב שַׁבָּת לְעֶרֶב שַׁבָּת.
[6] יְהוּדָה בְּרֵיהּ דְּרַבִּי חִיָּיא, חַתְנֵיהּ דְּרַבִּי יַנַּאי, הֲוָה אָזֵיל וִיתֵיב בְּבֵי רַב, [7] וְכָל בֵּי שִׁמְשֵׁי הֲוָה אָתֵי לְבֵיתֵיהּ. [8] וְכִי הֲוָה אָתֵי, הֲוָה קָא חָזֵי קַמֵּיהּ עַמּוּדָא דְנוּרָא. [9] יוֹמָא חַד מְשַׁכְתֵּיהּ שְׁמַעְתָּא. [10] כֵּיוָן דְּלָא חָזֵי הַהוּא סִימָנָא, אֲמַר לְהוּ רַבִּי יַנַּאי: ״כְּפוּ מִטָּתוֹ, [11] שֶׁאִילְמָלֵי יְהוּדָה קַיָּים, לֹא בִּיטֵּל עוֹנָתוֹ״. [12] הֲוַאי ״כִּשְׁגָגָה שֶׁיֹּצָא מִלִּפְנֵי הַשַּׁלִּיט״ וְנָח נַפְשֵׁיהּ.

LITERAL TRANSLATION

[1] When is the conjugal obligation of Rabbinic scholars?

[2] Rav Yehudah said in the name of Shmuel: Every Friday night (lit., "from the eve of Shabbat to the eve of Shabbat").

[3] "That brings forth its fruit in its season." [4] Rav Yehudah said, and some say [it was] Rav Huna, [5] and some say [it was] Rav Naḥman: This [refers to] one who has sexual relations every Friday night.

[6] Yehudah the son of Rabbi Ḥiyya, [and] the son-in-law of Rabbi Yannai, would go and sit in the Academy, [7] and every [Friday evening at] dusk he would come to his house. [8] And when he came, he [Rabbi Yannai] would see before him a pillar of fire. [9] One day his studies engrossed him. [10] Since he did not see that sign, Rabbi Yannai said to them: "Overturn his bed, [11] for if Yehudah were alive, he would not have neglected his conjugal obligation." [12] It was "as an error which proceeds from the ruler," and he died.

RASHI

מערב שבת כו׳ — שהוא ליל תענוג, ושביתה, והנאת הגוף. **כפו מטתו** — כדת המתאבלים, דחייבין בכפיית המטה.

SAGES

יְהוּדָה בְּרֵיהּ דְּרַבִּי חִיָּיא Yehudah the son of Rabbi Ḥiyya. He and Ḥizkiyah were twin sons of Rabbi Ḥiyya. They were Amoraim of the first generation. They are often mentioned together, both in stories told about them and also in relation to Halakhic issues that they dealt with together.

Yehudah the son of Rabbi Ḥiyya became the son-in-law of Rabbi Yannai and was highly regarded by his father-in-law both for his greatness as a Torah scholar and for his piety, which is described in a number of places in the Talmud.

Since he died a young man, not many of his teachings have been preserved, but some Halakhic and Aggadic remarks are recorded in his name.

NOTES

מֵעֶרֶב שַׁבָּת לְעֶרֶב שַׁבָּת Every Friday night. In the Jerusalem Talmud, Rav adduces support for this position from the Mishnah below (64b), which states that a woman whose husband is away all week, and who is being supported by him through a third party while he is gone, is entitled to eat with her husband once a week on Friday night — the reference to "eating" being understood as a euphemism for sexual relations.

Rashi explains that a Rabbinic scholar should engage in sexual relations with his wife once a week on Friday night,

HALAKHAH

עוֹנָה שֶׁל תַּלְמִידֵי חֲכָמִים The conjugal obligation of Rabbinic scholars. "A Rabbinic scholar must cohabit with his wife once a week, and it is the practice of Rabbinic scholars to engage in sexual relations on Friday nights," following Shmuel (see *Ḥelkat Meḥokek* and *Pitḥei Teshuvah*). (*Rambam, Sefer Nashim, Hilkhot Ishut* 14:1; *Shulḥan Arukh, Even HaEzer* 76:2.)

[1]רַבִּי אִיעֲסַק לֵיהּ לִבְרֵיהּ בֵּי רַבִּי חִיָּיא. [2]כִּי מְטָא לְמִיכְתַּב כְּתוּבָּה, נָח נַפְשָׁהּ דְּרְבִיתָא. [3]אָמַר רַבִּי: ״חַס וְשָׁלוֹם, פְּסוּלָא אִיכָּא?״ [4]יְתִיבוּ וְעַיְּינוּ בַּמִּשְׁפָּחוֹת. [5]רַבִּי אָתֵי מִשְּׁפַטְיָה בֶּן אֲבִיטַל, [6]וְרַבִּי חִיָּיא אָתֵי מִשִּׁמְעִי אֲחִי דָּוִד.

[7]אָזֵיל אִיעֲסַק לֵיהּ לִבְרֵיהּ בֵּי רַבִּי יוֹסֵי בֶּן זִימְרָא. [8]פָּסְקוּ לֵיהּ תַּרְתֵּי סְרֵי שְׁנִין לְמֵיזַל בְּבֵי רַב. [9]אַחְלְפוּהָ קַמֵּיהּ, אֲמַר לְהוּ:

LITERAL TRANSLATION

[1]Rabbi was occupied with [marrying off] his son into the family (lit., "house") of Rabbi Ḥiyya. [2]When he reached the writing of the ketubah, the girl died. [3]Rabbi said: "Is there, God forbid (lit., 'forbearance and peace'), a blemish?" [4]They sat and investigated [the genealogies of] the families. [5]Rabbi was descended (lit., "came") from Shefatyah ben Avital, [6]and Rabbi Ḥiyya was descended from Shim'i the brother of David.

[7]He went [and] occupied himself [with marrying off] his son into the family of Rabbi Yose ben Zimra. [8]They agreed that for twelve years he should go to the Academy. [9]They passed her before him, [and] he said to them:

TRANSLATION AND COMMENTARY

רַבִּי אִיעֲסַק לֵיהּ לִבְרֵיהּ [1]The Gemara continues with a story relating to **Rabbi** Yehudah HaNasi, who **was** once **occupied with marrying off his son to** a girl from **the family of Rabbi Ḥiyya.** [2]**When he went** to Rabbi Ḥiyya's house **to write the ketubah,** he found that **the girl,** Rabbi Ḥiyya's daughter, **had died.** [3]Sensing that the girl's premature death was Heaven's way of preventing the marriage, **Rabbi** Yehudah HaNasi **said: "Is there, God forbid, a blemish** in one of our families which makes that family unfit to establish a marital tie with the other?" [4]**They investigated the genealogies of the** two **families.** [5]They discovered that **Rabbi** Yehudah HaNasi **was descended from Shefatyah ben Avital,** the wife of King David, [6]**and** that **Rabbi Ḥiyya was descended from Shim'i, the brother of** King **David.** Rabbi Yehudah HaNasi was therefore a direct descendant of King David, whereas Rabbi Ḥiyya could trace his lineage only to the brother of the king. Thus they understood that Rabbi Ḥiyya's daughter was an unfit match for Rabbi Yehudah HaNasi's son, and that the marriage had been prevented by divine intervention.

אָזֵיל אִיעֲסַק לֵיהּ לִבְרֵיהּ [7]Rabbi Yehudah HaNasi then **went and occupied himself with marrying off his son to** a girl from **the family of Rabbi Yose ben Zimra.** [8]The parties **agreed** between them **that** Rabbi Yehudah HaNasi's son **would go for twelve years to the Academy,** and afterwards he would marry Rabbi Yose ben Zimra's daughter. [9]The bride **was passed before** the bridegroom, and after he had seen her, Rabbi Yehudah

SAGES

רַבִּי יוֹסֵי בֶּן זִימְרָא **Rabbi Yose ben Zimra.** One of the last Tannaim, Rabbi Yose ben Zimra was a priest and a younger contemporary of Rabbi Yehudah HaNasi, whose son married his daughter. Rabbi Yose ben Zimra lived a long life, and most of his teachings were transmitted by the Amoraim Rabbi Yoḥanan and Rabbi Elazar. Some of the statements by Rabbi Yose ben Zimra are Halakhic, but most of them (reported in both the Babylonian Talmud and the Jerusalem Talmud, and in the Midrashim) are Aggadic.

RASHI

איעסק לבריה — להשיא בתו של רבי חייא. **איכא פסולא** — שלא היו מהוגנים לזוג אחד. **שפטיה בן אביטל** — בן דוד היה, אביטל שם אשת דוד. ורבי חייא אתי משמעי, וזהו הפסול: שרבי היה מבית דוד, ולא היתה בת הבאה משמעי הוגנת לבנו, שלא היתה בת מלכים. **פסקו ליה תרתי סרי שנין** — קודם שיכנוס. **אחלפוה קמיה** — העבירו הנערה לפני החתן.

NOTES

because Friday night is the time set aside for physical rest and pleasure. *Rivan* adds that Friday night is not a time that is usually devoted to Torah study, and thus the scholar's cohabitation with his wife does not require him to neglect his studies. The *Zohar* deals with this issue in numerous places, explaining the mystical significance of sexual intercourse on Friday night, and suggesting that a Rabbinic scholar is actually forbidden to engage in sexual relations with his wife at any other time. The later codifiers deal with the matter in great detail.

יְתִיבוּ וְעַיְּינוּ בַּמִּשְׁפָּחוֹת **They sat and investigated the genealogies of the families.** Our commentary follows *Rashi*, who explains that the results of the investigation proved that Rabbi Ḥiyya's daughter was an unfit match for Rabbi Yehudah HaNasi's son, for Rabbi Yehudah HaNasi was a direct descendant of King David, whereas Rabbi Ḥiyya could only trace his lineage to the brother of the king. Some authorities (*Maharsha* and *Rabbi Ya'akov Emden*) ask: Even the kings of the House of David themselves were not particular about not marrying anybody outside the royal family. Why, then, should Rabbi Ḥiyya's daughter have been an unsuitable match for Rabbi Yehudah HaNasi's son? Rather, the Gemara should be understood as follows: Rabbi Ḥiyya and Rabbi Yehudah HaNasi sat down and investigated the genealogies of both families, but found no blemish on either side. On the contrary, they discovered that both were descended from Jesse, the father of King David. Thus there must have been some other reason for the girl's premature death (see also *Rivan*).

רַבִּי אָתֵי מִשְּׁפַטְיָה **Rabbi was descended from Shefatyah.** The Geonim raise a question concerning Rabbi Yehudah HaNasi's genealogy: The Gemara maintains here that Rabbi Yehudah HaNasi was descended from Shefatyah ben Avital, and was thus a direct descendant of King David. But according to the Jerusalem Talmud (*Ketubot* 12:3), Rabbi Yehudah HaNasi was descended from the tribe of Benjamin and could only trace his roots back to the House of David through his female ancestors. Some argue that the matter of Rabbi Yehudah HaNasi's genealogy was in dispute between the two Talmuds. Others answer simply that Rabbi Yehudah HaNasi was indeed a direct descendant of King David, but not through his male ancestors.

TRANSLATION AND COMMENTARY

HaNasi's son **said:** [1]**"Let it be** only **six years** that I must study in the Academy before I can take this girl as my wife." [2]The bride **was passed before** the bridegroom a second time, and after seeing her again Rabbi Yehudah HaNasi's son **said to** his father and to his father-in-law: [3]**"I will marry her** now, **and then I will go** away to study." [4]**He was embarrassed to face his father,** because he thought that the latter would criticize him for his impatience to be married. [5]But his father **said to him: "My son, you share the viewpoint of your Maker.** How so? [6]**At first the verse says** (Exodus 15:17): **'You shall bring them in and plant them** in the mountain of your inheritance, in the place, O Lord, that You have made for Yourself to dwell in.' This verse shows that God's original intention was that the Jewish people would first enter Eretz Israel and only afterwards build Him a Temple. [7]**But later** another **verse says** (Exodus 25:8): **'And they shall make Me a sanctuary and I will dwell among them.'** This verse shows that God commanded them to build the Sanctuary in the desert even before they reached the Promised Land. Thus we see that God Himself had intended to put off his 'wedding' with the Jewish people until after they were settled in Eretz Israel, but as a result of His heightened affection for His 'bride,' He suggested that the 'wedding' be brought forward. Hence, my son, you did nothing to be ashamed of, for God Himself acted in much the same way." [8]After Rabbi Yehudah HaNasi's son was married, **he went** away from home **and sat for twelve years in the Academy** studying Torah intensively. [9]**By the time he returned** home, **his wife had become infertile.** [10]**Rabbi** Yehudah HaNasi **said: "What should we do?** [11]**If** we allow him to **divorce her,** people **will say** that **this poor woman waited in vain.** [12]And **if** we allow him to **marry another woman** in addition to his first wife in order to fulfill his religious duty to have children, [13]people **will say** that **this** second woman **is his** real **wife,** for she is the mother of his children, **and** Rabbi Yose ben Zimra's daughter **is** merely **his mistress** whom he maintains solely for sexual relations." [14]Rabbi Yehudah HaNasi's son **prayed for** his wife, **and she was cured.**

[1]״נֶיהֱווּ שִׁית שְׁנִין״. [2]אַחְלְפוּהָ קַמֵּיהּ, אֲמַר לְהוּ: [3]״אִיכְנִיס, וַהֲדַר אֵיזִיל״. [4]הֲוָה קָא מִכְסִיף מֵאֲבוּהּ. [5]אֲמַר לֵיהּ: ״בְּנִי, דַּעַת קוֹנְךָ יֵשׁ בְּךָ. [6]מֵעִיקָּרָא כְּתִיב: ׳תְּבִאֵמוֹ וְתִטָּעֵמוֹ׳. [7]וּלְבַסּוֹף כְּתִיב: ׳וְעָשׂוּ לִי מִקְדָּשׁ וְשָׁכַנְתִּי בְּתוֹכָם׳״. [8]אָזֵיל יְתֵיב תַּרְתֵּי סְרֵי שְׁנֵי בְּבֵי רַב. [9]עַד דַּאֲתָא, אִיעַקְּרָא דְּבֵיתְהוּ. [10]אֲמַר רַבִּי: ״הֵיכִי נַעֲבֵיד? [11]נְגָרְשָׁהּ, יֹאמְרוּ: עֲנִיָּה זוֹ לַשָּׁוְא שִׁימְּרָה. [12]נִינְסֵיב אִיתְּתָא אַחֲרִיתֵי, [13]יֹאמְרוּ: זוֹ אִשְׁתּוֹ, וְזוֹ זוֹנָתוֹ״. [14]בָּעֵי עֲלָהּ רַחֲמֵי וְאִיתַּסִּיאַת.

LITERAL TRANSLATION

[1]"Let it be six years." [2]They passed her before him [again], [and] he said to them: [3]"I will marry [her], and then I will go." [4]He felt embarrassed in front of his father. [5]He said to him: "My son, you have the mind of your Maker in you. [6]At first it is written: 'You shall bring them in and plant them.' [7]And at the end it is written: 'And they shall make Me a sanctuary and I will dwell among them.'" [8]He went [and] sat [for] twelve years in the Academy. [9]By the time he came [back], his wife had become barren. [10]Rabbi said: "How should we act? [11][If] he divorces her, they will say: This poor woman waited in vain. [12][If] he marries another woman, [13]they will say: This is his wife, and this is his mistress." [14]He besought mercy for her and she was cured.

RASHI

דעת קונך יש בך – שאמר להרחיק זמן חופתו, וחזר וקרבה מרוב חיבת כלתו. **מעיקרא כתיב תביאמו ותטעמו בהר נחלתך מכון לשבתך** – שיבאו לארץ ואחר כך יבנו לו מקדש. **ולבסוף אמר ועשו לי מקדש** – במדבר. **איעקרא** – נעשית עקרה. כן דרך העומדות עשר שנים בלא בעל.

NOTES

דַּעַת קוֹנְךָ יֵשׁ בְּךָ You have the mind of your Maker in you. *Maharsha* elaborates on this comparison, noting that the Midrash likens the giving of the Torah on Mount Sinai to a deed of betrothal which the bridegroom hands over to his bride, and the resting of the Divine Presence on the Sanctuary to the completion of the marriage. God originally intended to put off His marriage with the Jewish people until after they entered Eretz Israel, but He later advanced the wedding date to enable the people to atone for the sin of the golden calf.

וְזוֹ זוֹנָתוֹ And this is his mistress. *Rabbi Ya'akov Emden* notes that Rabbi Yehudah HaNasi was not concerned that people would come to think of Rabbi Yose ben Zimra's daughter as his son's mistress simply because he married another woman in addition to his first wife, for polygamy was permitted during the Talmudic period and it was not unknown for people to have more than one wife. Rather, Rabbi Yehudah HaNasi was concerned that people would view his son's first wife as his mistress because she could not provide him with children, and people might think that he kept her as his wife only for sexual relations.

SAGES

רַבִּי חֲנַנְיָה בֶּן חֲכִינַאי Rabbi Ḥananyah ben Ḥakhinai. A Tanna of the fourth generation, Rabbi Ḥananyah (or Ḥanina) ben Ḥakhinai, was one of Rabbi Akiva's most distinguished students. His Halakhic teachings are cited in the Mishnah, the Tosefta, the Halakhic Midrashim and the Talmud. One source states that Rabbi Ḥananyah was one of the ten martyrs (עֲשֶׂרֶת הֲרוּגֵי מַלְכוּת) murdered by the Romans at the time of the Bar Kokhba revolt (c.135 C.E.).

רַבִּי חָמָא בַּר בִּיסָא Rabbi Ḥama bar Bisa. A member of the last generation of Tannaim, Rabbi Ḥama bar Bisa lived in Lydda (Lod), where he served as a local Rabbinical judge. Most Talmudic passages refer to him as "Rabbi Ḥama the father of Rabbi Oshaya," for the latter was one of the outstanding scholars of his time and the editor of important Baraita collections. One Talmudic source (*Bava Batra* 59a) speaks of Rabbi Ḥama's father, Rabbi Bisa, endorsing the ruling of his grandson, Rabbi Oshaya, against the ruling of his son, Rabbi Ḥama.

TRANSLATION AND COMMENTARY

רַבִּי חֲנַנְיָה בֶּן חֲכִינַאי [1] It was further related that **Rabbi Ḥananyah ben Ḥakhinai was** about to **go to the Academy at the end of** the festivities of **Rabbi Shimon ben Yoḥai's wedding.** [2] Rabbi Shimon ben Yoḥai **said to him: "Wait for me until** the festivities are over and **I will come with you** to the Academy." [3] But Rabbi Ḥananyah was eager to leave and **he did not wait for** Rabbi Shimon to accompany **him.** [4] **He went** away **and sat for twelve years in the Academy.** [5] **By the time** Rabbi Ḥananyah **came back, the streets of his** home **town had changed,** [6] **so that he did not know how to find his** own **house.** [7] **He went and sat on the bank of the river,** [8] and there **he heard** people **calling** out **to a certain girl** who was walking nearby: [9] **"Daughter of Ḥakhinai, daughter of Ḥakhinai, fill your jug and come with us."** [10] Rabbi Ḥananyah **said** to himself: "Surely I may **infer from this that this girl is my** own daughter whom I no longer recognize after our being apart for so many years." [11] **He** decided to **follow her** home. [12] When he arrived at his house, he found **his wife sitting** there **sifting flour.** [13] **She lifted up her eyes and looked at him,** and immediately **recognized** that it was her husband who was standing before her. [14] Overwhelmed with emotion, **she fainted and died.** [15] Rabbi Ḥananyah appealed to his Maker and **said to Him: "Master of the Universe, this poor woman** who waited so patiently all these years for my return, **is this her** fitting **reward?"** [16] **He prayed for her, and** miraculously **she came back to life.**

רַבִּי חָמָא בַּר בִּיסָא [17] The Gemara continues with a story relating to **Rabbi Ḥama bar Bisa,** who **went and sat for twelve years in the Academy** studying Torah. [18] **As he was returning** home, **he said** to himself: **"I will** take care **not** to **do what** Rabbi Ḥananyah **the son of Ḥakhinai did** and I will not shock my wife by my sudden reappearance." [19] When Rabbi Ḥama reached his home town, **he went in and sat** down **in the** local **Academy, and sent a message to his house** informing his family of his return. [20] As he was sitting there, **Rabbi Oshaya his son came** in **and sat** down **before him,** but Rabbi Ḥama did not recognize him. [21] Rabbi Oshaya **asked Rabbi Ḥama** questions **about the subject he was studying, and Rabbi Ḥama understood** from the young man's observations **that he knew the**

[1] רַבִּי חֲנַנְיָה בֶּן חֲכִינַאי הֲוָה קָאָזֵיל לְבֵי רַב בְּשִׁילְהֵי הִלּוּלֵיהּ דְּרַבִּי שִׁמְעוֹן בֶּן יוֹחַאי. [2] אֲמַר לֵיהּ: ״אִיעַכַּב לִי עַד דְּאָתֵי בַּהֲדָךְ״. [3] לָא אִיעַכְּבָא לֵיהּ. [4] אֲזַל יְתֵיב תְּרֵי סְרֵי שְׁנֵי בְּבֵי רַב. [5] עַד דְּאָתֵי, אִישְׁתַּנּוּ שְׁבִילֵי דְּמָתָא, [6] וְלָא יָדַע לְמֵיזַל לְבֵיתֵיהּ. [7] אֲזַל יְתֵיב אַגּוּדָא דְּנַהֲרָא. [8] שְׁמַע לְהַהִיא רְבִיתָא דְּהָווּ קָרוּ לָהּ: [9] ״בַּת חֲכִינַאי, בַּת חֲכִינַאי, מְלִי קוּלְתֵךְ וְתָא, נֵיזִיל״. [10] אֲמַר: ״שְׁמַע מִינָּהּ הַאי רְבִיתָא דִּידָן״. [11] אֲזַל בַּתְרָהּ. [12] הֲוָה יְתִיבָא דְּבֵיתְהוּ קָא נָהֲלָה קִמְחָא. [13] דָּל עֵינָהּ חֲזִיתֵיהּ, סָוֵי לִבָּהּ, [14] פְּרַח רוּחָהּ. [15] אָמַר לְפָנָיו: ״רִבּוֹנוֹ שֶׁל עוֹלָם, עֲנִיָּיה זוֹ, זֶה שְׂכָרָהּ?״ [16] בְּעָא רַחֲמֵי עֲלָהּ וְחַיָּיה.

[17] רַבִּי חָמָא בַּר בִּיסָא אָזֵיל יְתֵיב תְּרֵי סְרֵי שְׁנֵי בְּבֵי מִדְרָשָׁא. [18] כִּי אֲתָא, אֲמַר: ״לָא אִיעֲבִיד כִּדְעָבֵיד בֶּן חֲכִינַאי״. [19] עָיֵיל יְתֵיב בְּמִדְרָשָׁא, שָׁלַח לְבֵיתֵיהּ. [20] אֲתָא רַבִּי אוֹשַׁעְיָא בְּרֵיהּ, יְתֵיב קַמֵּיהּ. [21] הֲוָה קָא מַשְׁאִיל לֵיהּ שְׁמַעְתָּא, חֲזָא דְּקָא מִתְחַדְּדֵי שְׁמַעְתֵּיהּ.

LITERAL TRANSLATION

[1] Rabbi Ḥananyah ben Ḥakhinai was going to the Academy at the end of Rabbi Shimon ben Yoḥai's wedding. [2] He said to him: "Wait for me until I come with you." [3] He did not wait for him. [4] He went [and] sat [for] twelve years in the Academy. [5] By the time he came [back], the streets of the town had changed, [6] and he did not know how to go to his house. [7] He went [and] sat on the bank of the river. [8] He heard them calling to a certain girl: [9] "Daughter of Ḥakhinai, daughter of Ḥakhinai, fill your jug and come, let us go." [10] He said: "Infer from this [that] this girl is ours." [11] He went after her. [12] His wife was sitting sifting flour. [13] She lifted up her eyes [and] looked at him, her heart recognized [him], [14] [and] her spirit fled. [15] He said before Him: "Master of the Universe, this poor woman, is this her reward?" [16] He besought mercy for her and she revived.

[17] Rabbi Ḥama bar Bisa went [and] sat [for] twelve years in the study hall. [18] When he came [back], he said: "I will not do what the son of Ḥakhinai did." [19] He went in [and] sat in the study hall, [and] sent [a message] to his house. [20] Rabbi Oshaya his son came, [and] sat before him. [21] He asked him [Rabbi Ḥama] about his studies, [and Rabbi Ḥama] saw that he knew his studies well.

RASHI

בשילהי הלוליה דרבי שמעון — סוף ימי חופתו. **איעכב לי** — המתן לי עד שיכלו ימי חופתי, ואלך עמך לבי רב. **אישתנו שבילי דמתא** — שנבנו בעיר בניינים חדשים, ונסתמו בה מבואות. **לההיא רביתא** — נערה. **סוי לבה** — ראה לבה, כלומר: נדמה ללבה פתאום שזה בעלה. **לא איעביד כדעבד בר חכינאי** — שנכנס לביתו פתאום. **יתיב קמיה** — ולא היה האב מכירו. **חזיא** — לבריה דמחדדן שמעתתיה.

TRANSLATION AND COMMENTARY

material very **well.** [1]Rabbi Ḥama **became distressed,** regretting his prolonged absence from home. [2]**He said** to himself: **"Had I been here** all these years, I could have taught my own son Torah and **I** too **would have had a son** as accomplished **as this** young man." [3]Satisfied that his family was prepared for his arrival, Rabbi Ḥama **went in to his house. His son,** Rabbi Oshaya, **went in** after him. [4]**Rabbi Ḥama stood up before him** to show respect to the young scholar, **thinking that** Rabbi Oshaya **wanted to ask him** a further question **about his studies.** [5]Rabbi Ḥama's **wife** then **said to him: "Is there a father who stands up before his son?"** [6]The Gemara notes that **Rami bar Ḥama applied to** Rabbi Oshaya the verse (Ecclesiastes 4:12) which says: **"But a threefold cord is not quickly broken."** [7]Rami bar Ḥama explained that **this** verse refers to **Rabbi Oshaya, the son of Rabbi Ḥama bar Bisa.** This family produced three generations of great Torah scholars — Rabbi Bisa, Rabbi Ḥama, and Rabbi Oshaya — and the grandfather, Rabbi Bisa, lived long enough to see his grandson develop into a famous Rabbinic Sage.

רַבִּי עֲקִיבָא [8]It is further related that before **Rabbi Akiva** became a great scholar, he **was an** unlearned **shepherd** employed by **Kalba Savu'a,** one of the wealthiest men in Jerusalem. [9]Kalba Savu'a's **daughter,** Rachel, **saw that** this shepherd Akiva **was** both **modest and outstanding,** and recognizing his great potential she wanted to be his wife. [10]**She said to him: "If I** agree to **become betrothed to you, will you** agree to **go to the Academy** and devote yourself to the study of Torah?" [11]**He said to her: "Yes."** [12]Rachel **became secretly betrothed to** her father's shepherd, without her father's permission, **and she sent** her husband **away** to the Academy to fulfill his part of the agreement. [13]**Her father** was very angry when he **heard** what had happened, **and** he **banished** his daughter **from his house and forbade her by a vow from deriving any benefit from his**

[1]חָלַשׁ דַּעְתֵּיהּ, [2]אֲמַר: ״אִי הֲוַאי הָכָא, הֲוָה לִי זֶרַע כִּי הַאי״. [3]עָל לְבֵיתֵיהּ, עָל בְּרֵיהּ. [4]קָם קַמֵּיהּ, הוּא סָבַר לְמִשְׁאֲלֵיהּ שְׁמַעְתְּתָא קָא בָּעֵי. [5]אָמְרָה לֵיהּ דְּבֵיתְהוּ: ״מִי אִיכָּא אַבָּא דְּקָאֵים מִקַּמֵּי בְּרָא?״ [6]קָרֵי עֲלֵיהּ רָמֵי בַּר חָמָא: ״הַחוּט הַמְשֻׁלָּשׁ לֹא בִמְהֵרָה יִנָּתֵק״. [7]זֶה רַבִּי אוֹשַׁעְיָא, בְּנוֹ שֶׁל רַבִּי חָמָא בַּר בִּיסָא.

[8]רַבִּי עֲקִיבָא רַעְיָא דְּבֶן כַּלְבָּא שָׂבוּעַ הֲוָה. [9]חֲזִיתֵיהּ בְּרַתֵּיהּ דַּהֲוָה צְנִיעַ וּמַעֲלֵי. [10]אָמְרָה לֵיהּ: ״אִי מִקַּדְּשְׁנָא לָךְ, אָזְלַתְּ לְבֵי רַב?״ [11]אֲמַר לָהּ: ״אִין״. [12]אִיקַּדְשָׁא לֵיהּ בְּצִינְעָה, וּשְׁדַרְתֵּיהּ. [13]שְׁמַע אֲבוּהּ אַפְּקָהּ מִבֵּיתֵיהּ, אַדְּרָהּ הֲנָאָה מִנִּכְסֵיהּ.

LITERAL TRANSLATION

[1]He was distressed, [2][and] said: "If I had been here, I would have had a son like this." [3]He went in to his house, [and] his son went in. [4]He [Rabbi Ḥama] stood up before him, [for] he thought that he wanted to ask him about his studies. [5]His wife said to him: "Is there a father who stands up before his son?" [6]Rami bar Ḥama cited (lit., "read") regarding him: "But a threefold cord is not quickly broken." [7]This is Rabbi Oshaya, the son of Rabbi Ḥama bar Bisa.

[8]Rabbi Akiva was the shepherd of Ben Kalba Savu'a. [9]His daughter saw [in] him that he was modest and outstanding. [10]She said to him: "If I become betrothed to you, will you go to the Academy?" [11]He said to her: "Yes." [12]She became betrothed to him in secret, and she sent him away. [13]Her father heard [and] banished her from his house [and] forbade her with a vow from [deriving any] benefit from his property.

RASHI

אי הואי הכא – אילו הייתי כאן כשהנחתי בני קטן והלכתי – הייתי מלמדו תורה. והיה חכם כזה. **כלבא שבוע** – שם אחד מעשירי ירושלים, שכל הנכנס לביתו רעב ככלב היה יוצא שָׂבֵעַ.

BACKGROUND

בֶּן כַּלְבָּא שָׂבוּעַ Ben Kalba Savu'a. The family of Kalba Savu'a was one of the wealthiest and most powerful in Jerusalem at the time of the destruction of the Second Temple. Rabbinic sources relate that his family was one of three that owned enough food to supply all of Jerusalem during the siege. Kalba Savu'a was descended from Caleb the son of Yefunneh, one of the two spies in Moses' time who spoke favorably about Eretz Israel (see Numbers 13:30). Kalba Savu'a supposedly received his name (literally, "satiated dog") because anyone who entered his house as hungry as a dog left satiated. Elsewhere, the Gemara describes the hard life that Rabbi Akiva and his wife endured for many years while they were fobidden to benefit from Kalba Savu'a's property.

NOTES

הַחוּט הַמְשֻׁלָּשׁ A threefold cord. *Tosafot* explains that while there were other families that produced three successive generations of great Torah scholars, this family stood out in that Rabbi Bisa was still alive when his grandson Rabbi Oshaya was recognized as an important scholar, for we find elsewhere (*Bava Batra* 59a) that Rabbi Oshaya and Rabbi Ḥama disagreed about a certain issue, and Rabbi Bisa was approached to express his opinion on the matter. *Maharsha* adds that this family was singled out as a threefold cord that is not quickly broken, because it was Rabbi Bisa who taught his grandson Rabbi Oshaya and made him into such an accomplished scholar while Rabbi Ḥama was away at the Academy.

צְנִיעַ וּמַעֲלֵי Modest and outstanding. The Rishonim ask: What did Kalba Savu'a's daughter see in her father's shepherd that led her to conclude that he was modest and outstanding? Surely Rabbi Akiva later testified about himself (*Pesaḥim* 49b) that when he was still an unlearned man, he used to say that if a Rabbinic scholar were to fall into his hands, he would treat him most severely!

Ritva suggests that Rabbi Akiva's confession refers to an earlier period of his life, and that by the time he was

TRANSLATION AND COMMENTARY

property. [1]Akiva the shepherd **went** away **and sat for twelve years in the Academy,** and developed into one of the greatest Sages of his generation. Twelve years later, [2]**when he** decided to **return** home, **he brought with him** an entourage of **twelve thousand disciples.** [3]As he was about to reveal himself to his wife, **he heard an old man saying to her: "For how long** [63A] **will you** continue to **behave like a widow during her husband's lifetime?** How much longer will you tolerate your husband's prolonged absence?" [4]**She said to him:** "I have no complaints or regrets about this arrangement. **If he would listen to me,** [5]**he would stay there twelve more years** and continue his studies, and I would continue to wait for him." [6]Hearing this, Rabbi Akiva **said** to himself: **"I am acting with** my wife's **permission,"** [7]and **he went back and sat twelve more years in the Academy.** [8]**When** Rabbi Akiva **returned** home after this second twelve-year absence, **he brought with him twenty-four thousand disciples.** [9]When **his wife heard** that her husband was coming home, **she went out to greet him.** Because of the rift between her and her father, she had been forced to live a life of poverty. Seeing that she was going out in tattered clothes to greet a great visiting scholar, [10]**her neighbors said to her: "Borrow some** clothes **to wear, and dress yourself** properly!" [11]**She answered them** with the following verse (Proverbs 12:10): **"'A righteous man knows the life of his beast.'** Surely a righteous man like Rabbi Akiva will understand that I mean no disrespect when I appear before him in my ordinary clothes." [12]**When she reached** her husband, [13]**she fell on her face** before him **and kissed his feet.** [14]Rabbi Akiva's **attendants were** about to **push her away,** [15]**when he said to them: "Leave her** alone. [16]**Whatever I** have accomplished **and** whatever **you** have accomplished **is** all on account **of her."** [17]**Her father,** Kalba Savu'a, **had heard that a great man had come to town,** but he did not realize that the visiting scholar was his own son-in-law. Regretting the vow that he

[1]אֲזִיל יְתֵיב תְּרֵי סְרֵי שְׁנִין בֵּי רַב. [2]כִּי אֲתָא, אַיְיתֵי בַּהֲדֵיהּ תְּרֵי סְרֵי אַלְפֵי תַּלְמִידֵי. [3]שַׁמְעֵיהּ לְהַהוּא סָבָא דְּקָאָמַר לַהּ: "עַד כַּמָּה [63A] קָא מְדַבַּרְתְּ אַלְמְנוּת חַיִּים?" [4]אָמְרָה לֵיהּ: "אִי לְדִידִי צָיֵית, [5]יְתֵיב תְּרֵי סְרֵי שְׁנֵי אַחֲרִינֵי". [6]אֲמַר: "בִּרְשׁוּת קָא עָבֵידְנָא". [7]הֲדַר אֲזִיל וִיתֵיב תְּרֵי סְרֵי שְׁנֵי אַחֲרִינֵי בְּבֵי רַב. [8]כִּי אֲתָא, אַיְיתֵי בַּהֲדֵיהּ עֶשְׂרִין וְאַרְבָּעָה אַלְפֵי תַּלְמִידֵי. [9]שָׁמְעָה דְּבֵיתְהוּ, הֲוַת קָא נָפְקָא לְאַפֵּיהּ. [10]אָמְרוּ לַהּ שִׁיבָבְתָּא: "שְׁאִילִי מָאנֵי לְבוּשׁ וְאִיכַּסַּאי!" [11]אָמְרָה לְהוּ: "יוֹדֵעַ צַדִּיק נֶפֶשׁ בְּהֶמְתּוֹ". [12]כִּי מְטְיָא לְגַבֵּיהּ, [13]נָפְלָה עַל אַפָּהּ, קָא מְנַשְּׁקָא לֵיהּ לְכַרְעֵיהּ. [14]הֲווּ קָא מְדַחְפֵי לַהּ שַׁמָּעֵיהּ, [15]אֲמַר לְהוּ: "שִׁבְקוּהָ. [16]שֶׁלִּי וְשֶׁלָּכֶם שֶׁלָּהּ הוּא". [17]שְׁמַע אֲבוּהּ דְּאָתָא גַּבְרָא רַבָּה לְמָתָא, אֲמַר:

LITERAL TRANSLATION

[1]He went [and] sat [for] twelve years in the Academy. [2]When he came [back], he brought with him twelve thousand disciples. [3]He heard an old man saying to her: "For how long [63A] will you behave like a widow during [her husband's] lifetime?" [4]She said to him: "If he would listen to me, [5]he would sit [there] twelve more years." [6]He said: "I am acting with permission." [7]He went back and sat twelve more years in the Academy. [8]When he came [back], he brought with him twenty-four thousand disciples. [9]His wife heard [and] went out to [greet] him. [10]The neighbors said to her: "Borrow something to wear and dress yourself!" [11]She said to them: "A righteous man knows the life of his beast." [12]When she reached him, [13]she fell on her face, [and] she kissed his feet. [14]His attendants were pushing her away, [15][but] he said to them: "Leave her. [16]What is mine and what is yours is hers." [17]Her father heard that a great man had come to town, [and] he said:

RASHI

קא מדברת – את מתנהגת. שיבבתא – השכינות. שלי ושלכם שלה הוא – תורה שלמדתי אני ושלמדתם אתם – על ידה הוא.

NOTES

working for Kalba Savu'a he had already repented and developed into a modest and outstanding person, although he was still unlearned. After he married, he devoted himself entirely to the study of Torah and became a great scholar. *Tosafot* argues that even in his youth Rabbi Akiva was modest and outstanding in his personal behavior. Even then he did not really hate Rabbinic scholars, but resented their condescending attitude toward the unlearned and their tendency to distance themselves from anybody who was not a member of the scholarly class.

"יוֹדֵעַ צַדִּיק נֶפֶשׁ בְּהֶמְתּוֹ" "A righteous man knows the life of his beast." Two possible interpretations of this quotation from Proverbs are suggested in the commentary to *Nedarim* (50a) attributed to *Rashi*: Either Rabbi Akiva's wife knew that the visiting scholar was her husband and that he would not be offended by her appearance, or she was,

[1]״אֵיזִיל לְגַבֵּיהּ. [2]אֶפְשָׁר דְּמֵפֵר נִדְרַאי״. [3]אֲתָא לְגַבֵּיהּ, אֲמַר לֵיהּ: [4]״אַדַּעְתָּא דְּגַבְרָא רַבָּה מִי נָדְרַתְּ״? [5]אֲמַר לוֹ: ״אֲפִילּוּ פֶּרֶק אֶחָד, וַאֲפִילּוּ הֲלָכָה אַחַת״. [6]אֲמַר לֵיהּ: ״אֲנָא הוּא״. [7]נָפַל עַל אַפֵּיהּ וּנְשַׁקֵיהּ עַל כַּרְעֵיהּ, וְיָהֵיב לֵיהּ פַּלְגָא מָמוֹנֵיהּ. [8]בְּרַתֵּיהּ דְּרַבִּי עֲקִיבָא עָבְדָא לֵיהּ לְבֶן עַזַּאי הָכִי. [9]וְהַיְינוּ דְּאָמְרִי אֱינָשֵׁי: ״רְחֵילָא בָּתַר רְחֵילָא אָזְלָא״. [10]כְּעוֹבָדֵי אִמָּהּ, כָּךְ עוֹבָדֵי בְּרַתָּא.

LITERAL TRANSLATION

[1]"I will go to him. [2]Perhaps he will invalidate my vow." [3]He came to him, [and Rabbi Akiva] said to him: [4]"Would you have vowed had you known (lit., 'with the intention') [that he would be] a great man?" [5]He said to him: "Even one chapter, and even one law." [6]He said to him: "I am he." [7]He fell on his face and kissed his feet, and gave him half of his money.

[8]Rabbi Akiva's daughter acted in this way toward Ben Azzai. [9]And this is what people say: "A lamb follows a lamb." [10]Like the actions of the mother, so are the actions of the daughter.

TRANSLATION AND COMMENTARY

had taken twenty-four years previously, **he said** to himself: [1]**"I will go to** this Sage. [2]**Perhaps he will** find a way to **invalidate my vow,** so that I can once again provide for my daughter." [3]Kalba Savu'a **came before** Rabbi Akiva, and requested the dissolution of his vow. **Rabbi Akiva said to him:** [4]**"Would you have taken this vow had you known that** your son-in-law **would be a great man?"** [5]Kalba Savu'a **said to him:** "Had he known **even one chapter, or even one law,** I would never have taken the vow." [6]Rabbi Akiva **said to** his father-in-law: "In that case you are released from your vow, for **I am he."** [7]Kalba Savu'a **fell on his face** before him **and kissed his feet, and gave him half of his property.**

בְּרַתֵּיהּ דְּרַבִּי עֲקִיבָא עָבְדָא [8]As a footnote to this story, the Gemara adds: **Rabbi Akiva's daughter acted in the same way toward** the famous Tanna Shimon **ben Azzai** as her mother had acted toward her father. She too made her betrothal conditional upon her bridegroom devoting himself to Torah study. [9]This corresponds to the idea expressed by **the popular proverb,** which **states: "A lamb follows a lamb."** [10]**The actions of a mother are** closely **paralleled by the actions of her daughter.**

BACKGROUND

רְחֵילָא בָּתַר רְחֵילָא אָזְלָא **A lamb follows a lamb.** This statement is a double entendre. Not only was Rabbi Akiva a shepherd in his youth (and hence his wife and his daughter are compared to lambs), but the Aramaic word for "lamb" (רְחֵילָא) sounds like "Rachel," Rabbi Akiva's wife's name.

עָבְדָה לֵיהּ לְבֶן עַזַּאי הָכִי **She acted in this way toward Ben Azzai.** Little is known about Ben Azzai's personal life. This passage implies that Ben Azzai did not dedicate himself totally to Torah study (as is indicated by other passages) until Rabbi Akiva's daughter persuaded him to do so. Later, after Ben Azzai had become one of the outstanding scholars of his generation, he apparently divorced Rabbi Akiva's daughter. (*Tosafot* suggests that he may have divorced her while they were betrothed.) The Gemara (*Sotah* 4b) quotes Ben Azzai as explaining that he was not married, saying: "What can I do, for my soul longs for the Torah?"

NOTES

unaware of his identity, as was her father, but she assumed that a great scholar would not humiliate her on account of her clothing. *Maharsha* adds that when Rabbi Akiva's wife cited this verse, she was alluding to her husband's past, when he served as her father's shepherd.

אַדַּעְתָּא דְּגַבְרָא רַבָּה **Had you known that he would be a great man.** A number of Rishonim deal with a Halakhic difficulty that arises from this story: A vow can be dissolved if it is shown that it was not made with full intent and knowledge. But a vow cannot be dissolved on grounds of lack of intent and knowledge, if the person who vowed failed to foresee a situation that could not have been predicted when the vow was taken. How, then, could Rabbi Akiva have dissolved his father-in-law's vow on the grounds that when he took it, he did not know that his son-in-law would become a great scholar? Surely Rabbi Akiva's transformation into a Torah scholar could not have been predicted when the vow was taken!

Tosafot suggests that since Rabbi Akiva had already left to study Torah when his father-in-law took the vow, his becoming a Rabbinic scholar is not considered unpredictable, for someone who devotes himself to Torah study often develops into a great scholar. Along similar lines, *Meiri* maintains that it can be predicted that someone with the intellectual potential to acquire knowledge will do so. Alternatively, argues *Tosafot*, when Kalba Savu'a took his vow, he stated that he was depriving his daughter of benefiting from his property because she had accepted betrothal from someone who was not a Rabbinic scholar. Thus the regulations regarding unpredictable developments do not apply, for such a statement is treated as a condition.

Ritva argues that even before Rabbi Akiva went away to the Academy, he was not a totally unlearned man. Thus his father-in-law's vow was not made with full knowledge, for at the time of the vow Rabbi Akiva had already begun to study Torah. Alternatively, Kalba Savu'a was released from his vow because it was made without the knowledge that his daughter had made her betrothal conditional on her husband's going away to study Torah, for he would certainly not have penalized her had he known about that condition. It is also possible that Kalba Savu'a explicitly stated that his vow would be binding only as long as his son-in-law was an unlearned man. Thus, the vow did not require nullification, for it was automatically nullified when Rabbi Akiva acquired his learning. This also explains why the Gemara does not actually say that Rabbi Akiva nullified his father-in-law's vow. *Rivash* explains that Rabbi Akiva did not in any case nullify the vow himself, because he had a personal interest in the matter.

עָבְדָא לֵיהּ לְבֶן עַזַּאי **Acted in this way toward Ben Azzai.** *Tosafot* addresses the question of whether Ben Azzai was ever actually married to Rabbi Akiva's daughter, for elsewhere (see *Sotah* 4b) the Gemara states that Ben Azzai never married and that he failed to fulfill the obligation to procreate. *Tosafot* suggests that he may have been married to Rabbi Akiva's daughter for a short period but then left her. Alternatively, he betrothed her but never completed the marriage.

[1]רַב יוֹסֵף בְּרֵיהּ דְּרָבָא שְׁדַרֵיהּ אֲבוּהִי לְבֵי רַב לְקַמֵּיהּ דְּרַב יוֹסֵף. [2]פָּסְקוּ לֵיהּ שִׁית שְׁנֵי. [3]כִּי הֲוָה תְּלָת שְׁנֵי מְטָא מַעֲלֵי יוֹמָא דְּכִפּוּרֵי, [4]אֲמַר: "אֵיזִיל וְאִיחֲזֵינְהוּ לְאֱינָשֵׁי בֵּיתִי". [5]שְׁמַע אֲבוּהִי, שְׁקַל מָנָא, וּנְפַק לְאַפֵּיהּ. [6]אֲמַר לֵיהּ: "זוֹנָתְךָ נִזְכַּרְתָּ"? [7]אִיכָּא דְּאָמְרִי אֲמַר לֵיהּ: "יוֹנָתְךָ נִזְכַּרְתָּ?" [8]אִיטְרוּד, לָא מָר אִיפְסִיק וְלָא מָר אִיפְסִיק.

מִשְׁנָה [9]הַמּוֹרֶדֶת עַל בַּעְלָהּ, פּוֹחֲתִין לָהּ מִכְּתוּבָּתָהּ שִׁבְעָה דִּינָרִין בְּשַׁבָּת. [10]רַבִּי יְהוּדָה אוֹמֵר: שִׁבְעָה טְרַפָּעִיקִין. [11]עַד מָתַי הוּא

TRANSLATION AND COMMENTARY

רַב יוֹסֵף [1]The Gemara concludes this series of anecdotes with the following story: **Rav Yosef, the** married **son of Rava, was sent by his father to the Academy to study with** the Sage **Rav Yosef.** [2]**It was agreed** that he would stay away **for six years,** and devote himself exclusively to Torah study. [3]**Three years passed, Yom Kippur Eve arrived,** and Rav Yosef the son of Rava longed to see his family. [4]**He said:** "I have been away long enough. **I must go** now **and see the members of my household."** [5]**His father heard** about his son's impending arrival, **took a weapon** in his hand as if he were about to fight a battle, **and went out to** confront **him.** [6]According to one version of the story, **he** met his son and angrily **said to him: "Have you** returned home because you **remembered your mistress?** Were you so unable to control your physical desires?" [7]**There are some who** report this story in a slightly different manner. They **say that** Rava did not refer to his daughter-in-law as his son's mistress, but that **he said to** his son as follows: **"Have you** returned home because you **remembered your dove?"** [8]In any event, the father and son **quarreled** so vehemently that on this occasion **neither the one nor the other ate the last meal** before the Yom Kippur fast as required.

MISHNAH הַמּוֹרֶדֶת עַל בַּעְלָהּ [9]**If a woman rebels against her husband** (the Gemara will clarify the nature of this rebellion), **we** penalize her by **deducting from her ketubah seven dinarim for each week** that she persists in her rebellion. [10]**Rabbi Yehudah** disagrees and **says:** Her ketubah is diminished by **seven tropaics** (half-dinarim) each week. [11]The Mishnah asks: **How long** must the husband continue to keep the rebellious

LITERAL TRANSLATION

[1]Rav Yosef the son of Rava was sent by his father to the Academy [to study] before Rav Yosef. [2]They agreed on six years for him. [3]When three years had passed [and] the eve of Yom Kippur arrived, [4]he said: "I will go and see the members of my household." [5]His father heard, took a weapon, and went out to him. [6]He said to him: "Have you remembered your mistress?" [7]There are [some] who say [that] he said to him: "Have you remembered your dove?" [8]They quarreled, [and] neither did this Sage eat the last meal nor did that Sage eat the last meal.

MISHNAH [9][If] a woman rebels against her husband, we deduct from her ketubah seven dinarim per week. [10]Rabbi Yehudah says: Seven tropaics. [11]Until when does he

RASHI

שקל מנא – כלי זיין, כאילו בא להלחם. **איטרוד** – באותה מריבה. **לא מר איפסיק ולא מר איפסיק** – לא אכלו סעודת יום הכפורים שמפסיקין בה אכילה להתענות. סעודה אחרונה של ערב תשעה באב ויום הכיפורים קרי סעודה המפסקת, שמפסיקים בה, במסכת תענית (ל,א).

משנה המורדת על בעלה – בגמרא מפרש ממאי. **טרפעיקין** – בגמרא מפרש.

LANGUAGE

טְרַפָּעִיקִין **Tropaics.** From the Greek τρόπαικος, *tropaikos* (*victoriatus* in Latin), a coin worth half a dinar.

CONCEPTS

מוֹרֶדֶת **A rebellious woman.** A woman who refuses to fulfill her obligations towards her husband (particularly, a woman who refuses to have conjugal relations with her husband). Such a woman may be fined by having money deducted from her ketubah, and her husband may force her to accept a divorce. A husband who "rebels" against his wife may also be subject to monetary fines that increase the amount of his wife's ketubah.

NOTES

שְׁקַל מָנָא **He took a weapon.** It has been suggested that Rava was particularly angry with his son Rav Yosef, because unlike many other young scholars who were sent away to the Academy for twelve years (as we have seen in the stories related above), it was agreed that Rav Yosef would study in the Academy for only six years, and yet he was unable to resist the temptation to return home before completing his course of studies (*Ramat Shmuel*).

Maharsha prefers the reading found in some manuscripts and printed versions, זוּגָתְךָ ("your mate"), over the standard reading, זוֹנָתְךָ ("your mistress"). The alternative version יוֹנָתְךָ, ("your dove"), expresses the same idea, for doves are known for the affection they show their mates.

שִׁבְעָה דִּינָרִין ... שְׁלֹשָׁה דִּינָרִין **Seven dinarim ... three dinarim.** The question that immediately arises is why seven dinarim are deducted from a woman's ketubah for every week that she persists in her rebellion against her husband, but only three dinarim are added to her ketubah for every week that her husband rebels against her. The Gemara below (64a) explains that the woman's weekly seven-dinar penalty is based on a penalty of a dinar a day. The husband's three-dinar penalty is based on a daily penalty of half a dinar, multiplied by six for the six weekdays. The Gemara explains (64b) that the woman is entitled to a daily increment to her ketubah when her husband rebels against her that is only half as large as the penalty to which she is liable when she rebels against him, because she suffers less from her husband's rebellion than he does from hers.

The Jerusalem Talmud (see also *Bereshit Rabbah* 52) explains the matter differently: The seven-dinar penalty imposed upon a rebellious wife corresponds to the seven tasks that a woman is obligated to perform for her husband (see above, 59b), and the three-dinar penalty

TRANSLATION AND COMMENTARY

woman as his wife, and **deduct** a certain amount each week from her ketubah, before he is entitled to divorce her? [1] The Mishnah answers: He must keep her as his wife **until** nothing at all remains of **her ketubah**, after which he may divorce her without a ketubah. [2] **Rabbi Yose** disagrees and **says:** The husband may keep the rebellious woman as his wife even after nothing at all remains of her ketubah, and **may continue forever to deduct** seven dinarim (or seven tropaics) for each week that she persists in her rebellion. [3] The penalty remains in effect, **so that if she becomes the beneficiary of an inheritance,**

LITERAL TRANSLATION

deduct? [1] Until [an amount] corresponding to her ketubah. [2] Rabbi Yose says: He continues to deduct forever, [3] so that if an inheritance falls to her from somewhere else, he collects from it.

[4] And similarly if a man rebels against his wife, we add to her ketubah three dinarim per week. [5] Rabbi Yehudah says: Three tropaics.

פּוֹחֵת? ¹עַד כְּנֶגֶד כְּתוּבָּתָהּ. ²רַבִּי יוֹסֵי אוֹמֵר: לְעוֹלָם הוּא פּוֹחֵת וְהוֹלֵךְ, ³עַד שֶׁאִם תִּפּוֹל לָהּ יְרוּשָׁה מִמָּקוֹם אַחֵר, גּוֹבֶה הֵימֶנָּה.

⁴וְכֵן הַמּוֹרֵד עַל אִשְׁתּוֹ, מוֹסִיפִין עַל כְּתוּבָּתָהּ שְׁלֹשָׁה דִינָרִין בְּשַׁבָּת. ⁵רַבִּי יְהוּדָה אוֹמֵר: שְׁלֹשָׁה טַרְפָּעִיקִין.

RASHI

עד כדי כתובתה — ואחר כך נותן לה גט ויוצאה בלא כתובה. אבל אינו משהה לפחות על הנכסים שנפלו לה מבית אביה ולהפסידה ממנה. שלשה דינרים — בגמרא מפרש מאי שנא הוא מינה דידה.

her husband **may collect** the accumulated penalty **from** the estate that has come into her possession.

וְכֵן הַמּוֹרֵד עַל אִשְׁתּוֹ [4] The Mishnah continues: **And similarly if a man rebels against his wife, we** penalize the husband by compelling him to **add three dinarim to her ketubah for each week** that he persists in his rebellion. [5] **Rabbi Yehudah** disagrees and **says:** Her ketubah is increased by **three tropaics** (half-dinarim) for each week that her husband's rebellion continues.

NOTES

imposed upon a rebellious husband corresponds to the husband's three obligations toward his wife — food, clothing, and conjugal relations. *Tosafot* argues that the two Talmuds disagree with each other. But others have noted that the Jerusalem Talmud also offers the explanation of the Babylonian Talmud that a man suffers more from his wife's rebellion than a woman suffers from her husband's rebellion. The Jerusalem Talmud's first explanation appears to follow the opinion of Rabbi Yose the son of Rabbi Ḥanina that a rebellious wife is one who refuses to carry out the various tasks that a woman is obligated to perform for her husband, whereas the second explanation fits the viewpoint of Rav Huna that a rebellious wife is one who refuses to engage in sexual relations with her husband (*Ra'ah*).

Ra'ah asks: Since a married woman has eight obligations — the seven tasks that she must perform for her husband and her duty to cohabit with him — why is she penalized only seven dinarim a week and not eight? He answers that the seven obligations mentioned in the Jerusalem Talmud include the woman's duty to cohabit with her husband, but not her obligation to spin wool, for if a woman refuses to spin wool for her husband she is not considered a rebellious wife, but we deduct from her ketubah whatever loss in earnings she causes her husband to suffer.

עַד כְּנֶגֶד כְּתוּבָּתָהּ **Until an amount corresponding to her ketubah.** The Rishonim disagree about what the Mishnah

means when it says that a rebellious wife is penalized seven dinarim a week until she forfeits her entire ketubah. All agree that the woman forfeits her ketubah — both the basic portion and the additional portion — as well as her dowry, her *tzon barzel* property, that part of her property that is transferred to her husband while they are married but whose full value as fixed in the ketubah must be returned to her should she be divorced or widowed. They disagree about the woman's *melog* property, that part of her property that remains in her ownership even while she is married, during which time her husband is entitled to the property's usufruct. *Rashba* maintains that the rebellious wife does not forfeit her *melog* property, whereas *Ramban*, *Ritva*, and others maintain that she does, the dispute being based on two different interpretations of the Jerusalem Talmud dealing with the issue. According to *Rashba*, the anonymous first Tanna of the Mishnah and Rabbi Yose disagree not only about the property that the woman may inherit after she begins her rebellion, but also about the *melog* property in her possession before her rebellion began. According to the others, the Tannaim disagree only about an inheritance that came into her possession after she began her rebellion. The anonymous first Tanna maintains that the Rabbis did not extend her penalty to such property, for it is unusual for a woman to inherit property.

HALAKHAH

הַמּוֹרֵד **If a man rebels.** "If a man rebels against his wife, saying that he is ready to maintain her but refuses to cohabit with her, we penalize him by adding to his wife's ketubah thirty-six barley-grains of silver each week (following the anonymous first Tanna of the Mishnah). The penalty remains in effect as long as the husband persists in his refusal to cohabit with his wife and the wife does not demand a divorce. Even though the wife's ketubah contin-

ues to increase, the husband violates the negative commandment against diminishing his wife's conjugal rights each time he refuses to fulfill his marital duty. If the wife wishes the marriage to be dissolved, we compel the husband to divorce her immediately and to pay her her ketubah." (*Rambam*, *Sefer Nashim*, *Hilkhot Ishut* 14:15; *Shulḥan Arukh*, *Even HaEzer* 77:1.)

TRANSLATION AND COMMENTARY

GEMARA מוֹרֶדֶת מִמַּאי? [1] The Gemara first seeks to define the term "rebellious wife." In order to be categorized as **a woman who rebels** against her husband, **what** marital duties must she refuse to fulfill?

רַב הוּנָא אָמַר [2] **Rav Huna said:** A woman is regarded as a rebellious wife if she refuses to engage in **sexual relations** with her husband. [3] **Rabbi Yose the son of Rabbi Ḥanina said:** A woman is regarded as a rebellious wife if she refuses to carry out the various **tasks** that a woman is obligated to perform for her husband.

תְּנַן [4] The Gemara now considers these two opinions in the light of what **we learned** in the final clause of our Mishnah, which stated: **"And similarly if a man rebels against his wife,** we penalize the husband by compelling him to add three dinarim to her ketubah for each week that he persists in his rebellion." [5] **According to** Rav Huna, **who said** that a woman is regarded as a rebellious wife if she refuses to engage in **sexual relations,** the concluding clause of our Mishnah regarding a rebellious husband **is understandable.** "Rebellion" here means refusal to have sexual relations, no matter which spouse refuses. [6] **But according to** Rabbi Yose the son of Rabbi Ḥanina, **who said** that a rebellious wife is one who refuses to perform the **tasks** that a woman is obligated to perform for her husband, the parallel case of the rebellious husband is difficult to understand. [7] Are there any specific tasks that a man **is obligated to** perform for his wife?

גמרא [1]מוֹרֶדֶת מִמַּאי? [2]רַב הוּנָא אָמַר: מִתַּשְׁמִישׁ הַמִּטָּה. [3]רַבִּי יוֹסֵי בְּרַבִּי חֲנִינָא אָמַר: מִמְּלָאכָה. [4]תְּנַן: "וְכֵן הַמּוֹרֵד עַל אִשְׁתּוֹ". [5]בִּשְׁלָמָא לְמַאן דְּאָמַר מִתַּשְׁמִישׁ, לְחַיֵּי. [6]אֶלָּא לְמַאן דְּאָמַר מִמְּלָאכָה, [7]מִי מְשׁוּעְבַּד לַהּ?

LITERAL TRANSLATION

GEMARA [1] She rebels regarding what? [2] Rav Huna said: Regarding sexual relations. [3] Rabbi Yose the son of Rabbi Ḥanina said: Regarding work. [4] We have learned: "And similarly if a man rebels against his wife." [5] Granted according to the one who said regarding sexual relations, it is well. [6] But according to the one who said regarding work, [7] is he obligated to her?

NOTES

מוֹרֶדֶת מִמַּאי **She rebels regarding what?** The Gemara initially explains that, according to Rav Huna, a woman is only considered a rebellious wife if she refuses to engage in sexual relations with her husband, whereas according to Rabbi Yose the son of Rabbi Ḥanina she is only considered a rebellious wife if she refuses to do the various tasks that a wife is obligated to perform for her husband. The Gemara will later conclude that if a woman refuses to engage in sexual relations with her husband, all agree that she is considered a rebellious wife. Rav Huna and Rabbi Yose the son of Rabbi Ḥanina disagree only about whether or not a woman who refuses to perform the tasks that she is obligated to do is also treated as a rebellious wife.

The Rishonim disagree about which case is in dispute between the Amoraim. *Tosafot* and others maintain that the Amoraim disagree about a woman who refuses to perform the seven tasks listed in the Mishnah earlier in the chapter (59b): Grinding flour, baking, doing the laundry, cooking, nursing her infant, making her husband's bed, and spinning wool. Rav Huna follows his own opinion (58b), that a woman may say to her husband that she will not exercise her right to be maintained by him, nor will she do any handiwork for him. Thus a woman who refuses to perform the tasks imposed upon a married woman is not considered a rebellious wife. Rabbi Yose the son of Rabbi Ḥanina follows the viewpoint of Resh Lakish, that a woman can be compelled to produce handiwork for her husband, and therefore a woman who refuses to do so is treated as a rebellious wife.

Ra'avad asks: How can Rav Huna possibly maintain that a woman who refuses to do the household tasks imposed upon her is not considered a rebellious wife? How can her husband be required to maintain her when she refuses to fulfill her marital obligations? Moreover, the Gemara ruled earlier (59b) on the basis of a Baraita that a woman can be compelled to nurse her infant child. How can she be compelled to nurse her child except by being penalized by reducing her ketubah week by week for as long as she persists in her rebellion?

Ra'avad concludes that Rav Huna and Rabbi Yose the son of Rabbi Ḥanina are in full agreement that the woman's refusal to perform the first six tasks mentioned in the Mishnah is considered as rebellion. Rav Huna and Rabbi Yose the son of Rabbi Ḥanina disagree only about a woman who refuses to spin wool, the former maintaining that a woman may decide not to produce handiwork for her husband, and the latter maintaining that she may be compelled to do the handiwork that the Rabbis imposed upon her.

Ramban, *Ra'ah*, *Rashba*, and others maintain that Rav Huna and Rabbi Yose the son of Rabbi Ḥanina disagree only about the first six tasks mentioned in the Mishnah. According to Rav Huna, a woman who refuses to fulfill those obligations is treated as a rebellious wife, whereas according to Rabbi Yose the son of Rabbi Ḥanina, she is not. But both agree that a woman who refuses to produce handiwork is not regarded as a rebellious wife, for they both accept that a woman can waive her right to maintenance

HALAKHAH

מוֹרֶדֶת מִמַּאי **She rebels regarding what?** "A woman who refuses to cohabit with her husband is regarded as a rebellious wife, following Rav Huna (and Rabbi Yose the son of Rabbi Ḥanina, according to the Gemara's conclusion)." (*Rambam, Sefer Nashim, Hilkhot Ishut* 14:8; *Shulḥan Arukh, Even HaEzer* 77:2.)

LITERAL TRANSLATION

[1]Yes, when he says: [2]"I will not maintain [her] and I will not support [her]."

[3]But surely Rav said: [If] someone says: "I will not maintain [her] and I will not support [her]," [4]he must divorce [her] and give [her her] ketubah!

[5]But is it not necessary to consult with him?

[1]אִין, בְּאוֹמֵר: [2]"אֵינִי זָן וְאֵינִי מְפַרְנֵס".

[3]וְהָאָמַר רַב: הָאוֹמֵר: "אֵינִי זָן וְאֵינִי מְפַרְנֵס", [4]יוֹצִיא וְיִתֵּן כְּתוּבָּה!

[5]וְלָאו לְאִמְלוּכֵי בֵּיהּ בָּעֵי?

RASHI

גמרא באומר איני זן – דהיינו תחת מלאכה. **והאמר רב יוצא** – ומתניתין "מוסיפין" תנן, ואינו מוציא לאלתר. **ולאו אימלוכי ביה בעי** – שמא יחזור בו. ובתוך זמן שאנו נמלכין בו, ומחזירין עליו שיחזור בו – מוסיפין על כתובתה.

TRANSLATION AND COMMENTARY

אִין [1]The Gemara answers: **Yes**, we can understand the last clause of the Mishnah even according to Rabbi Yose the son of Rabbi Ḥanina. A man is considered rebellious **when he says:** [2]**"I will not maintain** my wife **and I will not provide for her support."** So a husband's "rebellion" may also be economic rather than sexual.

וְהָאָמַר רַב [3]The Gemara raises an objection: **But surely Rav said: If someone says: "I will not maintain** my wife **and I will not provide for her support,"** [4]**he must divorce her** immediately **and pay her her ketubah!** But our Mishnah teaches us that a rebellious husband must add a certain amount each week to his wife's ketubah, yet he is not required to divorce her immediately.

וְלָאו [5]The Gemara explains: Even though Rav said that a husband who refuses to maintain his wife must divorce her immediately, **does he not** agree that the court **must consult with him** to see whether he can be persuaded to provide for her support? Rav may maintain that the husband is penalized during the period of consultation by adding to his wife's ketubah for each week that he fails to maintain her. If the

NOTES

and stop producing handiwork for her husband.

As for *Ra'avad's* argument that Rav Huna must agree that a woman can be compelled to perform the various household tasks that were imposed upon her, the Rishonim suggest various other ways she can be compelled to fulfill her obligations. *Rambam* (*Hilkhot Ishut* 21:10) maintains that a woman can be compelled by the court to perform the tasks imposed upon her, even with a whip. *Ri Migash* maintains that she may be placed under a ban until she agrees to fulfill her duties. *Ramban* suggests that her husband can withhold her maintenance or can deny her conjugal rights.

Ra'ah distinguishes between the penalties imposed for rebellion, and the compensation that must be made for the monetary damage caused by the rebellious spouse. Rav Huna and Rabbi Yose the son of Rabbi Ḥanina disagree only about the definition of a rebellious wife, who may be penalized by deducting seven dinarim a week from her ketubah. But even Rav Huna agrees that if a woman refuses to perform the household tasks imposed upon her, her husband may hire a maid and deduct his expenses from his wife's ketubah. Similarly, Rabbi Yose the son of Rabbi Ḥanina maintains that the husband may deduct the cost of hiring household help from his wife's ketubah, in addition to deducting the weekly penalty imposed upon her.

וְהָאָמַר רַב **But surely Rav said.** The Gemara raises an objection against Rabbi Yose the son of Rabbi Ḥanina from the ruling of Rav. But Rav's ruling poses a difficulty for Rav Huna as well, for how can a woman who refuses to perform the various tasks imposed upon a married woman not be regarded as a rebellious wife, whereas a man who refuses to support his wife can be compelled to divorce her immediately?

Ramban answers that if a woman refuses to perform the various tasks that she is obligated to do for her husband, there are various ways the husband can compel her to fulfill her obligations. For example, he can withhold her maintenance or deny her conjugal rights. But if a man refuses to maintain his wife, there is little that the wife can do about it, and therefore the husband can be compelled to divorce her immediately. Moreover, if a woman refuses to fulfill her obligations, her husband suffers a loss, but he and his household are not placed in jeopardy. But if a man refuses to provide his wife with maintenance, she cannot wait until he agrees to support her, for she will starve, and this is why the courts can compel the man to grant her an immediate divorce and pay her her ketubah.

וְלָאו לְאִמְלוּכֵי בֵּיהּ בָּעֵי **But is it not necessary to consult with him?** Our commentary follows *Rashi*'s reading: "Is it not necessary to consult with *him*?" The Gemara assumes that before the husband can be compelled to divorce his wife, the court must consult with him and and see whether he can be persuaded to provide for her support. Several Rishonim (see *Ra'ah*, *Ritva*, and *Rivan*) point out the difficulties with this reading and interpretation. First, the Gemara should have explained how long the consultations must continue before the husband can be compelled to divorce his wife. In general, when the courts give a person the opportunity to effect a change, they give him thirty days to do so, but perhaps the law is different here. Second, why is it so obvious to the Gemara that such consultations are necessary? And third, why is the husband penalized during the period of consultations? Consequently, these other Rishonim prefer the reading: "Is it not necessary to consult with *her*, the woman?" This reading does not give rise to a contradiction between the Mishnah and Rav's ruling, for we consult with the woman whose husband refuses to support her, and find out how she wishes to proceed in the matter. If she wants a divorce, we compel the husband to grant her the divorce and pay her her ketubah immediately, as stated by Rav. And if she does not want an immediate divorce, we penalize him by compelling him to add to her ketubah for each week that he fails to maintain her, following the Mishnah.

TRANSLATION AND COMMENTARY

consultations fail, he is then required to divorce her and to pay her the increased ketubah.

מֵיתִיבֵי [1]**An objection was raised** against the viewpoint of Rav Huna from the following Baraita: "As for a rebellious wife, **the same law applies whether she is betrothed** to her husband and refuses to complete the marriage process **or** she is already **married** to him and fails to fulfill her marital obligations. [2]The same law applies **even** if she is **menstruating, and even** if she is **sick, and even** if she is a widow whose husband has died childless and she **is waiting for her** *yavam* (her husband's brother) to perform levirate marriage." [3]**According to** Rabbi Yose the son of Rabbi Ḥanina, **who said** that a woman is considered a rebellious wife if she refuses to perform the **tasks** that a woman is obligated to perform for her husband, this Baraita **is understandable.** [4]**But according to** Rav Huna, **who said** that a woman is considered a rebellious wife if she refuses to engage in **sexual relations** with her husband, how can a menstruating woman ever be categorized as a rebellious wife? [5]**Is a menstruating woman fit to have sexual relations?** What difference does it make to her husband that she refuses to cohabit with him when she is in any case forbidden to him?

[1]מֵיתִבֵי: "אַחַת לִי אֲרוּסָה וּנְשׂוּאָה, [2]וַאֲפִילּוּ נִדָּה, וַאֲפִילּוּ חוֹלָה, וַאֲפִילּוּ שׁוֹמֶרֶת יָבָם". [3]בִּשְׁלָמָא לְמַאן דַּאֲמַר מִמְּלָאכָה, שַׁפִּיר. [4]אֶלָּא לְמַאן דַּאֲמַר מִתַּשְׁמִישׁ, [5]נִדָּה בַּת תַּשְׁמִישׁ הִיא?

LITERAL TRANSLATION

[1]They raised an objection: "It is the same to me [whether she is] betrothed or married, [2]and even a menstruating woman, and even one who is sick, and even one who is waiting for [her] *yavam*." [3]Granted according to the one who said regarding work, it is well. [4]But according to the one who said regarding sexual relations, [5]is a menstruating woman fit for sexual relations?

RASHI

אחת לי — כולן שוות בתורת מרד, ואפילו שהיא נדה או חולה והיא מורדת. **ארוסה** — שאמרה: לא אנשא. הכי גרסינן: בשלמא למאן דאמר מתשמיש — שפיר. אלא למאן דאמר משום מלאכה, חולה בת מלאכה היא? בשלמא למאן דאמר מתשמיש — שפיר, ואי משום נדה דלאו בת תשמיש היא — אינו דומה מי שיש לו פת בסלו כו׳, כדלקמן. אלא למאן דאמר כו׳.

NOTES

בִּשְׁלָמָא לְמַאן דְּאָמַר מִמְּלָאכָה **Granted according to the one who said regarding work.** The Rishonim ask: Why does the Gemara say that the Baraita's mention of a menstruating woman is understandable according to Rabbi Yose the son of Rabbi Ḥanina, who said that a woman is considered a rebellious wife if she refuses to perform the tasks that a woman is obligated to perform for her husband? Surely the Baraita is also difficult according to Rabbi Yose, for it should not have said "*even* a menstruating woman," since regarding work a menstruating woman is no different from any other woman!

Ritva suggests that we might have thought that a menstruating woman who refuses to cook or bake for her husband is not treated as a rebellious wife, for a menstruating woman usually avoids the kitchen so as not to impart ritual impurity.

Tosafot argues that we might have thought that a menstruating woman is exempt from the tasks that a woman is obligated to perform for her husband, because she is considered to be slightly ill. Or alternatively, we might have thought that she is not treated as a rebellious wife, because she is forbidden to engage in the intimate tasks that a woman is obligated to perform for her husband, such as pouring his wine and washing his hands and face. Some Rishonim adopt alternative readings on account of the difficulties presented by the passage (see *Rashi*).

HALAKHAH

אַחַת לִי אֲרוּסָה וּנְשׂוּאָה **It is the same to me whether she is betrothed or married.** "If a woman is betrothed to be married, and when the time set for her marriage arrives, she refuses to complete the marriage in order to cause her bridegroom distress, she is treated as a rebellious wife (see Ḥelkat Meḥokek and Bet Shmuel regarding a betrothed woman who refuses to complete the marriage process by claiming incompatibility)." (*Rambam*, *Sefer Nashim*, *Hilkhot Ishut* 14:12; *Shulḥan Arukh*, *Even HaEzer* 77:2.)

וַאֲפִילּוּ נִדָּה, וַאֲפִילּוּ חוֹלָה **And even a menstruating woman, and even one who is sick.** "If a woman refuses to engage in sexual relations with her husband, even if she is menstruating or is ill and therefore not fit for such relations, she is treated as a rebellious wife. *Rema* notes that the authorities disagree about whether a distinction must be made between a woman who began her rebellion before she became ill or started menstruating and a woman who began her rebellion only after she was already ill or forbidden to her husband on account of her menstruation." (*Rambam*, *Sefer Nashim*, *Hilkhot Ishut* 14:11; *Shulḥan Arukh*, *Even HaEzer* 77:2.)

וַאֲפִילּוּ שׁוֹמֶרֶת יָבָם **And even one who is waiting for her *yavam*.** "According to some authorities, a widow whose husband died childless and who refuses to marry her brother-in-law in order to cause him distress is treated as a rebellious wife (see below, 64a)." (*Rambam*, *Sefer Nashim*, *Hilkhot Ishut* 14:11; *Hilkhot Yibbum* 2:10; *Shulḥan Arukh*, *Even HaEzer* 77:2.)

TRANSLATION AND COMMENTARY

אָמַר לָךְ [1] The Gemara answers: Rav Huna **can say to you: One who** is fasting and **has** a loaf of **bread** ready for him **in his basket is not like one who** is fasting and **does not** have a loaf of bread ready for him in his basket. A man whose wife would agree to engage in sexual relations with him, but is forbidden to do so on account of her menstruation, suffers far less than a man whose menstruating wife says that she would refuse to cohabit with him even if she were permitted to him. Thus a woman is regarded as a rebellious wife even if she refuses to cohabit with her husband when she is menstruating and is in any case forbidden to him.

אִיכָּא דְּאָמְרִי [2] **There are others who say** that the objection raised from the Baraita was directed at Rabbi Yose the son of Rabbi Ḥanina: **According to** Rav Huna, **who said** that a woman is regarded as a rebellious wife if she refuses to engage in **sexual relations** with her husband, [3] we can understand **why** the Baraita **teaches** us that the laws pertaining to a rebellious wife apply even to **a sick woman.** Even if she is unable to do the tasks that a married woman is ordinarily obliged to perform, she may still be able to engage in sexual relations with her husband, and therefore her refusal to cohabit with him renders her a rebellious wife. [63B] [4] **But according to** Rabbi Yose the son of Rabbi Ḥanina, **who said** that a rebellious wife is one who refuses to perform those **tasks** that a wife is obligated to perform for her husband, how can a sick woman ever be characterized as a rebellious wife? [5] **Is a sick woman fit to work?** Surely she cannot be penalized as rebellious if she is physically unable to do the work ordinarily undertaken by a married woman!

אֶלָּא [6] **Rather,** answers the Gemara, the dispute between Rav Huna and Rabbi Yose the son of Rabbi Ḥanina is to be understood as follows: **If** a woman persistently **refuses** to engage in **sexual relations** with her husband, [7] then **all agree** — both Rav Huna and Rabbi Yose the son of Rabbi Ḥanina — **that she is** regarded as a **rebellious** wife. [8] **They disagree** only **regarding** a woman who refuses to do the **tasks** that she is obligated to perform for her husband. [9] **The one Sage** — Rav Huna — **maintains** that **if** a wife **refuses** to perform these obligatory **tasks,** [10] **she is not** regarded as a **rebellious** wife. [11] **And the other Sage** — Rabbi Yose the son of Rabbi Ḥanina — **maintains** that **if** a wife **refuses** to perform these **tasks** for her husband, **she too is** treated as a **rebellious** wife, and is penalized for each week that she persists in her rebellion.

[1] אָמַר לָךְ: אֵינוֹ דּוֹמֶה מִי שֶׁיֵּשׁ לוֹ פַּת בְּסַלּוֹ לְמִי שֶׁאֵין לוֹ.
[2] אִיכָּא דְּאָמְרִי: בִּשְׁלָמָא לְמַאן דַּאֲמַר מִתַּשְׁמִישׁ, [3] הַיְינוּ דְּקָתָנֵי חוֹלָה. [63B] [4] אֶלָּא לְמַאן דַּאֲמַר מִמְּלָאכָה, [5] חוֹלָה בַּת מְלָאכָה הִיא?
[6] אֶלָּא, מִתַּשְׁמִישׁ, [7] כּוּלֵּי עָלְמָא לָא פְּלִיגֵי דְּהָוְיָא מוֹרֶדֶת. [8] כִּי פְּלִיגֵי, מִמְּלָאכָה. [9] מָר סָבַר: מִמְּלָאכָה, [10] לָא הָוְיָא מוֹרֶדֶת. [11] וּמָר סָבַר: מִמְּלָאכָה, נַמִי הָוְיָא מוֹרֶדֶת.

LITERAL TRANSLATION

[1] He can say to you: One who has bread in his basket is not like one who does not.

[2] There are [others] who say: Granted according to the one who said regarding sexual relations, [3] this is why it teaches [about] a sick woman. [63B] [4] But according to the one who said regarding work, [5] is a sick woman fit for work?

[6] Rather, [if she rebels] regarding sexual relations, [7] all agree (lit., "the whole world does not disagree") that she is rebellious. [8] When they disagreed, [it was] regarding work. [9] The one Sage maintains: [If she rebels] regarding work, she is not rebellious. [10] And the other Sage maintains: [11] [If she rebels] regarding work, she also is rebellious.

RASHI

אלא מתשמיש כולי עלמא לא פליגי דהויא מורדת – והך מתניתא במורדת מתשמיש.

NOTES

מִי שֶׁיֵּשׁ לוֹ פַּת בְּסַלּוֹ One who has bread in his basket. The Jerusalem Talmud distinguishes between a woman who refused to cohabit with her husband before the onset of her period and a woman who began to rebel against her husband during her period, when she was already forbidden to him. The former continues to be treated as a rebellious wife even while she is menstruating, and her ketubah continues to be diminished accordingly. But the latter is not treated as a rebellious wife, for she declared her refusal to cohabit with her husband while she was in any case forbidden to him. According to *Rosh*, the Babylonian Talmud does not accept this distinction. Even if a woman began her rebellion while she was menstruating, she is treated as a rebellious wife, for a man whose wife is forbidden to him on account of menstruation knows that in another few days she will undergo ritual immersion and be permitted to him. But if the woman announced that she would not cohabit with her husband even if she were permitted to him, her husband's suffering from his forced abstinence increases.

הַיְינוּ דְּקָתָנֵי חוֹלָה This is why it teaches about a sick woman. *Ritva* asks: Why does the Gemara not ask about a woman who is betrothed? According to Rabbi Yose the son of Rabbi Ḥanina, a rebellious wife is one who refuses

1 גּוּפָא: 2 ״הַמּוֹרֶדֶת עַל בַּעְלָהּ, פּוֹחֲתִין לָהּ מִכְּתוּבָּתָהּ שִׁבְעָה דִּינָרִים בְּשַׁבָּת. 3 רַבִּי יְהוּדָה אוֹמֵר: שִׁבְעָה טְרַפָּעִיקִין. 4 רַבּוֹתֵינוּ חָזְרוּ וְנִמְנוּ 5 שֶׁיְּהוּ מַכְרִיזִין עָלֶיהָ אַרְבַּע שַׁבָּתוֹת זוֹ אַחַר זוֹ, 6 וְשׁוֹלְחִין לָהּ בֵּית דִּין: הֱוִי יוֹדַעַת שֶׁאֲפִילּוּ כְּתוּבָּתֵיךְ

LITERAL TRANSLATION

[1]Returning to the statement quoted above (lit., "the thing itself"): [2]"[If] a woman rebels against her husband, we deduct from her ketubah seven dinarim per week. [3]Rabbi Yehudah says: Seven tropaics. [4]Our Rabbis went back and decided (lit., 'were counted') [5]that [the court] proclaims about her for four Sabbaths one after the other, [6]and the court sends her [a warning, saying]: Know that even if your ketubah

TRANSLATION AND COMMENTARY

Thus both Rav Huna and Rabbi Yose the son of Rabbi Ḥanina can interpret the Baraita as referring to a sick woman who refuses to engage in sexual relations with her husband, for even Rabbi Yose the son of Rabbi Ḥanina agrees that such a woman is regarded as a rebellious wife.

גּוּפָא [1]The Gemara now proceeds to quote in greater detail the Baraita cited above. **Returning to the statement quoted above,** we see that it states: [2]**"If a woman rebels against her husband, we** penalize her by **deducting from her ketubah seven dinarim for each week** that she persists in her rebellion. [3]**Rabbi Yehudah** disagrees and **says:** The ketubah of a rebellious wife is diminished by **seven tropaics** each week. [4]But **the later Rabbis went back and decided** that a different procedure should be adopted in order to persuade a woman to end her rebellion. [5]They enacted **that the court should** publicly **announce on four consecutive Sabbaths** that the woman is refusing to fulfill her marital obligations, to exert pressure on her to end her rebellion. [6]In addition, **the court must send her a warning, saying: Know that even if your**

BACKGROUND

רַבּוֹתֵינוּ חָזְרוּ וְנִמְנוּ Our Rabbis went back and decided. In other words, the later Sages discussed the regulation again and reached a conclusion (after a vote, as indicated by the word נִמְנוּ, meaning "they were counted") that there was need for another regulation to resolve the problem of the rebellious wife.

RASHI

חזרו ונמנו — שלא ישהו אותה לפחות מעט מעט, אלא יפסידוה כל כתובתה לאחר ארבע שבתות של הכרזה.

NOTES

to perform those tasks that a woman is obligated to perform for her husband. Why, then, do the laws pertaining to a rebellious wife apply to a betrothed woman? Surely a betrothed woman is not obligated to work for her bridegroom!

Ritva answers: The Baraita refers to a case where the time set for the woman's marriage has come, but she is not yet married. Such a woman is entitled to maintenance from her bridegroom, and in return she is obligated to give him her handiwork, and perhaps even to perform the household tasks imposed upon a married woman. Alternatively, the Baraita is referring to a case where the betrothed woman refuses to complete the marriage. Since a woman becomes obligated to perform certain household tasks for her husband when she is married, her refusal to complete the marriage is tantamount to a refusal to perform those tasks that were imposed upon a married woman.

שֶׁיְּהוּ מַכְרִיזִין That the court proclaims. *Rid* explains that the court makes a public announcement regarding the woman's refusal to fulfill her marital obligations, in order to embarrass her publicly and cause her to end her rebellion. Moreover, the matter is made public so that her friends and relatives will hear about it and will join the effort to persuade her to put an end to her rebellion.

אַרְבַּע שַׁבָּתוֹת Four Sabbaths. Almost all the Rishonim explain the Baraita according to its plain sense — that the court makes its public announcements once a week on Shabbat for four consecutive weeks. *Ritva* notes that a careful reading of the Baraita supports this understanding, for if "four Sabbaths" means every day for four weeks, there would have been no reason for the Baraita to say "one after the other," for unless stated otherwise, "four weeks" means four consecutive weeks. Moreover, *Tosafot* and *Ran* cite a Tosefta which states explicitly that the court's announcements are made once a week. *Rambam* disagrees with the rest of the Rishonim and explains the Baraita as meaning that the court makes its announcements every day for four consecutive weeks. *Maggid Mishneh* explains *Rambam*'s ruling: The Baraita stated that the announcements are made on four consecutive "Sabbaths." According to Rava, this supports Rami bar Ḥama's ruling that those announcements are made specifically in the synagogues and in the study halls. Since the announcements are made only in the synagogues and in the study halls, they must be made every day for four consecutive weeks. But if the announcements were made in the streets and marketplaces as well, it would not have been necessary to make them so frequently.

אֲפִילּוּ כְּתוּבָּתֵיךְ Even if your ketubah. This could mean that no penalty is imposed on the woman during the four-week period of announcements and warnings. If she persists in her rebellion even after the court's announcements and warnings, she forfeits her entire ketubah, but if

HALAKHAH

רַבּוֹתֵינוּ חָזְרוּ וְנִמְנוּ Our Rabbis went back and decided. "If a woman rebels against her husband, the court makes a public announcement on the matter every day for four weeks, declaring that the woman is refusing to cohabit with her husband. *Rema* notes that according to some authorities (*Tosafot, Ran,* and others), the court's announcements are not made every day but once a week on Shabbat. Afterwards, the court sends the woman a warning that if she persists in her rebellion, she will forfeit her entire ketubah. If she does persist in her rebellion, she loses her entire ketubah," following the opinion of the later Rabbis. (*Rambam, Sefer Nashim, Hilkhot Ishut* 14:9-10; *Shulḥan Arukh, Even HaEzer* 77:2.)

TRANSLATION AND COMMENTARY

ketubah — the basic portion and the additional sum — **is** as much as **a hundred maneh, you will lose it** all if you do not resume your marital duties. If the woman persists in her rebellion even after the court's announcements and warnings, she forfeits her entire ketubah and her husband has the right to divorce her immediately. [1]**The same law applies whether she is betrothed** to someone and refuses to complete the marriage process **or** she is already **married** to him and refuses to comply with her marital obligations. [2]The same law applies **even** if she is **menstruating, and even** if she **is sick, and even** if she is a widow whose husband died childless and she **is waiting for the** ***yavam*** to perform levirate marriage."

אֲמַר לֵיהּ [3]The Gemara now repeats the objection raised earlier against this Baraita, and offers the same resolution. **Rabbi Ḥiyya bar Yosef said to Shmuel: Is a menstruating woman fit to have sexual relations?** What difference does it make to her husband that she refuses to cohabit with him when she is in any case forbidden to him?

אֲמַר לֵיהּ [4]Shmuel **said to** Rabbi Ḥiyya bar Yosef: **One who** is fasting and **has** a loaf of **bread** ready for him **in his basket is not like one who** is fasting and **does not have** a loaf of **bread** ready for him **in his basket.** Similarly, a man whose wife is temporarily forbidden to him on account of her menstruation suffers far less from the abstinence forced upon him when he knows that his wife would otherwise agree to engage in sexual relations with him than when he knows that his wife would refuse to cohabit with him even if she were permitted to do so.

אֲמַר רָמִי בַּר חָמָא [5]**Rami bar Ḥama said: The court makes** its public **announcements about** the rebellious wife **only in the synagogues and in the study halls,** but not in the streets and marketplaces.

אֲמַר רָבָא [6]**Rava said:** A **precise** examination of the wording of the Baraita **also** provides support for the ruling of Rami bar Ḥama, **for** the Baraita **states:** [7]"The court makes its public announcements on **four consecutive Sabbaths,"** on days of rest, when people are not found in the streets and marketplaces but in the synagogues and study halls. [8]The Gemara accepts Rava's argument and says: It is indeed correct to **draw this conclusion from** the Baraita.

מֵאָה מָנֶה, הִפְסַדְתְּ. [1]אַחַת לִי אֲרוּסָה וּנְשׂוּאָה, [2]אֲפִילּוּ נִדָּה, אֲפִילּוּ חוֹלָה, וַאֲפִילּוּ שׁוֹמֶרֶת יָבָם״.

[3]אֲמַר לֵיהּ רַבִּי חִיָּיא בַּר יוֹסֵף לִשְׁמוּאֵל: נִדָּה בַּת תַּשְׁמִישׁ הִיא?

[4]אֲמַר לֵיהּ: אֵינוֹ דּוֹמֶה מִי שֶׁיֵּשׁ לוֹ פַּת בְּסַלּוֹ לְמִי שֶׁאֵין לוֹ פַּת בְּסַלּוֹ.

[5]אָמַר רָמִי בַּר חָמָא: אֵין מַכְרִיזִין עָלֶיהָ אֶלָּא בְּבָתֵּי כְנֵסִיּוֹת וּבְבָתֵּי מִדְרָשׁוֹת.

[6]אֲמַר רָבָא: דַּיְקָא נַמִי, דְּקָתָנֵי: [7]״אַרְבַּע שַׁבָּתוֹת זוֹ אַחַר זוֹ״. [8]שְׁמַע מִינָּהּ.

LITERAL TRANSLATION

is a hundred maneh, you have lost it. [1]It is the same to me [whether she is] betrothed or married, [2]even a menstruating woman, [and] even one who is sick, and even one who is waiting for her *yavam*."

[3]Rabbi Ḥiyya bar Yosef said to Shmuel: Is a menstruating woman fit for sexual relations?

[4]He said to him: One who has bread in his basket is not like one who does not have bread in his basket.

[5]Rami bar Ḥama said: [The court] does not proclaim about her except in the synagogues and in the study halls.

[6]Rava said: It is also precise, for it teaches: [7]"Four Sabbaths one after the other." [8]Conclude from this.

RASHI

דיקא נמי דקתני ארבע שבתות — ימים שאינם של מלאכה, והכל מצוין בבתי כנסיות ובבתי מדרשות.

NOTES

she ends her rebellion, she is still entitled to the entire amount recorded in her ketubah. The Rishonim argue that if this were so, a woman could rebel against her husband repeatedly for periods of three weeks at a time, without being penalized in any way. *Ra'ah* concludes from this that the woman's ketubah is diminished by seven dinars a week even during the period of announcements and warnings. The later Rabbis did not abolish that penalty altogether, but enacted that after four weeks of public announcements and warnings the rebellious wife immediately forfeits whatever remains of her ketubah. Others argue that according to the enactment of the later Rabbis a woman is given four weeks to reconsider her rebellion, during which time no penalty is imposed. But if she rebels again, she forfeits her entire ketubah immediately, for she was given four weeks of announcements and warnings the first time she rebelled against her husband (see *Ran*).

HALAKHAH

אֵין מַכְרִיזִין עָלֶיהָ אֶלָּא בְּבָתֵּי כְנֵסִיּוֹת The court does not proclaim about her except in the synagogues. "The public announcements regarding a woman's refusal to cohabit with her husband are made only in the synagogue or in the study hall," following Rami bar Ḥama. (*Rambam, Sefer Nashim, Hilkhot Ishut* 14:9; *Shulḥan Arukh, Even HaEzer* 77:2.)

LANGUAGE

בּוּרְכָא Absurdity. *Arukh* explains this word as being an expanded form of the word **בור** ("empty," "uncultivated"), and that it means "a senseless thing," "an absurdity." This meaning is attested to in other Talmudic passages as well. But other authorities derive it from a Persian word meaning "something disgusting."

TRANSLATION AND COMMENTARY

אָמַר רָמִי בַּר חָמָא [1] **Rami bar Ḥama** now clarifies a second point mentioned in the Baraita. **The court twice sends** the rebellious wife **a warning** that she is liable to forfeit her entire ketubah if she does not resume her marital obligations — [2] **once before the** court's public **announcement** regarding her rebellion **and once after the** public **announcement.** If the woman persists in her rebellion after she has received her final warning, she forfeits her entire ketubah and her husband is entitled to divorce her immediately.

דָּרַשׁ רַב נַחְמָן [3] **Rav Naḥman bar Rav Ḥisda stated: The Halakhah is in accordance with the** later **Rabbis,** who said that the procedure to be adopted in connection with a rebellious wife involves a series of announcements and warnings regarding her rebellion and its consequences.

אָמַר רָבָא [4] **Rava said: This** statement **is** patently **absurd.**

אָמַר לֵיהּ [5] **Rav Naḥman bar Yitzḥak said to** Rava: **What is the absurdity** of Rav Naḥman bar Rav Ḥisda's statement? [6] **I** myself **told him** that the Halakhah is in accordance with the later Rabbis, **and I reported** that ruling **to him in the name of a great authority.** [7] **And who is that** great authority? [8] It is **Rabbi Yose the son of Rabbi Ḥanina.**

[1] אָמַר רָמִי בַּר חָמָא: פַּעֲמַיִם שׁוֹלְחִין לָהּ מִבֵּית דִּין — [2] אַחַת קוֹדֶם הַכְרָזָה וְאַחַת לְאַחַר הַכְרָזָה.

[3] דָּרַשׁ רַב נַחְמָן בַּר רַב חִסְדָּא: הֲלָכָה כְּרַבּוֹתֵינוּ.

[4] אָמַר רָבָא: הַאי בּוּרְכָא.

[5] אָמַר לֵיהּ רַב נַחְמָן בַּר יִצְחָק: מַאי בּוּרְכָתֵיהּ? [6] אֲנָא אֲמָרִיתָהּ נִיהֲלֵיהּ, וּמִשְּׁמֵיהּ דְּגַבְרָא רַבָּה אֲמָרִיתָהּ נִיהֲלֵיהּ. [7] וּמַנּוּ? [8] רַבִּי יוֹסֵי בְּרַבִּי חֲנִינָא.

LITERAL TRANSLATION

[1] Rami bar Ḥama said: Twice they send her [a warning] from the court — [2] once before the proclamation and once after the proclamation.

[3] Rav Naḥman bar Rav Ḥisda expounded: The Halakhah is in accordance with our Rabbis.

[4] Rava said: This is an absurdity.

[5] Rav Naḥman bar Yitzḥak said to him: What is its absurdity? [6] I said it to him, and I said it to him in the name of a great man. [7] And who is he? [8] Rabbi Yose the son of Rabbi Ḥanina.

RASHI

בורכא — דבר שאינו הגון.

NOTES

פַּעֲמַיִם שׁוֹלְחִין לָהּ Twice they send her a warning. Most Rishonim explain that a rebellious wife is sent a warning once before the court makes its first public announcement regarding her rebellion and again after it makes its last announcement. But *Talmidei Rabbenu Yonah* maintains that she is sent two warnings with each announcement, one before and one after, so that she receives a total of eight warnings before she forfeits her ketubah.

הֲלָכָה כְּרַבּוֹתֵינוּ The Halakhah is in accordance with our Rabbis. The Rishonim interpret this passage in various ways. Our commentary follows *Rashi, Ri Migash,* and others, who explain that Rav Naḥman bar Rav Ḥisda agrees with the later Rabbis who rule that a rebellious wife forfeits her entire ketubah after the four weeks during which the court issues a series of announcements and warnings regarding her rebellion. But Rava disagrees, saying that the law is in accordance with our Mishnah that a rebellious wife is made to pay seven dinarim a week for as long as she persists in her rebellion. The Gemara goes on to explain that Rava agrees with Rav Sheshet, who rules that we consult with the rebellious wife and try to persuade her to resume her marital obligations. Meanwhile, her ketubah is reduced each week that she persists in her rebellion, as is stated in the Mishnah. There are two main difficulties with this explanation: First, why does the Gemara seek support for Rava? Surely he is ruling in accordance with the Mishnah! And second, why does Rav Sheshet add the new element that the Halakhah is that we consult with the rebellious wife? He should state simply that the Halakhah is in accordance with the viewpoint of the Mishnah.

Rabbenu Tam offers a different interpretation of this discussion. He explains that both Rav Naḥman bar Rav Ḥisda and Rava agree that the Halakhah is in accordance with the viewpoint of the later Rabbis as opposed to the viewpoint of the Mishnah. Rav Naḥman bar Rav Ḥisda says that the Halakhah follows the later Rabbis literally, and the court sends the rebellious woman a single warning after the public announcements are completed. Rava disagrees and says that the Halakhah is in accordance with Rami bar Ḥama that the warning must be issued twice, once before the public announcement and once after. The Gemara goes on to explain that Rava follows the viewpoint of Rav Sheshet that we consult with her and we warn her again that she is liable to lose her ketubah.

Ra'avad suggests a third interpretation: Rav Naḥman bar Rav Ḥisda rules that the law is in accordance with the viewpoint of the later Rabbis that after four weeks a

HALAKHAH

פַּעֲמַיִם שׁוֹלְחִין לָהּ Twice they send her a warning. "Before the court makes its public announcement regarding the rebellious wife, it sends her a warning that she is liable to forfeit her entire ketubah if she persists in her rebellion. And similarly at the end, after the final announcement is made, the court sends the woman a second such warning." (*Rambam, Sefer Nashim, Hilkhot Ishut* 14:9-10; *Shulḥan Arukh, Even HaEzer* 77:2.)

TRANSLATION AND COMMENTARY

וְאִיהוּ כְּמַאן סָבַר [1] Satisfied that Rav Naḥman bar Rav Ḥisda's ruling was stated on good authority, the Gemara now seeks to understand why Rava rejected Rav Naḥman's ruling outright. The Gemara asks: **With whose** viewpoint **does Rava agree?**

כִּי הָא דְּאִתְּמַר [2] The Gemara answers: We can understand Rava's viewpoint **in the light of the following statement** that the later Amoraim disagreed about the matter: **Rava said in the name of Rav Sheshet:** [3] **The Halakhah is** that the husband does not have the right to divorce his rebellious wife immediately and without having to pay her her ketubah. Instead, **we** continue to **consult with her** and we try to persuade her to resume her marital obligations; meanwhile her ketubah is reduced each week that she persists in her rebellion. [4] **Rav Huna bar Yehudah said in the name of Rav Sheshet:** [5] **The Halakhah is** that **we do not** continue to **consult with her** about ending her rebellion, and her ketubah continues to be reduced each week that she fails to fulfill her marital obligations. Thus both Rava and Rav Huna bar Yehudah agree that the law does not follow the later Rabbis but agrees with the Mishnah — that the rebellious wife's ketubah is decreased week by week until nothing remains, and only then is her husband entitled to divorce her without paying her her ketubah.

הֵיכִי דָּמְיָא מוֹרֶדֶת [6] Having clarified the procedures to be adopted with respect to a rebellious wife, the Gemara now asks: **How** precisely **do we visualize the case of a rebellious wife?**

אֲמַר אֲמֵימַר [7] **Amemar said:** The regulations governing a rebellious wife apply only in a case **where she says:** [8] **"I want** to remain married to **him, but** we have quarreled and **I wish to cause him distress** by refusing to cohabit with him." [9] **But** in a case **where she says:** "I cannot bring myself to cohabit with my husband,

[1] וְאִיהוּ כְּמַאן סָבַר?
[2] כִּי הָא דְּאִתְּמַר: רָבָא אָמַר רַב שֵׁשֶׁת: [3] הֲלָכָה: נִמְלָכִין בָּהּ.
[4] רַב הוּנָא בַּר יְהוּדָה אָמַר רַב שֵׁשֶׁת: [5] הֲלָכָה: אֵין נִמְלָכִין בָּהּ.
[6] הֵיכִי דָּמְיָא מוֹרֶדֶת?
[7] אֲמַר אֲמֵימַר: דְּאָמְרָה: [8] "בָּעֵינָא לֵיהּ, וּמְצַעַרְנָא לֵיהּ".
[9] אֲבָל אָמְרָה: "מְאִיס עֲלַי",

LITERAL TRANSLATION

[1] And with whom does he [Rava] agree?

[2] In accordance with this that was stated: Rava said in the name of Rav Sheshet: [3] The Halakhah is: We consult with her. [4] Rav Huna bar Yehudah said in the name of Rav Sheshet: [5] The Halakhah is: We do not consult with her.

[6] How do we visualize the case of (lit., "how is it like") a rebellious woman?

[7] Amemar said: If she says: [8] "I want him, but I [wish to] cause him distress." [9] But [if] she says: "He is repulsive to me,"

RASHI

ואיהו כמאן סבר — רבא דאמר בורכא היא, כמאן סבר? **נמלכין בה** — משהין את גיטה, ומחזירין עליה שתחזור בה ובתוך כך פוחתין מכתובתה שבעה דינרין בשבת. **היכי דמיא מורדת** — דכופין אותה, דמשהין גיטה ופוחתין כתובתה. **דאמרה בעינא ליה כו׳** — שיש לכופה על ידי פחיתת כתובתה. **אבל אמרה מאיס עלי** — לא הוא ולא כתובתו בעינא.

NOTES

rebellious wife immediately forfeits her entire ketubah, and against the viewpoint of our Mishnah that a weekly penalty is imposed on a woman who rebels against her husband. Rava disagrees and says that the later Rabbis never set out to invalidate the ruling found in the Mishnah. Rather, they added to it and allowed the rebellious wife to be judged in accordance with their ruling should she so desire. The Gemara goes on to explain that Rava follows the viewpoint of Rav Sheshet that we consult with the rebellious wife and we ask her whether she wishes to be judged according to the law of the Mishnah that seven dinarim a week are to be deducted from her ketubah, or according to the viewpoint of the later Rabbis that she loses her entire ketubah immediately after the four-week procedure of announcements and warnings is completed.

"מְאִיס עֲלַי" **"He is repulsive to me."** There are two fundamental positions regarding the law that applies to a woman who refuses to cohabit with her husband because she finds him repulsive. *Rambam* (and *Rashi*, according to many Rishonim) maintains that if a woman claims that she is unable to bring herself to have sexual relations with her husband because she finds him repulsive, her husband can

HALAKHAH

נִמְלָכִין בָּהּ **We consult with her.** "If a rebellious wife persists in her rebellion even after she has been warned about the possible consequences, we consult with her. If she remains adamant in her rebellion, she forfeits her entire ketubah," following Rava in the name of Rav Sheshet. (*Rambam, Sefer Nashim, Hilkhot Ishut* 14:10; *Shulḥan Arukh, Even HaEzer* 77:2.)

"בָּעֵינָא לֵיהּ, וּמְצַעַרְנָא לֵיהּ" **"I want him, but I wish to cause him distress."** "If a woman rebels against her husband in order to cause him distress, saying that she is doing so on account of something he did, or because of some quarrel between them, she is governed by all the laws pertaining to a rebellious wife. *Rema* notes that the same laws apply to a woman who refuses to cohabit with her husband because she claims she finds him repulsive, if she demands a divorce and payment of her ketubah," following *Bet Yosef* in the name of *Ran*, and *Rashi*. (*Rambam, Sefer Nashim, Hilkhot Ishut* 14:9; *Shulḥan Arukh, Even HaEzer* 77:2.)

"מְאִיס עֲלַי" **"He is repulsive to me."** "If a woman rebels

SAGES

רַב חֲנִינָא מְסּוּרָא Rav Ḥanina of Sura. A Babylonian Amora of the fifth generation, Rav Hanina of Sura was a colleague of Mar Zutra, Rav Mari, and Rav Pappi. His rulings are quoted in a number of places in the Talmud.

for **he is repulsive to me,"** [1] **we do not compel her** to remain his wife. No public announcement is made about her rebellion, nor is any warning sent to the woman regarding the consequences of her refusal to fulfill her marital obligation. Her husband may divorce her immediately without having to pay her her ketubah. [2] **Mar Zutra said:** Even in a case where the woman claims that

[1] we do not compel her. [2] Mar Zutra said: We compel her.

[3] There was an incident, and Mar Zutra compelled her, [4] and Rabbi Ḥanina of Sura resulted (lit., "came out") from it. [5] But it is not so.

¹ לָא כָּיְיפִינַן לָהּ. ²מָר זוּטְרָא
אָמַר: כָּיְיפִינַן לָהּ.
³הֲוָה עוּבְדָא, וְאַכְפָּהּ מָר
זוּטְרָא, ⁴וּנְפַק מִינֵּיהּ רַבִּי
חֲנִינָא מְסּוּרָא. ⁵וְלָא הִיא.

RASHI

לא כייפינן לה — להשהותה, אלא נותן לה גט, ויוצאה בלא כתובה.

she and her husband are incompatible, **we compel her** to remain his wife. If she persists in her refusal to cohabit with him, she too is treated as a rebellious wife.

הֲוָה עוּבְדָא [3] The Gemara relates that **there was** indeed **an incident** in which a woman refused to cohabit with her husband, arguing that she found him repulsive, **and Mar Zutra compelled her** to remain with her husband. In that case, the decision compelling the wife to remain with her husband had positive results, for a great Sage, [4] **Rabbi Ḥanina of Sura, was born from** this union. The Gemara adds that we might have thought that this incident proves that a woman who claims that she and her husband are incompatible should in fact be compelled to remain with him, [5] **but it is not** really **so.**

NOTES

be compelled to divorce her without delay, for a woman is not a captive who must submit to sexual relations with someone repulsive to her. *Rabbenu Tam* (in his *Sefer HaYashar*, and as cited by *Tosafot*) raises a series of objections against this position. His main argument is that if we compel a husband to divorce his wife when she claims that she finds him repulsive, then whenever a woman wants a divorce because she finds another man more attractive, she can simply put forward the claim that she finds her husband repulsive and get what she wants. Moreover, our Gemara nowhere states that the husband can be compelled to divorce his wife if she claims that he is repulsive. Thus we can infer that the husband cannot be compelled to divorce his wife, even if she claims that she finds him repulsive. All that the Gemara is saying here is that the penalties and the procedure of warnings and announcements described in the Mishnah and the Baraita do not apply in such a case (see also next note). Most of the Rishonim (*Ramban, Rashba, Ra'ah, Rosh, Ran,* and others) accept the interpretation of *Rabbenu Tam*.

The law regarding a woman who claims that she finds her husband repulsive underwent a change during the Geonic period with the passing of an enactment known as "The Law of the Academies." In order to prevent a woman who wanted a divorce from applying to a non-Jewish court to compel her husband to grant her the divorce (in which case the validity of her divorce and the legitimacy of her children from a later marriage would be in question), the Geonim enacted that if a woman claims that she finds her husband repulsive, her husband can be compelled to give her a divorce, and the woman is entitled to at least part of her ketubah. The Rishonim disagree about whether this enactment was meant to be established as the law or whether it was an emergency measure intended only for the period in which it was enacted. Most authorities limit the cases to which the enactment may be applied.

לָא כָּיְיפִינַן לָהּ We do not compel her. The Rishonim offer different interpretations of this passage in line with the position they take about the more fundamental issue of whether or not a husband can be compelled to divorce his wife if she claims that she finds him repulsive. According to *Rashi* and *Rambam,* Amemar said that we do not compel the woman to remain his wife, and the husband must grant her an immediate divorce without payment of her ketubah. Mar Zutra disagreed, saying that we compel the woman to remain her husband's wife. She too is treated as a rebellious wife, whose ketubah is reduced week by week, according to the Mishnah, or forfeited immediately after four weeks of announcements and warnings, according to the Baraita.

Rabbenu Tam explains Amemar's position as follows: If a woman claims that she finds her husband repulsive and that she is willing to forfeit her ketubah in order to obtain a divorce, we do not compel her to remain his wife by saying that she does not really mean to waive her ketubah, a decision that would deter her husband from divorcing her. Mar Zutra disagreed and said we compel the woman to remain married by saying that her waiver is not valid, so that her husband will not agree to divorce her.

Ra'ah argues that Amemar's view must be understood as follows: If a woman claims that she finds her husband repulsive, we cannot compel him to divorce her and pay her her ketubah, because we cannot be certain that she is telling the truth. But we do not take any steps to compel the woman to desist from her rebellion. In other words, we do not penalize her by diminishing her ketubah week by week or all at once, for she may indeed be telling the truth, and a woman who finds her husband repulsive is forbidden to cohabit with him. Thus the court does not address the case at all. Mar Zutra disagreed and said that we compel the woman to desist from her rebellion by treating her as a rebellious wife and by diminishing her ketubah. There is

HALAKHAH

against her husband, claiming that she is unable to bring herself to engage in sexual relations with him because she finds him repulsive, her husband may divorce her without

paying her her ketubah," following *Rabbenu Tam,* against *Rambam.* (*Rambam, Sefer Nashim, Hilkhot Ishut* 14:8; *Shulḥan Arukh, Even HaEzer* 77:2.)

TRANSLATION AND COMMENTARY

[1] **There,** in the case of Mar Zutra, **there was** special **divine assistance** which helped to bring about the happy ending to the story. But as a rule no good can come from a union to which one of the parties objects.

כַּלְתֵיהּ דְּרַב זְבִיד [2] It was related that **the daughter-in-law of Rav Zevid rebelled** against her husband and refused to cohabit with him. [3] **She took possession of a silk garment** that she had brought into the marriage as part of her dowry, and she claimed that she was still entitled to keep the garment. [4] **Amemar, Mar Zutra, and Rav Ashi were sitting** together discussing the validity of her claim, **and Rav Gamda was sitting with them.** [5] The first three Sages **sat and said: If** a woman **rebels** against her husband, **she loses** her entire ketubah and also **the clothing** she brought into the marriage as part of her dowry and **which is** now **worn** out **but still in existence** at the time of her rebellion. Thus Rav Zevid's daughter-in-law must give up the silk garment that is still in her possession. [6] When he heard this ruling, **Rav Gamda said to** his three colleagues: Is it **because Rav Zevid is a great man** that **you favor him** in your Halakhic ruling? [7] **Surely Rav Kahana said: Rava asked this** very **question** as to whether a rebellious wife forfeits the clothing she brought into the marriage, **and he was unable to answer it!** Yet here you have decided that a rebellious wife does indeed forfeit such clothing, and have ruled in Rav Zevid's favor!

אִיכָּא דְּאָמְרֵי [8] **There are some who report** this incident in a slightly different way. The three Sages, Amemar, Mar Zutra, and Rav Ashi **sat** discussing the case of the rebellion of Rav Zevid's daughter-in-law **and** they

[1] הָתָם סַיַּיעְתָּא דִּשְׁמַיָּא הֲוָה. [2] כַּלְתֵיהּ דְּרַב זְבִיד אִימְרְדָא. [3] הֲוָה תְּפִיסָא חַד שִׁירָא. [4] יְתִיב אֲמֵימָר, וּמָר זוּטְרָא, וְרַב אַשִׁי, וִיתִיב רַב גַּמְדָּא גַּבַּיְיהוּ. [5] יָתְבִי וְקָאָמְרִי: מָרְדָה, הִפְסִידָה בְּלָאוֹתֶיהָ קַיָּימִין. [6] אֲמַר לְהוּ רַב גַּמְדָּא: מִשּׁוּם דְּרַב זְבִיד גַּבְרָא רַבָּה, מַחֲנִיפִיתוּ לֵיהּ? [7] וְהָאָמַר רַב כָּהֲנָא: מִיבַּעְיָא בָּעֵי רָבָא, וְלָא פְּשִׁיט! [8] אִיכָּא דְּאָמְרִי: יָתְבִי וְקָאָמְרִי:

LITERAL TRANSLATION

[1] There there was divine assistance.

[2] The daughter-in-law of Rav Zevid rebelled. [3] She took possession of one silk garment. [4] Amemar, Mar Zutra, and Rav Ashi were sitting, and Rav Gamda was sitting with them. [5] They sat and said: [If] she rebelled, she has lost her worn clothes that [still] exist. [6] Rav Gamda said to them: Because Rav Zevid is a great man, do you show favor to him? [7] But surely Rav Kahana said: Rava asked [this] question, but did not resolve [it]!

[8] There are [some] who say: They sat and said:

RASHI

כלתה דרב זביד אימרידא — ואמרה: מאיס עלי. **הוה תפיסא חדא שירא** — מעיל אחד שהכניסה לו בכתובה. **הפסידה בלאותיה קיימין** — אפילו בגדיה שהכניסה לו בנדונייתה ושמאוס עליו בכתובתה, ועדיין הבלאות קיימין — תפסיד אותם. **מיבעיא בעי** — אם הפסידה בלאותיה אם לאו.

SAGES

רַב גַּמְדָּא **Rav Gamda.** A Babylonian Amora of the fifth and sixth generations, Rav Gamda was a disciple of Rava and transmitted several teachings in his name. Though he was not one of the judges of the central House of Study, he was highly respected, and other great Sages, sitting in judgment, took his opinions into consideration.

Nothing is known of his private life beyond the account (in *Nedarim* 50b) that a miracle took place for him and he became a wealthy man.

NOTES

no concern that she will violate the prohibition against engaging in sexual relations with a man that she despises, for if she does in fact return to him, it must be because she no longer finds him repulsive.

Some Rishonim cite a variant reading: "But if she says: 'He is repulsive to me,' we do not compel *him.*" *Ra'ah* explains that if a woman says that she finds her husband repulsive, there is little chance that she will be persuaded to return to him, and therefore we do not compel him to maintain her as his wife and to diminish her ketubah week by week. Instead, we allow him to divorce her immediately without payment of her ketubah. Mar Zutra disagreed with Amemar and said that even if the woman claims that she finds her husband repulsive, he may not divorce her immediately without paying her her ketubah. Instead, we reduce her ketubah week by week in the hope that she will agree to resume her marital obligations.

הָתָם סַיַּיעְתָּא דִּשְׁמַיָּא הֲוָה There there was divine assistance. According to one manuscript reading, the divine assistance that was granted in this case was due to the special merit of Mar Zutra, who issued the ruling. But other authorities cannot rely on such assistance and should refrain from issuing a similar ruling.

כַּלְתֵיהּ דְּרַב זְבִיד אִימְרְדָא The daughter-in-law of Rav Zevid rebelled. *Rashi* and others explain that the daughter-in-law of Rav Zevid refused to cohabit with her husband, claiming that she found him repulsive. Thus we are dealing with a case in which the laws pertaining to a rebellious wife do not apply. The Rishonim explain that *Rashi* understood the case in this way, because if Rav Zevid's daughter-in-law had refused to cohabit with her husband because she wanted to cause him distress, then surely she would not have been entitled to the silk garment, for a rebellious wife forfeits her entire ketubah, including her dowry. *Ra'ah* and others argue that the Gemara's formulation — "the daughter-in-law of Rav Zevid *rebelled*" — implies that she rebelled in order to cause her husband distress. According to the Mishnah, a rebellious wife forfeits her dowry, but here the Gemara is discussing the issue according to the later Rabbis, who were more lenient.

חַד שִׁירָא One silk garment. The standard text — חַד שִׁירָא — can also be interpreted to mean "one bracelet." *Rashi* follows the reading חֲדָא שִׁירָאָה, which he understands as "one garment." The discussion that follows regarding the rebellious wife's worn clothing supports *Rashi's* reading.

[1]מָרְדָה, לֹא הִפְסִידָה בְּלָאוֹתֶיהָ קַיָּימִין. [2]אֲמַר לְהוּ רַב גַּמְדָּא: [64A] [3]מִשּׁוּם דְּרַב זְבִיד גַּבְרָא רַבָּה הוּא, [4]אַפְכִיתוּ לֵיהּ לְדִינָא עִילָּוֵיהּ? [5]הָאָמַר רַב כָּהֲנָא: מִיבָּעֲיָא בָּעֵי לָהּ רָבָא, [6]וְלָא פָּשֵׁיט!

[7]הָשְׁתָּא דְּלָא אִתְּמַר לָא הָכִי וְלָא הָכִי, [8]תָּפְסָה, לָא מַפְּקִינַן מִינָּהּ; [9]לָא תָּפְסָה, לָא יָהֲבִינַן לָהּ.

LITERAL TRANSLATION

[1] [If] she rebelled, she does not lose her worn clothes that [still] exist. [2] Rav Gamda said to them: [64A] [3] Because Rav Zevid is a great man, [4] do you overturn the law upon him? [5] Surely Rav Kahana said: Rava asked [this] question, [6] but did not resolve [it]! [7] Now that it was not stated either this [way] or that [way, [8] if] she seized [something], we do not remove [it] from her; [9] [if] she did not seize [anything], we do not give [anything] to her.

RASHI

משום דרב זביד גברא רבה הוא — ולא יערער על דברינו, מחמת ענותנותו. **מפכיתו דינא** — לחובתו.

TRANSLATION AND COMMENTARY

said: [1] **If** a woman **rebels** against her husband, **she does not lose the clothing** she brought into the marriage as part of her ketubah and **which is** now **worn** out **but still in existence** at the time of her rebellion. Thus Rav Zevid's daughter-in-law may keep the silk garment that is still in her possession. [2] Responding to their ruling, **Rav Gamda said to them:** [64A] [3] Is it **because Rav Zevid is a great man**, and you know that he will not protest against an unfavorable judgment, [4] that **you turn the law against him?** [5] **Surely Rav Kahana said: Rav asked this** very **question** as to whether a rebellious wife forfeits the clothing she brought into the marriage as part of her dowry and which is now worn but still in existence, [6] **and he was unable to answer it!** Yet you have ruled against Rav Zevid that a rebellious wife does not forfeit such clothing!

הָשְׁתָּא [7] The Gemara concludes: **Now that** the law **has not been decided either this way or that way,** the law in practice is as follows: [8] **If** the woman **has** already **seized an article** that originally belonged to her, the court **does not remove it from her** possession. [9] But **if she has not** yet **seized the article**, the court **does not hand it over to her.** Since the law is in doubt, it is preferable to leave the article in the hands of the party in physical possession of it.

NOTES

מִשּׁוּם דְּרַב זְבִיד גַּבְרָא רַבָּה הוּא Because Rav Zevid is a great man. *Rashi* explains that Rav Gamda asked his colleagues whether they had ruled against Rav Zevid because they knew him to be a man of great modesty, who would not object to their ruling. It may be added that while the verse states (Leviticus 19:15): "And you shall not honor the person of the mighty," thus forbidding a judge from favoring a man of high standing in his Halakhic rulings, it is similarly forbidden to rule *against* such a person just because he is who he is.

הָשְׁתָּא דְּלָא אִתְּמַר Now that it was not stated. *Tosafot* and others ask: What does the second version of Rav Gamda's question mean? It is precisely because Rava was unable to resolve the issue that Rav Zevid's daughter-in-law should be entitled to keep the garment she has in her possession! They answer that Amemar, Mar Zutra, and Rav Ashi ruled that the woman could keep all her clothing, even what was not now in her possession, and Rav Gamda objected that since Rava was unable to resolve the issue, she should not be entitled to the clothing in her husband's possession. But this leads to another difficulty, for if this is the position of Rav Gamda, then the Gemara should not have concluded with the formula, "Now that it was not stated, etc." It should have said that the law is in accordance with Rav Gamda.

Rashba and *Ritva* suggest that according to Amemar and his colleagues, a woman's *tzon barzel* property is always viewed as being in her possession, and a rebellious wife can reclaim such property even if it is now in her husband's possession. Rav Gamda disagreed and said that *tzon barzel* property is always viewed as being in her husband's possession, and a rebellious wife is not entitled to such property, even if she has already seized it from her husband. The Gemara concludes that, since the law was not stated either way, the court may not remove from the woman's possession what she has seized from her husband; but nor may the court hand over to her what she has not yet seized from her husband.

תָּפְסָה, לָא מַפְּקִינַן If she seized something, we do not remove it from her. The issue of a rebellious wife's right to reclaim property that she brought into the marriage as her dowry is also discussed in the Jerusalem Talmud, which records conflicting opinions on the matter. The practical conclusions that can be drawn from our passage are largely dependent on the two opinions regarding the case involving Rav Zevid's daughter-in-law. According to *Rashi*,

HALAKHAH

הָשְׁתָּא דְּלָא אִתְּמַר Now that it was not stated. "When a man divorces his wife who rebelled against him in order to cause him distress, she must return everything that belongs to him. As for the dowry that she brought into the marriage, whatever is in her possession we do not take away from her, but whatever is in her husband's possession we do not hand over to her. *Rema* notes that she may reclaim any real estate that she brought into the marriage as *tzon barzel* property. Similarly, she may reclaim all of her *melog* property. The Aḥaronim disagree about a woman who rebelled against her husband, because she claimed that she found him repulsive. According to some authorities, if

TRANSLATION AND COMMENTARY

וּמַשְׁהִינַן לָהּ [1] The Gemara now mentions another ruling on the matter of a rebellious wife. If a woman rebels against her husband, **we make her wait twelve months for her bill of divorce**, in the hope that she will resume her marital obligations. [2] **During these twelve months** the rebellious wife **has no** claim of **maintenance against her husband,** for she forfeited her right to maintenance when she refused to engage in sexual relations with him.

[1] וּמַשְׁהִינַן לָהּ תְּרֵיסַר יַרְחֵי שַׁתָּא אַגִּיטָּא, [2] וּבְהָנָךְ תְּרֵיסַר יַרְחֵי שַׁתָּא לֵית לָהּ מְזוֹנֵי מִבַּעַל.

LITERAL TRANSLATION

[1] And we make her wait twelve months of the year for [her] bill of divorce, [2] and during those twelve months of the year she has no maintenance from [her] husband.

RASHI

ומשהינן לה – אולי תחזור בה. **תריסר ירחי שתא** – ותו לא.

NOTES

it was a case of a woman claiming that she found her husband repulsive, and therefore nothing can be learned from this passage regarding a woman who rebels against her husband in order to cause him distress. According to *Rambam*, Rav Zevid's daughter-in-law was the usual type of rebellious wife, and therefore the case of a woman who finds her husband repulsive was not discussed in the Gemara.

As was mentioned above (63b), the laws pertaining to a rebellious wife underwent a change during the Geonic period with the enactment of "the Law of the Academies." According to that enactment, a rebellious wife may reclaim her dowry, both her *tzon barzel* and *melog* property, even what is currently in her husband's possession. Some Rishonim find support for this enactment in the Jerusalem Talmud, which says that in those places where it is customary to include conditions in the ketubah document regarding the eventuality that one of the spouses may rebel against the other, the conditions are valid, as are all conditions regarding monetary matters (*Meiri*). Thus the Geonim enacted that all ketubot are to be treated as if they include certain conditions regarding the wife's right to her ketubah and her dowry if she rebels against her husband. But most Rishonim were opposed to the enactment, which they saw as directly contradicting Talmudic law, and it was only in special cases that it was put into practice.

וּמַשְׁהִינַן לָהּ תְּרֵיסַר יַרְחֵי שַׁתָּא אַגִּיטָּא And we make her wait twelve months of the year for her bill of divorce. The Rishonim disagree about the case to which this ruling applies. According to *Rashi*, who explains the entire passage as referring to a wife who refuses to cohabit with her husband on the grounds that she finds him repulsive, this ruling also applies to such a woman. We delay her bill of divorce for twelve months in the hope that she will desist from her rebellion. If she resumes her marital obligations during those twelve months, no penalties are imposed on her.

Ri Migash and *Rambam* explain that this ruling applies to a wife who rebels against her husband in order to cause him distress. Such a woman forfeits her ketubah after four weeks of announcements and warnings, but her husband is not required to divorce her until twelve months have passed. But if the woman rebels against her husband on the grounds that she finds him repulsive, we compel the husband to give her an immediate divorce without payment of her ketubah.

Some Rishonim maintain that this ruling applies in both cases, whether the woman rebels against her husband because she finds him repulsive or because she wants to cause him distress.

According to *Rosh*, this ruling stems from an enactment instituted by the later Amoraim. It often happened that a woman rebelled against her husband on the grounds that she found him repulsive, her husband would then grant her an immediate divorce without payment of her ketubah, and soon afterwards the woman would regret that she had ever asked for a divorce. Therefore, the later Amoraim enacted that the husband must wait for twelve months before divorcing his wife without paying her ketubah. During that time the woman may reconsider and resume her marital obligations. Since they enacted that we delay the woman's divorce in a case where she claims that she finds her husband repulsive, they enacted a similar delay in a case where she rebels against her husband in order to cause him distress, thus abolishing the whole procedure of announcements and warnings mentioned in the Baraita.

Ra'ah agrees that this enactment applies in both cases, even where the woman rebelled against her husband in order to cause him distress. Even though the woman has already forfeited her entire ketubah after the four-week procedure of announcements and warnings has been completed, she cannot be divorced until after twelve months have passed. The Rabbis sought to penalize the woman by not allowing her to remarry for a year. Alternatively, the enactment was made for the woman's benefit, so that she would have time to reconsider her decision. Even though the woman does not regain her ketubah, even if she resumes her marital obligations, the Rabbis wished to spare her the shame of divorce.

וּבְהָנָךְ תְּרֵיסַר יַרְחֵי שַׁתָּא And during those twelve months of the year. The Rishonim disagree about whether the

HALAKHAH

the woman is able to satisfy the court that she rebelled against her husband for a valid reason, we invoke "the Law of the Academies." In such a case, the husband must return to her all of her *tzon barzel* property (or pay her for what he is unable to return), and all of her *melog* property that is still in existence. If she cannot convince the court that she had a good reason to rebel against her husband, but there is no evidence of fraud, she may reclaim her *melog* property and keep the *tzon barzel* property that is in her possession. If the court suspects that the woman is involved in an attempt to defraud her husband, it may even reclaim the *tzon barzel* property in her possession and return it to her husband." (*Rambam, Sefer Nashim, Hilkhot Ishut* 14:13; *Shulḥan Arukh, Even HaEzer* 77:3.)

וּמַשְׁהִינַן לָהּ תְּרֵיסַר יַרְחֵי שַׁתָּא And we make her wait twelve months of the year. "If a woman rebels against

SAGES

רַב טוֹבִי בַּר קִיסְנָא Rav Tovi bar Kisna. A Babylonian Amora of the second generation, Rav Tovi bar Kisna was a disciple of Shmuel and transmitted rulings in his teacher's name.

רַב תַּחְלִיפָא בַּר אֲבִימִי Rav Taḥlifa bar Avimi. A Babylonian Amora of the second generation, Rav Taḥlifa bar Avimi was a disciple of Shmuel. He was apparently very attached to his teacher, and his rulings are mentioned in various places in the Babylonian Talmud.

BACKGROUND

אִגֶּרֶת מֶרֶד A document of rebellion. This was a document issued by a Rabbinical Court regarding a rebellious husband or wife. Once the court had decided that the case was to be regarded as one of rebellion, it delivered an appropriate document to the injured party, so that money could be collected or the ketubah reduced according to the instructions of the court. The writing of such a document was necessary to provide legal proof if the matter was brought before another court to decide the amount of the ketubah settlement that was due to the woman when she received a bill of divorce from her husband.

[1]אָמַר רַב טוֹבִי בַּר קִיסְנָא אָמַר שְׁמוּאֵל: [2]כּוֹתְבִין אִגֶּרֶת מֶרֶד עַל אֲרוּסָה, [3]וְאֵין כּוֹתְבִין אִגֶּרֶת מֶרֶד עַל שׁוֹמֶרֶת יָבָם.

[4]מֵיתִיבֵי: ״אַחַת לִי אֲרוּסָה וּנְשׂוּאָה, [5]אֲפִילּוּ נִדָּה, אֲפִילּוּ חוֹלָה, וַאֲפִילּוּ שׁוֹמֶרֶת יָבָם״.

[6]לָא קַשְׁיָא. [7]כָּאן שֶׁתָּבַע הוּא; [8]כָּאן שֶׁתָּבְעָה הִיא. [9]דַּאֲמַר רַב תַּחְלִיפָא בַּר אֲבִימִי אָמַר שְׁמוּאֵל: תָּבַע הוּא נִזְקָקִין לוֹ;

LITERAL TRANSLATION

[1]Rav Tovi bar Kisna said in the name of Shmuel: [2]We write a document of rebellion against a betrothed woman, [3]but we do not write a document of rebellion against a woman who is waiting for [her] *yavam*.

[4]They raised an objection: "It is the same to me [whether she is] betrothed or married, [5]even a menstruating woman, [and] even one who is sick, and even one who is waiting for [her] *yavam*."

[6]There is no difficulty. [7]Here [it is] where he claimed [her]; [8]here [it is] where she claimed [him]. [9]For Rav Taḥlifa bar Avimi said in the name of Shmuel: [If] he claimed [her], we pay attention to him;

RASHI

שתבע הוא — והיא מורדת. **תבעה היא** — והוא מורד.

TRANSLATION AND COMMENTARY

אָמַר רַב טוֹבִי בַּר קִסְנָא [1]The Gemara continues its discussion of the regulations governing a rebellious wife. **Rav Tovi bar Kisna said in the name of Shmuel:** [2]The court **writes a document of rebellion against a betrothed woman** who refuses to complete the marriage process, recording the court's decision that her husband is entitled to divorce her without paying her ketubah. [3]**But it does not write a document of rebellion against a widow** whose husband died childless and **who is waiting for her brother-in-law** to perform levirate marriage, but refuses to marry him, because the laws relating to a rebellious wife do not apply in such a case.

מֵיתִיבֵי [4]**An objection** to Shmuel's ruling **was raised** from the Baraita cited earlier, which stated: **"The same law applies whether** the rebellious woman **is betrothed** to her husband and refuses to complete the marriage, **or** is already **married** to him and refuses to comply with her marital obligations. [5]The same law applies **even** if she is **menstruating, and even if she is sick, and even** if she is a widow whose husband died childless and **is waiting for her** husband's brother (the ***yavam***) to perform levirate marriage, and she refuses to marry him." Thus the Baraita states explicitly that the regulations governing a rebellious wife apply to a woman who refuses levirate marriage to her brother-in-law, contrary to the ruling of Shmuel cited above.

לָא קַשְׁיָא [6]The Gemara answers: **There is** really **no difficulty,** because the Baraita is referring to a case different from that discussed by Shmuel. [7]**Here** in the Baraita we are referring to a case **where** it was the man who **demanded** that the marriage take place, and it was the woman who refused. [8]But **here** Shmuel is referring to a case in which it was the woman who **demanded** that the marriage take place, and it was the man who refused to marry her. Regarding such a case, Shmuel distinguishes between a betrothed woman and a widow awaiting levirate marriage. The court writes a document of rebellion on behalf of the betrothed woman entitling her to an increase in her ketubah, but it does not write a document of rebellion on behalf of the widow awaiting levirate marriage. [9]**For Rav Taḥlifa bar Avimi said in the name of Shmuel: If** a man **demands** to perform levirate marriage with his brother's widow, and she refuses to marry him,

NOTES

husband is required to divorce his rebellious wife after the twelve months have passed. According to some authorities, the husband is then compelled to divorce his wife without payment of her ketubah. *Rabbenu Yonah* argues that the husband should indeed divorce his wife, and if he fails to do so he is treated as a sinner, but he cannot be compelled to grant her a divorce. *Rabbenu Tam* maintains that while the husband is advised to divorce his wife, he is not regarded as a sinner if he refuses to do so.

אִגֶּרֶת מֶרֶד עַל אֲרוּסָה A document of rebellion against a betrothed woman. According to the *Geonim,* who maintain that a betrothed woman is not entitled to a ketubah

HALAKHAH

her husband in order to cause him distress, we delay her bill of divorce for twelve months. During those twelve months she is not entitled to maintenance from her husband, and she may keep her handiwork for herself. But her husband is still liable for her ransom and for her burial, and if she dies, he inherits her estate. If the woman rebels against her husband, claiming that she finds him repulsive, he may divorce her immediately (following *Rambam,* though we do not accept his viewpoint that the husband can be compelled to do so). Most authorities maintain that even in this case we delay the woman's bill of divorce for twelve months (see *Bet Shmuel*)." (*Rambam, Sefer Nashim, Hilkhot Ishut* 14:10; *Shulḥan Arukh, Even HaEzer* 77:2.)

תָּבַע הוּא If he claimed her. "If the *yavam* wishes to marry his brother's widow and she refuses, she is treated as a rebellious wife, following the viewpoint of the earlier

TRANSLATION AND COMMENTARY

the court **pays attention to him,** and draws up a document of rebellion against her. [1]But **if** a widow **demands** to marry her late husband's brother, and he refuses to marry her, the court **does not pay attention to her** and does not draw up a document of rebellion against him.

בְּמַאי [2]The Gemara objects to this interpretation of Shmuel's ruling: **How have you interpreted Shmuel's statement?** [3]If you are right that Shmuel is referring to a case **where** it is the woman who **demands** to be married, and it is the man who refuses to marry her, then a difficulty arises. [4]**Can this** interpretation be reconciled with the wording of Shmuel's statement: "The court **writes a document of rebellion** ***against*** **a betrothed woman,**" which implies that it is the woman who is being penalized? [5]If Shmuel was referring to the case of a rebellious husband, **he should have said:** "The court writes a document of rebellion ***on behalf of*** **a betrothed woman,**" thus entitling her to a larger ketubah if her bridegroom refuses to complete the marriage!

הָא לָא קַשְׁיָא [6]The Gemara rebuts this objection: **This,** too, **does not present a difficulty,** [7]for the text should **read** as follows: "The court writes a document of rebellion ***on behalf of*** **a betrothed woman,**" entitling her to a larger ketubah.

מַאי [8]The Gemara now seeks to understand Shmuel's distinction between a betrothed woman and a widow awaiting levirate marriage: **Why is a widow who is awaiting levirate marriage** treated **differently** from a betrothed woman, **in that** the court **does not write a document of rebellion on** the widow's **behalf** against her brother-in-law, whereas the court does write such a document on behalf of the betrothed woman against her bridegroom? [9]You may perhaps suggest that the widow is treated differently **because we can say to her: "Go** on your way; since you are a woman, **you are not commanded** to have children, for the obligation of procreation falls exclusively upon men." [10]But this poses a problem, for **regarding a betrothed woman** whose bridegroom refuses to marry her, we should **also** be able to **say to her:** [11]**"Go** on your way, for **you are not commanded** to have children." Why, then, does the court pay attention to her and write a document of rebellion on her behalf?

[1]תָּבְעָה הִיא, אֵין נִזְקָקִין לָהּ. [2]בְּמַאי אוֹקִימְתָּא לְהָא דִשְׁמוּאֵל? [3]בְּשֶׁתָּבְעָה הִיא? [4]הָאי ״כּוֹתְבִין אִגֶּרֶת מֶרֶד עַל אֲרוּסָה״? [5]״לַאֲרוּסָה״ מִיבָּעֵי לֵיהּ!
[6]הָא לָא קַשְׁיָא. [7]תְּנֵי: ״לַאֲרוּסָה״.
[8]מַאי שְׁנָא שׁוֹמֶרֶת יָבָם דְּלָא? [9]דְּאָמְרִינַן לָהּ: ״זִיל, לָא מִפַּקְדַתְּ״. [10]אֲרוּסָה נַמִי, נֵימָא לָהּ: ״זִיל, [11]לָא מִפַּקְדַתְּ״!

LITERAL TRANSLATION

[1][if] she claimed [him], we do not pay attention to her.

[2]How have you interpreted this [ruling] of Shmuel? [3]Where she claimed [him]? [4]Is this [formula,] "We write a document of rebellion *against* a betrothed woman," [correct]? [5]He should have [said:] *"On behalf of* a betrothed woman"!

[6]There is no difficulty. [7]Read (lit., "teach"): *"On behalf of* a betrothed woman."

[8]Why is a woman who is waiting for [her] *yavam* different, in that [we do] not [write a document of rebellion on her behalf]? [9]Because we say to her: "Go, you are not commanded." [10][Regarding] a betrothed woman too, let us say to her: [11]"Go, you are not commanded"!

RASHI

אין נזקקין לה – לכתוב לה אגרת מרד להוסיף על כתובתה. ולקמן מסיק פירושא ואזיל: משום דלא מפקדא אפריה ורביה. **לארוסה מבעי ליה** – וכותבין אגרת על הבעל. **דלא מפקדת** – בפריה ורביה, כדאמרינן ביבמות (סה,ב).

NOTES

unless the bridegroom drew up a ketubah in her favor at the time of betrothal, we are dealing here with a case in which the bridegroom drew up such a document for his bride. According to *Rashi*, who maintains that a betrothed woman is automatically entitled to a ketubah, even if her bridegroom has not drawn up such a deed, the Gemara's discussion applies to all betrothed women (*Ritva*).

נֵימָא לָהּ: ״זִיל, לָא מִפַּקְדַתְּ״ Let us say to her: "Go, you are not commanded." The Rishonim ask: If this argument is valid, why does the court draw up a document of rebellion on behalf of a married woman whose husband refuses to cohabit with her? Let us say to her: "Go on your way; you are not commanded to have children." They answer that a married woman does not base her claim on the obligation to have children. She comes to court demanding her conjugal rights, which her husband became obligated to satisfy when he married her (*Ramban*, *Rashba*, and *Ritva*).

HALAKHAH

Mishnah. According to some authorities, she is not treated as a rebellious wife if she refuses to marry her *yavam*, in accordance with the viewpoint of the later Mishnah." (*Rambam, Sefer Nashim, Hilkhot Yibbum* 2:10; *Shulḥan Arukh, Even HaEzer* 165:1.)

SAGES

רַבִּי פְּדָת Rabbi Pedat. A Palestinian Amora of the third generation, Rabbi Pedat was the son and disciple of the great Amora Rabbi Elazar (ben Pedat). He transmitted several rulings of Rabbi Yoḥanan, who was his father's (and possibly his own) teacher. Rabbi Pedat was Rabbi Assi's interpreter (מְתוּרְגְּמָן) and later he became one of the most important Amoraim of his generation. His teachings are recorded in both the Babylonian Talmud and the Jerusalem Talmud.

[1]אֶלָּא, בְּבָאָה מֵחֲמַת טַעֲנָה, [2]דְּאָמְרָה: ״בָּעֵינָא חוּטְרָא לְיָדָא, וּמָרָה לִקְבוּרָה״. [3]הָכִי נַמִי שׁוֹמֶרֶת יָבָם, [4]בְּבָאָה מֵחֲמַת טַעֲנָה!

[5]אֶלָּא, אִידִי וְאִידִי שֶׁתָּבַע הוּא, [6]וְלָא קַשְׁיָא. [7]כָּאן לַחֲלוֹץ; [8]וְכָאן לְיַיבֵּם. [9]דַּאֲמַר רַבִּי פְּדָת אָמַר רַבִּי יוֹחָנָן: [10]תָּבַע לַחֲלוֹץ, נִזְקָקִין לוֹ; תָּבַע לְיַיבֵּם, אֵין נִזְקָקִין לוֹ.

LITERAL TRANSLATION

[1]Rather, [it is] where she comes with a claim, [2]for she says: "I want a staff for [my] hand, and a hoe for [my] burial." [3]The same should apply (lit., "so also") [to] a woman who is waiting for [her] *yavam*, [4]where she comes with a claim!

[5]Rather, in both cases (lit., "this and that") [it is] where he claimed [her], [6]and [yet] there is no difficulty. [7]Here [he claims her] to perform *ḥalitzah*; [8]and here [he claims her] to perform levirate marriage. [9]For Rabbi Pedat said in the name of Rabbi Yoḥanan: [If] he claimed [her] to perform *ḥalitzah*, we pay attention to him; [10][if] he claimed [her] to perform levirate marriage, we do not pay attention to him.

TRANSLATION AND COMMENTARY

אֶלָּא [1]**Rather,** continues the Gemara, when Shmuel said that the court writes a document of rebellion on behalf of a betrothed woman whose bridegroom refuses to marry her, he must have been referring to a case **where** the woman **came** to court **with a** valid **claim,** [2]**saying:** "Though I am not commanded to have children, **I want a staff for my hand and a hoe for my burial.** I want to raise a family so that I will have someone to care for me in my old age and make arrangements for my funeral when I die." Thus the court recognizes her claim and takes action to compel her bridegroom to complete the marriage. [3]But if this is the case, **the same should apply to a woman who is awaiting levirate marriage** but whose brother-in-law refuses to marry her. [4]Here, too, Shmuel must have been referring to a case **where** the woman **came** to court **with a** valid **claim,** arguing that she wanted children to care for her in her old age. Why, then, did Shmuel rule that the court does not write a document of rebellion on her behalf to compel her brother-in-law to take her as his wife?

אֶלָּא [5]The Gemara now suggests an alternative solution to the contradiction between Shmuel's ruling and the Baraita cited above. **Rather,** says the Gemara, **both** the Baraita and Shmuel's ruling refer to a case **where** it was the man who **put forward the demand,** and it was the woman who refused him. [6]**And yet** the Baraita **poses no difficulty** for Shmuel, for the two are dealing with different cases. [7]**Here** in the Baraita it is referring to a case in which the brother of the deceased **demanded to perform *ḥalitzah*** and thereby free himself and his brother's widow from the obligation to marry, and the widow refused to participate in the ceremony, insisting that her brother-in-law take her in levirate marriage. In such a case, the woman is treated as a rebellious wife and a document of rebellion is drawn up against her. [8]**But here** Shmuel is referring to a case in which the brother of the deceased **demanded to perform levirate marriage,** and the woman wanted him to perform *ḥalitzah* and thereby free her from the levirate bond. In such a case, the woman is not treated as a rebellious wife and a document of rebellion is not drawn up against her. [9]This distinction is in conformity with what **Rabbi Pedat said in the name of Rabbi Yoḥanan: If** the brother of the deceased **demands to perform *ḥalitzah*** and the widow refuses to participate in the ceremony, the court **pays attention to him** and draws up a document of rebellion against her. [10]But **if** the brother-in-law **demands to perform levirate marriage** and the widow refuses to marry him, the court **does not pay attention to him** and does not draw up a document of rebellion against her.

RASHI

חוטרא לידא — רוצה אני שיהא לי בן שיחזיק בידי בזקנותי, ואשען עליו, וביום מותי יקברני. **תבע לחלוץ** — והיא אינה רוצה אלא להתייבם — נזקקין לו לכתוב אגרת מרד עליה. **אין נזקקין לו** — לפי שאין מתכוין לשם מצוה. וכמשנה אחרונה. ואמרינן ליה: זיל נסיב אחריתי.

NOTES

בְּבָאָה מֵחֲמַת טַעֲנָה Where she comes with a claim. Most Rishonim explain that the Gemara is suggesting that the court does not write a document of rebellion on behalf of the betrothed woman unless she produces a valid claim to justify such action. According to *Ra'ah*, the woman need not actually put forward the claim. Since the woman has a valid claim, if she fails to present it we put forward the claim on her behalf. A woman may argue that she wishes to raise a family so that she will have someone to take care of her in her old age (and the court may present such a claim on her behalf), even if she already has children, for she does not know which of her children will actually take care of her when she is unable to take care of herself.

HALAKHAH

תָּבַע לַחֲלוֹץ If he claimed her to perform *ḥalitzah*. "If the *yavam* wishes to perform *ḥalitzah*, and his brother's widow does not want to participate in the ceremony, she is treated as a rebellious wife." (*Rambam, Sefer Nashim, Hilkhot Yibbum* 2:16; *Shulḥan Arukh, Even HaEzer* 165:3.)

TRANSLATION AND COMMENTARY

מַאי [1] **Why,** asks the Gemara, **is** the law in the case **where** the brother of the deceased **demands to perform levirate marriage different in that** the court **does not pay attention to him** and does not write a document of rebellion against her? [2] You may perhaps suggest that the brother who demands to perform levirate marriage is treated differently **because we can say to him: "Go and marry another woman."** [3] **But** this poses a problem, for in a case where the brother of the deceased **demands to perform *ḥalitzah*** and the widow refuses to participate, **we should also** be able to **say to him:** [4] **"Go and marry another woman."** Why should the court pay attention to him and draw up a document of rebellion against the widow?

[1] מַאי שְׁנָא לְיַיבֵּם דְּלָא? [2] דְּאָמְרִינַן לֵיהּ: ״זִיל וּנְסֵיב אִיתְּתָא אַחֲרִיתֵי״. [3] לַחֲלוֹץ נַמִי, נֵימָא לֵיהּ: [4] ״זִיל וּנְסֵיב אִיתְּתָא אַחֲרִיתֵי״! [5] אֶלָּא, דְּאָמַר: ״כֵּיוָן דַּאֲגִידָא בִּי, [6] לָא קָא יָהֲבוּ לִי אַחֲרִיתֵי״. [7] הָכָא נַמִי: ״כֵּיוָן דַּאֲגִידָא בִּי, [8] לָא קָא יָהֲבוּ לִי אַחֲרִיתֵי״! [9] אֶלָּא, אִידֵי וְאִידֵי שֶׁתָּבַע לְיַיבֵּם, [10] וְלָא קַשְׁיָא. [11] כָּאן כְּמִשְׁנָה רִאשׁוֹנָה; [12] כָּאן

LITERAL TRANSLATION

[1] Why is [where he claims her] to perform levirate marriage different in that [we do] not [pay attention to him]? [2] Because we say to him: "Go and marry another woman." [3] [But where he claims her] to perform *ḥalitzah* also, let us say to him: [4] "Go and marry another woman"!

[5] Rather, [it is] because he can say: "Since she is tied to me, [6] they will not give me another [wife]." [7] Here too [he can say]: "Since she is tied to me, [8] they will not give me another [wife]"!

[9] Rather, in both cases [it is] where he claimed [her] to perform levirate marriage, [10] and [yet] there is no difficulty. [11] Here [it is] like the earlier (lit., "first") Mishnah; [12] here [it is]

אֶלָּא [5] The Gemara now suggests that the distinction between the two cases should be understood differently. **Rather,** says the Gemara, the reason why the court pays attention to the brother who demands to perform *ḥalitzah* **is because he can say: "As long as** my late brother's widow **is** still **bound to me** by the levirate bond, [6] **nobody** else **will give me another woman** in marriage." Any potential bride will be concerned that one day he will take his sister-in-law in levirate marriage. This being a strong argument, the court pays attention to him and writes the widow a document of rebellion in order to induce her to participate in the *ḥalitzah* ceremony, thereby freeing the brother-in-law to find himself another wife. [7] But this explanation is difficult, for **here too** in the case where the brother of the deceased demands to perform levirate marriage and the widow refuses, **he should be able to say: "As long as** my late brother's widow **is** still **bound to me** by the levirate bond, [8] **nobody** else **will give me another woman** in marriage." Thus the court should pay attention to him as well, and should write a document of rebellion against the woman!

אֶלָּא [9] The Gemara now suggests a third solution to the contradiction between Shmuel's statement and the Baraita. **Rather,** says the Gemara, **both** the Baraita and Shmuel's ruling refer to a case **where** the brother of the deceased **demanded to perform levirate marriage** with his brother's widow and the woman refused to marry him. [10] **And yet** the Baraita **poses no difficulty** for Shmuel, for it reflects an earlier stage of the Halakhah, whereas Shmuel follows the accepted viewpoint of a later period. [11] The Baraita **here,** which rules that a woman who refuses levirate marriage is regarded as a rebellious wife and that a document of rebellion is drawn up against her, **is in accordance with** the viewpont of **the earlier Mishnah.** [12] But Shmuel's ruling **here,**

NOTES

דְּאָמְרִינַן לֵיהּ: ״זִיל וּנְסֵיב אִיתְּתָא אַחֲרִיתֵי״ Because we say to him: "Go and marry another woman." The Rishonim object: Why does the Gemara not ask this same question in the case of a betrothed woman? If this is a valid argument, why does the court write a document of rebellion against a betrothed woman who refuses to complete the marriage? Let us tell her bridegroom to go and marry a different woman! They answer that the Gemara prefers to point out the difficulty arising from Rabbi Yoḥanan's distinction between the case where the brother of the deceased demanded to perform levirate marriage and where he demanded to perform *ḥalitzah*, rather than raise an objection from a ruling about a different case. Alternatively, the argument is valid only with respect to a *yavam*, whose sister-in-law became bound to him by the levirate bond through an act of Heaven, his brother's death. Since the *yavam* did not choose his sister-in-law to be his wife, he can be told to go and marry someone else. But this argument cannot be used with respect to an ordinary bridegroom, who chose a particular woman to be his wife (*Ra'ah*, *Ritva*).

כָּאן כְּמִשְׁנָה רִאשׁוֹנָה Here it is like the earlier Mishnah. Shmuel's ruling is also cited in the Jerusalem Talmud, and there too an objection is raised from the same Baraita. The Jerusalem Talmud offers two answers: The first is identical with the answer given in the Babylonian Talmud — that the Baraita's ruling follows the earlier Mishnah, whereas Shmuel's ruling follows the later Mishnah. According to the second answer, both rulings follow the later Mishnah that the commandment of *ḥalitzah* takes precedence over the commandment of levirate marriage. Shmuel is referring to a case in which the *yavam* wishes to marry his

REALIA

אִסְתִּירָא *Istira.*

An istira minted during the rule of the Roman Emperor Decius (c. 250 C.E.).

LANGUAGE

אִסְתִּירָא Istira. This word is derived from the Greek στατήρ, *stater*, a Greco-Roman coin which was minted from various metals and alloys (gold, silver, and electrum). An istira was worth half a dinar.

TRANSLATION AND COMMENTARY

that a woman who refuses levirate marriage is not treated as a rebellious wife, **is in accordance with** the viewpoint of **the later Mishnah.** [1]**For we have learned** elsewhere in a Mishnah (*Bekhorot* 13a): "A man whose brother dies childless is obliged by Torah law to marry his deceased brother's widow or to grant her *ḥalitzah*. [2]**The commandment of levirate marriage takes precedence over the commandment of *ḥalitzah*;** in other words, it is preferable that the brother of the deceased marry the widow, rather than free her to marry someone else by performing *ḥalitzah*. [3]**This** ruling **applied in the beginning, when** the parties **entered levirate marriage with the intention of fulfilling the** Biblical **commandment.** [4]But **now that** the parties **do not enter levirate marriage with the intention of fulfilling the** Biblical **commandment,** but for other reasons, such as for monetary benefit, [5]**the Sages say: The commandment of *ḥalitzah* takes precedence over the commandment of levirate marriage,** for a man who marries his brother's widow for any reason other than to fulfill the commandment of levirate marriage is guilty of incest." The Baraita follows the viewpoint that the commandment of levirate marriage takes precedence, and this is why the court pays attention to the brother of the deceased if he wishes to marry his brother's widow although she refuses. Shmuel follows the viewpoint that the commandment of *ḥalitzah* takes precedence, and this is why the court does not take any action to compel a woman to agree to levirate marriage.

עַד מָתַי [6]The Gemara now proceeds to analyze the next clause of our Mishnah, which stated: **"How long** must the husband continue to keep the rebellious woman as his wife, and **deduct** a certain amount each week from her ketubah, before he is entitled to divorce her?" And it is stated there that, according to Rabbi Yehudah, the woman's ketubah is reduced by seven tropaics per week. [7]The Gemara asks: **What are tropaics?**

אָמַר רַב שֵׁשֶׁת [8]**Rav Sheshet said** in reply: A tropaic is equivalent to an **istira.** [9]**And how much is an istira? Half a zuz** (dinar). Thus the penalty imposed on the rebellious wife according to Rabbi Yehudah

כְּמִשְׁנָה אַחֲרוֹנָה. [1]דִּתְנַן: [2]"מִצְוַת יִבּוּם קוֹדֶמֶת לְמִצְוַת חֲלִיצָה. [3]בָּרִאשׁוֹנָה, שֶׁהָיוּ מִתְכַּוְּונִין לְשׁוּם מִצְוָה. [4]עַכְשָׁיו שֶׁאֵין מִתְכַּוְּונִין לְשׁוּם מִצְוָה, [5]אָמְרוּ: מִצְוַת חֲלִיצָה קוֹדֶמֶת לְמִצְוַת יִבּוּם".

[6]"עַד מָתַי הוּא פּוֹחֵת, וכו׳?" [7]מַאי טְרַפָּעִיקִין?

[8]אָמַר רַב שֵׁשֶׁת: אִסְתִּירָא. [9]וְכַמָּה אִסְתִּירָא? פַּלְגָא דְּזוּזָא.

LITERAL TRANSLATION

like the later (lit., "last") Mishnah. [1]For we have learned: [2]"The commandment of levirate marriage takes precedence over the commandment of *ḥalitzah*. [3][This applied] in the beginning, when they intended [to perform levirate marriage] for the sake of [fulfilling] the commandment. [4]Now that they do not intend [to perform levirate marriage] for the sake of [fulfilling] the commandment, [5]they [the Sages] said: The commandment of *ḥalitzah* takes precedence over the commandment of levirate marriage."

[6]"Until when does he deduct, etc.?" [7]What are tropaics?

[8]Rav Sheshet said: An istira. [9]And how much is an istira? Half a zuz.

RASHI

אסתירא — סלע מדינה. **פלגא דזוזא** — זוז לורי, שהוא שש מעה כסף, נמצא טרפעיק שלש מעות.

NOTES

sister-in-law, and she wishes him to perform *ḥalitzah*. The Baraita is referring to a case in which the woman does not wish to marry the *yavam*, and is not willing to participate in the *ḥalitzah* ceremony (*Pnei Moshe*).

מִצְוַת יִבּוּם וּמִצְוַת חֲלִיצָה The commandment of levirate marriage and the commandment of *ḥalitzah*. The Rishonim disagree about whether the law follows the earlier Mishnah or the later Mishnah. The *Geonim*, *Rif*, and *Rambam* all rule that the law is in accordance with the earlier Mishnah — that the commandment of levirate marriage takes precedence over the commandment of *ḥalitzah*. *Rashi*, *Rabbenu Tam*, and most of the Tosafists rule that the law is in accordance with the later Mishnah — that the commandment of *ḥalitzah* takes precedence over the commandment of levirate marriage. Arguments in favor of one or the other ruling are brought from various passages in the Talmud, including the discussion found in our Gemara.

HALAKHAH

מִצְוַת יִבּוּם וּמִצְוַת חֲלִיצָה The commandment of levirate marriage and the commandment of *ḥalitzah*. "The commandment of levirate marriage takes precedence over the commandment of *ḥalitzah*, following the earlier Mishnah (*Rif*, *Rambam*, and others). According to some authorities, the commandment of *ḥalitzah* takes precedence over the commandment of levirate marriage, following the later Mishnah (*Rashi*, *Rabbenu Tam*, and others)." (*Rambam*, *Sefer Nashim*, *Hilkhot Yibbum* 1:2; *Shulḥan Arukh*, *Even HaEzer* 165:1.)

TRANSLATION AND COMMENTARY

(seven tropaics or three-and-a-half dinarim per week) is half the penalty imposed on her according to the first Tanna of the Mishnah (seven dinarim). And similarly, the penalty imposed on the rebellious husband according to Rabbi Yehudah (three tropaics per week) is half the penalty imposed on him according to the first Tanna of our Mishnah (three dinarim).

תַּנְיָא [1] The Gemara notes that **the same thing was also taught** in the following Baraita: [2] **"Rabbi Yehudah says:** The weekly penalty imposed on a rebellious husband is **three tropaics, which are nine ma'ahs,** [3] or **a ma'ah-and-a-half** for **each weekday** that he persists in his rebellion."** Thus we see that a tropaic is equivalent to three ma'ahs, or half a dinar (a dinar being equivalent to six ma'ahs).

אָמַר לֵיהּ [4] **Rabbi Ḥiyya bar Yosef said to Shmuel: In what way is** a husband **different** from a wife, in **that we give** the husband **a reduction for Shabbat,** [5] but **we do not give** the wife **an addition for Shabbat?** If a woman rebels against her husband, she is penalized seven dinarim (or seven tropaics, according to Rabbi Yehudah) per week. Now, it stands to reason that she is penalized one dinar (or tropaic) for each day, including Shabbat, that she persists in her rebellion. But if a man rebels against his wife, he is penalized only three dinarim (or three tropaics, according to Rabbi Yehudah) per week. Neither Rabbi Yehudah in the Baraita nor the first Tanna of our Mishnah penalizes the man for his refusal to cohabit with his wife on Shabbat.

אִיהִי [6] The Gemara explains: **In the case of a woman** who rebels against her husband, **we deduct** a certain amount from her ketubah for each day that she persists in her rebellion. [7] Thus the penalty imposed on her for refusing to cohabit with her husband on Shabbat **does not look like** the payment of forbidden **Shabbat wages,** for when a rebellious wife is penalized, her husband's obligation regarding her ketubah is reduced, but he is not paid anything extra. [8] But **in the case of a man** who rebels against his wife, **we** penalize the husband by compelling him to **add** a certain amount to her ketubah for each day that he refuses to cohabit with her. [64B] Thus the penalty imposed on the man for his refusal to engage in sexual relations with his wife on Shabbat would **look like** the payment of forbidden **Shabbat wages,** for the woman would be paid a larger ketubah as a result. This is why the rebellious wife is penalized for each

LITERAL TRANSLATION

[1] It was also taught thus: [2] "Rabbi Yehudah says: Three tropaics, which are nine ma'ahs, [3] a ma'ah-and-a-half for each day."

[4] Rabbi Ḥiyya bar Yosef said to Shmuel: [In] what [way] is he different that we give him [a reduction] for Shabbat, [5] and [in] what [way] is she different that we do not give her [an addition] for Shabbat? [6] In her case (lit., "she"), since we deduct, [7] it does not look like Shabbat wages. [8] In his case (lit., "he"), since we add, [64B] [9] it looks like Shabbat wages.

תַּנְיָא נַמִי הָכִי: [2] "רַבִּי יְהוּדָה אוֹמֵר: שְׁלֹשָׁה טְרַפְּעִיקִין, שֶׁהֵן תֵּשַׁע מָעִין, [3] מָעָה וָחֵצִי לְכָל יוֹם."

[4] אָמַר לֵיהּ רַבִּי חִיָּיא בַּר יוֹסֵף לִשְׁמוּאֵל: מַאי שְׁנָא אִיהוּ דְּיָהֲבִינַן לֵיהּ דְּשַׁבְּתָא, [5] וּמַאי שְׁנָא אִיהִי דְּלָא יָהֲבִינַן לָהּ דְּשַׁבְּתָא?

[6] אִיהִי, דְּמִיפְחַת קָא פָּחֵית, [7] לָא מִיחֲזֵי כִּשְׂכַר שַׁבָּת. [8] אִיהוּ, דְּאוֹסוּפֵי קָא מוֹסְפָא, [64B] [9] מִיחֲזֵי כִּשְׂכַר שַׁבָּת.

RASHI

מעה וחצי ליום – לְשֵׁשׁ יְמֵי הַמַּעֲשֶׂה, וּמִשַּׁבָּת לֹא יָהֲבִינַן לָהּ, כִּדְאָמַר לְקַמָּן. מַאי שְׁנָא אִיהוּ דְּיָהֲבִינַן לֵיהּ **דְּשַׁבְּתָא** – כְּשָׂכִיא מוֹרְדַת עָלָיו, דְּהָא שִׁבְעָה טְרַפְעֵיקִיס, טְרַפְעֵיק לַיּוֹם. **כִּשְׂכַר שַׁבָּת** – [כְּמוֹ שֶׁמִּשְׁתַּכֵּר בְּשַׁבָּת], גְּזֵרָה מִשּׁוּם מִקָּח וּמִמְכָּר וּשְׂכִירוּת.

SAGES

רַבִּי חִיָּיא בַּר יוֹסֵף **Rabbi Ḥiyya bar Yosef.** A second generation Babylonian Amora who later immigrated to Eretz Israel, Rabbi Ḥiyya bar Yosef was one of Rav's outstanding students and transmitted many of his teachings. After Rav's death, Rabbi Ḥiyya studied with Shmuel before leaving for Eretz Israel, where he became a student-colleague of Rabbi Yoḥanan (with whom he had many Halakhic discussions). He may also have served as a Rabbinical judge in Tiberias.

NOTES

מָעָה וָחֵצִי לְכָל יוֹם **A ma'ah and a half for each day.** *Ri Migash* points out that this penalty applies not only to a man of leisure, who is obligated to cohabit with his wife every day, but even to a sailor, whose conjugal obligation is once in six months (see above, 61b). Here, too, we invoke the argument that someone who has bread in his basket is not like someone who does not have bread in his basket. Since the woman refuses to cohabit with her husband, he is entitled to compensation for each day that she persists in her rebellion, even if for practical reasons they were unable to have sexual relations.

לָא מִיחֲזֵי כִּשְׂכַר שַׁבָּת **It does not look like Shabbat wages.** Even though the reduction of the woman's ketubah provides additional money for the husband, nevertheless since there is no actual transfer of money from the woman to her husband, the penalty imposed on the woman for her refusal to cohabit with her husband on Shabbat does not look like the payment of forbidden Shabbat wages (*Rivan*).

Ritva notes that in a case of true Shabbat wages, where wages are paid for work done on Shabbat, it makes no difference whether there is an actual transfer of money from the employer to the worker or only a reduction of a debt owed by the worker to his employer, for in both situations the Shabbat wages are forbidden. It is only here, where there is no real payment of Shabbat wages, but only a fine imposed by the Rabbis which may look like Shabbat wages, that we are more lenient in a case where there is no actual transfer of money.

BACKGROUND

שָׁלִישׁ A third party. This term is derived from the root שלש, and means a third man. But it has an additional meaning, that of a person in charge, a functionary, which is how it is most commonly used in the Bible. Here, too, the meaning is double: the husband appoints a special person as his שָׁלִישׁ, makes him responsible for satisfying his wife's financial needs, and reaches an agreement with him as to how to cover his expenses.

TRANSLATION AND COMMENTARY

day that she persists in her refusal, including Shabbat, whereas the rebellious husband is penalized for only six days of the week, but not for Shabbat.

אֲמַר לֵיהּ [1] The Gemara continues: **Rabbi Ḥiyya bar Yosef said to Shmuel: What is the** reason for the **difference** in law **between a rebellious husband and a rebellious wife,** in that the former is penalized half a dinar (or half a tropaic, according to Rabbi Yehudah) for each day that he refuses to cohabit with his wife, whereas the latter is penalized a full dinar (or a full tropaic) for each day that she persists in her rebellion?

אֲמַר לֵיהּ [2] Shmuel **said to** Rabbi Ḥiyya bar Yosef: The male sexual drive is stronger than that of the female, so a man suffers more from this deprivation than a woman does. You can **go out and learn** about the relative strengths of male and female desire **from** what takes place in **the market of prostitutes.** [3] **Who hires whom?** It is the man who usually hires the woman for the purpose of sexual intercourse, and not the woman who hires the man. [4] **Another explanation** may be offered as to why the penalty imposed on a woman who refuses her husband is twice as large as that imposed on a man who refuses his wife: A man's sexual **desire is** visible **externally,** [5] **whereas** a woman's **desire is** an entirely **internal** matter. The physiological changes associated with heightened male sexual desire are visible externally, and as such a man is liable to suffer public humiliation if his sexual impulses are frustrated by his wife's refusal to cohabit with him. Thus he is entitled to monetary compensation not only for the distress caused him by the forced abstinence, but also for the public embarrassment that this abstinence may cause him.

MISHNAH הַמַּשְׁרֶה אֶת אִשְׁתּוֹ [6] Among the duties imposed on a husband by virtue of his marriage is the obligation to maintain his wife and to provide her with food and clothing. This Mishnah lists the specific

[1] אֲמַר לֵיהּ רַבִּי חִיָּיא בַּר יוֹסֵף לִשְׁמוּאֵל: מַה בֵּין מוֹרֵד לְמוֹרֶדֶת? [2] אֲמַר לֵיהּ: צֵא וּלְמַד מִשּׁוּק שֶׁל זוֹנוֹת. [3] מִי שׂוֹכֵר אֶת מִי? [4] דָּבָר אַחֵר: זֶה יִצְרוֹ מִבַּחוּץ; [5] וְזוֹ יִצְרָהּ מִבִּפְנִים.

משנה [6] הַמַּשְׁרֶה אֶת אִשְׁתּוֹ עַל יְדֵי שָׁלִישׁ,

LITERAL TRANSLATION

[1] Rabbi Ḥiyya bar Yosef said to Shmuel: What is [the difference] between a rebellious husband and a rebellious wife?

[2] He said to him: Go out and learn from the street of prostitutes. [3] Who hires whom? [4] Another explanation (lit., "thing"): His desire is external; [5] but her desire is internal.

MISHNAH [6] [If] someone provides for his wife through a third party,

RASHI

מה בין מורד למורדת — מאי שנא כשהוא מורד אינו נותן אלא חצי טרפעיק ליום, וכשהיא מורדת נותנת טרפעיק? **מי שוכר את מי** — הוי אומר האיש שוכר את האשה, שמע מינה — צערו מרובה. **ויצרו מבחוץ** — קשויו ניכר, ומתגנה.

משנה המשרה את אשתו על ידי שליש — שנותן לה מזונותיה בבית אפוטרופוס, ואינה מתגלגלת עמו. **המשרה** — המַכְרֶה. "ויכרה להם כירה" מתרגמינן שירותא (מ"ב ו).

NOTES

מַה בֵּין מוֹרֵד לְמוֹרֶדֶת What is the difference between a rebellious husband and a rebellious wife? The Rishonim cite this passage as the most convincing proof that the law is in accordance with the opinion of Rav Huna that a rebellious wife is one who refuses to cohabit with her husband, and not one who refuses to perform the tasks that a married woman is obliged to perform for her husband. The two answers given by the Gemara do not account for the difference between the penalty imposed upon a rebellious husband and that imposed upon a rebellious wife according to Rabbi Yose the son of Rabbi Ḥanina, but only according to Rav Huna. On the contrary, the financial hardship caused to a woman by her husband who refuses to maintain her is much greater than the distress caused to a man by his wife's refusal to perform her obligatory tasks (*Ramban, Rashba, Ritva*, and others).

מִי שׂוֹכֵר אֶת מִי Who hires whom. The Jerusalem Talmud explains the difference between a rebellious husband and a rebellious wife in a similar manner — that a man suffers more from his wife's refusal to engage in sexual relations with him than vice versa. It supports this explanation with what the Sages said about Samson and Delilah (regarding the verse [Judges 16:16], "When she pressed him ... so that his soul was vexed to death"), that Delilah caused Samson great distress by abstaining from sexual relations with him.

זֶה יִצְרוֹ מִבַּחוּץ His desire is external. Our commentary follows *Rashi*, who explains this expression as referring to the externally visible manifestations of a man's heightened sexual desire. *Rid* takes these words as a figure of speech referring to the fact that verbally expressing one's desire to engage in sexual relations ("his desire is external") is distinctly male behavior. This behavioral norm, argues the Gemara, reflects the fact that the male sexual drive is stronger than that of the female, and as a result a man suffers more than a woman when his drive for sexual gratification is frustrated.

הַמַּשְׁרֶה If someone provides. *Rashi* and *Rivan* explain that the term הַמַּשְׁרֶה is derived from the same root as the Aramaic word שֵׁירוּתָא, meaning "meal," for the Mishnah refers to a husband who provides his wife with her meals through a third party. *Talmidei Rabbi Yonah* associates the term with the Aramaic word מַשְׁרִיתָא, meaning "camp." The husband "camps" his wife with another person, who supplies her with all her needs.

הַמַּשְׁרֶה אֶת אִשְׁתּוֹ If someone provides for his wife. It would appear from *Rambam*'s ruling (*Hilkhot Ishut* 12:12)

TRANSLATION AND COMMENTARY

amounts of food and clothing that the husband must provide for his wife: If a man is living apart from his wife — an arrangement that is permitted under certain circumstances — and **he is providing for her** support **through a third party,** [1] **he must not give her less than two *kabbin* of wheat or four *kabbin* of barley** each week. [2] **Rabbi Yose said: Nobody awarded** a woman such a large allowance of **barley except Rabbi Yishmael, who lived close to Edom.** [3] In addition to the grain, the husband must **give** his wife **half a *kav* of beans, half a *log* of oil** for food and lighting, **and** either **a *kav* of dried figs, or a *maneh* of pressed figs.** [4] **If he does not have** dried or pressed figs, **he must give her a corresponding amount of fruit of another kind.**

וְנוֹתֵן לָהּ מִטָּה [5] In addition to food, the husband **must give** his wife **a bed, a** soft **mattress, and a** firm **mat.**

LITERAL TRANSLATION

[1] he must not give her less than two *kabbin* of wheat or four *kabbin* of barley. [2] Rabbi Yose said: Nobody granted her barley except Rabbi Yishmael, who was close to Edom. [3] And he gives her half a *kav* of beans, and half a *log* of oil, and a *kav* of dried figs, or a *maneh* of pressed figs. [4] And if he does not have, he grants her a corresponding amount of fruit from another place.
[5] And he gives her a bed, a mattress,

[1] לֹא יִפְחוֹת לָהּ מִשְּׁנֵי קַבִּין חִטִּין אוֹ מֵאַרְבָּעָה קַבִּין שְׂעוֹרִין. [2] אָמַר רַבִּי יוֹסֵי: לֹא פָּסַק לָהּ שְׂעוֹרִין אֶלָּא רַבִּי יִשְׁמָעֵאל, שֶׁהָיָה סָמוּךְ לֶאֱדוֹם. [3] וְנוֹתֵן לָהּ חֲצִי קַב קִיטְנִית, וַחֲצִי לוֹג שֶׁמֶן, וְקַב גְּרוֹגָרוֹת, אוֹ מָנֶה דְּבֵילָה. [4] וְאִם אֵין לוֹ, פּוֹסֵק לְעוּמָּתָן פֵּירוֹת מִמָּקוֹם אַחֵר.
[5] וְנוֹתֵן לָהּ מִטָּה, מַפָּץ,

RASHI

לא יפחות לה — בשבת. **לא פסק שעורים כו'** — בגמרא מפרש לה. **גרוגרות** — תאנים יבשין. **דבילה** — תאנים דרוסות בעיגול, ונמכרות במשקל. **מפץ** — רך ממחצלת.

BACKGROUND

שֶׁהָיָה סָמוּךְ לֶאֱדוֹם Who was close to Edom.

As may be inferred from here and from other sources, Rabbi Yishmael lived for some time in the southern part of Judea, though he was also active both in the Academy in Yavneh and in Usha in Galilee. The land of Edom is in the southern Judean desert, where there is very little rain and the soil is of poor quality. Therefore the people there were accustomed to eating bread made from barley, whereas in most of Judea barley was mainly used as animal feed.

NOTES

that a man is permitted to live apart from his wife, provided that he supplies her through a third party with the maintenance to which she is entitled, and that he eats with her once a week on Friday night. Many Rishonim raise the objection that the Mishnah implies otherwise, for elsewhere (below, 70a–71b) it is taught that if a husband forbids his wife by a vow from benefiting from him, then for up to thirty days he must appoint an administrator to provide for her needs, but after that he must divorce her and pay her her ketubah. The Gemara (below, 70b) explains that after thirty days the husband must divorce his wife, for by then the matter must already have become public knowledge, and the woman is suffering humiliation as a result. How, then, can a person be permitted to make a permanent arrangement according to which he may live apart from his wife and provide for her needs through a third party?

Most Rishonim (*Ra'ah, Rashba, Ritva*, and others) follow the Jerusalem Talmud, which explains that our Mishnah is referring to a case in which the wife agreed to the arrangement whereby she would be maintained by her husband through a third party. But if she does not agree to the arrangement, her husband must return home after thirty days and personally provide for her maintenance, or else he must divorce her and pay her her ketubah.

Ra'avad and *Rid* explain that our Mishnah is referring to a case of a worker employed in another city, who is permitted to live apart from his wife all week, for she married him on the understanding that he would only be home on weekends. *Meiri* points out that even according to *Rambam* the husband may not arrange for his wife to be maintained against her will in someone else's house, but only that she be maintained in her husband's house through a third party.

מִשְּׁנֵי קַבִּין חִטִּין Less than two *kabbin* of wheat. The question is asked: When the Israelites were provided with manna in the wilderness, each person received an *omer*'s worth each day, an *omer* being equivalent to slightly less than two *kabbin* — how, then, can a woman maintain herself on only two *kabbin* of wheat per week?

The Geonim (cited by *Rid* and others) answered: Our Mishnah lists the minimum amounts of food which even the poorest person must provide for his wife. In the wilderness the Israelites were maintained liberally, in accordance with the highest standard of nearly two *kabbin* a day.

וְנוֹתֵן לָהּ חֲצִי קַב קִיטְנִית And he gives her half a *kav* of beans. The Rishonim note that our Mishnah records the foodstuffs that a man must provide for his wife as part of his duty to maintain her. The Tosefta (*Ketubot* 5:7) adds that the husband must also provide his wife with the utensils with which to prepare the food, such as a lamp, a cup, and a pot (*Rashba, Ritva*).

HALAKHAH

לֹא יִפְחוֹת לָהּ מִשְּׁנֵי קַבִּין חִטִּין He must not give her less than two *kabbin* of wheat. "How much food must a husband provide for his wife? During the week, he must supply her with bread that suffices for two meals a day, and side dishes together with the bread, and on Shabbat he must provide her with three meals, following the Mishnah and the Gemara. *Rambam* adds that the husband must provide his wife with the type of food that is customarily eaten in that particular locality, whether it be wheat or barley, rice or millet, or food of any other kind." (*Rambam, Sefer Nashim, Hilkhot Ishut* 12:10; *Shulḥan Arukh, Even HaEzer* 70:3.)

וְנוֹתֵן לָהּ מִטָּה And he gives her a bed. "A husband must provide his wife with new clothing worth fifty zuz (six-and-a-quarter dinarim in Tyrian coins) each year. He must give her the new clothing during the winter, and she continues

REALIA

מַפָּץ A mattress. This mattress, like the reed-mat (מַחֲצֶלֶת) mentioned below, was woven from reeds, although the latter was apparently manufactured from whole reeds, while the "mattress" was made of parted reeds (perhaps from their soft interiors), and was softer.

וּמַחֲצֶלֶת, [1]וְנוֹתֵן לָהּ כִּפָּה לְרֹאשָׁהּ, וַחֲגוֹר לְמָתְנֶיהָ, [2]וּמִנְעָלִים מִמּוֹעֵד לְמוֹעֵד, [3]וְכֵלִים שֶׁל חֲמִשִּׁים זוּז מִשָּׁנָה לְשָׁנָה. [4]וְאֵין נוֹתְנִין לָהּ לֹא חֲדָשִׁים בִּימוֹת הַחַמָּה, [5]וְלֹא שְׁחָקִים בִּימוֹת הַגְּשָׁמִים. [6]אֶלָּא נוֹתֵן לָהּ כֵּלִים שֶׁל חֲמִשִּׁים זוּז בִּימוֹת הַגְּשָׁמִים, [7]וְהִיא מִתְכַּסָּה בִּבְלָאוֹתֵיהֶן בִּימוֹת הַחַמָּה. [8]וְהַשְּׁחָקִים שֶׁלָּהּ.
[9]נוֹתֵן לָהּ מָעָה כֶּסֶף לְצוֹרְכָּהּ. [10]וְאוֹכֶלֶת עִמּוֹ מִלֵּילֵי שַׁבָּת לְלֵילֵי שַׁבָּת. [11]וְאִם אֵין נוֹתֵן לָהּ מָעָה כֶּסֶף לְצוֹרְכָּהּ, מַעֲשֵׂה יָדֶיהָ שֶׁלָּהּ.

LITERAL TRANSLATION

and a mat, [1]and he gives her a cap for her head, and a girdle for her loins, [2]and shoes from Festival to Festival, [3]and clothing worth fifty zuz from year to year. [4]And we do not give her new [clothes] in the summer (lit., "in the days of the sun"), [5]nor worn [ones] in the winter (lit., "in the days of the rains"). [6]Rather, he gives her clothing worth fifty zuz in the winter, [7]and she dresses in them when they are worn out during the summer. [8]And the worn [clothes] are hers.

[9]He gives her a silver ma'ah for her needs. [10]And she eats with him every Friday night (lit., "from the nights of Shabbat to the nights of Shabbat"). [11]And if he does not give her a silver ma'ah for her needs, her handiwork is hers.

TRANSLATION AND COMMENTARY

[1]**He must give her a** new **cap for her head and a** new **girdle for her waist** once a year, [2]**and** he must give her a new pair of **shoes for each** of the three **Festivals,** Pesah, Shavuot, and Sukkot. [3]He must also provide her with new **clothing worth fifty zuz each year.** [4]A husband **must not give** his wife **new clothes during the summer,** for new clothing is heavier and thus warmer than clothing that has already been worn for some time. [5]**Nor** may he give her **worn** clothing **during the winter,** for it is then that she needs new clothing to keep her warm. [6]**Rather, he must give her** new **clothing worth fifty zuz during the winter,** [7]**and she** continues to **dress in the** same **worn** clothing **during the** following **summer.** [8]When a man buys his wife new clothing, **the worn clothing** that she still has from the previous year **is hers** to keep.

נוֹתֵן לָהּ מָעָה כֶּסֶף [9]In addition to providing her with food and clothing, the husband **must** also **give** his wife a weekly allowance of **a silver ma'ah** (one-sixth of a dinar) which she may spend **on** the extra things that **she needs.** Even when a man is permitted to live apart from his wife, [10]she is entitled to **eat with** her husband once a week **on Friday night.** [11]**If** a man **does not give** his wife **a silver ma'ah** to spend **on her** personal **needs, her** surplus **handiwork is hers** to keep. The Rabbis enacted that the husband is required to give his wife a weekly allowance for her personal expenses, in return for which he is entitled to her earnings from those tasks that she is not legally required to perform for him.

RASHI

כפה — לעיף אחד משנה לשנה. **ממועד למועד** — אמנעלים קאי, מנעלים חדשים לכל שלשת רגלים. **חדשים** — קשים לה בימות החמה, לפי שהם חמים, ויפים לה בימות הגשמים. **אלא נותן לה כלים** — חדשים, של חמשים זוז בימות הגשמים כו׳. **והשחקים שלה** — אף כשיקנה לה חדשים. ובגמרא מפרש למאי מיבעי לה. **ונותן לה מעה כסף** — לכל שבת לדברים קטנים. **מעשה ידיה** — אוקימנן לעיל כתובות (נח,א) מותר מעשה ידיה. **ואוכלת עמו לילי שבת** — שהוא ליל עונה.

LANGUAGE

מָנֶה ***Maneh.*** Here this term refers to a unit of weight, not to a type of coin, as it does in some cases. Our Mishnah probably refers to the Italian *maneh*, which weighed 327 grams.

REALIA

כִּפָּה **A cap.**

From a Greek illustration. Married women used to wear large caps made of wool or other material, which covered most of their hair. Usually, a woman would not appear in public in a cap; instead, she would cover her hair with a veil, a kerchief, or a hat.

HALAKHAH

to wear the worn clothing during the following summer. Whatever clothing remains at the end of the year is hers to keep. He must give her a girdle for her waist and a covering for her head once a year, and a new pair of shoes for each of the Festivals. He must also provide his wife with household utensils and furniture, including a bed and a mattress or matting. *Rambam* notes that the quantities mentioned in the Mishnah applied only in Eretz Israel during the Mishnaic period. In other places and at other times we follow the underlying principle that a husband is required to provide his wife with clothing that is appropriate for winter and for summer in accordance with the standards set by the most simply dressed women in that particular locality." (*Rambam, Sefer Nashim, Hilkhot Ishut* 13:1-3; *Shulḥan Arukh, Even HaEzer* 73:1.)

מָעָה כֶּסֶף **A silver ma'ah.** "A husband must provide his wife with a weekly allowance of a silver ma'ah for her to spend on her personal needs." (*Rambam, Sefer Nashim, Hilkhot Ishut* 12:10; *Shulḥan Arukh, Even HaEzer* 70:3.)

וְאוֹכֶלֶת עִמּוֹ **And she eats with him.** "If a husband wishes to provide his wife with the maintenance to which she is entitled, but to live apart from her and to take his meals without her, he is permitted to do so, provided that he eats with her once a week on Friday night, following Rav Naḥman's interpretation of the Mishnah [below, 65b]. *Rema* notes that according to many authorities the husband cannot arrange for his wife to eat apart from him, unless she willingly accepts such an arrangement." (*Rambam, Sefer Nashim, Hilkhot Ishut* 12:12; *Shulḥan Arukh, Even HaEzer* 70:2.)

TRANSLATION AND COMMENTARY

וּמַה הִיא עוֹשָׂה לוֹ [1] The Mishnah continues: **What** is the set amount of handiwork that a woman **must do for** her husband? [2] If a woman spins the long, thin threads that are used for the **warp**, she must spin wool **weighing five Judean sela'im, which are** equivalent to **ten Galilean sela'im.** [3] And if she spins the short, thick threads that are used for the **woof**, which are easier to produce, she must spin wool **weighing ten Judean sela'im, which are** equivalent to **twenty Galilean sela'im.** [4] **But if** a woman **is nursing, we reduce** the amount of **handiwork** she must produce, [5] **and we add to the** amount of **maintenance** that her husband must provide for her.

בַּמֶּה דְּבָרִים אֲמוּרִים [6] The Mishnah concludes: **In what circumstances do the** standards set in our Mishnah **apply?** [7] These are the minimal standards, and they **apply to the poorest man in Israel.** [8] **But** in the case of **a person of higher social standing,** the husband's obligation regarding his wife's maintenance is determined **according to his** means and **social position,** for a wife is entitled to the standard of living to which her husband is accustomed.

GEMARA מַנִּי מַתְנִיתִין [9] We learned in the Mishnah that a man who provides for his wife's support through a third party must give her no less than two *kabbin* of wheat each week. The Gemara asks: **Whose opinion does our Mishnah follow?** [10] At first glance it would appear that the opinion expressed anonymously in the Mishnah corresponds **neither** to the known view **of Rabbi Yoḥanan ben Beroka, nor** to **that of Rabbi Shimon**, the Tanna who disagrees with him. [11] **For we have learned** in another Mishnah (*Eruvin* 82b): "A person is forbidden to walk more than two thousand cubits from his home on Shabbat. Nevertheless, the entire city in which he lives is considered as his 'place of residence,' and the two thousand cubits are counted from its limits. There is a Halakhically accepted way of extending the limit of two thousand cubits. If, before Shabbat, one places a specified amount of food somewhere within one's two-thousand-cubit limit (even at its furthest edge), one establishes the location of that food as one's 'place of residence' for Shabbat, and the two thousand cubits are counted from there. This placing of food in order to extend the distance that one is permitted to walk on Shabbat is called *eruv teḥumin* [lit., 'the joining of Shabbat borders']. If more than one person wishes to extend the two-thousand-cubit limit, enough food for each person must be placed at the site of the *eruv*. [12] **What is the measure** of food needed for the *eruv*? [13] Enough **food for two meals**

[1] וּמַה הִיא עוֹשָׂה לוֹ? [2] מִשְׁקַל חָמֵשׁ סְלָעִים שְׁתִי בִּיהוּדָה, שֶׁהֵן עֶשֶׂר סְלָעִים בַּגָּלִיל, [3] אוֹ מִשְׁקַל עֶשֶׂר סְלָעִים עֵרֶב בִּיהוּדָה, שֶׁהֵן עֶשְׂרִים סְלָעִים בַּגָּלִיל. [4] וְאִם הָיְתָה מֵנִיקָה, פּוֹחֲתִין לָהּ מִמַּעֲשֵׂה יָדֶיהָ, [5] וּמוֹסִיפִין לָהּ עַל מְזוֹנוֹתֶיהָ. [6] בַּמֶּה דְּבָרִים אֲמוּרִים? [7] בְּעָנִי שֶׁבְּיִשְׂרָאֵל. [8] אֲבָל בִּמְכוּבָּד, הַכֹּל לְפִי כְּבוֹדוֹ.

גמרא [9] מַנִּי מַתְנִיתִין? [10] לָא רַבִּי יוֹחָנָן בֶּן בְּרוֹקָא, וְלָא רַבִּי שִׁמְעוֹן. [11] דִּתְנַן: [12] "וְכַמָּה שִׁיעוּרוֹ? [13] מְזוֹן שְׁתֵּי סְעוּדוֹת

LITERAL TRANSLATION

[1] And what does she do for him? [2] The weight of five sela'im of warp in Judea, which are ten sela'im in Galilee, [3] or the weight of ten sela'im of woof in Judea, which are twenty sela'im in Galilee. [4] And if she was nursing, we reduce her handiwork, [5] and we add to her maintenance.

[6] In what [case] are these things said? [7] Regarding the poorest man in Israel. [8] But regarding a respected person, all is according to his dignity.

GEMARA [9] Whose [opinion] is our Mishnah? [10] Not [that of] Rabbi Yoḥanan ben Beroka, and not [that of] Rabbi Shimon. [11] For we have learned: [12] "And how much is its measure? [13] Food for two meals

RASHI

שתי — קשה לטוותו כפלים כשל ערב. משקל של יהודה כפלים כשל גליל.

גמרא הכי גרסינן: **מני מתניתין לא רבי יוחנן בן ברוקא ולא רבי שמעון. כמה הוא שיעורו** — של עירובי תחומין.

REALIA

שְׁתִי וָעֵרֶב Warp and woof. Cloth is woven on looms; fixed vertical threads (the warp) are strung on the loom, through which are inserted the horizontal threads (the woof, or filling).

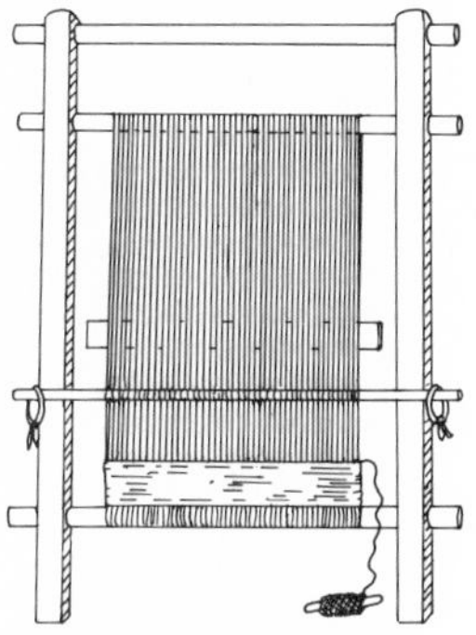

Since the warp serves as the basis of the cloth, it is usually much stronger than the woof (even though the threads are often thinner). Therefore the warp must be spun much more carefully than the woof, and a woman who spun woof threads was expected to spin twice as much as one who only spun the warp.

HALAKHAH

וְאִם הָיְתָה מֵנִיקָה And if she was nursing. "As long as a woman is nursing, the amount of handiwork she must produce is reduced, and the amount of maintenance to which she is entitled is increased," following the Mishnah. (*Rambam, Sefer Nashim, Hilkhot Ishut* 21:11; *Shulḥan Arukh, Even HaEzer* 80:11.)

בַּמֶּה דְּבָרִים אֲמוּרִים? בְּעָנִי שֶׁבְּיִשְׂרָאֵל In what case are these things said? Regarding the poorest man in Israel. "The standards set in the Mishnah regarding the husband's duty to maintain his wife were stated with respect to a very poor person. But if the husband is a wealthy man, he must provide his wife with food and clothing in accordance with his means and social position." (*Rambam, Sefer Nashim, Hilkhot Ishut* 12:11, 13:5; *Shulḥan Arukh, Even HaEzer* 70:3, 73:4.)

וְכַמָּה שִׁיעוּרוֹ? And how much is its measure? "When a person arranges an *eruv*, he must place two meals for each person who wishes to participate in the *eruv*," following Rabbi Yoḥanan ben Beroka, whose viewpoint is attributed to the Sages in *Eruvin*. (*Rambam, Sefer Zemanim, Hilkhot Eruvin* 1:9, 6:7; *Shulḥan Arukh, Orah Ḥayyim* 386:6, 409:7.)

REALIA

פּוּנְדְּיוֹן **Dupondius.**

A dupondius from Talmudic times.

LANGUAGE

פּוּנְדְּיוֹן **Dupondius.** The source of the Hebrew word פּוּנְדְּיוֹן, *pundyon,* is the Latin *dupondius,* a coin worth two isars.

REALIA

סְאִין וְקַבִּין ***Se'ahs* and *kabbin.*** The *se'ah* was the basic unit of volume in the Bible and the Talmud. One *se'ah* equals six *kabbin;* thus four *se'ahs* equal twenty-four *kabbin;* and the loaves of bread mentioned here weighed half a *kav* each.

TRANSLATION AND COMMENTARY

for each person participating in the *eruv.* When the Mishnah states that a person must set aside two meals for his *eruv,* [1]it means that he must set aside enough **food for** two **weekday** meals, **but not for** two **Shabbat** meals. [2]**This is the opinion of Rabbi Meir.** [3]**Rabbi Yehudah** disagrees and **says:** The Mishnah means that a person must set aside enough food **for** two **Shabbat** meals, **but not for** two **weekday** meals. [4]**And both** Rabbi Meir and Rabbi Yehudah **intend to be lenient** in their rulings. Rabbi Meir maintains that a person eats more bread on Shabbat than during the week, and therefore he sets the amount required for an *eruv* in accordance with the lesser amount that a person eats during the week. Rabbi Yehudah maintains that one eats less bread at his Shabbat meals than he does at his weekday meals, and therefore he sets the amount required for an *eruv* in accordance with the lesser amount that a person eats on Shabbat. [5]**Rabbi Yoḥanan ben Beroka says:** There is a fixed amount of food that a person must set aside when he arranges his *eruv.* The two meals that he sets aside must be made up of **a loaf** of bread **that is bought for a dupondius, when four *se'ahs*** of wheat **sell for a sela.** Four *se'ahs* are equivalent to twenty-four *kabbin,* and a sela is equivalent to forty-eight dupondii. Thus we are dealing with a case in which a *kav* of wheat sells for two dupondii, and a loaf bought for one dupondius is made from a half a *kav* of wheat. According to this calculation, a half-*kav* loaf suffices for two meals, or alternatively each meal requires a quarter of a *kav.* [6]**Rabbi Shimon** disagrees and **says:** It is sufficient for the person who is arranging his *eruv* to set aside two meals made up of **two-thirds of a loaf** of bread, **when three loaves** are made **from a *kav*** of wheat. When three loaves are made from a *kav* of wheat, each loaf is made from one-third of a *kav.* And if two-thirds of one of those loaves suffices for two meals, then each meal requires one-third of the loaf, or one-ninth of a *kav* of wheat. Having made reference to loaves costing a dupondius and to loaves made from one-third of a *kav* of wheat, the Mishnah adds that such loaves and fractions of them are also used as measures in other Halakhic contexts: [7]The time it takes to eat **half of** such a loaf (costing a dupondius, according to Rabbi Yoḥanan ben Beroka, or made from one-third of a *kav* of wheat, according to Rabbi Shimon) **is the unit** of time that a person may remain in **a house afflicted with leprosy** before his clothing contracts ritual impurity. A leprous house renders a person ritually impure as soon as he enters it, but the clothing he is wearing becomes ritually impure only after he has been in the house for the time that it takes to eat half of the loaf mentioned here. [8]**Half of half of** such a loaf, i.e., a quarter of

לְכָל אֶחָד וְאֶחָד, [1]מְזוֹנוֹ לַחוֹל
וְלֹא לַשַּׁבָּת. [2]דִּבְרֵי רַבִּי מֵאִיר.
[3]רַבִּי יְהוּדָה אוֹמֵר: לַשַּׁבָּת וְלֹא
לַחוֹל. [4]וְזֶה וְזֶה מִתְכַּוְּונִין
לְהָקֵל. [5]רַבִּי יוֹחָנָן בֶּן בְּרוֹקָא
אוֹמֵר: כִּכָּר הַלָּקוּחַ בְּפוּנְדְּיוֹן,
מֵאַרְבַּע סְאִין לְסֶלַע. [6]רַבִּי
שִׁמְעוֹן אוֹמֵר: שְׁתֵּי יָדוֹת
לְכִכָּר, מִשָּׁלֹשׁ כִּכָּרוֹת לְקַב.
[7]חֶצְיָהּ לְבַיִת הַמְנוּגָּע, [8]וַחֲצִי

LITERAL TRANSLATION

for each person, [1]his food for a weekday and not for Shabbat. [2][These are] the words of Rabbi Meir. [3]Rabbi Yehudah says: For Shabbat and not for a weekday. [4]And both this [Sage] and that intend to be lenient. [5]Rabbi Yoḥanan ben Beroka says: A loaf that is bought for a dupondius, when four *se'ahs* [sell] for a sela. [6]Rabbi Shimon says: Two-thirds of a loaf, when there are three loaves to a *kav.* [7]Half of it [is the measure] for a house afflicted with leprosy, [8]and half of

RASHI

מתכוונין להקל — רבי מאיר היה רגיל לאכול פת בשבת יותר מבחול, שהיה ממשיך פת לכל מינים הבאין לפניו. ורבי יהודה היה אוכל פת בחול יותר מבשבת, שהיה שבע במיני מעדנים. **רבי יוחנן בן ברוקא** — נתן שיעור קלוב: ככר הלקוח בפונדיון, כשלוקחין ארבע סאין בסלע, הן שתי סעודות. וקסלקא דעתך חצי קב, שהרי הסלע ארבעים ושמונה פונדיונין, שש מעה כסף דינר, ומעה שני פונדיונין — הרי שנים עשר לדינר, וארבעה דינר לסלע — הרי ארבעים ושמונה. וארבע סאין עשרים וארבעה קבין, ארבעים ושמונה חצאי קבין, נמצא לרבי יוחנן לחצי קב שתי סעודות. **רבי שמעון אומר** — שתי סעודות הן שתי ידות של ככר משלש ככרות לקב, ונמצא הקב תשע סעודות, שלש סעודות לככר ושלש ככרות לקב. **חציה** — של ככר. **לבית המנוגע** — השוהה בבית המנוגע כדי אכילת פרס. חצי ככר —

NOTES

חֶצְיָהּ לְבַיִת הַמְנוּגָּע **Half of it is the measure for a house afflicted with leprosy.** The Torah states regarding someone who enters a leprous house (Leviticus 14:47): "And he that lies in the house shall wash his clothes; and he that eats in the house shall wash his clothes." The Sages derive from this verse that a person's clothing does not contract

HALAKHAH

חֶצְיָהּ לְבַיִת הַמְנוּגָּע **Half of it is the measure for a house afflicted with leprosy.** "A person who enters a leprous house contracts ritual impurity immediately, but the clothing he is wearing remains ritually pure as long as he has not been inside the house for longer than the time that it takes to eat half a loaf of wheat bread." (*Rambam, Sefer Tohorah, Hilkhot Tum'at Tzara'at* 16:6.)

חֶצְיָהּ לִפְסוֹל אֶת הַגְּוִיָּה, [1]וַחֲצִי חֲצִי חֶצְיָהּ לְקַבֵּל טוּמְאַת אוֹכָלִין״. [2]מַנִּי? [3]אִי רַבִּי יוֹחָנָן בֶּן בְּרוֹקָא, תְּמָנֵי הָוְיָין; [4]וְאִי רַבִּי שִׁמְעוֹן, תְּמָנֵי סְרֵי הָוְיָין! [5]לְעוֹלָם רַבִּי יוֹחָנָן בֶּן בְּרוֹקָא, וּכְדַאֲמַר רַב חִסְדָּא: [6]צֵא מֵהֶן

LITERAL TRANSLATION

half of it [is the measure] to render the body ritually impure, [1]and half of half of half of it [is the measure] to contract the ritual impurity of foods." [2]Whose [opinion is it]? [3]If [it is that of] Rabbi Yoḥanan ben Beroka, they are eight; [4]and if [it is that of] Rabbi Shimon, they are eighteen!

[5]In fact, [it is that of] Rabbi Yoḥanan ben Beroka, and [it is] as Rav Ḥisda said: [6]Deduct from them

TRANSLATION AND COMMENTARY

the loaf, **is the** smallest **unit** of ritually impure food, the eating of which **disqualifies a** priest from partaking of terumah before he purifies himself by means of ritual immersion. [1]**And half of half of half of** such a loaf, i.e., an eighth of the loaf, **is the** smallest **unit** of food that is capable **of contracting the ritual impurity of foods."** Returning to its analysis of our Mishnah, the Gemara asks: [2]**Whose opinion does** our Mishnah **follow**? Our Mishnah states that a man must provide his wife with two *kabbin* of wheat each week. [3]Now **if** the Mishnah **follows the opinion of Rabbi Yoḥanan ben Beroka** that a meal requires a quarter of a *kav* of wheat, then the two *kabbin* suffice for only **eight** meals, and surely a wife must be provided with at least two meals a day — fourteen meals a week! [4]**And if** our Mishnah **follows the opinion of Rabbi Shimon** that a meal requires only a ninth of a *kav* of wheat, then the two *kabbin* suffice for **eighteen** meals, which is more than a wife needs!

לְעוֹלָם רַבִּי יוֹחָנָן בֶּן בְּרוֹקָא [5]The Gemara answers: **In fact,** the Mishnah **follows the viewpoint of Rabbi Yoḥanan ben Beroka,** which must be understood **as Rav Ḥisda explained** it: Rabbi Yoḥanan ben Beroka was not referring to a half-*kav* loaf, but rather to a loaf costing a dupondius, in a place where half a *kav* of wheat sells for a dupondius. Even though half a *kav* of wheat sells for a dupondius, a dupondius buys a loaf of bread which consists of only one-third of a *kav* of wheat, [6]for **a third** of the dupondius

RASHI

מטמא בגדים. כדכתיב "והאוכל בבית יכבס בגדיו", כששוהה שיעור אכילה הכתוב מדבר. כדתניא בתורת כהנים. ואף על גב דגבי סעודת עירוב אמרנו שלש סעודות בככר אין בו אלא שתי סעודות בינוניות, ושל עירוב שיעורו להקל, ובמצומצמות. והיינו דאמרינן אכילת פרס בכל שיעור שהיית סעודה, לפי ששיערוהו כחצי הככר. **וחצי חציה לפסול את הגוייה** — האוכל שיעור חצי פרס אוכלים טמאים נפסל גופו מלאכול בתרומה עד שיטבול. והוא שתי ביצים. שהככר של שלש לקב — שמונה ביצים הוא, שהקב עשרים וארבע ביצים, ארבעה לוגין חציה של ככר — ארבע ביצים, חצי חציה — שתי ביצים. **תמני סעודות הויין** — קביים חטים דמתניתין, וארבע עשרה סעודות היא צריכה לשבת. **ואי רבי שמעון** — דאמר תשע סעודות לקב. **שמונה עשר הויין** — והיא אינה צריכה אלא ארבע עשרה.

NOTES

ritual impurity as soon as he enters the leprous house, but only after he has been in the house for a certain time — the time it takes to eat a meal consisting of half a loaf of bread.

Rashi notes that even though Rabbi Shimon says that a third of a loaf of bread suffices for a single meal, he only says this with respect to an *eruv*. Regarding an *eruv*, the Rabbis were lenient and only required that a person set aside two very modest meals, each of which consists of a third of a loaf. But regarding all other matters, a meal is defined as half a loaf of bread, the precise measure of which (whether it is the bulk of three eggs or the bulk of four eggs) was the subject of disagreement between Rabbi Yoḥanan ben Beroka and Rabbi Shimon.

לִפְסוֹל אֶת הַגְּוִיָּה **To render the body ritually impure.** *Riva* (see *Tosafot*, and, at much greater length, *Tosefot Rabbenu Shimshon of Sens*) identifies the Rabbinic decree disqualifying a priest from eating terumah if he has eaten ritually impure food as being one of the eighteen decrees delivered at the end of the Second Temple period (see *Shabbat* 13b). The Gemara explains that the Rabbis decreed that a person who has eaten ritually impure food may not partake of terumah, lest the ritually impure food in his mouth impart ritual impurity to the terumah that he drinks to wash down the food.

Rabbenu Tam is of the opinion that the decree mentioned in our Gemara is a much earlier enactment. The Rabbis decreed that ritually impure food disqualifies a person from eating terumah, lest people think that just as there is no problem with terumah coming into contact with ritually impure food inside the priest's body, there is likewise nothing wrong with terumah coming into contact with ritually impure food outside his body.

לְקַבֵּל טוּמְאַת אוֹכָלִין **To contract the ritual impurity of foods.** *Rivan* has the following reading: "And half of half of half of it to *impart* the ritual impurity of foods." This is

HALAKHAH

וַחֲצִי חֶצְיָהּ לִפְסוֹל אֶת הַגְּוִיָּה **And half of half of it is the measure to render the body ritually impure.** "If a priest eats ritually impure foods, he does not disqualify himself from eating terumah unless he eats the equivalent of a quarter of a loaf of bread." (*Rambam, Sefer Tohorah, Hilkhot Tum'at Okhlin* 4:1.)

וַחֲצִי חֲצִי חֶצְיָהּ לְקַבֵּל טוּמְאַת אוֹכָלִין **And half of half of half of it is the measure to contract the ritual impurity of foods.** "Ritually impure food does not impart ritual impurity to other food or to liquids or to hands unless it contains the bulk of an egg without its shell." (*Rambam, Sefer Tohorah, Hilkhot Tum'at Okhlin* 4:1.)

TRANSLATION AND COMMENTARY

must be deducted for the shopkeeper's expenses and profit. [1] **Here too**, then, we must **add** another **third into** the calculation regarding the number of meals that can be prepared from two *kabbin* of wheat. If a third-of-a-*kav* loaf suffices for two meals, it follows that each meal requires a sixth of a *kav*. Thus the two *kabbin* of wheat that the husband must provide each week for his wife suffice for twelve meals, and not eight meals as was understood above.

אַכַּתִּי [2] The Gemara objects: But how can the Mishnah follow the viewpoint of Rabbi Yoḥanan ben Beroka? Even if a third is added, two *kabbin* of wheat **still** suffice for only **twelve** meals, and a wife is entitled to two meals a day, or fourteen meals a week!

אוֹכֶלֶת עִמּוֹ [3] The Gemara answers: We learned in the Mishnah that even when a man is permitted to live apart from his wife, she is entitled to **eat with him** once a week **on Friday night.** Thus the husband is not required to provide his wife with enough wheat to suffice for fourteen meals a week, for her Friday night dinner does not enter into the calculation.

הָנִיחָא [4] The Gemara raises another objection: **Granted according to the authority who says** (below, 65b) **that** when the Mishnah states that the wife is entitled to eat with her husband once a week on Friday, it means the word **eating** to be understood **literally.** Since the woman is entitled to eat with her husband on Friday nights, he is not required to provide her with sufficient grain for fourteen meals. [5] **But according to the authority who says** that the Mishnah means the word **eating** to be taken euphemistically as referring to **sexual relations, what is there to say?** According to this interpretation, the Mishnah rules that even when a man is permitted to live apart from his wife, she is still entitled to cohabit with him once a week on Friday night, but it says nothing about her Friday-night dinner. Thus the Mishnah cannot follow the viewpoint of Rabbi Yoḥanan ben Beroka, for it rules that the husband must provide his wife with two *kabbin* of wheat per week, and according to Rabbi Yoḥanan ben Beroka, two *kabbin* of wheat do not suffice for the fourteen meals that the woman needs each week. [6] **Moreover,** even if we deduct the woman's Friday-night dinner from the calculation, she still needs **thirteen** other meals each week, and according to Rabbi Yoḥanan ben Beroka, two *kabbin* of wheat suffice for only twelve!

אֶלָּא [7] **Rather,** answers the Gemara, the Mishnah does indeed follow the viewpoint of Rabbi Yoḥanan ben Beroka, but that viewpoint must be understood **as Rav Ḥisda explained** it: When Rabbi Yoḥanan ben Beroka spoke of the quantity of food that a person must set aside for his *eruv*, he did not refer to a half-*kav* loaf, but rather to a loaf costing a dupondius, in a place where half a *kav* of wheat sells for a dupondius. Even though half a *kav* of wheat sells for a dupondius, a dupondius buys a loaf of bread which is only one-quarter of a *kav* in volume, [8] for **a half** of the dupondius **must be deducted for the shopkeeper's** expenses and profit. [9] **Here too**, then, we must **add** another **half** into the calculation regarding the number of meals that can be prepared from two *kabbin* of wheat. Since a quarter-of-a-*kav* loaf suffices for two meals, it follows that each meal requires an eighth of a *kav*. Thus the two *kabbin* of wheat that the husband must

שְׁלִישׁ לַחֶנְוָונִי. [1] הָכָא נַמִי, אַיְיתֵי תִּילְתָּא שְׁדֵי עֲלַיְיהוּ. [2] אַכַּתִּי תַּרְתֵּי סְרֵי הָוְיָין! [3] אוֹכֶלֶת עִמּוֹ לֵילֵי שַׁבָּת. [4] הָנִיחָא לְמַאן דַּאֲמַר אֲכִילָה מַמָּשׁ. [5] אֶלָּא לְמַאן דַּאֲמַר אֲכִילָה תַּשְׁמִישׁ, מַאי אִיכָּא לְמֵימַר? [6] וְעוֹד, תְּלֵיסַר הָוְיָין! [7] אֶלָּא, כְּדַאֲמַר רַב חִסְדָּא: [8] צֵא מֵהֶן מֶחֱצָה לַחֶנְוָונִי. [9] הָכָא נַמִי, אָתְיָא פַּלְגָּא וּשְׁדֵי עֲלַיְיהוּ.

LITERAL TRANSLATION

a third for the shopkeeper. [1] Here too, bring a third [and] add to them.

[2] Still they are twelve!

[3] She eats with him on Friday nights.

[4] Granted according to the one who says [that] eating [is meant] literally. [5] But according to the one who says [that] eating [means] sexual relations, what is there to say? [6] And furthermore, they are thirteen!

[7] Rather, [it is] as Rav Ḥisda said: [8] Deduct from them a half for the shopkeeper. [9] Here too, bring a half and add to them.

RASHI

צא מהן שליש לחנווני — רבי יוחנן לא שיער בחצי קב אלא בככר הלקוח בפונדיון מן החנווני, והוא לקח ארבע סאין חטין בסלע, ומשתכר שליש בטורח, נמצאו בחצי קב שלש סעודות. השתים הוא מוכר בפונדיון שנתן, והשלישית משתכר. **אכתי** — קביס דמתניתין תרתי סרי הוין. **ומשנינן אוכלת עמו לילי שבת** — כדתנן במתניתין. **הניחא כו'** — פלוגתא לקמיה בשמעתין.

NOTES

consonant with the viewpoint of *Rashi*, *Rambam*, and others, that an item of food cannot impart ritual impurity unless it has the bulk of an egg. But food can contract ritual impurity no matter how small it is, even if it only has the bulk of a mustard seed.

קַשְׁיָא דְּרַב חִסְדָּא אַדְּרַב חִסְדָּא! [1]

לָא קַשְׁיָא. [2] הָא בְּאַתְרָא דְּיָהֲבֵי צִיבֵי. [3] הָא בְּאַתְרָא דְּלָא יָהֲבֵי צִיבֵי. [4]

אִי הָכִי, שִׁיתְּסָרֵי הָוְיָין! [5]

כְּמַאן? [6] כְּרַבִּי חִידְקָא, דְּאָמַר: [7] אַרְבַּע סְעוּדוֹת חַיָּיב אָדָם לֶאֱכוֹל בְּשַׁבָּת? [8]

אֲפִילּוּ תֵּימָא רַבָּנַן. [9] דַּל חֲדָא לְאָרְחֵי וּפָרְחֵי. [10]

LITERAL TRANSLATION

[1] There is a contradiction between Rav Ḥisda and Rav Ḥisda!

[2] There is no difficulty. [3] This [applies] in a place where they give wood. [4] This [applies] in a place where they do not give wood.

[5] If so, they are sixteen! [6] In accordance with whom? [7] [Is it] in accordance with Rabbi Ḥidka, who said: [8] A man is obliged to eat four meals on Shabbat?

[9] You can even say [it is in accordance with] the Rabbis. [10] Deduct one for guests and passing visitors.

TRANSLATION AND COMMENTARY

provide each week for his wife suffice for sixteen meals, more than enough to satisfy the woman's weekly needs.

קַשְׁיָא [1] The Gemara notes: **There is a contradiction between the two** statements of **Rav Ḥisda,** for he was quoted above as saying that a third of what is paid for a loaf of bread must be deducted for the shopkeeper's expenses and profit, and now he says that the shopkeeper's expenses and profit amount to half of what is paid for the loaf!

לָא קַשְׁיָא [2] The Gemara answers: **There is** really **no difficulty** in reconciling this seeming contradiction, for Rav Ḥisda's two statements refer to different cases. When he said that a third of the retail price of bread covers the shopkeeper's expenses and profit, [3] he was referring **to a place where** the customer **provides the wood** used to fire the oven in which the bread is baked. And when he said that the shopkeeper's expenses and profits amount to half of what is paid for the bread, [4] he was referring **to a place where** the customer **does not provide the firewood,** so that the cost of the wood must be added to the price of the bread.

אִי הָכִי [5] The Gemara raises another objection: **If** indeed **it is true** that a quarter-of-a-*kav* loaf suffices for two meals, and the husband must provide his wife with two *kabbin* of wheat, it turns out that the husband must provide his wife with wheat that will suffice for **sixteen** meals each week, which is more than two meals a day, or fourteen meals a week! [6] **Whose** opinion, then, does our Mishnah follow? [7] **Is it** necessary to say that it is **in accordance with** the viewpoint of **Rabbi Ḥidka, who said:** [8] **A person is obliged to eat four meals on Shabbat?** For according to Rabbi Ḥidka, the husband is required to provide his wife with sixteen meals a week — two meals for each of the six weekdays, and four meals on Shabbat.

אֲפִילּוּ [9] The Gemara answers: **You can even say** that our Mishnah **is in accordance with** the viewpoint of **the Rabbis** who disagree with Rabbi Ḥidka and say that a person is only obliged to eat three meals on Shabbat. A husband must provide his wife with two *kabbin* of wheat a week, which suffice for sixteen meals. [10] **Deduct one** meal that must be reserved **for guests and passing visitors,** and you are left with fifteen meals for the woman herself — two meals on each of the six weekdays, and three on Shabbat.

RASHI

באתרא דיהיב ציבי — מי שמוכר חטים לחנווני לעשות ככרות ולמכור בשוק, במקום שהוא נותן לחנווני עצים לאפות — אינו משתכר אלא שליש, ובמקום שאינו נותן עצים — מעכב לעצמו מחצה, שממעט הככרות למכור ביוקר כדי יציאת העצים. **כמאן כרבי חידקא** — בתמיה, נימא כרבי חידקא סתם לה מתניתין, דאמר ב״כל כתבי הקדש״ ארבעה סעודות לשבת?

NOTES

דְּיָהֲבֵי צִיבֵי Where they give wood. The Rishonim note that in addition to the amount of wheat specified in the Mishnah, the husband must also provide his wife with the wood used to fire the oven in which she bakes her bread. In any event, the Mishnah's list is incomplete, for it only mentions the food that a man must provide for his wife, but not the utensils she needs in order to prepare it. Elsewhere it is stated that the husband must provide his wife with such items as a lamp, a cup, and a pot.

אִי הָכִי, שִׁיתְּסָרֵי הָוְיָין If so, they are sixteen. Most Rishonim (*Ramban, Rashba, Ritva,* and others) explain that the Gemara's question assumes that the Mishnah's reference to the wife's right to eat with her husband on Friday night is a euphemism for sexual relations. For according to that opinion, if the husband is required to provide his wife with two *kabbin* of wheat each week, and a quarter-of-a-*kav* loaf suffices for two meals, it turns out that he must provide her with sixteen meals a week. But according to the authority who maintains that the woman is entitled to eat her Friday night meal with her husband, the husband

HALAKHAH

לֶאֱכוֹל בְּשַׁבָּת To eat on Shabbat. "A person is obligated to eat three meals on Shabbat, one at night, one in the morning, and one in the afternoon, following the opinion of the Sages who disagree with Rabbi Ḥidka." (*Rambam, Sefer Zemanim, Hilkhot Shabbat* 30:9; *Shulḥan Arukh, Oraḥ Ḥayyim* 291:1.)

REALIA

שְׁעוֹרִין אֲדוֹמִיּוֹת Edomite barley. Barley resists inclement weather better than wheat, and it grows even in dry areas. Generally, however, the less water there is, the smaller the crop (and the smaller the individual grains). This was apparently why the barley that grew in southern Judea (near Edom) was inferior to other barley. It is also possible that a special type of barley was cultivated there, which, though better suited to the local climatic conditions, was less tasty and nutritious than other barley.

[1] הָשְׁתָּא דְּאָתֵית לְהָכִי, [2] אֲפִילּוּ תֵּימָא רַבִּי שִׁמְעוֹן. [3] לְרַבָּנַן, דַּל תְּלָת לְאָרְחֵי וּפָרְחֵי. [4] לְרַבִּי חִידְקָא, דַּל תַּרְתֵּי לְאָרְחֵי וּפָרְחֵי.

[5] ״אָמַר רַבִּי יוֹסֵי: לֹא פָּסַק שְׂעוֹרִין, וכו׳״. [6] אֶלָּא בֶּאֱדוֹם הוּא דְּאָכְלִין שְׂעוֹרִים, [7] בְּכוּלֵּי עָלְמָא לָא אָכְלֵי?

[8] הָכִי קָאָמַר: לֹא פָּסַק שְׂעוֹרִים כְּפְלַיִם בְּחִטִּין אֶלָּא רַבִּי יִשְׁמָעֵאל, שֶׁהָיָה סָמוּךְ לֶאֱדוֹם, [9] מִפְּנֵי שֶׁשְּׂעוֹרִין אֲדוֹמִיּוֹת רָעוֹת הֵן.

[10] ״וְנוֹתֵן לָהּ חֲצִי קַב קִיטְנִית״. [11] וְאִילּוּ יַיִן לָא קָתָנֵי. [12] מְסַיֵּיע לֵיהּ לְרַבִּי אֶלְעָזָר, דְּאָמַר רַבִּי אֶלְעָזָר: [65A] [13] אֵין פּוֹסְקִין

LITERAL TRANSLATION

[1] Now that you have come to this, [2] you can even say [that it is in accordance with] Rabbi Shimon. [3] According to the Rabbis, deduct three for guests and passing visitors. [4] According to Rabbi Ḥidka, deduct two for guests and passing visitors.

[5] "Rabbi Yose said: Nobody granted [her] barley, etc." [6] But is it [only] in Edom that they eat barley, [7] [and] in the whole world do they not eat?

[8] This is what he says: Nobody granted [her] twice as much barley as wheat except Rabbi Yishmael, who was close to Edom, [9] because Edomite barley is of poor quality.

[10] "And he gives her half a *kav* of beans." [11] But wine it does not teach. [12] This supports Rabbi Elazar, for Rabbi Elazar said: [65A] [13] We do not grant

RASHI

רבי שמעון — דאמר תמני סרי הויין. **ואי כרבנן** — סבירא ליה לתנא דידן בסעודות שבת דל תלת יתירתא לארחי ופרחי. **אין בית דין פוסקין**

TRANSLATION AND COMMENTARY

הָשְׁתָּא [1] The Gemara concludes: **Now that you have come to this** explanation, that the husband must provide his wife with enough food to feed not only herself but an occasional guest or passing visitor as well, [2] **you can even say** that the Mishnah **is in accordance with** the viewpoint of **Rabbi Shimon,** according to whom two *kabbin* of wheat suffice for eighteen meals, an amount of food that considerably exceeds the woman's personal needs each week. [3] **According to the Rabbis,** who maintain that a person is only obliged to eat three meals on Shabbat, **deduct three** meals that must be reserved **for guests and passing visitors,** and you are left with fifteen meals for the woman herself — twelve meals for the six weekdays and three meals for Shabbat. [4] **According to Rabbi Ḥidka,** who maintains that a person must eat four meals on Shabbat, **deduct two** meals **for guests and passing visitors,** and you are left with sixteen meals — twelve meals for the six weekdays and four meals for Shabbat.

אָמַר רַבִּי יוֹסֵי [5] We learned in our Mishnah: "If a man is providing for his wife's support through a third party, he must not give her less than two *kabbin* of wheat or four *kabbin* of barley each week. **Rabbi Yose said: Nobody awarded** a woman such a large allowance of **barley** except Rabbi Yishmael, who lived close to Edom." [6] The Gemara asks: **But is it only in Edom that people eat barley?** [7] **Do people not eat** barley **in the rest of world?** Surely barley is a poor man's food everywhere!

הָכִי קָאָמַר [8] The Gemara answers: **This is what** Rabbi Yose **said: Nobody awarded** a woman **twice as much barley as wheat except Rabbi Yishmael, who lived close to Edom,** [9] **because Edomite barley is of poor quality.** But in other places, where the barley is of higher quality, the husband needs to give his wife only slightly more barley than wheat, in accordance with what the court determines.

וְנוֹתֵן לָהּ [10] The Gemara now proceeds to the next clause of our Mishnah, which stated: "In addition to the grain, the husband must also **give** his wife **half a *kav* of beans,** half a *log* of oil, and either a *kav* of dried figs or a *maneh* of pressed figs." The Gemara notes: The Mishnah speaks of grain, beans, oil, and fruit. [11] **But it does not state** that the husband must provide his wife with **wine.** [12] **This supports** the opinion of **Rabbi Elazar, for Rabbi Elazar said:** [65A] [13] **A wife is not to be awarded wine,** for alcohol tends to intensify

NOTES

is obligated to provide his wife with seventeen meals a week — the sixteen meals that she prepares from the two *kabbin* of wheat, as well as her Friday-night dinner!

Ra'avad argues that the Gemara asks this question even according to the authority who explains the Mishnah literally as referring to the Friday-night meal. For even he agrees that the Mishnah does not mean to say that the husband is required to provide his wife with extra food for the meal, but only that the woman is entitled to eat in her husband's company. Thus her Friday-night dinner is included in the sixteen meals that must be prepared from the two *kabbin* of wheat that the woman receives each week from her husband. Other Rishonim point out that the Jerusalem Talmud states explicitly that according to the authority who explains the Mishnah literally, the husband must provide the food for the meal.

TRANSLATION AND COMMENTARY

a woman's sexual appetite. [1]**And if you argue** that the verse says (Hosea 2:7): **"I will go after my lovers, who give me my bread and my water, my wool and my flax, my oil and my drink,"** and that the meaning of the word שִׁקּוּיַי (translated here as "drink") is "alcoholic beverages," thus implying that alcohol is among the things with which a woman is provided, I can answer you that the verse is to be understood differently. [2]The word שִׁקּוּיַי must be interpreted **as referring to** those **things that a woman longs for** (from the root שקק, meaning "to long for"). [3]**And what are** those things? **Jewelry.** Wine, by contrast, should not be given to a woman.

דָּרַשׁ רַבִּי יְהוּדָה אִישׁ כְּפַר נְבִירַיָא [4]The Gemara now adduces Scriptural support for its ruling that a wife should not be awarded wine: **Rabbi Yehudah of Kfar Neviraya, and some say** that **he was from Kfar Nefor Ḥayil, expounded:** [5]**From where do we derive that a wife is not** to be **awarded wine?** [6]**For the verse says** (I Samuel 1:9): **"And Hannah arose after she had eaten in Shiloh, and after he had drunk** [שָׁתָה]." [7]The verse says **"he had drunk,"** and this implies that only Hannah's husband, Elkanah, drank, **and** that Hannah **herself did not drink.** This point is emphasized in the verse in order to teach us that it is improper for a woman to be given intoxicating beverages.

אֶלָּא מֵעַתָּה [8]The Gemara asks: **If it is true** that the words "he had drunk" imply that it was only Elkanah who drank, and that Hannah did not drink, **does** the expression **"she had eaten" imply** that it was only Hannah who ate, [9]**and** that her husband, Elkanah, **did not eat?**

אֲנַן [10]The Gemara explains: When **we argued** that an inference can be drawn from the words "he had drunk," it was **because the verse** itself **changed its wording.** [11]**Since** the verse **is dealing with** Hannah — "Hannah arose after she had eaten" — and the passage continues with a description of Hannah's encounter with the High Priest, Eli, we would have expected the verse to continue: "And she had drunk." [12]**Why,** then, **does** the verse suddenly **change** its subject and mention that it was Elkanah who had drunk? [13]We must **conclude from** the way the verse is worded that the expression **"he had drunk"** implies that it was only Elkanah who drank, [14]**and** that Hannah **herself did not drink,** because it is improper for a woman to be given intoxicating beverages.

יֵינוֹת לְאִשָּׁה. [1]וְאִם תֹּאמַר: "אֵלְכָה אַחֲרֵי מְאַהֲבַי, נֹתְנֵי לַחְמִי וּמֵימַי, צַמְרִי וּפִשְׁתִּי, שַׁמְנִי וְשִׁקּוּיָי", [2]דְּבָרִים שֶׁהָאִשָּׁה מִשְׁתּוֹקֶקֶת עֲלֵיהֶן. [3]וּמַאי נִינְהוּ? תַּכְשִׁיטִין. [4]דָּרַשׁ רַבִּי יְהוּדָה אִישׁ כְּפַר נְבִירַיָא, וְאָמְרִי לַהּ אִישׁ כְּפַר נְפוֹר חַיִל: [5]מִנַּיִן שֶׁאֵין פּוֹסְקִין יֵינוֹת לְאִשָּׁה? [6]שֶׁנֶּאֱמַר: "וַתָּקָם חַנָּה אַחֲרֵי אָכְלָה בְשִׁלֹה, וְאַחֲרֵי שָׁתֹה". [7]"שָׁתָה", וְלֹא שָׁתַת. [8]אֶלָּא מֵעַתָּה, "אָכְלָה" [9]וְלֹא אָכַל הָכִי נָמֵי? [10]אֲנַן מִדְּשַׁנֵּי קְרָא בְּדִבּוּרֵיהּ קָאָמְרִינַן. [11]מִכְּדִי בְּגַוָּהּ קָא עָסֵיק וְאָתֵי, [12]מַאי טַעְמָא שַׁנֵּי? [13]שְׁמַע מִינָּהּ: "שָׁתֹה", [14]וְלֹא שָׁתַת.

LITERAL TRANSLATION

wine to a woman. [1]And if you say: "I will go after my lovers, who give me my bread and my water, my wool and my flax, my oil and my drink," [2][this refers to] things that a woman longs for. [3]And what are they? Jewelry.

[4]Rabbi Yehudah of Kfar Neviraya expounded, and some say [he was] of Kfar Nefor Ḥayil: [5]From where [do we derive] that we do not grant wine to a woman? [6]For it is said: "And Hannah arose after she had eaten in Shiloh, and after he had drunk." [7]"He had drunk," but she did not drink.

[8]If so, [does] "she had eaten" [9][imply] also that he did not eat?

[10]We say [this] because the verse changed its wording. [11]Now since it is dealing with her, [12]for what reason does it change? [13]Conclude from this: "He had drunk," [14]but she did not drink.

RASHI

יינות לאשה — שהיין מרגילה לתאות תשמיש.

SAGES

רַבִּי יְהוּדָה אִישׁ כְּפַר נְבִירַיָא Rabbi Yehudah of Kfar Neviraya. Only one other saying by this Sage is recorded in the Talmud (*Megillah* 18a). It is not clear whether he was among the last of the Tannaim or the first of the Palestinian Amoraim.

BACKGROUND

נְבִירַיָא Neviraya. This village apparently went by several other names, e.g., Nevorya, Nevor Ḥayil, Nefor Ḥayil, as well as Gevorya and Gevor Ḥayil. It was located north of Safed. Today, only the ruins of this village and the ancient synagogue there are extant.

NOTES

אֵין פּוֹסְקִין יֵינוֹת We do not grant wine. A similar discussion regarding the propriety of giving wine to a woman is found in the Jerusalem Talmud. There, the ruling that wine should not be given to a woman is supported by the verse (Hosea 4:11): "Harlotry and wine and new wine take away the heart," which points to the connection between intoxicating beverages and promiscuity.

וְשִׁקּוּיָי And my drink. If the word שִׁקּוּיָי is taken to mean "my drink," then it surely refers to wine, for water is mentioned explicitly earlier in the verse (*Rivan*). *Maharsha* adds that the juxtaposition of "my drink" and "my oil" teaches us that the drink referred to here is wine, just as three verses later (verse 10), when the metaphor of the adulterous woman is explained, wine and oil are mentioned together. That later verse which explains the metaphor also supports the Gemara's suggestion that the term שִׁקּוּיַי is to be understood as jewelry, for the verse states: "And I multiplied silver and gold for her, which they used for the

SAGES

רַב חִינָּנָא בַּר כָּהֲנָא Rav Ḥinnana (or Ḥanina) bar Kahana. A Babylonian Amora of the second generation, this Sage was a student of Rav, but he also transmitted the teachings of other Amoraim of the first generation — Shmuel and Rav Assi. His teachings, mainly in the area of Halakhah, are found in several places in the Talmud.

BACKGROUND

צִיקֵי קְדֵירָה Meat sauce. Some authorities explain this expression as referring to what remains in pots after meat has been cooked and removed. These remnants have a special taste and are used as the basis for sauces served with other dishes. The root of the word is apparently יצק, meaning "to mold" or "to pour," implying that these remnants are poured out of the pot after the main dish has been removed.

TRANSLATION AND COMMENTARY

מֵיתִיבִי [1] **An objection** to this ruling **was raised** from a Baraita, which states: **"If a woman is accustomed to wine, she may be given** wine to drink."

רְגִילָה [2] The Gemara answers: **If** a woman **is accustomed** to wine, the law **is different,** because she is less likely to get drunk. [3] The Gemara supports this answer by citing what **Rav Ḥinnana bar Kahana said in the name of Shmuel:** [4] **If** a woman **is accustomed** to wine, **she may be given one glass;** [5] but **if she is not accustomed** to wine, **she may be given two glasses.**

מַאי קָאָמַר [6] The Gemara expresses its astonishment at this ruling: **What does** Shmuel **mean?** This ruling as it stands runs counter to logic!

אָמַר אַבַּיֵי [7] **Abaye said: This is what** Shmuel **means:** [8] If a woman **is accustomed** to wine, then when she is **in the presence of her husband she may be given two glasses** to drink, [9] but when she is **not in the presence of her husband, she may be given** only **one glass.** [10] But **if she is not accustomed** to wine, then when she is **in the presence of her husband she may be given only one glass,** [11] and when she is **not in the presence of her husband, she may not be given any** wine **at all.**

וְאִי בָּעֵית אֵימָא [12] The Gemara now suggests another interpretation of the Baraita that ruled that wine may be given to a woman who is accustomed to it. **If you wish,** you can **say** that this is what the Baraita means: [13] **If** a woman **is accustomed** to wine, **she may be given** wine — not to drink, but **to** add flavor to **her meat sauce.** [14] This interpretation is supported by what **Rabbi Abbahu said in the name of Rabbi Yoḥanan: There was** once **a case involving the daughter-in-law of Nakdimon ben Guryon in which the Sages granted her two *se'ahs* of wine every Friday for** her to add to her **meat sauce.** Pleased with this ruling, Nakdimon's

[1] מֵיתִיבִי: ״רְגִילָה, נוֹתְנִין לָהּ״! [2] רְגִילָה, שָׁאנֵי, [3] דְּאָמַר רַב חִינָּנָא בַּר כָּהֲנָא אָמַר שְׁמוּאֵל: [4] רְגִילָה, נוֹתְנִין לָהּ כּוֹס אֶחָד; [5] שֶׁאֵינָהּ רְגִילָה, נוֹתְנִין לָהּ שְׁנֵי כּוֹסוֹת.

[6] מַאי קָאָמַר?

[7] אָמַר אַבַּיֵי: הָכִי קָאָמַר: [8] רְגִילָה, בִּפְנֵי בַעְלָהּ שְׁנֵי כּוֹסוֹת; [9] שֶׁלֹּא בִּפְנֵי בַעְלָהּ נוֹתְנִין לָהּ כּוֹס אֶחָד. [10] אֵינָהּ רְגִילָה, בִּפְנֵי בַעְלָהּ אֶלָּא כּוֹס אֶחָד; [11] שֶׁלֹּא בִּפְנֵי בַעְלָהּ אֵין נוֹתְנִין לָהּ כָּל עִיקָּר.

[12] וְאִי בָּעֵית אֵימָא: [13] רְגִילָה, נוֹתְנִין לָהּ לְצִיקֵי קְדֵירָה. [14] דְּאָמַר רַבִּי אַבָּהוּ אָמַר רַבִּי יוֹחָנָן: מַעֲשֶׂה בְּכַלָּתוֹ שֶׁל נַקְדִּימוֹן בֶּן גּוּרְיוֹן שֶׁפָּסְקוּ לָהּ חֲכָמִים סָאתַיִם יַיִן לְצִיקֵי קְדֵירָה מֵעֶרֶב שַׁבָּת לְעֶרֶב שַׁבָּת.

LITERAL TRANSLATION

[1] They raised an objection: "[If] she is accustomed [to wine], we give her"!

[2] [If] she is accustomed, it is different, [3] as Rav Ḥinnana bar Kahana said in the name of Shmuel: [4] [If] she is accustomed, we give her one glass; [5] [if] she is not accustomed, we give her two glasses.

[6] What does he say?

[7] Abaye said: This [is what] he says: [8] [If] she is accustomed, in the presence of her husband [we give her] two glasses; [9] not in the presence of her husband we give her one glass. [10] [If] she is not accustomed, in the presence of her husband [we give her] only one glass; [11] not in the presence of her husband we do not give her at all.

[12] And if you wish, say: [13] [If] she is accustomed, we give her for meat sauce. [14] For Rabbi Abbahu said in the name of Rabbi Yoḥanan: [There was] a case involving the daughter-in-law of Nakdimon ben Guryon [in] which the Sages granted her two *se'ahs* of wine for meat sauce from Friday to Friday.

RASHI

רגילה שאני — כיון דאינו חידוש לה, ככר דשה בו ואינו מזיק לגה. לציקי קדרה — להטעים תבשיל.

NOTES

Ba'al." *Maharam Schiff* notes that even though the verse in Hosea refers to an adulterous woman, the Gemara thinks that it is legitimate to infer from this verse that wine may also be given to a faithful wife, for the verse speaks of "my drink," meaning "the drink to which I am entitled from my husband."

מַעֲשֶׂה בְּכַלָּתוֹ There was a case involving the daughter-in-law. The Jerusalem Talmud relates a similar anecdote regarding Marta the daughter of Boethus. She, too, appeared before the Rabbis, claiming that she was entitled to receive wine as part of her maintenance. The Rabbis ordered that she be provided with two *se'ahs* of wine each day for cooking. Thinking that she was entitled to more, Marta began to curse the judges, saying: "May your own daughters be treated in this fashion." The Rabbis who thought that their award was quite generous responded by saying "Amen," hoping that their own daughters would indeed be maintained in such a fashion. (See also below, 66b, for another such incident involving the daughter of Nakdimon ben Guryon.)

TRANSLATION AND COMMENTARY

daughter-in-law blessed the Sages, [1] **saying to them: "May the same be given to your** own **daughters."** [2] **A Sage taught** a Baraita that fills in a number of details of the story: "At the time of this incident, Nakdimon ben Guryon's daughter-in-law **was waiting for her brother-in-law** [the *yavam*] to perform levirate marriage, her husband having died childless. [3] Hence the Sages **did not respond 'Amen'** to the blessing she bestowed on them, because they did not want their daughters ever to find themselves in such a situation."

תָּנָא [4] The Gemara now continues its discussion of the propriety of a woman drinking intoxicating beverages. **A Sage taught** the following Baraita: **"One glass** of wine **is good for a woman,** [5] but a **second** glass of wine **is a disgrace**, because such a quantity of alcohol causes her to begin to lose her social inhibitions. [6] After a **third** glass of wine, she is so under the influence of the intoxicating liquor that **she** is liable to **ask openly** for sexual relations. [7] And after a **fourth** glass, **she** is ready to **ask** to have sexual relations **even** with **an ass in the marketplace,** because she is so drunk that **she no longer cares** about the identity of her sexual partner.

אָמַר רָבָא [8] **Rava said: This** ruling that a woman is not to be given wine **was only taught** regarding a situation **when** the woman's **husband is not with her.** A woman must not be given wine to drink if her husband is not present, lest she behave promiscuously in her intoxicated state. [9] **But if her husband is with her, there is no concern,** for if she is overcome with sexual desire, her husband is there to satisfy her.

וְהָא חַנָּה [10] The Gemara objects: **But surely in the case of Hannah, her husband** Elkanah **was with her!** And since we derived the ruling that wine should be withheld from a woman from the story about Hannah, it follows that this ruling applies even if the woman's husband is present.

אַכְסְנַאי שָׁאנֵי [11] The Gemara answers: The law applying to **a guest is different.** [12] **For Rav Huna said: From where do we derive** the ruling **that a guest is forbidden to engage in sexual relations?** [13] **For the verse says**

[1] אָמְרָה לָהֶן: "כָּךְ תִּפְסְקוּ לִבְנוֹתֵיכֶם". [2] תָּנָא: "שׁוֹמֶרֶת יָבָם הָיְתָה, [3] וְלֹא עָנוּ אַחֲרֶיהָ: 'אָמֵן'".

[4] תָּנָא: "כּוֹס אֶחָד יָפֶה לְאִשָּׁה. [5] שְׁנַיִם נִיוּוּל הוּא. [6] שְׁלֹשָׁה, תּוֹבַעַת בַּפֶּה. [7] אַרְבָּעָה, אֲפִילּוּ חֲמוֹר תּוֹבַעַת בַּשּׁוּק, וְאֵינָהּ מַקְפֶּדֶת".

[8] אָמַר רָבָא: לֹא שָׁנוּ אֶלָּא שֶׁאֵין בַּעְלָהּ עִמָּהּ. [9] אֲבָל בַּעְלָהּ עִמָּהּ, לֵית לָן בָּהּ.

[10] וְהָא חַנָּה, דְּבַעְלָהּ עִמָּהּ הֲוַאי!

[11] אַכְסְנַאי שָׁאנֵי, [12] דְּאָמַר רַב הוּנָא: מִנַּיִן לְאַכְסְנַאי שֶׁאָסוּר בְּתַשְׁמִישׁ הַמִּטָּה? [13] שֶׁנֶּאֱמַר:

LITERAL TRANSLATION

[1] She said to them: "Grant the same to your daughters." [2] [A Sage] taught: "She was waiting for [her] *yavam*, [3] and they did not answer after her: 'Amen.'"

[4] [A Sage] taught: "One glass is good for a woman. [5] Two is a disgrace. [6] Three, she solicits openly (lit., 'with her mouth'). [7] Four, she solicits even an ass in the marketplace, and she does not care."

[8] Rava said: They only taught [this] when her husband is not with her. [9] But [if] her husband is with her, we have no [concern] about it.

[10] But surely [in the case of] Hannah, her husband was with her!

[11] A guest is different, [12] for Rav Huna said: From where [do we derive] that a guest is forbidden to engage in sexual relations? [13] For it is said:

RASHI

תובעת בפה — תשמיש.

NOTES

אֲבָל בַּעְלָהּ עִמָּהּ, לֵית לָן בָּהּ But if her husband is with her, we have no concern about it. *Rid* explains that there is no reason to be concerned about giving a woman wine to drink if her husband is with her, because he will ensure that she does not engage in promiscuous behavior.

Rivan explains the matter in a slightly different manner: A woman may be given wine if her husband is present, for if she loses her inhibitions and demands to engage in sexual relations, she can do so with her husband. According to this second explanation, we can understand the Gemara's argument that a woman may not be given wine, even if she is with her husband, if the couple are guests in someone else's house, for a guest is forbidden to engage in sexual relations.

HALAKHAH

מִנַּיִן לְאַכְסְנַאי שֶׁאָסוּר בְּתַשְׁמִישׁ הַמִּטָּה From where do we derive that a guest is forbidden to engage in sexual relations. "A man is forbidden to engage in sexual relations with his wife while they are staying in someone else's house. But if the host provides the couple with their own room, sexual relations are permitted, provided that they bring their own bedding and bedclothes." (*Rambam, Sefer Kedushah, Hilkhot Issurei Bi'ah* 21:15; *Shulḥan Arukh, Oraḥ Ḥayyim* 240:13; *Even HaEzer* 25:7.)

TRANSLATION AND COMMENTARY

(I Samuel 1:19): **"And they rose up early in the morning and they bowed before the Lord, and they returned and they came to their house to Ramah; and Elkanah knew Hannah his wife, and the Lord remembered her."** [1]Now that Elkanah was at home, he was **indeed** permitted to engage in sexual relations with his wife; [2]but **earlier,** while they were guests in Shiloh, he was **not** permitted to cohabit with her. Wine was therefore withheld from Hannah in Shiloh, even though she was there with her husband. But if a woman is at home with her husband, she may indeed be given wine to drink, as Rava stated.

חוּמָא דְּבֵיתְהוּ דְּאַבַּיֵי [3]The story is told that **Ḥoma the widow of Abaye came before Rava,** [4]and **said to him:** "Please instruct my husband's heirs to **provide me with maintenance** from his estate." [5]**He awarded her** maintenance as she had requested. [6]**She** then **said:** "Please instruct my husband's heirs to **provide me with wine** as well." [7]Rava **said to her: "I know that Naḥmani** [another name by which Abaye was known] **did not drink wine.** Since you were not accustomed to be given wine during your husband's lifetime, you cannot claim wine from his heirs." [8]Ḥoma then **said to him: "I swear to you that he used to give me to drink out of drinking horns** as big **as this!"** And she demonstrated with her hands the size of the drinking horns that Abaye used. [9]**As she was** lifting her arms to **show** Rava how wine was drunk in Abaye's home, her sleeve slipped a little and part of **her arm was exposed.** [10]Ḥoma's beauty was so great that when her arm was uncovered, **a light filled the** entire **courtroom.** [11]The sight of Ḥoma's arm aroused **Rava,** who **got up, went into his house, and asked** his wife, **Rav Ḥisda's daughter,** to engage in sexual relations with him. [12]**Rav Ḥisda's daughter** realized that something must have aroused her husband, and she **asked him: "Who appeared** before you **in court today?"** [13]Rava **said to her: "Ḥoma the widow of Abaye."** [14]In a jealous rage, Rava's wife **went** out **after** Ḥoma, **and struck her with the lock of a chest until she drove her out of Meḥoza.**

"וַיַּשְׁכִּמוּ בַבֹּקֶר וַיִּשְׁתַּחֲווּ לִפְנֵי ה׳, וַיָּשֻׁבוּ וַיָּבֹאוּ אֶל בֵּיתָם הָרָמָתָה; וַיֵּדַע אֶלְקָנָה אֶת חַנָּה אִשְׁתּוֹ, וַיִּזְכְּרֶהָ ה׳". [1]הָשְׁתָּא — אִין; [2]מֵעִיקָּרָא — לָא.

[3]חוּמָא דְּבֵיתְהוּ דְּאַבַּיֵי אֲתַאי לְקַמֵּיהּ דְּרָבָא. [4]אָמְרָה לֵיהּ: "פְּסוֹק לִי מְזוֹנֵי". [5]פָּסַק לָהּ. [6]"פְּסוֹק לִי חַמְרָא". [7]אֲמַר לָהּ: "יָדַעְנָא בֵּיהּ בְּנַחְמָנִי דְּלָא הֲוָה שָׁתֵי חַמְרָא". [8]אָמְרָה לֵיהּ: "חַיֵּי דְּמָר, דְּהָוֵי מַשְׁקֵי לֵיהּ בְּשׁוּפְרָזֵי כִּי הַאי"! בַּהֲדֵי דְּקָא מַחֲוְיָא לֵיהּ, [9]אִיגְלֵי דַּרְעָא, [10]נָפַל נְהוֹרָא בְּבֵי דִּינָא. [11]קָם רָבָא, עָל לְבֵיתֵיהּ, תְּבָעָהּ לְבַת רַב חִסְדָּא. [12]אָמְרָה לֵיהּ בַּת רַב חִסְדָּא: "מַאן הָוֵי הָאִידָּנָא בְּבֵי דִּינָא?" [13]אֲמַר לָהּ: "חוּמָא דְּבֵיתְהוּ דְּאַבַּיֵי". [14]נָפְקָא אַבַּתְרָהּ, מַחְתָא לָהּ בְּקוּלְפֵי דְּשִׁידָּא עַד דְּאַפְּקָה לָהּ מִכּוּלֵּי

LITERAL TRANSLATION

"And they rose up early in the morning and they bowed before the Lord, and they returned and they came to their house to Ramah; and Elkanah knew Hannah his wife, and the Lord remembered her."

[1]Now — yes; [2]at first — no.

[3]Ḥoma the wife of Abaye came before Rava. [4]She said to him: "Grant me maintenance." [5]He granted her. [6][She said:] "Grant me wine." [7]He said to her: "I know that Naḥmani did not drink wine." [8]She said to him: "By the life of the Master, [I swear] that he used to give me to drink out of drinking horns like this!" [9]As she was showing him, her arm was exposed, [10][and] a light fell on the court. [11]Rava got up, went into his house, and solicited the daughter of Rav Ḥisda. [12]The daughter of Rav Ḥisda said to him: "Who was in the court today?" [13]He said to her: "Ḥoma the wife of Abaye." [14]She went out after her, [and] struck her with the lock of a chest until she drove her out of all

RASHI

ויבאו אל ביתם — והדר "וידע אלקנה את חנה". **חומא** — זה שמה. **שופרזי** — גביעים ארוכים שקורין *מדירני"ש [פליידריי"ן]. **כי האי** — כמדת אמתי וזרועי. **תבעה לבת רב חסדא** — תבע את אשתו לתשמיש. **בקולפי דשידה** — במנעול של ארגז.

BACKGROUND

חוּמָא Ḥoma. Ḥoma was the daughter of Issi the son of Rav Yitzḥak the son of Rav Yehudah. She was originally married to Raḥavah of Pumbedita; after he died, she married Rav Yitzḥak the son of Rabbah bar Bar Ḥanah, and after his death, she married Abaye, who also died while married to her. Rava's wife was apparently concerned that other men (including her own husband) might want to marry Ḥoma because she was so beautiful and because of her distinguished ancestry.

בַּת רַב חִסְדָּא The daughter of Rav Ḥisda. Rav Ḥisda's daughter was Rava's second wife and their mutual affection and respect were profound. Rava had known her in the home of his teacher, Rav Ḥisda, when they were both children. She first married Rami bar Ḥama, but after she became a widow she waited for many years so that she could marry Rava. Elsewhere in the Talmud it is told that, after their wedding, their relationship was very close and they were seldom apart. She bore him a child, and Rava depended greatly on her advice.

LANGUAGE

שׁוּפְרָזֵי Drinking horns. The etymology of this word is unclear. *Arukh* explains it as meaning "long glass." Some authorities claim that the word is cognate to the Hebrew שׁוֹפָר, meaning "horn," and thus it denotes "horn-shaped drinking vessels."

קוּלְפֵי Lock. Some authorities derive this word from the Greek κόλαφος, *kolaphos*, meaning "a blow." Others read קוּפְּלָא, and claim that the word is related to the Persian *kopel*, meaning "broad stick," or "club."

LANGUAGE (RASHI)

מדירני"ש* None of the explanations of this word is fully satisfactory, but it apparently means "goblets," judging from the way *Rashi* uses it elsewhere.

NOTES

יָדַעְנָא בֵּיהּ בְּנַחְמָנִי I know that Naḥmani. Elsewhere (*Shabbat* 33a), Rava said about Abaye that he knew him to be a person who starved himself. Abaye was apparently a poor man, and this gave Rava good reason to think that he had not been accustomed to drinking wine. How can Rava's assessment be reconciled with the contrary testimony offered by Abaye's widow, Ḥoma, that he was indeed accustomed to drinking and offering her wine in large quantities? Perhaps Abaye grew more prosperous in his later years and indulged in wine, or, alternatively, he may have been accustomed to drinking wine for medical reasons.

בְּקוּלְפֵי דְשִׁידָא With the lock of a chest. Our translation follows the reading and interpretation of *Rashi* and others. *Arukh* had the reading קוּלְפָא דְשִׁירָאֵי, which he understood as referring to a strap made from a silk garment knotted at its end.

TRANSLATION AND COMMENTARY

[1] She **said to** Ḥoma: **"You have** already **killed three** men; [2] **are you now coming to kill another?!** You have been married three times, and each of your three husbands has died. And now you come to flaunt your beauty, hoping to attract my husband Rava to take you as his wife!"

דְּבֵיתְהוּ דְּרַב יוֹסֵף [3] A similar story was told about **the widow of Rav Yosef the son of Rava.** She once **came before Rav Neḥemyah the son of Rav Yosef,** [4] **and said to him:** "Please instruct my husband's heirs to **provide me with maintenance** from his estate." [5] Accepting her claim, Rav Neḥemyah **awarded her** maintenance. [6] The widow then said: "Please instruct the heirs to **provide me with wine."** [7] Once again, Rav Neḥemyah received her claim favorably and **awarded her** an allowance of wine. [8] Justifying his decision, Rav Neḥemyah **said to her: "I know that** as a rule **the people of Meḥoza drink wine.** Thus you must have been accustomed to drinking wine during your husband's lifetime, and therefore you are entitled to receive an allowance of wine from his heirs."

דְּבֵיתְהוּ דְּרַב יוֹסֵף בְּרֵיהּ דְּרַב מְנַשְּׁיָא מִדְּוִיל [9] The Gemara concludes the discussion of this topic with a story about **the widow of Rav Yosef the son of Rav Menashya from Dvil** who **came before Rav Yosef,** [10] **and said to him:** "Please instruct my husband's heirs to **provide me with maintenance** from his estate." Rav Yosef **awarded her** maintenance. [11] The widow then submitted another claim, saying: "Please instruct the heirs to **provide me with wine."** Once again, Rav Yosef ruled in her favor and **awarded her** wine. [12] The widow then put forward a third claim, saying: "Instruct the heirs to **provide me with silk garments."** [13] Rav Yosef **said to** the widow: **"Why** do you need **silk garments?"** [14] **She said to him:** "So that I will not be embarrassed to appear **before you, and your friends, and your friends' friends.** Just because I am a widow, there is no reason for me to dress less elegantly than when I was married."

מְחוֹזָא. [1] אָמְרָה לָהּ: ״קָטְלַתְּ לֵיךְ תְּלָתָא, [2] וַאֲתַתְּ לְמִיקְטַל אַחֲרִינָא!?״

[3] דְּבֵיתְהוּ דְּרַב יוֹסֵף בְּרֵיהּ דְּרָבָא אֲתַאי לְקַמֵּיהּ דְּרַב נְחֶמְיָה בְּרֵיהּ דְּרַב יוֹסֵף. [4] אָמְרָה לֵיהּ: ״פְּסוֹק לִי מְזוֹנֵי״! [5] פָּסַק לָהּ. [6] ״פְּסוֹק לִי חַמְרָא״. [7] פָּסַק לָהּ. [8] אֲמַר לָהּ: ״יָדַעְנָא בְּהוּ בִּבְנֵי מְחוֹזָא דְּשָׁתוּ חַמְרָא״.

[9] דְּבֵיתְהוּ דְּרַב יוֹסֵף בְּרֵיהּ דְּרַב מְנַשְּׁיָא מִדְּוִיל אֲתַאי לְקַמֵּיהּ דְּרַב יוֹסֵף. [10] אָמְרָה לֵיהּ: ״פְּסוֹק לִי מְזוֹנֵי״. פָּסַק לָהּ. [11] ״פְּסוֹק לִי חַמְרָא״. פָּסַק לָהּ. [12] ״פְּסוֹק לִי שִׁירָאֵי״. [13] אֲמַר לָהּ: ״שִׁירָאֵי לָמָּה״? [14] אָמְרָה לֵיהּ: ״לָךְ, וּלְחַבְרָךְ, וּלְחַבְרוּרָךְ״.

LITERAL TRANSLATION

Meḥoza. [1] She said to her: "You have killed three, [2] and [now] you come to kill another?!"

[3] The wife of Rav Yosef the son of Rava came before Rav Neḥemyah the son of Rav Yosef. [4] She said to him: "Grant me maintenance." [5] He granted her. [6] "Grant me wine." [7] He granted her. [8] He said to her: "I know that the people of Meḥoza drink wine."

[9] The wife of Rav Yosef the son of Rav Menashya from Dvil came before Rav Yosef. [10] She said to him: "Grant me maintenance." He granted her. [11] "Grant me wine." He granted her. [12] "Grant me silk garments." [13] He said to her: "Why silk garments?" [14] She said to him: "For you, and for your friends, and for your friends' friends."

RASHI

קטלת לך תלת – שכבר נישאת לשלשה ומתו. כדאמר ביבמות בפרק ״הבא על יבמתו״ (סד,ב). **למיקטל אחרינא** – שבאת להראות יופיך, שיקפוץ איש עליך. **לחברך ולחברורך** – שלא אתבזה על הבריות מכבודי הראשון, לא בפניך ולא בפני חביריך.

BACKGROUND

בְּנֵי מְחוֹזָא **The people of Meḥoza.** Meḥoza was a prosperous city on the Tigris, and its inhabitants were known for their wealth. They were used to drinking wine at home, so that the women of Meḥoza were also accustomed to it.

NOTES

לָךְ, וּלְחַבְרָךְ **For you, and for your friends.** *Rivan* and *Talmidei Rabbenu Yonah* explain that the widow wished to be provided with silk garments because she was interested in remarrying, and she thought that if she was dressed in fine clothing, she would be more attractive to people like Rav Yosef and his friends. An objection was raised against this interpretation — that if this was indeed the reason that the widow wanted the silk garments, then Rav Yosef should not even have awarded her maintenance, for elsewhere (above, 54a) Rav Yosef rules that if a woman uses cosmetics to make herself more attractive to potential suitors, she is no longer entitled to maintenance from her late husband's estate.

Our commentary follows *Rashi* and others, who explain that the widow wanted the silk garments so that she could proudly present herself before distinguished people like Rav Yosef and his colleagues. *Talmidei Rabbenu Yonah* explains that the widow asked for silk garments because people like

HALAKHAH

פְּסוֹק לִי חַמְרָא **Grant me wine.** "In a place where it is customary for women to drink wine, a man must provide his wife with a small amount of wine." (*Rambam, Sefer Nashim, Hilkhot Ishut* 12:10; *Shulḥan Arukh, Even HaEzer* 70:3.)

[1] ״וְנוֹתֵן לָהּ מִטָּה וּמַפָּץ, וכו׳״. [2] מַפָּץ וּמַחֲצֶלֶת לָמָּה לָהּ דִּיהַב לָהּ? [3] אֲמַר רַב פַּפָּא: בְּאַתְרָא דִּנְהִיגִי דְּמָלוּ פּוּרְיָא בְּחַבְלֵי דִּמְבַגֵּר לָהּ. [4] תָּנוּ רַבָּנַן: ״אֵין נוֹתְנִין לָהּ כַּר וְכֶסֶת. [5] מִשּׁוּם רַבִּי נָתָן אָמְרוּ: נוֹתְנִין לָהּ כַּר וְכֶסֶת״. [6] הֵיכִי דָּמֵי? אִי דְּאוֹרְחָהּ, מַאי טַעֲמָא דְּתַנָּא קַמָּא? [7] וְאִי דְּלָאו אוֹרְחָהּ, מַאי טַעֲמָא דְּרַבִּי נָתָן? [8] לָא, צְרִיכָא, כְּגוֹן דְּאוֹרְחֵיהּ דִּידֵיהּ וְלָאו אוֹרְחָהּ דִּידָהּ.

LITERAL TRANSLATION

[1] "And he gives her a bed and a mattress, etc." [2] Why does she need him to give her a mattress and a mat?

[3] Rav Pappa said: [This applies] in a place where they are accustomed to fill in the bed with ropes that hurt her.

[4] Our Rabbis taught: "We do not give her a cushion or a pillow. [5] In the name of Rabbi Natan they said: We give her a cushion and a pillow."

[6] How do we visualize the case (lit., "what is it like")? If it is her custom, what is the reason of the first Tanna? [7] And if it is not her custom, what is the reason of Rabbi Natan?

[8] No, it is necessary, for example, where it is his custom but it is not her custom.

TRANSLATION AND COMMENTARY

״וְנוֹתֵן לָהּ מִטָּה וּמַפָּץ״ [1] The Gemara now proceeds to analyze the next clause of the Mishnah, which stated: "In addition to food, the husband **must give** his wife **a bed, a** soft **mattress,** and a firm mat." [2] The Gemara asks: If the husband provides his wife with a bed, **why does she** still **need him to give her a mattress and a mat?**

אֲמַר רַב פַּפָּא [3] **Rav Pappa said** in reply: The Mishnah's ruling **applies in a place where it is customary to construct a bed by weaving ropes** across a frame. If the woman were to lie directly on top of the ropes, they would cut into her and **hurt her.** This is why the husband is required to provide his wife with a mattress or mat to place across the ropes, so that her bed will be comfortable.

תָּנוּ רַבָּנַן [4] **Our Rabbis taught** the following Baraita: "A man **is not required to give** his wife **a cushion or a pillow.** [5] **In the name of Rabbi Natan it was reported:** A man **is required to give** his wife **a cushion and a pillow."**

הֵיכִי דָּמֵי? [6] The Gemara asks: **How do we visualize the case? If it is the custom in the woman's** family to sleep with a cushion and a pillow, **why does the** anonymous **first Tanna** exempt the husband from providing his wife with the comforts to which she was accustomed before she married? There is a general rule that a married woman is not required to accept a decline in her standard of living below the level she enjoyed before she married. [7] **And if it is not the custom in her** family to sleep with a cushion and a pillow, **why does Rabbi Natan** require the husband to provide her with these things?

לָא, צְרִיכָא [8] The Gemara answers: **No, it was necessary** for the Baraita to state the disagreement between the anonymous first Tanna and Rabbi Natan **where it is the custom in the husband's** family to sleep with a cushion and a pillow, **but it is not the custom in the wife's** family to do so.

RASHI

מפץ ומחצלת למה לה – הרי עור שטוח על מטה טוב מן המפץ! ומשני: באתרא דמלו פוריא בחבלי – במקום שאין רגילין לעשות שטיח עור למטה, אלא סירוגי חבלים. **ומבגר לה** – מלערי לה ומזקינין אותה, לשון בוגרת. **אי דאורחה** – דרך בנות משפחתה. **אורחיה** – דרכו לישן על כרים וכסתות. ואנן קיימא לן: עולה עמו.

BACKGROUND

דְּמָלוּ פּוּרְיָא בְּחַבְלֵי To fill in the beds with rope. In ancient times, beds were made by stretching nets of rope over the bed frame, and the mattress was laid on top of them. However, in some places the bed was "filled with ropes," because the ropes were placed so close to one another that there was no need for a mattress, although the ropes themselves were uncomfortable to sleep on, being hard and rough.

LANGUAGE

דִּמְבַגֵּר לָהּ That hurt her. *Rashi* and some modern lexicographers suggest that the root בגר is used here in its usual sense of "age"; thus the Gemara means that the ropes cause the woman pain and make her age. Alternatively, בגר might be cognate to the Syriac פגר meaning "to cut," since the ropes cut the skin. Others suggest that the word is related to the Persian *baghr,* meaning "wound."

NOTES

Rav Yosef and his friends and their wives were likely to visit her to honor the memory of her husband, and it would be a mark of respect to her husband if she was dressed appropriately for the occasion.

כְּגוֹן דְּאוֹרְחֵיהּ דִּידֵיהּ For example, where it is his custom. Several Rishonim ask: There is a general rule that a woman "goes up with her husband" and is entitled to a standard of living in accordance with his means and social standing. Thus, if it is the custom in the husband's family to sleep with a cushion and a pillow, then his wife should be entitled to the same, even if that is not customary in her own family. Why, then, does the first Tanna of the Baraita rule that the woman is not entitled to a cushion and a pillow, and why does Rabbi Natan grant her those items only so that she can have them available for her husband's use when he comes home?

According to *Ramban*, this difficulty led *Rif* to rule in accordance with the viewpoint of Rabbi Natan that the woman is provided with a cushion and a pillow, although not for the reason he gave, but rather because she "goes up" with her husband.

Ramban explains that the Baraita is not dealing with a case where it is the custom in the husband's family to sleep with a cushion and a pillow, for in such circumstances his wife would indeed be entitled to those items, because she "goes up" with him. Rather, the Baraita is referring to a case where only the husband is used to sleeping with a cushion and a pillow, and in such circumstances the rule that a woman "goes up with her husband" does not apply. Thus, if the woman is entitled to a cushion and a pillow, it can only be for the reason Rabbi Natan gave .

Rashba and *Ritva* suggest that the Baraita is referring to a case where the husband is a pauper. If it is customary

TRANSLATION AND COMMENTARY

תַּנָּא קַמָּא [1]**The** anonymous **first Tanna maintains** that the husband **can say to** his wife: "I am accustomed to sleeping with a cushion and a pillow, but you are not. [2]So **when I go** away for a while, **I will take** my cushion and my pillow with me; [3]**and when I return** home, **I will bring them** back **with me."** [4]**But Rabbi Natan maintains** that the wife **can say to** her husband: [5]**"Sometimes it will happen that you will return** home **at dusk** on a Friday **and you will not be able to bring** your cushion and your pillow with you because it is forbidden to carry on Shabbat, [6]**and you will take mine and make me sleep on the ground.** Thus I must have a set of bedding ready for you when you return home."

״וְנוֹתֵן לָהּ כִּפָּה״ [7]We learned in our Mishnah: "In addition to food and bedding, the husband **must give** his wife **a** new **cap** and a new girdle once a year, and a new pair of shoes for each of the three Festivals." [8]**Rav Pappa said to Abaye:** [65B] [9]**The Tanna** of our Mishnah creates a situation in which the wife, according to the popular saying, is **stripped naked, but wearing shoes!** How can he rule that she must wear the same clothes for an entire year and yet be given new shoes three times a year?

אֲמַר לֵיהּ [10]Abaye **said to** Rav Pappa: **The Tanna** of our Mishnah **is referring to** a woman living in **a hilly**

[1]תַּנָּא קַמָּא סָבַר: אֲמַר לָהּ: [2]״כִּי אָזֵילְנָא, שָׁקֵילְנָא לְהוּ; [3]וְכִי אָתֵינָא, מַיְיתִינָא לְהוּ בַּהֲדַאי״. [4]וְרַבִּי נָתָן סָבַר: אָמְרָה לֵיהּ: [5]״זִימְנִין דְּמִיתְרְמֵי בֵּין הַשְּׁמָשׁוֹת, וְלָא מָצֵית מַיְיתֵי לְהוּ, [6]וּשְׁקַלְתְּ לְהוּ לְדִידִי וּמַגְנֵית לִי עַל אַרְעָא״.

[7]״וְנוֹתֵן לָהּ כִּפָּה״. [8]אֲמַר לֵיהּ רַב פַּפָּא לְאַבַּיֵי: [65B] [9]הַאי תַּנָּא שְׁלִיחַ עַרְטְלַאי וְרָמֵי מְסָאנֵי!

[10]אֲמַר לֵיהּ: תַּנָּא בִּמְקוֹם הָרִים

LITERAL TRANSLATION

[1]The first Tanna maintains: He can say to her: [2]"When I go, I will take them; and when I come, [3]I will bring them with me." [4]But Rabbi Natan maintains: She can say to him: [5]"Sometimes it will happen [that you come] at dusk, and you will not be able to bring them, [6]and you will take mine and you will make me sleep on the ground."

[7]"And he gives her a cap." [8]Rav Pappa said to Abaye: [65B] [9]This Tanna [has her] stripped naked but wearing shoes!

[10]He said to him: The Tanna refers to (lit., "stands on") a hilly place,

RASHI

כי אזילנא — ואני משרה אותך על ידי שליש, שקילנא להו בהדאי. **וכי אתינא** — ותשכבי עמי, מייתינא להו. **ושקלת לדידי** — מפץ שלי, או אם אקנה כר וכסת משלי. **האי תנא שליח ערטילאי ורמי מסאני** — מופשט וערום, שאין לו חליפות בגדים אלא משנה לשנה, ומנעלים קאמר ממועד למועד. ושאר בגדים לא תחליף במועד. ״והפשיט״ מתרגמינן ״וישלח״ (ויקרא א).

NOTES

in his wife's family to sleep with a cushion and a pillow, the husband is obligated to exert himself and provide her with the same, so that she does not suffer a decline in the standard of living to which she has been accustomed. But since this is the custom only in the husband's family, he is not required to exert himself so that she can live in accordance with the standard of the rest of his family.

Tosafot (cited by *Ritva* and others) argues that the rule that a woman goes up with her husband applies only if she is living with him. But the Baraita is dealing with a case where the husband is living apart from his wife and supporting her through a third party.

Ra'avad suggests that the first Tanna and Rabbi Natan agree that the woman must be provided with a cushion and a pillow, if that is the custom in the husband's family. They only disagree about whether the woman must be provided with an additional cushion and pillow for her husband's use when he returns home.

וּשְׁקַלְתְּ לְהוּ לְדִידִי וּמַגְנֵית לִי עַל אַרְעָא And you will take mine and you will make me sleep on the ground. *Rashi* offers two explanations of this argument: If the husband fails to bring his cushion and his pillow with him, he will either take his wife's mattress or he will take the cushion and the pillow she has acquired on her own. In either case the woman will be forced to sleep on the ground. Both explanations present difficulties: (1) If we are concerned that the husband will take his wife's mattress, why do we require him to provide her with a cushion and a pillow? Let him give her an extra mattress! *Tosafot* and others explain that an extra mattress will not suffice. Since the husband is accustomed to sleeping with a cushion and a pillow, when he comes home without them he will take both mattresses for his own use and will make his wife sleep on the ground. (2) If we are concerned that the husband will take the cushion and the pillow that his wife acquired on her own, why are we worried that she will have to sleep on the ground? She can always sleep on the mattress that her husband provided for her! *Ritva* explains that once the woman becomes used to sleeping with the cushion and the pillow she bought for herself, she will consider sleeping on a mattress like sleeping on the ground. Alternatively, we are concerned that when she buys herself the cushion and the pillow, she will sell her mattress and will be left with nothing when her husband comes home without his own cushion and pillow.

תַּנָּא בִּמְקוֹם הָרִים קָאֵי The Tanna refers to a hilly place. According to *Rambam* (*Hilkhot Ishut* 13:1-2), the specific regulations mentioned in our Mishnah regarding the husband's duty to provide his wife with clothing did not apply in all places at all times, but were limited to Eretz Israel during the Mishnaic period. In other places and at other times, the husband's obligation was determined by local

TRANSLATION AND COMMENTARY

region where the rough terrain causes her shoes to wear out very quickly. [1]In such a case, **she cannot manage with less than three** new **pairs of shoes** a year. [2]**And** the Tanna **tells us incidentally that** it is preferable that **he give her** a new pair of shoes **on** each of **the** three **Festivals,** Pesaḥ, Shavuot, and Sukkot, [3]**so that she can enjoy** her new shoes on the Festival. There is a positive Torah commandment to rejoice during the three Festivals. Included in this commandment is the duty of a husband to gladden the heart of his wife by presenting her with new clothing in honor of the Festival. Since the husband is obligated to provide his wife with three new pairs of shoes a year, it is recommended that he give her a new pair on each of the three Festivals and thereby fulfill his obligation to make his wife happy on the Festival.

"וְכֵלִים שֶׁל חֲמִשִּׁים זוּז" [4]Our Mishnah continues: "The husband must also provide his wife with new **clothing worth fifty zuz** each year." [5]**Abaye said:** When the Mishnah speaks here of fifty zuz, it means **fifty provincial zuz,** each provincial zuz being worth only one-eighth of a Tyrian zuz. During the time of the Mishnah and the Talmud, a number of different coins shared the same name, because two different systems of coinage were in use: (1) Tyrian money, which was roughly equivalent to the coins mentioned in the Torah, and according to which the values mentioned in the Torah were calculated. (2) Provincial money, which had units bearing the same names as those in Tyrian money, but whose value was only one-eighth of that of the corresponding Tyrian coins. According to Abaye, the fifty zuz that the husband must spend annually on his wife's clothing is calculated in provincial zuz. [6]**How do we know this?** [7]**From** the fact **that the Mishnah states: "In what circumstances do** the standards set in our Mishnah regarding a wife's right to food and clothing **apply?** [8]These are the minimal standards, and they apply to **the poorest man in Israel.** [9]**But** in the case of **a person of higher social standing,** the husband's obligation regarding his wife's maintenance is determined **in accordance with his** means and **social position."** [10]**Now if it should enter your mind** to say **that** when the Mishnah speaks of fifty zuz, **it means fifty** Tyrian **zuz literally,** there is a difficulty: A poor man is defined by the Halakhah as someone who does not have two hundred provincial zuz to his name. [11]**From where,** then, **does a poor man have fifty** Tyrian **zuz** (which are the equivalent of four hundred provincial zuz) to spend on his wife's clothing? [12]**Rather, infer from this** that when the Mishnah speaks of fifty zuz, it means **fifty provincial zuz.**

קָאֵי, [1]דְּלָא סַגְיָא בְּלָא תְּלָתָא זוּגֵי מְסָאנֵי. [2]וְאַגַּב אוֹרְחֵיהּ קָא מַשְׁמַע לָן דְּנֵיתְבִינְהוּ נִיהֲלָהּ בַּמּוֹעֵד, [3]כִּי הֵיכִי דְּנֶיהֱוֵי לָהּ שִׂמְחָה בְּגַוַּיְיהוּ.

[4]"וְכֵלִים שֶׁל חֲמִשִּׁים זוּז". [5]אֲמַר אַבַּיֵי: חֲמִשִּׁים זוּזֵי פְּשִׁיטֵי. [6]מִמַּאי? [7]מִדְּקָתָנֵי: "בַּמֶּה דְּבָרִים אֲמוּרִים? [8]בְּעָנִי שֶׁבְּיִשְׂרָאֵל. [9]אֲבָל בִּמְכוּבָּד, הַכֹּל לְפִי כְּבוֹדוֹ". [10]וְאִי סָלְקָא דַּעְתָּךְ חֲמִשִּׁים זוּז מַמָּשׁ, [11]עָנִי חֲמִשִּׁים זוּז מְנָא לֵיהּ? [12]אֶלָּא שְׁמַע מִינָּהּ: חֲמִשִּׁים זוּזֵי פְּשִׁיטֵי.

LITERAL TRANSLATION

[1]where she cannot manage without three pairs of shoes. [2]And incidentally he teaches us that he should give them to her on the Festival, [3]so that she will have joy from them.

[4]"And clothing worth fifty zuz." [5]Abaye said: Fifty provincial (lit., "simple") zuz. [6]From where [do we know this]? [7]From what [the Mishnah] teaches: "In what [case] are these things said? [8]Regarding the poorest man in Israel. [9]But regarding a respected person, all is in accordance with his dignity." [10]And if it should enter your mind [that it means] fifty zuz literally, [11]from where does a poor man have fifty zuz? [12]Rather, deduce from this: Fifty provincial zuz.

RASHI

זוזי פשיטי — זוזי מדינה, שהן שמינית שבזוזי צורי. כל כסף מדינה אחד משמונה בכסף צורי, כדאמרינן לעיל סלע מדינה פלגא דזוזא, שהוא אחד משמונה בסלע.

TERMINOLOGY

וְאַגַּב אוֹרְחֵיהּ קָא מַשְׁמַע לָן And incidentally he teaches us. An expression indicating that a particular subject is not the main purpose of a scholar's argument, although we are able to derive a law relating to it from the way he framed his statement.

LANGUAGE

פְּשִׁיטֵי Provincial. Some scholars interpret this word literally as meaning "simple" (cf. the Hebrew word פָּשׁוּט). Thus זוּזֵי פְּשִׁיטֵי are "simple coins," i.e., copper coins. Others suggest that the word is related to the Middle Persian *pasec,* meaning "small coin."

REALIA

זוּזֵי פְּשִׁיטֵי Provincial zuz. Two principal types of currency were used during the Talmudic period. One, based on silver, was called "Tyrian coin" (this is the currency mentioned in the Torah). The other type of currency, "provincial currency," consisted of coins with the same names as their Tyrian counterparts, although they were worth only one-eighth of the corresponding Tyrian coins. The use of similar names for coins of different values was common in ancient times (and still is in certain places), particularly since some coins were made of gold. This is why the Gemara had to explain precisely what type of coins the Mishnah was referring to — whether to silver dinarim or to "provincial zuz."

NOTES

custom in conjunction with the basic principles underlying our Mishnah's rulings. *Kesef Mishneh* adduces support for *Rambam*'s viewpoint from the Gemara's statement that it is only in a hilly region that the husband must provide his wife with three new pairs of shoes each year.

חֲמִשִּׁים זוּזֵי פְּשִׁיטֵי Fifty provincial zuz. Elsewhere (*Kiddushin* 11b) the Gemara states that wherever a sum of money is mentioned in connection with a Rabbinic obligation, it is calculated according to provincial currency. But even so, the Gemara finds it necessary to justify Abaye's statement that when the Mishnah speaks of the husband's obligation each year to provide his wife with clothing worth fifty zuz, it is referring to provincial zuz. *Rashba* and *Ritva* suggest that the Gemara finds it preferable to support Abaye's interpretation of the Mishnah with internal proof from the Mishnah itself. Moreover, the Gemara wishes to justify Abaye's interpretation of the Mishnah even according to those who may disagree with the opinion recorded in *Kiddushin* that Rabbinic obligations are always calculated according to provincial currency.

TRANSLATION AND COMMENTARY

וְאֵין נוֹתְנִין [1] The Gemara now proceeds to analyze the next clause of the Mishnah, which stated: "A husband **must not give** his wife **new clothes** during the summer, nor may he give her worn clothing during the winter." When a man buys his wife new clothing, she may keep the worn clothing she already has. [2] **Our Rabbis taught** a related Baraita, which states: **"The surplus of maintenance belongs to the husband.** If a woman does not make use of all the food that her husband has provided for her, she must return to him whatever remains. [3] But **the surplus of** her **worn clothing belongs to the woman.** She is not required to return it to her husband."

מוֹתַר בְּלָאוֹת לָאִשָּׁה [4] The Gemara seeks to understand our Mishnah's ruling in the light of this Baraita. If the husband provides his wife with new clothing, **why should she need** to keep her **worn clothing?**

אָמַר רַחֲבָה [5] **Raḥavah said** in reply: The woman may need to keep her worn clothes in order to **wear them during menstruation,** when she is forbidden to have sexual relations with her husband. She may prefer to set aside a special set of clothes to wear then, [6] **so as not to be repulsive to her husband** when she is once again permitted to him.

אָמַר אַבַּיֵי [7] **Abaye said: We have the** following authoritative **tradition** [8] that **the surplus of worn clothes** provided to **a widow** from her late husband's estate **belongs to** the husband's **heirs.** A widow is entitled to receive from her husband's estate the same maintenance that she received from her husband during his lifetime. Thus she is entitled to receive fifty zuz worth of clothing from the estate each year. But unlike a woman whose husband is alive, a widow must return to her husband's heirs any worn clothing remaining from the previous year. Abaye explains why the law that applies to a widow is different: [9] **There,** while the woman's husband is still alive, she may keep her worn clothing for use during menstruation, **so as not** to **be repulsive in** her husband's **presence** after her menstruation is over. [10] But **here,** where her husband is dead, **it makes no difference if she is repulsive,** for there is no need for her to make a favorable impression on his heirs.

[1] ״וְאֵין נוֹתְנִין לָהּ לֹא חֲדָשִׁים, וכו׳״. [2] תָּנוּ רַבָּנַן: ״מוֹתַר מְזוֹנוֹת לַבַּעַל. [3] מוֹתַר בְּלָאוֹת לָאִשָּׁה״.

[4] ״מוֹתַר בְּלָאוֹת לָאִשָּׁה״. לָמָּה לָהּ?

[5] אָמַר רַחֲבָה: שֶׁמִּתְכַּסָּה בָּהֶן בִּימֵי נִדָּתָהּ, [6] כְּדֵי שֶׁלֹּא תִּתְגַּנֶּה עַל בַּעְלָהּ.

[7] אָמַר אַבַּיֵי, נָקְטִינַן: [8] מוֹתַר בְּלָאוֹת אַלְמָנָה לְיוֹרְשָׁיו. [9] הָתָם הוּא דְּלָא תִּתְגַּנֵּי בְּאַפֵּיהּ. [10] הָכָא, תִּתְגַּנֵּי וְתִתְגַּנֵּי.

LITERAL TRANSLATION

[1] "And we do not give her new [clothes], etc." [2] Our Rabbis taught: "The surplus of maintenance [belongs] to the husband. [3] The surplus of worn clothing [belongs] to the woman."

[4] "The surplus of worn clothing [belongs] to the woman." Why does she [need it]?

[5] Raḥavah said: Because she wears them during the days of her menstruation, [6] in order that she not be repulsive to her husband.

[7] Abaye said: We maintain: [8] The surplus of the worn clothing of a widow [belongs] to his heirs. [9] There [the reason is] so that she not be repulsive in his presence. [10] Here, let her be very repulsive (lit., "repulsive and repulsive").

RASHI

מותר מזונות — כגון אשה שמזונות האמורים במשנתנו עודפין לה, שאינה רעבתנית. **שלא תתגנה על בעלה** — בימי טהרתה, כלובשת בגדים שלבשה בימי נדות. **מותר בלאות** — אלמנה הניזונת מנכסי יתומים, ועליהן ליתן לה כלים של חמשים זוז משנה לשנה.

SAGES

רַחֲבָה **Raḥavah.** A Babylonian Amora of the third generation, Raḥavah was a disciple of Rav Yehudah and reported many Halakhic teachings in his name. We also find him quoted in the Talmud in discussions with other Sages of his generation. Raḥavah was famous for the precision with which he reported teachings, so that when the Sages wished to express praise for someone's precision they would say he was as accurate and precise as "Raḥavah of Pumbedita." His two sons, Efah and Avimi, were famous Sages, known as חֲרִיפֵי דִּפּוּמְבְּדִיתָא — "the sharp-witted scholars of Pumbedita."

NOTES

מוֹתַר בְּלָאוֹת אַלְמָנָה **The surplus of the worn clothing of a widow.** The Baraita rules about the surplus of maintenance and worn clothing in the case of a married woman, and Abaye speaks about the surplus of worn clothing in the case of a widow. But nobody discusses the surplus of maintenance in the case of a widow. Most Rishonim follow *Rambam* (*Hilkhot Ishut* 18:4), who rules that the surplus of maintenance provided for a widow from her late husband's

HALAKHAH

מוֹתַר מְזוֹנוֹת לַבַּעַל **The surplus of maintenance belongs to the husband.** "If a woman is provided with maintenance, but does not consume all of the food that has been assigned to her, whatever is left over belongs to her husband. According to some authorities (see *Tosafot, Nazir* 24b), this ruling applies only if the cost of food has gone down and there is money left over from the funds set aside for the woman's maintenance. But if the woman eats less food, then whatever is left over belongs to her. Some Aharonim follow this view (see *Pithei Teshuvah*)." (*Rambam, Sefer Nashim, Hilkhot Ishut* 12:13; *Shulhan Arukh, Even HaEzer* 70:3.)

מוֹתַר בְּלָאוֹת לָאִשָּׁה **The surplus of worn clothing belongs to the woman.** "A married woman who is given clothing by her husband may keep that clothing after it has become worn out." (*Rambam, Sefer Nashim, Hilkhot Ishut* 13:1; *Tur, Even HaEzer* 73.)

מוֹתַר בְּלָאוֹת אַלְמָנָה **The surplus of the worn clothing of**

[1]״נוֹתֵן לָהּ מָעָה כֶּסֶף, וכו׳״. [2]מַאי ״אוֹכֶלֶת״? [3]רַב נַחְמָן אָמַר: אוֹכֶלֶת מַמָּשׁ. [4]רַב אַשִׁי אָמַר: תַּשְׁמִישׁ. [5]תְּנַן: ״אוֹכֶלֶת עִמּוֹ לֵילֵי שַׁבָּת״. [6]בִּשְׁלָמָא לְמַאן דַּאֲמַר אֲכִילָה. [7]הַיְינוּ דְּקָתָנֵי ״אוֹכֶלֶת״, [8]אֶלָּא לְמַאן דַּאֲמַר תַּשְׁמִישׁ, [9]מַאי ״אוֹכֶלֶת״? [10]לִישָּׁנָא מַעַלְיָא, כְּדִכְתִיב: [11]״אָכְלָה, וּמָחֲתָה פִיהָ, וְאָמְרָה, לֹא פָעַלְתִּי אָוֶן״.

LITERAL TRANSLATION

[1]"He gives her a silver ma'ah, etc." [2]What is [meant by] "she eats"? [3]Rav Naḥman said: She eats literally. [4]Rav Ashi said: Sexual relations.

[5]We have learned: "She eats with him [on] Friday nights." [6]Granted according to the one who says [that it means] eating. [7]This is why it states: "She eats." [8]But according to the one who says [that it means] sexual relations, [9]what is [meant by] "she eats"? [10][It is] elevated language, as it is written: [11]"She eats, and wipes her mouth, and says, I have done no wickedness."

TRANSLATION AND COMMENTARY

נוֹתֵן לָהּ מָעָה כֶּסֶף, וכו׳ [1]Our Mishnah continues: "In addition to providing his wife with food and clothing, the husband **must** also **give her** a weekly allowance of **a silver ma'ah,** which she may spend on the extra things that she needs. Even when a man is permitted to live apart from his wife, she is entitled to eat with her husband once a week on Friday night." [2]The Gemara asks: **What** does the Mishnah **mean** when it says that the woman is entitled to **eat** with her husband on Friday nights?

רַב נַחְמָן אָמַר [3]Two answers are given to this question. **Rav Naḥman said:** The expression **"she** is entitled to **eat"** is meant to be understood **literally.** The woman is entitled to partake of her Friday-night dinner in the company of her husband. [4]But **Rav Ashi said:** The expression "she is entitled to eat" is meant to be taken as an allusion to **sexual relations.**

תְּנַן [5]The Gemara now argues that the plain meaning of the Mishnah supports Rav Naḥman. **We have learned** in the Mishnah: **"She eats with him on Friday nights."** [6]**It is understandable, according to** Rav Naḥman, **who says that** the Mishnah **speaks of eating,** [7]**why it states: "She eats** with him on Friday nights." [8]**But according to** Rav Ashi, **who says that** the Mishnah **is referring to sexual relations,** [9]**why does** the Mishnah **state: "She eats"?** Let it state explicitly that the woman is entitled to engage in sexual relations with her husband on Friday nights!

לִישָּׁנָא מַעַלְיָא [10]The Gemara explains that "she eats" **is** to be understood as **a euphemistic reference** to sexual intercourse, similar to the euphemisms used in **the** following **verse** (Proverbs 30:20) which **says** with regard to an adultress: [11]"Such is the way of an adulterous woman; **she eats, and wipes her mouth, and says, I have done no wickedness."** Just as the verse refers to sexual relations in a euphemistic manner, so too does our Mishnah refer to intercourse when it uses the term "she eats."

TERMINOLOGY

לִישָּׁנָא מַעַלְיָא **Elevated language.** Although the Sages of the Talmud never refrained from discussing any subject necessary for understanding the Torah and deciding the Halakhah, they did make a point of using refined language. In many instances they made delicate allusions or used metaphors in discussing certain subjects, especially those related to sex. Although this use of language is not entirely clear, they preferred it, provided that the meaning was understood by their students.

NOTES

estate belongs to the husband's heirs. This seems logical, for if in the case of a married woman, where the surplus of worn clothing belongs to the woman, the surplus of maintenance belongs to her husband, then certainly in the case of a widow, where the surplus of worn clothing belongs to her late husband's heirs, the surplus of maintenance should also belong to those heirs. But *Ra'avad* follows the Jerusalem Talmud, which states explicitly that the surplus of maintenance belongs to the widow.

Ritva and others reject *Ra'avad*'s position, arguing that either the text in the Jerusalem Talmud must be revised to make it agree that the surplus of maintenance belongs to the husband's heirs, or the Jerusalem Talmud disagrees with the viewpoint of the Babylonian Talmud and the law is in accordance with the latter. (See Halakhah for a different view regarding the surplus of maintenance in general.)

מַאי ״אוֹכֶלֶת״ **What is meant by "she eats"?** A similar dispute as to whether the term "she eats" is to be understood literally or as a euphemistic reference to sexual relations is also found in the Jerusalem Talmud.

Ritva suggests that, even according to Rav Naḥman, the term "she eats" is a euphemism for sexual relations. The dispute between Rav Ashi and Rav Naḥman must therefore be understood as follows: Rav Ashi maintains that "she eats" refers only to sexual relations, whereas according to Rav Naḥman the term is to be taken in its literal sense as well, so that it refers to the woman's Friday-night dinner, which she is entitled to eat in the company of her husband. *Ramban* seems to share this view, for he

HALAKHAH

a widow. "A widow's leftover worn-out clothing belongs to her late husband's heirs." (*Rambam, Sefer Nashim, Hilkhot Ishut* 18:4; *Shulḥan Arukh, Even HaEzer* 95:5.)

אוֹכֶלֶת מַמָּשׁ **She eats is meant literally.** "Even if a man is living apart from his wife and is providing for her support through a third party, he is still required to have dinner with her once a week on Friday night, following Rav Naḥman (and in accordance with the reading that his disputant was Rav Assi and not Rav Ashi)." (*Rambam, Sefer Nashim, Hilkhot Ishut* 12:12; *Shulḥan Arukh, Even HaEzer* 70:2.)

TRANSLATION AND COMMENTARY

מֵיתִיבֵי [1] The Gemara **raises an objection** from a related Baraita against Rav Ashi's understanding of our Mishnah. [2] The Baraita states: **"Rabban Shimon ben Gamliel** disagrees with our Mishnah and **says:** A woman whose husband is living apart from her is entitled to **eat** with her husband both **on Friday night and on Shabbat** during the day." [3] **It is understandable, according to** Rav Naḥman, **who says that** the Mishnah **speaks of eating,** [4] **why** the parallel Baraita **states:** "She is entitled to eat with her husband on Friday night **and on Shabbat** during the day." [5] **But according to** Rav Ashi, **who says that** the Mishnah **is referring to sexual relations,** there is a difficulty. [6] Is it permitted to engage in **sexual relations on Shabbat** during the day? [7] **Surely Rav Huna said:** The people of **Israel are holy, and refrain from engaging in sexual relations during the day,** for modesty forbids intercourse in daylight!

[1] מֵיתִיבֵי: [2] ״רַבָּן שִׁמְעוֹן בֶּן גַּמְלִיאֵל אוֹמֵר: אוֹכֶלֶת בְּלֵילֵי שַׁבָּת וְשַׁבָּת״. [3] בִּשְׁלָמָא לְמַאן דְּאָמַר אֲכִילָה. [4] הַיְינוּ דְּקָתָנֵי ״וְשַׁבָּת״. [5] אֶלָּא לְמַאן דְּאָמַר תַּשְׁמִישׁ, [6] תַּשְׁמִישׁ בְּשַׁבָּת מִי אִיכָּא? [7] וְהָאָמַר רַב הוּנָא: יִשְׂרָאֵל קְדוֹשִׁים הֵן, וְאֵין מְשַׁמְּשִׁין מִטּוֹתֵיהֶן בַּיּוֹם! [8] הָאָמַר רָבָא: בְּבַיִת אָפֵל מוּתָּר.

[9] ״וְאִם הָיְתָה מֵנִיקָה״. [10] דָּרֵשׁ רַבִּי עוּלָּא רַבָּה אַפִּיתְחָא דְּבֵי נְשִׂיאָה: [11] אַף עַל פִּי שֶׁאָמְרוּ אֵין אָדָם זָן אֶת בָּנָיו וּבְנוֹתָיו כְּשֶׁהֵן קְטַנִּים, [12] אֲבָל זָן קְטַנֵּי קְטַנִּים.

LITERAL TRANSLATION

[1] They raised an objection: [2] "Rabban Shimon ben Gamliel says: She eats [on] Friday nights and [on] Shabbat." [3] Granted according to the one who says [that it means] eating. [4] This is why it states: "And [on] Shabbat." [5] But according to the one who says [that it means] sexual relations, [6] are there sexual relations on Shabbat? [7] But surely Rav Huna said: Israel are holy, and they do not engage in sexual relations during the day!

[8] Surely Rava said: In a dark house [intercourse] is permitted!

[9] "And if she was nursing." [10] Rabbi Ulla the Great expounded at the entrance of the Nasi's house: [11] Even though they said [that] a man does not [have to] maintain his sons and his daughters when they are minors, [12] yet he must maintain [them when they are] very young.

SAGES

רַבִּי עוּלָּא רַבָּה **Rabbi Ulla the Great.** Some authorities believe that the reference here is to the famous Amora known generally as Ulla (see *Ketubot*, Vol. I, p. 103), and that he was given the epithet "the Great" to distinguish him from another Sage named Rabbi Ulla, a Palestinian Amora of a later generation.

הָאָמַר רָבָא [8] The Gemara answers: There is really no difficulty, for **surely Rava** has limited this ruling by **saying** that if the couple are **in a dark room, it is permitted.** Thus both the Mishnah and Rabban Shimon ben Gamliel's dissenting view in the Baraita can be understood as referring to the woman's right to cohabit with her husband during Shabbat.

״וְאִם הָיְתָה מֵנִיקָה״ [9] We learned in our Mishnah: **"But if** a woman **is nursing,** we reduce the amount of handiwork she must produce, and we add to the amount of maintenance that her husband must provide for her." [10] **Rabbi Ulla the Great expounded at the entrance of the Nasi's house:** [11] **Even though** the Sages **said that a man is not** legally **obliged to maintain his sons and his daughters while they are minors** (unless the father is wealthy, in which case he can be compelled to maintain his children until they reach majority, the obligation flowing from the laws of charity), that ruling applies only with respect to children who have already reached a certain minimum age. [12] **But** the father **is** legally **obliged to maintain** his children **when they are very young.**

NOTES

explains that, according to Rav Naḥman, the woman is entitled to eat with her husband on Friday night, because eating dinner together will lead to greater intimacy, and Friday night is the preferred time for sexual relations. *Rambam* (*Hilkhot Ishut* 12:12) appears to understand that, according to Rav Naḥman, the Mishnah speaks only of the woman's right to eat together with her husband and makes no reference to her conjugal rights.

בְּלֵילֵי שַׁבָּת וְשַׁבָּת **On Friday nights and on Shabbat.** *Ra'ah* asks: Assuming that both the Mishnah and the Baraita are referring to the woman's right to engage in sexual relations with her husband during Shabbat, what is the basis of the dispute between the Tanna of the Mishnah and Rabban Shimon ben Gamliel? Were not the woman's conjugal rights clearly established earlier in the chapter (61b)?

Ra'ah answers that we are dealing here with a worker who would ordinarily be obliged to cohabit with his wife twice a week. But since the man is living apart from his wife with his wife's permission, his conjugal obligation, according to the Tanna of our Mishnah, is reduced to once a week on Friday night. Rabban Shimon ben Gamliel disagrees and says that the husband must make up for his absence during the week and cohabit with his wife both on Friday night and on Shabbat during the day.

זָן קְטַנֵּי קְטַנִּים **He must maintain them when they are very young.** From the fact that the Gemara connects this

HALAKHAH

אֲבָל זָן קְטַנֵּי קְטַנִּים **Yet he must maintain them when they are very young.** "Just as a man is liable by Torah law for his wife's maintenance, so too is he liable for his children's maintenance until they reach the age of six. From then

LITERAL TRANSLATION

[1] Until when? [2] Until they are six, as Rav Assi [said]. [3] For Rav Assi said: A child who is six goes out by means of his mother's eruv.

[4] From where [do we know this]? From what [the Mishnah] teaches: [5] "[And] if she was nursing, we reduce her handiwork, [6] and we add to her maintenance." [7] What is the reason? [8] Is it not because [the child] must eat with her?

[1] עַד כַּמָּה? [2] עַד בֶּן שֵׁשׁ, כִּדְרַב אַסִי. [3] דְּאָמַר רַב אַסִי: קָטָן בֶּן שֵׁשׁ יוֹצֵא בְּעֵירוּב אִמּוֹ.

[4] מִמַּאי? מִדְּקָתָנֵי: [5] "הָיְתָה מֵנִיקָה, פּוֹחֲתִין לָהּ מִמַּעֲשֵׂה יָדֶיהָ, [6] וּמוֹסִיפִין לָהּ עַל מְזוֹנוֹתֶיהָ". [7] מַאי טַעֲמָא? [8] לָאו מִשּׁוּם דְּבָעֵי לְמֵיכַל בַּהֲדָהּ?

RASHI

יוצא בערוב אמו — ערבה אמו לצפון ואביו לדרום — אמו מוליכתו אצלה, ואין אביו מוליכו אצלו. שעדיין הוא צריך לאמו, ובתרה שדיוהו רבנן. אלמא: עד שש צריך סיוע מאמו, וכשם שהבעל זן אותה — כך זן אותו עמה.

הדרן עלך אף על פי

TRANSLATION AND COMMENTARY

עַד כַּמָּה? [1] The Gemara asks: **Until when** is a child considered to be very young? [2] The Gemara answers: **Until** the child **is six** years old, **as Rav Assi said** in a different context. [3] **For Rav Assi said:** If a woman places an eruv beyond the northern edge of the city to enable her to walk more than two thousand cubits north of the city on Shabbat, and her husband places an eruv beyond the southern edge of the city to enable him to walk more than two thousand cubits south of the city on Shabbat, their **child who is in his sixth year** or less **may go out** northward **beyond his mother's eruv.** A child who is less than six years old is still attached to his mother, and so his "place of residence," which determines how far he is permitted to walk on Shabbat, is dictated by that of his mother. Thus we see that until a child reaches the age of six, he is viewed by the law as being inseparably attached to his mother. And it stands to reason that during that period the child's father must give his wife sufficient maintenance to provide both for the woman and for the child. But once the child reaches the age of six, he is viewed as being independent of his mother, and his father does not have to maintain him.

מִמַּאי [4] The Gemara asks: Accepting that a very young child is attached to his mother, **from where do we know** that his father is legally obliged to maintain him? [5] The Gemara answers: We can infer this **from what is stated in our Mishnah: "But if** a woman **is nursing, we reduce** the amount of **handiwork** that she must produce, [6] **and we add to** the amount of **maintenance** that her husband must provide for her." [7] **Why** must the husband increase his wife's maintenance while she is nursing? [8] **Is it not because the child must eat with** its mother, and therefore the husband must provide his wife with sufficient food for both of them? And just as the father must add to his wife's maintenance while she is nursing, so too must he maintain his young child as long as the child is attached to its mother, until the age of six.

NOTES

law with Rav Assi's ruling concerning the determining of a child's "place of residence" regarding an eruv, it would appear that a father is obligated to maintain his very young child, because that child is inseparably attached to his mother (see *Ri Migash* and *Meiri*). Thus the father's obligation to maintain his very young child derives from his obligation to maintain the child's mother. Just as a man is required to maintain his wife, he is likewise required to maintain his very young child who is totally dependent upon her. *Ran* concludes from this that a father is only obliged to maintain his very young child if he is obliged to maintain the child's mother. But if he is not required to maintain the mother (for example, if she is no longer alive), he is also exempt from maintaining his child. But most authorities disagree and maintain that the father's obligation toward his very young child is independent of his obligation toward the child's mother.

לָאו מִשּׁוּם דְּבָעֵי לְמֵיכַל בַּהֲדָהּ Is it not because the child must eat with her? The Rishonim ask: If this is really the Mishnah's reasoning, why does it limit its ruling to a case where the woman is nursing her infant? It should have stated the matter in more general terms — that if a

HALAKHAH

on, he should continue to maintain them until they reach majority, in accordance with the Rabbinic enactment passed at Usha, but he cannot be compelled to do so." (*Rambam, Sefer Nashim, Hilkhot Ishut* 12:14; *Shulḥan Arukh, Even HaEzer* 71:1.)

בֶּן שֵׁשׁ יוֹצֵא בְּעֵירוּב אִמּוֹ A child who is six goes out by means of his mother's eruv. "A child who is in his sixth year or less is permitted to walk more than 2,000 cubits beyond the city limits on the basis of the eruv placed by his mother. Some Aḥaronim (see *Mishnah Berurah*, in the name of *Eliyahu Rabbah*) rule in accordance with the more stringent view of *Rosh* and *Tur* that if the child's father is in the city, then even if the child is only four or five years old, he may not go beyond the 2,000-cubit boundary on the basis of his mother's eruv, unless an eruv has been placed for the child as well." (*Rambam, Sefer Zemanim, Hilkhot Eruvin* 6:21; *Shulḥan Arukh, Oraḥ Ḥayyim* 414:2.)

LITERAL TRANSLATION

[1]But perhaps [it is] because she is ill?

[2]If so, let it teach: "If she was ill." [3]What is [meant by] "if she was nursing"?

[4]But perhaps he teaches us this — [5]that in general nursing women are ill?

[6]It was stated: Rabbi Yehoshua ben Levi said: [7]We add wine for her, for wine is beneficial for [her] milk.

[1]וְדִלְמָא מִשּׁוּם דְּחוֹלָה הִיא? [2]אִם כֵּן, לִיתְנֵי: "אִם הָיְתָה חוֹלָה". [3]מַאי "אִם הָיְתָה מֵנִיקָה"?

[4]וְדִלְמָא הָא קָא מַשְׁמַע לָן — [5]דִּסְתָם מֵנִיקוֹת חוֹלוֹת נִינְהוּ? [6]אִיתְּמַר: אָמַר רַבִּי יְהוֹשֻׁעַ בֶּן לֵוִי: [7]מוֹסִיפִין לָהּ יַיִן, שֶׁהַיַּיִן יָפֶה לֶחָלָב.

הדרן עלך אף על פי

TRANSLATION AND COMMENTARY

וְדִלְמָא [1]The Gemara now suggests that this is not the only way to understand the Mishnah's ruling: **Perhaps** the husband must increase his wife's maintenance while she is nursing, not because he has any obligation toward the child, but **because** his wife **is** treated as if she were **ill** on account of the physical strain of nursing a child! Perhaps the husband must add to his wife's maintenance specifically for her benefit.

אִם כֵּן, לִיתְנֵי [2]The Gemara raises an objection to this suggestion: But **if** this is **so,** the Mishnah **should have stated** the law in more general terms, saying: **"If** a nursing woman **is ill,** we add to the amount of maintenance that her husband must provide for her." [3]**What does** the Mishnah **mean by** saying: **"If** a woman **is nursing,** we add to her maintenance"? Surely the Mishnah was formulated in this way in order to inform us that the husband must add to the maintenance provided for his wife while she is nursing, not because he is required to take care of someone who is ill, but because he is obliged to provide for his child!

וְדִלְמָא הָא [4]The Gemara rejects this last argument: **Perhaps** what the Tanna of our Mishnah wishes to **teach us** is **this** — [5]**that nursing women are assumed to be ill** and in weakened condition. But we cannot infer from this ruling whether a father is obliged to maintain his very young child.

אִיתְּמַר [6]The chapter concludes with the following ruling: **It was stated** that **Rabbi Yehoshua ben Levi said:** [7]If a woman is nursing, **we add wine** to the list of foods that her husband must provide for her, **for wine is beneficial for her milk.**

REALIA

שֶׁהַיַּיִן יָפֶה לֶחָלָב **For wine is beneficial for her milk.** This can be explained in several ways. First, wine contains alcohol and sugar, whose calories provide nutrition important for a nursing woman. Moreover, wine tends to speed up the secretion of body fluids, including milk.

NOTES

woman has a very young child, her husband is obliged to add to her maintenance!

Rashba and *Ritva* suggest that the Mishnah is referring specifically to a nursing woman because it also wishes to teach us the law that the amount of handiwork expected from the woman is reduced, and that law applies only to a woman who is nursing, and not to every mother with a very young child.

שֶׁהַיַּיִן יָפֶה לֶחָלָב **For wine is beneficial for her milk.** *Rivan* and *Ri Migash* explain that Rabbi Yehoshua ben Levi's statement is a continuation of the previous discussion, for it shows that the husband must add to his wife's maintenance while she is nursing because he is obliged to provide for his very young child, and not that his wife is treated as a sick woman whose physical strength must be maintained. Rabbi Yehoshua ben Levi says that a nursing woman must be given wine, because wine is good for her milk, benefiting the child, not its mother. Thus Rabbi Yehoshua ben Levi's statement supports the ruling of Rabbi Ulla the Great that a man is responsible for his children's maintenance while they are very young.

HALAKHAH

מוֹסִיפִין לָהּ יַיִן **We add wine for her.** "As long as a woman is nursing a child, her husband must add wine and other things to her maintenance that are beneficial for her milk." (*Rambam, Sefer Nashim, Hilkhot Ishut* 21:11; *Shulḥan Arukh, Even HaEzer* 80:11.)

Conclusion to Chapter Five

The Talmud concludes that whereas a man may add as much as he wishes to the minimum amount of his wife's ketubah, he may not fix her ketubah at less than the legal minimum, even if she agrees to the reduction. If the husband sets his wife's ketubah at less than the legal minimum, his stipulation is invalid, but his cohabitation with her is regarded as an act of prostitution. A woman may collect the addition to her ketubah as well as the basic portion if she is divorced or widowed after marriage, but if she is divorced or widowed after betrothal, she may collect only the basic portion of her ketubah, but not any extra sum added by the husband on his own initiative.

Unless specified otherwise, the betrothed bride and bridegroom are given a set amount of time from the date when the bridegroom asks for his bride in marriage, in order to prepare themselves for the wedding. Once the time set for the wedding has arrived, the bridegroom is responsible for his bride's support, even if the wedding has not yet taken place. For various reasons, however, the Rabbis decreed that a woman who is betrothed to a priest may not eat terumah until she and her bridegroom actually enter the bridal chamber for marriage.

With regard to a married woman's household duties, the Talmud concludes that a woman is obliged to perform certain household tasks related to preparing food and to childcare, and she must also produce a certain amount of handiwork in order to contribute to the family income. But she is entitled to waive her right to be maintained by her husband, and thus deprive him of his right to her handiwork. Moreover, a woman is freed from some or all of her domestic obligations if she brings into her marriage a dowry that is sufficient for the purchase of maidservants who can do the work in her stead, or if it is not the custom of both her family and her husband's family that a wife performs these tasks for her husband. However, even the wealthiest woman is required to perform for her husband certain intimate tasks that endear her to him. She must also engage in a certain minimum amount of work so that idleness will not lead her to sexual promiscuity. According to the Gemara's conclusion, a husband cannot consecrate his wife's handiwork.

The Sages established the husband's conjugal obligations in accordance with his occupation and the frequency with which he is found at home. A man may not reduce his conjugal obligations without his wife's permission. But a Rabbinic scholar is permitted to leave home for an extended period in order to study Torah, even though he will be unable to fulfill his marital obligations during this period. The obligation to cohabit with one's spouse is so central to the marital tie that if a husband refuses to cohabit with his wife, he can be compelled to grant her a divorce and to pay her her ketubah; and if it is the wife who refuses to engage in sexual relations with her husband, she can be divorced without a ketubah. The law distinguishes between a woman who refuses to cohabit with her husband because of a quarrel, and a woman who refuses to cohabit with her husband because she finds him repulsive. Different procedures were adopted in order to induce a "rebellious" spouse to fulfill his or her marital obligations, including warnings, public announcements, and financial penalties.

The Sages fixed the minimum amount of food and clothing that a husband must provide for his wife in order to fulfill his duty to maintain and clothe her. Like other obligations arising from the conditions contained in the ketubah, the husband's duty to provide his wife with maintenance depends in part upon local custom. And as is the case with other stipulations included in the ketubah, the husband's obligations can be altered by mutual consent.

List of Sources

Aḥaronim, lit., "the last," meaning Rabbinic authorities from the time of the publication of Rabbi Yosef Caro's code of Halakhah, *Shulḥan Arukh* (1555).

Arba'ah Turim, code of Halakhah by Rabbi Ya'akov ben Asher, b. Germany, active in Spain (c. 1270-1343).

Arukh, Talmudic dictionary, by Rabbi Natan of Rome, 11th century.

Avnei Nezer, novellae on the Talmud by Rabbi Avraham Bornstein of Sokhochev, Poland (1839-1908).

Ayelet Ahavim, novellae on *Ketubot* by Rabbi Aryeh Leib Zuenz, Poland, 19th century.

Ba'al HaMa'or, Rabbi Zeraḥyah ben Yitzḥak, Spain, 12th century. Author of *HaMa'or*, Halakhic commentary on *Hilkhot HaRif*.

Baḥ (Bayit Ḥadash), commentary on *Arba'ah Turim*, by Rabbi Yoel Sirkes, Poland (1561-1640).

Ba'er Hetev, commentary on *Shulḥan Arukh, Ḥoshen Mishpat*, by Rabbi Zeḥaryah Mendel of Belz, Poland (18th century).

Bereshit Rabbah, Midrash on the Book of Genesis.

Bet Aharon, novellae on the Talmud, by Rabbi Aharon Walkin, Lithuania (1865-1942).

Bet Shmuel, commentary on *Shulḥan Arukh, Even HaEzer*, by Rabbi Shmuel ben Uri Shraga, Poland, second half of the 17th century.

Bet Ya'akov, novellae on *Ketubot*, by Rabbi Ya'akov Lorberboim of Lissa, Poland (1760-1832).

Bet Yosef, Halakhic commentary on *Arba'ah Turim* by Rabbi Yosef Caro (1488-1575), which is the basis of his authoritative Halakhic code, *Shulḥan Arukh*.

Birkat Avraham, novellae on the Talmud, by Rabbi Avraham Erlinger, Israel (20th century).

Bnei Ahuvah, novellae on *Mishneh Torah*, by Rabbi Yehonatan Eibeschuetz, Poland, Moravia, and Prauge (c.1690-1764).

Derishah and *Perishah*, commentaries on *Tur* by Rabbi Yehoshua Falk Katz, Poland (c. 1555-1614).

Eliyah Rabbah, commentary on *Shulḥan Arukh, Oraḥ Ḥayyim*, by Rabbi Eliyahu Shapira, Prague (1660-1712).

Eshel Avraham, by Rabbi Avraham Ya'akov Neimark, novellae on the Talmud, Israel (20th century).

Even HaEzer, section of *Shulḥan Arukh* dealing with marriage, divorce, and related topics.

Geonim, heads of the academies of Sura and Pumbedita in Babylonia from the late 6th century to the mid-11th century.

Giddulei Shmuel, by Rabbi Shmuel Gedalya Neiman, novellae on the Talmud, Israel (20th century).

Gra, Rabbi Eliyahu ben Shlomo Zalman (1720-1797), the Gaon of Vilna. Novellae on the Talmud and *Shulḥan Arukh*.

Hafla'ah, novellae on *Ketubot*, by Rabbi Pinḥas HaLevi Horowitz, Poland and Germany (1731-1805).

Haggahot Mordekhai, glosses on the *Mordekhai*, by Rabbi Shmuel ben Aharon of Schlettstadt, Germany, late 14th century.

Halakhot Gedolot, a code of Hakhic decisioons written in the Geonic period. This work has been ascribed to Sherira Gaon, Rav Hai Gaon, Rav Yehudai Gaon and Rabbi Shimon Kayyara.

Ḥatam Sofer, responsa literature and novellae on the Talmud by Rabbi Moshe Sofer (Schreiber), Pressburg, Hungary and Germany (1763-1839).

Ḥaver ben Ḥayyim, novellae on the Talmud by Rabbi Ḥizkiyah Ḥayyim Ploit, Lithuania, 19th century.

Ḥelkat Meḥokek, commentary on *Shulḥan Arukh, Even HaEzer*, by Rabbi Moshe Lima, Lithuania (1605-1658).

Ḥoshen Mishpat, section of *Shulḥan Arukh* dealing with civil and criminal law.

Ittur, Halakhic work by Rabbi Yitzḥak Abba Mari, Provence (1122-1193).

Iyyun Ya'akov, commentary on *Ein Ya'akov*, by Rabbi Ya'akov bar Yosef Riesher, Prague, Poland, and France (d. 1733).

Kesef Mishneh, commentary on *Mishneh Torah*, by Rabbi Yosef Caro, author of *Shulḥan Arukh*.

Korban HaEdah, commentary on the Jerusalem Talmud by Rabbi David ben Naftali Frankel, Germany (1707–1762).

Magen Avraham, commentary on *Shulḥan Arukh, Oraḥ Ḥayyim*, by Rabbi Avraham HaLevi Gombiner, Poland (d. 1683).

Maggid Mishneh, commentary on *Mishneh Torah*, by Rabbi Vidal de Tolosa, Spain, 14th century.

Maharal, Rabbi Yehudah Loew ben Betzalel of Prague (1525–1609). Novellae on the Talmud.

Maharam Schiff, novellae on the Talmud by Rabbi Meir ben Ya'akov HaKohen Schiff (1605–1641), Frankfurt, Germany.

Maharsha, Rabbi Shmuel Eliezer ben Yehudah HaLevi Edels, Poland (1555–1631). Novellae on the Talmud.

Maharshal, Rabbi Shlomo ben Yeḥiel Luria, Poland (1510–1573). Novellae on the Talmud.

Meiri, commentary on the Talmud (called *Bet HaBeḥirah*), by Rabbi Menaḥem ben Shlomo, Provence (1249–1316).

Mekhilta, Halakhic Midrash on the Book of Exodus.

Melekhet Shlomo, commentary on the Mishnah by Rabbi Shlomo Adeni, Yemen and Eretz Israel (1567–1626).

Melo HaRo'im, commentary on the Talmud by Rabbi Ya'akov Tzvi Yolles, Poland (c. 1778–1825).

Mishnah Berurah, commentary on *Shulḥan Arukh, Oraḥ Ḥayyim*, by Rabbi Yisrael Meir HaKohen, Poland (1837–1933).

Mitzpeh Eitan, glosses on the Talmud by Rabbi Avraham Maskileison, Byelorussia (1788–1848).

Mordekhai, compendium of Halakhic decisions by Rabbi Mordekhai ben Hillel HaKohen, Germany (1240?–1298).

Nimmukei Yosef, commentary on *Hilkhot HaRif*, by Rabbi Yosef Ḥaviva, Spain, early 15th century.

Or Sameaḥ, novellae on *Mishneh Torah*, by Rabbi Meir Simḥah HaKohen of Dvinsk, Latvia (1843–1926).

Oraḥ Ḥayyim, section of *Shulḥan Arukh* dealing with daily religious observances, prayers, and the laws of the Sabbath and Festivals.

Perishah, see *Derishah*.

Pitḥei Teshuvah, compilation of responsa literature on the *Shulḥan Arukh* by Rabbi Avraham Tzvi Eisenstadt, Russia (1812–1868).

Pnei Moshe, commentary on the Jerusalem Talmud by Rabbi Moshe ben Shimon Margoliyot, Lithuania (c. 1710–1781).

Pnei Yehoshua, novellae on the Talmud by Rabbi Ya'akov Yehoshua Falk, Poland and Germany (1680–1756).

Porat Yosef, by Rabbi Yosef ben Rabbi Tzvi Hirsch, novellae on tractate *Ketubot* (19th century).

Ra'ah, see *Rabbi Aharon HaLevi*.

Ra'avad, Rabbi Avraham ben David, commentator and Halakhic authority. Wrote comments on *Mishneh Torah*. Provence (c. 1125–1198?).

Rabbenu Gershom, commentator and Halakhic authority, France (960–1040).

Rabbenu Ḥananel (ben Ḥushiel), commentator on the Talmud, North Africa (990–1055).

Rabbenu Shimshon (ben Avraham of Sens), Tosafist, France and Eretz Israel (c. 1150–1230).

Rabbenu Tam, commentator on the Talmud, Tosafist, France (1100–1171).

Rabbenu Yeḥiel, French Tosafist (d. 1268).

Rabbenu Yehonatan, Yehonatan ben David HaKohen of Lunel, Provence, Talmudic scholar (c. 1135–after 1210).

Rabbenu Yonah, see *Talmidei Rabbenu Yonah*.

Rabbi Aharon HaLevi, Spain, 13th century. Novellae on the Talmud.

Rabbi Akiva Eger, Talmudist and Halakhic authority, Posen, Germany (1761–1837).

Rabbi Avraham ben Isaac of Narbonne, French Talmudist (c. 1110–1179).

Rabbi Cresdas Vidal, Spanish Talmudist and commentator, 14th century.

Rabbi Yosef of Jerusalem, French Tosafist of the twelfth and thirteenth centuries, France and Eretz Israel.

Rabbi Moshe the son of Rabbi Yosef of Narbonne, French Talmudist of the twelfth century.

Rabbi Shlomo of Montpellier, French Talmudist of the thirteenth century.

Rabbi Shmuel HaNagid, Spain (993–1055 or 1056). Novellae on the Talmud found in *Shittah Mekubbetzet*.

Rabbi Ya'akov Emden, Talmudist and Halakhic authority, Germany (1697–1776).

Radbaz, Rabbi David ben Shlomo Avi Zimra, Spain, Egypt, Eretz Israel, and North Africa (1479–1574). Commentary on *Mishneh Torah*.

Rambam, Rabbi Moshe ben Maimon, Rabbi and philosopher, known also as Maimonides. Author of *Mishneh Torah*, Spain and Egypt (1135–1204).

Ramban, Rabbi Moshe ben Naḥman, commentator on Bible and Talmud, known also as Naḥmanides, Spain and Eretz Israel (1194–1270).

Ran, Rabbi Nissim ben Reuven Gerondi, Spanish Talmudist (1310?–1375?).

Rashash, Rabbi Shmuel ben Yosef Shtrashun, Lithuanian Talmud scholar (1794–1872).

Rashba, Rabbi Shlomo ben Avraham Adret, Spanish Rabbi famous for his commentaries on the Talmud and his responsa (c. 1235–c. 1314).

Rashbam, Rabbi Shmuel ben Meir, commentator on the Talmud, France (1085–1158).

Rashbatz, Rabbi Shimon ben Tzemaḥ Duran, known for his book of responsa, *Tashbatz*, Spain and Algeria (1361–1444).

Rashi, Rabbi Shlomo ben Yitzḥak, the paramount commentator on the Bible and the Talmud, France (1040–1105).

Rav Aḥa (Aḥai) Gaon, author of *She'iltot*. Pumbedita, Babylonia and Eretz Israel, 8th century. See *She'iltot*.

Rav Hai Gaon, Babylonian Rabbi, head of Pumbedita Yeshivah, 10th–11th century.

Rav Natronai Gaon, of the Sura Yeshivah, 9th century.

Rav Sherira Gaon, of the Pumbedita Yeshivah, 10th century.

Rema, Rabbi Moshe ben Yisrael Isserles, Halakhic authority, Poland (1525–1572).

Remah, novellae on the Talmud by Rabbi Meir ben Todros HaLevi Abulafiya, Spain (c. 1170–1244). See *Yad Ramah.*

Ri, Rabbi Yitzḥak ben Shmuel of Dampierre, Tosafist, France (died c. 1185).

Ri HaLavan, French Tosafist (12th century).

Ri Migash, Rabbi Yosef Ibn Migash, commentator on the Talmud, Spain (1077–1141).

Rid, see *Tosefot Rid.*

Rif, Rabbi Yitzḥak Alfasi, Halakhist, author of *Hilkhot HaRif*, North Africa (1013–1103).

Rishonim, lit., "the first," meaning Rabbinic authorities active between the end of the Geonic period (mid-11th century) and the publication of *Shulḥan Arukh* (1555).

Ritva, novellae and commentary on the Talmud by Rabbi Yom Tov ben Avraham Ishbili, Spain (c. 1250–1330).

Rivan, Rabbi Yehudah ben Natan, French Tosafist, 11th–12th centuries.

Rivash, Rabbi Yitzḥak ben Sheshet, Spain and North Africa (1326–1408). Novellae on the Talmud mentioned in *Shittah Mekubbetzet.*

Rosh, Rabbi Asher ben Yeḥiel, also known as Asheri, commentator and Halakhist, Germany and Spain (c.1250–1327).

Sefer HaYashar, novellae on the Talmud by Rabbenu Tam. France (c. 1100–1171).

Sefer Mikkaḥ U'Mimkar by Rav Hai Gaon. Treatise on the laws of commerce.

Sha'ar HaTziyyun, see *Mishnah Berurah.*

Shakh (Siftei Kohen), commentary on *Shulḥan Arukh* by Rabbi Shabbetai ben Meir HaKohen, Lithuania (1621–1662).

She'iltot, by Aḥa (Aḥai) of the Pumbedita Yeshivah, 8th century. One of the first books of Halakhah arranged by subjects.

Shittah Mekubbetzet, a collection of commentaries on the Talmud by Rabbi Betzalel ben Avraham Ashkenazi of Safed (c. 1520–1591).

Shulḥan Arukh, code of Halakhah by Rabbi Yosef Caro, b. Spain, active in Eretz Israel (1488–1575).

Sifrei, Halakhic Midrash on the Books of Numbers and Deuteronomy.

Sukkat David, by Rabbi David Kviat, novellae on tractate *Ketubot,* America (20th century).

Talmidei Rabbenu Yonah, commentary on *Hilkhot HaRif* by the school of Rabbi Yonah of Gerondi, Spain (1190–1263).

Taz, abbreviation for *Turei Zahav.* See *Turei Zahav.*

Terumot HaDeshen, responsa literature and Halakhic decisions by Rabbi Yisrael Isserlin, Germany (15th century).

Tiferet Yisrael, commentary on the Mishnah by Rabbi Yisrael Lipshitz, Germany (1782–1860).

Tosafot, collection of commentaries and novellae on the Talmud, expanding on Rashi's commentary, by the French-German Tosafists (12th and 13th centuries).

Tosafot Yeshanim, one of the editions of the *Tosafot* on the Talmud, 14th century.

Tosefot HaRosh, an edition based ot *Tosefot Sens* by the *Rosh,* Rabbi Asher ben Yeḥiel, Germany and Spain (c. 1250–1327).

Tosefot Rid, commentary on the Talmud by Rabbi Yeshayahu ben Mali di Trani, Italian Halakhist (c. 1200–before 1260).

Tosefot Sens, the first important collection of *Tosafot,* by Rabbi Shimshon of Sens (late 12th–early 13th century).

Tosefot Yom Tov, commentary on the Mishnah by Rabbi Yom Tov Lipman HaLevi Heller, Prague and Poland (1579–1654).

Tur, abbreviation of *Arba'ah Turim*, Halakhic code by Rabbi Ya'akov ben Asher, b. Germany, active in Spain (c. 1270–1343).

Turei Zahav, commentary on *Shulḥan Arukh* by Rabbi David ben Shmuel HaLevi, Poland (c. 1586–1667).

Yoreh De'ah, section of *Shulḥan Arukh* dealing mainly with dietary laws, interest, ritual purity, and mourning.

Zuto Shel Yam, by Rabbi Moshe Leiter, glosses on the Aggadah in the Talmud (20th century).

About the Type

This book was set in Leawood, a contemporary typeface designed by Leslie Usherwood. His staff completed the design upon Usherwood's death in 1984. It is a friendly, inviting face that goes particularly well with sans serif type.